THE VICTORIA HISTORY
OF THE
COUNTIES OF ENGLAND

—

A HISTORY OF
STAFFORDSHIRE

VOLUME VIII

THE VICTORIA HISTORY
OF THE
COUNTIES OF ENGLAND

EDITED BY R. B. PUGH

THE UNIVERSITY OF LONDON
INSTITUTE OF
HISTORICAL RESEARCH

Oxford University Press, Amen House, London, E.C.4

GLASGOW NEW YORK TORONTO MELBOURNE WELLINGTON
BOMBAY CALCUTTA MADRAS KARACHI LAHORE DACCA
CAPE TOWN SALISBURY NAIROBI IBADAN ACCRA
KUALA LUMPUR HONG KONG

PRINTED IN GREAT BRITAIN
AT THE UNIVERSITY PRESS, OXFORD
BY VIVIAN RIDLER
PRINTER TO THE UNIVERSITY

INSCRIBED TO THE

MEMORY OF HER LATE MAJESTY

QUEEN VICTORIA

WHO GRACIOUSLY GAVE THE TITLE TO

AND ACCEPTED THE DEDICATION

OF THIS HISTORY

VIEW OF LONGTON FROM THE NORTH

From a water-colour drawing by R. G. Haggar

A HISTORY OF THE COUNTY OF
STAFFORD

EDITED BY J. G. JENKINS

VOLUME VIII

PUBLISHED FOR
THE INSTITUTE OF HISTORICAL RESEARCH
BY THE
OXFORD UNIVERSITY PRESS
AMEN HOUSE, LONDON
1963

CONTENTS OF VOLUME EIGHT

LIST OF ILLUSTRATIONS

Thanks are due to Mrs. W. J. B. Blake, Mr. S. A. H. Burne, Mr. R. G. Haggar, Mr. T. Pape, Mr. S. K. Smith, Mr. E. J. D. Warrillow, Miss Phoebe Wedgwood, the Trustees of the British Museum, the Trustees of the William Salt Library, Stafford, the City of Stoke-on-Trent Central Library, the City of Stoke-on-Trent Museum and Art Gallery, the Borough of Newcastle-under-Lyme Museum and Art Gallery, and the National Buildings Record for permission to reproduce paintings, drawings, photographs, maps, and other works or for the loan of prints and photographs; and to W. T. Copeland & Sons Ltd. for lending the block of the illustration facing p. 204.

LIST OF ILLUSTRATIONS

LIST OF MAPS AND PLANS

The maps have been drawn by G. R. Versey and are based on Ordnance Survey maps with the sanction of the Controller of H.M. Stationery Office, Crown Copyright reserved. The plans of workers' terraced housing on p. 115 were measured and drawn by M. Edwards.

EDITORIAL NOTE

This volume, the fourth in the Staffordshire series to appear, is, like its predecessors, Volumes IV and V, the outcome of a partnership between the University of London and a group of Local Authorities in Staffordshire. For some explanation of the nature of that partnership the reader is referred to the Editorial Note prefixed to Volume IV, published in 1958. The partnership has continued unaltered since that time, and the University of London takes pleasure in renewing its gratitude to the Staffordshire Local Authorities for their friendly co-operation. This gratitude is more specially due because the Authorities have meanwhile generously increased the scale of their grants.

Until early in 1961 the local editorial arrangements remained the same as they were in 1958, except that in 1960 Mrs. Barbara Young (*née* Donaldson) resigned her post on marriage. In 1961 Mr. M. W. Greenslade, then assistant local editor, was promoted local editor and Mr. J. G. Jenkins was given the title of associate local editor with a responsibility confined to the unpublished general volumes. At the same time Mr. D. A. Johnson was appointed assistant local editor. A second assistant local editor, Miss A. J. Kettle, was appointed in 1962. Mr. Jenkins retired at the end of 1962.

The present volume has greatly benefited from the generous assistance given by a large number of people. Among these particular mention should be made of Mr. G. J. V. Bemrose (formerly Curator of the Stoke-on-Trent Museum and Art Gallery) and his staff; Mr. H. Dibden (Chief Education Officer of Stoke-on-Trent) and his staff; Mr. N. Emery (Horace Barks Reference Librarian at the Stoke-on-Trent Central Library); Mr. M. B. S. Exham (Lichfield Diocesan Registrar); Mr. R. G. Haggar; Mr. J. G. Hall (Education Officer of Newcastle-under-Lyme) and his staff; Mr. D. G. P. Harnaman and Mr. P. J. Bemrose (successively curators of the Newcastle-under-Lyme Museum and Art Gallery); Mr. C. J. Morton (Town Clerk of Newcastle-under-Lyme); Mr. S. O. Stewart (Librarian of the University of Keele); and Mr. F. B. Stitt (Librarian of the William Salt Library, Stafford, and County Archivist) and his staff.

STAFFORDSHIRE
VICTORIA COUNTY HISTORY COMMITTEE

as at 1 January 1963

Mr. G. C. W. Jones, Chairman   *Representing the West Bromwich County Borough Council*

Alderman H. Barks, o.b.e., Vice-Chairman   *Representing the Stoke-on-Trent City Council*

Alderman John F. Amery, o.b.e.
Alderman F. A. Dale
Alderman T. A. W. Giffard, m.b.e.
Alderman H. J. Hall
Alderman Sir Alfred Owen, c.b.e.
Alderman F. J. Oxford
Councillor N. Bayliss   *Representing the Staffordshire County Council*
Councillor Miss G. Joules
Mr. S. A. H. Burne
Mr. J. S. Roper
Mr. H. V. Thompson
Mr. N. W. Tildesley

Alderman J. W. Clark   *Representing the Burton-upon-Trent County Borough Council*

Alderman F. W. Perry   *Representing the Smethwick County Borough Council*

Mr. K. D. Miller   *Representing the Stoke-on-Trent City Council*

Mr. A. Marshall
Mr. R. H. Malbon   *Representing the Walsall County Borough Council*

Alderman H. E. Lane
Councillor H. Bagley   *Representing the Wolverhampton County Borough Council*
Mr. F. Mason

Co-opted members

The Rt. Hon. the Earl of Harrowby, d.l.   Mr. P. Styles
The Rt. Hon. the Lord Stafford   Professor M. J. Wise, m.c.
Professor J. W. Blake   Mr. H. Wallace-Copland, Her Majesty's
Mr. F. B. Stitt   Lieutenant for Staffordshire

Mr. R. B. Pugh   Editor, *Victoria History of the Counties of England*

Mr. T. H. Evans, c.b.e., d.l.   Hon. Secretary

Mr. J. J. Green   Hon. Treasurer

Editorial Sub-committee

Mr. G. C. W. Jones   Professor S. E. Finer
Alderman H. Barks, o.b.e.   Mr. F. B. Stitt
Professor J. W. Blake   Mr. P. Styles
Mr. S. A. H. Burne   Professor M. J. Wise, m.c.

Mr. R. B. Pugh   General Editor

Mr. T. H. Evans, c.b.e., d.l.   Hon. Secretary

Mr. J. J. Green   Hon. Treasurer

LIST OF CLASSES OF DOCUMENTS IN THE
PUBLIC RECORD OFFICE
USED IN THIS VOLUME
WITH THEIR CLASS NUMBERS

Chancery
C 1 Proceedings, Early
C 2   ,,   Series I
C 3   ,,   Series II
C 60 Fine Rolls
C 66 Patent Rolls
C 78 Decree Rolls
Inquisitions Post Mortem, Series I:
C 133   Edw. I
C 135   Edw. III
C 137   Hen. IV
C 138   Hen. V
C 139   Hen. VI
C 140   Edw. IV and V
C 142   Inquisitions Post Mortem, Series II

Court of Common Pleas
C.P. 25 (2) Feet of Fines, Series II
C.P. 43 Recovery Rolls
C.P. 45 Remembrance Rolls

Ministry of Education
Ed. 7 Elementary Education, Public Elementary Schools, Preliminary Statements
Ed. 21 Elementary Education, Public Elementary School Files

Exchequer, Treasury of Receipt
E 34 Miscellaneous Books

Exchequer, King's Remembrancer
E 134 Depositions taken by Commission
E 150 Inquisitions Post Mortem, Series II

Exchequer, Augmentation Office
E 301 Certificates of Colleges and Chantries
E 308 Particulars for the Sale of Fee-farm Rents
E 317 Parliamentary Surveys

Ministry of Health
M.H. 13 General Board of Health and Local Government Act Office, Correspondence
M.H. 30 Poor Law Commission, Poor Law Board and Local Government Board, County Registers, Correspondence and Papers

Home Office
H.O. 45 Correspondence and Papers, Domestic and General, Registered Papers
H.O. 129 Various, Census Papers, Ecclesiastical Returns

Court of King's Bench (Crown Side)
K.B. 28 Crown Rolls

Duchy of Lancaster
D.L. 1 Equity Proceedings, Pleadings
D.L. 3 Depositions and Examinations, Series I
D.L. 4   ,,   ,,   Series II
D.L. 5 Equity Proceedings, Entry Books of Decrees and Orders, Administrative, Financial, &c.
D.L. 12 Warrants (under Privy Seal, &c.)
D.L. 14 Drafts and Particulars for Leases
D.L. 29 Ministers' Accounts
D.L. 30 Court Rolls
D.L. 42 Miscellaneous Books
D.L. 43 Rentals and Surveys

Special Collections
S.C. 6 Ministers' and Receivers' Accounts

Board of Trade
B.T. 6 General, Miscellanea

LIST OF CLASSES OF OFFICIAL DOCUMENTS
IN THE STAFFORDSHIRE RECORD OFFICE
USED IN THIS VOLUME
WITH THEIR CLASS NUMBERS

County Council
  CC/V   County Council, various.

Court of Quarter Sessions
  Q/AH   Highways and Locomotives (Amendment) Act, 1878.
  Q/APs   Police, police stations.
  Q/RHd   Highways, diversion, closing and widening.
  Q/RPl   Parliamentary Elections, land tax assessments.

Q/RRp   Religion, papists.
Q/RRr   Religion, recusancy rolls.
Q/RUm   Public Undertakings, plans of schemes.
Q/RUo   Public Undertakings, acts and orders.
Q/RUt   Public Undertakings, turnpike trusts.
Q/SB   Sessions Bundles, 1768 and after.
Q/SBe   Early Sessions Bundles, to 1767.
Q/SM   Sessions Minute Books.
Q/SO   Sessions Order Books, main series.
Q/SR   Sessions Rolls.

NOTE ON ABBREVIATIONS

Among the abbreviations and short titles used the following may require elucidation:

Boro. Mus.	Borough of Newcastle-under-Lyme Museum and Art Gallery.
C.J.	*Journals of the House of Commons.*
Coulam, *Newcastle*	J. T. Coulam, *History of Newcastle-under-Lyme* (Newcastle-under-Lyme, 1908).
Eve. Sentinel	*Evening Sentinel.*
G.R.O.	General Register Office, Somerset House.
H.C.	House of Commons.
H.L.	House of Lords.
H.Mus.	City of Stoke-on-Trent Museum and Art Gallery (at Hanley).
H.R.L.	Horace Barks Reference Library (at the City of Stoke-on-Trent Central Library, Hanley).
Ingamells, *Newcastle Dir.*	J. Ingamells, *Directory of Newcastle-under-Lyme with Historical Records of the Ancient Borough* (Newcastle-under-Lyme, 1871).
Jewitt, *Ceramic Art*	Ll. Jewitt, *The Ceramic Art of Great Britain* (1883 edn.).
L.J.	*Journals of the House of Lords.*
Lich. Dioc. Regy.	Lichfield Diocesan Registry.
Mankowitz and Haggar, *Eng. Pottery*	W. Mankowitz and R. G. Haggar, *The Concise Encyclopedia of English Pottery and Porcelain.*
Meigh, 'Staffs. Potters'	A. Meigh, MS. List of the Potters of the Staffordshire Potteries (at the Victoria and Albert Museum).
Pape, *Med. Newcastle*	T. Pape, *Medieval Newcastle-under-Lyme.*
Pape, *Tudor and Stuart Newcastle*	T. Pape, *Newcastle-under-Lyme in Tudor and Early Stuart Times.*
Pitt, *Staffs.*	W. Pitt, *A Topographical History of Staffordshire* (Newcastle-under-Lyme, 1817).
S.H.C.	Staffordshire Record Society (formerly William Salt Archaeological Society), *Collections for a History of Staffordshire.*
S.R.O.	Staffordshire Record Office.
T.N.S.F.C.	North Staffordshire Field Club, *Transactions.*
Trans. Birm. Arch. Soc.	Birmingham and Midland Institute: Birmingham Archaeological Society, *Transactions and Proceedings.*
U.C.N.S.	University College of North Staffordshire (now University of Keele).
W.S.L.	William Salt Library, Stafford.
Ward, *Stoke*	J. Ward, *The Borough of Stoke-upon-Trent* (London, 1843).
Warrillow, *Etruria*	E. J. D. Warrillow, *History of Etruria.*
Warrillow, *Stoke*	E. J. D. Warrillow, *A Sociological History of the City of Stoke-on-Trent.*

ANALYSIS OF SOURCES
PRINTED IN *STAFFORDSHIRE HISTORICAL COLLECTIONS*
AND USED IN THIS VOLUME

Vol.	*Pages*	*Subject-matter or title of article*
i	1–144	Pipe Rolls, 1130, 1155–89.
,,	145–240	Liber Niger Scaccarii, 1166.
ii (1)	1–177	Pipe Rolls, 1189–1216.
,,	177–276	Staffs. Deeds, 1072–*c.* 1237.
iv (1)	1–217	Pleas coram rege, de banco, and before itinerant justices, 1219–72.
,,	218–63	Final Concords, 1218–72.
v (1)	123–80	Pleas of the Forest, 1262–1300.
v (2)		Heraldic Visitations.
vi (1)	1–28	Stone Priory Cartulary.
,,	37–300	Pleas coram rege, de banco, and before itinerant justices, 1271–94.
vii (1)	1–192	Pleas coram rege, de banco, and before itinerant justices, 1293–1307.
,,	193–255	Subsidy Roll, 1327.
vii (2)		'History of the Swynnerton family.'
x (1)	1–78	Pleas coram rege, de banco, and before itinerant justices, 1307–26.
,,	79–132	Subsidy Roll, 1332–3.
xi	127–292	Final Concords, 1327–1547.
,,	293–336	Cartulary of Augustinian Priory of Trentham.
xii (1)	1–173	Pleas de banco and before itinerant justices, 1341–59.
,,	177–235	Final Concords, mixed counties including Staffs., 1492–1558.
xiii	1–204	Pleas de banco and before itinerant justices, 1360–87.
,,	207–300	Final Concords, 1559–73.
xiv (1)	165–217	,, 1573–80.
xv	1–126	Pleas de banco and before itinerant justices, 1387–1412.
,,	129–98	Final Concords, 1580–9.
xvi	1–94	Extracts from the Chester Plea Rolls, 1329–1411; pleas coram rege and before itinerant justices, 1385–1412, with Gaol Delivery Rolls, *c.* 1334–*c.* 1357, Indictments *c.* 1366, and Coroners' Roll 1–13 Henry IV.
,,	95–226	Final Concords, 1589–1603.
xviii (1)	1–21	,, mixed counties including Staffs., 1589–1602.
New Series i		'The Gresleys of Drakelowe.'
New Series iii	1–70	Final Concords, 1607–12.
,,	71–120	'Notes on earlier Swynnertons of Eccleshall and Chell.'
New Series iv	1–28	Final Concords, mixed counties including Staffs., 1603–25.
New Series vi (1)	1–60	,, 1616–18.
,,	89–162	Pleas coram rege and de banco, 1474–85.
New Series vii	191–236	Final Concords, 1619–21.
New Series viii		Second Register of Bishop Robert de Stretton, 1360–85.
New Series ix	1–241	Chancery Proceedings, 1558–79 (A–D)—arranged alphabetically under names of petitioners.
,,	245–68	'Parentage of Sir James de Audley.'
New Series x (1)	11–70	Final Concords, 1622–5.
,,	71–188	Star Chamber Proceedings, temp. Henry VII–VIII.
New Series x (2)		Lichfield Episcopal Register, *sede vacante* and Bishop Robert de Stretton, 1358–85.

NEWCASTLE-UNDER-LYME

NEWCASTLE-UNDER-LYME, a market-town and parliamentary borough in the northern division of Pirehill hundred,[1] is situated in the north-west of the county in the undulating country which forms the head-waters of the River Trent. The town grew up around the 12th-century castle which stood in an extensive tract of water fed by the Lyme Brook and other streams descending from the eastern and western ridges. It is on these ridges, rising to a height of 500 ft., that the ancient borough has expanded in modern times, more particularly on the escarpment of the eastern ridge in the direction of the Potteries. The land to the north of the town is also hilly, but towards the south there is a shallow valley through which the Lyme Brook flows to join the Trent at Trent Vale. Geologically Newcastle is situated on a wide strip of barren measures let down by the Apedale Fault, and therefore differs from the contiguous Potteries area.[2] These measures do, however, contain sandstone once used for building (e.g. St. Giles's church tower),[3] clays and marls, and ironstone, which have contributed to the town's economic development.[4] Coal is found principally in the areas to the north and west of the old town which were added to it in 1932.[5]

In earlier times the town was well supplied with streams, which have now mostly disappeared. The Lyme Brook itself is no longer observable in the urban area, but in the 1870's its course could still be followed for most of the way through the town.[6] The stream crossed the northern boundary of the old borough just south of Hempstalls, and, after passing under the old canal, itself formed part of that boundary for a short distance.[7] It continued its course between the east side of Liverpool Road and Hempstalls Lane, passed under the railway from Newcastle to Market Drayton behind a row of houses in Wilson Street, and then under land occupied in part by a timber yard. Subsequently it flowed, mainly through culverts, under Liverpool Road, Bridge Street, and Froghall and past the paper-mill in Holborn. Having entered a culvert by the pool side, it joined near the Pool Dam coalyard another stream running from Ashfield.[8] This stream, known as the Ashfield Brook, entered the town on Knutton Road and passed parallel with Silverdale Road to the south-west of the castle mound and under the road known as Pool Dam leading to the Higherland. The combined streams, thereafter known as the Lyme Brook, flowed by the Well Steps in a southerly direction to join the Trent, 2½ miles from the town.[9] Other streams from the Rotterdam to the west and Deansgate to the south helped to maintain the level of the castle pool in medieval times and could still be traced in the 1870's.[10]

The old borough consisted of 554 acres[11] and when the new parish of Newcastle was constituted in 1807[12] the parochial limits were made to coincide with the municipal boundary. On the east the town was bounded by the parish of Stoke, on the north and west by Wolstanton parish, and on the south by Trentham parish. On the north-west, however, a wedge-shaped area, representing a detached portion of Stoke parish, comprised the castle mound and pool and terminated just beyond Pool Dam, the extreme southern end of which was within the borough. Although under the Reform Act of 1832 this area was included in the parliamentary borough,[13] it was not until 1875 that this part of Stoke parish was added to the borough for municipal purposes.[14] In 1877 so much of the township of Clayton Griffith in Trentham parish as adjoined the municipal boundary, being the area now (1959) occupied by the cemetery and the isolation hospital, was also added to the borough, but an attempt at the same time to include a part of Wolstanton was unsuccessful.[15]

In 1901 an unsuccessful attempt was made to bring within the borough the rest of Clayton, Silverdale, parts of Keele, and Wolstanton, comprising in all 4,772 acres.[16] In 1921 small portions of Keele (26 acres) and of Clayton (217 acres) were added to the borough, though the corporation had wished to extend the boundaries to include, in addition, Wolstanton, Silverdale, and Chesterton.[17] In 1927 further parts of Keele and Clayton were incorporated.[18]

In 1932 a great extension took place, resulting in the absorption of Wolstanton, Chesterton, Silverdale, the rest of the parish of Clayton, and parts of Audley and Keele parishes.[19] The existing borough thus at a single stride extended its area to 8,882 acres.[20] Much of it consisted of collieries, brickworks, and tileries, and much of it of agricultural land, some of which has been absorbed by the housing development of the 1930's and of the period after the Second World War.[21] The borough is now (1959) bounded on the north by the Urban District of Kidsxxv.

[1] Until 1834 Newcastle was in the southern division of Pirehill hundred, but in that year, by order of Staffs. Quarter Sessions, it was placed, for legal purposes, in the northern division: *Staffs. Advertiser*, 26 April 1834.
[2] *V.C.H. Staffs.* i. 277.   [3] See p. 20.
[4] See p. 50.   [5] See p. 53.
[6] *Newcastle-under-Lyme Almanack, 1874* (copy in H.R.L.). In the borough as enlarged in 1932 (see below) a small section of the brook can still be traced in the area between Cross Heath and Hempstalls Lane.
[7] O.S. Map 6″ Staffs. xi SE., xvii SE. (1890).
[8] *Newcastle Almanack, 1874*. In his description the author called Lyme Brook Ashfield Brook and vice versa.
[9] Ibid.
[10] O.S. Map 6″ Staffs. xvii SE. (1890); R. Malabar, *Plan of Newcastle-under-Lyme*, undated but *c.* 1860.
[11] *Rep. Com. Municipal Corps.* H.C. 116, p. 1955 (1835),

[12] Stoke Rectory Act (1807), 47 Geo. III, sess. 2, c. 114 (local and personal).
[13] *Parly. Boundaries Act*, 1832, 2 & 3 Wm. IV, c. 64.
[14] Local Govt. Bd.'s Poor Law Prov. Orders Act, 1875, 38 & 39 Vic. c. 168 (local).
[15] Newcastle Corp. Act, 1877, 40 & 41 Vic. c. 172 (local and personal).
[16] *Representation to Min. of Health* (1919), re boro. extension (copy in Boro. Mus.).
[17] Min. of Health Prov. Order Confirmation (Newcastle Extension) Act, 11 & 12 Geo. V, c. 68 (local).
[18] Min. of Health Prov. Order Confirmation (Newcastle Extension) Act, 1927, 17 & 18 Geo. V, c. 47 (local).
[19] Min. of Health Order no. 75877, Boro. of Newcastle (Extension) Order, 1931.
[20] *Census*, 1931, Staffs.   [21] See pp. 37–38, 53.

grove, on the west by the parishes of Audley and Keele, on the south by Whitmore and Swynnerton parishes, and on the east by the city of Stoke-on-Trent.

The geographical and economic importance of Newcastle arises in the main from its position on the great trunk road which links London and Birming-

and then crossed the Cheshire border at Lawton. That part of the road between Tittensor and Talke had become so ruinous that in 1714 a Turnpike Act for its repair and maintenance was passed, and among the trustees were many Newcastle burgesses, including the mayor.[22] In 1735 the turnpike trust was renewed for a further term of twenty-one years and

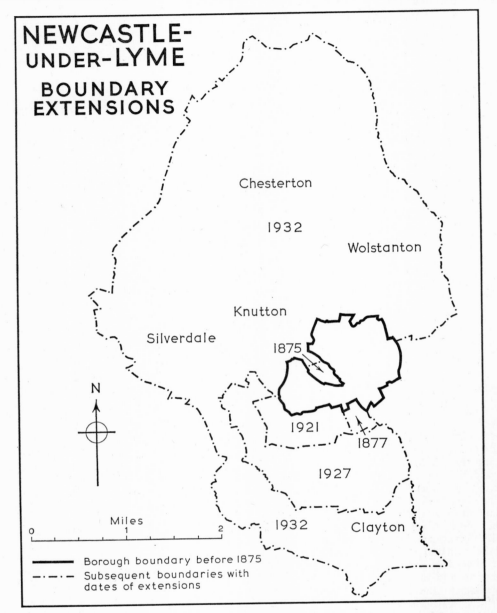

NEWCASTLE-UNDER-LYME
BOUNDARY EXTENSIONS

Chesterton
1932
Wolstanton
Knutton
Silverdale
1875
1921
1877
1927
N
1932
Clayton

Miles
0   1   2

———— Borough boundary before 1875
–·–·– Subsequent boundaries with dates of extensions

ham with Manchester and the North. It is also on the route from the north-east Midlands and the Potteries to Shrewsbury, Chester, and North Wales. No main railway passes through the town and its development has been to a large extent conditioned by the needs of road traffic on which its viability has largely depended.

In the early 18th century the post road from London to Lichfield, Chester, Liverpool, and the North ran through Newcastle to Talke-on-the-Hill

the trustees included the mayor, justices, and recorder of Newcastle.[23] When provision was made for further renewal in 1752, the town clerk was added to the list of trustees.[24] In this way Newcastle was strongly represented on the managing body of the road.

By the middle of the century the town had become the terminal point of five other roads, three of them passing through the growing Pottery towns. The first was the Newcastle–Leek road passing through

[22] *Statutes of the Realm*, ix. 995–9.
[23] Tittensor Turnpike Act, 1735, 8 Geo. II, c. 5.

[24] Tittensor Turnpike Act, 1752, 25 Geo. II, c. 16.

Wolstanton and Burslem; the second went through Cobridge and Sneyd Green before joining the Newcastle–Leek road at Endon; the third, the Newcastle–Uttoxeter road, linked Stoke, Fenton, and Longton with the town.[25] On the southern side two roads existed, one through Seabridge, Whitmore, and Drayton in Hales to Shrewsbury, and the other through Keele, Madeley, and Woore to Chester.[26] In 1823 or shortly afterwards a new road was constructed from Blackfriars Road (known as Victory Place in the early 1830's[27]) to Clayton, Beech, and Eccleshall.[28]

Until 1763 the flint and clay used in china manufacture, after being landed at Liverpool or Chester, was brought in via Lawton and the turnpike road to Newcastle, whence it proceeded by way of Wolstanton to Burslem and the other Pottery towns. The manufacturers were obliged to use the same roundabout route in the reverse direction for their finished goods. In that year authority was obtained for the creation of a new road from Lawton to Burslem, despite the opposition of Newcastle Corporation which was naturally concerned to preserve the monopoly of the Talke to Tittensor turnpike.[29]

In 1759 the Newcastle–Uttoxeter road was turnpiked and access to the seaport of Hull was thus made easier for the pottery manufacturers.[30] In 1779, as a result of an extension of the Tittensor–Talke road, it became possible to journey from London to Stoke, Burslem, and other places in the Potteries on turnpike roads without touching Newcastle.[31] With the opening of the Trent and Mersey Canal in 1777[32] yet another means of communication became available to the Pottery towns, so that by the end of the century Newcastle had ceased to play an important part in the economic life of the Potteries. It however still retained its importance as a market and coaching town, to which its road system largely contributed. Even the disappearance of the stage coach in the 1830's did not materially weaken its economic status as a marketing centre for a large rural area.

Newcastle was not walled in the Middle Ages. The early settlers no doubt relied on the castle for protection, and it may be that their habitations grew up originally within the outer bailey of the castle. The sites and names of Upper Green and Lower Green give some support to the possibility, and the open character of the former suggests further that it was the site of a primitive market.[33] The medieval church of St. Giles on its hill above the castle provided another focal point of settlement. A guildhall, presumably in High Street, existed at the end of the 13th century[34] and the street itself is definitely mentioned in 1326,[35] while Lower or Nether Street is met with in 1316.[36] Penkhull Street, the main entrance to the town from the south, appears at least by 1450[37] as also does Dog Lane, which traversed Merrial Street and the Ironmarket;[38] the latter was in existence by the middle of the 14th century.[39] Its width and that of High Street may indicate market sites. At the eastern end of the Ironmarket marshland, The Marsh of later times, and a large expanse of water known as Colleswaynes Lake[40] effectively prevented the development of the town in an easterly direction during the Middle Ages.

From a rental of 1608,[41] compiled to exhibit the chief rents payable to the borough, it appears that at that date the greatest number of houses were to be found in High Street, closely followed by the Ironmarket and Lower or Nether Street, with a substantial number in Penkhull Street. Other streets named in the rental, but containing only a small number of houses, were Bridge Street, Merrial Street, The Green, and Salters Lane—the last known as Hickman Street since at least 1875.[42] It seems, therefore, that by the beginning of the 17th century most of the town population had moved away from the low-lying neighbourhood of the castle to the higher ground to the east.

In August 1636 Henry, Earl of Huntingdon, passed through Newcastle and noted it as 'a long town, the street [presumably High Street] very broad, ill paved and houses poor thatched and very few either tiled or slated'. He thought the Guildhall 'a fair reasonable town house', but the church 'neither fair nor handsome'.[43] A plan made in 1691 shows the town to be compact and small, with most of the streets identifiable with their modern equivalents and with the market cross apparently sited in the middle of the High Street.[44]

For most of the 18th century the street plan was not significantly changed owing in the main to the existence of the circumambient open fields. In one direction, however, within the eastern sector of the old borough boundary, a measure of planned development was achieved. In 1782 the first steps were taken to reclaim The Marsh by enclosing its 23 acres of waste land described as being in a ruinous state.[45] As a result of the operations of the Marsh Trust the waterlogged area at the eastern end of the Ironmarket was drained to become the existing Nelson Place, from which new streets radiated eastwards and southwards. On the east were Queen Street, King Street, and Brunswick Street, and on the south Bagnall Street, now (1959) Barracks Road. By 1818 all these streets were in existence, as also was Water Street, linking the eastern ends of King and Brunswick Streets, and occupied for most of its length by a large brewery.[46] By 1834 Hanover Street, joining Queen Street with Hassell Street and traversing

[25] See pp. 83–84, 108–9, 177–8, 208, 228.
[26] *New Map of Staffs.* (1747). Printed for Jas. Smith, bookseller, Newcastle; see p. 76.
[27] T. Hargreaves, *Map of Staffs. Potteries and Newcastle* (1832), reproduced facing p. 5.
[28] See p. 76.
[29] Act for repairing road from Lawton to Burslem and Newcastle, 3 Geo. III, c. 45; *S.H.C.* 1934 (1), 65–72.
[30] Uttoxeter Turnpike Act, 1759, 32 Geo. II, c. 60.
[31] Tittensor Turnpike Act, 1779, 19 Geo. III, c. 119; *S.H.C.* 1934 (1), 72.
[32] Coulam, *Newcastle*, 143.
[33] See p. 46.
[34] Pape, *Med. Newcastle*, 142.
[35] *S.H.C.* 1913, 233.

[36] Ibid. 232.
[37] B.M. Add. Ch. 53619.
[38] S. Jackson, *Plan of Newcastle-under-Lyme, 1815* (copy in H.R.L.); Pape, *Tudor and Stuart Newcastle*, 241. By the beginning of the 19th cent. the name had been changed to Fog Lane: Parson and Bradshaw, *Dir. Staffs.* (1818).
[39] Pape, *Med. Newcastle*, 127.
[40] Ibid. 157.
[41] Pape, *Tudor and Stuart Newcastle*, 236–42.
[42] O.S. Map 6″ Staffs. xvii SE. (1890).
[43] Hist. MSS. Com. *Hastings*, iv. 338–9.
[44] See plate facing p. 8.
[45] See p. 50 and Malabar's *Plan* for the area of the Trust property.
[46] Parson and Bradshaw, *Dir. Staffs.* (1818).

King Street and Brunswick Street, had been constructed.[47]

Until the end of the 18th century the main thoroughfare of the town was not, as might have been expected, the High Street. The highway from Stone and the South entered the town at Stubbs Gate and then proceeded along Goose Street, Lower Street, Holborn, Lower Green, and Upper Green, and thence to the road to Congleton and the North.[48] This route effectively by-passed the centre of the town, where trade was concentrated, the markets were held, and the principal coaching inns situated. After the Improvement Act of 1819[49] the main thoroughfare was re-routed by constructing London Road at the southern approach to the town and Liverpool Street (later Road) at the northern exit, and by 1826–7 the reconstruction had been completed.[50] Thereafter, in the next fifty years, many buildings, chiefly working-class houses, were put up along and behind these two roads.[51]

The Inclosure Act of 1816 also affected the geographical development of the town.[52] The portions of the old open fields allotted to the burgesses in so far as they lay within the old municipal boundary were to the north and west of the town, with a smaller section to the south-east. No building development could take place on these extensive tracts of land[53] so long as the pasture rights of the burgesses remained intact, and although the 1859 Act[54] empowered the trustees of the burgesses to grant building leases, they were loth to do so. In the mid-1870's much of this burgess land was allotment gardens, and this description still remained true in the late 1920's.[55] In those parts of the town where inclosure had taken place the opportunity was seized to lay down streets and build houses, and this was particularly true of the north-east quarter. From the mid-19th century the high ground known as The Brampton was developed as the main residential quarter for the professional classes of Newcastle, and many of the villas then built in spacious grounds still survive, though not now occupied in most instances as dwellings.[56]

During the earlier 19th century when the population of the town doubled[57] some fifty new streets, most of them consisting of small working-class dwellings, were constructed.[58] Most of this new development was concentrated in the Liverpool Road area and eastwards from Marsh Parade to the borough boundary.[59] The latter includes the area between George Street and Mount Pleasant, where the layout of the narrow streets, named after the Royal Dukes, was on the gridiron plan.[60] The scheme had been started by 1832[61] and was evidently intended as a small self-contained unit with shops and public houses at the street corners and a market-place in the centre. The buildings were almost entirely demolished in 1958. At a slightly earlier period streets of working-class houses were also laid out in the Higherland, particularly on the northern side.[62] During the 20th century the inhabited area of Newcastle has greatly expanded, particularly since the extension of the borough in 1932. In recent years two major alterations in the centre of the town may be mentioned. For centuries the western end of the Ironmarket had been almost blocked by two large buildings, allowing access to High Street by two narrow lanes, Lad Lane and New Street, but shortly before the outbreak of the Second World War these were removed and an adequate junction with High Street secured. Also at the southern end of High Street buildings have been removed to achieve greater width in the main highway from the South and a more impressive approach to the town.

Changes in street names came into force on 1 January 1954. The principal street through the town from London Road in the south to Liverpool Road in the north had hitherto consisted of Penkhull Street, Market Square, High Street, Red Lion Square, and part of Bridge Street. The whole length of this thoroughfare was renamed High Street and the properties fronting on it were renumbered accordingly. At the same time lower Penkhull Street was included in Brook Lane, Merrial Street was extended to Nelson Place, eliminating the former Marsh Street, and Barracks Road was continued northwards to include Bagnall Street.[63]

The increase in population and the extension of the built-up area emphasized the need of open spaces for public recreation. Under the Inclosure Act of 1816 5 acres were allotted in The Brampton and The Stubbs to be converted into public walks by the trustees for the burgesses and maintained by them.[64] The Town Walks, as they were denominated in the Act, were to be laid out into broad footpaths with a plantation of trees and shrubs on each side.[65] Brampton Walks (now [1959] known as Station Walks) and Stubbs Walks were vested in the corporation in 1835.[66] In 1877 Stubbs Walks, part of which extends across the city boundary of Stoke-on-Trent, were enlarged,[67] and ten years later the borough council erected a bandstand there.[68] In 1897 about 4,000 sq. yds. of freehold land at the south-eastern end of the Ironmarket were bought by public subscription and vested in the corporation.[69] The area has been known successively as Queen's Garden[70] and Queen's Gardens.[71]

Public transport within the borough dates from 1882 when it was decided that the town should be

[47] Boro. Mus., Improvement Commrs.' Min. Bk. 1819–34, p. 190.
[48] *Newcastle-under-Lyme Almanack, 1874*; Coulam, *Newcastle*, 140.
[49] 59 Geo. III, c. 71 (local and personal).
[50] Imp. Commrs.' Min. Bk. 1819–34, pp. 93, 97.
[51] O.S. Map 6″ Staffs. xvii NE. (1890).
[52] See p. 49.　　　　[53] Malabar, *Plan*.
[54] 22 & 23 Vic. c. 103 (local and personal).
[55] O.S. Map 6″ Staffs. xvii NE. (1890); *Kelly's Dir. Staffs*. (1928).
[56] See p. 10.
[57] *V.C.H. Staffs*. i. 329.
[58] Lists of streets in Parson and Bradshaw, *Dir. Staffs*. (1818) and *Jones's Com. Dir. of Pottery Dist*. (1864).

[59] Malabar, *Plan*.
[60] Ibid.
[61] Hargreaves, *Map of Staffs. Potteries and Newcastle* (1832).
[62] Ibid.
[63] Ex inf. Boro. Surveyor's Office.
[64] 56 Geo. III, c. 33 (priv. act); see p. 49.
[65] 56 Geo. III, c. 33 (priv. act).
[66] *Representation to Local Govt. Bd*. (1901), re boro. extension, p. 17 (copy in Boro. Mus.).
[67] Ibid.
[68] *Kelly's Dir. Staffs*. (1936).
[69] *Repn. to Loc. Govt. Bd*. (1901), p. 7.
[70] Ibid.; Coulam, *Newcastle*, 147.
[71] *Newcastle Official Guide* [current edn.].

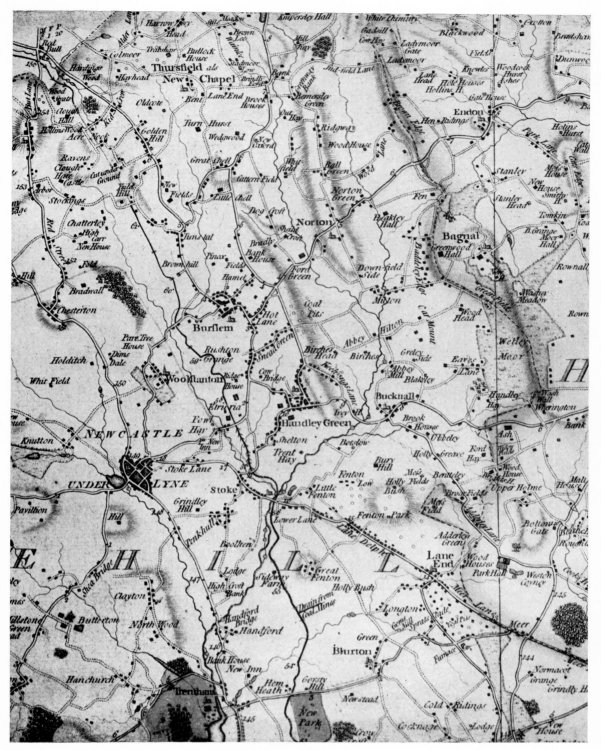

NEWCASTLE-UNDER-LYME AND THE POTTERIES

From a map of 1775 by W. Yates

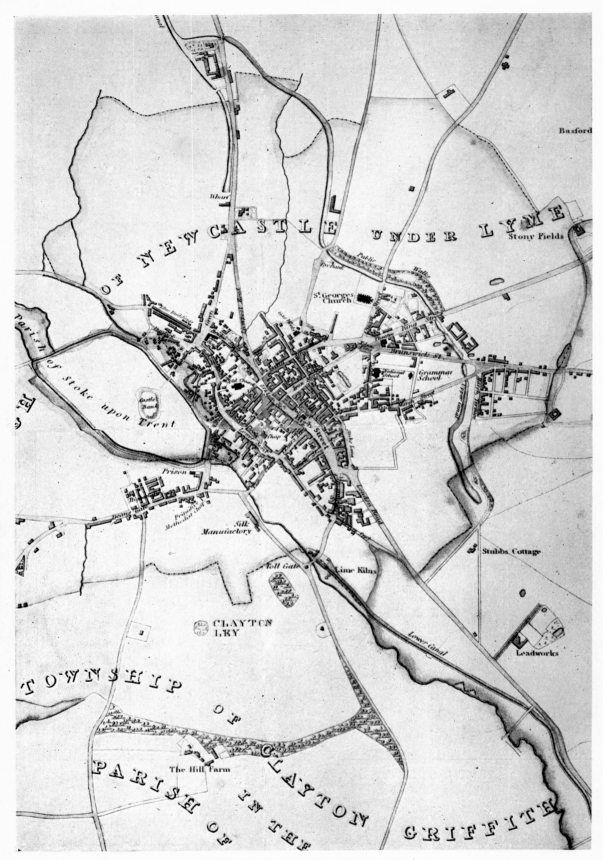

NEWCASTLE-UNDER-LYME
From a map of 1832 by T. Hargreaves

served by trams, though there was great division of opinion whether they should be horse-drawn or steam-driven.[72] The decision was in favour of steam with the result that the North Staffordshire Tramways Co. extended to Newcastle[73] the steam tramcar system already in operation in the Pottery towns.[74] One route entered the borough at the eastern end of Brunswick Street and then proceeded via Nelson Place, Ironmarket, New Street, High Street, and Penkhull Street to its termination in London Road. The second, from the junction in Nelson Place, followed a north-easterly course through Queen Street, Brampton, May Bank, Wolstanton, Port Hill, and Longport to Burslem. A third line went from Pool Dam to Silverdale.[75]

In 1886 the abandonment of the tramways was authorized, presumably in consequence of the substitution of electrical for steam motive power.[76] By 1901 an electric tram service was in operation over the old routes and also to Chesterton.[77] The trams were still running in 1926, though by then the Chesterton and Silverdale lines were being removed.[78] By 1928 the tramways had been abandoned and had been replaced by buses.[79] A bus station was erected at The Beeches, Liverpool Road, in 1932.[80]

Very little information about the population of Newcastle is available before the 19th century. In 1327 a tax on movables was paid by 50 inhabitants, those possessing goods worth less than 10s. and the women and children being exempt.[81] Five years later another tax list shows 55 payers on movable goods, the exemption limit on this occasion being 6s. instead of 10s.[82]

In 1563 a Lichfield episcopal return gives the number of households in the town as 78.[83] The rental of 1608[84] probably lists most houses, mentioning about 150. In February 1641/2 289 male inhabitants of Newcastle of the age of eighteen and upwards[85] took the Protestation Oath.[86] The Hearth Tax return of 1666[87] provides a list of 279 householders, 175 chargeable to tax and 104 exempt. The Compton Census of 1676,[88] supposedly restricted to persons aged sixteen and over, gives an estimate of 1,000 conformists and 5 nonconformists in Newcastle.

During the 19th century the population steadily increased. In 1801 it was 4,604 and this figure had been doubled by 1841. In 1891 the number of inhabitants was 17,805, nearly four times the 1801 figure.[89]

Since 1901 the population figures have been: 1911, 20,289; 1921, 20,549; 1931, 23,246; 1951, 70,036.[90]

When the boundary was extended in 1932 the distribution of the population was as follows: Newcastle municipal borough, 23,246 and the added areas, Chesterton, 6,861; Silverdale, 8,662; Wolstanton, 15,002; Clayton, 264; Keele (part of), 478; Audley (part of), 226; giving a total of 54,739.[91] The population was thus more than doubled, and by 1951, as a result of the development of housing estates, it had increased by a further 15,000. The distribution in 1951 was: Newcastle, 36,198; Silverdale and Knutton Heath, 4,773; Wolstanton, 16,275; Chesterton, 8,017; Knutton, 4,773.[92]

The position of the town on one of the main routes from London and Birmingham to Liverpool, Manchester, and the North inevitably led to its development as an important coaching station, especially towards the end of the 18th century when the growth of the industrial towns of the Midlands and the North stimulated the movement of passengers and goods. In the early years of the century there were probably no regular stage-coach services to and from Newcastle; in a 1707 list of stage-coach departures from London none was scheduled for Newcastle, though there is mention of a carrier leaving for the town each Monday.[93] By 1738 a wagon, carrying goods and passengers, was leaving Newcastle every Saturday for London, and in 1756 James Pickford was conveying goods and passengers weekly between London and Manchester via Newcastle.[94] By the end of the century six coaches, including two mail coaches, passed daily through the town on the London–Liverpool route and four on the Manchester–Birmingham route four days weekly. The Derby Fly on two days a week linked Newcastle with Lincoln through Uttoxeter, Derby, and Nottingham.

In the early 19th century coach services increased rapidly and the advent of the railway saw the stage-coach traffic at its peak. On 6 November 1830 no fewer than 29 coaches passed through Newcastle.[95] Thereafter coach travel rapidly declined and by 1838 the mail coaches had ceased to pass through the town.[96] But as late as 1839 the London–Manchester coach and the London–Liverpool coach were still stopping *en route* at the Castle Hotel. A coach also ran thrice weekly to Derby, but a notification in the same year that an omnibus called there at various hours 'on its way to the rails', i.e. to Whitmore station five miles distant, indicated that the horse-drawn long-distance coach was then almost obsolete.[97]

The first Newcastle canal was a small local affair. In 1775 Sir Nigel Gresley, Bt., and his son were empowered to make a canal from their coal-mines at

[72] *Newcastle Guardian*, 7 Jan. 1882.
[73] Ibid. 14 Jan. 1882.
[74] Tramway Orders Confirmation (No. 1) Act, 1881, 44 & 45 Vic., c. 105.
[75] Ibid.
[76] Tramway Orders Confirmation (No. 1) Act, 1886, 50 Vic., c. 10.
[77] *Repn. to Loc. Govt. Bd.* (1901), p. 13; N. Staffs. Tramways Act 1902, 2 Edw. VII, c. 229.
[78] *Representation to Min. of Health* (1926), re boro. extension, p. 17 (copy in Boro. Mus.).
[79] J. Wentworth Day, *Wheels of Service, The Story of P.M.T. 1898–1958* (copy in H.R.L.).
[80] *Staffs. Advertiser*, 23 Apr. 1932.
[81] *S.H.C.* vii (1), 205–6.
[82] Ibid. 81.
[83] Ibid. 1915, p. lxxii.
[84] See p. 3.

[85] *C.J.* ii. 389.
[86] H. of L. Rec. Office, H.L. Papers, 1641–2, Protestation Rets.
[87] *S.H.C.* 1921, 99–105.
[88] W.S.L., S. MS. 33.
[89] *Census*, 1891, Staffs.; *V.C.H. Staffs.* i. 329.
[90] *Census*, 1911–51, Staffs.
[91] Ibid. 1931, Staffs.
[92] Ibid. 1951, Staffs.
[93] J. Stow, *Survey of London and Westminster* (1720 edn.), ii, App. 142.
[94] *S.H.C.* 1934(1), 137.
[95] B.M. Add. MS. 36663, f. 558; and see White, *Dir. Staffs.* (1834) where the list differs slightly from that given in Allbut, *Newcastle and Pottery Dir.* (1822–3).
[96] Post Office map in *1st Rep. Sel. Cttee. on Postage*, H.C. (278), pp. 508–9 (1837–8), xx(1).
[97] I. Cottrill, *Police Dir. for Newcastle* (1839).

Apedale to Newcastle to feed the town with coal.[98] For a period of 21 years after the completion of the canal the coal was to be sold to the inhabitants of the town and of that part of the parish of Stoke-upon-Trent adjoining the Mill Pool at not more than 5s. per ton, and for a further term of 21 years at 5s. 6d. per ton. Since the beginning of the second term (in 1796) the price in fact had been raised to 6s. per ton.[99] By 1812 both Gresleys were dead and the coal-mines were nearly exhausted. In that year new arrangements were sanctioned.[1] Commissioners appointed under the Act were empowered to make by-laws rendered necessary by the 'great riots, injuries, and disturbances' that had arisen at the coal wharf over the delivery of the coal.[2] For six years from 31 July 1812 coal was to be supplied to Newcastle from the Bignall Hill Mines in Apedale at 7s. 6d. per ton and from Ham's Mines, also in Apedale, at 6s. per ton.[3]

When the Trent and Mersey Canal Bill was under consideration by the House of Commons in 1765, the borough petitioned for a branch to be constructed from the new canal to the town.[4] The attempt was unsuccessful, presumably for the geographical reason that the high ground between Stoke and Newcastle would have raised serious technical difficulties and the project would have been extremely costly. Thirty years later, however, the link with the Trent and Mersey Canal was effected when the Newcastle Canal Company was formed to make a canal from Stoke to Newcastle.[5] The new branch left the main canal at Stoke, turned southward and then westward at the end of the hill ridge between the two towns, and finally followed a northward course to its termination in Newcastle at the southern end of the present Brook Lane.[6] The canal was closed in stages after 1921.[7]

In 1797 the borough council approved a plan for the construction of a Junction Canal from the Newcastle or Lower Canal to pass through The Stubbs, The Marsh, and The Brampton to join Sir Nigel Gresley's canal 'near the house called the Gate',[8] and in the following year, an Act having been obtained,[9] the canal was cut.[10] The Act also authorized the cutting of a branch canal from Gresley's canal at Apedale to the coal and other works at Partridge Nest and Bignall End. The proprietors, among whom were Josiah Spode and Josiah Wedgwood, were empowered to erect a steam-engine for supplying the canal with water, while special powers were given to them to take the canal through The Marsh and to construct a wharf there; so long as Gresley's undertaking to supply the inhabitants of Newcastle with coal at a limited price persisted (see above), he was allowed to charge an extra 1½d. per ton for freight

in respect of coal sold at the wharf.[11] From its terminal point in Stubbs Field, now Stubbs Walks, near the top of Occupation Street, an inclined railway was made to link up with the head of the Lower Canal.[12] In this way direct canal communication was effected between the collieries to the west of Newcastle and the Pottery towns.

In 1846 the North Staffordshire Railway Company was empowered to construct a branch line from the main line near Stoke which was to end near the Silverdale Iron Works of Ralph Sneyd.[13] In 1849 and 1850 Sneyd, seeing no possibility that the Silverdale branch would be brought beyond Newcastle, constructed his own line from his ironworks to Pool Dam, and ten years later it was recognized as a public railway, under the name of the Silverdale and Newcastle Railway.[14] It was claimed that the establishment of the line had led to the erection of industrial plants and to a great increase in the population of Silverdale.[15] Half a mile to the south of the Pool Dam terminus was the head of the Newcastle Canal and it was natural that a junction between railway and canal should be sought. Accordingly, between 1850 and 1859 an extension railway was constructed by the canal company between the two points, the wagons containing coal, iron, and ironstone being drawn by horses.[16]

In 1852 the North Staffordshire Railway brought their line from Stoke via Newcastle to join the Silverdale and Newcastle Railway at Knutton Junction. For a quarter of a mile from Newcastle station the railway was laid on the bed of Robert Heathcote's canal (formerly Gresley's), which had been taken over by the N.S.R., and the goods yard at Newcastle was also made on part of the canal bed.[17] The passenger station in King Street was opened in September of that year.[18] In 1856 the Apedale branch from the Silverdale line was opened to serve important collieries to the north and north-west of the town.[19] In 1864 the canal company agreed to lease their canal and the canal extension railway to the N.S.R.,[20] which had already in 1860 become lessee of the Silverdale and Newcastle Railway.[21] In the same year the N.S.R. completed its control over the transport facilities in the Newcastle area by taking over the Audley mineral lines and obtaining power to lease Sneyd's railway.[22] In 1881 the N.S.R. obtained statutory authority for the removal of the restriction whereby horse haulage only should be used on the canal extension railway.[23]

In the initial stages of the construction of canals and railways the prime consideration had been to facilitate the transit of the heavy mineral traffic of the area, and it was not until 1864 that the needs of passengers were given some priority, apart from the

---

[98] 15 Geo. III, c. 16 (priv. act).
[99] 52 Geo. III, c. 77 (local and personal).
[1] Ibid.
[2] Ibid. For location of coal wharf, see Malabar's *Plan*.
[3] 52 Geo. III, c. 77 (local and personal).
[4] *S.H.C.* 1934(1), 113.
[5] 35 Geo. III, c. 87; see p. 179.
[6] T. Hargreaves, *Map of Staffs. Potteries and Newcastle* (1832).
[7] See p. 180.
[8] Boro. Mus., Corp. Order Bk. 1768–1800, f. 175b.
[9] 38 Geo. III, c. 29 (local and personal).
[10] *S.H.C.* 1934(1), 114.
[11] 38 Geo. III, c. 29.
[12] Coulam, *Newcastle*, 144.
[13] 9 & 10 Vic. c. 85 (local and personal).

[14] 22 & 23 Vic. c. 114 (local and personal).
[15] Ibid.
[16] Ibid.; 'Manifold', *N. Staffs. Rlwy.* 48.
[17] 22 & 23 Vic. c. 114; 'Manifold', op. cit. 48, and schedule between pp. 128 and 129.
[18] Ex inf. Brit. Rlwys., London Midland Region.
[19] 'Manifold', op. cit. 49.
[20] 27 & 28 Vic. c. 118 (local and personal).
[21] 23 & 24 Vic. c. 42 (local and personal).
[22] 'Manifold', op. cit. 53. Sneyd's Rlwy. was not the Silverdale and Newcastle Rlwy., but a second private line which Ralph Sneyd had been empowered to build (24 & 25 Vic. c. 66, local and personal) and which in conjunction with the Audley Mineral lines gave access to the mines round Talke.
[23] 43 & 44 Vic. c. 191 (local).

short line from Stoke to Newcastle. In that year the N.S.R. was empowered to extend the Silverdale line to Madeley and thence to Nantwich and Market Drayton and the London & North Western Railway.[24] A halt where the line crosses Liverpool Road was opened in May 1905 and is still in use.[25] The line has now (1959) been closed to passenger traffic except for the section from Stoke to Silverdale.

About 1911 a loop railway was projected to run from Trentham along the course of the old Newcastle Canal to connect with the Pool Dam branch.[26] The First World War held up construction and the project was finally abandoned in 1922.[27] All that had been built was a bridge carrying the line across the London Road and this was removed for scrap c. 1940.[28]

The earliest known post office in Newcastle is mentioned in 1734. It was then at the Swan Inn, the innkeeper presumably acting as postmaster.[29] Other postmasters are mentioned in 1771 and 1781.[30] In 1791 a post office is mentioned, though not its location.[31] By 1822 there was a post office in High Street opposite the Guildhall,[32] probably at no. 41 where in 1836 a postmistress was living.[33] In 1851 the post office was at 49 High Street[34] but by 1860 had been moved to Merrial Street.[35] Until 1854 Newcastle was the head post office of the whole of the Potteries district, but in that year the head office was transferred to Stoke.[36] From 1835 Tunstall, Burslem, Cobridge, Longport, Hanley, Shelton, Stoke, Longton, and Fenton were served by horse-posts from Newcastle, while foot-posts to Longton, Tunstall, and Cobridge were established in the same year.[37] In 1884 a new office was erected at the corner of High Street and the Ironmarket. By 1888 the old Merrial Street building had been demolished. By 1888–9 the office accommodation was increased by the addition of the adjoining shop, no. 1 High Street.[38] Since 1914 the General Post Office has stood at the eastern end of the Ironmarket.[39]

Apart from a royalist plundering raid in May 1644,[40] Newcastle was not subjected to any military assault during the Civil War, although North Staffordshire formed a narrow gap between the main royalist areas of the West and North which meant that defensive forces had to be concentrated in the neighbourhood of Stone and Newcastle.[41] The political excitement evoked by the Exclusion Bill produced a strong reaction in Newcastle where the corporation made it clear to the borough members of Parliament that they were in favour of disabling James, Duke of York, and all other Popish pre-

tenders.[42] In the reaction which followed the failure of the attempt to exclude James from the succession, Newcastle remained impenitent and was the only Staffordshire borough that did not present a loyal address.[43] In line with their attitude to the Exclusion Bill was the welcome given by the borough to the Duke of Monmouth when he toured the county in 1682. In September he visited the town where, it was reported to the government, 'his reception was above that at any other place . . . for the gentry and young freemen of the town all went on horseback out of town to meet him, and the mayor and aldermen and the rest of the town received him at the town's end on foot. The bells rang all night and many bonfires were made, but [no] wonder, for that town has ever been seditious and there are small hopes of amendment.'[44]

By 1715 Jacobite sympathizers were in control of the borough council, and in the riot of that year when the dissenters' meeting-house was burnt down[45] the authorities were thought to have dealt too leniently with the rioters. Henry Hatrell, a Newcastle attorney,[46] reported that 'the present mayor hath taken very poor bail for the rioters at Newcastle, all not worth £10, and I am told the said mayor charged the constables to take them before nobody but himself'.[47] This outburst of violence stirred the government to action, and the mayor and the two justices of the peace were arrested and detained in London for some months.[48] For the rest the borough seems to have concerned itself exclusively with its domestic affairs. If one can detect in its history a leaning towards reform and libertarian movements generally, it is perhaps worthy of remark that as early as 1863 the inhabitants petitioned the House of Commons in favour of votes for women.[49]

In 1930 the continuance of the borough as a separate entity was endangered by the promotion of the Stoke-on-Trent Extension Bill[50] which sought to incorporate Newcastle within the limits of that city. Despite strong local opposition—a postcard poll of the local government electors showed a majority of 97·84 per cent against the Bill—the measure was passed by the House of Commons,[51] only to be rejected by the House of Lords.[52] In recognition of their part in promoting opposition to the Bill the freedom of the borough was conferred on Lord Dartmouth and Col. J. C. Wedgwood (later Lord Wedgwood), M.P. for Newcastle.[53]

The best-known natives of Newcastle are Thomas Harrison, the regicide (1606–60), son of Richard Harrison (d. 1653), butcher and four times mayor,[54] and Philip Astley (1742–1814), the founder of the

[24] 27 & 28 Vic. c. 309 (local and personal).
[25] Ex inf. Brit. Rlwys., L.M.R.
[26] 'Manifold', op. cit. 114.
[27] 11 & 12 Geo. V, c. 117 (local).
[28] 'Manifold', op. cit. 114.
[29] Boro. Mus., Poll Bk., 1734.
[30] S.H.C. 1934 (1), 120.
[31] Univ. Brit. Dir. (1791), iv. 101.
[32] Allbut, Newcastle and Pottery Dir. (1822–3).
[33] Cottrill, Newcastle Police Dir. (1836).
[34] White, Dir. Staffs. (1851).
[35] Malabar, Plan.
[36] Warrillow, Stoke, 118.
[37] 1st Rep. Sel. Cttee. on Postage, H.C. 278, pp. 508–9 (1837–8), xx (1); H. Robinson, Brit. Post Office, A History, 216.
[38] Repn. to Local Govt. Bd. (1901), p. 12.
[39] Staffs. Advertiser, 29 Dec. 1914; and see p. 22.

[40] Cal. S.P. Dom. 1644, 177.
[41] S.H.C. 4th ser. i, p. lxv.
[42] S.H.C. 1920 and 1922, 152.
[43] Ibid.
[44] Cal. S.P. Dom. 1682, 416.
[45] See p. 56.
[46] T. Pape, Restoration Govt. and Corp. of Newcastle-under-Lyme, 52.
[47] B.M. Stowe MS. 750, f. 139a.
[48] Boro. Mus., Q. Sess. Min. Bk. 1664–1717, f. 158b.
[49] Petition in Boro. Mus.
[50] C.J. clxxxv. 156, 164, 373, 400.
[51] Ibid. 413.
[52] L.J. clxii. 455.
[53] Staffs. Advertiser, 4 Oct. 1930.
[54] D.N.B.; Sir Chas. Firth, 'Life of Thos. Harrison' (Proc. of American Antiquarian Soc. (1893), iv, no. 11), p. 123.

modern circus.[55] Newcastle has produced a few inventors of note. In 1713 Thomas Benson invented a flint-grinding machine which was supposed to obviate lung disease among pottery workers,[56] and Edward Massey (b. 1768) is known as the inventor in 1802 of the patent log for measuring the speed of ships.[57] A. W. Harrison, late-19th-century photographer, is credited with having produced the first X-ray photographs in this country.[58]

Joseph Mayer (1803–86), the antiquarian collector, was born at Thistleberry House, the son of Samuel Mayer, mayor in 1833. Although his major benefactions were made to Liverpool, where his extensive collections form part of the public museum, and to Bebington (Ches.) where he established a free library, his native town was not forgotten,[59] for he founded three university exhibitions tenable by pupils of the High School.[60] In 1882 he presented to the School of Art a good collection of drawings and prints of the old buildings of the town.[61]

BUILDINGS. By 1960 the almost wholesale demolition of buildings in Goose Street, Lower Street, Holborn, and the surrounding area had obliterated any traces, if such survived, of the early development of the town on the low-lying ground between the castle site and the High Street. Among houses still standing or partly demolished in this area, one or two are of the early 18th century. They include the Pomona Inn, which retains a brick façade of c. 1700 and a semicircular door-hood on carved brackets. It was also in this area, in Lower Street, that a house of Dominican friars, established by 1277,[62] stood. At the dissolution (1538) the domestic buildings included a hall called Kingsley Hall and 'the New Chamber'.[63] With some lands nearby they were granted in 1540 to John Smith, yeoman of the guard, with remainder to his son Richard for life.[64] In 1578 John Somer held them,[65] and in 1705 Ralph Beech of Newcastle.[66] At the second date they were decayed and had 'lately' been partly used for a kiln and malthouse. The foundations were discovered in 1870–1 when the cattle market was being constructed.[67] Further excavations in 1881 revealed some skeletons and a large sepulchral slab which was removed to St. Giles's churchyard.[68]

The only medieval domestic structure which has been found within the area of the ancient borough is the Star Inn on the south side of Ironmarket.[69] This is a timber-framed building consisting of a two-bay hall parallel with the street, the bays being divided by an open truss with chamfered timbers and an arch-braced tie beam. West of the hall is a two-storied cross wing, its ground floor now occupied by a shop.

The upper story probably contained the solar of the medieval house. Subsequent alterations to the building include an inserted ceiling to provide bedrooms in the upper part of the hall and a yard entry driven through its eastern bay. These may well have been made early in the 17th century. There are later brick additions at the back of the house.

In the Newcastle area timber construction appears to have been superseded by brick about the middle of the 17th century and there is no evidence that stone was in general use for early domestic buildings. It was said in 1911, however, that red sandstone from the demolished castle was to be found in the foundations of older houses, notably of the Lamb Inn in High Street,[70] rebuilt in 1925. Newcastle has always been noted for the number of its taverns and public houses, 65 being listed in 1839, exclusive of 32 beer-retailing establishments.[71] Several, of which early mention is made, have now disappeared, including the 'Angel' in High Street (in existence by 1569),[72] and the 'Eagle and Child' in Bridge Street (in existence by 1647).[73] By the 20th century nearly all the buildings in the town dating from before 1700 were, or had formerly been, licensed houses. Several were timber-framed structures but were not, except for the 'Star', known to incorporate medieval work. In High Street they include the 'Red Lion' (Penkhull Street), refronted with the adjoining house in the 18th century, and the Wine Vaults (Red Lion Square), much altered in both the 18th and 19th centuries. At the corner of Friars Street a timber-framed building, at one time partly occupied by the Market Inn, was demolished in 1958. Soon afterwards the 'Three Tuns' (Red Lion Square) was taken down, together with the adjoining shop on the corner of Church Street which had formed one of the two gabled cross-wings of the original building. The 'Three Tuns' first appears under this name in 1793,[74] although the building is much older, and it became one of the smaller coaching inns of Newcastle. Both the 'Old Bull's Head' and Hinds Vaults in Lad Lane, the latter facing High Street, are timber-framed buildings. Hinds Vaults has a double-gabled front, later faced with brickwork and given two projecting bay windows surmounted by cast-iron balustrades. These alterations were probably made in 1843, the date which appears on a barrel sign above the central doorway.[75] In 1960 the only timber building to retain something approaching its original front was the former 'Golden Ball' in High Street, formerly nos. 7 and 9 Bridge Street. This has an overhanging upper story and two gabled half-dormers. The Rainbow Inn on the east side of High Street, first mentioned by this name in 1851,[76] is a mid-17th-century brick structure with a later stucco frontage.

[55] D.N.B.
[56] Newcastle—Yesterday, To-day, Tomorrow (Knutton Co. Sec. Mod. Sch.), 12.
[57] Ibid.; Encycl. Brit. (1911 ed.), xvi. 864.
[58] Newcastle—Yesterday, To-day, Tomorrow, 12.
[59] D.N.B.
[60] Pape, Educ. End. of Newcastle-under-Lyme, 132.
[61] Newcastle Guardian, 15 Apr. 1882. The collection is now in the Boro. Mus.: ex inf. Principal, Newcastle Sch. of Art.
[62] Pape, Med. Newcastle, 65; Knowles and Hadcock, Med. Religious Houses, 186. An acct. of the house will be included in a later volume of V.C.H. Staffs.
[63] Letters re Suppression of the Monasteries, ed. T. Wright (Camd. Soc. 1843), 204; Pape, Med. Newcastle, 72.

[64] L. & P. Hen. VIII, xvi, p. 715; Pape, Med. Newcastle, 72.
[65] C 66/1169.
[66] W.S.L., H. M. Bourne papers.
[67] Pape, Med. Newcastle, 73.   [68] Ibid.
[69] The 'Star' in Ironmarket was an inn at least by 1734: Boro. Mus., Poll Bk. 1734.
[70] Staffs. Advertiser, 8 Apr. 1911.
[71] Cottrill, Police Dir. (1839).
[72] Pape, Tudor and Stuart Newcastle, 198.
[73] C 3/462, no. 4.
[74] Boro. Mus., Poll Bk. 1793.
[75] Boro. Mus., view of High St., &c. by J. Hulse (1800) showing the front before alteration; Jas. Hinds was the licensee by 1834: White, Dir. Staffs. (1834).
[76] White, Dir. Staffs. (1851).

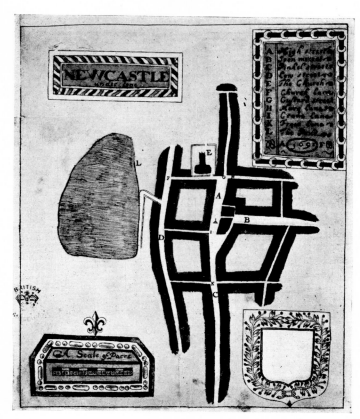

Plan, 1691

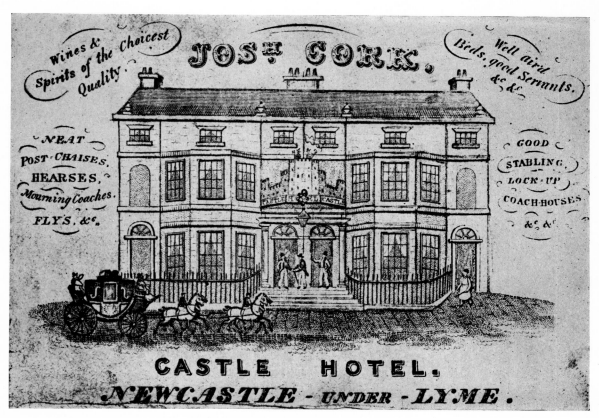

Advertisement of the Castle Hotel, 1839

NEWCASTLE

NEWCASTLE HIGH STREET, 1839

looking north-west

As the principal road through the town High Street contained several important coaching inns by the beginning of the 19th century. The most notable at this period was the 'Roebuck'[77] which Lord Torrington described in 1792 as the largest inn of the town but at the same time as 'one of the most savage, dirty alehouses' he had ever entered.[78] In 1839 the owner of the Castle Hotel opposite announced that he had acquired 'the horses, chaises, flys, hearses etc.' from the 'Roebuck's' late proprietor.[79] By 1842 the 'Roebuck' had closed,[80] but it appears to have opened again for a short period in the 1860's.[81] The building, which still stands on the west side of High Street, dates from the late 18th century and includes a large assembly room at the rear. Its three-story front, pierced by a carriage entrance, has been converted into shops and much altered. The Castle Hotel, the only coaching house to have survived until 1960, appears to have opened c. 1820,[82] but the building may be a little older. The stucco front of three stories has a central doorway flanked by large two-storied bay windows. The space between the bays on the first floor was formerly occupied by an elaborate castle sign.[83] An extension to the south of the building is of comparatively recent date.[84] Other coaching inns were the 'King's Head', the 'Three Tuns', the 'Woolpack', the 'Talbot', and the 'Globe'.[85] The 'Woolpack' stood at the junction of Red Lion Square and Lad Lane,[86] forming part of a block of buildings since reconstructed. A 'Talbot' is mentioned in High Street as early as 1608[87] and the coaching house was also there in 1851,[88] but the present inn of that name is a later building standing in Church Street. The 'Globe' first appears in Red Lion Square in 1834.[89] It was demolished c. 1898 when Globe Chambers, an early steel-framed building with an elaborate terra-cotta front, was erected on the site.[90]

In Ironmarket rather more than half the buildings are of the Georgian period. Most of these date from the end of the 18th century and have plain brick frontages of two or three stories. Many have the characteristic stone window lintels of the district, either with fluted keystones or with their moulded heads stepped up in the centre. There is less uniformity in High Street which contains a higher proportion of older buildings and where more reconstruction took place in the late 19th and the

20th centuries. Apart from the coaching inns there are several imposing late-18th-century houses. A good example is the building standing immediately south of the former 'Roebuck'. This has a brick front of three stories with a dentil cornice, a central pediment, and stone dressings to the windows. A later shop-front occupies the ground floor. A tall brick house on the east side of the former Penkhull Street was considerably altered when it became the National Provincial Bank early in the present century. It was originally known as 'Steps', the first house on the site being built by John Fenton in 1700-2.[91] The present building was a reconstruction by Thomas Fletcher soon after 1784.[92] Nos. 5 and 7 High Street (formerly 12 and 14 Bridge Street) have rainwater heads dated 1747 with initials 'I.B.' Modern shops have been inserted on the ground floor but the two upper stories are unaltered and the parapet retains four stone vases. Two other houses near the centre of the town have dated rainwater heads. The first, Bank House in the lower part of Bridge Street (1752), is a square detached brick house, now empty and derelict, said to have been the home of William Willett (d. 1778), a noted Unitarian minister and brother-in-law of Josiah Wedgwood.[93] The second, the Hawthorns in Merrial Street (1769 with initials 'W.B.'), has been occupied since c. 1874 by the Conservative Club,[94] together with the slightly later house adjoining it. Other 18th-century buildings in the town include the Unitarian Meeting House north-west of St. Giles's Church (1717),[95] the former Wesleyan Chapel above Lower Street (1790),[96] and the Albemarle Almshouses in Bridge Street (1743).[97]

The draining of The Marsh in the late 18th century was followed by development at the east end of Ironmarket,[98] and a rather hesitant attempt was made to provide a formal layout where the six roads radiate from Nelson Place. In 1787-8 the Royal Theatre was built by John Pepper[99] in the segment between King Street and Brunswick Street.[1] The building was converted into a cinema in 1910[2] and is now unused, but the remnants of a good frontage to Nelson Place can still (1960) be distinguished. This has a treatment of recessed panels and a central pedimented gable, flanked by ball finials. It bears a relief medallion of Shakespeare which has been attributed to John Flaxman.[3] A house of c. 1800 with an

[77] For much of the 18th cent. there were 2 inns of this name in Newcastle, sometimes referred to as the 'Old Roebuck' and the 'New Roebuck': Boro. Mus., Poll. Bks. 1734, 1774. Pape considers that the earlier 'Roebuck' was originally the 'Angel' and occupied part of the island site on the E. side of High St.: *Staffs. Advertiser*, 8 Apr. 1911. In 1785 the 'New Roebuck' was sold: W.S.L., H. M. Bourne papers.

[78] *Torrington Diaries*, iii. 127-8.

[79] Cottrill, *Police Dir.* (1839), 69.

[80] *Newcastle Election Petition*, H.C., p. 115 (1842), viii.

[81] *P.O. Dir. Staffs.* (1860, 1868); *Jones's Com. Dir. of Pottery Dist.* (1864); Malabar, *Plan*. The former Roebuck sign is now (1960) mounted on a pedestal outside the Trentham Hotel, Trentham.

[82] Allbut, *Newcastle and Pottery Dir.* (1822-3); the 'Castle' does not appear in Parson and Bradshaw, *Dir. Staffs.* (1818).   [83] See plate facing p. 8.

[84] Ibid.; Boro. Mus., photo of c. 1870 showing a low gabled building in this position.

[85] Allbut, *Pottery Dir.* (1822-3); White, *Dir. Staffs.* (1834); Cottrill, *Police Dir.* (1839).

[86] Boro. Mus., view of High St. by J. Hulse (1800); Corp. Order Bk. 1786-1833, 119.

[87] Pape, *Tudor and Stuart Newcastle*, 240.

[88] White, *Dir. Staffs.* (1851).

[89] Ibid. (1834).

[90] Date on building.

[91] W.S.L., D. 1788, P. 67, B. 5; *Staffs. Advertiser*, 8 Apr. 1911.

[92] F. R. Twemlow, *The Twemlows* (1910), 217; plans, &c. at Aqualate Hall.

[93] E. Meteyard, *Life of Wedgwood*, ii. 430-1. This house should not be confused with Bank House, Etruria, built for Thos. Bentley in 1767. The name Bank House refers to the elevated ground on which the house stands. For W. Willett see p. 64.

[94] *Kelly's Dir. Staffs.* (1880).

[95] For an acct. of the building see p. 64.

[96] See p. 59.

[97] See p. 71.

[98] See p. 3.

[99] T. Pape, 'Royal Theatre at Newcastle' (*Staffs. Sentinel Summer No. 1910*); see p. 54.

[1] See map facing p. 5.

[2] Town Clerk's Office, Boro. Counc. Min. Bk. No. VII.

[3] *Staffs. Advertiser*, 8 Apr. 1911; Meteyard, *Life of Wedgwood*, ii. 532, fig. 140.

impressive stucco front of five bays (now the borough treasurer's office) faces Nelson Place between Barracks Road and Ironmarket. In the tympanum of its central pediment is a niche containing a portrait bust of Lord Nelson. The segment between King Street and Queen Street is occupied by a three-storied red-brick terrace of early-19th-century houses and there are some dignified buildings of this date or a little earlier at the lower ends of both Queen Street and King Street. In particular no. 6 Queen Street (Public Health Dept.) has two good pedimented doorways, the more elaborate having Ionic columns and an enriched frieze with a pictorial panel in the centre. North of this is Brampton House, a square detached brick building of the early 19th century. On the north side of Ironmarket, between the Municipal Buildings and Nelson Place, are some well-designed early- and mid-19th-century brick frontages. The large detached houses on the high ground beyond Nelson Place date mostly from the mid- and late 19th century. Many are Italianate in style and there are several Gothic examples from the later period. On the west side of the town Thistleberry House, occupied in the 19th century by the Mayer family, was demolished c. 1955.[4] A three-storied brick tower in the grounds, erected by Samuel Mayer (d. 1838), was already ruinous by 1911 and the statuary and shell decorations which it contained had been mutilated.[5]

The chief public building is the Guildhall standing on an island site in the middle of the High Street. It was built shortly after November 1713 when the borough council decided to demolish the earlier hall,[6] which in the early 17th century seems to have been to the north of the present Guildhall.[7] In its original form it was a two-storied rectangular brick structure with a hipped roof and an external treatment of stone pilasters, surmounted by a cornice and a balustraded parapet. The upper story was carried partly on open round brick arches, four on the long and two on the short sides, and partly on three central pillars.[8] The space thus provided on the ground floor, approached at the south end by a flight of steps, was used as a provision market[9] until the covered market was built in Friars' Street in the mid-19th century.[10] Originally, too, in the centre of the roof there was a weatherboarded turret surmounted by a gilded globe and a weather vane.[11] About 1830 this arrangement was altered by the erection of a clock-tower containing two transparent dials, which were first lit by gas in 1833.[12] On top of the clock-tower slender pillars sup-

ported a cupola on which rested the globe and vane.[13] Until 1860 the upper room, which contains portraits of local celebrities, was used for meetings of the borough council and its committees, for Quarter Sessions courts, and also for public assemblies.[14] The full council still (1959) meets there. In 1860–2 the building was much altered in order to increase the accommodation and to provide a new court-room.[15] The ground-floor arches were bricked in and a semicircular addition was made to the north end of the hall. At the same time the balustraded parapet was altered, the roof cupola and clock were removed, while at the south entrance a high pillared portico was built surmounted by a tower and four-dialled clock, the gift of J. A. Hall, a former mayor.[16] Near this entrance the old stocks are said to have stood.[17] In 1877 a small room was built over the vestibule[18] and is now (1959) used as the mayor's parlour.

The Municipal Buildings (or Hall) in Ironmarket were built as a Golden Jubilee memorial in 1888–90,[19] to satisfy a long-standing demand for a large public hall.[20] The expanding town had outgrown the accommodation of the Guildhall, which in any case after 1862[21] was needed entirely for municipal purposes. The building covers the site of a house which in the early 18th century had been occupied by the Ford family,[22] one of whom, John, is said to have been a counsel defending Lord Lovat[23] (d. 1746)[24] at his trial. Subsequently, as no. 45 Ironmarket, Ambrose Astle, a surgeon, long lived in it.[25] It then passed successively to Arthur Leech, member of a well-known Newcastle family in the 1870's who renamed it Arlington House,[26] and to W. S. Allen, M.P. for Newcastle, who sold it to the corporation in 1887.[27] Designed in the 'Flemish' style by Sugden & Sons of Leek, J. Blood of Newcastle, and Snape & Chapman of Newcastle,[28] the lofty building is of red brick with stone dressings, with an adjacent clock-tower. The Ironmarket façade is adorned with life-size figures emblematic of architecture, painting, music, and literature.[29] Two rainwater heads, inscribed 'H.F. 1724', taken from Arlington House, have been built into the wall.[30] The ground floor contains a 'council chamber', originally designed for meetings of the borough council,[31] and the School of Art,[32] which in 1958 moved from the basement into the quarters evacuated by the public library.[33] In the large hall on the first floor are hung eighteen shields of arms of families associated with the borough, including those of Lord Cadman and Lord

[4] Ex inf. Boro. Surveyor's office.
[5] *Staffs. Advertiser*, 8 Apr. 1911.
[6] Corp. Order Bk. 1712–67, f. 3a.
[7] Pape, *Tudor and Stuart Newcastle*, 248.
[8] M.H. 13/132, containing ground plan and elevation of Guildhall in 1859.
[9] *Representation to Local Govt. Bd.* (1901), re boro. extension, p. 9; Ingamells, *Newcastle Dir.* 63.
[10] See p. 11.
[11] Corp. Order Bk. 1712–67, f. 129a. In 1741 freedom of the borough was conferred on Mr. Platt for undertaking to regild the globe and vane at his own expense (ibid.); the original turret is shown on the reproduction of a late-18th-cent. drawing at Boro. Mus.
[12] White, *Dir. Staffs.* (1834).
[13] J. Wedgwood, *Hist. of Wedgwood Family*, 100, reproducing an old print; W.S.L., Staffs. Views, p. 102 (b) (J. Buckler, 1840); see plate facing p. 9.
[14] White, *Dir. Staffs.* (1851).
[15] *Repn. to Local Govt. Bd.* (1901) re boro. extension, p. 9;

Staffs. Times and Newcastle Pioneer, 14 July 1860.
[16] *Newcastle Official Guide*; inscription on building.
[17] Coulam, *Newcastle*, 145.
[18] Ingamells, *Newcastle Dir.* 63.
[19] Boro. Mus., Fenton MS., Bk. 42.
[20] Ingamells, *Newcastle Dir.* 63.
[21] See above.
[22] Boro. Mus., Fenton MS., Bk. 42.
[23] Ibid. See *State Trials*, xviii, where a Mr. Ford is named among the defending counsel.
[24] *D.N.B.*
[25] Boro. Mus., Fenton MS., Bk. 42.
[26] Ibid.
[27] *Newcastle Guardian*, 11 Oct. 1890.
[28] Ibid. 7 July 1888.
[29] *Kelly's Dir. Staffs.* (1928).
[30] Boro. Mus., Fenton MS., Bk. 42.
[31] *Newcastle Guardian*, 7 July 1888.
[32] Ibid.
[33] See p. 53.

Wedgwood. The building also contains a tablet commemorating Samuel Mayer (d. 1838), mayor in 1833, removed from the Mayer Gallery, Bebington (Ches.), in 1892,[34] and a marble bust by Matthew Noble of George Granville, Duke of Sutherland (d. 1861), erected at Wall Grange Waterworks in 1863 and removed here in 1935.[35]

The Militia Barracks in Barracks Road off Hassell Street was built in 1855.[36] The buildings are of dark red brick and are arranged round four sides of a courtyard. The front range, facing the street, is of two stories with a three-story tower at each angle. The windows have stone mullions and round-headed lights. The central archway, leading to the courtyard, is surmounted by a small machicolated turret. Until 1880 the barracks was the headquarters of the 3rd King's Own Staffordshire Rifle Regiment which assembled annually at Newcastle for training.[37] In 1882 the building was bought by W. H. Dalton, a major in the Staffordshire Rangers Volunteers,[38] and was settled in trust for use by the Rifle Volunteers of Newcastle.[39] In 1907 the Volunteers were replaced by the Territorial Force and in 1925 the corporation became trustees.[40] During the Second World War the premises were let and in 1952 a scheme, known as the Barracks Trust, was drawn up whereby the barracks was to be used by the Territorial Army as required; otherwise it was to be used or let by the corporation for the benefit of the borough.[41] Part of the building is now (1959) occupied by Remploy Ltd.

The Covered Market, designed by R. Chapman of Newcastle,[42] was built in 1853–4 on the site of the Crown Inn and some small cottages.[43] Its principal front was in Penkhull Street (since 1954 incorporated in High Street)[44] and the building extended down the steep incline of Friars' Street in three divisions separated by flights of steps. It is built in the 'Tudor' style of red brick, chequered with blue, and has dressings of Hollington stone. The front building, or first division, is of three stories and is surrounded by a castellated parapet. The ground floor is occupied by two shops and between them is the entrance to the market proper; the first and second floors are occupied by offices.[45] The first and second divisions are still (1960) used,[46] but the third, approached from Friars' Street by a cart entrance,[47] did not long persist. It was subsequently used as a riding school and by c. 1930 had been converted into a roller-skating rink.[48] It is now (1960) a corporation garage.

The medieval market cross was restored in 1579 by Randle Bagnall, mayor.[49] During the Interregnum banns of marriage were proclaimed at the market cross[50] and the Wolstanton Parish Register records the publishing of banns there on three successive market days.[51] In 1691 it stood in the centre of High Street, opposite the end of Ironmarket,[52] probably on its original site. By 1820 the five circular stone steps forming the base of the cross had been moved to the north end of the Guildhall, and in that year a lamp standard was erected above them.[53] This consists of a Roman Doric column, raised on a square pedestal and surmounted by a wrought-iron bracket carrying two lamps.

The Weights and Measures Office, a small octagonal stone structure of one story, was erected in High Street to the south of the Guildhall in 1835.[54] It had a low-pitched octagonal roof surmounted by a lamp. Its erection involved the removal of a stone pillar from the site to the centre of Red Lion Square.[55] By 1877 the building itself had been removed to Red Lion Square[56] but in 1926 it was demolished.[57] The Weights and Measures Office is now (1960) at 22 High Street.

A bronze statue of Queen Victoria stands in front of the former Royal Theatre in Nelson Place. It was presented by Sir Alfred Seale Haslam, M.P. (mayor of the borough) and unveiled by Grand Duke Michael of Russia in 1903.[58]

CASTLE. The New Castle below the elm forest[59] on the border between Cheshire and Staffordshire seems to have been originally a royal castle and included in the royal manor of Trentham.[60] Evidence for the close association between Newcastle and Trentham is found in the Worcestershire Pipe Roll of 1154–5 where William de Beauchamp as sheriff accounts for £15 as the farm of Newcastle for a half-year and in the following year for £30 as the farm of Trentham, suggesting that Newcastle was then included in the vill of Trentham.[61] Moreover, a Trentham Priory charter of 1162 refers to *quid(am) viculus Novi Castelli qui est de territorio parochie de Trentham*.[62] The date of the construction of the castle and the reason for the appellation 'new' are not precisely known. The earliest evidence of its existence is contained in a charter of Stephen, assigned to the year 1149,[63] in which the king granted to Ranulf de Gernon, Earl of Chester, among other lands and lordships, the *novum castellum de Staffordshira* with all its appurtenances[64] and it is reasonable to surmise, therefore,

[34] Inscription on tablet.
[35] Information on monument.
[36] *Keates's Potteries Dir.* (1882–3).
[37] Ibid.   [38] Ibid.
[39] Char. Com. Files.
[40] Ibid.
[41] Ibid.
[42] *Keates's Potteries Dir.* (1882–3).
[43] Boro. Mus., Boro. Council Min. Bk. 1844–55, pp. 326, 378.
[44] See p. 4.
[45] *Keates's Potteries Dir.* (1882–3).
[46] See p. 46.
[47] *Keates's Potteries Dir.* (1882–3).
[48] Inf. from Boro. Surveyor's Office.
[49] Pape, *Tudor and Stuart Newcastle*, 203.
[50] Coulam, *Newcastle*, 117.
[51] *Wolstanton Par. Reg.* (Staffs. Par. Reg. Soc.), i, p. xii; S. W. Hutchinson, *Archdeaconry of Stoke-on-Trent* (1893), 14. The Newcastle register provides one example in Jan. 1650: *Newcastle Par. Reg.* i. 112.

[52] See plate facing p. 8.
[53] Tablet on base. In 1841 it was restored at a cost of £40, said to have been forfeited by a transported felon: White, *Dir. Staffs.* (1851).
[54] See plate facing p. 9.
[55] *Staffs. Advertiser*, 2 May 1835.
[56] It is shown S. of the Guildhall in mid-19th-cent. views and in a photo. of c. 1870 (Boro. Mus.) but not in subsequent views: *Staffs. Times*, 7 June 1877.
[57] Photo. of demolition at Boro. Mus.
[58] Inscription on base of statue.
[59] E. Ekwall, *Oxford Dict. of Eng. Place-Names* (1960).
[60] *V.C.H. Staffs.* iv. 26.
[61] *Red Bk. Exch.* (Rolls Ser.), 656, 662.
[62] *S.H.C.* xi. 303; and see Pape, *Med. Newcastle*, 33 sqq.
[63] *E.H.R.* x. 89. See also *Registrum Antiquissimum* (Lincoln Rec. Soc. xxvii), i. 288, for a text of Stephen's charter, and Pape, *Med. Newcastle*, 1, 2, for a discussion of the dating.
[64] J. Tait, *Med. Manchester*, 136–74.

that a castle existed in the early 12th century. The reference in this charter to the new castle of Staffordshire has led one authority to put forward the view that the castle was built to replace, as the seat of royal power in the county, the castle at Stafford which by the middle of the 12th century had declined in strength and military importance.[65] Another theory assumes the existence of an older castle, of which there is some slight archaeological evidence, in Trentham itself and its replacement, possibly for strategic reasons, by a new stronghold some three miles to the north-west.[66]

The Earl of Chester's possessions were confirmed to him by Henry son of the Empress in the 'Treaty of Devizes' of 1153,[67] but Ranulf died the same year, leaving a son Hugh, a minor.[68] After Ranulf's death the castle appears to have remained with the Crown for many years.[69] In 1190–3 it was held by the sheriff *ut custos*.[70] In 1215 King John conferred it with the manor on Ranulf de Blundeville, Earl of Chester, Hugh's son, in tail, to be held as 1 knight's fee.[71] After the earl's death without issue in 1232,[72] the castle and manor were granted in fee-farm in the same year to Gilbert de Segrave at £20 yearly.[73] In June 1234 Gilbert's father, Stephen de Segrave, was directed to ensure that his son surrendered them because they were necessary for the 'march' between England and Wales and the land of Chester.[74] In the following month the king appointed Adam Esturmy as keeper of the castle.[75] In 1238 the castle and manor were granted to Henry de Audley at a yearly rent of £68 18s. 2½d.,[76] after an inquiry into their value conducted in the same year.[77] On Henry's death in 1246 the keepership was granted to Hugh de Frodsham, a king's serjeant,[78] who in 1250 was directed to hand over the town and castle to James de Audley to be farmed yearly at £80.[79] In 1264 the king and his eldest son Edward granted Newcastle,[80] among other manors, to Simon de Montfort, Earl of Leicester, the grant being confirmed on 20 March 1265,[81] but on 4 August following the earl was killed at Evesham.[82]

Newcastle, including presumably the castle and manor, was granted by Henry III in 1267 to his younger son Edmund, created Earl of Lancaster.[83] Thomas, son of Earl Edmund, succeeded to the castle and manor in 1296, but was executed for treason on 22 March 1322.[84] His widow, Alice, daughter of the Earl of Lincoln, thereupon received the manor, castle, and borough in dower,[85] which she held until her death in 1348.[86] Henry, Earl of Lancaster (created Duke in 1351),[87] succeeded and when he died in 1361[88] his numerous possessions were partitioned between his two daughters, the elder, Maud, wife of William, Duke of Bavaria, receiving *inter alia* the castle and manor[89] at a yearly rent of £86 13s. 4d.[90] After Maud's death in 1362,[91] her estates passed to her sister Blanche, the wife of John of Gaunt, who held them in right of his wife until his death in 1399.[92] In 1361 or 1362 the estate was leased to Sir Godfrey Foljambe for life at £127 yearly, with provision for a reduction by £7 if the issues did not amount to that sum, and for a further reduction if the tenants of the mills withheld their farm. Foljambe was to maintain the buildings and received an allowance of timber for so doing.[93] The lease was surrendered in 1374, and Foljambe, who died two years later,[94] was compensated with a pension of £40 out of the issues.[95]

With the accession of Henry IV the importance of the castle as a royal stronghold seems to have progressively diminished. Its situation on low-lying ground surrounded by hilly country had rendered it peculiarly vulnerable to the new methods of siege made possible by the invention of gunpowder and the development of artillery. Moreover, during this period Tutbury castle seems to have been the principal seat of Lancastrian power in the county. The result was that the military importance of Newcastle, and consequentially expenditure on its upkeep, declined.[96] With the advent of the Tudors, neglect led rapidly to the deterioration and ultimate destruction of the fabric, so much so that when Leland passed through Newcastle about 1541 he recorded that 'al the castel is doune save one great toure'.[97]

Constables of the castle met with during the medieval period include Hugh de Cha(r)nia, 1250;[98] Hugh de Frodsham, 1251;[99] William de Fenton, 1253;[1] Richard Aubyn, Robert le Venur, Adam de Lavendene (all *temp.* Edward I);[2] Roger de Tissington, 1318;[3] Stephen de Yrton, 1342;[4] John de Rocheford, 1356;[5] Walter de Staunton, 1374;[6] Oliver de Barton, 1374 (also steward of Newcastle);[7] Sir John Blount, 1408 (also steward);[8] John Kyngeley, 1420; Robert Whitgreve, 1438; Edward Ellesmere, 1447; Ralph Wolseley, 1461; Hugh Eggerton, 1474; Sir John Savage, the younger, 1485.[9]

At some unknown but very early date the defence

[65] *V.C.H. Staffs.* iv. 26.
[66] S. A. H. Burne, 'The site of the "old" castle' (*T.N.S.F.C.*, xlvii), 144–50.
[67] *S.H.C.* ii (1), 220–33.
[68] *Complete Peerage*, iii. 167.
[69] *S.H.C.* i. 17, 18.
[70] Ibid. ii (1), 2, 18, 24.
[71] *Rot. Chart.* (Rec. Com.), i. 216; *Complete Peerage*, iii. 167.
[72] *Complete Peerage*, iii. 168–9.
[73] *Cal. Chart. R. 1226–57*, 172.
[74] *Close R. 1231–4*, 567.
[75] *Cal. Pat. 1232–47*, 61.
[76] Ibid. 233.   [77] Ibid.
[78] Ibid. 493.   [79] Ibid. *1247–58*, 79.
[80] *Rec. Soc. Lancs. and Ches.* xiv. 88–89.
[81] *Cal. Chart. R. 1257–1300*, 54.
[82] *Complete Peerage*, vii. 546.
[83] Ibid. 381; *Cal. Chart. R. 1267–1300*, 78.
[84] *Complete Peerage*, vii. 395.
[85] *Cal. Pat. 1321–4*, 183; S.C. 6/1146/11.
[86] *Complete Peerage*, vii. 396.
[87] Ibid. 402.

[88] Ibid. 409.
[89] *Cal. Inq. p.m.* xii, p. 104; *Abbrev. Rot. Orig.* (Rec. Com.), ii. 263.
[90] *Cal. Fine R. 1356–68*, 165–6.
[91] *Complete Peerage*, vii. 410.
[92] S. Armitage-Smith, *John of Gaunt*, 407.
[93] *Cal. Pat. 1361–4*, 202.
[94] D.L. 42/13, f. 95b.
[95] *Cal. Inq. p.m.* xiv, p. 262.
[96] Pape, *Med. Newcastle*, 115.
[97] Leland, *Itin.* (ed. Toulmin Smith), v. 18. Coulam (*Newcastle*, 21) points out that many of the old houses have red sandstone foundations and instances the Lamb Inn in the Market Place.
[98] *S.H.C.* xi. 319.
[99] *Close R. 1247–51*, 431; *Cal. Lib. R. 1245–51*, 378.
[1] *S.H.C.* xi. 310.
[2] Ibid. 1913, 237.   [3] Ibid. xi. 331.
[4] Ibid. 1913, 237.
[5] R. Somerville, *Hist. of the Duchy of Lancaster*, i. 362.
[6] *John of Gaunt's Reg.* (Camd. Soc. 3rd ser. xxi), no. 613.
[7] Ibid.   [8] *S.H.C.* xvi. 84.
[9] Somerville, op. cit. 550.

of the castle had been entrusted to a group of ser-jeants, originally described as the king's sokemen, whose service was secured upon lands in (i) Knutton with Dimsdale, Hanchurch, Clayton, Hanford, and Whitmore, (ii) Hanley, (iii) Longton, (iv) Fenton, (v) Tunstall with Chatterley and Normacot, and (vi) Bradwell with Thursfield.[10] When the service was recorded in 1236, the tenants of (i)–(iv) were expected to render 40 days' service at the king's cost, and the tenant of (v) and (vi) to provide a bowman for eight days in wartime at his own cost.[11] The service due on (v) and (vi), except the Bradwell portion of it, is not traceable after 1236 and it was expressly declared in 1251 that Henry de Audley abolished the service arising in Normacot,[12] the vill he had acquired at least by 1227.[13] The service arising in Longton is last mentioned in 1251–2,[14] in Clayton and Knutton in 1254–5,[15] in Hanley in 1297,[16] and in Bradwell in 1322.[17] The Longton, Hanley, and Bradwell tenants were said in these respective years to be required to maintain armed men for 40 days at their own expense, obligations the statement of which differs in certain respects from those of 1236. The Knutton tenant was to provide an armed horse-man. It may be doubted whether these services were practically enforceable by the time they came to be recorded.

From at least 1166 until at least 1215 the core of the effective garrison consisted of a body of armed serjeants in receipt of yearly wages. Paid until 1190 out of the issues of Trentham[18] and thenceforth out of the *corpus comitatus*,[19] this militia acted from 1191 as serjeants of the peace, or, as the Pipe Rolls put it, *ad custodiam patrie pro malefactoribus*.[20] In the troubled year 1172–3 these serjeants were reinforced by 5 knights and 20 serjeants for 19 weeks and in addition the sheriff claimed £13 6s. 8d. *in auxilio tenendi milites et servientes in Novo Castello*.[21] In the following year 5 knights, 6 mounted serjeants, and 10 foot-serjeants were maintained in the castle for 134 days.[22] When after 1190 the old corps of ser-jeants was expressly assigned police duties, reinforce-ment was resumed and knights were again residing in the castle.[23] In 1192 ten mounted serjeants were paid for the whole year, but their connexion with Newcastle is not stated specifically.[24] In 1192–3 5 knights, 15 mounted serjeants, and 30 foot-serjeants

guarded the castle for 40 days,[25] and in 1195–6 10 knights and 18 mounted serjeants for 24 days.[26] In the same year a body of 180 footmen was hired, 9 of whom (or 1 in 20) were 'magistri', receiving 4d. a day each, and the rest 2d. a day.[27] The knights re-tained in the king's service in 1197 may have had no connexion with Newcastle, though the sum allowed for maintenance would have paid for 5 knights for 40 days at the rates of 1193.[28]

The castle enclosure was oval, the long axis pointing roughly NW.–SE. with the mound at its southern end. The various streams that flowed past the site were dammed in early times to form the castle pool which was the principal means of de-fence. In 1171 as much as £37 was spent upon the castle pool[29] and since in 1169 £6 was spent upon a bridge[30] it is not fanciful to conclude that the pool was being constructed or substantially reconstructed at that time. These payments are in fact the first that are known to have been made by the sheriff for the benefit of the castle. Other payments made in the late 12th and early 13th centuries give indications, often imprecise, of the nature and extent of the fortifications. The building of two 'houses' is men-tioned in 1174[31] and in 1189–90 considerable ex-penditure is recorded on 'bretasches' (or wooden platforms) for the defence of the castle walls[32] and on wooden palisades which presumably surrounded the bailey.[33] Remains of such palisades were dis-covered in 1935 in the north-west part of the bailey.[34] In 1191 repairs were done to the chapel and the king's 'houses'[35] while in the following year the stone tower, which stood on the mound, and the bridge were repaired,[36] the latter in 1193 being em-battled (*kernelando*) with stone.[37] In 1933–4 drainage work in Silverdale Road revealed masonry and stout oak balks, which, conjecturally, formed part of the bridge connecting the causeway across the pool and spanning the Ashfield Brook.[38] In 1934 excavation brought to light in the south-western part of the bailey the foundations of two rooms of a long rect-angular building with walls up to 3 feet in height, which, from the kitchen refuse found there,[39] were presumably the castle kitchens, repairs to which are mentioned in 1192.[40]

The importance of the pool in the defence scheme is again shown by the expenditure on its repair in

[10] The service is first recorded in 1212: *Bk. of Fees*, 143. That survey states only the rents that the sokemen owed but by comparing it with the next survey of 1236 in which both rents and services are expressed it is possible to deduce what the service was believed to be in the earlier year. The 1212 survey traces the tenures, perhaps exag-geratedly, to the Conquest. The whole subject of castle-guard at Newcastle is treated in detail in Pape, *Med. Newcastle*, 19–23.
[11] *Bk. of Fees*, 593–4.
[12] Ibid. 1285; *S.H.C.* 1911, 407–8.
[13] *Cal. Chart. R.* 1226–57, 36.
[14] *Bk. of Fees*, 1285.
[15] *S.H.C.* 1911, 124–5, 308.
[16] Ibid. 242–6.
[17] *Cal. Inq. p.m.* vi, no. 356.
[18] *S.H.C.* i. 55, *et passim*. Eyton's notes on the Pipe Roll of 1168–9 (ibid. i. 57) suggest that they formed a stipen-diary garrison at Trentham castle. Pape, however, con-siders that by Trentham Newcastle is meant: *Med. Newcastle*, 9, 10.
[19] *S.H.C.* ii (1), 10, 17, 166.
[20] Ibid. 10.
[21] Ibid. i. 67.
[22] Ibid. 70.
[23] Ibid. ii (1), 10, 11, 14, 15.

[24] Ibid. 18, 21.
[25] Ibid. 24, i.e. 1s., 6d., and 2d. a day respectively.
[26] Ibid. 54.
[27] Ibid.
[28] Ibid. 64. Other payments from the Staffs. Pipe Rolls for the army of Wales in 1199 (ibid. 78) and in 1205 (ibid. 129, 133) and 1207 (ibid. 142) for King John's armies presumably have no connexion with Newcastle.
[29] *S.H.C.* i. 62–63. Described as *in operacione vivarii de novo oppido*.
[30] Ibid. 55.
[31] Ibid. 70.
[32] Ibid. ii (1), 1, 2.
[33] Ibid.
[34] *T.N.S.F.C.* lxx. 72–74. A great deal of wood was no doubt used. In 1205 the sheriff was ordered to take wood from neighbouring woodlands, outside the royal forest, for the repair of the castle, and in the following year, he was asked to estimate how much timber was required for similar repairs: *Rot. Litt. Claus.* (Rec. Com.), i. 20, 67.
[35] *S.H.C.* ii (1), 11.
[36] Ibid. 17, 18.
[37] *Pipe R.* 1193 (P.R.S. n.s. iii), 83; *S.H.C.* ii (1), 24.
[38] *T.N.S.F.C.* lxviii. 170–2.
[39] Ibid. lxix. 68–70.
[40] *S.H.C.* ii (1), 17, 18.

1194 of the considerable sum of £4 17s.[41] and of an unspecified sum three years later.[42] The maintenance of the bridge, further repairs to which are mentioned in 1196,[43] was no doubt of vital importance as it was the connecting link between the castle and the mainland. The king's 'houses' were repaired in 1194, 1195, and 1197.[44] The work carried out in the 1190's was partly, no doubt, to meet the needs of the larger garrison instituted in that decade (see above).

During John's reign work on the castle substantially increased. In 1199 the gaol, which was presumably situated within the castle precinct, is mentioned for the first time, in conjunction with the one at Stafford, both being repaired at a total cost of 25s.,[45] while general works on the castle came to £9 10s.[46] In 1200 the gaol was further repaired, as also was the pool (vivarium).[47] A sum of £5 was spent on the gaol in 1201 and £11 on general works.[48] Expenditure in 1202 on the bridge, the 'bretasches', a chamber, the mill, and the mill-pond reached the considerable figure of £24 3s. 4d.[49] In 1203 the king's 'houses', mills, and mill-ponds were repaired at a cost of £14 16s., as also were the gaol and the bridge.[50] In the following year the cost of general works at the castle amounted to £37 and the gaol was again repaired as it was also during 1206.[51] In the later year £54 6s. 9d. was spent on unspecified general work.[52]

In March 1206 King John was at Newcastle[53] and the large expenditure on maintenance and repair about this time may reflect his personal interest in the upkeep of the castle. Possibly as a result of the royal visit expenditure on general works rose considerably in 1207 (£40),[54] 1208 (£20),[55] 1209 (£10, which included the repair of a gaol)[56] and 1214 (£5), while in the last-mentioned year money was spent on repairing the gaol again.[57] Some part of this general expenditure was probably allotted to the repair and maintenance of the gateway, which presumably stood to the north of the bridge on the landward side of the pool. In 1935 excavation in the garden of John of Gaunt's Cottage near Silverdale Road, where masonry and timber balks had been found in the previous year (see above), brought to light the end of the outer gateway, including the base of a large corner buttress. South of this and in continuation at a higher level a length of solid wall 6 feet thick was partially uncovered.[58]

In 1239 the constable of the castle was authorized to spend £10 in repairing the bank (kaii) of the king's mill-pond there,[59] and to repair the king's 'houses'.[60] In 1251 Hugh de Frodsham was allowed £15 2s. 3d. spent during his keepership (1246–50) in repairing the palisades round the castle, as well as the bridge, the mill-pond, and the 'bretasches'.[61] In 1251 James de Audley was authorized to spend £20 where it was most needed in repairs to the castle[62] and two years later he was commissioned to repair the castle pool.[63] The latter probably refers to palisading round the pool, which was again repaired in 1253.[64]

In the 14th and 15th centuries expenditure, much of it domiciliary in character, on the maintenance of the fabric seems to have dwindled considerably. In 1374 the constable was ordered to put the houses within the castle in as good a condition as when Maud had leased the manor and castle to Sir Godfrey de Foljambe thirteen years earlier.[65] In the same year John of Gaunt arranged for the sale of twenty oaks from the wood of Newcastle-under-Lyme to provide money for repairs to the castle.[66] The cost of repairs to the castle and its 'houses' was estimated at 100 marks in 1375,[67] and about the same time timber was granted for making 10,000 shingles as roofing material for the 'houses' within the castle.[68] In 1387 £3 2s. 1d. was spent in making windows for the entrance gates and repairs to three halls.[69]

In 1399,[70] 1423,[71] and 1451[72] the castle bridge was under repair. In 1428 £8 11s. 4d. was expended on a passage from the north part of the hall up to the kitchen, a new chimney for the lower room under the principal one, repairs to a 'house', and lead to cover the tower next the gates.[73] In the following year wages amounting to £3 19s. were paid for making the new great gates.[74] In 1446 the palisades of the pinfold, situated near the bridge, and the entrance gates were repaired.[75] In 1477 repairs to the pool cost £3 15s. 10d.[76] while in 1478[77] and 1480[78] a total sum of £1 5s. 6d. was spent on repairs to the pinfold. It will be noted that for the second half of the century expenditure on the main building seems to have ceased, and so it is not surprising that when Leland visited the site a hundred years later his report should have been as brief and negative as it was.[79]

In 1610 the castle, then 'altogether decayed', was leased to Ralph Sneyd for 21 years.[80] In 1650 his

[41] S.H.C. ii (1) 30.
[42] Ibid. 64.
[43] Ibid. 54.
[44] Ibid. 30, 64.
[45] Ibid. 79.
[46] Pipe R. 1199 (P.R.S. N.S. x), 163.
[47] S.H.C. ii (1), 91.
[48] Pipe R. 1201 (P.R.S. N.S. xiv), 49.
[49] Ibid. 1202 (P.R.S. N.S. xv), 182. The mill-pond (stagnum) would be presumably below the mills and distinct from the castle pool.
[50] Ibid. 1203 (P.R.S. N.S. xvi), 250.
[51] Ibid. 1204 (P.R.S. N.S. xviii), 209; S.H.C. ii (1), 134.
[52] Pipe R. 1205 (P.R.S. N.S. xix), 156.
[53] Rot. Litt. Pat. (Rec. Com.), i. 59.
[54] Pipe R. 1207 (P.R.S. N.S. xxiii), 7.
[55] Ibid. 1209 (P.R.S. N.S. xxiv), 149.
[56] Ibid. 1212 (P.R.S. N.S. xxx), 88.
[57] S.H.C. ii (1), 160. Most of the refs. to gaol expenditure include details of irons supplied for the prisoners and expenses attending judgement by ordeal.
[58] T.N.S.F.C. lxx. 74–75.

[59] Cal. Lib. 1226–40, 388.
[60] Ibid. 1240–5, 71.
[61] Cal. Pat. 1247–58, 79; Cal. Lib. 1245–51, 350.
[62] Cal. Lib. 1245–51, 378.
[63] S.H.C. 1911, 17, 18.
[64] Ibid.
[65] John of Gaunt's Reg. (Camd. Soc. 3rd ser. xxi), no. 1538.
[66] Ibid. no. 1547.
[67] Ibid. no. 1721.
[68] Ibid. no. 1724.
[69] D.L. 29/367/6144.
[70] D.L. 29/728/11987.
[71] D.L. 29/183/2904.
[72] D.L. 29/184/2924.
[73] D.L. 29/183/2907.
[74] D.L. 29/183/2908.
[75] D.L. 29/184/2921.
[76] D.L. 29/185/2933.
[77] Ibid.
[78] D.L. 29/185/2935.
[79] See p. 12.
[80] Ward, Stoke, App. xxii.

THE BOROUGH OF NEWCASTLE-UNDER-LYME

grandson Ralph was the lessee at a nominal rent.[81] In 1698 another Ralph Sneyd sublet the castle, lately occupied by Thomas Hemmings, to John Walley, a blacksmith of Newcastle, for 21 years for £1 yearly.[82] This lease, however, does not seem to have been in force for the full period, for in the time of Queen Anne the site was leased to William Burslem (d. 1716). In 1723 his son Thomas let the site to Samuel Proctor at £1 15s. yearly, the lessor retaining the right to shoot over the ground and to fish in the castle pool.[83] Thereafter, for about a century, the mound, the adjoining bailey, and the pool probably remained undisturbed, the haunt of the fisherman and the fowler.

In 1828 Walter Sneyd of Keele bought the site from the duchy for £170.[84] He is stated to have reclaimed the greater portion of the pool (i.e. more than 30 acres) from the influx of the stream, so that by 1843 it had been 'by embanking and draining converted, from a stagnant and offensive morass, which it had become, into good garden and meadow land'.[85] Whatever portion of the original pool was left after the reclamation seems to have been neglected, for in 1849 the local Improvement Commissioners requested Ralph Sneyd to see to the cleansing of the pool, for which he was alleged to be responsible.[86]

In 1855[87] the erection of the Castle Hill Iron Foundry to the north-west of the mound resulted in considerable disturbance of the whole site. The levelling of the ground to the south-east of what was formerly a section of the bailey led to the destruction of a part of the castle walls, the stones of which were used as a foundation for a brick wall round the foundry enclosure.[88] Subsequently the erection of a laundry immediately to the north of the mound and of a dye-works to the north-west effectively sealed off that area from any future archaeological investigation.

By 1935[89] the site of the castle and the land covering the area of the pool had been acquired by the corporation, presumably from the Sneyd family. In 1939 it was decided to convert the site into a public park[90] and to synchronize its opening with the 350th anniversary of the grant of the 1590 charter.[91] At the time complaint was made that part of the castle mound was being used as material for levelling the site of the proposed park.[92] Owing to the war the completion of the work was delayed and it was not until 1944 that the Queen Elizabeth Garden, comprising bowling and putting greens, was formally opened to the public.[93]

MANOR. Strictly the borough had little connexion with the manor of Newcastle-under-Lyme. The latter was centred on the castle which lay, not in the borough, but in a detached part of the ancient parish of Stoke. The need to maintain its garrison led to the creation of manorial tenures in Stoke and Wolstanton ancient parishes involving the payment of rent and the performance of castle-guard. The descent of the manor together with particulars of these tenures, in so far as they lay in the ancient parish of Stoke, is treated below[94] and the subject of castle-guard above.[95] The manorial history of Wolstanton is reserved for treatment under that parish.

That the borough was not included within the manor appears to be confirmed by the reply of Edmund, Earl of Lancaster, to the *quo warranto* inquiry of 1293 when, while claiming view of frankpledge, free warren, and other manorial incidents in the manor of Newcastle, he expressly claimed nothing from the borough apart from its *firma burgi* of 40 marks.[96]

To the question whether the borough was itself a manor it is not easy to give a definite answer. The charter of incorporation of 1590 granted to the mayor, bailiffs, and burgesses view of frankpledge of all the inhabitants of the borough, including those entirely and those not entirely resident. The view was to be held in the Common Hall called the Guildhall twice annually 'in like manner as hath been used from ancient time'.[97] The existence of leet jurisdiction over a long, though unspecified, period, while it constituted a normal concomitant of the rights and privileges claimed by a lord of the manor, did not of itself indicate manorial status. A further statement in the charter that the burghal lands, privileges, and jurisdictions were to be held by the mayor, bailiffs, and burgesses as of the honor of Tutbury does, however, give a stronger indication of a manorial relationship between the Crown and the borough.[98]

In the 17th century, when the inhabitants objected to grinding their corn and malt at the castle mills,[99] the claim of the borough to be a separate manor was brought forward to support their case. In 1608 and 1609 Ralph Sneyd, then the lessee of the castle mills, sued his sister-in-law Ann Sneyd for failing to send her grain to the mills and maintaining in the town a hand grist mill set up by her late husband George Sneyd. The defendant's case was that, while the king was seised of a manor consisting of four several townships, there was another manor, that of the town and borough of Newcastle. The king had no mills in the town manor, and the inhabitants, of whom she was one, were not bound to do suit at the king's mills. The court, however, could find no grounds for the distinction between the manor of Newcastle-under-Lyme and the supposed manor of the town. In its view the manor and the borough were but one manor and the borough parcel of the manor, and in consequence the inhabitants owed suit at the king's mills.[1]

Again, in the period 1664–79, when William Sneyd, the then farmer of the castle mills, sought redress

[81] E 317/Staffs. 38.
[82] U.C.N.S., Sneyd MSS., Box S.102.
[83] Boro. Mus., Fenton deeds.
[84] Coulam, *Newcastle*, 34.
[85] Ward, *Stoke*, 333.
[86] Boro. Mus., Improvement Commrs.' Order Bk. no. 2, 4 Aug. 1849.
[87] Pape, *Tudor and Stuart Newcastle*, 336.
[88] *T.N.S.F.C.* lxix. 69.
[89] Museums Cttee. Min. Bk. f. 40a.
[90] Housing Cttee. Min. Bk. 14 Mar. 1939.
[91] Gen. Purp. Cttee. Min. Bk. 10 Mar. 1939.

[92] *Eve. Sentinel*, 1 Jan. 1940, letter from B. B. Simms.
[93] Ibid. 23 June 1944.
[94] See pp. 184–6.
[95] See p. 13.
[96] *Plac. de Quo Warr.* (Rec. Com.), 718.
[97] Pape, *Tudor and Stuart Newcastle*, 63.
[98] Ibid. 64.
[99] See p. 48.
[1] D.L. 5/24, ff. 760, 790, 791. Subsequently, on the ground of her poverty and advanced age, the court allowed Ann Sneyd to maintain the hand mill for her own use during her lifetime: ibid. f. 895.

against the mayor and corporation who had erected a horse mill within the borough for the grinding of grain and malt,[2] the defendants pleaded that the mills were within the manor of Newcastle and not within the manor of the borough. They contended that the latter was a 'real and absolute manor held immediately of the King's Majesty . . . consisting of divers ancient messuages and burgages, common land, waste ground, chief rents, and other privileges and perquisites, as waifs, estrays, felons' goods, &c. The manor of the borough has its distinct Court Leet and Court Baron and no one in the borough owes suit or service to or appears at any of the courts of the manor of Newcastle.'[3] Finally William Sneyd withdrew his suit and the Duchy Court in consequence was not obliged to adjudicate on the question of the status of the borough manor.[4] This seems to be the last occasion on which the claim of the borough to be a separate manor was formally submitted, and indeed by that time its validity or otherwise had ceased to have more than an antiquarian interest.[5]

In recent times an alleged custom of the manor was the subject of litigation.[6] Newcastle Corporation, the owners in fee simple of land in Wolstanton, formerly copyhold of the manor, on which they had erected Wolstanton Fire Station, brought an action to restrain the owners of the minerals thereunder (the Duchy of Lancaster) and the lessees of the mining rights (Wolstanton Ltd.) from so working the mines as to cause subsidence and damage to the property. The defendants pleaded that there was a custom or a right by prescription to let down the surface without paying compensation. On appeal the House of Lords held that the usage was unreasonable and therefore could not form the foundation of a custom to be recognized by the courts as valid and that the same principle applied to the claim by prescription.

CHURCHES. The ecclesiastical history of Newcastle exhibits two peculiarities. First, though the borough rapidly developed into an important town as compared with the surrounding Pottery villages, its church from the mid-13th century until the beginning of the 19th was a chapel dependent upon the church of Stoke-upon-Trent. Secondly, from an early period the borough council exercised a measure of control over its affairs which became practically exclusive during the 17th century.

A chapel at Newcastle is first mentioned in an agreement made between 1175 and 1182 which terminated a long-standing dispute.[7] This agreement shows that before that time Trentham Priory had owned the chapels of Newcastle and Whitmore but had given them to Robert de Costentin. Later Robert shared his interest in Newcastle chapel with Vivian, the Rector of Stoke.[8] By the agreement Robert and Vivian surrendered their interest to the priory and Vivian received in exchange a life estate in Whitmore chapel. The next reference to the chapel of Newcastle, in 1297,[9] shows that by that date it was subordinate to Stoke, for in the inquisition taken in that year on the death of Edmund, Earl of Lancaster, the church of Stoke with Newcastle and other chapels was described as being in his gift. Newcastle remained a chapelry dependent on the church of Stoke until 1807 when a separate parish was constituted and a rectory established.[10]

The appointment of the chaplain or curate of Newcastle remained with the Rector of Stoke-upon-Trent, except during the 17th century when the borough council assumed the right to choose their 'minister'. When the rectory of Newcastle was constituted in 1807 the Rector of Stoke retained the right of patronage, but in 1815 the advowson was acquired by the Revd. Charles Simeon, whose trustees still (1959) own it.[11] In 1816 the Revd. Clement Leigh, who, since 1803, had been perpetual curate of Newcastle,[12] resigned his curacy and was forthwith presented to the living as rector.[13]

The first appointment of a minister by the borough council was in 1647 when 'the Company [i.e. the borough council] having received sufficient testimonies (and some of them having experience) of the abilities and faithfulness of Mr. Crofton in the ministry of the gospel', chose him as minister.[14] Thereafter, during the Interregnum and even until the end of the century, the borough council continued to appoint the incumbent and to be responsible, in part at least, for the payment of his salary.[15]

Nothing is known about the maintenance of the curate of Newcastle or the source of his emoluments until 1601, and the silence of the minute book on this point may imply that the borough council did not concern itself in the matter before that date. In 1601, however, the council agreed that 'our preacher' should be paid £26 13s. 4d. yearly,[16] £10 13s. 4d. from the town rents and from the fees due from the bellman,[17] the balance of £16 being represented by tithe.[18] In 1615 the council agreed to pay the minister £4 yearly 'to be gathered by the churchwardens', and in the following year four assessors were chosen to levy the sum.[19] Apparently the townspeople objected to the rate and in 1618, the stipend having fallen into arrear, the bellman was instructed to pay the minister,[20] presumably out of the toll corn.[21] In 1624 the minister's stipend, referred to as a gratuity, was suspended for over a year because he had criticized the government of the town.[22]

[2] Pape, *Tudor and Stuart Newcastle*, 329.
[3] D.L. 5/37, f. 433; U.C.N.S., Sneyd MSS. Box S.92.
[4] D.L. 5/39, f. 411; Sneyd MSS. Box S.92.
[5] In 1835 it was stated that the corporation were lords of the manor of Newcastle extending over about 554 acres, which was the area of the ancient borough: *Rep. Com. Mun. Corps.* H.C. 116, p. 1955 (1835), xxv.
[6] *Times Law Reports*, vol. lvi (1939–40), 794–9, Newcastle-under-Lyme *v.* Wolstanton Ltd. and Duchy of Lancaster. A similar case, with the like result, occurred in 1844 (Hilton *v.* Lord Granville): ibid.
[7] *S.H.C.* xi. 322–3, where the terminal date is given as 1180; but Bishop Richard Peche, before whom the agreement was made, died 1182: Le Neve, *Fasti*, i. 545.
[8] See p. 186.
[9] *Cal. Inq. p.m.* iii, p. 290; *S.H.C.* 1911, 246.

[10] 47 Geo. III, sess. 2, c. 114 (local and personal).
[11] Coulam, *Newcastle*, 120; *Clergy List* (1915).
[12] Pape, *Story of Parish Ch. of St. Giles*, 15.
[13] J. W. Dunne, 'The Rectors of Newcastle' (*Staffs. Weekly Sentinel*, 25 Dec. 1915).
[14] Pape, *Tudor and Stuart Newcastle*, 312. It is probable that earlier curates or ministers, A. Storer, 1601–2, Marsh, 1604, N. Richardson, 1615–46, were appointed by the boro. council, but the evidence is lacking.
[15] Ibid. 316, 325.
[16] Ibid. 230.
[17] See p. 45.
[18] *Trans. Derbs. Arch. Soc.* vi. 163.
[19] Pape, *Tudor and Stuart Newcastle*, 253.
[20] Ibid. 255.   [21] See p. 45.
[22] Pape, *Tudor and Stuart Newcastle*, 267, 270.

In 1647 the minister received £60 yearly and a rent-free house which he was to keep in repair.[23] In 1648 the hay tithe was collected by the town towards making up the stipend[24] and the borough council also settled what should be paid for the corn, oats, and barley tithes by tenants of the glebe land in Stubbs Field.[25] These tithes were apparently to be paid to the town on that occasion and it was laid down that subsequently the minister was to supervise the tithe himself.[26]

In 1649 it was decided to pay £20 due to the town in respect of toll corn and the town rent to the minister, Joseph Sond, the remainder of his stipend to be found from the hay and small tithes and a collection by way of benevolence from the inhabitants.[27] These arrangements were temporary pending the receipt of an augmentation. An augmentation of £64 had been granted in respect of his predecessor as from 30 September 1648 but was not authorized for Sond until 6 January 1650.[28] The minister appointed in 1654 received £60 yearly and a rent-free house[29] and in addition, in the following year, 'the fees belonging to the church'.[30] Furthermore, in 1657, he was granted an augmentation of £50 on the recommendation of the Trustees for the Maintenance of Ministers.[31]

The relatively generous financial provision made during the Interregnum did not continue. After the Restoration the rents of certain corporation premises were applied to the relief of the poor and the maintenance of the minister. The amount allotted to the latter was £20 yearly, but c. 1709 'on some disobligation' the stipend to the minister was held back.[32] Nevertheless, though in the early 18th century the corporation ceased to make a regular contribution to the curate's stipend, in 1713, 1714, and 1716 £20, charged on the profits of the toll corn, was in fact paid to him.[33] In 1718, however, the corporation informed the bishop that they were not in a position, for financial reasons, to pay at that time £20 yearly to the curate,[34] and the payment seems never to have been resumed.

In the later 17th century efforts made from time to time by the rectors of Stoke to assert their rights in Newcastle contributed to the financial insecurity of the curate. In 1684 the borough council allowed the minister a small sum representing the tithes of Lent corn for 12 day-works in Stubbs Field which had been collected by the Rector of Stoke.[35] When the rector died in 1692[36] his successor demanded of the Newcastle curate £12 as first fruits; the borough

council intervened in the dispute and offered to pay half the sum involved, leaving the minister to pay the other half.[37] Again, in 1705, another rector attempted to replace Egerton Harding, the then curate, by his own nominee,[38] but this attempt evidently failed as Harding remained curate until his death in 1717.[39]

During the 18th century the emoluments of the Newcastle curacy seem to have comprised[40] (a) tithes within the township and chapelry of Newcastle, Easter dues, and surplice fees; (b) a yearly modus in lieu of the tithe hay, namely 1s. 6d. in the winter fields and 1s. in the summer fields for every day-work[41] of land mown, all inclosures that were mown being charged with a modus according to the quantity; (c) the glebe, the Parson's Flat in Stubbs Field, consisting of 10 day-works of land;[42] and (d) the parsonage house.[43] In addition, there was in 1705[44] another house of the yearly value of 30s., the gift of Edward Orme (d. 1705).[45]

At the beginning of the 19th century the income of the curacy was described as small and insufficient,[46] and by the Act of 1807 the revenues of the living were at last established on a firm basis,[47] comprising the great and small tithes within the township of Newcastle, the glebe lands, Easter dues, surplice fees, donations, and pensions. Also the Rector of Stoke was required to pay to the Rector of Newcastle a yearly sum of £108 or, at the option of the latter, the value of 227 bushels of wheat based on the average price a bushel throughout the county in the preceding year.[48] In 1844 this rent-charge, then represented by £105 15s., was still being paid.[49]

The extensive inclosure of 1816, involving the greater part of the common fields, provided for the extinguishment of the tithe thereon after the allotments had been made and for appropriate compensation to be made to the Rector of Newcastle.[50] The yearly payment to the incumbent was to be on the basis of one-fifth of a quarter of the total annual value (this quarter representing the arable portion of the land inclosed) and of one-eighth of the remaining three-quarters of the annual value.[51] Provision was made for the variation of the rent-charge every seven years, according to the average price of wheat.[52]

The gross annual income of the benefice for the period 1828–31 was £352 (£285 net).[53] In 1841 the tithe on the remainder of the tithable acreage amounting to 140½ acres, inclusive of the glebe, was

[23] Ibid. 312.
[24] Ibid. 314.
[25] Ibid.
[26] Ibid.
[27] Ibid. 316.
[28] *S.H.C.* 1915, 256.
[29] Pape, *Tudor and Stuart Newcastle*, 325.
[30] Ibid. 327.
[31] *Cal. S.P. Dom.* 1656–7, 279.
[32] W.S.L., Parker Jervis Coll., bdle. 29.
[33] Corp. Order Bk. 1712–67, ff. 6b, 11b, 20b.
[34] Ibid. f. 26a.
[35] Ibid. 1669–1712, f. 33b.
[36] *S.H.C.* 1915, 249.
[37] Corp. Order Bk. 1669–1712, f. 81a.
[38] Ibid. f. 126a.
[39] Pape, *Story of Parish Ch. of St. Giles*, 15.
[40] Lich. Dioc. Regy., terrier, 29 May 1705.
[41] A day-work was 3 r. of land: Wright, *Dial. Dict.*
[42] Lich. Dioc. Regy., terrier, 29 May 1705. The glebe in 1807 was stated to be a little over 11 a. (47 Geo. III, c.

114, local and personal) and about the same in 1884 when it consisted of the rectory house, water (then converted into meadowland), a meadow in the Ironmarket (1½ a.), gardens in Well St. (6 a.), and a meadow in Wolstanton (1½ a.): Newcastle Ch. Vestry, terrier, 1884.
[43] See p. 22.
[44] Lich. Dioc. Regy., terrier, 29 May 1705.
[45] *Staffs. Advertiser*, 8 Apr. 1911.
[46] *C.J.* lxii 132.
[47] 47 Geo. III, c. 114 (local and personal).
[48] By Stoke Rectory Act, 7 & 8 Geo. IV, c. 41, S. 41 (priv. act), the Rector of Newcastle was to accept, as glebe, land bought by the Rector of Stoke in whole or part satisfaction of this rent-charge.
[49] Newcastle Ch. Vestry, terrier, 1884.
[50] Act for enclosing Lands in Parishes of Newcastle-under-Lyme, &c., 56 Geo. III, c. 33, S. 79 (priv. act).
[51] Ibid.
[52] Ibid. In 1884 the rent-charge was £84 8s. 9d. based on the price of wheat: Newcastle Ch. Vestry, terrier, 1884.
[53] *Rep. Com. Eccl. Rev.* H.C. 54, p. 491 (1835), xxii.

commuted for a yearly rent-charge of £81.[54] This sum was still being paid to the incumbent in 1887.[55]

In 1940 the living of St. Thomas, Butterton, in the parish of Stoke-upon-Trent, 3½ miles from Newcastle, was united to that of St. Giles, Newcastle.[56]

The earliest chantry was established in honour of St. Katherine in 1318 by William Swanild,[57] a Newcastle merchant,[58] who endowed it with five houses and a yearly rent of 14d. in Newcastle, for the maintenance of a priest to serve daily at the altar of St. Katherine.[59] At that time the houses were worth £2 13s. 4d. yearly.[60] The patronage was at first retained by the Swanild family,[61] but by 1360 was in the hands of Richard de Routhesleye, who still held it in 1369.[62] By 1395 it had passed to Henry de Swerkeston,[63] a member of the guild merchant.[64]

In the late 15th century the endowments of the chantry seem to have been acquired by the town council, for in 1476 the mayor, the Twenty-four, and the community agreed to an exchange with Trentham Priory surrendering *inter alia* land that a Thomas Samfeld had given to the 'divine service of St. Katherine' for two crofts near Friars' Wood and two other 'hays' called Androeshayes.[65] In 1546 the yearly rent was said to be £3 11s. 6d. and it was erroneously stated that the chantry had been founded by the mayor and brethren of Newcastle.[66] From the dissolution of the chantry in 1548 until *c.* 1561 John Fenton, the last chantry priest, received the yearly revenue as his pension.[67] Later in Elizabeth I's reign the chantry lands were held in fee-farm by Edward Thickness, but in 1598 they were leased to Edmund Page for 21 years.[68] In 1608 the chantry property was being farmed by Robert Oliver and Robert Thomlynson,[69] and in 1610 by Thomas Marbury and Richard Cartwright for £3 11s. 4d.,[70] and it was at sixteen years' purchase of this figure that in 1677 a contract of sale of the chantry lands was entered into with John Chase.[71] In 1647 it was stated that a burgage called the 'Eagle and Child', an orchard on the east side of Church Lane, and a croft in Clayton Field near a pasture called Frerewood had formerly belonged to the chantry.[72]

The date of the foundation of the chantry of St. Mary is not known, but in 1385 the borough minutes record the election by the Twenty-four of a priest to celebrate mass at its altar, for which he was to receive a jar (*amphora*) of wine in addition to his salary from the rent of the chantry lands.[73] In 1392 the chantry was endowed with 12 houses, 6 tofts, 2 acres of land, and 10s. rent in Newcastle.[74] The tolls and profits arising out of St. Leonard's Fair also belonged to it, and in 1556 were granted to the Hospital of the Savoy.[75] In 1620 they were stated to be worth 3s. 4d. yearly.[76]

During Elizabeth I's reign the chantry lands were let to Edward Thickness and subsequently, in 1598, to Edmund Page[77] at a rent stated to be £4 17s. 3d. in 1608,[78] when Philip Ghent and Richard Moore farmed them in fee.[79] In 1677 this rent was entered at £5 16s. 7d., this being the figure, at sixteen years' purchase, at which a contract of sale was made with John Chase.[80]

Of the third chantry, that of Holy Trinity, even less is known. Some time in the period 1538–44 the mayor and one of the bailiffs were sued by John Heywood of Stonnylowe, grandson and heir of John Parker, for false imprisonment and expulsion from a house and garden in Newcastle, which the defendants claimed to have been the subject of a bequest to maintain a priest for the service of the Holy Trinity.[81]

Another chantry, although not so described, seems to have been attached to the altar of St. Sunday[82] by the end of the 15th century. In 1493 four persons were appointed by the borough council to supervise St. Sunday's 'cote to be kept in the road seller[83] with the oversight of the priest that sings before Saint Sunday'; the overseers were to be changed yearly, and they were to take charge of one key while the priest retained the other.[84] In the church of that time there were two chancels or chapels, one dedicated to Our Lady and the other to St. Sunday.[85] In the 16th century the latter seems to have been the name sometimes given to the church itself, which can be the only explanation of Leland's remark when he visited Newcastle in 1541 that 'the town useth to come to a chapel of St. Sunday by the castle'.[86] The name survives in Sunday Wells situated below the church in Lower Street near the paper mill.

The control exercised by the borough over matters of church administration is exemplified in the appointment by the council over a long period of the churchwardens (or more correctly chapel-wardens) of Newcastle. The two *custodes corporis ecclesie ville* elected in 1376–7[87] and the two supervisors of the church and receivers of money collected in church appointed in 1407–8[88] may have been churchwardens. In 1490, however, John Leighton and

[54] Tithe Redemption Com., Tithe Appt. and Maps, Newcastle (1841).
[55] *Ret. of Tithes Commuted*, H.C. 214, p. 197 (1887), lxiv.
[56] *Lich. Dioc. Dir.* (1947–8).
[57] Lich. Dioc. Regy., Bp's. Reg. ii, f. 138b; *S.H.C.* 1911, 339.
[58] Pape, *Med. Newcastle*, 49.
[59] *S.H.C.* 1911, 339.   [60] Ibid.
[61] Lich. Dioc. Regy., Bp's. Reg. ii, ff. 146, 156b.
[62] *S.H.C.* N.S. x(2), 14, 126.
[63] Lich. Dioc. Regy., Bp's. Reg. v, f. 47a.
[64] Pape, *Med. Newcastle*, 164.
[65] *S.H.C.* xi. 329.
[66] E 301/40, no. 25. The chantry is described as being within the 'parish' church of Newcastle.
[67] *S.H.C.* 1915, 257.
[68] B.M. Add. Ch. 7062.
[69] D.L. 12/21, warrant for grant in fee-farm to Oliver and Thomlynson.
[70] E 308/6/42, no. 323; Pape, *Tudor and Stuart Newcastle*, 32, for a list of the chantry lands.
[71] *Cal. Treas. Bks.* 1676–9 (1), 514.
[72] C 3/462, no. 4.
[73] Pape, *Med. Newcastle*, 156–7.
[74] *Cal. Pat.* 1391–6, 175. And see p. 187, n. 25.
[75] C 66/917/27.
[76] D.L. 12/27, warrant for grant in fee-farm to Sir Jas. Ouchterlony, Kt., and Ric. Gurnard.
[77] B.M. Add. Ch. 7062.
[78] D.L. 12/21, warrant for grant in fee-farm to Ghent and Moore.
[79] E 308/6/42, no. 323.
[80] *Cal. Treas. Bks.* 1676–9 (1), 514.
[81] C 1/1011 (31–33).
[82] St. Sunday is a rendering of Sanctus Dominicus (St. Dominic) due to confusion with the Latin *dies dominica* = Sunday (*O.E.D.*).
[83] Possibly a chest located in the rood loft.
[84] Pape, *Med. Newcastle*, 180.
[85] Pape, *Tudor and Stuart Newcastle*, 215.
[86] Leland, *Itin.* ed. Toulmin Smith, v. 18, 19.
[87] Pape, *Med. Newcastle*, 149.
[88] Ibid. 173.

William Coldall were elected *gardiani ecclesie* by the borough council[89] and in the following year they presented their account to the mayor, bailiffs, and their brethren, being then styled *prepositi ecclesie*. On the same occasion other churchwardens rendered their account and it may be assumed that they had acted in the years immediately preceding 1490 and that the submission of their accounts had fallen into arrear.[90]

Throughout the Tudor and Stuart periods these officers, often called church reeves and occasionally *editui*, were elected by the borough council. Light is thrown upon their subordination to the borough authorities and on the nature of their duties by their oath of office. Its terms as set down in 1596[91] required them to 'be at your mayor's commandment in all causes lawful ... take regard to the good orders and behaviour within the church, collect and gather such sums of money as shall be due to be paid for burials within the church, and of the same make a true account'. Although not specifically mentioned, one of their principal duties was to ensure the maintenance of the church fabric and to this end to collect the rates, or 'lunes' as they are called, authorized fairly regularly by the borough council for the repair of the church from the beginning of the 17th century onwards; in 1630, for example, the minutes record the council's agreement that the churchwardens cause a lune of 20 nobles to be levied for the repair of the church.[92] After 1707 the appointment of churchwardens by the council ceased,[93] and thereafter presumably these officers were elected by the vestry.

The church clerk or sexton was also appointed by the borough council. In 1510–11 Edward Storrop was elected *clericus pro ecclesia*.[94] From the middle of the 17th to the middle of the 18th century the borough council minutes record appointments to the office of church clerk and the arrangements made for his salary. As late as 1745 the parish clerk was still the employee of the borough council, which in that year withdrew his salary and instead gave him the 'benefit of the bells and buryings' and £2 yearly for looking after the chimes and clock.[95] In 1834, a dispute having arisen whether the rector, the corporation, or the parishioners had the right to appoint the parish clerk, the matter was referred to counsel who was of the opinion that, despite the ancient practice, the right of appointment was vested in the rector.[96]

Early in the 17th century Puritan leanings can be detected among the parishioners.[97] For example, in 1628 the council decreed that the church bells were not to be rung without the consent of the mayor or his deputy, except for prayers and burials, and that sparingly.[98] Arthur Storer, the minister in 1601–2, is described as a preacher[99] and one of the sixteen preachers in the whole of Staffordshire.[1] He was followed by another preacher of the name of Marsh in 1604[2] but the period of his incumbency is unknown, the next name being that of Nicholas Richardson (1615–46).[3] During the Civil War and Interregnum Newcastle was served by Presbyterian ministers, whose relations with the borough council were not, however, always amicable.[4]

At the Restoration Newcastle was without a minister, the previous incumbent, Ralph Hall, having departed in 1659 after a dispute with the borough council.[5] After a brief incursion by George Long, a man of strong nonconformist views, *c.* 1659–62,[6] the borough council in 1663[7] appointed Thomas Oulton who, save for an interruption of three years (1685–7) held the living until 1698.[8] His ejection in 1685, however, was probably for political, not religious, reasons connected with the overthow of the old council.[9] On its return to power in 1688 Oulton was reinstated.[10] During his incumbency the church in Newcastle seems to have been in a strong position, for in 1676 it was recorded that there were 1,000 conformists in the town, only 5 dissenters, and no papists.[11]

The appointment of Egerton Harding in 1698 witnessed an attempt to raise the spiritual and moral life of Newcastle and its neighbourhood. He was a local correspondent of the newly established S.P.C.K. and he reported in 1700 that he, with about sixteen of the neighbouring clergy, held a monthly lecture in Newcastle for suppressing immorality and profaneness and that the magistrates and gentry had promised their constant attendance.[12] This promise seems to have been fulfilled, for in the following year Harding reported that there was a 'visible increase of piety and morality amongst them'.[13] At the same time he stated that there was a well-stocked library,[14] that the poor were well inclined, and that they attended the sacraments, which were administered monthly.[15] It is not known for how long or to what extent the religious fervour initiated by Harding was maintained, as his later correspondence with the S.P.C.K. cannot be traced.

The acquisition of the advowson in 1815 by Charles Simeon[16] ensured adherence to the evangelical principles upheld by him. In 1854, as in Harding's day, Communion was celebrated on the first Sunday in each month after morning service, and in 1856, and subsequently until 1873, after

[89] Ibid. 176.
[90] Ibid. 178.
[91] Pape, *Tudor and Stuart Newcastle*, 221.
[92] Ibid. 282.
[93] See Corp. Order Bk. 1669–1712.
[94] Pape, *Med. Newcastle*, 190.
[95] Corp. Order Bk. 1712–67, f. 141*b*.
[96] Newcastle Ch. Vestry, Counsel's Opinion, 1834.
[97] See p. 56.
[98] Pape, *Tudor and Stuart Newcastle*, 278.
[99] Ibid. 230.
[1] *Trans. Derbs. Arch. Soc.* vi. 163.
[2] *S.H.C.* 1915, 256.
[3] Pape, *Story of Parish Ch. of St. Giles*, 15.
[4] See Pape, *Tudor and Stuart Newcastle*, chap. xi; and see p. 56.
[5] Pape, *Tudor and Stuart Newcastle*, 128.
[6] Ibid. 129; and see p. 56.
[7] Corp. Order Bk. 1590–1669, p. 198.

[8] Pape, *Story of Parish Ch. of St. Giles*, 15.
[9] See p. 27.
[10] Corp. Order Bk. 1669–1712, f. 58*a*; Hist. MSS. Com. *14th Rep. App.*, Pt. ii, 407: letters from Mayor and Corp. to Sir Edwd. Harley praying him to permit Mr. Oulton, their ejected minister, to return to his former cure, and from Harley agreeing that Oulton should leave Brampton and return to Newcastle. Brampton Bryan (Herefs.) was the seat of the Harley family: *D.N.B. sub* Harley.
[11] W.S.L., S. MS. 33.
[12] Holy Trinity Ch., Marylebone Rd., London, N.W. 1., S.P.C.K. archives, Corresp. Bk., 1699–1701, f. 25, no. 102.
[13] W. O. B. Allen and Edmund McClure, *Two Hundred Yrs., the Hist. of the S.P.C.K.* (1898), 97.
[14] A library had been constructed at the W. end of the ch. *c.* 1679: see p. 20.
[15] Allen and McClure, *Two Hundred Yrs.*, 97.
[16] *D.N.B.*

evening service as well. From 1855 to 1860 there was, in addition, a monthly early morning communion during the summer quarter.[17] In 1874 there were four celebrations monthly, on the first Sunday in the morning, on the second Sunday in the afternoon, on the third Sunday in the evening, and on the fourth Sunday at 8.30 a.m. In 1877 the early morning celebration was discontinued and the thrice-monthly celebration continued until at least 1882.[18] At the present time (1959) there are an early celebration every Sunday, a morning celebration on the first Sunday of the month, and an evening one on the last Sunday of the month.[19]

When the official ecclesiastical census was taken on 30 March 1851, for some unknown reason no services were held in the parish church and so no attendance figures were given.[20] Thirty years later an unofficial census conducted by a local newspaper on Sunday, 18 December 1881, disclosed attendances of 376 at the morning and 586 at the evening service.[21]

Little is known architecturally of the church that stood on the hilly ground to the east of the castle. The whole of it, except its massive western tower, was removed in 1720–1 when a new church was built. The discovery in 1873, when foundations were being excavated for a second rebuilding, of a section of zigzag moulding suggests a church originally of late-12th-century date.[22] The pre-18th-century church had a chancel[23] and at least a north aisle.[24] In 1678–9 the corporation agreed to spend £90 on erecting a loft and library at the west end of the church.[25] During the whole of the 17th century the corporation was authorizing, almost annually, the levying of lunes for the repair of the church. Despite this deterioration of the fabric continued, so much so that in 1685 the corporation decided to present a petition for a brief for its repair.[26] In 1715 damage to the church, which may have resulted in part from the riot in that year,[27] amounted to more than £3,115,[28] the amount for which a brief was then issued.[29]

It is not surprising, therefore, that, on application made, a faculty was granted in 1719 for the old church to be taken down and for the erection of a new one, which was to have galleries on its north and south sides.[30] A contract was entered into between the corporation and William Smith to build a new church and chancel according to 'a model on draught'[31] for £1,366.[32] About £700 was subscribed, briefs brought in about £500, and the sale of pews about £200.[33] The expenditure included £6 13s. 8d. for an entertainment at 'the covering of the church',[34] and £8 12s. for an ironwork canopy over the mayor's pew.[35] Although under the faculty the old church was to be removed in its entirety, local sentiment presumably secured the preservation of the tower. The new church, with seating accommodation for 892 persons, was opened for service on 5 November 1721.[36] Described by a local historian in 1908[37] as 'a hideous brick monstrosity' the church nevertheless seems to have been a good example of the early Georgian period.[38] The building was of brick with stone dressings and consisted of a nave of four bays and an apsidal chancel. The round-headed windows were flanked by stone pilasters and had stone archivolts with projecting imposts and key blocks. Above them, probably to light the galleries, were circular windows with tall keystones reaching to a panelled parapet. Internally the apse was fitted with dado panelling, while between the windows were boards inscribed with the Ten Commandments.[39] There were fine wrought-iron gates at the east end of the churchyard.[40]

By 1872[41] the church was dilapidated and no doubt inadequate to the needs of an enlarged population. It was, therefore, demolished except for the tower, and a new church, designed by Sir Gilbert Scott, was completed in 1876.[42]

The present church of *ST. GILES* consists of an aisled and clerestoried nave, an aisled chancel, north and south porches, and a medieval west tower. The tower, which is 110 ft. high and built of red sandstone, still remains its dominant feature and is a notable landmark. In 1840 it was reported to need repair at an estimated cost of £80.[43] In 1894,[44] the stonework having deteriorated, it was entirely refaced, at the cost of Francis Stanier, so that the external details now show little sign of antiquity. The tower rises in four stages and has double buttresses for its full height at the two western angles. Owing to the fall in the ground the floor of the

[17] *St. Giles's Ch. Annual Reports*, 1854–73 (copy in Newcastle Boro. Libr.).
[18] *St. Giles's Ch. Annual Reports*, 1867–82 (copy in H.R.L.)
[19] *Newcastle-under-Lyme Par. Mag.*
[20] H.O. 129/15/369.
[21] *Newcastle Guardian*, 24 Dec. 1881.
[22] Coulam, *Newcastle*, 88.
[23] Pape, *Tudor and Stuart Newcastle*, 330, authorization, in 1657, of the sale of the lead over the chancel and substitution of a timber roof.
[24] Coulam, *Newcastle*, 95, quoting the building contract for the 1721 ch.; Pape, op. cit. 271.
[25] Corp. Order Bk. 1669–1712, ff. 14b, 15b; and see p. 19.
[26] Corp. Order Bk. 1669–1712, f. 38a.
[27] See p. 56.
[28] *S.H.C.* 1938, 242. The meeting-house, very near the church, was burnt down and the latter may have been damaged as a result. The large amount of the sum solicited, however, may indicate that complete rebuilding was then being planned.
[29] W. A. Bewes, *Ch. Briefs*, 305.
[30] Coulam, *Newcastle*, 94.
[31] There is a plan of the ch. in St. Giles's vestry.
[32] Coulam, *Newcastle*, 94–95; H.M. Colvin, *Biographical Dict. of Eng. Architects, 1660–1840*, where Wm. Smith

(1661–1724), brother of Francis Smith 'of Warwick', is described as the leading master builder in the W. Midland counties in the early 18th cent. and a designer of 'handsome and well-built churches, admirably adapted to the needs of Protestant worship'.
[33] W.S.L., D. 1788, P. 52, B. 4.
[34] Ibid.
[35] Coulam, *Newcastle*, 96. The canopy is now (1959) in the V. and A. Mus., S. Kensington.
[36] Coulam, *Newcastle*, 96, 97. In 1851 the no. of seats was returned as 818, of which 320 were free: H.O. 129/15/369.
[37] Coulam, *Newcastle*, 97.
[38] For views of the 18th-cent. ch. see W.S.L., Staffs. Views, vii, pp. 100, 102 (a), 103 (a and b); Boro. Mus., water-colour by H. Whessell (1843).
[39] See plate facing p. 54.
[40] W.S.L., Staffs. Views, vii, p. 102 (a); see plate facing p. 54.
[41] Coulam, *Newcastle*, 108.
[42] Ibid. 108–17 for a full acct. of the preliminary negotiations and progress of construction.
[43] *Staffs. Advertiser*, 12 Dec. 1840. A stone inserted near the base of the E. buttress of the tower bearing the date 1841 and the names of two churchwardens presumably records the work then done.
[44] Coulam, *Newcastle*, 116.

lowest stage is below that of the nave and is approached from the latter by four steps under the tower arch. The walls of this stage are 7 ft. thick, pierced on the west and south by lancet windows. These and the heavily moulded tower arch are typical 13th-century features. The west doorway has been rebuilt in the same style. An internal north doorway, now blocked, originally gave access to the stair turret at the north-west angle of the tower. The tall second stage, containing the ringing chamber, is lighted by two tiers of small lancets with trefoil heads, the upper ones having ogee arches, indicating that this work belongs to the 14th century. The third stage, or clock chamber, has two-light windows with tracery of the later 14th century. The ancient timber strutting supporting the bell frame is brought down to rest on these window sills. The highest stage, or belfry, is strengthened at the angles by internal piers of masonry, possibly to give support to a projected spire. The windows, of two and three lights, are of 15th-century character, as also is the embattled parapet with crocketted pinnacles at the angles.[45] Before the 19th-century restoration there were intermediate pinnacles on each face of the tower.[46]

The body of the church, dating from 1876, is built of Blythe Marsh stone and is in the style of the late 13th century. The windows contain Geometrical tracery and the clerestory windows are alternately pointed and circular. The interior is faced with Bath stone with the darker Blythe Marsh stone[47] used sparingly to give contrast. The nave arcades of six bays have alternate circular and octagonal piers, the hoodmoulds and the 'stiff-leaved' capitals being of Blythe Marsh stone. The same stone is used for the sedilia in the chancel and for the quatrefoil piers which divide the chancel from a chapel on the north side and an organ chamber on the south. The chancel projects beyond its aisles and has a large seven-light east window filled with Geometrical tracery. The extreme length of the 19th-century church from the east face of the tower to the buttresses at the east end is 150 ft., the width is 75 ft., and the height 64½ ft.[48]

The marble font, surmounted by a detachable moulded and heraldic cover, and given to the old church in 1733 by Samuel Bagnall, has been superseded by a more elaborate modern one[49] presented by Joseph Griffith in 1899.[50] Another relic of the old church survives in a fine representation in carved oak of the pelican in her piety, formerly a roof ornament over the altar, but now adapted as a lectern.[51] The old communion table, having been disposed of as rubbish, was subsequently recovered and is now used as a credence table.[52] At the south end of the nave against the east wall of the tower is a stone recumbent figure, clothed in a long robe, the left hand thought to be holding a sword and the right clasping a glove; it was discovered in 1848.[53]

The mural tablets are few. When the 18th-century church was pulled down, they were stored away in a chamber covered by a mound in the northern part of the churchyard. When in 1894[54] the tower was restored, the tablets of three former incumbents, Edward Orme (d. 1705), Robert Fenton (d. 1760), and Clement Leigh (d. 1853), and that of Thomas Sparrow (d. 1827), a former town clerk, were restored to the church.[55] The first three are now on the walls of the chancel and that of Sparrow in the tower. Of the remaining tablets the most noteworthy is that on the wall of the north aisle to John Bourne (d. 1764), the inscription thereon testifying that 'his zeal for the advancement of religion appeared from several new chapels erected and endowed in this neighbourhood chiefly at his expense'. There are also memorials to John Ford (d. 1753), William Kinnersley (d. 1788), and William Beard (d. 1789), a chief justice in Wales.

Under a Scheme of 1896 two-thirds of the yearly income of Sir Walter Wagstaff Bagot's charity was allotted for the repair and maintenance of the parish church.[56] In 1955 the charity was represented by an investment of £207[57] and in 1959 an income of £9 was still being received therefrom.[58] By the will of John Thomas Cooke of Newcastle (proved 1920) the income from an investment of £100 was to be applied for the maintenance of the fabric[59] and is still (1959) so paid.[60] By the will of Robert Cadwallader Trigger of Newcastle (proved 1927) the income from an investment of £250[61] was to be applied for the upkeep of the church fabric[61] and the income therefrom, £9, is still being paid.[62]

In 1553 the plate consisted of a silver chalice with paten; two brass candlesticks had been sold by Richard Morton the late churchwarden.[63] In 1558 there were two chalices and two patens.[64] The plate now (1959) consists of a silver chalice and a paten presented by Thomas Lynnis in thankfulness, as the inscription records, 'for his prosperous voyage and safe return from the East Indies, 19 October 1629'; a silver chalice with cover, a silver salver, and a silver paten, all inscribed as being the gift in 1680 of William Leveson-Gower to the corporation in token of his having been thrice elected to be one of their burgesses in Parliament; and a silver flagon and lid, the gift of Mrs. Alice Fenton, 1757. There is also a modern silver chalice.[65] The design of the Leveson-Gower chalice resembles closely that of the earlier Lynnis one. Although all the old plate is now correctly described as silver it seems from inspection that the vessels were originally silver gilt.

[45] The above acct. is partly taken from J. H. Beckett, 'Old Church Towers of Staffs.' (T.N.S.F.C. xlv), 181–4. A survey of the tower was made in July 1759 by Wm. Baker: Colvin, Dict. Eng. Architects, 55.
[46] See plate facing p. 54.
[47] Coulam, Newcastle, 115.
[48] Ibid.
[49] Pape, Story of Parish Ch. of St. Giles, 12, 14. The cover of the old font is now (1959) in the Boro. Mus. The font itself is in St. Andrew's Church, Westlands: ex. inf. the rector.
[50] Kelly's Dir. Staffs. (1940).
[51] Pape, Story of St. Giles, 14.
[52] Ibid.
[53] Ibid. 13; Kelly's Dir. Staffs. (1940).
[54] See p. 20.
[55] Pape, 'The Mural Tablets of the Church of St. Giles' (Staffs. Advertiser, 2 Dec. 1911).
[56] Char. Com. files, Newcastle United Char.
[57] Ibid.
[58] St. Giles's Par. Ch. Vestry, Trustees Min. Bk. The church receives the whole of the income from this charity. Under the United Charities Scheme (see p. 71) ⅓ of the income was to be paid to the Watch Cttee. in aid of the police rate, but in fact no payments were made for that purpose: ex inf. the town clerk.
[59] Char. Com. files.
[60] St. Giles's Par. Ch. Vestry, Trustees Min. Bk.
[61] Char. Com. files.
[62] St. Giles's Par. Ch. Vestry, Trustees Min. Bk.
[63] S.H.C. 1915, 251.
[64] Pape, Tudor and Stuart Newcastle, 194.
[65] Ex. inf. the rector.

In 1553 there were four bells.[66] There seem to have been five in 1628[67] and they certainly numbered five in 1665.[68] In 1732 they were recast by Abraham Rudhall, the Gloucester bell-founder, as eight[69] and this is the present number. They were rehung in 1894.[70]

A church clock is mentioned in 1589[71] and by 1664 there were chimes as well.[72] In 1888 a new clock was provided and the chimes were restored,[73] while in 1894 the clock was supplied with two new dials.[74]

The registers begin in 1563 and the entries from that date to 1770 have been printed.[75] The first register covers the period 1563 to 1620, and the second 1628 to 1653; there is also a gap in the second volume for the period 29 January 1631/2 to 28 October 1633.

Although the church was not parochial until 1807, a graveyard existed before 1800 for land was then provided for its enlargement.[76] It was again enlarged in 1835.[77] It was ordered to be closed in 1851[78] but the order does not seem to have been fully complied with, for a further order, to take effect in 1865, was subsequently issued.[79]

In 1898 the churchyard was further enlarged to provide space for levelling the mounds which contained human remains, and which had been piled up around the new church when its foundations were being excavated in 1873. It was said that the mounds, besides being unsightly, interfered with the view of the tower from the neighbouring streets.[80] In the large mound on the north side of the churchyard a bricked chamber was built in 1874 in which to store mural tablets from the old church, but in 1912 some of them were moved to the present church.[81]

The ministers appointed in 1647 and 1654 were provided with a rent-free house in addition to their stipends.[82] In 1698 Sir John Leveson-Gower granted a plot of land at the east end of the Ironmarket in trust for the benefit of the then curate of Newcastle and his successors.[83] The erection thereon of a house and barn seems to have owed much to Bishop Lloyd, whose position as Lord Almoner apparently made it possible for him to contribute towards the cost.[84] His translation from Lichfield to Worcester in 1699[85] and removal from the office of Lord Almoner put an end to his interest in the parsonage house, on which, in 1703, there still remained a debt of £160.[86] The first tenant of the house, to which was attached an extensive garden, was Egerton Harding (d. 1717). In 1854 the house, by then known as the rectory and

Glebe House, was extended and enlarged by the addition of a story[87] by the rector.[88] In 1910 it was completely restored.[89]

In 1895 the National schools were built on a part of the adjoining glebe land, while another part, in 1897, was converted into the Queen's Gardens.[90] The land next to the rectory was sold in 1910 and used as a site for a new post office.[91]

In 1926[92] the rectory and site were sold and the buildings, now consisting of three shops on the ground floor with the Rectory Chambers above, appear to have been entirely reconstructed. Date-stones of 1698 (with initials E.H. for Egerton Harding) and of 1854 have been incorporated in the front elevation. Since 1934 the rectory has been situated in Seabridge Road.[93]

A church or chapel dedicated to St. Mary at one time existed to the west of the Castle Pool. It is first mentioned in 1297 when it was described as being by the pool (vivarium) of Newcastle, and in the gift of Edmund, Earl of Lancaster.[94] There is no information about the date of its foundation, but it may be assumed that its primary purpose was to serve the needs of the garrison and thus it may have been erected soon after the castle was built. The exact site is not known. The chapel was apparently still in existence in 1544 when an undertaking was given to repair a highway from St. Mary's Church to Deans Bridge,[95] but in 1608 it was referred to as the late church, called St. Mary's Church beyond the water.[96] In depositions taken in 1667 in a mill dispute the question was asked whether there was once a church beyond the mills called St. Mary's Church, to which no answer seems to have been returned, but the terms of the question suggest that the building lay to the west of the pool, possibly in the Higherland.[97]

In 1501 Nicholas Lovat, who was one of its church- or chapel-wardens in 1498, endowed it with a small annual rent issuing from a meadow in Clayton.[98] A plot of land to the north-east of the Castle Pool was known as St. Mary's Flat at least until the middle of the 19th century, and this was probably part of the endowment of St. Mary's Church.[99] A town rental of 1608 included a tenement in the Ironmarket, once called 'the Iron Hall', which had formerly belonged to 'the service of Our Lady beyond the water',[1] and a tenement beyond the water and a barn and garden in Merrial Street, also once the property of St. Mary's.[2]

It was reported in the time of Mary and Eliza-

[66] S.H.C. 1915, 251.
[67] Pape, Tudor and Stuart Newcastle, 278.
[68] Newcastle Par. Reg. (Staffs. Par. Reg. Soc.), i. 131.
[69] Coulam, Newcastle, 98, 99, where details of the cost and of the subscribers are given. Of the total cost of £298, the corp. provided £125.
[70] Coulam, Newcastle, 99, 116.
[71] Pape, Tudor and Stuart Newcastle, 208.
[72] Coulam, Newcastle, 102.
[73] Ibid. 116.
[74] Ibid.
[75] Staffs. Par. Reg. Soc. (1931, 1939).
[76] Lich. Dioc. Regy., Newcastle churchyard docs.
[77] Ibid. Its consecration in Oct. 1835 by the bishop was made the occasion for the presentation to the rector, Revd. C. Leigh, of his portrait: Staffs. Advertiser, 31 Oct. 1835.
[78] Lond. Gaz. 1851, p. 2779.
[79] Ibid. 1862, p. 3661.
[80] Lich. Dioc. Regy., Newcastle churchyard docs.
[81] Pape, Story of St. Giles, 13.
[82] Pape, Tudor and Stuart Newcastle, 312, 325.
[83] Coulam, Newcastle, 119.
[84] Cal. Treas. Bks. 1703, 412.
[85] Le Neve, Fasti, i. 558.
[86] Cal. Treas. Bks. 1703, 412.
[87] J. W. Dunne, 'Annals of a Parsonage' (T.N.S.F.C. i), 85.
[88] Coulam, Newcastle, 119.
[89] Ibid.
[90] See pp. 4, 69.
[91] Dunne, op. cit. 78, 82, 84; and see p. 7.
[92] Date-stone on present building.
[93] Ex. inf. the rector.
[94] Cal. Inq. p.m. iii, p. 290.
[95] Pape, Tudor and Stuart Newcastle, 189.
[96] Ibid. 238.
[97] D.L. 4/110/20. In the early 15th cent. St. Mary Street is mentioned but its location is unknown: D.L. 42/4, f. 173b.
[98] Pape, Tudor and Stuart Newcastle, 21.
[99] Ibid.
[1] Ibid. 241.
[2] Ibid. 242.

beth I that there had once been in the chapel a chantry dedicated to St. Mary endowed with a rent of £1 7s. 7d. The last chantry priest received this amount as a pension from 1548 until 1566 or later.[3] In 1677 the rent was stated to be £1 2s. 7d. at which figure, at sixteen years' purchase, a contract of sale was entered into with John Chase.[4]

By 1888 a Mission Room attached to the parish church had been established,[5] but it seems to have existed for a short time only. By 1891 the Mission Rooms attached to St. Giles's were stated to be Stubbs Gate and Friars' Wood.[6] During the First World War Stubbs Gate ceased to be used as a Mission Room.[7] Friars' Wood was closed in 1940.[8] It was a small iron church in Friarswood Road and is now (1960) used as part of the adjoining school. In 1938 St. Andrew's Mission Church was established in Westlands,[9] where a new housing estate had been built. In 1955 the area served by the church became a conventional district. Thus St. Andrew's ceased to be a mission church.[10] The mission church of St. James in Clayton originated in a mission centre at Clayton school 1951–4.[11]

The growth of population in the early 19th century led to a demand for an additional church, and in 1820 the corporation approached the commissioners for building churches for a building grant and offered to provide a free site. The corporation also undertook to build a parsonage near the church, on condition that the right of presentation was vested in them.[12] The proposed condition was evidently unacceptable, for in 1824 the corporation informed the Rector of Newcastle that they were prepared to agree to the vesting of the right of presentation in the bishop and in that event would subscribe £500 to the new church.[13] This proposal, too, seems to have been refused and in the following year the corporation agreed to subscribe £500 unconditionally.[14] At the same time they again expressed their view, on this occasion to the Revd. C. Simeon, the patron of St. Giles's, that the patronage of the living should be in the hands of the bishop, and that a public meeting had been of the same opinion.[15]

In 1826 the corporation sold to the commissioners a piece of land called the Cherry Orchard in The Brampton.[16] Here the new church was built and consecrated on 18 September 1828.[17]

In 1844 St. George's was constituted a chapelry district and to it was assigned the northernmost and easternmost part of the parish of Newcastle.[18] By the New Parishes Act of 1856[19] it received full parochial status and the incumbent became a vicar; previously he had been a curate under the Rector of Newcastle, who now became patron of the living. In 1875 a part

of St. George's parish to the west and south-west was re-annexed to the parish of St. Giles.[20]

In 1832 the corporation granted £140 towards the erection of a parsonage,[21] but it is doubtful whether one was then built. By 1872 there was a vicarage house in Sidmouth Avenue,[22] and in the same year the Ecclesiastical Commissioners, having received a benefaction of £518 7s. in favour of the vicarage, supplemented it with £519 out of their common fund towards the cost of providing a vicarage.[23]

In 1841 the glebe consisted of an acre of meadow known as Church Croft, subject to a yearly rent-charge of 11s. payable to the Rector of Newcastle.[24] By 1887 there was no glebe.[25] At the outset the income of the incumbent was small, the net income in 1831 being £98 (£108 gross).[26] Grants were made from Queen Anne's Bounty in 1832 (£400) and 1836 (£200).[27] In 1878 the Ecclesiastical Commissioners endowed the living with £76 yearly out of their common fund.[28]

The church of *ST. GEORGE* occupies a commanding position on the upper slope of The Brampton. It was designed by Francis Bedford (1784–1858) in the Perpendicular style and is built of Chapel Chorlton stone.[29] It consists of an aisled nave, a chancel flanked by a north organ chamber and a south vestry, south and north-west porches, and a west tower. The tower, which has an unusually tall belfry stage lighted by Perpendicular windows, is surmounted by a pierced and embattled parapet with pinnacles, 14 ft. high, at the angles. The base of the tower forms an entrance lobby with a vestry on each side of it. Externally the nave has tall Perpendicular windows, alternating with pinnacled buttresses. Inside the church the lofty nave arcades consist of slender shafts supporting four-centred arches. Both nave and aisles have plaster vaulting with bosses at the intersection of the ribs. Originally the nave was of five bays, the chancel being formed by a shallow projection at its east end.

In 1851 the average attendance was stated to be, at the morning service, 260 with 200 Sunday school children and, in the afternoon, 450 with 600 Sunday school children. No service was held in the evening.[30]

In 1879–81 extensive alterations were made to the church. A desire to enlarge the chancel could not be met by building outwards, owing to the proximity of Queen Street. The problem was therefore solved by including the easternmost bay of the nave in the chancel and at the same time raising the floor by two steps. The corresponding bays of the aisles were converted into an organ chamber on the north side and a chapel on the south. The organ was previously in the west gallery which had originally projected into the nave; there had also been a children's gallery.

[3] S.H.C. 1915, 252, 253, 257.
[4] Cal. Treas. Bks. 1676–9 (1), 515.
[5] Lich. Dioc. Ch. Cal. (1888).
[6] Ibid. (1891).
[7] Ibid. (1917–18).
[8] Ex. inf. the rector.
[9] Ibid.   [10] Ibid.
[11] Lich. Dioc. Dir. (1952–3); see p. 68. A small brick building, the church was being extended in 1960.
[12] Corp. Order Bk. 1800–25, 281.
[13] Ibid. 335.
[14] Ibid. 336, 338.
[15] Ibid. 340.
[16] Ibid. 1825–35, 20; Rep. Com. Mun. Corps. H.C. 116, p. 1957 (1835), xxv.
[17] Coulam, Newcastle, 122.
[18] Lond. Gaz. 1844, p. 1680.
[19] 19 & 20 Vic. c. 104.
[20] Lond. Gaz. 1875, p. 5106.
[21] Corp. Order Bk. 1825–35, 145, 203.
[22] P.O. Dir. Staffs. (1872).
[23] Lond. Gaz. 1872, p. 2243.
[24] Tithe Redemption Com., Tithe Maps and Appt. Newcastle, 1841.
[25] Ret. of Glebe Lands. H.C. 307, p. 65 (1887), lxiv.
[26] Rep. Com. Eccl. Rev. H.C. 54, p. 491 (1835), lxiv.
[27] C. Hodgson, An Acct. of the Augmentation of Small Livings by the Governors of the Bounty of Queen Anne (1845), p. ccxcvi.
[28] Lond. Gaz. 1878, p. 527.
[29] Staffs. Advertiser, 20 Sept. 1828.
[30] H.O. 129/15/359.

Both were removed and a light gallery, extending only over the west lobby and the vestries, was substituted. High pews were replaced by benches of pitch pine. A reredos of mosaic, inlaid in alabaster, and a new east window with Geometrical tracery were inserted in the chancel.[31] As a result of the alterations the seating accommodation appears to have been reduced. This was stated to be 884[32] at the end of 1881 and on 18 December in that year attendance at morning service was 356 and at evening service 338.[33]

In 1887 a new bell was installed and in 1908 the chancel was extended eastwards as far as was geographically possible,[34] and new windows were inserted in its north and south walls. To commemorate the centenary of the church in 1928 a north-west porch was added.[35]

A new font, the gift of the Sunday schools, had been installed in 1881, but in 1950 this was replaced by an octagonal marble font of modern design in memory of A. E. Wenger. It provides a striking feature of the present interior, occupying the most westerly bay of the nave and having a carved oak cover, 20 ft. high, in the form of a spire.

In 1851 part of the churchyard was used as a burial ground, but the greater portion was fenced off and let as a field.[36] The burial ground was ordered to be closed as from 1 March 1865,[37] but closure was later postponed to 30 June 1866.[38] In 1886 the churchyard was levelled and a boundary wall and entrance gate were built.[39]

In 1841 the corporation granted the minister of St. George's the use of the dining room in the former workhouse for the purpose of a weekly lecture as well as for a Sunday school.[40] By 1877 a mission church had been established in St. George's School Room.[41] It was still in use in 1952[42] but in 1960 the building was sold.[43] Mount Pleasant Mission Room was constituted in 1881[44] but by 1887 it had apparently ceased to be used for that purpose.[45] On 18 December 1881 the attendance there was 78 at the evening service, no service being held in the morning.[46] St. John the Evangelist's Mission Church in Liverpool Road was consecrated on 27 December 1880[47] with accommodation for 300 persons.[48] On 18 December 1881 no morning service was held there, but the attendance at the evening service was 179.[49] The church is built of grey stone in the Early English style and consists of an undivided nave and chancel with a south-east porch. A bell turret surmounting the porch was demolished in 1959. The church is still (1960) in use. By 1887 the Iron Church[50] had been built in Victoria Road on the site now occupied by St. Paul's Church[51] and in the following year it was given that name.[52] When St. Paul's Church was built in 1905 the iron building was moved to stand beside St. George's School Room (see above) and was sold along with it in 1960.[53]

By 1900 Wilmore Row Mission Room and the Ragged School Mission had been established.[54] By 1914 the latter was known as St. George's Hall;[55] it stands on the east side of Upper Green and since 1952 has been used as a cotton waste store.[56] St. John's Mission Hall[57] adjoins St. John the Evangelist's and was built c. 1911.[58] It is still (1960) in use.

St. Paul's Church in Victoria Road was built in 1905 to serve the needs of a new ecclesiastical parish formed partly out of St. George's parish and partly out of Penkhull parish.[59] The first vicar was appointed in 1905, and the church consecrated on 29 April 1908.[60]

The church of *ST. PAUL* is of Hollington stone and was designed by R. Scrivener & Sons of Hanley in the Perpendicular style. It consists of a clerestoried and aisled nave, a chancel flanked by an organ chamber on the south and a vestry on the north, and a south transept containing a side chapel. A porch at the north-west angle of the church forms the base of a tall tower, surmounted by an elaborate octagonal spire with flying buttresses and two tiers of lights. The interior, providing sittings for 500, is faced with Hollington stone. The nave, of four bays, is divided from its narrow passage aisles by low four-centred arches. A projecting bay at the west end of the nave serves as a baptistery.

The cost was met by A. F. Coghill in memory of the Revd. R. Ward, Vicar of St. George's 1875–95. He also gave £3,000 to the building fund and £5,000 as an endowment fund,[61] the latter being placed with the Ecclesiastical Commissioners, who undertook to pay the incumbent £150 yearly.[62]

The living was endowed with 2 acres of glebe[63] known as Stubbs Lodge in Occupation Street, on which a vicarage was erected in 1920.[64] The right of presentation belonged originally to A. F. Coghill[65] and is now (1959) in the hands of trustees.[66]

By 1907 York Street Mission Room had been established,[67] but by 1910 this had been replaced by the Parish Hall,[68] which is still (1959) used as a mission church.

LOCAL GOVERNMENT AND PUBLIC SERVICES. In the Pipe Roll for 1172–3[69] Newcastle

[31] *Annual Rep. of St. George's Ch. 1881* (copy in H.R.L.); *Official Souvenir*, May 1925 (copy in W.S.L., Newcastle Pamph. Box); *Newcastle Guardian*, 26 Nov. 1881.
[32] *Newcastle Guardian*, 24 Dec. 1881.   [33] Ibid.
[34] *Official Souvenir*; ex inf. R. Scrivener & Sons, architects, Hanley.   [35] Tablet in porch.
[36] White, *Dir. Staffs.* (1851).
[37] *Lond. Gaz.* 1862, p. 3661.
[38] Ibid. 1864, p. 5185.
[39] Coulam, *Newcastle*, 123.
[40] Corp. Order Bk. 1835–44, 288.
[41] *Lich. Dioc. Ch. Cal.* (1877).
[42] *Lich. Dioc. Dir.* (1951–2, 1952–3).
[43] Ex inf. the Vicar of St. George's.
[44] *Newcastle Guardian*, 10 Dec. 1881.
[45] *Lich. Dioc. Ch. Cal.* (1887).
[46] *Newcastle Guardian*, 24 Dec. 1881.
[47] *Staffs. Advertiser*, 8 Nov. 1930.
[48] *Annual Rep. of St. George's Ch. 1881* (copy in H.R.L.).
[49] *Newcastle Guardian*, 24 Dec. 1881.
[50] *Lich. Dioc. Ch. Cal.* (1887).
[51] Ex inf. the Vicar of St. George's; and see below.
[52] *Lich. Dioc. Ch. Cal.* (1888).
[53] Ex inf. the Vicar of St. George's.
[54] *Lich. Dioc. Ch. Cal.* (1900).   [55] Ibid. (1914).
[56] Ex inf. proprietor of store.
[57] *Lich. Dioc. Ch. Cal.* (1915).
[58] Ex inf. the Vicar of St. George's.
[59] *Lond. Gaz.* 1905, p. 5456.
[60] Coulam, *Newcastle*, 123.
[61] Ibid. 124.
[62] *Lond. Gaz.* 1905, p. 5456.
[63] *Kelly's Dir. Staffs.* (1916).
[64] Lich. Dioc. Regy., conveyance of 25 Feb. 1920 to Eccl. Com. of site of parsonage.
[65] *Clergy List* (1915).
[66] *Lich. Dioc. Dir.* (1959).
[67] *Lich. Dioc. Ch. Cal.* (1907).
[68] Ibid. (1910).   [69] *S.H.C.* i. 69.

was referred to as a borough for the first time and it may well be that a royal charter recognizing this status was granted to the inhabitants in or about that year. It is certain that when in 1179 Henry II granted a charter to Preston (Lancs.), the Newcastle charter, of which there now remains no trace, was taken as the model and the burgesses of Preston were conceded the same liberties and free customs as had been given to the burgesses of Newcastle.[70]

For the grant of burghal status, and such privileges as accompanied it, the town appears to have incurred a debt to the king of £23 6s. 8d., that being the sum for which the sheriff accounted in 1173.[71] Paid in instalments, the debt was finally extinguished in 1186.[72] Under Henry III a notable step forward in recognition of Newcastle's importance as a trading community was achieved.[73] This was the issue in 1235 of a charter[74] establishing a guild merchant in the town, with all the liberties and free customs belonging to such a guild,[75] and adding the declaration, which may have been included in Henry II's charter, that Newcastle should be a free borough. The new charter omits any reference to Henry II's charter and so implies that the status was being conferred for the first time.[76] A further advance on the road to burghal autonomy was marked in 1251 by the issue of another royal charter, which gave the mayor (here mentioned for the first time) and burgesses the right to hold the town at a fee-farm rent, payable annually to the king's bailiff at Newcastle.[77] That payment of the fee-farm rent did not ensure freedom from external interference appears from a royal mandate of 1282 directing the local bailiffs to protect from interference the burgesses, good men, bakers, brewers, butchers, fishers, carriers, millers, or other artificers of Newcastle.[78]

Although the grant of charters guaranteeing their rights and liberties would seem to have placed the inhabitants of Newcastle in a strong position, it was by no means unassailable. When, in 1267, Edmund, Earl of Lancaster, upon acquiring the castle and manor,[79] seems to have secured a controlling interest in the affairs of the borough,[80] he was concerned to assert his authority and, though the stages of the dispute are not known, it is clear that the burgesses had finally to bow to his will. In 1293–6 the mayor and community, while they had claimed to farm the

borough for 40 marks, renounced this right and acknowledged that Edmund and his heirs should hold the borough and its appurtenances and dispose of them in future at will, subject, however, to the liberties granted to the borough by the charters of Henry III and Edward I.[81] It is probable that on the death of Edmund in 1296 the borough was able to regain its financial and other privileges; by 1322 it was paying a farm of £20, which was less than the original 40 marks and probably a good deal less than what had been exacted by Edmund.[82] In 1325 the burgesses were petitioning the king for confirmation of 40 marks as the fee-farm rent and exemption from attendance at outside inquests or assizes.[83] Nevertheless the farm remained at £20, though the borough was not always prompt in payment. In 1494 the corporation, being then £166 in arrear, was threatened by the duchy council with the deprivation of its liberties in default of settlement.[84]

The constitutional development of Newcastle may be traced from the records of its governing body inscribed in a series of minute books, beginning in 1369 and continuing, with a gap of eighty years, from 1411 to 1491, to the present day.[85] According to the earliest of these records supreme authority resided in the mayor and the community (communitas), but it appears that the day-to-day administration of the borough was carried on by the mayor, the bailiffs, and a body of 24 burgesses, first mentioned in 1371.[86] Nevertheless, for certain enactments touching the generality of burgesses, the participation and consent of the community as a whole were deemed advisable, as, for example, in 1379–80 when regulations were adopted for the fencing of the common lands and the building of houses;[87] and again in 1384–5 when approving an ordinance that no 'foreigner' (unless he was a burgess) should be permitted to set up as a brewer or baker.[88] From the point of view of the evolution of the borough council it is perhaps significant that in 1379–80 the Twenty-four are described as elders (seniores) and in 1382–3 as aldermen.[89] For most of the 15th century no minute books have survived so that the stages in the development of town government are not on record, but in 1498 the 'counsell of the towne' is definitely associated with the mayor and 'his brethren' in giving its consent to a proposal relating to the common lands.[90]

[70] A. Ballard, Brit. Boro. Charters, 1042–1216, 27.
[71] S.H.C. i. 69.
[72] Ibid. 125.
[73] From 1215 until his death in 1232, Ranulf de Blundeville, Earl of Chester, was in possession of the castle and manor, but there seems to be no evidence for Pape's statement that the grant to Ranulf included also the borough: T. Pape, Med. Newcastle, 41. Nevertheless his influence during this period may well have been dominant and some recognition of this may have been implied in the annual rent of 60s. payable out of the stewardship (prepositura) of the town of Newcastle granted by Henry III in 1232 to the Abbey of St. Werburgh, Chester, for the purpose of celebrating masses for the earl's soul: S.H.C. 1939, 114.
[74] For text, as enrolled on the Charter Roll, see Pape, Med. Newcastle, App. C.
[75] For the guild merchant and its trading privileges, see p. 44.
[76] In B.M. Harl. MS. 2112, f. 60, there is a 17th-cent. copy of what appears to have been a rejected first draft of the 1235 charter. In addition to the conferment of a guild merchant, the draft charter purports to grant to the burgesses privileges of a manorial and judicial character such as sac and soc, toll and team, infangtheof, hangwite, and frankthefe, &c., all implying the existence of a manorial court with wide criminal jurisdiction. Why the provisions

were omitted from the definitive charter is unknown. The Chancery clerk may have copied them from Henry II's original charter and then it may have been decided to leave them out as being irrelevant to the subject matter of the charter about to be issued.
[77] Cal. Chart. R. 1226–57, 367.
[78] Cal. Pat. 1281–92, 29.
[79] See pp. 12, 184.
[80] Complete Peerage, vii. 381; Cal. Chart. R. 1257–1300, 78. The town had been definitely granted to Simon de Montfort in 1265 (ibid. 54) and although not specifically mentioned in the gift to Edmund was presumably implied therein.
[81] Pape, Med. Newcastle, 142. The charters referred to would presumably be those of 1235 and 1251, and Edward I's charter of 1281 granting a fair at Holy Trinity (see p. 47).
[82] D.L. 29/1146/11.
[83] Rot. Parl. i. 418.
[84] R. Somerville, Hist. of Duchy of Lancaster, i. 265.
[85] The min. bks. down to 1855 are in the custody of the Boro. Mus. For a description of the borough minute books see Pape, Tudor and Stuart Newcastle, App. I, 177.
[86] Pape, Med. Newcastle, 146.
[87] Ibid. 152–3.
[88] Ibid. 157.
[89] Ibid. 152, 154.
[90] Ibid. 185.

This body is presumably identifiable with the 'twelve' who both before and after 1498 assented *pro communitate* to borough business.[91] That the 'twelve' were representative of the burgesses as a whole is attested by the appearance of their names in 1496–7 as giving 'a whole assent and consent of the cominaltie' to action taken by the mayor and his brethren.[92]

In 1547–8 the minutes record the names of twenty persons as constituting the 'counsell of the towne',[93] indicating an enlargement of the earlier body of twelve. By 1572–3 the 'counsell' had increased to 24[94] and at that figure it remained until the grant of the new charter in 1590. Election to this council was in the hands of a committee of eight, four chosen from the Twenty-four and four from the council itself.[95]

1590 CHARTER. By patent of 18 May 1590, granted at the instigation of Robert, Earl of Essex, the town was incorporated and certain constitutional changes, which formed the basis of the government of Newcastle for the next two and a half centuries, were promulgated.[96] Henceforth the governing body, to be called the Common Council,[97] was to consist of the mayor, the bailiffs, and 24 'of the more discreet and better men' of the borough, to be called the capital burgesses. The members of the council so set up were nominated in the charter itself and consisted of the then mayor, the 2 bailiffs, and the 24 burgesses, comprising 6 ex-mayors, 7 ex-bailiffs and 11 members of the last 'counsel of the towne'. Power was given to the mayor, bailiffs, and capital burgesses to make ordinances regarding the method of election to the council and the filling of vacancies. In exercise of this power the council in 1596 enacted that vacancies in the capital burgesses should be filled by a majority of the capital burgesses themselves,[98] and again in 1599 that the election of the borough officers was to lie with the mayor, bailiffs, capital burgesses, and so many other 'of the beste sorte of the commonaltye' as should bring up the total of the electing body to thirty-two, in addition to the mayor and bailiffs.[99] When it is realized that the eight additional electing members were chosen by the council, it will be apparent that the ordinary inhabitants had no voice in the government of the borough, a state of affairs which remained unchanged until the Municipal Corporations Act of 1835. In fact, such meagre acknowledgement of the right of the 'commonalty' to have a say in the election of their masters as had been conceded in the ordinance of 1599 was later withdrawn, for in 1620 it was ordered that in future the election of officers should be made solely by the mayor, bailiffs, and 24 capital burgesses without the participation of the 'commonalty'.[1]

While the 1590 charter chiefly deals with the above changes in the governing body, it contains many other provisions which in the main are declaratory of existing custom and practice as exhibited in the minute books of the earlier period. From them a picture of the mayor as the chief administrative and judicial officer clearly emerges; in the 1590 charter his pre-eminence is amply recognized and the clerkship of the market was then added to his other functions.[2] Next to the mayor in the official hierarchy stood the two bailiffs whose chief duty it was to collect and pay the farm rent due from the borough. From 1490 to 1590 one bailiff was elected to represent the Twenty-four and the other to represent the community.[3] The other officers elected annually were the common serjeant (a second serjeant to serve the mayor appears to have been appointed by 1490),[4] two wardens of the assize of bread and ale,[5] two constables, two receivers of money, and two churchwardens.[6] The 1590 charter also provides for the appointment of a town clerk, an official who must have existed before, though references to him in the early minutes are curiously scanty; in 1379–80 there is a reference to 'communis clericus',[7] who presumably exercised functions roughly corresponding to those of a town clerk, while in 1383–4 there is included an item of 6s. 8d. 'pro feodo clerici ville'.[8]

The charter also provided for the holding of three borough courts: a tri-weekly 'court of record' before the mayor, bailiffs, and steward, to deal with trespasses and actions for debt and contract up to £40; a twice-yearly view of frankpledge; and a court of piepowder at the Monday market and the St. Giles, Trinity, and Easter fairs.[9] Apart from view of frankpledge, which was to be held 'in the manner as hath been used from ancient time', it is not known how far these courts already existed before 1590.

THE POST-RESTORATION BOROUGH. The restoration of the monarchy in 1660 heralded the beginning of an attack on the independence of the boroughs which was to continue, in the case of Newcastle, until the Revolution of 1688. The detailed story of the attempts of the Crown to obtain control of the borough with the principal object of influencing the election of the borough representatives to Parliament has already been told.[10] Briefly, a new charter was granted in 1664 which the borough council was in effect forced to accept.[11] The charter's most significant innovation was the insistence that royal approval should be obtained for the election or appointment of the recorder and the town clerk, the object being to safeguard and promote through these two important officers the interest of the Crown in the borough. In January 1684 when the mayor and corporation wanted to appoint John Turton as steward or recorder, the king did not approve and the borough was obliged to elect the royal nominee Peter Broughton of the Middle Temple 'though unknown to them'.[12] The charter also provided for the

[91] Pape, *Med. Newcastle*, 176, 179, 180, 184, 189.
[92] Ibid. 183.
[93] Pape, *Tudor and Stuart Newcastle*, 190.
[94] Ibid. 200.
[95] Ibid. 199, 200, 206.
[96] Ibid. chap. vi; *Cal. S.P. Dom.* 1581–90, 665.
[97] In 1596 the name was changed by the council itself to 'the Company of the Council or Capital Burgesses': Pape, *Tudor and Stuart Newcastle*, 67.
[98] Ibid. 218.
[99] Ibid. 228.
[1] Ibid. 257.

[2] Ibid. 62.
[3] Pape, *Med. Newcastle*, 176.
[4] Ibid.   [5] Ibid. 143–75.
[6] Ibid. 176. See pp. 18–19 for the control exercised by the corporation over these last officials.
[7] Pape, *Med. Newcastle*, 152.
[8] Ibid. 155.
[9] Pape, *Tudor and Stuart Newcastle*, 62–64; and see pp. 39, 40, 47.
[10] T. Pape, *Restoration Govt. and the Corp. of Newcastle-under-Lyme* (Manchester Univ. Press, 1940).
[11] Ibid. 26.   [12] *Cal. S.P. Dom.* 1683–4, 234.

appointment of three justices of the peace, namely the mayor and two capital burgesses,[13] and confirmed the power of a majority of the borough council to fill casual vacancies and the place of anyone (including the recorder and town clerk) removed from office for bad behaviour.[14] In the same year Newcastle, like other boroughs, found itself the target of an even more determined attack by the Crown on the entrenched position of the ancient corporations. In October the council minutes record the decision to surrender their charters to the king,[15] but before doing so the corporation prudently granted to a body of local trustees the town lands and rents on trust to permit the mayor, bailiffs, and capital burgesses to dispose of the rents and profits for the maintenance of their church minister and for the relief of the poor. While negotiations were going forward in London for the grant of a new charter, Charles II died (6 February 1685). The charter of James II granted in the following month provided for a complete reconstitution of the governing body. The new council was to consist of a mayor, twelve aldermen (the mayor being one), and fifteen capital burgesses, out of whom the two bailiffs were to be chosen. There was also to be a high steward,[16] a recorder, and a common clerk. The charter nominated those who were to be members of the corporation and office-holders, and these were clearly chosen for their amenability to the policy of the Crown. Even so the Crown reserved to itself the power at any time to remove any member of the council or any of the before-mentioned officials from office. The duration of this charter was brief. James thought it advisable, as with other boroughs, to try to placate local antipathy towards him by restoring the *status quo* and rehabilitating the old pre-1685 council; the change was effected by an Order in Council of 4 December 1687,[17] under the power reserved to the Crown in the 1685 charter. Under general proclamation of 17 October 1688, the charter of 1685 was itself annulled and constitutionally the borough regained the liberties and privileges it had enjoyed under the charter of 1664.

Nevertheless, though James's interference with the borough had been unsuccessful and of brief duration, it brought in its train two evils, namely financial difficulties and dissension among the burgesses. Considerable expenditure had been incurred in connexion with the surrender of the charters and the grant of the new charter in 1685.[18] To meet their difficulties, the council had recourse to borrowing, £220 from a Mr. Allen in April 1685 and £400 from William Sneyd in May 1685,[19] but this expedient also produced its problems, for succeeding minutes illustrate the council's difficulty in discharging its

debts.[20] In fact, it is clear that between 1683 and 1688 the affairs of the town were in a very disordered state, to which the bitter political and personal rivalry of two opposing factions in large measure contributed. When the old council was reinstated in 1688 its resentment against its predecessors found expression in an attack upon Thomas Hemings, mayor in 1686–7, and in January 1689 it was agreed that he and all other persons who had intermeddled with the rents, money, or stock of the town, or received any of the same by virtue of the late charter, should be called to account.[21] Proceedings against Hemings and some of his colleagues were instituted, and in 1693–4 and 1695–6 two separate suits appear to have been in progress simultaneously.[22] How these actions were finally determined is unknown and there is no further reference to them in the council minutes. It is probable that the death of Thomas Hemings on 30 November 1698[23] put an end to what must have been protracted and costly litigation.

Throughout the 18th century the government and administration of the borough preserved its oligarchical pattern and it was not until 1827 that the right of the council to elect the mayor without the participation of the general body of the burgesses was questioned. By a decision of the Court of King's Bench[24] it was held that the council's ordinance of 1620[25] was illegal, and consequently in 1833 the mayor and bailiffs were elected by the burgesses at large. A curious result of the decision was that, the former mayoral elections having been held to be bad, several of the capital burgesses were liable to be ousted as having been elected under bad presiding officers, which had the further consequence that vacancies in the council could not be filled because eligible persons refused to accept office for fear of legal proceedings.[26]

THE BURGESSES.[27] Such, in outline, is the history of the governing body. Something must, however, be added about the qualifications for burgess-ship. In origin the burgesses were presumably the holders of burgages, of which there were 160 in the early 13th century.[28] From 1369, when the minute books begin, ample information is provided about the election of burgesses, the conditions attached thereto, and the fees payable for admission to the freedom of the borough. The usual conditions required the burgess to reside in the town and to follow his trade or occupation there. Burgess-ship for life only could be conferred on 'foreigners', i.e. those living outside the borough. Regulations regarding such burgesses were made in 1596.[29] In the medieval period the fee payable for admission varied considerably up to a

[13] See p. 39.
[14] Pape, *Restoration Govt.* 27.
[15] Corp. Order Bk. 1669–1712, f. 34b.
[16] Charles, Earl of Shrewsbury, was appointed (Pape, *Restoration Govt.* 35), but the office ceased with the annulment of the charter. It was revived by the borough council in 1901 when Jas. Lovatt was appointed Lord High Steward to be succeeded in the following year by the Grand Duke Michael of Russia who held the office until his death (1929). Subsequent holders have been the Earl of Harrowby and Lord Webb-Johnson (d. 1958).
[17] Pape, *Restoration Govt.* 50, 51.
[18] Particular items mentioned in the min. book were £120 due to Thos. Hemings, an attorney practising in the town and a member of the new council, and 40 guineas to the recorder 'for his pains in soliciting for a new charter'.

Some of the expenditure might have been avoidable, e.g. £17 2s. 10d. to Ralph Walker 'for the entertainment of the gents at the reception of the new charter': Corp. Order Bk. 1669–1712, f. 37a.
[19] Ibid. ff. 36a, 37a.
[20] Ibid. ff. 38a, sqq.
[21] Ibid. f. 64b.
[22] E 134/5 Wm. and Mary, Mich./57, and 7 Wm. III Mich./44.
[23] *Newcastle Par. Reg.* i. 249 (Staffs. Par. Reg. Soc.).
[24] K.B. 28/512/6–7, and 28/520, Md. 6668.
[25] See p. 26.
[26] *Rep. Com. Mun. Corps.* H.C. 116, p. 1951, (1835), xxv.
[27] For the post-1835 position of the burgesses see p. 50.
[28] *Bk. of Fees*, 143.
[29] Pape, *Tudor and Stuart Newcastle*, 219.

maximum of 40s. In the earlier 16th century the usual fee on election was 10s., raised to 20s. in 1560, to £2 in 1577, and to £5 in 1589, at which figure it remained until 1835, apart from the two years 1608 and 1609 when 20 marks were exacted.[30] Apprentices who had served their seven-year term with a burgess in trade paid a smaller fee which from the first quarter of the 17th century was usually fixed at 33s. 4d.[31] Those who were wholly excused payment of admission fees included free-born burgesses if resident within the borough, and usually the persons elected to represent Newcastle in Parliament.[32] The last burgess admitted without payment to enjoy the full privileges was Josiah Wedgwood on 30 April 1831.[33] Honorary freedom of the borough without the full privileges is still bestowed in special cases.

Occasionally the burgess-ship was granted, not for a monetary payment, but as a consideration for the rendering of a special service. Thus in 1589 Humphrey Smith was made free for life on condition that he provided ropes for the church bells and clock. Again, in 1614 Humphrey Liversage, and after him his son Tnomas in 1622, were admitted to their liberties so long as they maintained the windows of the church, school house, and steeple in sufficient repair, for which they were also to receive 6s. 8d. from the town yearly.[34] In 1627 Richard Ashe and his son William were likewise admitted on condition that Richard should flag and pave the ground under the New hall[35] over a period of five years.[36]

While the records are for the most part silent about the privileges attached to burgess-ship, the obligations incurred thereby are clearly revealed. The efficient government of the urban community depended upon the co-operation of the burgesses who were required voluntarily to undertake such offices as that of bailiff, town serjeant, constable, receiver of town money, churchwarden, overseer of the poor, and surveyor of the highways.

A burgess, if elected a capital burgess, was required to undertake the office or submit to a pecuniary penalty, which could be substantial; in 1797 James Breck was fined 50 guineas for refusing to take up office.[37] In the sphere of trade regulation, in addition to the usual assize lookers, as they are termed, for bread and ale, and also for meat and fish,[38] from 1631 two burgesses were appointed to

act as searchers and sealers of leather.[39] Their duty was to ensure that all leather brought into the town for sale was properly tanned and to seize all footwear made of leather mixed with horse hide or other leather prohibited by law.[40] Recalcitrant burgesses and those who showed disrespect towards the mayor, by no means a negligible number, were punished by loss of their burgess rights, which, however, seem to have been restored after an interval and on payment of a fine.[41]

POST-1835 CONSTITUTION. Under the Municipal Corporations Act of 1835, the corporation was styled the Mayor, Bailiffs, and Burgesses of Newcastle-under-Lyme,[42] and the borough council was reconstituted to consist of six aldermen and eighteen councillors elected by the ratepayers.[43] For the purpose of municipal elections the borough was divided into two wards,[44] increased to twelve in 1932.[45] From that year, when the borough boundaries were extended,[46] the council has consisted of 48 members, namely 12 aldermen and 36 councillors, but the total is increased by one if the mayor is not an elected member.[47] These added parts were predominantly mining and industrial districts and, although at the time of the extension, membership of the council appears to have been largely on a non-party basis,[48] since the end of the Second World War municipal elections have been contested between candidates supporting the aims and policies of the Labour party on the one hand and mainly Independent candidates on the other. In the period 1947–49 the council was controlled by Independent members. Since that date Labour has been generally in control.[49]

The new council elected under the 1835 Act met in the first week of January 1836[50] and proceeded to establish committees to enable it to discharge its wider functions of government. As required by the Act,[51] a Watch Committee was constituted forthwith, followed by a Markets and Tolls Committee,[52] a Highways Committee, and in the following year, a Finance Committee.[53] As the work of the council expanded, so did the number of its committees. In 1849 a Sanitary Committee was formed[54] and by 1880 there were, in addition to those already mentioned, a Burial Board, and Lighting, Fire Brigade,

[30] Pape, *Med. Newcastle*, Apps. F & G *passim*; Pape, *Tudor and Stuart Newcastle*, App. I *passim*, and p. 94.

[31] Pape, *Tudor and Stuart Newcastle*, 95. When in 1804 the Newcastle Volunteer Infantry prepared to march from home for a lengthy period of service so as to improve their discipline, the apprentices enrolled in the corps were not to lose their rights of freedom by reason of such absence: Corp. Order Bk. 1800–25, p. 51.

[32] Pape, *Tudor and Stuart Newcastle*, 206, 223, 273, 276.

[33] Corp. Order Bk. 1825–35, f. 133a.

[34] Pape, *Tudor and Stuart Newcastle*, 208, 253, 263.

[35] Presumably the market house built c. 1626 (see p. 46).

[36] Pape, *Tudor and Stuart Newcastle*, 274.

[37] Corp. Order Bk. 1768–1800, f. 178a.

[38] Pape, *Tudor and Stuart Newcastle*, 221.

[39] Ibid. 286, *et passim*. They were not appointed after 1820: Corp. Order Bk. 1800–25.

[40] Pape, *Tudor and Stuart Newcastle*, 90.

[41] Exemption from unpopular duties could be bought and from the end of the 17th cent. the borough min. books contain many references to this practice. Thus in Nov. 1678 Rich. Cooke, apothecary, paid £30 for life exemption from serving all offices, watch and ward only excepted.

[42] Municipal Corps. Act, 5 & 6 Wm. IV, c. 76. By the Mun. Corps. Act, 1882, 45 & 46 Vic. c. 50, the style was

altered to the mayor, aldermen, and burgesses.

[43] 5 & 6 Wm. IV, c. 76.

[44] Ibid.

[45] Boro. of Newcastle-under-Lyme (Extension) Order, 1931.

[46] See pp. 1–2.

[47] Boro. of Newcastle-under-Lyme (Extension) Order, 1931.

[48] *Staffs. Advertiser*, 7 May 1932. The enlarged council was then stated to consist of Independent 39, Labour 6, Independent Labour 1, Co-operative 1, Communist 1.

[49] For the period 1946–9, the composition was as follows (Independent figures first): 1946–7, 26 : 22; 1947–8, 25 : 23; 1948–9, 26 : 22; and for the period 1949–58 (Labour figures first): 1949–50, 27 : 21; 1950–1, 27 : 21; 1951–2, 27 : 21; 1952–3, 34 : 14; 1953–4, 34 : 14; 1954–5, 34 : 14; 1955–6, 33 : 15; 1956–7, 28 : 20; 1957–8, 28 : 20. In 1958–9, each party had 24 members and in 1959–60 the composition was Labour 25, Independent 23: ex inf. the town clerk.

[50] Boro. Counc. Min. Bk. 1835–44, p. 7.

[51] Mun. Corps. Act, 5 & 6 Wm. IV, c. 76, § 76.

[52] Boro. Counc. Min. Bk. 1835–44, p. 30.

[53] Ibid. pp. 42, 81.

[54] Improvement Commrs.' Order Bk. No. 2, 4 Aug. 1849.

and Building Committees;[55] in the following year the Gas Works Management Committee was established.[56] In 1890 it was found necessary to effect a reorganization of the committee structure. Highways, Sewerage, Town Walks and Lighting, General Purposes, and Watch were made committees of the whole council, while the other committees constituted were Finance, Gas Works Management, Markets and Fairs, Corporation Estates, Burial Board, Sanitary, Building, Fire Brigade, Public Buildings, and Library.[57] In 1958 the total number of committees was still the same as in 1890, but changes in individual committees had taken place, brought about by the discharge of old responsibilities and the assumption of new ones: Sewerage, Town Walks and Lighting, Gas Works Management, Fire Brigade, and Public Buildings had given way to Allotments, Baths, Education, Rating, and Town Planning.[58] In 1850 the council constituted itself a local Board of Health and appointed its first medical officer.[59] The board remained in existence until 1876.[60]

At first the chief executive officer of the new council, as he had been of the old council, was the town clerk who was paid a yearly salary of £40;[61] before 1801 he had received no salary, but in that year his emoluments were fixed at £20 yearly, raised to £40 in 1827.[62] The office, a part-time one, was filled by a local solicitor who was also able to practise privately. So things remained until 1933, when, following the extension of the borough, the appointment was made a full-time one.[63]

A treasurer was one of the officers of the Improvement Commissioners[64] and it was no doubt his appointment that was continued by the new council.[65] Although by 1871 a borough treasurer was included among the officers of the corporation,[66] his was probably only a part-time appointment, and as late as 1914 the treasurer was the manager of a local bank.[67] The genesis of the borough surveyor is presumably to be found in the office of Surveyor of Works, a paid official of the Improvement Commissioners.[68]

When the reformed council met in the first week of January 1836,[69] the finances of the town were in jeopardy. The expensive litigation of the period 1827-32[70]—the legal expenses had amounted to more than £4,000[71]—had played havoc with the borough finances and when the new council took office the balance in hand amounted to 2s. 10½d.[72] Investigation was clearly called for and a Revenue Committee appointed for that purpose quickly reported that there had been slackness in the collection of rents from corporation property, the arrears amounting to £258.[73] The appointment forthwith of a Markets and Tolls Committee[74] also reflected the council's concern about the financial position, as the income of the corporation consisted largely of the tolls and stallage duties of the fairs and markets.[75] In 1833 £431 out of a total revenue of a little over £600 came from this source.[76]

The Improvement Commissioners under the 1819 Act had been empowered to levy highway, lighting, and improvement rates and had done so fairly frequently.[77] Under the 1835 Act, however, the council was authorized to levy a general rate to meet its expenditure under all heads.[78] In 1838 a borough rate was levied for the first time and the total required was £301 9s. assessable on a rateable value of £21,128.[79] Fifty years later the rateable value was nearly £50,000 and the product of the borough rate £3,759.[80] In 1891 the rateable value was £60,705 and this had risen by 1901 to £69,217,[81] while in the decade from 1901 to 1910 the total borough rate levied rose from £5,000 to £6,980.[82] The extension of the borough in 1932 led temporarily to a slight diminution in the rate: in 1931 it was 15s. 6d.,[83] in 1932 14s. 6d.,[84] and in 1933 15s.,[85] but by 1937 it had risen to 15s. 6d.[86] In 1943 the borough rate was 17s. in the £, in 1947 23s. 10d., in 1951 20s., in 1955 24s., the highest figure so far reached; in 1956, 1957, and 1958, the rates were 16s. 6d., 19s., and 19s. 6d.[87] From 1901 to 1921 the rateable value did not change appreciably, but by 1931 it had risen to £98,470.[88] The extension of the borough in 1932 resulted in a substantial accretion to the rateable value, which in that year rose to £216,758.[89] By 1955 it was £366,258 and in the following year, as a result of a revaluation of rateable properties, the rateable value reached £728,107.[90]

In addition to rates, the markets have continued to be a source of income. In 1901 the rent received from market dues was £650 yearly.[91] The leasing of the market tolls, with the exception of those arising in the cattle market, ceased in 1926[92] and from that date the corporation has collected its own tolls. In 1958 the gross receipts from this source amounted to nearly £8,000.[93]

OTHER ORGANS OF LOCAL GOVERNMENT. In addition to the borough council, both the guild merchant and the court leet in early times shared in the government of the town, though the records relating

55 Town Clerk's Office, Boro. Counc. Min. Bk. vol. v.
56 Ibid. 4 Aug. 1881.
57 Ibid. pp. 479-81.
58 Counc. Year Bk. (1957-8).
59 Boro. Mus., Fenton MS. Bk. 86.
60 Boro. Mus., Bd. of Health Report Bk. 1874-6.
61 Staffs. Advertiser, 2 Jan. 1836.
62 Rep. Com. Mun. Corps. H.C. 116, p. 1953 (1835), xxv.
63 Town Clerk's Office, Gen. Purp. Cttee. Min. Bk., 11 Nov. 1932.
64 Improvement Commrs'. Min. Bk. 1819-34.
65 See p. 31.
66 Ingamells, Newcastle Dir.
67 Staffs. Advertiser, 30 May 1914.
68 See p. 31.
69 Boro. Counc. Min. Bk. 1835-44, p. 7.
70 See p. 43.
71 Rep. Com. Mun. Corps. p. 1957.
72 Staffs. Advertiser, 19 Dec. 1835.
73 Ibid. 20 Feb. 1836.

74 Boro. Counc. Min. Bk. 1835-44, p. 30.
75 See pp. 31, 45-46.
76 Rep. Com. Mun. Corps. p. 1955.
77 See pp. 31, 35, 36.
78 Municipal Corps. Act, 5 & 6 Wm. IV, c. 76, § 92.
79 Boro. Counc. Min. Bk. 1835-44, p. 128.
80 Ibid. vol. v.
81 Repn. to Local Govt. Bd. (1901), re boro. extension, p. 5.
82 Town Clerk's Office, Boro. Counc. Min. Bk. vol. vii.
83 Staffs. Advertiser, 14 May 1932.
84 Ibid. 15 Apr. 1933.   85 Ibid.
86 Evening Sentinel, 7 Apr. 1937.
87 Newcastle Boro. Counc. Abstracts of Accts.
88 Municipal Year Bk.
89 Newcastle Boro. Counc. Abstracts of Accts.
90 Ibid.
91 Repn. to Local Gov. Bd. (1901), p. 11.
92 Repn. to Min. of Health (1926), p. 16.
93 Ex inf. markets inspector.

to these bodies are very fragmentary. Of the former the only extant records are of three meetings noted in the earliest borough council minute book;[94] these took place in Whitsun week, in 1382,[95] 1389,[96] and 1396.[97] The record of the proceedings provides little more than a skeletal view of the guild organization. The officers of the guild, namely, steward, clerk, two door-keepers, two treasurers, and two butlers (*pincerne*), are mentioned as also are the names of the members of two bodies known as the Prima Duodena and the Secunda Duodena, in whom, it may be surmised, was vested authority to manage the affairs of the guild and to promulgate its regulations. The guild officers were for the most part members of one or other of these two bodies. The sole mention of the statutes of the guild occurs in 1372–3 when, in the case of a John de Wygan who had 'rebelled' against the mayor and other officers a second time, it was ordained by the mayor, the Twenty-four, and the statutes of the guild (*per majorem et xxiiii^{or} et statuta Gilde*) that if he offended a third time he would be fined 20s. and lose his liberty for ever.[98]

The business transacted at the assemblies of 1389 and 1396, as recorded in the minute book, was limited to the admission of a number of the inhabitants to their liberty, but as the guild met for three successive days in Whitsun week[99] it is obvious that much more must have taken place than it was thought necessary or fitting to insert in a book used for recording the official acts of the borough. In fact, it would seem that the guild merchant was, in the matter of admitting persons to the liberty of the town, i.e. the burgess-ship, performing a function of the borough council, for in the form of admission, the fee, and the requirement of pledges there is nothing to distinguish the procedure of the guild from that of the borough council at this period. The closeness of the relationship between the two bodies is illustrated by the case of John Bikley of Cheshire, who in 1409–10 was elected by the borough council to the liberty of the town so long as he remained resident there but with the additional proviso 'that if at some future time some guild or leet should change the rules about liberty then John and his heirs would have to conform to the rules as amended by the guild.'[1] But whereas John Bikley paid his admission fee to the receivers of town payments, the burgesses admitted by the guild paid their fees to the receivers of guild payments; they may have been town receivers as well, for it is a fact of some importance that in 1389 and 1396 there are no recorded meetings of the borough council. Though the evidence is scanty it seems reasonably clear that there was some overlapping of the functions of the two bodies at this time; it may even be that at an early period of the borough's

history the guild merchant was the governing body out of which the borough council developed, but no evidence exists to support this possibility.

In the 15th and 16th centuries nothing is known of the history of the guild merchant and it may be supposed that in Newcastle, as in other towns, it slowly disintegrated, its function of guarding and supervising the trade monopoly being superseded by the activities of craft guilds and by the growing control of the central government over matters of trade and commerce. It is of some significance, however, that as late as 1502 the borough council disfranchised four burgesses because they had disobeyed the guild rule[2] and that in 1588 a burgess was disfranchised for bringing an action against another burgess contrary to an ordinance contained in the guild book, thus suggesting that some at least of the old guild statutes were still in force.[3] Two years later when the borough was granted its charter of incorporation[4] the grant specifically confirmed the liberties, exemptions, and customs of Henry III's charter of 1235 but mention of the guild merchant itself was significantly omitted.[5]

With regard to leet jurisdiction the council minute books in the 15th and 16th centuries[6] record a series of enactments in which the law-making body is described as 'the mayor and his brethren with the great inquest and the small',[7] though this formula is at times subject to slight variation. The judicial and administrative business effected by this body showed a wide range and it seemed on occasion to be discharging the undifferentiated functions of a court baron, a court leet, a guild merchant, and a borough council. In 1491 the court made regulations about the common gaps and gates for entry into the common fields of the town as a court baron might do, but at the same court the mayor was enjoined to see that no man bore any unlawful weapon.[8] The names of the two sets of jurors are given, twelve each for the *inquisitio magna* and *inquisitio parva*. Leet jurisdiction seemed to be involved in 1496 when it was laid down that an arrested man should be released only on giving his bond[9] and again in 1497 when rules for the levying of distress were promulgated.[10] The court performed the functions of a guild merchant in 1502 (Uttoxeter men to be allowed to trade only on payment of toll),[11] in 1510 (regulations for butchers),[12] and in 1540 (free entry of merchants).[13] But on the last-mentioned occasion the court also concerned itself, as a court baron would, with laying open of the Holt Fields after harvest. And finally, the great and small inquest participated in what appears to be purely borough business such as the elections to the borough council by the sworn men in 1571,[14] the payment of the school master in 1567,[15] and the readmittance of a disfranchised burgess in 1581.[16] It would seem, therefore, that the court,

[94] Printed in Pape, *Med. Newcastle*, App. F.
[95] Ibid. 153.
[96] Ibid. 160.
[97] Ibid. 164.
[98] Ibid. 146.
[99] Ibid. 160, 164.
[1] Ibid. 174.
[2] Ibid. 187.
[3] Pape, *Tudor and Stuart Newcastle*, 207.
[4] See p. 26.
[5] Pape, *Tudor and Stuart Newcastle*, 62.
[6] Transcribed and printed for the period 1369–1411 and 1490–1510 in Pape, *Med. Newcastle*, Appendixes F. and G.

(pp. 142–90) and for the period 1511–1660 in Pape, *Tudor and Stuart Newcastle*, App. I (pp. 177–335).
[7] Pape, *Med. Newcastle*, 176, 180, 184, *et passim; Tudor and Stuart Newcastle*, 181, 188, 195.
[8] Pape, *Med. Newcastle*, 176.
[9] Ibid. 183.
[10] Ibid. 184.
[11] Ibid. 187.
[12] Ibid. 189.
[13] Pape, *Tudor and Stuart Newcastle*, 188.
[14] Ibid. 199.
[15] Ibid. 197.
[16] Ibid. 204.

while at times transacting manorial business, at the same or other times concerned itself with mercantile or municipal affairs.

The nomenclature of the court as exhibited in the minute book shows considerable variation and it is notable that in the later entries there is a greater tendency to employ manorial terminology than in the earlier. In 1531, 1532, and 1581 it is styled simply the great court,[17] though in the last-named year the term great leet is also used synonymously. In 1583, 1588, and 1590 the court is referred to as the great leet,[18] while in 1635 and 1637 it is described as the court leet.[19] At all these courts the business transacted, or at least recorded, concerned the admission or readmission of burgesses or the imposition of penalties on those who had proved recalcitrant. It is not until 1653 that those customary officers of a medieval manor court, the 'afferers' or assessors of the amercements due for offences presented by the jury, are found, and at a second court in that year a shoemaker was fined for refusing to allow his wares to be searched by the sworn 'afferers'.[20] It is possible that the persistence of such medieval terminology into the 16th and 17th centuries is of no great significance and that what is noteworthy is the continued use of the jury of presentment, even into a period when its functions had been absorbed by the borough council and borough Quarter Sessions.

There was evidently a parish vestry in Newcastle in the 18th century at least, although almost nothing is known of its activities before the 19th century.[21] The functions of the vestry were in large measure discharged by the borough council, which for a considerable period exercised control over the appointment of parochial officers. The election of church- or chapel-wardens by the council dates from at least 1490[22] and continued until 1707.[23] Its election of overseers of the poor is first recorded in 1622[24] and it was still appointing them in the 18th century.[25] The election of two 'supervisors' of the highways began in 1626[26] and the council made annual appointments down to the end of the 18th century when the borough court of Quarter Sessions appointed them until 1819, at which date the Improvement Commissioners assumed responsibility in this sphere.[27]

Because, in the words of the Act,[28] the borough was 'very populous, a place of considerable trade, and also a great thoroughfare for travellers', a body of Improvement Commissioners was set up in 1819 who were made responsible for paving, lighting, watching, cleansing, regulating, and improving

the town. They consisted of the mayor, the recorder, the borough justice of the peace, the bailiffs, the capital burgesses, and the town clerk, and were to be assisted by a staff of officials including a clerk, a treasurer, and a surveyor of works.[29] Under the Municipal Corporations Act of 1835[30] the reformed borough council took over the functions exercised by the commissioners, the decisions taken by the council in that capacity being recorded, not in the council minutes, but in the order books of the commissioners; this procedure continued until 1850.[31]

RELIEF OF THE POOR. In Newcastle the parochial responsibility for the relief of the poor seems to have devolved upon the borough council early in the 17th century. It was the council which thereafter undertook the organization and distribution of relief, including many of the charities, the appointment of overseers, and the maintenance of a workhouse. This lasted until 1838 when the Newcastle Poor Law Union, consisting of Newcastle and eight neighbouring parishes, was created and control vested in a board of eighteen guardians, six of them representatives of the borough.[32]

Until the later 18th century the corporation was successful in finding expedients to avoid the need for poor rates, though very occasionally, as in 1630[33] and 1699,[34] a levy was imposed. Special income was sometimes assigned to the poor—part of a fine imposed for contempt of the mayor in 1623,[35] fines for defective chimneys in 1689,[36] the fees paid by two newly admitted burgesses in 1729.[37] But the first main source of relief during this period was the borough malt mill erected c. 1657 to provide for the maintenance of the poor.[38] The mill was formally settled in trust for the poor in 1687 specifically in order that a poor rate should not be necessary; if the income from the leasing of the mill proved insufficient the poor were to have also £12 a year out of the toll of corn ground there.[39] Although the arrangement at first achieved its purpose,[40] the need for new sources of revenue had arisen again by 1730 and it was then agreed to inclose some 8 acres of The Marsh and use the rents in lieu of a rate.[41] It is not clear whether this scheme was ever carried out, but by a Chancery decree of 1740 the proceeds of the mill, £45 a year charged on the market tolls, stallage, and profits from admissions of burgesses, the £30 annual income from Lord Ward's charity, and the rents from land bought with other charity money were devoted to poor relief by the corporation in satisfaction for all gifts made to them for the poor and as a further means of avoiding a poor rate.[42] The

[17] Ibid. 184, 185, 204.
[18] Ibid. 205, 207, 208, 212.
[19] Ibid. 294, 298.
[20] Ibid. 321-2.
[21] Corp. Order Bk. 1712-67, f. 184a; see p. 32.
[22] Pape, *Med. Newcastle*, 176; and see pp. 18-19.
[23] Corp. Order Bk. 1669-1712, f. 137a.
[24] Pape, *Tudor and Stuart Newcastle*, 263; and see p. 32.
[25] See p. 32.
[26] Pape, *Tudor and Stuart Newcastle*, 271.
[27] Boro. Mus., Q.S. Min. Bk. 1718-1811, ff. 221b et *passim*; Improvement Commrs.' Min. Bk. *passim*.
[28] 59 Geo. III, c. 71 (local and personal).
[29] Ibid.
[30] 5 & 6 Wm. IV, c. 76, § 72; Improvement Commrs'. Order Bk. No. 2, p. 13.
[31] The mins. of the Improvement Commrs. end on 9 Aug. 1850 (Order Bk. No. 2). In the Boro. Mus. are the

min. book 1819-34 and two order books covering the period 1835-50.
[32] The min. books 1838-1948 and the ledgers 1843-1927 are in the Staffs. Record Office.
[33] Pape, *Tudor and Stuart Newcastle*, 282.
[34] Corp. Order Bk. 1669-1712, f. 102a.
[35] Pape, *Tudor and Stuart Newcastle*, 264.
[36] Q.S. Min. Bk. 1664-1717, f. 28b.
[37] Corp. Order Bk. 1712-67, f. 77a.
[38] Pape, *Tudor and Stuart Newcastle*, 329, 330, 333; and see p. 48.
[39] Pape, *Restoration Govt. and the Corp. of Newcastle-under-Lyme*, 46-49.
[40] Ibid. 53; Corp. Order Bk. 1669-1712, f. 58b.
[41] Corp. Order Bk. 1712-67, f. 78a.
[42] *13th Rep. Com. Char.* H.C. 349, pp. 303-4 (1825), xi. In fact several charities continued to be distributed to the poor by the corporation: see p. 71.

charity land was sold *c.* 1795 and the proceeds were applied to parochial purposes.[43] The money arising from the sale of the malt mill in 1796, however, was assigned to the poor,[44] and the £45 and £30 were still paid to the overseers of the poor in 1903.[45]

By 1774, however, the corporation was in debt to the amount of £1,600 on account of the poor, and a rate was thenceforth imposed in addition to the other charges.[46] In 1775–6 the product of this rate amounted to £584.[47] In 1782 23 acres of The Marsh were inclosed[48] and, leased out as building plots, produced an income which was used to subsidize the rates; this amounted to £131 19s. 6d. in 1835–6.[49] The average annual rate in 1783–5 had dropped to £563 19s. 6d., but in 1802–3 the poor 'and other rates', assessed at 1s. 3d. in the £, totalled £964 7s. 6d.[50]

The first reference to overseers of the poor occurs in 1622 from which time they were appointed— usually two a year—by the corporation.[51] If a person chosen was unwilling to serve he was required to find an approved substitute or pay a fine.[52] In 1720 it was decided to create the two paid offices of standing 'supervisor' and standing overseer; the fines for exemption were to be £1 10s. and £2 respectively, and appointment was to be in the hands of the mayor and aldermen.[53] At first only one official, described as an overseer, was appointed,[54] but, after the repetition of the order in 1727,[55] an overseer and a supervisor were elected in 1728 and 1729[56] and two overseers in 1730.[57] From 1731 there seems to have been only one overseer,[58] but, from at least 1786, there were again two.[59] In 1759 it was resolved by the corporation that a Mr. Cartwright was to be elected overseer for the following year at a salary of £10.[60] Payments to the poor by the overseers had been under the direction of the corporation from at least 1661.[61] In 1685 the amount of the allowances dispensed was placed under the control of the bailiffs, the churchwardens, and four others.[62] The corporation was paying the overseers a minimum of £3 10s. from 1720,[63] £10 by 1759,[64] and £12 with a further

allowance of £2 a year for help in collecting the toll of corn in 1771.[65] In 1766 the overseer was ordered to present accounts each week of the bills for goods bought on the corporation's behalf; the overseer's accounts were to be inspected once a month by the mayor, the justices, and four others.[66] At the beginning of 1771 the accounts were laid before the whole corporation.[67] The vestry were electing the two overseers and passing their accounts by the 1830's.[68] When by the Rating and Valuation Act of 1925 the office of overseer was abolished, the Newcastle overseers' functions were transferred to the rating committee of the borough council.[69]

The relief, apart from charities,[70] granted to the poor of Newcastle at various times from the later 17th century onwards included weekly and occasional money grants;[71] grants in kind;[72] whole or part payment of rent;[73] grants for apprenticing;[74] and the provision, during the 1730's and 1740's at least, of medical attention, the doctor being given two bags of malt a year and in 1741 admission 'to the rights and privileges of the borough'.[75] The total expenditure on poor relief in 1775–6 was £577 10s.[76] In 1802–3 £574 5s. 7d. was spent on out-relief within the borough for 153 adults, 62 children under 15, and 23 persons requiring only occasional help; £223 8s. 1d. was spent on the workhouse, into which 18 adults and children were admitted that year.[77]

From the later 17th century, however, there was a steady stiffening in the corporation's attitude towards poor relief. In 1685 the overseers' expenditure was placed under stricter control (see above). In 1686, eleven years before the statute requiring such measures, the corporation ordered that anyone in receipt of weekly pay from the borough should wear a badge of red cloth in the shape of a castle on pain of losing the pay;[78] in 1717 the form of the badge was altered to the letters NP in red.[79] By the early 18th century the corporation order books indicate a reduction in the scale of relief.[80] A fine of 10s. was imposed in 1707 on all those who relieved vagrants and beggars,[81] and the following year a salaried

43 *13th Rep. Com. Char.* 304.
44 Corp. Order Bk. 1768–1800, f. 165b.
45 Boro. Counc. Mins. 1835–44, pp. 80–81; Char. Com. files.
46 *Rep. Com. Mun. Corps.* p. 1955.
47 *Return on Maintenance of Poor, 1803,* H.C. 175, p. 474 (1803–4), xiii.
48 See p. 50.
49 *S.H.C.* 1931, 92, 97; *Staffs. Advertiser,* 2 Apr. 1836; Char. Com. files, which show the income as still paid to the boro. counc. in 1930.
50 *Maintenance of Poor, 1803,* 474.
51 Pape, *Tudor and Stuart Newcastle,* 263, 271, 280–334 *passim* (although the entries are regular only from 1629); Corp. Min. Bk. 1368–1684 (entries from 1636 to 1683); Corp. Order Bk. 1669–1712 *passim* (although the appointments are not consistently recorded); ibid. 1712–67, ff. 7a–35a *passim.*
52 Corp. Order Bk. 1669–1712, ff. 42b. 160b.
53 Ibid. 1712–67, f. 35b.
54 Ibid. ff. 37a–66b *passim.* The intention seems to have been that one person should hold both offices: ibid. f. 35b.
55 Ibid. f. 67b.
56 Ibid. ff. 71a, 76b.
57 Ibid. f. 81a; no supervisor was then elected. In June 1731 a Mr. Raisebeck occurs as standing overseer and master of the new workhouse (ibid. f. 83b), but neither of the two overseers appointed the previous Oct. was of this name.
58 Ibid. ff. 86a, 90b, 93a, 121a, 146a; Boro. Mus., Newcastle Char. 1760.
59 Corp. Order Bk. 1768–1800, f. 102a; ibid. 1800–25,

p. 115; *Staffs. Advertiser,* 28 Mar. 1835, 2 Apr. 1836, 1 Apr. 1837.
60 Corp. Order Bk. 1712–67, f. 184a.
61 Ibid. 1590–1669, pp. 183–236 *passim.*
62 Ibid. 1669–1712, ff. 38a, 50a.
63 Ibid. 1712–67, ff. 35b, 67b.
64 Ibid. f. 184a.
65 Ibid. 1768–1800, f. 20b.
66 Ibid. 1712–67, ff. 212a, 212b–213a.
67 Ibid. 1786–1800, f. 20a.
68 *Staffs. Advertiser,* 28 Mar. 1835, 2 Apr. 1836, 1 and 8 Apr. 1837.
69 Char. Com. files.
70 See p. 71.
71 Corp. Order Bk. 1590–1669, pp. 183, 192, 193, 200; S.R.O., Newcastle Union Mins. 1838–9, *passim.*
72 Corp. Order Bk. 1669–1712, ff. 3a, 19b, 66b; Union Mins. 1838–9, *passim.*
73 Corp. Order Bk. 1590–1669, pp. 183, 232; ibid. 1669–1712, ff. 28b, 42b, 44a, 101a, 120b, 153a; ibid. 1712–67, f. 44a.
74 Ibid. 1590–1669, pp. 210, 236; ibid. 1669–1712, f. 91b.
75 Ibid. 1712–67, ff. 84a, 94b, 124b, 144a.
76 *5th Rep. of Cttee. on Poor Laws, 1777 (Reps. of Cttees. of H.C.,* 1st ser. ix), 459.
77 *Maintenance of Poor, 1803,* 474–5.
78 Corp. Order Bk. 1669–1712, f. 40b.
79 Ibid. 1712–67, f. 22b.
80 It may, on the other hand, be that orders for grants of relief were no longer so fully minuted. Also the charities were increasing in number: see pp. 71 sqq.
81 Corp. Order Bk. 1669–1712, f. 133b.

official was appointed to arrest and punish vagrants and beggars.[82] In 1731 the poor who were not in the newly established workhouse had their weekly pay cut by half.[83] In the same year the corporation ordered that all clothing given to the poor should be of blue cloth;[84] the colour was fixed in 1742 as green for men and boys and yellow for women and girls, 'that it may be visible who are clothed by the town'.[85] In 1745 it was ordered that no medical help was to be given unless on the instructions of the overseer.[86] The town clerk was directed in 1756 to strike off the roll of freemen any who were paupers or in receipt of pay for themselves or their families,[87] and in 1774 the corporation decided that too much was being spent on the poor and that in future no part of their revenue should go to the poor except what was assigned under the decree of 1740.[88]

In 1731, following a report from an exploratory committee and the unanimous approval of a public meeting, the corporation resolved that 'the houses in Ireland [Higherland] be immediately repaired and converted into a workhouse'.[89] The standing overseer was ordered to remove all the poor into the workhouse and to 'employ them in a proper manner and provide necessaries for them'; he was to receive a salary of 4s. a week as master of the workhouse.[90] In 1732 a George Alker was appointed to teach the poor to spin cotton.[91] The master was still paid 4s. a week in 1739, and his appointment included the stipulation that he should live in the workhouse.[92] The capacity of the workhouse was 40 in 1776.[93] In 1786 the corporation gave it into the control of the churchwardens and overseers on a 99-year lease at a rent of £5 10s. a year.[94] The overseers were given notice to quit in 1808 and a 21-year lease was granted to the parish vestry at a rent of £10.[95] The period was extended to 99 years in 1809 on condition that the parish should spend £300 on repairs and that the governor should take charge of debtors committed to gaol as well as paupers.[96] In 1838 the workhouse was temporarily taken over for the able-bodied poor of the new union by the guardians[97] who on inspection found the house 'extremely clean and well-regulated' with 'provisions of the best kind'.[98] There were 64 inmates, 29 of them children, and the accommodation included 12 sleeping-rooms, with 33 beds, a laundry, a bakehouse, stabling for a horse and a cow, and a recreation yard

each for the men and the women.[99] After the building of the union workhouse in 1838–9 (see below), the corporation regained possession of the old workhouse[1] but had sold it by 1849 to the trustees of Orme's Charity, from whom in that year the union clerk was ordered to secure its use for cholera victims.[2]

The union workhouse, a building in the Elizabethan style, was erected in the Keele road, east of the old workhouse, in 1838–9 with accommodation for 350 paupers.[3] An infirmary was added c. 1842.[4] In 1885–6 a new infirmary was built, the earlier building being converted into wards for the old and infirm.[5] The west wing of the workhouse, occupied by the women and girls, was burnt down in 1890[6] and rebuilt in 1892–3.[7] The casual wards were closed in 1914, the responsibility being transferred to Stoke.[8] The building was closed and demolished in 1938.[9]

PUBLIC HEALTH. The history of sewage disposal in Newcastle seems to date from the appointment, in 1635, of a common warder whose duties, in addition to those of acting as scavenger and carting the refuse to a convenient place, included the oversight of the town fields and hedges, the removal of cattle from those fields, cleansing the church gutters, and whipping dogs out of church.[10] In 1670 the council decided to appoint a common scavenger[11] but none filled the office until 1682.[12] In 1685 every inhabitant was ordered to clean twice a week the street in front of his house to the pavement channel and also all causeways against every house. The refuse was to be laid in a heap and carried away by the occupiers within ten days. In default the scavenger was to perform the task and to levy 4d. on the offender.[13] In 1723[14] and again in 1755[15] the cleansing of the streets was included in the bellman's duties. In 1726 the making of 'middens' in the streets was prohibited and those already in existence were to be removed.[16] In 1813, on the recommendation of the vestry, the governor of the workhouse was appointed town scavenger at a salary of £10 yearly.[17] In 1821 street cleansing was placed in the charge of the Improvement Commissioners[18] and ten years later their Surveyor of Works was appointed scavenger also, with the injunction to use extraordinary exertions to keep the streets free and

[82] Ibid. f. 145b.
[83] Ibid. 1712–67, f. 84b.
[84] Ibid. f. 85a.
[85] Ibid. f. 130a.
[86] Ibid. f. 144a.
[87] Ibid. f. 175a.
[88] Ibid. 1768–1800, f. 41b.
[89] Ibid. 1712–67, ff. 82b, 83b.
[90] Ibid. f. 83b. In fact some poor continued on out-relief at a severely reduced rate.
[91] Ibid. f. 92b.
[92] Ibid. f. 121a.
[93] 5th Rep. of Cttee. on Poor Laws, 1777, 459.
[94] Corp. Order Bk. 1768–1800, f. 102a.
[95] Ibid. 1800–25, pp. 115, 120.
[96] Ibid. pp. 128–9; White, Dir. Staffs. (1834).
[97] Boro. Counc. Mins. 1835–44, pp. 146, 148; S.R.O., Newcastle Union Mins. 1838–9, pp. 6, 63, the workhouse at Audley being temporarily retained for the old and infirm of the union.
[98] Union Mins. 1838–9, p. 9.
[99] Ibid.
[1] Boro. Counc. Mins. 1835–44, pp. 206, 207, 223, 235–6, 288.

[2] Union Mins. 1848–56, p. 104.
[3] Ibid. 1838–9, pp. 40, 41, 88, 94, 100; V.C.H. Staffs. i. 300; White, Dir. Staffs. (1851).
[4] White, Dir. Staffs. (1851); S.R.O., Union Mins. 1842–4, p. 10.
[5] Union Mins. 1884–9, pp. 26–27, 38, 44, 88, 227, 250, 251, 333–4.
[6] Ibid. 1889–93, p. 152. Pending the rebuilding, the girls were transferred to Stoke at the invitation of the Stoke guardians: ibid. p. 153.
[7] Ibid. pp. 232, 235, 267, 272, 279, 315; ibid. 1893–6, pp. 39, 43–44, 95, 114.
[8] H.R.L., Stoke Union Mins. 1913–15, Feb. 1914.
[9] Ex. inf. Staffs. County Counc. Welfare Officer.
[10] Pape, Tudor and Stuart Newcastle, 294–5, 304.
[11] Corp. Order Bk. 1669–1712, f. 3a.
[12] Ibid. f. 30b.
[13] Ibid. f. 39b.
[14] Ibid. 1712–67, f. 50a.
[15] Ibid. f. 172b.
[16] Ibid. f. 61a.
[17] Corp. Order Bk. 1800–25, p. 185.
[18] Improvement Commrs.' Order Bk. 1819–34, 21 Mar. 1821, p. 150.

clear from all kinds of nuisance.[19] In 1845 the streets were being cleaned twice weekly, but the courts and alleys inhabited by the poorer people were not brought within the scope of public scavenging. In them the refuse was flung into promiscuous heaps near each property and was only removed 'at the capricious pleasure of the occupants or landlords'.[20]

The first attempt to deal with sewerage seems to date from 1801 when the corporation contributed towards the cost of two common sewers, one in Red Lion Square and another from the end of Swinnerton's Lane (?now Hassell Street) on the east side of the Market Hall, to join a third common sewer opening into Friars Lane.[21] But such measures were inadequate. The Commissioners inquiring into the state of large towns drew attention, in 1845, to a widespread lack of sanitation. It was stated that while in some parts of the town the necessaries emptied into drains and cesspools, generally they had confined receptacles behind them which required frequent emptying and carrying away. In the courts and lower parts of the town there were no public necessaries; there were some used in common by inhabitants of certain courts which were in a filthy, neglected state. Even in the modern-built part of the town no public sewers had at that time been constructed and the refuse was thrown into water courses; it either soaked into the sub-soil or remained stagnant on the surface. The general insanitary conditions were aggravated by the over-crowded state of the lodging-houses, where, it was stated, men, women, and children were huddled together indiscriminately upon straw or in five or six beds packed together in one room; the inhabitants of these lodging-houses were said to be Irish 'of whom we have 600 of the lowest order'.[22]

Outbreaks of fever in 1847 and of cholera in 1832 and 1849[23] with heavy loss of life caused general concern[24] and the Improvement Commissioners admitted in 1847 that the provisions regarding sanitation contained in the Act of 1819[25] had not been fully carried out and that the condition of the town was unsatisfactory.[26] In the following year orders were issued for the removal of nuisances and for the provision of a main covered drain in The Marsh.[27] In 1849 all members of the borough council were constituted a Sanitary Committee to investigate the health of the town and to report thereon to the council quarterly.[28] The Local Board of Health created in 1850[29] forthwith took in hand a complete system of drainage, the sewage being conveyed some distance from the town to fertilize the land.[30] In 1851 these measures were reflected in the more encouraging account given by the board's medical officer. He reported that attention had been given to the crowded and unhealthy state of lodging houses situated in the most densely populated parts and to the filthy condition of dwelling houses in the same districts, namely Lower Street, Pool Dam, Upper and Lower Green, Fletcher Street, Dunkirk, Leech's Row, Holborn, Holborn Brook, Penkhull Street, and the cross streets in Higherland. Good results were expected from the intended enclosing of public wells.[31]

The problem of sewage disposal still remained unsolved. In 1861 an order was served on the borough, on behalf of the Duke of Sutherland, to restrain the corporation from turning sewage into the Lyme Brook.[32] Apparently the nuisance was not satisfactorily abated, for in 1875 the duke obtained an order for the sequestration of the borough rates, the execution of which was suspended on an undertaking by the corporation to deal effectively with the sewage.[33] Sewage works on about 30 acres between Clayton Road and Stone Road[34] were constructed in 1877[35] and four years later a lease was obtained of meadows near the works, as a result of which the council hoped that both the duke and the Rivers Pollution Commissioners would be satisfied.[36]

In 1891 and again in 1894 the County Medical Officer of Health reported unfavourably on the sewerage arrangements, particularly in the Ashfield district, a new part of the town with a population of over 1,000, but by the time of his second report this area had been connected with the general sewerage system. But in the greater part of the town the disposal of excrement and refuse still remained highly unsatisfactory and the report gave strong support to the view of the borough medical officer that the privy system should be abolished on the ground that, apart from the great sanitary improvement thus effected, excrement could be dealt with at the sewage works with a very trifling increase of cost and that the cost of collecting night-soil would be saved.[37]

In 1919 it was reported that since 1902 1,547 privies had been converted into water closets but there were still 91 privies and 27 pail closets in the town.[38] By 1926 these figures had been reduced to 4 and 10 respectively.[39] In 1926 90 ashpits were still in use, though these were gradually being done away with.[40] The industrial areas added to the borough in 1932 presented the borough council with further sanitary problems and in 1951 out of a total number of 20,637 households there were 83 without a piped water supply and 299 without water-closets.[41]

In 1906 a sewage disposal plant was erected at a cost of £24,800.[42] In 1932, by agreement with Stoke-on-Trent, arrangements for the sewage of the en-

[19] Improvement Commrs.' Order Bk. 1819–34, 21 Mar. 1821, p. 150.
[20] 2nd Rep. of Com. inquiring into State of Large Towns and Populous Districts, H.L., p. 49 (1845), xxvi.
[21] Corp. Order Bk. 1800–25, p. 19.
[22] 2nd Rep. State of Large Towns, pp. 48, 49.
[23] White, Dir. Staffs. (1851); C. Creighton, Hist. of Epidemics in Brit. ii. 822, 844.
[24] M.H. 13/132 for resolution of public meeting in Aug. 1849.
[25] Newcastle Improvement Act, 59 Geo. III, c. 71 (local and personal).
[26] Improvement Commrs.' Order Bk. No. 2, 6 Nov. 1847.
[27] Ibid. 27 Oct. and 9 Nov. 1848.
[28] Ibid. 4 and 29 Aug. 1849.

[29] See p. 29.
[30] White, Dir. Staffs. (1851). The main drainage system is shown in detail on Malabar, Plan.
[31] M.H. 13/132.
[32] Ingamells, Newcastle Dir. (1881), 69.
[33] Ibid.
[34] O.S. Map 6″ Staffs. xvii NE. (1890).
[35] Repn. to Local Govt. Bd. (1901), re boro. extension, p.8.
[36] Boro. Counc. Min. Bk. 25 Oct. 1881.
[37] M.H. 30/235.
[38] Repn. to Min. of Health (1919), re boro. extension, p. 10.
[39] Ibid. (1926), p. 11.
[40] Ibid.
[41] Census, 1951, Staffs.
[42] Repn. to Min. of Health (1919), p. 6.

larged borough to be dealt with at the city works at Strongford were completed,[43] though the scheme encountered much local opposition as many thought that the transfer of sewage disposal to Stoke would be used as an argument for a further attack on Newcastle's independence.[44]

In 1845 it was reported that there were no public baths in the town but that every facility existed for public bathing in the canals, without causing a nuisance.[45] Public baths in School Street on the site now (1959) occupied by the Public Library were opened in 1852.[46] They comprised covered and open swimming baths and slipper, vapour, and shower baths.[47] They were not, however, well supported, and in view of an annual deficit they were closed in 1856.[48] Four years later the premises were sold to the Wesleyan Society for school building.[49] The King Edward VII Memorial Baths in Brunswick Street were erected in 1906. They then consisted of two swimming baths and a Turkish bath.[50] Alterations were made in 1921, 1938–9, and 1946.[51]

The inadequacy of the burial grounds attached to St. Giles's and St. George's churches[52] led to the corporation's being empowered in 1863 to provide burial places,[53] and in 1866 a cemetery was opened between Priory Road and Clayton Road.[54] It was extended in 1897[55] and 1931.[56] In 1932 Silverdale Cemetery came under the control of the borough council and was added to in 1938.[57] In September 1954 the council assumed control of Chesterton churchyard.[58]

A corrugated iron isolation hospital for 27 patients was built beside the cemetery in 1874.[59] At first it was used for smallpox patients only, but in 1890 it began to be used for other infectious cases as well.[60] In 1901 the building was replaced by a new hospital, consisting of an administrative block and two pavilions; at the same time a third pavilion, the result of a private benefaction, was added.[61]

OTHER PUBLIC SERVICES. It was not until the early 17th century that the borough council actively concerned itself with the maintenance of its streets and highways. By 1609 'lunes' or rates were being levied for their repair,[62] and occasionally the highways or area to be repaired are mentioned: 'Brompton' (Brampton), the lane above the 'Hart's Head', Knutton bridges, and Pool Field in 1628,[63] and the last two again in 1630, together with the way to Chesterton.[64] During the 18th century the highway rates were authorized by the borough court of

Quarter Sessions on application by the surveyors[65] and occasionally the latter found it necessary to ask for a considerable levy, as, for example, £40 in 1723 for making a cart causeway in Pool Field leading to Keele.[66]

Although the town thus tried to improve and maintain its streets, there is little doubt that in the later 18th century the increased number of turnpike roads[67] and the heavier flow of traffic created difficulties which the old system was ill adapted to meet. It is not clear how far the turnpike trusts were expected to maintain their roads within the borough limits. In 1798 the Tittensor Turnpike trustees repaired the road at the junction of Penkhull Street with The Stubbs, and in the following year widened the footway in Bridge Street and built a stone wall along the new road by the side of Stubbs Field. Also, they widened the pavement near the Guildhall and the entrance into Penkhull Street, the narrowness of which had caused frequent accidents.[68] These may have been isolated instances and were possibly due to the fact that many Newcastle officials and burgesses were to be found among the trustees.[69] When, however, in 1763[70] new arrangements were being made in connexion with the important Newcastle–Uttoxeter turnpike road, relief was specifically granted to the inhabitants of Newcastle by limiting the obligation for statute work on this road to one day (or a money composition in lieu) because the maintenance of other roads was a heavy burden to them.

Under the 1819 Act[71] considerable powers were granted to the Improvement Commissioners to regulate and improve the roads and streets within the confines of the borough, and they were required to appoint surveyors of highways.[72] They could acquire by purchase and demolish those buildings, scheduled in the Act, which impeded the flow of traffic. Their re-routing of the main thoroughfare has already been mentioned,[73] while their order books provide information about substantial street improvements during the early part of the century. The considerable expenditure involved was met by an improvement rate of 6d. in the £ levied at the first meeting of the Commissioners in 1819[74] and repeated in 1832, 1833, and 1834.[75] A highway rate was also levied from 1821 to 1834.[76]

The first attempt to provide a communal water-supply was made in 1727 when the borough council levied a rate for a water-work, which two of the inhabitants, Burton and Bourne, were authorized to

43 Town Clerk's Office, Gen. Purp. Cttee. Mins., 21 Nov. 1932.
44 *Staffs. Advertiser*, 3 Sept. 1932.
45 *2nd Rep. State of Large Towns*, 49.
46 Ingamells, *Newcastle Dir.* 70.
47 *Staffs. Advertiser*, 10 July 1860.
48 Boro. Mus., Report Bk.; Ingamells, *Newcastle Dir.* 70.
49 Ingamells, *Newcastle Dir.* 70; and see p. 59.
50 *Repn. to Min. of Health* (1919), p. 11.
51 *Evening Sentinel*, 6 Oct. 1938, 4 May 1939; *Newcastle Official Guide* [1948].
52 See pp. 22, 24.
53 *Lond. Gaz.* 1863, p. 2323.
54 *Repn. to Local Govt. Bd.* (1901), p. 7.
55 Ibid.
56 Town Clerk's Office, Burial Bd. Cttee. Min. Bk. 1921–36.   57 Ibid. 1937–46.
58 Town Clerk's Office, Allotments, Parks and Cemeteries Cttee. Min. Bk.
59 *Repn. to Local Govt. Bd.* (1901), p. 8; *Kelly's Dir. Staffs.* (1928).

60 M.H. 30/235.
61 *Repn. to Local Govt. Bd.* (1901), p. 8; *Kelly's Dir. Staffs.* (1928).
62 Pape, *Tudor and Stuart Newcastle*, 243.
63 Ibid. 277.
64 Ibid. 283.
65 Boro. Mus., Q.S. Min. Bk. 1718–1811, ff. 13a, 16a, 37b, et passim.
66 Ibid. f. 13a.
67 See p. 3.
68 H.R.L., Tittensor Turnpike Trustees' Min. Bk., pp. 101, 106, 112, 122.
69 See p. 2.
70 Uttoxeter Turnpike Act, 1763, 3 Geo. III, c. 57.
71 59 Geo. III, c. 71 (local and personal).
72 Ibid. S. xxxix.
73 See p. 4.
74 Improvement Commrs.' Min. Bk., 3 July 1819.
75 *Staffs. Advertiser*, 20 Feb. 1836.
76 Improvement Commrs.' Min. Bk., 21 Mar. 1821; *Staffs. Advertiser*, 20 Feb. 1836.

construct on a waste piece of ground below the churchyard to supply Lower Street with water.[77] The town generally was well supplied with springs and wells and the provision of iron pumps was no doubt thought to be adequate.[78]

In 1795 a more ambitious project was embarked on, when Joseph Tilstone was given the right to lay pipes in the borough to carry water from the spring called Browning's Wells.[79] He is stated to have laid down lead and other pipes under some of the streets and to have erected an engine to pump the water[80] to two reservoirs in Merrial Street.[81] But this was only a partial answer to the problem, accentuated by the town's growing population. In 1811 the council decided to have Saint Sunday's Wells cleaned and the water therein made available for the benefit of the town and neighbourhood,[82] a clear indication that the system of piped water already in existence was quite inadequate. Over 30 years later it had to be admitted that of 2,039 houses in the town water was laid on in only 215.[83] For the accommodation of the poor, however, there were fourteen stand pipes in different streets, each on the average supplying twelve houses; for this service each house had to pay 1d. weekly. Those who could not pay so much were supplied by pumps, of which there were seventeen, and from open shallow wells.[84]

The supply from the water-works, for which the yearly charge to private houses varied from 5s. to 21s., and to public houses and hotels was up to £4, was irregular and water was only available from 9 a.m. to 3 p.m.[85] The problem of an adequate water-supply was one that affected not only Newcastle but the whole of the Potteries area, and in 1847 statutory authority was obtained for the formation of the Staffordshire Potteries Water Works Company to provide water for all parts of the Potteries and Newcastle.[86] The water-works were established at Wall Grange near Leek, and the supply was extended to Newcastle in 1850.[87]

Since 1925 the water-supply of the area has been the concern of the Staffordshire Potteries Water Board, of which the corporation is a constituent member,[88] and in that year a main was laid from Hanchurch reservoir to Nelson Place.[89] In 1932 the number of corporation members on the board was increased from three to seven.[90]

Newcastle was among the first provincial towns to institute a system of communal street lighting. In 1799 the corporation presented the town with 80 lamps, for the maintenance of which the inhabitants had already agreed to subscribe annually.[91] By the Act of 1819 the Improvement Commissioners were empowered to light the streets,[92] and at their first meeting in the same year levied a lighting rate of 6d. in the £.[93] The Newcastle Gaslight Company was formed and a gas-works erected in Rye Croft to supply gas for both public and private consumption.[94]

In 1827 the Gaslight Company took over the work of collecting the lighting rate.[95] In 1833, the commissioners contracted with Cooper, lessee of the gas-works, to light the town for three years at £260 yearly; the lessee was to collect and retain the rate of 6d. in the £.[96] In 1842 the council complained of poor street lighting, but Cooper retaliated by threatening to place the town in complete darkness unless he was paid money owing to him by the council.[97]

In 1855 the company transferred its base of operations to Brook Lane, where a larger installation was established,[98] rendered necessary by the extension of the supply to cover, in addition to Newcastle, Trentham, Stoke-upon-Trent, Keele, Wolstanton, Silverdale, Knutton, Chatterley, and Chesterton.[99]

Under powers conferred by a local Act of 1877,[1] the corporation bought the undertaking in 1880,[2] and in the same year debentures to the amount of £67,625 were issued in connexion with the purchase.[3] Under the management of the corporation, the length of mains was increased from 13 miles in 1877 to 33 miles in 1901, while the price of gas, 5s. per 1,000 ft. in 1874, had been reduced by 1900 to 2s. 10d. per 1,000 ft.[4] Between 1882 and 1899 £20,000 (or £1,222 yearly) was paid out of the net profits of the undertaking in aid of the borough rates.[5] At the end of the century the annual cost of public lighting in the town was £1,139 which was charged on the profits of the undertaking in exoneration of the borough rates.[6]

In 1906 the main pipes of the Corporation Gas Works in the parishes of Wolstanton, Silverdale, and Knutton were bought by the Wolstanton United Urban District Council.[7] In 1932, following the extension of the borough, the Wolstanton United Gas Undertaking was transferred to the corporation.[8] In 1937 the corporation was empowered to supply gas for industrial purposes.[9] In 1949 the gas industry was nationalized and the supply of gas to Newcastle has since that time been provided by the West Midlands Gas Board.[10]

In 1899 the corporation set up its own electricity

[77] Corp. Order Bk. 1712–67, f. 66a.
[78] In 1736 the Ironmarket pipe was converted into a leaden one and 2 leaden pumps were erected in Lower St. and at the Malt Mill: ibid. f. 110a.
[79] Ibid. 1768–1800, f. 160b.
[80] White, *Dir. Staffs.* (1851).
[81] *Pure and Wholesome Water for 100 years, 1849–1949* (copy in H.R.L.), 9. These reservoirs were stated in 1911 to be ruinous (*Staffs. Advertiser*, 8 Apr. 1911) and about 1935 were demolished in the course of road-widening operations: *Pure and Wholesome Water*, 9.
[82] Corp. Order Bk. 1800–25, p. 143.
[83] *2nd Rep. State of Large Towns*, 49.
[84] Ibid.   [85] Ibid.
[86] Staffordshire Potteries Waterworks Act, 10 & 11 Vic. c. 204 (local).
[87] *Pure and Wholesome Water*, 13. Nevertheless as late as 1878 petitions (in Boro. Mus.) were presented locally for and against the removal of the Butchery Pump in the Ironmarket.
[88] *Pure and Wholesome Water*, 19.   [89] Ibid. 18.

[90] Boro. of Newcastle-under-Lyme (Extension) Order, 1931.   [91] Corp. Order Bk. 1768–1800, f. 191a.
[92] 59 Geo. III, c. 71 (local and personal).
[93] Boro. Mus., Improvement Commrs.' Min. Bk.
[94] *Repn. to Local Govt. Bd.* (1901), p. 5.
[95] Improvement Commrs.' Min. Bk.
[96] *Staffs. Advertiser*, 2 Jan. 1836.
[97] Ibid. 12 and 19 Nov. 1842.
[98] Ingamells, *Newcastle Dir.* 65.
[99] 18 & 19 Vic. c. 77 (local).
[1] 40 & 41 Vic. c. 172 (local).
[2] *Repn. to Local Govt. Bd.* (1901), p. 5.
[3] Boro. Counc. Min. Bk., 4 Aug. and 12 Nov. 1881.
[4] *Repn. to Local Govt. Bd.* (1901), p. 5.
[5] Ibid. p. 6.   [6] Ibid.
[7] 6 Edw. VII, c. 43 (local); *Repn. to Min. of Health* (1919), p. 21.
[8] Boro. of Newcastle-under-Lyme (Extension) Order, 1931.
[9] 1 Edw. VIII & 1 Geo. VI, c. 75 (local).
[10] *Newcastle Official Guide*.

upply works in Friarswood Road,[11] and the supply of electricity began in 1904. In 1912–13 the works was remodelled and brought up to date.[12] By 1919 the system had been linked with that of Stoke-on-Trent and the corporation agreed to take a minimum of 60,000 units yearly from Stoke.[13] In 1921 a diesel generating set, the engine having come from a German submarine, was installed, and in 1927 the power station was enlarged.[14] Electricity supply was installed in Chesterton and Silverdale in 1935.[15] Nationalization in 1948[16] led to the creation of the Newcastle District of the West Midlands Electricity Board, covering an area of 50 square miles and including the Wolstanton and May Bank areas of the borough. In 1953 a grid sub-station was established at Holditch.[17]

The risk of fire in what was largely a thatch-roofed town[18] began to be met by the borough authorities in 1623 when every capital burgess was required to provide himself with a leather bucket and every alderman with a hook and bucket.[19] In 1666 three fire-lookers were appointed[20] and in 1689 the fire-lookers, by then two in number, gave notice to the inhabitants to repair their chimneys on pain of a 40s. fine.[21] In 1678 the inhabitants were forbidden to place 'any kidels of gorse in any stacks' except in covered and walled buildings,[22] and in 1753 a man was indicted for laying 10,000 'thids' or faggots of gorse so as to 'endanger' fire.[23] About 1734 the corporation acquired a manual fire pump.[24] In 1819 it was enacted that thatch was not to be used as a roofing material.[25]

In 1845[26] it was stated that there were two well-appointed engines with a brigade of 24 firemen under the superintendence of the chief constable.[27] In the event of fire a full supply of water was said to be available from numerous pumps and there were also four fire-plugs.[28] The organization of a municipal fire brigade seems to have produced successful results, for in the previous five years there had been only three small fires.[29] No doubt by this time tiles had replaced thatch as roofing material.[30] In 1848 a new fire-engine was bought[31] and in 1851 the borough possessed one large and two small fire-engines.[32]

In 1880 the brigade consisted of a captain, who was also the police superintendent, and eleven firemen, together with fourteen members of the police

force.[33] The close association with the police force was broken in 1888 when a volunteer brigade was formed consisting of a captain, lieutenant, and twelve men. The fire-engine was housed in the barracks[34] and the barrack square was used for drilling.[35]

By 1901 the fire station, the freehold property of the corporation, was, and still (1959) is, situated in King Street.[36] It was decided to acquire a motor fire-engine in 1919.[37] Since the transfer of the fire service to the county council in 1948[38] Newcastle has been the headquarters of the northern division.[39]

During the 20th century housing has become one of the major activities of the borough council. Notwithstanding the Acts of 1882[40] and 1890,[41] it was not until 1900 that the provision of houses began with the purchase by the corporation of some land in Lower Green and with the gift by Ralph Sneyd of other land in the same area. This building land was offered for sale but only five sites were disposed of, and consequently the corporation evolved its own scheme.[42] In February 1914 plans for twelve workmen's dwellings in Lower Green were approved and in the following month approval was given for a further seventeen to be built on corporation land in Castle Hill Road and Stanier Street.[43] By September 1915 the new houses,[44] which replaced 65 buildings in the same area, many of which were in a dilapidated and unhealthy state, were finished and tenanted.[45]

The First World War interrupted the execution of further plans, but by 1926 the corporation had erected or were in course of erecting 331 houses, 168 in Liverpool Road, 104 in Westlands, and 59 in Stanier Street; a further 213 had been built by private enterprise.[46] By 1930 a large housing estate had been developed at Poolfields on the north side of the Keele road[47] and in the same year, in order to rehouse people displaced from Fletcher Street and Shoreditch, the borough council compulsorily purchased from the Burgesses Trust land in Ashfield and also additional land beyond the railway bridge on the west side of Liverpool Road.[48]

The expansion of the borough in 1932 brought under the aegis of the council the heavily industrialized districts of Wolstanton, Chesterton, Silverdale, and Knutton, in many parts of which clearance and rehousing were urgently needed. Moreover, a large amount of land, both in this area and to the

[11] Electric Lighting Orders Confirmation Act, 62 & 63 Vic. c. 137 (local).
[12] *Repn. to Min. of Health* (1919), p. 22.
[13] Ibid.
[14] Ex inf. Newcastle District Manager.
[15] Ex inf. Newcastle District Manager.
[16] Electricity Act (1947), 10 & 11 Geo. VI, c. 54.
[17] Ex inf. Newcastle District Manager.
[18] See p. 3.
[19] Pape, *Tudor and Stuart Newcastle*, 263.
[20] Corp. Order Bk. 1590–1668, p. 226.
[21] Q.S. Min. Bk. 1664–1717, f. 28b.
[22] Corp. Order Bk. 1669–1712, f. 15a.
[23] Q.S. Min. Bk. 1664–1717, f. 84a.
[24] Newcastle Boro. Libr., Local Hist. Cuttings, Bk. I, f. 56a. This appliance was on show at the Newcastle Festival of Britain Exhibition in 1951.
[25] Newcastle Improvement Act, 59 Geo. III, c. 71, S. 79 (local).
[26] *2nd Rep. State of Large Towns*, 49.
[27] Isaac Cottrill described himself as 'Chief Officer of Police, Billet Master, Inspector of Weights and Measures, and of the Public Pastures, and Conductor of Fire Brigade': Cottrill, *Police Dir.* (1839).
[28] *2nd Rep. State of Large Towns*, 49.
[29] Ibid.
[30] See illustration of High St. facing p. 9.
[31] Boro. Mus., Improvement Commrs.' Order Bk. No. 2; Corp. Order Bk. 1844–55, p. 96.
[32] White, *Dir. Staffs.* (1851).
[33] Town Clerk's Office, Watch Cttee. Min. Bk.
[34] See p. 11.
[35] *Newcastle Guardian*, 8 and 22 Dec. 1888.
[36] *Repn. to Local Govt. Bd.* (1901), p. 11.
[37] *Repn. to Min. of Health* (1919); Town Clerk's Office, Fire Brigade Cttee. Min. Bk. 1908–33.
[38] Fire Services Act (1947), 10 & 11 Geo. VI, c. 41.
[39] *Boro. Counc. Year Bk.* (1957–8).
[40] Municipal Corps. Act (1882), 45 & 46 Vic. c. 50, S. 111.
[41] Housing of Working Classes Act (1890), 53 & 54 Vic. c. 70.
[42] *Staffs. Sentinel*, 23 Sept. 1915.
[43] Town Clerk's Office, Building and Housing Cttee. Mins.
[44] Known as 'Corporation Cottages' and dated 1915.
[45] *Staffs. Sentinel*, 23 Sept. 1915.
[46] *Representation to Min. of Health* (1926), re boro. extension, p. 26.
[47] *Staffs. Advertiser*, 4 Jan. 1930; ex inf. Housing Manager, Newcastle.
[48] *Staffs. Advertiser*, 15 Nov. 1930.

south of the old borough, by this extension of the borough boundaries became available for housing development schemes. By 1938 the corporation had acquired by purchase 200 acres of the Bradwell Hall estate in Wolstanton on which by the middle of that year nearly 200 houses had been erected.[49] By 1938, too, in the Clayton area much agricultural land represented by Seabridge Road farm, Hill farm, and Roe Lane farm, as well as land bordering on Clayton Road, had been acquired for further housing development.[50]

At the outbreak of the Second World War nearly 3,000 houses had been built by the council.[51] About 90 clearance orders had been issued, most of them concerned with the lower and older parts of the borough[52] but some also with Chesterton, Knutton, Silverdale, and Ravensdale, while some 1,700 families from the demolished areas had been rehoused.[53]

Since 1945 nearly 5,000 council houses, including 234 prefabricated buildings and 77 bungalows, have been built, the greatest concentration being in the Clayton area. Much new building has also taken place at Bradwell, at Chesterton (Hollow farm, Beazley House, Crackley Bank), at Silverdale on the extreme western boundary of the borough, and at Knutton on the land once occupied by Knutton farm and in the area to the north of the main street. Smaller housing schemes have been accomplished at Basford, Lower Milehouse, and Cross Heath. Slum clearance continued in the post-war period and up to 1959 730 families had been moved from cleared areas into the new housing estates.[54]

From the outset the work of planning the new estates and designing the houses was carried out by the Bournville Village Trust, but from 1955 the borough surveyor has been responsible for an increasing share of the work.[55]

It is noteworthy that, whereas before the Second World War, two-thirds of the houses built were of the three-bedroom type, since its close less than half of them have been; there has been a great increase in the demand for two-bedroom houses, maisonettes, and small flats.[56] In 1959 28 bungalows specially designed for old people together with a communal meeting hall were being built at Porthill Green.[57] Although the borough boundary still encloses much open land, a large part of it overlies coal-mines, and the consequent risk of subsidence renders its suitability for building doubtful.

SEALS, INSIGNIA, AND CIVIC OFFICERS.
The common seal, of which the brass matrix survives, is round, $1\frac{3}{4}$ inch, and depicts on waves a low embattled wall above which rises an embattled tower with 3 gabled projections in front and 2 gable-ends at each side.[58] On the tower is a banner flanked by 2 men-at-arms, one holding a battle-axe and the other blowing a horn. On the frieze below the battlements are 3 shields bearing shields of arms: (i) a lion rampant contourné within a bordure charged with roundels, probably for Edmund, Earl of Cornwall, (ii) ? England, and (iii) ? Chester. Legend, Lombardic:

SIGILLUM COMUNE BURGENSIUM NOVI CASTELLI

The seal, which is still (1960) in use, has been assigned to the 13th century[59] and was probably appended to the surrender of privileges by the mayor and burgesses in 1293–6[60] but that document exists no longer.

The seal recorded at the heralds' visitation of 1583[61] differs slightly from the foregoing in architectural and other details. Legend:

SIGILLUM COMUNE BURGI NOVI CASTRI SUBTUS LYME

No document bearing this seal has been traced.[62]

Another common seal[63] cast in 1687 is round and depicts an embattled castle. Legend, humanistic:

NEWCASTLE UNDER LINE[64]

The seal was appended to a series of deeds relating to the free school from 1698 to 1746.[65] Its introduction is perhaps connected with the grant of the new charter in 1685.[66]

A seal of unknown purpose, round, $\frac{7}{8}$ inch, bears the same design as the first common seal. Legend, black letter: NEWCASTLE UNDER LYME.[67] The form of the lettering suggests a mid-19th-century date.

In 1844 Joseph Mayer presented to the borough, for use by the Chief Officer of Police for the time being, a seal engraved on a cornelian, mounted in silver, with an ebony handle.[68] The design is that of the common seal. Legend:

SIGILLUM CONSTABULARII NOVI CASTRI SUBTUS LYMAM
1179

A seal for the recognizance of statute merchant debts was granted by the charter of 1664.[69] As was customary it was to be of two pieces, one to be kept by the mayor and the other by the clerk. Impressions have not been traced.

The insignia of the borough include two silver (originally silver gilt) maces presented in 1680 by William Leveson-Gower.[70] Previously the maces are said to have been of wrought iron.[71] In 1507 it was ordered that the town serjeant should pay 8d. and the mayor's serjeant 6d. towards their repair.[72] The insignia also include the high constable's oak staff

---

[49] *Evening Sentinel*, 16 June 1938.
[50] Ibid.
[51] Ex inf. housing manager.
[52] In particular, Upper Green (1937 and 1939); Paradise St. (1938; date tablet 1810 now in Boro. Mus.); Hassell St. (1938); Holborn (1939); Lower St. (1939); Goose St. (1939); Hick St. (1939); Bath St. (1938–40): ex inf. Boro. Surveyor's Office.
[53] Building and Housing Cttee. Mins.
[54] Ibid; and ex inf. housing manager.
[55] Building and Housing Cttee. Mins.
[56] Ex inf. housing manager.
[57] Ibid.
[58] W. de G. Birch, *Cat. of Seals in B.M.* ii, no. 5190; photograph in *S.H.C.* 1913, p. 300.
[59] Birch, *Cat. of Seals in B.M.* ii, no. 5190.
[60] See p. 25.

[61] B.M. Harl. MS. 1570.
[62] *T.N.S.F.C.* lii. 58.
[63] Birch, *Cat. of Seals in B.M.* ii, no. 5192.
[64] The legend according to no. 5192 above is NEWCASTLE UNDER LYNE but this is incorrect.
[65] W.S.L., S.D. 1/2/45.
[66] See p. 27.
[67] Birch, *Cat. of Seals in B.M.* ii, no. 5191.
[68] Boro. Counc. Min. Bk. 1835–44, pp. 353–4. The matrix is in the Boro. Mus.
[69] C 66/3069, no. 5.
[70] The maces bear the same inscription as the plate presented to the church by the donor: see p. 21.
[71] Ll. Jewitt, *Corp. Plate and Insignia of Office of Cities and Towns of Eng. and Wales*, 318.
[72] Pape, *Med. Newcastle*, 188.

surmounted by a crown beneath which is the cipher of George II and the date 1732.[73] The mayoral chain was given to the mayor by the burgesses and inhabitants in 1851 and is so inscribed. The chain incorporates a medallion embossed with a portrait of

THE BOROUGH OF NEWCASTLE-UNDER-LYME.
Or, rising from a base barry wavy of four pieces argent and azure charged with three fishes swimming proper, a castle of three towers gules; on a chief azure a lion passant guardant between two fleurs-de-lis all gold. [Granted 1951]

Queen Victoria and around the edge is inscribed: 'Made of California gold by Joseph Mayer, goldsmith, Liverpool.'[74]

No complete list of mayors seems to exist. Ingamells gives a list of mayors from 1318 to 1880,[75] and there is a list from 1900 in the Council Year Book. Ingamells also records the town clerks from the reign of Elizabeth I to 1880.[76] The names of high constables are extant from 1770.[77]

ADMINISTRATION OF JUSTICE. During the medieval period the preservation of the public peace within the borough was based on the system of frankpledge; in the 1590 charter specific reference is made to the ancient standing of the view of frankpledge.[78] The body responsible for holding the view seems to have been, in the 15th century at least, the great and small inquest, whose activities are occasionally recorded in the borough minutes.[79]

Under the 1590 charter the mayor was appointed a justice of the peace[80] and at the court of record then set up all trespasses committed within the borough or its precincts 'by force and arms' were dealt with at its three-weekly meetings.[81] At the same time the continuance of the leet jurisdiction or view of frankpledge was provided for,[82] so that there seems to have been some overlapping of the functions of the two courts. However, the court of record appears to have soon become a court for the recovery of debts and it is probable that misdemeanours and minor criminal offences were dealt with by the court leet which was still in existence in 1655.[83] As late as 1710 the borough council appointed a steward to preside at a meeting of the court.[84]

In 1594 the borough council set up courts of trial.[85] They were held four times yearly, were presided over by the mayor, and attended by the steward and all the aldermen, and thus appear to have been quarterly sessions of the peace. These arrangements were carried a step further by the 1664 charter which appointed the mayor and two capital burgesses as justices and thus gave a formal basis to the borough commission of the peace.[86] The capital burgesses were in practice chosen by the borough council and they with the mayor formed the borough court of Quarter Sessions, which was normally afforced by the recorder or steward as assessor.[87] It was held in 1835 that the county magistrates had concurrent jurisdiction with the borough magistrates but did not in practice exercise it.[88] By the same date petty sessions were being held every Monday.[89] The Municipal Corporation Commissioners considered that three magistrates were insufficient. They also recorded a current suspicion that the magistracy was animated by political bias.[90]

The Municipal Corporations Act (1835) preserved the borough commission of the peace and gave it a statutory basis. It was to consist of the mayor and his predecessor in office for one year after the termination of his mayoralty.[91] The borough council, however, thought two justices insufficient and in 1836 appointed three additional ones.[92] In 1958 there were six or seven magistrates who sat in turn, under the mayor, every week-day if necessary. They acted as licensing justices both for public houses and public entertainments.[93]

The Municipal Corporations Act did not empower the magistrates to sit as a court of Quarter Sessions and the old court met for the last time in April 1836.[94] It authorized the council, however, to petition for the re-establishment of the court and the council took advantage of this opportunity. Its petition to the King in Council was lodged in 1836[95] and granted by patent in 1837,[96] when the new court sat for the first time under the recorder.[97] Thenceforth it has sat regularly except when lack of business has led to cancellation; in 1914, for example, it was reported that no meetings had been held for two and a half years.[98]

In the mid-19th century petty sessional courts were being held at the police office in High Street.[99] Quarter Sessions met at the Guildhall until 1953. Since then both Petty and Quarter Sessions have met at the court house next to the police station in Water Street.[1]

A borough coroner was appointed in 1837 under the Municipal Corporations Act.[2] The office survives.

[73] *Coronation Souvenir Brochure* (1953). The date on the staff may indicate the first appointment to the office which was, and remains, honorific.
[74] The date is erroneously engraved MDCCCXXXXXI. On the links of the chain are inscribed the names of successive mayors from 1851.
[75] Ingamells, *Newcastle Dir.* 77–81.
[76] Ibid. 83.
[77] Ibid. 81–82; Mayor's Christmas Card for 1943 (copy in W.S.L. Pamphs. *sub* Newcastle).
[78] Pape, *Tudor and Stuart Newcastle*, 63.
[79] Pape, *Med. Newcastle*, 176, 180, 183, 184, 187–9.
[80] Ibid. 62.
[81] Ibid. 63.
[82] Ibid.
[83] Ibid. 327.
[84] Corp. Order Bk. 1669–1712, f. 151b.
[85] Pape, *Tudor and Stuart Newcastle*, 216, 225.
[86] C 66/3069, no. 5. The min. bks. of the court and of its

successor from 1664 to 1890 are in the custody of the Boro. Mus.
[87] *Rep. Com. Mun. Corps.* H.C. 116, p. 1954 (1835), xxv.
[88] Ibid.
[89] Changed to Thursday by 1851: White, *Dir. Staffs.* (1851).
[90] *Rep. Com. Mun. Corps.* pp. 1954, 1959.
[91] 5 & 6 Wm. IV, c. 76; Mun. Corps. (Consolidation) Act, 45 & 46 Vic. c. 50.
[92] Boro. Counc. Min. Bk. 1835–44, p. 35.
[93] *Counc. Year Bk.* (1957–8).
[94] Q.S. Min. Bk. 1834–46.
[95] Boro. Counc. Min. Bk. 1835–44, p. 76.
[96] C 66/4509/4/17.
[97] *Staffs. Advertiser*, 18 Nov. 1837.
[98] Ibid. 31 Oct. 1914.
[99] *P.O. Dir. Staffs.* (1850).
[1] Ex inf. the town clerk; Q.S. Min. Bks.
[2] Boro. Counc. Min. Bk. 1835–44, p. 114.

In the sphere of civil actions, the court of record set up by the 1590 charter was empowered to determine actions for debt and contract up to £40[3] (increased to £50 by the 1664 charter).[4] Small debts of less than 40s. were, however, at the first meeting of the town council after the receipt of the 1590 charter, transferred to the jurisdiction of a monthly court of conscience set up 'to hear and determine the causes of poor burgesses', though the charter apparently gave no authority for the creation of additional courts.[5] That may have been the reason why the existence of this court was brief, for in 1594 it was abolished by ordinance of the town council,[6] and actions for debts under 40s. were to be tried by a court of wager of law 'in the same manner and form as the same court was holden in this borough before our last grant [i.e. the 1590 charter] or confirmation'.[7] There exists apparently no other reference to this somewhat antiquated type of court with its archaic use of the oaths of compurgators in place of the usual forms of legal evidence.

The steward under the 1590 charter who, with the mayor and bailiffs, presided over the court of record received a fee of 40s. yearly for his attendance at the meetings of the court.[8] The person, often referred to as the learned steward, chosen for this office, would normally possess a legal qualification and in fact he was sometimes consulted by the council on matters calling for a knowledge of the law.[9] Although it appears that the creation of the office of steward was consequential upon the establishment of the court of record, there is mention of an official bearing that title in earlier records though his status and function are doubtful. In the early minute book, in 1556–7, there is reference to a steward of the mayor's court.[10] From 1590 the steward was chosen by the mayor, bailiffs, and burgesses, though their rights in this respect were later challenged by the Crown.[11]

By the beginning of the 19th century the court of record was falling into disuse,[12] and in 1835 it was reported that in the preceding six years only 27 actions had been instituted.[13] Under the Municipal Corporations Act of that year specific provision was made for the continuance of the court of which the judge was to be the recorder or such officer of the borough as had been designated in the granting charter.[14] The court was to be held under the same conditions and at the same times as before.[15]

Early in 1836 the borough council decided on the continuance of the court, as constituted by the 1590 charter, and to that end appointed two bailiffs who

with the mayor and steward (or recorder)—or any two of them, the mayor or steward being one—should hold and be judges of the court.[16] With the reconstitution of the Quarter Sessions court in 1837[17] under the presidency of the recorder, it was natural that that officer should be regarded as the presiding judge of the court of record. Nevertheless, the attempt to revive the ancient court was short-lived and in 1839, on the ground that the recorder was non-resident and could not be expected to attend to hear every petty case, the borough council decided against its continued existence.[18]

In 1847 a county court for Newcastle and the surrounding district was formed[19] and by 1851 was sitting monthly at the Guildhall.[20]

A town prison is first mentioned in 1490–1 and the serjeant was then its keeper.[21] In 1524–5 one of the serjeants (for by that time there were two) was still the keeper[22] and so it was in 1558–9.[23] In 1590 the bailiffs were declared to be responsible for the imprisonment, presumably in the borough gaol, of debtors.[24] The prison house, in 1612, was stated to be under the hall. In 1617 it is called the Stone House.[25] The Stone House apparently stood in High Street on the north side of its junction with the Ironmarket[26] and may have been so called in contrast to the brick or wooden buildings in the rest of the town. By 1628 the use of the Stone House as a prison seems to have ended as in that year the corporation leased the premises to Thomas Hunt,[27] but references to a common gaol or prison, of unspecified location, and its keeper are frequent in the late 17th century.[28] In 1612 a 'Cage', presumably a temporary lock-up for misdemeanants, is mentioned.[29]

Nothing further is known about a prison until 1799 when it was decided to erect a prison for offenders in the workhouse garden in the Higherland[30] and this had been built by 1802 when it was referred to as a house of correction.[31] In 1809, when the workhouse had been leased to the vestry,[32] the governor of the workhouse was given charge of a prison for debtors. Criminals and all other prisoners were to be in the charge of the constables, who were to have no access to the workhouse.[33] In 1811 a plan for the erection of a wall to enclose the prison courtyard was approved and also for the building of an additional room and two cells, the cost of the work amounting to £164.[34] In 1817 William Whitaker, master of the workhouse, was appointed keeper of the prison at a yearly salary of £5, which in 1826 the borough was asking the county treasurer to pay.[35]

[3] Pape, *Tudor and Stuart Newcastle*, 62–63.
[4] Pape, *Restoration Govt. and the Corp. of Newcastle-under-Lyme*, 27.
[5] Pape, *Tudor and Stuart Newcastle*, 208.
[6] Ibid. 216.
[7] Ibid.
[8] Ibid. 216, 284. Pape's statement (p. 73) that the steward was to have 40s. travelling expenses is probably due to a misconception of the word 'travell' (meaning travail) in the 1594 minute (p. 216). When a steward lived outside the borough, as in the case of the regicide John Bradshaw of Congleton, the council agreed to defray his travelling expenses (p. 324).
[9] Ibid. 288, 292.
[10] Ibid. 193.
[11] See p. 26.
[12] The min. bks. of the court from 1715 to 1830 are in the Boro. Mus. Four folios of minutes for the year 1635 have been inserted at the beginning of Corp. Order Bk. 1669–1712.
[13] *Rep. Com. Mun. Corps.* p. 1954.

[14] 5 & 6 Wm. IV, c. 76, S. 118.
[15] Ibid.
[16] Boro. Counc. Min. Bk. 1835–44, p. 22.
[17] See p. 39.
[18] *N. Staffs. Mercury*, 7 Dec. 1839.
[19] *Lond. Gaz.* 1847, p. 1012.
[20] White, *Dir. Staffs.* (1851).
[21] Pape, *Med. Newcastle*, 176.
[22] Pape, *Tudor and Stuart Newcastle*, 182.
[23] Ibid. 194.   [24] Ibid. 209.
[25] Ibid. 248, 255.
[26] Ibid. 312; and see 18th-cent. print in Boro. Mus.
[27] Pape, *Tudor and Stuart Newcastle*, 279.
[28] Q.S. Min. Bk. 1664–1717, ff. 36a, 51b, *et passim*.
[29] Pape, *Tudor and Stuart Newcastle*, 248.
[30] Corp. Order Bk. 1768–1800, f. 185a.
[31] Q.S. Min. Bk. 1718–1811, f. 231a.
[32] See p. 33.
[33] Corp. Order Bk. 1800–25, p. 128.
[34] Ibid. pp. 141, 142, 144.
[35] Q.S. Min. Bk. 1811–27, ff. 22a, 69a.

The situation of the prison in the Higherland had one serious disadvantage. In order to reach it from many parts of the borough it was necessary to pass through an isolated part of Stoke parish,[36] where the borough constables had no power to act, with the result that rescues of prisoners on their way to prison took place.[37]

The prison consisted of four cells described in 1819 as accommodating 8 prisoners[38] and in 1833 16.[39] The room for debtors was seldom required; there were only 2 in 1818, 1 in 1830, none in 1831, and 2 in 1832.[40] An allowance of 6d. a day for the maintenance of the prisoners was received from the county treasurer.[41] In the early 19th century the prison seems to have been nothing more than a place of temporary confinement pending trial by Quarter Sessions or the magistrates.[42]

In 1835 the Report on Municipal Corporations animadverted upon the state of the two prisons.[43] The prison for criminal offenders, attached to the workhouse, was described as small and inconvenient; it consisted of four small rooms with unglazed windows and without fire-places or means of heating. The building was so insecure that constables had to be placed outside to prevent escapes and instances were known of prisoners breaking out through the roof. This lack of security probably accounted for the committal of prisoners before and after trial to the county gaol.[44] The debtors' prison, also attached to the workhouse, was in somewhat better condition, having fire-places and glazed windows in its two rooms, and a yard for exercise.[45]

Although in 1838, as a result possibly of the report, a revolving *chevaux de frise* was ordered to be put up around the interior of the prison yard,[46] the prison was probably still ineffective.[47] In 1840, on receipt of a memorial from the magistrates on the insufficiency of the prison accommodation, the council agreed to the provision of an adequate prison with twenty cells, as well as temporary lock-ups.[48] In the same year it was decided to acquire from the Duke of Sutherland land in Friars' Wood on which to erect a new gaol. Government sanction for its building was refused in 1842[49] and, although in 1843–4 £58 was spent on the gaol and the maintenance of the prisoners,[50] it may be surmised that shortly afterwards the borough ceased to be responsible for the custody of offenders apart from those accommodated in the lock-up attached to the police office in the High Street.

From the time when the minute books begin a serjeant was annually elected,[51] and, although his duties were not particularized, his function was no doubt that of executing the judicial orders of the great and small inquest. He was required to find pledges for his good conduct, and in 1490–1 he was placed under oath to guard the prisoners and gaol under penalty of £5.[52] In the same year the practice of appointing two constables began.[53] From 1501–2 two serjeants were regularly selected, known, from 1507, as the town serjeant and the mayor's serjeant,[54] and it was to the former in 1524–5 that the custody of the town gaol was assigned.[55]

In 1596 the borough council settled the form of oath to be administered to the serjeants and constables and this is informative of the duties to be performed by these officers. The serjeants were responsible for levying distraints, serving court orders, and guarding the prisoners.[56] The constables, besides being required to collect subsidies and to provide post horses for royal messengers, were to assist in the preservation of the peace by raising the hue and cry against, and making search for, felons, and by setting the watch.[57] By 1599, however, the custody of prisoners seems to have been removed from the serjeants and transferred to the bailiffs.[58] In addition to the part played by these officers in the maintenance of law and order, the age-old obligation of the burgesses to give their aid when required remained. Thus in 1607 every burgess was required to provide himself with a club 'or good balke staffe' and to be ready upon all occasions to assist the authorities in maintaining the king's peace.[59]

During the 18th century the duty of maintaining order remained with the serjeants and constables who, as elected part-time officers, progressively found the task beyond them. It is true that in 1734[60] the borough council relieved their burden to a limited extent by adding to the bellman's duties the taking up of vagrants, and that by 1736[61] there existed a night bellman, but it was not until 1819 that the Improvement Commissioners, then appointed, were empowered to employ watchmen.[62] They do not seem to have taken speedy advantage of the power thus given, and it was not until 1831 that four night patrols, furnished with staves, lanterns, and rattles were appointed. These operated, with some intermission, until 1834.[63]

In that year the first step towards the establishment of a permanent police force was taken with the appointment of a full-time constable at a salary of £150 yearly and of two under-constables at £1 weekly.[64] Even so, the town clerk stated in the following year that the police were too few and incompetent.[65]

The Watch Committee,[66] set up under the Muni-

[36] See plate facing p. 5.
[37] Boro. Counc. Min. Bk. 1785–1833, p. 107.
[38] *Returns of Gaols, 1818,* H.C. 135, pp. 42–43 (1819), xvii.
[39] *Returns of several Places of Confinement,* H.C. 484, p. 39 (1833), xxviii.
[40] *Returns of Gaols, 1818,* 42–43; *Returns of Places of Confinement which do not come under the Gaol Act,* H.C. 485, p. 70 (1833), xxviii, which contains a plan of the prison.
[41] *Returns of Places of Confinement,* 70.
[42] Ibid.
[43] *Rep. Com. Mun. Corps.* p. 1955.
[44] Ibid.
[45] Ibid.
[46] Boro. Counc. Min. Bk. 1835–44, p. 149.
[47] *3rd Rep. of Inspectors of Prisons,* H.C. 141, p. 317 (1837–8), xxx, showing no prisoners. In subsequent reports the prison is not mentioned.

[48] Boro. Counc. Min. Bk. 1835–44, p. 206.
[49] Ibid. pp. 236, 291, 292, 301.
[50] *Rep. Sel. Cttee. on Burdens affecting Real Property,* appendix to mins. of evidence, H.C. 411–xi, p. 99 (1846), vi (2).   [51] Pape, *Med. Newcastle, passim.*
[52] Ibid. 176.   [53] Ibid.
[54] Ibid. 187, 188.
[55] Pape, *Tudor and Stuart Newcastle,* 182.
[56] Ibid. 221.
[57] Ibid. 220.   [58] Ibid. 225.
[59] Ibid. 234.
[60] Corp. Order Bk. 1712–67, f. 103a.
[61] Ibid. f. 110a.
[62] 59 Geo. III, c. 71 (local and personal).
[63] Boro. Mus., Improvement Commrs.' Min. Bk.
[64] Boro. Counc. Min. Bk. 1825–35, p. 197.
[65] *Rep. Com. Mun. Corps.* p. 1954.
[66] See p. 28.

cipal Corporations Act,[67] reappointed the existing police officer, Isaac Cottrill, and two constables.[68] Cottrill actively assisted in the suppressing of the Chartist riots in 1842,[69] but was subsequently found to have misapplied funds voted for the fire brigade, and in 1849 was dismissed for drunkenness.[70]

In 1858 the force, which had been threatened with extinction in 1843,[71] consisted of a superintendent and four constables,[72] which was criticized then[73] and later[74] by the Home Office as inadequate. By 1874 it numbered 15,[75] by 1881 17,[76] and by the beginning of the present century 18.[77] The extension of the borough in 1932 called for an expansion of the force which had risen to 58 in 1938.[78] In 1947 the county council became the police authority.[79]

In the mid-19th century the police office stood in High Street.[80] A new police station was opened in 1936 in Merrial Street,[81] and the old building pulled down soon after to make way for Lancaster Building. In 1939 a new station at Chesterton was approved, on the completion of which the police were to vacate Chesterton Hall, previously used as a police station.[82]

PARLIAMENTARY REPRESENTATION. One of the burghal privileges, not perhaps always valued as such in the early years, was that of electing two of their number as their representatives in Parliament. The first Newcastle burgesses are met with in the Parliament of 1354 and thereafter the names of those elected are fairly complete.[83] How or by whom elections were carried out in the later 14th century is unknown and it is noteworthy that the early minute books contain no references to burgess representatives. It may be significant that often during this period one of the two Newcastle members either was or had been the mayor or one of the bailiffs, which suggests nomination by the governing body of the borough. From the beginning of the 15th century it seems that at least one of the members was usually a nominee of the Chancellor of the Duchy of Lancaster,[84] and that elections were controlled from Tutbury.[85] While the early representatives were burgesses living in or near the town, in time the desire of the local gentry for a seat in Parliament brought about a change in the character of the borough representation as can be seen in the elections to the

later Tudor Parliaments.[86] Their ambitions in this respect sometimes conflicted with the wishes of the borough as happened in the case of the election to the Reformation Parliament (1529–36). In 1533 Thomas Bradshawe, Mayor of Newcastle, and his brethren complained to the Lord Chancellor that John Peassall of Eccleshall had contrived to get the sheriff to return him as one of the borough members, whereas Bradshawe maintained that Richard Robynson, the then mayor (1529–30), had been chosen 'by assent of the hoole commons of the seid towne'.[87] Another example of the intervention of a local magnate is provided by an entry in the borough minute books in 1596 to the effect that the mayor and capital burgesses had bestowed the freedom and burgess-ship of the borough upon Sir Walter Leveson for life and had elected him a parliamentary burgess, an election incidentally that began a parliamentary connexion between the borough and the Leveson family of Trentham which was to continue for two and a half centuries.[88]

During the Tudor and Stuart periods[89] the most significant aspect of the development of borough representation lies in the attempt to obtain electoral control, whole or partial, whether by a local influential family, by a great territorial magnate, or by the Crown itself. Representatives of the first category were the Bagnalls, the Chetwynds, the Levesons, the Mainwarings, and the Bowyers. Of the second, Queen Elizabeth's favourite, the Earl of Essex, lord lieutenant of the county 1588–1600, furnishes an example. Having been the chief promoter of the 1590 charter, the earl considered it reasonable to demand the nomination of one at least of the Newcastle members.[90] His interference in Staffordshire elections until his death in 1601 does not seem to have been so successful in Newcastle[91] as in other parts of the county, and indeed during the 16th and 17th centuries the burgesses showed a spirit of independence which at times proved too strong for those who wished to intermeddle in its parliamentary affairs. Even the Crown was not always successful in securing the acceptance of its nominees. When in 1605 Secretary Cecil, on the death of Sir John Bowyer, one of the sitting members, asked Ralph Sneyd of Keele to influence the mayor and burgesses in the matter of filling the

[67] 5 & 6 Wm. IV, c. 76.
[68] *Staffs. Advertiser*, 9 Jan. 1836.
[69] Boro. Mus., Watch Cttee. Min. Bk.
[70] Ibid.
[71] Boro. Counc. Min. Bk. 1835–44, pp. 322, 323; *N. Staffs. Mercury*, 21 Jan. 1843.
[72] Watch Cttee. Min. Bk.
[73] Ibid.
[74] Ibid.
[75] *Return of Expenditure on Police*, H.C. p. 370 (1822), liv.
[76] *Newcastle Guardian*, 10 Dec. 1881.
[77] *Repn. to Local Govt. Bd.* (1901), p. 11.
[78] *Evening Sentinel*, 19 Oct. 1937.
[79] Police Act, 1946, 9 & 10 Geo. VI, c. 46.
[80] White, *Dir. Staffs.* (1851); R. Malabar, *Plan of Newcastle*, c. 1860.
[81] Watch Cttee. Min. Bk.
[82] *Evening Sentinel*, 12 Aug. 1939.
[83] See lists for period 1354–1660 in Pape, *Med. Newcastle*, 92–96, and *Tudor and Stuart Newcastle*, 52, 151–2.
[84] R. Somerville, *Hist. of Duchy of Lancaster*, i. 326–7; C. H. Parry, *Parls. and Councs. of Engl.* 265–6.
[85] May McKisack, *Parl. Representation of the Eng. Boros. during the Middle Ages*, 115.
[86] The following Newcastle M.P.s were also landed pro-

prietors: in the 1558 Parl., Ric. Hussey of Longdon and Thos. Egerton of Wall Grange, Leek; in the 1571 Parl., Sir Ralph Bagnall of Dieulacres and Sir Ralph Bourchier of Benningborough, Yorks., and Haughton, Staffs.; in the 1584–5 Parl., Sir Peter Warburton of Grafton Hall, Ches., and Sir Walter Chetwynd of Ingestre; in the 1586–7 Parl., Jas. Colyer of Darlaston; in the 1597–8 Parl., Sir Walter Leveson of Lilleshall and Trentham and Sir John Bowyer of Sideway; and in the 1601 Parl., Edw. Mainwaring of Whitmore and Thos. Trentham of Rocester: *S.H.C.* 1917–18, 352 *et passim*; Pape, *Tudor and Stuart Newcastle*, chap. v. [87] C 1/862 (11–14).
[88] Pape, *Tudor and Stuart Newcastle*, 223. It seems probable that in the case of the local member, as distinct from the duchy nominee, it was the rule to confer burgess-ship at the time of election, if the candidate was not already a burgess. The boro. min. bk. in 1585 records that Jas. Colyer was elected a parliamentary burgess and 'therefore was admytted to the burgisshipp of this towne': Pape, op. cit. 206.
[89] For a detailed account of the parliamentary history of Newcastle in the 16th and 17th cents., see Pape, *Tudor and Stuart Newcastle*, chaps. v and xii; also *S.H.C.* 1917–18 and 1920 and 1922.
[90] Pape, op. cit. 48.
[91] Ibid. 131–2.

vacancy, the short reply he received was that the borough had already promised the election to Rowland Cotton, who was in fact elected.[92]

The first contested election occurred in 1624 and was followed by a petition to the House of Commons by the defeated candidate John Keeling. The report of the House on this petition is important for its declaration first that the custom of vesting the right of election in the mayor, two bailiffs, aldermen, and capital burgesses was not prescriptive, and secondly that in the time of Edward IV all the burgesses had the right of election.[93] As a consequence, thereafter the right of the general body of burgesses to take part in parliamentary elections went unchallenged.[94]

During the Interregnum the representation of Newcastle fluctuated. In the Parliament of 1653 no representative of the borough was summoned to attend, while as a result of the changes made by the Instrument of Government Newcastle in the Parliaments of 1654–5 and 1656–8 was represented by one member only.[95] The two-member basis was restored in the 1659 Parliament, and thereafter Newcastle continued to send two members to Parliament, until in 1885 its representation was reduced to one.[96]

With the election of William Leveson-Gower as one of the Newcastle members in 1675 begins the control of its parliamentary representation by the Leveson-Gower family which only came to an end in 1820.[97] One method noted in 1835[98] by which this control was exercised was the lease of 60 cottages by the corporation at a nominal rent to Lord Gower, which enabled him to exercise great influence over the poorer freemen, by whom the cottages were principally occupied; also much of the Gower property in the borough was held by members of the borough council at very inadequate rents. The borough minute book attests the granting of a 21-year lease of these cottages at an annual rental of ten guineas in September 1734.[99] At the election held in that year the tenants had 'disobliged' Lord Gower and on acquiring control of the cottages he ejected those who were opposed to him.[1] Ten years later the power of the corporation to make such a lease having been challenged, Lord Gower spent more than £600 in the resulting lawsuit in support of the corporation. In consideration thereof and of his lordship's having in 1743 erected a hospital for the reception of twenty poor widows,[2] the corporation granted him a new 99-year lease on the same terms as before.[3] In 1790, when an election petition was submitted by Thomas Fletcher[4] and Clement Kynnersley against the sitting members Sir Archibald Macdonald and John Leveson-Gower, it was stated in evidence that a great part of the borough was the property of the Marquess of Stafford, whose influence directed the

choice of the electors; and that it was customary for the electors to live ten, fifteen, and twenty years in their respective houses without paying any rent.[5] The election in 1812 of Sir John F. F. Boughey, Bt., in opposition to the patron, marks the beginning of the decline of the Gower interest in the borough, and 'by 1826 the House of Trentham had retired politically from Newcastle'.[6]

Although the Gower influence in parliamentary elections during the 18th century was paramount, nevertheless the electors of Newcastle could on occasion make known to their representatives their opinions on political matters in the expectation that those opinions would be acted upon. In 1719, for example, Bryan Broughton, one of the Newcastle members, excusing himself for not voting for the Peerage Bill, wrote: 'So violent is the prejudice of the people here against the bill that should I venture to appear in favour of it, I must from that time disclaim all hopes of ever serving His Majesty in Parliamentary station again, in this county at least.'[7] Again, in 1742 the local electors decided to make representations to their members of Parliament, Baptist Leveson-Gower and Randle Wilbraham, 'for their instruction and in voting in national affairs and their conduct as our representatives', and in the same year a remonstrance was addressed to these same members 'setting forth our and other national grievances . . . in order to have such national grievances redressed'.[8]

The unreformed corporation, being committed to the support of the Gower interest, when that interest was on the wane in the early 19th century, attempted by manipulation of the franchise to arrest its decline. The method adopted was the creation of honorary burgesses who could be depended upon to vote for the Gower nominee. In December 1815 28 honorary burgesses were elected, in July 1816 12, while before the general election of 1818, when polling began on 18 June, 32 were created on 9 June and 10 added as late as 13 June. In fact, between the elections of 1815 and 1818 the corporation added 202 names to the electoral roll, more than 30 per cent. of the total poll in 1818.[9] These activities, however, did not pass unchallenged and the corporation found itself involved in the period 1827–32 in long and expensive litigation as a result of which the illegality of its electoral practices was established.[10] Even as late as 1841 the 'objectionable' long-standing practice 'of distributing money under the appellation of "Market Money", "Dinner Money" or some other local term to the poorer voters after the election'[11] still prevailed.

By the Reform Act of 1832[12] the Newcastle constituency was defined as comprising the old borough and that part of the parish of Stoke-upon-Trent as

[92] Hist. MSS. Com. *Salisbury (Cecil) MSS.*, *XVII*, 358. For cases where Crown nominees were elected to represent Newcastle, see Pape, op. cit. 133–43.

[93] Pape, op. cit. 132.

[94] The right of burgesses or freemen resident to participate in the election of borough members was reaffirmed by the House of Commons in 1704 and 1706: *S.H.C.* 1933 (1), 35.

[95] Pape, op. cit. 146; *S.H.C.* 1920 and 1922, 96. In the 1656–8 Parliament Bowyer, the elected member, was not allowed to take his seat: ibid. 101.

[96] 48 and 49 Vic. c. 23.

[97] *S.H.C.* 1920 and 1922, 128. It should be mentioned that for Jas. II's single Parliament of 1685 there was a contested election in which 2 royal supporters were returned and Leveson-Gower was defeated.

[98] *Rep. Com. Mun. Corps.* p. 1957.

[99] Corp. Order Bk. 1712–67, f. 102*b*.

[1] W.S.L., Parker Jervis Collection, bdle. 29.

[2] See p. 71.

[3] Corp. Order Bk. 1712–67, f. 139*a*.

[4] 'The Fletcher family represented the constant and finally successful opposition to the Gower interest at Newcastle and in the county': *S.H.C.* 1933 (1), 7n.

[5] T. H. B. Oldfield, *Representative Hist. of Gt. Brit. and Ireland.* iv. 517.   [6] *S.H.C.* 1950–1, 293.

[7] E. Porritt, *Unreformed House of Commons*, i. 276.

[8] Corp. Order Bk. 1712–67, ff. 130*b*, 133*b*.

[9] *S.H.C.* 1950–1, 276.   [10] Ibid. 297–9.

[11] *Rep. of Sel. Cttee. on Newcastle-under-Lyme Election Petition*, H.C. 250, p. 6 (1842), viii.

[12] 2 & 3 Wm. IV, c. 65.

was surrounded partly by the boundary of the old borough and partly by the boundary of Knutton township, i.e. the detached portion of Stoke which lay in the Pool Dam area. In 1885 the parliamentary borough was enlarged to include the parishes of Tunstall, Wolstanton, Chesterton, and Silverdale.[13] In 1901 the total electorate was 9,360, made up as follows: Newcastle 3,065 (including 586 freemen), Tunstall 2,760, Wolstanton 1,288, Chesterton 995, and Silverdale 1,252.[14]

For some years after the Reform Act (1832), Newcastle returned Conservatives to Parliament, but from about the middle of the century, one Conservative M.P. and one Liberal seems to have been the general pattern until the enlargement of the electorate in 1885. Thereafter the single member was usually a Liberal. From 1906 to 1942 J. C. Wedgwood (afterwards Lord Wedgwood) represented the borough uninterruptedly, first as a Liberal and from 1922 as a member of the Labour party, since when Labour members have continued to be returned until the present time.[15]

ECONOMIC HISTORY. The beginnings of Newcastle-under-Lyme as an urban community must have followed very closely upon the establishment of the castle; the presence of a permanent garrison would attract traders and craftsmen whose settlement near the stronghold would be dictated both by the hope of gain and by the desire for protection. As early as 1166–7 the *novum oppidum cum soca sub Lima* was collectively amerced[16] and in the following year a man of the town was required to pay the considerable sum of 34s. for the horses that he had in the forest.[17] In 1168–9 the men of Newcastle as a whole contributed £4 6s. 8d. to an aid, compared with £4 13s. 4d. by Penkhull, £2 13s. 4d. by Wolverhampton, £1 10s. by Tettenhall, £1 6s. 8d. by Walsall, and £1 by Cannock.[18] In 1187 a tallage was levied on the royal demesnes and escheats in Staffordshire and the town's assessment of £15 4s. 8d. exceeded that of any other borough or estate in the county.[19] In 1191 the men of Newcastle contributed £6 13s. 8d. 'as a gift', which may be compared with £6 10s. from Stafford and 15s. from Tamworth.[20] These contributions give some indication of the level of economic development reached in the later 12th century. During the remainder of Richard I's reign the taxation of the town seems to have been on a lighter scale, 41s. in 1195[21] and 8 marks in 1199.[22] Under John a heavy tallage of £9 17s. was levied in 1205,[23] a sum not equalled by any other borough or town in the county. The sum paid in 1206 was 7 marks[24] and in 1214 35 marks.[25]

GUILDS. Although a market was apparently in existence by the beginning of the 13th century at least,[26] the first definite recognition of the town as

a trading community is contained in Henry III's charter of 1235 granting its burgesses a guild merchant and freedom to buy and sell their merchandise in all parts of the country free of tolls and other customs.[27] What kind of organization was set up to give effect to the royal concession is unknown and it is not until towards the end of the century that some light is thrown on the actual operations of the guild. In 1280 William de Pykestoke, a burgess of Stafford, sued eight Newcastle men who had deprived him of some cloth. Their defence was that they were burgesses of Newcastle where there was a guild of merchants and that according to the custom of the borough appertaining to the guild it was not lawful for anyone but a burgess to cut cloth or to sell by the ell or, unless he was a member of the guild, to keep a shop. William admitted having done all these things and relied on a charter of privileges that King John had granted to Stafford. In 1285 the case was decided in favour of the plaintiff on the ground that until seven years previously he and other burgesses of Stafford had been accustomed to cut cloth and sell it by the ell and likewise to sell wool by the fleece and to keep shops in Newcastle.[28] It emerges from the pleadings that the Newcastle guild was primarily concerned to protect its monopoly of retail trade within the borough; no objection was raised to wholesale trading by strangers, for example, in wool if sold by large weight and in sacks, but not by the fleece. This point was emphasized in another suit in 1280 when several burgesses of Newcastle were summoned by a Stafford baker for seizing ten fleeces belonging to him. In justification they asserted that by the liberty of their guild the custom of the borough was that no one, unless a member of the guild, could buy or sell wool in the borough, except by sacks or some great weight.[29] At the same time other liberties of the guild were stated to comprise prohibitions on the cutting of cloth to be sold in the town, the cutting up of meat and fish, and the buying of fresh leather.

The place of meeting of the guild, the Guildhall, is first mentioned in a charter of 1293–6.[30] In 1375–6 a number of the townspeople contributed sums totalling £9 13s. 6d. *pro communi aula*, which may have been for the building or rebuilding of the Guildhall;[31] the reference in the 1590 charter to the 'Common Hall called the Gildhall'[32] indicates that either appellation could be used for the same building, where not only guild but also borough business was transacted. From 1590 the place of assembly of the borough council has always been the Guildhall.[33]

The earliest craft guild of which we have any information was that of the butchers, which was in existence at least by 1510. In that year the mayor and his brethren, with the consent of the great and small inquests, laid down certain rules for the guild which reflect the trading and devotional aspects of the fraternity. No butcher was to set up in trade without

[13] Redistribution of Seats Act, 1885, 48 & 49 Vic. c. 23.
[14] *Repn. to Local Govt. Bd.* (1901), p. 4.
[15] *S.H.C.* 1933 (1), 78, 91, 101; *Dod's Parl. Companion*, passim.
[16] *S.H.C.* i. 48.
[17] Ibid. 55.
[18] Ibid. 56.
[19] Ibid. 130.
[20] *Pipe R.* 1191, 1192 (P.R.S. N.S. ii), 150.
[21] *S.H.C.* ii(1), 47.
[22] Ibid. 83.

[23] *Pipe R.* 1205 (P.R.S. N.S. xix), 158.
[24] Ibid. 1206 (P.R.S. N.S. xx), 114.
[25] *S.H.C.* ii(1), 162.
[26] See p. 45.
[27] *Cal. Chart. R.* 1225–57, 213.
[28] *S.H.C.* vi(1), 111; Pape, *Med. Newcastle*, 47–49.
[29] C. Gross, *Gild Merchant*, ii. 177; Pape, *Med. Newcastle*, 47.
[30] Pape, *Med. Newcastle*, 142.
[31] Ibid. 148.
[32] Pape, *Tudor and Stuart Newcastle*, 63.
[33] Ibid. 209 sqq.

the consent of the guild and the payment of an appropriate fee. No meat was to be offered for sale except the butcher's own, and shops were not to be opened at the times of church services. Two wardens were to be appointed yearly. The guild was required to equip itself with a banner and also to provide a light before St. Mary's altar in the church of St. Giles.[34]

There seems also to have been a guild of smiths, for in 1522 the mayor and his brethren, together with the great and small inquests, agreed to allow the smiths to maintain a light in the church as had been their former custom.[35]

MARKETS AND FAIRS. The right to hold a market was presumably one of the privileges granted in the lost royal charter.[36] That a market was in existence in the early 13th century is evidenced by the fact that in 1203 the market-day was changed from Sunday to Saturday, for which the burgesses had to pay a fine to the king.[37] It is not known how long the market continued to be held on a Saturday and it may be that the day remained unchanged until 1590 when under Elizabeth I's charter the market-day was declared to be Monday[38] and so it has remained. Additional market-days have, however, been instituted from time to time. In 1592 the borough council ordered, for some undeclared reason, that badgers should 'every Thursday bring their malt and other grain into the High Street unto the market place there to be sold and not in houses or other private places' instead of on the usual Monday.[39] How long this separate corn market lasted is unknown but it was certainly still in existence in 1639.[40] At the end of the 18th century Monday was still recorded as the only weekly market-day[41] but at the beginning of the 19th, to meet the demands of a larger population, a Saturday market for provisions was added.[42] In 1890 it was stated that a market was held also on Wednesday.[43] At the present time (1959) the market-days are Monday, Friday, and Saturday.[44]

Until 1251, when the burgesses were given the right to hold the town at a fee-farm rent,[45] the market tolls were payable into the royal exchequer and, according to a survey made about that time, these, together with pleas, fairs, and other perquisites, amounted to £12 15s.[46] Thereafter, tolls on produce brought to market were fixed and collected by the borough authorities as part of the town revenue. In 1502 the mayor and his brethren together with the great and small inquests declared that the men of Uttoxeter should not be free to buy

and sell unless they paid toll,[47] which suggests that they had been in the habit of using the market facilities without paying their dues. During the Middle Ages restrictions were placed on the use of the market by outside merchants,[48] but in 1540–1 it was made lawful for all persons to enter the borough with any kind of merchandise provided they paid toll.[49] This decree may have been promulgated following a Chancery suit[50] brought by the Newcastle bailiffs against two strangers who at the end of 1540 had sold goods by retail in the town; the goods had been seized but they had recovered possession, and so the town had sued them. The result is not known but it may have been unfavourable and thus have led to a change of policy towards strangers.

While it may be assumed that before 1590, when by the instrument of incorporation the clerkship of the market was attached to the office of mayor,[51] its general regulation fell within the duties of the mayor and bailiffs, no evidence to that effect is to be found in the borough council minute books, and it is possible that the supervision of the market was the responsibility of the guild merchant. The minutes record the election of two *supervisores marcatorum et assisarum sub majore* in 1509–10[52] and for the subsequent four years[53] but how far their duties exceeded those normally attached to the tasters of bread and ale, usually referred as 'syse-lookers', is not known. From the end of the 16th to the end of the 17th century, the official most concerned with the detailed affairs of the market was the bellman or town crier. He was authorized in 1596 to collect toll on all corn and grain brought for sale in the town either on market-day or any other week day and to retain it for his own use.[54] For this privilege he was required to pay an annual sum into the town chest—26s. 8d. in 1565,[55] £8 in 1613,[56] £12 in 1617,[57] £14 in 1637,[58] £18 in 1640,[59] £20 in 1649;[60] the upward grading of the farm rent during the period may point to Newcastle's advance as a centre of trade, but currency inflation may also have been a contributory factor. The importance of the corn toll was demonstrated in May 1637 when the assembly decided that in future the profit of the corn toll should be assigned to the mayor, a decision reversed three months later when it was realized that without the corn rent the town revenues would be placed in serious jeopardy. Accordingly the system of renting the corn toll to the bellman was resumed,[61] and continued until 1686. In that year he was allowed £6 yearly for collecting the toll and helping the persons appointed to sell it.[62] In 1710 the toll corn was leased to William Sharman on payment of

[34] Pape, *Med. Newcastle*, 189–90.
[35] Pape, *Tudor and Stuart Newcastle*, 181; and see p. 51.
[36] See p. 25. In the Pipe Roll for 1173–4 the sheriff accounts under Trentham for 40s. for a new market (*pro novo foro*) which was presumably located in the newly established borough: *S.H.C.* i. 71.
[37] *Abbrev. Plac.* (Rec. Com.), 43; Pape, *Med. Newcastle*, 41.
[38] Pape, *Tudor and Stuart Newcastle*, 63.
[39] Ibid. 214.
[40] Ibid. 302.
[41] *Univ. Brit. Dir.* (1791), iv. 101.
[42] White, *Dir. Staffs.* (1834).
[43] *Rep. Com. Market Rights and Tolls* [C. 6268–vi], p. 246, H.C. (1890–1), xxxix.
[44] *Newcastle Official Guide* [1951].
[45] See p. 25.
[46] *Cal. Inq. Misc.* i, p. 153.

[47] Pape, *Med. Newcastle*, 187.
[48] See p. 44.
[49] Pape, *Tudor and Stuart Newcastle*, 188.
[50] Ibid. 32.
[51] Ibid. 62.
[52] Pape, *Med. Newcastle*, 189.
[53] Pape, *Tudor and Stuart Newcastle*, 177–8.
[54] Ibid. 219–20.
[55] Ibid. 197.
[56] Ibid. 252.
[57] Ibid. 254.
[58] Ibid. 297–8. From the wording of the min. book entry it is not clear whether the £14 is a quarterly or yearly rent but probably the latter was intended.
[59] Ibid. 303.
[60] Ibid. 315.
[61] Ibid. 297–8.
[62] Corp. Order Bk. 1669–1712, f. 42b.

a lump sum of 40 guineas and a yearly rent of £40.[63] At first he kept the corn he collected in the old town hall but in 1715 he was no longer allowed to use the 'arks' in the town hall for that purpose.[64] A new lessee in 1752 was called upon to pay £86 yearly[65] but when five years later the lease was surrendered the corporation decided to keep the toll corn in their own hands.[66]

While the council insisted on the payment of corn toll by strangers and badgers,[67] its policy towards the burgesses showed inconsistency. In 1614 it was laid down that burgesses must pay toll on corn which they had bought in other markets and then offered for sale in the Newcastle market.[68] Five years later the burgesses were freed from toll,[69] but in 1625 they were again subjected to the levy.[70] In 1645, and again in 1648, 'foreign' burgesses[71] were required to pay the corn toll, which may indicate that by that date the ordinary burgess had been freed from the toll.[72]

Another important item of market revenue was that derived from stallages. Burgesses were entitled to set up stalls in the market free of toll[73] but by 1889 not more than four burgesses were exercising the right.[74] At this time, and probably earlier, the corporation, to save itself the trouble of employing a collector, leased out the market tolls, a practice which continued until 1926 when the corporation took over the tolls, with the exception of those arising in the cattle market.[75]

The exact location of the market in the Middle Ages is unknown, but so long as the castle remained a centre of activity, it is reasonable to suppose that the trade of Newcastle was carried on in its immediate neighbourhood. It has already been suggested[76] that the main thoroughfare of the town in the medieval period ran from Stubbs Gate through Lower Street and Holborn to Upper Green, the last-named being a large open space, suitable for a market. Although there is no documentary or other evidence to support this identification of Upper Green with the ancient market-place, it may be noted that in a list of openings into the common fields drawn up in 1561–2 one is described as 'the gap at Ashe in the old market leading into Ashfield', which could have been near Upper Green.[77] A reference in 1280 to the old market may indicate that by then a new market-place had been established as distinct from the old one.[78]

With the decay of the castle, the centre of burghal activity shifted eastwards to the higher and better-drained ground now traversed by the High Street

and Ironmarket, and it is at the junction of these two principal streets that the location of the buildings connected with government and trade are to be sought. The name Ironmarket, met with in the mid-14th century,[79] suggests a specialized market at which, possibly, local iron ware was sold.[80] At the end of the 17th century a plan of the town shows at the intersection of the two streets two large buildings, together with a market cross, one of which certainly represented the Guildhall and the other probably the market house.[81]

A market house is definitely mentioned in 1622 when the borough council nominated some of their number to assist the mayor in 'the surveying and overseeing of the work now in hand, being the building of our market house'.[82] It was apparently completed c. 1626 for in that year a rate of 20 marks or thereabouts was levied on the capital burgesses and other inhabitants for the 'finishing of the market house'.[83] The building seems to have been of two stories, the lower one being open and the upper supported by pillars.[84] This was probably not the first market house. In 1628 after the completion of the new building, the borough council granted a lease of the Stone House and Old Hall.[85] If these were separate buildings, the former, in 1617 at least,[86] was evidently the town gaol, while the latter, referred to in 1654 as 'the buildings heretofore called the Old Hall'[87] may have been an earlier market hall. Moreover, the Old Hall may have been identical with the Bothall (i.e. Booth Hall) which, with the profits from stalls and tolls, was reported in 1649 to have belonged to the former chantry of St. Katherine in the parish church.[88]

While the market house would be used for the administrative business of the market, particularly in relation to the collection of toll, the market itself was, and is, carried on to a considerable extent in the open market-place in High Street by means of booths and stalls.[89] The inconvenience and congestion caused by this practice engaged the attention of the council and in 1853 a covered market was built and opened in the following year.[90] It consisted of three divisions, the first two being used for the sale of butter, eggs, poultry, fruit, and general merchandise, and the third for the sale of meat. The fish market was held in Penkhull Street and High Street.[91] The market is still (1960) held on Mondays and Saturdays,[92] but the butchers' market no longer exists.[93]

Surrounded by a large agricultural district,[94] Newcastle was, and is, a natural centre for trading

[63] Corp. Order Bk. 1669–1712, f. 153b.
[64] Ibid. 1712–67, f. 18b.
[65] Ibid. f. 165b.
[66] Ibid. f. 177a.
[67] Pape, *Tudor and Stuart Newcastle*, 220, 254, 269, 273.
[68] Ibid. 252.
[69] Ibid. 256.
[70] Ibid. 269.
[71] See p. 27.
[72] Pape, *Tudor and Stuart Newcastle*, 310, 315.
[73] *Rep. Com. Mun. Corps.* H.C. 116, p. 1957 (1835), xxv.
[74] *Rep. Com. on Market Rights and Tolls* [C. 6268–xi], p. 171, H.C. (1890–1), xxxviii.
[75] *Repn. to Min. of Health* (1926), re boro. extension, p. 16.
[76] See p. 4.
[77] Pape, *Tudor and Stuart Newcastle*, 195.
[78] D.L. 42/2, f. 90.
[79] See p. 3.   [80] See p. 50.

[81] See plate facing p. 8.
[82] Pape, *Tudor and Stuart Newcastle*, 262.
[83] Ibid. 271.
[84] Ibid. 287, 296.
[85] Ibid. 279.
[86] See p. 40.
[87] Pape, *Tudor and Stuart Newcastle*, 323–4.
[88] Ibid. 179.
[89] *Rep. Com. Market Rights and Tolls* [C. 6268–vi], p. 246, H.C. (1890–1), xxxix.
[90] See above, p. 11.
[91] *Rep. Com. Market Rights and Tolls*, 244.
[92] Ex inf. markets inspector.
[93] See p. 11.
[94] Newcastle was the headquarters of the Newcastle and Pottery Agricultural Society established in 1800 for the encouragement of local husbandry: *Rules of Newcastle-under-Lyme and Pottery Agric. Soc.* (Smith, Newcastle; copy in boro. libr.).

in cattle. At the end of the 18th century 'a great beast market every Monday fortnight was held',[95] but in the later 19th century the number of cattle fairs was stated to be fourteen.[96] In 1871 a Smithfield Cattle Market was laid out in Blackfriars Road on land leased by the Duke of Sutherland.[97] The cattle market is now (1959) held every Monday.

In 1281 the borough received from Edward I, at the instance of his brother Edmund, the right to hold a fair to last for three days, namely on the eve, day, and morrow of the feast of Holy Trinity.[98] In 1336 a second fair to be held on the Tuesday following the Octave of Easter was granted,[99] but by 1438 its incidence had apparently been changed to Low Sunday,[1] while that of the earlier fair had become restricted to the Monday after Trinity.[2] In that year, because the town was laid waste (vastata) and its inhabitants impoverished, a third fair was granted to be held on St. Leonard's Day (6 Nov.).[3]

The charter of 1590, besides reciting in its preamble the grants of the Trinity and Easter fairs, also established a fair on the Monday after the feast of St. Giles the Abbot (1 Sept.).[4] Prompted by the reform of the calendar in 1752, the borough council in the following year decided that this fair should in future be held on Monday after 11 September.[5]

By the end of the 18th century the number of fairs had increased to six.[6] In 1840 there were seven fairs, namely Newmarket (13 Jan.), Shrove Fair (2 Mar.), Easter Fair (20 Apr.), Whit Monday Fair (8 June), Wool Fair (13 July), Wakes Fair (14 Sept.), and Cold Fair[7] (2 Nov.); in addition there were six cattle fairs.[8] At the beginning of the 20th century this list remained unchanged,[9] but none of the traditional fairs is now (1959) held. In fact, by the end of the 19th century the only fairs held seem to have been the cattle fairs and these assumed the names given to the old fairs; for example, in 1888 the July cattle and horse fair held in the Smithfield was known as the Wool Fair and a similar fair in November as the Cold Fair.[10]

In the 17th century and possibly earlier the practice of 'walking the fairs' by the senior members of the borough council was followed, and in 1637 it was decreed that aldermen, bailiffs, and ex-bailiffs should wear their gowns when performing this duty.[11] In 1641 the capital burgesses as a body were also required to take part in the ceremony and to provide themselves with gowns on pain of a fine of 20s. for each default.[12] In 1652 the fairs were to be walked by the mayor, bailiffs, and capital burgesses 'and by such others of the sergeants and burgesses as Mr. Mayor shall upon view of the suit roll think fit'.[13] This walking of the fairs by the mayor and burgesses may have been a vestige of the court of pie powder granted by the 1590 charter.[14] Apparently the custom in an attenuated form still persisted in the early 19th century until 1836 when it was decided that the customary procession of the council at the Whit Monday Fair should be discontinued.[15]

Fairs were a source of considerable revenue to the borough in the shape of tolls and stallage rents and the influx of many strangers into the town no doubt benefited its general trade. While confusion and a certain amount of disorder resulted from the periodic holding of fairs in the main streets—'a perfect pandemonium', as it was described—yet, so far as the pleasure fairs were concerned, in the late 19th century most of the inhabitants favoured their continuance.[16]

MILLS. From early times until at least the mid-18th century[17] the castle mills, situated at the outflow from the Pool Dam,[18] played an important part in the economic life of the town. A mill is first mentioned in 1193,[19] and in 1202 and 1203 mill and pond were repaired at a cost of over £17.[20] During the period 1246–50 further repairs were done to the 'mills'[21] and in 1249 the value of the castle mill amounted to the considerable sum of £16 yearly.[22] By 1279 there were definitely two mills. An inquiry then showed that a breach of the pool by floods reduced the output of the mills by three-quarters.[23] In 1285 Edmund, Earl of Lancaster, granted his Newcastle mills to the burgesses at a yearly rent of 70 marks (£46 13s. 4d.).[24] In 1322 the burgesses were farming the mills from the Earl of Lancaster at £16 13s. 4d.[25] In 1343 Henry, Earl of Lancaster, in consideration of the loss sustained by the town on the farm of 'the mill below the castle' granted them Kingsmeadow in his Newcastle manor, on which they could build a mill if they wished to, at a yearly rent of 20s.[26] Whether a mill was built is not known, but in 1428–9 the 20s. rent was being paid for Kingsmeadow.[27] By 1361 there were three water-mills farmed by the burgesses for £40 yearly[28] and although the mills remained under the control of the borough for another hundred years difficulty was frequently experienced in paying the stipulated rent. In 1405[29] the sum of 20 marks was respited on the ground of poverty and the rebate was increased to

[95] Univ. Brit. Dir. (1791), iv. 101.
[96] Rep. Com. Market Rights and Tolls, 170.
[97] Rep. to Local Govt. Bd. (1901), re boro. extension, p. 11; Rep. Com. Market Rights and Tolls, 172.
[98] Cal. Chart. R. 1257–1300, 252.
[99] Ibid. 1327–41, 359.
[1] Ibid. 1427–1516, 4.
[2] Ibid.
[3] Ibid.
[4] Pape, Tudor and Stuart Newcastle, 63.
[5] Corp. Order Bk. 1712–67, f. 167b.
[6] 1st Rep. Com. on Market Rights and Tolls [C. 5550], p. 203, H.C. (1889), i.
[7] The tolls of this fair, bought by the corporation in 1805, were charged with the yearly payment of 12s. to Thos. Bagnall's Charity: Corp. Order Bk. 1800–25, p. 342; Rep. Com. Mun. Corps. p. 1955; see p. 72.
[8] Cottrill, Newcastle Police Dir. (1839), giving list for 1840.
[9] Repn. to Local Govt. Bd. (1901), p. 11.
[10] Newcastle Guardian, 14 July, 10 Nov. 1888.
[11] Pape, Tudor and Stuart Newcastle, 298.

[12] Ibid. 306.
[13] Ibid. 320.
[14] See p. 26.
[15] Boro. Counc. Min. Bk. 1835–44, p. 9.
[16] Evidence on Market Rights, p. 174.
[17] U.C.N.S., Sneyd MSS., Box S. 92.
[18] The embanked roadway on the S. side of Pool Dam suggests an early mill site, and a brick building, probably of 18th-cent. date, formerly a marine store and now (1960) a garage, may represent one of the mills: Staffs. Advertiser, 8 Apr. 1911 (T. Pape, 'Memories of Old Newcastle').
[19] S.H.C. ii (1), 24.
[20] Ibid. 108, 114.
[21] Cal. Pat. 1247–58, 79; Cal. Lib. 1245–51, 350.
[22] S.H.C. 1911, 145.
[23] Cal. Close, 1272–9, 544.
[24] D.L. 42/2, f. 89.
[25] S.C. 6/1146/11.
[26] D.L. 42/2, f. 89.
[27] Pape, Med. Newcastle, 191.
[28] C 135/160.
[29] Pape, Med. Newcastle, 107, 171.

£20 during much of the 15th century.[30] In 1445–6 the mills were thoroughly repaired at a total cost of £10 17s. 1½d.[31] and in the following year the mill-houses were thatched, and wood and iron were used to repair the water-wheels.[32]

By 1476 the farmer of the mills was Hugh Egerton,[33] and in 1485[34] and again in 1493[35] he was granted short-term leases of the two water-mills under one roof, together with the fishery within the dam. The next lessee of the mills appears to have been Thomas Clayton, followed by William Sneyd who was granted a 20-year lease from 1537,[36] thus beginning a long and litigious connexion of the Sneyd family with the Newcastle mills. Once the mills had passed out of their control the burgesses showed reluctance to send their grain to the castle mills and already in 1520 they had decided on the erection of a malt mill in the town.[37] By 1557 they were maintaining that they had always ground their corn not at the castle mills but at other mills in the neighbourhood.[38] In 1574 Ralph Sneyd and Richard Smith, farmers of the castle mills, brought an action against some of the inhabitants for withdrawing their suit from the mills;[39] and again in 1596,[40] on behalf of the then farmers, Ralph Sneyd and Ralph Smith, royal proclamation was issued to ensure the compliance of the inhabitants, who, it was stated, not only withdrew their suit from the mills and ground at other mills, but also procured strange millers to come to the manor and town, who with horses carried away the mulcture, corn, and grains to other mills in other places.[41] By 1607 Ralph Sneyd was the sole lessee,[42] and in the following year he sued a number of the inhabitants, including his sister-in-law Ann Sneyd, for failure to grind at his mills.[43] In 1611 the king granted two water corn mills, under one roof, with the fishpond, and two other mills there under the same roof that Ralph Sneyd and Ralph Smith had built, to Felix Wilson and Robert Morgan in socage at an annual rent of £14 6s. 8d.[44] In the following year the latter conveyed the mills to William Sneyd in fee subject to the payment of the same rent to the king.[45] On William's death without issue in 1613 the mills passed to his brother and heir Ralph.[46] He, too, found the inhabitants unwilling to grind at the castle mills and in 1634 began an action against William Hunt, a capital burgess, who had set up his own hand mill or quern in the borough.[47] The borough council decided to support Hunt, regarding the case as one that affected the town as a whole,[48] but without avail, for the verdict was in favour of

Sneyd. On this occasion the court had no doubt that the borough was part of the manor and as such its inhabitants owed suit at the mills.[49]

During the Civil War the mills were sequestered on behalf of the Parliament and the Committee at Stafford ordered the inhabitants of Newcastle to grind their corn at the mills as formerly.[50] In 1656 the borough council decided that a horse mill to grind malt should be set up for the maintenance of the poor and four burgesses were appointed overseers for its erection.[51] All the burgesses were enjoined to grind their malt at the horse mill on pain of a 10s. fine.[52] As a result of the establishment of the malt mill, William Sneyd after the Restoration made strenuous efforts to re-establish the *status quo* and prolonged litigation took place, ending finally in 1679 with victory for the borough.[53] The corporation was thereafter free to make its own arrangements for the grinding of corn and malt. In 1696 a project was approved for the erection of a windmill on Brampton Bank,[54] but even so the borough may have found the number of mills under their control inadequate which would explain the action of the borough council in 1698 of hiring Captain Sneyd's water-mill for one year at a rent of £40.[55]

In 1701 it was ordered that all those who, having signed an obligation to grind their corn at the Town Mills, had broken their agreement, should be prosecuted,[56] and in the same year the council, in appointing new millers for the New Inn Mill (mentioned for the first time) and the Malt Mill, decided that the toll should be one-twentieth part of the grain.[57] In the late 18th century the malt mill was still apparently in use and burgesses were still required to grind their malt there.[58] The mill was said to have stood on the site of the Globe Inn[59] and the horse employed to turn the mill was kept in the field which subsequently became part of the burial ground of St. George's Church.[60]

The subsequent history of the castle mills is not known, though it appears that they were still being used in the mid-18th century. In 1751 it was stated that the upper part of the pool had been recovered by the corporation and converted into sound land. This had had the effect of diverting the flow of water through an opening lower than the dam with the result that the mills had been deprived of a sufficient supply of water.[61] It seems likely that these difficulties led to their rapid disuse, but one of these mills remained in existence until the middle of the 19th century, when it was sold by Ralph Sneyd to Samuel Mayer.[62]

[30] D.L. 29/183/2904, 2907; ibid. 184/2923, 2929.
[31] D.L. 29/184/2921.
[32] D.L. 29/184/2922.
[33] D.L. 29/184/2932. He was sheriff of the county in 1458–9 and 1476–7, and Mayor of Newcastle in 1490–1: Pape, *Med. Newcastle*, 128–9.
[34] D.L. 42/21, p. 110d.
[35] Ibid. p. 113d.
[36] D.L. 1/10/78, S 4.
[37] Pape, *Tudor and Stuart Newcastle*, 180–1.
[38] D.L. 1/36, S 6.
[39] *Ducatus Lancastriae (Pars Quarta)* (Rec. Com.), 27.
[40] D.L. 42/98, f. 278.
[41] One such was Thos. Bagnall who had set up a horse mill in Stoke where he ground not only his own corn but that of divers tenants and inhabitants of Newcastle: D.L. 42/98, f. 278b.
[42] U.C.N.S., Sneyd MSS., Box S. 102.
[43] D.L. 5/24, ff. 760, 790, 791; and see p. 15.
[44] C 66/8 James I, pt. 19, no. 5.

[45] U.C.N.S., Sneyd MSS., Box S. 102.
[46] C 142/338/86.
[47] D.L. 5/32, f. 201a.
[48] Pape, *Tudor and Stuart Newcastle*, 292.
[49] D.L. 5/32, f. 201b; and see p. 15.
[50] *S.H.C.* 4th ser. i. 143.
[51] Pape, *Tudor and Stuart Newcastle*, 329; and see p. 31.
[52] Pape, *Tudor and Stuart Newcastle*, 333.
[53] D.L. 4/110/20; ibid. 5/37, f. 433; ibid. 5/39, f. 411; U.C.N.S., Sneyd MSS., Box S. 92; and see pp. 15–16.
[54] Corp. Order Bk. 1669–1712, f. 90a.
[55] Ibid. f. 99b.   [56] Ibid. f. 108a.
[57] Ibid. f. 111a. In 1703 the town gave up its interest in the New Inn Mill: ibid. f. 116a.
[58] *Newcastle-under-Lyme Almanack, 1874* (copy in H.R.L.).
[59] Malabar, *Plan*; and see p. 9.
[60] *Newcastle Almanack, 1874.*
[61] U.C.N.S., Sneyd MSS., Box S. 92.
[62] Boro. Mus., Indenture dated 20 Dec. 1859.

COMMON LANDS AND INCLOSURES. As in most ancient boroughs, the burgesses of Newcastle combined farming with trade, and indeed, judging from the frequency with which regulations about the use and cultivation of the common fields appear in the minute books, the former seems to have been, in the earlier period at least, their predominant activity.[63] Until the early 19th century the common fields of the borough were six in number and surrounded it on all sides, their names then being Brampton (usually referred to as Brompton), Ashfield, King's Field, Pool Field, Clayton Field, and Stubbs.[64] Not all the fields were within the boundary of the borough, as it was later defined. Much of Ashfield lay in the neighbouring parish of Wolstanton, part of Clayton Field was in Clayton Griffith, a detached portion of Trentham parish until 1896 when it became part of Clayton civil parish,[65] and part of Stubbs in Stoke.[66]

Before the 14th century it can only be surmised, in the absence of documentary evidence, that the burgesses held strips in the common fields which they cultivated on a three-field system and possessed grazing rights in the pastures set apart for cattle. In the late 14th century some information becomes available, but not enough for any definite picture of this side of burghal life to be formed. The fact that in 1375 the governing body declared that in disputes about land within the liberty between a burgess or a stranger and the community of the town the claimant must produce a valid title or evidence suggests that attempts were being made to hold land in the common fields in severalty or to secure squatters' rights.[67] Three years earlier Adam de Prestbury had paid the town 20s. for the right to have a separately inclosed croft within the Red Field.[68] In 1379 occupiers of land in the common fields were required to inclose their holdings by Martinmas in the case of the summer field and by 25 April in the case of the lenten field.

Arable husbandry seems to have persisted until the early 19th century; in 1801 it was reported to the borough council that great loss was occasioned to corn and grass crops because the common fields were kept open so long in the spring and autumn, and orders were given that thereafter the winter common fields, usually inclosed at Old Michaelmas Day (11 October) should be inclosed each year on 29 September and the summer fields on 25 March instead of Old Lady Day (6 April).[69] But it is probable that some parts or even whole fields were set aside for the pasturing of cattle, and it seems clear that in the late 16th and early 17th centuries, three of the fields only, Brampton, Pool Field, and Stubbs, were under crop cultivation.[70] At this period, too, the mention of sheep and, in 1633,[71] the appointment of a town shepherd suggest that the burgesses were finding more profit in sheep farming, so much so

that complaints about the surcharging of the common fields and commons by sheep and cattle were voiced from time to time. In 1590 stinting was introduced based on the status of the owner in the community; accordingly the mayor was allowed 16 beasts, aldermen 14, bailiffs or ex-bailiffs 12, capital burgesses (or ex-members of the common council) 10, and common burgesses 6.[72] Evidently the problem of over-pasturing was a recurrent one, for in 1636 the stint was reduced to 12 for the mayor, 10 for aldermen, 8 for bailiffs and the rest of the council, and 4 for common burgesses.[73] In 1649 a similar process of diminution took place, the mayor and aldermen being allowed 8 and bailiffs and capital burgesses 6, while the figure for common burgesses remained unchanged.[74] Even as late as 1799 the system was still in operation when it was decided that in future the mayor should be allowed 4 beasts or 20 sheep, capital burgesses 3 beasts or 15 sheep, and all other common burgesses 2 beasts or 10 sheep.[75]

By the early 19th century, the pressure of an increasing population and the lessening need for a local agrarian economy led to a demand for a new approach to the problem and in 1816 a petition to the House of Commons by several owners of estates in which the common fields lay urged the inclosure of the common fields, Knutton Heath, and certain waste grounds.[76] The move was successful and in the same year an Inclosure Act was passed. It was alleged in support of it that while the common fields, heath, and waste grounds were incapable of material improvement, their contiguity to the increasingly populous town of Newcastle would enhance their value if they were inclosed, discharged of the rights of common, and specific parts for stinted pastures allotted to trustees for the burgesses.[77] Out of the total area of the six common fields of 600 acres five parcels amounting in all to 205 acres were to be allotted to the burgesses by commissioners appointed under the Act. The allotment in any common field was not to be less than 30 acres and in Clayton Field it was not to be more than 60 acres.

The award of the commissioners has not survived but it appears that the area allotted to the burgesses lay in four large fields, Ashfield, Stubbs, St. Anthony's Flat (part of Clayton Field), and Pool Field, over which they had the right of free pasture.[78] The property was managed by trustees who were empowered to let a portion for the purpose of raising money for the repair of fences, payment of taxes and tithes, and supporting the public walks in Brampton and Stubbs,[79] the making of which had been authorized by this Act.

The continued growth of the town and the demand for building plots led to a further Act in 1859 whereby the general management of the burgess lands was vested in 24 trustees chosen by the resident

[63] In 1341 it was stated that the greater part of the inhabitants were engaged in sheep farming: *Inq. Non.* (Rec. Com.), 131.

[64] Newcastle Inclosure Act, 1816, 56 Geo. III, c. 33 (priv. act). In 1372 there is mention of 'le Redefeld' and in 1491 of the 'redde feilde' and the 'redde flatt': Pape, *Med. Newcastle*, 146, 177.

[65] See p. 76.

[66] Malabar, *Plan*, with whole of lands held in trust for the burgesses.

[67] Pape, *Med. Newcastle*, 148.

[68] Ibid. 146.

[69] Corp. Order Bk. 1800–25, p. 15.

[70] Pape, *Tudor and Stuart Newcastle*, 210, 230.

[71] Ibid. 289.

[72] Ibid. 210.

[73] Ibid. 296.

[74] Ibid. 316.

[75] Corp. Order Bk. 1768–1800, ff. 187b, 188a.

[76] *C.J.* lxxi. 37.

[77] 56 Geo. III, c. 33 (priv. act).

[78] Cottrill, *Newcastle Police Dir.* (1836), 11; and see Malabar, *Plan.*

[79] See p. 4.

burgesses. These had power to subdivide the lands to provide gardens and fields for tillage and pasture for cattle; and to let the estate at rack-rent from year to year or for not more than 21 years. They were also empowered to let any mines or minerals for a period not exceeding 31 years, but they could set apart land for building purposes only if a majority of the burgesses was in favour.[80] Apparently it was this proviso that put a brake on building development. In 1873 it was reported that 'a majority of the burgesses are unwilling to sell an inch of their estate under any circumstances and thus retain possession of a vast quantity of building land which is much wanted.'[81] By 1892, however, the attitude of the burgesses had changed—'the spell has been broken and they [the burgesses] are beginning to be quite anxious to lease their land for building purposes'.[82] The process, however, seems to have been slow. In 1908 it was stated that up to that date only about 18 acres had been sold for building.[83]

The Act of 1835[84] put an end to the creation of new burgesses, though the rights of existing burgesses were preserved. Burgess-ship could be taken up by the son of a burgess or by anyone who had served his apprenticeship in the borough. Continued residence or occupation of property within the borough boundary (i.e. the boundary as enlarged in 1932) is a necessary condition for the retention of burgess rights, while absence from the town for a year and a day forfeits them irrevocably.[85] The burgesses, so defined, were and still are entitled under the 1859 Act to share the surplus income of the Burgess Trust. They are necessarily a diminishing number: 710 in 1873,[86] 557 in 1919,[87] about 200 in 1956.[88]

The borough owned the waste land known as The Marsh and also enjoyed rights over the manorial waste of Knutton Heath. The Marsh, consisting in 1782 of 23 acres,[89] was situated at the east end of the town in the area now occupied by Nelson Place, Queen Street, King Street, and Brunswick Street. As early as 1698 the borough council had attempted to have The Marsh inclosed but apparently without success,[90] and it was not until 1782 that an Inclosure Act was obtained,[91] whereby the land was inclosed and leased out, the profits being applied in aid of the borough poor rate.[92] In the following year a further Act[93] permitted the trustees to let the land on building leases and full advantage was taken of the permission so gained. The theatre and almost all the houses in Nelson Place, Queen Street, King Street, and Brunswick Street as far as the railway, and the old breweries in Water Street were built as a result of the Act.[94] In 1861 an Act provided for the incorporation of 24 trustees and they were given the power of sale as well as letting over the land, while the balance of the income of the trust fund was still to be applied in relief of the poor.[95] In exercise of their powers the trustees were responsible for the creation of North Street, West Street, and part of Victoria Road.[96] At the end of 1899 a capital sum of £9,739 stood to the credit of the trust.[97] In 1937 the lands, then amounting to about 4 acres, and the trust funds were transferred to the corporation and the trust came to an end.[98]

The Inclosure Act of 1816 dealt also with 100 acres of waste land on Knutton Heath in the Manor of Knutton on which presumably the burgesses had claimed rights of common over a long period. The Act took note, however, only of the fact that for many years previously part of Knutton Heath had been used for the annual horse races conducted by the borough, and the allotment was restricted to what was considered necessary for that activity, namely 6 acres, the grand stand, and two buildings used as a starting chair and distance chair, for which the borough council was to pay a yearly rent of £13 13s. to the lord of the manor of Knutton at his manor-house in Great Dimsdale.[99]

INDUSTRIES. Newcastle's earliest industry seems to have been ironworking; one of its principal streets bears the name of the Ironmarket.[1] References to John Andrew, 'ferrour', in 1421[2] and to Thomas Blomer, 'blomer' (presumably a worker in or owner of a bloom smithy) in 1456[3] indicate that the iron ore was being smelted locally and the iron used in local manufacturing. The principal product seems to have been nails. Sporadic references to nailers are met with from the 14th to the early 19th centuries, e.g. in 1380,[4] 1476,[5] 1490,[6] 1591,[7] 1602,[8] 1651, 1669, 1673,[9] 1822,[10] 1836,[11] and 1840.[12] In 1560 Ralph Leighton was seised of a tenement with a nail smithy.[13] At the end of the century a John Smith was an iron worker in Newcastle and in his will dated 1619, by which his wife was to have the

---

[80] Newcastle-under-Lyme Burgess Lands Act, 1859, 22 and 23 Vic., c. 103 (local and personal).
[81] *Keates's Potteries Dir.* (1873–4).
[82] Ibid. (1892–3).
[83] Coulam, *Newcastle*, 74.
[84] Municipal Corporations Act, 1835, 5 & 6 Wm. IV, c. 76.
[85] Boro. Libr., Local Hist. Bk. no. 1—explanatory note by A. V. Swann, Clerk to the Trust, 1951.
[86] *Keates's Potteries Dir.* (1873–4).
[87] *Repn. to Min. of Health* (1919), re boro. extension, p. 5.
[88] *Barrett's Stoke-on-Trent Dir. with Newcastle-under-Lyme* (1955–6), 424. [89] *S.H.C.* 1931, 92.
[90] Corp. Order Bk. 1670–1712, f. 101a.
[91] Newcastle-under-Lyme Marsh Inclosure Act, 1782, 22 Geo. III, c. 29 (priv. act).
[92] See p. 32.
[93] Newcastle-under-Lyme Marsh Inclosure (Amending) Act, 1783, 23 Geo. III, c. 10 (priv. act).
[94] Boro. Mus., Marsh Trust Min. Bk.
[95] Newcastle-under-Lyme Marsh Lands Act, 24 & 25 Vic., c. 43 (local and personal). The area of the land under the control of the trustees is delimited on Malabar's *Plan*.

[96] Marsh Trust Min. Bk.
[97] *Repn. to Local Govt. Bd.* (1901), re boro. extension, p. 12.
[98] Act for transfer of Marsh Lands to Corporation, 1 Edw. VIII & 1 Geo. VI, c. 75 (local and personal).
[99] 56 Geo. III, c. 33 (priv. act); *Staffs. Gaz. and Newcastle and Pottery Advertiser*, 16 Aug. 1814 (copy in H.R.L.). The corporation gave up its tenancy of the race course in 1849: Boro. Council Min. Bk. 1844–55, p. 140.
[1] See pp. 3, 46.
[2] *Cal. Pat.* 1416–22, 292.
[3] Ibid. 1452–61, 325.
[4] Pape, *Med. Newcastle*, 153, for the name Hen. Nayler.
[5] *S.H.C.* N.S. vi (1), 100–1.
[6] Pape, *Med. Newcastle*, 178.
[7] *S.H.C.* 1930, 119.
[8] Ibid. 1935, 466.
[9] *Newcastle Par. Reg.* (Staffs. Par. Reg. Soc.), 1563–1705.
[10] Allbut, *Newcastle and Pottery Dir.* (1822–3).
[11] Cottrill, *Newcastle Police Dir.* (1836).
[12] *Newcastle Register of Electors, 1840* (copy at Inst. of Hist. Research, London).
[13] *S.H.C.* 1938, 30.

use of his furnace, his forge is mentioned.[14] Also the mention in 1608 of a tenement in the Ironmarket 'sometime called the yron hall' may indicate the meeting-place of a guild of ironsmiths.[15] In 1663 Richard Booker, a native of the town,[16] claimed payment for ironmongery to the value of £80 delivered to Dublin Castle.[17] In 1822 the name of Joseph Poole, ironfounder, of Penkhull Street, is found,[18] and in 1825 an indictment was preferred against Joseph Lovat for creating a nuisance in erecting a nail manufactory in the town 'thereby occasioning divers noisome and unwholesome smokes, smells, and stenches'.[19] As late as 1861 there were 26 persons engaged in nail manufacture in Newcastle and its urban district.[20]

To Plot we owe the information that John Holland of Newcastle was one of the two frying-pan makers in England.[21] He is supposed to have had a forge not far from Keele Hall where flat round iron plates were hammered out; they were then brought to his forge at Newcastle to be worked into the conventional shape.

The most notable industry in Newcastle during the 17th and 18th centuries was the making of felt hats. As early as 1570 a hatter, Richard Norton, is met with and another in 1612, John Riggs.[22] The existence of hatters presupposes that of feltmakers, of whom, in the 17th century, there was a considerable number as may be gathered from parish register entries.[23] Late in the century the trade encountered difficulties because 'servants and others of inferior quality' had ceased to wear felt hats; at that time (1699) it was stated that there were numerous master hat-makers in the town who each employed nine or ten journeymen and many other persons, i.e. feltmakers, in producing the materials for hat making.[24] Despite temporary setbacks the hat industry continued to flourish. At a borough election in 1734 out of 436 burgesses on the roll 159 were described as hatters.[25] In the late 18th century the number of hat manufacturers totalled 27,[26] while in 1822 out of 1,000 householders in the borough, 307 were described as hat manufacturer, feltmaker, or hatter.[27] In the early 19th century machinery was introduced, in particular a carding machine and a blowing machine for the separation of short and coarse hairs from the wool or nap. The latter was the invention of James Astley Hall, a native of Newcastle and one of the chief hat manufacturers.[28] Although in 1844 the chief manufacture of the town was still described as that of hats

which were prepared for the finishers in London,[29] the growing popularity of the silk hat for the upper and middle classes and of the cloth cap for industrial workers brought about a decline in the demand for felt hats. By 1850 the number of hat manufacturers in Newcastle had fallen to nine[30] and 40 years later there were only two.[31] By the early 20th century the local manufacture of hats had ceased.[32] The fact that in 1836 there were three straw-hat makers[33] and in 1851 twelve[34] may indicate an attempt to establish an alternative, though short-lived, headgear industry of a very different kind.

Another pristine Newcastle industry was the making of clay tobacco pipes.[35] By 1637 pipe-making was already established in the town,[36] and towards the end of the century entries relating to pipe-makers in the parish register attest its continued existence.[37] Plot, with what seems to be the enthusiasm of a confirmed smoker, describes Charles Riggs of Newcastle as making 'very good pipes of three sorts of clay—a white and blue which he has from between Shelton and Hanley Green, whereof the blue burns the whitest, but not so full as the white, i.e. it shrinks more; but the best sort he has is from Grubber's Ash [2 miles north-west of the town], being whitish mixed with yellow. It is a short brittle sort of clay, but burns full and white; yet he sometimes mixes it with the blue before mentioned.'[38] Throughout the 18th century the manufacture persisted,[39] and in 1817 one Bellamy was indicted for causing a nuisance from the smoke and stench of the burning of clay pipes near the churchyard.[40] Two or three practitioners of the craft are met with during the earlier 19th century;[41] in 1861 there were still a dozen people, one of them a woman, whose occupation was that of tobacco-pipe-maker,[42] but by 1876 there was only one pipe-maker left in the town.[43]

In the early 19th century the new industry of silk throwing appeared. By 1822 the firm of Henshall & Lester, silk throwsters, had established itself in Marsh Parade.[44] In 1828 the competition of imported foreign thrown silks incited the managers, mill-men, and others employed in the silk mills of Newcastle and its neighbourhood to petition Parliament for an increase in the duty on these imports,[45] and in the following year a petition with the same object was addressed to the Board of Trade on behalf of 700 persons employed in four silk-throwing factories at Newcastle in which £30,000 had been invested.[46] The petitioners protested against the policy of the

[14] T. Pape, 'Early Iron Workers of Newcastle-under-Lyme' (T.N.S.F.C. lxxxix), 41.
[15] Pape, Tudor and Stuart Newcastle, 241; and see p. 45.
[16] Pape, Tudor and Stuart Newcastle, 335.
[17] Hist. MSS. Com. 8th Rep. (Pt. i), App. 544b.
[18] Allbut, Newcastle and Pottery Dir. (1822–3).
[19] Boro. Mus., Q.S. Min. Bk. 1811–27, f. 63a.
[20] Census, 1861, Staffs.
[21] Nat. Hist. of Staffs. (1686), 335–6; he d. 24 Sept. 1690: Newcastle Par. Reg. 1563–1705, 225.
[22] Pape, Tudor and Stuart Newcastle, 198, 249.
[23] Newcastle Par. Reg. 1563–1705.
[24] C.J. xii. 551.
[25] Anon. Hist. Sketch of Newcastle-under-Lyme (Bate, Hanley, 1841), 10.
[26] Univ. Brit. Dir. (1791), iv. 102–4.
[27] Allbut, Newcastle and Pottery Dir. (1822–3).
[28] Anon. Hist. Sketch Newcastle, 10; Newcastle Register of Electors, 1840 and 1845 (copies at Inst. of Hist. Research, London).
[29] Parl. Gaz. (1844).

[30] White, Dir. Staffs. (1851).
[31] Keates's Potteries Dir. (1892–3).
[32] Potteries, Newcastle and District Dir. (Staffs. Sentinel, 1912).
[33] Cottrill, Newcastle Police Dir. (1836).
[34] White, Dir. Staffs. (1851).
[35] See account in Pape, Tudor and Stuart Newcastle, 102–4.
[36] Ibid. 298.
[37] Newcastle Par. Reg. 1563–1705, sub 1670, 1673, 1674, 1675.
[38] Nat. Hist. Staffs. 121.
[39] Pape, Tudor and Stuart Newcastle, 103.
[40] Ibid.
[41] Allbut, Newcastle and Pottery Dir. (1822–3); Newcastle Reg. of Electors, 1840; White, Dir. Staffs. (1851).
[42] Census, 1861, Staffs.—Occupations.
[43] P.O. Dir. Staffs. (1876).
[44] Allbut, Newcastle and Pottery Dir. (1822–3).
[45] C.J. lxxxiii. 428.
[46] B.T. 6/175.

East India Co. in forbidding the exportation of raw silks from their territories and begged for the re-introduction of a protective duty of 7s. 6d. a lb. on foreign thrown silks. In 1833 there were three silk mills,[47] but by 1851 the number of silk throwsters and manufacturers was two,[48] their mills being situated in Friarswood Road and Hemstalls Lane.[49] In 1861 there were over 100 persons, most of them women, engaged in silk manufacture in Newcastle,[50] employed at the Brampton Mill (Bridgett & Co.), Friars Road Mill (J. and T. Brocklehurst & Sons) and by W. H. Walker of Silverdale.[51] By 1868 the only silk throwster left in the district was G. Walker & Co. of Silverdale,[52] which was at that date outside the borough boundary, and this firm was still operating in 1876;[53] but by the end of the century the industry no longer existed in Newcastle.

Although bordering on the Pottery towns, New-castle has never been a centre of the pottery industry, though during the later 19th century a few, never more than half a dozen, potters are to be found in the borough.[54] In the early 18th century one potter, Samuel Bell of Lower Street, has been the subject of recent investigation as being the maker of a certain type of red glazed ware, of which he has been claimed to be the inventor.[55] When, in 1750, Dr. Pococke visited Newcastle which he described as 'the capital of the Pottery villages', he found a few potters, but his account of their activities is brief, vague, and conflicting.[56] Tile-making does not seem to have been one of the old-established industries of the town, though Plot commends Thomas Wood of Newcastle for making tiles by some method, un-disclosed, which ensured a durability hitherto un-known.[57]

The manufacture of paper has been carried on for over a century at the Holborn Paper Mill in Hol-born,[58] by the Lamb family until about 1928.[59] Until the early 1930's tissues for the pottery industry were made there. After remaining vacant for about twenty years it is now (1960) producing paper re-quired in connexion with food distribution.[60]

One of the older industries of the town was that of tanning, though it was never a large one. A Chancery suit c. 1545 deals with the burning of 'a bark-house' in Nether Street, in which Ralph Kelynge and his son John were implicated.[61] In 1603 there is a reference to the 'trade or mystery' of a tanner carried on by Thomas Keeling, alderman, and his tanyard was situated in Lower Street.[62] A tanyard, presumably the same one, was still in

existence at the end of the century,[63] while in the later 18th century there were three tanners in the town.[64] During the whole of the 19th century the number of tanners varied from one to three, while in 1861 there were seventeen people engaged in the industry.[65]

One important industry of a somewhat specialized kind which was established in the late 19th century still exists. This is the manufacture of uniforms, carried on at the Enderley Mills in Liverpool Road. The factory was erected in 1881[66] by Richard Stan-way who seems to have concentrated on the supply of uniforms for the army, judging from the fact that two years later a group of army officers wished to convert the business into a limited company, with Stanway as managing director.[67] Nothing came of the project owing to Stanway's bankruptcy in 1884.[68] During his brief tenure the factory, employing about 700 workers, won the approval of the Government Inspector as being a model one; it included a surgery, crêche, and nursery department, a reading room, and a savings bank. Prizes were given for good work.[69] On Stanway's bankruptcy the business was acquired by John Hammond & Co. of Manchester in whose hands it still (1959) remains.[70] The scope of its activities has greatly increased and uniforms are supplied for police forces, fire brigades, and governments in this country and overseas.[71]

A glance at the census figures from 1801 to 1901 shows that the population of Newcastle in-creased fivefold during that period, which might suggest steady industrial expansion, whereas in fact, as has been shown above, by the late 19th century the old industries of the town had disappeared or shrunk to small proportions and had not been re-placed by new ones. The explanation is that New-castle had become a dormitory town, housing large numbers of people whose places of work were to be found in the heavily industrialized areas on its eastern and northern boundaries. In 1921, for example, out of a total number of occupied persons in Newcastle of 9,500, over 5,000 were working outside the town, the great majority of them in Stoke-on-Trent.[72] The statement made in 1908[73] that Newcastle was a resi-dential rather than an industrial town and was to be regarded as a suburb of the whole of the pottery dis-trict remained broadly true until the extension of the borough boundary in 1932 when the iron and coal industries of Chesterton, Silverdale, Knutton, and Wolstanton were brought within the borough.[74] The centre of Newcastle still retains the aspect of a

[47] *1st Rep. Factories Com.* H.C. 450, B2, pp. 2, 27, 78 (1853), xx.
[48] White, *Dir. Staffs.* (1851).
[49] O.S. Map 1" lxxii (1837); Malabar, *Plan.*
[50] *Census*, 1861, Staffs.—Occupations.
[51] *P.O. Dir. Staffs.* (1860).
[52] Ibid. (1868).
[53] Ibid. (1876).
[54] *Keates and Ford's Potteries Dir.* and *Keates's Potteries Dir.* (1865–6 to 1892–3).
[55] A. T. Morley Hewitt, 'Bell's Pottery, Newcastle-under-Lyme' (*Trans. Eng. Ceramic Circle*, iv, pts. 1 and 2); T. Pape, 'Newcastle-under-Lyme Pottery' (*T.N.S.F.C.* lv), 46–50.
[56] *Travels through Eng. of Dr. Rich. Pococke* (Camd. Soc. N.S. xlii), 7.
[57] *Nat. Hist. Staffs.* 336.
[58] Lewis, *Topog. Dict. Eng.* iii. 354.
[59] *Newcastle Register of Electors, 1840; P.O. Dir. Staffs.* (1860, 1876); *Cox's Potteries Annual and Year Bk.* (1924);

Kelly's Dir. Staffs. (1928).
[60] *Classified Telephone Dir. (Stoke-on-Trent Area),* 1958; ex. inf. the present proprietor.
[61] C 1/1160/65.
[62] Pape, *Tudor and Stuart Newcastle*, 232, 237.
[63] E 134/1 Wm. & Mary, Mich./20.
[64] *Univ. Brit. Dir.* (1791), iv. 102–4.
[65] Lewis, *Topog. Dict. Eng.* iii. 354; White, *Dir. Staffs.* (1851); *Census*, 1861, Staffs.—Occupations; *Keates and Ford's Potteries Dir.* and *Keates's Potteries Dir.* (1865–6 to 1892–3).
[66] *Newcastle Guardian*, 4 June 1881.
[67] Ibid. 2 June, 28 July 1883.
[68] Ibid. 26 July 1884.
[69] Ibid. 26 Apr. 1884.
[70] Ibid. 26 July 1884.
[71] *Newcastle Official Guide* [1951].
[72] *Census*, 1921, Staffs.—Workplaces.
[73] *V.C.H. Staffs.* i. 278.
[74] See p. 1.

market town though during the present century a number of light industries have established themselves, chiefly on its outskirts.

During the Second World War two large munition factories were established in the Cross Heath area and after the war continued in industrial use. One became the largest manufacturer of motor-car harness in the country and the largest producer of telephone and microphone cords, and is also engaged in the manufacture of fluorescent lighting equipment.[75] The other manufactures fractional h.p. motors, loom motors for the cotton industry, and electric lamps.[76]

Among other light industries are the manufacture of glue at the Waterloo Works, of leather goods in London Road, of silica in Sutton Street and at Rose Vale, Chesterton, of tires in Liverpool Road, and of pottery in the Ironmarket and at Chesterton.[77]

In the area covered by the enlarged borough, coal-mining is predominant, the chief centres being Chesterton, Silverdale, Apedale, and Wolstanton. Tile-making, made possible by the abundance of Etruria and Keele marls, is perhaps the most important local industry and the borough is credited with being the largest single production area in the country of clay roofing tiles. The local clay is also utilized for the manufacture of bricks and fireplaces.[78]

Iron-founding is carried on at Silverdale, galvanizing at Pool Dam and Chesterton, and welding at May Bank, while the cotton-spinning factory at the Cross Heath Mills in Liverpool Road has been in operation since at least 1860.[79]

SOCIAL LIFE. The Newcastle Literary and Scientific Institution was established in 1836[80] and in its premises in Brunswick Street, formerly the Shakespeare Inn, assembled a large library and the nucleus of a museum.[81] Part of the library consisted of books formerly belonging to a subscription library begun in 1812.[82] At the outset it attracted considerable interest and support, but this was not maintained, and after languishing for many years it finally came to an end in 1867 when the building was sold.[83]

A School of Art was established in 1853[84] and was housed in the building of the Literary and Scientific Institution. On its sale in 1867 the school moved to King Street[85] and remained there until 1890 when accommodation was provided in the new Municipal Buildings.[86] The school had the surprisingly large number of 200 pupils in 1882 and 245 in 1883; it was then known as the School of Science and Art.[87] In 1888 Albert Toft (1862–1949), the sculptor, was a pupil.[88]

The first public library in the town dated from 1876, when a reading room and museum were set up in Lad Lane. About two years later it was moved to the Savings Bank premises in Penkhull Street.[89]

A public library, supported out of the rates, was opened in the Municipal Buildings in 1891.[90] In 1958 it moved to a building in School Street, formerly used as a Wesleyan school.[91] In 1921 the library comprised more than 10,000 volumes, a part of which had been acquired by purchase from the then extinct library in Penkhull Street.[92] In 1959 the stock in the central library consisted of nearly 35,000 volumes.[93] There were then branch libraries at Victoria Street, Chesterton, High Street, Silverdale, Bradwell Lane, Wolstanton, Dartmouth Avenue, Clayton, and at Knutton.[94]

The present borough museum began its existence in 1941 with one room, subsequently increased to three rooms, in Lancaster Building in High Street. In 1956 the borough council acquired a large villa, The Firs, in Brampton Park, and opened it as a museum and art gallery.[95] It houses *inter alia* a valuable collection of old pictures of Newcastle and most of the borough records. In another and contiguous villa is the Arts Centre, opened in 1949.[96] Among the local societies meeting in it is the Newcastle-under-Lyme Antiquarian Society, founded in 1947.[97]

In the early 19th century Newcastle had its own local newspaper. This was the *Staffordshire Gazette*, first issued on Tuesdays, from 6 April 1813,[98] the printers and publishers being J. Smith[99] and J. Wilson in Lower Street. In 1814 the title was changed to the *Staffordshire Gazette and Newcastle and Pottery Advertiser*. From 9 January 1819 the title was once again changed to the *Newcastle and Pottery Gazette and Staffordshire Advertiser*, and Saturday became the day of publication.[1] Its subsequent history is unknown, but it had apparently ceased to exist by 1834.[2]

The next weekly paper was the *Newcastle Journal*, which began publication in 1855 and continued under that title until 28 June 1856, then as the *Newcastle and North Staffordshire Pioneer* from 5 July 1856 to 29 January 1859, then as the *Staffordshire Times and Newcastle Pioneer* from 5 February 1859 to 27 June 1868, then as the *Staffordshire Weekly Times* from 4 July 1868 to 21 November 1874, and lastly as the *Staffordshire Times* from 28 November 1874 to 10 June 1882.[3] The progressive changes of title may indicate a widening of the area which the newspaper attempted to cover; this may have led to its cessation. At all events, on 23 April 1881, publication in Newcastle began of a new weekly paper, the *Newcastle Guardian*, which, while giving some space to news from the Pottery towns, concentrated mainly on the affairs of Newcastle itself.[4] In politics

[75] *Barrett's Stoke-on-Trent Dir. with Newcastle-under-Lyme* [1958].
[76] Ibid.
[77] Ibid.; *Classified Telephone Dir.* (*Stoke-on-Trent Area*), 1959; *Newcastle Official Guide.*
[78] *Barrett's Stoke-on-Trent Dir.* [1958].
[79] *P.O. Dir. Staffs.* (1860).
[80] White, *Dir. Staffs.* (1851).
[81] Ibid.
[82] Ibid.
[83] *Keates's Potteries Dir.* (1882).
[84] Ibid.   [85] Ibid.   [86] See p. 10.
[87] *Newcastle Guardian*, 16 Feb. 1884.
[88] Ibid. 26 May 1888; *Dict. of Brit. Sculptors* (1953).

[89] *Keates's Potteries Dir.* (1882).
[90] Boro. Mus., Fenton MS. Bk. 42.
[91] See p. 69.   [92] *Kelly's Dir. Staffs.* (1928).
[93] Ex inf. boro. librarian.
[94] Ex inf. boro. librarian.
[95] *Staffs. Sentinel*, 3 Sept. 1956.
[96] Ex inf. boro. librarian.
[97] Ex inf. hon. secretary.
[98] H.R.L. possesses the 1813 and 1814 issues.
[99] He was the printer of Pitt's *Topog. Hist. of Staffs.* (1817).   [1] *Staffs. Advertiser*, 2 Jan. 1819.
[2] White, *Dir. Staffs.* (1834).
[3] B.M. Index of Newspapers, Colindale Repository.
[4] Ibid.

it was originally Liberal, but later described itself as independent.[5] It ceased publication in April 1909[6] and since that date no newspaper has been published in Newcastle. Mention should also be made of the *Newcastle-under-Lyme Free Press* which was issued free every Saturday by its proprietor, A. P. Bayley. It began in 1882[7] and came to an end *c.* 1908.[8] The only daily newspaper to be published in the town seems to have been the short-lived *Staffordshire Daily Times* of which there were ten issues only, from 1 to 14 October 1875.[9]

Though there are references to strolling players from 1610[10] and to a mountebank in 1730,[11] regular visits of acting companies do not seem to have been taking place until the close of the 18th century. In 1775 the council agreed to allow players to use 'the hall', presumably the Guildhall.[12] The Guildhall, however, was clearly inadequate for theatrical performances and the need for a permanent building was met in 1787–8 by the erection of the Royal Theatre[13] in Nelson Place by a company of shareholders.[14] From 1804 to at least 1829 licences were issued to Charles Stanton, comedian, to give performances in the theatre, sometimes from the beginning of July but more often from the beginning of August.[15] In 1829 Stanton's choice of play was restricted to such performances as might be lawfully acted in theatres in the City of Westminster.[16] The theatre season coincided with the Newcastle annual race-meeting[17] and in 1824 performances were billed to begin at 7.30 p.m. 'or as soon as the race is over'.[18] Prices of admission at that date were, box 3*s.*, pit 2*s.*, gallery 1*s.*, and the season ended on 22 September when Stanton took his benefit.[19] The rise of the Theatre Royal at Hanley is supposed to have been inimical to the continued existence of the Newcastle theatre and it was rarely used after 1880.[20] In 1910 the theatre was converted into a cinema.[21]

In the realm of outdoor recreation, though little is known of the sports and pastimes enjoyed by the inhabitants of Newcastle in medieval times, there is evidence that bear-baiting at least was one of them. In 1372 John of Gaunt in a letter to his steward, Godfrey Foljambe, confirmed the right of William de Brompton and Margery his wife to levy 4*d.* on each minstrel coming to the town at the Feast of St. Giles, and the same sum in respect of each bear

pour estre chace un cours.[22] This appears to be the only reference to bear-baiting in Newcastle, but in 1686 permission given to Thomas Hemings to extract limestone from the Bear Pits seems to indicate a definite location for the sport.[23] On the other hand, according to a local tradition, the bear ring was situated near the Butchery Pump in the Ironmarket, while a bull ring was said to have been in what was later Nelson Place.[24]

In April 1876 a skating rink was opened in a field near the railway station where Sidmouth Avenue is now situated. It was 150 ft. × 60 ft. and was specially designed for summer skating, but the venture was not a success.[25] About 1930 roller-skating was practised in a disused part of the Covered Market.[26]

The custom of the election by the populace of a mock mayor at the same time as the official mayoral ceremony took place was described in the mid-19th century as 'ancient', but the statement then made that it had prevailed for more than 230 years seems to be baseless.[27] The theory has been advanced[28] that this ceremony, characterized, in the 19th century at least, by a good deal of ribaldry and horse-play,[29] arose in protest at the exclusion of the ordinary burgesses from any part in the choice of the mayor.[30] While this may be true, the fact remains that the earliest reference is an inscription on a mould for a china bowl which runs 'Jatty Mayson, Mock Mayor of Newcastle, was legally chosen the 2nd. October 1792'.[31] In 1841 there were two mock mayors put up by the workpeople at two of the principal hat manufactories.[32] The custom had sunk into abeyance by the beginning of the present century.

ROMAN CATHOLICISM.[33] In the earlier 18th century there seems to have been a Roman Catholic centre at Chesterton Hall, the seat of the Macclesfield family,[34] and there is a tradition that in the early 19th century Mass was said in a room in the Shakespeare Hotel, Brunswick Street, Newcastle, by the *emigré* priest at Ashley and by Louis Gerard, the priest at Cobridge (1813–42).[35] About 1826 the Newcastle mission was taken over by Edward Daniel, the priest at Longton,[36] and in 1831 by James Egan who moved to Newcastle from Ashley.[37] Egan built the present church of Holy Trinity in London Road in

[5] *Newspaper Press Dir.* (1888).
[6] Ibid. (1909).
[7] Ibid.
[8] Ibid.
[9] *Tercentenary Handlist of Eng. and Welsh Newspapers, 1620–1920* (The Times, 1920), 266.
[10] Pape, *Tudor and Stuart Newcastle*, 244.
[11] Corp. Order Bk. 1712–67, f. 65*b.*
[12] Ibid. 1768–1800, f. 49*b.*
[13] See p. 9.
[14] White, *Dir. Staffs.* (1851).
[15] Q. S. Min. Bk. 1718–1811, ff. 241*a*, 244*a*, 247*b*, 253*a*, 260*a*, 263*b*, 268*b*, 271*b*, and Min. Bk. 1811–27 *passim*.
[16] Ibid. 1827–34, p. 60.
[17] See p. 50.
[18] *T.N.S.F.C.* lix. 191.
[19] Ibid.
[20] T. Pape, 'Royal Theatre at Newcastle' (*Staffs. Sentinel Summer No.* 1910).
[21] See p. 9.
[22] *John of Gaunt's Reg.* ed. S. Armitage-Smith (Camd. Soc. 3rd ser. xxi), no. 1105; Bodl. MS. Ashmole 833.
[23] Pape, *Restoration Govt.* 46.
[24] *Newcastle-under-Lyme Almanack* (T. Bailey, Newcastle, 1874).

[25] Ingamells, *Newcastle Dir.* 70; O.S. Map, 6″ Staffs. xvii SE. (1890)
[26] See p. 11.
[27] J. Mayer, 'Ancient Custom of electing a Mock Mayor at Newcastle-under-Lyme' (*Proc. Hist. Soc. of Lancs. and Ches.* 1850–1), 126–31.
[28] Ibid.; T. Pape, 'The Mock Mayor' (*Staffs. Advertiser,* 19 Oct. 1912).
[29] Mayer, op. cit.   [30] See p. 26.
[31] *Staffs. Advertiser,* 19 Oct. 1912; Wedgwood Mus., Barlaston.
[32] *Staffs. Advertiser,* 19 Oct. 1912.
[33] This article covers the area of the present borough.
[34] 'Cath. Chapels in Staffs.' (*Cath. Mag.* v), 661; E. E. Estcourt and J. O. Payne, *Eng. Cath. Nonjurors of 1715,* 251; 'Penal Laws under Queen Elizabeth' (*Rambler, a Cath. Jnl. and Review,* x, 1852), 305–6.
[35] *Programme of Celebration of Centenary of Cath. Emancipation, Hanley, 1929,* 19; T. M. Leith, Records of the Mission of St. Peter's, Cobridge (MS. at St. Peter's, Cobridge), f. 64*a*; *Cath. Mag.* v. 662. The French priest was presumably M. de Laistre who was at Ashley by 1804: Abp.'s Ho., Birmingham, Eccl. Diary 1803–33.
[36] *Laity's Dir.* (1827, 1831).
[37] Holy Trinity Bapt. Reg., note dated 18 Feb. 1831.

Red Lion Square in 1854

Church of St. Giles: interior before the rebuilding of 1876

NEWCASTLE

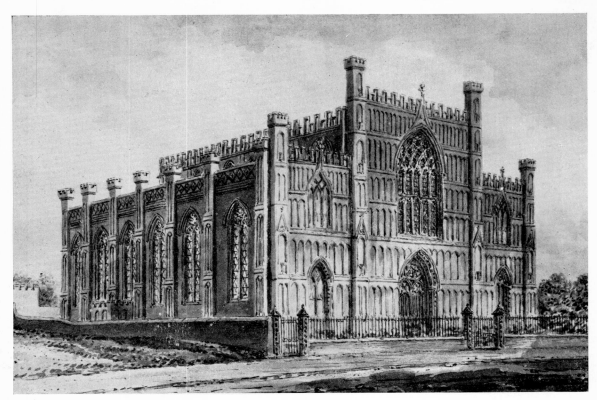

Roman Catholic Church of the Holy Trinity in 1840

Albemarle Almshouses

NEWCASTLE

1833-4,[38] and it was probably no coincidence that in the middle of 1834 two preachers touring under the auspices of the Reformation Society held a public meeting at Newcastle to denounce the Church of Rome.[39] The south aisle of the new church was at first used as 'a commodious residence for the priest' pending an increase in the congregation, but the aisle was incorporated in the church with the building of a presbytery to the north in 1849.[40]

The church of *HOLY TRINITY* is built in the Gothic style and consists of an aisled and clerestoried nave of six bays with a gallery at its west end and a shallow projecting chancel with an east window modelled on a window at York Minster.[41] Egan acted as his own architect and it is said that, having received an offer from a local brickmaker of all the bricks he might require, he designed the church accordingly, including the moulds for the bricks.[42] The result was described at the time as 'the finest modern specimen of ornamental brickwork in the kingdom'.[43] The west front, for which vitreous bricks were used, is particularly striking, the whole surface being covered with arcaded panels and the door and window openings to the nave, together with corresponding blind openings to the aisles, having heavily moulded surrounds. The building is surmounted by embattled parapets and small turrets. The church was restored in 1886, a sacristy being then added,[44] and in 1896 a new organ was installed.[45]

The first foundation from Holy Trinity was the church of the Sacred Heart, Silverdale, which was opened in a former school in Victoria Street in 1889.[46] A resident priest was appointed in 1916.[47] The present church of the Sacred Heart in High Street, an aisleless brick building with purple-brick dressings and a curved roof, was opened in 1925.[48]

There is a local tradition that Mass was said in a miners' hostel at Chesterton *c.* 1900.[49] The first regular Mass-centre in Chesterton was opened in a hut in Liverpool Road belonging to the Soldiers' and Sailors' Association in 1923 and served from Holy Trinity where a curate had been appointed for the purpose. In 1926 a hall at the north end of Castle Street was acquired and a chapel dedicated to St. John the Evangelist opened there.[50] A resident priest was appointed in 1948, and in 1956 St. John's Hall, a brick building used as both church and hall, was built at the junction of London Road and Loomer Road.[51]

From the time of the First World War Mass was said in private houses in Wolstanton first by a Belgian refugee priest and later by the priest from St. Joseph's, Burslem, who by 1923 had opened a Mass-centre at the school in Ellison Street.[52] In 1924 a small temporary church was erected in Dimsdale Parade East, and it continued to be served from Burslem until the appointment of a resident priest in 1927.[53] The present church of the Sacred Heart and St. Wulstan in Barkers Square off Church Lane was opened in 1959.[54] It is a simple red-brick building with round-headed windows.

The present chapel-of-ease to Holy Trinity at St. Mary's School, Stanier Street, Newcastle, was opened in 1938.[55]

A Mass-centre served from Silverdale was opened at the County Secondary School, Knutton, in 1942. It was replaced in 1953 by the present church of Our Lady of Sorrows, a small brick building in Cotswold Avenue, and a resident priest was appointed in 1957.[56]

A Mass-centre served from Holy Trinity was opened at the Clayton Lodge Hotel at Easter 1957 and a resident priest appointed soon afterwards.[57] The present church of Our Lady and St. Werburgh in Seabridge Lane was opened in 1957; it has a presbytery attached.[58]

The Sisters of Mercy opened a convent in a small rented house in Newcastle in 1892, moving to the larger Brook House, now the presbytery of Holy Trinity, in 1893.[59] This also proved too small and towards the end of the year the sisters bought the present St. Bernard's Convent, also in London Road, where a new wing was built in 1900 and a school opened.[60] St. Joseph's Convent in Silverdale Road, Wolstanton, also a house of the Sisters of Mercy, was opened in 1937.[61]

In 1767 there were said to be 5 papists in Newcastle and 11 in Wolstanton and in 1780 20 in Newcastle and 2 in Wolstanton.[62] The population attached to Holy Trinity in 1834 was about 300,[63] and on 30 March 1851 365 people attended Mass there.[64] By 1868 there was a large Irish element within the borough.[65] In 1959 the number of Roman Catholics in the central part of Newcastle was estimated as 2,500, in Silverdale 500, in Chesterton 500, in Wolstanton 1,300, in Knutton 500, and in Clayton 450.[66]

---

[38] White, *Dir. Staffs.* (1834); *Staffs. Advertiser*, 17 May 1834; Boro. Mus., Quarter Sessions Min. Bk. 1827–39, p. 240.

[39] M. G. Beresford, *Letter to Revd. J. Egan*, 2 (copy among W.S.L. pamphs. *sub* Newcastle). Newcastle borough and the Wolstanton area had petitioned Parliament against Catholic Emancipation in 1829, although there was some opposition to the petition in Newcastle: *Staffs. Mercury*, 10 Jan., 31 Jan., 7 Feb. 1829.

[40] White, *Dir. Staffs.* (1834, 1851); *Guide to Cath. Truth Conf., Hanley, 1896* (Cath. Truth Soc.), 30. The house still (1957) stands but was replaced by the present presbytery in 1893 when the Sisters of Mercy moved out: ex inf. Fr. D. Kelly, Holy Trinity (1957).

[41] White, *Dir. Staffs.* (1834).

[42] T. Pape, *Old Memories of Newcastle* (1911), 11.

[43] White, *Dir. Staffs.* (1834); see plate on facing p. In a more developed form it contains features to be found in the earlier church at Ashley, also the work of James Egan.

[44] *Kelly's Dir. Staffs.* (1892).

[45] Ibid. (1900).

[46] Ibid. (1896); *Cent. of Cath. Emanc.* 27.

[47] *Cath. Dir.* (1916); *Cent. of Cath. Emanc.* 27.

[48] Worship Reg. no. 49703; *Cent. of Cath. Emanc.* 27.

[49] Ex. inf. Fr. Kelly; note at beginning of St. John's Reg.

[50] Account by Fr. Kelly at beginning of St. John's Reg. (printed in *Holy Trinity Par. Mag.* Aug. 1948).

[51] *Birmingham Archdioc. Dir.* (1958).

[52] Ibid. (1960), 196; *Cath. Dir.* (1924).

[53] *Cath. Dir.* (1925, 1928); *Cent. of Cath. Emanc.* 29; ex inf. Fr. Kelly.

[54] *Birm. Archdioc. Dir.* (1960), 196.

[55] Ibid. (1958).

[56] Ex inf. the parish priest, Sacred Heart, Silverdale (1957).

[57] *Birm. Archdioc. Dir.* (1959), 230.

[58] Ibid. 230–1. The present church is intended to be used ultimately as a church hall, with a larger church on an adjoining site; a primary school is also planned: ibid. 231.

[59] *Cent. of Cath. Emanc.* 39.

[60] Ibid.

[61] Ex inf. Fr. Kelly.

[62] H.L., Main Papers, Rets. of Papists 1767, 1780. Wolstanton ancient parish included a large area not within the present Newcastle boundary.

[63] *Cath. Mag.* v. 662.

[64] H.O. 129/15/369.

[65] Boro. Mus., folder containing election handbills and addresses.

[66] *Birm. Archdioc. Dir.* (1960).

PROTESTANT NONCONFORMITY.[67] In 1672 two houses in Newcastle-under-Lyme, owned by William Beard and Susanna Sond, were registered for Presbyterian worship.[68] Although these registrations are the first definite evidence of a regular nonconformist meeting, opinion in the borough appears to have favoured puritanism, possibly even before the Civil War. The noted puritan, John Ball, when he was incumbent of Whitmore from 1610 to 1640 is said to have found many of similar opinions in the neighbourhood.[69] Newcastle was strongly Parliamentarian on the outbreak of the Civil War,[70] and during the Interregnum the corporation appointed men of Presbyterian views to the curacy of Newcastle.[71] Zachariah Crofton (incumbent 1647–9) and his successor Joseph Sond (incumbent 1649–54) were among the 36 Staffordshire clergy who subscribed to the declaration against toleration made by the Presbyterian clergy in 1648, commonly known as the Testimony of the Ministers.[72] Ralph Hall (incumbent 1654–9), although he incurred the council's disapproval in other matters,[73] was apparently also averse to toleration, since in 1658 Richard Hickock, a Quaker from Chester, reported that when he preached at Newcastle 'the people flocked in both nights to the house where I was and many of the town were forced to confess the truth and have contended for it before the mayor of the town and withstood him and the priest who have laboured to hinder our meetings there'.[74] A Humphrey Wolrich, a native of the borough and hitherto a Baptist, became a Quaker at this time.[75] In 1683 he and other Newcastle inhabitants were fined for attending a Quaker conventicle at Keele.[76] There was also Quaker activity at Wolstanton and Knutton in 1669[77] but no further records of Quaker meetings in the borough at this period have survived.

In 1662 George Long (incumbent from *c.* 1659) was ejected from the living of Newcastle.[78] He remained there to minister to the Presbyterians of the borough but was subsequently forced to leave after being indicted under the Five Mile Act (1665).[79] From then until 1672 (see above) there is no trace of regular nonconformist worship in the borough. In that year, also, Jane Machin, widow, licensed her house at Seabridge as a Presbyterian meeting-place.[80] In 1689, under the Toleration Act, William Beard and three others, George Wood, William Lawton, and Rose Bagnall, registered their houses for nonconformist worship.[81] George Long then returned as minister to the Presbyterian congregation and a meeting-house was built soon after, probably in 1694,[82] when a 'building standing on a piece of ground called the Fulatt' was registered.[83]

During the reigns of Charles II and James II dissenting participation in local government had to some extent been controlled by changes in royal policy and royal intervention in the government of the borough. Thus in 1662[84] and in 1685 members of the borough council who were dissenters, including in the latter year the mayor, were removed, with other councillors, from office,[85] but in 1687 after James II's Declaration of Indulgence William Beard was appointed mayor by royal mandate and at least two other dissenters were placed on the council.[86] The bill of 1702 against occasional conformity does not appear to have had any adverse effect on dissenting influence in Newcastle politics but the failure of the Sacheverell case had its echo in a virulent sermon against dissent preached in Newcastle Church in 1711.[87] By the end of Anne's reign the council was led by the High Church and Tory party and the last local outburst of this political and religious animosity occurred in 1715 when the meeting-house was burnt by a 'French and Popish mob' aided and abetted by the mayor and justices of the peace.[88] Compensation for the damage was assessed at £310 and by 1717 the present chapel had been built.[89]

John Wesley first preached in Newcastle in 1768 some eight years after the establishment at Burslem of the first Methodist group in the area;[90] he was very favourably impressed by the state of religious opinion

[67] This article covers the area of the present borough.
[68] A. G. Matthews, *Cong. Chs. of Staffs.* (1924), 91. Susanna Sond may have been related to Joseph Sond, minister of Newcastle (1649–54), who was ejected from the living of Swynnerton at the Restoration: *Newcastle Par. Reg.* (Staffs. Par. Reg. Soc.), i, p. iv; *Calamy Revised*, ed. A. G. Matthews.
[69] Anthony Wood, *Athenae Oxonienses*, ii. 670–2; *D.N.B.*; Whitmore Par. Reg. 1558–1765, where Ball first signs in 1610 and then regularly until 1639. And see above, p. 19.
[70] Matthews, *Cong. Chs. of Staffs.* 4–5.
[71] *Newcastle Par. Reg.* (Staffs. Par. Reg. Soc.), i, p. iv. They were Zachariah Crofton (1647–*c.* 1649), Joseph Sond (1649–54), Ralph Hall (1654–9), and Geo. Long (*c.* 1659–62). They were all ejected from their livings at the Restoration: *Calamy Revised*, ed. Matthews.
[72] Matthews, *Cong. Chs. of Staffs.* 18.
[73] *Newcastle Par. Reg.* (Staffs. Par. Reg. Soc.), i, p. iv.
[74] Matthews, *Cong. Chs. of Staffs.* 39.
[75] Ibid.
[76] S.R.O., Q/SR, Trans. 1683.
[77] Matthews, *Cong. Chs. of Staffs.* 89.
[78] *Calamy Revised*, ed. Matthews.
[79] Ibid.; Matthews, *Cong. Chs. of Staffs.* 87; G. Pegler, *Hist. of the Old Meeting House, Newcastle-under-Lyme*, 3 (copy among W.S.L. pamphs. *sub* Newcastle); *Calamy Revised*, ed. Matthews.
[80] Matthews, *Cong. Chs. of Staffs.* 91.
[81] Boro. Mus., Q. Sess. Min. Bks., Epiphany 1689; G.R.O., Worship Rets. 1852, vol. 8, Newcastle-under-Lyme.
[82] Pegler, *The Old Meeting House*, 4; *Calamy Revised*, ed. Matthews.

[83] Worship Rets. 1852, vol. 8, Newcastle-under-Lyme.
[84] Pape, *Restoration Govt.* 19–20, 30, 39. In 1662 there were at least 2 dissenters removed from the council, Wm. Beard and Thos. Bagnall. There can be no doubt that this Wm. Beard was the dissenter of that name since only one occurs in the parish register at this time: *Newcastle Par. Reg.* i. 152, 155, 158, 177, 186. Thos. Bagnall's mother, Rose Bagnall, registered her house for nonconformist worship in 1689: see above; *Newcastle Par. Reg.* (Staffs. Par. Reg. Soc.), i. 141; Pape, *Restor. Govt.* 19, 30.
[85] In 1685 the mayor was Geo. Wood who registered his house for nonconformist worship in 1689 (see above) and the other 2 dissenting councillors then removed were Wm. Lawton who also registered his house in 1689 (see above) and Humphrey Burrows.
[86] Pape, *Restor. Govt.* 50–51. The 2 councillors were Wm. Lawton (see above n. 85) and John Riley. Riley was one of the 2 dissenters who witnessed the will of the Revd. Edward Orme: Pegler, *The Old Meeting House*, 5; T. Pape, *Educ. Endowments of Newcastle-under-Lyme*, 76–77. Wm. Lawton and Hen. Hatrell, another dissenter, were prominent in arranging the displacement of the former council: Pape, *Restor. Govt.* 52.
[87] John Naden, M.A., *A sermon to reduce dissenters preached in Newcastle Ch. in Staffs., 24 June, 1711* (copy in Birmingham Ref. Libr.).
[88] W.S.L., S. MS. 370, vol. viii (2), 478–81; Pegler, *The Old Meeting House*, 4; *S.H.C.* 1920 and 1922, 221. The building was probably of wood as one of the rioters is described as 'having burnt the materials of the meeting-house after the others had pulled it down'.
[89] Pegler, *The Old Meeting House*, 5; and see p. 64.
[90] See p. 290.

in Newcastle, the congregation being so large that he had to preach in the open.[91] On his next visit, in 1774, he was invited to stay with the mayor and again preached in the open air because of the size of the congregation.[92] Opinion in the borough seems to have been favourable to the various evangelical movements of the late 18th century and the Methodists were shortly followed by the Independents, led by Captain Jonathan Scott, whose first church was formed by 1777.[93] The Baptists were not so successful; an ephemeral society of Particular Baptists was established in 1814 but no lasting Baptist church was started until 1832.[94] Meanwhile, on the formation of the Methodist New Connexion in 1797,[95] a society of that denomination had been established in Newcastle,[96] followed in 1823 or 1828 by a Primitive Methodist chapel.[97] Despite the favourable reception of Wesley and Scott, Newcastle never became an area of great nonconformist, and more particularly Methodist, activity as did the neighbouring Pottery towns. By 1851 there were seven chapels in the borough belonging to the Wesleyan Methodist Church, the Methodist New Connexion, the Primitive Methodist Connexion, the United Methodist Free Church, the Baptists, the Congregationalists or Independents, and the Christian Brethren. The population of the borough at this date was over 10,000; average attendance at the five chapels which made a return in the census of 1851 totalled slightly less than one-sixth of the population.[98] During the next 50 years the population of the borough increased to over 19,000; although the existing chapels extended or rebuilt their premises, only two new chapels were opened in the borough, the Wesleyan chapel at Ashfield and the Primitive Methodist chapel in Boundary Street, the former serving the development at Upper Green and the latter the development between Mount Pleasant and George Street. The Salvation Army and various missions were also established in Newcastle in this period, but no great expansion in the number of nonconformist places of worship took place.

The Methodist Union of 1932 brought about an immediate amalgamation of the circuits of the various churches, the new Newcastle Circuit being divided geographically in 1942 into Brunswick (now Wolstanton and Audley) and Ebenezer (now Newcastle) Circuits. The first of these contained in the main the chapels in the eastern and northern parts of the present borough and chapels in Audley, the second most of the Newcastle chapels and the chapels in the western part of the present borough.[99] The movement of its congregation out to the newer suburbs and the consequent decline in membership caused the closing in 1956 of one of the main chapels in Newcastle, Brunswick Chapel.[1]

Although Newcastle itself did not become very nonconformist, four of the outlying areas now in the borough, Silverdale, Chesterton, Red Street, and Knutton, did. Silverdale, which developed rapidly as an industrial village in the 19th century, had three chapels by 1851, a Wesleyan, a Methodist New Connexion, and a Primitive Methodist. These had increased to six by 1876 by the addition of Welsh Wesleyan, United Methodist Free Church, and Congregational chapels. The Salvation Army established itself there in 1883. The Welsh Wesleyan chapel closed before the end of the century but in the 1930's chapels of the Bethel Evangelistic Society, Elim Four Square Gospel Alliance, and Assemblies of God were opened there. The other three villages, with a similar history of industrial development, also show a similar concentration of nonconformist places of worship in the last hundred years, although after the Methodist Union of 1932 some of the Methodist chapels were closed and their congregations amalgamated.

Wolstanton, which developed as a dormitory suburb of Newcastle and Stoke-on-Trent, has or has had chapels of most major denominations, St. John's Wesleyan Church being the strongest. Nonconformity in Basford also expanded as the area developed as a suburb of Newcastle while the Methodist church on the new Westlands estate received most of the members of Brunswick Chapel after its closure in 1956.

Baptist Churches

NEWCASTLE. In 1814 a building near Bagnall Street, formerly used as a warehouse, was registered by Joseph Taylor as a meeting-house for Particular Baptists.[2] This society does not appear to have flourished long, for in 1832 there was no Baptist meeting-place and Thomas Carryer, a pawnbroker, registered a house and premises in or near the Ironmarket for that purpose.[3] The Revd. L. J. Abington, of New Street Baptist Church, Hanley, conducted the services.[4] It was still in use in 1834.[5] In 1839 the Shakespeare Assembly Room in Brunswick Street, presumably a room in the Shakespeare Hotel,[6] was registered as a meeting-place for Particular Baptists by William Berrisford, a hatter,[7] and in 1844 a small chapel was built in Bridge Street.[8] The congregation was small in 1851, averaging 50 people, and there was also a small Sunday-school class.[9] The society was extinct by 1854.[10] Preaching was restarted at the beginning of 1868 in a room in Hassell Street.[11] Later a site in London Road was bought; an iron church and school were erected there and opened in 1871.[12] The church was formally constituted in the following year;[13] it then had 18 members.[14] This chapel seated 200, and by 1900 the church had 72

[91] J. Wesley, *Journal*, 24 Mar. 1768.
[92] Ibid. 29 Mar. 1774.
[93] See p. 58.
[94] See below.
[95] See p. 276.
[96] See p. 61.
[97] Ibid.
[98] The Christian Brethren and the Methodist Free Church made no return but both probably had a small congregation. Attendance figures on 30 Mar. 1851 have been used for the New Connexion Chapel since it gave no average. Total average attendance for Newcastle was 1,680.
[99] Ex inf. the Supt. Minister, Wolstanton and Audley Circuit (1957).
[1] Ex inf. the supt. minister.

[2] G.R.O., Worship Rets. 1852, vol. 8, Newcastle-under-Lyme.
[3] Ibid.; *Records of an Old Association* (1905), 160–7.
[4] *Recs. Old Assoc.* 160–7.
[5] White, *Dir. Staffs.* (1834).
[6] See p. 54.
[7] Worship Rets. 1852, Newcastle.
[8] H.O. 129/15/369; White, *Dir. Staffs.* (1851).
[9] H.O. 129/15/369.
[10] *Recs. Old Assoc.* 167.
[11] Ibid.
[12] Ibid. It was not registered until 1875: Worship Reg. no. 22355.
[13] *Bapt. Handbk.* (1900); *Recs. Old Assoc.* 167.
[14] *Recs. Old Assoc.* 167.

members while the Sunday school had an average attendance of 200.[15] About 1912 the Baptist Union made a grant of £750 from the Twentieth Century Fund towards the cost of a new chapel,[16] the foundation stone of which was laid in 1914.[17] This replaced the former chapel in 1915[18] and is situated in London Road at the corner of Vesey Terrace. The membership of the church had dropped to about 60 people by 1935,[19] and has since remained more or less constant.[20] The Sunday school had declined in numbers from 200 in 1900[21] to about 90 in 1956.[22] It was rehoused in a new brick building erected by the side of the chapel in 1952.[23] The present chapel is in Gothic style and is a red-brick building with stone dressings.

CHESTERTON. A Baptist chapel was built in Victoria Street in 1876 to seat 200.[24] In 1883 the church had 17 members and Sunday-school attendance averaged 75.[25] It was still in use in 1893[26] but was acquired by the Congregationalists in 1894 when it was stated that the Baptists had recently ceased to use it.[27] It is described elsewhere.[28]

Bethel Evangelistic Society

SILVERDALE. The Bethel Evangelistic Society first met in the Silverdale Dance Hall in 1931.[29] The members then built the Bethel Temple in The Rookery which was opened in 1932.[30] The meeting was still held there in 1958.

Christadelphians or Brethren of Christ

The Stoke-on-Trent and Newcastle (Staffs.) group of this church is treated under Stoke.[31]

Christian Brethren

NEWCASTLE. The Christian Brethren probably established themselves in a chapel in Bow Street in 1842.[32] They registered Bridgman's Schoolroom in Bow Street, on the site of the later National schools,[33] as a place of worship in 1855. It had ceased to be used by 1866.[34] Part of a house in Merrial Street was registered for worship by the Brethren in 1856 possibly in succession to Bridgman's Schoolroom. It had ceased to be used by 1866.[35]

RED STREET. There was a society of Christian Brethren at Red Street in 1859.[36]

Church of Christ

NEWCASTLE. A Christian Meeting House at 10 Penkhull Street, Newcastle, was registered in 1893.[37] The registration was cancelled in 1925 on the revision of the official list.[38]

CHESTERTON. A Church of Christ in Heath Street had been opened by 1916.[39] It was still in use in 1958.

Church of Christ Scientist

NEWCASTLE. The second floor of a building in High Street was registered for public worship in November 1939 by a group of Christian Scientists.[40] In 1957 they moved to the first floor of 46 Ironmarket.[41]

Church of the Seventh Day Advent

NEWCASTLE, BASFORD. An Advent Church in Victoria Street, Basford, was registered for worship in 1948.[42]

Congregational Churches

NEWCASTLE. The history of Congregationalism may be traced back to the open-air preaching of Captain Jonathan Scott c. 1776.[43] By 1777 a church had been formed[44] and seven years later Scott bought some land on The Marsh, later King Street, on which he built 'The Marsh Chapel'.[45] This was described in 1834 as 'a handsome brick edifice'[46] and in 1851 seated nearly 500.[47] Average attendance in the first three months of that year was 200 and at the Sunday school 130.[48] In 1859 a new chapel was built, again in King Street, at a cost of £3,000.[49] It is a Gothic building of yellow and blue brick with a spired turret at the west corner. A new school was erected in 1912 at a cost of £1,150.[50] This chapel seats 500 and the membership in 1957 was 116.[51]

CLAYTON. A Congregational chapel to seat 250 was built in 1952 in Stafford Avenue, Clayton.[52] Proceeds from the sales of Copeland Street Chapel, Stoke-upon-Trent, and the chapel at Milton, helped to meet the cost of the new Clayton building.[53]

SILVERDALE. The Congregational Church at Silverdale originated in the work of an evangelist sent by the Staffordshire Congregational Union c. 1868.[54] The congregation first met in a room at 13 Bridge

---

[15] *Bapt. Handbk.* (1900).
[16] *Recs. Old Assoc.* 171–2; *Bapt. Handbk.* (1912). The cost of the proposed building was then assessed at £1,320.
[17] Tablet *in situ*.
[18] G.R.O., Worship Reg. no. 46518.
[19] *W. Midland Bapt. Assoc. Yr. Bk.* (1935).
[20] Ibid. (1935 and subseq. edns. to 1957); *Bapt. Handbk.* (1935 and subseq. edns. to 1957).
[21] *Bapt. Handbk.* (1900).
[22] Ibid. (1956).
[23] Part of the cost of the new Sunday sch. was met by a gift from the trustees of the former Burslem Bapt. Ch., the money being part of the proceeds of the sale of the site of that ch.: *W. Midland Bapt. Assoc. Yr. Bk.* (1953).
[24] *Baptist Handbk.* (1883).
[25] Ibid.
[26] Ibid. (1893). It was not then in a Baptist Association, so that attendance figures, &c., are lacking.
[27] A. G. Matthews, *Cong. Chs. of Staffs.* 238.
[28] See p. 59.
[29] Worship Reg. no. 53251.
[30] Ibid. no. 53638; local inf.
[31] See p. 283.
[32] G.R.O., Worship Rets. 1852, vol. 8, Newcastle-under-Lyme.

[33] Pegler, *The Old Meeting House*, 8.
[34] Worship Reg. no. 6529. The Supt. Registrar certified that it was disused.
[35] Ibid. no. 7690. The Supt. Registrar certified that it was disused.
[36] *Unit. Hist. Soc.* vi. 14–28.
[37] Worship Reg. no. 34046.   [38] Ibid.
[39] *Kelly's Dir. Staffs.* (1916). It was not registered until 1930: Worship Reg. no. 52314.
[40] Worship Reg. no. 59022.
[41] Ibid. no. 66170.
[42] Ibid. no. 62091.
[43] Matthews, *Cong. Chs. of Staffs.* 132.
[44] Baptismal Reg. at G.R.O.
[45] Matthews, *Cong. Chs. of Staffs.* 132. The original trust deed is dated 1794: Char. Com. files.
[46] White, *Dir. Staffs.* (1834).
[47] H.O. 129/15/369.
[48] Ibid.
[49] Matthews, *Cong. Chs. of Staffs.* 234.
[50] Ibid. 246.
[51] *Staffs. Cong. Yr. Bk.* (1957), 2.
[52] Ibid. (1952), 2.
[53] Inf. from Staffs. Cong. Union; see pp. 285, 287.
[54] Matthews, *Cong. Chs. of Staffs.* 227–8.

Street under the leadership of Mr. Smith, the village schoolmaster,[55] and later moved to the Temperance Hall, rented for £8.[56] In 1875 a building scheme was launched and the present church in Victoria Street was subsequently erected.[57] It seats 480 and membership in 1957 was 30.[58] The chapel is a red-brick building with a turret. The Sunday school, built in 1932,[59] stands behind it.

WOLSTANTON. A Congregational church was started in 1902 when G. W. Garlick purchased the necessary land and an iron building transported from Hanley Park was opened as a school-chapel, registered as the Congregational Sunday School, Watlands View.[60] It was superseded in 1908 by another building.[61] The present church was erected on an adjoining site in 1922.[62] It has a seating capacity of 450. Membership in 1957 numbered 150.[63]

CHESTERTON. The Staffordshire Congregational Union started a Congregational meeting at Chesterton in 1894, obtaining possession of a disused Baptist chapel in Victoria Street.[64] In 1901 the churches at Chesterton and Silverdale came together under the ministry of George Nicholls, afterwards M.P. for Northamptonshire. In 1912 a Sunday school was built,[65] and was superseded in 1937 by a new school costing £1,200.[66] The seating capacity of the chapel is 250 and in 1957 there were 70 members.[67] The chapel is a red-brick building with blue-brick dressings.[68]

Elim Four Square Gospel Alliance[69]

SILVERDALE. The branch of the Elim Four Square Gospel Alliance at Silverdale was formed by a secession from the Bethel Temple there.[70] In 1938 a splinter group from that church registered Emmanuel Chapel, Park Road, for worship.[71] In 1939 the group, which by then had joined the Four Square Gospel Alliance,[72] moved into a new brick chapel in Albert Street,[73] which is still in use.[74]

Labour Church

NEWCASTLE. The Old Meeting House[75] was let to the Labour party for one year from 1896 to 1897 for use as a Labour church.[76]

Wesleyan Methodist Church[77]

NEWCASTLE. In the autumn of 1777 a house at Lee's Croft was registered for worship by John Bourne and Joseph Smith of Tunstall[78] and John Glenn of Newcastle.[79] In December of the same year John Glenn registered what may have been the first Methodist chapel in Newcastle, 'a piece of building erected on part of a croft adjoining the bottom of Penkhull Street, called Hayes Croft'.[80] This was probably at the corner of London Road and Penkhull Street nearly opposite the present Roman Catholic church. In 1788 another chapel was built on roughly the same site,[81] Wesley recording that in March of that year he 'preached in the shell of a new chapel at Newcastle-under-Lyme'.[82] In 1799 this chapel was replaced by one in Lower Street,[83] licensed the following year at the request of Samuel Thomason.[84] The chapel, a large square red-brick building with a pyramidal hipped roof and two tiers of round-headed windows, was still standing in a dismantled condition in 1960. There were formerly two doorways with pedimented doorcases approached by a double flight of curved steps and surmounted by a bust of Wesley on the front and bearing the date May 1799. Internally there is a contemporary panelled gallery on cast-iron supports. In 1851 it seated 468 and had an average congregation of 250.[85] Shortly before 1859 a site was acquired for a new chapel in Brunswick Street;[86] the foundation stone was laid in 1860 in the name of the Holy Trinity[87] and the chapel opened for worship in 1861.[88] The Lower Street Chapel was sold in 1863[89] to the United Methodist Free Church.[90] In 1860 Sunday schools were erected on the site of the public baths in School Street.[91] A minister's house was purchased between 1875 and 1880.[92] About 1884 the Brunswick Lecture Hall was completed at a cost of £2,000, the gift of a Mrs. Gibson.[93] Additional vestries were also built at this date.[94] In 1940 Brunswick, which was head of the Wesleyan Circuit, and, after the Methodist Union, of Newcastle Circuit, seated 850.[95] After the division of Newcastle Circuit in 1942, Brunswick Chapel was head of the circuit covering part of Newcastle, Basford, Wolstanton, and Chesterton.[96] However, as

[55] Ibid.; ex inf. Mr. H. Jones, Helern, Highway Lane, Keele.
[56] Ex inf. Mr. H. Jones. It was not the Wesleyan chapel as stated by Matthews, *Cong. Chs. of Staffs.* 227–8. The Temperance Hall stood on the S. side of Victoria St. about 150 yds. farther E. than the Roxy Cinema, formerly the Market Hall. It was burnt down some years ago.
[57] Ex inf. Mr. H. Jones.
[58] *Staffs. Cong. Yr. Bk.* (1957).
[59] Ex inf. Mr. H. Jones.
[60] Worship Reg. no. 39366; Matthews, *Cong. Chs. of Staffs.* 244.
[61] Worship Reg. no. 42871; Matthews, *Cong. Chs. of Staffs.* 244.
[62] Worship Reg. no. 48448; Matthews, *Cong. Chs. of Staffs.* 244.
[63] *Staffs. Cong. Yr. Bk.* (1957), 2.
[64] See p. 58. The actual church was formed in 1896: Matthews, *Cong. Chs. of Staffs.* 238.
[65] Matthews, *Cong. Chs. of Staffs.* 238.
[66] Ibid. 246.
[67] *Staffs. Cong. Yr. Bk.* (1957), 2.
[68] It is the original Baptist chapel: ex inf. Mr. S. A. Cooper, Sec., Chesterton Cong. Ch.
[69] See p. 287.   [70] See p. 58.
[71] Worship Reg. no. 58066.
[72] Ibid. no. 58606.   [73] Ibid. no. 60434.
[74] Local inf.   [75] See p. 64.

[76] Pegler, *The Old Meeting House*, 11.
[77] The various 'divisions and unions' in the Methodist Church, in so far as they affect this area, are examined on pp. 276–9.   [78] S.R.O., Q/SB, Mich. 1777.
[79] Both were at this time prominent Tunstall Methodists, and Smith later helped Bourne and Clowes in founding the Primitive Methodist Connexion.
[80] G.R.O., Worship Rets. 1852, vol. 8, Newcastle-under-Lyme.
[81] J. Wesley, *Journal*, 20 Mar. 1788; *Newcastle-under-Lyme Dir.* (1871), 41.
[82] Wesley, *Journal*, 20 Mar. 1788.
[83] *Newcastle-under-Lyme Dir.* (1871), 41–42; G.R.O., Worship Rets. 1852, vol. 8, Newcastle-under-Lyme; H.O. 129/15/369/2/1.
[84] Boro. Mus., Q. Sess. Min. Bk. 1718–1811, f. 224b.
[85] H.O. 129/15/369/2/1.
[86] *Wes. Chap. Cttee. Rep. 1860*.   [87] Ibid.
[88] Char. Com. files; *Wes. Chap. Cttee. Rep. 1863*.
[89] *Wes. Chap. Cttee. Rep. 1863*; *Newcastle-under-Lyme Dir.* (1871), 42.
[90] *Newcastle-under-Lyme Dir.* (1871), 42.
[91] Ibid.; and see p. 35.
[92] *Wes. Chap. Cttee. Reps. 1875, 1880*.
[93] Ibid. *1884*.   [94] Ibid.
[95] *Meth. Ch. Buildings* (1947), 253.
[96] Ex inf. the Supt. Minister, Wolstanton and Audley Circuit (1957).

the central Newcastle chapels were losing strength, partly because of a population shift to the suburbs, Brunswick was closed in 1956 because it had a smaller congregation than Ebenezer Chapel. Many of the congregation joined the Westlands Methodist church.[97] Brunswick was sold to the corporation as an extension to the public swimming baths.[98] The former Brunswick Chapel, of red brick in Gothic style with blue-brick bands and stone dressings consisted of a nave and two aisles.

An iron chapel, Ashfield Wesleyan Mission Chapel, also known as Newcastle Home Mission Chapel, was opened in 1875 as a chapel and Sunday school.[99] It was subsequently replaced by a brick building and in 1940 seated 265.[1] There was also a school building by this date.[2] In 1957 the chapel had 50 members.[3] It is situated in Mortimore Street and is a red-brick building with round-headed windows. Westlands Methodist Church in Pilkington Avenue on the Westlands housing estate was registered for worship in 1939.[4] In 1940 it seated 100[5] and is a brick building.

CLAYTON. From at least 1876 a group of Wesleyan Methodists used the Board school for worship. It was still meeting there in 1940[6] but now has a hut off Clayton Road.

SILVERDALE. A Wesleyan Methodist chapel was erected at Silverdale (Knutton Heath) in 1824 and enlarged in 1834.[7] In 1851 it seated 200 and on 30 March of that year attendance was reported as 200 in the morning and 194 in the afternoon.[8] This chapel was replaced by a new building in Church Street in 1857.[9] A Sunday school was built adjoining it in 1858 and further extensions were added in 1869 and 1900.[10] In 1940 Wesley Chapel seated 380[11] and in 1957 had 42 members.[12] There was a Welsh Wesleyan chapel at Silverdale in 1876.[13] It was still in use in 1884 but had closed by 1892.[14] In 1867 a Wesleyan chapel was erected at Knutton.[15] This was closed by 1932 because of the dwindling of its congregation.[16] It is a small brick building standing beside Elim Church in Black Bank Road.

WOLSTANTON. There is a tradition that a Wesleyan group was meeting at Wolstanton by 1806,[17] and the

house of a Samuel Goodfellow, registered as a meeting-house for Protestant dissenters in 1795, may possibly have been used by Methodists.[18] The first chapel was built in 1813 or 1814[19] in Wedgwood Street and by 1829 had 59 members.[20] In 1851 it seated 220 and attendance on 30 March of that year was reported as 51 in the morning and 86 in the evening.[21] In 1865 the foundation stones of a new chapel in High Street were laid and the chapel was opened in 1867.[22] New Sunday-school buildings were started in 1868[23] and completed by 1891.[24] Between 1860 and 1890 the population of Wolstanton grew rapidly; the membership of the chapel increased to 170 in 1894 and it became necessary to extend or rebuild.[25] In 1894 the decision was taken to demolish the chapel and rebuild on the same site. The new chapel was opened in 1895.[26] In 1940 it seated 750.[27] It became head of the circuit on the closing of Brunswick Chapel, Newcastle, in 1956.[28] Membership increased with the closing of the Methodist New Connexion chapels at Wolstanton and Waterloo Road, Burslem,[29] and in 1957 stood at 367.[30] St. John's Church is a large brick structure in Perpendicular style, with a nave, transepts, and a square tower. The organ, originally built in 1896, was rebuilt in 1952.[31] A church hall behind the Sunday school was built in 1928.[32]

CHESTERTON. A Wesleyan chapel was built in 1785.[33] In 1851 it seated 158 and on 30 March of that year had a congregation of 40 in the morning and 70 in the evening. There was also a Sunday school.[34] In 1857 a new chapel was built, the former chapel being first used in 1858 as a poor relief station[35] and then passing to the Welsh Wesleyans.[36] The 1857 chapel was in turn replaced by another chapel in 1875, the 1857 chapel then being converted into a schoolroom.[37] In 1940 the chapel seated 420.[38] It is a large red-brick building in Gothic style with bands of blue brick and stone sills and copings. Between 1858 and 1868 a Welsh Wesleyan congregation began to meet in the old Wesleyan chapel.[39] This group continued to meet until at least 1904, but had dispersed by 1912.[40]

RED STREET. Wedgwood Chapel, Wedgwood Place, Red Street, lies just over the boundary in

97 Ex inf. the supt. minister.
98 Ibid.
99 *Newcastle-under-Lyme Dir.* (1871); *Wes. Chap. Cttee. Rep. 1875*; Worship Reg. no. 22553, where the denomination was wrongly entered as United Meth.
1 *Meth. Ch. Buildings* (1947), 253.
2 Ibid.
3 Circuit Plan, 1st Qr. 1957 (Newcastle Circuit).
4 Worship Reg. no. 58787.
5 *Meth. Ch. Buildings* (1947), 253.
6 *P.O. Dir. Staffs.* (1876); *Kelly's Dir. Staffs.* (1940).
7 H.O. 129/15/370/1/2.
8 Ibid.
9 Tablet *in situ*; *Wes. Chap. Cttee. Rep. 1857*.
10 Tablets *in situ*; *Wes. Chap. Cttee. Rep. 1858*.
11 *Meth. Ch. Buildings* (1947), 253.
12 Circuit Plan, 4th Qr. 1957 (Newcastle Circuit).
13 *P.O. Dir. Staffs.* (1876).
14 *Kelly's Dir. Staffs.* (1884, 1892).
15 Tablet *in situ*; *Wes. Chap. Cttee. Rep. 1869*.
16 Local inf.
17 *St. John's Ch. Wolstanton, Diamond Jubilee Celebrations* (copy in W.S.L.).
18 S.R.O., Q/SB, Trans. 1795, no. 124.
19 It is said to be 1813 in the census return of 1851: H.O. 129/15/370/1/1. The diamond jubilee leaflet gives 1814 as the date. There are registrations at Lichfield of a meeting-house in 1813 and a chapel in 1814: Lich. Dioc. Regy., Bp.'s Reg. Bk. F, pp. 187, 229.

20 *St. John's, Wolstanton, Jub. Celeb.*
21 H.O. 129/15/370/1/1.
22 *St. John's, Wolstanton, Jub. Celeb.*; Worship Reg. no. 17955.
23 *St. John's, Wolstanton, Jub. Celeb.*
24 *Wes. Chap. Cttee. Rep. 1891.*
25 *St. John's, Wolstanton, Jub. Celeb.*
26 Ibid.; Worship Reg. no. 35063.
27 *Meth. Ch. Buildings* (1947), 253.
28 Ex inf. the Supt. Minister, Wolstanton and Audley Circuit (1957).
29 *St. John's, Wolstanton, Jub. Celeb.*
30 Circuit Plan, 1st Qr. 1957.
31 *St. John's Wolstanton, Jub. Celeb.*
32 Local inf.
33 H. Mus., Heathcote papers, xi. 2; *Wes. Chap. Cttee. Rep. 1875*, where the date is wrongly given as before 1775. It was then said to be the oldest Methodist chapel still standing in N. Staffs.
34 H.O. 129/15/370/1/1.
35 H.R.L., Wolstanton and Burslem Union Mins. 1854–8, p. 486.   36 See below.
37 *Wes. Chap. Cttee. Rep. 1875*.
38 *Meth. Ch. Buildings* (1947), 254.
39 *Wes. Chap. Cttee. Rep. 1875*; *P.O. Dir. Staffs.* (1868). It was used as a poor relief station in 1858 when it was described as the old Wes. Chap.: H.R.L., Wolstanton and Burslem Union Mins. 1854–8, p. 486.
40 *Kelly's Dir. Staffs.* (1904, 1912).

Audley Urban District, but serves Red Street within the present borough of Newcastle. The house of James Hughes at Red Street was registered for worship by Protestant dissenters in 1808[41] and in 1833 the Wesleyan chapel was built.[42] A new chapel was built by the side of it in 1889.[43] In 1940 this seated 200[44] and in 1957 had 37 members.[45] The old chapel is a small building of ashlar bearing the inscription 'J.W. 1833'. The present one is of red brick.

BASFORD. A Wesleyan Methodist chapel had been built at Basford by 1902 to serve this rapidly developing suburb of Newcastle.[46] It is a brick building in Basford Park Road and in 1940 seated 250.[47] In 1957 it had a membership of 66.[48]

WOLSTANTON. Bradwell Methodist Church in Bradwell Lane on the Bradwell housing estate was registered for worship in 1949.[49]

Methodist New Connexion

NEWCASTLE. There was a Methodist New Connexion society at Newcastle by September 1797.[50] At first it met in premises in Fogg Lane (now Fogg Street), between the Ironmarket and Marsh (now Merrial) Street.[51] In 1799 a chapel, named Ebenezer by 1803,[52] was built in Marsh Street.[53] A school building was added in 1822 and the chapel was enlarged in 1823.[54] In 1851 it seated 550. Attendance on 30 March of that year was reported as 250 in the morning and 400 in the evening, while Sunday-school attendance on the same day was 230 in the morning and 480 in the afternoon.[55] The building of a new chapel was begun in 1857 on the same side of Merrial Street, but farther east, and completed in 1858.[56] The manse was built on the west side of this chapel in 1869.[57] In 1872 Ebenezer Chapel became head of the newly formed Newcastle Circuit[58] and in 1897 altered its designation to Ebenezer Church.[59] A vestry at the rear of the church was converted in 1944 into a small chapel.[60] The church seated 842 in 1941[61] and in 1957 had 220 members.[62] The old chapel has been used as schoolrooms and an assembly hall since 1858.[63] It is a two-story building with Classical features. Ebenezer Church is a well-proportioned two-story brick building with a stone portico and a pediment. The interior has a pillared gallery, elliptical in form.

SILVERDALE. There was a Methodist New Connexion society at Silverdale (Knutton Heath) by September 1797.[64] A chapel registered in 1808[65] may have been for this society or for the Wesleyan Methodists. The first chapel to be definitely associated with this group was built in 1834 and was called Bethel.[66] This seated 160 in 1851 and had an attendance on 30 March of that year of 80 in the afternoon and 60 in the evening. There was also a Sunday school with an attendance of 62.[67] This chapel stood on Bethel Bank, opposite the 'Sneyd Arms'.[68] It was replaced in 1856 by a chapel, also called Bethel, erected at the corner of Church and Chapel Streets.[69] This seated 400 in 1940[70] and had a membership of 97 in 1957.[71] It is a red-brick building with a white stone portico, pilasters of Staffordshire blue brick at the front, and round-headed windows with white keystones. The Sunday school is a smaller building in Chapel Street.

WOLSTANTON. Providence Chapel was built in 1828.[72] In 1851 it seated 70 and had an attendance of 29 in the afternoon and 54 in the evening on 30 March of that year. There was also a Sunday school with an attendance on that date of 44 in the morning, 32 in the afternoon, and 18 in the evening.[73] A new chapel in New Street was built in 1877.[74] This seated 300 in 1940[75] but was closed in 1953.[76]

CHESTERTON. A Methodist New Connexion chapel was built here between 1860 and 1868.[77] A new chapel, called Grove, in London Road was built in 1879.[78] In 1940 it seated 180[79] and had a membership of 71 in 1957.[80] The chapel is a red-brick building with round-headed windows and is dressed with Staffordshire blue brick.

BASFORD. A Methodist New Connexion chapel, registered for worship in 1878,[81] was started at Basford from Ebenezer Chapel, Newcastle.[82] It was closed in 1922.[83]

Primitive Methodist Church

NEWCASTLE. A Primitive Methodist chapel at Higherland later said to have been built in 1823[84] was registered in 1828.[85] In 1851 it seated 280 and attendance on 30 March 1851 was returned as 106 in the morning, 108 in the afternoon, and 351 in the evening. The Sunday school was also large, its

[41] Lich. Dioc. Regy., Bp's. Reg. E, p. 374.
[42] Inscription *in situ*.
[43] Tablet *in situ*; Worship Reg. no. 31725.
[44] *Meth. Ch. Buildings* (1947), 249.
[45] Circuit Plan, 4th Qr. 1957 (Tunstall Circuit).
[46] Worship Reg. no. 38893.
[47] *Meth. Ch. Buildings* (1947), 253.
[48] Circuit Plan, 1st Qr. 1957 (Brunswick and Audley Circuit).
[49] Worship Reg. no. 62479.
[50] *Handbk., 5th Annual Conf. United Meth. Ch. 1912* (copy in H.R.L.).
[51] *150th Anniversary Ebenezer Meth. Ch., Newcastle* (copy among W.S.L. pamphs. *sub* Newcastle), p. 8.
[52] S.R.O., Q/SB, Mich. 1799, no. 113, the licence being issued at the petition of John Ridgway; *150th Ann. Ebenezer Meth. Ch. 8*.
[53] *150th Ann. Ebenezer Meth. Ch. 8*.
[54] Ibid. 10.
[55] H.O. 129/15/369/2/1.
[56] *150th Ann. Ebenezer Meth. Ch. 11–12*; Worship Reg. no. 8356.
[57] *150th Ann. Ebenezer Meth. Ch. 17*.
[58] *Handbk., 5th Ann. Conf. United Meth. Ch. 1912*.
[59] *150th Ann. Ebenezer Meth. Ch. 14*.
[60] Ibid. 15.
[61] *Meth. Ch. Buildings* (1947), 253.

[62] Circuit Plan 4th Qr. 1957 (Newcastle Circuit).
[63] Ex inf. the Minister, Ebenezer Ch. (1957).
[64] *Handbk., 5th Ann. Conf. United Meth. Ch. 1912*.
[65] Lich. Dioc. Regy., Bp.'s Reg. E, p. 382.
[66] H.O. 129/15/370/1/2.
[67] Ibid.
[68] Local inf.
[69] Tablet *in situ*.
[70] *Meth. Ch. Buildings* (1947), 253.
[71] Circuit Plan, 4th Qr. 1957 (Newcastle Circuit).
[72] H.O. 129/15/370/1/3.
[73] Ibid.
[74] Tablet *in situ*.
[75] *Meth. Ch. Buildings* (1947), 253.
[76] Worship Reg. no. 23443; ex inf. the supt. minister (1957).
[77] *P.O. Dir. Staffs.* (1868). It is not mentioned in *P.O. Dir. Staffs.* (1860).
[78] Tablet *in situ*.
[79] *Meth. Ch. Buildings* (1947), 253.
[80] Circuit Plan, 1st Qr. 1957 (Brunswick and Audley Circuit).
[81] Worship Reg. no. 24261.
[82] *Handbk., 5th Ann. Conf. United Meth. Ch. 1912*.
[83] Worship Reg. no. 24261.
[84] H.O. 129/15/369/2/2.
[85] Lich. Dioc. Regy., Bp.'s Reg. G, p. 414.

attendance on the same day being 306 in the morning, 316 in the afternoon, and 351 in the evening. Presumably the evening service was a joint meeting of the chapel and Sunday school.[86] As these figures show, the chapel was too small to contain the congregation and in 1853 it was rebuilt.[87] A large Sunday-school building was added behind the chapel in 1856.[88] The chapel seated 460 in 1940,[89] and had 115 members in 1957.[90] The present chapel is of blue and red brick and has round-headed windows and doorway. A Primitive Methodist chapel had been built in Boundary Street by 1884.[91] In 1940 it seated 230.[92] It was closed in 1953.[93]

SILVERDALE. A Primitive Methodist chapel was erected at Silverdale (Knutton Heath) in 1838.[94] In 1851 it seated 120 and the congregation on 30 March of that year was said to be 120 also.[95] A new chapel, called Zion, was built in 1864[96] and in 1869 a Sunday-school building was added in Earl Street.[97] The chapel seated 750 in 1940[98] and in 1957 had a membership of 101.[99] It stands in High Street and is a red-brick building with round-headed windows.

KNUTTON. A Primitive Methodist chapel was erected in High Street, Knutton, between 1851 and 1880.[1] This stood on the west side of the present public house, the 'Mason's Arms', and was demolished in 1880 on the building of a larger chapel in High Street.[2] This was closed on the union of 1932.[3] It is a large red-brick building and is now in use as a school kitchen.

BLACK BANK. A Primitive Methodist chapel at Black Bank was registered for worship in 1861.[4] The registration was cancelled in 1940.[5] The chapel is a small building of red and blue brick and stands on the north side of Black Bank Road at Black Bank. In 1957 it was in use as a barn.

CROSS HEATH. A Primitive Methodist church in Liverpool Road was registered for worship in 1912.[6] It seated 300 in 1940 and had school buildings attached.[7] In 1957 it had 52 members.[8]

WOLSTANTON. The house of John Hancock at the Cotton Works[9] was registered for worship by a group of Primitive Methodists including James Nixon in February 1812.[10] Later in the same month the

Cotton Works appears on the Primitive Methodist preaching plan.[11] In 1822 the society apparently moved to another building called the Schoolroom which was registered[12] by Thomas Thompson, one of the original group.[13] The first chapel was opened in 1830 and seated 126 in 1851. Attendance on 30 March of that year was returned as 40 in the afternoon and 50 in the evening, while the Sunday school had an attendance of 50 in the afternoon and 20 in the evening.[14] This chapel lay in Chapel Lane[15] and was replaced in 1879 by Jubilee Methodist Church in High Street.[16] A Sunday-school building was added in 1884.[17] In 1940 this chapel seated 425[18] and in 1957 had 105 members.[19] It is a large building of red brick. A Primitive Methodist chapel in Peel Street, Longbridge Hayes, was built in 1879.[20] In 1940 it seated 128[21] and it was still in use in 1957.[22]

CHESTERTON. The first Primitive Methodist chapel at Chesterton was erected in 1834 and seated 146 in 1851.[23] Attendance on 30 March of that year was returned as 15 in the afternoon and 40 in the evening. There was also a Sunday school at which attendance on the same day was 40 in the afternoon and 10 in the evening.[24] This chapel stood in Wedgwood (later Calver) Street.[25] In 1872 a new chapel was built in London Road.[26] In 1875 Sunday-school buildings were added.[27] The chapel seated 500 in 1940[28] and had 41 members in 1957.[29] It is a large red-brick building with blue and yellow brick dressings.

RED STREET. A Primitive Methodist chapel was opened at Red Street between 1872 and 1876.[30] It is said to have belonged to a Mr. Cope. It ceased to be used as a chapel in 1933, and was then sold to a local builder who converted it into houses.[31]

United Methodist Free Church

NEWCASTLE. Newcastle Methodist Reform Church was the result of a secession from Lower Street Wesleyan Methodist Chapel in 1849.[32] From 1854 to 1863 this group worshipped in a chapel in Church Street,[33] then in the latter year purchased Lower Street Chapel from the Wesleyan Church.[34] Lower Street Chapel was closed in 1939.[35]

SILVERDALE. A United Methodist Free Church

[86] H.O. 129/15/369/2/2.
[87] Tablet *in situ.*
[88] Tablet *in situ.*
[89] *Meth. Ch. Buildings* (1947), 253.
[90] Circuit Plan, 4th Qr. 1957 (Newcastle Circuit).
[91] *Kelly's Dir. Staffs.* (1884).
[92] *Meth. Ch. Buildings* (1947), 253.
[93] Ex inf. the Supt. Minister, Wolstanton and Audley Circuit (1957).
[94] H.O. 129/15/370.   [95] Ibid.
[96] Tablet *in situ.*
[97] Tablet *in situ.*
[98] *Meth. Ch. Buildings* (1947), 253.
[99] Circuit Plan, 4th Qr. 1957 (Newcastle Circuit).
[1] Local inf. It does not occur in the census returns of 1851.
[2] Tablet *in situ*; local inf.   [3] Local inf.
[4] Worship Reg. no. 13702. This registration was cancelled on 1 Apr. 1879 on a certificate of disuse but re-registered on the same day: ibid. no. 24484.
[5] Ibid. no. 24484.
[6] Ibid. no. 45250.
[7] *Meth. Ch. Buildings* (1947), 253.
[8] Circuit Plan, 4th Qr. 1957 (Newcastle Circuit).
[9] Presumably the Cotton Works of Ric. Thompson and Son, Liverpool Rd., Wolstanton: Parson and Bradshaw, *Dir. Staffs.* (1818), 17; White, *Dir. Staffs.* (1834).
[10] Lich. Dioc. Regy., Bp.'s Reg. F, p. 81.
[11] H. B. Kendall, *Hist. of Prim. Meth. Ch.* i. 134.

[12] Lich. Dioc. Regy., Bp.'s Reg. G, p. 535.
[13] Ibid. F, p. 81.   [14] H.O. 129/15/370/1/2.
[15] Worship Reg. no. 20225.
[16] Ibid. no. 24975; tablet *in situ.* The foundation stone was laid the previous year: tablet *in situ.*
[17] Tablet *in situ.*
[18] *Meth. Ch. Buildings* (1947), 253.
[19] Circuit Plan, 1st Qr. 1957 (Brunswick and Audley Circuit).
[20] *Kelly's Dir. Staffs.* (1912 and later edns. to 1940); Worship Reg. no. 24974.
[21] *Meth. Ch. Buildings* (1947), 249.
[22] Circuit Plan, 4th Qr. 1957 (Burslem Clowes Circuit).
[23] H.O. 129/15/370/1/1.   [24] Ibid.
[25] Worship Reg. no. 12708.
[26] Ibid. no. 20669; tablet *in situ.*
[27] Tablet *in situ.*
[28] *Meth. Ch. Buildings* (1947), 253.
[29] Circuit Plan, 1st Qr. 1957 (Brunswick and Audley Circuit).
[30] *P.O. Dir. Staffs.* (1872, 1876).
[31] Local inf.
[32] *Handbk., 5th Conf. United Meth. Ch. 1912* (copy in H.R.L.).
[33] Worship Reg. no. 6130.
[34] *Wes. Chap. Cttee. Rep. 1803; Newcastle-under-Lyme Dir.* (1871), 42; see p. 59.
[35] Ex inf. the Supt. Minister, Wolstanton and Audley Circuit (1957).

chapel was built here in 1876.[36] In 1940 it seated 600[37] and in 1957 had 53 members.[38] It is a large red-brick building in High Street.

KNUTTON. A United Methodist Free Church chapel was erected in Paradise Street (now Cemetery Road) in 1862.[39] In 1867 this was replaced by a larger chapel, called Elim Chapel, which stands at the end of Black Bank Road.[40] This seated 266 in 1940.[41] It was still in use in 1958.

WOLSTANTON. A United Methodist Free Church chapel at May Bank was erected by 1872.[42] The present chapel which stands in Moreton Parade was probably built c. 1932[43] and seated 350 in 1940.[44] It was still in use in 1957.[45]

CHESTERTON. A United Free Church chapel was built in High Street, in 1861.[46] In 1940 it seated 450[47] and in 1957 had a membership of 58.[48] It is a large brick building with round-headed windows.

Missions[49]

NEWCASTLE. By 1882 there was a Total Abstinence Society in Newcastle,[50] which in 1886 erected a Temperance Hall in Bridge Street.[51] It ceased to be used as a Temperance Hall in 1910[52] and in 1944 was sold to the Salvation Army.[53] The Children's Special Service Association registered a mission room in Bow Street for worship in 1883. It had ceased to be used by 1896.[54] The Borough Mission registered a Borough Mission Hall in Church Street for worship in 1887. This registration was cancelled in 1888.[55]

SILVERDALE. There was a Temperance Mission in Silverdale in the later 19th century. Its hall, which stood in High Street,[56] was subsequently leased to the Congregationalists.[57]

CROSS HEATH. The Newcastle Borough Mission registered a mission room at Cross Heath for worship in 1898. This had ceased to be used by 1937.[58]

Reformed Episcopal Church

CHESTERTON. A Reformed Episcopal church, dedicated to St. Mary, at Churchfield, was registered for worship in 1910. The registration was cancelled in 1914.[59]

Salvation Army

NEWCASTLE. The Bowling Green, no. 35 Salters Lane, was registered for worship by the Salvation Mission in June 1883. It had ceased to be used by 1889,[60] and was superseded by the Malthouse, also in Salters Lane, registered for worship in November 1883.[61] It continued in use until 1917 when the former Temperance Hall in Bridge Street was taken over.[62] This was still in use in 1958.[63] A Junior Soldiers' Barracks in Croft Street was registered for worship in 1883. It was closed in 1930.[64]

SILVERDALE. A Salvation Workshop in Newcastle Street was registered for worship in 1883, but had ceased to be used by 1896.[65] A Barracks was registered in Albert Street in 1888.[66] In 1898 the present (1958) Barracks, a brick building in Vale Pleasant, was built.[67]

CHESTERTON. The Salvation Miners' Hall in Heathcote Street was registered for worship in 1882.[68] It was superseded by a hall in Sandford Street in 1922.[69] It had ceased to be used by 1954.[70] In 1954 the Salvation Army Hall, in Albert Street, was registered for worship.[71] It was still in use in 1958.

Society of Friends

NEWCASTLE. The Friends Meeting House in Priory Road was opened in 1951 to replace the Thomas Street Meeting House, Stoke-upon-Trent. It was still in use in 1958.[72]

KNUTTON. A Quaker conventicle was reported in 1669 at the house of John Bodily.[73]

WOLSTANTON. A Quaker conventicle at the houses of William Burslem and William Marsh was reported in 1669 at which one of the attenders was George Hanson.[74]

Spiritualist Churches

NEWCASTLE. A Spiritualist Free Church meeting, held at 4 Fogg Street, was registered in 1905. The house had ceased to be used for this purpose by 1906.[75] A First Christian Spiritualist church held at 47a Bridge Street was registered in 1931. It had ceased to meet by 1954.[76] A Light of Christ Spiritualist church in Hassell Street was registered in 1935. It had closed by 1954.[77]

SILVERDALE. A Spiritualist church in Wheat Sheaf Yard, Church Street, was registered in 1934. It had ceased to be used by 1954.[78]

[36] Tablet in situ; P.O. Dir. Staffs. (1876).
[37] Meth. Ch. Buildings (1947), 253.
[38] Circuit Plan, 4th Qr. 1957 (Newcastle Circuit).
[39] Local inf.; board at Elim Chap.
[40] Tablets in situ; local inf.
[41] Meth. Ch. Buildings (1947), 252.
[42] P.O. Dir. Staffs. (1872).
[43] The style of the building suggests that the chapel has been rebuilt. The Meth. Ch., Moreton Parade, was registered for worship in 1932: Worship Reg. no. 54159.
[44] Meth. Ch. Buildings (1947), 250.
[45] Circuit Plan, 4th Qr. 1957 (Wolstanton and Audley Circuit). [46] Tablet in situ.
[47] Meth. Ch. Buildings (1947), 253.
[48] Circuit Plan, 1st Qr. 1957 (Brunswick and Audley Circuit).
[49] This does not include missions attached to churches treated elsewhere in this article.
[50] Char. Com. files.
[51] Kelly's Dir. Staffs. (1892). It is there said to have cost £700, the total cost being borne by a Dr. Warham. F. E. Kitchener of Oulton Hall, Stone, advanced money towards the cost of erecting the hall and by will proved in 1915 he bequeathed to the trustees all money owing to him, the mortgage thus being liquidated: Char. Com. files.
[52] Worship Reg. no. 35619.
[53] Char. Com. files. The Salvation Army had occupied it since 1917: see below.
[54] Worship Reg. no. 27301.
[55] Ibid. no. 30291. [56] Local inf.
[57] See p. 59.
[58] Worship Reg. no. 36701.
[59] Ibid. no. 44370.
[60] Ibid. no. 27145.
[61] Ibid. no. 27420.
[62] Ibid. no. 47139; Kelly's Dir. Staffs. (1940).
[63] Worship Reg. no. 31189.
[64] Ibid.; ex inf. H.Q., N. Staffs. Division, the Salvation Army (1958). [65] Worship Reg. no. 27505.
[66] Ibid. no. 30740.
[67] A tablet in situ gives the date 1898. The registration was altered in 1906: Worship Reg. nos. 30740, 41753.
[68] Worship Reg. nos. 26204, 41476.
[69] Ibid. no. 48473.
[70] Ibid. no. 64388. [71] Ibid.
[72] Ex inf. the Clerk, Staffs. Monthly Meeting of the Soc. of Friends.
[73] G. L. Turner, Orig. Recs. of Nonconformity, i. 61.
[74] Ibid. [75] Worship Reg. no. 40872.
[76] Ibid. no. 53053.
[77] Ibid. no. 55745.
[78] Ibid. no. 55043.

Unitarians

Unitarianism in Newcastle dates from the mid-18th century when the old meeting-house[79] was under the ministration of William Willett until his resignation in 1776.[80] The congregation thereafter dwindled and the chapel was closed *c.* 1805[81] to be reopened for a brief period from 1808 to 1810.[82] Shortly afterwards the Rector of Newcastle obtained possession of the chapel and removed most of its pews to repair those of the parish church.[83] In 1820 the chapel was reopened under the leadership of Mary Byerley, niece of the first Josiah Wedgwood, and with the support of the second Josiah Wedgwood, who was one of the trustees.[84] In the following year Richard Cooper became joint minister of Hanley and Newcastle.[85] From 1831 to 1837 and from 1842 to 1845 there was no minister at Newcastle,[86] while in the 1840's there was some connexion with the Christian Brethren.[87] The congregation was re-organized in 1854 with Francis Wedgwood as chairman[88] and a regular minister was appointed in 1858.[89] There was again no minister from 1869 to 1872 and the chapel was closed for the next four years.[90] With the appointment of a minister in 1877, its fortunes revived.[91] In 1887 the congregation moved to two rented rooms at 25 King Street; it was hoped that a location in the centre of the town would attract more members, Lower Street by this date having ceased to be a main thoroughfare.[92] In 1892, however, the congregation returned to the chapel but was without a minister.[93] From 1896 to 1897 the building was occupied by the Labour party as a Labour church.[94] In 1898, after renovation, it was reopened by the Unitarians and in 1906 they obtained a minister.[95] The chapel was again renovated in 1907.[96] From 1913 to 1916 the chapel was once more without a minister[97] and in 1960 had a lay pastor but no regular minister. The minister of the chapel benefited under the charity of Humphrey Burrows, founded before 1740, and under that of Ralph Cartwright, founded by will of 1776.[98] The latter, and probably the Burrows Charity also, lapsed in 1805.[99]

There was a library at the meeting-house in the 1840's but it was falling into disuse by 1848 and the books were then lent to the Christian Brethren Preachers' Library in Market Street, Hanley.[1] The records of the meeting-house consist of a book of memoranda covering the period 1819–98 and a minute book, 1854–64.[2]

The meeting-house is a plain rectangular building, of which the door and window openings are probably original. It is now roughcast externally and has an upper story, added in 1926. The only original fittings internally are the panelled oak gallery front and a staircase with turned balusters. The pulpit was removed from its central position in 1959; some of the woodwork may be of 18th-century date. There are two inscribed slabs commemorating Hannah Astbury (d. 1729) and Lydia Borrow (d. 1731) on the floor of the chapel beneath the gallery.

SCHOOLS.[3] There is some justification for the claim, made 50 years ago, that Newcastle had been the educational centre of North Staffordshire for three and a half centuries.[4] It had produced in the Grammar School and the Orme School, re-formed after 1872 as the High School, the main means of secondary education for most of the area, including the Potteries.[5] The early history of the Grammar School falls within the scope of another volume, but its later history after the merging of all the educational endowments of the town in 1872[6] is treated here. The first mention of a schoolmaster in the town occurs in 1565[7] and the Grammar School arose from various endowments, not becoming in effect a grammar school until the end of the 17th century.[8] Until then it was the town school.[9]

The Orme School was founded under the will of the Revd. Edward Orme (d. 1705), at one time master of the borough school, who left various lands in trust, the revenue to be applied to educating and apprenticing the poor children of Newcastle.[10] After his term as master of the borough school the character of the school had been altered by William Cotton's endowment of 1692 from that of an English school to a grammar school, and Orme's endowment was designed to remedy the lack of a school where more elementary education could be provided.[11] The school was established in the Presbyterian meeting-house near St. Giles's Church,[12] but after the burning of the meeting-house by rioters in 1715, a separate school building was erected in the chapel yard.[13] Meanwhile, in 1708 a scheme for regulating the school had been drawn up by John Fenton.[14] One of the regulations required the teaching of the

[79] See p. 56.
[80] G. Pegler, *Hist. of the Old Meeting House, Newcastle-under-Lyme*, 6 (copy among W.S.L. Pamphs. *sub* Newcastle).
[81] Ibid.
[82] Ibid.
[83] Ibid. 7–8; Lilian Beard, 'Unitarianism in the Potteries from 1812' (*Unitarian Hist. Soc.* vi), 14–28.
[84] His father, the first Josiah Wedgwood, who took an active interest in the chapel, is said to have given it its communion cup.
[85] Pegler, op. cit. 8; *Unit. Hist. Soc.* vi. 14–28.
[86] Pegler, op. cit. 8.
[87] Ibid. The Christian Brethren approached Unitarianism in their beliefs.
[88] Pegler, op. cit. 8; *Unit. Hist. Soc.* vi. 14–28.
[89] Pegler, op. cit. 8; *Unit. Hist. Soc.* vi. 14–28.
[90] Pegler, op. cit. 10.
[91] Ibid. 10–11.
[92] Ibid. 10; Worship Reg. no. 29908; and see p. 4.
[93] Pegler, op. cit. 10.
[94] Ibid. 11.
[95] Ibid.
[96] Ibid.

[97] Ibid. 13.
[98] Pegler, op. cit. 6; see p. 75. As well as loaves for the poor, the Cartwright Charity provided 30s. yearly for the minister. The Burrows Charity provided for the schooling of 3 children and also the yearly interest on £20 towards maintaining the minister: *13th Rep. Com. Char.* H.C. 349, p. 307 (1825), xi.
[99] The Cartwright Charity lapsed in 1805: *13th Rep. Com. Char.* 306, 307.
[1] Pegler, op. cit. 8; *Unit. Hist. Soc.* vi. 14–28.
[2] In possession of Mr. D. S. Malbon, lay pastor.
[3] This article covers only schools supported by charitable endowments or out of public funds within the area of the present boro.
[4] T. Pape, *Educ. Endowments of Newcastle*, 1.
[5] With the possible exception of Longton: see p. 307.
[6] Pape, *Educ. End. Newcastle*, 112–19
[7] Pape, *Restoration Govt. and the Corp. of Newcastle-under-Lyme*, 197.
[8] Pape, *Educ. End. Newcastle*, 1–32.
[9] Ibid. 32.
[10] Ibid. 73.
[11] Ibid. 74.
[12] Ibid. 75; see p. 56.
[13] Pape, *Educ. End. Newcastle*, 84.
[14] Ibid. 78.

Church Catechism. Reading, writing, and accounting, however, constituted the greater part of the curriculum.[15] In 1709 the trustees invested part of the funds in the purchase of a farm at Knutton.[16]

In 1715 dissension arose over Henry Hatrell's administration of the trust, particularly over the expense incurred in building the new school and schoolhouse. New trustees were ordered to be appointed in 1727, but the order was subsequently set aside on legal grounds.[17] In 1773 the school received further endowments under the will of John Cartwright.[18] The endowments of the school in 1825 were reported to consist of a farm at Knutton (48 acres), a close at Knutton (2 acres), a malthouse at Newcastle (£21 p.a.), land in the recently inclosed Pool Field (2 roods), land in the recently inclosed Stubbs Field (3 acres), land at Knutton (2 acres), a small allotment upon the recently inclosed Knutton Heath (1 acre), and the school and schoolhouse in Newcastle, the total yearly income being £165. The number of pupils was then reported as being 50 annually since 1797, and the syllabus covered reading, writing, and arithmetic.

The accounts of the charity were in such confusion by 1825 that in the Charity Commissioners' opinion the funds could not be further expended without a Chancery order.[19] The school was closed from the date of the inquiry for twenty years[20] while a suit about the financial difficulties of the trust was in progress, until finally in 1845 new trustees were appointed in Chancery.[21] A new trust scheme was drawn up in 1847[22] under which the trustees sold the former school and built a new one on the site of the former corporation workhouse in Higherland bought by them in 1846.[23] The Orme School reopened in the new building in 1851.[24] Total receipts of the trust in 1847 amounted to £292 and by 1856 the amount invested was £2,673. The mineral rights of the Knutton farm were by this date providing a valuable additional income in royalties, amounting in 1856 to £1,882, in 1857 to £2,420, and in 1858 to over £7,000. The investments of the charity exceeded £15,000 by 1862 and £22,000 by 1866, and by 1872 were just under £29,000.[25]

Meanwhile the size of the school grew as it increased in prosperity. Until the end of 1855 the average number of pupils had been about 70. In December 1855 50 new boys were entered following the appointment of an additional master. From 1856 until the end of 1863 there were 120 pupils, increased to 150 in 1864 after the appointment of another master.[26] Extensions to the buildings were proposed in 1868, and in 1869 an inquiry into their necessity was held by the Charity Commissioners. Almost immediately after the report appeared the Endowed Schools Act[27] was passed. This gave the commis-

sioners the right to alter the purpose of and to consolidate educational trusts.[28] On the basis of a report made in 1868[29] by T. H. Green, the philosopher, the entire system of secondary education in the borough was revised.

Although the Orme School at this date was flourishing, the Grammar School had declined. Green reported of it that 'an impression that the school is unwholesome has definitely prevented boys from being sent to it' and 'the professional men seemed to have quite given up using the Grammar School.'[30] He further reported that 'among the more educated inhabitants of the Potteries [he] found a general sense of the want of a good middle and grammar school.'[31] Hitherto pupils in the Orme School had been nominated to the school by the trustees, not especially on grounds of poverty, and had usually come from the National and British schools. Green recommended that instead of this system pupils be admitted on merit, so that the Orme School would become superior to these two schools. Further, exhibitions from the Orme School to the Grammar School should be provided if the latter were reorganized.[32]

A third endowed school, 'a dame school for young children', existed in the borough by 1694.[33] Founded under the will of John Cowell (codicil dated 1655) and further endowed by Thomas Bagnall, by will dated 1675, and by Ralph Keeling, by will dated 1704, the school had started by 1694 when Jane Fernihough was appointed as school dame. In 1721 she was discharged and it was laid down that the dame should teach only children selected by the mayor, justices, and aldermen of the borough.[34] In 1825 there were only about 20 children in the school and when the then dame died in 1827 (aged 77) no successor was appointed.[35]

In 1871 the Charity Commissioners proposed the amalgamation of all the educational charities of Newcastle and the foundation of three schools, an upper school for boys called the High School, a lower school for boys called the Middle School, and a school for girls to be called the Orme Girls' School.[36] Despite strong local opposition this scheme was carried out in 1872.[37] The Middle School was housed in the Orme School buildings in Higherland and new buildings were erected for the High School and the Orme Girls' School. The scheme was amended in 1898 and 1907[38] to meet changing conditions in education. Under the 1872 scheme[39] the curriculum of the High School, which had an upper age limit of nineteen years, was the normal grammar-school curriculum with emphasis on experimental chemistry because of the trade and manufactures of the district. Not more than 10 per cent. of the pupils were to be foundation scholars, of whom one-third

[15] Ibid. 79–80.
[16] Ibid. 85–86.
[17] Ibid. 80–87.
[18] Ibid. 87.
[19] *13th Rep. Com. Char.* H.C. 349, pp. 284–93 (1825), xi, where a full report of the endowments and state of the charity is given.
[20] Pape, *Educ. End. Newcastle*, 94.
[21] Ibid. 96–98.
[22] Ibid. 100–2.
[23] Ibid. 98–100.
[24] Ibid. 102.
[25] Ibid. 105.
[26] Ibid. 106–7.

[27] End. Schs. Act, 32 & 33 Vic. c. 56.
[28] Pape, *Educ. End. Newcastle*, 108–9.
[29] Ibid. 109.
[30] Ibid.
[31] Ibid.
[32] Ibid. 109–11.
[33] Ibid. 59–64.
[34] Ibid. 63.
[35] Ibid. 64.
[36] Ibid. 114.
[37] Ibid. 115–19.
[38] Ex. inf. the solicitors to the Newcastle Endowed Schools Trust.
[39] Copy in possession of Boro. Educ. Officer, Newcastle-under-Lyme.

to one-half were to come from the Middle School. The Middle School was open to boys between the ages of eight and sixteen. All pupils were charged tuition fees and were required to pass an entrance examination in reading, writing, and arithmetic. The curriculum included writing, arithmetic, algebra, geometry, mensuration and land surveying, English, history, geography, political economy, at least one branch of the natural sciences, French, Latin, drawing and music, with special attention to drawing and chemistry as these subjects had most bearing on the manufactures of the district. There were a certain number of exhibitions to it, half of which were to be given to boys at elementary schools in the school district of Newcastle. Arnold Bennett was a pupil of this school and in June 1885, shortly after leaving, passed the London Matriculation Examination in the first division.[40] The Orme Girls' School was open to girls between the ages of eight and seventeen and the curriculum consisted of English, Latin or French or German, or any two of these, arithmetic and mathematics, history, geography, drawing, music, at least one branch of the natural sciences, domestic economy, needlework, and any other subjects which the governors might add. Half of the exhibitions to this school were to be open only to children from the elementary schools of Newcastle school district.

As at the same time the governors of the endowed schools paid £2,500 to the Newcastle-under-Lyme School Board towards the erection of public elementary schools and £300 p.a. for providing free places in these schools and various other amenities, by the end of 1872 a system of graded education had been established in Newcastle whereby children could by means of scholarships and exhibitions acquire a grammar-school education. The majority of the pupils at the endowed schools would, however, be paying fees.[41]

The first unendowed school, St. Giles's, was established in 1825. It was affiliated to the National Society. St. Patrick's Roman Catholic School followed in 1833, Newcastle British School in 1834, affiliated to the British and Foreign Schools Society, and a second National school, St. George's, in 1835. These four schools provided elementary education within the borough at a small fee until 1870. All were aided by government grants. In the area which later became part of the borough there were National schools at Chesterton, established in 1814, Silverdale (then called Knutton Heath) established 1847, and Wolstanton, established 1841. The Church of England was mainly responsible, therefore, for primary education in the borough proper and the surrounding area until 1870.

An unexpected result of the Education Act of that year was an immediate increase in the number of church and nonconformist schools. Longbridge Hayes National School was established in 1871, Red Street National School in 1872, Cross Heath Church School in 1876, Chesterton (Dunkirk) Church School in 1876, Knutton Church School in 1874, Wolstanton Wesleyan School in 1871, Silverdale Primitive Methodist School in 1872, and Newcastle Wesleyan School in 1871. Two school boards were formed covering the area of the present borough with the exception of Clayton, Newcastle School Board in February 1871[42] and Wolstanton School Board in March 1874.[43]

The first Newcastle School Board (1871–4) did little of its own accord to further primary education. Using the £2,500 given by the Endowed Schools Trust, it built Ryecroft Schools, costing £3,868 and accommodating 800.[44] The second board (1874–7) did more, taking over the British school in 1876,[45] which became Friarswood School, and Newcastle Wesleyan School in 1877 for which new buildings in Hassell Street were erected in 1881. No schools were erected by subsequent Newcastle School Boards. The first Wolstanton School Board (1874–7) opened schools at Silverdale (1875) and Chesterton (1876). In 1881 the Wolstanton Wesleyan School was taken over by the Wolstanton School Board. Thus in July 1903 on the formation of the Newcastle Education Committee[46] there were three local authority elementary schools in the area and two independent schools, St. Giles's and St. George's Church of England School, and St. Patrick's Roman Catholic School. In Wolstanton, where an education committee was formed in 1905,[47] there were two public elementary schools at that date, Ellison Street Schools and May Bank School, and two church schools, Wolstanton and Cross Heath.

Various areas had been detached from Wolstanton for educational purposes after the Education Act of 1902 and there were county elementary schools at Silverdale and Chesterton (two). Clayton School had also been transferred to the county from Stoke School Board.[48] There were church schools at Silverdale, Knutton, Red Street, and Chesterton.

Between the formation of Newcastle and Wolstanton Education Committees and their merger in 1932, no new school was built by the former and only one by the latter, namely Watlands Infants' School to replace Wolstanton Church of England Infants' School. In the same period the county built a school at Knutton in 1914 to take the children formerly in the infants' department of Knutton Church of England School.

In the 1930's, however, Newcastle began to put into effect the proposals of the Hadow Report (1926) and separated children over the age of 11 from those younger. In 1931 the Orme Boys' Senior School was opened in the buildings of the Orme Middle School, purchased by the committee in 1928,[49] to take senior boys from Hassell Street and Ryecroft Schools.[50] Broadmeadow Senior School at Chesterton was opened in 1931, taking senior pupils from Chesterton Church School and Albert Street School.[51] Knutton Senior School was opened in the following year to take seniors from the Knutton and Silverdale area, from both church and county schools.[52] Westlands Senior Girls' School to take the senior girls from the central Newcastle schools was not opened until 1936, however.[53] Reorganization on these lines

[40] Univ. of London, Senate Mins. 1885–6.
[41] Newcastle End. Schs. Scheme, 20 Feb. 1872 (copy in poss. of boro. educ. officer).
[42] Kelly's Dir. Staffs. (1880).
[43] Ibid.
[44] Ibid. (1892).
[45] See p. 69; P.O. Dir. Staffs. (1876).
[46] Kelly's Dir. Staffs. (1908).
[47] Ibid.
[48] In 1896 when Clayton parish was formed.
[49] Ex inf. boro. educ. officer (1959).
[50] Ex inf. boro. educ. officer.
[51] See pp. 67, 68.
[52] Ex inf. boro. educ. officer.
[53] Ex inf. boro. educ. officer.

had been completed by the end of 1936 with the exception of St. Giles's and St. George's Church School and the Roman Catholic schools. The Roman Catholic senior pupils were separated in 1938. In the field of elementary education, however, Newcastle was expanding only slightly in the 1930's to meet the needs of new housing areas. Priory Road Infants' school was built in 1934. The need for increased elementary education had been eased by the building of the new senior schools or, where these were housed in the existing buildings of an elementary school, by the provision of a new school for the juniors and infants.[54]

In the field of grammar-school education Newcastle made great advances in the period between the two world wars. The endowed grammar schools continued to be aided on a *per capita* basis by the county and Stoke-on-Trent.[55] The Orme Middle School, condemned in 1923 by the Board of Education,[56] was closed by 1927, and in 1928 the buildings were bought by Newcastle Education Committee.[57] The school was replaced in the same year by the erection of a new local authority Grammar School at Wolstanton.[58] It was designed for 500 boys and laid out on a double quadrangle plan. The school is open to boys from the county area and adjacent parts of Cheshire.[59]

Under the 1944 Education Act Newcastle was made an excepted district. In the post-war period the chief problem has been to find school accommodation for the growing child population of Newcastle. The education committee has had to provide much temporary accommodation and also has frequently had to house children from one school in another.[60] New primary schools have been built to meet the need for schools in new housing areas: Bradwell C.P. School (1951), Broadmeadow C.P.

School (opened as such 1958), Crackley Bank C.P. School (1956), Hempstalls C.P. School (1953), Langdale C.P. School (1954), and an independent school, St. Wulstan's R.C. Aided Primary School (1959).

One new secondary modern school has been built, Bradwell County Secondary Modern School, the senior schools established in the 1930's having been converted into secondary modern schools as a result of the Education Act of 1944.[61] The local authority in 1948 opened a girls' grammar school at Clayton Hall while the two endowed grammar schools, the High School and the Orme Girls' School, not having an income sufficient to qualify them as direct grant schools, became specially aided schools under the terms of the Act. The trust maintains the fabric of the main buildings and the local authority provides for the general running costs.

About one-third of the children in the four grammar schools now come from the county area. Roughly 360 children are admitted to the grammar schools each year, between 20 and 30 from Stoke,[62] 220 from Newcastle, and 110 from the county. Provision is made in each of the boys' grammar schools for technical education, since there is no technical school in the borough. At the secondary modern schools there is a 4th-year commercial course for selected pupils. Entrance to the grammar schools is by the 11-plus examination, but pupils are later transferred from secondary modern schools to the grammar schools and vice versa, the number affected each year being about 15 to 20. In the secondary modern schools there is a leaving examination assessed by the Education Department of the University College of North Staffordshire but at the present time (1960) there is no provision for taking the General Certificate of Education examination.[63]

TABLE I

List of Schools[64]

C.P. = County Primary   C.S. = County Secondary   C.E. = Church of England   C.E.V.P. = Church of England Voluntary Primary   C.E.V.C. = Church of England Voluntary Controlled   R.C. = Roman Catholic   R.C.A.P. = Roman Catholic Aided Primary   R.C.V.S. = Roman Catholic Voluntary Secondary
B = Boys   G = Girls   J = Junior   I = Infants   JM = Junior Mixed   M = Mixed   / = Separate departments

School	Date of opening	Changes in organization	Buildings
ALBERT STREET C.P. SCHOOLS,[65] Chesterton	1876	Opened as B/G/I. Senior pupils transferred 1931 to Broadmeadow Senior School. Boys' department became Broadmeadow C.P. School in 1958.	Opened in Primitive Methodist Sunday School buildings. New buildings later in 1876. Girls' school erected 1877, infants' school 1891. Annexes to girls' school erected 1949, annexe to boys' school at Broadmeadow C.S. School 1953. Infants in former boys' school since 1958 when girls' school took over former infants' buildings. For boys after 1958 see Broadmeadow C.P. School.

[54] As at the Watlands Sch.: see above.
[55] Ex inf. solicitors to Newcastle End. Schs. Trust (1959).
[56] Ex inf. boro. educ. officer.
[57] Ex inf. boro. educ. officer.
[58] Ex inf. boro. educ. officer.
[59] Ex inf. boro. educ. officer.
[60] Ex inf. boro. educ. officer.
[61] Ex inf. boro. educ. officer.
[62] This is a considerable decrease on the numbers before the war from Stoke: ex inf. boro. educ. officer.
[63] Ex inf. boro. educ. officer.
[64] The list includes all schools except nursery and grammar schools existing in 1959; it also includes schools that had closed before 1959.
[65] Ed. 7/111; *Kelly's Dir. Staffs.* (1884); Newcastle Educ. Cttee., Rep. on sch. premises (1953, unpub. ret.); 'Boro. of Newcastle-under-Lyme, 1959 List of Schools' (T/S); ex inf. boro. educ. officer.

School	Date of opening	Changes in organization	Buildings
BRADWELL C.P. SCHOOL,[66] Cauldon Ave., Bradwell Estate, Porthill	1951	Built to serve Bradwell housing estate; see also Watlands C.P.S.	Aluminium building. Since 1953 2 classes housed at Hempstalls C.P. School.
BROADMEADOW COUNCIL SCHOOL,[67] Hodgkinson St., Chesterton	1904	Infants' school. JM/I by 1912. Became Broadmeadow Senior School in 1931 (q.v.) when infants and juniors transferred to Albert Street Schools.	
BROADMEADOW C.P. SCHOOL,[68] Hodgkinson St., Chesterton	1958	Albert St. junior boys transferred to these buildings Dec. 1958.	Occupies former Broadmeadow School buildings (ground floor).
BROADMEADOW C.S. SCHOOL,[69] Hodgkinson St., Chesterton	1931	Secondary mixed from 1931 to 1958 when girls transferred to Chesterton C.S. School.	Occupies former Broadmeadow Council School buildings. Upper story added 1931.
CHESTERTON C.P. SCHOOL,[70] Church St., Chesterton	1931	Former National School. Became infants' only in 1931.	Former National School buildings.
CHESTERTON NATIONAL SCHOOL,[71] Church St., Chesterton	1814	Opened as a charity Sunday school and leased as a day school. M/I until 1855. B/G/I from 1855, when it benefited under Betton's Charity. In 1931 school taken over by L.E.A. as infants' school (see Chesterton C.P. School). Other pupils sent to Albert St. C.P., and Broadmeadow C.S. Schools.	Possibly rebuilt 1847. Girls' school erected 1855.
CLAYTON C.P. SCHOOL,[72] Clayton Rd., Clayton	1874	Opened as mixed all-age. Infants only by 1953. Closed 1954.	Enlarged 1892. Used St. James's Church also 1951–4. Since 1954 used as annexe to Langdale C.P. School.
COOPER STREET BOARD SCHOOL,[73] Wolstanton	1875	Closed, date unknown.	Used buildings of St. John's Wesleyan Sunday School.
CRACKLEY BANK C.P. SCHOOL,[74] Chesterton	1956		Extended 1958.
CROSS HEATH C.E.V.P. SCHOOL,[75] Liverpool Rd., Cross Heath	1876	Established as mixed all-age school.	Former mission church of St. Michael and All Angels. Church hall also used by 1953.
DUNKIRK C.E. SCHOOL,[76] Heath St., Dunkirk, Chesterton	1876	Founded as GI. Closed, date unknown.	Held in mission church.
ELLISON STREET C.P. SCHOOLS,[77] Wolstanton	1881	Formerly Wolstanton Wesleyan (q.v.). Taken over by School Board in 1881 when BG/I. Since 1932, when seniors transferred to Watlands Senior School (q.v.), run as separate JM/I schools.	Used Wolstanton Wesleyan School buildings till 1895 when present buildings completed. In 1953 using St. John's Sunday School, and St. Andrew's Church Hall.
FRIARSWOOD C.P. SCHOOL,[78] Friarswood Rd., Newcastle	1876	Formerly Newcastle British School (q.v.). Taken over by School Board 1876. Mixed all-age school till at least 1924.	Former buildings of the Newcastle British School (q.v.). Alterations made in 1877. Rooms at Higherland Methodist Church used as temporary accommodation from c. 1928. In 1948 permanent annexe at Blackfriars, formerly Royal Navy buildings, acquired.
HASSELL STREET C.P. SCHOOLS,[79] Newcastle	1877	Formerly Newcastle Wesleyan School (q.v.). Taken over in 1877. Until 1881 M/I. After 1881 B/G/I until 1931 when senior boys transferred to Orme Boys C.S. School and G/I until 1936 when senior	Used former Wesleyan School (q.v.) buildings in School Street. Present buildings erected 1881.

[66] Rep. on sch. premises (1953); '1959 List of Schs.'
[67] Ed. 7/111; Kelly's Dir. Staffs. (1916); Rep. on sch. premises (1953).
[68] Ex. inf. boro. educ. officer; '1959 List of Schs.'
[69] Ex inf. boro. educ. officer; Rep. on sch. premises (1953).
[70] Rep. on sch. premises (1953); '1959 List of Schs.'
[71] Ed. 7/111; White, Dir. Staffs. (1851); Rep. on sch. premises (1953).
[72] Ed. 7/108; Kelly's Dir. Staffs. (1896); Rep. on sch. premises (1953).
[73] Ed. 7/113.
[74] Rep. on sch. premises (1953); '1959 List of Schs.'; ex inf. boro. educ. officer.
[75] Ed. 7/111; Rep. on sch. premises (1953); Kelly's Dir. Staffs. (1916); '1959 List of Schs.'
[76] Ed. 7/111.
[77] Ed. 7/111; Kelly's Dir. Staffs. (1916); Rep. on sch. premises (1953); ex inf. boro. educ. officer; '1959 List of Schs.'
[78] Ed. 7/111; Rep. on sch. premises (1953); ex inf. boro. educ. officer; '1959 List of Schs.'
[79] Ed. 7/111; Rep. on sch. premises (1953); ex inf. boro. educ. officer; '1959 List of Schs.'

School	Date of opening	Changes in organization	Buildings
		girls transferred to Westlands C.S. School.	
HEMPSTALLS C.P. SCHOOL,[80] Collard Ave., Cross Heath	1953		Buildings erected 1953.
KNUTTON C.E.V.P. SCHOOL,[81] High St., Knutton	1874	Opened as M/I. Infants transferred to Knutton Temporary Council School in 1913. Seniors transferred to Knutton C.S. School in 1932.	Enlarged 1878 and 1895. Since 1949 used two classrooms at Knutton C.S.M. School, and since 1947 a Y.M.C.A. hut.
KNUTTON C.P. SCHOOL,[82] High St., Knutton	1914	Took infants from Knutton Temporary Council School. In 1953 was retaining 1st year of Knutton C.E.V.P. school due to overcrowding there.	Enlarged 1938. Used one classroom in Knutton C.S. School temporarily in 1953.
KNUTTON C.S. SCHOOL,[83] High St., Knutton	1932	Took senior pupils from Knutton C.E.V.P. and Silverdale C.E.V.P. Schools and Silverdale C.P. School.	Erected 1932, extended 1936, 1949.
KNUTTON TEMPORARY COUNCIL SCHOOL,[84] Black Bank Rd., Knutton	1913	Took infants of Knutton C.E.V.P. School 1913. Closed 1914 and pupils transferred to Knutton C.P. School.	Used United Methodist Sunday School, Knutton.
LANGDALE C.P. SCHOOL,[85] Langdale Rd., Clayton	1954		
LONGBRIDGE HAYES NATIONAL SCHOOL,[86] John St., Longbridge Hayes	1871	Used for girls and infants.	Mission church.
MAY BANK C.P. SCHOOL,[87] High St., May Bank	1903		Extended 1927.
NEWCASTLE BRITISH SCHOOL,[88] Friarswood Rd., Newcastle	1834	Associated with British and Foreign Schools Society from at least 1846. Taken over by Newcastle School Board 1876, and reopened as Friarswood School (q.v.).	Site given by Duke of Sutherland. Received government building grant.
NEWCASTLE WESLEYAN SCHOOL,[89] School St., Newcastle	1871	Opened as M/I school, closed in 1877 when taken over by School Board (see Hassell Street Schools).	Used Sunday-school buildings of Brunswick St. Wesleyan Chapel.
ORME BOYS C.S. SCHOOL,[90] The Higherland, Newcastle	1931	Took senior boys from Hassell St. and Ryecroft Schools (q.v.)	Using buildings of former Middle School (see pp. 65, 66).
PRIORY ROAD C.P. SCHOOL,[91] Newcastle	1934		Temporary weather-board additions, 1939.
RED STREET C.E.V.P. SCHOOL,[92] Chesterton	1872	Founded as an all-age National School.	Mission church.
RYECROFT C.P. SCHOOL[93]	1872	Opened as B/G/I. Senior boys transferred to Orme Boys C.S. School 1931, girls to Westlands C.S. School in 1936.	Opened in Methodist New Connexion Sunday School. New buildings 1874, enlarged 1891.
ST. GEORGE'S NATIONAL SCHOOL,[94] Liverpool Rd., Newcastle	1835	Opened in Holborn as infants' school. Moved to Liverpool Road 1854–60, when it became BG/I. Closed between 1872 and 1876 when merged with St. Giles's National School.	
ST. GILES'S AND ST. GEORGE'S C.E.V.C. SCHOOL,[95] Bow St., Newcastle	1825	Opened as St. Giles's National School. Benefited under Hatrell, Bagnall, and Cowell Charities. B/G/I until 1948 when B/G merged into one department containing JM section and SM section.	Original infants' school in School Street and original boys' and girls' school in Bath Street. Present buildings erected 1895. In 1947 two huts erected and additional accommodation used in St. John's Sunday School,

[80] Rep. on sch. premises (1953); '1959 List of Schs.'
[81] Ed. 7/111; Rep. on sch. premises (1953); ex inf. boro. educ. officer; '1959 List of Schs.'
[82] Ed. 7/111; Rep. on sch. premises (1953); ex inf. boro. educ. officer; '1959 List of Schs.'
[83] Ex inf. boro. educ. officer.   [84] Ed. 7/111.
[85] Rep. on sch. premises (1953); ex. inf. boro. educ. officer; '1959 List of Schs.'   [86] Ed. 7/113.
[87] Ed. 7/111; Rep. on sch. premises (1953); '1959 List of Schs.'   [88] Ed. 7/111.   [89] Ed. 7/111.
[90] Ex inf. boro. educ. officer.

[91] Rep. on sch. premises (1953); ex inf. boro. educ. officer; '1959 List of Schs.'
[92] Ed. 7/111; Rep. on sch. premises (1953); ex inf. boro. educ. officer; '1959 List of Schs.'
[93] Ed. 7/111; Kelly's Dir. Staffs. (1916); Rep. on sch. premises (1953); ex inf. boro. educ. officer; '1959 List of Schs.'
[94] '1959 List of Schs.'; White, Dir. Staffs. (1851); P.O. Dir. Staffs. (1854, 1860).
[95] Ed. 7/111; White, Dir. Staffs. (1851); Pape, Educ. End. of Newcastle, 65–67; Rep. on sch. premises (1953); ex inf. boro. educ. officer; '1959 List of Schs.'

School	Date of opening	Changes in organization	Buildings
			Liverpool Road. In 1948 former Domestic Science centre at Ryecroft School acquired as additional accommodation and from 1950 St. George's Institute has been used.
St. Luke's C.E.V.C. School,[96] Church St., Silverdale	1847	Opened as National School for B/G. Evening School for boys in 1855. Subsequently B/G/I. In 1932 senior children were transferred to Knutton Senior School and school reorganized as JM, I.	Land given and school built by Ralph Sneyd. Buildings enlarged 1894.
St. Mary's R.C.A.P. School,[97] Stanier St., Newcastle	1938	Annexe to infants' school opened in Wolstanton in 1953 (and see St. Wulstan's School).	
St. Patrick's R.C. School,[98] London Rd., Newcastle	1833	Started as mixed school. B/GI from 1865. In 1938 juniors and infants transferred to St. Mary's R.C.A.P. School (q.v.), this school becoming St. Patrick's R.C.V.S. School (q.v.).	Original school under same roof as church. New buildings 1864. Extensions 1883, 1895–1910. New infants' school 1897.
St. Patrick's R.C.V.S. School,[99] London Rd., Newcastle	1938		Used buildings of former St. Patrick's R.C. School.
St. Wulstan's R.C.A.P. School,[1] Church Lane, Wolstanton	1959	Took children from Wolstanton annexe of St. Mary's Infants' School and children from St. Mary's Junior School.	
Silverdale C.P. School,[2] Mill St., Silverdale	1875	Formerly Silverdale Primitive Methodist School (q.v.). B/G/I until 1932 when seniors transferred to Knutton C.S. School and school reorganized as JM/I.	New buildings erected 1877. Infants' department erected 1886 on opposite side of road. Extensions to junior school in 1909. Infants' school requisitioned 1939–45 by Civil Defence.
Silverdale Primitive Methodist School[3]	1872	All-age school. Taken over by Wolstanton School Board 1875 (see Silverdale C.P. School).	Primitive Methodist Sunday School buildings.
Watlands Council School,[4] Garnett Rd. West, Porthill	1913	Took children from Wolstanton C.E. Infants' School which then closed. Pupils transferred to Watlands C.P. School in 1932.	
Watlands C.P. School,[5] Loring Rd., Porthill	1932		Temporary accommodation provided 1949–51 to house infants living in Bradwell area until opening of Bradwell C.P. School, 1951.
Watlands C.S. School,[6] Garnett Rd. West, Porthill	1932	Took senior children from Ellison Street Schools and Wolstanton C.E. School in 1932.	Used buildings of former Watlands Council School.
Westlands C.S. School,[7] Abbots Way, Newcastle	1936	Took senior girls from Hassell Street and Ryecroft Schools (q.v.).	
Wolstanton C.E.V.C. School,[8] High St., Wolstanton	1841	Opened as all-age National School. Infants transferred to Watlands Council School in 1913. Seniors transferred to Watlands C.S. School in 1932.	Rebuilt 1872.
Wolstanton Wesleyan School,[9] Wolstanton	1871	Opened as B/G/I. Closed 1881 when taken over by School Board (see Ellison Street Schools).	Using Sunday School buildings of St. John's Wesleyan Church.

[96] Ed. 7/111; Rep. on sch. premises (1953); *Kelly's Dir. Staffs.* (1916); ex inf. boro. educ. officer; '1959 List of Schs.'
[97] Rep. on sch. premises (1953); '1959 List of Schs.'
[98] Ed. 7/111; *Kelly's Dir. Staffs.* (1916); Rep. on sch. premises (1953); ex inf. boro. educ. officer; '1959 List of Schs.'
[99] Rep. on sch. premises (1953); '1959 List of Schs.'
[1] Rep. on sch. premises (1959).

[2] Ed. 7/111; Rep. on sch. premises (1953); '1959 List of Schs.'
[3] Ed. 7/111.
[4] Ed. 7/111; ex. inf. boro. educ. officer.
[5] Ed. 7/111; ex inf. boro. educ. officer.
[6] Ex. inf. boro. educ. officer.
[7] Ex. inf. boro. educ. officer.
[8] Ed. 7/111; *Kelly's Dir. Staffs.* (1916); Rep. on sch. premises (1953); ex inf. boro. educ. officer; '1959 List of Schs.'
[9] Ed. 7/111.

CHARITIES FOR THE POOR. As will be seen from the table below, the corporation, either at the express wish of the donor or by its acquisition of the charity lands,[10] administered from the 17th century onwards an increasing number of the borough charities. Some of these were applied in relief of the poor rate under the decree of 1740.[11] From 1807 seventeen of the charities which were by then vested in the corporation were consolidated with ten in the hands of the churchwardens. The annual income from the former was £12 12s. (by at least 1824) and from the latter £13 5s. 4d. and was expended in bread and money doles on St. Thomas's Day (21 December).[12] The distribution, organized by the churchwardens and overseers, was held at the parish church and elsewhere in the town and attended by the rector and leading residents.[13] In 1896 all surviving Newcastle charities for the poor were vested as the United Charities in a body of trustees on which the corporation had five representatives. The moneys were thenceforward applied in general benefits to the poor of the borough,[14] often in large grants to the charitable organizations of the district.[15] In 1952 £47 10s. was distributed in money at Christmas to 47 poor.[16] In 1955 the United Charities, the funds of the District Nursing Association, and the charities of Eliza Hinds and Richard Mountford were vested as the Amalgamated Charities in a body of twelve trustees, six of them nominated by the borough council and six co-opted. Apart from sums reserved for special purposes such as sermons and, in the case of the Nursing Association, the sick poor of the borough, the income was to be applied in general relief, including weekly doles of between 2s. 6d. and 10s., to the poor of the borough 'as constituted from time to time'.[17]

By 1663 the corporation had at its disposal several almshouses.[18] An order was made in 1667 for their repair at the expense of the borough, although in one case the inmate was expected to contribute towards the cost under pain of ejection.[19] A house near the Castle Pool was taken into the corporation's hands in 1684 and converted into further almshouses.[20] The corporation almshouses seem to have been superseded by the workhouse[21] in 1731.[22]

By the will of Christopher Monck, Duke of Albemarle (d. 1688), a sum of £1,500 was bequeathed for the erection of almshouses for 20 widows, not necessarily from Newcastle, with a further £4,500 as endowment. As a consequence of disputes about the testator's property, it was not until 1743 that his heirs, Grace, Countess Granville, John, styled Lord Gower, and Bernard Granville, erected the 20 almshouses. They also agreed to keep them in repair and provide £160 annually for the maintenance of the widows; out of this sum £20 was to be spent each Michaelmas on gowns and petticoats of blue cloth which were to be worn by the inmates whenever they were in public. Each of the three above-mentioned heirs, with their heirs after them, was to present six of the widows and appoint the remaining two in rotation. By 1824 clothing had not been provided for some years, and the whole £160 was paid in money at the rate of 3s. a week to each widow with an additional 4s. each about Christmas time. The inmates were still chosen from other districts besides Newcastle.[23] The right of presentation, as well as that of appointing the trustees, remained in the Leveson-Gower family (dukes of Sutherland from 1833) until 1940 when the 5th duke settled a sum of £6,400 stock in redemption of the annual £160 and his responsibility to maintain the premises. By 1914 the 20 sets were occupied by 19 almswomen and a matron; most of the inmates then came from Newcastle, but some were widows of tenants on the Trentham estate. Since the site was required for road purposes, the building was bought in 1940 by the Ministry of Transport for £4,500 which was invested to meet the cost of new premises. Owing to the war, demolition was not carried out, and by agreement ten of the almshouses remained with the trustees rent-free for needy widows and the rest were taken over by the borough for housing.[24]

The building, which stands at the junction of Bridge Street and Lower Green, is of red brick with a hipped roof and consists of two ranges at right angles to one another. The range facing Bridge Street contains three cross-passages with staircases, each giving access to four sets of rooms, two on each floor. The individual sets consist of living room, bedroom, and pantry. The shorter range facing Lower Green has two entrances and contains eight sets of rooms, similarly arranged. On both façades the doorways and casement windows are surmounted by stone lintels with raised keystones, the upper windows having stone aprons below the sills. The doors and windows at the rear are contained in plain brick openings. In the centre of the Bridge Street front is an open pediment supported on stone console brackets, below which is an inscribed tablet, now (1960) almost illegible.[25]

[10] E 134/5 Wm. and Mary/Mich., no. 57; E 134/7 Wm. III/Mich., no. 44.
[11] See p. 31.
[12] *13th Rep. Com. Char.* H.C. 349, pp. 298–302 (1825), xi; Corp. Order Bk. 1800–25, pp. 341–2.
[13] *13th Rep. Com. Char.* 302.
[14] Char. Com. files, Scheme of 22 Sept. 1896.
[15] *Staffs. Advertiser*, 6 Jan. 1912.
[16] Char. Com. files.
[17] Ibid.
[18] Corp. Order Bk. 1590–1669, pp. 203–7.
[19] Ibid. p. 229.
[20] Ibid. 1669–1712, ff. 32b, 33b, 116b; Ward, *Stoke*, app., p. lxiii.

[21] It is possible that the houses in Higherland converted into the workhouse were almshouses: see p. 33.
[22] See p. 33.
[23] Boro. Mus., foundation deed (copy), printed in *13th Rep. Com. Char.* 295–6; W.S.L., Hand Morgan Coll., Bourne Papers, building account and copy of deed; Corp. Order Bk. 1712–67, f. 138a.
[24] Ex inf. Mr. F. Morris, a trustee (1957); Char. Com. files.
[25] See plate facing p. 55. The inscription reads: 'Erected at the expence of the Right Honourable Grace Countess Granville, John Lord Gower, and Bernard Granville, Esq. in completion of the Will of the most noble Christopher Duke of Albemarle, Anno 1743'.

TABLE II

Charities for the Poor

Founder	Instrument	Endowment	History
John Barker[26]	Will of 1607	£40 at discretion of his brother Ralph.	In 1612 paid by Ralph to corporation; laid out in purchase of rent-charge of £2 6s. 8d. for distribution to 10 poor on St. Thomas's Day (21 Dec.); by 1760 distributed in Lent in sums of 2s.; by 1824 part of general distribution of bread and money on St. Thomas's Day; one of United Charities from 1896 and still in force 1955 but then no longer vested in corporation.
John Bagnall[27]	Deed of 1619	6s. 8d. rent-charge vested in corporation.	Among United Charities from 1896 and still in force 1955.
Ralph Brereton of London[28]	Will of 1630	£100	Laid out by corporation in 1639 in purchase of an estate let for £5. Income distributed in bread every Sunday, and remainder on first market-day after Christmas, to 20 poor. In 1740 consolidated with other money in the corporation's hands in aid of poor rate; £4 6s. 8d., however, continued to be distributed in 20 loaves each week until corporation treasurer stopped the practice in 1820.
Alice, widow of Thomas Clayton[28]	Unknown but by 1639	£10	
Randle Astbury of Trentham[28]	Unknown but by 1639	£10	
Unknown[28]	Unknown but by 1639	£5	
Henry Smith of London[29]	Deed of 1641 putting into effect various deeds made in and after 1620	£12 rent-charge, vested in churchwardens and overseers but by 1729 in corporation.	By 1729 distributed in clothing; by 1824 allowed to accumulate for periodic distribution in clothing; among United Charities from 1896 and still in force 1955.
Sir John Bowyer of Knypersley[30]	Deed of 1661	£5 8s. rent-charge for apprenticing 2 children (£2 10s. each) of poor burgesses and buying them each a bible.	At first one apprentice selected by Sir John and his heirs and the other by corporation; by early 19th century mayor selected both; among United Charities from 1896 but lapsed by 1953.
Thomas Bagnall[31]	Will of 1675	12s. rent-charge on Cold Fair tolls for bread for 12 poor on 12 Sundays after Cold Fair (8 Nov.) through corporation.	By 1824 part of St. Thomas's Day distribution; among United Charities from 1896 and still in force 1955.
Richard Heath, alderman[32]	Will of 1685	10s. interest on £10 for bread, vested in corporation.	By 1760 distributed on Sunday after Cold Fair; by 1824 part of St. Thomas's Day distribution; among United Charities from 1896 and still in force 1955.
John Lowe of Marston Montgomery (Derb.)[33]	Deed of 1685	10s. rent-charge for bread on Quadragesima and Palm Sundays.	Among United Charities from 1896, by which time it was vested in corporation, and still in force 1955.
William Beard[34]	Deed of 1690	10s. rent-charge vested in corporation for bread for poor attending sermon on St. Mark's Day.	Among United Charities from 1896 and still in force 1955.
Sir William Leveson-Gower (d. 1691)[35]	Unknown	£2 12s. rent-charge for bread every Sunday, vested in churchwardens.	Rent-charge redeemed 1861; income 1888 £2 11s. 2d. interest on stock; among United Charities from 1896 and still in force 1955.
John Colclough of Trentham[36]	Will of 1699	Interest on £5 for bread on Sunday after 11 Oct.	Distribution at executor's discretion; apparently in hands of corporation by 1746; lapsed by 1760.

[26] *13th Rep. Com. Char.* H.C. 349, p. 293 (1825), xi; Pape, *Tudor and Stuart Newcastle*, 245–6; Boro. Mus., List of Newcastle Char. 1760, no. 40; Char. Com. files.

[27] *13th Rep. Com. Char.* 302–3; Pape, *Tudor and Stuart Newcastle*, 79; Char. Com. files; *Newcastle Par. Reg.* i. 72 (Staffs. Par. Reg. Soc.).

[28] *13th Rep. Com. Char.* 303–4; Pape, *Tudor and Stuart Newcastle*, 113–14, 301, 304; Boro. Mus., Corp. Order Bk. 1712–67, f. 53b, which states that Brereton added another £20.

[29] *13th Rep. Com. Char.* 307; *8th Rep. Com. Char.* H.C. 13, pp. 660–4 (1823), viii; *4th Rep. Com. Char.* H.C. 312, p. 448 (1820), v; Char. Com. files.

[30] *13th Rep. Com. Char.* 297; Corp Order Bk. 1590–1669, f. 200a; Char. Com. files.

[31] *13th Rep. Com. Char.* 301; Char. Com. files.

[32] *13th Rep. Com. Char.* 300; Newcastle Char. 1760, no. 13; Corp. Order Bk. 1669–1712, f. 69a.; Char. Com. files; *Newcastle Par. Reg.* i. 208.

[33] *13th Rep. Com. Char.* 282–3, 305; Char. Com. files.

[34] *13th Rep. Com. Char.* 299–300; Char. Com. files.

[35] *13th Rep. Com. Char.* 300; Char. Com. files; Burke, *Peerage* (1949), 1942.

[36] *13th Rep. Com. Char.* 307; Corp. Order Bk. 1712–67,

Founder	Instrument	Endowment	History
Francis Wells[37]	Unknown but by 1700	£1 interest on £20 for 40 loaves yearly.	In hands of corporation by 1725; by 1760 distributed on Easter Day; by 1824 part of St. Thomas's Day distribution; among United Charities by 1896 and still in force 1955.
Mr. Cotton[38]	Unknown but by 1701	£5 probably for apprenticing.	In 1701 corporation ordered charity to be used in apprenticing poor boys at discretion of justices 'out of the liberty of the town'; nothing further known.
John Baddeley[39]	Will of 1701	6s. 8d. rent-charge for bread, vested in churchwardens.	By 1760 distributed on Shrove Tuesday and by 1824 on St. Thomas's Day; among United Charities from 1896 but lapsed by 1955.
Richard Bagnall[40]	Deed of 1703	£1 rent-charge for bread, vested in mayor and other trustees.	Between at least 1746 and 1821 applied in apprenticing; distributed in money by 1866 but apparently lapsed by 1896.
Revd. Edward Orme (d. 1705)[41]	Will of 1705	£5 rent-charge for apprenticing 2 children under corporation's supervision.	By 1824 spent by custom on clothing for boys chosen; among United Charities from 1896 and transferred to control of Ministry of Education on formation of Amalgamated Charities in 1955; still applied in apprenticing in 1958.
John Mare[42]	Will proved 1708	5s. rent-charge for bread on Christmas Day, vested in churchwardens.	By 1824 part of St. Thomas's Day distribution; among United Charities from 1896 and still in force 1955.
Ralph Bailey of Normacot Grange, Stone[43]	Will—date unknown but by 1711	£2 12s. rent-charge vested in minister and churchwardens.	Distributed in Lent by 1760 in sums of 2s.; lapsed 1806.
Katherine, Dowager Lady Gower (d. 1723)[44]	Unknown	£1 interest on £20 for bread.	In hands of corporation by 1725; by 1760 distributed in August; by 1824 part of St. Thomas's Day distribution; among United Charities from 1896 and still in force 1955.
Nathaniel Beard[45]	Unknown but by 1725	10s. rent-charge for bread on Sunday after St. Luke (18 Oct.), vested in churchwardens.	By 1824 part of St. Thomas's Day distribution; lapsed 1861.
Samuel and Obadiah Rock[46]	Unknown but by 1725	10s. interest on £10 for bread on Sunday after 22 May.	In hands of corporation by 1740; formed part of St. Thomas's Day distribution by 1824; among United Charities from 1896 and still in force 1955.
Samuel Sunderland[47]	Unknown but by 1725	10s. interest on £10 for bread on Sunday after 13 May.	In hands of corporation by 1725; part of St. Thomas's Day distribution by 1824; among United Charities from 1896 and still in force 1955.
Isabel, wife of Samuel Sunderland[48]	Unknown but by 1725	5s. interest on £5 for 20 loaves on Sunday after 13 May.	In hands of corporation by 1725; part of St. Thomas's Day distribution by 1824; among United Charities from 1896 and still in force 1955.
John Browne (or Bourne)[49]	Unknown but by 1725	£1 interest on £20 for bread in November, vested in corporation.	Part of St. Thomas's Day distribution by 1824; among United Charities from 1896 and still in force 1955.
Samuel Bell[50]	Will—date unknown but by 1725	5s. rent-charge for bread, vested in churchwardens.	By 1760 distributed c. 20 January and by 1824 part of St. Thomas's Day distribution; among United Charities from 1896; by then vested in corporation, and still in force 1955.

ff. 55a, 146a. It does not appear in the list of 1760.

[37] *13th Rep. Com. Char.* 300; Corp. Order Bk. 1669–1712, f. 106a; Newcastle Char. 1760, no. 12; Char. Com. files.

[38] Corp. Order Bk. 1669–1712, f. 109a.

[39] *13th Rep. Com. Char.* 298; Newcastle Char. 1760, no. 16; Char. Com. files.

[40] *13th Rep. Com. Char.* 297–8; Corp. Order Bk. 1712–67, f. 146b; *Staffs. Endowed Char.* H.C. 91, pp. 38–39 (1869), xlv; Char. Com. files, where in a letter of 1896 it is said to have lapsed.

[41] *13th Rep. Com. Char.* 284, 288; Corp. Order Bk. 1669–1712, f. 128a; Char. Com. files; ex inf. Min. of Educ.; *Newcastle Par. Reg.* i. 267; see p. 64.

[42] *13th Rep. Com. Char.* 299, 321; Char. Com. files.

[43] *13th Rep. Com. Char.* 304–5; Newcastle Char. 1760, nos. 7, 41; Char. Com. files, vestry clerk's list of lapsed charities, 1889.

[44] *13th Rep. Com. Char.* 300; Corp. Order Bk. 1712–67, f. 55b; Newcastle Char. 1760, no. 24; Char. Com. files.

[45] *13th Rep. Com. Char.* 299; Corp. Order Bk. 1712–67, f. 54b; Char. Com. files, vestry clerk's list of lapsed charities, 1889.

[46] *13th Rep. Com. Char.* 300, 301; Corp. Order Bk. 1712–67, f. 55a; Char. Com. files.

[47] *13th Rep. Com. Char.* 300, 301; Corp. Order Bk. 1712–67, f. 55a; Char. Com. files.

[48] *13th Rep. Com. Char.* 300, 301; Corp. Order Bk. 1712–67, f. 55a; Char. Com. files.

[49] *13th Rep. Com. Char.* 300; Corp. Order Bk. 1712–67, f. 55a; Char. Com. files.

[50] *13th Rep. Com. Char.* 299; Corp. Order Bk. 1712–67, f. 55a; Newcastle Char. 1760, no. 24; Char. Com. files.

Founder	Instrument	Endowment	History
William Boughey[51]	Unknown but by 1725	10s. interest on £10 for bread on Easter Day, vested in churchwardens.	Lapsed 1806; revived after 1824; finally lapsed 1856.
John Boughey[52]	Unknown but by 1725	10s. rent-charge for bread on Whit-Sunday.	Lapsed 1806; revived after 1824; finally lapsed 1856.
Bridget Cook[53]	Unknown but by 1725	10s. rent-charge.	By 1760 distributed probably by church-wardens in bread; by 1824 part of St. Thomas's Day distribution; among United Charities by 1896, by which date vested in corporation, and still in force 1955.
Samuel Collier[54]	Unknown but by 1725	10s. interest on £10 for bread on St. Thomas's Day, vested apparently in corporation.	Among United Charities from 1896 and still in force 1955.
Hannah Bagnall[55]	Will of 1727	£1 interest on £20 for bread on 2nd Sunday in Lent, vested in corporation.	By 1824 part of St. Thomas's Day distribution; among United Charities from 1896 and still in force 1955.
John Ward, cr. Viscount Dudley and Ward 1763[56]	Deed of 1 Oct. 1730	£30 interest on £600.	Consolidated with charities in aid of poor-rate 1740.
John Smith[57]	Will of 1729	10s. interest on £10 for bread on 1 January.	In hands of corporation from 1734; by 1824 part of St. Thomas's Day distribution; among United Charities from 1896 and still in force 1955.
William Annion of Clayton (d. 1736)[58]	Will of 1736	£1 interest on £20 for bread on Easter and Christmas Days, vested in corporation.	By 1824 part of St. Thomas's Day distribution; among United Charities from 1896 and still in force 1955.
Mary Lowe[59]	Unknown: between 1725-40	5s. interest on £5 for bread in November.	In hands of corporation by 1740; part of St. Thomas's Day distribution by 1824; among United Charities from 1896 and still in force 1955.
John Fenton[60]	Deed of 1742	£1 interest on £20 for 20 loaves on each Sunday in Lent, vested in corporation.	Part of St. Thomas's Day distribution by 1824; among United Charities from 1896 and still in force 1955.
John (or William) Horderne[61]	Will of 1753	10s. interest on £10 for bread, vested in corporation.	By 1760 distributed on St. Thomas's Day; among United Charities from 1896 and still in force 1955.
John Hulme[62]	Will of 1757	£1 interest on £20 for bread on Sunday after 29 December, vested in corporation.	By 1824 part of St. Thomas's Day distribution; among United Charities from 1896 and still in force 1955.
Ann Hulme[63]	Will of 1757	£1 interest on £20 for bread on 1st Sunday after 14 August, vested in corporation.	By 1824 part of St. Thomas's Day distribution; among United Charities from 1896 and still in force 1955.
John Bourne[64]	Probably deed: probably 1758	£5 interest on £100, vested in corporation and distributed by churchwardens.	Among United Charities from 1896 and still in force 1955.
James Taylor[65]	Will: between 1725 and 1760	£1 rent-charge for bread on 1st Sunday after 22 May, vested in corporation.	By 1824 paid direct to churchwardens and part of St. Thomas's Day distribution; among United Charities from 1896, by when vested in corporation, and still in force 1955.

[51] *13th Rep. Com. Char.* 306; Corp. Order Bk. 1712-67, f. 55b; Char. Com. files, vestry clerk's list of lapsed charities, 1889.

[52] *13th Rep. Com. Char.* 306; Corp. Order Bk. 1712-67, f. 55b; Char. Com. files, vestry clerk's list of lapsed charities, 1889.

[53] *13th Rep. Com. Char.* 299; Corp. Order Bk. 1712-67, f. 55b; Newcastle Char. 1760, no. 27; Char. Com. files.

[54] *13th Rep. Com. Char.* 300, 301; Corp. Order Bk. 1712-67, f. 55b; Newcastle Char. 1760, no. 28; Char. Com. files.

[55] *13th Rep. Com. Char.* 300; Corp. Order Bk. 1712-67, f. 77b; Char. Com. files.

[56] *13th Rep. Com. Char.* 304; Char. Com. files; List of Charities, 1779, in poss. of Town Clerk; *S.H.C.* 1920 and 1922, 233-4; *Complete Peerage*, iv. 487-8.

[57] *13th Rep. Com. Char.* 300, 301; Boro. Mus., Bond from Corp. to Joshua Lawton of Knutton, 26 July 1734; Char. Com. files.

[58] *13th Rep. Com. Char.* 300, 301; Char. Com. files; Boro. Mus., release from corp. to execs. of Wm. Annion, 1736; *Stoke Par. Reg.* iii. 460 (Staffs. Par. Reg. Soc.).

[59] *Abstract of Ret. of Charitable Donations, 1786-8,* H.C. 511, pp. 1144-5 (1816), xvi (2); *13th Rep. Com. Char.* 301; Char. Com. files. It does not appear in the 1725 list in Corp. Order Bk. 1712-67, ff. 53b-55b; Char. Com. files.

[60] *13th Rep. Com. Char.* 301; Corp. Order Bk. 1712-67, f. 131b; Char. Com. files.

[61] *13th Rep. Com. Char.* 301; Newcastle Char. 1760, no. 32; Char. Com. files; *Newcastle Par. Reg.* ii. 234.

[62] *13th Rep. Com. Char.* 301; Char. Com. files; *Newcastle Par. Reg.* ii. 256.

[63] *13th Rep. Com. Char.* 301; Char. Com. files.

[64] Corp. Order Bk. 1712-67, f. 183a; *13th Rep. Com. Char.* 302; Char. Com. files.

[65] *13th Rep. Com. Char.* 298-9; Newcastle Char. 1760, no. 34; Char. Com. files. It does not appear in the 1725 list in Corp. Order Bk. 1712-67, ff. 53b-55b.

Founder	Instrument	Endowment	History
Ralph Cartwright[66]	Will of 1776	£1 10s. rent-charge for bread for 20 poor on 2 January.	Paid through the Presbyterian minister until 1805 when it lapsed; by 1896 it had been revived and vested in corporation; and thenceforward among the United Charities, being still in force 1955.
Thomas Fletcher (d. 1783)[67]	Will of 1781	£1 interest on £20 for bread on Sunday after 2 February, vested in rector.	By 1824 customarily distributed to 20 poor widows; by 1896 paid as interest on £40 stock and still in force as such 1955.
Richard Mountford of Tottenham High Cross (Mdx.)[68]	Will proved 1833	£100 for bread on Sunday after 25 March, vested in overseers of the poor.	As £98 10s. stock it formed part of the Amalgamated Charities from 1955.
Henry Dobbs of Norwood (Surrey)[69]	Probably deed of 1841	£1 10s. interest on £30 for bread, vested in corporation and distributed through rector and churchwardens.	First distribution in 1842; lapsed by 1896.
Eliza Hinds of Newcastle[70]	Will proved 1899	Residual estate to establish the Eliza Hinds Fund for poor and distressed of Newcastle or for charitable institutions there.	Income 1953–4 £60 9s. 2d. interest on £2,015 6s. 3d. stock; then, and for some years before, distributed in sums of 10s., with £1 1s. also to St. George's Parish Poor Fund; among Amalgamated Charities from 1955.
Edward Turner of Newcastle[71]	Will proved 1904	£1,000 to be called the Maria Turner Charity; income to be distributed in money and kind at Christmas by rector and churchwardens of St. Giles to poor of parish.	Income 1951–2 £28 2s. 4d., distributed in 36 5s. grocery tickets, in gifts of £2 or more, and in sending patients to convalescent homes.
Mayor's Poor Relief Fund[72]		Public subscription in 1921 and transfer of £251 16s. 3d. from other charity funds. Alleviation of distress caused by miners' strike in first instance.	Between 1921 and 1950 £476 18s. 2d. distributed by successive mayors to persons in distress; assets in 1950 consisted of £774 16s. 3d. in stock and cash, and the fund is used for occasional relief e.g. grants towards maintenance of the almshouses.
Annie Dutton of Sidmouth (Devon)[73]	Will proved 1933	One-third of residual estate for Christmas gifts for poor of St. George's parish.	In 1958 still distributed at the vicar's discretion at Christmas and, where funds are available, during the year as required.

CLAYTON

THE civil parish of Clayton was created in 1896 out of the townships of Clayton, Seabridge, and Clayton Griffith.[1] Clayton and Seabridge formed the western part of the parish of Stoke-upon-Trent, and Clayton Griffith to the north was a detached portion of Trentham parish.[2] At first 1,807 acres in extent,[3] Clayton was gradually reduced in size between 1921 and 1932 when it was taken into the borough of Newcastle-under-Lyme in three stages, in 1921, 1927, and 1932.[4]

The district is an upland area lying mainly around the 400- and 500-ft. contours above the Lyme Brook on the east and the Park Brook (formerly the Hanchurch Brook)[5] on the south. There is a dip in the level north of Clayton village where a stream runs down to the Lyme Brook. The soil is clay and the subsoil sandstone gravel.[6] The southern part of the area is still (1960) largely rural, with Clayton village lying in the south-east on the Newcastle–Eccleshall road and the hamlet of Seabridge in the south-west near the Newcastle to Market Drayton road. Most of the farms and cottages are of the 19th century and later. To the west of Clayton Lodge is a partly timber-framed house, probably of 17th-century date. Clayton Lodge, now an hotel, is a small late-Georgian house much altered and enlarged at subsequent periods; most of it is about to be rebuilt. In the northern part of the former parish there are extensive housing estates representing the southward development of Newcastle. In Clayton

[66] 13th Rep. Com. Char. 306; Char. Com. files; see p. 64.
[67] 13th Rep. Com. Char. 305; Char. Com. files; Burke, Peerage (1949), 231.
[68] Char. Com. files.
[69] Ibid; Boro. Mus., Counc. Mins. 1835–44, pp. 248, 323. It does not appear in 1896 list of United Char.
[70] Char. Com. files.
[71] Ibid.   [72] Ibid.
[73] Ibid.; ex inf. the Vicar of St. George's (1958).
[1] See p. 76.

[2] There was also a small detached portion of Trentham parish on either side of the road near Roe Lane Farm in Seabridge township: T. Hargreaves, Map of Staffs. Potteries and Newcastle (1832). The history of Clayton Griffith is reserved for treatment under the parish of Trentham in a future volume.
[3] Census, 1901, Staffs.
[4] See p. 1.
[5] Ward, Stoke, app. p. lxii.
[6] Kelly's Dir. Staffs. (1928).

Griffith, taken into the borough of Newcastle in 1921, the corporation built the Westlands estate, comprising 104 houses by 1926.[7] It bought agricultural land in Clayton in the 1930's for housing,[8] and before 1939 another council estate had been built to the north of Clayton Lane; a smaller estate in Northwood Road in Clayton village itself also dates from the 1930's. An estate was built in Clayton Lane after 1945, and another has recently been completed in Seabridge Lane. In recent years there has been much private building in Seabridge which has given it something of a middle-class residential character. The aircraft hangars in Northwood Road, Clayton, were built during the Second World War for the Fleet Air Arm, which also occupied Clayton Hall; the hangars were subsequently converted into a Royal Navy motor transport depot which was closed in 1959.[9]

Clayton was inhabited by 4 villeins and 6 bordars in 1086; it then included Clayton Griffith also, the separation of which probably took place in the 13th century.[10] Seabridge occurs on the Pipe Roll of 1199–1200.[11] There were 11 persons in Clayton and Seabridge assessed to the subsidy of 1332,[12] and c. 1680 there were '12 or 14' houses in Clayton and '10 or 12' in Seabridge;[13] in 1701 the population was 105 and 77 respectively.[14] Clayton Griffith by the late 17th century, and probably by the early 16th century, centred on the estate called Hill farm,[15] the house of which was still in existence in the early 1920's.[16] In 1834, however, the township was described as having 'a few scattered houses near the canal'.[17] The population of Clayton in 1821 was 152, of Seabridge 140, and of Clayton Griffith 34.[18] The population of the civil parish, comprising all three, was 269 in 1901, 312 in 1911, and 349 in 1921; in 1931, after the transfer of part of the parish to Newcastle (see above), the population was 264.[19]

The main road from Newcastle to Eccleshall passes through Clayton village as Clayton Road, with a side road, Northwood Lane, running from the village to Trentham. This stretch of the main road was constructed under the Turnpike Act of 1823,[20] and by 1832 there was a toll-gate where Clayton Road meets Friarswood Road and Brook Lane near the former Newcastle boundary.[21] Before 1823 the way to Newcastle was the present Clayton Lane which runs

north-eastwards from the village down to the Newcastle–Stone road at Spring Fields.[22] The southern end of Clayton Lane was diverted to its present more northerly course evidently in connexion with the rebuilding of Clayton Hall in the 1840's.[23] The road from Newcastle to Market Drayton runs through the western part of the area as Whitmore Road. Its course was straightened to its present line in the 1830's or 1840's.[24] It originally ran farther east along what is now called Harrowby Drive, past Roe Lane Farm and through Seabridge hamlet to Butterton, in Trentham ancient parish. This Seabridge–Butterton stretch, mentioned in 1483 when Thomas Swynnerton of Butterton was fined for stopping it up,[25] can still be traced as a sunken way down the slope between Seabridge Hall and Seabridge Farm, as an embankment on the north side of the Park Brook, and as a further sunken way up the slope on the south side of the brook. The Newcastle–Market Drayton road was turnpiked under an Act of 1769,[26] and by 1820 there was a toll-gate at its junction with Seabridge Lane which ran then as now from Clayton Road north of Clayton village.[27] The foundations of the bridge carrying the old road over the Park Brook between Seabridge and Butterton are still (1960) visible a little to the west of the present footbridge below Seabridge Farm.[28] A parish rate was levied for the repair of the bridge at the end of the 17th century when it was known as Butterton Bridge.[29]

For parochial purposes the townships of Clayton and Seabridge lay within the parish of Stoke-upon-Trent.[30] Clayton came within the jurisdiction of the Stoke Improvement Commissioners established in 1839 but did not form part of the borough of Stoke as incorporated in 1874.[31] In 1894 both Clayton and Seabridge were included in the new civil parish of Stoke Rural, but in 1896 they were combined with the detached portion of Trentham parish known as Clayton Griffith to form the civil parish of Clayton.[32] Between 1921 and 1932 the parish was gradually absorbed into the borough of Newcastle.[33] As part of Stoke parish Clayton and Seabridge were included in 1836 in the poor law union of Stoke-upon-Trent;[34] after 1896, however, the civil parish of Clayton was assigned to Newcastle Union.[35] Manorially Clayton and Seabridge were part of Newcastle manor from the 13th century and were represented at the court

[7] See p. 37.
[8] See p. 38.
[9] Local inf.; see p. 78.
[10] V.C.H. Staffs. iv. 56, no. 259; see p. 77.
[11] S.H.C. ii (1), 95.
[12] Ibid. x (1), 82.
[13] Ibid. 1919, 258.
[14] W.S.L., D. 1742, bdle. 55.
[15] Ward, Stoke, 520, 524; R. Plot, Map of Staffs. (1682); S.C. 6/Hen. VIII/3352, m. 4.
[16] O.S. Map 6" Staffs. xvii NE. (1925). The site now forms part of the Westlands housing estate.
[17] White, Dir. Staffs. (1834).
[18] Census, 1821, Staffs. Seabridge was described as including part of Swynnerton parish.
[19] Ibid. 1901, 1911, 1921, 1931.
[20] Act for repairing roads in Staffs. and Shrops., 4 Geo. IV, c. 47 (local and personal). C. and J. Greenwood, Map of Staffs. (1820), shows 2 adjacent roads from Newcastle to Clayton, one of them a turnpike road, but at that date these could only have been projected roads.
[21] Hargreaves, Map of Staffs. Potteries.
[22] W. Yates, Map of Staffs. (1775), reproduced facing p. 4.
[23] See p. 78.

[24] Presumably under Act for repairing road from Newcastle to Drayton, 2 & 3 Wm. IV, c. 85 (local and personal) The old line is shown on O.S. Map 1" lxxii NW. (1837) and lxxiii NE. (1833) and the new line on Tithe Redemption Com., Tithe Maps, Stoke-upon-Trent (Clayton, 1849).
[25] S.H.C. vii (2), 133.
[26] Act to repair road from Shawbury to Drayton and Newcastle, 9 Geo. III, c. 55. In the Annual Turnpike Acts Continuance Act, 35 & 36 Vic. c. 85, it was scheduled to be disturnpiked on or after 1 Jan. 1873.
[27] S.R.O., Q/SB, Mich. 1820; Hargreaves, Map of Staffs. Potteries.
[28] These remains were identified in T.N.S.F.C. lxxviii, p. A254. For other remains by the footbridge see p. 79.
[29] T.N.S.F.C. lxxvii, p. A221; Ward, Stoke, app. p. lxii.
[30] Ward, Stoke, 467–8, 494; Hargreaves, Map of Staffs. Potteries.
[31] See p. 194.
[32] Census, 1901, Staffs.; Kelly's Dir. Staffs. (1900). Part of Clayton Griffith had been taken into the borough of Newcastle in 1877: see p. 1.
[33] See p. 1.
[34] See p. 199.
[35] Kelly's Dir. Staffs. (1900).

leet by three frankpledges by at least 1335.[36] They lay within the constablewick of Penkhull.[37]

The history of Clayton's Anglican, Roman Catholic, and Nonconformist churches and chapels and of its schools is treated under Newcastle.[38]

MANOR. *CLAYTON* was held by Seagrim, a free man, before the Conquest and by Richard the Forester, with Nigel de Stafford as his tenant, in 1086; it was then assessed at ½ hide.[39] By the middle of the 13th century Clayton had been divided. Great Clayton, the southern portion, had been absorbed into the royal manor of Newcastle, of which it continued to form a part.[40] Clayton Griffith or Little Clayton, lying between Great Clayton and Newcastle, was held by the Griffin family of the lord of Knutton (in Wolstanton).[41] This second manor is historically a detached portion of the ancient parish of Trentham and is reserved for treatment there.

Part at least of Seabridge was included in the Keele estate by the end of the 17th century.[42]

OTHER ESTATES. The Dawson family had settled in the Clayton area by the early 15th century when Thomas Dawson held an estate there in succession to William Dawson.[43] A Robert Dawson succeeded his brother John in a messuage and lands in Stoke parish during the first half of Elizabeth I's reign.[44] The family held an estate in Clayton between at least 1599 and the death of John Dawson in or shortly before 1775 when the farm belonged to John Fenton.[45] They held another in Seabridge between at least 1599 and 1692 when William Sneyd of Keele granted to Thomas Dawson of Seabridge a 21-year renewal of the lease of Biddles Tenement where Thomas was then living.[46] It is possible that the Seabridge estate may be identifiable with Long Hay farm which in 1761 was a 61-acre property owned by Ralph Sneyd and in the tenure of Thomas Wiggin.[47]

In 1681 Lawrence Wellington and his wife Jane held 2 messuages in Clayton, with lands there and in Seabridge.[48] In 1704 Lawrence (by then of Coal-brookdale, Salop.), conveyed these farms, both held by tenants, to his son John, who by will of 1708 left them to his brother Lawrence.[49] In 1717 Lawrence sold one of them to Thomas Fenton of Penkhull in whose family it remained, still held by tenants, until at least 1785 when Thomas Fenton of Newcastle held it.[50] This farm is probably identifiable with Clayton farm held in 1811 by the Bougheys who had inherited lands from the Fentons through the marriage of Anne, sister and coheir of Thomas Fenton of Newcastle.[51] Clayton farm remained in the Boughey family until at least 1844.[52]

In 1223 the Earl of Chester gave 2 virgates of land in Seabridge to the Prior of Kenilworth in return for the prior's acknowledgement of the earl's right to the advowson of a moiety of Stoke church.[53] This land evidently passed to Stone Priory, a daughter-house of Kenilworth, since in 1291 the Prior of Stone held a carucate of land in Seabridge.[54] This remained part of the priory's estates until the Dissolution,[55] and in 1552 the Crown granted the priory's messuage and lands in Seabridge to Lord Clinton and Say as part of a large grant of former church property.[56] The estate was then in the tenure of Ralph Machin,[57] who had evidently been living there by 1547,[58] and a branch of the Machin family continued to hold a house and lands at Seabridge[59] until at any rate the early 18th century when Samuel Machin (d. 1719–23) was living there.[60]

By 1763 the Swynnertons of Butterton (in Trentham) held an estate in Seabridge and Clayton.[61] By 1818 this estate evidently included Seabridge House, for Elizabeth Swynnerton, one of the three daughters and coheirs of Thomas Swynnerton of Butterton, was then living there.[62] It included most of Seabridge by 1834, although the house was then held by Henry Townend.[63] On Thomas's death in 1836 the property passed to Mary, another of his daughters and the wife of Sir William Pilkington of Chevet (Yorks.).[64] The estate then descended in the Pilkington family (Milborne–Swinnerton–Pilkington from 1854) until its sale in the 1950's, although the house was not occupied by them.[65]

What is now Roe Lane farm is probably identifiable with the Roefields estate of the 17th and 18th

---

[36] D.L. 30/228/1.
[37] S.H.C. 1921, 154, 156.
[38] See pp. 23, 55 sqq.
[39] V.C.H. Staffs. iv. 56, no. 259.
[40] S.H.C. 1911, 146, 244; Cal. Pat. 1321–4, 182; D.L. 30/228; D.L. 30/250; D.L. 42/4, ff. 174a–177b; see p. 184.
[41] S.H.C. 1911, 123. In 1212 Ralph de Knutton held lands in Clayton, Knutton and elsewhere as a royal sokeman by ancient right (Bk. of Fees, 143), but whether this was the whole or only part of Clayton is not clear.
[42] See Dawson family's estate below.
[43] D.L. 42/4, f. 176b.
[44] C 3/50 (90).
[45] Stoke Churchwardens' Accts. (T.N.S.F.C. lxxiii), pp. A7, 37, 40, 41, 47, 52, 56; ibid. lxxiv, pp. A61 (including Seabridge), 84, 86; W.S.L., D. 1742, bdle. 46, book of 1740; W.S.L., D. 1788, P. 44, B. 8; ibid. P. 67, B. 32.
[46] T.N.S.F.C. lxxiii, pp. A7, 37, 40, 41, 47, 52, 56; ibid. lxxiv, p. A61; U.C.N.S., Sneyd MSS., Stoke Deeds (Jan. 1691/2).
[47] U.C.N.S., Sneyd MSS., Stoke Deeds (Jan. 1761).
[48] W.S.L., D. 1788, P. 33, B. 2.   [49] Ibid.
[50] Ibid.
[51] Ibid. P. 55, B. 10; Ward, Stoke, 422.
[52] W.S.L., D. 1788, P. 6, B. 19; ibid. P. 56, B. 23; ibid. P. 58, B. 8; ibid. P. C. 1 (m).
[53] S.H.C. iv (1), 223; vi (1), 5; see p. 188.

[54] Tax. Eccl. (Rec. Com.), 252. Stone Priory had been granted the advowson of the moiety about the mid-12th cent.: see p. 188.
[55] Inq. Non. (Rec. Com.), 128; Valor Eccl. (Rec. Com.), iii. 113.
[56] Cal. Pat. 1550–3, 372.   [57] Ibid.
[58] C 1/1120/12, 13. D.N.B. sub 'Machin, John', states that the family held the estate from 1531.
[59] S.H.C. xiii. 208; xvi. 134; Stoke Churchwardens' Accts. (T.N.S.F.C. lxxiii), pp. A7, 13, 37, 41, 47, 52, 56; ibid. lxxiv, pp. A61, 85; S.H.C. vii (2), 170. Theirs was the only family in Seabridge which Gregory King mentioned by name in his survey c. 1680: ibid. 1919, 258. John Machin (1624–64), a nonconformist preacher and minister who worked in Staffs., Ches., and Warws. from 1649 to 1664, was born at Seabridge and died there: D.N.B.
[60] Stoke Churchwardens' Accts. (T.N.S.F.C. lxxvii), p. A226; W.S.L., D. 1788, P. 43, B. 4.
[61] W.S.L. 27/9/42, 27/11/42, 11/32/45.
[62] Parson and Bradshaw, Dir. Staffs. (1818); S.H.C. vii (2), 141.   [63] White, Dir. Staffs. (1834).
[64] S.H.C. vii (2), 125, 141.
[65] Ibid. 141; Ward, Stoke, 525; White, Dir. Staffs. (1851); P.O. Dir. Staffs. (1872); Kelly's Dir. Staffs. (1932); Burke, Peerage (1949), 1791–2; ex inf. owner of Seabridge Farm (1960). Mary, who brought Butterton Hall also into the Pilkington family, had taken the name Milborne-Swinnerton: Burke, Peerage, 1791.

centuries. In 1653 John Machin and a Mr. Graston both paid parish rates on land of that name.[66] In 1739 Roefield House and lands attached were held of the lord of Newcastle manor by John Clewlow who in that year conveyed the estate to John Fenton.[67] Roe Lane farm formed part of the Pilkington family's property in Seabridge by the late 1840's when it was occupied by Edwin Booth.[68] By 1938 it had been bought by Newcastle Corporation with other agricultural land in the Clayton area for housing purposes,[69] but a tenant-farmer is still (1960) in occupation.

The Clayton family are said to have settled at Clayton before the end of the 14th century,[70] and they continued to hold an extensive estate there until the death of John Clayton in the mid-17th century.[71] His lands then passed to his two nieces and coheirs, daughters of Thomas Clayton, Elizabeth wife of Thomas Lea and Mary wife of John Wynser.[72] A Clayton Lea was living at Clayton in 1657[73] and was taxable on five hearths there in 1666.[74] The Leas were one of the two notable families living there c. 1680[75] and were still at Clayton in 1740.[76] Before the end of the 18th century, however, they had moved to Shropshire, and their house in Clayton, called Clayton Hall in 1817 when it was in a dilapidated state, was let as a farm.[77] On the death of the Revd. John Lea of Acton Burnell (Salop.) in 1812, the family lands were divided between his three nieces, daughters of his deceased younger brother Thomas Lea of Chester.[78] The site of the house may be that of the present Barn Farm on the western side of the main road, a building of 1878 which replaced one of 1688.[79]

The Lovatt family had settled in the Clayton area by the early 15th century,[80] and a Nicholas Lovatt seems to have held land there in 1501.[81] The family estate may have passed to the Trentham branch of the Lovatts which married into the Clayton family and had come to Clayton by 1567.[82] The Lovatts continued to hold extensive property in Clayton and c. 1680 were the only notable inhabitants apart from the Leas.[83] In 1785 Thomas Lovatt bought some

of the estates which had passed in the mid-17th century to the Leas and Wynsers after the death of John Clayton[84] (see above). On the death of Thomas in 1803 his property in Clayton, including Clayton Hall, passed to his daughter Anne (d. 1824), the wife of Hugh Booth of Cliff Bank, Stoke, a potter (d. 1831).[85] Mary Booth, their only child, married John Ayshford Wise in 1837, and the Clayton estate remained in the Wise family until after 1916, although the hall was in the hands of James Heath by 1892 and of Frederick Johnson between at least 1900 and 1916.[86] By 1924 the hall and estate had been sold to a Mrs. Johnson, apparently the tenant,[87] and in 1940 they were the home and property of the Misses Johnson.[88] The hall was taken over during the Second World War as a training centre for the Fleet Air Arm, and since 1948 it has been occupied as a girls' grammar school which continues to use also several of the outbuildings erected for the Fleet Air Arm.[89]

The hall, described c. 1840 as 'a mansion venerable for its antiquity', was a low, gabled building standing east of Clayton Road near its former junction with Clayton Lane and dating probably from the late 16th or early 17th century.[90] It was rebuilt on a site farther east in the 1840's, and Clayton Lane was diverted to its present more northerly course to enable the grounds of the hall to be enlarged.[91] The hall is a large stucco house in the Classical style with Italianate features standing in well-planted grounds on the ridge above the Lyme Brook and commanding a fine view to the south-east.

ECONOMIC HISTORY. The Clayton area is still largely rural except for the extensive suburban development of Newcastle in the northern part. In 1940 there were at least 11 farms in Clayton and Seabridge, all below 150 acres in extent. The chief crops were oats and wheat, and some land was under pasture.[92]

In 1086 Clayton, held by Richard the Forester

[66] *Stoke Churchwardens' Accts.* (*T.N.S.F.C.* lxxiv), p. A114.

[67] W.S.L., D. 1788, P. 43, B. 4. It was in the hands of a tenant.

[68] Tithe Redemption Com., Tithe Maps and Appt., Stoke-upon-Trent (Clayton); Hargreaves, *Map of Staffs. Potteries.*

[69] See p. 38.

[70] Ward, *Stoke,* 521.

[71] Ibid. 521 and app., p. xlviii. John Clayton granted lands there to his nephew Thos. Swynnerton of Butterton c. 1454: *S.H.C.* vii (2), 132. Ward states that the male line died out in 1633, but John Clayton was still living there in 1650: E 317/38 Staffs. No male member of the family was there in 1666: *S.H.C.* 1921, 154.

[72] Ward, *Stoke,* 521; Pitt, *Staffs.* 389, where it is also stated that Thos. Clayton d. c. 1659.

[73] *Stoke Churchwardens' Accts.* (*T.N.S.F.C.* lxxiv), p. A126.

[74] *S.H.C.* 1921, 154.

[75] Ibid. 1919, 258. The other was the Lovatts: see below.

[76] W.S.L., D. 1742, bdle. 46 (book of 1740).

[77] Pitt, *Staffs.* 389.

[78] Ibid.

[79] A tablet on the house gives the date of rebuilding while another is dated 1688 and bears the initials T L H. A tablet on the barn to the N. is dated 1740 and has the initials S L M. In the 1840's the farm was owned by the Pilkington family and occupied by Wm. Machin: Tithe Redemption Com., Tithe Maps and Appt., Stoke-upon-Trent (Clayton); see above.

[80] D.L. 42/4, ff. 176b, 177a.

[81] T. Pape, *Newcastle-under-Lyme in Tudor and Early Stuart Times,* 21.

[82] Ward, *Stoke,* 523; *S.H.C.* 1930, 9; *Stoke Churchwardens' Accts.* (*T.N.S.F.C.* lxxiii), p. A7; P. W. L. Adams, *Adams Family,* 400; *Newcastle Par. Reg.* (Staffs. Par. Reg. Soc.), i. 4.

[83] Ward, *Stoke,* 522–4 and app. p. xlviii; *S.H.C.* 1919, 258; W.S.L., D. 1742, bdle. 46 (book of 1740); W.S.L., D. 1788, P. 33, B. 2. In 1664 Nich. Lovatt bequeathed 2 messuages in Clayton and one in Seabridge to 3 different members of the family: ibid.

[84] Ward, *Stoke,* 521.

[85] Ibid. 521, 524; see p. 203.

[86] Ward, *Stoke,* 521, 524; White, *Dir. Staffs.* (1851); *P.O. Dir. Staffs.* (1854, 1876); *Kelly's Dir. Staffs.* (1880, 1892, and later edns. to 1916).

[87] *Kelly's Dir. Staffs.* (1924). Fred. Johnson was tenant between at least 1900 and 1916: ibid. (1900, 1908, 1912, 1916).

[88] Ibid. (1940).

[89] Ex inf. the head mistress (1958); see p. 76.

[90] Ward, *Stoke,* 521 and illus. facing; Hargreaves, *Map of Staffs. Potteries.*

[91] The new house, not mentioned in Ward, *Stoke,* published in 1843, and the new course of the road are both shown on Tithe Redemption Com., Tithe Maps, Stoke-upon-Trent (Clayton, 1849).

[92] *Kelly's Dir. Staffs.* (1940). There were 2 lime-burners and a brickmaker in Clayton Griffith in 1834 (White, *Dir. Staffs.,* 1834) and a brick and tile maker there in the middle of the 19th cent.: ibid. (1851); *P.O. Dir. Staffs.* (1854).

and valued at 10s., contained land for 3 ploughs; ½ plough was in demesne, and the 4 villeins and 6 bordars had a plough and a half.[93] There was also woodland 1 league by ½ league in area.[94] By the end of the 12th century Seabridge, and presumably Clayton as well, lay within the 'new forest'[95] which was in existence by 1167 and evidently extended from the north-east of Newcastle southward down both sides of the Trent to Tixall and eastward to the river Blythe.[96] In the mid-13th century the men of Clayton held 4 virgates of land there of the manor of Newcastle at a rent of 15s. 4d.[97] Some 50 years later there were 9 customary tenants holding 16 bovates in Clayton at 12d. a bovate and also commuting labour services for 40d. a year; in addition there were 16 acres at 8d. an acre and 80 acres at 6d. an acre and 5 cottages yielding a total of 2s. 6d. in rents. In all, Clayton was rendering £3 13s. 6d. to the lord of Newcastle manor.[98] The men of Seabridge held 1 virgate of the manor in the mid-13th century at a rent of 4s. and assarts for which they rendered 12s. 4d.[99] At the end of the century there were 4 bovates in Seabridge held by 6 customary tenants at 12d. a bovate, labour services being commuted by a six-monthly payment of 5d.; in addition the men of Seabridge and Newcastle held 82 acres there at 6d. an acre and 33½ acres at 12d. an acre,

and one cottage was yielding 2d. a year. With 20s. from the mill (see below) the total income from Seabridge was £4 16s. 0½d.[1] In the early 17th century all the land in Clayton and Seabridge held of Newcastle manor was evidently copyhold.[2]

The open fields in Seabridge included Over Field, Rowley Field, and Brook Field in the 17th century;[3] Over Field at least was still uninclosed in 1717.[4] Clayton also seems to have shared Stubbs Field with Newcastle and Penkhull. It was inclosed by an Act of 1816.[5] In the early 17th century the tenants of Clayton had pasture rights in a common called Northwood in Trentham manor.[6]

There was a water-mill at Seabridge, presumably on the Park Brook, by the mid-13th century when the men of Seabridge held it of the manor of Newcastle for 1 mark a year, a rent which had risen to 20s. before the end of the century.[7] The mill was being farmed for £1 6s. 8d. before 1387 when it was described as 'totally devastated'.[8] It appears, however, to have been in use again by 1428.[9] A sidestream and the remains of a sluice by the footbridge over the Park Brook below Seabridge Farm may indicate a mill site.[10]

Clayton had its own pound-keeper in 1839,[11] and the pinfold still stood on the southern part of the Green in the late 1870's.[12]

[93] V.C.H. Staffs. iv. 56, no. 259.
[94] Ibid.
[95] S.H.C. ii (1), 95.
[96] Ibid. i. 47–49; ibid. 1923, 294, 296, 302.
[97] Ibid. 1911, 147.
[98] Ibid. 244.
[99] Ibid. 146.
[1] Ibid. 244.   [2] Ward, Stoke, app. p. xlviii.
[3] D.L. 43/8/32, f. 26a; W.S.L., D. 1788, P. 33, B. 2. A 'Drybedfeld' was mentioned in the early 15th century as having 2 acres of waste inclosed out of it (D.L. 42/4, f. 177a); it may have lain in the Drybridge area in the NE. of the later civil parish: Hargreaves, Map of Staffs. Potteries.
[4] W.S.L., D. 1788, P. 33, B. 2.

[5] Ward, Stoke, app. p. xlv; S.H.C. 1941, 15; see pp. 49, 200.
[6] Ward, Stoke, app. p. xlii. The name still survives in an area on the Trentham side of the boundary.
[7] S.H.C. 1911, 146, 244.
[8] T. Pape, Medieval Newcastle-under-Lyme, 119.
[9] A nearby meadow was flooded that year 'per exaltacionem capitis stagni molendini': ibid. 191.
[10] The sluice is shown on O.S. Map 1/25,000 Staffs. xvii. 12. 2 (survey of 1877). The road between Seabridge and Butterton used to cross the brook near this point (see p. 76), and Hargreaves, Map of Staffs. Potteries (1832), shows a building at the S. end of the bridge.
[11] H.R.L., Stoke Commrs.' Mins. 1839–48, 7 Oct. 1839.
[12] O.S. Map. 1/25,000 Staffs. xvii. 12.2 (survey of 1877).

STOKE-ON-TRENT

ALTHOUGH Newcastle-under-Lyme and Stoke-on-Trent adjoin each other, their historical development has been strikingly dissimilar; the one has its roots deep in the past and exhibits the slow evolution of a burghal community, while the other is a town of the industrial age. Geologically the Potteries area can be described as an outcrop of quick-burning coals, clays, and marls, and it is this character of the subsoil that has favoured the growth of the local pottery industry. The story of Stoke is basically that of a community of potters, whose skill and business acumen have in the course of two centuries made Stoke the twelfth largest city in the United Kingdom and extended its reputation in the field of ceramics far beyond the shores of Britain.

The historical development of the 30 square miles of North Staffordshire moorland which today constitutes the city of Stoke-on-Trent can appropriately be described as a palimpsest whose original parochial pattern has been overlaid by a new complexus of civil government. The modern city has mainly evolved out of the ancient parishes of Stoke-upon-Trent and Wolstanton, both of which lie in the northern division of Pirehill hundred. Of the two Stoke has made by far the larger contribution. In early times the word 'Stoke' seems to have connoted no more than the location of a church. Its circumjacent parish, corresponding in size to but differing in composition from the city of today, comprised nearly a score of townships. These were Penkhull (with Boothen), Hanley (with Shelton), Fenton, Longton (with Lane End), Burslem, Newcastle, Whitmore, Norton, Bucknall (with Bagnall), Clayton (with Seabridge), Botteslow, and Hulton. Of these places Hanley, Fenton, Longton, and Burslem grew into separate parishes, each with an urban core, and Stoke itself, consisting partly of Penkhull and Boothen, made a fifth. Of the other components of the parish Newcastle, Whitmore, Norton-in-the-Moors, and Bucknall and Bagnall became separate parishes in 1807. Clayton and Seabridge, after inclusion in Stoke Rural in 1894, became a separate civil parish in 1896 and were incorporated into Newcastle between 1921 and 1932. Botteslow was transferred to Stoke Rural in 1894, and absorbed by Stoke in 1922. The lordship of Hulton, once part of Burslem parish, was divided in 1891 and 1894 and as a result of changes in the early 20th century and again in 1922, is now almost wholly within the city.

Most of the area covered by the modern city was once dominated by two manors: Tunstall embracing Burslem and Tunstall; and Newcastle, which included Penkhull and Boothen, Hanley and Shelton, Clayton and Seabridge, Botteslow, Longton, and part of Fenton. The rest of Fenton lay in Fenton Culvert manor. The development of the agrarian economy of the area and the maintenance of its leet jurisdiction remained under the control of the lords of Newcastle and Tunstall until well into the 19th century.

Yet a third pattern was imposed on the ancient parish of Stoke in the late 16th century as a result of the statutory obligation to make provision for the relief of the poor. The parish was divided into five units, Stoke, Burslem, Newcastle, Norton, and Whitmore, each of them being regarded as a separate parish for the purpose of poor relief. The first of these, Stoke, consisted of eight districts, each apparently a separate rating district, namely Penkhull with Boothen; Clayton and Seabridge; Shelton and Hanley; Fenton Culvert; Fenton Vivian; Longton; Bucknall; and Bagnall. Burslem was a separate parish for civil purposes, including poor relief, from the later 16th century, while Tunstall, as has been said, belonged to Wolstanton parish. By the early 17th century the eight districts of the Stoke area had been rearranged into four quarters: (1) Penkhull, Boothen, Clayton and Seabridge; (2) Shelton and Hanley; (3) the Fentons, Longton, and Botteslow; (4) Bucknall and Bagnall; and this territorial division was retained when the Stoke-upon-Trent Union was formed in 1836. Two years later Burslem became part of the Wolstanton and Burslem Union, as also did Tunstall. It will be seen, therefore, that in regard to the administration of the poor law the area was treated in a somewhat fortuitous manner and was unaffected by the creation of the new parishes in 1807.

By the beginning of the 19th century the Pottery villages had become towns or at least urban aggregates and new solutions had to be found to the problems of local government. A gradual evolution, beginning with *ad hoc* efforts to meet pressing needs, led slowly to the extrusion of new civil and ecclesiastical parishes, and thence to the formation of new boroughs and urban districts. In 1910 these were amalgamated to bring into existence the new borough of Stoke-on-Trent; the story of this amalgamation is related in the section headed 'The Federation of the Six Towns'.

In consequence of these various administrative complexities the article which follows discards the conventional framework of the ancient parish. Instead, each of the six towns—Tunstall, Burslem, Hanley, Stoke-upon-Trent, Fenton, and Longton—has been treated as though it were an ancient parish. To each a general introduction has been assigned and this is followed, in each case, by sub-sections on manors, other estates, churches, local government and public services, economic history, and social life. Botteslow and Hulton, most or all of which had been absorbed into Stoke by 1922, have been somewhat similarly handled. Four topics, however, have been treated in a way which ignores the division into towns. These are Roman Catholicism, Protestant nonconformity, schools, and charities for the poor. These four sections carry the story to the present day, as do all the sub-sections of the separate town histories. Developments since 1910, mainly in the sphere of local government, are traced in the section called 'Stoke-on-Trent since 1910'. The histories of Bucknall and Bagnall, Norton-in-the-Moors, Whitmore, and Wolstanton are reserved for treatment with the rest of Pirehill hundred.

TUNSTALL

TUNSTALL, the most northerly of the six towns incorporated in the new borough of Stoke-on-Trent in 1910, was at that time an urban district of 1,136 acres.[1] It extended to the Fowlea Brook on the west and to the ridge above the Scotia Brook on the east where from Great Chell the boundary ran down the west side of what is now the road to Smallthorne (High Lane). The boundary with the borough of Burslem, running just south of the town, was that of the ancient parish of Wolstanton of which Tunstall originally formed part. The northern boundary, though unrelated to geographical features, has, like the western, remained the boundary of this part of the city.[2]

This northern district of the Potteries consists of three main centres of population: Tunstall, the largest; Goldenhill, including parts of the old townships of Oldcott and Ravenscliffe; and Great and Little Chell, making up the township of Chell most of which by 1910 lay within the urban district. The Pitts Hill portion of Chell was added to the urban district in 1899.[3] Parts of Goldenhill and of the remainder of Chell were added in 1904.[4] Tunstall and Goldenhill are situated on the ridge between the valleys formed by the Fowlea and Scotia Brooks, and the main north–south road through the Potteries descends gradually from 700 ft. at Goldenhill, the highest point in the city, to 500 ft. below Tunstall. The Chells lie on the ridge east of the Scotia Brook, mainly around 600 ft., with Pitts Hill built on the road leading up to Great Chell. Despite extensive industrialization, there is still much open country in the area, particularly in the neighbourhood of Goldenhill. Some of it is wasteland but there still remain a number of farms.

The township of Tunstall covered the area of the urban district as first constituted in 1894[5] and included the hamlets of Sandyford, Newfield, and Furlong as well as Tunstall itself. It had an area of some 800 acres.[6]

The village of Tunstall was described in 1795 as 'the pleasantest village in the pottery'.[7] It developed rapidly after 1816 and c. 1840 was stated to have been built 'not altogether without a plan'.[8] The market-place was laid out in 1816 and formed the centre of the growing town.[9] Forty small houses in two terraces running west from the market-place were built in 1821 by the Tunstall Building Society.[10] The central area immediately east of the main road as far south as Rathbone Street had been developed by 1832 together with part of the Clayhills district to the north-west of the town and at least one street running south-west from the town-centre.[11] The streets immediately north-west of the market-place and the eastern end of King Street (now Madison Street) farther north appeared during the next eight years, and development continued south of Rathbone Street and in the Clayhills area.[12] The sidewalks of the new streets were paved with local blue brick, and the highway surveyors of the township contributed towards the cost of the paving.[13] By 1863 the south-western portion of the present central area had been built up as well as the group of streets around King Street.[14] Madeley Street, the streets between Goodfellow and America Streets, and the streets north of Sun Street (now St. Aidan's Street) were developed in the 1860's and 1870's.[15] Thus, while there had been 335 inhabited houses in Tunstall township in 1811, there were 520 in 1821, 725 in 1831, 1,306 in 1841, and 2,373 in 1871.[16] The area to the north-east of the town-centre was built up in the late 19th and early 20th centuries,[17] while Victoria Park, some 30 acres in extent, was laid out between 1897 and 1908.[18] The houses in King William Street on the south-eastern edge of the town were built at the end of the 19th century,[19] and an estate to the east of it was developed between the two world wars. By 1939 extensive slum clearance had been carried out in Watergate Street, and since 1945 council housing has been replacing many of the old cottages in the Clayhills area as well as in Ladywell, Roundwell, and America Streets.[20] There has been recent clearance in Butterfield Place (formerly Amicable Street),[21] and demolition is still (1960) in progress between Rathbone Street and Woodland Street.

Sandyford, at the junction of the Goldenhill and Holly Wall roads, and Newfield to the south, centring on the estate of that name, were already in existence in 1775[22] and expanded during the early

[1] *Census*, 1911, Staffs.
[2] For the boundaries see *Plan of Stoke-on-Trent and Newcastle-under-Lyme* (Geographia Ltd.); T. Hargreaves, *Map of Staffs. Potteries and Newcastle* (1832); O.S. Map 6″ Staffs. xi NE., xii NW. (1900).
[3] Local Govt. Board Order no. 39,185, 5 Nov. 1899, confirming Staffs. County Counc. Order 5 Nov. 1898 (copy of each with the Clerk of the Staffs. County Counc.).
[4] *Census*, 1911, Staffs., citing Local Govt. Board Order no. 43,817. The part of Goldenhill civil parish not added to Tunstall passed into Kidsgrove Urban District; and the part of Chell civil parish not added passed into Smallthorne U. D. Smallthorne was added to Stoke in 1922: see p. 259.   [5] See p. 95.
[6] White, *Dir. Staffs.* (1851).
[7] J. Aikin, *The Country around Manchester* (1795), 518.
[8] Ward, *Stoke*, 94.
[9] Ibid. 89.   [10] See p. 85.
[11] Hargreaves, *Map of Staffs. Potteries*; see p. 86.
[12] P. Kendall, *Map of Tunstall Town* (surveyed 1840; copy in W.S.L., S. 1909, ii); see p. 86.
[13] Ward, *Stoke*, 105.
[14] R. Malabar and Son, *Map of Tunstall Township* (sur-

veyed 1863; copy in W.S.L. 12/8/42). Warrillow, *Stoke*, 25, states that Keele St. was being laid out for building by Ralph Sneyd in 1857.
[15] Malabar, *Map of Tunstall Township*; O.S. Map 6″ Staffs. xi NE. (1890); date-stone of 1872 in Madeley St.
[16] *Census*, 1811, 1821, 1831, 1841, 1871.
[17] O.S. Map 6″ Staffs. xi NE. (1890, 1900); date-stones of 1892 and 1893 in Stanley St., 1892 and 1894 in Park Terrace, 1906 in The Boulevard, and 1910 in Victoria Park Rd.; H.R.L., Tunstall U.D.C. Mins. 1909–10, p. 57 (conveyance of building land in what is there called Victoria Rd., 1910); S.R.O., Q/RHd 95, where Queen's Ave. is described as 'a proposed new street'.
[18] *Kelly's Dir. Staffs.* (1912); *Staffs. Sentinel*, 8 June 1911; *Evening Sentinel*, 26 June 1945; P. W. L. Adams, *Adams Family*, 347.
[19] O.S. Map 6″ Staffs. xii NW. (1900).
[20] *City of Stoke-on-Trent Housing, 1919 to 1957*, 25, 30, 31, 51 (copy in H.R.L.). There are a few prefabricated bungalows off Watergate St.: ibid. 27.
[21] Ibid. 52.
[22] W. Yates, *Map of Staffs.* (1775), reproduced facing p. 4 (although they are not named there); see p. 92.

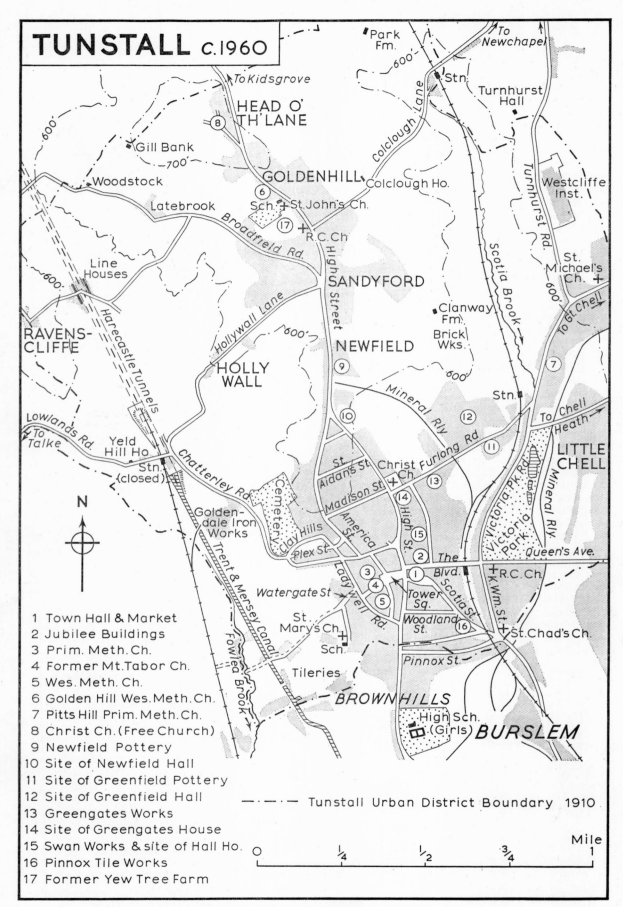

TUNSTALL c.1960

To Newchapel
Park Fm.
600
Stn
Turnhurst Hall
To Kidsgrove
HEAD O' TH' LANE
(8)
Gill Bank
700
Woodstock
Colclough Lane
GOLDENHILL
(6)
Colclough Ho.
Latebrook
Sch.
St. John's Ch.
(17)
R.C. Ch.
Broadfield Rd.
Turnhurst Rd.
Westcliffe Inst.
St. Michael's Ch.
600
To Gt. Chell
Line Houses
600
Hollywall Lane
SANDYFORD
Scotia Brook
Clanway Fm.
Brick Wks.
RAVENS-CLIFFE
Harecastle Tunnels
600
HOLLY WALL
NEWFIELD
(9)
600
Mineral Rly
Stn.
(7)
To Chell Heath
LITTLE CHELL
Lowlands Rd.
To Talke
Yeld Hill Ho
Stn. (closed)
Chatterley Rd
(10)
(12)
(11)
Mineral Rly
N
Golden-dale Iron Works
Cemetery
Clay Hills
St. Aidans St.
Madison St.
Christ Furlong Rd.
Ch.
(13)
(14)
Victoria Pk. Rd.
Victoria Park
Queen's Ave.
Trent & Mersey Canal
Fowlea Brook
Plex St.
America St.
High St.
(15)
The Blvd.
Scotia St.
R.C. Ch.
Wm. St.
Watergate St
(3)
(4)
(5)
(2)
(1)
Tower Sq.
Woodland St.
(16)
St. Chad's Ch.
St. Mary's Ch.
Sch.
Laddywell Rd.
Pinnox St.
Tileries
BROWN HILLS
High Sch. (Girls)
BURSLEM

1 Town Hall & Market
2 Jubilee Buildings
3 Prim. Meth. Ch.
4 Former Mt. Tabor Ch.
5 Wes. Meth. Ch.
6 Golden Hill Wes. Meth. Ch.
7 Pitts Hill Prim. Meth. Ch.
8 Christ Ch. (Free Church)
9 Newfield Pottery
10 Site of Newfield Hall
11 Site of Greenfield Pottery
12 Site of Greenfield Hall
13 Greengates Works
14 Site of Greengates House
15 Swan Works & site of Hall Ho.
16 Pinnox Tile Works
17 Former Yew Tree Farm

— · — · — Tunstall Urban District Boundary 1910

Mile
0   ¼   ½   ¾   1

The fine stipple indicates built-up areas.

19th century after the establishment of the Sandyford and Newfield pottery works.[23] Both now consist mainly of housing dating from the period between the two world wars. The Holly Wall area to the west is mainly agricultural. It undoubtedly owes its name to the holy well mentioned in the 12th century.[24] The hamlet of Smithfield on the road to Pitts Hill and Chell was built by Theophilus Smith in the early 1790's near his house and pottery works. It lay in the area earlier known as Furlong and consisted of about 40 cottages, a few shops, and an inn.[25] Smith was declared bankrupt in 1800, and in 1801 he committed suicide in Stafford Gaol while awaiting trial for attempted murder.[26] The village, like the estate, was renamed Greenfield in 1801,[27] but the name Furlong was in use again by the end of the 19th century.[28] The Greenfield housing estate, begun in 1945 and expanded later, occupies the site of Greenfield Hall and its park,[29] and another estate was still being built to the west in 1959 as an extension of the late-19th-century Clanway Street.[30]

The civil parish of Goldenhill, an area of 856 acres, included Goldenhill village and the hamlets of Latebrook and Line Houses.[31] Goldenhill village existed by 1670[32] and in 1775 was nearly as large as Tunstall village.[33] It increased in size throughout the 19th century, mainly to the east of the main road,[34] and, around the beginning of the present century, at Head o' th' Lane to the north of the village.[35] There is a large housing estate of the years between the world wars on the southern outskirts of the village on either side of the main road.[36] There was a furnace with five workmen's cottages on the Latebrook House estate west of Goldenhill in the mid-1820's,[37] and a few terraces of cottages had been built at Latebrook itself by the 1870's.[38] A little to the west is the hamlet of Line Houses situated on the hillside directly over the Harecastle tunnels and consisting mainly of terraced cottages in two parallel rows said to have been built to accommodate workers on the railway tunnel in the 1840's.[39] One block, however,

was in existence by 1839 and may have been built for workers on the canal tunnel in the 1820's.[40] Forty-eight houses and cottages and the village hall were sold on the break-up of the Williamson estate in 1950.[41] Ravenscliffe hamlet lies on the north-western boundary of the city.

The township of Chell, 740 acres in area by 1841,[42] was divided into Great and Little Chell, possibly a result of the division of the manor of Chell early in the 13th century.[43] Great Chell was the more developed of the two in 1775[44] and still contained most of the township's population, mainly potters, in 1841;[45] the recent development there lies mainly outside the 1910 boundary. Little Chell was still undeveloped at the end of the 19th century,[46] but large council estates were built there between the two world wars and after 1945.[47] Pitts Hill, situated on St. Michael's Road below Great Chell, occurs as the home of a branch of the Bourne family in 1678[48] and was developing c. 1800,[49] presumably in connexion with the Greenfield Pottery. There is a council estate of the years between the world wars on St. Michael's Road.[50]

In 1666 there were 17 households in Tunstall township liable for hearth tax.[51] In 1811 the population of the township was 1,677,[52] and during the 19th century it continued to rise: 1831, 4,673;[53] 1851, 9,566;[54] 1871, 13,540.[55] The township of Chell had 10 households liable for hearth tax in 1666[56] and a population of 356 in 1811,[57] 535 in 1831,[58] 953 in 1851[59] and 5,670 in 1871.[60] In 1901 the urban district of Tunstall had a population of 19,492 and the new civil parishes of Goldenhill and Chell had populations of 4,378 and 3,502 respectively.[61] The area of the urban district as extended in 1904 had a population of 22,494 in 1911[62] and 22,740 in 1921.[63]

The main road through the centre of Tunstall and Goldenhill runs north to Manchester and the north-west and south to Newcastle-under-Lyme and

[23] C. and J. Greenwood, *Map of Staffs.* (1820); White, *Dir. Staffs.* (1834); Lich. Dioc. Regy., Tithe Maps and Appt., Wolstanton; see pp. 99, 101.
[24] See p. 93.
[25] Adams, *Adams Family*, 345, 347, and view of 1794 facing p. 348; see pp. 91, 100.
[26] P. W. L. Adams, *Notes on Some N. Staffs. Families*, 80–82; W.S.L., D. 1723/4 (Reg. of Felons, Stafford Gaol), p. 44; *Staffs. Sentinel, summer number 1911*, 22. He was charged with the attempted murder of John Wainwright whom he suspected to be his wife's lover; before shooting himself Smith also shot his wife who was visiting him in the hospital of Stafford Gaol and who subsequently died of the wound.   [27] See p. 91.
[28] O.S. Map 6″ Staffs. xii NW. (1900); ibid. 1/25,000, SJ 85 (1952); Adams, *Adams Family*, 245. The area was called Furlong Lane in the 1870's: O.S. Map 6″ Staffs. xii NW. (1890).
[29] Date-stone on one of the houses; *Stoke-on-Trent Housing, 1919 to 1957*, 21; see p. 91.
[30] Date-stone of 1896 on one of the terraces.
[31] *Census*, 1901, Staffs.
[32] *Tunstall Ct. R.* (*T.N.S.F.C.* lxvi), 103, 126; R. Plot, *Map. of Staffs.* (1682).
[33] Yates, *Map of Staffs.* (1775).
[34] Greenwood, *Map of Staffs.*; O.S. Map 6″ Staffs. vi SE. (1900); xi NE. (1900); date-stones of 1851 in Drummond St. (with initials R.S.), 1852 in Alice St., 1856 in Temperance Place, 1867 and 1869 in Murray St., 1871 and 1874 in Heath St. where there is also a terrace inscribed 'Jubilee Cottages', and 1897 in Albert St. There has been some demolition to the north of Temperance Place.

[35] O.S. Map 6″ Staffs. vi SE. (1900, 1926).
[36] *Stoke-on-Trent Housing, 1919 to 1957*, 20, 22.
[37] See p. 103.
[38] O.S. Map 6″ Staffs. xi NE. (1890). There has been some demolition of cottages in this area.
[39] Local inf. There was a school there by 1854: see p. 312.
[40] Lich. Dioc. Regy., Tithe Maps and Appt., Wolstanton; see p. 84.
[41] Ex inf. Mr. C. Boden, Holly Wall (1960); *Williamson Estate Sale Cat.* (copy in Mr. Boden's possession).
[42] White, *Dir. Staffs.* (1851).   [43] See p. 88.
[44] Yates, *Map of Staffs.* (1775).
[45] White, *Dir. Staffs.* (1851).
[46] O.S. Map 6″ Staffs. xii NW. (1900).
[47] *Stoke-on-Trent Housing, 1919 to 1957*, 23, 24.
[48] *Wolstanton Par. Reg.* (Staffs. Par. Reg. Soc.), i. 135, 225; *Tunstall Ct. R.* (*T.N.S.F.C.* lxiii), 57; ibid. lxvi. 107, 123.
[49] Yates, *Map of Staffs.* (1775); Greenwood, *Map of Staffs.*
[50] *Stoke-on-Trent Housing, 1919 to 1957*, 26.
[51] *S.H.C.* 1921, 159–60.   [52] *Census*, 1811, Staffs.
[53] Ibid. 1831.   [54] Ibid. 1851.
[55] Ibid. 1871.
[56] *S.H.C.* 1921, 159.   [57] *Census*, 1811, Staffs.
[58] Ibid. 1831.
[59] Ibid. 1851.   [60] Ibid. 1871.
[61] Ibid. 1901. Part of Chell civil parish had already been taken into Tunstall Urban District in 1899: see p. 81.
[62] *Census*, 1911, Staffs. For the transfer of parts of Goldenhill and Chell to the urban district in 1904 see p. 81.
[63] *Census*, 1921, Staffs.

Burslem. It was turnpiked in 1763 as a result of the efforts of Josiah Wedgwood.[64] There was a toll-gate at Tunstall by 1778,[65] but in 1782 an order was made for its replacement by a gate and house near the Galloping Flash Inn.[66] Later in the same year a toll-house was erected near Tunstall pinfold at the junction with the road from Chell[67]—presumably Furlong Road, the Tunstall end of the turnpike road from Congleton (see below). The only toll-gate on the Tunstall stretch of the north–south road in 1836 was Sandyford Chain.[68] This presumably stood at the junction with Hollywall Lane. It was replaced in or soon after 1847 by a toll-gate at the junction with Colclough Lane (see below), but this too was discontinued in 1855.[69] In this year orders were given for the erection of a toll-gate at the north end of Joseph Heath's factory in High Street and a toll-house and side chain at King Street,[70] but neither of these existed in 1863.[71] On the winding up of the Lawton–Burslem Turnpike Trust in 1878 only one toll-house on the road lay in Tunstall.[72]

The road to Congleton through Biddulph, turn-piked in 1770,[73] left Tunstall along the present Fur-long Road where by 1839 there was a toll-gate near Christ Church.[74] The course of Furlong Road was straightened c. 1812.[75] By the end of the 18th century there was a toll-gate at Furlong where the Biddulph road was joined by the road from Little Chell.[76] Colclough Lane, still the name of the Goldenhill end of the road to Newchapel, was in existence by 1535.[77] The road between Little Chell and 'Fore-longe', which occurs in 1636,[78] was evidently the present road from Little Chell across Victoria Park to Furlong Road. The road running from Great Chell to Newchapel was mentioned in 1664.[79] In addition to these three, the present roads from Tunstall and Sandyford to Chatterley Station and the two from Goldenhill leading west over Harecastle Hill into Ravenscliffe were all in existence by 1775.[80]

By 1790 Tunstall was served by the same coaches as Burslem and had its own postmaster.[81] The coaching inns by the late 1820's were the 'Sneyd Arms' and the 'Swan with two Necks'—presumably the present Swan Inn—and there was also a post-office at the 'Sneyd Arms'.[82] Horse- and foot-posts connected with the Royal Mail at Newcastle-under-

Lyme from 1835 until 1854 when the station post-office at Stoke replaced Newcastle as the postal centre for the Potteries.[83] There was an omnibus service between the 'Sneyd Arms' and Longport Station by 1851 (see below). In 1900 the new Potteries Electric Traction Company extended the Potteries electric tramcar service from Burslem through Tunstall to a terminus at Head o' th' Lane where a depot was built; a service was also introduced between Tunstall and Trubshaw Cross, Long-port. Motor-buses were introduced from 1914 and gradually replaced the trams between 1926 and 1928, the depot becoming a bus garage.[84]

The Trent and Mersey Canal, begun in 1766 and opened in 1777,[85] runs along the Fowlea valley and enters the Harecastle tunnels to run underground for over a mile and a half to Kidsgrove. The shorter of the two tunnels was built at the same time as the canal by James Brindley, but the volume of traffic led to great delays, particularly as there was no towing path and boats had to be 'legged' through.[86] In 1808 the owners of the canal tried to secure authority for a new branch running above ground from the southern end of the Harecastle tunnel up the Fowlea valley and past Clough Hall to the northern end of the tunnel, but the attempt was unsuccessful.[87] However, a second tunnel with a towing path was built to the east of the first by Thomas Telford in 1824–7 and used by northbound traffic. Brindley's tunnel was reserved for southbound traffic, but the canal company rejected Telford's scheme for adding a towing path to it.[88] Brindley had constructed a branch canal connecting his tunnel with an underground wharf attached to a colliery in Goldenhill in which he had an interest; this branch had become unsafe by 1820 and on Telford's advice its use was discontinued after the opening of the second tunnel.[89] Haulage by horse through Telford's tunnel was replaced in 1914 by a system of electric tugs; the earlier tunnel then went out of use.[90] The introduction of diesel-driven barges made the tugs unnecessary, and they were withdrawn in the mid-1950's; a fan was then installed at the southern entrance of the tunnel to extract the diesel fumes.[91] By 1781 there was evidently a wharf at Tunstall Bridge,[92] and in 1832 there was a coal wharf below

[64] See p. 108.
[65] W.S.L. 88/1/41 (Lawton, Burslem, and Newcastle Turnpike Trust Mins. 1776–83), 9 Jan. 1778.
[66] Ibid. 12 July 1782.
[67] Ibid. 20 Dec. 1782.
[68] Staffs. Advertiser, 5 Mar. 1836.
[69] W.S.L. 88/2/41 (Turnpike Mins. 1828–59), pp. 168, 169, 218.   [70] Ibid. p. 217.
[71] Malabar, Map of Tunstall Township (surveyed 1863).
[72] W.S.L. 88/3/41 (Turnpike Mins. 1859–78), 23 Oct. 1878.
[73] Act for repairing the road from Tunstall to Bosley, 10 Geo. III, c. 66.
[74] Lich. Dioc. Regy., Tithe Maps and Appt., Wolstanton.
[75] J. Carey, New Map of Staffs. (1806), which shows the earlier course of the road; Greenwood, Map of Staffs., which shows it altered. The work was presumably done under an Act of 1812 enlarging the powers conferred by previous Acts: 52 Geo. III, c. 88.
[76] Yates, Map of Staffs. (1799).
[77] B.M. Add. Ch. 53605.
[78] Tunstall Ct. R. (T.N.S.F.C. lxv), 78. Although it is not clear why the inhabitants of Sneyd as well as those of Little Chell had to contribute to the upkeep of the road, this identification seems likely.
[79] Ibid. 100.   [80] Yates, Map of Staffs. (1775).

[81] Univ. Brit. Dir. (1791), iv. 105; Parson and Bradshaw, Dir. Staffs. (1818); see p. 109.
[82] Pigot's Nat. Com. Dir. (1828–9). These were still the posting-inns in 1860: P.O. Dir. Staffs. (1860).
[83] See p. 7.
[84] Warrillow, Stoke, 74; P.M.T. House Mag. (May–June 1958), 3, 6, 7 (copy in H.R.L.).
[85] S.H.C. 1934 (1), 109.
[86] Ibid. 110; S. Shaw, Staffs. Potteries (1829), 23–24; A. R. L. Saul, 'James Brindley' (T.N.S.F.C. lxxiii), 61.
[87] C.J. lxiii. 118–19; S.R.O., Q/RUm/42 and 44, the plan proposing a short tunnel either to the E. or the W. of Clough Hall or a continued course above ground to the E. The Act of 1809 authorizing other clauses in the petition makes no mention of the new branch: 49 Geo. III, c. 73 (local and personal).
[88] L.T.C. Rolt, Thos. Telford, 165–7.
[89] Shaw, Staffs. Potteries, 24–25; H. A. Moisley, 'Potteries Coalfield' (Leeds Univ. M.Sc. thesis, 1950), 71; T.N.S.F.C. lxxiii, 61–62; Rolt, Telford, 162–3, 167; see p. 102.
[90] 'Manifold', N. Staffs. Rlwy. 14, 150; Rolt, Telford, 167; Staffs. Sentinel, 12 Sept. 1913.
[91] Ex inf. the tunnel-keeper (1960).
[92] W.S.L. 88/1/41, 13 Dec. 1781, order for delivery of stone there. In 1782 an order was given for stone to be 'boated' to Tunstall Meadow: ibid. 24 Jan. 1782.

the southern end of the tunnels,[93] where there was still a wharf in 1863.[94] The New Wharf at Tunstall occurs in 1834.[95] The Colonial Wharf, to the south of the bridge below Watergate Street, was in use between at least 1924 and 1940,[96] but by 1959 it was derelict. At the southern end of Telford's tunnel a retaining wall of heavy rusticated masonry with a whitewashed cottage for the tunnel-keeper above it survives from Telford's time, but the entrance to his tunnel is now hidden by a brick building containing the fan mechanism. A little to the west is the old brick archway forming the entrance to Brindley's disused tunnel.

The railway from Stoke to Manchester and Crewe, a section of the former North Staffordshire Railway opened in 1848,[97] runs through the north-western part of the Tunstall area where the third Harecastle tunnel was built for it.[98] At first the nearest station to Tunstall was at Longport, with an omnibus between it and the 'Sneyd Arms' six times a day in 1851.[99] The station south of the tunnel mouth was opened in 1864 as Tunstall station and renamed Chatterley in 1873.[1] It was closed to passenger traffic in 1948.[2] The station in the centre of Tunstall was opened in 1873 with the building of the Potteries Loop Line which in the following year was extended to Pitts Hill and Goldenhill where stations were opened.[3] A mineral line, built under an Act of 1864 from the Loop Line north of Tunstall station to the New-field Pottery, was opened in 1874. Another built under the same Act from the main line near Long-port through Tunstall and Chell to the Chatterley-Whitfield Colliery was opened in 1875; a branch to the High Lane Colliery at Little Chell had ceased to exist by the end of the century.[4]

BUILDINGS. The market-place (now Tower Square) still forms the nucleus of the town. Several of the plain two-storied houses erected round it soon after 1816 survive as well as the former chapel of the Methodist New Connexion (1821)[5] at its west end. The original town hall in the centre of the square has been replaced by a clock tower of yellow brick, erected in 1893, and the east end of the square is now dominated by the ornate Renaissance façade of the second town hall dating from 1883–5.[6] This front is of nine bays, the lower story being of rusticated stone and the upper story of brick with stone dressings. Nearly all the buildings in the central part of High Street date from the late 19th and the 20th centuries. An exception is the Swan Inn, a low brick structure which though now faced with imitation

half-timbering may be of early-18th-century origin. The entrance to Copes Avenue north of the Swan Pottery is flanked by twin lodges, this being the drive entrance of the former Hall House. They date from the 1830's and are square buildings of yellow brick with low-pitched hipped roofs and round-headed doorways. Hall House was demolished early in the 20th century, and streets of houses were built over its ground.[7] In The Boulevard (formerly Station Road), the other principal street at the town centre, the two most impressive buildings are the covered market (1858) and the Jubilee Buildings (1889–90). The market, which stands at the rear of the town hall, was considerably reduced in size when the town hall was built.[8] It has single-story arcaded fronts with heavily rusticated round-headed entrances both from The Boulevard and from Butter-field Place. The Jubilee Buildings, erected in 1889–90 to commemorate the Golden Jubilee, originally contained the fire station and volunteers' armoury as well as the present Victoria Institute and public baths.[9] Designed by A. R. Wood of Tunstall,[10] the buildings are of red brick with stone and terracotta dressings in a style similar to that of the town hall but on a less elaborate scale.

Owing to Tunstall's late start as a pottery town, it was possible for the new streets of working-class houses to be laid out on largely open ground and there was no legacy of the sub-standard cottages arranged in courts or squares which were to cause such problems elsewhere. The earliest housing in Tunstall dates from c. 1820 when standards were very slowly beginning to improve. In spite of extensive clearance, particularly since the Second World War, many of the terraced streets laid out between 1820 and 1850 are still in existence. Specially noteworthy are the two terraces, each of 20 houses, which form the south side of Paradise Street and the north side of Piccadilly Street at the west end of Tower Square. They were built in 1821 by the Tunstall Building Society which had been formed in 1816 with 32 members, many of them working potters.[11] The houses may be fairly taken as representative of the local housing of the time. Each dwelling contains a front and a back room on each of the two floors with a privy and an ashpit in the diminutive walled yard at the rear. Wash-houses or sculleries appear to have been added beyond the back doors of many of the houses at a later date. A narrow cobbled footway runs between the yards of the two terraces and is crossed by a passage entered through an archway in the centre of each row. Above the arches are oval plaques bearing the street names and the date. In

[93] Hargreaves, *Map of Staffs. Potteries.*
[94] Malabar, *Map of Tunstall* (surveyed 1863).
[95] White, *Dir. Staffs.* (1834).
[96] *Kelly's Dir. Staffs.* (1924, 1940). There was a wharf on or near this site in the late 1870's: O.S. Map 6" Staffs. xi NE. (1890).
[97] 'Manifold', *N. Staffs. Rlwy.* 34–35.
[98] *Guide to N. Staffs. Rlwy.* (copy in W.S.L. Pamphs., vol. iv, no. 12), 11–12.
[99] White, *Dir. Staffs.* (1851); see p. 110. This service was still in operation in 1867: *Keates and Ford's Potteries Dir.* (1867).
[1] Ex inf. Brit. Rlwys. L.M.R. (1958).
[2] Ex inf. Brit. Rlwys.
[3] 'Manifold', *N. Staffs. Rlwy.* 54; *P.O. Dir. Staffs.* (1876).
[4] 'Manifold', *N. Staffs. Rlwy.* 53 and schedule between pp. 128 and 129; O.S. Map 6" Staffs. xi NE. (1890); xii

NW. (1890).
[5] See pp. 81, 296–7.   [6] See p. 95.
[7] The house, which was in existence by 1829 and probably by 1820, stood in its own grounds to the NE. of the Swan Works; it was the home of Ralph Hall, owner of the works and much of the surrounding land, until the 1860's: S. Shaw, *Staffs. Potteries*, 17; White, *Dir. Staffs.* (1834, 1851); *P.O. Dir. Staffs.* (1860); Greenwood, *Map of Staffs.* (1820); Hargreaves, *Map of Staffs. Potteries*; Malabar, *Map of Tunstall* (surveyed 1863). The house was still mentioned in *Kelly's Dir. Staffs.* (1900).
[8] See p. 98.
[9] *Staffs. Sentinel*, 31 Oct. 1891; see pp. 96, 97, 104.
[10] *Kelly's Dir. Staffs.* (1900).
[11] Ward, *Stoke*, 94–95; S. J. Price, *Building Societies*, 65; see p. 81; see plate facing p. 113 and plan on p. 115. The subscription was £1 1s. a share a month: Price, loc. cit. For building-society housing in Burslem see p. 114.

Rathbone Street a number of cottages of the same period survive, their doorways, like those in Paradise and Piccadilly Streets, having simple wood surrounds. Between Rathbone and Woodland Streets, where demolition was in progress in 1960, the houses date from *c.* 1840 and have the round-headed doorways with moulded archivolts and projecting keystones which appeared in such numbers in the Potteries at that period.[12] The layout also includes a series of short cul-de-sac streets, the general arrangement being similar to that of the Building Society terraces but on a slightly more generous scale; the projecting wash-houses and water-closets appear to be later additions.

MANORS. *TUNSTALL* manor, also called Tunstall Court from the 16th century,[13] covered an area which extended to the Cheshire border and included the following townships: Tunstall, Chell, Oldcott, and Ravenscliffe; Burslem and Sneyd; and Chatterley, Brieryhurst, Stadmorslow, Thursfield, Wedgwood, and Bemersley.[14] Much of it thus lay outside the area covered by this article; the history of the manor as a whole, however, will be traced here. Between 1212 and 1273 Tunstall, Bemersley, Burslem, Chatterley, Chell, Oldcott, and Thursfield, as well as Whitfield within the Bemersley portion of Tunstall manor, were mentioned as distinct manors or vills,[15] but all, except for Chell, had been merged within the manor of Tunstall by the end of the 13th century.[16]

In 1086 Tunstall may have formed part of Thursfield (in Wolstanton), of which Richard the Forester was overlord.[17] By *c.* 1200 Aline, daughter and heir of Richard's grandson Robert fitz Orm, and her husband Engenulph de Gresley were holding Tunstall,[18] apparently as tenants of the Earl of Chester whose family may well have acquired the overlordship by royal grant during the earlier 12th century.[19] Although Engenulph and Aline were later said to have given it to Adam de Audley, husband of Aline's cousin Emma,[20] Tunstall was not listed among the

possessions of Adam's son and heir Henry in 1212, and land was then held there of the king in socage by Henry de Verdon in right of his wife,[21] the widow of Engenulph's heir Robert.[22] By 1227, however, Henry de Audley was holding Tunstall, allegedly by gift of Engenulph and Aline; he had also been granted by the Earl of Chester rent there due to the earl, a gift which probably marked the termination of the earl's overlordship.[23] The king confirmed both these grants in 1227,[24] and in 1236 Henry was holding the vill of Tunstall of the royal manor of Newcastle-under-Lyme by service of castle-guard.[25] The overlordship was held in 1272, 1276, and 1283 by the Earl of Lancaster as lord of Newcastle.[26] However, Henry de Audley (d. 1276) successfully refused service at the earl's court at Newcastle,[27] and from 1299 to 1434 the overlordship was merely said to lie with the heirs of Engenulph and Aline de Gresley.[28]

The manor descended in the Audley family until the death of Nicholas de Audley in 1391,[29] and as he was childless his estates were divided among his three sisters or their heirs.[30] In 1392 one third passed to Margaret, one of these sisters, and her husband Roger Hilary.[31] In 1411, under a settlement of 1392, this share was united with that of the Tuchets, the heirs of Joan, another sister, and the holders of the Audley barony from 1405.[32] These two parts descended with the barony[33] until 1560 when Henry Lord Audley mortgaged what was then called the manor of Tunstall to Sir William Sneyd of Bradwell (in Wolstanton).[34] Sir William subsequently held the courts of this manor,[35] and it passed at his death in 1572 to his son Ralph[36] to whom George Lord Audley sold it in 1576.[37] The manor then remained in the Sneyd family,[38] lords of the other third part by the end of the 18th century (see below), and in 1940 such manorial rights as survived were held by Ralph Sneyd.[39]

The remaining third part of the manor resulting from the division after the death of Nicholas de Audley in 1391 was the share of Fulk FitzWarin as the grandson of Nicholas's third coheir.[40] It re-

---

[12] Houses in Plex St. with similar doorways are dated 1843.
[13] Ward *Stoke*, app., pp. viii, xxiv; *S.H.C.* 1941, 119, 162; S.R.O., Index to Gamekeepers' Deps.; U.C.N.S., Sneyd MSS., Ct. R. 7/41.
[14] *Tunstall Ct. R.* (*T.N.S.F.C.* lix–lxvi), *passim*. This article deals only with Tunstall, Chell, and the Goldenhill portion of the townships of Oldcott and Ravenscliffe. The remaining portion of these is reserved for treatment under Wolstanton. Burslem and Sneyd are treated in the article on Burslem Boro. in this volume. The other townships are reserved for treatment under the ancient parishes of Wolstanton and Norton-in-the-Moors.
[15] *Bk. of Fees*, 143, 594; *Cal. Chart. R. 1226–57*, 36, 409; *S.H.C.* vi (1), 58–59; ibid. N.S. xi. 242, 243.
[16] *S.H.C.* N.S. xi. 246–70; *Plac. de Quo Warr.* (Rec. Com.), 710, 777; *Tunstall Ct. R.* (*T.N.S.F.C.* lxvi), 140–2.
[17] *V.C.H. Staffs.* iv. 56, no. 254.
[18] *Cal. Chart. R. 1226–57*, 36; R. Eyton, *Domesday Studies, Staffs.* 89.
[19] *S.H.C.* i. 234–5.
[20] *Plac. de Quo Warr.* (Rec. Com.), 710; *S.H.C.* iv (1), 50; ibid. N.S. ix. 259; *Complete Peerage*, 'Audley'.
[21] *Bk. of Fees*, 143.
[22] *S.H.C.* N.S. i. 27, 30; Robt. had d. childless.
[23] *Cal. Chart. R. 1226–57*, 36; *S.H.C.* i. 234–5; A. Huntbach, 'Presidential Address' (*T.N.S.F.C.* lii), 18.
[24] *Cal. Chart R. 1226–57*, 36.
[25] *Bk. of Fees*, 594. The Earl of Chester held Newcastle manor from 1215 until 1232; see p. 184.
[26] *Cal. Inq. p.m.* ii, pp. 68, 121, 287; *S.H.C.* N.S. xi. 242.
[27] *S.H.C.* N.S. xi. 244; *Cal. Inq. p.m.* ii, p. 121.

[28] *Cal. Inq. p.m.* iii, p. 408; v, p. 29; vi, p. 42, where 'Alan' de Gresley should presumably read 'Aline'; C 137/67; C 139/65. There is an isolated ref. in 1641 to the overlordship of 'the heir of Alan de Gresley': C 142/702/36.
[29] *Complete Peerage*, 'Audley'; *Cal. Inq. p.m.* ii, pp. 68, 121, 287; iii, p. 408; v, p. 29; vi, p. 42; *Cal. Fine R. 1391–9*, 10.
[30] *Cal. Close R. 1389–92*, 468.
[31] Ibid.
[32] *Complete Peerage*, 'Audley'; C 137/73; *Cal. Close R. 1409–13*, 254; *S.H.C.* xi. 209.
[33] *Complete Peerage*, 'Audley'; U.C.N.S., Sneyd MSS. Ct. R. 7/3, 7/5–7/9; *Tunstall Ct. R.* (*T.N.S.F.C.* lx, lxi), *passim*; *L. & P. Hen. VIII*, i, p. 96; iv, p. 3183; v, p. 150.
[34] *S.H.C.* xiii. 211–12; C 142/162/142.
[35] *Tunstall Ct. R.* (*T.N.S.F.C.* lxi), 42; ibid. lxii. 59.
[36] Ibid. lxii. 65; C 142/162/142.
[37] U.C.N.S., Sneyd MSS., Tunstall Deeds (1574, 1576, 1577); *S.H.C.* xiv (1), 190.
[38] C 142/388/51; *Tunstall Ct. R.* (*T.N.S.F.C.* lxiii–lxvi), *passim*; S.R.O., Index to Gamekeepers' Deps.; White, *Dir. Staffs.* (1851); Burke, *Land. Gent.* (1952), 2355–6.
[39] *Kelly's Dir. Staffs.* (1940).
[40] *Cal. Close R. 1389–92*, 468. He was only 2 years old in 1391, and in 1393 his mother Eliz. m. Sir Hugh Courtenay as her 2nd husband (*Complete Peerage*, 'FitzWarin'); Sir Hugh tried to secure the wardship of the heir after Eliz.'s death in 1411: C 137/85; *Cal. Fine R. 1405–13*, 214; *Cal. Close R. 1409–13*, 399–400. This explains why this part of the manor was variously described as the king's and Courtenay's in 1405 (U.C.N.S., Sneyd MSS., Ct. R. 7/3) and 'recently Courtenay's' in 1416: ibid.

mained with Fulk's descendants (earls of Bath from 1536)[41] until 1620 when Francis, son and heir of Sir William Bowyer of Knypersley, bought this third of Tunstall manor from William Earl of Bath at Sir William Bowyer's direction.[42] Francis held the court baron as lord in 1620[43] but seems to have held this share of the manor jointly with his father.[44] He is not mentioned after 1632, however, and Sir William was holding the lordship at his death in 1641 with a son Richard as his heir.[45] Some interest in it seems to have remained with William Earl of Bath whose son and heir Edward was stated to be holding the third part of Tunstall at his death in 1637,[46] while two of Edward's daughters and coheirs made settlements of it in 1652.[47]

In 1652, however, this part of the manor was held by John Bowyer of Knypersley, younger son and heir of Sir William,[48] and John was succeeded by his son Sir John in 1666.[49] This John was followed by his son, also Sir John, in 1691 and he by his uncle, Sir William Bowyer, in 1701.[50] Sir William died in 1702 leaving four daughters and coheirs who still held the lordship jointly in 1725.[51] By 1728, however, it had passed to Sir Thomas Gresley, husband of Dorothy, one of the coheirs.[52] He was succeeded in 1746 by his son Sir Thomas and he in 1753 by his younger brother Sir Nigel,[53] whose son, Sir Nigel Bowyer Gresley, sold this third part of Tunstall manor soon after his succession in 1787 to Ralph Sneyd,[54] lord of the other two parts.

Although in 1317 the lord had no buildings in the vill of Tunstall,[55] he had a house at Holly Wall by the late 14th century,[56] and there was a capital messuage attached to the manor in 1431.[57] By 1547 'the chief house or hall of Tunstall' was in the hands of Sir William Sneyd, who in that year leased it for life to Robert Parker.[58] By 1683 this or a house on

the same site had evidently passed into the Child family and was doubtless the brick house in the centre of the town called the Manor House which was occupied by Thomas Child, yeoman, in the mid-18th century.[59] This house still stood in 1838 when it was described as 'ancient'.[60]

The division of the manor at the end of the 14th century was not simply territorial. The exact form of the tripartite division is not clear, although in 1405 lands within the manor were held of each of the lords separately.[61] After two of the shares had been united in 1411, however, all the copyhold tenements in the townships in the north-western part of the manor, Ravenscliffe, Oldcott, Brieryhurst, and Thursfield, were assigned to the lord of the third part along with some rents out of five of the other townships. The townships of Sneyd, Chell, and Wedgwood and the remainder of the divided rents were the share of the Audleys and the Sneyds after them.[62] The mills, commons, heriots, and mineral rights were not divided as such, but the proceeds were shared between the two lords in the proportion of two to one.[63] There may have been some formal confirmation of this whole division in the mid-16th century.[64] In one respect, however, the detailed administration of the manor remained tripartite, a reeve being appointed annually for each third.[65] By the mid-16th century there had been a hardening of the division of the manor,[66] and the practice of appointing two reeves at the court of the two-thirds part and one at the court of the third part was introduced.[67] With the enfranchisements of the early 17th century[68] the office of reeve disappeared.

Courts were being held for the manor by 1274,[69] and the view of frankpledge was first mentioned in 1283 when the income from it was 10s.[70] The court rolls, however, survive only from 1326.[71] The courts

[41] *Complete Peerage*, 'Bath', 'FitzWarin'; *Cal. Close* 1392–6, 73; *Cal. Fine R.* 1405–13, 214; C 138/52; C 139/51; C 139/65; C 142/129/31; *S.H.C.* N.S. iv. 11; U.C.N.S., Sneyd MSS., Ct. R. 7/3, 7/5–7/9; *Tunstall Ct. R.* (*T.N.S.F.C.* lxi), *passim*; ibid. lxii. 65; lxiii. 53.

[42] U.C.N.S., Sneyd MSS., Tunstall Deeds; W.S.L., D. 1788, P. 33, B. 7, where Francis is described as Sir Wm.'s son and heir. Francis does not, however, appear in the pedigrees given in *S.H.C.* v (2), 50.

[43] *Tunstall Ct. R.* (*T.N.S.F.C.* lxiv), 122.

[44] Wedgwood, *Wedgwood Family*, 316; U.C.N.S., Sneyd MSS., Tunstall Deeds, 18 June 7 Chas. I.

[45] U.C.N.S., Sneyd MSS., Tunstall Deeds, 20 May 10 Chas. I; C 142/702/36.   [46] C 142/570/140.

[47] C.P. 25(2)/616, 1652 Hil., 1652 Mich.

[48] W.S.L., D. 1798, bdle. 164; *S.H.C.* v (2), 50.

[49] *S.H.C.* N.S. i. 242; Hist. MSS. Com. *House of Lords*, N.S. iv. 310; *Tunstall Ct. R.* (*T.N.S.F.C.* lxvi), 124, 126.

[50] *S.H.C.* N.S. i. 242; Hist. MSS. Com. *House of Lords*, iv. 310.

[51] *S.H.C.* N.S. i. 242; *Tunstall Ct. R.* (*T.N.S.F.C.* lxvi), 139; U.C.N.S., Sneyd MSS., Ct. R. 7/34.

[52] U.C.N.S., Sneyd MSS., Ct. R. 7/34; *S.H.C.* N.S. i. 227.

[53] *S.H.C.* N.S. i. 227; U.C.N.S., Tunstall Deeds, rental of Sir Nigel Gresley 1756–7; Ward, *Stoke*, app., p. xxxvii.

[54] Ward, *Stoke*, 74 (where there is confusion between this Sir Nigel and his father); S.R.O., Index to Gamekeepers' Deps.; *S.H.C.* N.S. i. 228. Ralph Sneyd d. in 1793: Burke, *Land. Gent.* (1952), 2356.

[55] *S.H.C.* 1911, 337.

[56] *Tunstall Ct. R.* (*T.N.S.F.C.* lix), 64, 85.

[57] C 139/51.

[58] Ward, *Stoke*, 80 n., citing the lease, which seems to have been a renewal of a similar lease of 1537 or 1538; a condition of the 1547 lease was that Parker should accompany Sir Wm. 'this viage to serve the Kynge's Majestie in his warres in Scotland'.

[59] Ibid. 80 n., 92–93, and app. p. viii.   [60] Ibid. 93.

[61] U.C.N.S., Sneyd MSS., Ct. R. 7/3.

[62] Ibid., Keele Deeds, Sneyd *v.* tenants of Tunstall manor, nos. 11, 15; ibid., Tunstall Deeds, rental of Sir Nigel Gresley 1756–7; ibid., Ct. R. 7/3–7/6; *Tunstall Ct. R.* (*T.N.S.F.C.* lxi–lxiii), *passim*; ibid. lxiv. 100–23; lxvi. 140–2 (bounds, 1719). By the mid-18th century the lord of the third part was in receipt of rents from Sneyd township also, though no longer from Chatterley: rental of Sir Nigel Gresley (cited above).

[63] U.C.N.S., Sneyd MSS., Keele Deeds, Sneyd *v.* tenants of Tunstall manor, nos. 11, 15; ibid., Tunstall Deeds; *Tunstall Ct. R.* (*T.N.S.F.C.* lxii), 70; ibid. lxiii. 55; lxiv. 116.

[64] U.C.N.S., Sneyd MSS., Keele Deeds, Sneyd *v.* tenants of Tunstall manor, nos. 11, 15, which imply that the whole division took place by agreement between Lord Audley and the Earl of Bath. The evidence already cited from the ct. rolls shows the division to have been much earlier.

[65] J. C. and J. G. E. Wedgwood, *Wedgwood Pedigrees*, 17, 19, 20; U.C.N.S., Sneyd MSS., Ct. R. 7/3, 7/5, 7/7, 7/8; *Tunstall Ct. R.* (*T.N.S.F.C.* lx), 31.

[66] There were separate courts by 1537, and the Earl of Bath appointed his reeve at his own little court in 1551: *Tunstall Ct. R.* (*T.N.S.F.C.* lxi), 41. And see n. 64 above for the evidence of a formal confirmation of the division in the mid-16th cent.

[67] *Tunstall Ct. R.* (*T.N.S.F.C.* lxi), 30, 41, 44–45; ibid. lxiv. 116–18, showing a reeve for 'the lord's part' of the manor and a reeve for 'the lady's part', both apparently within the two-thirds part.   [68] See p. 97.

[69] *S.H.C.* N.S. xi. 242; *Cal. Inq. p.m.* ii, p. 68.

[70] *S.H.C.* N.S. xi. 247. An item called headborough silver appears in 1577: *Tunstall Ct. R.* (*T.N.S.F.C.* lxiv), 118.

[71] U.C.N.S., Sneyd MSS., Ct. R. 7/1–7/42. A selection down to 1719, omitting the 15th cent., has been printed in *T.N.S.F.C.* lix–lxvi.

of the divided manor were at first held jointly and the perquisites divided,[72] but from at least 1537 a separate court baron was held for the third part of the manor with what seems to have been a separate view of frankpledge in 1537 and 1551.[73] For 60 years after 1620, the Bowyers held no courts; as a result William Sneyd was claiming before 1680 that the right to hold courts belonged to his part of the manor only.[74] Probably in answer to this claim Sir John Bowyer held his own courts leet and baron, with a court of survey, in 1680 and a further court in 1681 additional to the Sneyds' view and court baron.[75] There were no further courts, however, for this third part of the manor until 1719 when the court leet for the whole manor and a court baron were held by the heirs of Sir William Bowyer.[76] This view and court baron continued to be held by the lords of the third part of Tunstall until at least 1728, but the Sneyds were holding the courts leet and baron again by 1749.[77] After 1813 the courts lapsed; they were revived in 1826 and thereafter were held each October for the audit of chief rents and the swearing of chief constables and headboroughs and also 'as a festive meeting and bond of connexion between the lord and his tenants'.[78] Tunstall court was still held in 1917.[79]

Until the 16th century the manor courts were always held at Tunstall,[80] but in 1537, after the division of the courts, the court for the third part of the manor was held 'at Parke', possibly the Park House in Oldcott.[81] In 1551 the Earl of Bath's great and small courts and view were held at Thursfield,[82] but the subsequent courts for this part of the manor were all held at Tunstall until their lapse in 1620;[83] with their revival in 1680 Newchapel (the former Thursfield) became the meeting-place.[84] Lord Audley's court was held at Burslem instead of Tunstall in 1549,[85] and thereafter the courts for this part were held variously at one or other of these two places.[86] By the mid-18th century they were always held at Burslem, presumably at the alehouse known as the Court House,[87] and met in the town hall by the beginning of the 19th century when they were convened by the constables of Burslem.[88] The revived court of 1826, summoned by the constables of Burslem and the headborough of Tunstall, met in the court house at Tunstall and during the next few years was held either there or in Burslem town hall.[89] Between at least 1834 and 1841, however, it was transferred to the 'Grapes' at Newchapel, the summons being issued through the constable of Thursfield and the headborough of Tunstall. The court-house in Cross Street, Tunstall, was pulled down in 1888.[90]

By c. 1200 CHELL, like Tunstall, was held by Engenulph de Gresley and his wife Aline, apparently of the Earl of Chester, and was conveyed by them to Adam de Audley, husband of Aline's cousin Emma.[91] The overlordship also had been remitted by the earl to Adam's son Henry by 1227.[92] In 1252 Henry's son James received a grant of free warren in his demesne lands in Chell.[93]

Before 1212 Chell had been divided by the lord between two tenants in unequal parts, and the names Great Chell and Little Chell may originate in this division.[94] It is not, however, possible to establish a clear link between these two parts and the later manors of Great and Little Chell. The title of manor was evidently applied to different estates at various times so that one single descent cannot be traced; all such estates were, however, held of the manor of Tunstall.

Henry de Audley (succ. by 1212) granted two-thirds of Chell to Richard of Hanley,[95] probably to be identified with Richard of Chell who, with his heir Richard, occurs c. 1230 holding land in Chell.[96] Richard's overlord, however, was his kinsman Robert de Swynnerton,[97] who, therefore, seems to have acquired an intermediate lordship in Chell. One or other of these Richards died c. 1251 leaving a daughter and heir Margery, the wife of Robert de Mere, and the family estate subsequently passed to their son, also Robert de Mere.[98] By 1263 this younger Robert had been succeeded by his cousin John de Swynnerton, who would also have been the holder of any mesne lordship as nephew and heir of Robert de Swynnerton.[99] John was succeeded in 1284 by his cousin Roger de Swynnerton who was holding four messuages and four bovates of land in Great Chell in 1286[1] and of whom Robert Chell, in succession to a brother Richard, was holding a messuage and virgate in Chell in 1290.[2] By 1319 a messuage and land in Chell with a court and mineral rights were in the hands of Richard de Whethales,[3] probably a member of a cadet branch of the Swynnerton family.[4] He or Sir Richard de Peshale, possibly his nephew, was the lord of Chell

---

[72] U.C.N.S., Sneyd MSS., Keele Deeds, Sneyd v. tenants of Tunstall manor, nos. 11, 15.
[73] *Tunstall Ct. R.* (*T.N.S.F.C.* lxi), 30, 31, 39, 40, 48; ibid. lxii. 65; lxiii. 53; lxiv. 104–16, 119–23.
[74] U.C.N.S., Sneyd MSS., Keele Deeds, Sneyd v. tenants of Tunstall manor, no. 15.
[75] *Tunstall Ct. R.* (*T.N.S.F.C.* lxvi), 113, 117, 124, 126.
[76] Ibid. 139.
[77] U.C.N.S., Sneyd MSS., Ct. R. 7/34, 7/35. There is a gap in the series between 1728 and 1749.
[78] Ward, *Stoke.* 77–78; W. Capey, 'Manor of Tunstall' (*T.N.S.F.C.* 1888), 86; U.C.N.S., Sneyd MSS., Ct. R. 7/41, 7/42; *Staffs. Advertiser*, 2 Nov. 1839.
[79] A. Huntbach, 'Presidential Address' (*T.N.S.F.C.* lii), 24.
[80] Adams, *Adams Family*, 9–17, passim; *Tunstall Ct. R.* (*T.N.S.F.C.* lix, lx), passim; ibid. lxi. 26, 30.
[81] *Tunstall Ct. R.* (*T.N.S.F.C.* lxi), 31.
[82] Ibid. 39, 40.
[83] Ibid. 48; lxii. 65; lxiii. 53; lxiv. 104–16, 119–23.
[84] Ibid. lxvi. 124, 126, 140; U.C.N.S., Sneyd MSS., Ct. R. 7/34.
[85] *Tunstall Ct. R.* (*T.N.S.F.C.* lxi), 32.

[86] Ibid. 42; lxii–lxvi, passim.
[87] U.C.N.S., Sneyd MSS., Ct. R. 7/35; Ward, *Stoke*, app., p. xxxiii and map facing p. 225.
[88] U.C.N.S., Sneyd MSS., Ct. R. 7/40.
[89] Ibid. 7/41, 7/42.
[90] Adams, *Adams Family*, 11 (with drawing); W. Scarratt, *Old Times in the Potteries*, 58 (with a different view on p. 61 from that given by Adams).
[91] *Cal. Chart R.* 1226–57, 56; *S.H.C.* 1911, 443–4; see p. 86.
[92] *Cal. Chart R.* 1226–57, 56.
[93] Ibid. 409.
[94] See p. 83
[95] *S.H.C.* 1911, 444; the bounds are given.
[96] Ibid. 445.
[97] Ibid.
[98] *S.H.C.* N.S. iii. 103–4.
[99] Ibid. 96, 103–4.
[1] Ibid. 104–5; *S.H.C.* vi (1), 166.
[2] Ibid. vi (1), 193.
[3] Ibid. 1911, 446–7.
[4] Ibid. N.S. iii. 106–7; N.S. ii. 98–99 and pedigree between.

in 1340,[5] and Sir Richard seems to have been in possession in 1342[6] and 1343,[7] but by 1344 the manor had passed to John, son of Adam de Wheth-ales and possibly brother of Sir Richard.[8]

The other third of Chell had been granted before 1212 by Adam de Audley to Robert Blund[9] and confirmed to him subsequently by Henry de Audley who added 14 acres 'in the wood between Chell and Thunstal'.[10] The Blunds are identifiable with that branch of the Chell family[11] which held an estate in Chell in the 13th and 14th centuries,[12] and it may have been a member of this family, Thomas son of Adam of Chell, who appears in 1344 as Thomas lord of Little Chell.[13] Nothing further, however, is heard at this time of such a lordship, and it is just possible, though highly conjectural, that Thomas was Thomas le Wolf whose son John, of Little Chell, married Margaret the daughter and heir of John of Chell,[14] very possibly the John son of Adam de Whethales[15] who was lord of Chell in 1344 (see above). The two lordships would thus have been united.

At any rate before the end of Edward III's reign Margaret was 'domina de Chell', and, by then a widow, she made a settlement of all her lands in the lordship of Chell.[16] She subsequently married John Byron (Burne, Bourne), and their son Geoffrey Bourne succeeded in 1415, after Margaret's death, to her freehold messuage and lands in Chell; he also had lands in Little Chell.[17] These estates descended in the Bourne family and were described by the early 16th century as the manor of Chell, which in 1536 was held by John Bourne, yeoman, of Little Chell.[18] Members of this branch of the family continued to hold a freehold estate in Little Chell until the end of the 18th century at least, although the title of manor was no longer given to it.[19] Another branch of the family, also descended from Margaret and John Bourne, held an estate in Great Chell.[20]

By the mid-16th century a manor had developed out of an estate in Great Chell owned by Robert Badger who by 1540 held a court baron there.[21] In 1580 he or another Robert Badger conveyed 'the manor of Chell otherwise Great Chell' to William Unwyn[22] who as William Unwyn of Chatterley conveyed it to Ralph Sneyd of Bradwell in 1587.[23] This manor of Great Chell thenceforward descended in the Sneyd family who from at least 1669 also had a manor of Little Chell,[24] possibly as lords of the Bourne estate there. In the early 19th century there was once more only the single manor of Chell, held by the Sneyds.[25] A court was held for the manor of Great Chell in 1679 when the bounds were given.[26]

OTHER ESTATES. A freehold estate in Oldcott called Broadfield was held by the Colclough family from at least 1549.[27] William Colclough moved to Burslem some time after his marriage into the Burslem family c. 1617[28] and between at least 1634 and 1673 a branch of the Rowley family held the lease of Broadfield House of the Colcloughs.[29] Margaret Colclough died there in 1711,[30] and the farm was held by John Colclough later in the 18th century.[31] John Gilbert of Clough Hall in Audley parish (d. 1812) later acquired the estate, rebuilt the house, and divided the farm into two.[32] In 1825 the house and some 28 acres were occupied by John Stubbs,[33] and the farm was held in 1834 by a Daniel Stubbs.[34] There were two houses in the Broadfield area in 1839 owned by Robert Williamson and held by tenants.[35] In 1956 the survivor of the two, Meadow House, with land attached, was bought from a Mr. Burgess by Alfred Meakin (Tunstall) Ltd. who demolished the house but still (1960) own the land.[36]

Chell Lodge on the south side of Little Chell Lane, also known as Little Chell Hall in the mid-19th century,[37] was built by Thomas Cartlich in the late 1830's and was his home until he moved to Woore Manor (Salop.) c. 1860.[38] Occupied by the Turner family from c. 1868 until c. 1892,[39] it was

[5] U.C.N.S., Sneyd MSS., Chell Deeds; *S.H.C.* N.S. ii, pedigree between pp. 98 and 99.
[6] *S.H.C.* xii (1), 10.
[7] Ibid. xi. 153.
[8] U.C.N.S., Sneyd MSS., Chell Deeds; *S.H.C.* 1911, 448.
[9] *S.H.C.* 1911, 443–4.   [10] Ibid. 444.
[11] Ibid. 446, where John Blund's seal is inscribed 'Joha*nn*is de Chelle'.
[12] Ibid. 445–6, 447; B.M. Add. Ch. 53592, giving Chell pedigree.
[13] *S.H.C.* 1911, 447; U.C.N.S., Sneyd MSS., Chell Deeds.
[14] W.S.L., Hadfield MSS., no. 25, p. 3, pedigree of Chell and le Wolf; B.M. Add. Ch. 53592, giving Chell pedigree; *S.H.C.* xi. 174. The two pedigrees do not agree, but neither is accurate.
[15] *S.H.C.* N.S. iii. 106–7.
[16] W.S.L., Hadfield MSS., no. 25, p. 2, which dates the settlement as 1362. John le Wolf was still alive, however, in 1363: *S.H.C.* xi. 174.
[17] W.S.L., Hadfield MSS., no. 25, pp. 2–3.
[18] Ibid. p. 3; B.M. Add. Ch. 53600–2, 53606–7.
[19] W.S.L., Hadfield MSS., no. 25, p. 3; *Tunstall Ct. R.* (*T.N.S.F.C.* lxiii), 58; ibid. lxvi. 112, 113; U.C.N.S., Sneyd MSS., Tunstall Deeds, Tunstall Ct. Rental 1621; ibid. Ct. R. 7/33; P. W. L. Adams, *Wolstanton*, 93, 94, 95; E 134/9 Geo. II Mich./17, m. 4; H.R.L., E.M.T. 10–795.
[20] W.S.L., Hadfield MSS., no. 25, p. 3; Adams, *Wolstanton*, 94; U.C.N.S., Sneyd MSS., Chell Deeds; ibid. Tunstall Deeds, Tunstall Rental 1621; Ward, *Stoke*, 127; *Tunstall Ct. R.* (*T.N.S.F.C.* lxvi), 107, 108, 109, 127, 137. A house in Biddulph Rd. at Gt. Chell opposite the junction with High Lane dated 1631 and still standing in 1914 is

said to have been a home of the Bournes: Adams, *Adams Family*, 304; Adams, *Wolstanton*, 104–5.
[21] U.C.N.S., Sneyd MSS., Chell Deeds, Ct. R. 1540, 1547; B.M. Add. Ch. 53609; *Cal. Inq. p.m. Hen. VII*, iii, p. 564, showing rent in Chell held of Chris. Bagger by Humph. Swynnerton of Swynnerton and Hilton c. 1505.
[22] *S.H.C.* xiv (1), 216; ibid. xv. 136.
[23] U.C.N.S., Sneyd MSS., Chell Deeds.
[24] C 142/388/51; C.P. 25(2)/724, 21 Chas. II East.; C.P. 43/812/rot. 43; U.C.N.S., Sneyd MSS., Chell Deeds; ibid. Tunstall Deeds, appointment of gamekeeper, 1794; S.R.O., D. 260/M/box 25, bdle. k, Royalist Compositions.
[25] U.C.N.S., Sneyd MSS., Chell Deeds, appointment of gamekeeper, 1812; *Kelly's Dir. Staffs.* (1884, 1940).
[26] U.C.N.S., Sneyd MSS., Ct. R. 7/27.
[27] *Tunstall Ct. R.* (*T.N.S.F.C.* lxi), 33; ibid. lxiii. 53, 69; lxiv. 108; *S.H.C.* 1947–8, 113.
[28] J. C. Wedgwood, *Wedgwood Family*, 77; Ward, *Stoke*, 194; *S.H.C.* N.S. vii. 215.
[29] *Wolstanton Par. Reg.* i. 21–116; Wedgwood, *Wedgwood Family*, 79, 80, 84, 87. A branch of the Colclough family lived at Latebrook during the 17th cent. at least: S.R.O., D. 260/M/T4/103.
[30] *Wolstanton Par. Reg.* i. 223.
[31] W.S.L. 93/27/41, f. 16.
[32] Ibid.   [33] Ibid.
[34] White, *Dir. Staffs.* (1834).
[35] Lich. Dioc. Regy., Tithe Maps and Appt., Wolstanton.
[36] Ex inf. Mr. C. Boden, Holly Wall (1960).
[37] White, *Dir. Staffs.* (1851); *P.O. Dir. Staffs.* (1854).
[38] P. W. L. Adams, *John Henry Clive*, 7 n., 31, 123 and n.; Lich. Dioc. Regy., Tithe Maps and Appt., Wolstanton.
[39] *P.O. Dir. Staffs.* (1868); *Kelly's Dir. Staffs.* (1892).

the home of William Bolton Clive from the early 20th century until his death in 1920.[40] The site is now occupied by a post-1945 housing estate.

A copyhold estate centring on a house called Clanway within the Audleys' part of Tunstall manor was the seat of a branch of the Bourne family from before 1575[41] until the early 17th century.[42] By 1619, when it was enfranchised as a farm of some 28 acres, it had been leased by John Bourne of Chesterton to Randolph Whitall[43] whose family may still have held it in 1635.[44] Henry Bourne was living there in 1662,[45] but by 1677 it had passed to William Baddeley who was then succeeded by another William Baddeley, still the occupant in 1685.[46] The estate was occupied in 1719 by a Mr. Astbury.[47] In 1829 it was owned by Thomas Wedgwood and was in the hands of a tenant.[48] Some 10 years later it was an 85-acre farm owned by Philip Egerton Wedgwood and still held by a tenant.[49] In 1851 it was occupied by John Henry Clive, formerly of Newfield and of Chell, and later in the century by his grandson William Clive.[50] The 19th-century farmhouse, the adjoining land, and the adjacent Clanway Brickworks were by 1958 owned by the Berry Hill Brickworks Ltd.[51]

A branch of the Bourne family was living at Colclough Lane in Oldcott probably by 1512[52] and certainly between 1535 and 1711.[53] Thomas Bourne, described as of Colclough, was granted the freehold of his lands in Oldcott and elsewhere in Sir William Bowyer's third of the manor in 1623.[54] Colclough Lane House was owned in 1781 by John Heathcote of Longton Hall and occupied by William Tunstall.[55] It was later the home of Thomas Tunstall who died in 1838 at the age of 89.[56] By the following year it was owned and occupied by Robert Williamson.[57] The three-storied brick house in Colclough Lane, now (1960) known as Colclough House, dates from the late 18th or early 19th century. Its frontage was altered in the present century when it was converted into two dwellings; parts of the stables and other outbuildings are occupied as cottages.

A house in Oldcott called Gill Bank with land attached was held by a branch of the Rowley family between at least 1603 and 1671.[58] John Rowley bought the freehold of all his copyhold land in the Bowyers' part of the manor (which included Oldcott)

in 1620.[59] In 1680 the estate was held by William Knight[60] and in 1728 by Thomas Barnet.[61] By 1755 half of Gill Bank belonged to Obadiah Lane whose son Obadiah succeeded in 1757.[62] About 1839 the 43-acre farm at Gill Bank was owned by Jervis Swynfen and occupied by John Nixon[63] whose family were still tenants in 1876. By 1880 the estate and house had been divided, the larger of the two farms being occupied by the Athertons and the smaller by the Wilsons.[64] In 1919 the smaller farm, still held by the Wilsons, was owned by the trustees of Mrs. Gladys Gooch of West Ilsley (Berks.), who sold it in that year to John Atherton, tenant of the other farm; it later passed to his daughter, Mrs. E. M. Reeves.[65] The other farm was owned in 1919 by Robert Heath of Biddulph Grange and his brothers Sir James and Arthur Heath and was sold by them soon afterwards to John Atherton's son, who sold it in 1926 to his sister's husband, Samuel Reeves.[66] The two farms were thus united in the Reeves family, but Mr. Reeves then demolished the part of the house attached to the larger farm and built the present farmhouse on a nearby site. Mrs. Reeves sold the smaller farm c. 1957 to Mr. R. F. Sutton who has carried out alterations to the remaining part of the old farmhouse. The larger farm is of 60 acres and the smaller of 20 acres.[67] The old farmhouse is a brick building probably dating from the earlier 18th century. Woodstock, a farmhouse to the south-west, is of the same type and carries a tile at its gable end with the date 1735 and the initials 'T B'.

An estate consisting of 2 copyhold messuages and 26 acres of land in Tunstall and Chatterley was held in 1539 by a Thomas Knight, and by 1615 had passed to his great-granddaughter Alice and her husband James Beech.[68] This was presumably the estate called Furlong, consisting of 2 messuages, 26 acres of land, and coal and ironstone mines, of which James and Alice acquired the freehold from Ralph Sneyd in 1619.[69] The Furlong estate was evidently held by William Beech and his wife Helen in 1661,[70] and by 1679 it had passed to Ann Beech of Great Chell, her sister Alice, and Alice's husband John Machin of Botteslow.[71] It evidently became the share of Alice since she was living there as a widow

40 Adams, *Clive*, 19, 124; *Kelly's Dir. Staffs.* (1912). He was the grandson of John Hen. Clive, who lived at Newfield Hall from c. 1813 till 1824 or 1825 (see p. 92), at Chell House after his second marriage in 1824 till the early 1840's (Adams, *Clive*, 19), and by 1851 at Clanway. Chell House, described as 'lately erected' in 1816 (*Staffs. Advertiser*, 18 Mar. 1816), stood to the W. of High Lane at its junction with the road from Tunstall to Biddulph.
41 U.C.N.S., Sneyd MSS., Tunstall Deeds.
42 *Tunstall Ct. R.* (*T.N.S.F.C.* lxiii), 41; W.S.L., D. 1788, P. 43, B. 2.
43 U.C.N.S., Sneyd MSS., Tunstall Deeds.
44 *Wolstanton Par. Reg.* i. 17; U.C.N.S., Sneyd MSS., Oldcott Deeds.
45 *Tunstall Ct. R.* (*T.N.S.F.C.* lxv), 96; Ward, *Stoke*, app., p. viii.
46 *Wolstanton Par. Reg.* i. 131, 132, 151.
47 *Tunstall Ct. R.* (*T.N.S.F.C.* lxvi), 142; *Wolstanton Par. Reg.* i. 225.
48 S.R.O., Q/RPl 1829.
49 Lichfield Dioc. Regy., Tithe Maps and Appt., Wolstanton. 50 Adams, *Clive*, 19, 123; see p. 92.
51 Ex inf. the tenant (1958); see pp. 247, 271.
52 *Tunstall Ct. R.* (*T.N.S.F.C.* lx), 31.
53 Ibid. lxiii, 54; lxv. 120; B.M. Add. Ch. 53605; *Wolstanton Par. Reg.* i. 26–220; *Burslem Par. Reg.* i. 58. A John Baggeley or Baddeley may have held the lease in 1666:

Ward, *Stoke*, app. p. viii.
54 W.S.L., D. 1788, P. 33, B. 7.
55 W.S.L., D. 788 (32), bdle. 8.
56 Ward, *Stoke*, 195.
57 Lich. Dioc. Regy., Tithe Maps and Appt., Wolstanton.
58 *Tunstall Ct. R.* (*T.N.S.F.C.* lxiii), 49; ibid. lxiv. 105, 107, 113; *Wolstanton Par. Reg.* i. 22, 57, 61, 110; Ward, *Stoke*, app. p. viii; S.R.O., D. 260/M/T4/103 (deed of 1646), which also shows Wm. Beech living at Gill Bank. Wm. d. there in 1673: *Wolstanton Par. Reg.* i. 116.
59 U.C.N.S., Sneyd MSS., Oldcott Deeds.
60 *Tunstall Ct. R.* (*T.N.S.F.C.* lxvi), 126.
61 U.C.N.S., Sneyd MSS., Ct. R. 7/34, Oct. 1728.
62 H. Mus., Heathcote Papers, xix. 1.
63 Lich. Dioc. Regy., Tithe Maps and Appt., Wolstanton; White, *Dir. Staffs.* (1834, 1851); *P.O. Dir. Staffs.* (1854 and later edns. to 1876).
64 *Kelly's Dir. Staffs.* (1880).
65 Ex inf. Mrs. Reeves (1958); W.S.L., Sale Cat. E/4/10.
66 Ex inf. Mrs. Reeves; Burke, *Land. Gent.* (1952), 1198–9. 67 Ex inf. Mrs. Reeves.
68 C 2/Jas. I, K 4/17.
69 Adams, *Adams Family*, 345; see p. 101.
70 C.P. 25(2)/723, 13 Chas. II Mich.
71 C.P. 25(2)/726, 31 Chas. II Trin.; Adams, *Adams Family*, 345. For the Machins of Botteslow see pp. 92, 212, 246.

in 1719[72] and in 1723 Thomas Machin of Botteslow and his wife Sarah sold the estate to Thomas Marsh of Bradwell (in Wolstanton) and Great Chell.[73] Members of the Machin family, however, were living there as tenants in 1730 and 1787.[74] In 1730 Thomas Marsh sold the estate to Richard Taylor of High Carr (in Wolstanton) who in 1756 conveyed the eastern part of it to Robert Clowes of Betley and his son William.[75] A Charles Clowes sold this part in 1788 to Theophilus Smith of Burslem who in 1787 had bought the other part, called the Oldershaws.[76] Smith demolished the house at Furlong and in 1791 built another on the Oldershaws to the north of Furlong Lane which he called Smithfield; he also built the village of Smithfield and in 1793 opened a pottery works there on the south side of the road.[77] He was declared bankrupt in 1800,[78] and in 1801 his assignees sold the whole estate to John Breeze who moved there from Burslem and renamed it Greenfield.[79] John's son Jesse succeeded in 1821, and in 1826 Jesse was succeeded by his daughters Jane, who in 1827 married William Adams (the son of William Adams of Bagnall and Fenton), and Mary, who in 1834 married William's brother Edward.[80] William and Jane lived at Greenfield after their marriage in 1827,[81] and by agreement between William and Edward and their wives in 1858 the Greenfield estate was assigned to the heirs of William and Jane.[82] In addition to working the factory and colliery there William farmed some 40 acres.[83] In 1902 his son William (succ. 1865) sold some land on the south-east of the estate to form part of the new Tunstall Park.[84] Shortly before 1908 the hall was demolished to make way for further coal mining.[85] The site of Greenfield Hall and its park is now occupied by a housing estate.[86] The hall, a brick building with two original wings and with additions of 1842, stood some 400 yards east of Christ Church, and the grounds were noted for their trees, lawns, and, in the time of Theophilus Smith, private swimming-bath.[87]

A house and 12 acres of land called the Will Flats on the south side of the present Furlong Lane were owned by the six daughters and coheirs of Thomas Child of Tunstall by 1735. In that year Jane the eldest sister and her husband George Booth bought up the other five interests.[88] By 1745 Booth had established a pottery works there but in that year sold the house, land, and works to John Bourne of Newcastle-under-Lyme who the following year sold the whole estate to Thomas Glass, a potter of Shelton.[89] Glass leased it to George Booth and his son Thomas and in 1757 sold it to John Kinsey of Cheshire.[90] After Kinsey's death in 1784 it was divided between his nephew Thomas Kinsey and another relative, Mary Hughes.[91] These two families, by various sales between 1784 and 1794, disposed of the estate to William Adams, a potter of Burslem, son of Edward Adams of Bagnall and tenant of the house and works from 1779.[92] Adams, having rebuilt the factory by 1786, had by the following year built the new Greengates House on a site to the west of the factory and opposite the later Christ Church.[93] The house, a solid three-story building, stood in wooded grounds.[94] William's youngest son, Benjamin Adams, who succeeded in 1805, sold the house and works to John Meir in 1822[95] and the property remained with the Meirs until 1896 when it became part of the Adams's family business.[96] Greengates House was bought in 1922 by the guardians of the Wolstanton and Burslem Union[97] who, however, shortly afterwards sold it to the Tunstall War Memorial Committee for conversion to a hospital.[98] This scheme, however, was abandoned,[99] and the house had been demolished by 1925.[1]

There were two farms at Holly Wall within the Sneyds' portion of Tunstall manor in at least the 17th and 18th centuries.[2] The first was held by William Bourne of Yew Tree in 1619 when it was enfranchised, and it was still in the Bourne family in 1735.[3] The second farm was held by the Broad family between at least 1642 and 1713[4] and probably by the Baddeley family in the early 1720's.[5] In 1839 Ralph Sneyd owned a 46-acre farm at Holly Wall which was then in the hands of a tenant.[6] Before the break-up of the Keele estate in 1950 it had been sold

[72] U.C.N.S., Sneyd MSS., Ct. R. 7/34 (1719). The family property divided in 1680 included Tunstall House in Tunstall which was assigned to John and Alice: H. Mus., Heathcote papers, xxi. 2, which does not, however, appear to mention the Furlong estate.
[73] Adams, *Adams Family*, 345.   [74] Ibid.
[75] Ibid. 346.   [76] Ibid.
[77] Ibid. 346–7 and plate facing p. 348; Ward, *Stoke*, 102. For the history of the pottery see p. 100.
[78] H. Mus., Heathcote papers, xviii. 15.
[79] Adams, *Adams Family*, 347–8; Adams, *N. Staffs. Families*, 67; see p. 83, n. 26. He may have been the tenant of the potworks by 1795: see p. 100, n. 74.
[80] Adams, *Adams Family*, 347 and pedigree between pp. 292 and 293; Adams, *N. Staffs. Families*, 72; Ward, *Stoke*, 88.
[81] Adams, *Adams Family*, 338, 342; most of their married life, however, was spent in Liverpool.
[82] Ibid. 344, 347, and additions and corrections p. G.
[83] Ibid. 341, 343. Neither pottery nor colliery was in operation in 1829: S. Shaw, *Staffs. Potteries* (1829), 20.
[84] Adams, *Adams Family*, 347; see p. 81.
[85] Adams, *Wolstanton*, 91.
[86] See p. 83.
[87] Adams, *Adams Family*, 343 and illustrations facing pp. 344, 348, 354; Ward, *Stoke*, 102; Shaw, *Staffs. Potteries*, 20; Hargreaves, *Map of Staffs. Potteries*.
[88] Adams, *Adams Family*, 374.
[89] Ibid. For the Greengates Pottery see p. 99.
[90] Adams, *Adams Family*, 374–5.

[91] Ibid. 375.   [92] Ibid. 374, 375.
[93] Ibid. and illus. facing p. 373.
[94] *William Adams*, ed. W. Turner (1923), 165–6. Ward, *Stoke*, 103, described it as 'handsome'.
[95] Adams, *Adams Family*, 382; Ward, *Stoke*, 103.
[96] Lich. Dioc. Regy., Tithe Maps and Appt., Wolstanton; White, *Dir. Staffs.* (1834, 1851); Adams, *Adams Family*, 382. The eldest surviving brother, Wm., d. a month after his father: ibid. pedigree between pp. 380 and 381.
[97] H.R.L., Wolstanton and Burslem Union Mins. 1919–22, pp. 398, 443.
[98] Ibid. p. 481; Warrillow, *Stoke*, 364.
[99] Warrillow, *Stoke*, 364. The funds raised were applied instead to the new Haywood Hospital, Burslem: ibid.; see p. 128.
[1] Ex inf. Wm. Adams & Sons (Potters) Ltd., Tunstall (1958).
[2] For the holy well and hermitage in the 12th cent. see p. 54, and for Lord Audley's house at Holly Wall in the 14th cent. see p. 87.
[3] W.S.L., D. 1798, bdle. 195; E 134/9 Geo. II Mich./17, mm. 1, 2, 7. It was leased out by the Bournes.
[4] Ward, *Stoke*, app. p. viii; *Wolstanton Par. Reg.* i. 73–186, *passim*; W.S.L. 305/40; W.S.L., D. 1788, P. 39, B. 4; P. 43, B. 2.
[5] U.C.N.S., Sneyd MSS., Hulton deeds, rentals of 1722 and 1723.
[6] Lich. Dioc. Regy., Tithe Maps and Appt., Wolstanton.

to a Mr. Davis and was bought from him in 1950 by Alfred Meakin (Tunstall) Ltd.[7] Other lands at Holly Wall were owned by the Williamsons in 1839.[8] On the break-up of the Williamson estate in 1950 a second farm there was bought by Meakin Ltd. which now owns over 150 acres in the Holly Wall area.[9]

The estate called Newfield was held in 1627 by Thomas Baddeley[10] whose family had land in Tunstall by the 13th century.[11] Newfield remained with the Baddeleys[12] until the death in 1770 of Thomas Baddeley who had settled it on his nephew Captain (later Admiral) Smith Child in 1764.[13] The admiral, who rebuilt the hall c. 1770,[14] died at Newfield in 1813,[15] and the estate, to which a pottery works had been added before 1800,[16] passed to his grandson Smith Child, a minor.[17] Newfield Hall was occupied from c. 1813 until 1824 or 1825 by John Henry Clive, later of Chell and of Clanway, who as the admiral's partner managed the estate and pottery works for the heir.[18] Although Smith Child was still living there in 1838,[19] the hall was divided into tenements soon afterwards and the timber in the grounds was cut down.[20] In 1858 the house and adjoining land were sold for mining purposes to William Adams [21] whose son bought the pottery works also in 1872.[22] Parts of the estate were sold by the family shortly before 1930,[23] but c. 1945 they still owned the hall. It was by then unoccupied and was demolished c. 1948.[24] The site is now (1958) occupied as a warehouse by Beresford Transport Ltd., who also use one of the outbuildings, probably the former stables, as a garage.[25] A view of Newfield Hall in 1770[26] shows it to have been a large three-storied house with a seven-bay side elevation and a five-bay entrance front, the latter approached by a carriage sweep.

The Park House in Oldcott and a freehold estate attached were granted to Richard, son of John Colclough, by Lord Audley in 1336 or 1337.[27] From at least 1514 the Rowley family were living at the Park (also known as Black Park at that time), but by 1544 the house and lands had passed to Thomas Burslem, the husband of Joan, daughter and heir of John Rowley of Black Park.[28] Other members of the Rowley family proceeded to challenge the claim first of Thomas Burslem and later of his son John, and it was not until 1574 that John secured final acknowledgement of his right.[29] John's son Thomas died in 1619 and the 84-acre Park estate passed to his second son Robert, who was living there in 1616.[30] Robert was succeeded in 1664 by his son John, and on John's death in 1680 the estate went to his daughter Elizabeth, the wife of Philip Machin of Botteslow.[31] Philip died in 1695.[32] A Thomas Machin was living there in 1709[33] and a 'Mr. Machin' in 1719,[34] presumably Thomas's son John who died there in 1733.[35] The estate passed into the Baddeley family of Newfield when Elizabeth daughter of Philip and Elizabeth Machin married Randle Baddeley in 1699. Afterwards it passed into the Child family.[36] The Park farm then descended in that family until its sale about the mid-1950's by Sir Smith Hill Child to Messrs. J. and F. T. McEllin Ltd., builders, of Bignall End.[37] It is still (1960) being worked as a farm. The present house appears to have been built in 1840 by Smith Child. The porch, which incorporates brick ornament similar to that at St. John's, Goldenhill, carries a date tablet with his initials.

Yeld Hill in Ravenscliffe, occupied by a Richard Turner in 1628,[38] was the home of the Tunstall family between at least 1632 and 1713.[39] In 1829 it was owned by Thomas Kinnersley.[40] Some ten years later it was a 70-acre farm owned by Edward Kinnersley and occupied by John Grey.[41] By 1932 it was owned by the Condliffe family who sold it c. 1958 to Mr. A. Hollins.[42] The farmhouse appears to date from the late 18th or early 19th century.

The Yew Tree estate to the south-west of what is

[7] Ex inf. Mr. C. Boden, Holly Wall (1960).
[8] Lich. Dioc. Regy., Tithe Maps and Appt., Wolstanton.
[9] Ex inf. Mr. Boden. He has a copy of the Williamson Estate Sale Catalogue (30 Aug. 1950) in his possession. Meakin Ltd. opened a new works nearby in 1957: see p. 101.   [10] Ward, Stoke, app. p. viii.
[11] Ibid. 87 (pedigree); Close R. 1268–72, 388; S.H.C. N.S. x (1), 17.
[12] Wolstanton Par. Reg. i. 15, 78; Tunstall Ct. R. (T.N.S.F.C. lxvi), 139.
[13] Ward, Stoke, 85–87; Adams, Wolstanton, 103; Wolstanton Par. Reg. ii. 389.
[14] Shaw, Staffs. Potteries, 20; Adams, Wolstanton, 103.
[15] Ward, Stoke, 85.
[16] See p. 101.
[17] Ward, Stoke, 85, 87; Adams, Clive, 18. Part at least of the family property was already in the hands of Admiral Smith Child's grandson John Child in 1807 but he d. in 1811: Ward, Stoke, 87; see p. 212.
[18] Adams, Clive, 3, 9, 18, 19; see p. 101.
[19] White, Dir. Staffs. (1834); Ward, Stoke, 85; Lich. Dioc. Regy., Tithe Maps and Appt., Wolstanton. Newfield Hall had been altered and modernized by 1838: Ward, Stoke, 102, where it is described as 'plain and unpretentious'.
[20] White, Dir. Staffs. (1851); W. Scarratt, Old Times in the Potteries, 43.
[21] Adams, Adams Family, 341.
[22] Ibid. 364; see p. 101.
[23] Adams, Adams Family, 78; the pottery was sold c. 1895.
[24] E. J. D. Warrilow, 'The Passing of Newfield Hall' (Staffs. Life, Feb. 1948); J. Jack, The Church on the Hill (1944), 17; Adams, Clive, 19; ex inf. Beresford Transport Ltd. (1958).
[25] Ex inf. Beresford Transport Ltd.

[26] H.R.L., S.I. 860.
[27] U.C.N.S., Sneyd MSS., Oldcott Deeds, endorsement on a grant by Francis Bowyer of Knypersley to Robt. Burslem of the Park, 2 Feb. 18 Jas. I, 'as by the original deeds appeareth'; S.H.C. v (2), 86.
[28] C 1/952/73; Tunstall Ct. R. (T.N.S.F.C. lx), 38, 46. In 1512 a Thos. Smith lived there: ibid. 33.
[29] C 1/952/73; C 1/1154/42–45; S.H.C. 1931, 195–6; S.H.C. xiv (1), 165.
[30] Wedgwood, Wedgwood Family, 69, 71–72, and pedigree following; Adams, Adams Family, 69–71; Tunstall Ct. R. (T.N.S.F.C. lxiii), 53, 82; ibid. lxiv. 110, 111, 121; S.H.C. N.S. vii. 215.
[31] Adams, Adams Family, 70–71; Tunstall Ct. R. (T.N.S.F.C. lxvi), 125.   [32] Wolstanton Par. Reg. i. 183.
[33] Adams, Adams Family, 345.
[34] U.C.N.S., Sneyd MSS., Ct. R. 7/34 (1719).
[35] Adams, Adams Family, 345; Wolstanton Par. Reg. i. 276. Thos. d. in 1716: ibid. 234.
[36] Adams, Adams Family, 70; Ward, Stoke, 87; Wolstanton Par. Reg. i. 190.
[37] Lich. Dioc. Regy., Tithe Maps and Appt., Wolstanton; Ward, Stoke, 127; Burke, Peerage (1949), 402–3; ex inf. the tenant (1958).
[38] W.S.L., D. 788 (32), bdle. 8.
[39] Wolstanton Par. Reg. i. 17 (where it is called Field Hill), 110, 119; S.H.C. 1919, 263; W.S.L., D. 1788, P. 33, B. 1; ibid. P. 43, B. 2. Thos. Cartwright of Yeld Hill occurs in 1675 and John Innsball (?Innshall) of Yeld Hill in 1692: Wolstanton Par. Reg. i. 125, 173.
[40] S.R.O., Q/RPl 1829.
[41] Lich. Dioc. Regy., Tithe Maps and Appt., Wolstanton; White, Dir. Staffs. (1834). Grey was still the tenant in 1851: ibid. (1851).
[42] Ex inf. Mrs. Hollins (1958); Kelly's Dir. Staffs. (1932, 1940).

now Goldenhill was the home of a branch of the Bourne family between at least 1569 and 1680, and was enfranchised by the Sneyds in 1619.[43] It was held in the early 18th century by Henry Bourne who leased it to a John Malkin;[44] from *c.* 1715 the tenant was Abraham Scott, a potter (d. 1737), whose widow Hannah was living there in 1742.[45] On the death of Henry Bourne after 1710 the estate passed to his daughter Elizabeth, wife of Robert Holt.[46] She was dead by 1725; her heir was Elizabeth, daughter of James Holt, who married James Rhode and, after his death in 1728 or 1729, a Davison, probably William Davison.[47] In 1742 William Davison agreed to sell the Yew Tree estate to Ralph Moreton.[48] In 1829 it was owned by Mary Moreton and held by George Mountford[49] and some ten years later the 96-acre farm was owned by Messrs. Sparrow and Moreton and occupied by Joseph Mountford,[50] still tenant in 1854.[51] The house and part of the farm were bought *c.* 1930 by the Vicar of Goldenhill for the extension of the burial ground attached to St. John's Church, but soon afterwards some of this land was incorporated in a new housing estate.[52] The 19th-century farmhouse, with brick barns probably of an earlier date, still (1960) stands as part of a scrap-metal yard.

CHURCHES. Tunstall, Oldcott, Ravenscliffe, and Chell originally formed part of the chapelry of Newchapel within the ancient parish of Wolstanton.[53] In the 12th century there was evidently a holy well and hermitage at Tunstall, the property of Trentham Priory, and this presumably lay in the district now known as Holly Wall.[54] By 1366 the lord of Tunstall manor had a chapel in his house at Holly Wall.[55] A graveyard at Chell was mentioned in 1569.[56] There does not, however, appear to have been a church in Tunstall before the 19th century.[57]

CHRIST CHURCH, Tunstall, was built in 1831–2; £3,000 of the total cost was provided by parliamentary grant and the remaining £1,000 by private subscription. The burial ground was given by Ralph Sneyd.[58] A parish consisting of Tunstall, Oldcott, and Ravenscliffe was created in 1837.[59] The living, a perpetual curacy until 1868 when it was styled a vicarage,[60] was in the gift of the Sneyds[61] until its transfer *c.* 1890 to the Bishop of Lichfield[62] who still holds it.[63] The benefice was augmented by a grant of £400 from Queen Anne's Bounty in 1837.[64] The church is built of Chell stone[65] and was designed by Francis Bedford[66] in a mixture of Gothic styles, the windows being single or paired lancets and the tower being surmounted by an embattled parapet, angle pinnacles, and an octagonal spire. The base of the tower forms the central bay of a vestibule stretching across the west end of the wide nave. Originally there was a small chancel and the nave had galleries on three sides.[67] In 1885–6 extensions were made at the east end of the church to the design of A. R. Wood.[68] They include two shallow transepts and a larger chancel flanked by a south chapel and by an organ chamber. The clock in the tower was given by the parishioners in 1916.[69] The single bell of 1833 was replaced in 1856 by a peal of six bells;[70] two more were added early in the 20th century,[71] and the whole peal was rehung in 1916.[72] The first vicarage house was built in Lyndhurst Street (now Hannah Street) in 1840, but having become unsafe through subsidence it was replaced by a new house in Church Street (now Dunning Street) *c.* 1889.[73] The present vicarage is Park House, Stanley Street.[74]

Five mission centres have been founded from Christ Church: Sandyford Mission *c.* 1880–*c.* 1901;[75] the Home Mission *c.* 1887–*c.* 1893,[76] which was evidently replaced by Lyndhurst Street (now Hannah Street) Mission opened *c.* 1893,[77] itself replaced in 1906 or 1907 by the present St. Aidan's Mission Church, Summerbank Road;[78] and Goodfellow Street Mission *c.* 1905–*c.* 1919.[79]

The church of *ST. JOHN THE EVANGELIST*

[43] *Tunstall Ct. R.* (*T.N.S.F.C.* lxii), 59; ibid. lxiii, lxiv, *passim*; *Wolstanton Par. Reg.* i. 14–140, *passim*; U.C.N.S., Sneyd MSS., Oldcott Deeds; W.S.L., D. 1798, bdle. 195.
[44] W.S.L., D. 1798, bdle. 195.
[45] Ibid.; E 134/9 Geo. II Mich./17, mm. 1, 2, 7; *Wolstanton Par. Reg.* i. 285, 315.
[46] W.S.L., D. 1798, bdle. 195.
[47] Ibid.; E 134/9 Geo. II Mich./17, m.1.
[48] W.S.L., D. 1798, bdle. 195.
[49] S.R.O., Q/RPl 1829.
[50] Lich. Dioc. Regy., Tithe Maps and Appt., Wolstanton.
[51] White, *Dir. Staffs.* (1851); *P.O. Dir. Staffs.* (1854).
[52] Jack, *The Church on the Hill*, 53; see p. 83.
[53] Newchapel Par. Reg., introd. n. on chapelry (from transcript in W.S.L., f. 4); *Wolstanton Par. Reg.* (Staffs. Par. Reg. Soc.), i, p. x. This chapelry had evidently been formed by 1534: *S.H.C.* 1915, 318, 320.
[54] *S.H.C.* xi. 303.
[55] *Tunstall Ct. R.* (*T.N.S.F.C.* lix), 64.
[56] Ibid. lxii. 64.
[57] The only possible evidence to the contrary is the former open field called Church Field, which evidently lay to the W. of the town, and the discovery at various times of human bones in that area: Ward, *Stoke*, 88; see p. 98.
[58] Ward, *Stoke*, 90–92; H.O. 129/15/370/2/8; Lich. Dioc. Regy. Bp.'s Reg. I, pp. 556–69.
[59] *Lond. Gaz.* 1837, p. 1194; *Census*, 1841.
[60] *Lich. Dioc. Ch. Cal.* (1868, 1869).
[61] Ibid. (1868, 1890); White, *Dir. Staffs.* (1834); Ward, *Stoke*, 92.
[62] *Lich. Dioc. Ch. Cal.* (1891); Lich. Dioc. Regy., Bp.'s Reg. 35, pp. 118, 184.
[63] *Lich. Dioc. Dir.* (1959).
[64] C. Hodgson, *An Acct. of the Augmentation of Small Livings by the Governors of the Bounty of Queen Anne* (1845), p. ccxcviii. [65] Ward, *Stoke*, 91.
[66] H. M. Colvin, *Biog. Dict. Eng. Architects*, 70.
[67] W.S.L., Staffs. Views, xi, p. 71 (view of E. end *c.* 1838); Lich. Dioc. Regy., Bp.'s Reg. I, p. 560.
[68] *Kelly's Dir. Staffs.* (1890); Lich. Dioc. Regy., Bp.'s Reg. S, pp. 725–8; *Lich. Dioc. Mag.* (1883), 174; Colvin, *Biog. Dict. Eng. Architects*, 70.
[69] Tablet at W. end of nave.
[70] Lich. Dioc. Regy., Bp.'s Reg. I, p. 560; C. Lynam, *Ch. Bells Staffs.* 58. It was transferred to the new church of St. Mary: see below.
[71] Between 1900 and 1908: *Kelly's Dir. Staffs.* (1900, 1908).
[72] Tablet at W. end of nave.
[73] W. J. Harper, *Bygone Tunstall*, 37 (copy among W.S.L. pamphs. *sub* Tunstall). The house used before 1840 was in the SW. part of the town near the later St. Mary's Church: ibid.
[74] Tablet *in situ*.
[75] *Lich. Dioc. and Ch. Cal.* (1881, 1901).
[76] Ibid. (1887, 1893).
[77] Ibid. (1894, 1906).
[78] Ibid. (1907); Lich. Dioc. Regy., Bp.'s Reg. 37, pp. 11–12; *Lich. Dioc. Dir.* (1959). Although the foundation stone of the church was laid in 1906 (inscription on stone), the church was not consecrated until 1914: *Staffs. Advertiser*, 10 Oct. 1914.
[79] *Lich. Dioc. Ch. Cal.* (1906, 1919). A mission of St. Barnabas is mentioned in its place in the list of missions in 1920: ibid. (1920).

at Goldenhill was built in 1840–1 at a cost of £2,000 which was met by subscription and a grant from the Lichfield Church Extension Society.[80] In 1843 a parish covering Oldcott and Ravenscliffe was formed out of Christ Church parish.[81] The right of appointing the minister, even before the creation of the parish, was granted to Smith Child of Newfield in recognition of his benefactions to the new church.[82] He retained the patronage of the perpetual curacy until 1853 when, as the condition of an augmentation of the endowment by the Ecclesiastical Commissioners, the right of presentation was transferred to the Bishop of Lichfield.[83] The bishop is still the patron.[84] The benefice has been styled a vicarage since 1868.[85] All pew-rents were abolished in 1884, and since the proceeds had formed part of the vicar's income a charge of £40 was made on the offertory instead.[86] The church is built of brick and externally has 'Norman' detail carried out in vitreous brickwork. The windows are round-headed with stone shafts in the jambs. The architect was 'Mr. Stanley of Shelton'.[87] The building consists of a wide nave with an organ gallery at its west end, a very small projecting chancel, and a spired west tower. A 'convenient' vestry was added in 1880[88] but was replaced by a new north-west vestry in 1891.[89] The vicarage house lies to the south of the church.

The present mission chapel at Ravenscliffe was opened from St. John's c. 1905.[90]

The church of *ST. MARY THE VIRGIN* in the south-western part of Tunstall was completed in 1859.[91] A parish was formed out of the parishes of Christ Church, Tunstall, and St. Paul, Burslem, in 1881.[92] The patronage of the vicarage has remained in the hands of the Bishop of Lichfield.[93] The building consists of an aisled and clerestoried nave with a west gallery, a chancel flanked by a north-east tower and south-east chapel, and a north porch. It is built in the 'Early English' style and is of dark red brick with blue-brick dressings and ornament. The tall

tower and broach spire, also of brick, were erected at the expense of John Wedg Wood of the Big House, Burslem, and the Woodlands Pottery, Tunstall (d. 1857).[94] The single bell, dated 1833, was transferred from Christ Church, Tunstall, in 1856.[95] To commemorate the jubilee of the church in 1909 the space below the gallery was enclosed as a vestry and the original south-east vestry was converted into a chapel.[96] The vicarage house opposite the church was built in 1883.[97]

A mission centre in Williamson Street was opened from St. Mary's c. 1884 but was evidently closed within a year.[98] In 1905 a new mission was opened in Williamson Street, apparently in a stable loft.[99] It was closed in 1906 when the present church of *ST. CHAD* was opened nearby in King William Street.[1] A conventional district was formed out of the parishes of Christ Church and St. Mary in 1920 under a curate-in-charge nominated by the bishop.[2] The church is of brick and consists of an aisleless nave and a shallow chancel with a Lady chapel on the south. There are two bells, one a memorial to Louisa Wain, the foundress of the church.[3] A new church was begun on a site to the south in 1931, but it was never completed beyond the shell. It was dismantled c. 1947 and the present church hall built on the site in 1954.[4]

Another mission-centre was founded from St. Mary's in Plex Street c. 1884 but was closed within a year. A new centre was opened there c. 1901 and remained in use until c. 1948.[5]

A mission room was established at Chell within the parish of St. James, Newchapel, in 1882. It was replaced in 1894 by the present church of *ST. MICHAEL AND ALL ANGELS* on an adjoining site.[6] The room was retained as a Sunday school.[7] A parish covering Great and Little Chell, Pitts Hill, Chell Heath, Turnhurst, and Fegg Hayes was formed out of the parish of St. James in 1925.[8] The living, a perpetual curacy, has remained in the gift of a

[80] Jack, *The Church on the Hill*, 10–11, 13; Lich. Dioc. Regy., Bp.'s Reg. M, pp. 1–23; H.O. 129/15/370; (C. Hodson, *An Acct. of the Augmentation of Small Livings by the Governors of the Bounty of Queen Anne* (1845), pp. xi, xxxix, xlix of 1856 supplement.
[81] Jack, *The Church on the Hill*, 14; *Wolstanton Par. Reg.* i, p. x. Part of the parish was assigned to the new parish of St. Thomas, Kidsgrove, in 1853: *Lond. Gaz.* 1853, p. 71.
[82] Lich. Dioc. Regy., Bp.'s Reg. L, pp. 378–80.
[83] Jack, *The Church on the Hill*, 14; Lich. Dioc. Regy., Bp.'s Reg. 30, p. 230. For the secession following Bp. Selwyn's presentation of a Tractarian in 1873 see p. 287.
[84] *Lich. Dioc. Dir.* (1959).
[85] Ibid.; *Lich. Dioc. Ch. Cal.* (1868; 1869).
[86] Harper, *Bygone Tunstall*, 76; Lich. Dioc. Regy., Bp.'s Reg. M, p. 7.
[87] *Staffs. Advertiser*, 14 Aug. 1841.
[88] *Lich. Dioc. Mag.* (Dec. 1880). At the same time the E. end was raised, a 'hot-water apparatus' was installed to heat the church and—'best alteration of all'—the doors of the pews were removed: ibid.
[89] Ibid. (1891), 219.
[90] *Lich. Dioc. Ch. Cal.* (1906); Jack, *The Church on the Hill*, 36; *Lich. Dioc. Dir.* (1959).
[91] *P.O. Dir. Staffs.* (1868); Lich. Dioc. Regy., Bp.'s Reg. Q, pp. 336–41. By 1881 there was accommodation for 900: *Lich. Dioc. Ch. Cal.* (1881).
[92] *Lond. Gaz.* 1881, p. 6819. Founded as a chapel-of-ease to Christ Church it could become a district church only after the next voidance of the mother church, which occurred in 1880: Lich. Dioc. Regy., Bp.'s Reg. Q, pp. 336–41. Another part of Christ Church parish was added in 1913: *Kelly's Dir. Staffs.* (1916).
[93] *Lich. Dioc. Ch. Cal.* (1883); *Lich. Dioc. Dir.* (1959).

[94] Tablet in church which also states that John Wedg Wood (d. 1857) subscribed to the building fund of the church and left money to it by will; F. Falkner, *Wood Family of Burslem*, pedigree; see p. 117. Extensive improvements to the church were carried out in 1885: *Lich. Dioc. Mag.* (1885), 164.
[95] Lynam, *Ch. Bells Staffs.* 58; Harper, *Bygone Tunstall*, 32.
[96] St. Mary's Vestry, Churchwardens' Acct. Bk. 1860–1918, 15 Apr. 1909. Other alterations were carried out in 1932: *Kelly's Dir. Staffs.* (1940).
[97] Date-stone on house; Lich. Dioc. Regy., Bp.'s Reg. S, p. 636. [98] *Lich. Dioc. Ch. Cal.* (1885).
[99] Ibid. (1905); Lich. Dioc. Regy., Bp.'s Reg. 36, pp. 469–70; *Evening Sentinel*, 9 Apr. 1947. Services are said to have been held in the kitchen of a house in Pinnox St. at some date before 1905: ibid.
[1] Lich. Dioc. Regy., Bp.'s Reg. 36, pp. 502–4; date on foundation stone.
[2] Lich. Dioc. Regy., Bp.'s Reg. 38, pp. 121–2, 318–19.
[3] Plaque in church.
[4] *Evening Sentinel*, 9 Apr. 1947; Char. Com. files. The hall was previously in Pinnox St.
[5] *Lich. Dioc. Ch. Cal.* (1885, 1902); *Lich. Dioc. Dir.* (1948–9).
[6] *Lich. Dioc. Mag.* (1893), 116–17; *Lich. Dioc. Ch. Cal.* (1884, 1895); *Staffs. Advertiser*, 10 Aug. 1929; date on foundation stone of the mission hall. The room was enlarged in 1887: *Kelly's Dir. Staffs.* (1892).
[7] *Staffs. Advertiser*, 10 Aug. 1929. New Sunday sch. premises were begun in that year (ibid.), and the room is now used as a parish hall.
[8] Lich. Dioc. Regy., Bp.'s Reg. 39, pp. 301–2; *Kelly's Dir. Staffs.* (1924, 1928).

group of trustees including the Bishop of Lichfield.[9] The church is of red brick and consists of a nave and chancel; it has lancet windows and a bell-cote containing one bell.

LOCAL GOVERNMENT AND PUBLIC SER-VICES. The area covered by the Tunstall Urban District in 1910 was parochially within Wolstanton and manorially part of Tunstall manor.[10] By the early 19th century the machinery of parochial and manorial government was inadequate for the needs of the growing town, particularly as the manorial court lapsed in 1813,[11] but it was only after 40 years of piecemeal experiment that a local board with general powers of government was set up.

The first experiment came in 1816 when the principal inhabitants of the area decided to elect one of themselves as chief constable mainly for purposes of policing—'to promote general good order and tranquillity and stop the increase of drunkenness and disorder'.[12] With the revival of the court leet in 1826 the chief constable seems to have been appointed annually by the court on the recommendation of the chief inhabitants until the establishment of the local board in 1855.[13] As an attempt at policing the experiment failed for lack of money,[14] but the first chief constable, J. H. Clive of Newfield Hall, was largely responsible for the laying out of the market-place and the building there of a town hall in 1816.[15] In 1832 the Tunstall Improvement Society was estab-lished to preserve public order and improve the streets, but this too soon failed for want of funds.[16] During the winter of 1837–8 more gas-lighting and watching of the streets was provided after a public meeting had authorized a rate for the purpose under the Watching and Lighting Act of 1830, but local opposition was able to bring even this small im-provement to an end in 1838.[17] A company was set up in 1840 to run the market,[18] and in 1847 a body of eighteen improvement commissioners equipped with rating powers was established for 'paving, lighting, watching, watering, cleaning, draining, and improving' the township of Tunstall and for the management of the market.[19] In 1855 the township was placed under the control of the Tunstall Local Board of Health consisting of twenty-four elected

members.[20] Government by the board, with the chair-man acting as chief bailiff, lasted until 1894 when the Tunstall portion of Wolstanton ancient parish be-came an urban district and the Goldenhill and Great Chell portions two civil parishes; Goldenhill com-prised the township of Oldcott, with that part of Ravenscliffe not in Kidsgrove Urban District, and Great Chell the townships of Chell and Wedgwood.[21] In 1895 the urban district was divided into two wards, North and South, with twelve members each. A new Chell ward with three members was added in 1900 after the transfer of Pitts Hill from Great Chell parish to the urban district in 1899. After the addi-tion of Goldenhill and most of Chell in 1904, there were four wards, North with nine members, South with ten, Chell with three, and Goldenhill with five.[22] By 1886 the Board of Health was working through four regular committees—finance, sewers (sanita-tion from 1888), highways, and library.[23] The urban district council had seven by 1904—finance and general purposes, highways and buildings, sanita-tion, public buildings, park, free library, and higher education; the last was replaced in 1905 by the education committee.[24] Tunstall formed three wards of the new county borough in 1910, with a represen-tation of three aldermen and nine councillors.[25]

The town hall and court house of 1816 in the market square consisted of two floors. The western end of the ground floor was used as a lock-up and a place for keeping two fire engines, while the arched eastern end provided storage space for the market stalls. The upper floor formed a hall for public business and by 1840 a subscription newspaper room also.[26] There was a partial rebuilding in 1857.[27] The present town hall was erected in High Street opposite the east end of Tower Square in 1883–5,[28] and the old hall was converted in 1885 into a free library and reading room.[29] It was demolished in 1891 or 1892,[30] and the site is now occupied by a clock tower erected in honour of Sir Smith Child in 1893.[31]

A chain of office for the chief bailiff and chairman of the urban district council was presented in 1897 by W. Boulton, chief bailiff and chairman 1896–7, to commemorate the Diamond Jubilee.[32]

Each of the townships in the Tunstall area was originally represented at the Tunstall leet by one frank-pledge or headborough appointed by the

[9] Lich. Dioc. Regy., Bp.'s Reg. 39, pp. 301–2; _Lich. Dioc. Ch. Cal._ (1926); _Lich. Dioc. Dir._ (1959).
[10] For the limits of the area here treated see p. 81. For the manorial hist. see pp. 86 sqq.
[11] See p. 88.
[12] Ward, _Stoke_, 93–94.
[13] Ibid. 78; U.C.N.S., Sneyd MSS., Ct. R. 7/41; _Staffs. Advertiser_, 2 Nov. 1839; White, _Dir. Staffs._ (1851).
[14] Ward, _Stoke_, 104.
[15] Ibid. 94, and app. pp. xi–xii; see pp. 81, 98.
[16] Ward, _Stoke_, 104.
[17] Ibid. 104–5.
[18] See p. 98.
[19] Tunstall Improvement Act 1847, 10 & 11 Vic. c. 252 (local and personal). A rate of 2s. 6d. in the £ could be levied if approved by 5 of the commissioners and a rate of 3s. 6d. if approved by a meeting of the ratepayers. The eligibility of electors and commissioners alike depended on property qualifications.
[20] The Public Health Supplemental Act, 1855, 18 & 19 Vic. c. 125.
[21] Local Govt. Board Order no. 31,833, 30 Oct. 1894, confirming Staffs. County Counc. Order 21 July 1894 (copy of each with the Clerk of the Staffs. County Counc.).
[22] Staffs. County Counc. Orders 18 May 1895 and 13 Mar. 1900 and Provisional Order 23 Feb. 1904 (copy of

each with the Clerk of the Staffs. County Counc.); H.R.L., Tunstall U.D.C. Mins. 1903–9, pp. 70–71, 315; see p. 81.
[23] H.R.L., Tunstall Board of Health Mins. 1886–92, pp. 1, 2, 3, 78–79, 107. There was also a Jubilee Cttee. set up to consider how to commemorate Queen Victoria's Golden Jubilee: ibid. 17; the building of the Jubilee Buildings was the result: see pp. 85, 104.
[24] H.R.L., Tunstall U.D.C. Mins. 1903–9, pp. 77–78, 164–5, 177. These were the council's cttees. during the remainder of its existence: ibid. 1909–10, pp. 1, 57.
[25] _Stoke Counc. Year Bk._ (1915).
[26] Ward, _Stoke_, 94; U.C.N.S., Sneyd MSS., Ct. R. 7/41, Oct. 1840.
[27] P. W. L. Adams, _Wolstanton_, 102. For a view of c. 1885 see plate facing p. 104.
[28] _Staffs. Advertiser_, 31 Oct. 1885; inscription on build-ing; see p. 85.
[29] See p. 104.
[30] _Staffs. Advertiser_, 12 Sept. 1891; Adams, _Wolstanton_, 102; H.R.L., Tunstall Bd. of Health Mins. 1886–92, pp. 378, 390.
[31] Inscription on tower.
[32] T. Pape, 'Early Armorials of the Pottery Towns' (_Cox's Potteries Annual_, 1925), 20. The chairman of the U.D.C. retained the old office of chief bailiff: Warrillow, _Stoke_, 213–14.

court.[33] However, Tunstall township had two headboroughs or constables between at least 1808 and the early 1840's, Chell two from 1837, and Oldcott two in 1840; by the 1830's it was the custom for the chief inhabitants of these townships to recommend suitable persons for election by the court.[34] The constablewick of Tunstall—or Tunstall Court—covered the same area as the manor,[35] and between at least 1603 and 1757 a chief constable for this district was elected annually by the court;[36] it is likely, however, that the office had lapsed by the early 19th century.

The chief constable was at first intended to have a salaried police officer under him, but for lack of money none was appointed.[37] The watching of the streets was one of the objects of the similarly unsuccessful scheme of 1837–8.[38] By 1851 Tunstall had a police force consisting of an inspector and four county policemen, with a station in High Street; by 1860 the station had been moved to a building in Market Street formerly a farmhouse, and this was replaced in 1959 by the present police station in Malpass Street erected on the site of cottages demolished that year.[39] The town hall of 1816 included a lock-up at the western end of the ground floor.[40] The stocks standing in front of the eastern end were removed c. 1857.[41]

A stipendiary magistrate was appointed for the whole Potteries area in 1839 with provision for weekly sessions at Tunstall town hall. Tunstall and the other parts of Wolstanton parish lying within the parliamentary borough of Stoke were constituted one of the six rating divisions formed to support the new system.[42] Tunstall was at first within the county court district of Hanley, constituted in 1847, and under an order of 1858 sessions of the court were held at Tunstall.[43] In 1880 Tunstall was formed into a separate county court district[44] which by 1896, however, had become part of the Burslem district.[45]

PUBLIC HEALTH. Cleansing and drainage were among the responsibilities of the commissioners of 1847. Their powers, however, were stated not to extend to 'existing processes' employed by the factories and mines which had brought prosperity to Tunstall, despite the fact that such processes might be 'a nuisance or injurious to the health of the inhabitants'. Interference, it was held, might well lead to unemployment and the destruction of the town's prosperity, reducing it 'to its former insignificance'; provided that the nuisances were mitigated the justices were to ignore complaints.[46] Sewers were evidently being laid down from the mid-1850's,[47] but by the 1860's sewage disposal was one of the local board's main problems. The use of the Fowlea Brook and the canal brought complaints of pollution and the threat of legal action, and although a sewage-disposal works was being planned by 1866, it was not until 1878 that a works was opened by the board. This was situated to the south-west of the town beyond the canal, just over the Burslem boundary.[48] By the 1890's mining subsidence and the growth of the town had made the works inadequate, and early in the 20th century the present works was opened on an adjoining site to the north.[49] The works off Boathorse Road south-west of Goldenhill had been built by the early 1920's.[50] The replacement of privies by water-closets was organized by the council from the first years of the 20th century,[51] and a scavenging department was created in 1901.[52]

Restrictions were imposed on burials in the churchyards of Tunstall and Goldenhill in 1856, and burials at Tunstall were further restricted in 1867.[53] In 1866 a burial board was set up, but at first there was some difficulty in finding a site for a cemetery.[54] The present cemetery in the Clayhills area was opened in 1868.[55] At first just under 7 acres in area, it was extended by another 14 acres at the beginning of the 20th century.[56]

The public baths in the north end of the Jubilee Buildings were built in 1889–90, with the sanitary committee of the local board as the baths committee.[57]

OTHER PUBLIC SERVICES. In the early 19th century Tunstall's water-supply depended on a defective public pump and a few springs; the names of two of these springs, Lady Well and Round Well, survive as street names in the western part of the town. A portion of the town was also supplied by a system owned by a Mr. Hargreaves, but the inadequacy of all these sources was made very clear during the drought of 1835.[58] The Potteries Waterworks Company, formed in 1847, probably began to supply Tunstall in 1849, and in 1854 the company built a pumping station in High Street, Tunstall, and a

[33] Tunstall Ct. R. (T.N.S.F.C. lix–lvi), passim.
[34] [C. Shaw], When I was a Child (1903), 31; U.C.N.S., Sneyd MSS., Ct. R. 7/40, 7/41. Oldcott nominated 3 headboroughs in 1836: ibid. 7/41.
[35] S.H.C. vii (1), 206; x (1), 94–95; 1921, 158–62.
[36] Adams, Wolstanton, 93–97; Tunstall Ct. R. (T.N.S.F.C. lxiii), 51, 61.
[37] Ward, Stoke, 93–94, 104.   [38] Ibid. 104.
[39] White, Dir. Staffs. (1851); P.O. Dir. Staffs. (1860); Harper, Bygone Tunstall, 99; S.R.O., Q/APs 1; Warrillow, Stoke, 406.
[40] See p. 95.
[41] Harper, Bygone Tunstall, 50–51, 52; Scarratt, Old Times in the Potteries, 74; [Shaw], When I was a Child, 41–42.
[42] Act for more effectual execution of office of J.P., 2 & 3 Vic. c. 15; White, Dir. Staffs. (1851).
[43] Lond. Gaz. 1858, p. 4094; see p. 159.
[44] Lond. Gaz. 1880, p. 6095.
[45] Kelly's Dir. Staffs. (1896, 1908).
[46] Tunstall Improvement Act 1847, 10 & 11 Vic. c. 252 (local and personal).
[47] Warrillow, Stoke, 183.
[48] Keates and Ford's Potteries Dir. (1867), 279–80; Staffs. Sentinel, 24 Nov. 1898; H.R.L., Stoke Commrs.' Mins. 1855–65, 2 Apr. 1862.
[49] Staffs. Sentinel, 24 Nov. 1898; H.R.L., Tunstall U.D.C. Sanitary Cttee. Mins. 1899–1905, pp. 2, 19, 20–21, 46–47, 61–62, 75, 105–6, 116, 194.
[50] O.S. Map 6″ Staffs. xi NE. (1925).
[51] H.R.L., Tunstall U.D.C. Sanitary Cttee. Mins. 1899–1905, pp. 58, 134–260; 1905–10, passim.
[52] Ibid. 1899–1905, pp. 103, 106–8.
[53] Lond. Gaz. 1857, p. 2907; 1865, p. 2691; 1867, 17, 2923, 5874.
[54] H.R.L., Tunstall Burial Bd. Mins. 1866–79, p. 1; Keates and Ford's Potteries Dir. (1867), 280.
[55] Lich. Dioc. Regy., Bp.'s Reg. R, pp. 345–8; Kelly's Dir. Staffs. (1884).
[56] H.R.L., Tunstall Burial Board Mins. 1896–1910, pp. 323, 349, 352, 357–8, 364, 388, 398, 440, 496, 500. Only 8 acres were at first laid out. The new area contains the site of Broomhill House, owned by the Clives in the mid-19th cent. and pulled down probably in the 1860's: P. W. L. Adams, John Henry Clive, 90, 100, 103, 106; Malabar, Map of Tunstall (1863), showing the house.
[57] Staffs. Advertiser, 2 Aug. 1890; date '1889' on building; H.R.L., Tunstall Board of Health Mins. 1886–92, pp. 98, 267.
[58] Ward, Stoke, 104; Pure and Wholesome Water for 100 Years, 1849–1949, 9 (copy in H.R.L.); Warrillow, Stoke, 160, 162.

reservoir in Goldenhill for the benefit of Goldenhill and Kidsgrove.[59]

Gas was supplied to Tunstall from the works of the British Gaslight Company at Shelton by 1837, and in the following winter more street lighting was provided out of the rate levied for improved lighting and watching. Although this improvement had to be discontinued because of local opposition, the private use of gaslighting was then spreading,[60] and in 1852 the British Gaslight Company opened a new works at Brownhills to serve the Tunstall area.[61] In 1857 or 1858 the company came to an agreement with the Burslem and Tunstall Gas Company whereby the latter waived its statutory rights in Tunstall, which it had not then used, and in return the British Gaslight Company sold to the other company all its installations in Burslem, other than the mains running to Tunstall.[62] Tunstall's gas supply thus continued in the hands of the British Gaslight Company until 1922 when the company was acquired by Stoke Corporation.[63]

Abortive efforts were made to supply electricity to Tunstall in 1890 and again in 1900.[64] In 1905 a supply became available from the new works of Burslem Corporation.[65]

After the building of the town hall in 1816 two fire engines were kept there,[66] and their maintenance was one of the aims of the unsuccessful Tunstall Improvement Society of 1832.[67] Responsibility passed to the local board[68] which opened a new station in the Jubilee Buildings in 1890 or 1891.[69] This station was closed in 1926 when the Tunstall area became the responsibility of the Burslem brigade.[70]

Originally the upkeep of the ancient highways in Wolstanton parish seems to have been the individual concern of each of the townships; certainly Tunstall township was responsible for its own roads by the late 1830's.[71] The local board and subsequently the urban district council each assumed highway responsibilities.[72]

RELIEF OF THE POOR. The poor of Tunstall were relieved by the officers of Wolstanton parish until 1838 when Tunstall became part of the new Wolstanton and Burslem Union.[73] The union workhouse was built in Turnhurst Road, Chell, c. 1838–9, 'a palatial structure' costing £6,200 and providing accommodation for 400 inmates.[74] A range was built to the south as a hospital in 1894.[75] The workhouse remained in use after the amalgamation with Stoke Union in 1922[76] and is now the Westcliffe Institution. The original structure, of yellow brick with stone dressings in the 'Tudor' style of the period, still forms part of the large group of buildings on the east side of Turnhurst Road.

ECONOMIC HISTORY. Until the 19th century the economy of Tunstall was predominantly agrarian. The soil, however, is heavy and cold, and the district has never been one of large and prosperous estates.[77] In 1680, for instance, the three largest farms in Sir John Bowyer's part of the manor were of only 41, 40, and 38 acres.[78] Yet despite increasing industrialization since the end of the 18th century several farms, devoted to arable and dairy farming, still survive.

At the end of the 13th century there were 15 freeholders and 58 customary tenants,[79] while by the early 17th century 61 acres in the manor were 'ancient freehold' and 1,660 acres copyhold.[80] In 1619, however, the Sneyds enfranchised most of the copyholds in their part of the manor,[81] and between 1620 and 1628 Sir William and Francis Bowyer enfranchised those within their share.[82] There was no copyhold land in the manor of Great Chell in 1679.[83]

In the last quarter of the 13th century the Audleys' demesne in Tunstall manor consisted of a carucate and meadow land.[84] Mentioned as 'a plot of land' in 1308[85] the demesne had disappeared by 1317.[86] Labour services were being commuted by this period.[87] 'The day works' of 18 serfs were valued at 10s. in 1283;[88] in 1308, however, the customary

[59] *Pure and Wholesome Water*, 12, 13, 14, 16, 27; White, *Dir. Staffs.* (1851).
[60] Ward, *Stoke*, 104–5; see p. 160. Ward mentions that many shopkeepers were using it.   [61] See p. 128.
[62] The British Gaslight Co. Ltd. (Staffs. Potteries) Act, 21 & 22 Vic. c. 33 (local and personal).
[63] See p. 161.
[64] The Electric Lighting Orders Confirmation (No. 7) Act, 1890, 53 & 54 Vic. c. 192 (local); H.R.L., Tunstall Board of Health Mins. 1886–92, pp. 334, 348; The Electric Lighting Orders Confirmation (No. 4) Act, 1900, 63 & 64 Vic. c. 48 (local).
[65] The Electric Lighting Orders Confirmation (No. 5) Act, 1905, 5 Edw. VII, c. 113 (local); H.R.L., Burslem Boro. Electricity Cttee. Mins. 1897–1910, *passim*; see pp. 128–9.   [66] Ward, *Stoke*, 94.
[67] Ibid. 104; see p. 95.
[68] H.R.L., Tunstall Board of Health Mins. 1886–92, pp. 9, 10. The board was planning the purchase of a steam fire engine in 1886: ibid. p. 4.
[69] *Staffs. Advertiser*, 2 Aug. 1890, 31 Oct. 1891. The council contracted for a new fire engine in 1909: H.R.L., Tunstall U.D.C. Mins. 1909–10, p. 19.
[70] See p. 267.   [71] Ward, *Stoke*, 105.
[72] H.R.L., Tunstall Board of Health Mins. 1886–92, p. 2; Tunstall Board of Health Lighting and Improvement Cttee. Mins. 1881–94, *passim*; Tunstall U.D.C. Highways and Buildings Cttee. Mins. 1900–9, *passim*.
[73] Tunstall originally formed part of the northern division of the parish, but the N. and S. divisions were eventually amalgamated and the rates paid into a common fund: Ward, *Stoke*, 121; White, *Dir. Staffs.* (1834).

[74] Ward, *Stoke*, 271; White, *Dir. Staffs.* (1851). For a picture of life in the workhouse soon after it was established see [Shaw], *When I was a Child.*
[75] *Kelly's Dir. Staffs.* (1900); inscription on building.
[76] *Kelly's Dir. Staffs.* (1924, 1940); see p. 129.
[77] H. A. Moisley, 'The Potteries Coalfield' (Leeds Univ. M.Sc. thesis, 1950), 30, 31.
[78] *Tunstall Ct. R.* (*T.N.S.F.C.* lvi), 124–6; these farms were, respectively, Philip Machin's (Park House: see p. 92), Thos. Wood's at Goldenhill, and John Bourne's (Yew Tree: see p. 93).
[79] *S.H.C.* n.s. xi. 252–3, 261–2.
[80] U.C.N.S., Sneyd MSS., Tunstall Deeds, list of copyhold tenures (undated, but probably 1619); ibid., Keele Deeds, Sneyd v. tenants of Tunstall manor, no. 15.
[81] Ibid., Tunstall Deeds, Burslem Deeds; Wedgwood, *Wedgwood Family*, 271, 275, 320; *Tunstall Ct. R.* (*T.N.S.F.C.*, lxiv), 127. Some copyhold still survived in the Sneyds' part in 1653: ibid. lxiv. 128; lxv. 87. For the division of the manor see pp. 86–87.
[82] U.C.N.S., Sneyd MSS., Oldcott Deeds, Ravenscliffe Deeds, Tunstall Deeds; ibid., Ct. R. 7/34, record of enfranchisement (undated), signed by purchasers of copyholds; ibid., Keele Deeds, Sneyd v. tenants of Tunstall manor, no. 15; S.R.O., D. 260/M/T4/103; *Tunstall Ct. R.* (*T.N.S.F.C.* lxvi), 124–6.
[83] U.C.N.S., Sneyd MSS., Ct. R. 7/27.
[84] *S.H.C.* n.s. xi. 242, 245. In 1299 only the meadow was given as demesne: ibid. 252. In 1283 the demesne included a 'grange': ibid. 246.   [85] Ibid. 261.
[86] *S.H.C.* 1911, 337; ibid. n.s. xi. 238.
[87] Ibid. n.s. xi. 235–7.   [88] Ibid. 247.

tenants paid 12s. 10d. in lieu of autumn works,[89] and in 1363 and 1378 they were paying 44s. 4½d. in lieu of winter works, the same for summer works, and 8s. 8d. for spring works.[90] By 1278 a further due, called 'coustout', was paid triennially on Ascension Day by the copyholders,[91] and, variously called 'stuth' and 'stuffe', this charge survived until at least 1620.[92] The copyholders also paid an annual aid of 20s. to the lord by 1278,[93] probably the forerunner of the regular tallage of £7 at Martinmas in force 100 years later.[94] It is not clear whether the 28s. 7¾d. 'serjeanty' paid by the copyholders in 1308[95] was another version of this due or a commutation of a service, possibly the castle guard which the Audleys had formerly had to perform at Newcastle-under-Lyme.[96]

By the early 17th century there were six open fields around Tunstall hamlet: Church Field (19 acres), Lower Tunstall Field (21 acres and ½ day work), Whitteley (9 acres), Great Clanwall (6½ acres), Over Tunstall Field (16½ acres), and Lyme Heath (24 acres and 1 day work). These were enclosed by agreement in 1613.[97] In Chell there are references to open field arable in the 13th century.[98] The Town Meadow in Tunstall, mentioned in 1653, was evidently then uninclosed.[99]

The pinfold was apparently situated at the junction of Furlong Lane and the road north from Tunstall to Lawton in 1782,[1] but by 1840 it had been moved to the west end of Clayhills Road where it still stood in 1860.[2] The pinner for Tunstall manor was chosen in the 1830's at the court leet on the nomination of the chief inhabitants. There was also one pinner for the townships of Chell and Wedgwood in 1837–8, nominated by the inhabitants of Chell, and in 1839 a pinner was appointed for Chell, Wedgwood, and Bemersley 'as a matter of convenience'.[3]

MARKETS. The appointment of a market-reeve by the manor court in 1525[4] is the only indication of the existence of an early market in Tunstall manor. In 1816 a market square of nearly an acre (now Tower Square) was laid out on land called Stony Croft which was leased from the lord of the manor, and small-scale markets began to be held,[5] the stalls being stored at the eastern end of the new town hall. Management was vested in a body of shareholders, and it was stipulated that for two years the market-place and buildings were to be available free but that after that time rents were to be charged.[6] By the late 1830's these rents were farmed out by the shareholders whose income from this source was then £150.[7] By this time the chief market was held on Saturday, with a smaller one on Monday, and the scope had been enlarged to include the sale of meat and vegetables.[8] In 1840 the system of management was legalized by an Act of Parliament which created the Tunstall Market Company,[9] but by the Improvement Act of 1847 management was vested in the Improvement Commissioners, who set up a hay market in addition to the general market.[10] A covered market known as the Shambles was established in 1858 on a site to the east of the market square, but by 1880 the building was found to be too large as well as structurally faulty.[11] Part of the site was assigned for the new town hall, opened in 1885,[12] and the covered market is now held in the remaining portion of the older building.[13] The market-days became Wednesday, Friday, and Saturday about the mid-1950's in line with those of the rest of the city.[14]

MILLS. There were two water-mills within the manor of Tunstall in the late 13th and early 14th centuries.[15] As their location was not specified it is not possible to link them definitely with the later mills of the area, but they may be identifiable with those at Burslem[16] and Little Chell (see below).

A corn mill in Tunstall formed part of the estate held by a William Lawton in the Earl of Bath's portion of the manor in 1615, and a John Lawton of Staffordshire and Cheshire compounded for a water-mill in Tunstall in 1645.[17] A William Lawton held it in 1667.[18]

By 1820 there was a windmill in Peel Street (now Robert Street).[19] It was demolished c. 1855, although the corn-room continued to be used for some years as a practice-room by a drum and fife band.[20]

A steam-driven corn mill was erected in 1826 in

---

[89] S.H.C. N.S. xi. 262.
[90] Tunstall Ct. R. (T.N.S.F.C. lix), 58, 84.
[91] S.H.C. N.S. xi. 245.
[92] Ibid. 235, 247, 262; C 139/51; Tunstall Ct. R. (T.N.S.F.C. lix), 58, 81, 84; ibid. lxiv. 117, 118; U.C.N.S., Sneyd MSS., Oldcott Deeds, Francis Bowyer to Wm. Bourne 20 Dec. 18 Jas. I, endorsement.
[93] S.H.C. N.S. xi. 245. It was 40s. by 1283: ibid. 246.
[94] Tunstall Ct. R. (T.N.S.F.C. lix), 58, 84.
[95] S.H.C. N.S. xi. 262.
[96] See p. 86.
[97] Ward, Stoke, app. pp. ix–xi.
[98] S.H.C. 1911, 446: '3 selions between Middelfurlong and Wallenefeld'. 'The assart of Swinescroft in Chell' occurs c. 1223 and was evidently arable during the following cent.: ibid. 445–6, 447.
[99] Tunstall Ct. R. (T.N.S.F.C. lxv), 87.
[1] W.S.L. 88/1/41 (Lawton, Burslem, and Newcastle Turnpike Trust Mins. 1776–83), 20 Dec. 1782, when it was ordered that all coal brought from the collieries at Chell through the gate at Tunstall pinfold was to be exempt from tolls.
[2] Kendall, Map of Tunstall Town (surveyed 1840); Malabar, Map of Tunstall Township (surveyed 1863); Harper, Bygone Tunstall, 106.
[3] U.C.N.S., Sneyd MSS., Ct. R. 7/41; Staffs. Advertiser 2 Nov. 1839.

[4] Tunstall Ct. R. (T.N.S.F.C. lix), 58.
[5] Ward, Stoke, 94–95; see p. 81.
[6] Ward, Stoke, app. pp. xi–xii.
[7] Ibid. 95; Lich. Dioc. Regy., Tithe Maps and Appt., Wolstanton.
[8] Ward, Stoke, 95.
[9] Ibid. 595–6; 3 & 4 Vic. c. 63 (local and personal).
[10] White, Dir. Staffs. (1851); see p. 95.
[11] Harper, Bygone Tunstall, 49, who, however, gives the date of the building as 1867, in contradiction of Malabar, Map of Tunstall Township (surveyed 1863), and Kelly's Dir. Staffs. (1892).
[12] Harper, Bygone Tunstall, 49–50; Staffs. Advertiser, 31 Oct. 1885; see p. 85.
[13] See p. 85 for a short description of the building.
[14] Stoke Official Handbk. [1958 and previous edn.].
[15] S.H.C. N.S. xi. 246, 252, 261; ibid. 1911, 337.
[16] See p. 131.
[17] Tunstall Ct. R. (T.N.S.F.C., xiv), 111; Royalist Composition Papers (from transcript in W.S.L., S. MS. 339 (iv), pp. 97–98).
[18] C.P. 25(2)/724, 19 Chas. II East.
[19] C. and J. Greenwood, Map of Staffs. (1820); Harper, Bygone Tunstall, 24; White, Dir. Staffs. (1851). The Windmill House within Tunstall manor, mentioned in 1733 (Adams, Wolstanton, 96), was probably in Tunstall.
[20] Harper, Bygone Tunstall, 25.

what is now The Boulevard, but by 1851 it had been converted into the present Soho flint-grinding mill.[21] The building was extended in 1874.[22]

A water-mill in Little Chell, presumably situated on the Scotia Brook near what is now the south-east corner of Victoria Park, was held by the Colclough family for several generations before 1539[23] when it was settled on Richard Colclough of Little Chell.[24] By 1612 it had passed into the Knight family[25] who seem also to have held the Furlong (later Greenfield) estate with which the mill and a house attached then descended until after the early 18th century.[26] John son of John and Alice Machin was living at the house in 1738, although the mill itself was then in the hands of a tenant, Joseph Wallburton of Burslem.[27] John died in 1746[28] and his widow Rachel, who continued to live at the mill-house, leased the mill as a flint mill, along with a kiln, to their eldest son Thomas, a potter.[29] In 1753, as Thomas Machin of Beeches Mill, he sold the estate to Thomas Baddeley of Newfield[30] who in 1757 employed James Brindley to fit the mill with machinery for grinding flint and also pumping water out of a neighbouring mine.[31] The grinding apparatus was later removed but the mill continued to drain the mine until the demolition of Brindley's water-wheel early in the 19th century.[32] In 1764 Thomas Baddeley settled the mill and the Mill farm, of about 50 acres, with the Newfield estate on Smith Child,[33] whose youngest son Baddeley inherited the mill and farm on the division of the family estates in 1819.[34] Only the farm survived in 1832.[35]

POTTERY INDUSTRY. There is evidence that a small-scale pottery industry existed in the Tunstall area by the 14th century. In 1348 William the potter paid 6*d*. to the lord of the manor for licence to make earthen pots,[36] and in 1369 Robert the potter paid 12*d*. for a year's licence to dig earth for making pots.[37] Coarse ware is said to have been made at Goldenhill during the 16th century,[38] and in 1603 Gervase Griffye of Ravenscliffe occurs as a dish-maker.[39] In 1635 it was presented in the manor court that three men of Tunstall 'dug in the ways and waste land and carried off clay',[40] and in 1683 the court ordered the filling in of pits made at Pitts Hill Bank.[41] A Thomas

Moss is said to have been making pottery at Golden-hill in 1700.[42]

By 1800 pottery-making in the Tunstall area, though still on a small scale compared with other parts of the Potteries, was becoming an industry of importance. Its development was helped by the turnpiking of the main road in 1763 and the construction of the Trent and Mersey Canal in 1766–77.[43] About 1750 Enoch Booth had introduced improved techniques at his Tunstall works (see below), mixing local clay with clay from Devon and Dorset and with flint and pioneering a fluid glaze.[44] At the beginning of the 19th century there were 3 potteries in the village itself, 2 in Furlong Road, and 2 in the Newfield area. At Goldenhill there were 6 works.[45]

In the course of the 19th century the concentration of works in the area shifted to the fast-growing town of Tunstall. By 1818 there were 10 in Tunstall township, including Greengates, Greenfield, New-field, and Sandyford, but only 4 at Goldenhill.[46] By 1834 Tunstall township had 13 potteries and Goldenhill two.[47] Some four years later there were 17 in Tunstall township, including the new works at Sandyford built by James Beech nearly opposite his older works in 1838, known as the Lion Works by 1845, and occupied as the Boston Pottery since at least 1913. Of these 17, 12 made earthenware only, 3 earthenware and china, and 2 china toys and Egyptian black ware.[48] By 1863 the township had 19 potteries. Most of them were in the town itself, but there were 2 in Furlong Road, 1 at Newfield, 2 at Sandyford, and 1 by the canal.[49] There seems to have been only 1 works at Goldenhill, the Collinsons', and that closed c. 1864.[50] Another occurs at Pitts Hill in 1887.[51] In 1900 there were 13 larger works in Tunstall Urban District.[52] The number in the area had dropped to 11 by 1959, all of them making earthenware. Vitrified ware also was produced at W. H. Grindley's Woodland Pottery, red ware at Lingard and Webster's Swan Pottery, and bone china at the Weetman Figures Works at Sandyford.[53]

Of the major potteries in the district the Green-gates Works seems to have had the earliest origin since it grew out of a pottery owned by George Booth in 1745 as part of an estate in Furlong Road. The works then passed with the estate through

[21] Shaw, *Staffs. Potteries*, 18; date on building; White, *Dir. Staffs.* (1851), where the occupant is Wm. Malpas, a corn-miller in 1834 (ibid. 1834). The street was known as Mill St. in 1840 (Kendall, *Map of Tunstall Town*, surveyed 1840), but this may derive from its earlier name, Mill Lane, which in turn derived from the fact that it led to Mill farm in Little Chell: Hargreaves, *Map. of Staffs. Potteries*; see below for Mill farm.

[22] Date on chimney.

[23] C 1/756/2; B.M. Add. Ch. 53603, 53604.

[24] *S.H.C.* xi. 208.

[25] Ibid. N.S. iv. 37.

[26] Ibid. 74; N.S. xii. 42; *Wolstanton Par. Reg.* i. 47, 132; Ward, *Stoke*, app. p. viii; W.S.L., D. 1788, P. 44, B. 8; C.P. 25(2)/723, 13 Chas. II Mich.; C.P. 25(2)/726, 31 Chas. II Trin.; C.P. 25(2)/966, 9 Anne Trin.; H. Mus., Heathcote Papers, xxi. 2; see p. 90.

[27] H. Mus., Heathcote Papers, xxi. 2.

[28] *Wolstanton Par. Reg.* i. 309.

[29] H. Mus., Heathcote Papers, viii. 19.

[30] Ibid. xxi. 2. In 1749 Rachel was still living at the mill-house which by 1753 had been divided into two and was occupied by Thos. Machin and Wm. Gater: ibid. For Baddeley's succession to the property of the Machins of Botteslow see pp. 92, 212, 246.

[31] S. Smiles, *James Brindley*, 146; Ward, *Stoke*, 164.

[32] Smiles, *Brindley*, 147; Ward, *Stoke*, 164.

[33] H. Mus., Heathcote Papers, viii. 15.

[34] Ibid. viii. 15; xxi. 2.

[35] Hargreaves, *Map of Staffs. Potteries*.

[36] *Tunstall Ct. R.* (*T.N.S.F.C.* lix), 48.

[37] Ibid. 70.

[38] S. Shaw, *Staffs. Potteries*, 22.

[39] *Tunstall Ct. R.* (*T.N.S.F.C.* lxiii), 46.

[40] Ibid. lxv. 75.

[41] Ibid. lxvi. 123.

[42] Meigh, 'Staffs. Potters', 146.

[43] See p. 84.

[44] Mankowitz and Haggar, *Eng. Pottery*, 28.

[45] Allbut, *Staffs. Pottery Dir.* (1802). There was also an unoccupied works at Pitts Hill.

[46] Parson and Bradshaw, *Dir. Staffs.* (1818).

[47] White, *Dir. Staffs.* (1834).

[48] Ward, *Stoke*, 100. For the potteries at Sandyford see Meigh, 'Staffs. Potters', 21, 22, 29, 44, 51, 62, 81, 122, 129, 152, 160, 177, 179, 197, 217, 218; Jewitt, *Ceramic Art*, 564. Jas. Beech was one of the managers at Greengates under Benjamin Adams: Adams, *Adams Family*, 382.

[49] Malabar, *Map of Tunstall* (1863).

[50] Meigh, 'Staffs. Potters', 57. One E. Ellerton occurs as a potter in Goldenhill in 1864: ibid. 76.

[51] Ibid. 20.

[52] *Kelly's Dir. Staffs.* (1900).

[53] *Pottery Gaz. Dir.* (1960).

various hands and in 1784 was sold to William Adams, earth-potter of Burslem and tenant since 1779. Within two years Adams had rebuilt the factory,[54] then the largest in the Tunstall area, and in the period up to his death in 1805 he produced there blue-printed ware, fine stone ware, jasper, Egyptian black (basalte), and, for the first time, 'mocha' (white or cream ware).[55] Benjamin Adams, William's youngest son and heir, was only 17 in 1805 and the works seems to have been run by his managers and his elder sister Mary until he took over in 1809.[56] The manufacture of jasper ware was a family secret and therefore ceased during these four years; it was not resumed on a large scale and Benjamin concentrated on stone, blue-printed, and useful ware.[57] Not as gifted as his father, and, though never enjoying the best health, very fond of sport, he spent less time in the factory; it was also a period of general decline in the pottery trade.[58] In 1822 he sold the Greengates Works and estate to John Meir who already had a small pottery in Tunstall,[59] and the property remained in the hands of the Meirs until 1896 when it was bought by the senior branch of the Adams family.[60] The pottery, still worked by William Adams and Sons (Potters) Ltd., was largely rebuilt in 1929[61] and was enlarged to accommodate the production of the Greenfield factory which was transferred there in 1956 (see below). The making of jasper ware, which ceased again when Benjamin Adams sold the works, was revived soon after the Adams family regained possession.[62] The Meirs had a flint mill at the works from at least 1851.[63]

The works established by Enoch Booth about the mid-18th century[64] presumably stood in the centre of the town to the north of the later Market Square and on the site of the Phoenix Works which replaced it. Occupied in the late 1770's by Charles Bagnall,[65] it had passed by 1781 to Anthony Keeling, Enoch Booth's son-in-law, who rebuilt it and began to make 'Queen's ware in general, blue-painted, and enamelled Egyptian black'; he also built Calver House for himself nearby in Well Street in 1793.[66] By 1802 he was in partnership with Enoch Keeling and running a second works in the centre of Tun-

stall,[67] but his success declined and in 1810 or 1811 he retired to Liverpool where he died in 1815.[68] In 1812 the pottery was held by Read and Goodfellow[69] and between at least 1828 and 1854 by Thomas Goodfellow, in whose time it was known as the Phoenix Pottery and who was employing 200 hands by the early 1830's; his executors held it in 1860.[70] It was described in 1841 as a 'dirty, sloppy, ill-ventilated, and inconvenient factory'.[71] It was in the hands of Bridgwood and Clarke in 1863 and 1864 and of Edward Clarke between 1865 and 1877[72] and was pulled down soon afterwards.[73]

In 1793 Theophilus Smith opened a potworks in his newly built village of Smithfield lying along Furlong Road east of the Greengates Works. In 1801 after Smith's bankruptcy John Breeze bought the whole Smithfield estate, including the works, and renamed it Greenfield,[74] but he passed most of the management of the works over to his son Jesse.[75] The ware produced by the Breezes was porcelain, cream, green-glazed, blue-printed, and Egyptian black.[76] A west front was added to the factory in 1818.[77] John died in 1821 and Jesse in 1826; Jesse's two daughters succeeded and in 1827 and 1834 married respectively William and Edward Adams, sons of William Adams of Bagnall and Fenton.[78] The works was first let to Wood and Challinor of Brownhills, but in 1834 it was added to the Adams's family business.[79] The main product until the time of William's death in 1865 was white granite ware (ironstone china), first made at Greenfield in 1842; other products were sanitary ware, printed ware, and sponged and painted ware for the East.[80] A second west range was added in 1904 and the north front was rebuilt in 1920 and 1925.[81] In 1956 the factory was closed and production transferred to the enlarged Greengates Works; the Greenfield premises were sold for development purposes in 1959.[82] By 1960 most of the buildings were derelict but the west front of 1818 still retained a pedimented central feature with its Venetian window and date-tablet. Crate-makers' shops were still in use in the south-east of the main buildings. The Breezes had a flint mill at Greenfield in which steam-driven machinery was installed in 1806,

54 Adams, *Adams Family*, 375; see p. 91.
55 *William Adams*, ed. W. Turner (1923), 14, 15–16, 25–38, 40–64, 79–88.
56 Adams, *Adams Family*, 381–2 and pedigree between pp. 380 and 381.
57 Ibid. 382; *Wm. Adams*, 19–21, 89–91.
58 *Wm. Adams*, 21–22.
59 Adams, *Adams Family*, 382; Parson and Bradshaw, *Dir. Staffs.* (1818).
60 See p. 91. The works was up for sale in 1891: *Staffs. Advertiser*, 26 Sept. 1891.
61 An inscription on the N. front states that the factory was then rebuilt; the W. front, however, seems older.
62 *Bi-centenary of Richard Adams*, 23 (copy among W.S.L. pamphs. *sub* Ceramics).
63 White, *Dir. Staffs.* (1851); *Kelly's Dir. Staffs.* (1884).
64 Ward, *Stoke*, 49; Meigh 'Staffs. Potters', 32, giving the date 1750–7.
65 Meigh, 'Staffs. Potters', 11.
66 Ibid. 120; Mankowitz and Haggar, *Eng. Pottery*, 120, 268, 269, 274; Ward, *Stoke*, 93; S.R.O., Q/RPl 1781, 1783. Porcelain was made at Keeling's works in 1781 by the company of which he was a member and which in 1782, after a disagreement leading to his withdrawal, moved to New Hall, Shelton: see p. 166. Calver House was used as a workingmen's club from at least 1876 until the early 1880's: *P.O. Dir. Staffs.* (1876); *Kelly's Dir. Staffs.* (1880, 1884).

67 Allbut, *Staffs. Pottery Dir.* (1802).
68 Ward, *Stoke*, 93; Meigh, 'Staffs. Potters', 120.
69 Meigh, 'Staffs. Potters', 165.
70 Ibid. 88; White, *Dir. Staffs.* (1834); *1st Rep. Factories Com.* H.C. 450, p. B2, 39 (1833), xx. Goodfellow was living at Calver House between at least the late 1830's and 1854: Ward, *Stoke*, 93; *P.O. Dir. Staffs.* (1854).
71 *2nd Rep. Com. Employment of Children* [431], p. c80, H.C. (1843), xiv.
72 Meigh, 'Staffs. Potters', 41, 54; Malabar, *Map of Tunstall*; Jewitt, *Ceramic Art*, 564.
73 Jewitt, *Ceramic Art*, 564. It was still shown on O.S. Map 1/2,500 Staffs. xi. 8 (1879; surveyed 1878).
74 See p. 91. John Breeze is said to have been working the pottery from 1795 on the evidence of acct. bks. of the time (Adams, *Adams Family*, 348; *Wm. Adams*, 146), but he is not shown as tenant by the land tax returns: S.R.O., Q/RPl 1795–1800.
75 *Wm. Adams*, 145–6.
76 Ibid. 146–7; Adams, *Adams Family*, 348.
77 P. W. L. Adams, *Notes on some N. Staffs. Families*, 72.
78 See p. 91.
79 *Wm. Adams*, 148; White, *Dir. Staffs.* (1834); see p. 119. It was still to let in Sept. 1828: *Staffs. Advertiser*, 13 Sept. 1828.
80 *Wm. Adams*, 148–9.
81 *Bi-cent. of Ric. Adams*, 23; inscriptions on building.
82 Ex inf. W. Adams and Sons (Potters) Ltd. (1959).

causing much local interest; the mill was pulled down c. 1926.[83]

There was a pottery attached to the Newfield estate on the main road between Tunstall and Goldenhill towards the end of the 18th century when it was worked by John and Caleb Cole.[84] By 1802 it was in the hands of Caleb and his brother-in-law William Adams of Greengates and was apparently held by William alone at the time of his death in 1805.[85] It was then advertised as being to let, but by 1806 it was being worked by the owner of the Newfield estate, Admiral Smith Child, from 1809 in partnership with John Henry Clive. After the Admiral's death in 1813 Clive managed both estate and works on behalf of the heir, Smith Child, probably until c. 1824.[86] The products of Child and Clive included good quality cream ware.[87] Until 1872 the pottery remained in the hands of tenants, including Joseph Heath and Company from 1824 until at least 1841 and Podmore, Walker, and Company between at least 1848 and 1853. In 1872 Smith Child sold it to William Adams of Greenfield, the tenant since at least 1860.[88] It was worked by W. H. Grindley and Company from at least 1880 until 1891 and was taken over by T. Rathbone and Company in 1892.[89] Since 1918 it has been in the hands of Alfred Meakin (Tunstall) Ltd., who also work the Royal Albert and Victoria Potteries in Parsonage Street and opened a new works on a site off Hollywall Lane in 1957.[90]

✳ COAL MINING. The large number of disused coal shafts still visible in the undeveloped areas around Tunstall town in the later 19th and early 20th centuries indicate the extensive although mainly small-scale mining that has been carried on in this district of abundant coal.[91] There are numerous references to coal mining within Tunstall manor from the late 13th century onwards,[92] while from the late 18th century, with improving communications and the growing needs of the pottery industry, several bigger

undertakings were launched. However, except in the 19th century, the more important mining operations within the large manor of Tunstall seem always to have been outside the Tunstall–Goldenhill area. Since the early 20th century there has been little mining there, although there are several large collieries throughout the surrounding district. It was a peculiarity of Tunstall manor that the lord granted leases in a row (or seam) independently of the land above, so that in a given piece of land the mineral rights and the surface rights were often held by different tenants. This custom was possibly borrowed from the similar practice in the lead mines of the High Peak.[93]

Within Tunstall township there were coal and ironstone mines on the Furlong (later Greenfield) estate by 1619,[94] and about the beginning of the 19th century John Breeze was working 14 or 15 small pits there and in the vicinity, partly to supply his Greenfield Pottery.[95] When the Adams family succeeded to the estate they continued to work the pits at intervals until 1902, employing 22 men below ground and 4 above in 1894.[96] The Childs sank shafts at Clanway east of their Newfield estate c. 1800, and the Clanway Colliery (coal and ironstone) remained in operation until 1902, with 127 employees below ground and 45 above in 1896.[97] There was a colliery at Greengates by 1832 which was worked as the Tunstall Colliery (coal and ironstone) by Meir and Heath by 1841 and by Henry Meir by 1872.[98] There were coal and ironstone mines at Newfield in the mid-19th century, owned then by the Newfield Colliery Company and later by Thomas Adams and Company; as a result of the spread of flooding from the Pinnox and Scotia Collieries at Burslem most of these Newfield pits had been closed by 1870 but some remained in operation for a few years longer.[99] Thomas Peake was working a coal and ironstone mine at his tileries south-west of the town by 1856; the last of the pits at this Tileries Colliery was abandoned in 1891.[1] There was

[83] Wm. Adams, 15, 147–8; Adams, Adams Family, add. and corr., p. L.

[84] Mankowitz and Haggar, Eng. Pottery, 271; see p. 92.

[85] Adams, Adams Family, 375, 378; Allbut, Staffs. Pottery Dir. (1802).

[86] P. W. L. Adams, John Henry Clive, 18; see p. 92.

[87] Adams, Clive, 18.

[88] Meigh, 'Staffs. Potters', 2, 104, 157. He built a flint mill on the N. side of Parsonage St. in 1859, and this side of the business was run separately by the Tunstall Mill Co. until 1896 when Wm. sold the mill to Mears and Green, a local firm of borax refiners: Wm. Adams, 152; Malabar, Map of Tunstall; Kelly's Dir. Staffs. (1896); H.R.L., EMT 15–895.

[89] Meigh, 'Staffs. Potters', 92, 164.

[90] Ex inf. Alfred Meakin (Tunstall) Ltd. (1959). The first part of the Royal Albert Pottery was built on the S. side of Parsonage St. by Turner, Goddard & Co. in 1866 and the second on the opposite side of the street by Alfred Meakin in 1883; the whole was amalgamated, apparently by 1892, with the Victoria Works to the E., opened by John Tomkinson in 1858, and a further block in Bank St. was added in 1911: Meigh, 'Staffs. Potters', 140, 197, 198; Jewitt, Ceramic Art, 565; Kelly's Dir. Staffs. (1884, 1892); Malabar, Map of Tunstall; O.S. Map 1/2,500 Staffs. xi. 4 (1879); inscriptions on buildings.

[91] O.S. Map 6″ Staffs. vi SE. (1890, 1926); xi NE., xii NW. (1890, 1925); Pitt, Staffs. 393, 394.

[92] S.H.C. N.S. xi. 246, 261, 269; Tunstall Ct. R. (T.N.S.F.C. lix), 44, 48, 58, 84; W.S.L., D. 1490/33; S.C. 6/Hen. VII/679, m. 5; C 2/Jas. I/S 9/22; C.P. 43/409, rot. 203. It is not always possible to relate the mines mentioned to a specific part of the manor. For mining at Burslem and Sneyd see

pp. 138–9.

[93] J. U. Nef, Rise of Brit. Coal Industry, 300–1. It is there suggested that the same custom may have existed in the neighbouring manor of Newcastle also. In the 14th cent. the lord of Tunstall sometimes granted leases of 'picks' in the mines (T.N.S.F.C. lix. 44, 48), while there is a ref. to a 'werke' in the ironstone mine in Tunstall Field in the 15th cent.: see p. 102, n. 29.

[94] Adams, Adams Family, 345.

[95] Wm. Adams, 156; Adams, Adams Family, 348. In 1808 mines belonging to Smith Child of Newfield were being worked by Breeze and Young: ibid.

[96] Adams, Adams Family, 341–2, 365; Rep. Insp. Mines, N. Staffs., 1894 [C. 7667], p. 43, H.C. (1895), xxii; Rep. Insp. Mines, Stafford, 1902 [Cd. 1590], p. 267, H. C. (1903), xv; see p. 101. About 1850 Wm. and Edw. Adams were also working mines leased from the Cartlich family: Adams, Adams Family, 341–2.

[97] Adams, Adams Family, 157; Adams, Clive, 18; Pigot's Nat. Com. Dir. (1828–9); Ward, Stoke, 102; White, Dir. Staffs. (1851); Kelly's Dir. Staffs. (1884, 1896); O.S. Map 6″ Staffs. xi NE. (1900); Rep. Insp. Mines, N. Staffs., 1896 [C. 8450], p. 55, H.C. (1897), xx; Rep. Insp. Mines, Stafford, 1902, 26.

[98] Hargreaves, Map of Staffs. Potteries; Pigot's Nat. Com. Dir. (1841); P.O. Dir. Staffs. (1872). Ward, Stoke, 102, mentions the colliery of Jos. Heath & Co. at Botany Bay, identifying Botany Bay with Greengates on p. 103.

[99] White, Dir. Staffs. (1851); P.O. Dir. Staffs. (1872); Staffs. Advertiser, 22 Jan. 1870; Adams, Adams Family, 364–5; O.S. Map 6″ Staffs. xi NE. (1890); see p. 138.

[1] Rep. Insp. Mines, 1856 [2270, sess. 2], p. 81 (1857), xvi; Rep. Insp. Mines, N. Staffs., 1890 [C. 6346], p. 28,

a colliery (coal and ironstone) at what is now the southern end of Victoria Park by the 1870's with another beyond the mineral line to the east.[2]

In the Goldenhill area Randle Baddeley was digging coal 'in the lane in Oldcott between Broadfield and Gill Bank' in or before 1719, while George Sparrow was working in Colclough Lane at the same time.[3] During the early 1730's Sparrow was mining 'coal, cannel, and ironstone' on the Yew Tree Farm estate in partnership with Thomas Hatherton and others. Despite great demand for the products operations were not on a large scale, six workmen being the maximum number employed at any one time. Great expense was incurred in drainage, and there were several old workings, 14 yards and more deep and some 150 yards long, which the partners cleared of the dirt and rubbish filling them.[4] James Brindley had an interest in a colliery at Goldenhill to which he constructed a branch canal from the main Trent and Mersey Canal inside the Harecastle Tunnel; this branch was closed in the late 1820's.[5] In 1793 Thomas Tunstall was working seams of 'the big cannel row and little cannel row' on his Colclough Lane estate,[6] and in the late 1820's William and James Tunstall were mining at Goldenhill.[7] The Goldenhill Colliery (coal and ironstone) in Colclough Lane was being worked by Robert Williamson in 1841, but though still in operation in the early 1920's it had been closed by 1931.[8] There was a small colliery at Gill Bank in the early 1890's[9] and opencast mining on 30 acres of Gill Bank farm from 1943 to 1948.[10] There was still small-scale mining in the Gill Bank area in the late 1950's.[11]

There was a coal mine at Ravenscliffe in 1348 when Simon Keeling paid the lord of Tunstall manor 12d. for one pick there for a year.[12] John Gilbert of Clough Hall (d. 1812) owned a colliery at Ravenscliffe which was closed in 1797.[13] A colliery at Goldendale worked by Robert Williamson between at least the early 1830's and the early 1850's[14]

may be identifiable with the Ravenscliffe Colliery (coal and ironstone) to the west of Chatterley station worked in 1862 by Williamson Brothers and later by the Goldendale Iron Company.[15] Though the scale of operations at the Ravenscliffe Colliery was expanding during the 1890's, work ceased there in 1902.[16] Williamson Brothers were also working the Yeld Hill Colliery (coal and ironstone) nearby in 1862, and this remained in operation until 1889 or 1890.[17] There was some small-scale mining in this area in the late 1950's.[18]

There was evidently coal and ironstone mining at Chell by the 1340's,[19] and a coal mine there was leased out by the lord of Tunstall in 1377 for 32s. a year.[20] Collieries there were in operation in 1782.[21] By 1851 Robert Beswick was working a colliery (coal and ironstone) at Great Chell to the east of the workhouse in Turnhurst Road, where by 1894 the Chell Colliery Company was employing 61 men below ground and 23 above; work ceased in 1901 evidently as a result of flooding.[22] In the 1870's there was a colliery east of the main road at Pitts Hill.[23]

IRON MINING AND WORKING. It has been suggested that the mining of ironstone in the Tunstall area may date from pre-Roman times,[24] but firm evidence of an iron industry there dates only from the Middle Ages. The lords of Tunstall were mining ironstone in the manor from at least the 1280's,[25] while the lord of Chell evidently had ironstone mines by the 1340's (see above). John of Sneyd seems to have been smelting iron within Tunstall manor early in the 14th century,[26] underwood for charcoal was in demand in the 1370's,[27] and there was evidently iron-working at Chell early in the 15th century.[28] There was an ironstone mine in Tunstall Field by the 1460's, normally worked by the lords of the manor themselves in the later 15th century but farmed out by the mid-16th century.[29] In the

---

H.C. (1890–1), xxii; ibid. *1891* [C. 6625], p. 25, H.C. (1892), xxiii. There was a colliery at Clayhills in 1855 owned by J. Booth: *Rep. Insp. Mines, 1855* [2132], p. 106, H.C. (1856), xviii. ² O.S. Map 6″ Staffs. xii NW. (1890).
³ *Tunstall Ct. R.* (*T.N.S.F.C.* lxvi), 139; E 134/9 Geo. II Mich./17, mm. 1, 2, 6.
⁴ E 134/9 Geo. II Mich./17, m. 6.
⁵ A. R. L. Saul, 'James Brindley' (*T.N.S.F.C.* lxxiii), 61–62; see p. 84.
⁶ W.S.L., D. 788(32), bdle. 8; see p. 90.
⁷ *Pigot's Nat. Com. Dir.* (1828–9).
⁸ Ibid. (1841); *Rep. Insp. Mines* [1845], p. 145, H.C. (1854), xix; *Keates's Potteries Dir.* (1873–4, 1892–3); O.S. Map 6″ Staffs. vi SE. (1926); xi NE. (1890, 1925); S.R.O., CC/V 4 (map of Stoke collieries, 1931).
⁹ *Rep. Insp. Mines, N. Staffs., 1890*, 28; ibid. *1896*, 25. Six men were employed below ground and 2 above in 1894: ibid. *1894*, 42.
¹⁰ Ex inf. Mrs. Reeves, Gill Bank Farm (1959), who also stated that old footrail workings were discovered in the process.
¹¹ The Gill Bank Colliery Ltd., Latebrook, have been working a footrail near Acres Nook for some years, and were employing 16 men below ground and 6 above in 1957: *Guide to the Coalfields* (1960); ex inf. Mrs. Reeves (1959). The Windmill Colliery Co., Goldenhill, employing 3 men, was also listed among the licensed mines: *Guide to the Coalfields* (1960).
¹² *Tunstall Ct. R* (*T.N.S.F.C.* lix), 48.
¹³ W.S.L. 93/23/41, f. 9a; H.R.L., Wolstanton Vestry Mins. 1793–1801, 28 May 1800, when Gilbert claimed rating relief for the closed colliery.
¹⁴ C.P. 25(2)/1561, 3 Wm. IV Trin.; White, *Dir. Staffs.* (1851). Williamson and Gilbert were among the 4 co-

parceners of an estate at Goldenhill including mines in 1786: W.S.L. 93/23/41, f. 9a.
¹⁵ O.S. Map 6″ Staffs. xi NE. (1890); *Slater's Com. Dir.* (1862).
¹⁶ *Rep. Insp. Mines, N. Staffs., 1894*, 46, showing 48 men employed below ground and 19 above; ibid. *1896*, 59, showing 88 men below ground and 17 above; *Rep. Insp. Mines, Stafford, 1902*, 269.
¹⁷ O.S. Map 6″ Staffs. xi NE. (1890); *Rep. Insp. Mines, 1862* [3252], p. 69, H.C. (1864), xxiv (1); *Rep. Insp. Mines, N. Staffs., 1890*, 25.
¹⁸ The Lowlands Colliery Ltd., Chatterley, had a licensed mine, Ravenscliffe No. 4, employing 20 men below ground and 10 above in 1957: *Guide to the Coalfields* (1960).
¹⁹ Sneyd MSS., Chell Deeds (1340, 1344); *S.H.C.* 1911, 448. ²⁰ *Tunstall Ct. R.* (*T.N.S.F.C.* lix), 84.
²¹ W.S.L. 88/1/41 (Lawton, Burslem, and Newcastle Turnpike Trust Mins. 1776–83), 20 Dec. 1782.
²² White, *Dir. Staffs.* (1851); O.S. Map 6″ Staffs. xii NW. (1890); *Rep. Insp. Mines, N. Staffs., 1894*, 42; *Rep. Insp. Mines, Stafford, 1902*, 25.
²³ O.S. Map 6″ Staffs. xii NW. (1890).
²⁴ *Wm. Adams*, 155. For evid. of c. A.D. 100 see J. M. T. Charlton, 'Excavations at the Roman site at Holditch 1957–1959' (*N. Staffs. Journal of Field Studies*, i).
²⁵ *S.H.C.* N.S. xi. 246, 252, 261, 269; *Cal. Close 1307–13*, 27; *S.H.C.* xiii. 17; C 139/51/54. For the division of the mineral rights between the lords of the various parts of the manor see p. 87. ²⁶ *Tunstall Ct. R.* (*T.N.S.F.C.* lix), 40.
²⁷ Ibid. 80. ²⁸ B.M. Add. Ch. 53595.
²⁹ W.S.L., D. 1490/33; S.C. 6/Hen. VII/679, m. 5d; *Tunstall Ct. R.* (*T.N.S.F.C.* lxi), 35 (surrender of a 'werke' in the mine); *S.H.C.* 1931, 183.

later 1550's Lord Audley leased other ironstone mines in Tunstall lordship, with five iron mills, to Robert Lucy of London, a lease which was assigned after Lucy's death to Sir Thomas Lodge (Lord Mayor of London, 1562–3); by 1563, however, Ursula Unwyn was working the mine in Tunstall Field under a lease which she stated had been granted to her deceased husband Edward c. 1550, and she evidently maintained her right against Sir Thomas who claimed that his lease included that mine also.[30] In 1561 Henry Lord Audley leased or granted ten ironstone mines in the Tunstall portion of Wolstanton parish to Sir William Sneyd, to whom he had already mortgaged his share of the manor,[31] but George Lord Audley's grant of this part of the manor to Ralph Sneyd in 1576 excluded the iron mines in or near Tunstall township.[32] In 1579 Lord Audley granted an iron mine in Tunstall along with Heley Castle and other local estates to Gilbert Gerard[33] whose son Thomas Lord Gerard was holding iron mines in Tunstall in 1611.[34] On Thomas's death in 1617 these passed, with a furnace and forge in Tunstall, to his son Gilbert,[35] to whom the Earl of Bath leased his rights in the third part of the ironstone mines in Tunstall, including the mine in Tunstall Field, in 1620.[36] Gilbert's descendants still held this mine in Tunstall Field in the 1680's.[37] Meanwhile, in 1596, Ralph Sneyd had granted an ironstone or 'boylem' stone mine to William Bowyer on a 300-year lease, but in 1643 this mine was no longer worked.[38]

Ironstone as well as coal was being mined on the Furlong estate in 1619 (see above). A century later Randle Baddeley was digging ironstone 'in the lane in Tunstall between Newfield and Yew Tree Hollow',[39] while the mining operations on the Yew Tree estate in the 1730's produced ironstone as well as coal (see above). In the same way many of the 19th-century collieries raised ironstone. There was a large furnace on the Latebrook House estate by the mid-1820's with five workmen's cottages attached.[40]

The present Goldendale Ironworks between Chatterley Road and the canal had been opened by Williamson Brothers by 1848, and there were then two furnaces in blast.[41] The brothers also worked the nearby coal and ironstone mines at Ravenscliffe and Yeld Hill (see above). The Ravensdale Iron-

works to the south had been opened by the early 1850's when it was owned by Joseph Bull;[42] some ten years later the owner was William Bates.[43] By 1870 Bates had failed and the works had passed to his largest creditor, Robert Heath, whose firm was still operating there in 1908.[44] The site is now largely obliterated by the slag heap of the Goldendale Ironworks.[45] The Goldendale Iron Foundry on the opposite side of the road near Holly Wall was in operation in the 1870's.[46]

OTHER INDUSTRIES. The iron-impregnated clay on the slope descending to the Fowlea Brook west of Tunstall was used from about the mid-18th century for making tiles. By 1817 Tunstall was noted for its manufacture of 'a superior kind of blue tile, the clay found here being favourable for the purpose; it is little inferior, in appearance, to common slate'.[47] Blue bricks also were produced by then and were used in paving the side-walks of the new streets.[48] Thomas Peake in Watergate Street and Robert Shufflebotham at Clayhills were making bricks and tiles by the late 1820's.[49] By 1834 there were 5 such manufacturers, 3 at Clayhills, 1 at Flash, and 1, Peake's, in Watergate Street. Peake's works, which by then was producing ornamental garden pottery as well as bricks, tiles, and pipes, was the largest and was equipped with steam-driven engines 'for crushing and preparing the clay'.[50] Peake's son John Nash Peake (1837–1905) succeeded his father in the management of the tileries in 1861. By the time of his own death he had doubled their size so that with their 35 ovens and kilns they were one of the largest tileries in the country. He was also a notable public figure in the district and was the leader of the Liberal party in North Staffordshire for many years.[51] There were some seven brick and tile works in the area in the early 1890's.[52] In the late 1950's there were brickworks at Clanway and Colclough Lane and two tileries on the slope to the west of Tunstall (including Thomas Peake Ltd.), while tiles were also made at the Boston Pottery at Sandyford and at Goldenhill.[53] The biggest tile works in the Tunstall area, however, is that belonging to Richards Tiles Ltd. The business was founded by Alfred and Edward Corn, potters of Longport. In 1903 they moved to the Pinnox Works in Woodland Street, Tunstall, in

[30] S.H.C. 1931, 182–3; C 78/30/14, mm. 16, 17. Lodge described the mines leased to him as in 'Tunstall lordship and parish': S.H.C. 1931, 183. He did not specify where the 5 mills were. Property in Tunstall and Brieryhurst conveyed to Edward Unwyn by a Sir Lawrence Smith in 1550 included a workshop : ibid. xii (1), 205.

[31] S.H.C. xiii. 215; see p. 86.

[32] U.C.N.S., Sneyd MSS., Tunstall Deeds.

[33] S.H.C. xiv (1), 204.

[34] Ibid. N.S. iii. 60; Complete Peerage, v, 'Gerard'.

[35] S.H.C. N.S. vi (1), 42–43, 60; ibid. 1917–18, 390 note 3; C 142/368/119.

[36] S.H.C. N.S. vii. 207; U.C.N.S., Sneyd MSS., Tunstall Deeds; S.R.O., D. 260/M/T4/103.

[37] Plot, Nat. Hist. Staffs. 158; C.P. 43/409, rot. 203. An ironstone mine at Tunstall was supplying the forge at Lawton (Ches.) in 1696–7: B. L. C. Johnson, 'The Iron Industry of Ches. and N. Staffs. 1688–1712' (T.N.S.F.C. lxxxviii), 40, 54.

[38] U.C.N.S., Sneyd MSS., Tunstall Deeds, 11 Mar. 38 Eliz. I, and endorsement.

[39] Tunstall Ct. R. (T.N.S.F.C. lxvi), 139.

[40] Shaw, Staffs. Potteries, 23; Staffs. Advertiser, 9 Dec. 1826; Sale Notice of Latebrook, Goldenhill, and Ravenscliffe Estates, 1826 (copy in H.R.L.). An ironstone mine at Latebrook had been supplying the forge at Lawton in

[41] R. Meade, Coal and Iron Industries of U.K. (1882), 506; H. Mus., Heathcote papers, x. 17. In 1920 Hugh Henshall Williamson sold the Goldendale Colliery, mining rights at Latebrook, Broadfield, and Ravenscliffe, and calcining hearths at Latebrook and Broadfield to the Goldendale Ironstone Mines Ltd.: ibid.

[42] Slater's Birmingham District Dir. (1852–3). Keates's Potteries Dir. (1892–3), 73, states that it was erected c. 1846 by Geo. Dawes.

[43] Slater's Nat. Com. Dir. (1862); Malabar, Map of Tunstall; Keates and Ford's Potteries Dir. (1865–6). He had another forge to the SW. just outside the Tunstall boundary.

[44] Anon. 'Hist. of Staffs. Iron Industry' (T/S in H.R.L.), Keates and Ford's Potteries Dir. (1869–70); Kelly's Dir. Staffs. (1908).

[45] Anon. 'Hist. of Staffs. Iron Industry'.

[46] Ibid.; O.S. Map 6″ Staffs. xi NE. (1890).

[47] Ward, Stoke, 100; Pitt, Staffs. 394.

[48] Ward, Stoke, 100; see p. 81.

[49] Pigot's Nat. Com. Dir. (1828–9).

[50] White, Dir. Staffs. (1834); Ward, Stoke, 100–1.

[51] Staffs. Sentinel, 1 May 1905.

[52] Keates's Potteries Dir. (1892–3).

[53] Barrett's Stoke-on-Trent Dir. [1959].

order to concentrate entirely on the manufacture of glazed tiles and sanitary ware. A new factory adjoining the Pinnox Works was opened in 1911, the main works was reconstructed in the early 1920's, and in 1933–4 the factory on the main road at Brownhills was built. This was almost doubled in size in 1938 and again extended after the Second World War. The Hallfield Brick Works in Hanley was acquired by the company in 1947 and is used for the production of unglazed floor tiles, while two new factories have been built since 1954 at Adderley Green near Longton. The company have also worked the flint mill off Scotia Road, Burslem, since c. 1910 through the Burslem Mills Company.[54]

A millstone quarry within Tunstall manor was being worked in the later 13th and early 14th centuries,[55] and there were two such quarries in the manor in the early 1490's, both leased out.[56] In 1585 Sir Gilbert Gerard held 20 quarries in Tunstall.[57] The stone for Christ Church, Tunstall, built in 1831–2, came from quarries at Chell.[58]

A chemical laboratory for the production of crystallized salts was opened by Roylance Child in 1826 in the former Clayhills Pottery on the east bank of the canal; the building was used as a pottery again from c. 1853.[59] The Staffordshire Chemicals Ltd. has a sulphuric acid plant by the canal below Watergate Street.

SOCIAL LIFE. In 1829 Tunstall had 'a very respectable literary society, unassuming in character but assiduous in research'; a second society was founded in 1845.[60] A third society, of longer life than the other two, was the Tunstall Athenaeum and Mechanics' Institute, established in 1850, with premises in Wesley Place.[61] The town hall of 1816, where a subscription newspaper room had been opened by 1840,[62] was converted into a free library and reading-room in 1885 after the opening of the

present town hall in High Street.[63] The Athenaeum was evidently closed at this time; its books were transferred to the new library.[64] In 1891 the library was moved into the new Victoria Institute (see below) where it has since remained.

The Victoria Institute in The Boulevard is housed in the Jubilee Buildings, erected in 1889–90 to commemorate the Golden Jubilee. Schools of art and science were opened in the Institute in 1890, the public library was moved there in 1891, and a museum was added in 1897. The school of art was closed in 1926, and the museum has been transferred to the City Museum at Hanley, opened in 1956; the Institute still, however, houses a technical school and the library.[65]

Tunstall Wakes were held on the first Sunday after the feast of St. Margaret (20 July), the saint to whom Wolstanton church is dedicated.[66] The wakes were abolished in 1879 as a result of a memorial to the Home Secretary from the Tunstall Local Board. This was part of a movement to limit wakes in the Potteries to the first week in August when Stoke Wakes were held, but its success was shortlived, and Tunstall Wakes were soon revived.[67] A wakes fair is still (1960) held in July on waste ground off Furlong Road.[68]

The Prince of Wales Theatre, later known as the Theatre Royal and apparently as St. James's Hall also, was built in 1863 on Booth's Fields at the junction of Sneyd Street (now Ladywell Street) and Victoria Street (now Harewood Street). Despite its initial success it eventually failed and was closed c. 1880. In 1882 the dilapidated building was taken over by the Salvation Army.[69] The Regent Hall in High Street, built in 1883–4 and still standing in 1900, was used for concerts and lectures.[70]

'A tradesmen's association for the prosecution of felons' was founded at Tunstall in 1826. It still existed in 1851.[71]

[54] *Richards 1837–1953* (copy among W.S.L. pamphs. *sub* Trade); *Richards* (Christmas, 1951), 2–5 (copy in H.R.L.); Meigh, 'Staffs. Potters', 62, 103; inf. from Richards Tiles Ltd. (1959), who also state that a third unit is being built at Adderley Green; see p. 170. The Pinnox Works was built by Edw. Challinor in 1842: Meigh, 'Staffs. Potters', 51.

[55] *S.H.C.* N.S. xi. 242, 246, 252, 261.

[56] S.C. 6/Hen. VII/679, m. 5.

[57] *S.H.C.* xv. 160.

[58] Ward, *Stoke*, 90–91; see p. 93.

[59] Ward, *Stoke*, 101–2; *Pigot's Nat. Com. Dir.* (1828–9); White, *Dir. Staffs.* (1834, 1851); Meigh, 'Staffs. Potters', 7, 54, 77, 126; Hargreaves, *Map of Staffs. Potteries*. It had been opened as a pottery early in the 19th cent. by Thos. Knight, a Burslem grocer, and closed in 1819; it was still worked as a pottery in 1900: Ward, *Stoke*, 102; Meigh, 'Staffs. Potters', 54, 123.

[60] Shaw, *Staffs. Potteries*, 18; White, *Dir. Staffs.* (1851).

[61] R. G. Haggar, *Some Adult Educ. Institutions in N. Staffs.* (*Rewley House Papers*, iii, no. 6), 6; *P.O. Dir. Staffs.* (1854, 1860). For the Burslem and Tunstall Literary and Scientific Society see p. 141.

[62] Ward, *Stoke*, 94; see p. 95.

[63] *Staffs. Advertiser*, 31 Oct. 1885; see p. 95.

[64] *Staffs. Advertiser*, 31 Oct. 1885; *Kelly's Dir. Staffs.* (1884).

[65] *Staffs. Advertiser*, 2 Aug. 1890, 31 Oct. 1891, 24 Nov. 1898; *Kelly's Dir. Staffs.* (1900); R. G. Haggar, *A Cent. of Art Educ. in the Potteries*, 29; H.R.L., Tunstall Board of Health Free Libr. Cttee. Mins. 1885–1910, pp. 64, 65; *Stoke Official Handbk.* (1960); see p. 270. For the Jubilee Buildings see p. 85.

[66] Ward, *Stoke*, 108.

[67] *Lond. Gaz.* 1879, p. 4281; *Keates's Potteries Dir.* (1892–3), 100; see p. 141.

[68] Local inf. (1960).

[69] W. Scarratt, *Old Times in the Potteries*, 33; Harper, *Bygone Tunstall*, 103–4; *Kelly's Dir. Staffs.* (1880); O.S. Map 1/2,500 Staffs. xi. 8 (1879); see p. 305. Booth's Fields was the usual site for circus tents: Harper, *Bygone Tunstall*, 102–3. There were also 2 music halls, in America St. and Sneyd St.: ibid. 103.

[70] *Kelly's Dir. Staffs.* (1884, 1900).

[71] White, *Dir. Staffs.* (1851). For the Burslem and Tunstall society, founded by 1813, see p. 142.

TUNSTALL: THE TOWN HALL *c.* 1885
(demolished in 1891 or 1892)

COBRIDGE: WATERLOO ROAD *c.* 1870
showing the former toll-house

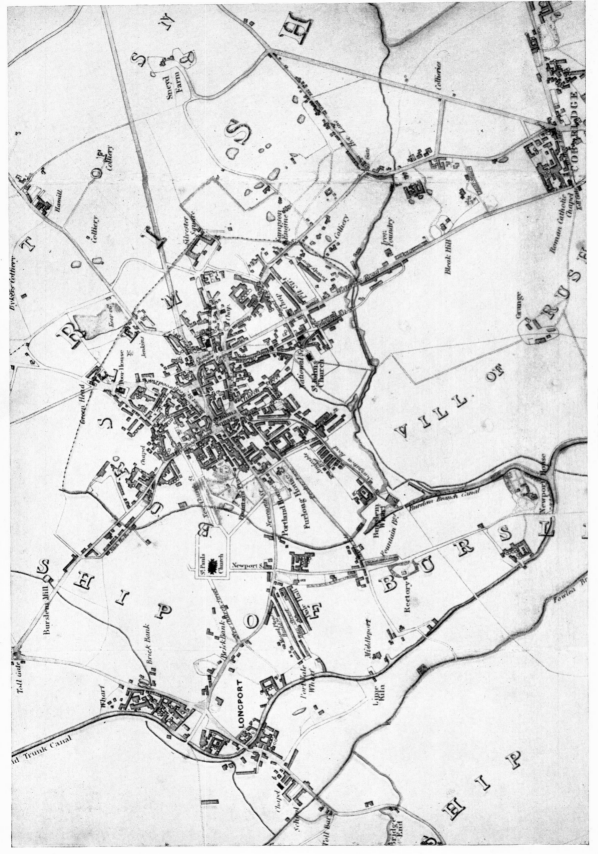

BURSLEM

From a map of 1832 by T. Hargreaves

BURSLEM

THE borough of Burslem consisted by 1910 of the townships of Burslem[1] and Sneyd, Cobridge (formerly the vill of Rushton Grange), and 166 acres of the Sneyd Green portion of the lordship of Hulton, which were added to the borough in 1891.[2] This area of 1,862 acres[3] was bounded on the north by the urban district of Tunstall, on the south by the borough of Hanley, on the west by the parish of Wolstanton, where the Fowlea Brook formed the boundary then as now, and on the east by the urban district of Smallthorne.[4]

The eastern part of the borough lay along a north–south ridge between 600 and 700 feet above sea-level; a coal seam runs north-west through this high ground with considerable outcropping, and the area has long been the main scene of Burslem's coal and ironstone mining.[5] From this ridge two spurs slope westwards to below 400 ft. along the Fowlea Brook, with Burslem built on the northern spur and Cobridge on the southern. Sneyd and Sneyd Green lie at the junction of these spurs with the main ridge. The Scotia (or Sytch) Brook crosses the lower ground between Burslem and Tunstall, and another stream, probably the Cobridge Brook of 1691[6] and the Hot Lane Brook of 1833,[7] flows between Burslem and Cobridge; both of them are tributaries of the Fowlea Brook, but their courses have been partly covered over by building. The Burslem district, with its distinctive bottle ovens, a typical though vanishing feature of the Potteries scene, presents a built-up industrial landscape interspersed with several tracts of wasteland.

Burslem lies at the intersection of roads from Newcastle and from the north-east of the county and the road running north and south through the Potteries. The Newcastle–Leek road runs through Cobridge and the road from Great Chell to Hanley runs as High Lane along the high ground in the eastern part of the former borough. The course of Grange Street and Sneyd Street probably represents the western end of a road connecting Hulton Abbey with Rushton Grange.[8]

Burslem village grew up around the road junction on the slope falling westwards to the Fowlea Brook, northwards to the Scotia Brook and southwards to the Cobridge Brook. It had fewer than 70 houses c. 1680[9] and in the mid-18th century was still an isolated moorland settlement, mainly agrarian in its pursuits apart from small-scale pot-making. By then, however, the ground-plan of the modern town was already distinguishable. It consisted of what are now called Swan Square, Queen Street, St. John's Square, Market Place, Wedgwood Street, Greenhead Street, and Bournes Bank running down to St. John's Church.[10] The development of this 'scattered town on the top of a hill',[11] based on its position and its industry, began in the later 18th century, and by 1817 several new streets had been laid out, with houses built of local brick,[12] while Waterloo Road running south from the town was opened in that year.[13] In 1829 it was stated that the many wide new streets had 'nearly doubled the size of the town within the present quarter of a century'.[14] Some of this development was in the Sytch Hollow below the north-western slope of the town, more to the south-east of the town and around Waterloo Road and St. John's Church, and most to the south-west. Even in this last area, however, John Riley's Portland House (still standing as a county technical school) and John Ward's Furlong House (no longer in existence) represented the farthest point of development.[15] The appearance of the town centre between the old town hall and Shoe Lane (now Wedgwood Street) was considerably altered in the 1830's when the new market hall and the extension of the market-place replaced a potworks and cottages there.[16]

The next big expansion came in the third quarter of the 19th century. New streets of terraced cottages brought the town to its present extent on the south-east. Others were laid out on the south at the Burslem end of Waterloo Road and around St. John's Church, and on the south-west towards the expanding suburbs of Longport and Middleport (see below).[17] On the western slope of the town new streets covered most of the Fountain Place Works, its mansion and grounds.[11] The Sytch Hollow was also being developed during the third quarter of the 19th century;[19] although many of the cottages there have been demolished, some remain, and there is also housing of the inter-war years and later above the former mill.[20] The area

[1] Burslem township included Burslem village, Longport, Middleport, and Brownhills. For the parish of Burslem, covering a different area from both borough and township, see p. 125.

[2] Local Govt. Board's Provisional Orders Confirmation (no. 15) Act, 1891, 54 & 55 Vic. c. 223 (local); S.R.O., copy of map of Burslem Borough as extended in 1891.

[3] Census, 1901, Staffs.

[4] Plan of Stoke-on-Trent and Newcastle-under-Lyme (Geographia Ltd.).

[5] See p. 139. There is outcropping coal in the cellars of the Red Lion Inn in Moorland Road.

[6] Tunstall Ct. R. (T.N.S.F.C. lxvi), 134.

[7] U.C.N.S., Sneyd MSS., Ct. R. 1/2.

[8] Ward, Stoke, 273; W. Yates, Map of Staffs. (1775), reproduced facing p. 4; William Adams, ed. W. Turner, pl. no. lxii.

[9] S.H.C. 1919, 259. The figure doubtless applied to the whole Burslem area, excluding Cobridge which is mentioned separately.

[10] J. C. Wedgwood, Wedgwood Family, map facing p. 121. The map is a 19th-cent. reconstruction: see p. 130, n. 49. Brick House Lane (now St.) connecting Queen St. and Market Place was built by John Adams of Newcastle-

under-Lyme before 1840: P. W. L. Adams, Adams Family, 126, 127, and add. and corr. p. X. For the naming of Queen St. see p. 133.

[11] Wesley's description in 1760: Ward, Stoke, 32.

[12] Pitt, Staffs. 396.

[13] See p. 108. The Act there cited, under which Waterloo Rd. was built, also made provision for a new road to Burslem Church, evidently the present Baptist St. (formerly Regent St. West).

[14] S. Shaw, Staffs. Potteries, 26.

[15] Ibid. 32–33; T. Hargreaves, Map of Staffs. Potteries and Newcastle (1832), reproduced on facing p.; see pp. 121, 315.

[16] Ward, Stoke, 256–7 and plan facing p. 225; see pp. 130, 135.

[17] O.S. Map 6″ Staffs. xii SW. (1890); Ward, Stoke, 260; date-stone of 1852 in Helen Street. Holy Trinity Ch., Nile St., was built in 1851–2 to serve the new parish of Sneyd estab. in 1844: see p. 124.

[18] F. Falkner, The Wood Family of Burslem, 82; O.S. Map 6″ Staffs. xii SW. (1890); see pp. 135–6. For the R.C. ch., presbytery, and sch. built on the Hall St. part of the site in 1897–1903, see p. 275.

[19] O.S. Map 6″ Staffs. xii NW., SW. (1900).

[20] See p. 131.

known as the Jenkins to the north-east of the town centre where James Brindley built the flint-grinding windmill for the Wedgwoods of the Big House c. 1750[21] was still a public recreation ground in the late 1870's,[22] but the present terraced streets were built there during the next 20 years.[23]

During the first half of the 20th century new public buildings have been erected, and retail shops have multiplied. In the period before and after the Second World War some of the terraced cottages were demolished. In 1957 the market hall of 1835–6 was pulled down,[24] leaving an open space between the public library—the old town hall of 1854–7—and Wedgwood Street. This space was being laid out in 1960 as a garden and car park to mark the golden jubilee of Federation, the work being undertaken by the city in collaboration with the Civic Trust. The layout, designed by Mischa Black, includes a formal approach to the east entrance of the mid-19th century town hall.[25] Even so the Burslem of today is still recognizable as the 'Bursley' of 1872 described by Arnold Bennett:

. . . On a little hill in the vast valley was spread out the Indian-red architecture of Bursley—tall chimneys and rounded ovens, schools, the new scarlet market, the grey tower of the old church, the high spire of the Evangelical church, the low spire of the church of genuflexions, and the crimson chapels, and rows of little red houses with amber chimney pots, and the gold angel of the blackened town hall topping the whole.[26]

Before the cutting of the Trent and Mersey Canal in 1766–77 there were only a few cottages around Longbridge where the road to Wolstanton and Newcastle crossed the Fowlea Brook.[27] At Trubshaw Cross to the east, where this road was joined by a track leading from Brownhills and Tunstall, there stood an ancient stone cross.[28] The name Longport was adopted in 1777,[29] the year when the canal was completed. Several factories, some with large houses attached, were built there, the earliest c. 1773.[30] Princes Square, near the site of the later Longport station, was built in 1807, possibly for workers at the nearby Davenport factory. By 1832 there were several streets of houses off Newcastle Street in the Dale Hall area. Union Buildings in Newport Lane had been erected by 1817; Mount Pleasant Buildings in Reid Street dated from 1819; and Fountain Build-

ings in Newport Lane were built by Enoch Wood's workers in 1824.[31] In the late 1830's Church Square, Newport Lane north of Newcastle Street, and Lyndhurst Street were being laid out around St. Paul's Church, Dale Hall (built in 1828–31).[32] Longport, however, remained distinct from Burslem, even in 1851 when Dale Hall stood isolated between the two places.[33] In the third quarter of the century streets were constructed on both sides of Newcastle Street, and the area around Longport station, opened in 1848, was developed.[34] The streets laid out over the Davenports' Longport Hall estate were being planned by 1885.[35] By the late 1950's several of the terraces off Newcastle Street had been demolished or abandoned, and a new estate was being built on the site of those in the area around Port Vale Street.[36]

Middleport and Newport to the south of Longport grew in similar fashion with the erection of factories and large houses after the opening of the canal. There was also some development in the late 1830's: in 1838 Navigation Street, Wharf Street, and Bridge Street (now Milvale Street) by the canal occur as proposed new streets. Streets of terraced houses were built in the third quarter of the 19th century.[37] Middleport Park was laid out in 1908 on ground that had been the garden of the former St. John's rectory house.[38]

The Brownhills area lies to the north of the road from Longport to Tunstall, and while in effect a continuation of Tunstall it remains (1960) separated from Burslem by the belt of undeveloped land along the Scotia Brook and the mineral line to the Chatterley–Whitfield Colliery. Brownhills was the name of a plot of pasture owned by the Burslem family at the end of the 16th century[39] and was an inhabited area by the mid-18th century, developing over the next century around the potteries there.[40] It consists of factories, housing of the period between the world wars on either side of the Tunstall–Longport road, and a girls' high school built in the grounds of the late-18th-century Brownhills House and incorporating the house itself.[41] There is also extensive wasteground to the west running down to the canal and Westport Lake beyond.

Sneyd township, also called the Hamil by the 18th century from the name of the principal part (see below), occupied the north-east of the borough and amounted to some 550 acres in area.[42] Although its

---

[21] See p. 134.
[22] O.S. Map 6″ Staffs. xii NW., SW. (1890).
[23] Ibid. (1900).   [24] See p. 130.
[25] News Chron. and Daily Dispatch, 29 Mar. 1960.
[26] Clayhanger, bk. i, chap. i. 'The new scarlet market' was in fact not built until 1878–9: see p. 131. 'The Evangelical church' is St. Paul's, 'the church of genuflexions' Holy Trinity, Nile St.
[27] J. Aikin, The Country around Manchester (1795), 518; Ward, Stoke, 155; see p. 108.
[28] See p. 113.
[29] W.S.L. 88/1/41 (Lawton, Burslem, and Newcastle Turnpike Trust Mins. 1776–83), 17 July 1777.
[30] Aikin, Country around Manchester, 518; Ward, Stoke, 156; Allbut, Staffs. Pottery Dir. (1802); see p. 136. The house of c. 1773 later became St. Paul's rectory-house; see p. 124.
[31] Hargreaves, Map of Staffs. Potteries; see p. 114.
[32] H.R.L., EMT 1–839 (a); see pp. 114, 123.
[33] H.O. 129/15/370/3/1; Lich. Dioc. Regy., Tithe Maps and Appt., Burslem.
[34] O.S. Map 6″ Staffs. xi SE. (1890); tablet inscribed 'Church Street 1850' in Ellgreave St. (1958); see p. 110.
[35] H.R.L., Burslem Boro. Mins. 1882–90, pp. 180, 183.

The hall itself was used as the premises of the Burslem Endowed School for Boys in the early 1880's: Warrillow, Stoke, 287–8, 295.
[36] City of Stoke-on-Trent Housing, 1919 to 1957, 30, 52 (copy in H.R.L.).
[37] Hargreaves, Map of Staffs. Potteries; H.R.L., EMT 1–839 (a); Lich. Dioc. Regy. Tithe Maps and Appt., Burslem; O.S. Map 6″ Staffs. xi SE., xii SW. (1890); Burslem Bd. of Health Rep. 1857, 17 (copy in H.R.L.). The house at Newport, S. of Middleport, near the junction of the Burslem branch canal with the main canal belonged to the Davenports, who used it as an 'occasional residence' about the mid-19th cent.: Ward, Stoke, 160; Lich. Dioc. Regy., Tithe Maps and Appt., Burslem.
[38] Warrillow, Stoke, 382; see p. 123.
[39] Ward, Stoke, 152; Tunstall Ct. R. (T.N.S.F.C. lxiii), 78.
[40] Ward, Stoke, 154–5; Burslem Par. Reg. (Staffs. Par. Reg. Soc.), i. 214; iii. 651–816, passim; see p. 137.
[41] See pp. 113, 118.
[42] Ward, Stoke, 207, 211; Wedgwood, Wedgwood Family, map facing p. 121. The boundary of the township ran within 200 yds. of Burslem market-place: Ward, Stoke, 207.

name suggests a Saxon forest clearing,[43] it was apparently still a woodland area, at least in part, in the early 13th century.[44] There were at least three farms in Sneyd in the early 16th century, all owned by Hulton Abbey.[45] By the 18th century the principal part of the township was around the Hamil, situated at what is now the north-east corner of Burslem Park.[46] Hot Lane farther south, mentioned in 1669,[47] was extensively built up on both sides by 1775,[48] although most of the buildings there have been demolished. Moorland Road was constructed in 1820.[49] There was little further development in the Sneyd area until the later 19th century, but from then until the 1930's the housing in Hamil Road, in Moorland Road opposite the Sneyd Colliery, and in the streets between the two and to the north of Hamil Road were being built; the housing in the corresponding stretch of High Lane is of the same period, and the roads to the east are all of the 20th century.[50] Houses were built in Macclesfield Street by Stoke Corporation in the early 1920's to rehouse families moved from Massey Square in Burslem, the first slum-clearance project in Stoke-on-Trent.[51] Miners' Hall at the corner of Park Road and Moorland Road was opened in 1893 for meetings of the North Staffordshire Miners' Federation.[52] Burslem Park, laid out on some 22 acres of waste land between Hamil Road and Moorland Road, was opened in 1894.[53] The housing in Scotia Road dates from the last quarter of the 19th century onwards.[54] The extensive waste in the northern part of the Sneyd district, which in the 19th century was an area of collieries and small-scale industrial undertakings,[55] is partially occupied by the large Stanfield council estate dating from the years between the world wars.[56]

Land at 'Smallthorneheede' lay within Sneyd township in 1569,[57] and land called Smallthorne in Sneyd was held with the Overhouse estate by 1666.[58] The 19th-century development of the Smallthorne area, however, was on the Norton side of the borough boundary.

The Cobridge district was formerly the vill of Rushton Grange, an area of 420 acres[59] centring on the farm of that name. Rushton ('Rushy Tun') was presumably an early settlement near the Fowlea Brook,[60] and there is known to have been a vill of Rushton by 1086. The grange was established on the eastern slope above the brook by the Cistercians of Hulton by 1235.[61] Cobridge Gate[62] on the hill-top to the east of the farm was already an inhabited area by the mid-17th century.[63] It had three or four small houses c. 1680[64] and a century later was developing around the potteries there.[65] In 1817 Cobridge was said to have a 'considerable' population and to be 'a prosperous and increasing place'.[66] By 1832 building was spreading from the Burslem end of Waterloo Road,[67] and in the later 19th century there appeared streets of cottages between this road and Elder Road, and also the middle-class houses and terraces of Waterloo Road.[68] This was 'Bleakridge', the 'residential suburb of Bursley', described by Arnold Bennett in Clayhanger, These Twain, The Card, and other novels and stories. In the mid-1850's Lord Granville built 'a little town' for his workers—two rows of superior cottages at the southern end of Waterloo Road and more in several new streets to the east.[69]

The western part of this Cobridge area around the former Grange farm is still (1960) largely waste, much of it being occupied by the workings of the disused Grange Colliery.[70] There are two council housing estates in this district. One was laid out off Commercial Street south of St. John's Church in the years between the world wars. The other, south of it, dates from after 1945.[71] Demolition of the cottages around the Bleak Hill Pottery between Waterloo Road and Elder Road was in progress in 1958 and cottages in Waterloo Road west of Christ Church had been pulled down before the end of 1959. Cobridge Park (9 acres), between Elder Road and the railway, was opened in 1911.[72]

Sneyd Green, formerly part of the lordship of Hulton, was an inhabited area before the end of the 16th century,[73] and the courts of Hulton manor were being held there by 1733.[74] The present Sneyd Street, running from Hanley Road to Cobridge and

[43] E. Ekwall, Oxford Dict. Eng. Place-names.
[44] Dugdale, Mon. v. 715; S.H.C. 1911, 444.
[45] S.C. 6/Hen. VIII/3353, mm. 12, 12d; L. & P. Hen. VIII, xviii (1), p. 200.
[46] St. John's, Burslem, Churchwardens' and Overseers' Accts. 1700-95, pp. 133, 137, 140; S.R.O., Q/RUt 3, Great Chell to Shelton Turnpike Accts. 1829-30; Ward, Stoke, 210.
[47] Tunstall Ct. R. (T.N.S.F.C. lxvi), 30.
[48] W. Yates, Map of Staffs. (1775).
[49] See p. 109.
[50] The terrace called Providence Buildings at the top of Hamil Rd. is dated 1888, Roseberry Cottage in High Lane 1889, and Park Terrace in Park Rd. 1892. Much of this housing figures in Arnold Bennett's The Card as the terra-cotta housing erected by Alderman Cotterill in the later 19th cent. The Acreswood Rd. area to the E. of High Lane is a council estate of the years between the world wars; Stoke-on-Trent Housing, 1919 to 1957, 18.
[51] Housing in Stoke-on-Trent (Soc. for Socialist Inquiry and Propaganda, N. Staffs. Branch), 10 (copy in H.R.L.).
[52] Kelly's Dir. Staffs. (1896).
[53] Staffs. Advertiser, 1 Sept. 1894, pp. 5, 7; Staffs. Sentinel, 12 June 1911. The lake disappeared in 1921 when the covering of an old colliery shaft beneath the water collapsed: Staffs. Advertiser, 4 June 1921.
[54] O.S. Map 6" Staffs. xii NW. (1890, 1900).
[55] Hargreaves, Map of Staffs. Potteries; O.S. Map 6" Staffs. xii NW. (1890).
[56] Stoke-on-Trent Housing, 1919 to 1957, 26.

[57] Tunstall Ct. R. (T.N.S.F.C. lxii), 62.
[58] Wedgwood, Wedgwood Family, 98, 112; see p. 120.
[59] Ward, Stoke, 274.
[60] Ekwall, English Place-names, interprets Rushton in Ches. in this way.   [61] See p. 116.
[62] So called from a gate across the road: Adams, Adams Family, 129, 185.
[63] S.H.C. 4th ser. ii. 94.
[64] Ibid. 1919, 258.
[65] Yates, Map of Staffs. (1775); Adams, Adams Family, add. and corr. p. K; Allbut, Staffs. Pottery Dir. (1802); see pp. 137-8.   [66] Pitt, Staffs. 399.
[67] Hargreaves, Map. of Staffs. Potteries.
[68] Date-stones of 1851 on Elder Place, 1866 and 1880 in Church Terrace, 1868 in Remer St., 1882 in Rushton St., the 1880's and 1890's in the central part of Waterloo Rd., and the 1890's in several of the side-streets; H.R.L., Burslem Boro. Mins. 1878-82, p. 166 (plans for laying out streets on the Cobridge Villa estate 1879); see p. 112. Brownfield Terrace in the southern part of Waterloo Rd. is dated 1889.
[69] Burslem Board of Health Rep. 1853, 13; W. Scarratt, Old Times in the Potteries, 143; see p. 114.   [70] See p. 140.
[71] Stoke-on-Trent Housing, 1919 to 1957, 26.
[72] Staffs. Sentinel, 19 May 1911. The southern portion of the land was bought by the Burslem town council in 1909; the northern portion was still being laid out at the time of the opening.
[73] S.H.C. 1929, 238; 1930, 102, 107; 1932, 79.
[74] See p. 249.

probably forming part of an old way from Hulton Abbey to Rushton Grange,[75] was built up by 1775,[76] and c. 1840 Sneyd Green had 'a considerable population, chiefly of colliers and other cottagers'.[77] Apart from some later-19th-century housing around and near the junction of North Road and Leek New Road,[78] there was not much further expansion in the area before the 20th century. The council estate stretching from Sneyd Street and Milton Road over to Leek New Road dates from the years between the world wars and also includes housing at the eastern end built since 1945. The large estate south of Milton Road at the foot of the hill leading down from Hanley Road was built in the late 1950's.[79]

In 1086 Burslem was inhabited by a villein and four bordars.[80] There were 41 persons in the township chargeable for hearth tax in 1666.[81] The population was 12,631 in 1841 and 20,971 in 1871.[82] Sneyd township had 15 persons chargeable for hearth tax in 1666[83] and a population of 1,328 in 1841 and 1,292 in 1871.[84] The population of Cobridge (formerly the vill of Rushton Grange) was 1,584 in 1841 and 3,299 in 1871.[85] The population of the area contained in the new borough was 28,249 in 1881, 38,766 in 1901 (after the addition of much of Sneyd Green in 1891), 41,566 in 1911, and 42,442 in 1921.[86]

The road running north and south through the Potteries was at first only a side way from the main road from Cheshire to Lichfield through Newcastle and Stone.[87] In 1763, however, it was turnpiked as far south as Burslem—a triumph for Josiah Wedgwood and the potters over the vested interests of Newcastle.[88] The road from Brownhills to Trubshaw Cross (presumably the stretch known in the 17th century as Smallbridge Bank) was also turnpiked under this Act, and so was the road from Burslem to Trubshaw Cross (Pack Horse Lane). Thus

Tunstall and Burslem were linked with Newcastle.[89] The line of the road from Burslem to Trubshaw Cross was subsequently altered so that it became the present Newcastle Street, and in 1828 the old road was sold. Enoch Wood bought the part which ran through his Fountain Place Works;[90] the eastern end of this stretch, running from Westport Road down to the entrance of Ford and Sons' pottery, still survives and retains the name of Pack Horse Lane. The course of the road through Longport was diverted in 1848 to run on its present more southerly line, and a bridge was built over the newly opened railway.[91] In 1858 a new canal bridge was built at Longport and the road there widened.[92] In 1765 Wedgwood secured the extension of the turnpike road from Burslem along Nile Street and Elder Road to Cobridge and thence to Shelton. Thus he achieved his original plan for a north–south turnpike road through the Potteries.[93] The 1765 extension was straightened by the building of Waterloo Road in 1815–17 from Burslem to Cobridge; the southern part of this road, from Cobridge to Hanley, already existed in 1814.[94] The road from Burslem to Tunstall, now Scotia Road, was called 'a new carriage road' in 1825,[95] but it was still only a private road in the later 19th century although it was then being developed.[96] The first toll-house and gate on the Burslem section of this road system was that built between 1777 and 1780 at the north side of Longbridge south of the canal.[97] It was replaced in 1782 by a new house to the west of Fowlea Brook at the end of the road from Longbridge Hays.[98] A toll-house and gate was erected in Newport Street at Dale Hall between 1848 and 1851 to cover traffic using Port Vale Wharf.[99] By 1828 there was a toll-gate and weighing machine at Brownhills at the junction of the roads from Burslem and Longbridge.[1] There were also gates at the junction of Nile Street and Hot Lane and the junction of Waterloo Road and Grange Street in 1832, cover-

[75] See p. 105.
[76] Yates, Map of Staffs. (1775). It now contains houses of the 19th cent., the 1920's and 1930's, and later; some of the housing there was the object of slum clearance plans in 1955: Stoke-on-Trent Housing, 1919 to 1957, 52.
[77] Ward, Stoke, 283.
[78] O.S. Map 6" Staffs. xii SE. (1890); date-stone of 1887 on Jubilee Terrace.
[79] Stoke-on-Trent Housing, 1919 to 1957, 29, showing it had begun by 1957; it was finished by the following year.
[80] V.C.H. Staffs. iv. 50, no. 177.
[81] S.H.C. 1921, 158. The number of households in the chapelry of Burslem (including Sneyd) in 1563 was 32; the number of conformists given in the Compton Census of 1676 for Burslem chapelry was 427 and the number of papists 17: ibid. 1915, p. lxxii.
[82] Census, 1841, 1871, Staffs. The census of 1871 is the last to give township figures for Burslem parish; the subsequent arrangement is by wards of the boro. It should be noted that the population figures given for Burslem 1801–1901 in V.C.H. Staffs. i. 324, differ from those given in the present section since the earlier volume is treating the whole of Burslem par. [83] S.H.C. 1921, 159.
[84] Census, 1841, 1871, Staffs. The population dropped to 1,254 in 1851 and 1,128 in 1861: ibid. 1861. For the population of Rushton in 1086 see pp. 247–8.
[85] Census, 1841, 1871.
[86] Ibid. 1881, 1901, 1911, 1921.
[87] Brownhills Lane, described as 'the king's way' from the 16th cent. (Tunstall Ct. R. (T.N.S.F.C. lxi), 37; ibid. lxvi. 127; U.C.N.S., Sneyd MSS., Ct. R. 7/33), was probably part of it.
[88] Act for repairing road from Lawton to Burslem and Newcastle, 3 Geo. III, c. 45; S.H.C. 1934 (1), 65–70; see p. 3.

[89] S.H.C. 1934 (1), 69; Tunstall Ct. R. (T.N.S.F.C. lxvi), 109.
[90] Ward, Stoke, 260; W.S.L. 88/2/41 (Lawton, Burslem, and Newcastle Turnpike Trust Mins. 1828–59), pp. 8, 11–12.
[91] Staffs. Advertiser, 14 Oct. 1848; Lich. Dioc. Regy., Tithe Maps and Appt., Burslem; W.S.L. 88/2/41, p. 180.
[92] Burslem Board of Health Rep. 1858, 13 (copy in H.R.L.).
[93] Act for repairing road from Newcastle to Hassop, 5 Geo. III, c. 84; S.H.C. 1934 (1), 70–71.
[94] Act to continue Acts for repairing road from Lawton to Burslem, &c., 55 Geo. III, c. 19 (local and personal); Ward, Stoke, 238; S.R.O., Q/RUt 5/16.
[95] Act for regulating markets in Burslem, &c., 6 Geo. IV, c. 131 (local and personal).
[96] H. J. Steele, 'Social Conditions in Burslem during the 17th and 18th cents.' (T.N.S.F.C. lxxviii), 31; see p. 107.
[97] W.S.L. 88/1/41 (Lawton, Burslem, and Newcastle Turnpike Trust Mins. 1776–83), 13 May 1777, 19 Jan. 1780.
[98] Ibid. 12 July, 27 Sept. 1782; Hargreaves, Map of Staffs. Potteries.
[99] W.S.L. 88/2/41, pp. 173, 183, 200, 213, 218. This was to replace Longport toll-gate, presumably in connexion with the diversion of the road in 1848; a toll-house near Longport station, however, was demolished on the winding-up of the trust in 1878: W.S.L. 88/3/41 (turnpike mins. 1859–78), 23 Oct. 1878.
[1] W.S.L. 88/2/41, p. 5; and see plate facing p. 105. Orders were given for the disposal of the weighing machine in 1831 and for the demolition of the toll-house in 1878: W.S.L. 88/3/41, 23 Oct. 1878. For view see 88/2/41, p. 30; Warrillow, Stoke, 18, plate 1, and photograph of c. 1868 in H.R.L.

ing the links between the Newcastle to Lawton and the Newcastle to Hassop roads.[2]

The road from Burslem to Leek may originally have run along Hamil Road to the Smallthorne area,[3] but by 1775, possibly as a result of the turnpiking of the road from Burslem to Cobridge, the Leek road ran along Nile Street and then up Hot Lane to Smallthorne.[4] Moorland Road was built in 1820 to provide a more direct route from the town-centre to Smallthorne.[5]

The road from Newcastle to Leek originally ran via Cobridge along Elder Road and Sneyd Street to Sneyd Green, continuing thence to Milton and Endon. There it joined the road from Burslem to Leek.[6] The course of the road had been altered by 1775 (probably under the Act of 1765 turnpiking the road from Newcastle to Leek and Hassop) to run from Cobridge along Elder Road to Hot Lane where it joined the road from Burslem to Leek.[7] By the end of the century Sandbach Road had been built, providing a more direct route to Smallthorne from the Cobridge end of Elder Road.[8] This road from Cobridge to Leek was, however, superseded when the present Leek New Road was built c. 1839. This leaves the old turnpike road at a point to the north of the junction of Elder Road with Sneyd Street and passes under High Lane north of the Sneyd Green cross-roads. North Road (now North Street) was built from Hot Lane toll-gate to link Burslem town with this new road.[9]

The road from Great Chell to Hanley, which runs as High Lane through the eastern part of the area, was turnpiked in 1770.[10] Toll-gates were erected at the junctions with Hamil Road,[11] with the road from Newcastle to Leek at Nettlebank near Smallthorne,[12] and with Sneyd Street at Sneyd Green.[13]

The Long Bridge, carrying the pack-horse road between Burslem and Newcastle over the Fowlea Brook and the marshes around it, was described in 1624 as 'a great passage out of the north parts unto divers market towns within the county'.[14] It was built or rebuilt c. 1544 when John Adams of the 'Bruckehouse' in Wolstanton bequeathed 3s. 4d. towards its construction.[15] It was in a bad state of repair by 1624 when the inhabitants of Tunstall Court, who were responsible for its upkeep, petitioned the justices in Quarter Sessions for help to-

wards the cost of repair; the justices granted £20 and appointed four overseers to supervise the work.[16] By the mid-18th century the crossing consisted of a range of stepping-stones making 'a kind of bridge which ran about 100 yards parallel with the water'; with the development of the area after the cutting of the canal a raised highway was built over the swamps.[17] 'The foot-bridge across the brook between Crocketts Meadow and the common footway from Tunstall and Wolstanton' was mentioned in 1689 and 1690.[18] This was presumably Small Bridge which carried the road from Tunstall to Wolstanton over Scotia Brook near Burslem Mill and the widening of which was ordered by the turnpike trustees in 1782.[19] In 1833 it was stated that the footpath through Hot Lane Brook in Hulton manor, presumably where Elder Road crossed a stream south of the junction with Hot Lane, required planks and a handrail to be passable in times of flood.[20]

By 1790 Burslem was served by daily mail coaches between London and the North, evidently from the Legs of Man Inn where daily coaches between London and Liverpool called by 1802.[21] These ran from the 'Leopard' also by 1818, and there were then coaches between Birmingham and Liverpool three times a week from these inns.[22] By 1834 there were return coaches to Birmingham and Manchester each weekday.[23] By 1824 there was a local 'safety coach' between Hanley, Burslem, and Leek once a week,[24] and by 1851 there were omnibuses from the posting-inns to the station at Longport and to Hanley, Stoke, and Longton.[25] From 1862 the Potteries Tramroad Company was running horse-drawn tramcars between Burslem market-place and Hanley along a 'street railway' built by George Train of Boston, Mass.[26] These were replaced by the North Staffordshire Tramway Company's steam-driven cars in 1882 when the Stoke to Longton tramway was extended to Hanley and Burslem.[27] Electricity was substituted for steam in 1899 after the Potteries Electric Traction Company had taken over the trams, and lines were opened from Burslem to Smallthorne along Moorland Road in 1899, to Tunstall and Goldenhill in 1900, and to Newcastle in 1905.[28] Services were also begun between Trubshaw Cross and Tunstall in 1900 and between Sneyd

[2] Hargreaves, *Map of Staffs. Potteries*; *Evening Sentinel*, 9 Oct. 1946. For a view of the toll-house in Waterloo Rd. see plate facing p. 104.

[3] J. Smith, *New Map of Staffs.* (1747).

[4] Yates, *Map of Staffs.* (1775).   [5] Ward, *Stoke*, 238.

[6] Smith, *New Map of Staffs.*

[7] Yates, *Map of Staffs.* (1775); Act for repairing road from Newcastle to Hassop, 5 Geo. III, c. 84.

[8] Yates, *Map of Staffs.* (1799), showing it running into Hot Lane; C. and J. Greenwood, *Map of Staffs.* (1820), showing it running into High Lane as now.

[9] T. Roberts, 'Old Roads of Burslem' (*Stoke-on-Trent Bi-monthly Review*, Feb. 1953), 4. It was originally planned to start from Waterloo Rd. half-way between Burslem and Cobridge and to follow a more northerly course: S.R.O., Q/RUt 5/82.   [10] See p. 146.

[11] Hargreaves, *Map of Staffs. Potteries*.

[12] Ibid. It had been erected by 1788: *S.H.C.* 1934 (1), illustration facing p. 54.

[13] Hargreaves, *Map of Staffs. Potteries*. This gate at the NE. corner of the junction evidently replaced, between 1780 and 1784, a gate erected in 1770: U.C.N.S., Sneyd MSS., Ct. R. 1/2, 1/3.

[14] *S.H.C.* 1934 (1), 47.   [15] Ibid. 1910, 247.

[16] Ibid. 1934 (1), 47; S.R.O., Q/SO 2, f. 63b.

[17] Aikin, *Country around Manchester*, 518; S. Shaw, *Staffs. Potteries*, 34; see p. 106.

[18] *Tunstall Ct. R.* (*T.N.S.F.C.* lxvi), 130, 131.

[19] W.S.L. 88/1/41, 2 May 1782. The name Small Bridge was still used c. 1840: Ward, *Stoke*, 156.

[20] U.C.N.S., Sneyd MSS., Ct. R. 1/2; Hargreaves, *Map of Staffs. Potteries*.

[21] *Univ. Brit. Dir.* (1791), iv. 106; Allbut, *Staffs. Pottery Dir.* (1802).

[22] Parson and Bradshaw, *Dir. Staffs.* (1818).

[23] White, *Dir. Staffs.* (1834), giving the 'Leopard' and the Waterloo and American Hotel as posting-houses. The Blue Ball Inn in Nile St. was given as the only posting-inn in 1850 and 1860, but in 1854 the Royal Hotel at Hill Top and the New Inn in St. John's Sq. were also mentioned: *P.O. Dir. Staffs.* (1850, 1854, 1860).

[24] Warrillow, *Stoke*, 44.

[25] White, *Dir. Staffs.* (1851). According to Warrillow, *Stoke*, 56, the Burslem–Longton service started in 1842. There was still an omnibus service between Longport and the tram terminus in the centre of Burslem in 1867: *Keates and Ford's Potteries Dir.* (1867).

[26] C. Lee, 'English Street Tramways of George Francis Train' (*Jnl. of Transport Hist.* i), 106; *Staffs. Advertiser*, 16 Jan. 1862; W.S.L. 88/3/41, p. 10.

[27] *Kelly's Dir. Staffs.* (1900); S.R.O., Q/RUo 30 and 39 (a, b); Warrillow, *Stoke*, 74.

[28] *P.M.T. House Mag.* (May–June 1958), 3 (copy in H.R.L.); Warrillow, *Stoke*, 69–75.

Green and Hanley in 1905.[29] Motor-buses were introduced from 1914 and gradually replaced the trams between 1926 and 1928.[30]

The landlord of the 'Legs of Man' was postmaster by 1790,[31] and by 1834 there were post-offices at Longport and Cobridge as well as Burslem.[32] There was a horse-post from Newcastle to Burslem, Longport, and Cobridge and a foot-post also to Cobridge from 1835 until 1854 when the station post-office at Stoke replaced Newcastle as the postal centre of the Potteries.[33]

The first sod of the Trent and Mersey Canal, opened in 1777, was cut below Brownhills in 1766 by Josiah Wedgwood, one of its most strenuous promoters.[34] A branch canal was completed in 1805 from the main canal at Newport to the end of Navigation Road which was run from the town centre.[35] Public wharves were built at Longport (by 1790),[36] at Small Bridge (apparently by 1802),[37] at the end of the Burslem branch canal,[38] and at Port Vale (by 1832);[39] all four were in use c. 1840 in addition to several private wharves.[40] By 1854 the public wharves in use were those at Longport, Port Vale, and on the branch canal,[41] but by 1860 only the last two remained, together with a wharf at Brownhills.[42] The Port Vale wharf ceased to be used early in the 20th century,[43] but the Brownhills wharf continued until at least 1940.[44] The wharf on the branch canal at the end of Navigation Road was the only wharf in use in this part of the city by 1958, although the branch canal was by then liable to minor subsidence.[45]

The railway from Stoke to Crewe and Manchester touches the western boundary of Burslem at Longport where a station was opened in 1848.[46] The small station building in the 'Tudor' style with Dutch gables and dark brick ornament is characteristic of its period. The Potteries Loop Line was completed as far as Burslem in 1873 with stations there and at Cobridge; the station on the main line was then named Longport instead of Burslem.[47] Waterloo Road Station on the Loop Line at the southern end of Waterloo Road was opened in 1900 and closed in 1943.[48] A mineral line built from the main line at Etruria to the Shelton Colliery at Hanley c. 1848 crosses the southern end of Waterloo Road near Granville Place.[49] Two further mineral lines were built from the main line under an Act of 1864; one, opened in 1875, from Longport through the Sytch area, Tunstall, and Great Chell to the Chatterley-Whitfield Colliery, with a branch, which has now disappeared, from the Sytch to the High Lane Colliery in Chell; the other, opened in 1872, from Etruria to the Grange Colliery and Commercial Street.[50]

BUILDINGS. More buildings have survived from before the middle of the 19th century in Burslem than in any of the other Pottery towns. The market-place, dominated in the centre by the former town hall, is still mainly Georgian in scale and contains many brick and stucco frontages of the late 18th and early 19th centuries. At its north-west corner the front of a chemist's shop retains its original glazing-bars and fluted Doric pilasters. On the south side several houses which have been refronted appear to be of early or mid-18th-century origin; among them is the Leopard Hotel[51] where the central doorway is flanked by three-storied semicircular bays probably added in the 1830's. A little farther west is a tall frontage of stone ashlar, built in 1836 'in the Italian stile' for what was then the new Commercial Bank.[52] The original Venetian windows to the ground floor have been replaced by modern shop fronts, making it hard to recognize that this was once 'the most striking private building in the centre of the town, indeed almost the only one having the character of elegance'.[53] At the south-east corner of the market-place, its front facing Moorland Road, is the fine mid-18th-century building now occupied by the Midland Bank but formerly known as the Big House. Built by the brothers Thomas and John Wedgwood in 1751[54] it was, as its name suggests, the most important residence in the town at that period. It is still the only house of any quality to survive from before the last years of the 18th century. The front, of red brick with stone dressings, is of three stories and five bays, the central bay projecting slightly and being surmounted by a pediment. The window-lintels are of rusticated stone and the central windows are emphasized by stone architraves; below them is a pedimented porch supported on Doric columns. A walled forecourt and entrance gates were removed in 1956.[55] Internally the house contains much contemporary panelling and a fine oak staircase with three turned balusters to each step. To the east of the Big House stands the Red Lion Inn, probably the oldest surviving house in Burslem. Its front carries an embossed tile[56] dated 1675 with initials R D S, but the roof line has been raised and a late-19th-century wing has been added at its western end. More recently the original brick front has been covered with plaster and imitation half-timbering.

[29] Warrillow, Stoke, 75.
[30] P.M.T. House Mag. (May–June 1958), 6–7; Warrillow, Stoke, 76–78.
[31] Univ. Brit. Dir. (1791), iv. 106.
[32] Parson and Bradshaw, Dir. Staffs. (1818); White, Dir. Staffs. (1834).   [33] See p. 7.
[34] Ward, Stoke, 154; E. Meteyard, Life of Josiah Wedgwood, i. 454; S.H.C. 1934 (1), 105–9.
[35] Ward, Stoke, 237. It was under construction by 1802: Allbut, Staffs. Pottery Dir. (1802).
[36] Univ. Brit. Dir. (1791), iv. 105.
[37] Ward, Stoke, 159; Allbut, Staffs. Pottery Dir. (1802).
[38] Parson and Bradshaw, Dir. Staffs. (1818).
[39] Hargreaves, Map of Staffs. Potteries.
[40] Ward, Stoke, 159.
[41] P.O. Dir. Staffs. (1854). What is there called Middleport Wharf is probably to be identified with the wharf at the end of Navigation Rd.   [42] Ibid. (1860).
[43] Kelly's Dir. Staffs. (1900) contains the last mention of it. The wharves at Port Vale in the early 1920's (O.S.

Map 6" Staffs. xii SW., 1926) were presumably private.
[44] Kelly's Dir. Staffs. (1940); O.S. Map 6" Staffs. xi SE. (1900, 1926).
[45] Ex inf. Brit. Transport Waterways, NW. Div. (1958).
[46] Ex inf. Brit. Rlwys., London Midland Region; Staffs. Advertiser, 14 Oct. 1848.
[47] 'Manifold', N. Staffs. Rlwy. 53–54; ex inf. Brit. Rlwys.
[48] Ex inf. Brit. Rlwys.   [49] See p. 147.
[50] 'Manifold', N. Staffs. Rlwy. 53 and schedule of lines between pp. 128 and 129; O.S. Map 6" Staffs. xii SW. (1890, 1900).
[51] An early meeting of the promoters of the Trent and Mersey Canal took place at the 'Leopard' in March 1765: E. Meteyard, Life of Josiah Wedgwood, i. 408.
[52] Ward, Stoke, 267.   [53] Ibid.
[54] See p. 117. The date appears with initials 'T J W' on a rainwater head.
[55] Ex inf. the Manager, Midland Bank (1959).
[56] For an illus. of the tile see Meteyard, Wedgwood, i. 123, fig. 41.

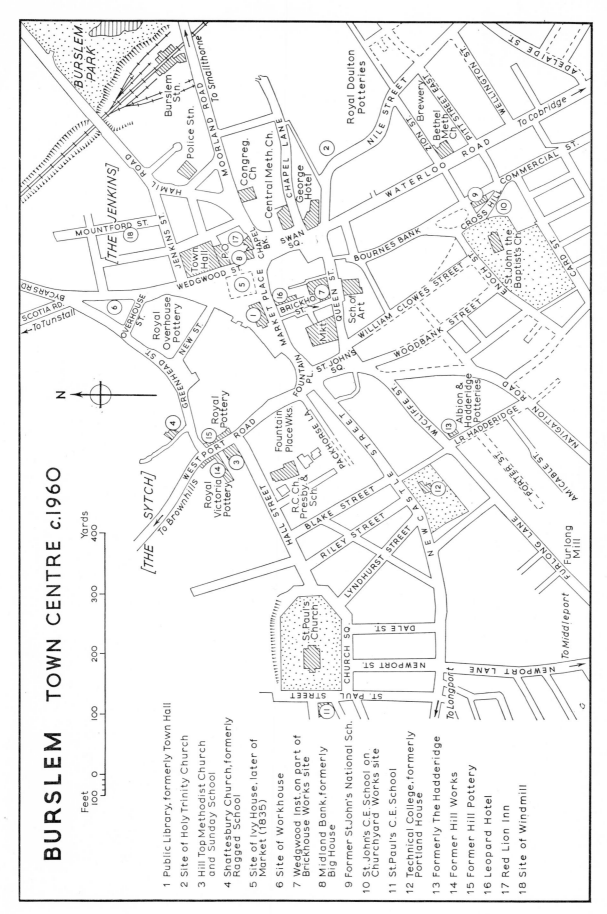

BURSLEM TOWN CENTRE c.1960

Feet
100 0   100   200   300   400
                                            Yards

1 Public Library, formerly Town Hall
2 Site of Holy Trinity Church
3 Hill Top Methodist Church and Sunday School
4 Shaftesbury Church, formerly Ragged School
5 Site of Ivy House, later of Market (1835)
6 Site of Workhouse
7 Wedgwood Inst. on part of Brickhouse Works site
8 Midland Bank, formerly Big House
9 Former St. John's National Sch.
10 St. John's C.E. School on Churchyard Works site
11 St. Paul's C.E. School
12 Technical College, formerly Portland House
13 Formerly The Hadderidge
14 Former Hill Works
15 Former Hill Pottery
16 Leopard Hotel
17 Red Lion Inn
18 Site of Windmill

To the west of the market-place one or two plain buildings of the late 18th and early 19th centuries survive in St. John's Square. These include the house and shop at the lower end of the square which Arnold Bennett used as the setting of *The Old Wives' Tale*. A three-storied brick range at the junction of Westport Road and Pack Horse Lane, although converted into modern shops, is still distinguishable as part of the frontage of Enoch Wood's Fountain Place Works (1789).[57] Farther north in Westport Road the imposing Classical façade of Samuel Alcock's Hill Top Pottery[58] forms a striking group with the Hill Works (1814)[59] and the Methodist Chapel (1837).[60]

The area immediately south of Newcastle Street, where some larger residential houses had been built by the early 19th century, was later in the century covered by streets of working-class housing. Furlong House, built before 1834 by John Ward, a solicitor of Burslem and the historian of Stoke-upon-Trent, and still occupied by him in the early 1840's,[61] has disappeared completely. The house formerly known as the Hadderidge[62] still stands at the junction of Wycliffe Street and Lower Hadderidge, but an extension of the modern factory which adjoins it has been built across the front of the ground floor. The appearance of the two upper stories suggests that it was a rather plain brick house of the late 18th century. Portland House, the home of the Riley family in the early 19th century[63] and one of the earliest residences to be built by a pottery owner away from his works, still stands in its own grounds. Now used as a county technical school, it is a square brick house of three stories, its front having flanking Venetian windows to the two lower floors and semicircular windows above; a stone bay window and a stone porch are later additions. Furlong Place in Furlong Lane, consisting of a pair of tall stucco houses dated 1836 and an adjoining brick pair of similar size, is an example of middle-class terraced housing rare in the Potteries until the later 19th century.

A long three-storied building which was erected in 1817 as a National school[64] is still standing to the east of St. John's churchyard and is now (1960) used as a printing works. In its original form it had a pediment on its west side and a cupola on the roof and was said to have 'the outside character of a cotton or silk factory'.[65]

At the east end of the town-centre Chapel Bank is dominated by the tall stone front of the Central Methodist Church, built in 1801 and refronted in 1870.[66] Farther south, at the junction of Queen Street and Waterloo Road, stands the late-18th-century brick house which, with its outbuildings, is the original of the printing establishment in Bennett's *Clayhanger*. The George Hotel—the 'Dragon' of Bennett's novels—was formerly an 18th-century building with a pair of two-storied semicircular bay windows; the present hotel, designed in the neo-Georgian style by Longden and Venables, dates from 1928–9 when it replaced several adjoining properties as well as the former inn.[67] During rebuilding parts of a still earlier structure were found on the site.[68] Opposite the hotel several late-18th-century brick frontages have survived at the upper end of Nile Street.

Waterloo Road, constructed in 1815–17,[69] contains much small-scale housing of that time at its northern end. Farther south, the older part of the front range of the Washington Works has a dignified treatment of recessed brick arcading dating from the 1830's. The three-storied bow window of the American Hotel opposite is similar in detail to those at the 'Leopard' and is probably of much the same date.[70] As Waterloo Road approaches Cobridge the houses become larger, more pretentious, and progressively later in date, representing the first middle-class area of 19th-century Burslem. The various mid-19th-century architectural styles include the gabled 'Tudor' of Camoys Terrace[71] and the Italianate stucco of the detached house now occupied as the Russell Hotel. At Cobridge itself a brick terrace dating from *c.* 1880 contains the double-fronted and bay-windowed house which was opened in 1960 as the Arnold Bennett Museum.[72]

There have been three town halls in Burslem. The first was erected in the centre of the market-place *c.* 1761 and was a rectangular brick building of two stories, having open arches to the ground floor and a large room with sash windows above. It was later coated with cement and surmounted by a balustraded parapet and a central clock turret with a bell cupola.[73] The building served as a lock-up and as a storage-place for market stalls; the eastern end was occupied by the police by 1834, and the remainder was used as a newspaper room, a hall for public business, and, after 1839, a court room. In 1851 the ground floor was converted into a fish market and the upper floor was extended.[74] A new hall, which is still in use as a public library, was built in 1854–7 on the site of the old one.[75] It is a massive stone building designed by G. T. Robinson of Wolverhampton in a mixture of Classical styles with features of the Greek Revival predominating. Above a rusticated and sharply battered base is an applied Corinthian order and a deep eaves cornice surmounted by acroteria. At the west end is a projecting portico with arched entrances below and free-

[57] See p. 136.   [58] See p. 135.   [59] See p. 135.
[60] See p. 301 and plate facing p. 294.
[61] Shaw, *Staffs. Potteries*, 33; Ward, *Stoke*, 267; Lich. Dioc. Regy., Tithe Maps and Appt., Burslem; R. Nicholls, *Hist. Stoke-on-Trent and Newcastle-under-Lyme*, preface. In 1840 he was chief constable of Burslem: Ward, op. cit. 599. In 1851 the house was occupied by Miss Susan Ward: White, *Dir. Staffs.* (1851).
[62] See p. 119.
[63] Ward, *Stoke*, 267.
[64] See Table IX.
[65] Ward, *Stoke*, 244; and see plate facing p. 136.
[66] See p. 290.
[67] Ex inf. Mr. H. Stockton, Burslem (1960): W. E. Tate, *Inns and Inn Signs in and near Burslem*, 25 (copy in H.R.L.). An inn on the site, known as the 'George and Dragon', evidently existed *c.* 1750: Wedgwood, *Wedgwood Family*, map facing p. 121. An inn was kept there by Thomas Daniel in 1647: Tate, op. cit., 25.
[68] H. J. Steele, 'Social Conditions in Burslem during the 17th and 18th Cents.' (*T.N.S.F.C.* lxxviii), 37.
[69] See p. 108.
[70] The Waterloo and American Hotel was a posting-house by 1834: see p. 109, n. 23.
[71] The terrace was probably built soon after 1839 when the barony of Camoys was recreated: see p. 116.
[72] See p. 142.
[73] Ward, *Stoke*, 235–6 and plate facing p. 257.
[74] See p. 126.
[75] *Burslem Board of Health Rep. 1853*, 3, 9; ibid. *1854*, 4–5, 6, 12; ibid. *1857*, 4. The foundation stone was laid by Wm. Davenport of Longport Hall in May 1854 and the hall was opened in Jan. 1857. Wm. Davenport gave a new organ in 1864: ibid. *1864*, 12; ibid. *1865*, 13.

St. Paul's Church, built 1828–31

Air view of town centre *c.* 1930, looking north-east

BURSLEM

Piccadilly Street, Tunstall (1821)

Beresford Street, Hanley (1878)

Penkhull Square (c. 1800)

Granville Street, Cobridge (1853)

WORKERS' HOUSING

standing Corinthian columns to the principal story. Above this an elaborate clock turret is supported by caryatid figures, the whole being crowned by a gilded angel. This angel, poised high above the surrounding buildings, is a noted Burslem landmark. Internally there is an impressive entrance hall at the west end, having tall cast-iron columns and a double staircase. In 1911 a third town hall was built,[76] occupying much of the east side of the market-place. It was designed by Russell and Cooper and has a long neo-Classical front of stone ashlar with a colonnaded portico near its north end.

The first covered market, designed by Samuel Ledward,[77] was built in 1835 on ground to the east of the town hall which had previously been occupied by a potworks and other old buildings. It was a single-storied stone structure in the Classical style, raised at the south end, where the ground fell away, on a rusticated base surmounted by iron railings. In the centre of the south front was a projecting Doric portico of three bays.[78] The building was demolished in 1957.[79] The present market hall between the market-place and Queen Street was erected in 1878-9.[80] It has a Gothic frontage of red brick with stone dressings facing Queen Street and incorporating shop fronts under pointed arches, now mostly altered. The interior contains fine cast-iron detail of the Gothic Revival period.

The Wedgwood Memorial Institute in Queen Street, built between 1863 and 1869, has an elaborate and remarkable front, mainly in the Venetian Gothic style. A competition for the design of the building was originally won by G. B. Nichols of Wolverhampton, but his elevation of 1860 was modified in 1863 to include terra-cotta panels and other decorative features. A further competition was held and designs submitted by Robert Edgar and John Lockwood Kipling, father of Rudyard Kipling, were adopted. The street front of the building is of two stories and twelve bays. The upper story consists of a blind arcade, the arches containing terra-cotta figures representing the months of the year designed and executed by Rowland Morris; above these are signs of the Zodiac carried out in mosaic. Between the stories is a series of ten panels depicting processes in the pottery industry, designed by Matthew Eldon and executed by Rowland Morris and others. The statue of Josiah Wedgwood, which stands above the richly ornamented central doorway, was completed in 1873 and is the work of Rowland Morris.[81] Opposite the Wedgwood Institute in Queen Street is the School of Art, which dates from 1906-7.

At Trubshaw Cross, Longport, where an ancient cross once stood, a modern stone cross was erected at the centre of the traffic roundabout in 1949. It stands on a base of 1750 which at one time formed part of a lamp standard set in the middle of the road junction.[82] To the north-west of the roundabout,

between Davenport Street and the canal, stood the factory buildings (recently demolished) and dwelling-house dating from about the close of the 18th century and at one time belonging to the Davenports; they were an example of a master potter's house with its works attached.[83] Another house, of slightly later date, became the Duke of Bridgewater Inn about the middle of the 19th century;[84] it stands in Station Street on the south side of the canal bridge and has a symmetrical three-storied brick front with altered ground-floor windows. Longport Hall, demolished in the 1880's, stood in its own grounds to the south of Trubshaw Cross.[85] A view of the garden front in 1843, when the hall was the residence of William Davenport, shows an early-19th-century house with a three-storied central block of three bays flanked by projecting two-storied wings of equal height; another wing is visible at the back.[86] Between later buildings on the south side of Newcastle Street stands a row of six cottages (nos. 119-29) apparently of 18th-century date.[87]

Brownhills House, now part of a girls' school, lies halfway between Burslem and Tunstall and dates from c. 1782.[88] It is built of red brick with stone window-lintels and is L-shaped on plan, its principal front facing south. There was originally a single bowed projection on its west side, but additions of 1830 appear to have included a stone bay window in the same wall and a stone porch at the centre of the south front.[89]

Rushton Grange, which occupied a site at Cobridge to the west of Waterloo Road, was demolished in the present century.[90] A view of the house in 1800 shows a long timber-framed front range with a thatched roof and dormer windows, a massive chimney at one end, and a projecting wing at the rear; at this period the building appears to have been divided into cottages but c. 1840 it was referred to as a farm-house and had been 'in a very slight degree modernised'.[91] A single-story structure, forming part of the front range, was used as a Roman Catholic chapel until the late 18th century.[92] The only buildings at Cobridge which have survived from before the 19th century appear to be part of a row of cottages with front gardens in Grange Street and the Black Boy Inn with an adjoining house in Cobridge Road.[93] Among older pottery buildings both Furnival's works in Elder Road (dating from the late 18th century) and the front range of the Soho Pottery in Waterloo Road (1848) are of architectural interest.[94]

Much of the early working-class housing in Burslem was considered generous by contemporary standards: in 1829 reference was made to the 'many wide and spacious new streets of excellent dwelling houses',[95] and in 1844 it was said that most of the houses had four rooms and were occupied by only one family and that 'there are few places in the king-

[76] Staffs. Advertiser, 12 Mar. 1910; Kelly's Dir. Staffs. (1912).
[77] Ward, Stoke, 257.
[78] See pp. 119, 130; Ward, Stoke, plate facing p. 257 and ground plan facing p. 225.
[79] Warrillow, Stoke, 400.   [80] See p. 131.
[81] R. G. Haggar, A Cent. of Art Educ. in the Potteries, 15, 17 (copy in H.R.L.); see p. 141 and plate facing p. 270.
[82] Ward, Stoke, 156; E. J. D. Warrillow, 'Burma Bell and Trubshaw Cross' (Staffs. Life, ii), 247; inscription on shaft.   [83] See p. 137.
[84] Tate, Inns and Inn Signs in and near Burslem, 35.

[85] See p. 106.
[86] Print at H.R.L., reproduced in Warrillow, Stoke, 295 (ii).
[87] Buildings are shown in this area by Yates, Map of Staffs. (1775).   [88] See p. 118.
[89] Ward, Stoke, 152 and plate facing p. 151.
[90] See p. 116.
[91] Ward, Stoke, 280 and plate on p. 287.
[92] Ibid. 280-1; see p. 272.
[93] The 'Black Boy' existed as an inn by 1808: Tate, Inns and Inn Signs in and near Burslem, 22.
[94] See pp. 137, 138.
[95] Shaw, Staffs. Potteries, 26.

dom where the poor have such ample house room'.[96] These comparatively good conditions were partly due to the existence of adequate open land around the town over which new streets could be built to accommodate the rapidly increasing population. Again, in contrast to older and larger industrial towns, there were scarcely any middle-class houses from which the occupants had moved to the outskirts and which had been taken over as tenements by the poorer workers. Near the town-centre, however, there were a few congested areas where older cottages had been hemmed in by potworks and later buildings. These included the Massey Square district between Moorland Road and Chapel Lane in which a collection of old courts containing 90 houses was cleared away in the early 1920's.[97] Another black spot was the so-called 'Hell Hole' near the junction of Waterloo Road and Nile Street, demolished between 1890 and 1900.[98] One who had lived there as a child some 50 years earlier remembered not only dilapidated cottages but also that 'drunkenness and semi-starvation, broken pavements, open drains, and loud-mouthed cursing and obscenity seemed its normal conditions'.[99]

The articles of the Burslem United and Amicable Building Society, founded in 1807,[1] included particulars of three types of proposed houses and specified that in all cases there should be passage-ways between every two houses and land for gardens at the rear. This was to ensure that each house had its own yard and back access and to eliminate the system of communal yards and shared privies which was then so general. The largest type of house included a parlour and a third bedroom, but the two smaller types appear to represent the standard four-roomed plan of the period, having a living room or 'house place' with a kitchen behind it, a pantry beside or under the staircase, and two 'lodging rooms' above. This arrangement persisted in the Potteries until well after the middle of the 19th century.[2] There appear to have been no 'back-to-back' houses, nor was it usual to build workers' houses with cellars or with more than two stories. In a few outlying areas of Burslem the terraced cottages had small front gardens but usually the front rooms opened straight on to the street. Examples of small planned groups, all of which were probably the work of building societies, were Amicable Buildings in Upper Hadderidge (1818), Union Buildings in Newport Lane (before 1817), and Mount Pleasant Buildings in Reid Street (1819).[3] Fountain Buildings in Newport Lane, also known as Tuppenny Row, consisted of terraced cottages flanking a central shop and were built by Enoch Wood's workers in 1824 through their own building society.[4] All these groups had

been demolished by 1960. The partly demolished Princes Square near Longport Station, a three-sided close of terraced cottages with small front gardens, was built in 1807, possibly for workers in the nearby Davenport factory; its former central range carried a dated pediment.

Another attempt to produce well-built workers' houses was made in the late 1830's when the trustees of William Adams of Cobridge Hall (d. 1831) were selling land to the south and east of St. Paul's Church to be laid out in accordance with conditions imposed by themselves. Thus in Church Square and Newport Lane, on land sold to John Mayer, a builder, and Samuel Mayer, the younger, a potter, the houses were to have 'dress bricks, sash windows and panelled doors' with a stone string course; they were to be set back two yards from the street and this space was to be 'enclosed with iron palisadoes'. Paved footpaths and water gullies were to be provided and the roadway was to be adequately surfaced.[5] A few of these houses at the north end of Newport Lane (now Newport Street) are still recognizable by the small enclosed spaces in front of them and by their well-designed details; these include round-headed doorways with moulded archivolts, decorative fanlights, and six-panelled doors.[6]

The provision of projecting wash-houses[7] opening out of the back rooms does not appear to have become general in the Potteries until the later 19th century. For example, at Elder Place in Cobridge, a terrace of superior cottages with long front gardens built in 1851,[8] the present back kitchens are obviously later additions. In this and hundreds of other cases they were probably added only when piped water became available. The privy (or later the water-closet) was sometimes built behind the wash-house but more often at the farther end of the yard.

The most striking advance in 19th-century housing in Burslem—or for that matter in the Potteries generally—was made on Earl Granville's Cobridge estate, built for his workers at the south end of Waterloo Road in the mid-1850's[9] and still standing in 1960. Most of the houses had front gardens, while all had wash-houses and yards with separate access. In several of the terraces superior houses, let at higher rents than usual, were planned with small entrance halls and a third bedroom. Private drainage works were completed in 1855 and by 1857 there were 126 water-closets on the estate, 116 of which were said to be in good order.[10] Apart from this scheme the first terraced houses to have passage halls and a third bedroom appear to have been those in Elm Street on the east side of Waterloo Road, evidently built c. 1880.[11] According to Arnold Bennett these 'lobbied cottages' were at once occupied and,

---

[96] Warrillow, *Stoke*, 176.
[97] O.S. Map 1/500 Staffs. xii. 9. 2 (1879); see p. 107.
[98] Warrillow, *Stoke*, 321–3.
[99] [C. Shaw], *When I was a Child*, 121–2.
[1] S. J. Price, *Building Societies*, 63–64. There is a copy of the articles in W.S.L. Pamphs. vol. xv, no. 16.
[2] This has been called the 'cottage' plan as distinct from the later 'tunnel-back' plan in which the maximum accommodation on a narrow frontage was obtained by building out a back wing containing domestic offices and sometimes a third bedroom; the latter remained the standard town-house plan all over the country until well into the 20th cent. For examples in Birmingham see *Bournville Village Trust 1900–1955*, 37–38.
[3] Ex inf. Mr. R. G. Haggar; see p. 106.

[4] Falkner, *Wood Family*, 82; ex inf. Mr. Haggar.
[5] H.R.L., EMT 1–839 (a).
[6] Larger houses with enriched doorcases at the S. end of the terraces may be slightly earlier in date.
[7] These were later used as back kitchens and are now often referred to as sculleries.
[8] Date on terrace. The round-headed doorways have typical moulded archivolts and projecting keystones.
[9] See p. 107.
[10] *Burslem Board of Health Rep. 1853*, 13; ibid. *1854*, 15; ibid. *1855*, 10; ibid. *1856*, 17; ibid. *1857*, 19; see plate facing p. 113 and plan on p. 115.
[11] The late appearance of such houses in the Potteries was commented on by E. Meteyard c. 1865: *Life of Josiah Wedgwood*, i. 201.

WORKERS' TERRACED HOUSING

SOME TYPICAL

19th - CENTURY PLANS

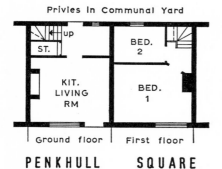

Privies in Communal Yard

PENKHULL SQUARE

STOKE c.1800

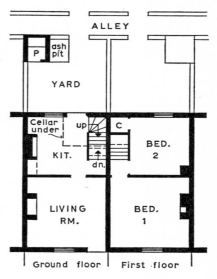

PICCADILLY · STREET

TUNSTALL 1821

0 5 10 20 30

scale of feet

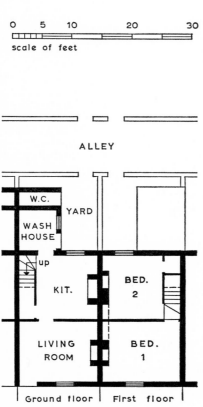

EARL GRANVILLE'S ESTATE

(SMALLER TYPE) COBRIDGE 1853

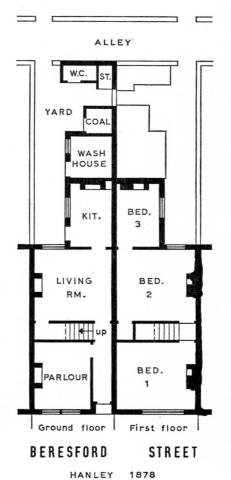

BERESFORD STREET

HANLEY 1878

as a consequence, cottage property in the centre of the town depreciated.[12] Nevertheless houses of the older type with their front doors opening straight into the living room continued to be built in most of the new streets at least until the end of the 19th century.

MANORS. *BURSLEM* was held before the Conquest by Alward, but by 1086 it had passed to Robert de Stafford and was then assessed at ⅓ hide.[13] By 1243 it was held of the Stafford barony as ½ knight's fee, and the overlordship remained with the barony until at least 1460.[14]

In 1086 Burslem was held of Robert de Stafford by Ulviet,[15] but by the beginning of the 13th century it had passed to Adam de Audley[16] (either the father or the son). The manor then remained in the Audley family,[17] but it had been absorbed into their manor of Tunstall by the end of the 13th century[18] and thereafter descended as part of that manor.[19] The courts for the two-thirds share of Tunstall manor were frequently held at Burslem from 1549.[20]

James de Audley received a grant of free warren in his demesne lands in Burslem manor in 1252.[21]

RUSHTON was held before the Conquest by Ulviet but had become part of Robert de Stafford's barony by 1086 when it was assessed with Hulton at ⅓ hide.[22] The overlordship descended in the barony until at least 1284 when Rushton and Hulton together formed ½ knight's fee.[23]

In 1086 the Saxon tenant was still in possession, holding of Robert de Stafford.[24] By 1223 the vill had passed to Henry de Audley who in that year included it among the endowments of Hulton Abbey.[25] By 1235 the abbey had established a grange at Rushton[26] which in 1291 consisted of 3 carucates worth £1 each.[27] In 1535 Rushton Grange consisted of arable, meadow, and pasture, together worth £4,[28] and on the dissolution of the abbey in 1538 it passed to the Crown.[29] The 'manor or grange' and its lands were granted to James Leveson of Wolverhampton in 1539 at a rent of £7 5s.,[30] and in 1540

James conveyed the grange to Richard Biddulph of Biddulph for £130 7s.[31] The estate then descended in the Biddulph family until 1835.[32] It was sequestrated by 1645;[33] in 1784 it was described as 'the manor or reputed manor of Rushton Grange' in the possession of John Biddulph, but much of the land was sold during the 17th and 18th centuries, the remainder being the estate centring on the Grange farmhouse.[34] This farm was leased by the Roman Catholic Biddulphs to the Bagnalls, also Roman Catholics, between at any rate the mid-17th century and the end of the 18th century,[35] and it had become a Roman Catholic centre by the 18th century.[36] One of the Bagnalls was making butterpots there in the early 18th century.[37]

On the death in 1835 of John Biddulph of Burton upon Trent, the last of the senior male line of the family, his estates were divided between his coheirs, Thomas Stonor (Baron Camoys, 1839) of Stonor Park (in Pyrton parish, Oxon.), and Anthony George Wright of Burton-upon-Trent who in 1837 assumed the name of Biddulph.[38] They still held it in 1840,[39] but by 1842 the 220-acre Grange estate[40] had passed to Lord Camoys,[41] whose grandson still owned it in 1885.[42] Although by 1829 the part of the farmhouse formerly used as a Roman Catholic chapel was 'a mere thatched shed',[43] the farm still existed in the early 1920's,[44] but by 1958 the site was occupied by a small demolition works, the disused workings of the Grange Colliery, and a post-1945 housing estate.

Henry de Audley's grant of Rushton Grange to Hulton Abbey in 1223 included land called 'Mannesmor'.[45] Meadow called 'Monsmore' was part of the estate in 1539,[46] and in 1838 Mansmore was a large piece of land, including meadow, to the west of the farmhouse and crossed by the Trent–Mersey Canal.[47]

OTHER ESTATES. Bank House in Sneyd within Tunstall manor was occupied by William Stevenson in 1619 when the property was enfranchised by the Sneyds.[48] William was probably living there by

[12] *Clayhanger*, bk. ii, chap. iii.
[13] *V.C.H. Staffs.* iv. 50, no. 177.
[14] *Bk. of Fees*, 967, 974; *Feud. Aids*, v. 3; C 139/180. In 1276 Theobald de Verdon was stated to be overlord: *Cal. Inq. p.m.* ii, p. 121.
[15] *V.C.H. Staffs.* iv. 50, no. 177. He held Rushton and Hulton T.R.E. and T.R.W.: see below and p. 249.
[16] *S.H.C.* 1911, 443, grant of a plot of land in Burslem by Adam de Audley to Robt. Blund; the Hospitallers of St. John of Jerusalem were in receipt of rent for this plot.
[17] *Bk. of Fees*, 967, 974; *S.H.C.* N.S. xi. 242, 244; *Cal. Close* 1272–9, 234; *Cal. Inq. p.m.* ii, p. 121; *Feud. Aids*, v. 3.
[18] See p. 86.
[19] *Tunstall Ct. R.* (*T.N.S.F.C.* lix–lxvi), *passim*; *S.H.C.* xii (1), 213; Hist. MSS. Com. *House of Lords*, N.S. iv. 310; S.R.O., Q/RPl 1781, 1801, 1820; see pp. 86–88.
[20] See p. 88.
[21] *Cal. Chart. R.* 1226–57, 409.
[22] *V.C.H. Staffs.* iv. 50, no. 176.
[23] See p. 249.
[24] *V.C.H. Staffs.* iv. 50, no. 176.
[25] Dugdale, *Mon.* v. 715.
[26] *Close R.* 1234–7, 35; *Cal. Chart R.* 1226–57, 458.
[27] *Tax. Eccl.* (Rec. Com.), 252.
[28] *Valor Eccl.* (Rec. Com.), iii. 107.
[29] *L. & P. Hen. VIII*, xiii (2), p. 147; S.C. 6/Hen. VIII/3353, m. 12d; ibid. 3354, m. 37.
[30] *L. & P. Hen. VIII*, xiv (2), p. 302; S.C. 6/Hen. VIII/3353, m. 12d.
[31] Ward, *Stoke*, 275 and n.

[32] Ibid. 275, 276, 278–9; *S.H.C.* xvi. 137; ibid. N.S. vi(1), 6; S.R.O., Index to Gamekeepers' Deps., where it is called a manor; Lich. Dioc. Regy., Tithe Appt., Burslem.
[33] S.R.O., D. 260/M/box 25, bdle. k, Royalist Compositions; *S.H.C.* 4th ser. i. 255.
[34] S.R.O., Q/RRp 4; S.R.O., D. 418/M 11, M 17, M 24; Ward, *Stoke*, 275–6, 280, 287; Adams, *Adams Family*, 128, 184, 185, 287, and add. and corr. p. C; see p. 118.
[35] S.R.O., Q/RRr, m. 3; ibid. Q/RRp 4; Ward, *Stoke*, 216, 280; *Burslem Par. Reg.* i, 229; ibid. iii. 662, 683; St. Peter's, Cobridge, Bapt. Reg. i, 15 Feb. 1797.
[36] See p. 272.
[37] Adams, *Adams Family*, 111.
[38] Ward, *Stoke*, 276; *Complete Peerage*, 'Camoys'.
[39] W.S.L. 136/40, f. 3.
[40] Lich. Dioc. Regy., Tithe Appt., Burslem.
[41] T. M. Leith, Recs. of the Mission of St. Peter, Cobridge (MS. at St. Peter's R.C. Church, Cobridge), f. 80a; White, *Dir. Staffs.* (1851).
[42] *Staffs. Sentinel*, 23 May 1885.
[43] Shaw, *Staffs. Potteries*, 37.
[44] O.S. Map 6" Staffs. xii SW. (1925). Rushton Grange is the Manor Farm described by Arnold Bennett at the beginning of *Clayhanger* as 'the astonishing farm, with barns and ricks and cornfields complete, seemingly quite unaware of its forlorn oddness in that foul arena of manufacture'. For a description of the house c. 1800 see p. 113.
[45] Dugdale, *Mon.* v. 715.
[46] S.C. 6/Hen. VIII/3353, m. 12d.
[47] Ward, *Stoke*, 282.
[48] U.C.N.S., Sneyd MSS., Burslem Deeds.

1598,[49] and he died there in 1653.[50] It was the home of his son William in 1657.[51] A Richard Badley was occupant in 1678,[52] but the Stevenson family were again living there between at least 1686[53] and 1704.[54] By 1742 it was held by Thomas Harrison[55] whose family remained there until at least 1807 when another Thomas Harrison died there.[56] It was on the same site that in 1828 Richard Riley built the present Bank House, 'a showy mansion on the summit of the ridge' above the Hamil, on the east side of the present High Lane.[57] Riley died before taking possession, and the house, though offered for sale in 1829,[58] was owned in 1848 with some 10 acres of land by Mary and Elizabeth Riley who had leased it out.[59] Still a private residence in 1916,[60] the house was taken over after the First World War by the Burslem Suburban Club and Institute,[61] its present (1960) occupants. It is a tall square stucco building with castellated parapets and angle turrets.

The Big House, which stands on the corner of Wedgwood Street and Moorland Road, was built in 1751 by Thomas and John Wedgwood, fifth and sixth sons of Aaron Wedgwood (d. 1743) and the first master-potters to make the manufacture of pottery a large-scale commercial undertaking rather than a domestic industry.[62] Thomas died childless in 1776 and John in 1780 when the Big House estate and potworks passed to Thomas, John's second son.[63] By 1816 Thomas had sold the Big House potworks, which was situated to the rear of the house,[64] but he continued to live at the house, dying unmarried in 1826.[65] It presumably passed to his elder brother John, of Bignall End, who died in 1838 and whose disputed inheritance eventually passed to the Woods of Brownhills, the heirs-at-law as descendants of John Wedgwood of the Big House.[66] The house was the home of his friend Enoch Wood's eldest son Enoch in 1829,[67] but by 1834 was in the hands of John Irvin Holden.[68] In the 1850's the house was occupied by John Wedg Wood of the Woodlands Pottery, Tunstall (d. 1857), a younger son of John Wood of Brownhills and a great-grandson of the John Wedgwood who built the Big House.[69] The home in 1860 of George Alcock,[70] the house had by 1879 become the premises of the Burslem Conservative Club,[71] which retained it until 1922 when the Midland Bank, the present occupants, took it over.[72]

The Birch House, on the west side of what was later Swan Square,[73] was occupied in 1569 by Richard Daniel[74] and was held of the Sneyds' manor of Tunstall by members of the Daniel family until at least 1677.[75] It was evidently enfranchised with most of the land in the Sneyds' part of Tunstall manor in 1619.[76] In 1742 the tenant was Urian Leigh[77] and c. 1750 Joshua Ball.[78] The house was still standing in 1838[79] but no longer exists.

The Brick House, on the east side of what was later St. John's Square, was occupied in 1657 by John Adams (d.1687), whose pottery there is said to have been the earliest important potworks in Burslem.[80] The house and works were owned by this branch of the Adams family until the 19th century, although in the hands of tenants (including Josiah Wedgwood from 1762 until 1770) for most of the period after the death of John Adams in 1757.[81] In 1836 the property was divided, part of it being sold as the site for the Independent Chapel opened in 1838, part leased to Beech and Jones, potters, and the rest divided among several other tenants.[82] In 1840 the plot east of Brickhouse Street was sold to the tenant, a plumber and glazier, and after changing hands several times was conveyed c. 1879 to the Burslem Corporation for the extension of the Wedgwood Institute.[83] The remainder, except for Deans's printing works, was sold to William Beech in 1846, and after his death in 1864 the potworks was run by Beech and Podmore.[84] In 1876 part of these premises was sold to the Burslem local board for the new covered market and the rest to a Mr. Beardmore.[85]

The house, which was probably built before the middle of the 17th century, when the use of brick instead of timber was unusual enough to account for its name, was a small rectangular building with end gables and dormer windows to the attic story.[86] The mullioned and transomed windows may have been of stone. By the 19th century the works consisted of a large irregular group of two-storied brick ranges surrounding five bottle ovens.[87] The name survives in Brick House Street, running north from

[49] *Burslem Par. Reg.* i. 12–24, *passim.*
[50] Ibid. 67.   [51] Ibid. p. iv.
[52] Ward, *Stoke*, app. p. viii.   [53] Ibid.
[54] *Burslem Par. Reg.* i. 136.
[55] Ward, *Stoke*, app. p. xxviii.
[56] *Burslem Par. Reg.* iii. 646, 653, 751, 789.
[57] Ward, *Stoke*, 210; Shaw, *Staffs. Potteries*, 33, where it is described as 'a very beautiful mansion'; Yates, *Map of Staffs.* (1775).
[58] Shaw, *Staffs. Potteries*, 32, 33; H. Wedgwood, *Staffs.: Up and Down the County*, ii. 20; Ward, *Stoke*, 210.
[59] Lich. Dioc. Regy., Tithe Maps and Appt., Burslem; Adams, *Adams Family*, 322, 324; White, *Dir. Staffs.* (1851).
[60] *Kelly's Dir. Staffs.* (1916), showing Sam. J. Simpson resident there. For a picture of the house at this period see Adams, *Adams Family*, plate facing p. 328.
[61] *Kelly's Dir. Staffs.* (1924).
[62] Wedgwood, *Wedgwood Family*, 153–4, 157; date and initials on rainwater head on E. wall; see p. 134. For a description of the house see p. 110.
[63] Wedgwood, *Wedgwood Family*, 157, 158.
[64] See p. 134.
[65] Wedgwood, *Wedgwood Family*, 158; Parson and Bradshaw, *Dir. Staffs.* (1818).
[66] Wedgwood, *Wedgwood Family*, 157–8 and pedigree facing p. 165; Adams, *Adams Family*, 163 n. 1.
[67] Shaw, *Staffs. Potteries*, 31; Wedgwood, *Wedgwood*

Family, 159; Falkner, *Wood Family*, pedigree.
[68] White, *Dir. Staffs.* (1834).
[69] Ibid. (1851); *P.O. Dir. Staffs.* (1854); Wedgwood, *Wedgwood Family*, 165 and Wood pedigree opposite.
[70] *P.O. Dir. Staffs.* (1860).
[71] Falkner, *Wood Family*, 93; *Kelly's Dir. Staffs.* (1880).
[72] *Evening Sentinel*, 20 Sept. 1956.
[73] Ward, *Stoke*, app. p. xxviii.
[74] *Tunstall Ct. R.* (*T.N.S.F.C.* lxii), 64.
[75] Ibid. lxv. 86, 95, 102; lxvi. 103, 107; *Burslem Par. Reg.* i. 23, 48, 51, 54, 59, 88; U.C.N.S., Sneyd MSS., Burslem Deeds, enfranchisement 17 Aug. 17 Jas. I; ibid. Ct. R. 7/26. The house in Burslem occupied by Thos. Daniel and Jane Daniel, widow, in 1698 (W.S.L. 57/37) may have been the Birch House.
[76] *Tunstall Ct. R.* (*T.N.S.F.C.* lxiv), 128; ibid. lxv. 102.
[77] Ward, *Stoke*, app. p. xxviii.
[78] Ibid. p. xxxii.   [79] Ibid.
[80] Ward, *Stoke*, app. p. xxviii; Adams, *Adams Family*, 108–9; see p. 132.
[81] Adams, *Adams Family*, 109–27.
[82] Ibid. 126.
[83] Ibid. 126–7; see p. 141.
[84] Adams, *Adams Family*, 127.
[85] Ibid.; see p 131.
[86] E. Meteyard, *Life of Josiah Wedgwood*, i. 331, fig. 74.
[87] Ibid. 455, fig. 91; H.R.L., old photographs of the so-called Bell Works before demolition.

Queen Street and indicating the approximate site of the buildings.

Brownhills House and a pottery nearby were built by John Wood, son of Ralph Wood, after his purchase in 1782 of the property from which the Brownhills district takes its name and which had descended first in the Burslem family from at least 1590 and later in a branch of the Wedgwood family.[88] John Wood was murdered in 1797 by Dr. John Oliver, the disappointed suitor of John's daughter Maria.[89] He was succeeded by his son John who in 1830 demolished the factory, enlarged the house, and laid out the grounds, so that c. 1840 it was considered that Brownhills House could 'for amenity of situation challenge any residence within the borough'.[90] A 20-acre estate in 1848,[91] the property was still owned by the Wood family in 1912,[92] but it is now (1960) occupied by a girls' high school.

Brownhills Villa, 'an elegant house' to the west, was built in the 1830's by Howard Haywood and his brother Richard Howard Haywood, who had a brick and tile factory nearby.[93] It remained their home for some 40 years[94] but is no longer in existence.

Bycars (or Bycroft) House and farm in Sneyd, lying to the north-east of Burslem town where the name still survives in Bycars Road and Bycars Lane, was the home of Thomas Mitchell in 1658[95] and of Daniel Nixon in 1742.[96] In 1760 an estate called 'the two Bicars', tenanted by Brindley and Rogers, was bought from Charles Crewe by John Wedgwood of the Big House.[97] The farmhouse had been pulled down by the 1830's when the name survived in the Bycars Colliery and Flint Mill.[98]

A house and lands to the south-east of Burslem church, the later Churchyard estate, were granted by one of the Audley barons to Thomas Crockett and his heirs apparently in the later 15th century. The rent of 20s. was to be paid to Burslem church to secure prayers 'for ever'.[99] By the early 16th century the estate had come into the hands of John Asbury whose son Thomas was curate of Burslem c. 1540–55 and lived in 'the priest's chamber' in the house.[1] The estate passed to John's daughter Elizabeth and John Shaw her husband.[2] John Shaw died in 1599,[3] and in 1639 his son John, sexton of Burslem (d. 1640), being childless, sold the estate to John Shaw, son of

his brother Thomas.[4] In 1640 the Rector of Stoke made an unsuccessful attempt to secure the estate as glebe; the 20s. rent was still being paid at this time.[5] John Shaw conveyed half the house and 50-acre estate, with the reversion of the other half, to his daughter Margaret and Thomas, son of Gilbert Wedgwood, on their marriage in 1653.[6] Thomas, who built the potworks attached to the estate,[7] died in 1679, and in fulfilment of the terms of his will his widow and his father-in-law conveyed the house and lands to his son John Wedgwood.[8] A further unsuccessful attempt was made in 1679 to secure the estate for the church, this time by the curate of Burslem,[9] who, however, married Thomas's eldest daughter in 1681.[10] The estate passed to John Wedgwood's younger brother Thomas in 1680 when their mother remarried and John moved to the Overhouse.[11] Thomas was succeeded in the Churchyard estate in 1716 by his second son Thomas[12] and he in 1739 by his son Thomas who later inherited the Overhouse and moved there.[13] The Churchyard estate, still of 50 acres, passed to Thomas's son Thomas in 1773.[14] In 1780 it was sold to Josiah Wedgwood of Etruria, who was uncle of this last Thomas.[15] Josiah had himself been born at the Churchyard House in 1730 and had served his apprenticeship to his eldest brother at the adjoining works from 1744 to 1749.[16] Thomas may have retained a lease of it, for in 1788, the year after his death, it was let to Joseph Wedgwood, a distant relative of Josiah and husband of his niece Mary. When Josiah died in 1795 the estate was sold to Thomas Green,[17] and the house was probably demolished at this time to allow for the extension of the factory buildings.[18]

Eliza Meteyard, writing c. 1865, gives an engraving of the building and a detailed description of its internal arrangements.[19] Much of her information is evidently based on memories handed down from a previous generation. It appears to have been a typical small farmhouse of the late 16th or early 17th century, timber-framed and with a thatched roof.

The Cobridge Gate estate was originally part of the Biddulphs' Rushton Grange property and was sold by them in 1672 to the Stevensons, who were already tenants.[20] In 1729 the Stevensons sold most of the estate, then in the tenure of Randall Bagnall, to John Adams of Birches Head and Ralph Taylor of the

[88] Ward, *Stoke*, 152; F. Falkner, *The Wood Family of Burslem*, 6; see p. 137.
[89] H. Wedgwood, *Staffs.: Up and Down the County*, iii. 47–68; *Burslem Par. Reg.* iii. 737.
[90] Ward, *Stoke*, 152–3; Lich. Dioc. Regy., Tithe Maps and Appt., Burslem, no. 794. For a description of the house see p. 113.
[91] Lich. Dioc. Regy., Tithe Maps and Appt., Burslem.
[92] Falkner, *Wood Family*, 5 and pedigree.
[93] Ibid. 154; Lich. Dioc. Regy., Tithe Maps and Appt., Burslem. By the early 1840's they had begun making 'architectural ornaments of terra cotta, especially adapted for edifices of the Elizabethan stile': Ward, *Stoke*, 154.
[94] Lich. Dioc. Regy., Tithe Maps and Appt., Burslem; *P.O. Dir. Staffs.* (1854, 1860, 1868, 1872); see p. 330.
[95] Ward, *Stoke*, app. p. viii.
[96] *Burslem Par. Reg.* i, pp. iv, v.
[97] Wedgwood, *Wedgwood Family*, 155.
[98] *Burslem Par. Reg.* i, p. v; Ward, *Stoke*, 210, and app. p. xxviii; Hargreaves, *Map of Staffs. Potteries*; Parson and Bradshaw, *Dir. Staffs.* (1818).
[99] Wedgwood, *Wedgwood Family*, 263, 265, and map facing p. 121.
[1] Ibid. 260, 263, 268; *S.H.C.* 1915, 251.
[2] Wedgwood, *Wedgwood Family*, 260, 263, 268.

[3] *Burslem Par. Reg.* i. 12.
[4] Wedgwood, *Wedgwood Family*, 256, 258, 263, 269; *Burslem Par. Reg.* i. 47.
[5] Wedgwood, *Wedgwood Family*, 255–62.
[6] Ibid. 256, 263–4, 269; *Burslem Par. Reg.* i. 68.
[7] See p. 133.
[8] Wedgwood, *Wedgwood Family*, 110, 111–12, 264.
[9] Ibid. 263–8.
[10] Ibid. 115.
[11] Ibid. 113–14, 117, 124, 126–7; *Burslem Par. Reg.* i. 107; see p. 120.
[12] Wedgwood, *Wedgwood Family*, 128, 129–30.
[13] Ibid. 130–1; *Burslem Par. Reg.* i. 206; see p. 120.
[14] Wedgwood, *Wedgwood Family*, 135, 136, 137.
[15] See p. 133.
[16] E. Meteyard, *Life of Josiah Wedgwood*, i. 222 and n.
[17] See p. 133.
[18] Ll. Jewitt, *The Wedgwoods*, 98, 99; Jewitt, *Ceramic Art*, 438. Jewitt states (ibid. 439) that a house near the works occupied by Joseph had been built by one of the Wedgwoods and still existed as the Mitre Hotel in 1883.
[19] Meteyard, *Wedgwood*, i. 200–2, and fig. 52 on p. 188.
[20] Adams, *Adams Family*, 184; H.R.L., EMT 10–672; see p. 116.

Old Hall, Hanley.[21] John Adams sold a small part of his share in 1750 to Joseph Warburton, husband of his distant relative Mary Adams,[22] and the remainder of this moiety was divided at John's death in 1753 between his two youngest sons, Joseph and Benjamin.[23] In 1769 Joseph's portion was bought by William Adams of the Brick House[24] who in the same year bought a potworks at Cobridge[25] and who in 1777 acquired Benjamin's share from Benjamin's son Thomas.[26] The Adams's moiety included Cobridge Gate House, cottages, lands, coal mines, and the Bull's Head Inn at Sneyd Green.[27] In 1790 William Adams also bought the other moiety from Ralph Taylor's nephew and great-nephews, the Heaths.[28] From c. 1769 to 1806 he was acquiring other land in Cobridge from the Daniel, Bourne, Hales, and Warburton families, and besides making pottery he was also mining extensively in Cobridge.[29] He demolished Cobridge Gate House c. 1780 and built on its site Cobridge Hall with gardens, a park, and a drive running up from what is now Vale Place, the southern extension of Waterloo Road.[30] He died in 1831[31] and the hall and a 31-acre estate remained the home of his unmarried sons and daughters, the youngest of whom, Mary, died in 1869.[32] This branch of the Adams family then came to an end, and most of the property passed to the descendants of Mary's aunt Lucy Daniel.[33] The hall was being demolished in 1913.[34]

Cobridge Cottage, situated off Elder Road in the area of the later Grange and Mawdesley Streets, was occupied by Ralph Stevenson, a potter, between at least 1803 and 1818.[35] In the 1820's it was a convent[36] and by the 1830's the home of Samuel Alcock, a potter.[37] Cobridge Cottage had been demolished by 1913.[38]

A house called the Hadderidge was built after the middle of the 18th century on land of that name which lay on the road leading south-west out of what was later St. John's Square.[39] The land had been in the Adams family since the 16th century or earlier,[40]

and in or after 1736 was leased with a potworks by Ralph Adams of the Brick House to his son-in-law John Shrigley, who moved away c. 1750.[41] Ralph's son William Adams sold the house, pottery, and much of the estate to his brother-in-law Thomas Heath in 1806.[42] Dying unmarried in 1829, Thomas was succeeded by his sister Sarah Adams (d. 1846), a widow from 1829; her sons for a time ran the Hadderidge works and later leased it out.[43] On the dissolution of the family partnership in 1853 William Adams, one of these sons, took over the Hadderidge and Greenfield (Tunstall) estates and works, having in 1836 bought the Lower Hadderidge—part of the Hadderidge estate not included in the 1806 sale—from the Cobridge Hall branch of the Adams family.[44] The estate passed to William's son William, who succeeded in 1865.[45] The name of the estate survives in the streets called Lower and Upper Hadderidge, and the house and works still stand.[46]

By the 1750's the Ivy House, with potworks attached, stood to the north-west of the Big House.[47] Owned by John and Thomas Wedgwood of the Big House, the property was leased in 1759 to Josiah Wedgwood, their distant relative, who then began working on his own account for the first time.[48] He gave up the house and pottery in 1762, moving to the Brick House,[49] but c. 1774 he made an offer to buy the Ivy House and works from the Big House Wedgwoods who, however, would not sell.[50] The property evidently passed with the Big House to John Wedgwood's son Thomas (d. 1826),[51] and it was sold in 1831 and 1834 to the market commissioners who demolished the buildings and incorporated the site in the new market-place.[52] The Ivy House itself appears to have been little more than a cottage, built of brick or stone and having stone mullioned windows. It probably dated from the later 17th century.[53]

A house and land called Jackfield in the Hamil in Sneyd were occupied by Richard Leigh in 1640.[54] This had probably been the Leigh family's home

[21] Adams, *Adams Family*, 128, 184; H.R.L., EMT 11–729. Part of the estate, in Shelton, passed to the Hales family: see p. 272.
[22] Adams, *Adams Family*, 284.
[23] Ibid. 128, 199.   [24] Ibid. 128, 215.
[25] See p. 137.
[26] Adams, *Adams Family*, 128–9, 220 n. 3; H.R.L., EMT 11–777(*b*).
[27] Adams, *Adams Family*, 127, 129, 185; H.R.L., EMT 14–790; see p. 140.
[28] Adams, *Adams Family*, 129; S.R.O., D. 239/M/1906.
[29] Adams, *Adams Family*, 131–2, 134–5, 136–8, 143, 157 and n.; see pp. 137, 140. John Bourne was his father-in-law and John Hales his step-father.
[30] Adams, *Adams Family*, 127–8, and plate facing p. 126; *William Adams*, ed. W. Turner (1923), 174–5; Hargreaves, *Map of Staffs. Potteries*.
[31] Adams, *Adams Family*, 165.
[32] Ibid. 162–3; Lich. Dioc. Regy., Tithe Maps and Appt., Burslem; *P.O. Dir. Staffs.* (1868). Wm.'s eldest and last surviving son, John, of Cobridge Hall and Newcastle, d. at Newcastle in 1847, while the other sons, Thos. and Wm., both of Cobridge Hall, had d. in 1835 and 1834.
[33] Adams, *Adams Family*, 164, 165.
[34] Ibid. 166.
[35] Ibid. 166–7; Ward, *Stoke*, 286; Parson and Bradshaw, *Dir. Staffs.* (1818), 47.   [36] See p. 272.
[37] White, *Dir. Staffs.* (1834); Ward, *Stoke*, 286, which also shows Ralph Stevenson's pottery in the hands of John and Geo. Alcock.   [38] Adams, *Adams Family*, 166.
[39] Ibid. 320 (although the statement that it was probably built by Wm. Adams of Cobridge Hall c. 1760 cannot be correct since Wm. was born only in 1748), and plate facing

p. 318. The map of Burslem c. 1750 (Wedgwood, *Wedgwood Family*, facing p. 121) shows the land but not the house.   [40] Adams, *Adams Family*, 93–94.
[41] Ibid. 116–17. For the history of the pottery see p. 134.
[42] Adams, *Adams Family*, 320, 321 note; P. W. L. Adams, *Notes on N. Staffs. Families*, 11.
[43] Adams, *Adams Family*, 330, 331, 340–1. She had m. her father's partner, Wm. Adams, in 1793: ibid., pedigree between pp. 292 and 293.
[44] Ibid. 340–1; see pp. 91, 100.
[45] Adams, *Adams Family*, 337, 352.
[46] For a short description of the house see p. 112.
[47] Wedgwood, *Wedgwood Family*, map facing p. 121; Jewitt, *The Wedgwoods*, 120–2; see p. 135.
[48] Wedgwood, *Wedgwood Family*, 156, 168, and pedigrees following pp. 136, 164. Josiah m. Sarah, niece of John and Thos.: ibid. 164, 168.
[49] Ibid. 156; see pp. 117, 133.
[50] Jewitt, *The Wedgwoods*, 123, 157.
[51] Ibid. 123.
[52] Ward, *Stoke*, 256; Jewitt, *The Wedgwoods*, 123; see pp. 130, 135. Jewitt's statement that Thos., descendant of the Big House Wedgwoods, sold the property is incorrect since Thos. d. in 1826, but presumably Thos.'s elder brother, John of Bignal End (d. 1838), is meant: ibid. 157–8.
[53] Meteyard, *Wedgwood* i, fig. 59. This view of the house and works is reproduced on a mug commemorating the Wedgwood bicentenary in 1959. See also Ward, *Stoke*, engraving at foot of p. 232.
[54] *Burslem Par. Reg.* i. 47. 'Jacparok', the name of arable land in Tunstall manor in 1408, has been identified as Jackfield: Adams, *Adams Family*, 13.

since at least the beginning of the century[55] and thus the estate in Sneyd held by Thomas Leigh which the Sneyds enfranchised as lords of Tunstall manor in 1619.[56] The Leighs remained there at least until the death in 1748 of Margaret Leigh, 'the Burslem witch',[57] and c. 1758 the estate was in the hands of Joseph Booth.[58] By 1760 it was held by the Bennett family,[59] and by the late 1830's John Bennett was evidently owner as well as occupier.[60]

Another estate at Jackfield was held in 1657 by John Malkin whose son Thomas succeeded him there in 1683.[61] Thomas Malkin, probably Thomas's son,[62] was making black and mottled pottery at the Hamil in the early 18th century.[63] In 1752 Jonah Malkin sold this Jackfield estate to his wife's brother, John Wedgwood of the Big House (d. 1780), who left it to his youngest son Richard (d. unmarried 1787).[64] It passed to John's eldest son John Wedgwood of Bignall End (d. 1838), and after a long dispute the ownership probably passed to the Woods of Brownhills as heirs-at-law of this branch of the Wedgwood family.[65] In 1848 the farm was held by John Dean who was still living at the Hamil in 1860 as a farmer, colliery agent, and brick and tile manufacturer.[66]

The whole Jackfield area is now occupied by housing of the late 19th and early 20th centuries.[67]

The Burslem family were living at Burslem by the end of the 13th century.[68] By the end of the 16th century their Burslem house was Dale Hall,[69] but they had also acquired the Park estate in Oldcott.[70] By 1616 they had moved their Burslem home to the Overhouse on Burslem Bank,[71] and on the division of the family estates in that year the Overhouse and Dale Hall were assigned to Thomas Burslem, his younger brother Robert taking the Park estate.[72] When Thomas died in 1628 both the Burslem properties passed to his younger daughter Katherine and her husband William Colclough.[73]

Katherine died at the Overhouse in 1669 and under the terms of the will of her son John Colclough (d. 1666) the house and some 100 acres in Burslem and Sneyd passed to her nephew Thomas

Wedgwood of the Churchyard House, second son of Katherine's elder sister Margaret and her husband Gilbert Wedgwood.[74] Thomas Wedgwood died in 1679 and on his widow's remarriage in 1680 the Overhouse passed to his son John[75] who died in 1705 with his daughter Katherine as his heir.[76] Thrice widowed, she died as Katherine Egerton at the Overhouse in 1756 and the house and some 160 acres in and near Burslem, 59 acres of it in hand, went to Thomas son and heir of her cousin Thomas Wedgwood of the Churchyard.[77] In 1742, however, Thomas was either already living at the Overhouse or working the pottery attached to the estate.[78] His son Thomas succeeded in 1773 and died in 1787 with a son Thomas, a minor, as his heir; the potworks was by then leased out.[79] In 1810, a year after the death of this next Thomas, the Overhouse estate was sold to a Christopher Robinson, and he later sold it to John Wood who in turn sold it to a Mr. Challinor c. 1860,[80] probably Edward Challinor who had bought the pottery in 1819.[81] The house, rebuilt as a small double-fronted structure of brick evidently in the late 18th or early 19th century on 'the site of the old timber-built manor-house',[82] was occupied by the Twigg family about the middle years of the century[83] and was still a private residence in 1924.[84] It still (1960) stands, though in an altered form, and is occupied as offices. The potworks is still in operation.

Dale Hall, in the tenure of a Thomas Robinson in 1666, passed on Katherine Colclough's death in 1669 to Burslem Wedgwood, her great-nephew.[85] He may have been living there in 1673,[86] but the hall had evidently been abandoned by the early 18th century.[87] The site is thought to be in the built-up area south-east of St. Paul's churchyard.[88]

Sneyd farm was in existence by 1657 when it was occupied by a Thomas Bayley.[89] By 1719 it was held of Tunstall manor by George Parker of Macclesfield (Earl of Macclesfield from 1732), who was then mining there.[90] The farm was in the hands of a tenant, William Baddeley, in 1742.[91] The house, called Sneyd House by the early 19th century,[92] and

[55] Tunstall Ct. R. (T.N.S.F.C. lxiii), 75; ibid. lxiv. 126.
[56] U.C.N.S., Sneyd MSS., Burslem Deeds.
[57] Ibid. 20 May, 15 Chas. II; ibid. Sneyd Green Deeds, 19 May, 1 Jas. II; Burslem Par. Reg. i, pp. iv, v, 48, 126, 127, 168, 231; Ward, Stoke, 223, and app. p. viii; Tunstall Ct. R. (T.N.S.F.C. lxvi), 142–3; E. J. D. Warrillow, 'The Burslem Witch' (Staffs. Life, i), 50; see p. 122. A low thatched building known as Molly Leigh's cottage was still standing in 1900: Staffs. Life, i. 50.
[58] Burslem Par. Reg. i, p. v.
[59] S.R.O., Roads and Bridges Index.
[60] Ward, Stoke, 210 and app. p. xxviii; see p. 128.
[61] Burslem Par. Reg. i, pp. iv, 112; Ward, Stoke, app. p. xxviii; P. W. L. Adams, Wolstanton, 95; Tunstall Ct. R. (T.N.S.F.C. lxvi), 120. Land on the S. side of the present Hamil Rd. was called Malkins Moor in the mid-18th cent.: Wedgwood, Wedgwood Family, map facing p. 121.
[62] Burslem Par. Reg. i. 115.
[63] Wedgwood, Wedgwood Family, 124.
[64] Ibid. 154, 157, and pedigree following p. 164. A younger son of the Churchyard Wedgwoods (see p. 118) m. into the Malkin family in 1719 and was apparently connected with the Hamil pottery: Wedgwood, Wedgwood Family, 205.
[65] Wedgwood, Wedgwood Family, 157–8; Lich. Dioc. Regy., Tithe Maps and Appt., Burslem; see p. 118.
[66] Lich. Dioc. Regy., Tithe Maps and Appt., Burslem; White, Dir. Staffs. (1851); P.O. Dir. Staffs. (1854, 1860).
[67] See p. 107.
[68] S.H.C. n.s. xi. 253; Wedgwood, Wedgwood Family, 59–62 and pedigree following p. 72.
[69] Ward, Stoke, 187; Wedgwood, Wedgwood Family, 67.
[70] See p. 92.
[71] Wedgwood, Wedgwood Family, 67, 71, 72, and map facing p. 121.
[72] Ibid. 69, 71–72; see p. 92.
[73] Wedgwood, Wedgwood Family, 72–77.
[74] Ibid. 78–79, 85–86; see p. 118.
[75] Wedgwood, Wedgwood Family, 110, 111–12, 117; Burslem Par. Reg. i. 107.
[76] Wedgwood, Wedgwood Family, 119, 120.
[77] Ibid. 120, 122, and pedigree following p. 136.
[78] Ibid. 134 and map facing p. 121; Jewitt, The Wedgwoods, 125–6; U.C.N.S., Sneyd MSS., Burslem Deeds, abstract of title deeds relating to Burslem estates of Thos. Wedgwood, f. 1; see p. 133.
[79] Wedgwood, Wedgwood Family, 137–8.
[80] Ibid. 138; Jewitt, The Wedgwoods, 127.
[81] See p. 133.
[82] Meteyard, Wedgwood, i. 181 n. 1 and fig. 49.
[83] White, Dir. Staffs. (1851); P.O. Dir. Staffs. (1860); Adams, Adams Family, 324.
[84] Kelly's Dir. Staffs. (1924).
[85] Wedgwood, Wedgwood Family, 80–81, 86, 97–98, and pedigrees following pp. 72, 100.
[86] Ward, Stoke, app. p. viii.
[87] Ibid. 188 n.
[88] Ibid. 187–8 and n.
[89] Ward, Stoke, app. p. xxviii.
[90] Ibid. 209, 599; Tunstall Ct. R. (T.N.S.F.C. lxvi), 143; C.P. 25 (2)/1003, 9 Geo. I. Hil.; Complete Peerage, 'Macclesfield'; see p. 139.
[91] Ward, Stoke, app. p. xxviii.
[92] Burslem Par. Reg. ii. 592; iii. 625.

a farm of 162 acres were owned by the Earl of Macclesfield in 1848 and tenanted by a William Heath.[93] The property was described *c.* 1838 as 'abounding, like all the rest of the hamlet, with mines of coal and ironstone'.[94] The house was still a private residence in 1940 when it was destroyed during an air-raid, and the site has since been taken over by the National Coal Board.[95]

James Tellwright ('Telryche') held a house and copyhold estate at Sneyd within the manor of Tunstall in 1549.[96] The house and land, known as Stanfields by the early 19th century and situated on the hillside below High Lane,[97] were enfranchised by the Sneyds in 1619[98] and remained in the occupation of the Tellwright family until the death in 1828 of John Tellwright, a coal master, 'a man of primitive speech and manners, wholly unalloyed by the refinements of modern times'.[99] Most of the property passed to his eldest son, William Tellwright of Biddulph, formerly a tilewright and *c.* 1838 described as 'a respectable yeoman'.[1] By 1848 the 33-acre Stanfields farm was held of him by Samuel Cork, still the tenant in 1854.[2] Some outbuildings still standing on the waste-ground north of Dolly's Lane (1958) may have belonged to this farm.

CHURCHES. By 1297 Burslem was a chapelry in the parish of Stoke-upon-Trent[3] and retained that status until 1809 when it was made parochial under the Stoke Rectory Act of 1807.[4] As a chapelry it was in the charge of a curate appointed by the Rector of Stoke.[5] In several respects, however, it had parochial status before 1809, and indeed from the late 16th century it was often called a parish.[6] It organized its own poor relief and highway maintenance,[7] and by 1553 it had its own churchwardens.

Under the Act of 1807 the living was made a rectory and the patronage vested in the trustees of William Robinson, rector and patron of Stoke.[8] The patronage was sold in 1809 to William Adams of Cobridge Hall,[9] who presented in 1811.[10] It is not clear why, on the resignation of his nominee in the same year, the next presentation was made by Josiah Spode as patron.[11] When William Adams died in 1831 the patronage passed to his son Thomas and on Thomas's death in 1835 to his sisters.[12] They had sold it by 1850 to Charles Hebert, rector 1850–8.[13] In 1858 John Armstrong became the rector and patron,[14] and after his death in 1869 the patronage passed to John Morris who presented Alfred Watton,[15] himself the patron by 1871.[16] Watton died in 1886 and his widow made the next presentation,[17] but shortly afterwards the patronage was acquired by Robert Heath, the younger, of Biddulph Grange.[18] From him it passed *c.* 1918 to the Church of England Trust Society,[19] which, as the Martyrs' Memorial and Church of England Trust, still holds it.[20]

By 1738 there had been assigned to the curate the tithes, fees, and dues arising within the chapelry.[21] By the Act of 1807 these revenues were legally secured to the new rectory, which was further endowed with 7½ acres of glebe in Burslem and an annual pension of £68 out of the revenues of Stoke rectory.[22] Much of the new parish was tithe-free, since it had once belonged to Hulton Abbey. This exempt area lay at Abbey Hulton and Rushton Grange and thus included Cobridge.[23] From *c.* 1815 the tithe was compounded at an average rate of 5*s.* an acre,[24] and in 1843 it was commuted for £400.[25] The glebe lay across the course of the present Waterloo Road and over the two decades from 1815, the year the construction of that road was begun, was largely sold for building plots. The proceeds were applied towards building the rectory-house and increasing the endowments of the church.[26] The rector's net annual income over the three years 1828–31 was £530 out of which he paid £158 to an assistant

[93] Lich. Dioc. Regy., Tithe Maps and Appt., Burslem.
[94] Ward, *Stoke,* 209.
[95] Ex inf. the Manager, Sneyd Colliery (1958).
[96] *Tunstall Ct. R.* (*T.N.S.F.C.* lix), 35. The family held land in Sneyd before the mid-15th cent. (Adams, *Adams Family,* 16), and Ward (*Stoke,* 203–4) suggests that the name is evidence of the early making of pottery in the area.
[97] Hargreaves, *Map of Staffs. Potteries* (1832); Ward, *Stoke,* 204.
[98] U.C.N.S., Sneyd MSS., Burslem Deeds.
[99] *Tunstall Ct. R.* (*T.N.S.F.C.* lix), 46; ibid. lxiii. 47, 64; ibid. lxvi. 142; Ward, *Stoke,* 204–5 and app. pp. viii, xxviii; *S.H.C.* 1947, 76; Parson and Bradshaw, *Dir. Staffs.* (1818).
[1] Ward, *Stoke,* 205.
[2] Lich. Dioc. Regy., Tithe Maps and Appt., Burslem; White, *Dir. Staffs.* (1851); *P.O. Dir. Staffs.* (1854).
[3] *S.H.C.* 1911, 246.
[4] Stoke Rectory Act, 47 Geo. III (sess. 2), c. 114 (local and personal). The act provided that the various chapelries should become parishes when the existing curates died or resigned.
[5] *S.H.C.* 1915, 251; Inst. Bks.; Lich. Dioc. Regy., Bp.'s Reg. 24, pp. 63–64.
[6] Ward, *Stoke,* app. pp. xvii, xxvii, xxix, xxxi; St. John's, Burslem, Churchwardens' and Overseers' Accts. 1700–95, *passim.*
[7] See pp. 125, 129.
[8] Stoke Rectory Act; Lich. Dioc. Regy., Bp.'s Reg. 28, p. 113.
[9] W.S.L. 11/158/4/1/50, 11/158/4/2/50, 11/158/4/12/50, 11/158/4/35/50. He insisted in 1809 that the rector was not to be absent for more than 30 days a year and was to live in the parish: Adams, *Adams Family,* 152.
[10] Lich. Dioc. Regy., Bp.'s Reg. 28, p. 142.

[11] Ibid. p. 156; Inst. Bks. Wm. Adams was patron in 1815: Burslem Glebe Act, 55 Geo. III, c. 57 (priv. act).
[12] Adams, *Adams Family,* 145; H.R.L., EM 25/1.
[13] S. W. Hutchinson, *Archdeaconry of Stoke-on-Trent,* 124; Lich. Dioc. Regy., Bp.'s Reg. 31, p. 213; Adams, *Adams Family,* 153, which gives the date of sale as 1853. Hebert, however, presented himself in 1850.
[14] Hutchinson, op. cit. 124; *Lich. Dioc. Ch. Cal.* (1859).
[15] Hutchinson, op. cit. 124; *Lich. Dioc. Ch. Cal.* (1870).
[16] *Lich. Dioc. Ch. Cal.* (1871).
[17] Ibid. (1887); Hutchinson, op. cit. 124; Lich. Dioc. Regy., Bp.'s Reg. 35, p. 72.
[18] *Lich. Dioc. Ch. Cal.* (1889); Hutchinson, op. cit. 124; Lich. Dioc. Regy., Bp.'s Reg. 36, p. 402. Presumably the Robt. Heath who succeeded his father Robt. in 1893 is meant: Burke, *Land. Gent.* (1952), 1199.
[19] *Lich. Dioc. Ch. Cal.* (1917–18, 1919); Lich. Dioc. Regy., Bp.'s Reg. 38, p. 129. This trust and the Martyrs' Memorial Patronage Trust amalgamated in 1922: Lich. Dioc. Regy., Bp.'s Reg. 38, pp. 289–300.
[20] *Lich. Dioc. Dir.* (1959).
[21] Ward, *Stoke,* app. pp. xxix–xxx, where the emoluments are listed.
[22] Stoke Rectory Act; A. L. Lumb, *Burslem Par. Church* (pamph. on sale in the ch.). Instead of the £68 the rector could demand a sum equivalent to 143 bushels of wheat if he wished.
[23] Lich. Dioc. Regy., Tithe Maps and Appt., Burslem; Ward, *Stoke,* 213. In the same way Rushton and part of Hulton were exempt from ch. rates: ibid. 212–13.
[24] Ward, *Stoke,* 214.
[25] Lich. Dioc. Regy., Tithe Maps and Appt., Burslem.
[26] Burslem Glebe Act, 55 Geo. III, c. 57 (priv. act), where the glebe is given as nearly 4 a.; Ward, *Stoke,* 224; see p. 112.

curate.[27] The pension of £68 was still being paid by the Church Commissioners in 1958.[28]

Burslem chapel had two churchwardens in 1553,[29] but by the mid-17th century one was appointed for each of the townships of Burslem, Sneyd, and Hulton, chosen from certain landholders in rotation.[30] This system of rotation was abandoned c. 1789, although one churchwarden continued to be chosen from each township, and by the early 19th century a fourth was appointed by the minister.[31] In 1789 the vestry decided to create a new office for the prevention of 'disorders and irregularities that arise from children playing in and daubing the seats in church on Sundays and other times' with a wage of 2s. a week to be paid out of the church rates; an official 'for keeping good order in the church on Sundays' was still being appointed in 1792.[32] By the early 19th century the organist's salary was paid out of the market tolls, a system which received official sanction in the Act of 1825 regulating the market[33] and remained in force until 1851 when the Burslem local board refused to continue the payments.[34]

One of the Audley barons, apparently in the later 15th century, gave a 20s. rent-charge to Burslem chapel to secure prayers 'for ever'.[35]

The church of *ST. JOHN THE BAPTIST*, lying below the southern slope of the ridge on which Burslem is built, consists of a nave, an apsidal chancel, and a low west tower flanked by vestries. The tower is of stone and was almost certainly built c. 1536.[36] It is entirely late Perpendicular in style and, in spite of claims made to the contrary, shows no signs of earlier work. In the west wall a low Tudor-arched doorway has a three-light window above it. The belfry stage is pierced by three-light Perpendicular windows and surmounted by an embattled parapet. The body of the church is of brick and is said to have been built in 1717 to replace an earlier timber-framed thatched structure which was burnt down in that year.[37] In 1788 the church, 'being too small for the number of inhabitants', was lengthened by the addition of the present chancel 'according to Mr. Thomas Sherwin's plan'.[38] The alterations, which appear to have been instigated by Enoch Wood, then churchwarden, cost £700.[39] They included the raising of the roof and probably the insertion of additional galleries. Externally the building is very plain, the nave being lighted on both sides by tall round-headed windows in brick reveals. Near both ends of the south wall and near the east end of the north wall are shorter windows with stone doorways below them. The chancel has an apsidal east end in which there is a stone Venetian window. It is possible that some of the original features were reinstated when the chancel was extended in 1788; the two pedimented doorways near the east end appear to belong to the early, rather than the late, 18th century. The doors give access to two vestibules flanking the chancel, which at one time contained gallery staircases.[40] It is known that there was formerly a gallery at the east end of the church on which an organ, erected by subscription in 1792, was mounted.[41] A west gallery, which still exists, is probably of the same period, and there may also have been side galleries. A new pulpit, a desk, and a 'singers' table' were installed c. 1789.[42] Under a vestry resolution of 1793 a brick vestry was added on the south side of the tower in the following year.[43]

In 1878 the nave was restored and refitted at a cost of £2,000.[44] A new organ was installed in the west gallery and the east gallery was probably cleared away at the same time. Alterations to the fittings at the east end were made in 1919.[45] The north-west vestry was added in the 1930's.[46]

The chancel contains a modern tablet commemorating various members of the Adams family who lived between the 15th and 17th centuries. Also in the chancel are two terra-cotta plaques, a figure of Christ and a Descent from the Cross, which were modelled by Enoch Wood (d. 1840), the first when he was fifteen years old and the second when he was eighteen. These, together with a bust of John Wesley and other ornaments (now in the vestry), had originally been placed in the Wood family vault.[47]

In the churchyard is a medieval stone coffin, said to have been brought from Hulton Abbey.[48] Near it stands a table-tomb set with its axis north and south. This is reputed to be the grave of Margaret Leigh (d. 1748). According to local legend she was a witch whose ghost could be laid only after her body had been exhumed and her grave reorientated.[49]

Because of 'the great increase of inhabitants' in the parish the churchyard had to be extended in 1804.[50] It was further extended in 1847[51] and 'improved' in

[27] *Rep. Com. Eccl. Rev.* H.C. 54, pp. 466–7 (1835), xxii.
[28] Ex inf. the Rector of Burslem (1958).
[29] *S.H.C.* 1915, 251.
[30] Ward, *Stoke*, 213.
[31] Ibid.; St. John's, Burslem, Churchwardens' and Overseers' Accts. 1700–95, p. 173; Lich. Dioc. Regy., Bp.'s Reg. E, p. 199.
[32] Churchwardens' and Overseers' Accts. 1700–95, pp. 146, 160, 161.
[33] Ward, *Stoke*, 254; see p. 125. The same custom prevailed at Hanley: see p. 162.
[34] *Staffs. Advertiser*, 4 Jan., 4 Feb., 8 Mar., 10 May 1851; *Burslem Board of Health Rep. 1851*, 18–19 (copy in H.R.L.). The organist twice sued the board for the continuation of the payment but without success: ibid. 19; ibid. *1853*, 4–5.
[35] See p. 118.
[36] Adams, *Adams Family*, 145 n. 2, John Tunstall's bequest towards the building of the steeple of Burslem ch., 1535 or 1536; *S.H.C.* 1910, 246.
[37] Ward, *Stoke*, 221; *Burslem Par. Reg.* i, p. iii. A note by J. Buckler on a drawing of St. John's in W.S.L., Staffs. Views, p. 160 (*b*), states 'body of the church built 1738'.
[38] Ward, *Stoke*, 221; Churchwardens' and Overseers' Accts. 1700–95, pp. 143, 153. 'The pillars' were removed

at the same time. The tower was repaired in 1791–2: ibid. pp. 161, 162.
[39] Lumb, *Burslem Par. Ch.*, citing a note by Enoch Wood in his copy of Shaw, *Staffs. Potteries*. For this copy see Falkner, *Wood Family*, 88.
[40] Traces of the staircase are still visible.
[41] Ward, *Stoke*, 222; *Kelly's Dir. Staffs.* (1880). The organ gallery was mentioned in 1793: Churchwardens' and Overseers' Accts. 1700–95, p. 165.
[42] Churchwardens' and Overseers' Accts. 1700–95, pp. 145, 151.
[43] *Burslem Par. Reg.* i, p. iii; Churchwardens' and Overseers' Accts. 1700–95, p. 156, where its position was fixed as 'at the south end of the steeple', the cost to be met out of the poor rate.
[44] *Kelly's Dir. Staffs.* (1880).
[45] Faculty, 10 Mar. 1919, copy inserted in Burslem Churchwardens' and Overseers' Accts.
[46] Local inf.
[47] Inscriptions in chancel; Lumb, *Burslem Par. Ch.*; Falkner, *Wood Family*, 41–44.
[48] Ward, *Stoke*, 223. [49] Ibid.; see p. 120.
[50] Lich. Dioc. Regy., Bp.'s Reg. E, pp. 199–201; Ward, *Stoke*, 223.
[51] Warrillow, *Stoke*, 179.

1878.[52] The older part of the churchyard is still surrounded by brick walls dating from the late 18th or early 19th century. Iron gates of the same period stand at the north and east entrances, the latter being the more elaborate and having an ironwork overthrow incorporating a lamp bracket.

The plate in 1553 included a silver chalice and paten.[53] It now includes a silver flagon of 1718, a silver chalice of 1723, and a silver paten of 1724, all the gift of Katherine Egerton of the Overhouse (d. 1756), and a silver chalice and paten of 1848, given by Mary, widow of John Wood of Brownhills, in 1850.[54] There were three bells and a sacring bell in 1553.[55] Four new bells were installed in 1720.[56] These were recast in 1827 when two more were added,[57] and all six were rehung in 1911.[58]

The surviving registers date from 1636; the earlier book, dating from 1578, was burnt in the fire of 1717 but there is a transcript of it made in 1701.[59] The registers from 1578 to 1812 have been printed.[60] There is also a book of churchwardens' and overseers' accounts dating from 1700 to 1795, with some vestry minutes.

About the mid-16th century the curate of Burslem, Thomas Asbury, occupied a room in the Churchyard House known as the Priest's Chamber, but it passed with the rest of the estate to his sister and her family.[61] The inhabitants of Burslem petitioned William Primrose, Rector of Stoke 1618–33, to secure the room for the curate or schoolmaster of Burslem but without success.[62] Katherine Egerton (d. 1756) left £200 for the purchase of a house and land for the curate of Burslem, and the property acquired, a house next to the Crown Inn, was occupied by two successive curates. The estate was then secured by Thomas Wedgwood of the Overhouse (d. 1787), Katherine's residuary legatee, since the property was not legally settled and the bequest was void.[63] Despite the provision in the Act of 1807 that a parsonage house should be erected as soon as possible,[64] it was not until 1827 that a house was built on land called Wilberstones given by the patron, William Adams, who also contributed £250 towards the cost. After years of neglect the house fell into decay and was sold and demolished in or soon after 1903, the grounds being used to form Middleport Park in 1908. A house in Waterloo Road was bought instead for the rector by the patron, Robert Heath,[65] and this is still the rectory house.

Three mission centres have been opened from St. John's: St. John the Baptist Mission Room c. 1901–c. 1902, evidently replaced by the mission chapel at St. John's National school c. 1902–c. 1927;[66] and the Rectory Room c. 1905–c. 1927.[67]

The church of ST. PAUL, Dale Hall, was built in 1828–31 as a chapel of ease to St. John's. The site, to the north of Newcastle Street, was given by William Adams of Cobridge, patron of the mother church, and at that time it lay in almost open country. The cost of erection was met by a parliamentary grant of £8,000 and subscriptions and parish rates amounting to £4,000. The Burslem Market Trustees voted £1,000 out of their future income for the purchase of another 2 acres and the laying out of this and the rest of the site as the churchyard.[68] A parish covering Dale Hall and Longport was created out of St. John's parish in 1845.[69] The patronage of the living, a perpetual curacy until 1868 when it became a vicarage, has remained in the hands of the Rector of Burslem.[70] The rector's net annual income in 1831 was £109,[71] but the benefice was augmented from Queen Anne's Bounty in 1832 (£400) and 1833 (£200).[72]

The church, which provided some 2,000 sittings, was built of Hollington stone and was designed by Lewis Vulliamy (1791–1871) in the Perpendicular style.[73] It consists of an aisled and clerestoried nave of six bays, a shallow projecting chancel, and a west tower, 115 feet in height. The tower, which was provided with one bell,[74] rises in four stages, the belfry stage having paired Perpendicular windows and being surmounted by tall angle pinnacles. The base of the tower and the area below the west gallery form a vestibule with a staircase at each end. The aisles are occupied by side galleries and there was originally a second west gallery above the present one. This was removed in 1835 to make room for an organ, erected in the lower gallery in that year and still in position. The pulpit, font, and choir stalls are of later date but the church retains its original box pews 'of good deal, wainscot . . . painted to resemble oak', as well as the gallery fronts 'of stucco, but painted in oil, in resemblance of pannelled Gothic wainscot'.[75] The mural tablets include one to Henry Davenport (d. 1835). The open space surrounding the church and its position on rising ground contribute to an impressive exterior view, but the condition of the fabric and of the churchyard had deteriorated by 1960.

[52] *Kelly's Dir. Staffs.* (1880).
[53] *S.H.C.* 1915, 251.
[54] Inscription on plate; *Burslem Par. Reg.* p. vii; S. A. Jeavons, 'Church Plate in the Archdeaconry of Stoke-on-Trent' (*Trans. Birm. Arch. Soc.* lxxvii), 69, 70, 83; see p. 120.   [55] *S.H.C.* 1915, 251.
[56] Ward, *Stoke*, 222.
[57] Ibid.; C. Lynam, *Ch. Bells Staffs.* 43; A. E. Garbett, 'Ch. Bells Staffs'. (*Trans. Old Stafford Soc.* 1953–4), 16.
[58] Lumb, *Burslem Par. Ch.*
[59] *Burslem Par. Reg.* i, pp. x and 1.
[60] Staffs. Par. Reg. Soc. (1915).
[61] Wedgwood, *Wedgwood Family*, 261; *S.H.C.* 1915, 251; see p. 118.
[62] Wedgwood, *Wedgwood Family*, 260; Hutchinson, *Archdeaconry of Stoke*, 120.
[63] *13th Rep. Com. Char.* H.C. 349, p. 261 (1825), xi; Ward, *Stoke*, 225; see p. 120.
[64] Stoke Rectory Act.
[65] Adams, *Adams Family*, 151–2; *Burslem Par. Reg.* p. vii; Churchwardens' and Overseers' Accts. 1700–95, n. added in 20th cent. on p. 177; see p. 106.
[66] *Lich. Dioc. Ch. Cal.* (1902, 1903, 1928).

[67] Ibid. (1906, 1928).
[68] White, *Dir. Staffs.* (1834); Ward, *Stoke*, 247–8, 251; Lich. Dioc. Regy., Bp.'s Reg. I, pp. 229–43; H.O. 129/15/370/3/1; Adams, *Adams Family*, 154. The foundation stone was laid in 1828 and the church was consecrated in 1831. In *Staffs. Advertiser*, 29 Jan. 1831, the cost is given as about £10,000 and the amount of private subscription as £2,000.
[69] *Lond. Gaz.* 1845, p. 205. Part of St. Paul's parish was assigned to the new parish of St. Mary, Tunstall, in 1881: see p. 94.
[70] White, *Dir. Staffs.* (1851); *Lich. Dioc. Ch. Cal.* (1868, 1869, 1917–18); *Lich. Dioc. Dir.* (1959).
[71] *Rep. Com. Eccl. Rev.* 466–7.
[72] C. Hodgson, *An Acct. of the Augmentation of Small Livings by the Governors of the Bounty of Queen Anne* (1845), p. ccxcviii.
[73] Ward, *Stoke*, 248; H.M. Colvin, *Biog. Dict. Eng. Architects*, 643; see plate facing p. 112.
[74] Lynam, *Ch. Bells Staffs.* 43; Lich. Dioc. Regy., Bp.'s Reg. I, p. 241.
[75] Ward, *Stoke*, 250. For a detailed acct. of the church written about 10 years after its completion see ibid. 248–52.

A house on the north side of Newcastle Street west of Ellgreave Street erected by John Brindley *c.* 1773 was bought as the parsonage house, William Adams and the trustees of Queen Anne's Bounty contributing towards the cost.[76] It was sold in 1858 and a new house was built on the south side of Newcastle Street with the proceeds of the sale.[77] This has been sold to the Heath Filtration Co. Ltd., and the present vicarage house, purchased in 1958, is on Porthill Bank on the Wolstanton side of the Fowlea valley.[78]

Three mission chapels have been opened from St. Paul's: the present Sytch Mission Chapel, Bodley Street, in 1879;[79] St. John's Mission Chapel *c.* 1883, evidently closed within a year;[80] and Hope Mission Chapel opened in 1886 in the former Congregational chapel in Newcastle Street and replaced in 1897 by a mission chapel in Shirley Street which was closed *c.* 1957.[81]

CHRIST CHURCH, Cobridge, was built in 1839–41 as a chapel of ease to St. John's at a cost of some £1,500, about half of which was met by the Incorporated Society and the Lichfield Diocesan Church Extension Society and the rest by subscription.[82] The Rector of Burslem, Edward Whieldon, who for some years had been trying to found a church in the area, contributed generously out of the revenues of his rectory.[83] A parish consisting of Cobridge, Sneyd Green, and Abbey Hulton was created out of St. John's parish in 1844.[84] The living, a perpetual curacy at first and a vicarage from 1868, has remained in the gift of the Rector of Burslem.[85] The church is built of yellow brick in a simple Gothic style and was designed by Lewis Vulliamy.[86] It consists of nave, chancel, and west tower and has an open wood roof and lancet windows. It was enlarged and 'beautified' in 1845–6,[87] and the chancel was extended in 1900.[88] There is an organ gallery at the west end with a vestry in the south-west corner under the gallery. The vicarage house to the west was built in 1851.[89]

Four mission chapels have been opened from

Christ Church: Cobridge Schoolroom *c.* 1873–*c.* 1893;[90] Cottage Lecture Room, Adams Square, *c.* 1893, evidently closed within a year;[91] Granville Mission Room *c.* 1897–*c.* 1900;[92] and St. Andrew's, Sneyd Street, Sneyd Green, built in 1908–9 in memory of George Bates, a pottery manufacturer of the Prospect Works in Sneyd Street, who had contributed towards the cost.[93] In 1955 St. Andrew's became the centre of a statutory district.[94] It benefits under a gift of £500 left by Harriet Bates of Endon by will proved in 1912.[95] It is a low-built brick structure with a bell-cote containing one bell. Extensions at the east end started in 1958[96] were still in progress in 1960. The minister's house to the southwest was built in 1946 and extended in 1956.[97]

A parish covering the Sneyd area was created out of St. John's parish in 1844.[98] Services were held in a room in Nile Street until the building of the church of *HOLY TRINITY* in the same road in 1851–2.[99] The cost was met partly by grants from the Incorporated Society, the Diocesan Church Extension Society, and the Peel Memorial Fund, and partly by subscription.[1] The church became unsafe through mining subsidence, and in 1956 the congregation and furnishings were transferred to St. Werburgh's in Hamil Road, which was reconsecrated as the church of Holy Trinity, Sneyd, in 1958.[2] The building in Nile Street was demolished in 1959. The patronage of the living, a perpetual curacy at first and a vicarage from 1868, was vested in the Crown and the Bishop of Lichfield, who present alternately.[3] The living is at present held jointly with that of St. Werburgh.[4] The former church of Holy Trinity was built in Gothic style to the designs of G. T. Robinson[5] and consisted of nave, chancel, aisles, and northeast tower with spire. A side-chapel and vestries were added in 1895.[6] The vicarage house in Waterloo Road has been occupied by the Rector of St. John's, Hanley, since 1958.[7]

The church of *ST. WERBURGH*, a red-brick building in Hamil Road, was erected in 1895[8] on land said to have been given by the Wood family.[9]

[76] Ward, *Stoke*, 156, 160; Lich. Dioc. Regy., Tithe Maps and Appt., Burslem: White, *Dir. Staffs.* (1851).
[77] Ll. Jewitt, *Ceramic Art of Gt. Britain*, ii. 283; *P.O. Dir. Staffs.* (1872); Adams, *Adams Family*, 155; O.S. Map 6″ Staffs. xi SE. (1890). The old house is no longer standing.
[78] Ex inf. the Vicar of St. Paul's (1958).
[79] *Kelly's Dir. Staffs.* (1880); *Lich. Dioc. Dir.* (1960).
[80] *Lich. Dioc. Ch. Cal.* (1884).
[81] Lich. Dioc. Regy., Bp.'s Reg. 35, p. 71; *Lich. Dioc. Mag.* (1886), 30; H. V. Stuart, *Reminiscences* (copy among W.S.L. pamphs. *sub* Stoke); date on Shirley Street chapel; *Kelly's Dir. Staffs.* (1892); *Lich. Dioc. Dir.* (1957).
[82] H.O. 129/15/370/3/1; White, *Dir. Staffs.* (1851); Lich. Dioc. Regy., Bp.'s Reg. M, pp. 24–42; inscription on W. front of church; C. Hodgson, *An Acct. of the Augmentation of Small Livings by the Governors of the Bounty of Queen Anne* (1845), pp. xxv, xxxix, xlix of 1856 supplement.
[83] H.O. 129/15/370/3/1; White, *Dir. Staffs.* (1834, 1851); Adams, *Adams Family*, 152. The project had been delayed by the death of Wm. Adams in 1831: ibid.
[84] *Lond. Gaz.* 1845, p. 205. Part of Christ Church parish was assigned to the new parish of St. Philip and St. James, Milton, in 1865: ibid. 1865, p. 4463.
[85] White, *Dir. Staffs.* (1851); *Lich. Dioc. Ch. Cal.* (1868, 1869, 1917–18); *Lich. Dioc. Dir.* (1959).
[86] Colvin, *Biog. Dict. Eng. Architects*, 644.
[87] White, *Dir. Staffs.* (1851); inscription on W. front of church.
[88] Lich. Dioc. Regy., Bp.'s Reg. U, pp. 430–3.
[89] White, *Dir. Staffs.* (1851).
[90] *Lich. Dioc. Ch. Cal.* (1874, 1893).

[91] Ibid. (1894).
[92] Ibid. (1898, 1900).
[93] Stone at W. end; Lich. Dioc. Regy., Bp.'s Reg. 37, pp. 113–14; *Fifty Years on the Green* (copy among W.S.L. pamphs. *sub* Burslem).
[94] *Fifty Years on the Green.* This was under an Order in Council of 1952.
[95] Char. Com. files. For her bequest to the poor of Cobridge see p. 330.
[96] Date on N. transept.
[97] *Fifty Years on the Green.*
[98] *Lond. Gaz.* 1844, p. 1889.
[99] White, *Dir. Staffs.* (1851); *P.O. Dir. Staffs.* (1854); *Staffs. Advertiser*, 5 July 1881; Lich. Dioc. Regy., Bp.'s Reg. Oᴬ, pp. 583–95.
[1] White, *Dir. Staffs.* (1851); *Staffs. Advertiser*, 1 Feb. 1851.
[2] Ex inf. the Vicar of Holy Trinity and St. Werburgh's (1958).
[3] White, *Dir. Staffs.* (1851); *Lich. Dioc. Ch. Cal.* (1868, 1869, 1917–18); *Lich. Dioc. Dir.* (1959).
[4] Ex inf. the Vicar of Holy Trinity and St. Werburgh's (1958).
[5] M. Port, *Six Hundred New Churches*, 64.
[6] *Lich. Dioc. Mag.* (1895), 169; Lich. Dioc. Regy., Bp.'s Reg. Oᴬ, p. 588; Lynam, *Ch. Bells Staffs.* 56; *Kelly's Dir. Staffs.* (1940). The aisles were restored in 1906: *Lich. Dioc. Mag.* (1906), 176.
[7] See p. 154.
[8] Stone *in situ*; *Lich. Dioc. Ch. Cal.* (1896); *Lich. Dioc. Mag.* (1895), 169.
[9] Char. Com. files.

At first a mission chapel within the parish of Holy Trinity, it became the centre of a conventional district in 1929[10] and a parish church in 1939 under a perpetual curate presented by the bishop.[11] A new church was built in 1953[12] on the corner of High Lane and Haywood Road. It is a large building of brown brick with stone dressings, consisting of wide nave with passage aisles and a projecting chancel. The west end of the nave serves as a baptistery and is lit by a tall lancet window. Externally this window is contained within a recessed panel of red brick, surmounted by a stone cross which rises above the low-pitched west gable. There is a bell in a bell-cote on the south face of the building. The vicarage house was built on an adjoining site in 1951, replacing the house in Minster Street (formerly York Street) sold in 1952.[13] The building in Hamil Road was used only as a Sunday school from 1953 until 1956[14] when the church of Holy Trinity, Sneyd, was transferred there.

The Good Shepherd Mission Room in the parish of Holy Trinity was opened c. 1895 and closed c. 1898.[15]

LOCAL GOVERNMENT AND PUBLIC SERVICES. Burslem, though anciently part of the parish of Stoke, was evidently an independent parish for civil purposes by the later 16th century.[16] The parish included the townships of Burslem and Sneyd, which manorially were part of Tunstall manor.[17] The lordship of Abbey Hulton, a distinct manor,[18] was part of Burslem parish for poor relief and highway maintenance by the 18th century[19] and doubtless earlier as well. Cobridge, formerly the liberty of Rushton Grange, continued to enjoy many of the extra-parochial immunities of the former Hulton Abbey until the mid-19th century.[20]

The first attempt to supplement the parochial and manorial system was the organization of the market under a body of trustees c. 1761,[21] but the first extensive change came in 1825[22] when new market trustees were appointed and a body of commissioners was set up to provide lighting and policing in the area. All inhabitants possessing a certain property qualification were automatically commissioners, while those with a higher qualification also became trustees. The latter were empowered to pave the market-place, defined as the area within a 200-yard radius of the hall, and its approaches, and were also given powers of compulsory purchase to enable them to extend the market-place eastwards. The commissioners had power to levy two rates of 6d. in the

£ for lighting and policing, and any surplus from the market tolls after the needs of the market had been met could also be applied to these purposes. Their lighting powers applied only to Burslem town itself, within carefully defined boundaries, but could be extended to Longport and Cobridge if 'the major part in value' of the property owners there wished it; the policing powers covered the townships of Burslem and Sneyd and the liberty of Rushton Grange but only the Sneyd Green portion of Abbey Hulton lordship; the commissioners could also insist on the paving of all new streets. They could appoint a chief constable and deputies each year as well as such regular officials as clerks and treasurers, and business could be transacted through committees. The Act stipulated that the rights of the lord of Tunstall manor were to be in no way prejudiced.[23]

At the first meeting of the commissioners Joseph Twigg was elected chairman and chief constable, a clerk and a treasurer were appointed, and a committee of 32 was set up to transact 'the general business of the Act'.[24] As such business increased the use of committees became more frequent: in December 1825, for instance, a committee of six to complete the contract with the British Gaslight Company;[25] in January 1827 a committee of seven to examine the accounts;[26] in June 1833 a rates committee of eight which in August of that year was ordered to sit monthly, a reflection of the difficulty that was being experienced in rate collection;[27] in June 1838 a regular finance committee.[28] Although the only specific powers which the Act gave the chief constable were those of suspending deputy constables and appointing a town crier, he in fact was from the first also chairman of the commissioners. He thus became 'an important civil officer placed in a middle position between the magistracy and the acting constabulary force'.[29] Two assistant chief constables were appointed in 1832, and there was one deputy chief constable in 1833-4 and 1834-5.[30]

Although in 1838 the commissioners were complaining that their powers were 'quite inadequate to the good government of the town' and that their expenditure was exceeding the amount they could levy under the Act of 1825,[31] the system lasted without alteration until 1850. In that year the Burslem Local Board of Health was set up with authority over the whole parish including Rushton Grange but excepting Abbey Hulton (and Sneyd Green as part of Abbey Hulton) and took over the powers of the market trustees, the commissioners, and the parochial highway surveyors. The board consisted of 15

[10] *Lich. Dioc. Ch. Cal.* (1896, 1929); Lich. Dioc. Regy., Bp.'s Reg. 39, pp. 326-7, licence of 1929 to the Vicar of Sneyd to perform divine service, holy communion, and baptism; ibid. p. 394, similar licence dated 1932.
[11] *Kelly's Dir. Staffs.* (1940); *Lich. Dioc. Dir.* (1946, 1959).
[12] Stone *in situ*. The site had been acquired by 1940 (*Kelly's Dir. Staffs.* 1940), so that building was evidently prevented by the Second World War.
[13] Char. Com. files.
[14] Ex inf. the Vicar of Holy Trinity and St. Werburgh's (1958).
[15] *Lich. Dioc. Ch. Cal.* (1896, 1898).
[16] See p. 129.
[17] For Tunstall manor see p. 86.
[18] See p. 249.
[19] See pp. 248-9.
[20] Ward, *Stoke*, 286-7. E.g. exemption from tithes, ch. rates and highway rates, although c. 1840 Cobridge was

paying poor rates and was subject to the policing powers of the Burslem Improvement Commrs. In 1850 it became subject to the new Burslem Local Board. For the mid-19th-cent. ch. at Cobridge see p. 124.
[21] Ward, *Stoke*, 235-6; see p. 130.
[22] 6 Geo. IV, c. 131 (local and personal). Occupiers of houses of less than £4 in value were exempted from the rates.
[23] H.R.L., Burslem Commrs.' Mins. 1825-50, pp. 2, 6.
[24] Ibid. p. 14.
[25] Ibid. p. 22.
[26] Ibid. p. 24.
[27] Ibid. pp. 55, 58-63.
[28] Ibid. p. 116.
[29] Ibid. *passim*; Ward, *Stoke*, 255. The chair was occasionally taken by one of the assistants or the deputy: Burslem Commrs'. Mins. pp. 52, 62, 64, 69.
[30] Burslem Commrs.' Mins. 1825-50, pp. 50, 53, 71.
[31] Ibid. p. 110.

members, 9 for Burslem, 3 for Sneyd, and 3 for Rushton Grange.[32] The board elected Elijah Hughes, the existing chief constable and a member of the board, as their chairman and the first chief bailiff.[33] A clerk was appointed at once, and Alcock's Bank which had acted as treasurer to the commissioners since 1838 was retained as treasurer until 1864 or 1865; the board's account was then transferred to the local branch of the Manchester and Liverpool District Bank whose manager became treasurer.[34] Six committees were set up: audit; by-laws; highways, lighting, and improvement; market; finance; sewers.[35] A general district rate of 2s. and a special lighting rate were imposed;[36] 15 years later the general rate was 2s. 3d. for Burslem (a 3d. increase on the previous year), 1s. 6d. for Rushton Grange, and 2s. 6d. for Sneyd, with an estimated yield of respectively £2,060 2s. 9d., £378 12s., and £572 14s.[37]

The area covered by the local board was incorporated as the borough of Burslem in 1878, with a council of 6 aldermen and 18 councillors, 6 for each of the three wards (North, South, and East).[38] At its first meeting the council elected Thomas Hulme, the last chairman of the local board, as mayor, and set up eight regular committees in place of the previous six: a watch committee consisting of the whole council; finance; town hall and fire brigade; sanitary; highways, lighting and improvement; gas; Wedgwood Institute; cemetery.[39] Burslem Borough formed 5 of the 26 wards of the new county borough in 1910 with a representation on the council of 5 aldermen and 15 councillors.[40]

The first town hall was built c. 1761. It served as a storage place for the market stalls and as a lock-up; the eastern end was occupied by the police by 1834 and the remainder was used as a newspaper room, a hall for public business, and, after 1839, a court room.[41] In 1851 the ground floor was converted into a fish market and the upper floor was extended.[42] It was replaced by a new hall built on the same site in 1854–7 and itself replaced by the present town hall in Wedgwood Street in 1911.[43]

The mayor's chain was presented in 1880 during the mayoralty of James Maddock by the widow and family of John Maddock, chief bailiff in 1852 and 1854. The mace was presented by Alderman Thomas Wood in 1892.[44]

As members of Tunstall manor, Burslem and Sneyd were each represented at the Tunstall court leet by one frankpledge from at least the early 14th century;[45] they also lay within the jurisdiction of the constable appointed by the court until at any rate the mid-18th century.[46] This system was obsolete by the early 19th century, and it was largely for police purposes that the commissioners were established in 1825. Their policing powers covered the whole of Burslem parish except for part of Abbey Hulton; the Sneyd Green portion of Hulton lay within their jurisdiction.[47]

A chief constable was appointed in September 1825; in October a head constable for Burslem, two under-constables for Burslem, a constable for Longport, and another for Cobridge were appointed. In addition three watchmen were engaged for Burslem for the winter months and one each for Longport, Brownhills, and Cobridge.[48] The appointment of two watchmen for the summer season also was introduced in 1828.[49] The watchmen were replaced by special constables from October 1832.[50] In January 1834, however, the immediate appointment of six paid watchmen was agreed, but it was also agreed that 'the respectable inhabitants of the parish be solicited to become captains or heads of the watch to attend in rotation each night'.[51] Two watchmen were appointed for three months in April, but in June a system of six paid assistant constables was instituted 'to keep a watch over the disorderly people particularly those assembled at the outskirts of the town' every Sunday for the ensuing four months.[52] These 'Sunday constables' continued to be used in addition to the watchmen for the next four summers, but in 1839 and 1840 winter watchmen only seem to have been appointed.[53]

Meanwhile the regular police force was being improved. In 1836 a head constable and under-constable were appointed for Burslem with five other constables, one each for Cobridge, Longport, Dale Hall, Brownhills, and Hot Lane.[54] In 1839 Burslem town was given three assistant constables, but this number dropped to two in 1842.[55] The head constable of Burslem was given the title of sergeant in 1840.[56] The police 'office' was at the east end of the upper story of the town hall by 1834.[57] The policing of the area was taken over, probably in 1843,[58] by a

[32] The Public Health Supplemental Act, 1850 (No. 3), 13 & 14 Vic. c. 108; Local Govt. Board's Provisional Orders Confirmation (no. 15) Act, 1891, 54 & 55 Vic. c. 223 (local); *Burslem Bd. of Health Rep. 1851*, 15 (copy in H.R.L.)
[33] *Burslem Bd. of Health Rep. 1851*, 15.
[34] Ibid.; ibid. *1865*, 9–10; Burslem Commrs'. Mins. 1825–50, p. 108.
[35] *Burslem Bd. of Health Rep. 1851*, 15. By 1872 the number had dropped to 4: finance, markets and town hall; sewers, scavenging and nuisance; highways, lighting and improvement; free libr. and Wedgwood Institute: ibid. *1872*, 4. The Wedgwood Institute Cttee. had become a regular cttee. in 1863 (when the foundation stone of the institute was laid), replacing the exploratory Wedgwood memorial cttee. set up some years before: ibid. *1863*, 9; *1864*, 5; see p. 141. By 1878 when the board was replaced by the borough council there were again 6 cttees.: finance; market and town hall; sanitary; highways, lighting and improvement; gas; Wedgwood Institute; general purposes: H.R.L., Burslem Board of Health Mins. 1878, 1 May 1878. [36] *Burslem Bd. of Health Rep. 1851*, 18.
[37] *Keates and Ford's Potteries Dir.* (1867).
[38] 39 & 40 Vic., c. 97 (local); H.R.L., Burslem Boro. Attendance Bk. 1878–89, list for 1878; *Woolley's Stoke Boro. Almanack* (1879); *Kelly's Dir. Staffs.* (1880, 1908).
[39] H.R.L., Burslem Boro. Counc. Mins. 1878–82, 28
Aug. 1878. By 1906 there were 13 regular cttees.: general purposes; markets, town hall, and baths; sanitary; sewage disposal; public libraries and museum; electric lighting; park and cemetery; gas; highways; finance; stores; isolation hospital; and, for the first time, education: ibid. 1898–1906, pp. 485–6, 487.
[40] *Stoke Counc. Yr. Bk.* (1915).
[41] Ward, *Stoke*, 234–6; White, *Dir. Staffs.* (1834).
[42] *Burslem Bd. of Health Rep. 1851*, 21–22; White, *Dir. Staffs.* (1851); *Staffs. Advertiser*, 4 Jan. 1851.
[43] See pp. 112–13.
[44] Burslem Boro. Mins. 1878–82, pp. 266–7; *Guide to Ch. Congress, 1911*, 136 (copy in H.R.L.), the chain and mace being included in an art exhibition on the occasion of the congress.
[45] *Tunstall Ct. R.* (*T.N.S.F.C.* lix–lxvi), passim.
[46] See p. 96.
[47] 6 Geo. IV, c. 131 (local and personal).
[48] H.R.L., Burslem Commrs.' Mins. 1825–50, p. 12.
[49] Ibid. p. 28.   [50] Ibid. pp. 50, 51, 54.
[51] Ibid. pp. 67, 68.   [52] Ibid. pp. 70, 72.
[53] Ibid. pp. 74, 76, 82, 88, 93, 96, 114, 122, 150, 163.
[54] Ibid. p. 84.
[55] Ibid. pp. 144, 180.   [56] Ibid. p. 156.
[57] White, *Dir. Staffs.* (1834); Ward, *Stoke*, 236.
[58] See pp. 195, 216.

body of the new county police, considered inefficient by the commissioners in 1845.[59] The force had a station in Market Place by 1851 at the north end of the market building; it was enlarged in 1854 and again in 1874 after the accommodation had been declared 'very inadequate',[60] and was replaced by the present station in Jackson Street in 1939.[61] There was a 'stone house' in 1826,[62] and by 1834 there were lock-ups attached to the watch house on the ground floor of the town hall.[63] A lock-up was built at Longport apparently in the late 1830's.[64] The stocks, mentioned in 1680 as in need of repair,[65] stood in front of the fire engine house at the town hall by 1851 when the local board ordered their removal.[66]

THE BOROUGH OF BURSLEM.

Gold and red quarters with two vertical and two horizontal stripes interlaced and counterchanged; in the first and fourth quarters a Portland Vase; in the second, a scythe; and in the third, a silver fret. [Granted 1878]

A stipendiary magistrate was appointed for the Potteries area in 1839, and the part of Burslem parish within the parliamentary borough of Stoke (i.e. all the parish except Abbey Hulton) formed one of the six rating divisions established for the support of the new system; the public room on the upper floor of the town hall provided a court room for the weekly sessions.[67] Burslem was at first within the Hanley county court district, and under an order of 1858 regular sessions of the court were held at Burslem town hall.[68] In 1880 Burslem was formed into a separate county court district.[69] The borough was granted a commission of the peace in 1900.[70]

PUBLIC HEALTH. By the Act of 1825 the market trustees and the commissioners were given certain public health powers; inspectors could destroy unwholesome meat in the market; no cattle were to be slaughtered there; scavengers were to be appointed to remove dirt from the market-place and its approaches; the streets could be watered by fire engines; privies were to be emptied only between midnight and 5 a.m.[71] In 1831 a temporary local board of health was set up to meet the cholera threat, recommendations regarding cleanliness and diet were published, and a scheme of house-to-house visits was established.[72] In the following year the inhabitants, 'in consequence of the probable approach of cholera into the neighbourhood', were urged to help the constables to arrest tramps, generally regarded as carriers of disease; the inhabitants were also recommended to remove nuisances or cause the constables to do so.[73]

The first important health measures, however, came only after the establishment of the local board in 1850. An officer of health was appointed at once, with an inspector of nuisances and two scavengers soon afterwards; the regular inspection of the common lodging houses of the district was also undertaken.[74] Some watering of the streets during the summer of 1851 was organized but only in Burslem township and a small part of Cobridge; and even for this the expense was met by public subscription.[75] In 1853 a deputation of the board toured other parts of the country in order to obtain information about drainage and water-supply systems, and among its recommendations was the replacement of privies and cesspools by 'closets with pans and syphons . . . of earthen or stoneware'.[76] This was endorsed by the officer of health,[77] but a personal inspection by the board in 1857 revealed extensive 'filth and nuisance'. This state of affairs, however, was to some extent remedied during the next year by the completion of public drainage works begun in 1855, by the progress of private drainage works, and by the extensive installation of water closets.[78] Yet the need for further closets was still being urged in 1886 when, in particular, Massey Square (between Chapel Lane and Moorland Road), the Hadderidge area, and Adams Square (off Sneyd Street) were noted as having sanitary arrangements 'of the most objectionable order'.[79] The completion of the drainage system raised the problem of sewage disposal, especially in connexion with the pollution of the Fowlea Brook.[80] It was not until 1879, however, that the sewage works at Bradwell Hall Farm on the Wolstanton side of the brook south of Middleport was opened; extensions on the Burslem side of the brook were completed in 1908.[81] A refuse destructor

[59] Burslem Commrs.' Mins. 1825–50, p. 209.
[60] White, *Dir. Staffs.* (1851); *Burslem Bd. of Health Rep. 1854*, 12; S.R.O., Q/APs 1 (including detailed plan of 1874 extensions); O.S. Map 1/500 Staffs. xii. 9.2 (1879).
[61] Date on foundation stone; *Kelly's Dir. Staffs.* (1940).
[62] Burslem Commrs.' Mins. 1825–50, p. 20. This was presumably the watch house at the E. end of the town hall mentioned by Arnold Bennett in 'The Elixir of Youth' (*Tales of the Five Towns*).
[63] White, *Dir. Staffs.* (1834).
[64] Burslem Commrs.' Mins. 1825–50, pp. 26, 93, 98, 101, 208.
[65] *Tunstall Ct. R.* (*T.N.S.F.C.* lxvi), 114, 115.
[66] *Staffs. Advertiser*, 4 Jan. 1851.
[67] Act for more effectual execution of office of J.P., 2 & 3 Vic. c. 15; Ward, *Stoke*, 236.
[68] *Burslem Bd. of Health Rep. 1858*, 13; *1859*, 5; *Lond. Gaz.* 1858, p. 4904. [69] *Lond. Gaz.* 1880, p. 6095.
[70] *Kelly's Dir. Staffs.* (1908).
[71] Act for regulating markets in Burslem, &c., 6 Geo. IV, c. 131 (local and personal).
[72] Printed copy of recommendations in H.R.L.
[73] Printed copy of recommendations in H.R.L.
[74] *Burslem Bd. of Health Rep. 1851*, 19; ibid. *1852*,

4, 7; ibid. *1853*, 14–16.
[75] Ibid. *1851*, 25. It was reported, however, that the crossings and footpaths in Rushton Grange were regularly swept and repaired.
[76] Original copy of the report in H.R.L.
[77] *Burslem Bd. of Health Rep. 1853*, 14.
[78] Ibid. *1855*, 5; *1858*, 5–6, 10–12, 17–18.
[79] *Staffs. Sentinel*, 18 Sept. 1886 (cutting in H.R.L., vol. of local govt. newscuttings relating especially to Burslem); Burslem Boro. Mins. 1878–82, p. 188; O.S. Map 1/500 Staffs. xii. 9. 19 (1879). For the sanitary arrangements of Earl Granville's new cottages at Cobridge see p. 114.
[80] *Burslem Bd. of Health Rep. 1862*, 8, 11; *1866*, 10; H.R.L., Stoke Commrs.' Mins. 1855–65, 7 Sept. 1859; see p. 196.
[81] *Staffs. Sentinel*, 21 Oct. 1898; *Kelly's Dir. Staffs.* (1880, 1912); *Souvenir of Opening of Burslem's New Sewage Disposal Works* (copy in the possession of the City Sewage Engineer in 1959); Burslem Boro. Mins. 1878–82, p. 249; O.S. Map 6" Staffs. xi SE., xii SW. (1900, 1925). The Boro. Sewage Farm Cttee. held its first meeting on 28 Nov. 1879: H.R.L., Burslem Boro. Farm Cttee. Mins. 1879–96.

was built in 1889 to avoid the need for refuse tips;[82] it was replaced by a new destructor in Scotia Road opened in conjunction with the electricity works there in 1905.[83]

The public baths in Moorland Road were opened by the corporation in 1894.[84]

Restrictions were placed on burials in the churchyards of St. John's and St. Paul's churches and in the ground attached to the Baptist chapel in 1856, while in 1881 both the churches were closed for burials and further restrictions were placed on the churchyards.[85] Meanwhile in 1872 a burial board had been set up consisting of all the members of the local board and it met for the first time in 1873.[86] A 28-acre site on the hillside at Nettlebank between Sneyd Hill and Leek Road was acquired for a cemetery, which was opened in 1879.[87]

The Haywood Hospital in Moorland Road was built in 1886–7 under the terms of Howard Haywood's bequest.[88] It was replaced by the present Burslem, Tunstall, and Haywood Memorial Hospital off High Lane built in 1927–30,[89] and the old building is now a county technical college. Stanfields Sanatorium on a site to the north was opened by the corporation as an isolation hospital in 1906 and from at least 1916 until 1956 was used as a sanatorium. It is now devoted to the care of chronic invalids.[90]

OTHER PUBLIC SERVICES. Until the end of the 18th century Burslem's water-supply evidently depended entirely on springs. One of these was by St. John's churchyard, but besides being very sluggish it was also liable to pollution from the graveyard.[91] Another spring at the Grange Farm was more healthy but very small.[92] About 1798 Enoch Wood built a conduit head outside the entrance to his pottery works in what is still called Fountain Place and, pumping water to it by means of an engine in the works, provided a free public supply. The conduit head was removed c. 1815,[93] but the site is still marked by a lamp-stand. From 1820 Burslem was supplied with water from John Smith's newly established water-works at Hanley,[94] and between 1832 and 1836 W. Walsh built a reservoir at the High Lane end of Sneyd hamlet, bringing water from

John Bennett's land at Jackfield and running pipes down to the town nearly a mile away. Walsh, however, received inadequate backing, and after his death in 1836 the scheme lapsed.[95] By 1840 the Hill Top Pottery as well as the Fountain Place Works was raising its own water-supply, but large quantities were required by the industry and in dry weather the town was short of water.[96] In 1844 Burslem's supply was stated to come from springs, from Bycars Mill, and from the reservoir at the Hill Top Works, whence the water was piped and sold to those wanting it; for people living in the Hamil area there was a supply from the Jackfield Colliery.[97] The Potteries Water Works Company was formed in 1847 and began supplying the Burslem area in 1849.[98] Its first main reservoir had been built on the high ground above Birches Head by 1849; for years an open reservoir, it was covered over in 1924 when another was built beside it.[99]

Gas lighting was supplied in Burslem town from the end of 1826 by the British Gaslight Company from its works at Shelton under a contract made between the company and the Burslem commissioners.[1] In 1837 the commissioners transferred the contract to the newly formed Burslem and Tunstall Gas Company, which had a works in Waterloo Road and opened the present works at Longport before 1851.[2] The commissioners extended their public lighting to Longport in 1838.[3] With the creation of the local board in 1850 the extension of public lighting throughout the area subject to the board was at once undertaken,[4] and by 1853 there were 182 public lamps in Burslem township, 33 in the vill of Rushton Grange, and 16 in Sneyd.[5] The local board acquired the Burslem and Tunstall Gas Company in 1877,[6] and the undertaking remained in the hands of the new borough until 1910 when it passed to the county borough of Stoke.[7] The British Gaslight Company opened the present works at Brownhills in 1852 for the supply of gas to Tunstall,[8] and by an agreement with the Burslem and Tunstall Gas Company in 1857 or 1858 it left the supply of the Burslem area to that company in return for a monopoly in Tunstall where the Burslem company had not yet begun to exercise its statutory rights.[9]

The borough opened the present electricity works

[82] Staffs. Sentinel, 21 Oct. 1898.
[83] H.R.L., Burslem Boro. Electricity Cttee. Mins. 1897–1910, pp. 62, 102.
[84] Staffs. Advertiser, 30 June, 4 Aug. 1894. A subscription bath was opened at Bycars Colliery in 1816 and was still in use in 1824: Pitt, Staffs. 396–7; Ward, Stoke, 210; Warrillow, Stoke, 372.
[85] Lond. Gaz. 1856, p. 2905; 1881, p. 5301. There was some relaxation in favour of St. Paul's churchyard in 1882: ibid. 1882, p. 483.
[86] Ibid. 1872, p. 3621; H.R.L., Burslem Burial Bd. Mins. 1873–8, p. 1.
[87] Burslem Burial Bd. Mins. 1873–8, passim; Burslem Boro. Mins. 1878–82, p. 218; Kelly's Dir. Staffs. (1880).
[88] See p. 330.
[89] Inscriptions on E. front of building; Warrillow, Stoke, 363–4.
[90] Kelly's Dir. Staffs. (1908, 1916); Warrillow, Stoke, 366.
[91] Warrillow, Stoke, 162, 177–8; W.S.L., Staffs. Views, ii, p. 159 (c), woodcut of women waiting at the spring for water to rise.
[92] Warrillow, Stoke, 162.
[93] Falkner, Wood Family, 81; U.C.N.S., Sneyd MSS., Burslem Deeds, notice concerning the removal of the vegetable market in 1816 to a spot 'below where the fountain lately stood'.

[94] See p. 160.
[95] Ward, Stoke, 268; see p. 120.
[96] Ward, Stoke, 268. Wood had made 'the fountain in his manufactory' available to the public free of charge during a shortage in the summer of 1826: Warrillow, Stoke, 163.
[97] Pure and Wholesome Water for 100 Years, 1849–1949, 6, 12, 13 (copy in H.R.L.).
[98] Ibid. 13; White, Dir. Staffs. (1851); Staffs. Weekly Sentinel, 20 July 1956; Warrillow, Stoke, 165.
[99] Pure and Wholesome Water, 13; White, Dir. Staffs. (1851); Staffs. Weekly Sentinel, 20 July 1956.
[1] H.R.L., Burslem Commrs.' Mins. 1825–50, 14, 21, 22; see p. 160.
[2] Ward, Stoke, 268; Act for incorporating the Burslem and Tunstall Gas Co. 20 & 21 Vic. c. 59 (local and personal); Burslem Commrs.' Mins. 1825–50, p. 121; White, Dir. Staffs. (1851).
[3] Burslem Commrs.' Mins. 1825–50, pp. 117–18, 119, 125–6.
[4] Burslem Bd. of Health Rep. 1851, 18, 27–28.
[5] Ibid. 1853, 13.
[6] Burslem Local Board Gas Act, 40 & 41 Vic. c. 208 (local).
[7] Local Govt. Board's Provisional Orders Confirmation (no. 3) Act, 8 Edw. VII, c. 144 (local); see p. 266.
[8] Warrillow, Etruria, 152, 154; White, Dir. Staffs. (1851).
[9] See p. 97.

in Scotia Road in 1905.[10] The works passed to the county borough of Stoke in 1910.[11]

By 1837 the Burslem commissioners maintained three fire engines, at Burslem, Longport, and Cobridge. In that year a committee appointed to report on the reorganization of the brigades recommended that each of these places should have a captain and 10 men, with a superintendent for the whole area; the commissioners agreed to carry out these recommendations.[12] By 1851 the brigades consisted of 36 men under the control of the superintendent of police, but within two years control had been transferred to the newly created inspector of nuisances.[13] The system was reorganized in the early 1880's when a single brigade was set up for the borough with a new station in the market-place housing a steam-powered engine.[14] By 1896 the station had been transferred to Baddeley Street[15] where it remained until the opening of the present station in Hamil Road in 1956.[16]

The townships of Burslem and Sneyd were individually responsible for the upkeep of their roads.[17] Under the Highways Act of 1835 Burslem township, having a population of over 5,000, increased the number of its highway surveyors to nine in 1836, probably from two; Sneyd at this time had two surveyors.[18] The vill of Rushton Grange was exempt from all highway rates until 1850,[19] and the resulting neglect of its roads is reflected in the comment of Thomas Campbell the poet, who visited Ralph Stevenson at Cobridge Cottage in 1805 and found the roads thereabouts 'so deep that one can hardly drag a pair of heavy shoes along them'.[20] But there was evidently neglect in Burslem township also where in 1795 'the common highways, bridges, causeways, and pavements' were 'so far out of order' that they could not be repaired by statute labour only and a special rate of up to 6d. had to be authorized by Quarter Sessions.[21] The local board, on taking over the powers of the surveyors of Burslem and Sneyd and assuming responsibility for Rushton Grange in 1850, found the roads generally in a bad state and immediately set about repairing

them.[22] The board's responsibility for the upkeep of the highways passed to the new borough in 1878.[23]

RELIEF OF THE POOR. Burslem relieved its poor through its own parish vestry, independently of the mother parish of Stoke.[24] There were three overseers of the poor, one each for Burslem, Sneyd, and Hulton, during most of the 18th century at least,[25] but in 1793 the vestry appointed a salaried overseer for the whole parish.[26] By 1835 there were four overseers with two paid assistant overseers.[27] With the establishment of the Wolstanton and Burslem Union in 1838 Burslem was given a representation of eight on the board of sixteen guardians.[28] In 1922 the ten civil parishes of the union joined with the five of Stoke Union to form the Stoke and Wolstanton Union.[29]

The expenditure on poor relief increased in the course of the 18th century. Thus in 1714 one levy raised £1 7s. 8d. from Hulton and 12s. 6d. from Sneyd;[30] in 1802–3 the parish rates, assessed at 10s. in the £ on houses and 20s. on land, brought in £2,125 11s. 10d., and the expenditure on the poor amounted to £1,726 14s. 5½d. in out-relief and £326 2s. 0¾d. in workhouse relief.[31] There was considerable fluctuation in expenditure in subsequent years: nearly £7,400 was spent in 1817–18, just over £2,500 in 1823–4, and just under £4,000 in 1836–7.[32] Burslem's contribution to the union in the first half of 1857 was fixed at £3,629 5s. 7d.;[33] its contribution for the second half of the financial year 1921–2, the last before the amalgamation with Stoke, was £9,520, out of a total £46,637 from the ten parishes then comprising the union.[34]

In the early 18th century the main form of relief was monthly or weekly pay. In 1707 there were 24 poor in the parish in receipt of such relief—14 in Burslem, 4 in Sneyd, and 6 in Hulton; the largest individual payment was 1s. 3d. a week.[35] Occasionally relief took the form of payment of rent.[36] In 1802–3 184 adults and 165 children under 15 were given out-relief, 413 persons occasional relief, and 39 work-house relief.[37] By 1834 there were two parish surgeons.[38] There was a parish workhouse by 1741,[39] with a

[10] H.R.L., Burslem Boro. Electricity Cttee. Mins. 1897–1910, pp. 62, 100, 102; Staffs. Advertiser, 12 Mar. 1910, supplement.

[11] Local Govt. Board's Provisional Orders Confirmation (no. 3) Act, 8 Edw. VII, c. 144 (local); see p. 266.

[12] Burslem Commrs.' Mins. 1825–50, pp. 93, 98, 101. The engine at Longport was mentioned in 1829 (ibid. p. 38) and that at Burslem in 1835: ibid. p. 76. The Act of 1825 (§ 72) stated that the commrs. could keep or contract for a fire engine.

[13] White, Dir. Staffs. (1851); Burslem Bd. of Health Rep. 1853, 15; 1858, 19; 1871, 17.

[14] Burslem Boro. Mins. 1878–82, pp. 305, 341, 407, 433, 474, 487, 493, 501; 1882–90, pp. 3, 7, 25, 29, 199.

[15] Kelly's Dir. Staffs. (1896).

[16] H.R.L., brochure of official opening, 17 May 1956; The Surveyor, 1 Sept. 1956 (copy in H.R.L.). For the organization of the fire service after 1910 see p. 267.

[17] St. John's, Burslem, Churchwardens' and Overseers' Accts. 1700–95, p. 97; Staffs. Advertiser, 26 Mar. 1836; Ward, Stoke, 211.

[18] Staffs. Advertiser, 26 Mar. 1836.

[19] Burslem Bd. of Health Rep. 1851, 5; Adams, Adams Family, 185.

[20] Staffs. Sentinel (Summer Number 1910), 40, where Stevenson's home is wrongly called Cobridge Hall; see p. 119.   [21] S.H.C. 1934 (1), 79.

[22] Burslem Bd. of Health Rep. 1851, 5, 15, 22.

[23] See list of cttees. on p. 126.

[24] Ward, Stoke, 217–18, 467, and app. pp. xxx–xxxi; St.

John's, Burslem, Churchwardens' and Overseers' Accts. 1700–95; Staffs. Advertiser, 28 Mar. 1835.

[25] Churchwardens' and Overseers' Accts. 1700–95, passim to p. 122. This evidence applies only to the first three-quarters of the 18th cent. but the same system was doubtless in force earlier since this was the ancient method of choosing the churchwardens: Ward, Stoke, app. pp. xxvii–xxviii. During the first year of the overseers' accounts, 1704–5, only the overseers of Burslem and Hulton are mentioned.

[26] Churchwardens' and Overseers' Accts. 1700–95, p. 156.   [27] Staffs. Advertiser, 28 Mar. 1835.

[28] Ibid. 8 Apr. 1838; H.R.L., Wolstanton and Burslem Union Mins. 1854–8, p. 36.

[29] Wolstanton and Burslem Union Mins. 1919–22, p. 32; see p. 199.

[30] Churchwardens' and Overseers' Accts. 1700–95, p. 21.

[31] Returns on Maintenance of Poor, 1803, H.C. 175, p. 468 (1803–4), xiii; the rates consisted of 'poor and other rates'.

[32] Rep. Sel. Cttee. on Poor Rate Returns, 1822, H.C. 556, p. 160 (1822), v; 1825, H.C. 334, p. 197 (1825), iv; 3rd Ann. Rep. Poor Law Com., H.C. 546, p. 174 (1837), xxxi.

[33] Wolstanton and Burslem Union Mins. 1854–8, p. 323.

[34] Ibid. 1919–22, p. 381.

[35] Churchwardens' and Overseers' Accts. 1700–95, p. 14.

[36] Ibid. p. 15.   [37] Maintenance of Poor, 1803, 469.

[38] Staffs. Advertiser, 28 Mar. 1835. There were still two for the parish after the union: ibid. 7 Apr. 1838.

[39] Burslem Par. Reg. i. 211, 212.

capacity of 60 in 1775.[40] A new workhouse was built at Greenhead in 1780[41] and was enlarged in the 1830's to hold 300.[42] It had only 152 inmates in 1838, but this figure was a large increase on the average for the previous few years.[43] The union workhouse in Turnhurst Road, Chell, was built c. 1838–9.[44] The old parish workhouse was leased out as an infantry barracks by the early 1850's[45] and was sold by the guardians in 1857 for £1,000 after several unsuccessful attempts to secure more. It was bought by James Vernon who converted it into the Scotia Pottery.[46] This was demolished in 1958.[47]

ECONOMIC HISTORY. Burslem was still a village in the later 17th century, even though its agrarian character was by then modified by the extensive, though small-scale, pottery industry; the potter, with his oven and sheds adjoining his house, was normally a farmer as well. Mining also had long been in progress on the high ground to the east of the village, largely in connexion with the needs of the potters.[48] In the mid-18th century the village still presented a pattern of inclosed fields, lanes, and small potworks.[49] There were then 23 such works in the village, but the few shops were those of a small agricultural community—4 smithies, 2 butcher's shops, a joiner's, a cobbler's, and a barber's; there were also 19 alehouses and a bakehouse.[50] During the later 18th century, with the reorganization of the pottery industry, the turnpiking of the roads, the building of the canal, and the establishment of a market, the evolution of modern Burslem began. The development of the outlying parts of the parish is a feature of the 19th and 20th centuries, and in the 1840's the parish, even excluding Rushton Grange and most of Hulton, had over 2,600 acres of arable, meadow, and pasture and only some 260 acres of buildings, roads, colliery workings, and waste.[51]

Burslem, valued at 10s. in 1086, then had land for 2 ploughs, and the villein and 4 bordars there had 1 plough. There were 2 acres of alder.[52] Rushton and Hulton were together valued at 10s. in 1086. They had land for 3 ploughs, and the 3 villeins and 3 bordars in the 2 vills had 1 plough. There was woodland 1 league long and ½ league broad attached to

the 2 vills.[53] In the early 13th century Hulton Abbey owned woodland at Rushton[54] and Sneyd.[55] Most of the land in Burslem was copyhold until the enfranchisement of much of Tunstall manor by the Sneyds in 1619 and the Bowyers between 1620 and 1628.[56] From the 17th century numerous 999-year and 500-year leases were granted by small proprietors for building purposes, but before the mid-19th century most of these had become freehold.[57] Inclosure of the open fields seems to have taken place during the 17th century. The 'Milnefield'—situated presumably on the northern side of the village near the mill—was evidently an open field in 1549, and open-field arable still existed in 1601.[58] By the mid-18th century, however, there were only inclosed fields.[59] As at Penkhull butts of arable were held in certain closes in Burslem during the 17th century.[60] Early in the 19th century some furlongs and meadows were still shared out in doles and dayworks among various proprietors, but most of these had been eliminated before the middle of the century by purchase and exchange.[61]

MARKETS AND FAIRS. An open-air meat and vegetable market was established in the area round the town hall about the time of the building of the hall c. 1761.[62] It steadily increased in importance, and before the end of the 18th century markets were being held every Monday and Saturday, that on Monday being the larger.[63]

In 1816 the vegetable market was moved 'to the open part of the town below where the fountain lately stood' (now St. John's Square) to ease congestion.[64] In 1824 more land near the town hall was leased from the lord of the manor for an extension of the market-place,[65] which for some years previously had been partially lit during the winter.[66] In 1825 the market was placed under a body of trustees with authority to make by-laws for its regulation and extension; these powers were taken over by the local board in 1850.[67] The market-place was extended on the east in 1831, and after the purchase in 1834 of most of the remaining buildings between the market-place and Shoe Lane a covered market-house with 124 places was erected on the site in 1835–6 for the butchers and provision-merchants.[68] It was demolished in 1957.[69] A Monday

[40] 5th Rep. Cttee. on Poor Laws, 1777 (Reps. of Cttees. of H.C., 1st ser. ix), 458.
[41] Churchwardens' and Overseers' Accts. 1700–95, p. 139; Ward, Stoke, 270, 271; Hargreaves, Map of Staffs. Potteries.
[42] Ward, Stoke, 271.
[43] Ibid.
[44] See p. 97.
[45] Wolstanton and Burslem Union Mins. 1854–8, pp. 2, 9, 204; White, Dir. Staffs. (1851). It may have been used as a works before that as White describes the barracks as a converted manufactory.
[46] Wolstanton and Burslem Union Mins. 1854–8, pp. 9, 12, 24, 46, 98, 143, 211, 215, 218, 296, 333–4, 365; Jewitt, Ceramic Art, 464.
[47] Warrillow, Stoke, 241, pl. 4.
[48] H. J. Steele, 'Social Conditions in Burslem during the 17th and 18th cents.' (T.N.S.F.C. lxxviii), 22–24; R. Plot, Nat. Hist. Staffs. (1686), 122; see pp. 138, 139.
[49] T.N.S.F.C. lxxviii, map facing p. 16; Ward, Stoke, 225–6 and map facing p. 225 (also reproduced in Wedgwood, Wedgwood Family, facing p. 121). The two maps are 19th cent. reconstructions: T.N.S.F.C. lxxviii. 29.
[50] Ward, Stoke, 235, map facing p. 225, and app. pp. xxxii–xxxvii.
[51] Lich. Dioc. Regy., Tithe Maps and Appt., Burslem;

Rushton Grange and much of Hulton were not tithable and so are not included.
[52] V.C.H. Staffs. iv. 50, no. 177.   [53] See p. 251.
[54] Close R. 1234–7, 35.   [55] See p. 251.
[56] T.N.S.F.C. lxxviii. 24; U.C.N.S., Sneyd MSS., Burslem Deeds; see p. 97.
[57] Ward, Stoke, 206.
[58] Tunstall Ct. R. (T.N.S.F.C. lxi), 35; ibid. lxiii. 44.
[59] Ibid. lxxviii, map facing p. 16.
[60] Wedgwood, Wedgwood Family, 315; see p. 200.
[61] Ward, Stoke, 206.
[62] Ibid. 235–6; U.C.N.S., Sneyd MSS., Burslem Deeds; see p. 126.
[63] Ward, Stoke, 236; J. Aikin, Country Around Manchester (1795), 519.
[64] U.C.N.S., Sneyd MSS., Burslem Deeds.
[65] Ward, Stoke, 252.
[66] Ibid. 253.
[67] Ibid. 253–6; White, Dir. Staffs. (1851). For details of these powers see p. 125.
[68] Ward, Stoke, 256–7, plate facing p. 257, and ground-plan facing p. 225; Staffs. Advertiser, 5 Dec. 1835; Act for regulating markets in Burslem, &c., 6 Geo. IV, c. 131 (local and personal); see p. 119.
[69] Warrillow, Stoke, 400. For a description of the building see p. 113.

corn market was established in 1848; a cattle market on alternate Tuesdays was started at the same time but had lapsed by 1851.[70] In 1851 the ground floor of the town hall was converted into a fish market, and improvements were also carried out at the covered market.[71] The present market-hall between Market Place and Queen Street was built for the vegetable market in 1878–9 with entrances in Market Place, Queen Street, and Brickhouse Street.[72] About this time there was also a pig market in Swan Square.[73] A Friday market had been added to the other two general markets by 1940,[74] but about the mid-1950's the market-days became Wednesday, Friday, and Saturday in line with those of the rest of the city.[75]

By the end of the 18th century cattle fairs were being held at Burslem on 22 March, 18 June, and 17 October.[76] The market trustees appointed in 1825 established six fairs, on the Saturdays before Shrovetide, Easter, and Whitsun, and on the Saturdays after Midsummer Day, 11 September, and Christmas Day.[77] These fairs seem never to have been well supported[78] and had evidently lapsed by 1851.[79] By 1908 there was a fair 'in private grounds' on the Saturday following 24 June[80] and this was still held in 1940.[81]

MILLS. Burslem (or Sytch) Mill stood on the Scotia Brook off the road between Burslem and Brownhills in the area known as the Sytch. It was owned by the lord of Tunstall manor in 1348[82] and is probably identifiable with the mill held by the Audleys in 1273.[83] It descended as part of Tunstall manor,[84] and while the manor was divided into two-thirds and one-third shares the profits of the mill were divided in the same proportion.[85] At some time after 1857 the Sneyds sold the mill to Charles Salt,[86] who was also working the Clanway Colliery, Tunstall.[87] The mill ceased to be worked in the 1880's.[88] Tenants of the mill included George Unwyn at the time of its lease in 1536 to Thomas Rowley of Chell,[89] Ralph Bourne to whom this or another Thomas Rowley transferred it in 1580,[90] Francis Fynney of Burslem in 1691,[91] Benjamin

Cartlich in 1719,[92] Ralph Wood (1676–1753), great-grandfather of Enoch Wood, probably in the early 18th century,[93] the Shrigley family from 1750 to 1813,[94] John Wood of Brownhills in 1816,[95] Jesse Finney by 1848,[96] Francis Hine in 1854,[97] and a Mr. Buckley in 1857.[98] It seems to have been in use as a flint mill during part of the 19th century.[99] A brick range of mill buildings probably dating from the early 19th century has for some years been occupied as a house and outbuildings; the former mill-stones have been made into a flight of steps leading up to no. 156 Westport Road, situated some 100 yards to the south-east and said to have been at one time the mill-house.[1]

Another mill on the Scotia Brook, at Small Bridge to the south-west, was in operation c. 1840, owned by John Wedg Wood and occupied by John Walker.[2] Apparently used as a colour mill c. 1878,[3] this mill had ceased to be worked by 1881.[4]

The Port Vale corn mill on the canal at Bridge Street (now Milvale Street), Middleport, dated 1844, was owned and operated by Samuel Fitton between at least 1848 and 1854.[5] It was in the hands of Robert Cliffe in the early 1860's.[6] By 1868 it was held by Fitton and Pidduck, a firm of flour millers which was still working the mill in 1924.[7] The building passed soon afterwards to Price and Son, bakers, still the occupants in 1940.[8] The lower floors are now (1960) used by The Five Towns Fireplaces Ltd., but the rest is derelict. The tall brick building of five stories formerly had hoists both above the canal and on the street frontage. Near the south entrance the date 1844 and the names of John Cliffe and Anne Fitton are scratched on the brickwork; a third name, now illegible, was probably that of Samuel Fitton.

There was a mill in the Lower Hadderidge area by 1860.[9] Its situation was given as Luke Street in 1892,[10] and a corn mill there is now (1960) run by Malkin Brothers.

POTTERY INDUSTRY. The earliest pottery works so far discovered in the Burslem district was situated at Sneyd Green. Two kilns dating from the 13th

[70] White, Dir. Staffs. (1851).
[71] Ibid.; Staffs. Advertiser, 4 Jan. 1851; Burslem Bd. of Health Rep. 1851, 21.
[72] Kelly's Dir. Staffs. (1880); H.R.L., Burslem Boro. Mins. 1878–82, p. 25.
[73] Burslem in Days Gone By (copy in H.R.L.), stating, c. 1932, that many people then remembered this market.
[74] Kelly's Dir. Staffs. (1940).
[75] Stoke Official Handbk. [1958 and previous edn.].
[76] Aikin, Country Around Manchester, 519; Univ. Brit. Dir. (1791), iv. 105–6.
[77] Ward, Stoke, 258. In 1834 the dates were given as 8 Feb., 29 Mar., 17 May, 28 June, 13 Sept., and 26 Dec.: White, Dir. Staffs. (1834).   [78] Ward, Stoke, 258.
[79] They are not mentioned in White, Dir. Staffs. (1851).
[80] Kelly's Dir. Staffs. (1908).   [81] Ibid. (1940).
[82] Tunstall Ct. R. (T.N.S.F.C. lix), 76.
[83] S.H.C. N.S. xi. 242.
[84] Tunstall Ct. R. (T.N.S.F.C. lix), 46, 83, 84; ibid. lxi. 32; U.C.N.S., Sneyd MSS., Burslem Deeds; W.S.L., D. 1790/33, compotus of Audley, Horton and Tunstall 10–11 Edw. IV.
[85] U.C.N.S., Sneyd MSS., Keele Deeds, Sneyd v. tenants of Tunstall Manor, no. 15.
[86] Harper, Bygone Tunstall, 70.
[87] Ibid.; see p. 101.
[88] Harper, Bygone Tunstall, 71; H. Wedgwood, Staffs.: Up and Down the County (1881), iii. 51, 67, mentions the mill as no longer in use.

[89] Tunstall Ct. R. (T.N.S.F.C. lxi), 32.
[90] U.C.N.S., Sneyd MSS., Burslem Deeds.
[91] Ibid.
[92] Tunstall Ct. R. (T.N.S.F.C. lxvi), 142.
[93] F. Falkner, The Wood Family of Burslem, 80; Ralph worked Bell's Mill at Shelton and a mill at Cheddleton at the same time, spending 2 days a week at each of the 3 mills.
[94] U.C.N.S., Sneyd MSS., Burslem Deeds.
[95] Ibid.
[96] Lich. Dioc. Regy., Tithe Maps and Appt., Burslem.
[97] P.O. Dir. Staffs. (1854).
[98] Staffs. Advertiser, 22 Aug. 1857.
[99] Parson and Bradshaw, Dir. Staffs. (1818); Keates's Potteries Dir. (1873–4, 1875–6); Burslem Bd. of Health Rep. 1857, 13.   [1] Local inf.
[2] Lich. Dioc. Regy., Tithe Maps and Appt., Burslem; Ward, Stoke, 160.
[3] O.S. Map 6" Staffs. xi SE. (1890).
[4] Wedgwood, Staffs.: Up and Down the County, iii. 51.
[5] Lich. Dioc. Regy., Tithe Maps and Appt., Burslem; White, Dir. Staffs. (1851); P.O. Dir. Staffs. (1854).
[6] P.O. Dir. Staffs. (1860); Keates and Ford's Potteries Dir. (1865–6).
[7] P.O. Dir. Staffs. (1868); Kelly's Dir. Staffs. (1924).
[8] Kelly's Dir. Staffs. (1928, 1940); local inf.
[9] P.O. Dir. Staffs. (1860), sub Williams; (1876), sub Jones; Kelly's Dir. Staffs. (1880), sub Jones.
[10] Kelly's Dir. Staffs. (1892), sub Jones.

century and fragments of pottery of the same period have been unearthed to the north-west of the junction of Sneyd Street and Crossway Road.[11] Potter was a family name at Hulton early in the 15th century,[12] but otherwise the Adams family are the earliest identifiable potters in the Burslem area. William and his brother Richard were fined in 1448 for digging clay by the road between Burslem and Sneyd,[13] and Thomas Adams of Burslem was evidently making pottery before 1563.[14] His grandson William Adams was described in his will of 1617 as a master potter—one of the first master potters who can be identified—and William's son Thomas was also so described in his will of 1629.[15] The Daniel family of Burslem were making pottery there before the end of the 16th century;[16] the name occurs on fragments of 17th-century butter pots unearthed to the north of the town hall,[17] and Thomas Daniel of Burslem, a potter, was accused in 1682 of engrossing the butter pots made in Burslem, Hanley, and Stoke.[18] A works of the mid-17th century specializing in tygs has been traced on a site adjoining the 'Marquis of Granby' in the market place,[19] while near the former meat-market fragments of 17th-century tygs of unusual form have been found, with remains of unglazed red-clay butter pots below them.[20] The Wedgwoods of Burslem had begun to produce pottery by the 1650's,[21] and in the later part of the century a pottery in operation on the site of the medieval works at Sneyd Green where fragments of unusual white and brown slipware tygs of the period have been found.[22] In all, Burslem had by this time achieved its status as 'mother of the Potteries', and Plot recorded that 'the greatest pottery they have in this county is carried on at Burslem near Newcastle-under-Lyme where for making their several sorts of pots they have as many different sorts of clay which they dig round about the town all within half a mile's distance'.[23]

About 1710 there are said to have been 35 potworks at Burslem (2 of them not then worked), 4 at Cobridge, 1 at Rushton Grange, 2 at Sneyd Green, and 1 at Holden Lane;[24] there seems also to have

been a pottery at Brownhills c. 1700 in the hands of one of the Wedgwoods.[25] With the turnpiking of the main roads in 1763 and 1765 and the building of the Trent and Mersey Canal in 1766–77 the industry received fresh encouragement, while the new district of Longport, at first entirely one of factories, grew up near the point where the Tunstall to Newcastle and Burslem to Newcastle roads converge and cross the canal.[26] About 1800 there were 30 potworks at Burslem, 5 at Longport, 1 at Newport on the canal to the south, 1 at Brownhills, and 8 at Cobridge.[27] About 1840 there were 24 at Burslem (5 of them unoccupied), 2 at Longport, and 10 at Cobridge.[28] There were 26 major works at Burslem, Middleport, and Newport in 1959, 3 at Longport, 2 at Brownhills, 1 in Scotia Road, and 7 at Cobridge; the main product was earthenware with a certain amount of vitrified ware and redware, but only 4 works were producing bone china.[29] One factory was making sanitary ware.[30]

The oldest pottery which can be identified over any length of time is the Knowle Works. This stood at the west end of Hamil Road adjoining what was later the Big House estate and can be traced back to 1651 when it was in the hands of the Malkin family.[31] Richard Malkin was making black and mottled ware there c. 1710.[32] The pottery was bought by John Breeze in 1793 and let to the firm of Enoch Wood and James Caldwell in 1818,[33] but in 1827 the ownership of the works, then in the tenure of Enoch Wood and Sons, had passed with that of the Greenfield estate into the Adams family by marriage.[34] Some ten years later the pottery was unoccupied but subsequently passed through various hands.[35] It seems to have been demolished by the end of the 19th century.[36]

The works attached to the Brick House between the later St. John's Square and Queen Street[37] can be traced back nearly as far as the Knowle Works. John Adams, who was living at the Brick House in 1657 and died in 1687, is said to have produced the black and mottled ware that has been found on the site.[38] His son John was making black and mottled

[11] T.N.S.F.C. lxxxix. 84–85; xci. 85–86; exhibits at the City Mus., Hanley.
[12] Procs. before J.P.s in 14th and 15th Cents. ed. Bertha Putnam, 305, 317.
[13] Adams, Adams Family, 15. An old kiln and very coarse saggars were found in a field near the Hamil early in the 18th cent.: Shaw, Staffs. Potteries, 7. No evidence is given for the statement by Adams (op. cit. 15) that the monks of Hulton Abbey produced pottery and that their works was taken over by the Adams family at the Dissolution.
[14] In his will proved 1563 he left his best 'yron chymney' to his son Wm. and his other chimney to his daughter Ellen: Adams, Adams Family, 56.
[15] Ibid. 57, 58.   [16] Ibid. 104.
[17] T.N.S.F.C. xci. 94. These fragments are preserved in the City Mus., Hanley. Another branch of the Daniel family was making pottery at the Nook on the S. side of what was later Queen Street by the mid-17th cent.: S.H.C. 4th ser. ii. 94.   [18] S.R.O., Q/SR Trans. 1682.
[19] T.N.S.F.C. xci. 95.
[20] Ibid. lxxiv. 66–67. A mug with hard-fired coarse body very recently found on this site may date from c. 1600: Evening Sentinel, 17 Feb. 1960.
[21] Wedgwood, Wedgwood Family, 88, 89.
[22] T.N.S.F.C. lxxxix. 85–86.
[23] R. Plot, Nat. Hist. Staffs. (1686), 422.
[24] Adams, Adams Family, 111.
[25] Meigh, 'Staffs. Potters', 207.
[26] See pp. 106, 108, 110.
[27] Allbut, Staffs. Pottery Dir. (1802).

[28] Ward, Stoke, 159, 259, 264–6, 286.
[29] Pottery Gaz. Dir. (1960).
[30] Ibid.
[31] P. W. L. Adams, Notes on Some N. Staffs. Families, 77; Adams Family, 348. This end of Hamil Rd. was called Knowle St. in 1832: Hargreaves, Map of Staffs. Potteries. See p. 120 for the Malkins' Jackfield estate.
[32] Wedgwood, Wedgwood Family, map facing p. 121. A Robt. Malkin, potter, was in trouble in 1679 for 'digging and making caverns in the waste of the lord' and removing the soil from the road at Small Bridge Bank: Tunstall Ct. R. (T.N.S.F.C. lxvi), 109. Isaac Malkin had a pottery at Greenhead c. 1710 (Wedgwood, Wedgwood Family, 125 and map facing p. 121) and Thos. Malkin another at Jackfield: see p. 120. Sam. Malkin (1688–1741) had a pottery in Nile St., apparently by 1712, and this was called the Knowle Works about the time of his death: Mankowitz and Haggar, Eng. Pottery, 139; Wedgwood, Wedgwood Family, map facing p. 121, which, however, shows in Hamil Rd. only a house belonging to a Joseph Malkin. Samuel's work can be seen in the City Mus., Hanley.
[33] Adams, Adams Family, 348; Jewitt, Ceramic Art, 438.
[34] Adams, N. Staffs. Families, 74; Adams Family, 348; see p. 91.
[35] Meigh, 'Staffs. Potters', 74, 75, 77, 78, 170, 218.
[36] O.S. Map 6" Staffs. xii SW. (1900).
[37] Adams, Adams Family, 126–7; Wedgwood, Wedgwood Family, map facing p. 121; see p. 117.
[38] Adams, Adams Family, 108–9, where it is also stated that John's father Robt. (d. 1654) established the works.

ware at the Brick House c. 1710.[39] This John's second son Ralph enlarged the works after succeeding his father in 1727 and conveyed it in 1747 to his son John as part of his marriage settlement.[40] John died in 1757 leaving a minor William as his heir, and the works as well as the house was evidently then let.[41] Josiah Wedgwood was tenant of the Brick House Works from 1762 to 1770, and during that period achieved his first fame as a potter. He perfected his cream-coloured ware and black Etruscan ware and in 1765 worked for Queen Charlotte; the cream ware thereafter became known as Queen's ware.[42] It is to commemorate this royal patronage that Queen Street is so named.[43] It is said that the pottery became known as the Bell Works during Wedgwood's tenancy from his new method of summoning his workmen, by bell instead of by horn.[44] William Adams, of age in 1769, occupied the house and works from 1770 to 1774, making 'cream colour ware and china glazed ware painted and printed, the most advanced styles of pottery of that time'.[45] The works was regularly leased out from 1774 when William turned all his attention to his Cobridge works. Although the property was divided in 1836 the pottery remained in operation until its demolition in 1876.[46]

The Churchyard Works on the south-east side of St. John's churchyard was built shortly before 1679 by Thomas Wedgwood of the adjoining Churchyard House, evidently as a replacement for an earlier pottery which he had been working by 1657. He also had a horse-driven mill at his new works, presumably for pugging the clay.[47] The works then descended in this branch of the Wedgwood family and in 1780 was bought by a younger son, Josiah Wedgwood of Etruria.[48] By 1773, when Josiah's eldest brother died, the works had been mortgaged, and Josiah established his brother's son and heir Thomas in business there. Thomas died in 1787, and Josiah let the whole Churchyard estate including the works from 1788 to 1793 to Joseph Wedgwood, the husband of his niece Mary and a distant relative.[49] On Josiah's death in 1795 the property passed to five of his children and was sold to Thomas Green.[50] On Green's bankruptcy in 1811 the works passed to a Mr. Joynson (probably P. J. Joynson) and in 1812

to John Mosley who subsequently leased it out 'in small holdings to different potters'.[51] In the 1850's the whole works was taken over by Jesse Bridgwood of Tunstall who by 1860 had been joined by Edward Clarke, and under this partnership the buildings were greatly improved and extended.[52] For most of the period between Bridgwood's death in 1864 and 1880 Clarke let the works, but from 1880 until at least 1889 he was again at the Churchyard Works producing mainly for the American market. His wares included white granite and a fine white earthenware called 'royal semi-porcelain'.[53] The works had been demolished by 1896 when St. John's School was rebuilt on the site.[54]

The Overhouse Pottery in Wedgwood Place has the longest history of any in Burslem, having been worked continuously for at least 250 years. There may have been a works attached to John Colclough's Overhouse estate at the time of his death in 1666.[55] At any rate in 1667 John's mother Katherine Colclough of the Overhouse leased out a building of two bays in Burslem 'used for pothouses', a pot oven, and a smokehouse, with the right to dig clay and marl on the site.[56] However, Thomas Wedgwood, the Colcloughs' successor at the Overhouse, makes no mention of any such works in his will of 1678.[57] His son John, who succeeded him in 1679, had a pottery at Greenhead c. 1680[58] which may be identifiable with the Overhouse Works. In 1691 he leased part of a 'serviceyard' to Richard, youngest son of Aaron Wedgwood, who seems subsequently to have run the Overhouse Works. In 1708 Richard married Katherine Wedgwood, his relative and by then the owner of the Overhouse. He died in 1718.[59] By 1742 the works may have been held on lease by Thomas Wedgwood of the Churchyard who succeeded Katherine in the Overhouse property in 1756. His son Thomas followed him in 1773,[60] and the products of this Thomas included 'cream-coloured ware and china glazed ware painted with blue'.[61] When he died in 1787 he left a minor, also Thomas, as his heir, and the works was leased to Read and Goodfellow.[62] After the death of this last Thomas in 1809, the pottery was sold to Christopher Robinson in 1810[63] and to Edward Challinor in 1819.[64] Challinor leased it out from the 1820's[65] and in 1869

[39] Ibid. 111.
[40] Ibid. 114, 115, 118.
[41] Ibid. 122, 124. Ralph lived until 1766: ibid. 118.
[42] Ibid. 125, 126; Wedgwood, Wedgwood Family, 168; Mankowitz and Haggar, Eng. Pottery, 186, 233.
[43] Adams, Adams Family, 127.
[44] Ibid.   [45] Ibid. 125–6.
[46] Ibid. 126–7; Jewitt, Ceramic Art, 441; Meigh, 'Staffs. Potters', 21, 22, 35, 36, 207; photographs before demolition at H.R.L.
[47] Wedgwood, Wedgwood Family, 88, 89, 108, 111, 112 and n., and map facing p. 121.
[48] See p. 118.
[49] E. Meteyard, Life of Josiah Wedgwood, ii. 272 and n. 2; Wedgwood, Wedgwood Family, 136, 137, 175, and pedigrees following pp. 136, 164; Burslem Par. Reg. ii. 461.
[50] Ll. Jewitt, The Wedgwoods, 99, but the statement there quoted that Josiah's brother John owned the works from 1787 is wrong since John d. 1767 (Wedgwood, Wedgwood Family, 132); Stoke-upon-Trent Par. Reg. iii. 794; Wedgwood, Wedgwood Family, 175.
[51] Jewitt, Ceramic Art, 439; Meigh, 'Staffs. Potters', 91, 115, 116, 119, 146, 175, 192, 200, 214. The works was unoccupied c. 1840: Ward, Stoke, 266.
[52] Jewitt, Ceramic Art, 439–40; Meigh, 'Staffs. Potters', 40, 41. They also worked the Phoenix Pottery in Tunstall: ibid. 41.

[53] Jewitt, Ceramic Art, 440; Meigh, 'Staffs. Potters', 54, 77, 125, 214, 217.   [54] See p. 315.
[55] His will mentions 'the serviceyard and the kilneyard': Wedgwood, Wedgwood Family, 81. For the estate see p. 120.
[56] Adams, N. Staffs. Families, 50. The Malkins had a house and potworks at Greenhead, near the Overhouse, early in the 18th cent.: Wedgwood, Wedgwood Family, 125, and map facing p. 121.
[57] Wedgwood, Wedgwood Family, 111–14.
[58] Ibid. 110; Meigh, 'Staffs. Potters', 207.
[59] Wedgwood, Wedgwood Family, 117, 118, 120. It is not clear from the list of Burslem potters c. 1710 (ibid. 124–5) whether the works was that held by Ric. and described as in the centre of the town, that held by Thos. Taylor and described as 'later Mrs. Wedgwood's', or that not then being worked but with the name John Wedgwood attached to it, John of the Overhouse having died in 1705 and not having mentioned a potworks in his will of that year: ibid. 119. Ric. and his brother Thos. are said to have introduced flint into Burslem pottery: see n. 70 below.
[60] See p. 120.
[61] Jewitt, Ceramic Art, 433.
[62] Wedgwood, Wedgwood Family, 137.
[63] Ibid. 138.
[64] Tablet on façade.
[65] Jewitt, Ceramic Art, 459; Meigh, 'Staffs. Potters', 7, 51, 157.

rebuilt it.[66] Soon afterwards the Overhouse Pottery passed to Ralph Hammersley, of the Church Bank Works, Tunstall, and the firm of Ralph Hammersley and Sons ran it from 1883 until c. 1905.[67] It is now known as the Royal Overhouse Pottery, worked by Barratts of Staffordshire Ltd.[68]

Aaron Wedgwood (c. 1624–1700), fifth surviving son of Gilbert Wedgwood of Burslem, was evidently a potter of note by 1693 when with his sons Thomas and Richard he was in some kind of association with John and David Elers of Fulham. Probably he was supplying them with red Staffordshire clay and so was partly responsible for the Elers brothers' coming to Bradwell.[69] It is not clear whether this 17th-century works is identifiable with a works on the east side of what is now Wedgwood Street where Aaron's second surviving son Aaron was producing dipped and black ware c. 1710.[70] When this younger Aaron died in 1743 this pottery passed to his younger sons Thomas (1703–76) and John (1705–80) who re-built it and ran it as a large-scale enterprise instead of the usual domestic industry. They employed their own travellers and traded direct with London and Liverpool instead of relying on the itinerant hawk-ers.[71] Their products were cream-coloured ware and fine white salt-glazed stoneware; they also invented a pyrometer and employed James Brindley to build a windmill at the Jenkins for grinding flint c. 1750.[72] This mill was apparently in use in 1832, and the derelict base still stood in the 1860's.[73] The brothers built the Big House in front of their works facing Chapel Bank in 1751.[74] In 1780 the Big House pot-tery passed to John's second son Thomas whose products included 'cream-coloured ware and china glazed ware painted with blue'.[75] He had sold it by 1816, and though it was worked by the younger Enoch Wood in 1829[76] it was unoccupied some ten years later.[77] Between at least the 1860's and 1880's it was being used as a builder's premises.[78]

By c. 1736 a pottery had been built on the Adams family's Hadderidge estate south-west of Burslem town and was leased with the estate by Ralph Adams of the Brick House to his son-in-law John Shrigley.[79] In the early 1790's the pottery was sold to Thomas Lakin and John Ellison Poole, who re-built it. From 1795 it was worked by Lakin, Poole, and a Thomas Shrigley and then by Poole and Shrigley until their bankruptcy in 1797.[80] Thomas Heath had bought the works as well as much of the estate by 1806.[81] He was succeeded in 1839 by his sister Sarah Adams (d. 1846), and for a time her sons William, Edward, Lewis, and Thomas carried on the pottery with their Stoke works. Later, however, they leased it out.[82] On the dissolution of the family partnership in 1853 William Adams took over the Hadderidge and Greenfield (Tunstall) works, al-though the former continued in the hands of tenants.[83] It was held by the firm of Edwards by the end of the 19th century, passing from them c. 1918 to Sheldon and Buckley Ltd. who were succeeded some ten years later by J. S. Maddock.[84] In 1932 the works passed to the present owners, W. R. Midwinter Ltd., who had already acquired the nearby Albion Pottery from Edwards in 1916.[85]

Before 1715 Thomas Mitchell had a works in Rotten Row (now Greenhead Street) which by 1715 was no longer in operation.[86] In 1726, however, a Thomas Mitchell of Burslem is described as an earth-potter.[87] By 1736 John Mitchell, a noted manu-facturer of salt-glazed stoneware and later a patron of John Wesley, was working at Hill Top where in 1743 the young Aaron Wood became his employee.[88] Mitchell had failed by the 1780's, and by 1786 the works was in the hands of John Robinson who eventually took over the old Methodist chapel also. This had been built in 1766 on an adjoining site given by John Mitchell and was turned into a ware-house by Robinson.[89] By the early 1830's the pottery had passed from the Robinson family to Samuel Alcock who incorporated it with two neighbouring potworks and reorganized the whole as the Hill Pottery; 400 hands were employed there by that

[66] Tablet on façade; Jewitt, *Ceramic Art*, 459.
[67] Jewitt, *Ceramic Art*, 459, where it is also stated that Hammersley started at the new works on its opening in 1870; Meigh, 'Staffs. Potters', 9, where Hammersley's first date is given as 1880, with (p. 171) Robinson, Kirkham & Co. in 1870–2. Gater, Hall & Co. were there by 1907: ibid. 84.
[68] *Pottery Gaz. Dir.* (1959).
[69] Wedgwood, *Wedgwood Family*, 142. In 1688 Thos. son of Aaron Wedgwood was in trouble for digging pits at Brownhills: *Tunstall Ct. R.* (*T.N.S.F.C.* lxvi), 127.
[70] Wedgwood, *Wedgwood Family*, 125, 151, and map facing p. 121; Hargreaves, *Map of Staffs. Potteries*. Aaron the elder had left all his potworks to his youngest son Ric., tenant of the Overhouse, who was working 'in the middle of the town' c. 1710: Wedgwood, *Wedgwood Family*, 125. The eldest son Thos. (who had bought the Red Lion Inn next to the potworks of Aaron the younger) or his son Thos. (who later became noted for his salt-glazing) at this time held the lease of a works nearby on the W. side of the present Wedgwood St.: ibid. 125, 146–7, 149–50. According to Josiah Wedgwood Thos. of the 'Red Lion' and Ric. of the Overhouse introduced flint into Burslem pottery, using it in their white ware which was fired in an oven on the Bournes' estate at Chell: ibid. 324.
[71] Wedgwood, *Wedgwood Family*, 151, 153–6.
[72] Ibid. 154, 155, and map facing p. 121; Meteyard, *Wedgwood*, i. 181, 277–82, although the date 1758 appears to be too late.
[73] Hargreaves, *Map of Staffs. Potteries*; Meteyard, *Wedgwood*, i. 281.
[74] See p. 117.
[75] Wedgwood, *Wedgwood Family*, 157, 159; Jewitt,

Ceramic Art, 442.
[76] Wedgwood, *Wedgwood Family*, 159; Meigh, 'Staffs. Potters', 215.
[77] Ward, *Stoke*, 266.
[78] Jewitt, *The Wedgwoods*, 160; Jewitt, *Ceramic Art*, 442.
[79] See p. 119.
[80] Mankowitz and Haggar, *Eng. Pottery*, 124; Jewitt, *Ceramic Art*, 443–4; Adams, *Adams Family*, add. and corr., p. X; Adams, *North Staffs. Families*, 11, where the date of sale is given as 1793; Meigh, 'Staffs. Potters', 123, 158; H.R.L., EMT 11–793 (a, b), 11–795.
[81] Adams, *Adams Family*, add. and corr., p. X. The pottery was held by a Wm. Dawson c. 1800: Allbut, *Staffs. Pottery Dir.* (1802).
[82] Adams, *Adams Family*, 328, 330, 331, 340–1; Meigh, 'Staffs. Potters', 100, 155, 216. It seems to have been known as the Furlong Pottery at this time: ibid. 100, 155.
[83] Jewitt, *Ceramic Art*, 466; Meigh, 'Staffs. Potters', 29, 36, 104; H.R.L., EMT 15–863.
[84] Meigh, 'Staffs. Potters', 74, 75, 131, 178.
[85] Ex inf. W. R. Midwinter Ltd. (1959); *Survey of Stoke-on-Trent* (*Brit. Bull. of Commerce*, Nov. 1954), 27 (copy in H.R.L.); *Pottery Gaz. Dir.* (1959).
[86] Adams, *Adams Family*, 111.
[87] W.S.L., D. 1788, P. 34, B. 1.
[88] Mankowitz and Haggar, *Eng. Pottery*, 155; F. Falkner, *The Wood Family of Burslem*, 26–27; H. Wedgwood, *Staffs.: Up and Down the County*, ii. 20, 27–28; Wedgwood, *Wedgwood Family*, map c. 1750 facing p. 121, which, however, shows Thos. Mitchell at Hill Top and John on the adjoining site to the E.
[89] Wedgwood, *Staffs.: Up and Down the County*, ii. 28, 31, 32; Meigh, 'Staffs. Potters', 170; see p. 290.

time.[90] The works itself was described in the early
1840's as 'one of the largest and best conducted in
the Potteries'.[91] Samuel Alcock and Company, who
made good porcelain, bisque figures, and parian
vases and figures, failed in 1859, and in 1860 the
works was taken over by Sir James Duke and
Nephews (J. and C. Hill) who sold it in 1865 to
Thomas Ford; he in turn sold it in 1866 to the
Earthenware and Porcelain Company.[92] This operated for a year as the Hill Pottery Company and was
then liquidated, Thomas Ford buying the works
back in 1867.[93] The china department was in that
year taken over by Alcock and Diggory (Bodley and
Diggory in 1870), and as the Crown Works it was in
the hands of the firm of Bodley from 1871 until at
least 1892.[94] The earthenware department passed in
1867 to Burgess and Leigh who held it until at least
1889.[95] The whole works is now part of the Royal
Pottery of J. Steventon and Sons Ltd. The large
Classical building still standing on the east side of
Westport Road (formerly Liverpool Road) on the
crest of the hill represents the front range of the
pottery completed in 1839 by Samuel Alcock on the
site of the Robinsons' works. It was considered at
the time to be 'the most striking and ornamental
object of its kind within the precincts of the borough'
(i.e. Stoke).[96] This admiration was evidently shared by
Arnold Bennett. The building appears in *Clayhanger*
as the Sytch Pottery and encouraged the young
Edwin in his desire to become an architect.[97] The
building, which is now largely derelict, is of brick
with stone dressings and has three stories and a basement. Its ten-bay front incorporates much heavy
Classical detail used in an unconventional manner.
The imposing central feature consists of a 'Venetian'
doorway approached by seven steps and flanked by
paired Ionic columns bearing entablatures on which
stand large vases (one of them now missing). Above
the doorway is a balustrade and a Venetian window
with rusticated quoins and voussoirs. Other first-
floor windows are emphasized by moulded stone or
pedimented heads, giving the effect of a *piano nobile*.
The façade has a central pediment, below which
stone triglyphs are set into the brickwork.

By the 1750's there was a pottery attached to the
Ivy House estate which was owned by the Wedgwoods of the nearby Big House. It was as tenant of
this works from 1759 to 1762 that Josiah Wedgwood,
a distant relative of the Big House Wedgwoods, first
worked on his own account. His attempt to buy the
whole property *c.* 1774 was unsuccessful, and the
works evidently remained with the Big House branch

of the family until its demolition to make way for the
new market in the 1830's.[98]

The Hill Works (now the Royal Victoria Pottery)
on the opposite side of Westport Road from the Hill
Pottery was held in 1784 by Enoch and Ralph Wood
who produced 'useful and ornamental ware, Egyp-
tian black, cane and various colours, also black
figures, seals and syphers'.[99] Still held by Ralph
Wood in 1802[1] the works subsequently passed to
John Taylor and in 1814 was rebuilt by John and
Richard Riley who made china, earthenware, and
Egyptian black.[2] The Rileys both died in the late
1820's, and the works passed first to Alcock and
Keeling and by 1834 to Samuel Alcock and Com-
pany.[3] About 1851 it was taken over by Barber and
Son, in 1860 by Morgan, Wood and Company
(Wood and Baggaley by 1870), by 1880 by Jacob
Baggaley and in 1887 by Dunn and Bennett who
were succeeded in 1938 by the present occupants,
Wade, Heath and Company.[4] The two-storied entrance front of the works as rebuilt by the Rileys in
1814 is set at an angle of 45 degrees to the main outside walls of the factory, which, as the ground slopes
away to the north-west, is of three and four stories.
The design of the entrance feature is one which was
much favoured in the Potteries in the late 18th and
early 19th centuries and which persisted in a modified form into Victorian times. An elliptical archway
with rusticated voussoirs is flanked by narrow windows—now altered—and is surmounted by a Venetian window which has a Tuscan order with a fluted
frieze. Above this is a dentil cornice and an open
pediment, the latter carrying an oval plaque inscribed 'Hill Works 1814'.

The Fountain Place Works, with a house and
grounds attached, was built in 1789 by Enoch Wood,
son of Aaron Wood the block-cutter and modeller;
the whole estate, incorporating the sites of four older
potteries, extended westwards down the hillside and
southwards to straddle Pack Horse Lane.[5] Wood was
in partnership with James Caldwell from 1790 to
1818, and from 1818 to 1846—six years after Wood's
death—the firm was known as Enoch Wood and
Sons. By the early 1830's 1,100 hands were employed at the works.[6] Wood's products included
blue-printed ware, jasper ware, black basaltes,
figures, and some experimental porcelain.[7] After
1846 the factory passed through various hands, but
from *c.* 1868 it was not in continuous occupation;
much of it was subsequently demolished to make
way for new streets and buildings.[8] The surviving
parts of the works are now (1960) in the hands of

[90] Ward, *Stoke*, 264–5; Mankowitz and Haggar, *Eng.
Pottery*, 6; Meigh, 'Staffs. Potters', 5, 170; inscription
'Hill Pottery' on building; *1st Rep. Factories Com.* H.C.
450, p. B2, 35 (1833), xx. The other two factories were
John Riley's Hill Works opposite and Wm. Taylor's works
situated apparently to the east. Ward (p. 265) mentions
the absorption or demolition of 'three of the better sort
of houses of the last century . . . to make room for buildings
of trade'.
[91] *2nd Rep. Com. Employment of Children* [431], p. *c* 53,
H.C. (1843), xiv.
[92] Mankowitz and Haggar, *Eng. Pottery*, 6, 7, 9; Jewitt,
Ceramic Art, 459.
[93] Jewitt, *Ceramic Art*, 459–60.
[94] Ibid. 460; Mankowitz and Haggar, *Eng. Pottery* 27;
Meigh, 'Staffs. Potters', 30.
[95] Jewitt, *Ceramic Art*, 460; Meigh, 'Staffs. Potters', 47.
[96] Ward, *Stoke*, 265 and plate facing.
[97] Bk. i, chap. xiv.   [98] See p. 119.

[99] Jewitt, *Ceramic Art*, 465; Mankowitz and Haggar,
Eng. Pottery, 242–3.
[1] Allbut, *Staffs. Pottery Dir.* (1802).
[2] Ward, *Stoke*, 264; Jewitt, *Ceramic Art*, 465; Mankowitz and Haggar, *Eng. Pottery*, 192; inscription on
building; see plate facing p. 294.
[3] Mankowitz and Haggar, *Eng. Pottery*, 192; Jewitt,
Ceramic Art, 465.
[4] Jewitt, *Ceramic Art*, 465; C. Bunt, *Brit. Potters and
Pottery To-day*, 54; Meigh, 'Staffs. Potters', 10, 217;
Pottery Gaz. Dir. (1959).
[5] Ward, *Stoke*, 259–60, 267; Mankowitz and Haggar,
Eng. Pottery, 242; see plates facing pp. 105, 136.
[6] Mankowitz and Haggar, *Eng. Pottery*, 243; *1st Rep.
Factories Com.* p. B2, 15.
[7] Mankowitz and Haggar, *Eng. Pottery*, 242.
[8] Meigh, 'Staffs. Potters', 14, 39, 54, 57, 84, 89, 108,
110, 138, 139, 155, 156, 174, 180; Falkner, *Wood Family*,
82; see p. 105.

Ford & Sons, a firm established in Newcastle by Thomas Ford in 1865.[9] The house was still standing in 1881 when it was offered as premises for the new Haywood Charity Hospital, but it was rejected as unsuitable.[10] Wood had at first had a windmill at the works for 'raising water and preparing the clay, ready for the hands of the potters, and for grinding glaze and colours', but by the early 1840's it had been replaced by steam power.[11] He and Caldwell also had a flint mill at Bycars to the north-east of the town from 1806, and this, still held by the Wood family in 1860, remained in use until at least 1882.[12] The works dated from 1789 but was probably extended in the early 19th century. It occupied the whole area between Hall Street on the north and Newcastle Street on the south and had a long east frontage to Liverpool Road (now Westport Road) and Fountain Place.[13] This frontage incorporated the entrance to Pack Horse Lane which served as an access road to part of the works. At the Fountain Place end of the lane it was spanned by a covered bridge and flanked by tall buildings which were continued for a considerable distance down the lane. On the north side some of these buildings are still standing, including a three-storied range with an angle entrance on the corner of Pack Horse Lane and a frontage of nine bays on Westport Road. In spite of the insertion of a shop front and the mutilation of the upper stories the original elevation on the angle can still be recognized. This formerly had an entrance arch flanked by small windows, a Venetian window to the first floor, and a three-light window above, the whole being surmounted by a pediment and a domed bell turret. Other original features which survive are the base of the windmill at the north-east corner of the site and the lodge gates—probably of the early 19th century—which stand at the blocked end of Pack Horse Lane. The square three-storied house built and occupied by Enoch Wood appears to have stood near the centre of the site; the factory buildings stood mostly above and behind it, and its gardens stretched westwards down the slope.[14] The numerous brick ovens and many of the walls originally had castellated parapets, so that a distant view of the works in its heyday must have given the impression of a hillside fortification.

The Royal Doulton Potteries in Nile Street incorporate a pottery worked at the beginning of the 19th century by John and Richard Riley which itself occupied the site of an earlier works.[15] The Rileys were succeeded after their removal to the Hill Works

c. 1814 by John Cormie.[16] The pottery is evidently identifiable with the Hole House works held between at least 1834 and 1851 by Mellor, Venables and Company, a firm in which Cormie's nephew Thomas Pinder was a partner.[17] Pinder's great-nephew Shadford Pinder was working there by 1862 under the name Pinder, Bourne and Company.[18] Sir Henry Doulton, of Messrs. Doulton, Lambeth, acquired the works from this firm in 1877, adding a new wing in 1884 for the manufacture of bone china.[19] Two other factories were subsequently added: the Kilncroft works in Chapel Lane dating from at least the early 19th century and the Sylvester Pottery which was in existence by the 1830's. There was also extensive new building in 1889. The number of employees increased rapidly during this period, from 300 in the early 1880's to 1,300 in 1893.[20] In recent years there has been large-scale modernization, and the factory is now one of the biggest pottery works in the world.[21]

The first pottery at Longport was built c. 1773 by John Brindley, a younger brother of James Brindley, the engineer, and was acquired by John Davenport in 1793 or 1794.[22] At first Davenport made earthenware only (cream-coloured, painted and transfer-printed), but early in the 19th century he began to make porcelain also. In 1797 he had begun the manufacture of a chemical preparation for use in glazing and from 1801 was also producing glass.[23] About 1810 he acquired a pottery at Newport founded c. 1795 by Walter Daniel.[24] Davenport's sons continued the business after his retirement c. 1830, enlarging the buildings and acquiring a factory at Longport built by Robert Williamson soon after Brindley's.[25] Another pottery also built about that time by Edward Bourne had been added to the Davenport works by the early 1840's so that the family then had four factories at or near Longport employing in all over 1,500 people.[26] The Newport Pottery passed in the 1850's to Cork and Edge (Cork, Edge, and Malkin 1860–70, Edge, Malkin and Company Ltd. 1870–1903). It was bought in 1920 by the present owners, the Newport Pottery Company Ltd.; as A. J. Wilkinson Ltd. they had moved in 1898 from the Central Pottery, Burslem, to the Mersey Pottery at Middleport, built by Anthony Shaw c. 1860.[27] The Davenport works in New Bridge Street passed in 1877 to Edward Clarke and Company, and the site is now occupied by the works of Pidduck and Beardmore Ltd., makers of fireplaces, stoves, and domestic fittings generally. The rest of the business remained in the Davenports'

[9] Survey of Stoke-on-Trent (Brit. Bull. of Commerce, Dec. 1954), 27 (copy in H.R.L.).
[10] Warrillow, Stoke, 363.   [11] Ward, Stoke, 260.
[12] Shaw, Staffs. Potteries, 31; Parson and Bradshaw, Dir. Staffs. (1818); P.O. Dir. Staffs. (1860); Keates's Potteries Dir. (1882).
[13] Ward, Stoke, view of E. front facing p. 267.
[14] Ibid., W. view facing p. 266; see plate on facing p.
[15] Jewitt, Ceramic Art, 448; Allbut, Staffs. Pottery Dir. (1802).
[16] Jewitt, Ceramic Art, 448; Mankowitz and Haggar, Eng. Pottery, 60.
[17] Jewitt, Ceramic Art, 448; Meigh, 'Staffs. Potters', 14, 169; W.S.L. 136/40.
[18] Jewitt, Ceramic Art, 448; Meigh, 'Staffs. Potters', 155. Pinder, Bourne and Hope were working there in 1860: ibid.
[19] Mankowitz and Haggar, Eng. Pottery, 76, 78.
[20] Meigh, 'Staffs. Potters', 31, 46, 74, 99, 109, 112, 135, 137, 152, 213; Jewitt, Ceramic Art, 456, 465, 466; Allbut,

Staffs. Pottery Dir. (1802); Descriptive Acct. of the Potteries (1893), 53 (copy in H.R.L.).
[21] Stoke Official Handbk. [1958], 95.
[22] Ward, Stoke, 156, giving 1794 as the date of Davenport's acquisition of the works; Jewitt, Ceramic Art, 467, giving 1793.
[23] Ward, Stoke, 156–7; Mankowitz and Haggar, Eng. Pottery, 67–68.
[24] Jewitt, Ceramic Art, 450; Ward, Stoke, 157; Mankowitz and Haggar, Eng. Pottery, 67. The works was for sale in 1804: ibid.
[25] Jewitt, Ceramic Art, 468; Ward, Stoke, 156.
[26] Ward, Stoke, 156, 157.
[27] Jewitt, Ceramic Art, 450; Meigh, 'Staffs. Potters', 61; Mankowitz and Haggar, Eng. Pottery, 80–81; Pottery Gaz. Dir. (1959); Survey of Stoke-on-Trent (Brit. Bull. of Commerce, Dec. 1954), 32 (copy in H.R.L.). A. J. Wilkinson had been in association with Davenport at Newport; his brother-in-law Arthur Shorter had taken over his business in 1894: ibid.

St. John's Church *c.* 1840; the National School appears on the left

West view of Fountain Place House and Works, *c.* 1840

BURSLEM

ARNOLD BENNETT AGED 23
from a drawing by M. Du Mayne

ENOCH WOOD AGED 62
self-portrait in biscuit pottery

THE WEDGWOOD FAMILY AT ETRURIA HALL, 1780
from a painting by George Stubbs

hands until its sale to Thomas Hughes in 1887 or 1888.[28] The group of buildings north-west of Trubshaw Cross represents part of the Davenport works.[29] The house, which dates from near the end of the 18th century, is built of brick and has a three-storied front of five bays. The windows have stone lintels with fluted keystones, and the central doorway is surmounted by a 'Gothic' fanlight and an open pediment. The factory buildings have recently been demolished. The entrance range to the works, of three stories, stood to the north of the house. Its central archway, above which was a pointed niche, was flanked by two projecting bays which rose to the full height of the building.

John Wood, son of Ralph Wood, built a pottery and house at Brownhills in or soon after 1782; the works was demolished by his son John in 1830 when the house and grounds were improved.[30] This was the only pottery at Brownhills at the beginning of the 19th century,[31] but from c. 1805 Joseph Marsh was making china there, with Samuel Marsh and Richard Haywood as his successors c. 1818.[32] This china works was taken over in the 1840's by George Bowers who began making earthenware there after 1851; he was succeeded by his son Frederick in the 1860's, but the business failed in 1871.[33] The works was then bought by James Eardley of Alsager (Ches.) and worked by the Brownhills Pottery Company,[34] passing about the turn of the century to George Clews and Company who still work it as the Brownhills Pottery.[35]

A pottery in Sneyd Street, Cobridge, was one of several in the neighbourhood worked by the Daniel family during the later 18th century. It was sold in 1769, two years after the bankruptcy of Sampson Daniel, to William Adams of the Brick House. About 1780 Adams built Cobridge Hall nearby.[36] At his Cobridge works he introduced into Staffordshire the manufacture of blue-printed ware and in 1775 the use of copperplate engraving.[37] By 1802 this pottery, with at least one other in Cobridge, had been let by Adams,[38] but it remained the property of this branch of the Adams family until after the death in 1869 of Mary Adams, the last of William's children.[39] The family trustees then sold it to Messrs. Furnival who apparently held the lease by 1850.[40] The pottery

had been pulled down by the mid-1920's.[41] A works on an adjoining site to the south was held by the Blackwells from c. 1780, by the Blackwells in partnership with the Dillons from c. 1822 until 1832, and then by the Dillons until 1843. Since at least 1848 it has remained in the hands of Messrs. Furnival.[42] The oldest surviving buildings of this last factory probably date from the late 18th century and include a warehouse range fronting on Elder Road with a dwelling house behind. The former has been altered and faced with stucco but retains a central archway with a Venetian window and a pediment above it. Over the pediment stands the original bell cupola, almost the only example of this feature—another is at the former Wedgwood works at Etruria—to survive in the Potteries. The house, now incorporated in the works, has a long front of seven bays and a pedimented doorcase and dates from the second half of the 18th century.

In 1802 William Adams was working two potteries opposite each other in Elder Road.[43] That to the west had to be partially demolished when Waterloo Road was built in 1815–17; the remainder of the site was occupied until recently by the Globe Pottery, now replaced by Ridgway's Portland Pottery.[44] The other has been identified as the works held by Stevenson and Dale in 1789, by Bucknall and Andrew Stevenson c. 1805. It was later worked by Stevenson alone who produced blue-printed ware at the pottery until it was closed in 1818.[45] It was soon reopened by Ralph and James Clews, but they went bankrupt in 1835.[46] Described in 1841 as having 'extensive rooms, better than common',[47] the works was held from 1836 by John Robinson, John Wood, and William Brownfield and from 1841 by Wood and Brownfield.[48] The Brownfields were sole owners from 1850, and in 1890 the works was reorganized as the co-operative Brownfield Guild Pottery, which failed soon afterwards.[49] It has been worked as the Alexandra Pottery by Myott, Son and Company since at least 1903[50] and is situated in Douglas Street and Arthur Street behind Furnival's works.

The Warburton family, who had factories in Hot Lane and at Cobridge during the 18th century, had two works in Elder Road near the junction with Hot Lane at the beginning of the 19th century.[51] One of

28 Jewitt, *Ceramic Art*, 468, 471; Meigh, 'Staffs. Potters', 66; *Pottery Gaz*. 1 Oct. 1881, 1 Feb., 2 July 1888.
29 Meigh, 'Staffs. Potters', 66; see plate facing p. 172.
30 See p. 118. Meigh, 'Staffs. Potters', 127, states that Littler was Wood's precursor there for a few years about the mid-18th cent. before he went to Longton Hall (see p. 239)   31 Allbut, *Staffs. Pottery Dir.* (1802).
32 Mankowitz and Haggar, *Eng. Pottery*, 141.
33 Ibid. 32; Jewitt, *Ceramic Art*, 470; Meigh, 'Staffs. Potters', 36.
34 Jewitt, *Ceramic Art*, 470–1; Meigh, 'Staffs. Potters', 44.
35 Meigh, 'Staffs. Potters', 44, 54; *Pottery Gaz. Dir.* (1959).
36 Adams, *Adams Family*, 136 and add. and corr., p. K; H.R.L., EMT 10–769, 10–783, 11–780; see p. 119. Another of Sampson's potworks at Cobridge was sold to Wm. in 1787: H.R.L., EMT 1–787(*b*). A Ralph Daniel of Cobridge introduced the use of plaster moulds to England c. 1745: Mankowitz and Haggar, *Eng. Pottery*, 66.
37 Adams, *Adams Family*, 127, 328.
38 Allbut, *Staffs. Pottery Dir.* (1802).
39 Adams, *Adams Family*, 142, 164, 165; H.R.L., EM 26–866, plan of 1866. Ric. Adams, belonging to another branch of the family, had a works at Cobridge c. 1759–90. He possibly learnt the art from his great-uncle at a works in Holden Lane: Adams, *Adams Family*, 315–17 and add. and corr., p. K.

40 Adams, *Adams Family*, add. and corr., p. C.
41 Ibid.
42 Mankowitz and Haggar, *Eng. Pottery*, 26, 72; Meigh, 'Staffs. Potters', 70.
43 Allbut, *Staffs. Pottery Dir.* (1802).
44 Adams, *Adams Family*, add. and corr., p. K; Meigh, 'Staffs. Potters', 15, 26, 29, 55, 56, 86, 100, 112; T. Roberts, 'Old Roads of Burslem' (*Stoke Bi-monthly Review*, Feb. 1953), 3, stating that there had been an alternative proposal to run Waterloo Rd. along the course of the present Remer St., thus saving the works.
45 Mankowitz and Haggar, *Eng. Pottery*, 210; Jewitt, *Ceramic Art*, 472; Adams, *Adams Family*, add. and corr., p. K. The Bucknall family were making pottery at Cobridge and possibly Hot Lane in the 18th cent: Meigh, 'Staffs. Potters', 46.
46 Ward, *Stoke*, 286; Mankowitz and Haggar, *Eng. Pottery*, 55; S.R.O., D. 206/M4.
47 *2nd Rep. Com. Employment of Children*, p. c58.
48 Mankowitz and Haggar, *Eng. Pottery*, 192.
49 Ibid. 38, 192.
50 Adams, *Adams Family*, add. and corr., p. K.; Meigh, 'Staffs. Potters', 148.
51 Meigh, 'Staffs. Potters', 204; Adams, *Adams Family*, add. and corr., p. K; Allbut, *Staffs. Pottery Dir.* (1802); Mankowitz and Haggar, *Eng. Pottery*, 230–1. Peter Warburton (1773–1813) built the Bleak Hill Works (still

these, the Villa Pottery, was in the hands of Thomas Hughes between at least 1822 and 1834. By 1834 he was evidently in partnership with Elijah Jones who by 1841 was working at the Villa Pottery with Edward Walley. The pottery was held by Walley alone from at least 1846 until 1865 when it passed to Wood, Son and Company (later Wood and Dunn).[52] William Cartlidge moved there from Bournes Bank in 1879 and was still working the pottery in 1892.[53]

A works in what is now the Cobridge part of Waterloo Road was held by the Stevenson family from at least 1775 until Ralph Stevenson's bankruptcy in 1835 and passed soon afterwards to John and George Alcock.[54] It was run as the Elder Pottery by Henry Alcock and Company from at least 1864 until 1910 when it was bought by the Soho Pottery Ltd. founded by S. J. Simpson at Tunstall in 1904.[55] It is still worked by this company—renamed Simpsons (Potters) Ltd. in 1942.[56] The range of buildings facing Waterloo Road has a simple but well designed brick front, the stone entrance-arch bearing the date 1848 and the initials 'J A' (John Alcock).

The mills at the Fountain Place Works, the Jenkins, and Bycars have been treated above. Burslem's other flint-grinding mills have included the Furlong Mills in Furlong Lane, built in 1843, enlarged in 1913, and run since 1926 by a subsidiary company of Alfred Meakin (Tunstall) Ltd.;[57] a mill off Scotia Road run since c. 1910 by the Burslem Mills Company, a subsidiary of Richards Tiles Ltd., Tunstall;[58] a mill in Adkins Street, Cobridge, worked since 1932 by the North Road Mill Company, a subsidiary of the Wade group;[59] two mills by the late 1820's at Longport where there was still a flint mill in 1940;[60] a mill in Bridge Street, Middleport, by 1896, worked since at least 1916 by the Middleport Mills Company;[61] two mills still in use at Newport—Mellor's, run by the North Staffs. Pulveriser Company between at least 1896 and 1940, and Oliver's dating from at least 1908;[62] Hoston Mill off Scotia Road, owned in 1834 by Hugh Henshall Williamson and in the 1870's, after his death, absorbed into the Pinnox Iron Works;[63] and a mill in Chester Street, Brownhills, built by George Bowers in or shortly before 1853 presumably in connexion with his nearby pottery (see above) and still in use in 1924.[64] The old corn mill at the Sytch seems to have been used as a flint mill for a time during the 19th century.[65]

MINING. Evidence of coal mining in Burslem goes back at any rate to the beginning of the 14th century[66] and probably to the 1280's.[67] From at least the later 14th century it seems to have been normal for the lords of Tunstall manor to lease out their Burslem mines.[68] By the later 15th century these included mines in the coal seams running north-west along the high ground from above Hulton and through the Hamil (Sneyd), with considerable outcropping.[69] Even by the later 17th century there were shafts around the Hamil ancient enough to contain fully grown oaks,[70] and 200 years later it was noted that to the east of Burslem town 'the face of the country is thickly scarred with marks of the old surface workings'.[71] During the 19th century there was deeper mining, and the rise in the population of Burslem township in the 1860's was attributed to the extension of mining operations, particularly of ironstone mining.[72] This was carried on in addition to the coal mining at many of the collieries. In 1869, however, the Pinnox and Scotia collieries fell into disuse on the death of the owner, H. H. Williamson, and were consequently soon flooded; the water spread, helped by very wet weather and the lack of concerted pumping operations on the part of the colliery owners, so that in several of the mines in the Burslem and Tunstall district output soon dropped and in the course of the next 20 years ceased altogether.[73] Sneyd Colliery, one of those which closed down, was reopened by William Heath in the early 1880's and since c. 1920 has been the only colliery in the Burslem area.

standing between Elder and Waterloo Roads) early in the 19th cent.: ibid. 231.

[52] Jewitt, *Ceramic Art*, 478; Meigh, 'Staffs. Potters', 112, 117, 119, 203, 217; White, *Dir. Staffs.* (1834).

[53] Jewitt, *Ceramic Art*, 478; Meigh, 'Staffs. Potters', 50.

[54] Mankowitz and Haggar, *Eng. Pottery*, 210; Ward, *Stoke*, 286; Meigh, 'Staffs. Potters', 5; H.R.L., EMT 1–836(a). In the early 1830's 600 hands were employed there: *1st Rep. Factories Com.*, p. B2, 20.

[55] Meigh, 'Staffs. Potters', 5, 185; *Survey of Stoke-on-Trent (Brit. Bull. of Commerce*, Dec. 1954), 15.

[56] *Brit. Bull. of Commerce*, Dec. 1954, 15.

[57] White, *Dir. Staffs.* (1851); *P.O. Dir. Staffs.* (1872); *Kelly's Dir. Staffs.* (1884, 1912); tablets on buildings; ex inf. Alfred Meakin (Tunstall) Ltd. Howard and Ric. Haywood and John Goodwin held a flint mill in Beech's Lane in 1844 (H.R.L., EMT 15–844), and Goodwin held the Furlong Mill in 1851.

[58] See p. 104.

[59] *Survey of Stoke-on-Trent (Brit. Bull. of Commerce*, vol. 16 N.S. no. 7), 11; *Kelly's Dir. Staffs.* (1932, 1940). A flint mill variously described as in Hot Lane, North Rd., and Flint St., was worked by Edw. Corn between at least 1865 and 1892: *Keates and Ford's Potteries Dir.* (1865–6); *Keates's Potteries Dir.* (1873–4, 1875–6, 1882, 1892–3).

[60] *Pigot's Nat. Com. Dir.* (1828–9); *P.O. Dir. Staffs.* (1872); *Kelly's Dir. Staffs.* (1884, 1896, 1924, 1940); O.S. Map 6" Staffs. xi SE. (1890, 1900, 1926).

[61] *Kelly's Dir. Staffs.* (1896, 1908, 1916); *Barrett's Stoke City Dir.* [1959]. Wm. Bowers had a mill at Middleport in 1851: White, *Dir. Staffs.* (1851).

[62] *Kelly's Dir. Staffs.* (1896, 1908, 1916, 1924, 1940); *Stoke City Dir.* [1959], which does not mention Mellor's; O.S. Map 6" Staffs. xii SW. (1900, 1926).

[63] White, *Dir. Staffs.* (1834, 1851); *Mining Jnl. and Commercial Gaz.*, 22 July 1871, 637 (copy in H.R.L.); Malabar, *Map of Tunstall*; O.S. Map 6" Staffs. xii NW. (1890).

[64] W.S.L., D. 1797; *Kelly's Dir. Staffs.* (1896, 1908, 1924); O.S. Map 6" Staffs. xi NE. (1925).

[65] See p. 131.

[66] *S.H.C.* N.S. xi. 261. For mining within Tunstall manor generally see p. 101.

[67] *S.H.C.* N.S. xi. 246, mentioning a mine in Tunstall manor in 1282.

[68] *Tunstall Ct. R.* (*T.N.S.F.C.* lix), 58, 84; W.S.L., D. 1490/33; S.C. 6/Hen. VII/679, m. 5; see p. 139.

[69] Bodl. MS. 36911, Thos. Endon's Plan of Coal Mines in Sneyd Hamlet, May 1683 (photostat copy in H.R.L.); Ward, *Stoke*, 209; Wedgwood, *Wedgwood Family*, 275, 290; C. J. Homer, 'N. Staffs. Coalfield' (*Trans. N. Staffs. Inst. Mining Engineers*, i), 105. The seams worked included the Great Row which provides a coal well suited to the needs of the pottery industry: [J. O'N. Millott], *Coal Seams of N. Staffs.* (D.S.I.R. Pamph., H.M.S.O. 1937), 44. For present-day outcropping in the centre of Burslem, see p. 105, n. 5.

[70] Wedgwood, *Wedgwood Family*, 308.

[71] *Staffs. Sentinel*, 26 Apr. 1890; O.S. Map 6" Staffs. xii SW. (1890, 1926).

[72] *Census*, 1871, Staffs.

[73] *Staffs. Advertiser*, 22 Jan., 23 July 1870; *Mining Jnl.* 11 May, 10 and 22 June, 4 Nov. 1871 (copy of relevant extracts in H.R.L.); *Staffs. Sentinel*, 26 Apr. 1890.

Although the bulk of the mining was carried on in the eastern part of this area, there were numerous disused shafts in the waste ground north of the town by the 1870's.[74] Williamson and Brindley's Scotia Colliery, probably situated to the west of Scotia Road, was in operation by 1818 and some ten years later was run by H. H. Williamson with his nearby Pinnox Colliery. Both ceased working in 1869 as a result of his death and were soon flooded.[75] By 1888 they had been taken over by the Chatterley Iron Company, although only Pinnox was then being worked.[76] The Dale Hall Colliery, in operation between at least the early 1860's and the early 1870's, is probably identifiable with the disused colliery just to the north of St. Paul's Church a few years later.[77] Robert Heath's Brownhills Colliery (coal and ironstone), west of Brownhills Road, was in operation by the early 1870's and was employing 182 below ground and 44 above in 1896; it was closed in 1902.[78] The Mill Hayes Colliery (coal and ironstone) east of the Sytch Mill was being worked by Cork, Ford and Company in the early 1860's and by Charles Salt as owner and manager between at least the mid-1870's and the early 1880's. It is probably identifiable with Thomas Wood's Sytch Croft Coal and Ironstone Works of c. 1863.[79]

It was Sneyd township, however, 'abounding . . . with mines of coal and ironstone',[80] that was the centre of Burslem's mining from at least the later 15th century. Among others the Adams family held mining leases there between at least 1467 and the early 17th century,[81] the Middletons between at least 1488 and 1665,[82] the Rowleys between at least 1513 and 1614,[83] the Daniels between at least 1578 and 1649,[84] the Burslems between at least 1619 and 1649,[85] and the Colcloughs by 1624. The Colcloughs took over the interests of the Daniels and the Burslems in 1649 and are said to have been the first to exploit the mines commercially.[86] The Wedgwoods

carried on the Colcloughs' operations for a few years from 1669.[87] In 1719 George Parker (created Earl of Macclesfield in 1732) ran a gutter from the mines on his Sneyd farm estate down to the low ground near St. John's Church, thus draining the mines without machinery.[88] By the 19th century at least the earls were leasing out the Sneyd Colliery, to which a brickworks had been added by the mid-1850's,[89] but flooding brought work to an end c. 1876. William Heath (through the Sneyd Colliery Company) took a lease in 1881, pumped out water some 600 feet deep, and reopened the colliery.[90] Since c. 1920 it has been the only colliery in the Burslem area.[91] In 1957 1,010 men were employed below ground there and 400 above.[92] Enoch Wood and James Caldwell were working the Bycars Colliery to the north-east of Burslem town by 1816,[93] and by 1834 it was held by John Wedg Wood, along with one of the two collieries at the Hamil which had been in operation by 1818.[94] Bycars and Hamil were in operation as coal and ironstone mines in the early 1880's, although the first effects of the flooding from the Pinnox and Scotia collieries in 1869 were felt at Bycars; both had been closed by 1888.[95] The Pinnox Colliery on the Tunstall boundary was worked by H. H. Williamson by the late 1820's and remained in operation until 1869 when it was abandoned as a result of his death and soon became flooded; an attempt to sell it by auction in 1870 failed.[96] By 1888, however, coal and ironstone were being mined there by the Chatterley Iron Company, but about this time it was again closed.[97] The Jackfield Colliery (coal and ironstone) was being worked by 1832 and the Stanfield Colliery by 1841, and both were closed because of flooding c. 1889;[98] the Bank Top Colliery off High Lane to the north-east, in operation by 1856, was closed for the same reason in the early 1880's.[99] All three had been acquired by the Sneyd Colliery Company by 1890, but since the flooded

[74] O.S. Map 6" Staffs. xii NW., SW. (1890).
[75] Parson and Bradshaw, Dir. Staffs. (1818); Pigot's Nat. Com. Dir. (1828–9); Staffs. Advertiser, 22 Jan. 1870; O.S. Map 6" Staffs. xii SW. (1890).
[76] Rep. Insp. Mines, N. Staffs., 1888 [C. 5779], p. 14, H.C. (1889), xxiv.
[77] Slater's Com. Dir. (1862); Jones's Potteries Dir. (1864); Keates's Potteries Dir. (1873–4); O.S. Map 6" Staffs. xii SW. (1890).
[78] Keates's Potteries Dir. (1873–4, 1892–3); Rep. Insp. Mines, Stafford, 1896 [C. 8450], p. 54, H.C. (1897), xx; ibid. 1902 [Cd. 1590], p. 265, H.C. (1903), xv; O.S. Map 6" Staffs. xii NW. (1890).
[79] Slater's Com. Dir. (1862); Jones's Potteries Dir. (1864); Keates's Potteries Dir. (1875–6; 1882); Rep. Insp. Mines, N. Staffs., 1888, 14, which describes it as 'standing'; Warrillow, Stoke, 330.
[80] Ward, Stoke, 209.
[81] Adams, Adams Family, 16–17, 18–19, 31, 33, 37–38; W.S.L., D. 1490/33; S.C. 6/Hen. VII/679, m. 5.
[82] Wedgwood, Wedgwood Family, 286.
[83] Ibid. 251–2, 253, 254, 273.
[84] Ibid. 252, 253, 275, 285.
[85] Ibid. 270–1, 279.
[86] Adams, Adams Family, 39; Wedgwood, Wedgwood Family, 78, 279, 285; U.C.N.S., Sneyd MSS., Hulton Deeds (4 Oct. 22 Jas. I); Bodl. MS. 36911.
[87] Wedgwood, Wedgwood Family, 78, 81–82, 85, 110, 114; U.C.N.S., Sneyd MSS., Burslem Deeds (29 July, 1 Aug. 1678).
[88] Ward, Stoke, 209, 599; see p. 120.
[89] Parson and Bradshaw, Dir. Staffs. (1818); Pigot's Nat. Com. Dir. (1828–9); Ward, Stoke, 210; White, Dir. Staffs. (1834, 1851); P.O. Dir. Staffs. (1854); Keates and Ford's Potteries Dir. (1865–6); Keates's Potteries Dir. (1873–4). A brickworks there was still mentioned in Kelly's Dir.

Staffs. (1940), but it is no longer in operation: Guide to the Coalfields (1960).
[90] Staffs. Sentinel, 26 Apr. 1890; S.R.O., D. 321/M/13/72. An old working 60 ft. deep was reopened by the co. in 1890 to obtain the pillars of coal left standing there: Staffs. Sentinel, 26 Apr. 1890.
[91] The Sandbach and Grange Collieries were closed about then.   [92] Guide to the Coalfields (1960).
[93] Ward, Stoke, 210. A subscription swimming-bath supplied with warm water from the colliery's engine was built nearby in 1816 but remained in use only a few years: ibid.
[94] White, Dir. Staffs. (1834); Parson and Bradshaw, Dir. Staffs. (1818). Two collieries at the Hamil are shown on Hargreaves, Map of Staffs. Potteries (1832).
[95] Keates's Potteries Dir. (1882); Staffs. Sentinel, 26 Apr. 1890; O.S. Map 6" Staffs. xii NW. (1890). They do not appear on the list of collieries in Rep. Insp. Mines, N. Staffs., 1888, 14. The Cobridge Brick and Sanitary Pipes Co. was digging fireclay at Bycars by 1902: Rep. Insp. Mines, Stafford, 1902, 265.
[96] Pigot's Nat. Com. Dir. (1828–9); White, Dir. Staffs. (1834, 1851); R. Malabar, Map of Tunstall (surveyed 1863); Keates and Ford's Potteries Dir. (1865–6); Staffs. Advertiser, 22 Jan., 23 July 1870.
[97] Rep. Insp. Mines, N. Staffs., 1888, 14. It does not occur in the list in Rep. Insp. Mines, N. Staffs., 1890 [C. 6346], H.C. (1890–1), xxii.
[98] Hargreaves, Map of Staffs. Potteries; Pigot's Nat. Com. Dir. (1841); White, Dir. Staffs. (1834, 1851); Ward, Stoke, 210; Keates's Potteries Dir. (1882); Rep. Insp. Mines, N. Staffs., 1888, 14; Staffs. Sentinel, 26 Apr. 1890.
[99] Rep. Insp. Mines, 1856 [2270], p. 79, H.C. (1857, sess. 2), xvi; Keates's Potteries Dir. (1882); Staffs. Sentinel, 26 Apr. 1890. It does not appear in Kelly's Dir. Staffs. (1884) or in the list in Rep. Insp. Mines, N. Staffs., 1888.

seams had been well worked already, new shafts were sunk with a view to opening up fresh seams nearly 600 feet below the old.[1]

The Adams family of Birches Head and the Heath family of Hanley and Burslem were mining at Cobridge after the sale of most of the Cobridge Gate House estate in 1729 to John Adams and to Thomas Heath's uncle Ralph Taylor.[2] It is alleged that the damage to his property in the area resulting from these operations led William Adams of the Brick House, Burslem, to set about buying up the estate; at any rate he acquired it, along with most of the mines, by various purchases and leases between 1769 and 1810 and for a time was more interested in mining than in potting.[3] After the middle of the 19th century his family sold the Cobridge mines, and others, to the Shelton Bar Iron Company.[4] In 1818 Baddeley and Company also were mining at Cobridge,[5] and their Cobridge Colliery was the only one in the neighbourhood open in 1834; passing through various hands it was worked until 1893 or 1894.[6] The Sandbach Colliery south of Rushton Grange had been opened by 1856 but seems to have been closed temporarily during the last decade of the century.[7] By 1902 it had 41 employees below ground and 17 above, but, though still in operation during the First World War, it had been closed by the early 1920's.[8] The Boothen Colliery to the north of the Hanley boundary at Vale Place was worked by Fox and Ward in the 1860's but by 1889 had been taken over by the Shelton Iron, Steel, and Coal Company; it was still in operation at the end of the century.[9] By the late 1860's Robert Heath had opened the Grange Colliery (coal and ironstone), also in the Rushton area, and operations there were greatly expanded at the end of the century. In 1894 149 were employed below ground and 50 above; in 1902 the numbers were respectively 431 and 183.[10] Closed about the same time as the Sandbach Colliery, it was then used as a pumping pit in connexion with the Racecourse Pits at Etruria, and when these closed c. 1937 it was dismantled.[11]

The iron industry in Burslem has been confined mainly to the mining of ironstone which, as already shown, was carried on side by side with coal mining at many of the collieries, at any rate during the 19th and early 20th centuries. Thus at the Jackfield Colliery in the 1830's much ironstone was raised, calcined on the spot, and then sent by canal to the south of the county for further working.[12] This practice was general in the Burslem area by 1856 when it was also stated that the ironstone mines were being worked on an unprecedented scale.[13] The rise in the population of Burslem in the 1860's was attributed mainly to the extension of ironstone mining in the area,[14] but by the early 1870's the industry was declining, largely because the shallow pits had been worked out to a considerable depth and because the price of iron had dropped by 50 per cent. and more.[15] In the 1890's, however, there were still three Burslem collieries raising ironstone—Brownhills, Sneyd, and Grange.[16]

OTHER INDUSTRIES. Bricks and tiles were produced in the Dale Hall area by at least 1761,[17] and the Basford family were making tiles there for at least 50 years from the 1830's.[18] There were some 8 brick and tile works in the area in the middle of the century,[19] some 11 towards the end,[20] and some 20 in the late 1950's.[21] The present tileries include the Wade Group's Flaxman Art Tile Works in High Street, opened by at least 1892,[22] and the Brownhills works of Richards Tiles Ltd., built in 1933–4.[23] The present brickworks include the Sneyd Brickworks in Nile Street, the brickworks between Waterloo Road and Sneyd Street, and the Brookfields Saggar Brick and Marl Works to the south-west, all dating from at least the 1870's;[24] the works of the Cobridge Brick and Marl Company off Leek Road has been in existence since at least the end of the 19th century.[25]

Burslem Brewery in Zion Street (formerly Regent Street East) had been opened by the mid-1860's.[26] On the merger with Ind Coope and Allsopp of

[1] *Staffs. Sentinel*, 26 Apr. 1890. The Bank Top site was being used as a brickworks by the end of the cent.: O.S. Map 6" Staffs. xii SW. (1890).

[2] Adams, *Adams Family*, 128–9, 138, 219–20; see p. 118. For mining in the Birches Head and Sneyd Green areas see p. 252.

[3] Adams, *Adams Family*, 128–9, 135, 138; H.R.L., EMT 11–786; U.C.N.S., Sneyd MSS., Burslem Deeds (28 Feb. 1810).

[4] Adams, *Adams Family*, 129 note. Ann and Mary were described as working a mine at Sneyd Green in 1852–3 (*Slater's Birmingham District Dir.* 1852–3), and the Misses Adams still owned a colliery on the Cobridge Hall Estate in 1857, although it was by then leased out: *Staffs. Advertiser*, 13 June 1857.

[5] Parson and Bradshaw, *Dir. Staffs.* (1818).

[6] White, *Dir. Staffs.* (1834, 1851); Pigot's *Nat. Com. Dir.* (1841); *Rep. Insp. Mines, 1857* [2433], p. 60, H.C. (1857–8), xxxii; *Keates and Ford's Potteries Dir.* (1865–6); *Keates's Potteries Dir.* (1873–4); *Rep. Insp. Mines, N. Staffs., 1893* [C. 7339], p. 32, H.C. (1894), xxiv; ibid. *1894* [C. 7667], p. 42, H.C. (1895), xxii.

[7] *Rep. Insp. Mines, 1856*, 79. It was last mentioned in *Rep. Insp. Mines, N. Staffs., 1889* [C. 6015], p. 48, H.C. (1890), xxiii, and was still closed in 1898; O.S. Map 6" Staffs. xii SW. (1900).

[8] *Rep. Insp. Mines, Stafford, 1902*, 269; *Kelly's Dir. Staffs.* (1916). It is not shown on O.S. Map 6" Staffs. xii SW. (1926).

[9] *Slater's Com. Dir.* (1862), where it is evidently identifiable with the Cobridge Colliery; *Jones's Potteries Dir.* (1864); *Keates and Ford's Potteries Dir.* (1865–6,

[9a] 1869–70); *Rep. Insp. Mines, N. Staffs., 1888*, 13; O.S. Map 6" Staffs. xii SW. (1890, 1900).

[10] *Keates and Ford's Potteries Dir.* (1869–70); O.S. Map 6" Staffs. xii SW. (1890); *Rep. Insp. Mines, N. Staffs., 1894*, 43; *Rep. Insp. Mines, Stafford, 1902*, 267.

[11] Ex inf. Mr. W. Jack, Norton-in-the-Moors (1959); *Kelly's Dir. Staffs.* (1916); O.S. Map 6" Staffs. xii SW. (1926). [12] Ward, *Stoke*, 210.

[13] *Burslem Bd. of Health Rep. 1856*, 7 (copy in H.R.L.).

[14] *Census*, 1871, Staffs.

[15] *Staffs. Advertiser*, 26 Apr. 1890. The extensive flooding of the collieries in the area (see above) affected the coal industry much more than the iron, presumably because the ironstone pits were much shallower than the coal pits: *Mining Jnl.* 1 Apr. 1871 (copy of relevant extract in H.R.L.).

[16] *Rep. Insp. Mines, N. Staffs., 1893*, 33, 37; ibid. *1894*, 41, 43, 47.

[17] Adams, *Adams Family*, 139–40. For the production of tiles at Hulton Abbey see p. 252.

[18] Jewitt, *Ceramic Art*, 457; White, *Dir. Staffs.* (1834, 1851); *P.O. Dir. Staffs.* (1872).

[19] White, *Dir. Staffs.* (1851).

[20] *Keates's Potteries Dir.* (1892–3).

[21] *Barrett's City of Stoke Dir.* [1959].

[22] Meigh, 'Staffs. Potters', 201. [23] See p. 104.

[24] O.S. Map 6" Staffs. xii SW. (1890). One was presumably worked by the Bryan St. Brick and Marl Co. of 1895, and perhaps the other also: *Rep. Insp. Mines, N. Staffs., 1895* [C. 8074], p. 61, H.C. (1896), xxii. For the brickworks at the Sneyd Colliery see p. 139.

[25] O.S. Map 6" Staffs. xii SW. (1900).

[26] *Keates and Ford's Potteries Dir.* (1865–6).

Burton-upon-Trent in 1949 it ceased production and has since been used as offices and a depot.[27]

SOCIAL LIFE. The Burslem and Tunstall Literary and Scientific Society was founded for 'all classes of society' in 1838.[28] It was refounded in 1849 as a mechanics' institute; Josiah Powell, later clerk to the local board and first town clerk of the borough, was the secretary.[29] The institute still existed in 1854.[30]

The foundation stone of the Wedgwood Memorial Institute in Queen Street was laid by W. E. Gladstone in 1863, and the building, containing a museum, a picture gallery, and lecture rooms, was opened by Lord de Grey and Ripon in 1869.[31] A reference library, reading-room, and school of art were added later in the same year, and in 1870 the library became a lending library.[32] A new wing containing a museum and picture gallery was opened in 1879.[33]

A 'Government School of Design' was opened in 1853 in the old assembly room of the Legs of Man Inn, 'a villainous room in a locality where no one having physical decency, to say nothing of health, would go'; it was closed in 1858.[34] There was a school of art at the Wedgwood Institute from 1869 (see above), and the present school on the opposite side of Queen Street was built in 1906–7.[35] With the amalgamation of the art schools of the various towns after Federation, the Burslem school became the principal of the Stoke-on-Trent Art Schools.[36]

There was a newspaper room at the town hall between at least 1834 and 1868.[37]

Burslem Wakes were held during the week following 24 June,[38] the feast of the Nativity of St. John the Baptist to whom the old church is dedicated. A custom of decorating the church with branches of trees and shrubs on Wakes Sunday survived until c. 1700.[39] With the coming of the industrial era attempts were made to restrict the wakes. 'Our men have been at play four days this week, it being Burslem Wakes', wrote Josiah Wedgwood on one occasion; 'I have roughed and smoothed them over and promised them a long Christmas, but I know it is all in vain, for Wakes must be observed though the world were to end with them'.[40] In 1852 the manu-

facturers and tradesmen were trying to change the date of Burslem Wakes to the beginning of August when Stoke Wakes took place,[41] and in 1879 the wakes were abolished by official order as a result of a memorial to the Home Secretary from Burslem Borough Council.[42] However, after a vote by the burgesses in 1880, the council decided to restore the wakes fair on the Sunday after 24 June, and despite a renewed attempt at abolition in 1906[43] it is still (1960) held. The wakes were formerly an occasion of wild exuberance. In *The Old Wives' Tale* Arnold Bennett describes the 'orgiastic carnival' of the 1860's, 'gross in all its manifestations of joy', during which 'Miss Chetwynd's school was closed, so that the daughters of the leading families might remain in seclusion till the worst was over'.[44]

Bull-baiting, bear-baiting, and cock-fighting were popular sports at Burslem until they were banned by law in 1837. The baiting evidently took place in St. John's Square early on Sunday mornings, and more frequently during the wakes, while the final cock-fight of the wakes was held on ground to the south-east of the town where the brewery was later built.[45] Bull-baiting and cock-fighting also took place at the 'Bull's Head', Sneyd Green, which formed part of the Cobridge Gate estate.[46] A maypole formerly stood in the centre of the space later to be Burslem market-place, but it had been removed by 1760.[47]

The Port Vale Association Football Club, deriving its name from Port Vale House in Alexandra Road (now Scott Lidgett Road), Longport, where it opened its first headquarters in 1876, had its first ground in the meadows nearby. It moved in 1881 to the area now covered by Westport Lake and in 1884 to Moorland Road. The club, which became professional in 1885 under the name Burslem Port Vale, moved in the following year to the ground that later became Cobridge Dog Track; wound up in 1907 and restarted in 1909, it settled at Hanley in 1911. In 1950 it moved to a plot of waste in Hamil Road which it had bought cheaply in 1944 and converted into the present Vale Park Ground.[48]

There was a music hall, The White Hart, in Liverpool Road in 1880[49] and another in Cleveland Street in the 1920's (later the Coliseum Super Cinema).[50] The theatre in Wedgwood Place that

[27] *Evening Sentinel Survey of Industry and Commerce, 1959*, 2 June 1959, p. xiv (copy in H.R.L.).
[28] *Rules and Orders of the Burslem and Tunstall Literary and Scientific Soc.* (copy in H.R.L.).
[29] R. G. Haggar, *Some Adult Educ. Institutions in N. Staffs.* (*Rewley House Papers*, iii, no. 6), 6 (copy in H.R.L.); White, *Dir. Staffs.* (1851); *P.O. Dir. Staffs.* (1854, 1872); *Kelly's Dir. Staffs.* (1880).
[30] *P.O. Dir. Staffs.* (1854).
[31] *Burslem Bd. of Health Rep. 1864*, 3, 18–21; *1869*, 8–10; *Staffs. Sentinel*, 17 Sept. 1892: R. G. Haggar, *A Cent. of Art Educ. in the Potteries*, 15, 17 (copy in H.R.L.).
[32] *Burslem Bd. of Health Rep. 1870*, 6; F. Falkner, *The Wood Family of Burslem*, 91; Haggar, *Cent. Art Educ. in Potteries*, 20, 23.
[33] *Staffs. Advertiser*, 13 Sept. 1879; H.R.L., Burslem Borough Mins. 1878–92, p. 217.
[34] Haggar, *Cent. Art Educ. in Potteries*, 10–11.
[35] Inscription on building; Falkner, *Wood Family*, 91.
[36] Haggar, *Cent. Art Educ. in Potteries*, 33–36.
[37] White, *Dir. Staffs.* (1834, 1851); *P.O. Dir. Staffs.* (1868).
[38] Ward, *Stoke*, 269.
[39] Ibid. 269–70.
[40] J. Leighton, 'Pots and Potters' (*T.N.S.F.C.* xci), 29.

[41] *Burslem Board of Health Rep. 1852*, 5.
[42] *Lond. Gaz.* 1879, p. 4089; *Keates's Potteries Dir.* (1892–3), 100, which misprints the date as 1870; *Charity: two sermons preached May 1879 by the Rector of Burslem* (copy in H.R.L., pamphlets vol. 45). See p. 104 for a similar move at Tunstall.
[43] H.R.L., Burslem Boro. Mins. 1878–82, p. 366; 1898–1906, pp. 465–6, 474, 478; *Keates's Potteries Dir.* (1892–3), 100; H. V. Stuart, *Reminiscences* (1926), 5 (copy among W.S.L. pamphlets *sub* Stoke).
[44] Book i, chap. iv.
[45] J. Edge, *Burslem of 50 Years Ago* (lecture given 1868), 20 (copy in H.R.L.); Ward, *Stoke*, 269; Arnold Bennett, 'The Elixir of Youth' (*Tales of the Five Towns*); *Burslem in Days Gone By* (copy in H.R.L.); printed description of Burslem Wakes in 1820 among W.S.L. Pamphs. (vol. xv, no. 13).
[46] Adams, *Adams Family*, 216; see p. 119.
[47] H. J. Steele, 'Social Conditions in Burslem during the 17th and 18th Cents.' (*T.N.S.F.C.* lxxviii), 28, 34; Wedgwood, *Wedgwood Family*, map facing p. 121.
[48] *Port Vale 1876–1950* (copy in H.R.L.); W. E. Tate, *Inns and Inn Signs in and near Burslem*, 28, 29 (copy in H.R.L.).   [49] *Kelly's Dir. Staffs.* (1880).
[50] Ibid. (1924, 1928).

141

appears in *Clayhanger* as 'The Blood Tub' was known as the Wedgwood Theatre by 1903. It was demolished to make way for the town hall of 1911 and rebuilt as Burslem Hippodrome. 'The home—in the inter-war-years—of popular variety' under the direction of Pat Collins, it had been closed by 1940 and was demolished in 1947–8.[51]

There was a choral society at Cobridge *c.* 1824.[52] In 1855 Josiah Powell founded his Burslem tonic sol-fa choir, an event which had much to do with the popularity of choral music in the Potteries later in the century.[53] The Burslem Orchestral Union existed by the end of the century and *c.* 1900 was taken over by John Cope, who until 1919, with the support of Madame Marie Reymond, tried unsuccessfully to arouse an enthusiasm for orchestral music in the Potteries.[54]

The Burslem, Cobridge, Longport, and Tunstall Society for the Prosecution of Felons was founded in 1813.[55] The present Burslem Association for the Prosecution of Felons dates from 1821.[56] Arnold Bennett stated that by the 1880's it had become 'a dining-club and little else' with an exclusive annual dinner 'admitted to be the chief oratorical event of the year'.[57]

Arnold Bennett (1867–1931), the novelist of 'the Five Towns,' was born in Hope Street, Hanley, the son of a solicitor who had formerly been a potter and a schoolmaster. He lived in Burslem from 1875 to 1878, first in Dane Street, and then in Newport Lane. The family moved to no. 198 Waterloo Road, Cobridge, in 1878 and later lived at no. 205 which since 1960 has been maintained by the city as a Bennett Museum. Bennett left the district in 1888, but his ashes are buried in his mother's grave in Burslem cemetery.[58]

HANLEY

THE borough of Hanley as it existed in 1910 covered an area of 1,957 acres[1] and comprised the township of Hanley, the township of Shelton (except for the former glebe land around Stoke station), the Birches Head area, and part of Sneyd Green; these last two districts had been added to the borough in 1905.[2] Hanley thus occupied the rough triangle formed by the Trent on the east, its tributary the Fowlea Brook on the west, and the irregular Burslem boundary on the north.

The ground rises from under 400 ft. along the two river valleys to over 600 ft. east of Hanley town and at Birches Head; the slope up from the Trent in this north-eastern part of the area is particularly steep. Shelton was the larger of the two townships, 995 acres to Hanley's 483,[3] and the boundary between the two ran along the present Bryan Street, then east of Stafford Street, across Lichfield Street, and down through Joiner's Square to the Trent.[4] Hanley township thus included the eastern half only of the town, with the Hope Street area, Piccadilly, Pall Mall, and Albion Street all lying in Shelton. The Hanley–Shelton area is crossed by three old roads, those between Newcastle and Cheadle, between Newcastle and Leek, and between Great Chell and Hanley. The mid-19th-century road from Stoke to Endon runs through the eastern part of the former borough along the low ground beside the Trent.

Except for the extreme north-eastern part, where the belt of farming land around Abbey Hulton be-

gins, there is nothing in the area to recall the moorland settlement which still survived in the early 18th century. Over the last 200 years the district has become solidly built up and industrialized, with the town of Hanley now the shopping and cultural centre of the Potteries.

Hanley existed as a vill in the early 13th century.[5] In the early 18th century it was still 'a humble collection of dwellings' which lay chiefly around Upper Green (at the junction of Keelings Lane and the present Town Road), and Lower Green (the later Market Square). The whole formed 'two small villages, half a mile apart'.[6] Hanley Green as an alternative name to Hanley was in use by the end of the 16th century, and its use still lingered in the middle of the 19th century.[7] By 1775 the built-up area had spread westwards into Shelton township and there was continuous building along what are now Town Road, Old Hall Street, Albion Street, and Marsh Street.[8] The growth of the town is reflected in the building of the church in 1738, its extension in 1764, and its rebuilding in 1787–90.[9] By the 1790's Hanley, though still smaller than Burslem, was 'an improving and spirited place'; it was, however, 'built so irregularly that, to a person in the midst of it, it has scarcely the appearance of anything beyond a moderate village; yet if the houses had been properly joined together, it would not only make a capital town but a well-built one'.[10]

In the first third of the 19th century the ground-

[51] H.R.L., Burslem Boro. Mins. 1898–1906, pp. 241, 430; *Kelly's Dir. Staffs.* (1912, where it is called the Wedgwood Theatre and Hippodrome, 1924, 1932, 1940): *Evening Sentinel*, 20 Dec. 1947; E. J. D. Warrillow, 'Bennett Memorials' (*Staffs. Life*, iii), 26; ex inf. Mr. R. G. Nettel (1960).
[52] *Hanley Jubilee Souvenir* (1907), 28.
[53] Ibid. 31–32; R. G. Nettel, *Music in the Five Towns, 1840–1914*, 9–10.
[54] Nettel, *Music in the Five Towns*, 71–72, 81–83.
[55] Warrillow, *Stoke*, 388–9.
[56] The articles were prepared in 1821 but not signed till 1826; the mins., however, date from 1822; inf. from the secretary (1962).   [57] *Clayhanger*, bk. iii, chaps. xiii and xv.
[58] *D.N.B.*; *Stoke Official Handbk.* (1960), 38, 39; *The Guardian*, 25 Mar. 1960; J. R. Ford, *Bennett Country* (H.R.L. Information Pamph., no. 5).

[1] *Census* 1911, Staffs.
[2] *Plan of Stoke-on-Trent and Newcastle-under-Lyme* (Geographia Ltd.); Local Govt. Board Provisional Order (no. 11) Act, 5 Edw. VII, c. 107 (local). For the glebe around Stoke station see pp. 158, 173, 194.
[3] Ward, *Stoke*, 364, 409.
[4] T. Hargreaves, *Map of Staffs. Potteries and Newcastle* (1832); and see plan opposite.
[5] See p. 151.
[6] Ward, *Stoke*, 348.
[7] *S.H.C.* 1929, 113, 117; Ward, *Stoke*, 348; Warrillow, *Stoke*, 397.
[8] W. Yates, *Map of Staffs.* (1775), reproduced facing p. 4.
[9] See p. 154.
[10] J. Aikin, *Country around Manchester* (1795), 520, 521.

plan of the present town-centre, including the area round Piccadilly and Pall Mall, was completed. The streets in the rectangle formed by Albion Street, Lichfield Street, Mollart Street (then Union Street), and Bethesda Street on the south side of the town, much of the area around Hope, Hanover, and Union Streets on the north side, and many of the streets on the eastern slope above the town had been laid out. Charles Street and Well Street represented the beginning of development in the Wellington area to the south-east.[11] In the 1830's Hanley was considered 'a large modern town', the largest in the Potteries and the second in Staffordshire; its streets 'generally spacious and well paved', its houses of 'neat appearance, and some of them, as well as the public edifices ... spacious and elegant'.[12] On the other hand much of the town was overcrowded and insanitary.[13] In 1850 it was noted that 'the principal streets have some good shops; and there has been lately finished a range of shops far above the standard of everything else in the Pottery district'.[14] There was a great rise in population in the early 1850's owing to the increased numbers employed at Lord Granville's pits.[15] By 1857 several groups of new streets had been laid out in the Wellington area, which was constituted a new ecclesiastical parish in 1845, and streets had also been laid out west of Bethesda Street and in the Bryans Wood area on the north side of the town.[16] In the course of the next 20 years new streets were built leading off both sides of Lichfield Street and the west side of York Street.[17] In this way Hanley town was solidly built up before 1880. Soon after this date, however, slum clearance was carried out in Old Hall Street and improvements were made to buildings in the Crown Bank area.[18] Extensive demolition of slum property was begun shortly before 1939 and has continued since the war, particularly in the Wellington area, the streets between Bucknall Old and New Roads, Bryan Street, and the area round Bethesda and Warner Streets.[19] Many of the cleared areas remain undeveloped spaces, but there has been some rebuilding from the late 19th century up to the present time.[20]

The district known as Joiner's Square existed by 1829 as a few houses and collieries south of the Caldon Canal on the east side of the track later to be

Lichfield Street. It was then already suffering from mining subsidence.[21] Leek Road, opened in the early 1840's,[22] still marked the limit of the area in 1857,[23] but in the course of the next 20 years or so there was further development including the terraced houses in Austin Street and Simpson Street on the south side of Leek Road.[24] New streets of houses between the road and the Trent continued to be built until recent years, including council estates dating from the years between the two world wars[25] and the period since 1945. The pottery works of Johnson Bros. was extended on both sides of the canal in Eastwood Road between 1888 and 1896.[26]

There was extensive building along Keelings Lane by 1775 as well as at Upper Green around the junction of the lane with what is now Town Road.[27] By 1829 William Ridgway of Northwood House (earlier known as Prospect House) had changed the area 'from a rude and demoralized part of Hanley into a beautiful, cleanly, well-ordered hamlet' which was known as Northwood by 1832. Not only had he 'converted his residence from a plain, unpretending house into an elegant suburban villa' but he had also 'cleared the neighbourhood of a number of unsightly cottages and objects which formerly surrounded it ... erected or improved some good neighbouring houses', and built a school and 'several neat almshouses for decayed widows'.[28] The church of Holy Trinity in Lower Mayer Street was built in 1848–9,[29] and the population of the new parish, 3,300 in 1850 and 'for the most part very poor', continued to increase.[30] Several new streets were built on the east side of Keelings Lane about this time. Others were laid out on the south side of Providence Square, the former Upper Green.[31] A new terrace was built in Lower Mayer Street in 1870.[32] In the last quarter of the 19th century new streets were built southward from Providence Square, joining those to the northeast of Hanley town. To the east of Providence Square the series of streets known as Birches Head was laid out around Grove House.[33] In the first decade of the 20th century the streets around Northwood Park were laid out; the park itself, some 11 acres in extent, was opened in 1907 as part of the jubilee celebrations of Hanley's incorporation.[34] There is housing of the years between the two world

[11] C. and J. Greenwood, *Map of Staffs.* (1820); Hargreaves, *Map of Staffs. Potteries*; W. Pitt, *Topog. Hist. Staffs.* 401; Mankowitz and Haggar, *Eng. Pottery*, 164; G. E. Stringer, *New Hall Porcelain*, 42. The part of John St. west of Bagnall St. bears the date 1807. Pall Mall existed as New St., Shelton, by 1818: A. Huntbach, *Hanley*, 110. Plans for making a road from Market Sq. to Piccadilly were made in 1826: H.R.L., Hanley Highway Surveyors' Mins. 1817–41, 31 Mar. 1826. In Windmill St. there are still terraces dated 1831 and 1834, the latter bearing the initials 'JC'.

[12] White, *Dir. Staffs.* (1834).   [13] See p. 159.

[14] *The Staffs. Potteries* (*The Land We Live In*, xxx), 30 (copy among W.S.L. pamphs. *sub* Pottery).

[15] *P.O. Dir. Staffs.* (1854).

[16] C. J. H. Homer, *Plan of Hanley and Shelton, 1857* (copy in S.R.O., Z/M/7); see p. 157.

[17] O.S. Map 6" Staffs. xii SW., xviii NW. (1890); datestones of 1874 in Jasper St. and of 1875 and 1876 at the southern end of Bethesda St.

[18] *Hanley Jubilee Souvenir* (1907), 44.

[19] *City of Stoke-on-Trent Housing, 1919 to 1957*, 10, 51, 52 (copy in H.R.L.).

[20] e.g. an estate of post-1945 prefabricated bungalows between Hanover St. and Union St. and a few houses of the late 1950's in Nelson Place: *Stoke-on-Trent Housing, 1919 to 1957*, 10, 27, 30, 52.

[21] S. Shaw, *Staffs. Potteries* (1829), 46; Hargreaves, *Map of Staffs. Potteries*.   [22] See p. 146.

[23] Homer, *Plan of Hanley and Shelton, 1857*.

[24] O.S. Map 1/500 Staffs. xvi. 4. 7 and 8 (1866); O.S. Map 6" Staffs. xviii NW. (1890); date-stone of 1878 in Botteslow St. A mission chapel was opened in the area c. 1870 (see p. 157), and the school in Hazelhurst St. is dated 1879.

[25] *Stoke-on-Trent Housing, 1919 to 1957*, 23.

[26] *Stoke Official Handbk.* (1960); O.S. Map 6" Staffs. xviii NW. (1900).

[27] Yates, *Map of Staffs.* (1775).

[28] Shaw, *Staffs. Potteries*, 43; Ward, *Stoke*, 382; Hargreaves, *Map of Staffs. Potteries*; see pp. 149, 331.

[29] See p. 156.

[30] *Staffs. Advertiser*, 9 Mar. 1850. The population of Northwood in 1841 was given as 700: *Census*, 1841, Staffs.

[31] Homer, *Plan of Hanley and Shelton, 1857*.

[32] Inscription on terrace: 'Prospect Place 1870'.

[33] O.S. Map 6" Staffs. xii SW. (1900); date-stones of 1876 in St. John St., 1887 in Dilke St., 1888 in Lockett St., 1892 in Turner St., 1895 in Harrop St., and 1896 and 1904 in Birches Head. A mission chapel was opened at Far Green c. 1876: see p. 156. For Birches Head farm on the eastern outskirts of the area see p. 152.

[34] *Hanley Jubilee Souvenir*, 47; Huntbach, *Hanley*, 89; *Staffs. Advertiser*, 18 and 25 May 1907; *Staffs. Sentinel Potteries, Newcastle and District Dir.* (1907).

wars around the junction of Keelings Lane and Bucknall Old Road, in Cromer Road to the north, in Birches Head Road, and to the west of Chell Street.[35] Housing of the late 1950's has replaced the old terraces in the streets immediately south of Providence Square, and new streets were still being laid out on the north side of Birches Head Road in 1959.

The development of Shelton township is partly, as already shown, the result of the south-westerly extension of Hanley town over the boundary of Hanley and Shelton townships. The original centre of Shelton was probably the area round Shelton Old Hall on the ridge to the east of the Stoke–Hanley road.[36] Before the end of the 16th century Snape Marsh—the present Marsh Street district of Hanley town—was an inhabited area.[37] By 1775 the main part of Shelton lay along the stretch of the road between Stoke and Hanley now known as Snow Hill and Broad Street, and in the Marsh Street area.[38] There was further development southwards later in the century. The Caldon Canal was constructed under an Act of 1776, and on its south bank were built the Chatterleys' Shelton Hall and the Ridgways' Cauldon Place house and pottery works.[39] By 1832 further development in Shelton included the group of streets running southwards off Broad Street to what is now Cannon Street, St. Mark's Church, built in 1831–4, a few streets north and west of the church, and Charles Meigh's Grove House farther west still. There had also been some development in the Etruria Vale area near Etruria Basin, and the present road from Shelton to Newcastle existed as far as the east bank of the Trent and Mersey Canal; there was already a terrace of cottages, several of them still (1960) inhabited, at the eastern end of the road.[40] The terraces on the north side of Bedford Street date from the early 1850's.[41] By 1857 the streets north of St. Mark's had been extended, including Sun Street linking Broad Street and the wharves at Etruria.[42] In the course of the next 20 years the streets on either side of Stoke Road north of the Caldon Canal were laid out, and terraces were built in Lower Russell Street,[43] now part of Shelton New Road. From c. 1876 the streets south of the Caldon Canal were being laid out, and by 1897 1,036

houses had been built in the area.[44] During this same period new streets were built in the Mousecroft area to the east of St. Mark's, and the housing between Rectory Road and Havelock Road and around the Etruria Vale end of Sun Street is also mainly of this period.[45] Hanley Park was laid out in 1892–7 on some 63 acres of Stoke Fields, waste ground lying on either side of Victoria Road and crossed by the canal.[46] Some large houses were built on the north side of the park about the turn of the century,[47] and a new church of St. Jude was built in Victoria Road in 1899–1901 in place of the nearby mission chapel of 1880.[48] Clough Street which now runs from Marsh Street through the Tinkersclough area to Etruria Vale Road still ran only as far as the railway goods yard in the early 1920's.[49] By 1939 there had been slum clearance at the west end of Sun Street[50] and by 1950 extensive clearance in the area north of St. Mark's.[51] There are housing estates of the period between the world wars to the east and south of Hanley Park, to the south of the cemetery, and round the junction of Etruria Vale Road and Sun Street.

There were three or four small houses around the Ridge House in the western part of Shelton township c. 1680,[52] but the village of Etruria nearby was the creation of Josiah Wedgwood after his purchase of the Ridge House estate in 1767[53]—'a colony newly raised where clay-built man subsists on clay'.[54] On the west bank of the Trent and Mersey Canal, then still under construction, and just off the Newcastle–Leek road, Josiah opened his pottery works in 1769; on the rising ground to the east of the canal he built Etruria Hall; and on either side of the main road between the Fowlea Brook and the canal he erected cottages for his workmen.[55] Seventy years later Etruria was in the main still a village of one street containing 'about 120 workmen's dwellings . . . with an inn and some houses of a better class for farmers, clerks and others'.[56] The first nonconformist chapel had been built in 1808, and the church of St. Matthew was opened in 1849.[57] In 1841 Lord Granville completed the first part of his ironworks in Mill Street (now Etruria Road);[58] the railway was opened in 1848.[59] Although Salem Street was in existence by 1845, it was apparently not then built up,[60] but there were terraces on both sides by 1857;[61]

[35] *Stoke-on-Trent Housing, 1919 to 1957*, 24, 27, 30, 31.
[36] See p. 153.
[37] *S.H.C.* 1932, 130; S.R.O., Q/RUt 5/80A and 82.
[38] Yates, *Map of Staffs.* (1775). The main road was formerly known as Snow Hill only between the present Cutts St. and Wood Terrace and as Broad St. from Wood Terrace to Victoria Sq.; it then continued as High St. up to the junction with Marsh St.: Hargreaves, *Map of Staffs. Potteries*.
[39] See pp. 147, 153, 167.
[40] Hargreaves, *Map of Staffs. Potteries*; Ward, *Stoke*, 384–6; *2nd Rep. Com. Employment of Children* [431], p. C12, H.C. (1843), xiv; inscription 'William Street 1818' in Yates St.; W.S.L. 4/45 (b); see p. 146. Bedford Chapel in Bedford Rd. (see p. 295) is dated 1834.
[41] Tablets bearing dates 1853 and 1855 and initials 'J.F.'.
[42] Homer, *Plan of Hanley and Shelton, 1857*.
[43] O.S. Map 6″ Staffs. xviii NW. (1890); date-stones of 1869 in Wellesley St. and Croston St. and 1877 in Pyenest St.
[44] *Lich. Dioc. Mag.* (1897), 166; Huntbach, *Hanley*, 64; O.S. Map 6″ Staffs. xviii NW. (1900); date-stone of 1882 in Boughey Rd.; see plate facing p. 113.
[45] O.S. Map 6″ Staffs. xii SW., xviii NW. (1900); date-stones of 1874 in Shirley Rd. and of 1881 and 1883 in Rectory Rd. Some of the housing off Havelock St. is earlier

(O.S. Map 6″ Staffs. xviii NW. 1890) and some is of the years between the world wars.
[46] *Staffs. Sentinel Potteries, Newcastle, and District Dir.* (1907); *Staffs. Sentinel*, 7 Dec. 1927; T. Mawson, *Hanley Park* (copy in H.R.L.). The section near Cauldon Place was opened in 1894 and the second portion of the park in 1897. An unsuccessful attempt had been made in 1857 to secure the land later used for the cemetery as a 'people's park': *Staffs. Advertiser*, 28 July 1894; see p. 160.
[47] O.S. Map 6″ Staffs. xii SW. (1900); date-stones of 1896 and 1901.
[48] See p. 157.
[49] O.S. Map 6″ Staffs. xii SW. (1890, 1926).
[50] *Stoke-on-Trent Housing, 1919 to 1957*, 31.
[51] The resulting drop in population led to the closing of the Broad St. Mission: Char. Com. files; see p. 155.
[52] *S.H.C.* 1919, 258.   [53] See p. 152.
[54] *Gent. Mag.* 1794, lxiv (2), 1078.
[55] Ward, *Stoke*, 443; Warrillow, *Etruria*, 22–23; see p. 152. The stretch of the road where the cottages were built was later known as Lord St.
[56] Ward, *Stoke*, 443; Hargreaves, *Map of Staffs. Potteries*; J. C. Wedgwood, *Wedgwood Family*, map facing p. 170.
[57] See pp. 155, 289.   [58] See p. 169.   [59] See p. 147.
[60] Wedgwood, *Wedgwood Family*, map facing p. 170.
[61] Homer, *Plan of Hanley and Shelton, 1857*.

by that time also the terraces at the northern end of Fold Street (now Etruscan Street) had been built.[62] By 1865 there were some 200 houses in the village, most of them still occupied by employees of the Wedgwoods.[63] Before 1880 a new terrace in Fold Street and the terraces at the Salem Street end of Cavour Street had been built, and there were terraces along Mill Street near Lord Granville's ironworks.[64] In the last quarter of the century streets of terraced housing were laid out between the west end of Mill Street and Etruria Vale Road and in the village itself Humbert Street was built.[65] Belmont Road and Dundee Road between the canal and Etruria Vale Road were in existence by 1888,[66] Ladysmith Road and Kimberley Road in the same area date from the turn of the century,[67] and Pretoria Road was added during the period between the world wars; during the same period the terraces in Dundee Road and Ladysmith Road were extended and the houses in Belmont Road built. The 11-acre Etruria Park at the junction of Etruria Road and Etruria Vale Road was opened in 1904.[68] Etruscan Street was extended past the new gasworks to Shelton New Road at Cliff Vale c. 1908.[69] The housing at the west end of Cavour Street dates from the 1930's after the street had been extended through the grounds of Etruscan Villa.[70] As a result of the growth of its industries,[71] Etruria lost its rural character. Etruria Grove, lining the main road eastwards from the canal bridge and said to have been planted by Josiah Wedgwood, disappeared in the 1870's,[72] and the landscape has long since been dominated by the iron and steel works and the gasworks. Brindley Bank, the open ground between the Hall and the main road, was levelled in 1951 by the Shelton Iron and Steel Company and now forms their sports ground.[73] From c. 1860 mining subsidence has been very extensive; the canal represents the original level of the area and its western side has had to be built up some 12 ft., while elsewhere the ground has dropped as much as 30 ft.[74] There has been extensive clearance of the cottages in the main street since 1956.[75]

By 1775 there was some building along the stretch of the main road where it climbs from Etruria up to Cobridge.[76] This included Cobridge House, the home of the Hales family from the late 17th century to the 19th century, which was replaced by the present St. Augustine's Home early in the 20th

century.[77] In 1832 the road was still tree-lined along its western side where it skirted the race-course east of Etruria Hall,[78] but with the opening of the pit on the course and of the ironworks on the opposite side of the road the trees disappeared (see above). The terraced cottages on the east side of the road below Cobridge had been built before 1880, and those on the north side of Century Road, the former Boothen Lane, date from the later 19th century.[79] Two more terraces had been built on either side of Cobridge Road by 1922.[80] There is extensive council housing of the years between the world wars and the period since 1945 partly in place of and partly behind the terraces on the east side of the road; some rebuilding was still in progress in 1959.

In 1666 there were 14 persons chargeable for hearth tax in Hanley township and 36 in Shelton,[81] while in 1701 the population of the two was respectively 326 and 499.[82] In 1811 Hanley township had a population of 4,481 and Shelton one of 5,487.[83] By 1861 the population of the new borough was 31,953—14,678 in the Hanley portion and 17,275 in the diminished Shelton portion.[84] In 1901 the population of the borough was 61,599,[85] and in 1911 the area of the former borough as extended in 1905 had a population of 66,255[86] and in 1921 one of 67,891.[87]

The road from Newcastle to Cheadle branched from the Newcastle–Uttoxeter road at Cliff Bank in Stoke and ran along the present Shelton Old Road and up the slope of Stoke Road, Snow Hill, and Broad Street to Hanley. This slope was 'formerly a deep cutting and a high footpath unpaved', frequently blocked by snow in winter and described in 1763 as 'in a ruinous condition, narrow and incommodious'. From Broad Street the road then followed the present Albion Street, Old Hall Street, and Bucknall Old Road, descending to the Trent and Bucknall by a hill 'so steep that the road on one side was paved with stone blocks'.[88] The portion from Cliff Bank to Snape Marsh at the north end of the present Broad Street was turnpiked in 1763 as an extension of the Newcastle to Uttoxeter turnpike;[89] the remainder was turnpiked in 1771.[90] A new road (the present Liverpool Road) was built from a point near Shelton Wharf into Stoke in 1791–2, continuing thence along the present London Road to the main Stone–Newcastle road.[91] By 1832 Bucknall New Road had been built from the end of Old Hall

[62] Ibid.
[63] Ll. Jewitt, *Josiah Wedgwood*, 197.
[64] O.S. Map 6″ Staffs. xii SW. (1890).
[65] Ibid. (1900); Warrillow, *Etruria*, 231, 327; date-stone of 1879 on terrace at the N. end of Etruria Vale Rd.
[66] Warrillow, *Etruria*, 185, 187; O.S. Map 6″ Staffs. xii SW. (1900). The northern end of Belmont Rd. by the church existed by 1857: Homer, *Plan of Hanley and Shelton, 1857*. There is some housing of the period between the world wars and of post-1945 date in Ladysmith Rd.
[67] Warrillow, *Etruria*, 327–8.
[68] Ibid. 145.
[69] Ibid. 163.
[70] Ibid. 79.
[71] See pp. 161, 169, 170.
[72] Warrillow, *Etruria*, 133–4, 136–40, 147, 163, 345; Hargreaves, *Map of Staffs. Potteries*.
[73] Warrillow, *Etruria*, 372–3.
[74] Ibid. 25, 91–92, 95, 125, 145, 157, 162, 185, 187, 230, 348–9; see pp. 156, 166.
[75] Mankowitz and Haggar, *Eng. Pottery*, 85.
[76] Yates, *Map of Staffs.* (1775).

[77] See p. 272.
[78] Hargreaves, *Map of Staffs. Potteries*.
[79] O.S. Map 6″ Staffs. xii SW. (1890, 1900).
[80] Ibid. (1926).   [81] *S.H.C.* 1921, 164.
[82] W.S.L., D.1742, list of inhabitants of Stoke parish, 1701. Yet c. 1680 Gregory King reported 70 or 80 houses in Hanley and only some 20 in Shelton with 3 or 4 at the Ridge House: *S.H.C.* 1919, 258, 259.
[83] *Census*, 1811, Staffs.
[84] Ibid. 1861. That part of Shelton around Stoke station, with a pop. of 1,056 in 1861 (ibid.), was never included in the boro. of Hanley but formed part of the boro. of Stoke when it was incorporated in 1874: see p. 194.
[85] *Census*, 1901, Staffs.
[86] Ibid. 1911; see p. 142.
[87] *Census*, 1921, Staffs.
[88] Yates, *Map of Staffs.*; *Hanley Jubilee Souvenir* (1907), 27; H. A. Moisley, 'Industrial and Urban Development and the N. Staffs. Conurbation' (*Trans. Inst. Brit. Geographers*, 1951), 6.   [89] See p. 178.
[90] Act for repairing road between Shelton and road between Cheadle and Leek, 11 Geo. III, c. 87.
[91] See p. 178.

Street,[92] thus avoiding the steep hill on Bucknall Old Road. The road from Shelton to Newcastle, which runs from Bedford Road near its junction with Stoke Road, was extended westwards from the Trent and Mersey Canal at Cliff Vale in the late 1830's as part of the Newcastle to Uttoxeter turnpike system.[93] By 1806 a toll-gate had been erected about $\frac{1}{4}$ mile to the north of Shelton Wharf opposite the present Cauldon Road,[94] and the toll-house, a plain double-fronted brick cottage, is now (1960) occupied as a shop. By 1831 there was also a toll-gate at the eastern junction of Bucknall Old and New Roads (the Ivy House Gate),[95] and this still stood in the 1870's.[96]

The Newcastle–Leek road, which crosses the Fowlea valley at Etruria and runs up to Cobridge along Cobridge Road, was turnpiked in 1765 when it was also joined to the road from Newcastle to Cheadle at Snape Marsh by the turnpiking of Boothen Lane (now Century Road) and Marsh Street. Hanley was thus linked with the Lawton, Burslem, and Newcastle system via Cobridge.[97] A more direct route to Burslem was provided by Waterloo Road, built from Vale Place as far as Cobridge by 1814 and extended to Burslem in 1815–17.[98] Mill Street (now Etruria Road) had been built from the eastern end of Etruria to the western outskirts of Hanley by 1832;[99] plans for its continuation into the centre of Hanley in 1835[1] and 1839[2] were not carried out, but it was being extended as Trinity Street to meet Stafford Street at Miles Bank in 1847.[3] Etruria Vale Road running from the east end of Etruria up to Bedford Road and so into Stoke Road was in existence by 1775.[4] There was formerly a toll-chain across the Newcastle–Leek road where it entered Etruria Village, and c. 1880 toll was taken there for charity on festive occasions.[5] By 1799 there was a toll-gate at the junction of the main road with Century Road, and this was still in use in the 1870's.[6] Another stood at the junction with Etruria Vale Road by 1832[7] and was still in use c. 1876, while the house was not taken down until 1904 when Etruria Park was laid out and the road widened.[8] By 1832 there were also toll-gates in Etruria Vale Road on the slope between Rectory Road and Sun Street

and in Vale Place at the end of Waterloo Road; both were still in use in the 1870's.[9]

The road running from Great Chell and Sneyd Green through the centre of Hanley to the Albion Inn on the Cheadle road was turnpiked in 1770.[10] There was a toll-gate at its junction with Keelings Lane at Upper Green by 1820, and there seems at some time to have been another a little to the south-west, presumably at the junction of what are now Hulton Street and Town Road.[11]

The road from Stoke to Endon was built between 1840 and 1842[12] and runs as Leek Road through the eastern part of the area. Lichfield Street was extended to Fenton at the same time (the present Victoria Road), crossing Leek Road at a point south-west of Joiner's Square. A toll-gate, still in use in 1857, was set up at the crossing.[13]

Bucknall Bridge carrying the road from Newcastle to Cheadle over the Trent was a county responsibility by 1830.[14] The bridges carrying this road, its Liverpool Road branch, and the road from Newcastle to Leek over the Fowlea Brook are described elsewhere.[15]

By 1802 there was a daily coach service to London and Liverpool from the Swan Inn in Market Square.[16] This inn was a building probably dating from the late 17th or early 18th century.[17] It was demolished in the 1840's to make way for the new market hall.[18] By 1818 the area enjoyed the same coaching facilities as Burslem and Stoke, two coaches daily between London and Liverpool and a third three times a week between Birmingham and Liverpool, all from the 'King's Head' at the west end of Piccadilly.[19] By 1824 there was also a 'safety' coach from the 'King's Head' to Leek via Burslem once a week and another three times a week through Stoke and Longton to Stafford and Birmingham.[20] By 1850 the posting-houses were the Albion Hotel in Old Hall Street and the 'Saracen's Head' in Stafford Row (now Stafford Street),[21] and by 1860 the 'Saracen's Head' and the 'King's Head'.[22] By 1851 there were omnibuses from the posting-inns to Stoke station seven times a day, and Hanley was also on the route of the Longton to Burslem omnibus, which called twice a day at the inns.[23] A horse-drawn tram

[92] Hargreaves, *Map of Staffs. Potteries.*
[93] See p. 178.
[94] S.R.O., Q/SB Trans. 1806; Hargreaves, *Map of Staffs. Potteries.*
[95] W.S.L. 130/47, f. 95; Hargreaves, *Map of Staffs. Potteries.*
[96] O.S. Map 6" Staffs. xii SW. (1890).
[97] Yates, *Map of Staffs.* (1775); see p. 108.
[98] S.R.O., Q/RUt 5/16; see p. 108.
[99] Hargreaves, *Map of Staffs. Potteries.*
[1] H.R.L., Hanley Highway Surveyors' Mins. 1817–41, 23 Sept. 1833.
[2] S.R.O., Q/RUt 5/82.
[3] Lich. Dioc. Regy., Bp.'s Reg. O^A, p. 202 and plan facing. In *Hanley Jubilee Souvenir* (1907), 26, it is claimed that the road was completed by the boro. council, i.e. in or after 1857.
[4] Yates, *Map of Staffs.*
[5] Warrillow, *Etruria*, 145.
[6] Yates, *Map of Staffs.* (1799 edn.); Warrillow, *Etruria*, 147; O.S. Map 6" Staffs. xii SW. (1890).
[7] Hargreaves, *Map of Staffs. Potteries.*
[8] Warrillow, *Etruria*, 144; Huntbach, *Hanley*, 109; O.S. Map 6" Staffs. xii SW. (1890).
[9] Hargreaves, *Map of Staffs. Potteries.*
[10] Act for repairing road from Tunstall to Bosley and from Gt. Chell to Shelton, 10 Geo. III, c. 66; S.R.O., Q/RUt 5/72.

[11] H.R.L., Hanley Highway Surveyors' Mins. 1817–41, p. 2; Hargreaves, *Map of Staffs. Potteries*; *Hanley Jubilee Souvenir* (1907), 27. One at least was still in use in 1840: H.R.L., Hanley Highway Surveyors' Mins. 1817–41, 19 Oct. 1840. [12] See p. 178.
[13] Act for improving roads from Newcastle-under-Lyme to Blythe Marsh, from Cliff Bank to Shelton, from Fenton to Hem Heath and from Shelton to Newcastle-under-Lyme and for making roads to communicate therewith, 3 and 4 Vic. c. 116 (local and personal); *Map of Stoke Boro. 1842* (in some copies of Ward, *Stoke*); Homer, *Plan of Hanley and Shelton*, 1857. The Hanley to Fenton road had originally been planned in the Act for repairing road from Tunstall to Bosley and Gt. Chell to Shelton and making a diversion to communicate therewith, 3 and 4 Wm. IV, c. 54 (local and personal).
[14] J. Potter, *List of Bridges which Inhabs. of County of Stafford are bound to repair* (1830), 7.
[15] See p. 179.
[16] Allbut, *Staffs. Pottery Dir.* (1802).
[17] It had a long low front with a central entrance below a gable and a projecting wing at each end: Warrillow, *Stoke*, 18 (iv).   [18] See p. 162.
[19] Parson and Bradshaw, *Dir. Staffs.* (1818).
[20] Warrillow, *Stoke*, 44.
[21] *P.O. Dir. Staffs.* (1850, 1854).
[22] Ibid. (1860).
[23] White, *Dir. Staffs.* (1851), 259, 286.

service was started between Hanley and Burslem in 1862, a 'street railway' built by George Train of Boston, Mass.[24] It was replaced by steam-driven trams in 1882 when the line from Longton to Stoke was extended to Hanley and Burslem.[25] Electricity was substituted for steam after the trams had been taken over by the Potteries Electric Traction Company in 1898 and new lines were then opened: to Etruria and Newcastle in 1900, to Fenton and Longton via Victoria Road in 1900, and to Sneyd Green via Town Road and Chell Street in 1905.[26] Motor buses, introduced from 1913, gradually replaced the trams between 1926 and 1928.[27] A new garage was opened in Clough Street in 1953.[28]

From 1835 there was a horse-post to Hanley and Shelton from Newcastle, the postal centre for the Potteries. Stoke became the postal centre in 1854 with the opening of the station post office there.[29] By 1790 Hanley had its own postmaster and Shelton a postmistress.[30] There was a post-office at Etruria by 1834[31] and one at Northwood by 1860.[32] The general post office in Tontine Street was opened in 1906.[33]

The Trent and Mersey Canal built in 1766–77[34] passes to the west of Shelton and through Etruria. There was a wharf at Etruria by 1783, probably at Etruria Basin in Etruria Vale, where a wharf was certainly in existence by 1802.[35] There was a wharf at Shelton by 1791, probably on the south side of Stoke Road; there was another on the north side of the road by 1802.[36] By 1816 the canal company had a tramway for goods from the wharf at Etruria Basin to Miles Bank in the centre of Hanley;[37] by the 1870's it ran only as far as the goods station in Etruria Road.[38] By 1851 the public wharves in use were those at Shelton south of the main road, at Etruria Vale, and in Etruria itself.[39] Shelton Wharf was evidently closed c. 1870,[40] that in Etruria Vale continued in use until at least the 1870's,[41] and Etruria Wharf, off Belmont Road, is still used.[42] The Caldon Branch Canal was built from the main canal near Etruria Basin to Froghall under an Act of 1776.[43] There were two wharves on this branch near

Joiner's Square by 1832, one of which, to the east of the Lichfield Road bridge, was still in use in the 1870's.[44] The Caldon Wharf of 1851 may have been one of these or else a wharf attached to the Cauldon Place Pottery where there was certainly a wharf in the 1870's. There was then also a wharf to the east, on the opposite side of Chatterley Bridge, belonging to the canal company, and by 1907 this was the property of the borough council and known as Town Wharf; the site was occupied in 1959 by Podmores (Engineers) Ltd.[45] There was a third wharf in this part of Shelton in the 1870's, near the Russell Street bridge.[46] Pottery materials continue to be conveyed from the Cockshott railway sidings on the main canal south-east of Hanley cemetery to Joiner's Square.[47]

The main railway line from Stoke to the north runs along the Fowlea valley and has a station at Etruria. When the line was opened in 1848 Etruria Station lay on the north side of the main road just over the Wolstanton boundary where the Loop Line now branches off.[48] It was rebuilt on its present site south of the main road—on the Stoke side of the former Hanley–Stoke boundary—when the first part of the Loop Line was opened in 1862.[49] The Loop Line began as a branch to Hanley where a station was built on the south side of Etruria Road,[50] opposite the site now occupied by the Grand Hotel. With the extension of the line as far as Burslem in 1873 the station was moved to its present site on the north side of the road; it was rebuilt c. 1916.[51] Lord Granville's mineral lines to his ironworks in Etruria and the line to his Shelton Colliery north of Hanley town were built under an Act of 1847 about the same time as the main line, from which they branched at Etruria.[52] The line from Stoke to Biddulph and to Leek which runs under Bucknall Road to the west of Bucknall was opened for mineral traffic in 1860; Bucknall and Northwood station off Bucknall Road was opened for passenger services in 1864.[53]

BUILDINGS. The centre of Hanley preserves the irregular layout of the late-18th-century village[54] and

[24] C. Lea, 'English Street Tramways of George Francis Train' (*Jnl. of Transport Hist.* i), 106; *Staffs. Advertiser*, 16 Jan. 1862. At first the Hanley terminus was in Fountain Sq., but it was moved to the Trinity St. end of Foundry St. in 1863 to avoid the curve at the top of Hope St.: Warrillow, *Stoke*, 58, 61.

[25] *Kelly's Dir. Staffs.* (1884); S.R.O., Q/RUo 22, 30, 39, and 40; *Staffs. Advertiser*, 14 Jan. 1882.

[26] Warrillow, *Stoke*, 62, 74, 75; W. Campbell, *Street Map of Hanley, Burslem, Tunstall and Newcastle-under-Lyme* (1907; copy in H.R.L.).

[27] Warrilow, *Stoke*, 76-78.

[28] *P.M.T. House Mag.* (May–June 1958), 6 (copy in H.R.L.).

[29] See p. 7.

[30] *Univ. Brit. Dir.* iv. 108, 109.

[31] White, *Dir. Staffs.* (1834).

[32] *P.O. Dir. Staffs.* (1860).

[33] *Hanley Jubilee Souvenir* (1907), 27.

[34] *S.H.C.* 1934 (1), 109.

[35] Ward, *Stoke*, 445; Allbut, *Staffs. Pottery Dir.* (1802).

[36] Act . . . to make a road from the Black Lion to Shelton Wharf, 31 Geo. III, c. 129; Allbut, *Staffs. Pottery Dir.* (1802); Hargreaves, *Map of Staffs. Potteries*, which shows Shelton Wharf on the S. side of Stoke Rd.

[37] *Staffs. Advertiser*, 25 Mar. 1816; Shaw, *Staffs. Potteries*, 40; Hargreaves, *Map of Staffs. Potteries*.

[38] O.S. Map 6″ Staffs. xii SW. (1890).

[39] White, *Dir. Staffs.* (1851); Hargreaves, *Map of Staffs. Potteries*.

[40] It is shown on O.S. Map 1/500 Staffs. xvi. 3. 25 (1866) but not on O.S. Map 6″ Staffs. xviii NW. (1890; surveyed late 1870's). A freehold wharf at Shelton lately owned by the Spode family and held by the Bridgewater trustees in succession to Pickford & Co. was offered for sale in 1850: W.S.L., D. 1788, P. 2, B. 8.

[41] O.S. Map 6″ xii SW. (1890).

[42] Ex. inf. Brit. Transport Waterways, NW. Div. (1959). It was formerly on the opposite side of the canal: O.S. Map 1/500 Staffs. xi. 15. 24 (1866).

[43] Act to enable the proprietors of the navigation from the Trent to the Mersey to make a navigable canal from the said navigation to Froghall, 16 Geo. III, c. 32.

[44] Hargreaves, *Map of Staffs. Potteries*; O.S. Map 6″ Staffs. xii SW. (1890).

[45] White, *Dir. Staffs.* (1851); O.S. Map 6″ Staffs. xii SW. (1890); *Hanley Jubilee Souvenir*, 48.

[46] O.S. Map 6″ Staffs. xii SW. (1890).

[47] Ex inf. Brit. Transport Waterways.

[48] *Staffs. Advertiser*, 14 Oct. 1848; Warrillow, *Etruria*, 71.

[49] Warrillow, *Etruria*, 74, 126; 'Manifold', *N. Staffs. Rlwy.* 50–51.   [50] Warrillow, *Etruria*, 74.

[51] Huntbach, *Hanley*, 16; 'Manifold', *N. Staffs. Rlwy.* 118. The first station is now occupied as a warehouse: Warrillow, *Stoke*, 103.

[52] 'Manifold', *N. Staffs. Rlwy.* 33; Homer, *Plan of Hanley and Shelton, 1857*; O.S. Map 6″ Staffs. xii NW. (1890).   [53] Ex inf. Brit. Rlwys., L.M.R.

[54] See p. 142.

was described in 1960 as 'an archipelago of island sites'.[55] The buildings occupying these variously shaped islands have been replaced piecemeal from the early 19th century onwards and are now of widely different heights, styles, and materials. Because of Hanley's development as an important shopping centre and the large scale of its later com-

gregational chapel (1784),[56] now altered for use as a roller-skating rink, and its adjoining manse. In New Hall Street the Georgian front of Hope Congregational Church (1812)[57] is little changed. Immediately south of the town-centre parts of Pall Mall, Albion Street, and Bagnall Street are free of shop fronts and retain something of the scale of the

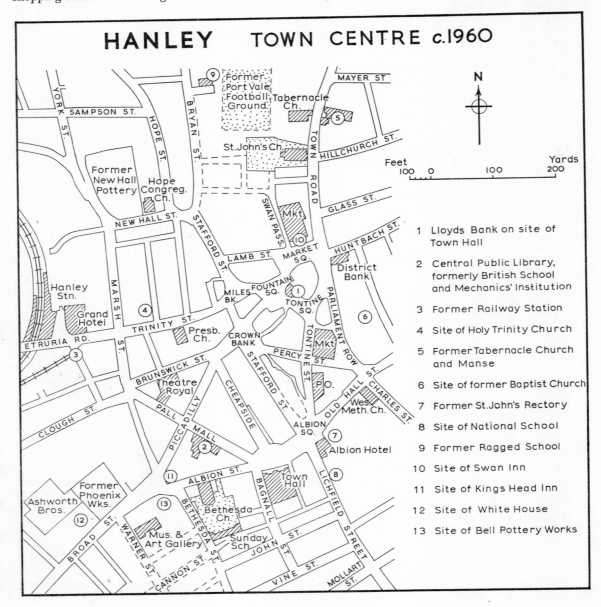

HANLEY TOWN CENTRE c.1960

1 Lloyds Bank on site of Town Hall

2 Central Public Library, formerly British School and Mechanics' Institution

3 Former Railway Station

4 Site of Holy Trinity Church

5 Former Tabernacle Church and Manse

6 Site of former Baptist Church

7 Former St. John's Rectory

8 Site of National School

9 Former Ragged School

10 Site of Swan Inn

11 Site of Kings Head Inn

12 Site of White House

13 Site of Bell Pottery Works

mercial buildings this lack of uniformity is even more pronounced than in the other Pottery towns. A few low-built brick houses dating from the first third of the 19th century have survived, notably in New Hall Street, Parliament Row, and Tontine Street. On the south side of Fountain Square the French Horn public house and the single-story shops adjoining it are of this type. Town Road (formerly High Street) contains some more substantial buildings of the same period, including the former Con-

early town. The most notable older building in this area is Bethesda Chapel, built in 1819 and altered in 1859 and 1887, together with its Sunday schools (1819) and graveyard.[58] The winding road leading south-westwards to Stoke, now known as Snow Hill, Howard Place, and Stoke Road, is still partly residential in character. To the south of St. Mark's Church there are some middle-class terraced houses as well as several larger houses in their own gardens, some of them dating from the early 19th century.

[55] *Sentinel Suppl.* iv, 17 May 1960, quoting Mr. J. W. Plant, City Reconstruction Officer.

[56] See p. 285.   [57] See p. 285.
[58] See pp. 294–5 and plate facing p. 294.

Near the Stoke boundary three tall ranges of late-19th-century pottery buildings (now occupied by Messrs. Grimwade and the Empire Porcelain Company) form an impressive group.

The former town hall at the upper end of Fountain Square, built in 1845, had a severely Classical two-storied stone front of seven bays with a central Ionic portico surmounted by a pediment.[59] Lloyds Bank, which had occupied the premises since 1886, rebuilt them in 1936.[60] The present town hall in Albion Square, built as the Queen's Hotel in 1869 and acquired for the town in 1884,[61] is a large three-storied brick building with stone dressings, its front having projecting wings in the centre and at both ends. Designed by Robert Scrivener, it is domestic rather than monumental in character with echoes of the French Renaissance in its high-pitched roof and dormer windows.

The covered market occupying a large island site between Tontine Street and Parliament Row was built as a shambles in 1831[62] and is a Classical stone structure, mostly of one story. The principal front, facing Tontine Street, has a central feature consisting of an arched entrance surmounted by a stone turret and cupola; this is connected by three-bay Doric colonnades to pedimented side wings. On the north side of Market Square the market opened in 1849 on the site of the Swan Inn[63] has an impressive stone façade of three stories with balustrades and a row of stone vases set above tall shop windows. These appear to have been the first of Hanley's more ambitious shop fronts;[64] the same elevational treatment, on a slightly smaller scale, has been taken round the eastern side of the block where it faces Town Road.

The District Bank to the west of Market Square was originally an early-19th-century building of pale brick, designed by T. W. Atkinson in 'the gabled or Tudor style of architecture'. It was noted c. 1840 that 'its elevation rises above all the neighbouring houses and makes it conspicuous at a considerable distance.[65] The bank was rebuilt in 1881[66] in a late-19th-century version of the same style.

The former British School and Art School in Pall Mall (1818),[67] now part of the city library, has an impressive brick front with neo-Classical stone dressings, retaining its twin doorways flanked by Doric pilasters and its contemporary cast-iron railings and gate-piers. Originally the building consisted of two tall stories, but a third was added in 1880.[68] The two painted barbotine portraits over the entrance to the eastern extension were executed by George Cartlidge, a ceramic craftsman and a teacher of painting at the Art School from 1897.[69] The adjoining part

of the library to the west was built as the Mechanics' Institution in 1859–61. Its stone front was designed by Robert Scrivener in the Classical style with a Tuscan order below and an Ionic order above.[70] The upper story eventually became unsafe and was taken down after the opening of the new museum in Broad Street in 1956.[71]

Of the dozen private dwelling houses 'of the first class' mentioned by Ward c. 1840[72] only a few remain and all of these have been put to other uses. The favoured residential districts at this period included Northwood, the area immediately east of the town-centre now represented by Old Hall Street and Albion Square, and the southern area around the road leading to Stoke. At Northwood the only traces of the improvements carried out by William Ridgway in the early 19th century are a few brick and stucco villas near Keelings Lane. Among them a two-storied stucco house with 'Gothic' features in Birch Street was once a school known as 'Alfieri's Academy'.[73] In Old Hall Street the former St. John's Rectory, dating from the 1840's, has recently been demolished.[74] On an adjoining site is the large house which was owned by the Chatterley family in 1849 and occupied by Joseph Clementson.[75] Bank House, on the site of which the Queen's Hotel (now town hall) was erected in 1869, was an impressive brick building standing in a walled garden and probably dating from the late 18th century. It had a pedimented doorway and consisted of a three-storied block with an adjoining two-storied wing; the forecourt was bounded by a low brick wall and iron railings.[76] Albion House,[77] a two-storied stucco building which stood opposite, was probably built in the 1830's. A plain two-storied brick house of the late 18th century which still stands in Cannon Street is now used as a local headquarters by the Royal and Antediluvian Order of Buffaloes; it has a modillion cornice and a central doorway surmounted by a Doric frieze and a segmental pediment. The dwelling house built by John Baddeley (d. 1772) which formerly stood in front of his pottery works[78] in Shelton High Street (now Broad Street) was described by Ward as 'a specimen of a first-rate house of the last century'. It was occupied in Ward's time by a Mr. Hicks (probably Richard Hicks, d. 1844), by Lydia Hicks between at least 1849 and 1854, and by Crapper and Company, dentists, by 1860. Known as the White House by 1876, it was offered for sale after Crapper's death in 1891.[79] In the 1840's William Yates was occupying an 18th-century house opposite the west end of St. Mark's Church where his family had been 'long seated'[80] but which has now disappeared. Grove House, altered and enlarged by Charles Meigh

[59] See plate facing p. 167.
[60] See p. 158.
[61] Staffs. Advertiser, 10 July 1886; see p. 158.
[62] See p. 162.
[63] For markets see p. 162; for the Swan Inn see p. 146.
[64] Probably those described in 1850 as 'far above the standard of everything else in the Pottery district': see p. 143.
[65] Ward, Stoke, 382; W.S.L., Staffs. Views, iv, p. 266.
[66] Warrillow, Stoke, 394.
[67] See pp. 171, 316.
[68] R. G. Haggar, A Century of Art Educ. in the Potteries, 24.
[69] Ibid. 24, 40. He is not to be confused with the head master of the Art School of the same name: ibid. 32, 40.
[70] Keates's Potteries Dir. (1892–3).   [71] See p. 171.
[72] Ward, Stoke, 382–6, from which the details which

follow are taken unless otherwise stated.
[73] Warrillow, Stoke, 290 (vi); see p. 143.
[74] See p. 154.
[75] Tithe Redemption Com., Tithe Maps and Appt., Stoke-upon-Trent (Hanley, 1849).
[76] Warrillow, Stoke, 290 (iv); see pp. 157, 158.
[77] Ward (p. 383) states that it was owned by W. Parker, importer of cobalt and zaffres, who also had a country residence at Rownall Hall.
[78] Now occupied by George L. Ashworth & Bros. Ltd.: see p. 164.
[79] Ward, Stoke, 383; Tithe Redemption Com., Tithe Maps and Appt., Hanley; White, Dir. Staffs. (1851); P.O. Dir. Staffs. (1854, 1860, 1876); W.S.L. 13/45; Warrillow, Stoke, 358 (i); see pp. 164, 295.
[80] Ward, Stoke, 384; Tithe Redemption Com., Tithe Maps and Appt., Hanley.

c. 1840 and at that time containing a fine collection of pictures, stood near the junction of Snow Hill and Bedford Road.[81] Cauldon Place, John Ridgway's 'elegant modern mansion' attached to his pottery works, appears to have been altered beyond recognition.[82] Shelton Hall opposite, dating from 1782, was demolished in 1959.[83] Shelton Old Hall, one of the few ancient buildings in the area, stood on the crown of the hill to the north-east until its destruction by fire in 1853.[84]

Etruria Hall, completed in 1770, was built by Josiah Wedgwood for his own occupation as part of his development of the former Ridge House estate on the western outskirts of Shelton.[85] His architect was Joseph Pickford of Derby.[86] The site chosen was on rising ground on the north side of the road to Newcastle, the house facing towards the Etruria Works which stood beyond the Trent and Mersey Canal about 300 yards away.[87] The intervening area was laid out and planted as ornamental grounds leading down to two small lakes near the canal. There appears to be no evidence for the suggestion that 'Capability' Brown was employed as a landscape gardener at Etruria;[88] it is more probable that, as in the design of the house and works, Wedgwood put many of his own ideas into practice. Owing to the gradual enlargement since 1858 of the Shelton ironworks, all traces of the gardens and parkland surrounding the hall have been obliterated, the last of Josiah Wedgwood's trees having been felled in the 1870's.[89] Etruria Hall was originally a square three-storied brick house with stone dressings, typical of its period, the three central bays of its five-bay front projecting slightly and being surmounted by a pediment.[90] Late in Wedgwood's life two flanking wings were added, both square blocks of two stories with single-story links connecting them to the original building. In 1844 the house was said to contain 34 rooms.[91] Below the building were vaulted cellars in which Wedgwood's private laboratory was situated.[92] The south wing was extended and the interior of the house largely remodelled *c.* 1916;[93] further alterations were made at subsequent dates. The only original fittings which remain appear to be a basket grate in a first-floor room and a balustrade in the 'Chinese Chippendale' style to a secondary staircase. In 1781 and 1784 Flaxman had supplied designs for decorative plasterwork and a painted ceiling but it is doubtful whether these were ever

executed.[94] Bank House, built for Wedgwood's partner Thomas Bentley but never occupied by him, served as a home for the Wedgwoods from November 1769 until the hall was completed in the following year.[95] It was a tall, square, three-storied house standing near the main road to the south of Etruria Hall.[96] The house was demolished in 1819 but an L-shaped range of outbuildings, at one time occupied as Grove Farm, still survived in the early 1950's.[97]

The former North Staffordshire Infirmary at Wood Hills, Etruria, was built in 1816–19 to the designs of Joseph Potter of Lichfield. It was enlarged at various periods and demolished after the infirmary was moved to Hartshill in 1869.[98] The buildings, which were faced with 'Roman' cement, consisted of several two- and three-storied ranges built on a slope and roughly enclosing a courtyard. The principal part had a central five-bay colonnaded portico, approached by a double flight of steps and recessed between two projecting gabled wings.[99]

The earliest houses in the Potteries known to have been put up expressly for workers in the industry were those at Etruria, built by Josiah Wedgwood in the late 1760's.[1] Apart from a row of six cottages forming an extension of the canal frontage of the works themselves, these were all built in terraced blocks on both sides of the road to Newcastle (now Etruria Road) and stretched westwards from the canal bridge.[2] They were mostly simple four-roomed cottages with small-paned casement windows and plain doorway openings, the floors to the lower rooms being of brick and the front doors opening straight into the living rooms. Apart from this last feature they were still considered to be well built and generously planned nearly a hundred years later.[3] Wells and pumps were provided for every few dwellings and there were several communal bakehouses where villagers could bake their bread for $\frac{1}{2}d.$ a loaf.[4] All the earliest cottages, with the exception of an altered example incorporated in the Etruria Works, had been demolished by 1960, most of them in the previous decade.[5]

The oldest terraced houses to survive in the centre of Hanley appear to be those in John Street, dated 1807. Some of these are superior houses with pedimented doorcases and long back yards, but all are built on the 'cottage' plan, back kitchens, where they exist, being later additions.[6] Several streets of terraced cottages to the north-west of St. Mark's

[81] In 1849 it was owned by Chas. Meigh sen. and occupied by Chas. Meigh jun.: Tithe Redemption Com., Tithe Maps and Appt., Hanley.   [82] See p. 167.
[83] See p. 153.   [84] See p. 153.
[85] See p. 152. For an estate plan see Wedgwood Mus., Barlaston, Plan of Etruria Estate by Chas. Heaton (1826).
[86] Meteyard, *Wedgwood*, i. 494; ibid. ii. 82.
[87] See p. 166.
[88] Meteyard, *Wedgwood*, ii. 129; Warrillow, *Etruria*, 36, 37. Although Wedgwood had met Brown in 1767 (Meteyard, *Wedgwood*, ii. 5 n. 2) and mentions him occasionally in other connexions in his correspondence with Bentley (Wedgwood Mus., Barlaston, Letters, i. 243, ii. 32, vii. 130, viii. 67, xii. 88, 109), there is no suggestion that he was employed at Etruria. Brown's biographer, Miss D. Stroud, has found no documentary evidence for such employment: ex inf. Miss Stroud.
[89] Warrillow, *Etruria*, 133–40.
[90] Meteyard, *Wedgwood*, ii. 129, fig. 19; Warrillow, *Etruria*, 46.
[91] Meteyard, *Wedgwood*, ii. 128; Warrillow, *Etruria*, 46, 56, 132, 306; see plate facing p. 166.
[92] Meteyard, *Wedgwood*, ii. 332 n. 3.

[93] Warrillow, *Etruria*, 53.
[94] Ibid. 39–45.
[95] Meteyard, *Wedgwood*, i. 485–6, 495; ibid. ii. 125–6, 189.   [96] Warrillow, *Etruria*, 52.
[97] Ibid. 33–36, 52.
[98] See p. 160.
[99] Warrillow, *Etruria*, 238; W.S.L., Staffs. Views, iv, p. 185. For plan see O.S. Map 1/500 Staffs. xi. 15. 24 and 25 (1866).   [1] See p. 144.
[2] Wedgwood Mus., Barlaston, Plans of Etruria Works (1805) and Etruria Estate (1826); Warrillow, *Etruria*, 23–25 and plates on pp. 41, 137, 143.
[3] Meteyard, *Wedgwood* i. 201 n. 1.
[4] Warrillow, *Etruria*, 23–25.
[5] Warrillow, *Stoke*, 133 and plates on p. 154. A row which still stands immediately W. of the canal bridge and includes the Bridge and Etruria Inns had not been built by 1805: Wedgwood Mus., Barlaston, Plan of Etruria Works (1805).
[6] Few terraces in Hanley had projections at the rear by 1849: Tithe Redemption Com., Tithe Maps, Hanley (1849). For the introduction of back kitchens in the Potteries see p. 114.

Church probably date from the first quarter of the 19th century, among the oldest being Yates Street (formerly William Street) where there is a date tablet of 1818. In the present St. Mark's Street a few cottages with small front gardens survive; most of this row and other early terraces disappeared when a large garage was built and the surrounding area levelled between 1955 and 1957.[7] In Windmill Street to the north-east of the central area a row of cottages with simple wood doorcases carries the date 1831 above an arched entry. Higher up the street on the opposite side another entry is dated 1834. In this case the houses have round-headed doorways with moulded archivolts and projecting keystones—an early use of this feature which was a favourite one in the Potteries for about 20 years.[8]

By 1850 there were several working-class areas in Hanley where the houses appear to have been built systematically round a series of communal courts. These were particularly noticed in Davis Street (between the Trent and Mersey and the Caldon Canals) while conditions were said to be very bad in William Street (now Yates Street) and the other streets to the north of St. Mark's Church.[9] As a contrast attention was drawn to a row of cottages belonging to John Ridgway, each let at £10 a year; 'the back yards are paved with brick, each house has a washhouse and a separate privy and a small garden; all is clean and comfortable'.[10]

By the end of the century Hanley's exceptionally rapid increase in population was causing serious overcrowding. Old property in the centre of the town, shut in by later buildings, had deteriorated and was attracting the poorest class of tenant by its lower rents. In 1901 the worst areas were said to be in the Hope and Etruria wards and in 'a quarter of the town not many minutes walk from Shelton Church'.[11] A typical 'dark spot' was a court off Marsh Street which contained twelve dwellings, each having one room downstairs with a small back-place (the latter without fireplace or sink) and two corresponding rooms above. They were arranged in two rows, one without back access, and opened upon a common yard where they shared one water tap, one dustbin, and five water-closets.[12]

In some parts of the town, however, conditions were better: in 1899 it was stated that good working-class houses in Hanley, containing two bedrooms, two dwelling rooms, a back kitchen, and a fair-sized yard, were let for between 5s. and 5s. 4d. a week including rates; sixteen new streets had been built in the past year.[13] By 1902 there were some superior houses with bathrooms which commanded a higher rent than the normal 5s. 3d.[14] In the same year a

scheme was submitted to the corporation for 270 cottages to be built on the Park Estate, each with a living room, a scullery, a bathroom, and three bedrooms.[15] There were also schemes for model lodging-houses and for two-storied blocks of flats.[16]

MANOR. William of Hanley held 3 virgates in the vill of Hanley in 1212 as a royal sokeman, paying the king 6s. rent.[17] Although in 1227 the Crown confirmed to Henry de Audley a grant of 'all the land of Hanlih' made by Richard son of Noel of Hanley,[18] William of Hanley was holding the vill of the king in 1236 for a rent of 6s. payable at Newcastle and for 40 days' castleguard there.[19] The overlordship thereafter descended with Newcastle until at least 1650.[20]

In 1297 Robert Auxtin, lord of Hanley, held Hanley by a rent of 6s., the provision of a foot-soldier at the castle for 40 days in war-time, and the usual services including suit at the three-weekly court of Newcastle; Robert also paid a fine of $\frac{1}{2}$ mark to enclose 31 acres of waste and with the other tenants of Hanley rendered 6d. an acre for the 70 acres of land which they held there.[21] In 1320 Robert Auxtin of Hanley granted his house and lands there to John de Kynnersley, clerk, a conveyance confirmed by Robert's son John, and in 1321 Stephen Auxtin of Hanley granted John de Kynnersley all his capital messuage and lands there.[22] What was called the manor of Hanley was conveyed in 1324 by Ralph, the son of William son of Thomas Swanild, to John de Kynnersley who the following year granted it to his great-nephew Nicholas de Kynnersley.[23] Before 1371 Nicholas, who died childless, had conveyed the manor to Sir Richard de Peshale. He in turn conveyed it to Richard de Colclough,[24] who represented Newcastle-under-Lyme in the parliament of 1360 and was mayor in 1374–5.[25] His son John, who represented Newcastle in 1384 and 1390,[26] had succeeded him in his lands by 1385, and the manor remained in the Colclough family for the next 300 years.[27] In 1687 Sir Caesar Colclough died unmarried and was succeeded by his sister Margaret who with her husband Robert Leigh (alias Colclough) mortgaged lands in Hanley and elsewhere in 1689 to Richard Bagnall of London, a younger son of the Bagnall family which had been prominent in the public life of Newcastle, and others.[28] Richard Bagnall evidently secured the ownership of the manor which then descended in his family, passing at the death of John Bagnall in 1785 to his sister Anna-Maria, wife of William Scott, later Lord Stowell.[29] She died in 1809, and her daughter

---

[7] Warrillow, *Stoke*, 35.
[8] For other dated examples see pp. 86 and n. 12, 114, n. 8.
[9] R. Rawlinson, *Rep. to Bd. of Health on Stoke Par.* (1850), 53 (copy in H.R.L.).   [10] Ibid. 71.
[11] *Housing of the People in Hanley* (1901), 3–4, 6, 9 (copy in H.R.L.).
[12] Ibid. 4. For slum clearance see pp. 143, 144, 145, 268, 269.
[13] *Hanley M.O.H. Rep. 1899* 32 (copy in H.R.L.).
[14] Ibid. *1902*, 17.
[15] T. H. Whittingham, *Schemes for Workmens' Dwellings and Model Lodging Houses* (1902; copy in H.R.L.).
[16] Ibid.; T. W. Harrison, *Municipal Dwellings for the Very Poor* (1902; copy in H.R.L.).
[17] *Bk. of Fees*, 143.   [18] *Cal. Chart. R. 1226–57*, 37.
[19] *Bk. of Fees*, 594; see pp. 13, 184.

[20] *S.H.C.* 1911, 245; Ward, *Stoke*, app. p. xliv; D.L. 42/4, f. 179a; E 317/Staffs./ 38, f. 8.
[21] C 133/81/6, the relevant portion of which is partially transcribed in *Cal. Inq. p.m.* iii, p. 220, and *S.H.C.* 1911, 245.   [22] W.S.L., D. 1733, bdle. 8.
[23] Ibid., bdles. 8, 13; *S.H.C.* xiii. 111.
[24] *S.H.C.* xiii. 87, 99, 111.
[25] Ibid. 1917–18, 102.
[26] Ibid. 102, 139.
[27] Ibid. xv. 54; xiii. 262; N.S. x (1), 31; Ward, *Stoke*, 340–1 and app. p. xliv; D.L. 42/4, f. 179a; E 317/Staffs./ 38, f. 8; W.S.L., D. 1742, bdle. 2.
[28] W.S.L. 439/35; Ward, *Stoke*, 346–7; C.P. 45/430, rot. 56.
[29] W.S.L. 31/47/42; W.S.L. 423/28: Adams, *Adams Family*, 194; Ward, *Stoke*, 345, 347; *Complete Peerage*, 'Stowell of Stowell Park'.

Marianne, who married Lord Sidmouth in 1823, succeeded her as lady of the manor.[30] Marianne died in 1842 and her son, the Revd. William Leonard, Viscount Sidmouth, held the manor in 1862.[31]

The manor-house is said to have been Hanley Hall which stood near the junction of Old Hall Street and Bucknall New Road and was the home of the Smith family in the 17th and 18th centuries.[32] The Old Hall Pottery stood on or near the site.[33]

OTHER ESTATES. Birches Head farm, situated within the manor of Hulton on the road from Hanley to Abbey Hulton, was the home of John Adams, youngest son of Thomas Adams of Burslem, by 1611.[34] It remained in the occupation of this branch of the Adams family until the death of Mabel, the widow of John Adams (d. 1753), in 1771.[35] The family also mined coal on the estate.[36] The farm was held by the Jacksons between at least 1834 and 1854.[37] The ownership remained with the Sneyds until 1951 when the 78-acre farm, tenanted by Mrs. L. Udall, was offered for sale on the break-up of the Keele estate.[38] Much of the land has been bought for building purposes, but in 1958 Mrs. Udall, who had then lived there for 21 years, was still farming 57 acres.[39] The brick farmhouse appears to date from the early 19th century with later additions, but masonry in the walls may be of 17th-century origin.

The Ridge House estate, which was probably the 66-acre copyhold estate in Shelton held by Ralph Homersley in 1615,[40] passed in 1620 to Robert Homersley[41] and was held by him and Balthazar Bell in 1649 when it was described as 'a farm of great yearly value'.[42] Bell, who was taxable on 4 hearths in 1666,[43] was apparently the sole occupant c. 1680.[44] In 1745 it was occupied by Ralph Leigh[45] and in 1767 by a Mrs. Ashenhurst.[46] She and her son sold the estate in that year for £3,000 to Josiah Wedgwood who proceeded to build the Etruria pottery

works, opened in 1769, Etruria Hall, finished in 1770, and rows of cottages for his employees.[47] Bank House on a site to the south of the hall on the opposite side of the main road from the present vicarage was completed for Josiah's partner Thomas Bentley in 1769 and was occupied by Josiah for nearly a year until the completion of the hall. In the event Bentley never lived in the house, which after Josiah's departure was occupied for a time by Hugh Henshall, James Brindley's brother-in-law.[48] After Josiah's death in 1795 the hall stood empty for some time, Josiah II living in the south of England and apparently staying at Bank House on his few visits to Etruria each year.[49] He lived at Bank House from 1806 to 1807 before moving to Maer Hall, but for several years after 1803 Etruria Hall was occupied by Thomas Byerley (d. 1810), his cousin and a partner in the pottery firm.[50] Josiah II was back at Etruria from 1812 until his return to Maer in 1819.[51] Bank House was then demolished.[52] The hall, a boarding-school in the mid-1820's and unoccupied c. 1829,[53] was the home of Francis Wedgwood, a younger son of Josiah II, by 1834.[54] Having inherited the Etruria estate on the death of his father in 1843, Francis settled at Barlaston in 1848 and sold Etruria Hall and much of the land.[55] The hall was sold to the Duchy of Lancaster and by 1854 had been let to John Lancaster[56] and by 1860 to Earl Granville[57] who in 1858 had established a new branch of the Shelton ironworks on a site to the west of the hall.[58] Between at least 1868 and 1872 the hall was the home of Colonel William Roden, Mayor of Hanley 1866–8 and one of the M.P.'s for Stoke in 1868.[59] Unoccupied in 1876,[60] it was let in tenements by 1880.[61] From at least 1892 it has been used as offices by the Shelton Iron, Steel and Coal Company[62] (since 1956 Shelton Iron and Steel Ltd.), which bought the hall from the Duchy in 1930.[63]

The Ivy House and lands belonging to it lay to the south of Bucknall Road near what is now the junc-

[30] Ward, *Stoke*, 345, 347. The manor was held by Anna's husband and another trustee in 1812: ibid. 361; her son Wm. Scott d. in 1835; ibid. 347.

[31] Huntbach, *Hanley*, 12; *Complete Peerage*, xi. 735.

[32] Ward, *Stoke*, 339 and app. p. xlvii; *S.H.C.* 1921, 164: W.S.L., D. 1742, list of inhabs. of Stoke parish, 1701; W.S.L., S.MS. 370, viii (2), p. 960 (transcripts from Dr. Burney's Newspaper Coll. in B.M.); W.S.L. 130/47, ff. 4, 5. Ralph Taylor was living there in 1729: Adams, *Adams Family*, 128.

[33] Ward, *Stoke*, 339; W. Scarratt, *Old Times in the Potteries*, 180; see p. 167.

[34] U.C.N.S., Sneyd MSS., Sneyd Green Deeds; Adams, *Adams Family*, pedigree between pp. 60 and 61.

[35] Adams, *Adams Family*, pedigree between pp. 180 and 181; U.C.N.S., Sneyd MSS., Tunstall Deeds, Burslem Deeds, Hulton Deeds, Sneyd Green Deeds; Ward, *Stoke*, app. p. xxviii; B.M. Campb. i, 29; W.S.L., D. 1788, P. 32, B. 6; *Burslem Par. Reg.* iii, 645.   [36] See p. 252.

[37] White, *Dir. Staffs.* (1834, 1851); *P.O. Dir. Staffs.* (1854).

[38] Adams, *Adams Family*, 171; W.S.L., Sale Cat. E/4/16.

[39] *Staffs. Weekly Sentinel*, 20 July 1958. She was still living there in 1960.

[40] Ward, *Stoke*, app. p. xlvi.   [41] C3/356/22.

[42] W.S.L., D. 1788, P. 44, B. 9.

[43] *S.H.C.* 1921, 155.

[44] Ibid. 1919, 258. There were 2 families of this name in Shelton in 1701: W.S.L., D. 1742, list of inhabs. of Stoke parish, 1701.

[45] Warrillow, *Etruria*, 15; E. Meteyard, *Life of Josiah Wedgwood*, i. 458 note.

[46] Meteyard, *Wedgwood*, i. 457–8, 494.

[47] Ibid. 457–8, 494–7; ii. 128–30, 189, 601–2; Ll. Jewitt,

Josiah Wedgwood, 191; Mankowitz and Haggar, *Eng. Pottery*, 85; see pp. 144, 150, 166. A 45-acre Ridge House farm still formed part of the Wedgwoods' Etruria estate in 1844: Warrillow, *Etruria*, 307, 310; J. C. Wedgwood, *Wedgwood Family*, map facing p. 170.

[48] Meteyard, *Wedgwood*, ii. 114, 125–6, 189; Warrillow, *Etruria*, 33–34, 52.

[49] Wedgwood, *Wedgwood Family*, 183–4 and note on map facing p. 170; Warrillow, *Etruria*, 48.

[50] Warrillow, *Etruria*, 48; Wedgwood, *Wedgwood Family*, 184, and pedigree between pp. 136 and 137.

[51] Wedgwood, *Wedgwood Family*, 184; it is not clear whether he lived at the hall or Bank Ho.

[52] Warrillow, *Etruria*, 34, 36, 52, 349; Ward, *Stoke*, 444; Wedgwood, *Wedgwood Family*, map facing p. 170; see p. 150.

[53] S. Shaw, *Staffs. Potteries*, 50; *Pigot's Nat. Com. Dir.* (1828–9); Warrillow, *Etruria*, 49; Warrillow, *Stoke*, 276.

[54] White, *Dir. Staffs.* (1834); Ward, *Stoke*, 444.

[55] Wedgwood, *Wedgwood Family*, 194. Warrillow, *Etruria*, 49, states that the property was put up for auction in 1844; according to *P.O. Dir. Staffs.* (1850) the hall was still the seat of Francis in 1850 but was occupied by Tom Wedgwood, presumably his cousin. In 1851 it was the home of Edw. Kinnersley: White, *Dir. Staffs.* (1851).

[56] *P.O. Dir. Staffs.* (1854).   [57] Ibid. (1860).

[58] Warrillow, *Etruria*, 49.

[59] *P.O. Dir. Staffs.* (1868, 1872); Warrillow, *Etruria*, 49, 259; A. Huntbach, *Hanley*, 123; *Members of Parl.*, H.C. 69, p. 485 (1878), lxii (2).

[60] *P.O. Dir. Staffs.* (1876).

[61] *Kelly's Dir. Staffs.* (1880).

[62] Ibid. (1892); Warrillow, *Etruria*, 49–50, 53.

[63] Ex inf. Shelton Iron and Steel Ltd.

tion with Bucknall New Road.[64] It was owned in 1716 by Elizabeth and Mary Vyse, daughters and coheirs of John Vyse, clerk, of London, and was then the home of John Ford, still the tenant in 1749.[65] In 1722 Elizabeth, Mary, and Mary's husband, Thomas Adams of Shifnal (Salop.), sold the estate to Thomas Heath of Hanley, a potter,[66] who in 1738 sold it with a flint mill on the Trent to Richard Hoskins of Stafford.[67] By 1770 the estate was occupied by John Wardle, except for the flint mill which was in the hands of Joseph Bucknall;[68] in that year Richard Hoskins's son Abraham, of Burton-upon-Trent, who had succeeded between 1749 and 1764, sold the estate to John Baddeley, a potter of Shelton, who was succeeded by his son Ralph in 1772.[69] The Ivy House was the home of Ralph's son Daniel by 1800,[70] but by the end of 1801 Ralph had given up his house and works in Shelton and in 1802 was living at the Ivy House, which had evidently been rebuilt shortly before.[71] The estate was sold in 1802 to Richard Mountford of Tottenham (Mdx.)[72] but in 1831 he sold it to Daniel Baddeley's three unmarried daughters who were then already living there.[73] Daniel himself was again living at the Ivy House in 1834.[74] In 1845 the survivor of the three daughters, then of Wootton, and Daniel's eldest son Whieldon Baddeley of Rocester sold the estate, including the flint mill, to Richard Mountford Baddeley, a barrister described then and in 1851 as living at Ivy Cottage.[75] Known as Ivy House Hall in 1872,[76] the house was still standing in 1911.[77] The site is now occupied by territorial army buildings, and what were probably out-buildings form part of a car-dealer's yard. The mill was used as a corn mill during the 1870's[78] but had been demolished by the end of the century.[79]

The house known as Shelton Old Hall was situated at the top of the slope above the present Wellesley Street to the south of St. Mark's Church. By 1680 it was the seat of John Fenton, coroner for Staffordshire, who died there in 1694; his son Elijah Fenton the poet was born there in 1683.[80] John's elder son and heir John moved to Newcastle in 1695,[81] but the house and lands in Shelton remained

the property of the family and were owned by Sir Thomas Fletcher Fenton Boughey of Aqualate in the mid-19th century.[82] By 1834 the half-timbered hall, 'built in the form of a long cross' and 'almost the only relic of ancient domestic architecture' in the Potteries district, was the homestead of Shelton (or Bank) farm and in the tenure of the Woodwards.[83] An engraving of c. 1840 shows a long rambling building with thatched roofs and much exposed timber framing; parts of it may well have been of medieval origin with additions of the 17th century.[84] In 1853, however, most of it was burnt down, although the ruins stood for many years afterwards.[85] The Woodwards continued to hold the farm from Sir Thomas Boughey until at least 1876,[86] and the farm itself was still in existence in the early 1920's.[87] Sir Thomas Boughey's nephew still owned land in Shelton in 1932.[88] A 19th-century farmhouse now (1960) forms part of the abattoir of J. Mayer and Sons (Hanley) Ltd.

The house variously known as Shelton Hall and Chatterley Hall was built on the south bank of the Caldon Canal west of the road between Stoke and Hanley by Charles and Ephraim Chatterley in 1782.[89] Ephraim was evidently living there c. 1790,[90] and after his death in 1811[91] the house remained the home of his widow Mary (d. 1832).[92] William Bishop, who married Charles Chatterley's daughter Mary Ann, died there in 1840,[93] and a William Bishop was living there in 1850.[94] Hanley cemetery was laid out over the southern part of the grounds in 1860,[95] but the hall itself remained standing between Cemetery Road and Caledonian Road until 1959 when it was in a ruinous state and was demolished.[96] It appears to have been a square three-storied building with a lower wing on its north side.[97]

The Amys family, who were living at Shelton by the early 14th century,[98] held Trent Hay farm by at least 1570.[99] Lands called Trent Hay were held by John Breeton in 1615.[1] The occupant of the farm in 1668 was a John Leigh,[2] who was dead by 1712. In 1718 his daughters and coheirs sold the farm to John Fenton[3] in whose family it then remained, though held by a tenant.[4] The farm was bought in the late

[64] Hargreaves, *Map of Staffs. Potteries.*
[65] W.S.L. 130/47 (Ivy Ho. abstract of title), ff. 1–2, 16.
[66] Ibid. ff. 2–3, 11, 14, 15.
[67] Ibid. ff. 11–16.   [68] Ibid. ff. 23, 24.
[69] Ibid. ff. 16, 17, 19–23; see p. 164. Ralph worked the mill in connexion with his pottery.
[70] W.S.L. 130/47, f. 36.
[71] Ibid. f. 42; see p. 164. It was then described as 'newly erected': W.S.L. 130/47, f. 42.
[72] W.S.L. 130/47, ff. 42–51.
[73] Ibid. ff. 89–97.
[74] White, *Dir. Staffs.* (1834). He was living at Abbots Bromley in 1807 (H.R.L., EMT 7–807, *b*), and at Hascombe, Surrey, in 1810: Adams, *Adams Family,* 138.
[75] W.S.L. 130/47, ff. 115–24, and agreement of 1846; *P.O. Dir. Birm., Staffs. and Worcs.* (1850); White, *Dir. Staffs.* (1851).
[76] *P.O. Dir. Staffs.* (1872); it was the home of Chas. Mottram Cox who was working the Ivy Ho. Colliery: see p. 169. By 1884 it was the home of C. J. Homer, engineer and coal master, who d. there in 1893: *Kelly's Dir. Staffs.* (1884); *Staffs. Advertiser,* 11 Nov. 1893.
[77] W. Campbell, *Street Map of Hanley, Burslem, Tunstall and Newcastle* (1912; copy in H.R.L.).
[78] O.S. Map 6″ Staffs. xii SW. (1890).
[79] Ibid. (1900).
[80] Ward, *Stoke,* 412–21; E. J. D. Warrillow, 'Shelton Old Hall' (*Staffs. Life,* i), 6; O.S. Map 6″ Staffs. xii SW. (1890, 1900).
[81] F. R. Twemlow, *The Twemlows,* 216.
[82] Ward, *Stoke,* 421–2; White, *Dir. Staffs.* (1851); *Illus.*

London News, 11 June 1853; W.S.L., D. 1788, vol. 270 (rental 1851–67).
[83] Ward, *Stoke,* 412; Shaw, *Staffs. Potteries,* 48; *Staffs. Life,* i. 6; White, *Dir. Staffs.* (1834, 1851). It was in a neglected state.
[84] Ward, *Stoke,* plate facing p. 409.
[85] *Staffs. Life,* i. 6–7; *Illus. London News,* 11 June 1853.
[86] *P.O. Dir. Staffs.* (1854 and edns. to 1876); W.S.L., D. 1788, vol. 270.
[87] O.S. Map 6″ Staffs., xviii NW. (1925).
[88] *Kelly's Dir. Staffs.* (1932); Burke, *Peerage* (1949), 231–2.
[89] Ward, *Stoke,* 386; Hargreaves, *Map of Staffs. Potteries;* S.R.O., Q/RUt 5/72; Huntbach, *Hanley,* 136.
[90] *Univ. Brit. Dir.* (1791), iv. 109.
[91] Tablet in St. John's Ch., Hanley.
[92] Parson and Bradshaw, *Dir. Staffs.* (1818); Adams, *Adams Family,* 195; Huntbach, *Hanley,* 137.
[93] Tablet in St. Peter's, Stoke; Adams, *Adams Family,* 195.   [94] *P.O. Dir. Staffs.* (1850).
[95] See p. 160.
[96] Warrillow, *Stoke,* 277, where it is also stated that the hall was a private school in the 1850's.
[97] Ibid. 358, pl. 2.   [98] *S.H.C.* vii (2), 199; x. 82.
[99] Ibid. N.S. ix. 23–24; Huntbach, *Hanley,* 109. The family seem still to have been living at Shelton in 1606: *S.H.C.* 1940, 297.   [1] Ward, *Stoke,* app. p. xlvi.
[2] S.R.O., Q/SR Mich. 1671, no. 20.
[3] W.S.L., D. 1788, P. 67, B. 11.
[4] Ibid. P. 12, B. 2; ibid. P. 61, B. 102; ibid. P. 67, B. 15; ibid. vol. 76.

1870's by Hanley Borough as the site of the new sewage disposal works, and the house was converted into two workmen's dwellings.[5]

CHURCHES. Hanley and Shelton lay within the parish of Stoke until the formation of new parishes in the area during the 19th century. The first Anglican chapel there, however, was built in 1738 in what is now Town Road. Its erection was due to the initiative of John Bourne, town clerk of Newcastle-under-Lyme, who gave £500 towards the cost and endowed the curacy; the rest of the cost was met by subscription, including £500 from Richard Hollins of Hanley, and the site was given by John Adams of Birches Head, Hollins's father-in-law.[6] The chapel seated about 400 but was enlarged by Bourne apparently in 1764, the year of his death.[7] It was a plain building with three windows on each side and a gallery round three sides of the interior.[8] By 1777 the fabric was so decayed, partly, it would seem, because of mining subsidence, that plans were then being made for rebuilding; with the continuing growth of population the chapel anyhow became too small.[9] Under an Act of 1787 it was pulled down and a new chapel, consecrated in 1790, was built a little to the east; it was to be, 'to all intents and purposes, the chapel of Hanley and Shelton'.[10] The cost, over £1,000, was defrayed by subscription and by the sale of additional pews.[11] Except for 80 free sittings, all the pews were privately owned, but there was also accommodation for 300 children in the aisles and galleries;[12] the total seating in 1851 was 1,200.[13]

The living was a curacy at first and a vicarage from 1868, but became a rectory with the creation of the parish in 1891 under the Stoke Rectory Act of 1889. The patronage was vested in a body of trustees until c. 1918 when it passed to the Bishop of Lichfield.[14] The benefice was united in 1941 with that of Holy Trinity, which was in the gift of the Crown and the bishop alternately. The bishop was then given the right of presentation for three turns out of four, and still (1959) shares the patronage with the Crown.[15] John Bourne endowed the curacy with a farm at Audley which was conveyed to the Governors of Queen Anne's Bounty and is evidently represented by two grants of £400 made from

the Bounty in 1740 and 1741.[16] Further grants were made from the Bounty in 1803 (£200), 1804 (£200), 1805 (£200), and 1810 (£300).[17]

The church of *ST. JOHN THE EVANGELIST*, on a commanding site west of the town-centre, is of brick with stone dressings and consists of a wide nave, a west tower of four stages, and a projecting chancel added in 1871.[18] The nave windows, arranged in two tiers, are slightly pointed and there are Gothic openings in the tower. The four entrances to the body of the church, one near each end of the north and south walls, are purely Classical, having stone Tuscan pilasters and pediments. Those near the east end give access to circular vestibules containing gallery staircases. The chancel of 1871[19] is built of brick in the Gothic style. The church was restored in 1885.[20] Surviving 18th-century fittings include galleries on three sides of the nave and two internal porches of panelled wood. The font dates from 1879, the organ from 1912, the reredos from 1930, and the other chancel fittings from 1935.[21] In 1880 the date-tablet of the original chapel (1738) was discovered and has been mounted in the north vestibule. The church contains several mural tablets, the earliest of which commemorates Ephraim Chatterley (d. 1811). The plate includes a silver chalice of 1750, the gift of Ralph Taylor, and a silver flagon and silver paten of 1788, the gift of the Hon. J. Fitzwilliam.[22] There are 10 bells, 8 dating from 1790 and the other 2 from the early 20th century.[23] The registers date from 1754.[24] The churchyard of the first chapel was less than an acre in extent, but land was added at the time of the rebuilding, bringing the area up to an acre.[25]

A house was built near the junction of Albion Street and Old Hall Street for the curate in 1813 with money raised by subscription and the mortgaging of the living. This was burnt down during the riots of 1842, and a new house was built soon afterwards in Old Hall Street, the rector receiving £2,000 compensation from the Hundred.[26] This site was sold to the city in 1958 for development, and the rector now lives at no. 204 Waterloo Road, Burslem, the former vicarage house of Holy Trinity, Sneyd.[27] The house in Old Hall Street, recently demolished, was a low two-story brick building with stone dressings set back in its own garden and adjacent to the Albion Hotel.

The following mission centres have been opened

[5] See p. 159. For views see Warrillow, *Stoke*, 164 (i, ii).
[6] Ward, *Stoke*, 348–9; A. Huntbach, *Hanley*, 60–61; Adams, *Adams Family*, 187, 301–2; original tablet dated 1738 in present church.
[7] Ward, *Stoke*, 349; White, *Dir. Staffs.* (1834), which incorrectly states that the chapel was built in 1764.
[8] Huntbach, *Hanley*, 61.
[9] B.M. Ch. Br. xvii. 8 and xxxi. 3; Act for rebuilding the chapel of Hanley, 27 Geo. III, c. 62.
[10] Ward, *Stoke*, 350, 358–9; Huntbach, *Hanley*, 61; Lich. Dioc. Regy., Bp.'s Reg. A, B, C, D, ff. 467a–477b; 27 Geo. III, c. lxii.
[11] Ward, *Stoke*, 358–9; the bells and organ cost another £1,000. [12] Ibid. 359.
[13] White, *Dir. Staffs.* (1851).
[14] 27 Geo. III, c. 62; Lich. Dioc. Regy., Bp.'s Reg. 28, p. 17; ibid. Reg. 31, p. 199; Reg. 33, pp. 106, 399; Reg. 34, p. 254; Reg. 35, pp. 351–2; Reg. 39, p. 112; Ward, *Stoke*, 359; Lich. Dioc. Ch. Cal. (1869, 1892, 1919); Huntbach, *Hanley*, 61, 62; see p. 187. The Act of 1889 not only created the new parish out of St. Peter's, Stoke, but also endowed it with £7,500 out of the Stoke revenues: R. Nicholls, *Stoke Ch.* 81, 90.
[15] *Lich. Dioc. Dir.* (1946, 1960).

[16] Ward, *Stoke*, 349; C. Hodgson, *An Acct. of the Augmentation of Small Livings by the Governors of the Bounty of Queen Anne* (1845), p. ccxcvii.
[17] Hodgson, *Queen Anne's Bounty*, p. ccxcvii.
[18] For early views of the church see W.S.L., *Staffs. Views*, iv, p. 267; Ward, *Stoke*, 358.
[19] Huntbach, *Hanley*, 62.
[20] *Lich. Dioc. Mag.* (1886), 13.
[21] Inscriptions in situ.
[22] S. A. Jeavons, 'Church Plate in the Archdeaconry of Stoke-on-Trent' (*Trans. Birm. Arch. Soc. lxxvii*), 72, 75.
[23] C. Lynam, *Ch. Bells Staffs.* 49; *Kelly's Dir. Staffs.* (1908); A. E. Garbett, 'Ch. Bells Staffs.' (*Trans. Old Stafford Soc. 1953–4*), 11.
[24] S. W. Hutchinson, *Archdeaconry of Stoke-on-Trent*, 129, which also states that much was burnt during the riots of 1842. There is a transcript 1789–1803 in W.S.L.
[25] Ward, *Stoke*, 359; Lich. Dioc. Regy., Bp.'s Reg. A, B, C, D, f. 473a, b. Pitt, *Staffs.* 402, describes it as enclosed with a wall and large iron gates.
[26] Huntbach, *Hanley*, 63–64; Ward, *Stoke*, 360, 586; W.S.L., H.M. Staffs. County 1, misc.; C. J. H. Homer, *Plan of Hanley and Shelton, 1857* (copy in S.R.O., Z/M/7).
[27] Local inf.

from St. John's: the Workmen's Refuge *c.* 1871–*c.* 1887,[28] possibly identifiable with the mission centre at the Workmen's Club mentioned from 1899 and closed *c.* 1928;[29] St. John's Mission Hall opened in the former Congregational chapel in Town Road in 1884 and closed *c.* 1897;[30] the Cross Street Mission Room *c.* 1887–*c.* 1947;[31] and the Boys' Club *c.* 1899–*c.* 1922.[32]

The church of *ST. MARK* in Broad Street, Shelton, was built in 1831–4 under the terms of the Stoke Rectory Act of 1827 allowing the sale of tithe and glebe belonging to Stoke Rectory for the endowment of new parishes; with a seating capacity of 2,100 it is said to be the largest parish church in the diocese.[33] The cost was met partly by subscription but in the main by a grant from the Church Building Commissioners.[34] A new parish was created out of Stoke parish in 1843.[35] The living, which has always been a rectory, was at first in the gift of Clotworthy Gillmoor, Commander R.N.,[36] but by 1857 the patronage had passed to the Revd. Charles Gillmoor.[37] By 1859 it was in the hands of the Revd. Francis Grant (rector 1845–65),[38] and in 1860 it was conveyed by Henry Birch 'and another' to the Revd. Alfred Peache, who in 1862 conveyed it to Wilberforce Heeles.[39] In 1864 Heeles 'and another' conveyed it to the Revd. S. T. Nevill (rector 1865–72 and appointed Bishop of Dunedin, New Zealand, in 1871), who mortgaged it in the same year.[40] It was held by successive rectors[41] until the resignation of the Revd. A. W. Carter (rector 1903–10), who retained it and by his will, proved in 1914, left it to the Bishop of Lichfield,[42] still the patron.[43]

The church, which was much admired at the time it was built, stands on high ground and is still a dominant feature in this part of the city. It is a stone building designed in the Gothic style by John Oates of Halifax and completed after his death by Matthew Oates and Thomas Pickersgill of York.[44] It consists of a tall aisled nave and a west tower 120 ft. high surmounted by an arcaded parapet and eight crocketted pinnacles. Originally there was a square-ended chancel, flanked by a porch and a vestry, with a triple lancet window at its east end;[45] the present apsidal chancel, designed by R. Scrivener and Sons, was added in 1866 when the church was restored.[46]

The nave is lighted on each side by seven lancet windows and has tall arcades supported on octagonal stone piers. There are galleries in the aisles and across the west end of the nave. The principal entrance to the church at its west end opens into a vaulted octagonal lobby occupying the lowest stage of the tower. This is flanked by vestibules containing the gallery staircases. The original pulpit had a sounding-board and was 'elevated on a pedestal shaft'.[47] The present pulpit was installed after the First World War.[48] There was originally one bell, dated 1833; a second was added in 1877.[49] The former rectory house in Rectory Road was built shortly before 1851;[50] Dean Woodhouse, Rector of Stoke 1814–31, had given £1,000 for this purpose.[51] The house is stone-fronted with two curvilinear gables and by the late 1950's was occupied as a social and welfare club. A smaller house had then been built for the rector on part of the site.

The following mission centres have been opened from St. Mark's: at Etruria in 1844, replaced by new parochial organization in the same year; Ashley Street School *c.* 1871–*c.* 1903;[52] St. Saviour's *c.* 1890–*c.* 1895;[53] St. Mark's Hall, Tinkersclough, *c.* 1895–*c.* 1912, evidently replaced by the present St. Mark's Mission Chapel built *c.* 1912 on an adjoining site and by the present centre at Shelton school, also opened *c.* 1912;[54] and Shelton New Mission *c.* 1908–*c.* 1912,[55] possibly replaced by Broad Street Mission Room opened *c.* 1912 and closed *c.* 1947.[56]

In 1844 services were held at Etruria, within the parish of St. Mark, Shelton, in a clubroom over the stable of the Etruria Inn.[57] A new parish was created in the same year,[58] and a chapel erected on the canal-side 'for the use of the boatmen employed on the Trent and Mersey Canal'.[59] In 1845 the bishop instructed that the schoolroom then being built should be used for services as soon as it was completed in place of 'the boatmen's chapel'.[60] The church of *ST. MATTHEW* was built in 1848–9 on a site given by the Duchy of Lancaster, the cost being met by subscription and grants from the Diocesan Church Extension Society, the Church Building Society, and the Ecclesiastical Commissioners.[61] The living, a perpetual curacy from the formation of the parish in

[28] *Lich. Dioc. Ch. Cal.* (1871, 1887).
[29] Ibid. (1899, 1928).
[30] *Lich. Dioc. Mag.* (1884), 73–74; *Lich. Dioc. Ch. Cal.* (1887, 1888, 1897); see p. 285.
[31] *Lich. Dioc. Ch. Cal.* (1888); *Lich. Dioc. Dir.* (1947–8).
[32] *Lich. Dioc. Ch. Cal.* (1900, 1922).
[33] Lich. Dioc. Regy., Bp.'s Reg. K, pp. 70–114; Ward, *Stoke*, 425; T. H. Brookes, 'St. Mark's Church, Shelton' (*Staffs. Life*, i), 107; see p. 187.
[34] Ward, *Stoke*, 425; White, *Dir. Staffs.* (1834).
[35] *Lond. Gaz.* 1843, p. 1659.
[36] Lich. Dioc. Regy., Bp.'s Reg. 30, p. 284; White, *Dir. Staffs.* (1851); *P.O. Dir. Staffs.* (1854).
[37] *Lich. Dioc. Ch. Cal.* (1857).
[38] Ibid. (1859); Hutchinson, *Archdeaconry of Stoke*, 130.
[39] Lich. Dioc. Regy., Bp.'s Reg. 38, p. 374.
[40] Ibid.; Hutchinson, op. cit. 130.
[41] Lich. Dioc. Regy., Bp.'s Reg. 38, pp. 374–6; Hutchinson, op. cit. 130. Nevill's mortgagees presented in 1875: Lich. Dioc. Regy., Bp.'s Reg. 33, p. 354.
[42] Lich. Dioc. Regy., Bp.'s Reg. 36, pp. 67–73; ibid. Reg. 38, pp. 376–83; *Lich. Dioc. Ch. Cal.* (1904, 1911, 1915).
[43] *Lich. Dioc. Dir.* (1959).
[44] M. Port, *Six Hundred New Churches*, 64; Ward, *Stoke*, 425; H. M. Colvin, *Biog. Dict. Eng. Architects*, 422; ex inf. Mr. Port (1960).
[45] Ward, *Stoke*, 424; W.S.L., Staffs. Views, viii. 170–1.

[46] Ex inf. R. Scrivener & Sons, Hanley; *Staffs. Life*, i. 107.   [47] Ward, *Stoke*, 425.
[48] Inscription in church.
[49] Lich. Dioc. Regy., Bp.'s Reg. K, p. 94; Lynam, *Ch. Bells Staffs.* 56.
[50] White, *Dir. Staffs.* (1851); O.S. Map 6" Staffs. xii SW. (1890).   [51] Ward, *Stoke*, 426.
[52] *Lich. Dioc. Ch. Cal.* (1872, 1903).
[53] Ibid. (1891, 1895).
[54] Ibid. (1896, 1912, 1913); *Hanley Jubilee Souvenir*, (1907), 38; *Lich. Dioc. Dir.* (1959); O.S. Map 6" Staffs. xii SW. (1900, 1926). The church is a brick building in what is now Clough St.   [55] *Lich. Dioc. Ch. Cal.* (1909, 1912).
[56] Ibid. (1913); Char. Com. files, which give its location as Slippery St. and state that it was founded by deed of gift dated 1915. The building was let to St. Mark's Youth Club in 1947 and sold in 1950: ibid.
[57] Warrillow, *Etruria*, 84, 138.
[58] *Lond. Gaz.* 1844, p. 1889.
[59] Lich. Dioc. Regy., Bp.'s Reg. 30, pp. 320–5, 326–7, 330; ibid. Reg. 31, pp. 8, 15; Warrillow, *Etruria*, 84. It stood between the canal bridge and the first lock towards Shelton, and the site was subsequently occupied by the Navigation Inn: ibid. 84–85.
[60] Lich. Dioc. Regy., Bp.'s Reg. 31, pp. 107–8.
[61] Ibid. Bp.'s Reg. OA, pp. 25–48; White, *Dir. Staffs.* (1851).

1844 and a vicarage from 1868, has remained in the alternate gift of the Crown and the Bishop of Lichfield.[62] Designed by Henry Ward and Son of Hanley[63] in the Early English style and built of sandstone from Caldon Low,[64] St. Matthew's consists of nave, aisles, chancel, and north-west turret. There were originally galleries on three sides.[65] The church, which was constantly subject to mining subsidence,[66] had to be restored in 1890,[67] 1894,[68] 1905,[69] and 1915,[70] and again in 1947–8 as a result of bombing.[71] By 1960 most of the walls were out of the perpendicular and had been secured by iron ties, while two of the stone arches of the nave were supported on wooden strutting. Basford Lodge on Basford Bank was at first used as the parsonage house,[72] but this was replaced by the present house c. 1857.[73]

Emmanuel Mission was opened from St. Matthew's c. 1909 and closed c. 1957.[74]

A new parish covering much of the central part of Hanley was created out of the parish of St. Mark in 1845.[75] A building known as the Museum, possibly part of the Mechanics' Institution in Frederick Street (now Gitana Street), was licensed for divine service in 1846.[76] The church of *HOLY TRINITY* was built in 1848–9 on a site at the junction of Trinity Street and Lower Foundry Street given by the Duchy of Lancaster; the cost was met by subscription and grants from various church building societies.[77] Abandoned in 1940, the church was demolished in 1952.[78] The living, at first a perpetual curacy and from 1868 a vicarage, remained in the alternate gift of the Crown and the Bishop of Lichfield[79] until the union of the benefice with that of St. John the Evangelist, Hanley, in 1941. Designed in the Romanesque style by Henry Ward and Son of Hanley,[80] the church consisted of nave, aisles, chancel, west gallery, and west tower.[81] The vicarage house was in Lichfield Street.[82]

The Church Mission Room in Paddock Street was opened from Holy Trinity c. 1888. It was replaced in 1897 by the present St. Chad's Mission Chapel, a brick building also in Paddock Street.[83]

A new parish covering the Northwood district was formed out of Stoke parish in 1845.[84] The church of *HOLY TRINITY* in Lower Mayer Street was built in 1848–9 on land given by Charles Smith of Elmhurst Hall near Lichfield.[85] The living, at first a perpetual curacy and from 1868 a vicarage, has remained in the alternate gift of the Crown and the Bishop of Lichfield.[86] The church, designed by J. Trubshaw,[87] is built of stone in the Early English style and consists of an aisled nave, a chancel, and a north-west porch surmounted by a tower with a stone broach spire. Seriously damaged by fire in February 1949, it was then restored and reopened in 1950.[88] The vicarage house, formerly at the west end of Cardwell Street,[89] has recently been moved to Cromer Road; the old house is now the Hollybush Inn.

The following mission centres have been opened from Holy Trinity, Northwood: Far Green Mission Room c. 1876–c. 1887;[90] the Iron Room, Queen's Road, c. 1891–c. 1913;[91] Peel Street Mission Room c. 1894, replaced c. 1908 by a brick chapel in the same street (now Perceval Street) which was closed c. 1946;[92] Butler Street Mission Room; and St. Matthew's, Birches Head.

The Butler Street Room was opened in 1896 for the 3,000 Welsh in Hanley Borough and had its own chaplain. It was replaced in 1899 by St. David's Chapel at the junction of Town Road and Broom Street. This had been sold by 1921 after the dispersal of the congregation.[93]

The mission chapel of *ST. MATTHEW* was an iron building in Leonard Road (now Birches Head Road) and was dedicated in 1899.[94] It was pronounced beyond repair in 1930, but plans for a new church were delayed by the Second World War and by the problem of mining subsidence on the proposed site.[95] The old church was demolished in 1956 to make way for the present church built in 1958–9;

[62] Lich. Dioc. Regy., Bp.'s Reg. 31, p. 15; ibid. Reg. 35, p. 177; Reg. 37, p. 413; *Lich. Dioc. Ch. Cal.* (1857, 1869); *Lich. Dioc. Dir.* (1959).
[63] White, *Dir. Staffs.* (1851).
[64] Warrillow, *Etruria*, 85.
[65] Lich. Dioc. Regy., Bp.'s Reg. OA, p. 33.
[66] Warrillow, *Etruria*, 91–92, 95; *Lich. Dioc. Mag.* (1893), 179, stating that the building had been declared unsavable.
[67] *Kelly's Dir. Staffs.* (1892).
[68] Ibid. (1896); £350 was then contributed towards the cost by the Duchy of Lancaster and the Shelton Iron, Steel and Coal Co.
[69] Ibid. (1908).   [70] Ibid. (1924).
[71] Warrillow, *Etruria*, 95–97.
[72] Ibid. 85.
[73] Lich. Dioc. Regy., Bp.'s Reg. P, p. 551.
[74] *Lich. Dioc. Ch. Cal.* (1910); *Lich. Dioc. Dir.* (1958).
[75] *Lond. Gaz.* 1845, p. 2533.
[76] Lich. Dioc. Regy., Bp.'s Reg. 31, 113; see p. 170.
[77] Lich. Dioc. Regy., Bp.'s Reg. OA, pp. 201–18; White, *Dir. Staffs.* (1851).
[78] Ex inf. the Church Commrs. (1959); ex inf. the Potteries Demolition Co., Hanley (1959). The site is now (1960) a car park.
[79] Lich. Dioc. Regy., Bp.'s Reg. 31, p. 35; ibid. Reg. 32, pp. 230, 274; Reg. 34, p. 224; Reg. 37, p. 429; Reg. 39, p. 492; *Lich. Dioc. Ch. Cal.* (1857, 1869); *Lich. Dioc. Dir.* (1938).
[80] White, *Dir. Staffs.* (1851).
[81] Lich. Dioc. Regy., Bp.'s Reg. OA, p. 209.
[82] O.S. Map 1/500 Staffs. xvi. 4. 2 (1866); *Kelly's Dir. Staffs.* (1932). In 1851 the incumbent was living at Northwood: White, *Dir. Staffs.* (1851).
[83] *Lich. Dioc. Ch. Cal.* (1889, 1896, 1897); *Lich. Dioc.*

Mag. (1897), 41; Lich. Dioc. Regy., Bp.'s Reg. 35, p. 426; foundation stone dated 1896.
[84] *Lond. Gaz.* 1845, p. 2535.
[85] Lich. Dioc. Regy., Bp.'s Reg. OA, pp. 62–85; C. Hodgson, *An Acct. of the Augmentation of Small Livings by the Governors of the Bounty of Queen Anne* (1845), pp. xxx, xxxix of 1856 supplement.
[86] Lich. Dioc. Regy., Bp.'s Reg. 31, pp. 35 (where the incumbent is called a minister or perpetual curate), 154; Reg. 33, p. 386; Reg. 35, p. 211; *Lich. Dioc. Ch. Cal.* (1857, where there is mention only of an incumbent, 1862, 1869); *Lich. Dioc. Dir.* (1959).
[87] Port, *Six Hundred New Churches*, 64.
[88] Tablet *in situ*.
[89] O.S. Map 1/500 Staffs. xi. 16. 13 (1866). The house still (1960) stands.
[90] *Lich. Dioc. Ch. Cal.* (1877, 1887).
[91] Ibid. (1892, 1913).
[92] Ibid. (1895); *Lich. Dioc. Dir.* (1946); date on foundation stone. John Walker of Hanley by will proved 1913 left £20 to the mission to provide a lay reader: Char. Com. files. It was also known as the Vincent St. Mission from the name of the street to the W. of Perceval St. By 1959 it was used as a furniture store.
[93] Lich. Dioc. Regy., Bp.'s Reg. 35, pp. 410–11; ibid. Reg. 36, pp. 23–24; Reg. 37, p. 27; Reg. U, pp. 244–51; Char. Com. files. There was a Welsh curate attached to Holy Trinity, Northwood, by 1865: *Lich. Dioc. Ch. Cal.* (1865).
[94] *Lich. Dioc. Mag.* (1899), 141–2; Lich. Dioc. Regy., Bp.'s Reg. 36, p. 40 (licence, 1900).
[95] *St. Matthew's Appeal Leaflet* (copy among W.S.L. pamphs. *sub* Hanley); Char. Com. files; *Kelly's Dir. Staffs.* (1940); *Staffs. Weekly Sentinel*, 20 July 1956.

services in the meantime were held in the church hall in Addison Street.[96] In 1954 the area served by St. Matthew's was made an ecclesiastical district.[97] The new church, designed by W. H. Homer of Jennings, Homer and Lynch of Brierley Hill,[98] is built of stone and yellow brick in a contemporary style. On the north side a Lady Chapel forms a short aisle and there is a small tower containing a bell. There are continuous clerestory windows, diagonally set windows lighting the chancel, and a wide covered approach on the south side. The vicarage house is opposite.

A new parish covering the Wellington district was formed out of Stoke parish in 1845[99] and services were held in a temporary church in Gate Street from 1848.[1] The church of *ST. LUKE* was built in 1853-4 by subscription and grants from various church building societies.[2] The living, at first a perpetual curacy and from 1868 a vicarage, has remained in the alternate gift of the Crown and the Bishop of Lichfield.[3] The stone church in the Gothic style, consisting of nave, north aisle, south transept, chancel, west gallery, and west turret, was designed by Henry Ward and Son of Hanley.[4] The first parsonage house was built in Lichfield Street in 1858 but was sold in 1935 when the present house near the church was bought.[5] Extensive restoration of the church was carried out in 1948-51.[6]

The following mission centres have been opened from St. Luke's: Joiner's Square Mission Room *c.* 1870, the predecessor of the present parish church of All Saints, Leek Road; Oldham Street Schools *c.* 1908, transferred to All Saints district *c.* 1911 and closed *c.* 1928;[7] and the mission chapel of St. Michael and All Angels. This is a brick building in Bucknall Road opened *c.* 1912. It was closed in 1946 despite the refusal of many of the congregation to acquiesce and attend St. Luke's.[8] The building is now (1959) occupied as a physical training centre.

A mission room was established at Joiner's Square in the parish of St. Luke, Wellington, *c.* 1870[9] and replaced by All Saints Mission Chapel in Leek Road in 1890.[10] A mission district was assigned to it *c.* 1906.[11] A Sunday-school hall nearby was licensed for divine service in 1911 pending the completion of the church of *ALL SAINTS* on an adjoining site.[12]

This church, begun in 1911, was completed in 1913,[13] and a new parish of All Saints was created in the same year out of the parishes of St. Luke, Wellington, and St. Jude, Shelton.[14] The vicarage has remained in the gift of the Bishop of Lichfield.[15] The church was designed by Gerald Horsley[16] in a Gothic style and is built of brick with stone dressings. It consists of clerestoried nave, north aisle, and chancel flanked by an organ chamber and a side chapel; there is an open-air pulpit, now (1960) dilapidated, at the west end. Structural provision was made for a south aisle but this addition was not carried out. The vicarage house is nearby in Leek Road.

The Sunday-school hall continued to be used as a mission room until *c.* 1945.[17]

The church of *ST. JUDE* in Beresford Road, Shelton, was opened as a mission chapel in Stoke parish. It was built to the designs of R. Scrivener and Sons, Hanley, in 1879-80 and enlarged by the addition of aisles in 1883 and 1885.[18] A new parish of St. Jude was created in 1895, and an endowment of £300 was granted out of the funds of Stoke rectory, with a further £30 a year in 1897.[19] A site for a new church and parsonage house in Victoria Road (now College Road) between Beresford and Seaford Streets was bought in 1897,[20] and the present church of St. Jude was built in 1899-1901.[21] The cost was met by grants from the Incorporated Church Building Society and the Diocesan Church Extension Society and by subscriptions.[22] The vicarage has remained in the gift of the Bishop of Lichfield.[23] The church, a building of brick with stone dressings designed in the Gothic style by R. Scrivener and Sons, consists of a nave, wide-aisled and clerestoried, with vestibules and a vestry across its west end, and a baptistery at the west end of the south aisle. The chancel is flanked by an organ chamber and a side chapel. Externally there are two west turrets, one of which contains a bell. The former mission church has been used as Shelton Repertory Theatre since the 1930's.[24]

LOCAL GOVERNMENT AND PUBLIC SERVICES.[25] In matters of parish government the townships of Hanley and Shelton lay within the ancient

[96] Ex inf. the minister (1959); *St. Matthew's Appeal Leaflet.*
[97] Ex inf. the minister.
[98] Ex inf. the minister.
[99] *Lond. Gaz.* 1845, p. 2535.
[1] *Centenary Handbk.: Ch. of St. Luke* (copy in H.R.L.); White, *Dir. Staffs.* (1851).
[2] Lich. Dioc. Regy., Bp.'s Reg. P, pp. 77-93.
[3] Ibid. Reg. 31, p. 73; Reg. 32, pp. 89-90; Reg. 39, pp. 107, 500; *Lich. Dioc. Ch. Cal.* (1857, 1869); *Lich. Dioc. Dir.* (1959).
[4] Port, *Six Hundred New Chs.* 66. The iron gates and railings in front of the church are said to have come from Bank House: W. Scarratt, *Old Times in the Potteries*, 146; see p. 149.
[5] *St. Luke's, Wellington: Centenary Yr. Bk. 1854-1954* (copy in H.R.L.).
[6] *Centenary Handbk.: Ch. of St. Luke*; stone *in situ.*
[7] *Lich. Dioc. Ch. Cal.* (1909, 1912, 1928).
[8] W. Campbell, *Street Map of Hanley, Burslem, Tunstall, and Newcastle* (1912; copy in H.R.L.); *Lich. Dioc. Ch. Cal.* (1914); *Staffs. Sentinel*, 15, 18, 20, 25 Nov. 1946.
[9] *Lich. Dioc. Ch. Cal.* (1871). It was called East Vale Mission Room in 1881 (ibid. 1881) and Eastwood Vale Mission in 1882: ibid. 1882.
[10] Lich. Dioc. Regy., Bp.'s Reg. T, pp. 373-81; O.S. Map 6″ Staffs. xviii NW. (1900).

[11] *Lich. Dioc. Ch. Cal.* (1907).
[12] Lich. Dioc. Regy., Bp.'s Reg. 37, pp. 177-8; *Kelly's Dir. Staffs.* (1912).
[13] *Kelly's Dir. Staffs.* (1916); date on foundation stone.
[14] *Lich. Dioc. Dir.* (1955-6), 132.
[15] *Lich. Dioc. Ch. Cal.* (1913); *Lich. Dioc. Dir.* (1959), where it is called a perpetual curacy.
[16] *Collins Guide to Eng. Par. Churches*, ed. J. Betjeman, 338.
[17] *Lich. Dioc. Dir.* (1946).
[18] Tablet in present church; Lich. Dioc. Regy., Bp.'s Reg. 34, pp. 136-7; *Lich. Dioc. Mag.* (Apr. 1880), 8; ibid. (1884), 11; ibid. (1885), 163, 164; ibid. (1897), 166.
[19] Lich. Dioc. Regy., Bp.'s Reg. U, pp. 116, 193.
[20] Ibid. p. 221; *Lich. Dioc. Mag.* (1897), 166. The house is in Seaford Street and lies to the east of the church.
[21] *Lich. Dioc. Mag.* (1899), 141; ibid. (1901), 157; Lich. Dioc. Regy., Bp.'s Reg. U, pp. 479-83.
[22] Lich. Dioc. Regy., Bp.'s Reg. U, p. 480.
[23] *Lich. Dioc. Ch. Cal.* (1896), where it is called a perpetual curacy; *Lich. Dioc. Dir.* (1959).
[24] *Kelly's Dir. Staffs.* (1900); ex inf. R. Scrivener and Sons; see p. 172.
[25] Since this account was written, minutes of the Improvement Commrs. 1847-58 and an extensive set of borough minutes from 1857 onwards have been found; they are now available at H.R.L.

parish of Stoke-upon-Trent and together formed the Shelton quarter of that parish.[26] Manorially Hanley and Shelton formed part of Newcastle manor.[27]

The first move towards a form of government better suited to the needs of the growing population was the establishment of a market, apparently in 1776; a body of trustees was set up in 1791 and given statutory authority by Act of Parliament in 1813,[28] the first Act concerned with local government in the Potteries. Of wider importance was the establishment of a body of Improvement Commissioners with policing and lighting powers in 1825, when a similar body was set up for Burslem also. Those inhabitants who satisfied a certain property qualification were, as at Burslem, automatically commissioners, and membership of the board was also extended to the officiating minister or ministers, representatives of the county justices, the Chancellor of the Duchy of Lancaster, and the Steward of Newcastle manor. The commissioners were empowered to levy a watching and lighting rate of 6d. in the £ on property worth between £4 and £6 a year, 9d. on property worth up to £8, and 1s. on property of higher value; property under £4, the North Staffordshire Infirmary, the market, and the free schools were exempt, and a graduated rebate was allowed for those inhabitants who were inadequately served by the public lamps. The whole of Hanley was covered by the Act, but certain parts of Shelton, namely Cobridge, Etruria, much of Josiah Wedgwood's land, and the Stoke glebe lands in the area later occupied by Stoke station, were exempted; these areas were to be included only if the commissioners and 'the major part in annual value' there agreed. The commissioners were empowered to appoint a chief bailiff, constables, and watchmen.[29] In 1828 the property qualification was modified and more elaborate provision made for the punishing of certain specified nuisances and obstructions, including the careless driving of carriages. Meetings of the inhabitants and of the commissioners were presided over by the chief bailiff.[30]

From this organization Hanley and Shelton in 1857 moved directly to borough status. The whole area, except the Stoke glebe lands, was then incorporated as the Borough of Hanley. The borough was divided into three wards, North, South, and East, with 9 councillors each for the North and East

wards and 6 for the South, and 2 aldermen for each ward.[31] In 1859, under the Local Government Act of the previous year, the mayor and corporation became the Hanley Local Board of Health,[32] to which the management of the market was transferred from the trustees in 1862.[33] In 1889 Hanley became a county borough.[34] The three wards were reorganized as eight in 1895—Etruria, Hope, Providence, Northwood, Wellington, Eastwood, Park, and Cauldon—with three councillors and an alderman each.[35] By at least 1886 the following committees had been set up: Watch; Markets; Sanitary; General Purposes; Town Hall; Works; Finance; Burial Board; Free Library.[36] There were 25 committees by the last year of the borough's existence, including an education committee which met for the first time in 1903.[37] The rateable value of the borough was £236,085 in 1900-1 and £247,652 in 1909-10.[38] Hanley Borough formed 7 of the 26 wards in the new county borough of Stoke-on-Trent in 1910 with a representation of 21 councillors and 7 aldermen.[39]

The first town hall, as distinct from the market halls, was opened in 1845 in Fountain Square on the site of the old butter market.[40] It was replaced in the mid-1880's when the Queen's Hotel in Albion Street, opened in 1869, was adapted and became the town hall;[41] this new hall still houses certain municipal offices. The town hall of 1845 was taken over by Lloyds Bank in 1886 and rebuilt in 1936.[42] The Victoria Hall was added at the rear of the new town hall in 1887-8.[43] A council chamber designed by R. Scrivener and Sons and Joseph Lobley, the borough surveyor, was used for the first time in March 1910, and the mayor then stated that it had been built in the hope that it would be used as the council chamber of the new county borough of Stoke, a hope which was not fulfilled.[44]

The mayoral chain was presented by Herbert Keeling of Shelton Hall in 1887 to commemorate Queen Victoria's Golden Jubilee.[45] Herbert Coates, mayor 1901-2, presented the mayoral robes and hat which he had worn at the coronation of Edward VII for use by his successors.[46]

By 1335 Hanley and Shelton were each represented at the Newcastle manor court leet by two frankpledges,[47] and by this period Hanley formed a constablewick with Fenton Vivian and Longton[48] while Shelton lay within Penkhull constablewick.[49]

---

[26] Ward, *Stoke*, 467-8. Shelton being the larger in the early 18th century, it then served the offices of churchwarden and overseer of the poor twice for every once that Hanley served: W.S.L., D. 1788, P. 67, B. 11.

[27] See pp. 151, 184-5.   [28] See p. 162.

[29] 6 Geo. IV, c. 73 (local and personal). For the Burslem Act see p. 125.

[30] 9 Geo. IV, c. 28 (local and personal).

[31] H.R.L., printed copy of the Charter of Incorporation of Hanley and Shelton 1857; *Staffs. Advertiser*, 22 Aug., 5 Sept 1857; *P.O. Dir. Staffs.* (1860). By an oversight the charter did not mention the exclusion of the Stoke glebe land in Shelton, and this area had to be excluded by a special Act: Act to amend the charter, 20 & 21 Vic. c. 10 (local and personal).

[32] *Lond. Gaz.* 1859, p. 415; *Staffs. Advertiser*, 11 May 1907; 21 & 22 Vic., c. 25. The execution of this Act was vested in local boards with powers for regulating sewerage, scavenging, buildings, highways, streets, markets, and water-supply; boroughs were empowered to adopt the Act.

[33] Act to confirm provisional orders under the Local Govt. Act, 25 & 26 Vic. c. 25 (local); see p. 162.

[34] K. D. Miller, *Brief Chronology of Local Govt. in Stoke-on-Trent* (1st edn.), 12-18; Local Govt. Act 1888, 51 & 52

Vic. c. 41; see p. 254.   [35] *Kelly's Dir. Staffs.* (1896).

[36] *Hanley Boro. Year Bk. 1886-7* (copy in H.R.L.).

[37] Ibid. *1903-4, 1909-10*.

[38] Ibid. *1900-1, 1909-10*. The rateable value for the general district rate was £229,416 in 1900-1 and £241,262 in 1909-10: ibid.

[39] *Stoke Counc. Year Bk.* (1915).

[40] *Ancient Corp. of Hanley*, ed. W. D. Spanton, 109; see p. 162. For a description see p. 149.

[41] *Ancient Corp. Hanley*, 111; *Staffs. Advertiser*, 24 Dec. 1869, 10 July 1886; *Staffs. Sentinel*, 21 May 1927; Ward, *Stoke*, 383. For a description of the building see p. 149.

[42] Warrillow, *Stoke*, 223.

[43] *Staffs. Advertiser*, 18 May 1907; ticket of admission to laying of foundation stone 1887 and programme of opening ceremony 1888 (copies in H.R.L.).

[44] *Staffs. Advertiser*, 12 Mar. 1910; see p. 259.

[45] T. Pape, 'Early Armorials of the Pottery Towns', *Cox's Potteries Annual* (1925), 21, 23.

[46] *Hanley Boro. Year Bk. 1903-4*, 8, 9.

[47] D.L. 30/228/1.

[48] *S.H.C.* x (1), 93-94; ibid. 1921, 164. The constablewick also included Lane End, Botteslow, and Normacot Grange: ibid.   [49] See p. 195.

By 1558 Hanley was represented at the court leet by one frankpledge and Shelton by two.[50]

The powers of the commissioners set up in 1825 were largely concerned with improved policing of the area and included the appointment of a chief bailiff, a head constable, assistant constables, and watchmen.[51] The old manorial system, however, was still sufficiently alive for the head constable and two assistants to be sworn at the October meeting of the Newcastle manor court in 1829.[52] There was a lock-up, the 'stonnus', adjoining the market hall of 1819 in Fountain Square, and the stocks stood outside.[53] By 1834 the police force consisted of a head constable, three acting constables, and six watchmen; the police office was in Trinity Street, and the stocks had by then been moved there.[54] After the Chartist riots of 1842 the local force was replaced by a body of county police, comprising a superintendent, an inspector, and 20 men by 1851, and when the new town hall in Fountain Square was opened in 1845 the police station was moved there.[55] A borough force was established in 1870, while the members of the fire brigade were required to act as special constables when necessary.[56] The station was moved in 1884 to the new town hall in Albion Street[57] where it has remained.

A stipendiary magistrate was appointed for the Potteries area in 1839 and held weekly sessions at Hanley or Shelton which together formed one of the six rating districts established to support the new system.[58] The Hanley County Court District established in 1847 originally covered the whole of the Potteries with the court meeting at Hanley Town Hall.[59] A commission of the peace was granted in 1859, and in 1880 a court of Quarter Sessions was set up.[60]

PUBLIC HEALTH. In the mid-19th century the state of public health in Hanley and Shelton was considered to be better than that in other parts of the Potteries because of the lofty situation of much of the area.[61] Even so conditions were bad enough. Little advantage was taken of the possibilities of the situation for drainage purposes. There was only one sewer worth the name, that running from the town hall in Fountain Square down to the Fowlea Brook, and in 1849 one doctor described the area as 'surrounded by a moat filled with decomposing filth'. Privies were few and filthy and there was little street cleaning. The burial ground attached to St. John's Church had been overcrowded for years (the nearby Tabernacle ground also was full), and in addition it

was 'a receptacle for all manner of nuisances' by day and a resort of prostitutes and thieves by night. Badly ventilated houses and unhealthy courts made matters worse. Thus the Chapel Fields area was fever-ridden and there was 'not an old inhabitant in the neighbourhood'. Far Green, Chell Street, and the area around Bryan Street suffered from open ditches behind the houses. The Marsh Street area was disease-ridden. The 'Royal' group of streets, so-called from their high-sounding names, between Broad Street and Cannon Street, were noted for poverty, filth, and crime. The streets north of St. Mark's were also very unhealthy. Etruria suffered from a low-lying situation, a ditch at the back of the houses on one side of the main street, and lack of drainage, while in Mill Street (now Etruria Road) the side-walks and channels were in a very poor state and there were open middens in the courts draining into the street passage. A further nuisance in the Mill Street area was caused by the calcining of ironstone in open heaps near the road, while the practice of firing chimneys in the Hanley district generally was noted as another nuisance.

Although the Shelton highway board built some new sewers early in the 1850's,[62] it was some years before the problem of sewage disposal was tackled in a thoroughgoing manner. In the meantime the use of the Fowlea Brook for this purpose by Hanley Borough, as also by Burslem and Tunstall, brought repeated complaints from Stoke, including the threat of legal proceedings in 1867.[63] A meeting of representatives from the Pottery towns and Newcastle organized by the Mayor of Hanley in 1870 to discuss possible solutions to the sewage problem failed to achieve anything.[64] In the late 1870's Hanley constructed a sewage-disposal works in Leek Road on the site of Trent Hay farm, the farmhouse being converted into two workmen's dwellings. Pollution of the Trent and the Fowlea Brook remained a problem, however, but extensions to the works were completed in 1907.[65] The replacement of privies by water-closets was in progress by 1887 when there were 374 of the latter in use, but in 1900 there were still 1,096 privies and 2,695 Rochdale pans in the borough. The rate of replacement, however, increased considerably during the next few years.[66]

Burials at Holy Trinity, Northwood, at St. John's, Hanley, at St. Matthew's, Etruria, and at Hope, Bethesda, Brunswick, and Tabernacle chapels were restricted from 1856, and at St. Mark's, Shelton, from 1857; in 1866 further restrictions were imposed

[50] D.L. 30/228/5.
[51] 6 Geo. IV, c. 73 (local and personal).
[52] Staffs. Advertiser, 10 Oct. 1829. This lists the constables, &c. for various parts of the manor who were 'sworn in or appointed'.
[53] Ward, Stoke, 362; Hanley Jubilee Souvenir (1907), 25–26, 47. Warrillow, Stoke, 386, states that the lock-up was established in 1790 and that the stocks formerly stood in front of St. John's Church.
[54] White, Dir. Staffs. (1834); Huntbach, Hanley, 14, 19.
[55] P.O. Dir. Staffs. (1854), which, however, wrongly gives the date of the riots as 1849; White, Dir. Staffs. (1851); Huntbach, Hanley, 14. For an acct. of the riots see Ward, Stoke, 584–9.
[56] Staffs. Advertiser, 11 May 1907; P.O. Dir. Staffs. (1872). The Hanley police themselves eventually became the fire brigade until the creation of a volunteer force in 1913: see pp. 161, 267.
[57] Kelly's Dir. Staffs. (1884).
[58] Act for more effectual execution of office of J.P., 2 and 3 Vic., c. 15.

[59] Lond. Gaz. 1847, p. 1012; White, Dir. Staffs. (1851).
[60] Staffs. Advertiser, 11 May 1907. The boro. court min. bks. 1864–6 and 1868–1915 and the registers of the court of summary jurisdiction 1880, 1887–8, 1893–4, and 1901 survive in S.R.O., D. 26/P/1–53.
[61] R. Rawlinson, Rep. to Bd. of Health on Stoke Par. (1850; copy in H.R.L.), on which the rest of this paragraph is based.
[62] Ibid. 45; ibid. (1853), 7.
[63] H.R.L., Stoke Commrs.' Mins. 1865–74, pp. 4, 8, 78, 149.
[64] Ibid. pp. 155–6, 159, 162–3.
[65] W. H. Makepeace, Hanley's Sewage Disposal Works (copy with the City Sewage Engineer, 1959); J. Lobley, Hanley Sewage Works (1878; copy in H.R.L. Pamphs., vol. 45); Rep. of Meeting of Assoc. of Municipal and Sanitary Engineers and Surveyors at Hanley, 1881 (copy in H.R.L. Pamphs., vol. 45); Warrillow, Stoke, 189; H.R.L., Stoke Boro. Mins. 1893–5, p. 34; 1895–8, p. 442; 1898–1900, pp. 531, 532; 1903–5, pp. 563–4.
[66] Hanley M.O.H. Reps. 1887, 1898–1907.

on all of these and also on Providence Chapel.[67] The borough council, in whom burial powers were vested in 1858,[68] opened a cemetery on 20 acres of the Shelton Hall estate on the west side of Stoke Road in 1860.[69] A further 7 acres was added in 1876, and early in the 20th century the area was increased to 30 acres.[70]

In 1849 the Eastwood Mill Company opened the Eastwood Baths, consisting of swimming and private baths and still in operation in 1851; there were also medical baths in Slack's Lane in 1851, run by a 'medical galvanizer'.[71] A public swimming bath, with private baths attached, was built in 1853–4 near Macaroni Bridge on the Trent and Mersey Canal about a quarter of a mile north of Etruria, water being supplied from the Fowlea Brook; the bath was still open in 1858.[72] The present public baths in Lichfield Street were built in 1873.[73]

A 'house of recovery' for the poor, consisting of a dispensary and a reception ward and supported by voluntary contributions, was built in 1803–4 at Etruria Vale north of the Bedford Street canal bridge; of brick and three stories high, it was designed by David Bellhouse of Manchester.[74] However, the site, of less than 2 acres, was not sufficient for the extensions which soon became necessary, and a new two-story building, known as the North Staffordshire Infirmary and designed by Joseph Potter of Lichfield, was erected in 1816–19 on 6 acres of land called Wood Hills, rising ground on the east side of Etruria Vale Road opposite the site of the later Etruria Park.[75] Fever wards were added in 1828–9, largely with the proceeds of a bazaar held at Newcastle, and wards for burns in 1852; a north wing was built in 1855 with money given by Charles Keeling of The White House, Newcastle.[76] The old infirmary building meanwhile remained standing until after its purchase in 1867 by the British Gaslight Company.[77] With the development of the ironworks and coal mines near the second building and the increasing danger from subsidence the area became unsuitable for a hospital, and in 1869 the infirmary was moved to Hartshill.[78] The second building was demolished soon afterwards, and new streets of cottages were built over the site.[79]

The Church and Institute for the Deaf and Dumb in Wellesley Street, Shelton, the headquarters of the North Staffordshire Deaf and Dumb Society, was built in 1936 and extended in 1949.[80]

PUBLIC SERVICES. Before 1820 Hanley's water-supply, whether fetched in a pitcher or bought from a higgler at ½d. a bucket, came chiefly from a spring called Woodwall Well near the present Well Street; this spring with a pump added was still in use in the 1840's, but the supply was by then 'impaired by recent robberies committed on its hidden streams'.[81] There was also a piped spring at the gasworks in Shelton where water was available free until c. 1875 when the spring ceased to flow.[82] In 1820 John Smith started his waterworks on a site next to the later Ivy House Paper Mill, pumping water from a disused colliery to a reservoir on the hill top above the town and supplying water not only to Hanley and Shelton but also to Burslem.[83] The supply, however, was not only of poor quality but also inadequate. In 1844 only 1,200 of the 4,700 houses in Hanley had water, which was anyhow available only three days a week.[84] Other springs in the Hanley area included one off Hillchurch Street, another north of the market place, Bryans Well excavated c. 1835 in the Bryan Street area, a spring below Etruria Woods, Washerwall Well, and a spring on Botteslow Farm where children were still bathed in the 1860's, because of the alleged curative properties of the water.[85] The Staffordshire Potteries Waterworks Company, formed in 1847, began to supply Hanley in 1849, and Smith was then bought out.[86] The company's first office was in Lamb Street, Hanley; this was replaced in 1858 by an office in Albion Street which was extended to its present size in 1889 by the acquisition of the bank building next door.[87]

The first gasworks in the district was built in 1825 between Lower Bedford Street and the Trent and Mersey Canal by the British Gaslight Company, a London concern established in 1824.[88] The works at first supplied gas to Hanley, Stoke, Burslem, Wolstanton (including Tunstall), and Norton-in-the-Moors, but the high prices charged led to the establishment of rival companies in the Potteries including one in Hanley, the Hanley Gas Consumers Company, formed in 1864. This, however, was wound up in the following year since the British Gaslight Company reduced its charges when threatened with competition from the new company. The campaign between these two companies found the town clerk, who was also legal adviser to the British Gaslight Company, and the borough surveyor on opposite sides. During an acrimonious council meeting in 1865 the clerk was accused of partiality by Clement Wedgwood who carried a motion in favour of the new Hanley company. In the same

[67] *Lond. Gaz.* 1856, p. 2904; 1865, p. 127.
[68] Ibid. 1865, pp. 127, 1880. [69] Ibid. 1858, p. 1842.
[70] *Ancient Corp. of Hanley*, 110; Lich. Dioc. Regy., Bp.'s Reg. Q, pp. 378–81; *Kelly's Dir. Staffs.* (1908).
[71] White, *Dir. Staffs.* (1851); Warrillow, *Stoke*, 372.
[72] Warrillow, *Stoke*, 372.   [73] Date on building.
[74] R. Hordley, *N. Staffs. Infirmary and Eye Hospital 1802–1902*, 8, 9 (copy in H.R.L.); Warrillow, *Etruria*, 153, 224–6, 232; Ward, *Stoke*, 390–2; Hargreaves, *Map of Staffs. Potteries*.
[75] Hordley, *N. Staffs. Infirmary*, 9–12; Warrillow, *Etruria*, 153, 226–30. A copy of the statutes of the infirmary, which describe it as estab. in 1815, is in W.S.L. Pamphlets (vol. v, no. 4).
[76] *Staffs. Advertiser*, 24 May, 22 Nov. 1828; Hordley, *N. Staffs. Infirmary*, 13, 14; Ward, *Stoke*, 390; Warrillow, *Etruria*, 230.
[77] Warrillow, *Etruria*, 156, 229; Ward, *Stoke*, 391–2.
[78] Hordley, *N. Staffs. Infirmary*, 15–17, 38; Warrillow, *Etruria*, 230–1; see pp. 169–70, 197. The move to Harts-

hill was originally planned in 1862 but opposition from subscribers in the northern part of the Potteries to the choice of a site in the south delayed the move until 1866: Hordley, op. cit. 22–23.
[79] Warrillow, *Etruria*, 228, 231; see p. 145. For a description of the building see p. 150.
[80] *The Deaf and Dumb in N. Staffs.* (copy in H.R.L.). A Roman Catholic chapel was opened there in 1957: *Hear Here* (Nov. 1957), 8 (copy in H.R.L.).
[81] Ward, *Stoke*, 378; *Pure and Wholesome Water for 100 Years, 1849–1949*, 7 (copy in H.R.L.).
[82] *Pure and Wholesome Water*, 8.
[83] Ibid. 7; Ward, *Stoke*, 377–8; Shaw, *Staffs. Potteries*, 42; Hargreaves, *Map of Staffs. Potteries*.
[84] Ward, *Stoke*, 378; *Pure and Wholesome Water*, 7.
[85] Warrillow, *Stoke*, 161.
[86] *Pure and Wholesome Water*, 12.
[87] Ibid. 11, 13.
[88] Warrillow, *Etruria*, 151–4; Ward, *Stoke*, 379–80; Hargreaves, *Map of Staffs. Potteries*.

year it was stated that some 4,000 of Hanley's 7,200 houses had no gas, and that, while the average town had one street lamp for every 60 inhabitants, Hanley had only one for every 107.[89] In 1866 restrictions were imposed on the British Gaslight Company in the public interest by Act of Parliament, and the maximum price of its gas was fixed at 3s. 6d. per 1,000 cubic feet;[90] in 1863, at the beginning of the campaign, the company had reduced its domestic charge from 4s. 6d. to 4s. 3d.[91] An Act of 1880 allowing the company to expand the works at Shelton imposed further restrictions on its activities,[92] while in 1895 Hanley Borough was empowered to appoint an auditor of the company's accounts and to inspect the quality of the gas supplied.[93] When the infirmary building, on the opposite side of Lower Bedford Street from the company's works, became vacant in 1867, the company bought it with the surrounding land and demolished it; new apparatus was erected there along with a new building, Gas House, still (1959) standing though unoccupied, and this was used as offices and the manager's house.[94] By 1900 the area had become affected by mining subsidence, and in that year the company bought land west of the Trent and Mersey Canal, opening the first part of the present works there in 1904.[95] The undertaking, which Hanley Borough had unsuccessfully tried to buy in 1877,[96] was sold to the Stoke-on-Trent Corporation in 1922 and officially inaugurated as the central works for the city by Stanley Baldwin in 1928.[97] The works has grown to be one of the largest in the country, covering an area of over 37 acres from Etruria Station to the Bedford Street canal bridge.[98] The two waterless gas-holders, one built before the Second World War and the other in 1946–9,[99] are a prominent feature of the landscape in this part of the city.

Hanley Borough opened its electricity works, the first in the Potteries, in the specially built Bethesda Road, north of Hanley Park, in 1894.[1] The undertaking passed in 1910 to the new county borough of Stoke.[2]

Hanley had its own fire brigade by 1853.[3] With the establishment of the borough police force in 1870 the members of the brigade had to act as special constables when required, and this probably explains why by 1907 the police themselves formed the fire brigade.[4] A private brigade belonging to the Wedgwood factory at Etruria and consisting of a captain and 10 men was also available to the public; its manual engine, installed in 1783, was used in 1915 to fight a fire at the works until the arrival of the brigades from Hanley and Stoke.[5]

By 1817 Hanley vestry was appointing two highway surveyors to maintain its roads and Shelton too had its own surveyors.[6] In 1823, however, a salaried standing surveyor for both Hanley and Shelton was appointed, in addition to the usual surveyors, by a joint meeting of the two townships; a committee of three was also appointed for each township to assist the surveyors.[7] In 1824 there was a return, at any rate in Hanley, to the former system of two elected surveyors only.[8] In 1826 there was again a salaried surveyor for the two townships, and in 1827 Hanley at least had its own salaried surveyor.[9] By 1829 the old system had once more been restored in Hanley,[10] but from 1832 a salaried overseer was again appointed there each year.[11] In 1837, under the Highways Act of 1835, the inhabitants of Hanley set up a board of repairs of eleven elected members[12] which appointed a salaried surveyor (called assistant surveyor from 1839).[13] A survey of the roads of Hanley, carried out immediately, revealed them as in a generally bad state.[14] A salaried rate collector, who also acted as clerk, was appointed in 1840.[15] Shelton also had its own board of repairs by 1839,[16] and in the middle of the century its 20 members were said to be mainly working men.[17] It was stated in 1849 that in most of the streets in Hanley and Shelton the crown of the road was macadamized with Macclesfield stone while the pavements were of blue brick.[18] The control of the highways passed to the borough council as the Hanley Local Board under the Act of 1858.[19] In 1879 the council requested the county justices to declare Hope Street, Stafford Street, Trinity Street, Brunswick Street, Piccadilly, Clough Street, and Sun Street main roads,[20] and thus to take over responsibility for them.

[89] Warrillow, *Etruria*, 152, 154, 155; White, *Dir. Staffs.* (1851); H.R.L., scrapbk. relating to Hanley Boro.'s gas transactions; see p. 128.

[90] 29 & 30 Vic. c. 119 (local and personal).

[91] *Staffs. Sentinel*, 21 Nov. 1863, which also pointed out that the equivalent charge in Liverpool was 3s. 5d., in Birmingham 3s. 4d., and in Wolverhampton 3s.

[92] 43 & 44 Vic. c. 120 (local).

[93] 58 & 59 Vic. c. 18 (local).

[94] Warrillow, *Etruria*, 156–7.

[95] Ibid. 157, 162–3.

[96] Ibid. 155, 162.

[97] Ibid. 165, 166; see p. 266.

[98] Warrillow, *Etruria*, 163, 165, 171, 181.

[99] Ibid. 172, 174, 176, 177.

[1] *Staffs. Advertiser*, 28 July 1894; *Staffs. Sentinel Potteries, Newcastle and District Dir.* (1907); *Stoke Official Handbk.* (1960), 63; J. Lobley, *Rep. on Hanley Lighting* (1893; copy in H.R.L. Pamphlets, vol. 38); Electric Lighting Orders Confirmation (no. 1) Act, 1891, 54 & 55 Vic. c. 49 (local); O.S. Map 6″ Staffs. xii SW. (1900). It was originally intended to link Bethesda Rd. with Bethesda St.: *Staffs. Advertiser*, 24 Feb. 1894.

[2] See p. 266.

[3] Warrillow, *Etruria*, 323.

[4] *Kelly's Dir. Staffs.* (1892); *Staffs. Advertiser*, 11 May 1907.

[5] Warrillow, *Etruria*, 320, 322.

[6] H.R.L., Hanley Highway Surveyors' Mins. 1817–41,

pp. 4, 5; Ward, *Stoke*, 364.

[7] H.R.L., Hanley Highway Surveyors' Mins. 1817–41, 22 Mar. 1823.

[8] Ibid. 22 Sept. 1824, 22 Sept. 1825.

[9] Ibid. 22 Sept. 1826 and accts. for 1826–7, 1827–8.

[10] Ibid. 22 Sept. 1829, 22 Sept. 1830 and accts. for 1828–9, 1829–30.

[11] Ibid. 22 Sept. 1832, 22 Sept. 1833, 22 Sept. 1834, 26 Oct. 1835, 25 Mar. 1836, and accts. for 1832–7.

[12] Ibid. 25 Mar. 1837. Except for a special meeting in 1839 at the Sea Lion Inn (where an adjourned meeting had been held in 1829: ibid. 22 Sept. 1829), the inhabs. met in the vestry at St. John's until at least 1840: ibid. 1838–40. The board at first met in the vestry but after March 1838 moved to 'The Sea Lion' and in 1839 to the police office: ibid. 3 Apr. 1837 and later; Huntbach, *Hanley*, 109.

[13] Hanley Highway Surveyors' Mins., 3 Apr. 1837, 5 Mar. 1838, 28 Mar. 1839, 31 Mar. 1840. In 1839 the general meeting of the inhabs. withdrew its confidence from the existing surveyor and a new official was appointed by the board: ibid. 25 and 28 Mar. 1839.

[14] Ibid. 3 and 17 Apr. 1837.

[15] Ibid. 31 Mar. 1840.

[16] Ibid. 8 May 1839; *P.O. Dir. Staffs.* (1854).

[17] Rawlinson, *Rep. to Bd. of Health* (1850), 45; ibid. (1853), 7.

[18] Ibid. (1850), 43.

[19] See p. 158.

[20] S.R.O., Q/AH, bdle. 3.

ECONOMIC HISTORY. Until the early 18th century the economic history of Hanley is that of a small moorland settlement whose inhabitants were engaged predominantly in agriculture. Thereafter the rise of the pottery and coal industries, followed by the development of the iron industry in the 19th century, brought about the complete industrialization of the town which has also become the social centre of the potteries.

In the mid-13th century the tenants of Newcastle manor in Shelton held $9\frac{1}{2}$ virgates of land at a rent of £1 8s. 7d.[21] In 1297 they held $10\frac{1}{2}$ 'warae' of land containing 42 bovates at a rent of 9d. a bovate, by socage—presumably villein socage—tenure, and paid 5s. 2d. in common in lieu of labour services; there were also over 60 acres of assarted land leased out at the will of the lord and 5 cottagers paying a total of 1s. 8d. for their holdings.[22] At Hanley in 1297 the mesne lord and the tenants there held 70 acres at 6d. an acre.[23] The total issues of Shelton were £4 14s. 5d. and of Hanley £2 8s. 8d.[24] The assized rents of both in 1386–7 were £7 11s. $1\frac{1}{2}d$.[25] and in 1422–3 £6 15s. $10\frac{1}{2}d$.[26] By 1615 the principal form of tenure in Hanley and Shelton was copyhold,[27] but in the 18th century with the development of the pottery industry many long leases of waste were made by the lords of Hanley manor, particularly around Lower Green (the present Market Square) and the freehold of most of these plots was eventually bought by the lessees.[28] The mixture of the two forms of tenure was causing considerable confusion by the mid-19th century.[29]

Inclosure from the waste was in progress in Shelton by the mid-13th century[30] and in Hanley also by 1297 when the lord of Hanley owed 6s. 8d. to the lord of Newcastle manor for 31 acres so inclosed.[31] In the early 17th century the tenants of Hanley and Shelton had common rights in Snape Marsh in Shelton and part of Hanley Green.[32] The open fields in Shelton township at this time included Rye Field (apparently shared with Penkhull) and Old Field and probably Woodcroft and Great Cotton also.[33]

Shelton pinfold stood to the east of Cleveland Passage c. 1880 and may be identifiable with the pinfold owned by the corporation in 1907.[34]

MARKETS AND FAIRS. A market-house was built by subscription apparently in 1776 on that part of Lower Green where the Angel Hotel now stands.[35] About 1790 the market day was stated to be Saturday and in 1795 Monday;[36] early in the 19th century the market was held every Wednesday and Saturday.[37] At the time of the establishment of the market the sale of corn was forbidden there as in the other markets of the Potteries in order to protect Newcastle's corn market, and this prohibition continued until at least the mid-19th century.[38] The market was given parliamentary sanction in 1813 by an Act which also authorized the trustees to provide more suitable premises, to improve the market-place, and to use profits for the benefit of the inhabitants of Hanley and Shelton.[39] The market-house was subsequently taken down as it was proving an obstruction in the street, and in 1819 a covered shed was built on a site enclosed for the purpose and known as Hadley's Pool, until then a stagnant pool and now Fountain Square; the poultry and butter section of the market was held under this cover, while the stalls of the open-air market held in Market Square were stored there.[40] The market-tolls which had produced only some 20 guineas in 1812 were let for £1,512 in 1840; the 20-guinea salary of the organist at St. John's, Hanley, was a charge on the tolls by 1812 and still remained so in 1861.[41] In 1831 the trustees built the Shambles in Tontine Street, a Classical building then used mainly as the meat market, and by 1834 a cattle market was being held on the second Tuesday of the month.[42] By 1840 Market Square, where the vegetable market was still held, had been paved and the streets leading to it widened as well as paved.[43] The town hall having been completed in 1845 on the site of the 1819 market hall in Fountain Square,[44] a covered hall in Swan Passage was opened for the fish and potato market in 1848. In the following year another larger hall for the vegetable market was opened to the east on the site of the Swan Inn which the market trustees had bought some years before.[45] In 1862 the powers of the trustees were vested in the corporation as the Hanley Local Board which bought the market premises from the lord of the manor in 1870.[46] The cattle market was held every other Tuesday by 1851,

[21] Cal. Inq. Misc. i, p. 153.
[22] Cal. Inq. p.m. iii, p. 290; S.H.C. 1911, 244–5. These are complementary versions of the relevant parts of C 133/81/6. For villein socage in Penkhull see p. 200.
[23] S.H.C. 1911, 245.
[24] Ibid.
[25] T. Pape, Medieval Newcastle-under-Lyme, 118.
[26] S.H.C. 1912, 218.
[27] Ward, Stoke, app., p. xlvi. In 1622 the Meire family's estate in Shelton and Hanley was described as part freehold and part copyhold: C 3/367/23. Shelton Mill was freehold.
[28] Ward, Stoke, 348; W.S.L. 423/28.
[29] Ward, Stoke, 348.
[30] Cal. Inq. Misc. i, p. 153. By 1297 over 60 a. of assart were held by tenants at will: see above.
[31] S.H.C. 1911, 245.
[32] Ward, Stoke, app. p. xlii.
[33] D.L. 43/8/32; see p. 200.
[34] Huntbach, Hanley, 109; Staffs. Advertiser, 18 May 1907. In 1893 there was a pound by the Trent near Havelock St., evidently on the Hanley side of the Stoke-Hanley boundary: H.R.L., Stoke Boro. Mins. 1893–5, p. 150.
[35] Huntbach, Hanley, 10. Ward, Stoke, 361, however, mentions only a lease of the site to trustees in 1791.
[36] Univ. Brit. Dir. (1791), iv. 107; J. Aikin, The Country around Manchester (1795), 520.

[37] Ward, Stoke, 362.
[38] Aikin, Country around Manchester, 520; Huntbach, Hanley, 13; White, Dir. Staffs. (1851). In Burslem, however, a corn mkt. was estab. in 1848: see p. 130.
[39] Ward, Stoke, 361–2; 53 Geo. III, c. 115 (local and personal). [40] Ward, Soket, 362.
[41] Ibid. 363 and n.; H.R.L., Hanley Market Trustees' Mins. 1845–62, 17 Oct. 1861. The custom of paying an organist's salary out of the market tolls also prevailed at Burslem: see p. 122.
[42] Ward, Stoke, 362–3; White, Dir. Staffs. (1834). For a description of the building see p. 149.
[43] White, Dir. Staffs. (1834); Ward, Stoke, 363.
[44] See p. 158.
[45] Hanley Market Trustees' Mins. 1845–62, pp. 2, 10, 20–21, 59, 81; White, Dir. Staffs. (1851); Ward, Stoke, 363; E. J. D. Warrillow, 'Two Old Inns' (Staffs. Life, ii), 140; Ancient Corp. of Hanley, ed. W. D. Spanton, 110; Staffs. Advertiser, 23 Apr. 1938. The 'Swan' had been chosen as the site of the meat market by 1829, but the owner had then refused to sell at the price offered: ibid. 30 May 1829. For a description of the 1849 market building see p. 149.
[46] Huntbach, Hanley, 12; Act to confirm orders under the Local Government Act of 1858, 25 & 26 Vic. c. 25 (local and personal); Hanley Market Trustees' Mins. 1845–62, 5 Sept. 1862.

alternating with that at Stone.[47] A hide and skin market was begun in 1852 or 1853 in a shed erected to the north of the potato market.[48] By 1858 the cattle market, held in the market-place, was proving an inconvenience there, but it was not until 1869 that the corporation transferred it, evidently with the hide and skin market, to a large site off Regent Road.[49] The cattle market was discontinued in the mid-1920's,[50] but a market is still held off Regent Road as part of the Hanley and Stoke Hide Market.[51] The hall to the west of Swan Passage was still used as the fish market in 1924,[52] but that market was moved soon afterwards to the Tontine Street hall,[53] where it is still (1960) held on Tuesdays. By the mid-1950's a Friday general market had been started, so that the markets, held in the large hall of 1849, now take place on Wednesdays, Fridays, and Saturdays.[54] Market Square was still the site of an open-air wholesale market in 1938, but a proposal was then made to remove it, in order to ease traffic congestion.[55] The space is now a car park, but part of it is still used as a plant market.

Fairs were held on 16 February, 6 April, and 25 May between at least 1834[56] and 1850.[57]

MILLS. There was a mill at Shelton by the mid-13th century held of the manor of Newcastle by the men of Shelton at a fee-farm rent of 13s. 4d.[58] This belies the tradition that it was enfranchised only after the accession of Henry VII who is alleged to have made the tenure freehold as a reward to the miller for supplying Henry's troops before the Battle of Bosworth.[59] In 1568 half the mill was leased by the Duchy to Richard Tunstall for 40 years at a rent of 6s., while in 1597 a quarter share was surrendered by John Amys to William Bolton for 40 years at a rent of 5s.[60] In 1615, however, 'the tenants of Shelton Mill' were said to be holding by the old fee-farm rent of 13s. 4d.,[61] and by 1633 the mill had been leased by the Duchy to William Hudson at the rent of 13s. 4d.[62] Soon afterwards it passed to John Bell who compounded for it as a delinquent

in 1643.[63] In 1679 Balthazar Bell of the Ridge House was stated to be holding a quarter of the mill.[64] In 1708 the mill was settled on John Astbury, John Walton, John Staner, and their wives.[65] Known as Bell's Mill by the mid-18th century it was still in existence on the south side of Mill Street (now Etruria Road) c. 1837.[66] Lord Granville's ironworks were begun on the opposite side of the road in 1839, and the mill estate was eventually bought by Lord Granville, the pool being filled in at the beginning of the 20th century.[67]

A windmill on the high ground beyond the east end of the present Windmill Street was built c. 1795.[68] Still in use c. 1837,[69] it had been converted by 1850 into William Dodd's Hallfield Observatory.[70] Dodd had evidently left by 1854,[71] although the observatory still stood in 1857.[72]

A corn mill known as the Borough Mills in Marsh Street below Holy Trinity Church was in use between at least the 1840's and the end of the century.[73] The Ivy House Mill on the Bucknall side of the Trent, formerly a flint mill, was used as a corn mill by the 1870's.[74] The Ridgway Flour Mills on the Trent and Mersey Canal off Shelton New Road were in operation from 1879 until at least 1924.[75] In 1958 there were mills at Birches Head (Dicksons) and Shelton (Leese and Son, Pyenest Street, and Staffordshire Farmers).[76]

POTTERY INDUSTRY. Pottery-making did not become an important industry in Hanley until the later 18th century, helped then by the opening of the Trent and Mersey Canal and its Caldon branch and by the turnpiking of the roads. The earliest known kiln there, however, was that worked by a Richard Broke c. 1540.[77] Slipware potters of the 17th century, possibly including Thomas Toft (d. 1689), seem to have worked at Hanley,[78] and butter pots were being made there by the 1680's.[79] By that time Shelton clay was used not only in the making of clay pipes at Newcastle[80] but also by Thomas Miles in the production of a brown and white stoneware at

[47] White, *Dir. Staffs.* (1851).
[48] Hanley Market Trustees' Mins. 1845–62, pp. 116, 126, 135, 143.
[49] Ibid. pp. 144, 154; *Ancient Corp. of Hanley*, 110; O.S. Map 1/500 Staffs. xi. 15. 10 (survey of 1866); O.S. Map 6" Staffs. xii SW. (1890), showing the hide and skin market there.
[50] It is mentioned in *Kelly's Dir. Staffs.* (1924) but not in the edn. for 1928.
[51] *Stoke Classified Telephone Dir.* (Dec. 1959); local inf. (1960); see p. 201.
[52] *Kelly's Dir. Staffs.* (1924).
[53] Ibid. (1928).
[54] *Stoke Official Handbk.* [1958 and previous edn.]
[55] *Staffs. Advertiser*, 23 Apr. 1938. The lack of alternative accommodation was 'an old and growing evil' even in 1910: Huntbach, *Hanley*, 12.
[56] White, *Dir. Staffs.* (1834).
[57] *P.O. Dir. Staffs.* (1850).
[58] *Cal. Inq. Misc.* i, p. 153; *Cal. Lib.* 1251–60, 436; D.L. 42/4, f. 179a.
[59] Ward, *Stoke*, 410–11.
[60] Ibid. app. p. xlvi.
[61] W.S.L., D. 1788, P. 44, B. 8 (copy of relevant court rolls).
[62] Public Rec. Office, MS. Calendar of Duchy of Lanc. Particulars for Grants, f. 50b—Round Room, 27 (94).
[63] S.R.O., D. 260/M/ box 25, bdle. k, f. 84b.
[64] W.S.L., D. 1788, P. 44, B. 8, endorsement on 1679 copy of ct. roll.
[65] C.P. 43/500, rot. 16.
[66] Ward, *Stoke*, 410; H. Wedgwood, *Romance of Staffs.*

86–87; Warrillow, *Etruria*, 190, 193; *Stoke-upon-Trent Par. Reg.* iii. 494, 594; O.S. Map 1", lxxii NW. (1837). It was one of the 3 mills worked by Ralph Wood, great-grandfather of Enoch Wood of Burslem, probably in the early 18th cent.: see p. 131 and n. 93.
[67] Warrillow, *Etruria*, 49, 190, 384; Wedgwood, *Romance of Staffs.* 86; O.S. Map 6" Staffs. xii SW. (1890); see p. 169. Homer, *Plan of Hanley and Shelton, 1857*, shows the mill apparently as part of the ironworks.
[68] J. T. Wilkinson, *Hugh Bourne*, 22 (Hugh Bourne being involved in its building); Hargreaves, *Map of Staffs. Potteries*.
[69] O.S. Map 1", lxxii NW. (1837).
[70] Huntbach, *Hanley*, 110; *P.O. Dir. Staffs.* (1850); White, *Dir. Staffs.* (1851). Dodd lived there.
[71] *P.O. Dir. Staffs.* (1854).
[72] Homer, *Plan of Hanley and Shelton, 1857*.
[73] *Descript. Acct. of the Potteries* (1893), 42 (copy in H.R.L.); *Kelly's Dir. Staffs.* (1896); Lich. Dioc. Regy. Bp.'s Reg. Oᴬ, p. 202 and plan facing (1847).
[74] See p. 153.
[75] *Kelly's Dir. Staffs.* (1924); date on building which is now occupied by a firm of woodworkers; Warrillow, *Etruria*, 199.
[76] *Barrett's City of Stoke Dir.* [1959].
[77] C 1/955/52.
[78] Mankowitz and Haggar, *Eng. Pottery*, 104, 222–3.
[79] S.R.O., Q/SR Trans. 1682. In 1679 John Stanley and John Bryan were presented at Newcastle manor court for digging holes, presumably for clay, in the 'common way' at Hanley: D.L. 30/242/3.
[80] R. Plot, *Nat. Hist. Staffs.* (1686), 121.

Miles Bank,[81] the junction of the present Stafford and Trinity Streets. There are said to have been seven potters at Hanley in the early 18th century, producing cloudy and mottled ware, black and mottled ware, 'small ware', 'a sort of dishes', milk pans, and butter, lamprey, and venison pots.[82] Thomas Astbury was apparently making pottery at Shelton c. 1690,[83] while he or a John Astbury is alleged to have introduced Devonshire clay and calcined flint into Staffordshire and to have built the flint mill near the Ivy House which was in use by 1738.[84] John Astbury (d. 1743) had a works in Shelton[85] which is said to have been on the site of the present Ashworth Brothers' pottery on the east side of Broad Street (see below). Joshua Twyford (1640–1729) was also working at Shelton by 1717, apparently in partnership with John Astbury.[86] John Middleton (d. 1744) was making pottery at Shelton by 1719 on a site lying south of a Joshua Astbury's house, while his son John, who was disowned by his father after a quarrel, had a secret share in the Bell Works in Albion Street[87] (see below). The New Hall Works, originating in Tunstall in 1781 and opened in Hanley the following year, was the first Staffordshire pottery to use Cornish clay in the manufacture of porcelain (see below).

By the early 19th century the number of potteries had risen to 20 in Hanley and 15 in Shelton including 1 at Boothen Brook, 1 at Etruria, and 1 at Vale Pleasant (Etruria Vale).[88] Some 40 years later there were only 24 large potworks in Hanley and Shelton, although there were several other smaller works producing in the main china toys and also some enamelling and gilding works.[89] This decline in numbers was partly the result of the concentration of the industry in fewer hands; in addition it was stated that 'several potworks of the olden time have been swept away by the besom of modern improvement'.[90] Most of the inhabitants of Hanley and Shelton then worked in the potteries and the subsidiary businesses, women and children being employed extensively.[91] Around the turn of the 19th and 20th centuries several new works were built

along the Caldon Canal between Hanley Park and Bucknall Road where, it was claimed, more ovens were then erected than anywhere else in the Potteries.[92] In 1959 there were 22 major potteries in the area, most of them producing earthenware only. In addition there were three makers of sanitary ware, including Twyfords of the Cliffe Vale Pottery, Shelton New Road, and the Etruria Works, Garner Street.[93] The Cliffe Vale Pottery was built by T. W. Twyford in 1887 and enlarged in 1911, 1936, and 1953; the Etruria Works, Garner Street, was opened in 1912 and extended in 1950.[94]

The oldest works in the district which can be traced over any period is said to have been that formerly in Upper Market Street (now Huntbach Street) which was held by John Glass between at least 1787 and 1834 and possibly by Joseph Glass who c. 1700 was making 'cloudy and a sort of dishes' at Hanley.[95] About 1840 the works was in the hands of Samuel Keeling, in the 1850's of Meakin Bros. (of the Eagle Works from 1859), and between at least 1862 and 1871 of Taylor Bros.; it was pulled down soon afterwards.[96]

Otherwise the works with the longest known history is Ashworth's in Broad Street. The Shelton works of John Astbury (d. 1743) (see above) is said to have passed to John Baddeley (d. 1772) and so would be identifiable with the pottery on the west side of High Street, Shelton (now Broad Street) where Baddeley made salt-glazed stone-ware and cream-ware rivalling Josiah Wedgwood's and in 1751 seems to have attempted to make porcelain.[97] He also bought the Ivy House estate, including the flint mill, in 1770.[98] His sons John and Ralph succeeded him; they increased the number of ovens from two to four and replaced the thatched roof of the works with tiles.[99] By the 1780's the works was held by Ralph alone, who was also using the Ivy House mill, but by 1801 the works and a house adjoining were unoccupied and for sale, Ralph evidently having retired to the Ivy House; the Shelton house and pottery were bought by Joseph Boon and Richard Hicks, who also secured the lease

[81] Jewitt, Ceramic Art, 480; Meigh, 'Staffs. Potters', 142; A. Huntbach, Hanley, 47. Mankowitz and Haggar, Eng. Pottery, 150 (following S. Shaw, Staffs. Potteries, 109), states that there were 2 potters of this name, one making brown ware at Miles Bank and the other white ware elsewhere in Shelton.
[82] E. Meteyard, Life of Josiah Wedgwood, i. 192.
[83] Meigh, 'Staffs. Potters', 8, which also mentions Wm. Astbury of Shelton c. 1720.
[84] Shaw, Staffs. Potteries, 126, 128–30; Staffs. Sentinel Summer No. 1911, 21; Huntbach, Hanley, 34–35; Mankowitz and Haggar, Eng. Pottery, 10. An entry in the commonplace book of Josiah Wedgwood (I) suggests a confusion or alias between Astbury and Heath in connexion with the introduction of flint (Wedgwood, Wedgwood Family, 324); the name, however, is given as Joshua Astbury or Heath (see note 87 below). It was certainly a Thos. Heath who owned the Ivy House flint mill in the early 18th cent.: see p. 153.
[85] Meigh, 'Staffs. Potters', 8; Mankowitz and Haggar, Eng. Pottery, 10; W.S.L., D. 1788, P. 45, B. 5.
[86] Jewitt, Ceramic Art, 480, 487; Mankowitz and Haggar, Eng. Pottery, 227; W.S.L., D. 1742/348. Both Astbury and Twyford are stated by Shaw, Staffs. Potteries, 119, to have secured the secrets of the Elers brothers at Bradwell Wood, Wolstanton, Astbury by feigning idiocy and Twyford indifference.
[87] Mankowitz and Haggar, Eng. Pottery, 150; W.S.L., D. 1788, P. 61, B. 41. A Joshua Astbury of Shelton, gent., son and heir of Joshua Astbury of Shelton, deceased, occurs

in 1740: ibid. P. 42, B. 11; and see n. 84 above.
[88] Allbut, Staffs. Pottery Dir. (1802).
[89] Ward, Stoke, 372–6, 443–4.
[90] Ibid. 373–4, 376.
[91] 2nd Rep. Com. on Employment of Children [431], pp. c12, 13, H.C. (1843), xiv.
[92] Huntbach, Hanley, 54.
[93] Pottery Gaz. Dir. (1960).
[94] Information from Twyfords Ltd. (1959); Stoke Official Handbk. (1960), 170, 171; dates on buildings. The Twyford family began making sanitary ware at a works in Bath St., Hanley, c. 1850: ex inf. Twyfords. The 1953 factory is in Etruscan St. opposite the main Cliffe Vale works.
[95] Mankowitz and Haggar, Eng. Pottery, 96–97; Huntbach, Hanley, 42; Meteyard, Josiah Wedgwood, i. 192. Meigh, 'Staffs. Potters', 86, gives c. 1670 as the earliest ref. to Joseph Glass.
[96] Ward, Stoke, 375; Jewitt, Ceramic Art, 487, 504; Meigh, 'Staffs. Potters', 139, 140, 193; B. Hollowood, J. and G. Meakin (copy in H.R.L.).
[97] Mankowitz and Haggar, Eng. Pottery, 12; Huntbach, Hanley, 35; Allbut, Staffs. Pottery Dir. (1802). A pottery in Shelton lately held by 'Widow Astbury' was let to a Thos. Taylor by John Fenton of Newcastle in 1749: W.S.L., D. 1788, P. 44, B. 9. Baddeley carried on a flint-grinding business at Stone: ibid. P. 27, B. 20, which also shows him bankrupt in 1761 and evidently extricating himself by a partnership with John Fletcher of Newcastle.
[98] See p. 153.
[99] Mankowitz and Haggar, Eng. Pottery, 12.

of the flint mill.[1] By 1807 the pottery was held by Hicks and Job Meigh (1784–1862), with a third partner named Johnson from 1822, and some 600 hands were being employed there by the early 1830's. The firm's products included transfer-printed and enamelled ware, china, and ironstone china.[2] In 1835 the pottery passed to Ridgway (William), Morley (Francis, Ridgway's son-in-law), Wear and Company; Morley became sole owner in 1845 and in 1851 bought the moulds of C. J. Mason, inventor of Mason's Ironstone China.[3] Morley was joined in 1857 by Taylor Ashworth (1839–1910), who bought the business for his sons on Morley's retirement in 1862 and built up the manufacture of durable ware, sanitary ware, and insulators. His sons' main interest, however, was the Lancashire wool and cotton industry, and with the slump in the woollen trade in 1893 the Broad Street works was sold to J. Goddard, whose descendants, trading as George L. Ashworth and Bros. Ltd., continue to produce durable ware to Mason's designs.[4] The oldest of the existing buildings, which are set back from the road on the west side of Broad Street to the rear of the Mitchell Memorial Theatre, appear to date from 1815.[5] The long front range of two low stories has a central Venetian window surmounted by a pediment, the window being finely detailed with a Tuscan order and a fluted frieze; there is a similar window at the south gable end of the range. Near the north end of the front elliptical stone archways, now filled in, probably represent the entrances to stables belonging to the former dwelling house which stood between the works and the road.[6] Behind the front range, which contains warehouse, showroom, and offices, are two lower parallel ranges with the ovens beyond them; a second two-storied wing runs at right angles across the northern end of the site. Although the buildings have been extended and altered, this probably represents the original layout of the works.

The Church Works in High Street, Hanley, some 200 yards north of St. John's Church, was built about the mid-18th century by Humphrey Palmer who produced Egyptian black (the clay for which came from the nearby Chapel Fields) and other ware in imitation of Josiah Wedgwood; so much so that he was eventually sued for infringement of Wedgwood's

patent covering the manufacture of Etruscan painted vases.[7] Enoch Wood served his apprenticeship at the Church Works under Palmer.[8] The business failed in 1778 but was saved by James Neale (1740–1814), Palmer's London partner or agent; Neale took various partners from 1780, and the works at this period produced cream, blue-painted, lustre and jasper ware, Egyptian black, marbled vases, and figures, often in imitation of Wedgwood.[9] James Wilson, partner from 1786, succeeded as sole owner in the early 1790's and was himself followed in 1801 by his brother David who took his sons into partnership; John, the last of these, went bankrupt in 1817.[10] The works was held from 1818 by Jacob Phillips and John Bagster or Baxster (d. 1825), and after the winding up of the firm in 1828 the pottery and a house adjoining were bought by Joseph Mayer (1775–1860), son of Elijah Mayer (1715–1813) who had built up another potworks in Hanley High Street.[11] In 1831 Joseph leased the Church Works to his cousin William Ridgway, retaining, however, an oven and other buildings where he stored some of his best stock until his death.[12] The works remained in the Ridgway family, in partnership with Leonard Abington (1785–1867), Radical, Baptist minister, and modeller to Jacob Phillips and Joseph Mayer, until Edward John Ridgway moved to his new Bedford Road works in 1866.[13] The Church Works then passed to Powell and Bishop (Powell, Bishop, and Stonier by 1880, Bishop and Stonier between at least 1896 and 1914).[14] It was demolished c. 1948,[15] and by 1959 the site was occupied partly by the King George VI Memorial Club and an Auxiliary Fire Service office, the remainder being used as a car park. By the early 1880's Powell, Bishop and Stonier had a large flint mill on the bank of the Caldon Canal near Nelson Place and their newly erected Waterloo Works, and this remained in use until at least 1896.[16]

The earliest known occupant of the Bell Works at the junction of Albion Street and Broad Street was Warner Edwards (d. 1759), who produced lead-ore glazed ware and fine enamel decorations there; for a time John Middleton the younger, the first curate of the new church, was a partner, though in secret.[17] By the early 1790's the works was in the hands of Job and George Ridgway and remained in that

[1] Ibid. 12–13 (1802 given as the date when Hicks and Boon took over), 27 (1805 being given as the date); Jewitt, *Ceramic Art*, 499; *Staffs. Advertiser*, 7 Nov. 1801, 27 Feb. and 6 Mar. 1802; W.S.L. 130/47, ff. 36, 42, 46, 91. Ralph Baddeley was still working the flint mill in 1792: W.S.L., D. 1792, bdle. 61.

[2] H.R.L., EMT 7–807 (b), showing Hicks and Meigh in possession of the works by 1807 and Hicks then living at the house; Mankowitz and Haggar, *Eng. Pottery*, 108, 148; Jewitt, *Ceramic Art*, 491; *1st Rep. Factories Com.* H.C. 450, pp. B2, 38, 42 (1833), xx. Hicks was still living at the house c. 1840 (Ward, *Stoke*, 383), and Mrs. Hicks was living there in 1850 and 1851: *P.O. Dir. Staffs.* (1850); White, *Dir. Staffs.* (1851).

[3] Mankowitz and Haggar, *Eng. Pottery*, 108, 142, 157; Jewitt, *Ceramic Art*, 491.

[4] Mankowitz and Haggar, *Eng. Pottery*, 9–10; *Pottery Gaz. Dir.* (1960).

[5] The date was found on a beam inside the front range.

[6] Ex inf. Mr. J. V. Goddard (1960); see p. 172.

[7] Jewitt, *Ceramic Art*, 481; Mankowitz and Haggar, *Eng. Pottery*, 169–70; Adams, *Adams Family*, 187, 197, and add. and corr. no. 3, p. 2. John Voyez, the modeller, who was brought to Staffs. from London by Wedgwood in 1768, was imprisoned in Stafford Gaol for 3 months in 1769 after being sacked by Wedgwood for stealing models,

clay and moulds, and worked for Palmer for a time after his release, subsequently returning to London; his work included imitations of Wedgwood, and he is said to have forged the mark of Wedgwood and Bentley: Mankowitz and Haggar, *Eng. Pottery*, 228–9; N. Hudson Moore, *Wedgwood and his Imitators*, 95–100; R. J. Charleston, 'Jean Voyez' (*Trans. Eng. Ceramic Circle*, v), 12.

[8] Mankowitz and Haggar, *Eng. Pottery*, 170.

[9] Ibid. 162–3; Jewitt, *Ceramic Art*, 481–2.

[10] Meigh, 'Staffs. Potters', 148, 213–14; Mankowitz and Haggar, *Eng. Pottery*, 162, 241; Jewitt, *Ceramic Art*, 482.

[11] Mankowitz and Haggar, *Eng. Pottery*, 145, 174; Jewitt, *Ceramic Art*, 482.

[12] Jewitt, *Ceramic Art*, 482; Huntbach, *Hanley*, 46.

[13] Jewitt, *Ceramic Art*, 482, 500; Mankowitz and Haggar, *Eng. Pottery*, 1, 191. The Bedford Rd. works was held by Ridgways until c. 1952: *Pottery Gaz. Dir.* (1953).

[14] Meigh, 'Staffs. Potters', 29, 160.

[15] Adams, *Adams Family*, add. and corr. no. 3, p. 2. A fragment of the early factory buildings is still (1960) standing.

[16] Jewitt, *Ceramic Art*, 498; *Kelly's Dir. Staffs.* (1896). Geo. Edwards also had a flint mill in Nelson Pl. between at least 1884 and 1912: ibid. (1884, 1912).

[17] Mankowitz and Haggar, *Eng. Pottery*, 81, 150; Jewitt, *Ceramic Art*, 480–1; see p. 164.

family until the dissolution of W. Ridgway and Sons in 1854.[18] In 1805 George built a house (now demolished) adjoining the works at the junction of Bethesda Street and Albion Street.[19] The pottery was bought in 1856 by Joseph Clementson, who had been working the Phoenix Pottery on the opposite side of Broad Street since 1832 (see below), and was held by Clementson Bros. from 1867 until at least 1916.[20] By 1922 the premises had been taken over by the Bell Pottery Company and by G. M. Creyke and Sons, both of whom were still working there in 1940.[21] The pottery was disused by 1950[22] and was demolished soon afterwards; the site is now occupied by the new City Museum and Art Gallery, opened in 1956,[23] and by a car park. Photographs show a long two-storied front to Broad Street with a pediment near its northern end.[24]

Josiah Wedgwood opened his works at Etruria in 1769, using the same architect as for Etruria Hall nearby, Joseph Pickford of Derby, but in fact working largely to his own designs.[25] In partnership with Thomas Bentley until the latter's death in 1780, he proceeded to improve all the types of ware which he had so far been making in Burslem, but he never produced porcelain or bone china.[26] A windmill for grinding materials had been built at Etruria by 1779 by Erasmus Darwin,[27] and between 1782 and 1784 a Boulton and Watt steam engine was installed for driving the clay, flint, and colour mills.[28] A new 10-horse-power engine was ordered in 1792,[29] and in 1802 Josiah Wedgwood (II) bought a 30-horse-power engine.[30] Bone china was made by him from 1812 to 1822, and its manufacture was revived in 1878.[31] Josiah Wedgwood and Sons Ltd. built a new works at Barlaston in 1938, completing it after the Second World War; the earthenware department was finished in 1940.[32] The company sold the Etruria works to the Shelton Iron, Steel, and Coal Company in 1943 but subsequently took a lease of the premises; in 1951 they sold the lease to the Dunlop Rubber Company and now (1960) occupy only a small part of the building as sub-tenants of Dunlop's.[33] Covering an area of about seven acres the Etruria works was laid out from the first in two distinct sections known as the Ornamental and the Useful Works; each had its separate buildings and ovens ranged round its own court or 'square'.[34] The site was bounded on the east by the canal which was here widened to form lay-bys and from which two branches were taken into the works. The long principal range of buildings fronting on the canal, originally at water level but now owing to subsidence about 12 feet below it, is of three stories. Its slightly projecting central feature has a ground-floor entrance with a semicircular three-light window above it, the whole being surmounted by a pediment and a bell cupola. The original cupola was replaced by a copy in 1923.[35] A row of cottages for employees formerly continued the line of the canal frontage to the south,[36] with a low circular tower, which is still standing, beyond them. The windmill appears behind the north end of the front range in a watercolour drawing of 1794,[37] while in 1805 the engine room was situated behind the Useful Works and the cratemakers' pool and shops lay to the south of it.[38] The china works, added early in the 19th century, was beyond the Ornamental Works at the northern end of the site.[39] Although much altered and partly derelict many of the original buildings, including the front range and several ovens, are still (1960) in existence. Almost all the early equipment has been dismantled, but Josiah Wedgwood's turning wheel, probably dating from 1769, is preserved at the City Museum and Art Gallery, Hanley.

A company consisting of Samuel Hollins, Anthony Keeling, Jacob Warburton, William Clowes, John Turner, and Richard Champion was formed in 1781 to work the patent for the manufacture of hard-paste porcelain from Cornish clay and stone, taken out by William Cookworthy of Plymouth in 1765 and transferred in 1774 to Richard Champion, then of Bristol.[40] The work was at first carried on at Keeling's pottery in Tunstall, but in 1782 after a dispute and the withdrawal of Keeling and Turner, as well as of Champion who had been offered the deputy-paymastership of the forces, the company moved to Shelton New Hall, apparently the site of a 17th-century potworks. The premises had been expanded by 1802 to include 3 messuages, 3 potworks, and over 100 acres of land, and in 1810 the company bought the hall and estate, possibly as a land speculation.[41] Although the patent expired in 1796 the firm continued to produce hard-paste porcelain until 1810 or 1812 when it changed to

[18] Mankowitz and Haggar, *Eng. Pottery*, 190–1; Meigh, 'Staffs. Potters', 167, 168.

[19] The house bore the inscription 'GR 1805': ex inf. Mr. R. G. Haggar (1960).

[20] Jewitt, *Ceramic Art*, 500; Meigh, 'Staffs. Potters', 54.

[21] Meigh, 'Staffs. Potters', 23, 62; *Kelly's Dir. Staffs.* (1924, 1940).

[22] O.S. Map 1/1,250, SJ 8847 SW. (1951, surveyed 1950).

[23] See p. 270.

[24] Warrillow, *Stoke*, 332 (ii, v.).

[25] See pp. 144, 150, 152.

[26] Mankowitz and Haggar, *Eng. Pottery*, 233, 234; see pp. 133, 135.

[27] Meteyard, *Josiah Wedgwood*, ii. 29–31, 210. Even in 1769, however, Darwin had been confident that it would be made obsolete by the use of steam power.

[28] J. Thomas, 'The Econ. Development of the N. Staffs. Potteries since 1730' (London Univ. Ph.D. thesis, 1934), 235–41.

[29] Ibid. 242–6.   [30] Ibid. 251–3.

[31] Mankowitz and Haggar, *Eng. Pottery*, 234–5. Jewitt, *Ceramic Art*, 526, gives 1808 or 1809 to 1815 as the dates when Josiah (II) was making bone china; Warrillow, *Etruria*, 124, gives 1812 to 1815.

[32] Mankowitz and Haggar, *Eng. Pottery*, 235; Warrillow, *Etruria*, 359–61.

[33] Ex inf. Josiah Wedgwood & Sons Ltd. (1959).

[34] For details of the original layout, buildings, and equipment see Meteyard, *Wedgwood*, i. 494–6; ii. 82–84, 110–14, 234–9; Warrillow, *Etruria*, chaps. ii and xiv; for plans see Wedgwood Mus. Barlaston, plans of 1805, 1826, 1844, and 1866; for views see Meteyard, *Wedgwood*, ii. 111, 235, 237, 238; Warrillow, *Etruria*, 24, 30, 40, 127; series of 26 drawings made 1947–51 by L. G. Brammer and now at Barlaston.

[35] Warrillow, *Etruria*, 26.

[36] Eight cottages were advertised in a sale catalogue of 1844: ibid. 311. All but one were replaced by a later extension to the works.

[37] See plate on facing page.

[38] Wedgwood Mus. Barlaston, Survey of Etruria Works made in 1805 by Adam MacPhail (20 ft. to 1 inch).

[39] Wedgwood Mus. Barlaston, Plan of Etruria Estate by Chas. Heaton (1826).

[40] Mankowitz and Haggar, *Eng. Pottery*, 47, 59, 163; G. E. Stringer, *New Hall Porcelain*, passim.

[41] Mankowitz and Haggar, *Eng. Pottery*, 164; Jewitt, *Ceramic Art*, 484; Stringer, *New Hall Porcelain*, 12, 56–57, 60; see p. 100. The name New Hall was used by at least 1801, presumably to avoid confusion with the Old Hall in Hanley and the other 2 halls in Shelton: Stringer, *New Hall Porcelain*, 42; see pp. 152, 153.

The works in 1794

The hall *c.* 1870, with the works in the foreground

ETRURIA

Bottle ovens (demolished *c.* 1960) at the Eastwood Pottery with the Caldon Canal in the foreground

Air view of the town centre *c.* 1930, looking north-east with the former town hall near the middle of the picture

HANLEY

bone china; it also supplied Cornish clay and stone to local potters.[42] The business closed down in 1835, and the premises were occupied by William Ratcliff from 1837 to 1840 'as a common potworks' making earthenware, by William and Thomas Hackwood (earthenware and jet) from 1842 to 1856 (Thomas alone from 1849), by Cockson and Harding (earthenware) from 1856 to 1862, and by W. and J. Harding (cream, painted, Egyptian black, Rockingham, and tinted) from 1864.[43] John Aynsley, a china manufacturer of Longton, bought the works in 1872, letting the back part to Thomas Booth and Son (earthenware) and selling the front in the same year to Henry Hall, a metal mounter and already the tenant; Aynsley sold more of the land in 1876.[44] Booth's portion was burnt down and rebuilt, passing in 1880 to Ambrose Bevington and Son (earthenware), in 1892 to Plant and Gilmore, and in 1899 to the New Hall Pottery Company. During the First World War the last of these bought back all the property sold by Aynsley.[45] The hall itself was demolished in 1920.[46] Production ceased in 1956 when the New Hall Pottery Company was liquidated.[47] A flint mill was built on the Booden Brook near the works in or soon after 1806; still held by the company in 1818, it was in the hands of a Thomas Crockett some ten years later and was still in use at the end of the century.[48] The company seem also to have mined their own coal on the site of the works.[49]

Charles and Christopher Whitehead were producing salt-glazed white stone-ware at a pottery on or near the site of Hanley Old Hall in the 1780's.[50] This works was replaced by another erected in 1790 by Job Meigh (1750–1817) whose second son and grandson, both named Charles, in turn produced earthenware there.[51] It was stated in 1841 that this works ranked 'with the first class in being extensive, well-situated in the highest part of the township of Hanley, well drained and ventilated. The rooms are more spacious than most others, cleanly and good; there is, however, one great defect and that is the close approximation of the two privies for males and females, and their indecent publicity'.[52] In 1862 the younger Charles formed the Old Hall Earthenware

Company—the first pottery limited liability company in North Staffordshire—and this was replaced in 1887 by the Old Hall Porcelain Works Company which ran the pottery until it was closed in 1902.[53] It was demolished in 1904.[54] A steam flint mill in Norfolk (now Meigh) Street nearby was acquired by the Old Hall Earthenware Company in 1863.[55]

The Cauldon Place Works, with a house attached, had been built by Job Ridgway by the early 19th century on the south bank of the Caldon Canal east of Stoke Road.[56] The pottery remained part of the family business, passing in 1830 to John Ridgway who produced earthenware and a fine porcelain there and became potter to Queen Victoria at the beginning of her reign.[57] The premises were described in 1841 as 'delightfully situated . . . apart from every other building. . . . The rooms are lofty, spacious, and in all respects clean and healthy; the children and people generally are orderly, regular in their work and respectful.'[58] The firm of Bates, Brown-Westhead and Moore (later Brown-Westhead, Moore and Company) succeeded John Ridgway in 1859 and subsequently added a new china works on the Cauldon Place site, continuing to produce china, earthenware, and parian there until 1920.[59] The works was then run by the Cauldon Potteries Ltd. (china) and F. and R. Pratt and Company (earthenware) until the later 1930's[60] when the premises were acquired by the corporation.[61] During the Second World War there was an A.R.P. station on the site.[62] Part of the old building is now (1960) occupied by the City College of Building and the catering department of the North Staffordshire Technical College.[63] By the end of the 19th century the firm had its own mill in the vicinity for preparing clay and colour.[64]

A works in High Street, Shelton, evidently known by 1845 as the Phoenix Works,[65] was held by the Hammersley family during the first quarter of the 19th century,[66] by Elizabeth Jones in 1831–2,[67] by Joseph Clementson in partnership with Jonah Read between 1832 and 1839, and by Clementson alone thereafter.[68] In 1841 the works was described as 'second rate, with small unventilated rooms . . . well

[42] Mankowitz and Haggar, *Eng. Pottery*, 164; Jewitt, *Ceramic Art*, 484–5; Stringer, *New Hall Porcelain*, 33–34, 58.
[43] Mankowitz and Haggar, *Eng. Pottery*, 164–5; Jewitt, *Ceramic Art*, 485; Ward, *Stoke*, 373.
[44] Jewitt, *Ceramic Art*, 485; Stringer, *New Hall Porcelain*, 42–43.
[45] Jewitt, *Ceramic Art*, 485; Mankowitz and Haggar, *Eng. Pottery*, 165; Stringer, *New Hall Porcelain*, 43.
[46] Stringer, *New Hall Porcelain*, 42.
[47] Mankowitz and Haggar, *Eng. Pottery*, 165.
[48] Stringer, *New Hall Porcelain*, 56; Parson and Bradshaw, *Dir. Staffs.* (1818); *Pigot's Nat. Com. Dir.* (1828–9); *Kelly's Dir. Staffs.* (1896). It was also a colour mill c. 1840: Ward, *Stoke*, 381. For the co.'s tenancy of the mill at Hulton see p. 252.
[49] Stringer, *New Hall Porcelain*, 57.
[50] Meigh, 'Staffs. Potters', 210–11; Jewitt, *Ceramic Art*, 488–9; see p. 152.
[51] Mankowitz and Haggar, *Eng. Pottery*, 148, 167.
[52] *2nd Rep. Com. on Employment of Children*, p. c29.
[53] Mankowitz and Haggar, *Eng. Pottery*, 167; Jewitt, *Ceramic Art*, 489, giving 1861 as the date of the formation of the Old Hall Earthenware Co.
[54] Huntbach, *Hanley*, 47–48.
[55] H.R.L., EMT 15–863.
[56] Jewitt, *Ceramic Art*, 492, stating that the business was founded c. 1794 and that the Cauldon Place Works was built in 1802; Mankowitz and Haggar, *Eng. Pottery*, 190–1, giving 1802 as the date of building. An inscription

on the building—apparently not placed there until much later as the date 1882 also appears—reads 'J R 1798' but no works on the site is shown on the map in Allbut, *Staffs. Pottery Dir.* (1802).
[57] Mankowitz and Haggar, *Eng. Pottery*, 190–1; Ward, *Stoke*, 375.
[58] *2nd Rep. Com. on Employment of Children*, p. c24.
[59] Mankowitz and Haggar, *Eng. Pottery*, 38, 191; Huntbach, *Hanley*, 39; Meigh, 'Staffs. Potters', 45, 51; *Staffs. Sentinel*, 15 July 1899.
[60] Meigh, 'Staffs. Potters', 51, 55, 161, 170, 205; Compton Mackenzie, *The House of Coalport*, 98. In 1924 the Cauldon Potteries Ltd. took over the Coalport China Co. whose works was moved from Salop. to Shelton in 1926 and to the present Crescent Works in Stoke c. 1936: ibid. 86, 98; Mankowitz and Haggar, *Eng. Pottery*, 56–57. For F. and R. Pratt at Fenton see p. 220.
[61] *Staffs. Sentinel*, 27 July 1938. A proposal to house the city museum there was rejected: ibid.
[62] *News Chron.*, 10 Nov. 1954 (copy of relevant article in H.R.L.).   [63] See p. 171.
[64] *Descript. Acct. of Potteries* (1893), 10 (copy in H.R.L.).
[65] A gilt phoenix was placed in the pediment of the 1845 frontage: see below and plate facing p. 172.
[66] Allbut, *Staffs. Pottery Dir.* (1802); Meigh, 'Staffs. Potters', 97.
[67] Meigh, 'Staffs. Potters', 117; Ward, *Stoke*, 375.
[68] Jewitt, *Ceramic Art*, 499–500; Mankowitz and Haggar, *Eng. Pottery*, 55.

drained but badly provided with conveniences for the sexes, being close together and much exposed,'[69] but it was extended in 1845 when the present Broad Street frontage was built.[70] In 1844 Clementson had bought an adjoining potworks to the west[71] which had been worked by John and Edward Baddeley by the 1780's[72] and which was probably amalgamated with the Phoenix Works after 1844. In 1867 the Phoenix Works passed to Clementson's sons with the Bell Works opposite[73] (see above) and remained in the hands of Clementson Bros. until at least 1916.[74] The present Clementson flint and colour mills on the north had been built by 1924.[75] The site of the factory was sold in 1960. The front range was then standing, but the rest of the buildings had been demolished and the area was used as a car park. The two-storied brick façade to Broad Street, although built in 1845, is purely Georgian in character and is a well-designed example in the local tradition. A central elliptical archway has rusticated quoins and voussoirs, and above it is a three-light window, both arch and window being flanked by recessed round-headed panels. In the pediment are a gilt phoenix, modelled in relief, and the date 1845 in raised lettering. At each side of the central feature are two-storied wings, each of five bays, the sash windows of the ground floor being set in a series of arcaded panels.

The mills at the Ivy House, in Nelson Place, and near the former Phoenix Works, and those attached to the Etruria works, the Old and New Hall Potteries, and the Cauldon Place Works have all been treated above.[76] Other mills connected with the pottery industry have included Upper Botteslow Mill, on the Trent, between at least 1759 and 1912, part of which still (1960) stands at the end of Trent-mill Road; Lower Botteslow Mill, a little way downstream, by 1792 and still in use in the early 1920's;[77] the Eastwood Mill, Botteslow Street, which was in operation by the beginning of the 19th century and the site of which has been occupied

since 1937 by Hargreaves Mill Ltd.;[78] the Meighs' Dresden Mill on the Caldon Canal between at least 1834 and 1851;[79] a flint mill at Etruria Vale from at least 1834 and still in use;[80] the Westwood flint mill on the Caldon Canal west of Lichfield Street from 1848 and still in use;[81] and John Bourne's bone mill in Cobridge Road by 1851, replaced by the Etruscan Bone and Flint Mill on the Caldon Canal in Lower Bedford Street which was built by his relative J. Shirley in 1857 and is still run by Jesse Shirley and Sons Ltd. as a mill for grinding bone, flint, colours, and glazes.[82]

The newly built Mellor Green Laboratories in Snow Hill belong to the British Ceramic Research Association.[83]

MINING. Although the Hanley–Shelton area abounds in coal,[84] the mining industry has never been as extensive there as in the northern part of the Potteries. Its records, however, go back nearly as far. In 1297 the possessions of the lord of New-castle manor included an 'underground coal mine' at Shelton worth 10s. a year.[85] A mine in the Great Row seam there which was being worked early in the 16th century was still in operation in 1612,[86] and a mine in the Small Row described as in Hanley and Shelton was being worked in 1561.[87] John Bell of Shelton Mill was mining at Hanley Green in 1643,[88] and in 1650 he held the lease of two mines in the Great Row and Cannel Row described as at Shelton and Hanley.[89] Coal mines at both places were listed among the possessions of the Duchy of Lancaster in 1675,[90] and a few years later Plot recorded the dig-ging of 'peacock' coal at Hanley Green.[91] Two coal mines in Hanley and Shelton, in the tenure of Thomas Fernihough in 1713, were leased by the Duchy of Lancaster to William Burslem of New-castle from 1717; in 1732 Lord Gower was granted the reversion of Burslem's lease, due to expire in 1743 or 1744,[92] and this evidently marks the beginning of the Leveson-Gower family's extensive

[69] *2nd Rep. Com. on Employment of Children*, p. c27.
[70] Mankowitz and Haggar, *Eng. Pottery*, 55; date on building.
[71] Jewitt, *Ceramic Art*, 499; H.R.L., EMT 7–844 (b), 7–846 (a, b).
[72] The Baddeleys had held it from at least the 1780's until 1807 when it was conveyed to Geo. Taylor; it passed on his death in 1811 to Hicks and Meigh, who also held the adjoining works to the W., formerly Ralph Baddeley's (now Ashworth's: see above), and it was held in the 1820's by John Mare: Mankowitz and Haggar, *Eng. Pottery*, 12, 13; Meigh, 'Staffs. Potters', 105, 133, 193; Allbut, *Staffs. Pottery Dir.* (1802); H.R.L., EMT 7–807 (b), 7–844 (b), 11–807, 11–844.   [73] Jewitt, *Ceramic Art*, 500.
[74] Meigh, 'Staffs. Potters', 54.
[75] O.S. Map 1/1,250, SJ 8847 SW. (1951); *Kelly's Dir. Staffs.* (1924); *Barrett's City of Stoke Dir.* [1959].
[76] In 1841 it was stated that 'there are three or four establishments on the outskirts of the town for boiling and calcining bones on a large scale, which frequently inundate the neighbourhood with very offensive odours'; it was added, however, that they had not been found to be a cause of disease: *2nd Rep. Com. on Employment of Children*, p. c12.
[77] W.S.L., D. 1788, vol. 95; W.S.L., D. 1742, bdle. 61; Yates, *Map of Staffs.* (1775, 1799); Hargreaves, *Map of Staffs. Potteries*; White, *Dir. Staffs.* (1834, 1851); *Kelly's Dir. Staffs.* (1884, 1896, 1908); O.S. Map 6" Staffs. xviii NW. (1890, 1925); W. Campbell, *Street Map of Hanley, Burslem, Tunstall and Newcastle-under-Lyme* (1912). The directories do not distinguish the 2 Botteslow mills, one of which was a bone mill in 1834 (White, *Dir. Staffs.* 1834), but both were again flint mills by the 1860's: O.S. Map 1/500 Staffs. xvi. 4. 8 (1866).

[78] Adams, *Adams Family*, 265; *Stoke Official Handbk.* (1960), 86, 133, 135; C. J. H. Homer, *Plan of Hanley and Shelton, 1857* (copy in S.R.O., Z/M/7).
[79] White, *Dir. Staffs.* (1834, 1851); Ward, *Stoke*, 381. The family held a steam-driven flint mill in Hill St. in 1818 and 1819: Parson and Bradshaw, *Dir. Staffs.* (1818); H.R.L., EMT 11–819. The Dresden Mill was a colour mill by the 1870's: O.S. Map 6" Staffs. xii SW. (1890).
[80] White, *Dir. Staffs.* (1834, 1851); *P.O. Dir. Staffs.* (1872); *Kelly's Dir. Staffs.* (1884, 1928); *Barrett's City of Stoke Dir.* [1959]; Warrillow, *Etruria*, 198–9.
[81] Sign on building; O.S. Map 6" Staffs. xviii NW. (1890); *Barrett's City of Stoke Dir.* [1959].
[82] Warrillow, *Etruria*, 196, 198; White, *Dir. Staffs.* (1851); tablet on building.
[83] For the Association's laboratories at Penkhull see p. 204.
[84] C. J. H. Homer, 'The N. Staffs. Coalfield' (*Trans. Inst. N. Staffs. Mining Engineers*, i), 105. Two or three cart-loads of surface coal were removed when a cellar was being excavated at the top of Piccadilly early in the present century: Huntbach, *Hanley*, 32.
[85] *S.H.C.* 1911, 245.
[86] Ibid. N.S. ix. 106; D.L. 5/25, ff. 566, 599.
[87] *S.H.C.* N.S. ix. 137.
[88] S.R.O., D. 260/M/box 25, bdle. k, Royalist Composi-tions, f. 84b.   [89] E 317/Staffs. 38, 39.
[90] *Cal. S.P. Dom.* 1675–6, 212.
[91] R. Plot, *Nat. Hist. Staffs.* (1686), 212. Shaw, *Staffs. Potteries*, 43, states that peacock coal was formerly dug on the Ivy House estate.
[92] D.L. 42/27, ff. 23b, 24a. Burslem's lease was for 26½ yrs. from Mich. 1717; the lease to Lord Gower, however, was to be for 19 yrs. from 25 Mar. 1743.

industrial undertakings in Hanley and Shelton. The family's mining operations, run by the Shelton Iron, Steel, and Coal Company from 1888, were in fact the main feature of the expansion of the coal industry in the Hanley district in the 19th century, particularly in the 1850's and 1860's.[93] During the 19th century the disused shafts of earlier workings were being built over and becoming a public danger and thus added to the nuisance of mining subsidence.[94] Soon after the creation of the borough in 1857 the borough council paid some £2,000 for a plan showing the whereabouts of these shafts. In fact it was not until 50 years later that any action was taken, following the disappearance of a man in 1904 owing to a sudden subsidence in John Street. Some 20 disused shafts, mostly boarded over, were then located and covered with brick.[95] Since c. 1937 Hanley has had only one colliery in operation, the Deep Pit, formerly only a part of Earl Granville's Shelton Colliery.

John Bell's two mines at Hanley and Shelton in the mid-17th century may well be identifiable with the two leased by the Duchy in the early 18th century to William Burslem and then to Lord Gower (see above) who himself leased 'a coal work' at Hanley Green, apparently in 1752, to Jeremiah Smith who was still the tenant in 1774.[96] These were presumably the operations which caused trouble when the foundations of the new St. John's Church were dug c. 1788, having also, it seems, been at least partly responsible for the ruinous state of the first church.[97] Lord Gower's grandson, the 4th Earl Granville, was mining at Shelton by at least 1818, and by the early 1830's his Shelton Colliery included coal and ironstone pits in the area between Mill Street and Brook Street and also south of Mill Street.[98] The number of these pits was increased to serve Lord Granville's ironworks nearby, opened in 1841 (see below), but most of them were closed c. 1889;[99] the two coal pits near Hanley goods station, however, were employing 681 below ground and 144 above in 1902 and remained in operation for a few years

longer.[1] The Shelton Colliery also included the Deep Pit at Far Green, opened by 1854; it was stated in 1869 to be the deepest pit in North Staffordshire, and in the early 20th century its workings were said to extend to Stoke on the south and Foxley on the north-west.[2] Employing 485 below ground and 118 above in 1894, 588 below and 209 above in 1902, and 750 below and 290 above in 1957,[3] it has remained the only colliery in operation in Hanley since production ceased at the Racecourse Pits c. 1937. These were opened by Lord Granville c. 1870 on the former racecourse to the north of Etruria Hall and in 1894 were employing 623 below ground and 193 above; one of the pits, devoted solely to ironstone mining, was closed in 1901.[4]

The Ivy House Colliery between Leek New Road and the Caldon Canal east of Ivy House Road was being worked by 1841 and was closed c. 1889.[5] The Hallfield Colliery (coal and ironstone) on the high ground at the end of Upper Market Street (now Huntbach Street), with a tramway running down to the Caldon Canal near Ivy House Road, was in operation by 1851.[6] Only coal was being mined there in 1858 because of the low price paid locally for ironstone,[7] and the colliery seems to have closed soon afterwards.[8] The Northwood Colliery north of the junction of Bucknall Old and New Roads was in operation by the mid-1860's; employing 430 below ground and 90 above in 1902, it was closed c. 1920.[9]

The mining at Birches Head and at the New Hall Pottery is described elsewhere.[10]

IRON-WORKING. Several attempts to establish iron foundries at Hanley and Shelton in the earlier 19th century met with little or no success.[11] In 1839, however, the 4th Earl Granville began to build three furnaces between Cobridge Road and Mill Street, an area rich in ironstone as well as coal where the earl was already mining, and first blew them in 1841.[12] His son the 5th earl (d. 1891) produced 7,280 tons of pig iron there in 1848[13] and in 1850 erected new furnaces on the bank of the Trent and Mersey

[93] Census, 1861, 1871, Staffs.; see p. 170.
[94] Staffs. Advertiser. 10 July 1886, reporting a meeting of the Association of Municipal and Sanitary Engineers; it was then said that 'almost the entire town is honey-combed'.
[95] W. Scarratt, Old Times in the Potteries, 163; Huntbach, Hanley, 31–32.
[96] W.S.L. 241/26, pp. 1, 11, 21, 37, [48], [62]. Smith's lease was for 29 yrs.
[97] B.M. Ch. Br. xxxi. 3; see p. 154.
[98] Parson and Bradshaw, Dir. Staffs. (1818); Staffs. Advertiser, 3 Oct. 1829; White, Dir. Staffs. (1834, 1851); Ward, Stoke, 379; Hargreaves, Map of Staffs. Potteries; Homer, Plan of Hanley and Shelton, 1857; O.S. Map 6" Staffs. xii SW. (1890). These pits included Bell's Mill Pit south of Mill St. where there was a strike in 1851, the men there receiving only 3s. 6d. a day and having to find their own tools and gunpowder, whereas the standard wage in N. Staffs. was 4s. as well as equipment; the men at other local pits came out in sympathy: The Lever, 27 Sept. 1851, 276–7 (copy in H.R.L.).
[99] Rep. Insp. Mines, N. Staffs., 1888 [C. 5779], p. 13, H.C. (1889), xxiv; 1889 [C. 6015], p. 13, H.C. (1890), xxiii; 1890 [C. 6346], p. 29, H.C. (1890–1), xxii. In 1888 there was a disused pit belonging to the earl at Joiner's Square where there had been a colliery in at least the 1820's and early 1830's: Shaw, Staffs. Potteries, 46; Hargreaves, Map of Staffs. Potteries.
[1] Rep. Insp. Mines, Stafford, 1902 [C. 1590], p. 270, H.C. (1903), xv; Scarratt, Old Times in the Potteries, 163; W. Campbell, Street Map of Hanley, Burslem, Tunstall, and Newcastle (1907; copy in H.R.L.). The tip at Tinkers-clough which resulted from these workings (Warrillow,

Stoke, 263) is still (1960) in existence.
[2] Rep. Insp. Mines [1994], p. 107, H.C. (1854–5), xv; Homer, Plan of Hanley and Shelton, 1857; T.N.S.F.C. (1869), 4–5; Scarratt, Old Times in the Potteries, 162. There was also the Clayholes Pit nearby, to the E. of Providence Sq.: Homer, Plan of Hanley and Shelton, 1857; O.S. Map 1/500 Staffs. xi. 16. 7 (1866).
[3] Rep. Insp. Mines, N. Staffs. 1894 [C. 7667], p. 46, H.C. (1895), xxii; Rep. Insp. Mines, 1902, 270; Guide to the Coalfields (1960).
[4] Scarratt, Old Times in the Potteries, 162, 169; Rep. Insp. Mines, N. Staffs. 1894, 46; Rep. Insp. Mines, Stafford, 1901 [Cd. 1062], p. 29, H.C. (1902), xvii; ex inf. Mr. W. Jack, Norton-in-the-Moors (1959).
[5] Pigot's Nat. Com. Dir. (1841); Slater's Birmingham District Dir. (1852–3); Rep. Insp. Mines (1854–5), 108; Rep. Insp. Mines, N. Staffs. 1888, 13. It does not occur in the list for 1890: ibid. 1890.
[6] White, Dir. Staffs. (1851); S.R.O., D. 321/M/B/62, 65, 66; Homer, Plan of Hanley and Shelton, 1857.
[7] S.R.O., D. 321/M/B/66.
[8] It was not mentioned in Keates and Ford's Potteries Dir. (1865-6). The Hallfield Brickworks had been established nearby by 1866: O.S. Map 1/500 Staffs. xi. 16. 13 (1866).
[9] Keates and Ford's Potteries Dir. (1865-6); S.R.O., D. 321/M/B/75; Rep. Insp. Mines, Stafford, 1902, 269; Kelly's Dir. Staffs. (1916); O.S. Map 6" Staffs. xii SW. (1890; 1926).   [10] See pp. 167, 252.
[11] Ward, Stoke, 378–9; Staffs. Advertiser, 25 Mar. 1816.
[12] Ward, Stoke, 379; Warrillow, Etruria, 179, 182, 203; Keates's Potteries Dir. (1892-3), 72–73.
[13] R. Meade, The Coal and Iron Industries of the U.K., 506.

Canal at Etruria west of the Wedgwood works; about two years later his new Shelton Bar Iron Company built a forge and mills in Mill Street to work the pig produced at the furnaces and in 1864 added a forge and mills at the Etruria site also.[14] It was these developments that were chiefly responsible for the rise in the population of Hanley and Shelton in the 1850's and 1860's.[15] In 1888 the company became the Shelton Iron, Steel, and Coal Company with Lord Granville as its first chairman, more new plant was then laid down, and the expansion of the works has continued during the 20th century. The company has operated since 1956 as Shelton Iron and Steel Ltd.[16]

OTHER INDUSTRIES. There were about five brick and tile works in the area in the early 1830's,[17] about eight 60 years later,[18] and about a dozen in the late 1950's.[19] The Hallfield Brick Works had been established near the site of the former Hallfield Colliery on the high ground east of the town by the mid-1860's,[20] but it had evidently been reopened on its present site in Festing Street by the end of the century.[21] It was purchased in 1947 by Richards Tiles Ltd. of Tunstall and is used for the production of unglazed floor tiles.[22]

The Ivy House paper mill on the north bank of the Caldon Canal west of what is now Ivy House Road was founded by G. H. Fourdrinier in 1827, after experiments in Hertfordshire, and contained machinery for making paper by the piece instead of the sheet. Despite stiff opposition from other paper manufacturers Fourdrinier built up a business producing tissue paper for pottery engraving as well as ordinary paper. It was taken over by Thomas Brittain in 1855, and in 1890 his grandson, Thomas Arthur Brittain, and two other members of the family bought a paper mill at Cheddleton and incorporated the two businesses as Brittains Ltd. Paper-making eventually ceased at the Ivy House Mill which was rebuilt and since 1906 has been devoted to paper coating and finishing.[23]

The Eastwood silk mill also on the Caldon Canal was built by James Baddeley in 1824 but failed soon afterwards. He was offering it for sale in 1829, and some ten years later it was being used by Joseph Fourdrinier as a workshop producing machines and parts for the paper-making trade generally.[24]

There were two breweries in the area by the early 1830's: in Vale Place, Hanley, and at the junction of Sun Street and Broad Street, Shelton.[25] The first survived until the early 20th century and the second until the 1930's.[26]

SOCIAL LIFE. The Pottery Subscription Library at Hanley was founded in 1790 by James Straphan, the first bookseller in the Potteries.[27] About 1840 the library, consisting of some 3,000 volumes, was housed in the shop of Thomas Allbut, who had succeeded Straphan as librarian and treasurer c. 1800; the membership was elective with an entrance fee of 2 guineas and an annual subscription of 1 guinea. The library was still in existence in 1860.[28] The Shelton Subscription Library was founded in 1814 and was still in existence in 1830, housed in Bethesda Schoolroom.[29] Between at least 1851 and 1876 there was a subscription newspaper room at the town hall.[30] The borough council established a free library in 1887, taking a lease of the whole building in Pall Mall belonging to the Mechanics' Institution (see below) except for the reading-room.[31] The city library is still housed there and since 1958 has also occupied the adjoining building which formerly housed the British School, Hanley, and the Russell Art Gallery.[32] A boys' library was formed as part of the free library in 1893, mainly at the instigation of the mayor, Edwin Hammersley.[33]

The Pottery Philosophical Society was established at the Red Lion Inn, Shelton, in 1820 with a largely middle-class membership; refounded in 1824, it continued to meet, in members' houses, until 1835.[34] The Mechanics' Institution was founded in 1826 for 'the promotion of useful knowledge among the working classes' at the instigation of Benjamin Vale, then curate of Stoke and later Rector of Longton, and with the support of Josiah Wedgwood and other leading local men.[35] Premises containing lecture-rooms and classrooms, a library, a laboratory, and a committee room were built in Frederick Street (now Gitana Street) in 1834–5, and c. 1840 the institution had a library of nearly 1,500 books, 'excluding polemical divinity and party politics'.[36] A museum known as the North Staffordshire Museum had been added by 1851, and probably by 1846.[37] The institution moved into a new building in Pall Mall in 1861.[38] With the exception of the reading-room, which is still in use, the rest of

[14] Keates's Potteries Dir. (1892–3), 73; Homer, Plan of Hanley and Shelton, 1857; O.S. Map 1/500 Staffs. xi. 15, 18 and 20 (1866).
[15] Census, 1861, 1871, Staffs.
[16] Keates's Potteries Dir. (1892–3); see p. 152.
[17] White, Dir. Staffs. (1834); Hargreaves, Map of Staffs. Potteries. [18] Keates's Potteries Dir. (1892–3).
[19] Barrett's City of Stoke Dir. [1959].
[20] O.S. Map 1/500 Staffs. xi. 16. 13 (1866).
[21] Ibid. 6″ Staffs. xii SW. (1900).
[22] See p. 104.
[23] Ward, Stoke, 376–7; Brittains Ltd., Paper Craftsmanship (copy among W.S.L. pamphs. sub Industries); inf. from Brittains Ltd. (1960); V. Brittain, Testament of Youth, chap. i; O.S. Map 6″ Staffs. xii SW. (1890).
[24] Ward, Stoke, 380; Staffs. Mercury, 4 Apr. 1829.
[25] White, Dir. Staffs. (1834, 1851); Keates and Ford's Potteries Dir. (1865–6); Keates's Potteries Dir. (1873–4, 1882 which also mentions the Etruria Brewery, Salem St., 1892–3).
[26] Kelly's Dir. Staffs. (1908, 1928 which shows the Shelton Brewery in the hands of Parker's Burslem Brewery, 1932); S.R.O., D. 206/4.

[27] Ward, Stoke, 408.
[28] Ibid.; P.O. Dir. Staffs. (1860).
[29] Rules and Catalogue of the Shelton Subscription Library (1830; copy in W.S.L. Pamphs., vol. vii, no. 19).
[30] White, Dir. Staffs. (1851); P.O. Dir. Staffs. (1876). There was a second newsroom in Piccadilly in 1860 (ibid. 1860), possibly identifiable with the Protestant Conservative Assoc.'s newsroom there in 1868: ibid. 1868.
[31] Staffs. Advertiser, 18 Dec. 1886; ibid. 14 Dec. 1887; Staffs. Sentinel, 1 and 15 Oct. 1892.
[32] See pp. 149, 270, 316.
[33] Staffs. Sentinel, 26 Oct. 1892; ibid. 17 Oct. 1893; 12 Mar. 1898.
[34] R. G. Haggar, Some Adult Educ. Institutions in N. Staffs. (Rewley Ho. Papers, iii, no. 6), 1 (copy in H.R.L.).
[35] Ibid. 3–4; Ward, Stoke, 392–3.
[36] Ward, Stoke, 393; Staffs. Advertiser, 10 Oct. 1835.
[37] White, Dir. Staffs. (1851); see p. 156. The museum was being planned c. 1838: Ward, Stoke, 393.
[38] Haggar, Some Adult Educ. Institutions, 9–10. There is a copy of a plan (never carried out) for the new building in H.R.L. For a description of the actual building see p. 149.

the building in Pall Mall has been occupied by the free library since 1887, and the museum became the nucleus of the borough museum.

In 1850 about 80 working men bought the former Primitive Methodist chapel in Brunswick Street and adapted it as the People's Hall for lectures and public meetings.[39] 'A majority of the share-holders', it was stated in 1851, 'are democratic, but they disclaim all party spirit in the use of the hall and permit nothing tending to immorality or inebriety'.[40] The venture seems not to have prospered,[41] and by 1854 the building was used as a theatre (see below).

The first move towards the establishment of an art school was made by the Mechanics' Institution in 1845, but the idea was taken up in the following year by certain master potters.[42] The Potteries Schools of Design were founded in 1847 under the auspices of the London School of Design and consisted of schools held in the British School building in Pall Mall, Hanley, and in Stoke town hall; the Hanley branch became an independent school in 1860.[43] The Mechanics' Institution continued to hold its own art classes until at least 1853, to some extent in rivalry with the new schools.[44] The building in Pall Mall was enlarged in 1880 by the addition of a new story, and, under the head masterships of Samuel Cartlidge (1882–1900) and his successor George Cartlidge, the Hanley School of Art reached a high standard of achievement.[45] With the amalgamation of the art schools of the various towns after Federation, however, the Hanley school gradually lost ground to its rival at Burslem and was closed in its centenary year, 1947.[46]

The North Staffordshire Technical and Art Museum established in the Mechanics' Institution building in Pall Mall by the North Staffordshire Chamber of Commerce in 1890 was transferred in 1891 to the borough council which also took over the museum belonging to the Mechanics' Institution. The North Staffordshire Natural History Museum, established in association with the North Staffordshire Naturalists' Field Club, was opened in the same building in 1908. The present City Museum and Art Gallery in Broad Street was opened in 1956, and the upper part of the Mechanics' Institution which had housed the museum was demolished.[47]

Two temporary buildings were erected in 1906 and 1908 for mining and pottery classes respectively on land at the south end of Victoria (now College) Road given by A. S. Bolton of Oakamoor as the site of a place of higher education. The Central School of Science and Technology was opened there in 1914; an extension was added at the Station Road end of the building in 1931 and an engineering workshop in 1939. The College of Ceramics on the opposite side of College Road was opened in 1957; the next year a new engineering department involving the completion of the Station Road wing was opened and the mining department rehoused.[48] The department of building, formed in 1946 and since 1957 existing independently as the City of Stoke-on-Trent College of Building, is situated at the former Cauldon Place Pottery where a new building was opened in 1960.[49] The technical college's department of catering also has premises on the Cauldon Place site.

The Hanley and Shelton Anti-slavery Society was founded in 1830 and received support from leading manufacturers of the area and local clergy. It was still meeting at the end of 1839.[50]

Being within Stoke parish Hanley took part in Stoke Wakes, held originally on the first Sunday of August and by the mid-19th century during the whole of the first full week of August.[51] The side-shows that filled the market square in Hanley and the streets around it were banned from the town-centre during the First World War; they were restored after the war to be banned once more in 1923.[52] Pat Collins in that year opened his Wakes Fair on a ground in Regent Road[53] where it is still (1960) held.

From 1824 horse-racing was held during the wakes over a mile-long course on a 50-acre field to the east of Etruria Hall; by 1840 a grandstand had been built on the east side of the course.[54] The last meeting was held in 1841,[55] and from 1850 races were held at Boothen near Stoke;[56] the Racecourse Pits were opened on the Etruria course c. 1870 by Earl Granville.[57] Port Vale Football Club moved from Cobridge in 1911 to a ground off Bryan Street below St. John's Church; this remained the club's home until the opening of its present ground in Hamil Road, Burslem, in 1950.[58] The Hanley ground and grandstand are now derelict. Hanley Swifts Football Club had a ground at Northwood c. 1910.[59] The present Sun Street greyhound track had been opened by 1940.[60] Cockfighting was held at the Cat Inn, Northwood, towards the end of the 18th century.[61]

[39] White, *Dir. Staffs.* (1851); *The Lever* (1851), p. 101 (copy in H.R.L.). Plans for a library, reading-rooms and classrooms had not been carried out: ibid. 23 Aug. 1851, pp. 225–6.   [40] White, *Dir. Staffs.* (1851).
[41] *The Lever* (1851), pp. 225–6, 253–4.
[42] R. G. Haggar, *A Cent. of Art Educ. in the Potteries*, 5.
[43] Ibid. 5–6, 12; *Staffs. Potteries Schs. of Design* (rep. of first annual general meeting of the friends of the Potteries Schools of Design; copy in W.S.L. Pamphs., vol. vi, no. 12).   [44] Haggar, *Art Educ. in the Potteries*, 8–9.
[45] Ibid. 24, 31–32, 40.
[46] Ibid. 33–35. For a description of the building see p. 149.
[47] H.R.L., Hanley Boro. Gen. Purposes Cttee. Mins., 24 July 1891; *Kelly's Dir. Staffs.* (1892); *Staffs. Sentinel*, 8 Nov. 1890; Huntbach, *Hanley*, 84; *Hanley Boro. Yr. Bk. 1908–9*; G. Bemrose, 'Some Notable Museums' (*The North-western Naturalist*, June 1936), 107 (copy in H.R.L.); inf. from the librarian, H.R.L. (1960). For the museum and art gallery since 1910 see p. 270.
[48] *Staffs. Sentinel*, 23 Sept. 1915; inscriptions on Station Rd. frontage and in hall of College of Ceramics; ex inf. the Principal, N. Staffs. Technical College (1959); *Staffs. Advertiser*, 25 Apr. 1914.
[49] *News Chron.* 10 Nov. 1954; ex inf. the Principal, N.

Staffs. Technical College (1959); local inf. (1960); see p. 167.
[50] H.R.L., Hanley and Shelton Anti-slavery Soc. Proc. 1830–9.
[51] See p. 205. A September wake, still held in 1822, was started in connexion with the founding of St. John's: *Staffs. Advertiser*, 14 Sept. 1822.
[52] *Hanley Jubilee Souvenir* (1907), 19; *Staffs. Sentinel*, 3 Mar. 1919; *Staffs. Advertiser*, 11 Aug. 1923.
[53] Warrillow, *Stoke*, 394.
[54] *Staffs. Advertiser*, 24 and 31 July, 7 Aug. 1824; ibid. 6 and 13 Aug. 1825; Ward, *Stoke*, 392, where 1825 is wrongly given as the first year; Warrillow, *Etruria*, 187–8, 315; *Hanley Jubilee Souvenir* (1907), 27–28; Hargreaves, *Map of Staffs. Potteries*.
[55] *Staffs. Advertiser*, 7 Aug. 1841; ibid. 13 Aug. 1842.
[56] See p. 205.   [57] See p. 169.
[58] *Port Vale 1876–1950* (copy in H.R.L.); O.S. Map 6" Staffs. xii SW. (1926); see p. 141.
[59] Huntbach, *Hanley*, 101.
[60] *Old and New Hall Potteries*, 2 (copy among W.S.L. Pamphs. *sub* Ceramics).
[61] Huntbach, *Hanley*, 99. There is a Cat Inn in Keelings Lane.

An attempt to establish a theatre in Hanley in 1824 was unsuccessful, and the only dramatic entertainment available before the middle of the 19th century was that provided by itinerants on ground at the rear of the Sea Lion Inn in High Street (now Town Road).[62] In the early 1850's, however, a theatre known as the Potteries Royal Theatre was established in the former People's Hall, Brunswick Street.[63] 'Dingy and inconvenient', it was replaced by the Theatre Royal which was opened on the same site in 1871 with its entrance in Pall Mall[64] and was enlarged in 1888 and partially reconstructed in 1894.[65] It was burnt down in 1949 and rebuilt in 1950–1.[66] A wooden hall in Glass Street (formerly Church Street), originally used by circuses, was the Victoria Music Hall by 1866 and in 1868 became the People's Music Hall; this venture failed and by 1869 the building was again used by circuses. As the Theatre Royal, Grand Opera House and Temple of Varieties, it presented a mixture of dramatic and music hall performances while the Theatre Royal was being built, but in 1873 it once more became a music hall. In 1878 it became the Imperial Circus and was also used as a hall by the newly formed Hanley and Shelton Philharmonic Society (see below) and other large gatherings. It was later rebuilt as the Imperial Mission Hall and in 1908 became a skating-rink.[67] A wooden building in Tontine Street on the site of the present post office was occupied by Batty's Circus c. 1880.[68] The Alexandra Music Hall opened in New Street (now Goodson Street) by 1880[69] had been renamed the 'Gaiety' by 1892[70] and the 'Empire' by 1900.[71] It was subsequently enlarged and in 1901 was reopened as the King's Palace Theatre.[72] This had been closed by 1924.[73] The Grand Theatre of Varieties at the junction of Trinity Street and Upper Foundry Street was opened in 1898 and closed c. 1932.[74] The Lyric Theatre in Marsh Street occurs in 1912 and 1916.[75] The amateur repertory theatre which occupies the former mission church of St. Jude in Beresford Street, Shelton, was opened in the 1930's.[76] The Mitchell Memorial Youth Centre in Broad Street containing a theatre and workshops was built in 1955–7 in memory of R. J. Mitchell, the designer of the Spitfire aircraft, who was born at Butts Lane, Kidsgrove, in 1895.[77]

There was a choral society at Shelton by 1824,[78] and the Hanley district was represented at the choral festival held at Stoke in 1833.[79] A music festival drawing on local talent was held in 1854 in St. Mark's Church, Shelton, and in Hanley town hall.[80] In 1878 the Hanley and Shelton Philharmonic Society was founded[81], and about the same time James Garner, an employee at the Meakins' Eastwood Vale Pottery and organist and choirmaster at the Eastwood Vale Baptist church, formed the Eastwood Vale Prize Choir; in 1882 it was renamed the Hanley Glee and Madrigal Society and soon became the most notable choir in the district.[82] The Etruscan Choral Society originated as part of a new social club at Etruria during the General Strike of 1926.[83] At first called the Etruscan Male Voice Choir, it was renamed when a mixed choir was added in 1931, and by 1935 it was achieving national fame.[84] Depleted after the war broke out in 1939 and disbanded in 1941 when Salem Chapel where it rehearsed was bombed, the choir was reformed in 1944, and in 1945 it opened new premises in Humbert Street in a hall formerly a school and a chapel and then reconstructed as the Etruria Philharmonic Hall.[85]

Until 1888 Hanley's concerts and recitals were held variously in the old town hall, St. Mark's Church, the covered market (where Jenny Lind sang), and the music hall in Glass Street.[86] In 1887–8 the Victoria Hall was built as an extension of the new town hall to the designs of the borough surveyor, Joseph Lobley; it is acoustically very fine, and all major concerts were thenceforward held there. Hanley's position as the musical centre of the Potteries was thus secure.[87] A series of five music festivals was held between 1889 and 1899 in imitation of other provincial towns; the first made a profit which was given to local hospitals but the other four ran at a loss.[88] Elgar conducted the first performance of 'King Olaf' at the 1896 festival and thereafter regularly came to Hanley to conduct.[89] Delius conducted at a concert in 1908, and the North Staffordshire District Choral Society gave the first performance of his 'Sea Drift' under Thomas (later Sir Thomas) Beecham in the same year.[90] A series of celebrity concerts endowed by George Meakin was

[62] Hanley Jubilee Souvenir (1907), 28; P. W. L. Adams, John Henry Clive, 53–54; S.R.O., Q/SB Trans. 1820, Q/SR East. 1830.
[63] P.O. Dir. Staffs. (1854); Scarratt, Old Times in the Potteries, 196; Homer, Plan of Hanley and Shelton, 1857; Hanley Jubilee Souvenir (1907), 28; Adams, Clive, 54–55.
[64] Ancient Corp. of Hanley, 111; Scarratt, Old Times in the Potteries, 196.
[65] Kelly's Dir. Staffs. (1896).
[66] Theatre Royal, Hanley: Brochure of Re-opening 1951 (copy in H.R.L.).
[67] Staffs. Sentinel, 16 Aug. 1820; Ancient Corp. of Hanley, 111; Hanley Jubilee Souvenir (1907), 31, 32; Huntbach, Hanley, 102; O.S. Map 1/500 Staffs. xi. 16. 2 (1866).
[68] Huntbach, Hanley, 101.
[69] Kelly's Dir. Staffs. (1880).
[70] Ibid. (1892).   [71] Ibid. (1900).
[72] Staffs. Advertiser, 13 Apr. 1901.
[73] Kelly's Dir. Staffs. (1924).
[74] Staffs. Advertiser, 27 Aug. 1898; Reg. of Defunct and other Companies removed from Stock Exchange Official Yr. Bk. 1956, 197. It occurs in Kelly's Dir. Staffs. (1932).
[75] Kelly's Dir. Staffs. (1912, 1916).
[76] Ibid. (1940); see p. 157.
[77] Staffs. Eve. Sentinel, Suppl. 28 Oct. 1957.
[78] Hanley Jubilee Souvenir, 28.
[79] Ibid. 31; see p. 205.

[80] Hanley Jubilee Souvenir, 31; Staffs. Sentinel Summer No., 1911, p. 51.
[81] Hanley Jubilee Souvenir, 32; H.R.L., News Cuttings, iv, pp. 80–81.
[82] R. Ship, Hanley Glee and Madrigal Soc. (copy in H.R.L.); Huntbach, Hanley, 82; R. Nettel, Music in the Five Towns, 1840–1914, 14–31, 60. Another important choir of the district was James Whewall's N. Staffs. District Choral Soc. which was formed in 1901 among the miners of Red Street and since 1944 has been called the City of Stoke-on-Trent Choral Soc.: ibid. 56–60, 89–93, 100–6; G. Thompson, City of Stoke-on-Trent Choral Soc. (copy in H.R.L.).
[83] Warrillow, Etruria, 234–7, 239.   [84] Ibid. 240–1.
[85] Ibid. 242, 245–6; see pp. 295, 307.
[86] Hanley Jubilee Souvenir (1907), 31, 32, 35; Nettel, Music in the Five Towns, 18, 20, 22.
[87] Nettel, op. cit. 37, 53; Hanley Jubilee Souvenir, 32.
[88] Nettel, op. cit. 37, 47–48; Staffs. Advertiser, 13 Oct. 1888; ibid. 16 Feb. 1889; 4 and 25 Oct. 1890; 28 Oct. 1899. The loss in 1890 was blamed partly on 'the unhappy want of unanimity of the various Pottery towns'; a rival concert was held at Tunstall, and Stoke like Newcastle was unsympathetic: ibid. 25 Oct. 1890.
[89] Nettel, op. cit. 41, 89, 94, 96. His last appearance in Hanley was in 1932 for a performance of 'King Olaf': ibid. 97.
[90] Ibid. 99, 100.

The adjoining works (demolished 1961)

Phoenix Works, Hanley, 1845 (demolished 1962)

Late-18th-century master potter's house at Longport

Boundary Works, Longton, 1819

ARCHITECTURE OF THE POTTERY INDUSTRY

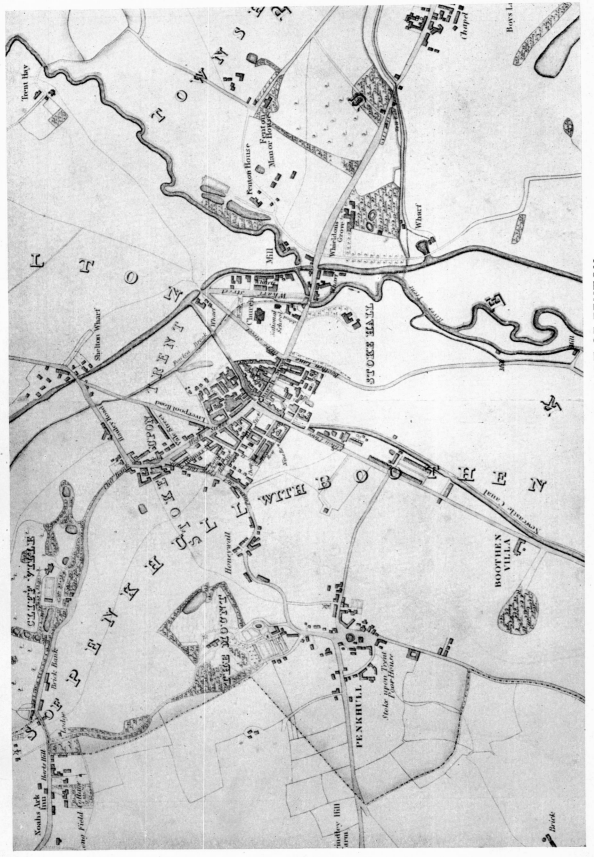

STOKE-UPON-TRENT AND PART OF FENTON
from a map of 1832 by T. Hargreaves

held in the Victoria Hall from 1888. Although the concerts were at first very popular, support dwindled after 1900 and they lapsed in 1908.[91]

In 1783, presumably as a protest against its lack of self-government, Hanley began the custom of appointing a mock mayor and corporation annually. The ceremony formed part of an annual venison feast, the Marquess of Stafford presenting half a buck and the qualification for membership of the corporation being the ability to drink a yard glass of ale at a draught.[92] 'So Hanley made its own charter of incorporation and municipal honours became as clay in the hands of a potter'.[93] The feast, described by the *Staffordshire Advertiser* in 1860 as 'a joke from beginning to end'[94] and by Arnold Bennett as 'a piece of elaborate machinery for dinner-eating',[95] is still (1960) held.[96]

The Hanley Association for the Prosecution of Felons evidently dates from 1792.[97] It still survives as a dining-club.[98]

STOKE-UPON-TRENT

THE borough of Stoke-upon-Trent as it existed in 1910 covered an area of 1,882 acres[1] and comprised the old township of Penkhull together with a small area of former glebe around Stoke railway station which had once been part of Shelton township.[2] The boundary was largely natural. On the west it followed the Lyme Brook down to the Trent at Hanford and then turned north-eastward along the Trent as far as the Fowlea Brook.[3] The township boundary then followed the Fowlea Brook north-west to Etruria, but the borough boundary continued up the Trent for about a mile and then swung north-westwards to rejoin the Fowlea Brook, thus including the railway station. From Etruria the boundary ran west along the Newcastle road as far as Basford, and it then curved round the south-eastern part of Newcastle borough to rejoin the Lyme Brook.[4]

The township of Penkhull thus formed the southern end of a ridge lying between the Fowlea and Lyme Brooks and dropping down to the Trent, of which both brooks are tributaries. The ground rises, steeply in places, from below 350 ft. along these rivers, and in Stoke town itself,[5] to over 525 ft. around Penkhull and Hartshill in the centre and northern part of the borough area. The road from Derby, Uttoxeter, and the south-eastern part of the Potteries to Newcastle-under-Lyme crosses the Trent near Stoke church. Other roads run to Hanley and Leek. The main road from London and Stafford to Newcastle and the north of England runs through the western part of the former Stoke borough. The

district is one of 19th-century urban development around Stoke church with Penkhull, Boothen, Hartshill, and Trent Vale as areas of suburban development dating from the early 19th century onwards.

In the Middle Ages the main centre of population was around Penkhull village, and Stoke itself then seems to have been nothing more than the place where the parish church was located. Even in the mid-18th century Stoke comprised little more than the church and the houses of the rector, curate, and parish clerk.[6] Already, however, there were at least three potworks a little to the west of the church,[7] and with the growth of the pottery industry in the later 18th century, the turnpiking of the road from Derby and Uttoxeter to Newcastle-under-Lyme in 1759, and the opening of the Trent and Mersey Canal in 1777, Stoke began to develop as a town.[8] Although it was still described as a village in 1795,[9] there was by then extensive building along both sides of the turnpike road from the church up to Cliff Bank.[10] By 1820 several new streets which had been laid out on the south side of this stretch of the road around the town hall of 1794 formed the nucleus of the growing town; buildings had also been erected in the Eldon Place stretch of London Road.[11] Glebe Street, Brook Street, and Wharf Street on the north side of the main road were built about the same time as the new church (1826–30).[12] The town was then described as 'pleasantly situated' on the Trent with 'many handsome houses, wharves, warehouses

[91] Ibid. 53; *Hanley Jubilee Souvenir*, 35; Huntbach, *Hanley*, 83.

[92] *Ancient Corp. of Hanley*; G. Huntbach, 'Origin of the famous Venison Feast' (*Staffs. Life.* 1949), 40–41, 43.

[93] *Ancient Corp. of Hanley*, 7.

[94] 12 Oct. 1860.

[95] 'The Revolver' (*The Matador of the Five Towns*).

[96] Ex inf. the librarian, H.R.L.

[97] Warrillow, *Stoke*, 387, 390; H.R.L., T/S of a declaration by the inhabs. of the Potteries for the founding of an association for the prosecution of felons, 1792.

[98] Ex inf. the librarian, H.R.L.

[1] *Census*, 1911, Staffs.

[2] Stoke-upon-Trent also gave its name to a large ancient parish which included most of the Potteries area (i.e. excluding Tunstall which was in Wolstanton parish), and to the parliamentary borough which was created in 1832 and covered all the main centres in the Potteries. It has been suggested that in 1086 Penkhull probably included Newcastle-under-Lyme and Shelton: Ward, *Stoke*, 510.

[3] E. of Boothen Old Road the boundary evidently followed what had been the course of the Trent before the straightening of the river c. 1880 and c. 1884: H.R.L.,

Stoke Boro. Sanitary Cttee. Mins. 1874–81, p. 332; 1881–92, pp. 28, 29, 152.

[4] T. Hargreaves, *Map of Staffs. Potteries and Newcastle* (1832); O.S. Map 6″ xvii NE., SE.; xviii NW. (1900), SW. (1901); *Plan of Stoke-on-Trent and Newcastle-under-Lyme* (Geographia Ltd.); Ward, *Stoke*, app., pp. lxii, lxiii, where the Lyme Brook is called Newcastle Brook (1689).

[5] The area around Stoke parish church was liable to flooding until c. 1881: see pp. 191, 196.

[6] Ward, *Stoke*, 450, 498.

[7] See pp. 177, 179.

[8] J. Aikin, *The Country around Manchester* (1795), 522; Ward, *Stoke*, 499.

[9] Act for making canal from Stoke to Newcastle, 35 Geo. III, c. 87.

[10] W. Yates, *Map of Staffs.* (1775 and 1799); see plate facing p. 4 for reproduction of part of 1775 edn. The main road is now known as Church St. at the E. end of Stoke and as Hartshill Rd. farther W.; the central section was formerly called High St.

[11] C. and J. Greenwood, *Map. of Staffs.* (1820); see p. 180.

[12] Hargreaves, *Map of Staffs. Potteries*, reproduced on facing page; Ward, *Stoke*, 498; see pp. 180, 183, 190.

and earthenware manufactories'.[13] Houses were built along Liverpool Road in the late 1820's,[14] and several shops were erected there by William Copeland in the next decade.[15] A new road to Leek was run from the end of Glebe Street in the early 1840's; the railway and station were opened in 1848.[16] To Charles Dickens in 1852 Stoke was 'a picturesque heap of houses, kilns, smoke, wharfs, canals and river lying (as was most appropriate) in a basin'.[17] The third quarter of the century saw the building of the terraced cottages east of Leek New Road near the station and of the Copeland Street area, a mixture of factories and terraced houses, linking Glebe Street and Liverpool Road.[18] The area around Lonsdale and Woodhouse Streets was also beginning to be built up, and it was further developed in the last decade of the century over the grounds of the former rectory-house, known in the 19th century as Stoke Hall.[19] The triangle of streets between Liverpool Road, Shelton Old Road, and Hartshill Road dates mainly from the last quarter of the 19th century.[20] The town-centre was thus completely built up by 1900.

The hill-top village of Penkhull may originally have been a British settlement. It has been suggested that the name is a compound of the British 'pencēt' ('end of the wood') and the Old English 'hyll'.[21] Also a cup, possibly of prehistoric origin, has been found there.[22] By 1086 the village was the centre of the district, and it retained this status until the development of Stoke town in the 19th century.[23] It still possesses a certain village quality in the area round the church, which in 1842 replaced a school on the open space in the centre of the village known as Penkhull Green.[24] The character of Penkhull was, however, being modified by the early 19th century. Until then it was a village of small farmers,[25] with apparently some pottery making c. 1600.[26] Josiah Spode (d. 1827), who in 1803 built The Mount, a mansion standing in extensive grounds to the north of the village,[27] also erected cottages at the Penkhull end of Penkhull New Road and at Penkhull Square on what is now called Trent Valley Road (formerly Brisley Hill).[28] At Honeywall to the east of the

village there were by 1829 'a number of houses, pleasantly situated on an elevated tract of land, possessing a fine view of the eastern side of the district.'[29] Penkhull was described in 1834 as 'a populous suburb of the town [Stoke], having many modern houses erected chiefly for the accommodation of the working-classes',[30] and c. 1840 as consisting 'of some farm-houses, a few genteel houses, and a number of modern workmen's dwellings'.[31]

Prince's Road, running from the west end of the street named Honeywall past The Mount to the Newcastle road at Hartshill, dates from the 1850's. It was laid out by Frederick Bishop, mainly with a better type of terraced housing, soon after he had acquired The Mount in the early 1850's.[32] By 1876 the roads to the east of Prince's Road were being laid out.[33] As a result of all this development some 1,300 more houses were standing in and near Penkhull in 1861 than in 1831.[34] The North Staffordshire Infirmary was moved from Etruria to the new buildings erected in 1866–9 on the northern part of the estate attached to The Mount. The remainder of the estate, including the house, was taken over by the North Staffordshire Blind and Deaf School in 1897.[35] Queen's Road, running from Penkhull round the west side of the infirmary to the north end of Prince's Road, was built c. 1884, mainly, it would appear, to give access to the new cemetery;[36] it contains a few houses at either end, mostly of the late 19th century, and also the laboratories of the British Ceramic Research Association.[37] The Trent Valley Road area south of the village is mainly a residential district dating from the late 19th century onwards.[38] The houses on the west side of the road for about half a mile below Penkhull Square were built as a garden suburb after 1910.[39] There is also extensive housing of the years between the world wars along Newcastle Lane and to the north of it, in St. Thomas Place, off the north end of Prince's Road, and to the west of the Cliff Bank end of Honeywall. A council estate begun between Honeywall and Penkhull New Road since 1945 is still (1960) growing; part of it is built on the site of the old cottages. Another post-1945 estate has been built

[13] Pigot's Nat. Com. Dir. (1828–9).
[14] S. Shaw, Staffs. Potteries (1829), 60.
[15] Ward, Stoke, 498.   [16] See pp. 178, 180.
[17] Reprinted Pieces (1858), 'A Plated Article'; reprinted from Household Words, 24 Apr. 1852.
[18] O.S. Map 6" Staffs. xviii NW. (1890); R. Nicholls, Township of Penkhull cum Boothen, 26–27; date-stones of 1854 and 1864 in Copeland St., the E. end of which, between Glebe St. and the canal bridge, existed by 1839: S.R.O., Q/RUt 5/80A.
[19] O.S. Map 6" Staffs. xviii NW. (1890, 1900); see p. 186.
[20] O.S. Map 6" Staffs. xviii NW. (1890; 1900). Vale St. existed by 1832: Hargreaves, Map of Staffs. Potteries.
[21] E. Ekwall, Concise Oxford Dict. Eng. Place-names.
[22] R. Nicholls, Hist. Stoke and Newcastle, 14 and plate facing p. 40; the caption of the plate wrongly gives Normacot as the place where the cup was found, but this has been corrected in the copy in W.S.L.
[23] V.C.H. Staffs. iv. 39, no. 17. It gave its name to the township, and from the mid-17th cent. to the early 19th cent. it was the meeting-place of Newcastle manor court: see p. 186.
[24] V. G. Aston, Hist. Penkhull, 41 (copy among W.S.L. pamphs. sub Stoke); see p. 192.
[25] One farm still remains, off Garden Street. Elm Tree House in this street bears the date 1694.
[26] See p. 202.
[27] Ward, Stoke, 502, 511; Aston, Penkhull, 35–36; Staffs. Advertiser, 8 May 1897, giving the date 1803. For

a description of the building see p. 183.
[28] See p. 184.
[29] Shaw, Staffs. Potteries, 60; Hargreaves, Map of Staffs. Potteries. Honeywall was an inhabited area by 1804: Stoke Par. Reg. (Staffs. Par. Reg. Soc.), iv. 1047, 1095.
[30] White, Dir. Staffs. (1834).
[31] Ward, Stoke, 510.
[32] Staffs. Advertiser, 14 May 1859; 3 Nov. 1860, 1 Dec. 1860, 21 Jan. 1905; P.O. Dir. Staffs. (1854). The Mount was occupied by Lewis Adams 1835–42 (P.W.L. Adams, Adams Family, 333) and by 1851 was a girls' boarding sch.: White, Dir. Staffs. (1851).
[33] H.R.L., SM 21J, plan of township of Penkhull with Boothen, 1876; O.S. Map 6" Staffs. xviii NW. (1890).
[34] Census, 1831, 1841, 1851, 1861, Staffs.
[35] See p. 197.
[36] Lich. Dioc. Regy., Bp.'s Reg. S, pp. 709–10, where in 1884, the year of the opening of the cemetery (see p. 197), mention is made of Queen's Rd. as an 'intended new road'. Its completion was ordered by the Borough Sanitary Committee within a fortnight in Jan. 1884: H.R.L., Stoke Boro. Sanitary Cttee. Mins. 1881–93, p. 145. It had been built by 1892: Kelly's Dir. Staffs. (1892).
[37] Date-stones of 1899; see p. 204. The house, converted for the Brit. Ceramic Assoc. in 1939, bears the date 1893.
[38] O.S. Map 6" Staffs. xviii NW. (1900); H.R.L., SM 24G, plan of Stoke parish, 1913. Most of the housing dates from between the wars.
[39] See p. 184.

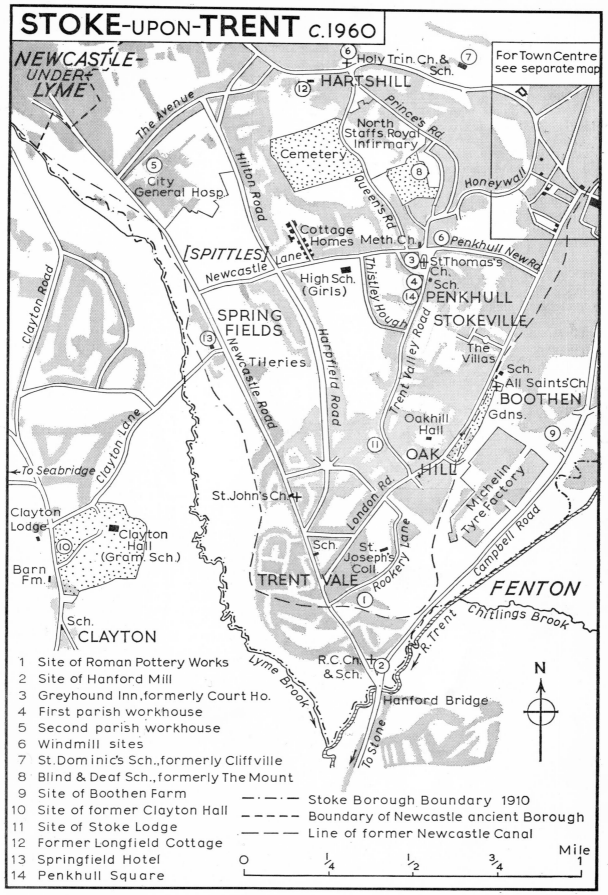

STOKE-UPON-TRENT C.1960

NEWCASTLE-UNDER-LYME

For Town Centre see separate map

Holy Trin. Ch. & Sch.

HARTSHILL

North Staffs. Royal Infirmary

The Avenue

Cemetery

Hilton Road

Honeywall

City General Hosp.

Prince's Rd

Queen's Rd

Clayton Road

Cottage Homes Meth. Ch.

[SPITTLES]

Newcastle Lane

Penkhull New Rd

St. Thomas's Ch.

Sch.

High Sch. (Girls)

PENKHULL

STOKEVILLE

SPRING FIELDS

Thistley Hough

The Villas

Sch.

All Saints' Ch.

Tileries

Newcastle Road

Harpfield Road

Trent Valley Road

BOOTHEN

Gdns.

Clayton Lane

Oakhill Hall

OAK HILL

Michelin Tyre Factory

To Seabridge

St. John's Ch.

London Rd

Clayton Lodge

Clayton Hall (Gram. Sch.)

Campbell Road

Barn Fm.

Sch.

St. Joseph's Coll.

Rookery Lane

FENTON

TRENT VALE

Chitlings Brook

CLAYTON

R. Trent

R.C. Ch. & Sch.

Lyme Brook

Hanford Bridge

To Stone

N

1 Site of Roman Pottery Works
2 Site of Hanford Mill
3 Greyhound Inn, formerly Court Ho.
4 First parish workhouse
5 Second parish workhouse
6 Windmill sites
7 St. Dominic's Sch., formerly Cliffville
8 Blind & Deaf Sch., formerly The Mount
9 Site of Boothen Farm
10 Site of former Clayton Hall
11 Site of Stoke Lodge
12 Former Longfield Cottage
13 Springfield Hotel
14 Penkhull Square

—·—·— Stoke Borough Boundary 1910
———— Boundary of Newcastle ancient Borough
— — — Line of former Newcastle Canal

0   ¼   ½   ¾   Mile   1

The fine stipple indicates built-up areas.

in the area around Hilton Road and Lodge Road north of Newcastle Lane,[40] and the estate in the Thistley Hough area off Trent Valley Road is still expanding.

Boothen had grown up as a smaller settlement on the Trent below Penkhull by the early 15th century.[41] The hamlet still existed in the early 1920's centring on Boothen Farm and the Plough Inn,[42] but already by the 1870's the development of Stoke town along London Road was reaching as far south as the Boothen area; several of the side streets off that road had been built up, notably the Stokeville area which extends between London Road and what is now Trent Valley Road.[43] In the early 1880's Campbell Road had been built as a continuation of Lonsdale Street as far as Boothen hamlet, cutting across the more circuitous old road.[44] By 1898 both Campbell Road and London Road were built up as far as the Boothen area, and Corporation Street had been made linking the two.[45] The centre of the district thus moved to London Road where the church, the school, and most of the shops are situated. The terraced houses in Birks Street, Lime Street, and Fielding Street, between the northern part of Campbell Road and the river, and the housing in Corporation Street and the streets to the north date from the end of the 19th century and the early years of the 20th century.[46] Campbell Road was continued south to the main Newcastle–Stone road at Hanford Bridge in 1923–4,[47] and the Michelin tyre factory was opened in 1927 to the south of Boothen hamlet.[48] There are now (1960) other smaller factories between Campbell Road and the river and off London Road. A large council estate in Water Street and Fletcher Road was completed in 1927.[49] The housing in Chamberlain Avenue and at the end of Penkville Street, both on the west side of London Road, is also of the years between the world wars.

The Oak Hill district around the junction of London Road and Trent Valley Road originally centred on the early-19th-century Oak Hill Hall[50] and the older Stoke Lodge to the west.[51] By 1820 there were several buildings on London Road by Oak Hill Hall and on what is now Racecourse Road opposite, including a soapworks.[52] Little more was built there during the rest of the 19th century,[53] but at the end of the century the triangle of streets on the south side of London Road was laid out; the streets

around the hall had also been begun, and they were completed in the course of the next 20 years or so.[54] A council estate on the site of Stoke Lodge was finished in 1924, and by 1939 further housing had been erected in both areas, including more new streets round Oak Hill Hall.[55]

In the first and second centuries A.D. there was a Roman potworks on the rising ground above the Trent near the present Trent Vale Brick Works.[56] The modern Trent Vale, however, extending along the Newcastle road from Hanford Bridge, developed as a residential district in the early 19th century.[57] By the 1830's there were several 'villa residences . . . snug, rural boxes', as well as brick and tile yards on the canal,[58] and in 1843–4 St. John's Church was built.[59] Although there are still some 19th-century cottages along the Newcastle road and in the Flash Lane area, Trent Vale consists mainly of extensive 20th-century housing,[60] with a strip of meadow land along the Lyme Brook. The area east of the church, including Harpfield Road and the streets around The Crescent, and most of the streets between London Road and Rookery Lane were built up by 1922, and by 1939 both these areas had been extended and new estates laid out between the Newcastle road and the Lyme Brook.[61] The years since 1945 have brought further development in the southern part of the area.[62]

Spring Fields to the north existed by 1775 as a group of houses around the junction of the road from Clayton with Newcastle Road.[63] There was a tilery on the site of the present works there by 1832.[64] Most of the present housing is of the years between the world wars and of the post-1945 period, and there is a post-1945 estate of pre-fabricated houses off Harpfield Road on the slope to the east.[65] There are two bakeries and several factories on the main road there. The group of streets in the Stubbs area to the east of the main road before it enters the borough of Newcastle had been built by the 1870's.[66]

Hartshill occurs as a name attached to land in Stoke parish c. 1600[67] and was an inhabited area by 1738.[68] In 1775 most of the building there was around the junction of what are now called Hartshill Road and Stoke Old Road.[69] It thus lay west of the present Hartshill which centres on the church. By 1820, however, the district was developing eastwards.[70] The larger houses included Cliffville above Cliff Bank, built in 1810,[71] and Longfield Cottage

[40] *City of Stoke-on-Trent Housing, 1919 to 1957*, 22, 30, 61 (copy in H.R.L.).
[41] D.L. 30/231/5.
[42] O.S. Map 6″ Staffs. xviii NW. (1925). The old Plough Inn stood in Sideway Rd., and the present inn of the same name at the junction of Campbell Rd. and Boothen Old Rd. is a modern rebuilding. Some cottages, probably of the early 19th cent., in Water St. and South Terrace are the only remains of the hamlet.
[43] O.S. Map 6″ Staffs. xviii NW. (1890); H.R.L., SM 21J, plan of Penkhull and Boothen, 1876; see p. 183.
[44] See p. 178.
[45] O.S. Map 6″ Staffs. xviii NW. (1900); *Staffs. Sentinel*, 1 Nov. 1898.
[46] H.R.L., SM 23A, plan of Stoke Boro. 1900; O.S. Map 6″ Staffs. xviii NW. (1925). [47] See p. 178.
[48] *Stoke Official Handbk.* [1958], 141.
[49] *Stoke-on-Trent Housing, 1919 to 1957*, 21, 27, 58.
[50] Greenwood, *Map of Staffs.*; Lich. Dioc. Regy., Bp.'s Reg. H, p. 545. The name 'Ochul' occurs in the 13th cent. as one of the open fields of Longton: see p. 237.
[51] Ward, *Stoke*, 513; Yates, *Map of Staffs.* (1775).
[52] Greenwood, *Map of Staffs.*

[53] O.S. Map 6″ Staffs. xviii NW. (1900).
[54] Ibid. (1925); H.R.L., SM 23A, plan of Stoke Boro. 1900; ibid., SM 24G, plan of Stoke Parish 1913.
[55] *Stoke-on-Trent Housing, 1919 to 1957*, 26, 57.
[56] See p. 202.
[57] White, *Dir. Staffs.* (1834); Ward, *Stoke*, 513; Yates, *Map of Staffs.* (1775); Hargreaves, *Map of Staffs. Potteries*.
[58] Ward, *Stoke*, 513; White, *Dir. Staffs.* (1834).
[59] See p. 193. [60] See pp. 268, 269.
[61] O.S. Map 6″ Staffs. xviii NW., SW. (1925); *Stoke-on-Trent Housing, 1919 to 1957*, 26, 28, 57.
[62] *Stoke-on-Trent Housing, 1919 to 1957*, 21, 24, 25, 26. This includes an estate of 95 single-story prefab. houses between Stone and Campbell Rds.
[63] Yates, *Map of Staffs.* (1775).
[64] Hargreaves, *Map of Staffs. Potteries*; see p. 204.
[65] *Stoke-on-Trent Housing, 1919 to 1957*, 26.
[66] O.S. Map 6″ Staffs. xvii NE. (1890).
[67] R. Nicholls, *Stoke Ch.* 60.
[68] *Stoke Par. Reg.* iii. 471.
[69] Yates, *Map of Staffs.* (1775).
[70] Greenwood, *Map of Staffs.*
[71] See pp. 183, 186, 273.

opposite the Noah's Ark Inn.[72] The latter was the birthplace in 1826 of Dinah Maria Mullock, later Mrs. Craik and author of *John Halifax, Gentleman.* Her grandmother, Jane Mellard, had moved there *c.* 1816, and the Mellards remained at Longfield Cottage until 1831[73] after which it was the home of Herbert Minton (d. 1858).[74] Minton built cottages for his workers on both sides of the main road near the church, and these are still occupied.[75] There were also several brick and tile yards in the Hartshill area by the 1830's.[76] Holy Trinity church was built in 1842.[77] Shelton New Road, built in the 1830's, joins Hartshill Road at the Stoke–Newcastle boundary,[78] and by 1850 there had been extensive building round this junction, representing the eastward spread of Newcastle.[79] There had also been some development north and south of the main road round Hartshill church by this time.[80] Victoria Street linking Hartshill Road at Harpfield with Etruria Road at Basford was constructed *c.* 1880.[81] The streets of terraced cottages south of Hartshill Road opposite the end of Victoria Street were laid out at the beginning of the 20th century.[82] The stretch of The Avenue in this area had been built by the early 1920's,[83] and this road, which serves a residential district as well as providing a south-eastern by-pass of Newcastle, had been extended to Newcastle Road by 1939. The housing estate on the north side of Hartshill Road, between Victoria Street and the 19th-century streets west of Hartshill church, dates from the years between the world wars. Some of the houses in this part of Stoke Old Road were rebuilt during this period, while the extension of Cumming Street to the north-east contains a post-1945 council estate.[84] Slum clearance and rebuilding were still in progress in the pre-1850 Steel Street area south of Hartshill church in 1959.[85]

Cliff Vale, apparently the whole area of low ground along the Fowlea Brook between Shelton Old Road and Etruria Road,[86] contained several brickworks at the northern end of Stoke Old Road (now Brick Kiln Lane) by 1832.[87] It began to be developed only towards the end of the 19th century when Garner Street was built from the Etruria Road end of Brick Kiln Lane down to Shelton New Road with several terraces of houses along its southern end.[88] A council estate was laid out during the years between the world wars on the north side of Shelton New Road between Brick Kiln Lane and Garner Street.[89] North Street, running from Shelton Old Road to Shelton New Road, was built in two stages in the later 19th century,[90] but contains only two groups of houses, both of the 20th century. The steeply rising ground on the Hartshill side of North Street is still (1960) undeveloped.

Basford lies on both the Stoke and the Wolstanton sides of Etruria Road which at this point was known as Basford Hill or Basford Bank by the 1830's.[91] There were then several brick and tile yards in the area, especially along Stoke Old Road (then Stoke Lane), and Stoneyfields House, still standing in the north-eastern extremity of the area, had also been built by then.[92] Several streets of larger houses were laid out on the Stoke side of Etruria Road in the third quarter of the 19th century,[93] and the streets in the Kingsfield area to the west date from *c.* 1900;[94] all these streets were continued southwards in the years between the world wars.[95]

The population of Penkhull in 1086 was recorded as 17 villeins and 6 bordars.[96] Only 13 inhabitants in the vill paid tax in 1332,[97] while in 1666 44 persons in the Penkhull, Boothen, and Stoke portion of Penkhull constablewick were chargeable for hearth tax.[98] There were 40 or 50 houses in this district *c.* 1680.[99] The population of Penkhull and Boothen township (including Stoke itself) was 419 in 1701[1] and 3,851 in 1811;[2] in 1831 the population of Penkhull was 5,876 and that of Boothen 121.[3] In 1871 the figures were 12,959 and 767 respectively, and the continuing increase was then attributed to the prosperity of the pottery industry and the facilities for building offered by clubs.[4] In 1901 the population of the borough was 30,458, and in 1911 the population of the same area was 36,375 and in 1921 37,935.[5]

The road from Derby and Uttoxeter through Stoke to Newcastle follows the course of the Roman Ryknield Street as far as Fenton and there turns west to cross the Trent at Stoke.[6] It was evidently in use by the 13th century,[7] and was turnpiked in 1759.[8] The stretch between Stoke and Newcastle, now Hartshill Road, is said formerly to have followed

[72] See p. 183.
[73] *Fenn's Stoke Boro. Almanack* (1901); A. L. Reade, *The Mellards,* 17, 53.
[74] White, *Dir. Staffs.* (1834); Ward, *Stoke,* 512.
[75] See p. 184.
[76] See p. 204.
[77] See p. 193.
[78] See p. 178.
[79] Lich. Dioc. Regy., Tithe Maps and Appt., Stoke.
[80] Ibid.
[81] Date-stone of 1880; O.S. Map 6″ Staffs. xvii NE. (1900).
[82] Coronation Rd. bears the date 1902 and the streets to the W. are in the same style.
[83] O.S. Map 6″ Staffs. xvii NE. (1926). A terrace there bears the date 1914.
[84] *Stoke-on-Trent Housing, 1919 to 1957,* 20.
[85] Ibid. 30. Some new houses had been completed by April 1959.
[86] The name now applies to the part of the district around Shelton New Rd. but North St. contains Cliff Vale Terrace and the former Cliff Vale School.
[87] Hargreaves, *Map of Staffs. Potteries.*
[88] O.S. Map 6″ Staffs. xviii NW. (1900).
[89] *Stoke-on-Trent Housing, 1919 to 1957,* 26.

[90] See p. 178.
[91] Hargreaves, *Map of Staffs. Potteries*; Ward, *Stoke,* 511. It occurs as Fowlea Bank in 1771: S.R.O., Roads Index.
[92] Hargreaves, *Map of Staffs. Potteries*; Ward, *Stoke,* 511, 513.
[93] O.S. Map 6″ Staffs. xvii NE. (1890).
[94] H.R.L., SM 220, plan of Stoke Parish 1901.
[95] This includes the Kingsfield council estate: *City of Stoke-on-Trent Housing, 1919 to 1957,* 23.
[96] *V.C.H. Staffs.* iv. 39, no. 17.
[97] *S.H.C.* x (i), 82.
[98] Ibid. 1921, 153–4.
[99] Ibid. 1919, 258.
[1] W.S.L., D. 1742, list of inhabs. of Stoke parish 1701.
[2] *Census,* 1811, Staffs. It should be noted that the population figures given for Stoke 1801–1901 in *V.C.H. Staffs.* i. 325, differ from those given in the present section since the earlier volume is treating a larger area.
[3] *Census,* 1831, Staffs.
[4] Ibid. 1871, Staffs.
[5] Ibid. 1901, 1911, 1921, Staffs.
[6] See p. 208.
[7] *S.H.C.* xi. 322–3.
[8] Act for repairing rd. from Derby to Newcastle, 32 Geo. II, c. 60; *S.H.C.* 1934 (i), 58–59.

a more northerly and direct line from a point near the Jolly Potters Inn, returning to the line of the present Hartshill Road along the western part of Stoke Old Road (formerly Stoke Lane).[9] Shelton Old Road, formerly Hanley Road,[10] was turnpiked from Cliff Bank to Shelton in 1763, the first stage of the link from the Derby–Newcastle turnpike to that from Lawton (Ches.) through the northern part of the Potteries.[11] This link was completed in 1765 along a side road from Shelton to Etruria as part of the turnpiking of the road from Newcastle to Hassop (Derb.) via Etruria and Cobridge.[12] The Etruria Road stretch of this road from Newcastle Hassop formed the northern boundary of Penkhull township. This portion was stated in 1780 to be in such a bad state of repair, despite considerable expenditure, 'that post-chaises from Newcastle-under-Lyme to Leek go another road two miles longer'.[13] By 1849 there was a toll-gate at the point where this road is joined by Stoke Old Road.[14] Shelton New Road which runs up from the Fowlea Brook at Cliff Vale to meet Hartshill Road at the Newcastle boundary was built in the late 1830's under an Act of 1823.[15] North Street was built from Shelton Old Road along the low ground by the Fowlea Brook during the third quarter of the 19th century and was continued to Shelton New Road before the end of the century.[16] The road from Stoke to Endon running from Church Street along Glebe Street had been built by 1842 under an Act of 1840.[17] At first it crossed the railway by a level crossing; the Improvement Commissioners' schemes for a bridge, drawn up in 1852, were thwarted for many years, evidently by the railway company, and the present railway bridge was not built until 1868.[18]

The western part of the area is crossed by the ancient highway from London to Carlisle.[19] The stretch in Penkhull township was turnpiked in 1714 as part of the road from Tittensor to Talke, the first Staffordshire turnpike.[20] By 1791 there was a toll-gate, known as Knappers Gate, at Spittles where a road from Penkhull, the present Newcastle Lane, joined the main road.[21] This still stood in 1878. A

hilly side road led from the highway along the present Rookery Lane just south of the Black Lion Inn at Trent Vale, up Brisley Hill (now Trent Valley Road) to Penkhull and thence down Honeywall to join the road from Derby to Newcastle at Cliff Bank; another road ran from the foot of Brisley Hill to Boothen, and thence to Stoke.[22] A new road, the present London Road, more direct than either of these, was built in 1791–2 under an Act of 1791 from the 'Black Lion' at Trent Vale and along the foot of the steep slope below Penkhull to meet the road from Derby to Newcastle at what is now Campbell Place; it was continued on the other side of this main road by the construction of Liverpool Road ('the new road to Shelton') to join Shelton Old Road near Shelton Wharf.[23] A toll-house was built in 1792 at the junction with Brisley Hill,[24] superseding an older toll-house nearby which was sold in 1793; the second house still stood in 1878.[25] A chain was placed across the Stoke end of the road, but proving unnecessary it was removed a few weeks later.[26] In the early 1880's Campbell Road, parallel to and east of London Road, was run from Lonsdale Street, Stoke, to Boothen, cutting across the more circuitous old road to Boothen which, however, still survives as Boothen Road and Boothen Old Road.[27] In 1923–4, as one of the unemployment relief works, Campbell Road was continued south to meet the Newcastle road at Hanford Bridge.[28]

There were two ancient bridges over the Trent within Penkhull township, Stoke Bridge on the road from Derby to Newcastle, and Hanford Bridge on the main highway south from Newcastle. Stoke Bridge was stated in 1568 or 1569 to be repairable by several of the neighbouring townships.[29] It was apparently repairable by Stoke parish in 1666,[30] but its upkeep was a county responsibility by 1668.[31] Repairs carried out in 1717, 1718, and 1720 included 'securing the arch',[32] and in 1792 the bridge was widened.[33] By 1864 it was a bridge of stone and brick with four arches.[34] Hanford Bridge was a structure of at least three arches by the late 17th century.[35] Its maintenance too was a county responsibility by 1625.[36]

[9] Nicholls, *Penkhull cum Boothen*, 26. Hargreaves, *Map of Staffs. Potteries* (1832), shows the present course through Hartshill, but it is not clear from the smaller-scale Yates, *Map of Staffs.* (1799), how it ran at the end of the 18th cent.

[10] Hargreaves, *Map of Staffs. Potteries*.

[11] 3 Geo. III, c. 57; *S.H.C.* 1934 (1), 67–71; see p. 145.

[12] 5 Geo. III, c. 84; *S.H.C.* 1934 (1), 71; see p. 108.

[13] *S.H.C.* 1934 (1), 94–95.

[14] Lich. Dioc. Regy., Tithe Maps and Appt., Stoke.

[15] 4 Geo. IV, c. 51 (local and personal); S.R.O., Q/RUt 5/80A (map of 1839 showing the road). It was not marked on O.S. Map 1", lxxii NW. (1837), but negotiations for the purchase of the land were in progress in 1834: S.R.O., D. 206/M/8.

[16] O.S. Map 6" Staffs. xviii NW. (1890; 1900).

[17] 3 & 4 Vic. c. 116 (local and personal); S.R.O., Q/RUt 5/80A, 5/84; *Map of Stoke Borough 1842* (printed by W. Dean and included in some copies of Ward, *Stoke*).

[18] H.R.L., Stoke Commrs.' Mins. 1848–55, Apr. 1852–Sept. 1854 *passim*; ibid. 1855–65, 3 July 1861; 1865–74, pp. 81, 118.

[19] It is shown on the Gough Map of *c.* 1360: E. J. S. Parsons, *The Map of Britain* (facsimile with introd.)

[20] 12 Anne, c. 14 (priv. act); *S.H.C.* 1934 (1), 56..

[21] H.R.L., Tittensor Turnpike Rd. Bk. 1791–1803, p. 5; Hargreaves, *Map of Staffs. Potteries*; H.R.L., Stoke Boro. Mins. 1874–81, p. 312.

[22] Yates, *Map of Staffs.* (1775); Nicholls, *Penkhull cum*

Boothen, 26, 27; *T.N.S.F.C.* xlv. 163; H.R.L., Tittensor Turnpike Rd. Bk. 1791–1803, p. 5; Hargreaves, *Map of Staffs. Potteries*.

[23] 31 Geo. III, c. 129; H.R.L., Tittensor Turnpike Rd. Bk. 1791–1803, pp. 1–25 *passim*.

[24] H.R.L., Tittensor Turnpike Rd. Bk. 1791–1803, pp. 21, 24, 27; O.S. Map 6" Staffs. xviii NW. (1890).

[25] H.R.L., Tittensor Turnpike Rd. Bk. 1791–1803, pp. 24, 38; H.R.L., Stoke Boro. Mins. 1874–81, p. 312.

[26] H.R.L., Tittensor Turnpike Rd. Bk. 1791–1803, pp. 24, 26.

[27] Ex inf. the Stoke-on-Trent City Surveyor (1959).

[28] Ex inf. the city surveyor.

[29] *S.H.C.* 1948–9, 82, the townships being Stoke, Newcastle, Wolstanton, Penkhull, Shelton, Hanley, Clayton, and Seabridge.

[30] *Stoke Churchwardens' Accts.* (*T.N.S.F.C.* lxxv), pp. A133, 147.

[31] S.R.O., Q/SR Mich. 1671, nos. 19–22; *S.H.C.* 1934 (1), 22.   [32] W.S.L., D. 1742, vouchers.

[33] *S.H.C.* 1934 (1), 89.

[34] W.S.L., Hand Morgan Coll., 31/15, County Surveyor's Notebk.

[35] The Stoke parish boundary was said to run through the middle arch in 1689: Ward, *Stoke*, app. p. lxii. By 1864 it was a stone bridge of 3 arches: W.S.L., Hand Morgan Coll., 31/15.

[36] S.R.O., Q/SO, f. 63b; S.R.O., Q/SR Mich. 1658; *S.H.C.* 1934 (1), 82.

Boothen Bridge, which was repairable by Stoke parish in the late 17th century,[37] may have been a bridge over the Trent leading to Fenton mill. Complaints were made in 1856 and again in 1869 about the dangerous state of the bridge carrying the footpath between Boothen and Fenton over the Trent,[38] and there is still a footbridge over the river near the site of the former Fenton mill.

There were two ancient bridges over the Fowlea Brook on the eastern boundary of the township, one carrying the road from Penkhull to Shelton via Cliff Bank and the other the road from Newcastle to Cobridge; a third was built at the end of the 18th century. The first seems to be identifiable with the 14th-century Wolfordbridge,[39] and it occurs in the 16th century as 'the bridge at the Fowle Ley going from Shelton to Penkhyll', for the repair of which Nicholas Adams of Sneyd (d. 1567) bequeathed a plank of wood.[40] It occurs variously as the Fowlea Bridge and the Lower Fowlea Bridge during the 17th century, when its maintenance was a regular charge on Stoke parish,[41] and as Fowlea Bridge in 1727 and 1728.[42] The Upper Fowlea Bridge carrying the Newcastle–Cobridge road over the brook is mentioned in 1660 as a parish responsibility[43] and by 1832 was known as Etruria Bridge.[44] It was a county bridge by 1864 when it was of brick with one arch.[45] A third bridge was built over the brook within Penkhull township when the turnpike road from Trent Vale to Shelton Wharf was constructed in 1791–2.[46] It was either this Liverpool Road Bridge or the Lower Fowlea Bridge that occurs in 1830 as Shelton Bridge, a new structure and the responsibility of the county.[47] In 1856 the Improvement Commissioners complained to the justices about the state of the Liverpool Road bridge.[48]

A bridge carrying the footway between Penkhull and Clayton over the Lyme Brook and another bridge nearby were stated in 1712 to be in need of repair.[49] The first was probably the bridge in what is now Clayton Lane.[50]

By 1790 Stoke was served by the same coaches as Burslem, the 'Wheatsheaf' being the coaching inn

by 1818. The town was on the route of a Hanley–Stafford–Birmingham coach by 1824, and by 1834 the thrice-weekly coach between Newcastle and Derby called at the 'Wheatsheaf'.[51] By 1851 there was an omnibus service from Stoke Station to Newcastle and to Hanley.[52] By 1854 there were omnibuses from the 'Wheatsheaf' to the railway station to meet each train, and there was also a service between Longton and Burslem which called at the 'Wheatsheaf'.[53] A steam tramway was started between Stoke and Longton in 1881 and extended to Hanley and Burslem in 1882.[54] A branch-line to Oak Hill was opened by 1892.[55] Tramway offices and sheds were built in Woodhouse Street in the 1890's, and electricity, generated from there, was substituted for steam by the Potteries Electric Traction Company in 1899.[56] A line was built to Newcastle in 1900–4, and the Oak Hill branch was extended to Trent Vale in 1899–1905.[57] Motorbuses, introduced from 1914, gradually replaced the tramcars between 1925 and 1928.[58]

By 1790 one of the innkeepers was the post-master of Stoke.[59] From 1835 Stoke was linked by a horse-post with Newcastle, the postal centre of the Potteries area. Stoke became the centre in 1854 when a head office for the Potteries was opened at the railway station.[60]

The Trent and Mersey Canal, opened in 1777,[61] runs through the north-eastern portion of the former borough, and a low aqueduct of three arches was built to carry it over the Trent.[62] By 1802 there was at least one public wharf in Stoke, and this, off Wharf Street, remains in use.[63] The Newcastle-under-Lyme branch was built in 1795–6 under an Act of 1795 from the main canal north-west of Glebe Street along the east side of London Road to Trent Vale where it passed under the main Newcastle road at the west end of Rookery Lane; it then ran north through the meadows by the Lyme Brook to Brook Lane in Newcastle.[64] Its purpose, according to the preamble of the Act, was to provide for Newcastle and the works near it a link with the main canal and to 'assist the agriculture of the neighbourhood of the said canal by a supply of lime at less expense'. It appears,

[37] Stoke Churchwardens' Accts. (T.N.S.F.C. lxxvi), pp. A172, 185, 187; ibid. lxxvii, p. A209.
[38] H.R.L., Stoke Commrs.' Mins. 1855–65, 4 and 11 June 1856; ibid. 1865–74, p. 125. Early in the 20th cent. the borough agreed to pay half the cost of a footbridge over the Trent at Boothen with a concrete path: H.R.L., Stoke Boro. Mins. 1905–8, pp. 498–9.
[39] Nicholls, Penkhull cum Boothen, 40–41; Ward, Stoke, app. p. lxvi.
[40] Adams, Adams Family, 31.
[41] Stoke Churchwardens' Accts. (T.N.S.F.C. lxxiv), pp. A77, 80, 81, 97; ibid. lxxv, pp. A134, 144, 156; lxxvi, p. A182; lxxvii, pp. A190, 194, 208. In 1699 it occurs as 'the Nether Fowley Bridge': ibid. p. A222.
[42] S.R.O., Roads Index.
[43] Stoke Churchwardens' Accts. (T.N.S.F.C. lxxv), p. A134; ibid. lxxvi, p. A165; lxxvii, pp. A202, 222; S.R.O., Roads Index.
[44] S.R.O., Bridges Index; S.R.O., Q/SB, Mich. 1832.
[45] W.S.L., Hand Morgan Coll., 31/15, County Surveyor's Notebk.
[46] H.R.L., Tittensor Turnpike Rd. Bk. 1791–1803, pp. 7, 24, 26.
[47] J. Potter, List of Bridges which Inhabs. of County of Staffs. are bound to repair (1830), 8. Shelton Bridge was found to be decayed in 1833 and 1838: S.R.O., Bridges Index. By 1864 it was a brick bridge of one arch: W.S.L., Hand Morgan Coll., 31/15, County Surveyor's Notebk.
[48] H.R.L., Stoke Commrs.' Mins. 1855–65, 5 Mar. 1856.
[49] W.S.L., D. 1788, P. 40, B. 7, the Lyme Brook still being called the Newcastle Brook as in 1689: see p. 173, n. 4.

[50] Hargreaves, Map of Staffs. Potteries, showing a footpath continuation of Clayton Lane to Penkhull.
[51] Univ. Brit. Dir. (1791), iv. 109; Parson and Bradshaw, Dir. Staffs. (1818); White, Dir. Staffs. (1834); see pp. 109, 146, 228.   [52] White, Dir. Staffs. (1851).
[53] P.O. Dir. Staffs. (1854).
[54] Kelly's Dir. Staffs. (1884); S.R.O., Q/RUo 30, 39 (a, b). This line was not extended to Tunstall until 1900: see p. 84.
[55] Kelly's Dir. Staffs. (1884, 1892).
[56] P.M.T. House Mag. (May–June 1958), 3 (copy in H.R.L.); see pp. 174, 186. A new block of offices was built there in 1937: Warrillow, Stoke, 79.
[57] Warrillow, Stoke, 75.
[58] P.M.T. House Mag. (May–June 1958), 6–7. The company was renamed the Potteries Motor Traction Co. in 1933: Warrillow, Stoke, 79.
[59] Univ. Brit. Dir. (1791), iv. 110.
[60] See p. 7.
[61] S.H.C. 1934 (1), 109.
[62] Aikin, Country around Manchester, 522; White, Dir. Staffs. (1834).
[63] Allbut, Staffs. Pottery Dir. (1802); Hargreaves, Map of Staffs. Potteries; ex inf. Brit. Transport Waterways, NW. Div. (1959). There seems to have been a wharf off Lytton St. also between at least 1884 and 1896: Kelly's Dir. Staffs. (1884; 1892; 1896).
[64] Act for making canal from Stoke to Newcastle, 35 Geo. III, c. 87; H.R.L., Tittensor Turnpike Rd. Bk. 1791–1803, pp. 81, 87–88; Hargreaves, Map of Staffs. Potteries; see p. 6.

however, never to have been a profitable venture,[65] and under an Act of 1921 the stretch from Newcastle to Trent Vale was filled in.[66] The remainder also had been filled in as far as a point just north of Church Street by 1938, when a further Act allowed the stopping up of the canal as far as its present termination at Aqueduct Street.[67] This left only a side arm from the main canal about 100 yards long, over which the main towpath and Copeland Street are carried on original hump-backed bridges. There was a wharf at the junction of the two canals by 1832, and this was still in use in 1916.[68] In 1960 the wharf and the short length of branch canal were being used by the Stoke-on-Trent Boat Club.

The railway between Stoke and Norton Bridge, the first part of the present London–Manchester line, was opened in 1848, some eighteen months after the cutting of the first sod at Stoke;[69] later in the year the line was extended to Crewe and to Congleton. There was at first a temporary station at Whieldon's Grove (in Fenton), but this was replaced later in the year by the present Stoke station built on land called Winton's Wood then in Shelton township.[70] Etruria station, on the main line from Stoke to the north, lies just within the boundary of Penkhull township.[71] The branch line from Stoke to Newcastle, tunnelling under the high ground north of Hartshill, was opened in 1852.[72] There is also a side line from the Michelin tyre factory to the main line at Sideway, south of Stoke.

BUILDINGS. Only a few of the buildings along the main street of Stoke survive from the early development of the town in the years immediately before and after 1800. Most of the frontages have been rebuilt, several of them in the different ornate styles of the late 19th and early 20th centuries. The Grapes public house, a substantial late-18th-century building on the corner of London Road, and probably the oldest house in the centre of Stoke, was demolished in 1960. Although altered, perhaps at the time of its conversion to an inn c. 1865,[73] it retained a Georgian façade of five bays with a central pedimented doorcase and a dentil cornice; there was also a plastered back wing with hipped dormer windows. The Wheatsheaf Hotel, facing the end of London Road, is still recognizable as the coaching house of c. 1820, although its long three-storied front was altered later in the 19th century. Farther west in the main street are three early-19th-century residential properties; the present offices of the City Registrar with its

original stable range beside it, the Clifton Hotel, and the stucco house now used as a presbytery for the Roman Catholic church. Near the corner of Vale Street a row of brick cottages with front gardens has survived from c. 1800.

The area of small streets lying south-west of the main street and surrounding the former town hall and market-place formed the nucleus of the town early in the 19th century. Apart from dwelling-houses, both terraced cottages and slightly larger double-fronted houses, the older buildings include the striking Wesleyan Methodist Chapel (1816 and later),[74] the chapel of the Methodist New Connexion (1816)[75] and the former Friends' Meeting House, built as an Independent chapel in 1823.[76] The original town hall, built in 1794 and demolished c. 1938, was on the usual pattern with an open arcaded market below and a meeting-room above.[77] Immediately to the west stands the covered market of 1835, still (1960) in use as a hide and skin market.[78] Where the ground falls away to the east it has a good brick front with stone dressings, the central projecting bay being surmounted by a pediment and flanked by arched entrances with iron grilles; the flights of stone steps leading up to them have been partly cut away. At the lower end of Honeywall a few early houses remain, although there has been much demolition of small property in this area. A Russian gun, presented to the town by W. T. Copeland in 1857 and erected opposite the 'Wheatsheaf' in 1858, was moved to a site in Hill Street by the old town hall c. 1874.[79]

The former National school,[80] occupying the south-east corner of St. Peter's churchyard, was built in 1815. It consists of a rectangular two-storied brick range of six bays, the ground-floor openings being pointed and having heavily moulded brick jambs and arches. A projecting feature surmounted by an octagonal turret at the south end of the building disappeared during later extensions[81] and a date tablet of 1815 has been re-set. Glebe Street and Brook Street, bounding the extended churchyard on the north and west and laid out with it shortly before 1830, were said soon afterwards 'to present an agreeable uniformity of character'.[82] Both streets are open to the churchyard, giving a certain spaciousness and dignity to this part of the town. Shop fronts have been inserted in the stucco terrace houses of Glebe Street but several original doorways with elliptical fanlights survive. Brook Street, containing a terrace of what was described c. 1840 as 'a superior class of houses of the bay window stile of architec-

---

[65] Shaw, *Staffs. Potteries*, 61; White, *Dir. Staffs.* (1851).
[66] N. Staffs. Rlwy. Act. 11 & 12 Geo. V, c. 117 (local); O.S. Map 6″ Staffs. xvii NE., SE. (1926).
[67] L.M.S.R. Act, 1 & 2 Geo. VI, c. 27 (local). The Coronation Gardens below All Saints' Church, Boothen, are laid out over part of the course of the canal: *Stoke Official Handbk.* [1958], 51.
[68] Hargreaves, *Map of Staffs. Potteries*; *P.O. Dir. Staffs.* (1860, and later edns. to 1876); *Kelly's Dir. Staffs.* (1880, and later edns. to 1916). It does not occur in White, *Dir. Staffs.* (1834, 1851).
[69] 'Manifold', *N. Staffs. Rlwy.* 26–30, 33–35. For the branch line through Fenton and Longton to Burton-upon-Trent opened in 1848 see p. 209.
[70] 'Manifold', *N. Staffs. Rlwy.* 34, 35; *Staffs. Advertiser*, 14 Oct. 1848; see p. 209. For a description see p. 182.
[71] See p. 147.
[72] See p. 6.
[73] The earliest reference to an inn of this name occurs in *Keates and Ford's Potteries Dir.* (1865–6).

[74] See p. 289.
[75] See p. 294.
[76] See p. 284.
[77] See pp. 194, 195. For a view of the building in 1840 W.S.L., Staffs. Views, x, p. 17.
[78] Ward, *Stoke*, 505; see p. 201.
[79] H.R.L., Stoke Commrs.' Mins. 1855–65, 18 Aug., 2 Sept. 1857, 3 Mar., 13 June 1858; ibid. 1865–74, p. 352; H.R.L., Stoke Boro. Mins. 1874–81, pp. 24, 27, 29, 33. It is no longer there. Another Russian gun from the Crimean War was erected outside Longton Court House in 1867: Warrillow, *Stoke*, 385 (no. 10). A Russian gun presented to Newcastle by Sam. Christy M.P. in 1857 (inscription on gun) still stands in the part of Stubbs Walks within the city (see pp. 4, 176).
[80] See p. 320.
[81] For a view of the sch. in 1840 see W.S.L., Staffs. Views, x. p. 15.
[82] Ward, *Stoke*, 498.

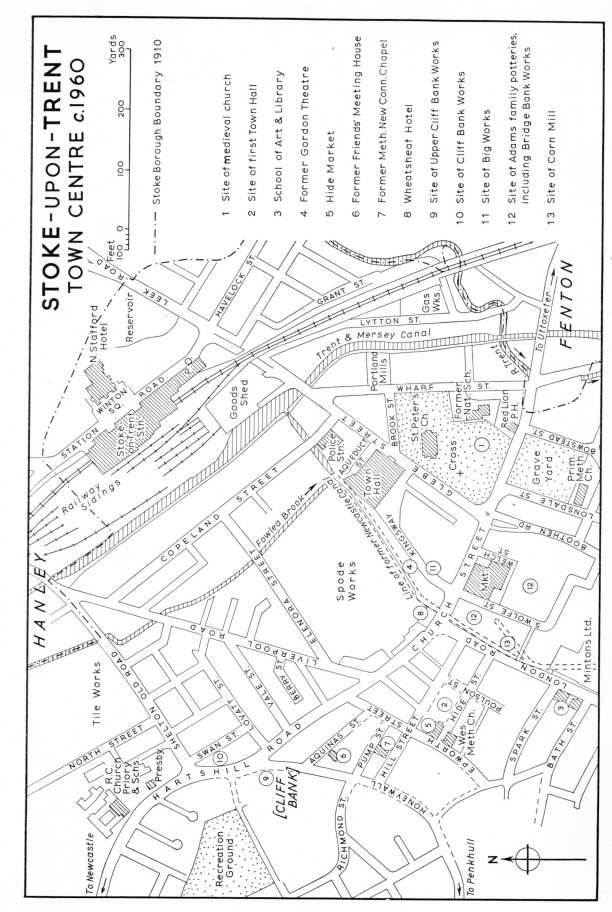

STOKE-UPON-TRENT
TOWN CENTRE c.1960

Yards
300
200
100
0

Feet
100 0

- - - - - Stoke Borough Boundary 1910

1 Site of medieval church
2 Site of first Town Hall
3 School of Art & Library
4 Former Gordon Theatre
5 Hide Market
6 Former Friends' Meeting House
7 Former Meth. New Conn. Chapel
8 Wheatsheaf Hotel
9 Site of Upper Cliff Bank Works
10 Site of Cliff Bank Works
11 Site of Big Works
12 Site of Adams family potteries, including Bridge Bank Works
13 Site of Corn Mill

FENTON

To Uttoxeter

HANLEY

To Newcastle

To Penkhull

N

ture',[83] is comparatively unaltered. The houses, now mostly occupied as professional offices, are of yellow brick and have 'Tudor' doorways and mullioned windows; the two end blocks are of somewhat later date. Farther north, on a wedge-shaped site between Glebe Street and Wharf Street, a striking Italianate stucco building was erected as a hotel in 1854[84] but is now used as offices; the angle is occupied by a circular staircase hall surmounted by a lantern.

The approach to the railway station represents one of the few attempts at a formal layout to be found in the Potteries. The station itself, built in 1848,[85] has a long two-storied brick front in the contemporary 'Tudor' style with a projecting gabled wing at each end. In the centre is a stone portico of seven arches, surmounted by a square bay ornamented with strapwork and other Jacobean detail. Directly opposite is the North Stafford Hotel, also dating from 1848[86] and built to resemble a tall Elizabethan manor house with 'Flemish' gables, stone dressings, and blue diaper ornament to the brickwork. Flanking it are lower buildings in the same style which, with the hotel, form three sides of Winton Square, the fourth side being occupied by the front of the station. In the centre of the square stands a bronze statue of Josiah Wedgwood, erected by subscription in 1863.[87]

Stoke town hall in Glebe Street is the largest and most imposing municipal building in the six towns. It was begun in 1834 to an ambitious Classical design by Henry Ward, but the north wing was not built until c. 1842 and the south wing was still unfinished in 1850.[88] The long stone front includes a main block of thirteen bays, having tall windows to the upper floor and a projecting central Ionic portico surmounted by blocking courses and a small pediment. The pedimented side wings also project and are of three stories. The whole is raised on a rusticated base containing round-headed windows and three central arched entrances in the centre. There was originally a space in the centre of the building used as a market-place, but in 1888, five years after the removal of the market to Church Street, the space was reconstructed to include the council chamber, mayor's parlour, and municipal offices, all formerly housed in the south wing.[89] The building was retained after 1910 for most of the new county borough's activities, and the King's Hall, seating 3,250, was erected behind it in 1910–11.[90] The extensions were designed in a free Classical style by T. Wallis and J. A. Bowden of London[91] and executed in stone. In 1935 the first-floor assembly room in the main building was reconstructed as the Jubilee Hall and the glazed tiles with which it had been lined, probably in 1888, were covered over by wood panelling.[92]

Public buildings to the south of Church Street include the market of 1883,[93] built of red brick in the Flemish style with curly gables and a central tower; the low front with its row of shops was apparently added in 1900.[94] In London Road the College of Art (1858–9 with later additions at the rear)[95] is Gothic in style and has ornamental terracotta bands and window-heads. The adjacent library and museum (1877–8)[96] is of strikingly original design, having circular windows to the principal floor and an upper story of timber with wide eaves and casement windows; between the two are decorative panels of tile and mosaic. On the opposite side of London Road is the most impressive of the industrial buildings in the town-centre. This factory, belonging to Mintons Ltd. and dating from about the middle of the 19th century, has a very long three-storied front, rising in the centre to four stories. Its line is continued to the south by the Campbell Tile Works, built by 1876 in much the same style.[97] Near the modern additions to the Minton factory at its northern end is a statue of Colin Minton Campbell, unveiled in 1887, the sculptor being Thomas Brock (1847–1922).[98] It originally stood in Campbell Place but was later moved to Kingsway to relieve traffic congestion; it was removed to its present site in 1954.[99] A Gothic drinking fountain at the angle of a factory building on the opposite side of London Road was presented by Colin Minton Campbell in 1859.[1]

The old village centre at Penkhull still contains several rows of rural cottages grouped round or near the triangular green on which stands the 19th-century church of St. Thomas. A single cottage row also survives among newer houses in the hamlet of Honeywall, lying on the winding road between Penkhull and Stoke. There do not appear to be any cottages dating from before the late 18th century. Penkhull also possesses several groups of workers' houses of a slightly later period, including those built by Josiah Spode II (d. 1827)[2] and those in Penkhull New Road known as 'Commercial Buildings'. The former Stoke-upon-Trent parish workhouse is a plain three-storied building with a plastered front standing on the south side of Penkhull Green and now used as several dwellings. It appears to have been rebuilt or much altered since the time when it ceased to be used as a workhouse.[3] On the west side of the green is the Greyhound Inn, incorporating the former court house of the manor of Newcastle-under-Lyme.[4] It was largely rebuilt in 1936 but parts of the original timber-framed structure, probably dating from the 16th century, were preserved. The main block, which is parallel with the road, and a small back wing are still of timber construction, but a two-storied cross-wing at the south end has

[83] Ward, Stoke, 498.
[84] Local inf. (1960); date on building.
[85] See p. 180.
[86] Ex inf. Brit. Rlwys. L.M.R.
[87] Inscription on base; see plate facing p. 204. The sculptor was E. Davis of London.
[88] White, Dir. Staffs. (1851); P.O. Dir. Staffs. (1850); Ward, Stoke, 508, 600; H.R.L., Stoke Commrs. Mins. 1839–48, 5 May, 10 Nov., 1 Dec. 1841, 5 Jan. 1842, 1 Feb. 1843. For an architect's drawing (undated) of the 'New Market and Town Hall' see plate facing p. 190.
[89] See p. 195.
[90] Kelly's Dir. Staffs. (1912); Staffs. Sentinel, 12 Mar. 1910, 3 Oct. 1911; foundation stone dated 1910. The scheme had been put in hand by the Stoke-upon-Trent boro. counc.: H.R.L., Stoke Boro. Mins. 1908–10, pp. 192,

240–1, 242–5, 303–4, 329–30, 348–50.
[91] Tablet on building.
[92] Stoke Official Handbk. (1960), 14; ex inf. the city architect (1960).
[93] See p. 201.
[94] Date above central entrance.
[95] See p. 205.
[96] See p. 204.
[97] See p. 204.
[98] Staffs. Advertiser, 8 Jan. 1887; Stoke Bi-monthly Review (Apr. 1954).
[99] Stoke Bi-monthly Review (Apr. 1954).
[1] Inscription above fountain.
[2] See pp. 174, 184.
[3] See p. 199.
[4] See p. 186.

been entirely rebuilt in brick. The massive chimney between this and the main block formerly had stone fireplaces with four-centred arches on both floors, but the one which survives in the central bar was moved from the room above in 1936. A small room at the north end of the building is lined with 16th- or early-17th-century panelling, partly reset. A court-room with oak benches round the walls and a seat for the presiding official is said to have been in existence until the alterations of 1936.[5] Elm Tree House in Garden Street, formerly a farm, has a dated tile of 1694 built into its front wall but the house has been much altered. A tile of the same date was recently removed from a brick outhouse in Newcastle Lane.[6] The Grove, known earlier as Beech Grove[7] and now altered and enlarged as a nursery school, stands in its own grounds at the junction of St. Thomas Place and Doncaster Lane. It is largely a brick building of the late 18th century but during reroofing in 1925 the timbers of three older gables were discovered at the back.[8] At the time of the riots in 1842 the house was occupied by the stipendiary magistrate whose servants were said to have saved the family silver by hiding it in a pig trough.[9]

The Mount, a large house standing half-way between Penkhull and Hartshill in what were formerly extensive grounds, has been incorporated in the North Staffordshire Blind and Deaf School since 1897. It was built in 1803 by Josiah Spode (II) and c. 1840 was said to hold 'acknowledged pre-eminence' among the mansions in the district.[10] The original tall two-storied west front is still visible between later additions. It is built of brick and has seven windows to each floor, the three central windows being contained in a bowed projection of stone surmounted by a dome. Part of a brick stable block belonging to the house stands in Greatbatch Avenue, while a small lodge with a Classical stone portico survives at the junction of Prince's Road and Mount Avenue. In the 1870's two ice-houses still existed in the grounds, one in the shrubbery north of the house and one near the north-east corner of the present cemetery.[11]

The house called Cliffville stands in a commanding situation north of Hartshill Road on the western outskirts of Stoke. It was said c. 1840 to be 'little inferior in any respect to the Mount' and its grounds to have 'attained a high degree of sylvan beauty'.[12] The house, occupied since the 1920's as a girls' school in connexion with the Dominican convent, was built in 1810 by John Tomlinson[13] and is a typical rectangular two-storied building of the period with a Classical porch at its east end. Longfield Cottage, opposite the 'Noah's Ark' at Hartshill, is a low-built early-19th-century stucco house which now houses the Hartshill Orthopaedic Hospital.[14]

Springfields Hotel, formerly Springfields House, which stands west of Newcastle Road at its junction with Clayton Lane, is a square brick building with stone dressings and a central pediment, dating from the later 18th century. The symmetrical two-storied front is of five bays, the windows having stone lintels with raised keystones. The central first-floor window is emphasized by a stone architrave, the doorway below it being flanked by Corinthian pilasters and surmounted by a semicircular fanlight and an enriched frieze.

In the Trent Vale and Oak Hill districts to the south of Penkhull, a favourite residential area in the earlier 19th century,[15] several larger detached houses of this date survive, including the present Jubilee Working Men's Club, the adjacent house in Newcastle Road, Oak Hill Hall, and a 'Tudor' villa known as New Lodge at the south end of Trent Valley Road. At Stokeville near Boothen is an isolated example of early middle-class suburban development dating from c. 1850 and known by at least 1880 as The Villas.[16] The stucco houses, both detached and in pairs, are laid out along three roads and are in a pronounced Italian style with small square towers, low-pitched pantile roofs, wide bracketed eaves, and round-headed windows.

Variations from the standard design in early working-class housing are to be found in Wharf Street, where a yellow-brick terrace dating from c. 1835 has 'Tudor' features, and in Elenora Street (formerly Peel Street), where the entrances to each pair of dwellings are combined to form a small recessed porch beneath a four-centred arch. In general the terraces were laid out on much the same lines as elsewhere in the Potteries,[17] but it is evident that the available sites were more restricted, owing partly to the position of the main roads, the river, and the two canals, and partly to the fact that much of the area was low-lying and liable to floods. By 1850 bad housing conditions and the absence of drainage were causing anxiety; among the black spots were 'the three Cliff Squares',[18] evidently a series of cramped courts on the sloping ground at Cliff Bank built by Josiah Spode.[19] In Copeland Street the privies were below the fronts of the houses, and in Lower Square only one was provided for 20 dwellings. In the outlying areas the cottages at Hartshill, although in a healthy situation, were said to be confined and without drainage.[20] A suggestion for installing piped water and drainage in the houses in Berry Street on the west side of Liverpool Road was made in 1849.[21] Unlike most of the houses in Stoke, those in Berry Street appear to have already been provided with projecting wash-houses or back kitchens at this date.[22]

The workmens' dwellings built by Josiah Spode (II) at Penkhull c. 1800[23] appear to have been of a minimum standard, even for the period. Penkhull Square, which was then in open country and which

[5] Ex inf. the licensee (1960); V. G. Aston, *Hist. Penkhull*, 17–19 (copy among W.S.L. pamphs. *sub* Stoke); R. Nicholls, *Township of Penkhull-cum-Boothen*, plate facing p. 15.
[6] Local inf. (1960).
[7] O.S. Map 1/500 Staffs. xviii. 5. 2 (1877).
[8] Ex inf. Miss E. M. Ashwell, granddaughter of Dr. M. H. Ashwell who bought the Grove in the 1880's.
[9] Ex inf. Miss Ashwell; Ward, *Stoke*, 586.
[10] Ward, *Stoke*, 511; see pp. 174, 197.
[11] O.S. Maps 1/1,250 Staffs. xviii. 1. 21 (1875), 1. 22 (1877).   [12] Ward, *Stoke*, 511–12.
[13] Ibid. 511; see pp. 186, 273.

[14] See pp. 176–7, 197.   [15] See p. 176.
[16] *Kelly's Dir. Staffs.* (1880).
[17] See, e.g., pp. 85, 114.   [18] See p. 196.
[19] *Fenn's Stoke Boro. Almanack* (1892).
[20] R. Rawlinson, *Rep. to Bd. of Health on Stoke Par.* (1850), 68 (copy in H.R.L.).
[21] Ibid., plans facing p. 78.
[22] Tithe Redemption Com., Tithe Maps, Stoke (1849).
[23] Abstract of Title of Trustees under will of Wm. Taylor Copeland, in poss. of Mrs. J. T. Townsend and Miss Lowe, The Views, Penkhull, whose family acquired the property in 1907; Aston, *Penkhull*, 31; Nicholls, *Penkhull cum Boothen*, 26, 27.

still stands on the west side of Trent Valley Road, consists of 20 cottages built round a courtyard and approached through an archway in the front range. Each dwelling originally contained a living-room and a small scullery with two corresponding bed-rooms above, one of them too small for a full-sized bed. The projecting sculleries at the backs of some of the houses, as well as the rows of water-closets on the site of a communal ashpit behind the square, are additions of c. 1907.[24] In Penkhull New Road two terraces of cottages, also built by Josiah Spode and known as Ten Row and Seven Row, have similar accommodation, although they, too, were sub-sequently enlarged. A new standard, both in size and external finish, appears to have been set by the terraces in Hartshill Road built by Herbert Minton (d. 1858) for his workpeople.[25] North of the road a deliberately picturesque row of six small cottages has bay windows at both ends and a continuous veranda between them; the upper rooms have gabled dormer windows with decorative barge-boards and finials. The terraces opposite are larger and probably of slightly later date. They are built of red brick with blue-brick and tile dressings and have elaborate gabled porches, gabled dormers, and Gothic win-dows. The gabled houses, with either red-brick or plastered walls and arranged in informal groups, on the west side of Trent Valley Road for about half a mile south of Penkhull Square were built as a garden suburb 'for working people and others' by a society (Stoke-on-Trent Tenants Ltd.) formed on co-partnership principles in 1910.[26]

MANORS. Before the Conquest *PENKHULL* was held by Alfgar Earl of Mercia. It had passed to the Crown by 1086 when it was assessed at 2 hides 'cum appendiciis'.[27] It is possible that part of the lands appurtenant to this manor became the nucleus of the manor of Newcastle, into which by at least the mid-13th century Penkhull had been absorbed.[28]

The manor of *NEWCASTLE-UNDER-LYME*, first mentioned in 1215,[29] developed in close asso-ciation with the castle situated in the detached part of Penkhull township in the ancient parish of Stoke. The manor no doubt arose out of the need for a castle garrison, and by 1236[30] a group of serjeants, called king's sokemen in 1212,[31] were holding land under the obligation of performing castle-guard and, in addition, paying a yearly rent. The manor then consisted of the vills of Knutton, Fenton Vivian,

Hanley, and Longton.[32] The manor also included a virgate of land in Shelton held by William Muriel by the serjeanty of guarding the king's 'hay' there, called Cliff Hay.[33] Henry de Audley's holding within the manor of the vills of Tunstall, Chatterley, Bradwell, Thursfield, and Normacot by serjeanty of castle-guard[34] still existed in 1236, but by mid-century these vills had ceased to form part of the manor.[35] By about the same time the manor included Penkhull, Wolstanton, Shelton, Clayton, and Sea-bridge.[36]

In 1215 the manor was granted to Ranulf de Blundeville, Earl of Chester, by King John, to be held as a knight's fee.[37] On Ranulf's death without issue in 1232 the manor reverted to the Crown.[38] In 1267 Henry III conferred it on his younger son, Edmund, then created Earl of Lancaster, to be held as a fourth of a knight's fee.[39] About the same time Edmund became possessed of the lands of the Ferrers family, whose chief seat was at Tutbury, whereupon the manor of Newcastle became part of the honor of Tutbury.[40] Apart from a lease for three years from 1270 to the Bishop of Coventry and Lichfield,[41] Edmund held the manor until his death in 1296.[42] Thereafter it remained with the Earldom, subsequently the Duchy, of Lancaster.

Under the Tudors the practice began of farming out the manor, and in this connexion the Bagnall family is frequently met with. It was as bailiffs, how-ever, that the Bagnalls seem to have been con-cerned initially with the manor, for in 1509 Richard Smyth of Newcastle complained that Ralph Bagnall, then bailiff of the manor, had trespassed on Smyth's land in Clayton Griffith, pulled down hedges, and carried away his fences.[43] The Bagnalls are first en-countered as farmers of the manor in Elizabeth I's reign when Sir Ralph Bagnall is referred to as farmer in court rolls for 1567-79.[44] His nephew, Sir Henry Bagnall, farmed the manor after his uncle's death in 1580[45] until 1595.[46] In 1596 he asked for the rever-sion of the manor, 'which he hath now in possession and hath been held from her Majesty by his an-cestors for a long time'.[47] The request, however, seems to have been unsuccessful, for in 1601–2 and in the early years of James I's reign (1603–9) the farmer was Thomas Crompton.[48] In 1609 the farm of the manor passed to Ralph Sneyd, of Keele; he, and later his son Ralph, retained it, possibly intermittently, until 1622;[49] for the next seventeen years the manor remained under the direct control of the duchy.[50] In 1639 Samuel Terrick, M.P. for Newcastle in 1645,[51] was the fee

---

[24] Inf. from Mrs. J. T. Townsend. See plate facing p. 113 for a view and see p. 115 for plan.

[25] *Staffs Weekly Sentinel*, 16 Mar. 1956. The parish hall is now situated in a former cottage at the end of one of the groups.

[26] *Prospectus etc. of Stoke-on-Trent Tenants Ltd.* (copy in H.R.L.).

[27] *V.C.H. Staffs.* iv. 39, no. 17.

[28] *Cal. Inq. Misc.* i, no. 459; *S.H.C.* 1911, 145. The 'manor' of Penkhull mentioned in 1305 and 1308 (*Cal. Fine R.* 1302–7, 252; *S.H.C.* ix (1), 16; *Cal. Close*, 1307–13, 86), does not in fact seem to have been a distinct manor.

[29] *Rot. Chart.* (Rec. Com.), i. 216.

[30] *Bk. of Fees*, 593–4.

[31] Ibid. 143; *S.H.C.* 1911, 379.

[32] *Bk. of Fees*, 593–4.

[33] Ibid. ; see p. 201.

[34] See p. 13.

[35] *S.H.C.* 1911, 145–6.   [36] Ibid.

[37] *Rot. Chart.* (Rec. Com.), i. 216.

[38] *Complete Peerage*, iii. 168–9; *Cal. Chart. R.* 1226–57, 172.   [39] *Cal. Chart. R.* 1257–1300, 78.

[40] Adam Coyne, bailiff and receiver of Newcastle in 1313–14, is listed as one of the officers of Tutbury manor: R. Somerville, *Hist. of Duchy of Lancaster*, i. 353.

[41] *Cal. Pat.* 1266–72, 428.

[42] *Complete Peerage*, vii. 395.

[43] D.L. 3/9/325.

[44] W.S.L., D. 1788, vol. 90.

[45] Pape, *Tudor and Stuart Newcastle*, 42.

[46] W.S.L., D. 1788, vol. 90.

[47] Hist. MSS. Com. *Cal. of MSS. Hatfield House*, Pt. vi. 545.

[48] *Ducatus Lancastriae* (Pars Quarta), *Cal. Pleadings* (1834), 448; W.S.L., D. 1788, vol. 90.

[49] W.S.L., D. 1788, vol. 90.

[50] Ibid.

[51] Pape, *Tudor and Stuart Newcastle*, 80.

farmer[52] and again in 1660.[53] In a survey made in 1650 Ralph Sneyd was named as lessee of the perquisites and profits of the manor court,[54] while in 1654 Thomas Harrison, a native of Newcastle and one of the regicides, was described as lord of the manor.[55] Queen Anne granted a 31-year lease of the perquisites of the manor court to William Burslem, a prominent Newcastle burgess.[56] In 1731, before its expiration, the manor was leased to John Lord Gower and thereafter continuously to members of the Gower family until 1876.[57]

By 1236 the yearly fee-farm rents payable in respect of Knutton, Fenton, Hanley, and Longton were £4 11s. 6d., 7s. 4d., 6s., and 5s., respectively.[58] By the end of the 14th century a consolidation of the manorial tenures, probably for administrative and financial reasons, had taken place, with the result that assessed rents were then receivable from (i) Knutton, (ii) Penkhull, (iii) Wolstanton, (iv) Clayton and Seabridge, and (v) Shelton and Hanley.[59] Knutton still paid its old fee-farm rent of £4 11s. 6d. but the rents of the remaining properties showed considerable advances on those exacted in the middle of the previous century.[60]

Information about the incidents of copyhold tenure is provided by an action in 1619 brought against certain of the copyholders with the object presumably of augmenting the royal revenue. The defendants were Sir Thomas Colclough, Sir Rowland Cotton, Sir William Bowyer, Ralph Sneyd, and other named copyhold tenants of Penkhull, Boothen, Clayton, Seabridge, Shelton, Hanley, and Wolstanton.[61] Grants of copyholds by custom of the manor had, it was alleged, been made by the stewards of the manor without the knowledge of the king or his court and were, therefore, void in law. Moreover, fines had always been uncertain and arbitrable at the will of the lord or his steward and so had provided good revenue to the king. But the copyholders, so it was said, had combined to defraud the king of the fines and had pretended that by the custom of the manor the fines were certain, namely, one year's rent for an estate of inheritance and a half-year's rent for a life interest. The rights of common in the waste and the right to dig in their holdings for coal, limestone, slate, gravel, clay, and stone marl, and to cut and sell timber were described as pretended customs. The copyholders claimed that their lands from time immemorial had been held by copyhold tenure and that the fines were not uncertain but had always been assessed on the basis of one year's rent. Nevertheless, they were obliged, or found it politic, to submit and to ask the duchy court to ratify the customs hitherto enjoyed, namely those above-mentioned and in addition the custom of 2s. farefee (or fairwell) to the lord on surrender and the customary payment of 24s. to the reeve. A composition was finally agreed to so that the holdings and customs

could be ratified.[62] Under it the copyholders were called upon to pay the considerable sum of £1,373 5s., being 40 years' purchase of their ancient yearly rent amounting to £34 6s. 7½d., together with £22 19s. 10d. representing arrears of fines, one-half to be paid at the date of the decree and the remaining half three months later on its confirmation by Parliament. The heavy financial burden resulting from these legal proceedings must have caused hardship to the copyholders and it seems probable that the full amount was never paid; 30 years later half the composition was still outstanding[63] and in 1660 Capt. Samuel Terrick was petitioning for a grant of the composition money.[64] At the same time the importance attached to the decree as confirmatory of title was such that those copyholders who had been excluded from the original composition successfully petitioned in 1640 for admission thereto.[65]

By the middle of the 19th century, with the acceleration of industrial development within the area, mineral rights had become a source of considerable profit, as the coal and ironstone mines under all the copyhold lands were still the property of the duchy and were extensively worked by Lord Granville and other lessees.[66] The legal transactions involved by changes in their use brought increased business to the manor court. In the five years 1880-4, for example, 227 courts were held and at them no fewer than 1,311 transfers of copyholds were effected. The purchase moneys paid on transfer amounted to nearly £757,000.[67]

The customs of the manor were set out in the decree of 1619 dealt with above. The payment of third borough silver referred to in a survey of 1650 is presumably identical with the 'frithborwesulver' met with in the 14th century.[68] The fullest declaration of the customary rights of the copyholders is contained in the proceedings of a court baron held at Penkhull in 1714.[69] Thereat the jury presented (i) that by the immemorial custom of the manor a copyholder could devise his holding by will without surrender, (ii) that heirs could bar the entail, (iii) that a copyholder, in the presence of two other copyholders, could lease for a term of three years, and (iv) that a copyholder could assign his copyhold estate. All this indicated that copyhold tenants had, or claimed to have, acquired rights of disposition over their holdings analogous to those of a freeholder.

At the same court the method of serving the office of reeve was declared. For this purpose the manor was divided into three: (i) Penkhull and Boothen, (ii) Shelton and Hanley, and (iii) Clayton, Seabridge, and Wolstanton. In each of the three parcels certain ancient messuages were designated to which the office of reeve had been incident time out of mind. In Penkhull and Boothen there were 17 such messuages, in Shelton and Hanley 10, and in Clayton, Seabridge, and Wolstanton 9. The office (or, as had

[52] Hist. MSS. Com. 5th Rep. App. 141.
[53] Cal. Treas. Bks. 1660-7, 44.
[54] E 317/Staffs./38.   [55] D.L. 30/240/4.
[56] D.L. 42/27, f. 26.
[57] Boro. Mus., Fenton MS. Bk., f. 100.
[58] Bk. of Fees, 593-4.
[59] D.L. 29/367/6144.   [60] Ibid.
[61] D.L. 5/28, ff. 456-61b. A somewhat inaccurate 19th-cent. copy is to be found in D.L. 42/232. For a rental giving the names, rents, and holdings of the copyholders who compounded with the commissioners, see W.S.L., D. 1788, P. 32, B. 6.

[62] In the customs as ratified it is noteworthy that the right to dig for coal was omitted.
[63] E 317/Staffs./38. As the decree does not appear to have been confirmed by Act of Parliament, this may have been the reason for non-payment of the other moiety.
[64] Cal. Treas. Bks. 1660-7, 44.
[65] Cal. S.P. Dom. 1640, 304.
[66] White, Dir. Staffs. (1851).
[67] Return of fees by Steward of Newcastle-under-Lyme Manor, H.C. 77, p. 351 (1886), xxxviii.
[68] Cal. Inq. p.m. xi, p. 104.
[69] W.S.L., D. 1788, P. 3, B. 7.

become the practice, a money payment in lieu) was discharged (or paid) by the occupant of each of these messuages in rotation so that the liability of the individual occupant occurred once every 36 years.

During the Middle Ages the castle was the meeting-place of the manorial courts and on its decay the meeting-place was moved to Stoke, where courts were being held in the middle years of Elizabeth I. They were held at Penkhull in the later 1580's. Stoke was again the usual meeting-place at the end of the reign and throughout James I's. At the beginning of Charles I's reign the courts met at one or other of these two places,[70] while from 1635 to at least 1817 all were normally held at Penkhull.[71] The old court-house forms the core of the Greyhound Inn opposite the west door of Penkhull church.[72] By 1829 courts were being held at the 'Wheatsheaf' in Stoke,[73] and by 1854 at Hanley;[74] they were still being held there in 1928.[75]

OTHER ESTATES. By 1086 the moiety of the rectory held by Robert de Stafford was endowed with half a carucate of land,[76] and there was evidently another half attached to the remaining moiety since by 1341 the rectory's endowments included a whole carucate.[77] Vivian of Stoke, who was presented to the rectory by Henry II,[78] held an estate at Stoke by 1167,[79] and by the early 15th century the rector held over 5 acres of arable and 8 acres of waste in Penkhull township.[80] The moated parsonage-house was known in the 19th century as Stoke Hall and lay south of the church beyond the road to Fenton.[81] This house, or another house on the same site, was in existence by the mid-15th century as the residence of James Moseley, the rector's proctor.[82] Occupied by the curate at the beginning of the 17th century,[83] the hall was again the rector's home in 1666 when John Mainwaring (rector 1633–92) was taxable on eight hearths there.[84] It was in the hands

of a tenant-farmer in 1818[85] and of the curate c. 1828 after the demolition of the curate's house in the churchyard.[86] 'A truly shabby house' by this time, it was repaired in 1829 out of money raised by the sale of tithes and glebe,[87] and was again occupied by the curate in 1851, the rector being non-resident.[88] Sir Lovelace Tomlinson Stamer (rector 1858–92) lived there until 1864 when Cliffville, the house built by John Tomlinson in 1810 on an estate of 70 acres near Hartshill, was acquired as the rectory-house along with 20 acres of land.[89] New streets were being laid out over part of the estate in 1877.[90] The hall was evidently let until 1891.[91] It was then demolished and tramway offices and sheds, now the P.M.T. offices and garage, were built on the site, while more streets were laid out over the estate during the next few years.[92] Under the Act of 1889 (see below) the sale of Cliffville was authorized and £4,000 assigned for a new rectory-house near the church.[93] The new house was built in Butler Street near the site of the old rectory before Stamer's departure in 1892[94] and was still occupied in 1916.[95] By 1928, however, the rector had again moved out to Hartshill and was occupying the present rectory-house in Prince's Road.[96]

The moiety of the rectory mentioned in 1086 was valued at 30s.,[97] and in 1291 Stoke church with its chapels was valued at £40.[98] In 1341 the rector's estate consisted of a carucate worth 40s., 20 acres of meadow worth 40s., rents of 40s., and tithes and other offerings worth £10.[99] In 1535 the value of the rectory was given as £41 0s. 8d. consisting of £4 10s. in glebe, £33 4s. in tithes, and £3 6s. 8d. in offerings.[1] At the end of the 16th century, however, the Rector of Stoke was described as 'the best man in the town' and his living as 'one of the best parsonages in the country'.[2] The net annual income of the rector during the three years 1828–31 was £2,717.[3]

The Act of 1807 dividing the parish[4] also allowed the rector to lease out 61 acres of glebe in Shelton

[70] D.L. 30/237/5, 18, 23, 25; W.S.L., D. 1788, vol. 90, copy of Newcastle Ct. R. 1588–1616.
[71] W.S.L., D. 1788, vol. 90; D.L. 30/241/50; R. Nicholls, *Penkhull cum Boothen*, 21–22; W.S.L. 2/40/42. The small court was held at Clayton in June 1679: D.L. 30/242/3.
[72] V. G. Aston, *Penkhull*, 18–19 (copy among W.S.L. pamphlets *sub* Stoke); see pp. 182–3.
[73] *Staffs. Advertiser*, 10 Oct. 1829; White, *Dir. Staffs.* (1851); Aston, *Penkhull*, 40.
[74] *P.O. Dir. Staffs.* (1854).
[75] *Kelly's Dir. Staffs.* (1928).
[76] *V.C.H. Staffs.* iv. 51, no. 191; see p. 188.
[77] *Inq. Non.* (Rec. Com.), 128.
[78] *S.H.C.* iv (1), 23.
[79] Ibid. i. 48; ii (1), 95, 110.
[80] D.L. 42/4, f. 173a.
[81] Hargreaves, *Map of Staffs. Potteries*; R. Nicholls, *Stoke Ch.* 38.
[82] C 1/44/226.
[83] Ward, *Stoke*, 482.
[84] *S.H.C.* 1921, 153; 5 more hearths had been stopped up.
[85] Parson and Bradshaw, *Dir. Staffs.* (1818).
[86] *Pigot's Nat. Com. Dir.* (1828–9); see p. 191.
[87] Ward, *Stoke*, 481–2; White, *Dir. Staffs.* (1834); Shaw, *Staffs. Potteries*, 60; Stoke Rectory Act, 7 & 8 Geo. IV, c. 41 (priv. act).
[88] White, *Dir. Staffs.* (1851), 239, 241; Stoke Hall farm was then held by a tenant. The rector had been living at the Hall in 1834: ibid. (1834).
[89] Nicholls, *Stoke Ch.* 82; Ward, *Stoke*, 511–12; *P.O. Dir. Staffs.* (1868, 1872, 1876); *Kelly's Dir. Staffs.* (1880, 1884, 1892); F. D. How, *Bp. Sir Lovelace Tomlinson Stamer*, 112, stating that Stamer moved to Cliffville at the

end of 1863; *Stoke Par. Mag.* (Dec. 1908).
[90] H.R.L., Stoke Boro. Sanitary Cttee. Mins. 1874–81, p. 165.
[91] *Kelly's Dir. Staffs.* (1880, 1884); Lich. Dioc. Regy., Bp.'s Reg. T, p. 353, conveyance of Stoke Hall by Jas. Pratt to Rector of Stoke to hold as part of the possessions of rectory (1891).
[92] Nicholls, *Stoke Ch.* 38, 39, 82, 116–17; O.S. Map 6″ Staffs., xviii NE. (1890, 1900); H.R.L., S.M 23A, Plan of Stoke Boro. 1900; ibid. Stoke Boro. Mins. 1893–5, pp. 2, 260, date-stones of 1892 on garage in Butler St., of 1893 on house opposite, and of 1896 in Stamer St.; see pp. 174, 179.
[93] Nicholls, *Stoke Ch.* 81. An acre of glebe had been reserved for a more centrally situated house when Cliffville was acquired: How, *Stamer*, 206. Cliffville then became a private house (*Kelly's Dir. Staffs.* (1892, and later edns. to 1916); *Fenn's Stoke Boro. Almanack*, 1900) and since the 1920's has been part of the Dominican convent sch.: see p. 273.
[94] H. V. Stuart, *Reminiscences*, 9 (copy among W.S.L. Pamphs. *sub* Stoke); H.R.L., SM. 23A, Plan of Stoke Boro. 1900.
[95] *Kelly's Dir. Staffs.* (1916).
[96] Ibid. (1928).
[97] *V.C.H. Staffs.* iv. 15, no. 191.
[98] *Tax. Eccl.* (Rec. Com.), 242. The annual value was given as 160 marks in 1293: *S.H.C.* vi (1), 267.
[99] *Inq. Non.* (Rec. Com.), 128.
[1] *Valor Eccl.* (Rec. Com.), iii. 120.
[2] Erdeswick, *Staffs.* ed. T. Harwood (1844), 20.
[3] *Rep. Com. Eccl. Rev.* H.C. 54, pp. 500–1, (1835), xii. The gross income was £3,000. Out of his net income the rector paid £195 to his assistant curate: see p. 189.
[4] See p. 188.

and Penkhull as building plots.[5] Having bought the advowson in 1817[6] John Tomlinson in the same year secured from the rector a lease of the tithes, many of which had by then been allowed to lapse.[7] Tomlinson then proceeded to revive most of these,[8] and in 1827 secured an Act of Parliament allowing the sale of the tithes and also part of the glebe in Shelton, Penkhull, and Fenton for building; the proceeds were to be used to increase the endowment of the rectory, improve the house, and endow two new churches.[9] The tithes were sold at an average price of between £10 and £15 an acre, and by c. 1840 some £50,000 had been raised by the sale of tithe and glebe; the annual income of the church rose from some £600 in 1807 to £3,000 in 1831.[10] The tithes of Stoke were commuted in 1849 as follows: Clayton and Seabridge £142 8s. 2d., Penkhull and Boothen £199 7s. 10d., Hanley and Shelton £205 12s. 3d., Fenton and Botteslow £183 0s. 1d., Longton £185 15s. 5d.[11] The average annual income from tithe rent-charges between 1885 and 1887 was some £770.[12] By 1889 the total realized by the sale of tithes and dues was over £80,000, while the accumulated fund for the purchase of further lands had reached over £16,000.[13] In 1889 the rector, Sir Lovelace Tomlinson Stamer, by then also Bishop of Shrewsbury, secured an Act which permitted the accumulated fund to be used by the Bishop of Lichfield for the purchase of the advowson. The Act also assigned nearly £34,000 stock out of the rectory's funds for increasing the endowments of Hartshill, Penkhull, Trent Vale, Fenton, Longton (St. John's), and a new parish in Hanley (St. John's), and a further £4,000 for building a rectory-house nearer Stoke church.[14]

The Fenton family were living at Boothen between at least 1579 and 1666.[15] In 1706 Thomas Fenton, who had succeeded his father Thomas in 24 customary acres in Penkhull and Boothen in 1701,[16] sold his house at Boothen, occupied by Lawrence Simcock, to John Bowyer,[17] whose family had held property at Penkhull from at least 1544.[18] In 1711 John Bowyer sold the Boothen estate with land at Penkhull to George Boughey of Audley.[19] The estate

then descended in the Boughey family, who in 1940 were still said to own most of the land in Boothen.[20] By the end of the 18th century most of the Bougheys' 174-acre Boothen estate consisted of Boothen farm, where the farmhouse had been rebuilt in or shortly before 1777.[21] Tenants of the farm included the Emery family from before 1733 until at least 1754[22] and the Bagnalls between at least 1819 and 1892.[23] The southern extension of Campbell Road, dating from 1923–4, and the Michelin Athletic Club, now occupy the site of the house and buildings.[24]

Three farms in Penkhull and lands and rents there and elsewhere, all forming the endowment of Our Lady's Chantry in Stoke church, were leased in 1548 by the Crown to Sir Ralph Bagnall, patron of Stoke rectory, for 21 years.[25] Ralph conveyed them to his sister Anne and her husband Roger Brereton of Stoke, and their son Roger alienated part of the estate to various persons after the death of Anne.[26] The Crown granted the endowments to Edward Kendall of Lincoln's Inn in 1612, but this grant seems to have been ineffective,[27] presumably because of the numerous alienations. The Crown attempted to recover part at least of the estate in 1618[28] and in 1628 made a grant of all the endowments to Henry Atkinson and William Clarke.[29]

Land in Stoke, described as given for a priest there, was granted by the Crown to Sir George Howard in 1559.[30]

Grindley Hill farm lay north of the road from Penkhull village to London Road by 1760 and was then owned by the Fenton family.[31] By 1797 it had passed to the Armitstead family in the right of Katherine, sister and coheir of Thomas Fenton of Newcastle and wife of the Revd. John Armitstead.[32] Thomas Fletcher, husband of Katherine's sister Anne, the other coheir, was then attempting to secure the farm by exchange with the Armitsteads, but Katherine's death in 1798 prevented the transaction.[33] By 1819 the farm was owned by Sir Thomas's son John (by then Sir John Fenton Fletcher Boughey)[34] and was still in existence in the early 1920's.[35] The site is now occupied by housing of the years between the world wars.[36]

[5] Nicholls, *Stoke Ch.* 78–79.
[6] See p. 199.
[7] Ward, *Stoke*, 458; W.S.L., D. 1788, P. 59, B. 14.
[8] Ward, *Stoke*, 458–9; W.S.L., D. 1788, P. 56, B. 23; ibid. P. 59, B. 14.
[9] Stoke Rectory Act, 7 & 8 Geo. IV, c. 41 (priv. act); Nicholls, *Stoke Ch.* 79. Churches were built at Longton and Shelton: see pp. 155, 234.
[10] Ward, *Stoke*, 459–60; Lich. Dioc. Regy., Bp.'s Reg. H, pp. 369–70, 540–6; ibid. K, pp. 9–11; W.S.L., D. 1788, P. C. 1(m); U.C.N.S., Sneyd MSS., Stoke Deeds. Thus tithes in Gt. Fenton and Boothen were sold to Thos. Allen of Gt. Fenton in 1829 for £1,052: W.S.L., D. 1742/345, 347.
[11] Tithe Redemption Com., Tithe Appt., Stoke.
[12] Nicholls, *Stoke Ch.* 82.   [13] Ibid. 81.
[14] Stoke Rectory Act, 52 & 53 Vic. c. 203 (local); Nicholls, *Stoke Ch.* 81–84, 88–90 (these latter pages based on How, *Stamer*, 202–18); see p. 189.
[15] *S.H.C.* 1926, 104; *Stoke Churchwardens' Accts.* (*T.N.S.F.C.* lxxiii), pp. A8, 37, 40; ibid. lxxv, p. A139; Ward, *Stoke*, app. p. xlv; *Stoke Par. Reg.* i. 75; *S.H.C.* 1921, 154.
[16] W.S.L., D. 1788, P. 4, B. 3.   [17] Ibid.
[18] C 1/936/195; *S.H.C.* 1921, 153; W.S.L., D. 1788, P. 56, B. 23; *Stoke Par. Reg.* ii. 352.
[19] W.S.L., D. 1788, P. 4, B. 3.
[20] Ibid. P. 4, B. 4, 5; P. 56, B. 23; ibid. P. C. 1(m); ibid. vol. 270; *Kelly's Dir. Staffs.* (1940); *V.C.H. Staffs.* iv. 106.

Their lands in Boothen had been sold by 1959: ex inf. Mrs. John W. Greene, Aqualate Hall (1959).
[21] W.S.L., D. 1788, P. 56, B. 23.
[22] Ibid. P. 4, B. 15; P. 56, B. 23; *Stoke Par. Reg.* iii. 553.
[23] W.S.L., D. 1788, P. 4, B. 4, 5; P. 56, B. 23; ibid. P. C. 1(m); ibid. vol. 270; *Kelly's Dir. Staffs.* (1884; 1892).
[24] O.S. Map 6" Staffs. xviii NW. (1925); see pp. 176, 178.
[25] D.L. 14/6/72; E 134/16 Jas. 1/Hil. 9; see p. 189. The estate in Penkhull, Hanley, and Shelton held by 'the procurator of St. Mary' early in the 15th cent. (D.L. 42/4, ff. 168a–174a passim, 178b), may be connected with these chantry lands or with those of the Chantry of Our Lady in St. Giles's, Newcastle: see p. 18.
[26] E 134/16 Jas. I./Hil. 9.
[27] Ibid.; C 66/2455, m. 2.   [28] E 134/16 Jas. I/Hil. 9.
[29] C 66/2455, mm. 1, 2, 5.
[30] *Cal. Pat.* 1558–60, 89.
[31] Yates, *Map of Staffs.* (1775). The name Grindley Hill occurs in 1651: W.S.L., D. 1788, P. 46, B. 2; ibid. vol. 76, rental 1760–71. In 1708 a house and lands in Penkhull including Grindley Hill Field were occupied by Wm. Shaw as tenant of John Bowyer: ibid. P. 4, B. 3.
[32] W.S.L., D. 1788, P. 2, B. 6; W.S.L., pedigree in introd. to catalogue of D. 1788.
[33] W.S.L., D. 1788, P. 2, B. 6.
[34] Ibid. P. 56, B. 23; *V.C.H. Staffs.* iv. 106.
[35] O.S. Map 6" Staffs. xvii NE. (1925).
[36] See p. 174.

The medieval hospital of St. Loye lay in the area still known in 1849 as Spittles at the junction of Newcastle Lane and the present Newcastle Road.[37] The hospital and its lands evidently remained with the Crown after the Dissolution until 1590 when they formed part of a large grant of former church land made by the queen to William Tupper and William Dawes.[38] There was an estate called Spittle in Stoke parish in 1653,[39] and in 1714 Roger Townsend held of Newcastle manor a copyhold messuage and lands in Penkhull called Spittle Houses.[40] In or shortly before 1741 Roger was succeeded by his grandson Joseph Townsend,[41] but no mention was made then of the Spittle Houses estate. An estate called the Spittles was bought from a James Goodwin by Josiah Wedgwood of Etruria (d. 1795)[42] and was still owned by his son Josiah in 1834.[43]

CHURCHES. There was a church at Stoke by 1086,[44] and for the next seven centuries and more this remained the mother church of a large parish. That parish included Newcastle, Clayton, and Seabridge on the west, the detached Whitmore, farther west still, Burslem, Hanley, Norton-in-the-Moors, Bucknall, and Bagnall in the north, and Lane End and Fenton in the east. Originally there was no centre of population around the church: there was no township called Stoke, and as late as the mid-18th century there were very few houses near the church.[45] During the Middle Ages six chapels of ease were built within the parish, all of which had cure of souls by 1563,[46] but the parish was not divided until 1807 when the surrounding chapelries were made into five rectories by an Act of Parliament.[47] The reduced parish of Stoke was further divided in the course of the next century by the creation of new parishes at Longton in 1839, Hartshill in 1842, Shelton in 1843, Penkhull in 1844, Trent Vale in 1844, Northwood, Hanley, in 1845, Wellington, Hanley, in 1845, Fenton in 1860, Hanley (St. John) in 1891, and Shelton (St. Jude) in 1895.[48] The history of only those churches and mission-centres within the borough of Stoke as it existed in 1910 will be treated in this section.

In 1086 a moiety of the church of Stoke was held by Robert de Stafford as part of his fee of Caverswall.[49] The other moiety may have been held by the king as lord of Penkhull.[50] The Stafford family's moiety subsequently passed to Walter of Caverswall who, with the consent of his overlord Robert de Stafford (II), gave it c. 1155 to Stone Priory.[51] Kenilworth Priory, the mother house of Stone, twice received confirmation of this grant from Henry II.[52] The other moiety probably passed from the Crown to the Earl of Chester with Newcastle manor[53] since in 1221 and 1222 the king and Earl Ranulf were suing the Prior of Kenilworth for his half-share as wrongfully alienated by Walter of Caverswall.[54] The prior eventually surrendered his claim to the earl in 1223 in return for land in Seabridge,[55] and both shares were thus united in the earl's hands.

The king evidently recovered the advowson of Stoke along with Newcastle manor c. 1232, and both were leased by the Crown to Gilbert de Seagrave in that year.[56] The king, however, was presenting regularly from 1235[57] until 1266 when the advowson of Stoke was granted with Newcastle manor to Edmund, Earl of Lancaster,[58] who by 1268 had leased the advowson to Hamon Lestrange.[59] It was held by Edmund in 1293 and at his death in 1296 and descended with Newcastle manor until 1547, passing to the Duchy of Lancaster in the 14th century.[60] During this time, however, grants were sometimes made of single presentations,[61] while in 1485 Richard III gave the advowson to the abbey of St. Mary de Pré, Leicester, with licence to appropriate the church.[62] This grant, however, does not seem to have taken effect since in 1493 Henry VII presented.[63] The Duchy of Lancaster continued to make grants of single presentations[64] and finally in 1547 conveyed the advowson to Sir John Russell, Keeper of the Privy Seal, who at once granted it to Ralph Bagnall.[65] In 1562 Ralph leased it to Francis Biddulph,[66] but by 1591 it was in the hands of Sir Henry Bagnall, Marshal of Ireland and nephew of Ralph Bagnall,[67] who conveyed it in 1597 to William Crompton.[68] William's son, Thomas Crompton of Stone, sold it in 1605 to Richard Barbour[69] who in

[37] Nicholls, *Penkhull cum Boothen*, 37; *S.H.C.* 1915, 250; Hargreaves, *Map of Staffs. Potteries*; Lich. Dioc. Regy., Tithe Appt. and Maps, Stoke. It is probably to be identified with the 'hospitalis sancti Lodowici juxta castrum nostrum subtus Lynam' which occurs in 1437: D.L. 42/18, f. 99a.
[38] C 66/1340, mm. 1, 8, 18.
[39] Stoke Churchwardens' Accts. (*T.N.S.F.C.* lxxiv), p. A113.
[40] W.S.L., D. 1788, P. 67, B. 26.
[41] Ibid., P. 67, B. 22.
[42] J. C. Wedgwood, *The Wedgwoods*, 174.
[43] Lich. Dioc. Regy., Bp.'s Reg. K, p. 9.
[44] *V.C.H. Staffs.* iv. 51, no. 191.
[45] See p. 173.   [46] *S.H.C.* 1915, 248.
[47] Ward, *Stoke*, 457–8; Stoke Rectory Act, 47 Geo. III, sess. 2, c. 114 (local and personal).
[48] *Lich. Dioc. Dir.* (1955–6), 131–2.
[49] *V.C.H. Staffs.* iv. 51, no. 191; Robt. was overlord of Caverswall and Ernulf de Hesding tenant. The suggestion has been made that Caverswall was then included in the parish of Stoke: Ward, *Stoke*, 450.   [50] See p. 184.
[51] *S.H.C.* ii (1), 236.
[52] *Cal. Pat.* 1476–85, 66; *Cal. Chart. R.* 1300–26, 277.
[53] See p. 184.
[54] *Curia Regis R.* x. 293; *S.H.C.* iv (1), 23, 25; *Rolls of Justices in Eyre, 1221–2* (Selden Soc. lix), pp. 466–7.
[55] *S.H.C.* iv (1), 223; *S.H.C.* vi (1), 5; see p. 77. It was

possibly this land that was meant when in 1292 Kenilworth released to Stone a moiety of Stoke ch., a grant confirmed in 1336 by the king: *Cal. Pat.* 1334–8, 308–9.
[56] *Cal. Chart. R.* 1226–57, 172; see p.
[57] *Cal. Pat.* 1232–47, 96 when, however, the presentation was described as being to 'a mediety of the church'; ibid. 1247–50, 127, 560; 1266–72, 738.
[58] *Cal. Inq. p.m.* vii, p. 62; *Plac. de Quo Warr.* (Rec. Com.), 712; *S.H.C.* vi (1), 245, 267; vii (1), 5.
[59] *Cal. Chart. R.* 1257–1300, 114.
[60] Lich. Dioc. Regy., Bp.'s Reg. 1, ff. 15b, 16a; 2, ff. 154a, 189b, 9, f. 50b; *Cal. Papal Regs.*, ii. 8; *Cal. Close*, 1360–4, 205; *Cal. Inq. p.m.* xi, p. 104; *S.H.C.* vi (1), 267; *S.H.C.* n.s. x (1), 105–49 *passim*; *S.H.C.* n.s. viii. 81; see p. 184.
[61] *Cal. Inq. p.m.* vii, p. 80; Lich. Dioc. Regy., Bp.'s Reg. 10, f. 16a; D.L. 42/22, ff. 230b, 245b–246a.
[62] *Cal. Pat.* 1476–85, 541; *V.C.H. Leics.* ii. 15.
[63] Lich. Dioc. Regy., Bp.'s Reg. 12, f. 143a.
[64] D.L. 42/22, ff. 230b, 245b; Lich. Dioc. Regy., Bp.'s Reg. 14, f. 21b.
[65] *Cal. Pat.* 1547–8, 4, 7; D.L. 42/23, f. 281b; Ward, *Stoke*, 346; *S.H.C.* 1917–18, 325–7. Bagnall was Sir Ralph 'late of Stoke' in 1557: *Cal. Pat.* 1553–7, 318.
[66] *Cal. Pat.* 1560–3, 393.
[67] *Acts of P.C.* 1591, 234; *S.H.C.* 1917–18, 347.
[68] *S.H.C.* xvi. 161.
[69] W.S.L., D. 1742, bdle. 12; *S.H.C.* xviii (1), 20.

1606 or 1607 sold it to Roger Brereton and his son Roger.[70] The Breretons, although accused of simony in 1636 over the presentation of John Mainwaring three years before,[71] retained the patronage[72] until 1656 when Ralph, a younger son of the elder Roger Brereton, sold it to Peter Birkened of London.[73] Sir James Edwards seems to have held the patronage in 1675, when he settled it on or conveyed it to a Thomas Whitley,[74] but by c. 1680 it had passed to a 'Mr. Spademan',[75] doubtless the John Spateman who in 1684 settled it on or conveyed it to Thomas Allen.[76] However, it was by a John Sidebotham that Dr. Thomas Allen was presented to Stoke rectory in 1697.[77] Dr. Allen held the patronage by 1732 when he settled both benefice and right of presentation on his son Thomas who succeeded him in the same year.[78] In 1742 the younger Thomas sold the patronage for £4,000 to James Robinson of Lichfield.[79] William Robinson presented in 1798[80] and his widow Ruth in 1801, when William Robinson, himself patron by 1807 and presumably her son, was given the rectory.[81] His trustee Spencer Madan presented on his death in 1812 and again in 1814,[82] and in 1817 the Robinsons' trustees sold the advowson to John Tomlinson of Cliffville, a solicitor formerly of Hanley.[83] He died in 1838 and under his will and that of his son John Wickes Tomlinson, rector from 1831 (d. 1857), the patronage was vested in trustees for its sale.[84] By the efforts of John Tomlinson's grandson, Sir Lovelace Tomlinson Stamer, 3rd baronet, rector from 1858 to 1892, an Act was passed in 1889 authorizing the transfer of the advowson to the Bishop of Lichfield, the purchase price being defrayed out of the funds of the rectory.[85] The bishop remains the patron.[86]

In 1380 the absentee rector was given leave by the bishop to farm his church while he was in attendance on the Duke of Lancaster.[87] By the 15th century it had become customary for the rector to appoint a parish priest and a deacon, the latter being responsible for looking after the church.[88] Failure to appoint a deacon over a period of more than ten years was

then leading to thefts from the church and disorder in the churchyard.[89] The rector evidently had one assistant 'curate' by the 16th century.[90] In 1602 the curate was paid £13 6s. 8d. from the small tithe,[91] and by 1828 his stipend was £195 a year.[92] By 1860 there were three assistant curates.[93]

There was a single churchwarden about the middle of the 15th century.[94] There were four churchwardens in 1553[95] but before the end of the 16th century only two.[96] The number seems to have remained at two except around the turn of the 18th and 19th centuries when there seems to have been only one.[97] It was stated in 1724 that one of these was chosen for the north side of the parish, consisting of Longton and Bucknall Quarters, and one for the south side, consisting of the Quarters of Penkhull and Shelton; the churchwardens were elected in turn from each of the two quarters comprising their area.[98]

By the Reformation there were two chantries in Stoke church, one of Our Lady and one of St. Nicholas and St. Katherine.[99]

At the time of its demolition in 1830[1] the former church of *ST. PETER AD VINCULA* consisted of an aisled nave, a chancel of three bays, a west tower, a south porch and a north vestry.[2] Although some older work was incorporated, much of the structure, including the chancel, had apparently been rebuilt early in the 13th century. The chancel was lighted by lancet windows and there was a priest's door on the south side.[3] The tower dated from the 14th century; it was of three stages with a west doorway, a tall west window above it, paired windows to the belfry, and an embattled parapet with angle pinnacles. Gargoyles at parapet level were probably those later incorporated in the end houses of the terrace in Brook Street.[4] The south porch was in existence by the 15th century.[5] Some of the buttresses may have been added about 1687.[6] A west gallery was installed in 1717,[7] and it was probably at this time that the pitch of the nave and aisle roofs was lowered, the parapet of the nave was

[70] W.S.L., D. 1742, bdle. 12.
[71] *Cal. S.P. Dom.* 1635–6, 478, 486, 496, 514.
[72] Inst. Bks.   [73] W.S.L., D. 1742, bdle. 12.
[74] C.P. 25(2)/725, 27 Chas. II Trin.
[75] *S.H.C.* 1919, 258.
[76] C.P. 25(2)/726, 36 Chas. II Trin.
[77] Lich. Dioc. Regy., Bp.'s Reg. 18, f. 31a. Sidebotham was also acting as patron in connexion with Norton chapel in the same year; W.S.L., D. 1742/340. In *S.H.C.* 1919, 258, it is stated that Sidebotham bought the advowson from the Breretons.
[78] W.S.L., D. 1742, bdle. 12.
[79] Ibid.; C.P. 25(2)/1206, 16 Geo. II Trin.; Inst. Bks.
[80] Lich. Dioc. Regy., Bp.'s Reg., 27, p. 17; Inst. Bks.
[81] Lich. Dioc. Regy., Bp.'s Reg., 27, p. 91; Inst. Bks.; Ward, *Stoke*, 457.
[82] Lich. Dioc. Regy., Bp.'s Reg. 28, pp. 169, 206; Inst. Bks.; Stoke Rectory Act, 47 Geo. III, sess. 2, c. 114 (local and personal).
[83] Ward, *Stoke*, 458, 511; Lich. Dioc. Regy., Bp.'s Reg. 29, pp. 244–5.
[84] R. Nicholls, *Stoke Ch.* 88; Adams, *Adams Family*, 145, 163; Lich. Dioc. Regy., Bp.'s Reg. M, p. 241; ibid. Bp.'s Reg. 32, 150; *Lich. Dioc. Ch. Cal.* (1889). The rector was non-resident in 1851: White, *Dir. Staffs.* (1851), 227, 239.   [85] See p. 187.
[86] Nicholls, *Stoke Ch.* 27; *Lich. Dioc. Dir.* (1959).
[87] *S.H.C.* n.s. viii. 81.
[88] C 1/44/226.   [89] Ibid.
[90] Nicholls, *Stoke Ch.* 109–10; *S.H.C.* 1915, 249–50; Stoke Churchwardens' Accts. (T.N.S.F.C. lxxviii), p. A248; Lich. Dioc. Regy., Bp.'s Reg. 18, f. 33a.

[91] *S.H.C.* 1915, 255.
[92] *Rep. Com. Eccl. Rev.* H.C. 54, pp. 500–1 (1835), xxii.
[93] Lich. Dioc. Ch. Cal. (1860).
[94] C 1/44/226.   [95] *S.H.C.* 1915, 249.
[96] Stoke Churchwardens' Accts. (T.N.S.F.C. lxxiii), A3; lxxviii, p. A234.
[97] Nicholls, *Stoke Ch.* 111–13; Lich. Dioc. Dir. (1957).
[98] W.S.L., D. 1788, P. 67, B. 11. This division is seen in the method of collecting the ch. rate in 1628: Stoke Churchwardens' Accts. (T.N.S.F.C. lxxiv), pp. A60–61, 63–64. Newcastle and Whitmore were the responsibility of the churchwarden for the S. side.
[99] *S.H.C.* 1915, 250; 1910, 246, bequests by Thos. Adams to the chantries 1536. For endowments see p. 187. The lands held by 'the procurator of St. Mary' early in the 15th cent. may have belonged to one of the Stoke chantries or to the chantry of Our Lady in St. Giles's, Newcastle: see p. 187, n. 25.
[1] *Staffs. Advertiser*, 11 Sept. 1830. Ward gives 1829 as the date of demolition: *Stoke*, 461.
[2] This architectural description is based on Ward, *Stoke* view on p. 462; *Staffs. Advertiser*, 5 Nov. 1881 and 21 Jan. 1905; Nicholls, *Stoke Ch.* 33–35; remains in churchyard. See also plate facing p. 190.
[3] A 'choir door' was mentioned in the 15th cent. C 1/44/226.
[4] Nicholls, *Stoke Ch.* 34. The gargoyles are still in Brook Street.   [5] C 1/44/226.
[6] Stoke Churchwardens' Accts. T.N.S.F.C. (lxxvi), p. A176: 'a view taken of the church wall, whether it would be supported by buttresses'.
[7] W.S.L., D. 1742, bdle. 55; Ward, *Stoke*, 489.

raised, and circular clerestory windows were inserted to light the upper part of the church. Other galleries may have been added later.[8] Square-headed aisle windows were possibly of 14th-century origin or, more probably, 18th-century insertions.[9]

After the completion of the new church the materials of the old building, including the internal fittings, were put up for sale.[10] Much of the stone was used to form the bed of a watercourse serving Boothen Mill and here it was discovered by Charles Lynam in 1881 when the mill was demolished and the watercourse was about to be filled in.[11] From the available worked stones and certain other fragments from the old building Lynam reconstructed two semicircular arches, a circular and an octagonal pier, parts of other arches and three semi-octagonal responds. These were set up on the site of the former church, the plan of which was said to be discernible from existing foundations.[12] At the same time the east end of the chancel was indicated by masonry and by placing in position the original altar slab which had been preserved in the new church (see below). With the exception of some stones bearing Norman zigzag ornament,[13] all the reused fragments appear to date from the first half of the 13th century. The evidence concerning the exact form of the original nave is conflicting: Lynam's reconstruction gives a four-bay nave arcade with semicircular arches while surviving views of the exterior suggest a nave of five bays.[14] One who remembered the old church wrote in 1881 that the nave arcades were of five pointed arches;[15] this type of arch would certainly seem more probable in association with the other early-13th-century features.[16]

The new church, on a site to the north of the old one, was begun in 1826 and consecrated in 1830.[17] It was the first of the new 19th-century churches to be built in the Potteries and consequently the laying of the foundation stones was attended by much ceremony and enthusiasm.[18] The list of subscribers illustrates the wide range of support given by this time to the building of new churches. The cost was over £14,000, and £15,000 was raised by means of a parliamentary grant of £641, a grant of £391 from the Incorporated Church Building Society, a parish rate of £3,400, and private benefactions including £3,300 from the rector, John Chappel Woodhouse (1814–32), £500 from Josiah Spode, £300 from John Tomlinson the patron, £250 from George IV out of the Duchy of Lancaster's revenues, £500

from 'the working-classes of Stoke proper', and £500 in the form of free help from parishioners.[19] The building, which is in the Perpendicular style, was designed by Trubshaw and Johnson[20] and carried out in red sandstone, now much blackened. It consists of a wide galleried nave of five bays, a chancel flanked by low vestries, and a west tower. The windows contain Perpendicular tracery, those in the nave having deep transomes to mask the backs of the side galleries. The tower rises in four stages and is surmounted by an embattled parapet and angle pinnacles. The hood-moulding of the west doorway rests on carved corbel heads, said to represent John Tomlinson and the Revd. John Woodhouse, respectively patron and rector of the church.[21] Flanking the tower are two vestibules containing the gallery staircases. The nave retains galleries on three sides, supported on buttressed stone piers and with fronts of panelled oak; the organ occupies its original position in the west gallery. The nave ceiling is spanned by cast-iron trusses and is divided into panels by moulded ribs and bosses. An unusual feature for the period is the comparatively long chancel, divided from the nave by a stone arch and said at the time to be 'unlike the mimick chancels of most modern churches'.[22] The east window of five lights contains contemporary stained glass which includes figures of the twelve apostles. Armorial bearings in the other chancel windows[23] have been replaced by later stained glass.

The interior of the church was renovated in 1888 to commemorate the consecration of the rector, Sir Lovelace Stamer, as Bishop of Shrewsbury. At this time the three-decker pulpit in the central aisle, the square family pews, and all the pew doors were removed, and the organ was reconstructed.[24] The present pulpit dates from 1894.[25] The old altar slab lay in the new church until 1881 when it was placed on its original site; it was taken back to the church in 1933, and after a short time in the Warrior's Chapel it has since been used as the high altar once again.[26] The reredos was given by Sir Lovelace Stamer in 1888 and the two side-panels were added by the parishioners in 1892 in memory of his work as rector.[27] A font was presented to the new church by John Tomlinson[28] and the old font, probably of Norman date,[29] was first removed to his garden at Cliffville and in 1876 placed in its former position on the site of the old church; it was transferred to the new church and rededicated in 1932.[30] A new

[8] Nicholls, *Stoke Ch.* 41.
[9] Ibid. 34; Ward, *Stoke*, 463.
[10] *Staffs. Advertiser*, 11 Sept. 1830.
[11] Ibid. 5 Nov. 1881.
[12] Ibid. 21 Jan. 1905; Nicholls, *Stoke Ch.* 33–35. The dimensions are given as: chancel 32 ft. by 18 ft.; nave 66 ft. by 18 ft.; aisles 8 ft. wide; tower 18 ft. square.
[13] Lynam believed them to be part of a Norman doorway: *Staffs. Advertiser*, 5 Nov. 1881.
[14] Ward, *Stoke*, 462; Nicholls, *Stoke Ch.* plate facing p. 33.
[15] Nicholls, *Stoke Ch.* 41.
[16] Dr. G. R. Rigby, formerly of Penkhull, has suggested that the arcades may have been altered when the 18th-cent. clerestory was inserted as was done at Caverswall church.
[17] Tablet in ch.; Ward, *Stoke*, 471–3; Lich. Dioc. Regy., Bp.'s Reg. I, pp. 134–56. The parish vestry was considering the question of rebuilding in 1807: H.R.L., report of rebuilding cttee., 1807.
[18] Ward, *Stoke*, 471–2.
[19] Tablet in ch.; Nicholls, *Stoke Ch.* 95–97; H.O. 129/15/ 371/3/1. The parl. grant took the form of a remission of duty on materials.
[20] Jas. Trubshaw of Haywood and Thos. Johnson of Lichfield: H. M. Colvin, *Biog. Dict. Eng. Architects*, 625–6; Ward, *Stoke*, 473; *T.N.S.F.C.* (1889), 58.
[21] Ward, *Stoke*, 474.   [22] Ibid.
[23] Ibid. 475.
[24] *Staffs. Advertiser*, 21 Jan. 1905; *Stoke Par. Mag.* (Dec. 1908), 3, 6; tablet at W. end of ch.
[25] Inscription on pulpit.
[26] Hartill, *Stoke Ch.* 6; Nicholls, *Stoke Ch.* 34. It was dropped and cracked during an excavation in the chancel in 1856. The communion table in use in the old church at the time of its demolition was evidently of the early 17th cent.: ibid.; *Stoke Churchwardens' Accts.* (*T.N.S.F.C.* lxxiii), p. A48: 'for a new communion table, xi*s.* iii*d.*' (1622).
[27] P. Hartill, *Stoke Ch.* 14.   [28] Ward, *Stoke*, 477.
[29] S. A. Jeavons, 'Fonts of Staffs.' (*Trans. Birm. Arch. Soc.*, lxviii), 15.
[30] Hartill, *Stoke Ch.* 5; W.S.L., C.B. Stoke-on-Trent, note on font.

St. Peter's Church *c.* 1824 (demolished in 1830)

The Town Hall: an architect's elevation of the proposed east front *c.* 1834

STOKE-UPON-TRENT

cover was then made out of oak taken from the beams of the bell-chamber of St. Peter's, Wolverhampton.[31] An ivory Spanish crucifix thought to be of the late 17th century and mounted on Genoese velvet of the same period was given by Ronald Copeland in 1933 and hangs above the pulpit.[32] A feature of the church is the large number of memorial tiles around the walls, introduced by Sir Lovelace Stamer in 1858.[33] Several of the existing mural tablets were moved from the old church including those to John Poulson (d. 1691), John Fenton (d. 1782) with members of his family, and Hugh Booth (d. 1789). In the chancel is a tablet to Josiah Wedgwood (d. 1795) with a portrait medallion in high relief by John Flaxman[34] and one to his wife Sarah (d. 1815) and his son Thomas (d. 1805). Tablets to members of the Spode family include those to Josiah (d. 1797),[35] Josiah (d. 1827), and Josiah (d. 1829), the last incorporating a mourning figure by William Behnes.[36] Opposite is a large tablet by Behnes with an angel in high relief, commemorating John Bourne (d. 1833). Also in the chancel are memorials to John Woodhouse (d. 1833), rector and Dean of Lichfield, and to John Tomlinson (d. 1838); both have portrait heads, the latter by Behnes. Other tablets in the church include those to William Adams (d. 1829), Thomas Wolfe (d. 1848), William Copeland (d. 1868), and the Revd. Sir Lovelace Tomlinson Stamer (d. 1908). There is also a modern tablet commemorating members of the Adams family (1775–1865).

In 1553 the plate consisted of a silver chalice and paten,[37] presumably the silver cup with a silver cover mentioned between 1606 and 1612 when both pieces were in the hands of the clerk.[38] They were evidently lost by 1613, for that year one of the churchwardens, after being cited before the Official at Caverswall because the church had no communion book or cup, bought a new silver cup and cover.[39] In 1615 the plate was said to consist of a silver 'peece' and a silver cup. A pewter flagon was added in 1616.[40] These three items still made up the church plate in 1627.[41] The church does not now possess any plate dating from before the early 19th century.[42]

There were three bells and a small bell, presumably a sanctus bell, in 1553.[43] There seem to have been at least four bells by 1615[44] in addition to the sanctus bell which was in the custody of Thomas Browne of Great Fenton between at any rate 1606

and 1627.[45] Some of the bells were recast at Congleton in 1611, 1617, and 1627.[46] There was also a clock by 1613.[47] There were five bells before the end of the 17th century,[48] and in 1697 there was mention of 'the little bell wheel'.[49] Before the end of the 18th century there were six bells.[50] Five of them were recast in 1831 and 1832 by William and John Taylor of Oxford and Bideford and the sixth was removed.[51] Three new bells were added at this time.[52]

The registers date from 1630. Those up to 1812 have been printed.[53]

The rectory estate and the successive parsonage houses are described elsewhere.[54] The assistant curate's house stood in about half an acre of ground at the south-west corner of the churchyard facing on the Fenton road by the early 19th century, but it was demolished when the new church was built.[55] The curate then moved to Stoke Hall,[56] the rector being Dean of Lichfield, and was living there again in 1851, John Wickes Tomlinson being non-resident.[57]

The churchyard had an alley or walk by the mid-15th century which was then used for processions.[58] In 1791 the extent of the churchyard was increased to 2 acres by the addition of glebe adjoining the church.[59] When the National school was built to the east in 1815 part of the churchyard was taken as a playground.[60] With the rebuilding of the church the area was again increased by the purchase of another 2 acres of glebe land, and the level was raised to avoid the flooding to which the ground had previously been liable.[61] In 1910 the churchyard was taken over as an open space by the corporation, and during the miners' strike in 1912 it was laid out by men on strike, part of the distress fund being used to meet the cost.[62]

Two fragments of a stone cross thought to date from c. 1000 were dug up in 1876 near the line of the south wall of the former church. They seem to have been partly cut away, and it has been suggested that they were used as the lintel of the priest's door in the old church. They were placed near the door to the clergy vestry in the new church, remaining there until 1935 when Percy Adams of Woore Manor had them placed in the churchyard, mounted on a base and railed round to commemorate George V's Silver Jubilee.[63]

The Red Lion Inn at the south-east corner of the churchyard belonged to the rector until 1925 when it was conveyed to Showell's Brewery. The inn

[31] Hartill, *Stoke Ch.* 5.
[32] Ibid. 17; plaque below crucifix.
[33] F. D. How, *Bp. Sir Lovelace Tomlinson Stamer*, 77–78.
[34] Ward, *Stoke*, 476.
[35] The tablet is of later date.
[36] The 3 memorials by Behnes are signed.
[37] *S.H.C.* 1915, 249. A maslyn cross on a maslyn foot was also mentioned.
[38] *Stoke Churchwardens' Accts.* (*T.N.S.F.C.* lxxiii), pp. A11, 17, 21.
[39] Ibid. p. A30.
[40] Ibid. pp. A34, 45.
[41] Ibid. lxxiv, p. A57.
[42] S. A. Jeavons, 'Church Plate in the Archdeaconry of Stoke-on-Trent' (*Trans. Birm. Arch. Soc.* lxxvii), 77; inf. from the rector.
[43] *S.H.C.* 1915, 249.
[44] *T.N.S.F.C.* lxxiii, p. A36.
[45] Ibid. pp. A12, 17, 21, 34, 45; ibid. lxxiv, p. A57.
[46] Ibid. lxxiii, pp. A15, 41, 56. The work was probably done by Geo. Lea at the Chapel Foundry: ibid. p. A2.
[47] Ibid. p. A23.

[48] Ibid. lxxvii, pp. A199, 210, 215, 226; lxxviii, p. A227.
[49] Ibid. lxxvii, p. A223.
[50] *Univ. Brit. Dir.* iv. 109.
[51] Nicholls, *Stoke Ch.* 34; C. Lynam, *Ch. Bells Staffs.* 57, 70; A. E. Garbett, 'Ch. Bells Staffs.' (*Trans. Old Stafford Soc.* 1953–4), 14.
[52] Lynam, *Ch. Bells Staffs.*, 57.
[53] Staffs. Par. Reg. Soc. (1914, 1918, 1925, 1926–7).
[54] See pp. 186–7.
[55] C. Lynam, 'Stoke Old Ch.' (*Stoke Par. Mag.*, Jan. 1880), p. 5; Parson and Bradshaw, *Dir. Staffs.* (1818); *Staffs. Advertiser*, 21 Jan. 1905; Ward, *Stoke*, 498; H.R.L., copy of plan of Stoke churchyard 1825.
[56] *Pigot's Nat. Com. Dir.* (1828–9).
[57] White, *Dir. Staffs.* (1851).
[58] C 1/44/226.
[59] Lich. Dioc. Regy., Bp.'s Reg. A, B, C, D, pp. 476–9; H.R.L., copy of plan of Stoke churchyard 1825.
[60] *Staffs. Advertiser*, 21 Jan. 1905, p. 7; see p. 320.
[61] H.R.L., plan of churchyard; *Gent. Mag.* 1830, c (1), 584. For the new burial ground on the opposite side of Church St. see p. 197.   [62] Char. Com. files.
[63] Nicholls, *Stoke Ch.* 36–37; Hartill, *Stoke Ch.* 4.

stands on the site of an earlier building, probably also an inn, which is said to have been given to the church to provide an income for the support of a curate by one of the Poulson family,[64] parish clerks between at least the 17th and the early 19th centuries.[65]

The parish church seems to have been used as a prison for the Scots in 1648 when 4s. 6d. was paid to the clerk 'for dressing and cleaning the church after the Scots were gone'.[66]

Fourteen mission centres have been opened from St. Peter's: Cliff Vale c. 1860–1957; Boothen 1870; Cliff Bank Square c. 1883–c. 1902;[67] Potts Ground c. 1883, now known as All Saints Mission as it is served from All Saints Mission Church, Boothen;[68] Queen Street (now Rebecca Street) c. 1883–c. 1911;[69] Welch Street c. 1883–c. 1898;[70] a mission room at Stoke Wharf for 'canal boat people' 1886–c. 1923;[71] Union Street c. 1886–c. 1889;[72] Frederick Avenue c. 1893 in two converted cottages, replaced in 1899 by the first part of the present mission church of St. Barnabas which was completed in 1906;[73] Bowstead Street c. 1898–c. 1903;[74] Oxford Street c. 1899–c. 1906;[75] Holy Trinity Mission, Birks Street, 1908, burnt down in 1952;[76] Dean Street c. 1911–c. 1928;[77] and St. Peter's Mission, Golding Street, c. 1950–c. 1958.[78]

At Cliff Vale services were held c. 1860 at the school in Shelton Old Road formed out of two converted cottages. This was replaced by an iron church which after a fire in 1865 was itself replaced in the same year by the school church in North Street. St. Andrew's Mission Church on the site of the Upper Cliff Bank Pottery at the junction of Honeywall and Hartshill Road was built in 1906. It was sold in 1957.[79]

At Boothen services were held from 1870 in the school church built that year. An iron mission church was built in 1877 and replaced by the present stone church of All Saints erected in 1887–8 on a site given by Sir Thomas Boughey. The Diocesan Church Extension Society gave £230 and the Incorporated Church Building Society £120, and £4,000 was raised by subscription. The church was designed by Charles Lynam and is in the Perpendicular style with nave, chancel, two aisles under separate gabled roofs, and a west turret.[80]

A school at Penkhull stated in 1835 to have been erected for the provision of religious instruction was licensed for divine service in 1836.[81] The church of *ST. THOMAS THE APOSTLE* was built on the same site at the south end of the village green in 1842. Most of the cost of erection and endowment was met by the Revd. Thomas Webb Minton (1791–1870), of Darlington (Co. Durham),[82] but £410 was contributed by the Diocesan Church Extension Society.[83] The right of appointing the incumbent, a perpetual curate from 1843 when the parish was formed and a titular vicar from 1868, lay with the founder[84] until his death in 1870 when it passed to his son, the Revd. Samuel Minton of Putney.[85] It passed c. 1883 from him to F. Bishop[86] and c. 1884 to the Rector of Stoke,[87] who is still the patron.[88] The Revd. A. Perry, vicar since 1956,[89] was Lord Mayor of Stoke in 1957–8 and was probably the first Anglican clergyman to be a lord mayor.[90]

The church, which is in the Early English style, was designed by George Gilbert (later Sir Gilbert) Scott and originally consisted of a nave, transepts, chancel, and west tower. The nave has an open roof, pierced by dormer windows, and the tower, which contains one bell dated 1843,[91] is surmounted by a broach spire. In 1892 the building was enlarged by the addition of north and south aisles which were continued westwards to form a vestry and a baptistery flanking the base of the tower. At the same time the organ gallery was moved from the west end to the south transept, a vestry being constructed

[64] Nicholls, *Stoke Ch.* 38, 79, 82. The inn was occupied by Sam. Poulson in 1818 (Parson and Bradshaw, *Dir. Staffs.* 1818) and was labelled 'Poulson's premises' on a plan of the churchyard of 1830 in Lich. Dioc. Regy., Bp.'s Reg. I, p. 137.

[65] Nicholls, *Stoke Ch.* 23, 47, 49, 50; *Stoke Churchwardens' Accts.* (*T.N.S.F.C.* lxxiv), p. A101; W.S.L., D. 1742, list of Stoke parishioners 1701; Parson and Bradshaw, *Dir. Staffs.* (1818); Ward, *Stoke*, 479. The tablet mentioned by Ward is still in position.

[66] *Stoke Churchwardens' Accts.* (*T.N.S.F.C.* lxxiv), pp. A97, 101; lxxviii, p. A254.

[67] *Woolley's Stoke Boro. Almanack* (1884); Lich. Dioc. Ch. Cal. (1902).

[68] *Woolley's Stoke Boro. Almanack* (1884); *Lich. Dioc. Dir.* (1959). It disappears from the *Lich. Dioc. Ch. Cal.* after 1928.

[69] *Woolley's Stoke Boro. Almanack* (1884); *Lich. Dioc. Ch. Cal.* (1911).

[70] *Woolley's Stoke Boro. Almanack* (1884); *Lich. Dioc. Ch. Cal.* (1898).

[71] *Lich. Dioc. Mag.* (1886), 164, 172; *Woolley's Stoke Boro. Almanack* (1887); *Lich. Dioc. Ch. Cal.* (1924), 265.

[72] *Lich. Dioc. Ch. Cal.* (1887, 1889).

[73] Ibid. (1893); *Lich. Dioc. Mag.* (1896), 28; *Woolley's Stoke Boro. Almanack* (1884); *Fenn's Stoke Boro. Almanack* (1900); Hartill, *Stoke Ch.* 15; Lich. Dioc. Regy., Bp.'s Reg. 36, p. 8. There is a bell in a bell-cote.

[74] *Lich. Dioc. Ch. Cal.* (1899, 1903).

[75] Ibid. (1900, 1906).

[76] *Stoke. Par. Mag.* (Dec. 1908), 13; Char. Com. files.

[77] *Lich. Dioc. Ch. Cal.* (1912, 1928). It is described as St. Peter's Church Army Mission in *Stoke Par. Mag.* (Jan. 1925).

[78] *Lich. Dioc. Dir.* (1950–1); ex inf. the secretary to the Rector of Stoke (1959).

[79] F. E. J. Wright, *The Schs. of the Par. of St. Peter ad Vincula*, 8–10 (copy in H.R.L.); Lich. Dioc. Regy., Bp.'s Reg. 33, p. 14; 36, p. 500; *Lich. Dioc. Mag.* (Dec. 1880), 10; Adams, *Adams Family*, add. and corr. no. 3, p. 3; Char. Com. files; see pp. 202, 319. The proceeds of the sale of the church, £1,250, were added to the Church Day-school Building Fund: Char. Com. files.

[80] Lich. Dioc. Regy., Bp.'s Reg. 33, p. 141; 34, pp. 26–27; ibid. Reg. T, pp. 190–5; *Lich. Dioc. Ch. Cal.* (1888), 51, 162; *Keates's Potteries Dir.* (1892–3); date-stone on N. side; Lynam, *Ch. Bells Staffs.*, 57; see p. 319.

[81] Lich. Dioc. Regy., Bp.'s Reg. 30, pp. 41–42; V. G. Aston, *Hist. Penkhull*, 40–41 (copy among W.S.L. pamphs. *sub* Stoke).

[82] Lich. Dioc. Regy., Bp.'s Reg. M, pp. 240–7, 250–60; Aston, *Penkhull*, 40–43; memorial tablet in N. aisle; Jewitt, *Ceramic Art*, 397, 398; C. Hodgson, *An Acct. of the Augmentation of Small Livings by the Governors of the Bounty of Queen Anne* (1845), pp. xii, xxiii, xxxix, xlix of 1856 supplement.

[83] Lich. Dioc. Regy., Bp.'s Reg. M, p. 243; H.O. 129/15/371/3/1.

[84] Lich. Dioc. Regy., Bp.'s Reg. M, p. 249; ibid., Reg. 32, pp. 185, 192; White, *Dir. Staffs.* (1851); Hutchinson, *Archdeaconry of Stoke*, 132; *Lich. Dioc. Ch. Cal.* (1869).

[85] Lich. Dioc. Regy., Bp.'s Reg. 33, p. 359; 34, p. 84; *Lich. Dioc. Ch. Cal.* (1871); *P.O. Dir. Staffs.* (1876).

[86] *Lich. Dioc. Ch. Cal.* (1883).

[87] Ibid. (1884).

[88] *Lich. Dioc. Dir.* (1959).

[89] Ibid.

[90] T. H. Brookes, 'Ch. of St. Thos. Penkhull' (*Staffs. Life*, ix), 9.

[91] Ibid. 8; Lynam, *Ch. Bells Staffs.*, 55.

beneath it; all pew rents were abolished at this period.[92] The Revd. Vernon Aston, vicar 1931–56, built the present stone arcades of three bays between the nave and aisles.[93] Extensive renewal of the fabric, including an almost complete rebuilding of the walls, was carried out in 1958.[94] The clock was given in memory of John Blow Ashwell by his widow and children in 1913.[95] A north aisle window is fitted with pictorial stained glass in memory of 292 Army Field Company R.E. Also in the north aisle is a tablet commemorating the Revd. Thomas Webb Minton (1791–1870), founder of the church, and his son the Revd. Samuel Minton (d. 1893), the first vicar. The churchyard includes the grave of the parents of Sir Oliver Lodge, F.R.S., who was born and baptized at Penkhull in 1851, the son of a railway clerk.[96] The portion of the churchyard on the north side of the church has been laid out by the city council as a garden. The vicarage-house seems to have stood at first at the junction of Penkhull New Road and East Street, but this house was soon replaced by the present vicarage in Doncaster Lane.[97]

A mission centre in Slaney Street was opened from St. Thomas's in c. 1894. It was closed c. 1898.[98]

The church of *HOLY TRINITY* at Hartshill was built and endowed in 1842 by Herbert Minton of Longfield Cottage (1792–1858). He also built the house for the incumbent to the west and the schools to the south and gave 2 acres of ground for the churchyard.[99] The right of nominating the incumbent, a perpetual curate from the creation of the parish in 1842 and a titular vicar from 1868, lay with the founder until his death in 1858 when it passed to his nephew Colin Minton Campbell.[1] On Campbell's death in 1885 it passed to John Fitzherbert Campbell[2] and c. 1911 to the Bishop of Lichfield[3] who is still the patron.[4] The church was designed by George Gilbert Scott[5] in the Early English style and consists of an aisled and clerestoried nave of five bays, a chancel, and a spired west tower. The chancel, which originally had two bays and a square east end,[6] was rebuilt in its present apsidal form at the expense of Colin Minton Campbell (d. 1885),[7] an organ chamber being added to the north and a chapel to the south of it. In the nave a continuous dado is formed by glazed memorial tiles. The origi-

nal fittings included one bell; a second bell was added in 1873.[8] A panelled reredos and a new organ (1948) serve as memorials to those who fell in the First and Second World Wars respectively.[9] In 1960 temporary scaffolding had been erected to protect the nave arcades from mining subsidence.

Three mission centres have been opened from Holy Trinity, all of them still in existence in some form. The earliest was at Kingscroft school where services were held from c. 1873. A few years later the iron church of St. Matthew was built at the junction of Kingscroft and Spring Street. It was enlarged in 1887. In 1922 it was replaced by the present St. Matthew's Mission Church nearby in Stoke Old Road.[10]

The second mission centre was in Sackville Street (now Bedford Street), at Basford, where the church of St. Mark was opened in 1878.[11] It was enlarged in 1884 and 1887.[12] In 1915 it was replaced by the present church of St. Mark in Basford Park Road (and thus within the bounds of the ancient parish of Wolstanton and of the present borough of Newcastle). A new parish was created out of Hartshill and Wolstanton in the same year. The living, a titular vicarage, has remained in the gift of the bishops of Lichfield.[13]

The third mission centre opened from Holy Trinity is in two converted cottages in Garner Street and dates from c. 1894.[14]

The church of *ST. JOHN THE EVANGELIST* in Newcastle Road, Trent Vale, was built in 1843–4 at a cost of £1,260, of which £255 was given by the Diocesan Church Extension Society and the rest raised by subscription.[15] It was made a parish church in 1844 shortly after its consecration.[16] The patronage of the living, a perpetual curacy until 1868 when it became a titular vicarage, has always been held by the Rector of Stoke.[17] The church, which is built of dark brick with stone dressings and has lancet windows, originally consisted only of a nave, a chancel, and a spired west tower with a bell,[18] the base of the tower forming an entrance porch. A south vestry was added in 1878.[19] In 1909 a new nave and chancel were built to the north, the original nave becoming a south aisle.[20] The present nave has a baptistery at its west end and is divided from the aisle by a stone

[92] Tablet in N. aisle; *Lich. Dioc. Mag.* (1892), 107; ibid. (1893), 28.
[93] *Staffs. Life*, ix. 8.
[94] Ibid. 9.
[95] Tablet at W. end.
[96] Aston, *Penkhull*, 27; *Staffs. Life*, ix. 8.
[97] Aston, *Penkhull*, 30, 35.
[98] *Lich. Dioc. Ch. Cal.* (1895, 1898); *Lich. Dioc. Mag.* (1897), 42.
[99] Lich. Dioc. Regy., Bp.'s Reg. M, pp. 185–211; Ward, *Stoke*, 513; memorial tablet in side chapel; Hodgson, *Queen Anne's Bounty* (1845), p. xlix of 1856 supplement. The benefice received grants from Queen Anne's Bounty in 1843 (£200), 1844 (£200), and 1845 (£200): ibid. p. ccxcvii, and pp. xi, xxxix of 1856 supplement.
[1] Lich. Dioc. Regy., Bp.'s Reg. M, pp. 202, 642–4; ibid., Reg. 30, p. 228; Reg. 32, pp. 91, 214, 333; *Lich. Dioc. Ch. Cal.* (1859, 1869).
[2] *Lich. Dioc. Ch. Cal.* (1888).
[3] Ibid. (1912).
[4] *Lich. Dioc. Dir.* (1959).
[5] *Staffs. Weekly Sentinel*, 16 Mar. 1956.
[6] Lithograph in church.
[7] Tablet in side chapel.
[8] Lynam, *Ch. Bells Staffs.*, 49; Lich. Dioc. Regy., Bp.'s Reg. M, p. 197.
[9] Inscription on organ case.

[10] *Lich. Dioc. Ch. Cal.* (1874, 1876, 1888); ex inf. Mr. E. G. Beckett, churchwarden of Holy Trinity (1960), who also states that the mission appears to have begun earlier with services in private houses; see p. 319.
[11] Lich. Dioc. Regy., Bp.'s Reg. 34, p. 50.
[12] *Lich. Dioc. Mag.* (1884), 11; *Lich. Dioc. Ch. Cal.* (1887), 147.
[13] Lich. Dioc. Regy., Bp.'s Reg. 37, 233–7, 454; *Lich. Dioc. Dir.* (1955–6), 132; ibid. (1959). The W. end is incomplete, and has been bricked across.
[14] *Lich. Dioc. Ch. Cal.* (1895). The ch. hall on the opposite side of the street was built in 1954: date on foundation stone; *Staffs. Weekly Sentinel*, 16 Mar. 1956.
[15] Lich. Dioc. Regy., Bp.'s Reg. N, pp. 64–69, 71–75, 78–84, 87–94; White, *Dir. Staffs.* (1851). For benefactions of 1848 see Hodgson, *Queen Anne's Bounty*, pp. xvi, xxxix of 1856 supplement.
[16] *Lond. Gaz.* 1844, p. 3212; Lich. Dioc. Regy., Bp.'s Reg. N, pp. 87–94.
[17] Lich. Dioc. Regy., Bp.'s Reg. N, p. 94; *Lich. Dioc. Ch. Cal.* (1917); *Lich. Dioc. Dir.* (1959). It is stated in White, *Dir. Staffs.* (1851), that the patronage was exercised by the bishop or the rector.
[18] Lynam, *Ch. Bells Staffs.*, 58.
[19] *Kelly's Dir. Staffs.* (1882); Lynam, *Ch. Bells Staffs.*, 58.
[20] *Kelly's Dir. Staffs.* (1912).

arcade of four bays. The vicarage-house is in Vicarage Lane on the opposite side of the main road.

The Bible and Domestic Mission Room was opened from St. John's c. 1888. It was closed c. 1904.[21]

LOCAL GOVERNMENT AND PUBLIC SERVICES.

By the 17th century the Penkhull–Boothen area was grouped for purposes of parish government with Clayton and Seabridge to form one of the four quarters of the ancient parish of Stoke-upon-Trent; from 1816 the government of the parish was conducted by a select vestry.[22] Manorially the area was part of Newcastle manor.[23]

In 1839, however, Stoke, like Longton, Fenton, and Trentham, was placed under a body of commissioners with powers of policing, lighting, and generally improving the streets. All the inhabitants satisfying a certain property qualification were to be commissioners, meeting monthly and having power to levy rates up to 1s. in the £ for general improvements and 8d. in the £ for lighting. Those inhabitants not well served by public lighting were exempt from the lighting rate. The commissioners' powers to widen and improve the streets did not include powers of compulsory purchase. A chief bailiff, watchmen, and beadles were to be appointed. The experience of the 14 years that had passed since the setting up of the Burslem and Hanley Improvements Commissioners may perhaps be seen in the more detailed powers given to the 1839 commissioners; they were specifically enabled, for instance, to ensure that cellar windows and gratings were secured and that door gates opened inwards, and to see to the naming of streets, the numbering of houses, and the destruction of mad dogs. Also the property qualification was lower than at Burslem and Hanley. The area for which the Stoke Commissioners were responsible included most of the township of Penkhull, the township of Clayton, and the part of Shelton township that was exempted from the jurisdiction of the Hanley commissioners. The small detached portion of Penkhull that lay to the northwest of Newcastle was not included and was taken into Newcastle in 1875. The portion of Shelton that was included consisted of the glebe land where Stoke Station now stands.[24]

At the first meeting of the commissioners held at the town hall on 4 July 1839, Lewis Adams was elected chief bailiff, and a clerk was appointed.[25] Thereafter monthly meetings were held at the town hall, with the chief bailiff in the chair. In 1860 the meeting-place was transferred to the Minton Memorial Building in London Road.[26] At first *ad hoc* committees were set up to deal with particular problems, such as policing,[27] lighting,[28] rating,[29] and drainage,[30] but by 1859 there were regular committees for lighting, finance, and improvement.[31] A rate committee was added in 1863,[32] a smoke-prevention committee for 1868 and 1869 only,[33] and a highway committee in 1873.[34] In 1859 the clerk was dismissed after 20 years' service as a result of a dispute over expenses, and a 'non-professional' clerk was appointed in his place.[35] He was, however, retained as legal adviser. The commissioners imposed the statutory improvement rate of 1s. in August 1839 and the lighting rate of 8d. in October 1840; in February 1841 the improvement rate was reduced to 8d. and in November to 6d., while the lighting rate was brought down to 6d. in August 1842.[36]

A proposal to form a local board of health covering the whole of Stoke parish produced strong local opposition and was dropped by the central Board of Health in 1851.[37] The commissioners' rule therefore lasted until 1874 when the whole of the Stoke District except Clayton was incorporated as the borough of Stoke-upon-Trent with a mayor, 5 other aldermen and 18 councillors, 6 for each of the 3 wards (East, West, and South).[38] Four committees were set up: general purposes; finance and rate; highways and sanitary; lighting and watch.[39] In November 1877 a market, baths, and free library committee was added.[40] By 1909–10, the last year of the council's existence, five other committees had been added: plans, gas, cemetery, electricity, and education.[41] The rateable value of the borough in 1890 was £72,208 8s. 1d. and the rate was 5s. 4d. in the £; ten years later the rateable value was £111,000 and the rate 7s. 9d.[42] With the creation of the new county borough of Stoke-on-Trent in 1910, the area covered by the old borough of Stoke-upon-Trent was formed into four wards represented on the new council by 4 aldermen and 12 councillors.[43]

The first town hall was built by subscription in Market Street (now Hill Street) in 1794, and was administered by trustees.[44] A market was eventually held in the lower part,[45] where by 1829 the fire engine also was kept.[46] The erection of the present town hall in Glebe Street was begun in 1834, but part was still unfinished in 1850.[47] The market was held on the ground floor of the central part by 1850, and the large hall above housed the Stoke-upon-

[21] *Lich. Dioc. Ch. Cal.* (1889, 1904).
[22] Ward, *Stoke*, 467–8, 492; see pp. 189, 198.
[23] See p. 184.
[24] 2 & 3 Vic. c. 44 (local and personal); see pp. 1, 158.
[25] H.R.L., Stoke Commrs.' Mins. 1839–48, 4 July 1839.
[26] Ibid. 1839–74 *passim*.
[27] Ibid. 14 Aug. 1839. [28] Ibid. 7 Oct. 1839.
[29] Ibid. 5 June 1840. [30] Ibid. 6 Oct. 1847.
[31] Ibid. 1855–65, 5 Jan., 7 Sept., 2 Nov. 1859, 12 June 1861.
[32] Ibid. 10 June 1863. It had been dropped by 1871: ibid. 1865–74, p. 213.
[33] Ibid. 1865–74, pp. 101–2, 105, 176.
[34] Ibid. p. 298.
[35] Ibid. 1855–65, 5 and 19 Jan., 6 and 20 July, 3 Aug. 1859. It was felt that the expenses, £72, should be covered by his salary, already reduced from £25 to £20. It was stressed, however, that there was no 'imputation on his professional character'. The new clerk's salary was £40.
[36] Ibid. 1839–48, 14 Aug. 1839, 7 Oct. 1840, 3 Feb., 3 Nov. 1841, 3 Aug. 1842.

[37] Ibid. 1848–55, 17 July 1850, 20 Feb., 2 Apr. 1851; R. Rawlinson, *Rep. to Bd. of Health on Stoke Parish* (1850), 8–9 (copy in H.R.L.).
[38] 36 & 37 Vic. c. 216 (local); H.R.L., Stoke Boro. Mins. 1874–81, pp. 1–2, 4, 5.
[39] Stoke Boro. Mins. 1874–81, pp. 8–10. The highways became the responsibility of the lighting cttee. in 1875 (ibid. p. 122), and in 1876, for a year only, the highway and lighting cttee. was amalgamated with the general purposes cttee.: ibid. pp. 180, 246.
[40] Ibid. p. 246. It had been set up as a market cttee. the previous Jan.: ibid. p. 198.
[41] Ibid. 1908–10, pp. 271–3; *Stoke Boro. and District Rate Estimates 1909* (copy in H.R.L., SP. 850.35). The education cttee. was not appointed along with the other cttees. at the Nov. meeting of the council.
[42] *Fenn's Stoke Boro. Almanack 1892, 1903.*
[43] *Stoke Counc. Yr. Bk.* (1915).
[44] Ward, *Stoke*, 505. For a short description see p. 180.
[45] See p. 201.
[46] Shaw, *Staffs. Potteries*, 50. [47] See p. 182.

Trent Athenaeum and the school of design; the ground floor of the north wing was occupied by the police force and the fire engine from 1843, while the large room above was used as a court room and for public meetings.[48] By 1876 the upper room in the central block was used as an assembly room, the Athenaeum having been moved to the south wing, which also contained the county court offices.[49] By 1880 the upper floor of the south wing contained the council chamber, the mayor's parlour, and municipal offices.[50] The market had been moved to a new building in 1883,[51] and five years later the vacated ground floor of the central block was reconstructed to include chamber, parlour, and offices, while the assembly room above was altered to hold 1,400.[52] The town hall was retained after Federation for most of the new county borough's offices,[53] and has been considerably extended since.[54] By the middle of the century the old hall in Hill Street was let for storage and subsequently was used at different times as a fire station and a drill hall;[55] it was demolished c. 1938.[56] The mayor's chain was presented by Colin Minton Campbell in 1874.[57]

As a member of Newcastle manor Penkhull township was represented at the court leet by three frankpledges by 1335[58] and was paying 'frithborwe-sulver' to the lord of Newcastle by 1361.[59] Penkhull also gave its name to a constablewick which by the early 14th century included the townships of Clayton, Seabridge, Wolstanton, and Shelton—all members of Newcastle manor—as well as Penkhull itself.[60] This system was evidently still in force in its essentials in 1829 when at the October court a chief constable, two headboroughs, and three assistant constables were appointed for Stoke and Penkhull.[61] There was a lock-up in Penkhull at this time, but at this October court the need for a lock-up in Stoke was urged on the ground that prisoners sometimes escaped while being conducted to Penkhull by the constables.[62]

The main policing power given to the commissioners established for the Stoke district by the Act of 1839 was the appointment of a chief bailiff, watchmen, and beadles. The organization of the police was to be the responsibility of the chief bailiff, and provision was made in the Act for the chief bailiffs of Stoke, Longton, Fenton, and Trentham to appoint a single superintendent of police with powers over all four districts.[63]

In August 1839 a superintendent and two policemen were appointed for the Stoke district and a house in Liverpool Road was leased for three months as a temporary station; in November the former parish office was taken as a temporary station and lock-up.[64] Two unpaid police officers were appointed for Trent Vale and Clayton in November; a year later it was agreed that one of the police should live at Trent Vale as soon as a house could be provided, and within two years of this decision Trent Vale had its own police officer and station.[65] The Chartist riots of August 1842 aroused great concern about the size of the police force and led to the establishment of a county force in Stoke in 1843, a measure which had been firmly opposed in 1839 and 1840 on the grounds of expense and the adequacy of the Stoke force.[66] In the meantime the chief bailiff was asked to appoint two paid temporary assistants to the police in August 1842, and in October it was agreed that he should set up a force of 10 men paid 2s. 6d. each a night and divided among five areas, with a volunteer superintendent for each area and a nightly horse patrol throughout the district; the cost of this additional policing was to be met by a 4d. rate and public subscription.[67] The police office and the chief bailiff's house at Penkhull had been attacked and damaged during the riots, while the superintendent of the Stoke police resigned apparently in dismay at the damage done to his personal property by the rioters. Some compensation was given to him and one of his men by the commissioners who also voted a £5 reward to James Hope, one of the force, for his conduct during the riots as well as 4 guineas for the expense which he had incurred in medical attention to his injuries; he was also appointed police officer for Trent Vale. At the same time the commissioners expressed their dissatisfaction with the conduct of another member of the force during the disturbances.[68] A police station for the county police in the new north wing of the town hall was completed in 1843,[69] and remained there until the building of the present station in Copeland Street in 1897.[70]

A stipendiary magistrate for the Potteries area was appointed in 1839 sitting once a week at Stoke town hall; Stoke and Penkhull formed one of the six rating areas established to support the new system.[71] Stoke was at first within Hanley county court district. In 1853 it was formed into a separate district including also Longton, Fenton, and Trentham parish; the court met monthly at Stoke town hall.[72] Stoke also had its own borough court from 1901.[73]

[48] P.O. Dir. Staffs. (1850); see pp. 198, 201, 204, 205.
[49] P.O. Dir. Staffs. (1876).
[50] Kelly's Dir. Staffs. (1880). The Athenaeum library and museum had been removed to London Rd. shortly before: see pp. 204–5.   [51] See p. 201.
[52] Kelly's Dir. Staffs. (1892); Fenn's Stoke Boro. Almanack 1894.
[53] See p. 259. The rest were housed in Hanley town hall.
[54] See p. 182.
[55] White, Dir. Staffs. (1851); see pp. 198, 201.
[56] Local inf. (1960).
[57] Stoke Ch. Congress, 1911, 136 (copy in H.R.L.). The chain was on view at the art exhibition held in connexion with the congress.
[58] D.L. 30/228/1. Boothen occurs, presenting jointly with Penkhull, from 1406: ibid. 231/5.
[59] Cal. Inq. p.m. xi, p. 104.
[60] S.H.C. vii (1), 199; x (1), 82; ibid. 1921, 153–7; 1932, 158; 1935, 352; 1941, 118–19.
[61] Staffs. Advertiser, 10 Oct. 1829.   [62] Ibid.
[63] Potteries Improvement Act, 2 & 3 Vic. c. 44 (local and personal).

[64] Stoke Commrs.' Mins. 1839–48, 4 and 24 July, 7 and 14 Aug., 23 Oct., 6 Nov. 1839.
[65] Ibid. 7 Oct. 1839, 4 Nov. 1840, 2 Nov. 1842.
[66] Ibid. 20 Nov. 1839, 8 July 1840, 3 Aug., 5 Sept. 1842, 14 Jan., 1 Feb. 1843.
[67] Ibid. 24 Aug., 7 Sept., 21 Oct. 1842. The rate was to be levied on those assessed at £10 and above. No volunteer was to have to serve more than once a fortnight. The horse patrol may have been from the military force then in the area: ibid. 5 Sept. 1842.
[68] Ibid. 2 and 10 Nov. 1842; Ward, Stoke, 586.
[69] Stoke Commrs.' Mins. 1839–48, 14 Jan., 1 Feb., 2 Aug. 1843.
[70] S.R.O., Q/APs 1; date on building.
[71] Act for more effectual execution of office of J.P., 2 & 3 Vic. c. 15; Stoke Commrs.' Mins. 1839–48, 4 Sept. 1839.
[72] Lond. Gaz. 1847, p. 1012; 1853, p. 3587; P.O. Dir. Staffs. (1854).
[73] Kelly's Dir. Staffs. (1908); S.R.O., D. 26/P/95–97 (Stoke Court of Summary Jurisdiction Mins. 1901–6, 1909–10).

PUBLIC HEALTH. The Stoke commissioners concerned themselves with matters of public health from the first. They made the inspector of police also the surveyor of nuisances, obstructions, and encroachments in 1839,[74] appointed a scavenger in 1840,[75] and arranged for the watering of the public streets in July 1842.[76] An inspector of nuisances was appointed in 1845 with responsibility for the suppression of nuisances, the watering of the streets, and the supervision of the lighting of the town.[77] A joint inspector and scavenger was appointed in 1849,[78] but soon afterwards the two offices were again divided; the scavenger was made responsible, subject to the supervision of the inspector whose salary was fixed at £20, for watering the streets at a salary of £72 and for removing ashes and night soil at 4d. a load.[79] A scavenger was appointed for Hartshill, Stoke Lane, and Basford in 1853.[80] The office of medical officer of health was created in 1877.[81]

The main problem, that of drainage, had by the late 1840's become very serious. Disease caused by inadequate and filthy privies and by accumulations of ashes and refuse was general, although Penkhull's high situation made it healthier than other parts of the district; Boothen Road, Welch Street, Wharf Street, the three Cliff Squares, Thomas Street, Pleasant Road, and the side streets off Liverpool Road were noted as particularly insanitary and fever-ridden.[82] The main streets, while generally macadamized and provided with flagged or bricked sidewalks, were not regularly cleaned, and, though the turnpike trustees had their roads scraped, the clerk to the commissioners considered that Stoke was 'badly off in this respect, worse than any other town in England'.[83] In the town itself these insanitary conditions were greatly aggravated by the existence of extensive waste land in the centre which was never dry, by the stagnant state of the Newcastle Canal, and by the flooding of the area 'by filthy water from the Foul-hay Brook' and water backed up from the Upper Boothen Mill on the Trent; cellars could not be drained so that as a result of this flooding several of them were perpetually wet, while the streets were always muddy.[84] There was only one main public sewer. This was the Boothen Drain, built earlier in the century by the parish at the suggestion of the rector to drain the glebe land and the churchyard and running down Glebe Street to the meadows by the Trent near the Lower Boothen Mill. Even this was not cleaned out.[85] In the late 1840's the sewer was cleaned and 'eye-holes' were inserted every 50 yards,[86] the beginning of a gradual improvement in the town's drainage. Efforts were made to keep the main and side drains clear;[87] another main public sewer was built in the 1850's along Liverpool Road to the Boothen Drain;[88] drainage work was begun at Trent Vale in 1852;[89] there were plans in 1854–5 for a new drain at Stoke Lane[90] and in 1864 for another from Penkhull churchyard down to Penkhull Terrace;[91] a sewer had been built from Hartshill to Stoke by the end of 1866;[92] orders were given for the cleansing of the Fowlea Brook in 1868 and 1869, including the clearance of the mud deposit at the junction with the Trent;[93] sewerage was provided for Oakhill in 1882–3;[94] Charles Lynam was appointed surveyor in 1860 at a salary of £20.[95] In 1879 the corporation bought the 60-acre Sideway farm on the Fenton side of the Trent and within three years had opened a sewage disposal works there.[96] An attempt by the commissioners in 1851 to buy and dismantle the Upper Boothen Mill was unsuccessful because of the high compensation demanded by the tenant,[97] but 30 years later the corporation concluded an agreement with the rector and the mill was bought and demolished.[98]

Other measures for improving public health included the opening of the baths in Park Street, London Road, in 1860 as part of the Herbert Minton Memorial Scheme and their extension in the early 1880's;[99] the replacement of privies by water closets —40 in 1897, 300 in 1900;[1] attempts from the 1850's onwards to deal with the smoke nuisance caused by factories;[2] the opening of a refuse destructor with the electricity works in 1904.[3] By 1909 there were 6,238 water closets and 1,565 cesspits; there were 2,739 covered ashpits, 4,876 dustbins, and 580 open pits.[4]

The pollution of the Fowlea Brook, the Lyme Brook, and the Trent presented a serious problem as the Potteries area developed. Parts of Wolstanton, Tunstall, Burslem, and Hanley discharged their sewage into the Fowlea Brook; Newcastle and the Stoke Union Workhouse discharged into the Lyme Brook; the Bucknall area and part of Hanley dis-

[74] Stoke Commrs.' Mins. 1839–48, 17 Oct. 1839.
[75] Ibid. 8 Jan. 1840.
[76] Ibid. 6 July 1842.
[77] Ibid. 14 May 1845.
[78] Ibid. 1848–55, 11 and 25 May 1849.
[79] Ibid. 1 Aug. 1849.
[80] Ibid. 2 Nov. 1853.
[81] Ibid. 1865–74, pp. 304–5.
[82] R. Rawlinson, *Rep. to Bd. of Health on Stoke Par.* 26–27, 37, 67–68 (copy in H.R.L.).
[83] Ibid. 41.
[84] Ibid. 26–27, 67–68.
[85] Ibid. 40 and map facing; Stoke Commrs.' Mins. 1839–48, 3 Nov. 1847; 1848–55, 16 Apr. 1851, 3 Mar. 1852.
[86] Rawlinson, *Rep. on Stoke Parish*, 27; Stoke Commrs.' Mins. 1839–48, 6 Oct., 3 Nov. 1847.
[87] Stoke Commrs.' Mins. 1848–55, 17 and 27 July, 1 Aug., 3 Oct. 1849.
[88] Ibid. 1839–48, 3 Nov. 1847; ibid. 1848–55, 7 Mar. 1849, 2 and 16 Apr., 4 June, 1 Sept. 1851; ibid. 1855–65, 3 Nov. 1858.
[89] Ibid. 1848–55, 16 Sept., 1 Dec. 1852.
[90] Ibid. 6 Sept. 1854, 7 Feb. 1855.
[91] Ibid. 1855–65, 1 June 1864.

[92] Ibid. 1865–74, p. 48.   [93] Ibid. pp. 107, 146.
[94] Stoke Boro. Mins. 1881–93, pp. 71, 73, 93.
[95] Stoke Commrs.' Mins. 1855–65, 1 Aug. 1860.
[96] *Staffs. Sentinel*, 1 Nov. 1898; *Fenn's Stoke Boro. Almanack, 1894*; Stoke Boro. Sanitary Cttee. Mins. 1874–81, pp. 237–438 *passim*; ibid. 1881–93, pp. 3, 9, 10–11, 22, 31. The sewage farm was let for a time: e.g. ibid. pp. 86, 87, 366.
[97] Stoke Commrs.' Mins. 1848–55, 16 Apr. 1851, 3 Mar. 1852. The tenant required £200 a year for the remainder of the lease.
[98] Stoke Boro. Sanitary Cttee. Mins. 1874–81, pp. 406, 412–13, 420; 1881–92, p. 43.
[99] Warrillow, *Stoke*, 373; *Fenn's Stoke Boro. Almanack, 1894*; R. G. Haggar, *A Century of Art Education in the Potteries*, 12–13.
[1] *Stoke M.O.H. Rep. 1904*, 62 (copy in H.R.L., S.P. 850.614).
[2] Stoke Commrs.' Mins. 1848–55, 13 Jan., 7 Sept. 1853; ibid. 1855–65, 2 July 1856; ibid. 1865–74, p. 94; Stoke Boro. Mins. 1895–8, p. 283; 1900–3, p. 435; 1905–8, p. 270. There was a smoke prevention cttee. in 1868 and 1869: see p. 394.
[3] *Stoke M.O.H. Rep. 1904*, 62.
[4] Ibid. *1909*, 23.

196

charged into the Trent. Stoke suffered particularly because of its situation on all three rivers downstream from these centres of population. The fact that Stoke's own drainage flowed into the Fowlea Brook and the Trent made matters worse. Even the building of various sewage-disposal works throughout the Potteries did not completely solve the problem, and Stoke's continual complaints to the various local authorities concerned persisted into the 20th century.[5]

Restrictions were placed on burials in the churchyards of St. Peter's, Stoke, and St. Thomas's, Penkhull, in 1856.[6] A burial board of nine members was set up by the ratepayers in 1867.[7] In 1868 2 acres of land on the opposite side of Church Street from St. Peter's were consecrated as a new burial ground. The land was given by the rector and the patron, and the cost of laying it out, £900, was met by a 7d. rate.[8] In 1882 both St. Peter's and Holy Trinity, Hartshill, were closed for burials and further restrictions were placed on their churchyards.[9] Burial powers were vested in the borough council in 1883,[10] and the corporation cemetery at Penkhull, 21 acres in area, was opened in the following year.[11] A further 3 acres was added in 1905.[12] The closing of the 1868 burial ground was ordered by the council in 1893.[13]

The North Staffordshire Infirmary was moved from Etruria to the Hartshill portion of The Mount estate in 1869. The foundation-stone of the new buildings was laid by the Prince of Wales in 1866. The infirmary was one of the first civil hospitals in the kingdom to be built on the pavilion system and it is said that this scheme was adopted on the advice of Florence Nightingale. With the development of the eye department the name was changed in 1890 to the North Staffordshire Infirmary and Eye Hospital,[14] and in 1925 the name was again changed to the North Staffordshire Royal Infirmary.[15] A temporary smallpox hospital was built at Penkhull by the Hanley, Stoke, and Fenton Joint Hospital Board in 1883, but it proved impossible to secure a renewal of the lease in 1886 and a new hospital was opened at Bucknall instead.[16] The North Staffordshire Blind and Deaf School was opened at the Penkhull end of The Mount estate in 1897.[17] The Cripples' Home opened at Hanchurch in 1911 was later moved to the Church Institute in Stoke and then to premises in Woodhouse Street. In 1918 it was reopened at Longfield Cottage in Hartshill Road as the Hartshill Orthopaedic Hospital.[18] The City General Hospital in London Road occupies the buildings of the former Stoke and Wolstanton Union workhouse, incorporating the buildings of the Stoke parish workhouse, erected in 1832–3.[19]

OTHER PUBLIC SERVICES. In the late 1840's Stoke's water-supply was dependent on two public pumps and a public well. A second well was destroyed by the building of the railway at this time.[20] A supply was laid on to part of the town in 1849 by the Potteries Waterworks Company established in 1847,[21] but there were frequent complaints of its inadequacy. Thus, when a fire broke out at 'The Noah's Ark', Hartshill, in 1856, the fire brigade was held up for two hours owing to lack of water in the mains.[22] Two years later the company was notified that there was frequently no supply to the fire plugs at Penkhull,[23] and in 1872 there was inadequate water for fighting a fire at Hartshill church.[24] In the same year the Local Government Board's inspector attributed the large increase in mortality in the Stoke area partly to the inadequate water-supply.[25] At the end of 1873 the waterworks company was asked to extend its mains to Boothen and to the part of Basford still without a supply; but in June 1876 Boothen at least still had no supply and was presumably still dependent on its 'town pump', the repair of which had been ordered in 1874 and whose water was declared unfit for drinking in 1881, and on the well which in 1881 was ordered to be closed as unfit for domestic use.[26] An old public well in Spring Meadow, Trentham Road, Penkhull, was still in use in the early 1880's;[27] a well in Honeywall was closed as unhealthy.[28]

Stoke town was at first supplied with gas from the British Gaslight Company's works at Shelton built in 1825, but in 1839 the commissioners accepted the tender for lighting the streets submitted by the new Stoke, Fenton, and Longton Gas Company which had a works off Wharf Street in the early 1840's and was soon supplying several factories, inns, and houses as well as the public lamps.[29] Public lighting was extended to Penkhull in 1849 when the company agreed to light 13 lamps there,[30] and by 1851 the

[5] Stoke Commrs.' Mins. 1855–65, 7 Sept. 1859, 2 Apr. 1862; 1865–74, pp. 2, 4, 8, 56, 78, 102, 149, 152; Stoke Boro. Mins. 1893–5, p. 34; 1895–8, pp. 282–3, 497; 1898–1900, pp. 531–2; 1903–5, pp. 563–4; 1905–8, p. 294; see p. 236. Petroleum products were polluting the Fowlea Brook in 1868: Stoke Commrs.' Mins. 1865–74, p. 107. There were various unsuccessful attempts by several of the authorities to deal with the problem of pollution jointly: e.g. ibid. pp. 149, 155–6, 159, 162–3; see p. 159.

[6] Lond. Gaz. 1856, p. 2904.

[7] H.R.L., Stoke Burial Bd. Mins. 1867–81, 15 Apr., 4 May 1867.

[8] Keates and Ford's Potteries Dir. (1867), 281–3; Keates's Potteries Dir. (1892–3), 423; Stoke Commrs.' Mins. 1865–74, p. 55; Stoke Burial Bd. Mins. 1867–81 passim; Lich. Dioc. Regy., Bp.'s Reg. R, pp. 144, 291–4.

[9] Lond. Gaz. 1882, pp. 3512–13.

[10] Ibid. 1883, p. 911.

[11] Keates's Potteries Dir. (1892–3); Lich. Dioc. Regy., Bp.'s Reg. S, pp. 709–12; H.R.L., SM 21, plan of proposed cemetery 1881.

[12] Lich. Dioc. Regy., Bp.'s Reg. U, pp. 685–6, 691–5.

[13] Stoke Boro. Mins. 1893–5, p. 21.

[14] R. Hordley, N. Staffs. Infirmary and Eye Hospital 1802–1902 (Newcastle-under-Lyme, 1903), passim (copy in H.R.L.).

[15] Warrillow, Stoke, 352.   [16] Ibid. 361–2.

[17] Staffs. Advertiser, 8 May 1897; Staffs. Life, i. 31.

[18] Warrillow, Stoke, 365. For the earlier history of Longfield Cottage see pp. 176–7.

[19] See pp. 199–200.

[20] Rawlinson, Rep. to Bd. of Health on Stoke Par. (1850), 35, 36; Stoke Commrs.' Mins. 1839–48, 3 Aug. 1842, 13 Aug. 1846.

[21] Pure and Wholesome Water for 100 Years, 1849–1949, 12, 13 (copy in H.R.L.).

[22] Stoke Commrs.' Mins. 1855–65, 5 Mar. 1856.

[23] Ibid. 2 June 1858.

[24] Ibid. 1865–74, pp. 244, 246.

[25] Ibid. p. 234.

[26] Ibid. p. 323; Stoke Boro. Mins. 1874–81, pp. 34, 161; H.R.L., Stoke Boro. Sanitary Cttee. Mins. 1874–81, p. 19; 1881–93, p. 34.

[27] Stoke Boro. Sanitary Cttee. Mins. 1881–93, p. 34, an order of 1881 for the restoration of the approach to the well after the closing of the way by the owner of the land.

[28] Ibid. p. 202.

[29] Stoke, Fenton and Longton Gas Act, 21 & 22 Vic. c. 40 (local); Stoke Commrs.' Mins. 1839–48, 7 and 12 Oct. 1839; Ward, Stoke, 506–7; White, Dir. Staffs. (1851); see p. 160.

[30] Stoke Commrs.' Mins. 1848–55, 7 Oct., 6 Nov. 1849.

Stoke area had 116 street lamps in use.[31] In 1878 the undertaking was bought by the Stoke borough council and the Fenton local board and run by a joint committee consisting of six representatives from each.[32] Differences arose between the two authorities, however, and in 1883 the committee was abolished. Stoke borough council took over the Wharf Street works but had to supply the Fenton area until the local board had built its own manufacturing plant.[33] The Stoke undertaking passed to the new county borough in 1910,[34] and the works continues in use as a holder station supplied from the main works for the whole city at Etruria.[35]

The borough council opened an electricity works in Bagnall Street (now Yeaman Street) in 1904.[36] Taken over by the new county borough in 1910[37] and extended in 1911,[38] it is now (1960) used as district office and depot of the Stoke South District of the Midlands Electricity Board. Stoke station, however, and part of the North Stafford Hotel were first lit by electricity as early as 1893.[39]

By 1829 Stoke had its own fire engine kept at the old town hall in Hill Street.[40] This remained the engine house until 1843 when premises were provided adjoining the police station in the new north wing of the town hall in Glebe Street.[41] A new engine was bought at the end of the year, and a committee was set up by the commissioners to enlist 'a corps of young active men of good character to be called the Stoke Fire Brigade'.[42] The headquarters of the brigade and the fire engine were moved back to the old town hall in the early 1880's; the brigade then consisted of a superintendent, who was also the superintendent of police in the late 1870's, a sergeant, a corporal, and 10 men.[43] A steam fire engine was bought in 1904.[44] About that time the old town hall became a drill hall and the brigade was moved to the Old Town Yard behind the new town hall; the King's Hall was opened there in 1910–11 and the brigade was installed in a wooden shed in South Wolfe Street behind the covered market. A fire station was opened in Welch Street in 1914 but went out of use when the city's fire service was reorganized in 1926.[45]

By the early 18th century there appears to have been a single supervisor of the highways for the south side of Stoke Parish (the Penkhull and Shelton quarters) and the office was served by the retiring churchwarden for that part of the parish.[46] By 1780, however, there was a surveyor for Penkhull 'liberty'.[47] The Penkhull and the Glebe highway boards, presumably set up under the Highways Act of 1835, were superseded in 1874 by the new borough council,[48] which in the same year also took over the roads maintained by the Darlaston turnpike trust, namely the main road between Hanford and Newcastle, London Road, and Liverpool Road. In 1876 the council took over the roads maintained by the Newcastle to Blythe Marsh turnpike trust, namely the main road from Stoke to Hartshill road, Shelton New Road, Shelton Old Road, Glebe Street, and Wharf Street. All these turnpike roads were in such a bad state of repair that a large amount had to be spent on their improvement, and in 1879 the borough applied to the justices for all of them to be declared main roads and so a county responsibility.[49]

Other activities of the Improvement Commissioners included the regulation from 1840 of the public clocks to the standard of the station clock at Whitmore, a service undertaken in collaboration with Burslem, Hanley, and Shelton;[50] the numbering of houses in 1844, and again in 1867;[51] and the constant approving of new buildings in accordance with standards laid down.[52]

RELIEF OF THE POOR. For the purposes of poor relief Stoke parish was divided by the late 16th century into five independent units, themselves parishes as far as relief was concerned: Stoke-upon-Trent, Burslem, Newcastle-under-Lyme, Norton in the Moors, and Whitmore. This section will deal with the area covered by Stoke-upon-Trent.

The Stoke-upon-Trent relief area consisted by 1570 of eight districts, each apparently separate for rating at least: Penkhull, with Boothen; Clayton and Seabridge; Shelton and Hanley; Fenton Culvert; Fenton Vivian; Longton; Bucknall; and Bagnall.[53] By the early 17th century, however, the area had been rearranged into four 'quarters', each under an overseer: Penkhull, Boothen, Clayton, and Seabridge; Shelton and Hanley; the Fentons, Longton, and Botteslow; and Bucknall and Bagnall.[54] This organization was unaffected by the creation of the new ecclesiastical divisions in 1807,[55] and there were still four overseers in 1836.[56] In 1816, however, the direction of all parish business including poor relief

---

[31] White, *Dir. Staffs.* (1851).
[32] Stoke-upon-Trent and Fenton Gas Act, 41 & 42 Vic. c. 131 (local).
[33] Stoke-upon-Trent and Fenton Gas Act, 46 & 47 Vic. c. 149 (local).
[34] See p. 266.
[35] *Stoke Official Handbk.* [1958], 47.
[36] *Kelly's Dir. Staffs.* (1912); Stoke Boro. Mins. 1903–5, pp. 62, 362, 383, 427; Electricity Lighting Orders Confirmation (No. 8) Act, 61 & 62 Vic. c. 207 (local); S.R.O. Q/RUm 632, 718.
[37] See p. 266.
[38] *Kelly's Dir. Staffs.* (1912)
[39] *Fenn's Stoke Boro. Almanack, 1895.*
[40] See p. 194.
[41] Stoke Commrs.' Mins. 1839–48, 5 May, 10 Nov., 1 Dec. 1841, 5 Jan., 1 Mar. 1842, 6 Dec. 1843; see p. 195.
[42] Stoke Commrs.' Mins. 1839–48, 6 Dec. 1843.
[43] *Woolley's Stoke Boro. Almanack, 1879, 1883, 1884, 1885.* The brigade evidently numbered 12 men by 1864: Stoke Commrs.' Mins. 1855–65, 1 June 1864.
[44] Stoke Boro. Mins. 1893–5, pp. 4, 102, 103; 1903–5, pp. 67, 97–98, 216, 219.
[45] *Staffs. Sentinel,* 11 Sept. 1913, 13 and 14 Jan. 1914;

Fenn's Stoke Boro. Almanack, 1903 (showing the brigade still at Hill St.); Stoke Boro. Mins 1898–1900, p. 293; see p. 267. The old hall was partially used as a drill hall in 1899: Boro. Mins. 1898–1900, p. 293.
[46] W.S.L., D. 1788, P. 67, B. 11.
[47] *S.H.C.* 1934 (1), 94.
[48] *Woolley's Stoke Boro. Almanack, 1884*; Keates and Ford's Potteries Dir. (1867), 283; Stoke Commrs.' Mins. 1865–74, *passim.* For the new council's highway cttee. and that set up by the commrs. in 1873 see p. 194.
[49] S.R.O., Q/AH, bdle. 2.
[50] Stoke Commrs.' Mins. 1839–48, 5 Feb. 1840, 6 Sept., 4 Oct. 1848.
[51] Ibid. 10 July 1844; ibid. 1865–74, p. 58.
[52] Ibid. 1839–74, *passim.* The new borough also passed by-laws in this matter in 1874: copy in H.R.L.
[53] Ward, *Stoke,* 467.
[54] Ibid. 467–8.
[55] Ibid. 466; see p. 188.
[56] *Staffs. Advertiser,* 26 Mar. 1836. A scheme, approved by the general vestry in 1828, to procure an Act of Parliament reducing the divisions to 3 and reapportioning the rates (ibid. 21 June 1828) was evidently never carried out. In 1833 4 overseers (for Hanley, Shelton, Lane End, and

was placed under the control of a select vestry,[57] and this gained closer control in 1834 when the one salaried assistant overseer was given the power of appointing annually, and paying, the governor of the workhouse and the six collectors, subject to the supervision of the overseers and the select vestry.[58] The Stoke-upon-Trent Union was formed in 1836 with a board of 24 guardians, but the area covered remained the same as that of the old organization.[59] After the local government reorganization of 1894 the union consisted of five civil parishes—Hanley, Stoke, Fenton, Longton, and Stoke Rural—each with its own overseers.[60] The number of guardians was increased to 32, all of them elected every three years.[61] In 1922 the union was amalgamated with the Wolstanton and Burslem Union to form the Stoke and Wolstanton Union with a board of 65 guardians elected every three years, 56 of them representing the county borough of Stoke-on-Trent (including Burslem and Tunstall).[62] The union was dissolved in 1930, and a public assistance committee was set up for the city of Stoke; the rest of the union became the responsibility of the Newcastle Area Guardians Committee.[63]

The total income from the rates of the eight districts of Stoke-upon-Trent in 1570 was £12 14s. 1d.[64] In 1640 2 lewns levied on 119 persons in the Penkhull Quarter produced £9 0s. 4d., in 1662 5 levied on 34 in the Shelton and Hanley Quarter produced £5 1s. 2½d., and in 1696 14 levied on 40 in the Longton and Fenton Quarter produced £40 19s. 6d.[65] Expenditure on the poor in 1648 amounted to £8 13s. 2d. in the Penkhull Quarter, £9 2s. 7d. (including 25s. due to Burslem under the plague order) in Shelton and Hanley, £7 10s. in Longton and Fenton, and £6 13s. 4d. in Bucknall and Bagnall.[66] The overseers' disbursements reached just over £1,000 in the financial year 1775–6.[67] In 1802–3, when the rate was assessed at 6s. 8d. in the £ on land and 3s. 4d. on houses, over £3,775 was spent on out-relief and nearly £1,200 on workhouse relief.[68] The overseers' expenditure reached over £8,000 on out-relief and over £1,200 on workhouse relief in 1832–3,[69] but a policy of retrenchment and

a more efficient administration had reduced the total amount spent on poor relief by nearly a third the following year.[70] In the first year of the new system, despite a severe depression in local trade, expenditure dropped to £5,460,[71] but by 1840–1 it was rising again.[72] A poor rate of 9d. in the £ was levied for the last half of 1877–8,[73] and about this time there were five rating districts—Hanley, Shelton, Stoke, Fenton, and Longton—with five collectors under a superintendent.[74] The total rate levied for the last half of 1910–11 was £29,800.[75] Weekly expenditure at the beginning of 1926 was just under £200, but with the depression of that year it had risen to over £4,700 by the summer. During the first three months of 1928 some £6,365 were spent on unemployment relief, some £15,444 on out-relief and £122,512 on relief in the two workhouses and the children's homes at Penkhull. The poor-rate for the following year was levied at 4s. 5d. in the £.[76]

The main form of poor relief was at first presumably weekly or monthly pay, but no overseers' accounts seem to have survived. Workhouse relief was provided in Stoke by the 18th century (see below). In 1802–3 246 adults and 445 children under 15 were given out-relief, while 195 persons received workhouse relief and 348 occasional relief.[77] The policy of retrenchment applied in 1833–4 included a stricter scrutiny of applicants for relief and the payment of some out-relief in the form of provisions instead of money.[78]

A workhouse for Stoke-upon-Trent parish had been built by 1735 at the southern end of Penkhull village at the junction of Penkhull Green and the road from Trentham (now Trent Valley Road); in 1776 it had a capacity of 80.[79] The inmates were being employed in the potworks of the area by the beginning of the 19th century.[80] In 1832–3 the vestry erected a new workhouse at the Spittals on London Road just south of the Newcastle-under-Lyme boundary.[81] The old workhouse was at first occasionally used as a marble factory but the parish decided in 1834 to sell it.[82] By 1902 it had been converted into cottages which are still standing.[83] The economies of 1833–4 included the 'farming' of the

Stoke) were elected with 2 unpaid assistant overseers for the Fentons and Bucknall: ibid. 23 Mar. 1833. There was at least one salaried assistant by 1824 and there were probably 2 from at least 1827: *Abstract of Stoke Par. Accts. 1832–3* (copy in H.R.L.), showing the amount spent on this item doubling in 1827–8.

[57] Ward, *Stoke*, 492.
[58] *Staffs. Advertiser*, 22 Mar. 1834.
[59] Ward, *Stoke*, 492, 493; White, *Dir. Staffs.* (1851). It has been stated that Stoke was the first manufacturing town to be placed under a board of guardians: W. H. Warburton, *Trade Union Organization in the Potteries*, 101 n.
[60] H.R.L., Stoke Union Mins. 1910–13, p. 1; *Kelly's Dir. Staffs.* (1896). Bagnall was transferred to Leek Union by Local Govt. Bd. Orders of 6 and 7 June 1906, having been transferred by the county council from Stoke R.D. to Leek R.D.
[61] *Staffs. Advertiser*, 21 July 1894.
[62] *Kelly's Dir. Staffs.* (1924); *Stoke Union Yr. Bk. 1929–30* (copy in H.R.L.).
[63] *Staffs. Advertiser*, 29 Mar. 1930; *Kelly's Dir. Staffs.* (1932).   [64] Ward, *Stoke*, 467.
[65] Ibid. 468.   [66] Ibid. 467.
[67] *5th Rep. Cttee. on Poor Laws, 1777* (*Reps. Cttees. of H.C.*, 1st ser. ix), 458.
[68] *Rets. on Maintenance of Poor, 1803*, H.C. 175, p. 470 (1803–4), xiii.
[69] *Staffs. Advertiser*, 22 Mar. 1834; *Stoke Par. Accts. 1832–3*. The 5 rates levied that year brought in £12,460

17s. 6d.
[70] *Staffs. Advertiser*, 22 Mar. 1834; 28 Mar. 1835.
[71] *3rd Annual Rep. Poor Law Com.*, H.C. 546, p. 174 (1837), xxxi; *Petition of Stoke Guardians, 1838* (copy in B.M, C.T. 244, no. 18).
[72] Ward, *Stoke*, 493.
[73] H.R.L., Stoke Union Mins. 1876–8, p. 111.
[74] *Kelly's Dir. Staffs.* (1880).
[75] Stoke Union Mins. 1910–13, p. 9.
[76] *Stoke Union Yr. Bk. 1929–30*. For the children's homes see p. 200.
[77] *Maintenance of Poor 1803*, 471.
[78] *Staffs. Advertiser*, 28 Mar. 1835.
[79] *Fenn's Stoke Boro. Almanack, 1902*; *Stoke-upon-Trent Par. Reg.* iii. 447; Yates, *Map of Staffs.* (1775); Hargreaves, *Map of Staffs. Potteries*; *5th Rep. Cttee. on Poor Laws, 1777*, 458.
[80] *Maintenance of Poor, 1803*, 471.
[81] Ward, *Stoke*, 492; *Stoke Par. Accts. 1832–3*, showing a building cttee. appointed Feb. 1832, with building costs in 1831–2 at £305 14s. 6d. as opposed to just under £22 in 1830–1 and just under £53 in 1832–3.
[82] *Staffs. Mercury*, 22 Mar. 1834. The net value of marbles made by inmates of the workhouse in 1832–3 was £15 13s. 8½d., after the deduction of the cost of raw clay (£8 8s. 11d.), while among the debts owing by the parish in Mar. 1833 was £6 0s. 10½d. for 'clay etc. for making marbles': *Stoke Par. Accts. 1832–3*.
[83] *Fenn's Stoke Boro. Almanack, 1902*; see p. 182.

poor in the workhouse to the governor at the rate of 2s. 5d. each a week, in place of the former weekly cost of 2s. 10d. each as well as the governor's salary of £60 a year.[84] With the formation of the union in 1836 the new workhouse, which had already cost about £3,000 to build, was altered to the requirements of the poor law commissioners at a further cost of some £3,500, its capacity being thereby increased from 270 to 500; at first, however, there were no more than 300 inmates at any one time.[85] The workhouse remained in use after the amalgamation of the Stoke Union with the Wolstanton and Burslem Union in 1922[86] and now forms part of the City General Hospital. Two low two-story ranges, one of which was built as a hospital in 1842,[87] and a large three-storied block to the rear, represent the earliest of the workhouse buildings. These two blocks stand at the north end of the present extensive site where further buildings have been added at all periods.[88]

The Penkhull Children's Homes were built c. 1900[89] and extended in 1924.[90] They are situated in St. Christopher Avenue to the west of Penkhull village and consist of a series of individual houses.

ECONOMIC HISTORY. The Stoke area was primarily agricultural until the late 18th century when the pottery industry was becoming established. Even in the early 20th century the district, largely industrialized around the town itself, still retained traces of its agrarian past, particularly around Penkhull and Boothen. After the First World War, however, this part of the city was used for extensive new housing estates which were laid out over much of the surviving agricultural land. New factories also were built there.[91]

Valued at £6 in 1086, Penkhull then possessed land for 11 ploughs and 2 acres of meadow, and there were 17 villeins and 6 bordars with 8 ploughs.[92] In 1169 Penkhull paid 7 marks as an aid for the marriage of the king's daughter,[93] and in 1195, 1199, 1205, and 1206 it contributed tallages of 20s., 4 marks, £9 9s. 4d., and £7 respectively. A comparison with similar contributions from other manors and towns in Staffordshire in these years emphasizes the relative wealth of Penkhull.[94] The manor was restocked with 16 oxen and 2 other draught animals, 25 cows, 1 bull, and 15 sows at a cost of £7 8s. in 1199, when four other royal manors in Stafford-

shire were similarly restocked.[95] By the mid-13th century, when the manor had been absorbed into Newcastle manor,[96] the royal demesne in Penkhull included a carucate of land leased to the men of the vill for 15s. and a field called 'Caldhole' leased for 11s. to William Muriel,[97] keeper of the royal woodland in the area (see below). The men of Penkhull also held 8½ virgates at a rent of 34s., while a further 8 bovates were held in villeinage at a rent of 20s. 8d.[98] At the end of the 13th century, when the demesne of 8 bovates was held by customary tenants at a rent of £2, 18 sokemen (presumably the villein sokemen found on manors of ancient demesne) held 34 bovates for £1 14s. and a further 144½ acres for £3 12s. 3d., and 8 customary tenants held 8 bovates in villeinage.[99] Labour services were being commuted by this time: the sokemen paid 7s. 6d. in lieu of customary works and the villeins 7s. with a further 4s. in lieu of mowing the lord's meadow and making his hay.[1] With further rents, mainly for meadow and pasture, the Earl of Lancaster's income from Penkhull by the end of the century was £13 9s. 8d.[2] Nearly a century later the assized rents were worth £15 10s. 9d.[3] and in 1650 £10.[4] Early in the 15th century most of the land in Penkhull township was held either by socage tenure (presumably villein socage tenure) or else by lease out of the lord's demesne; there had also been extensive inclosure from the waste by then.[5] Only a very small amount of land was still held in villeinage and the labour services due from it had been commuted; another parcel was described as lately enfranchised.[6] Most of the land at Penkhull seems to have been copyhold at the beginning of the 20th century.[7]

The open fields of Penkhull township in the early 15th century included Stubbs, Oldfield, and Woodfield and possibly Whatley also.[8] In 1615 the open fields included Stubbs, Rye Field (apparently shared with Shelton), Church Field, and Cherry Field;[9] butts of arable were also held in certain closes, as at Burslem.[10] Stubbs, which was shared with Newcastle borough, and evidently with Clayton also, was inclosed in 1816.[11] Boothen Green occurs in 1615 as 2 acres of common pasture belonging to the tenants of Boothen;[12] Penkhull Green, in the centre of Penkhull village, provided the site for a school and, in 1842, the church.[13]

In 1086 the woodland attached to Penkhull manor was 1 league long and 2 furlongs broad.[14] By the

[84] *Staffs. Advertiser*, 28 Mar. 1835.
[85] Ward, *Stoke*, 492; White, *Dir. Staffs.* (1851), 223.
[86] *Kelly's Dir. Staffs.* (1924, 1940).
[87] Inscription on building.
[88] Warrillow, *Stoke*, 354–5, 356–7.
[89] They are mentioned in *Fenn's Stoke Boro. Almanack 1902* but not in *Kelly's Dir. Staffs.* (1900).
[90] *Kelly's Dir. Staffs.* (1924).
[91] O.S. Map 6" Staffs. xvii NE., xviii NW. (1900); see pp. 174, 176, 182–3, 187.
[92] *V.C.H. Staffs.* iv. 39, no. 17.
[93] *S.H.C.* i. 56.
[94] Ibid. ii (1), 47, 83, 128, 137.
[95] Ibid. 79.
[96] See p. 184.
[97] *S.H.C.* 1911, 145.
[98] Ibid.
[99] Ibid. 242–3. For villein sokemen see P. Vinogradoff, *Villainage in England*, 16–26; F. Pollock and F. W. Maitland, *Hist. of English Law*, i. 389–405.
[1] *S.H.C.* 1911, 243. They shared this 4s. with 4 customary tenants in Wolstanton. The villeins' rents and commuted services amount to 20s. 8d. (13s. 8d. for the

bovates and 7s. for services), which is the figure given as rent for the 8 bovates c. 1250; this probably indicates commutation by the middle of the century.
[2] Ibid. 243.
[3] Pape, *Med. Newcastle*, 118.
[4] E 317/Staffs./38.
[5] D.L. 42/4, ff. 168a–174a. The survey is dated 2 Henry son of King Henry—either 1414–15 or 1423–4.
[6] Ibid. ff. 171b, 173b.
[7] S. A. H. Burne, 'Vanished Hunting-Grounds of N. Staffs.' (*T.N.S.F.C.* xlv), 174; Ward, *Stoke*, 511, 512. The Mount estate was freehold by 1861: R. Hordley, *N. Staffs. Infirmary and Eye Hosp.* 21.
[8] D.L. 42/4, ff. 172b, 173a, b.
[9] D.L. 43/8/32, ff. 5, 7, 8; see p. 162. Doles of land in Rye Field were mentioned in 1693: W.S.L., D. 1788, P. 56, B. 23.
[10] D.L. 43/8/32, f. 7; see p. 130.
[11] See pp. 49, 79. It was evidently known as Castle Stubbs also in the 17th cent.: D.L. 30/239/2 (May, 3 Chas. I).
[12] D.L. 43/8/32, f. 1. Thos. Fenton held ½ of it: ibid. f. 8.
[13] See p. 192. Nicholls, *Penkhull cum Boothen*, 41, cites a Newcastle court roll of 1558 as mentioning 'common land in le Grene in Penkhull and Boothen'.
[14] *V.C.H. Staffs.* iv. 39, no. 17.

1160's Penkhull evidently formed part of the 'new forest' which extended from the Newcastle area to Tixall and the Blythe.[15] When this was disafforested by King John in 1204, he exempted Cliff Hay.[16] It has been suggested that this hay, which extended into Wolstanton parish,[17] included the present Hartshill district: Park Lane and Park Meadow occur among the place-names of the area in 1827, while Parker's Close, three fields lying near the mouth of the railway tunnel, occurs in the mid-19th century; the names Cliff Bank, Cliff Vale, and Cliffville survived into the 20th century, and the Cliffville estate was freehold land in an area of extensive copyhold tenure early in this century.[18] As keeper of the hay William Muriel held a virgate in Shelton in 1236 and was succeeded, at any rate in the land, by his son John in 1253.[19] The only other known keeper was Roger Myson, who seems to have forfeited the office by 1263.[20] 'Boscum de le Clif' occurs in a charter of 1286,[21] while in 1361 'a little wood called le Clif in Newcastle' formed part of the estates of the Duke of Lancaster.[22] Grants of the herbage of what was called Castle Cliff were made at various times from at any rate the late 14th century.[23] In 1241 ten oaks out of 'the wood at Newcastle-under-Lyme' were assigned as building material,[24] presumably for work on the castle,[25] and in 1423 eight cart-loads of timber were taken to repair the bridge at the castle.[26] In 1438 or 1439 the hedges and posts of Castle Cliff were themselves repaired.[27] Presentments were made by the jurors of Newcastle manor in 1615 concerning recent thefts of trees from Castle Cliff.[28] By grant of John of Gaunt as Duke of Lancaster in 1364 40 acres of Castle Cliff passed to Hugh Bowyer of Newcastle who conveyed the land and the buildings there to Nicholas del Chambers in 1377 or 1378.[29] An inclosure of 8 acres in 'le Clyff' called 'Trumpeshey' was held by a tenant early in the 15th century[30] and in 1615 when there was also a 'Trumpers Hay Mede'.[31] Land called Trumpers Hays, owned by the Fentons in the 18th century,[32] was still part of the estate in the area belonging to their descendant Sir Thomas Fletcher Fenton Boughey in 1867.[33]

By 1333 the lord of Newcastle manor had fish-ponds at Penkhull.[34]

MARKETS AND FAIRS. The lower part of the town hall erected in Market Street (now Hill Street) in 1794 was intended for a market, but none was being held in 1800.[35] By 1818 there was a Saturday market,[36] but in 1834 it was said to be overshadowed by the market at Hanley.[37] A new market hall was built at the south-west corner of the market-place in 1835, extending back to Epworth Street (formerly Cross Street and earlier still Chapel Street).[38] In 1845 the market was formally established by Act of Parliament and transferred to the new town hall in Glebe Street where it was held on the ground floor of the central block.[39] By 1850 a small Wednesday market was being held in addition to the main market on Saturday; a fortnightly cheese market had just been established, but it evidently lapsed after a very short time.[40] By 1876 the Wednesday market also had been discontinued.[41] The present market hall on the south side of Church Street was built by the corporation in 1883; it stands on three sides of a square with a row of shops making up the fourth side on Church Street.[42] A Friday market was added in the 1920's and the Wednesday market was revived in the mid-1950's, so that there are now three market days.[43] The 1835 market hall in Cross Street was used as a shambles by 1859,[44] and by at least 1872 a hide and skin market was held there;[45] it now (1960) forms part of the Hanley and Stoke Hide Market and is also used by the North Stafford Butchers Hide, Skin and Fat Co. Ltd.[46]

About the mid-19th century there was a cheese fair on the last Wednesday in February and the last Wednesday in September.[47]

A pinfold for Penkhull township was erected by the Stoke Improvement Commissioners in 1839 or 1840,[48] and it was evidently transferred with the market in 1845 to Glebe Street where it stood in 1850.[49]

MILLS. There was a mill in Penkhull township by 1327,[50] probably the Stoke Mill of 1558, then

[15] S.H.C. 1923, 296–7, 301–2.
[16] Rot. Chart. (Rec. Com.), i. 122; S.H.C. v (1), 155; S.H.C. 1923, 301.
[17] D.L. 42/4, f. 182a.
[18] T.N.S.F.C. xlv. 173–4; Nicholls, Penkhull cum Boothen, 39; Stoke Par. Reg. ii. 430; Ward, Stoke, 512.
[19] Bk. of Fees, 594; Cal. Inq. p.m. i, p. 70.
[20] Cal. Inq. Misc. i, p. 96.
[21] B.M. Add. Ch. 43971.
[22] Cal. Inq. p.m. xi, p. 104.
[23] Pape, Med. Newcastle, 118, 191; D.L. 42/4, f. 183b; Ward, Stoke, app. p. xliv. In 1263 the area was described as 'the king's wood called the Clyf belonging to the castle of Newcastle-under-Lyme': Cal. Inq. Misc. i, p. 96.
[24] Close R. 1237–42, 381.
[25] Pape, Med. Newcastle, 26–27.
[26] Ibid. 122.   [27] Ibid. 123.
[28] Ward, Stoke, app. p. xlii. The Castle Cliff still occurs in 1677: D.L. 30/242/1.
[29] Ward, Stoke, app. p. lxvi.
[30] D.L. 42/4, f. 173b. It lay in the Harpfield area: Nicholls, Penkhull cum Boothen, 37, 38.
[31] D.L. 43/8/32.
[32] W.S.L., D. 1788, P. 67, nos. 4, 15.
[33] Ibid., vol. 270, rental 1851–67.
[34] Cal. Pat. 1330–4, 497.
[35] Ward, Stoke, 505; R. Nicholls, Penkhull cum Boothen, 28; see p. 194. For a brief description of the building see p. 180.

[36] Parson and Bradshaw, Dir. Staffs. (1818), p. xxxvii.
[37] White, Dir. Staffs. (1834).
[38] Ward, Stoke, 505; W.S.L. 47/20/43. See p. 180 for a description of the building.
[39] Stoke-upon-Trent Market Act, 1845, 8 & 9 Vic. c. 16 (local and personal); White, Dir. Staffs. (1851); Ward, Stoke, 505–6; see p. 194.
[40] P.O. Dir. Staffs. (1850). The cheese market is not mentioned in White, Dir. Staffs. (1851).
[41] Mentioned in P.O. Dir. Staffs. (1872) but not in that for 1876.
[42] Staffs. Advertiser, 22 Sept. 1883; 29 Sept. 1883. It occupies the site of the house built by Thos. Wolfe for his son-in-law Robt. Hamilton: P. W. L. Adams, 'Thos. Wolfe' (T.N.S.F.C. lviii), 38 and plate facing p. 35; Ward, Stoke, 502–3. See p. 182, for a brief description of the building.
[43] Kelly's Dir. Staffs. (1924, 1928); Stoke Official Handbk. [1958 and previous edn.]. There are now 3 throughout the city.
[44] H.R.L., Stoke Commrs.' Mins. 1855–65, 3 Aug. 1859.
[45] P.O. Dir. Staffs. (1872); Kelly's Dir. Staffs. (1940).
[46] Local inf. (1960); Stoke-on-Trent Classified Telephone Dir. (Dec. 1959); see p. 163.
[47] P.O. Dir. Staffs. (1850).
[48] H.R.L., Stoke Commrs.' Mins. 1839–48, 5 Dec. 1839, 8 July 1840.   [49] Ibid. 1848–55, 6 Feb. 1850.
[50] S.H.C. vii (1), 199, where Adam the miller occurs under Penkhull.

belonging to the rectory.[51] In 1699 the rector leased 'one pair of mills' on the rectory estate to Thomas Mellor of Sneyd Green for seven years, with the proviso that the lessor was either to have his corn ground free or be given £2 10s. instead.[52] There were two such glebe mills on the Trent at Boothen by 1760, the upper mill situated at what is now the southern end of Stoke football ground and the lower mill a short distance downstream.[53] Both had by then been converted into flint-mills[54] and were still in use as such in the 1870's.[55] In order to ease the flow of the river and so prevent flooding in the area round the church the corporation bought and demolished the upper mill in 1881,[56] but the lower mill was evidently still in use in 1909.[57]

Hanford Mill stood on the Trent to the east of the Newcastle road on the Stoke side of Hanford Bridge by 1775.[58] It was in use as a flint mill in 1792[59] and still existed in 1832.[60]

There was a corn-mill on the Newcastle Canal off Eldon Place, London Road, by 1828 when it was worked by John Pratt, still the miller in 1834.[61] It had passed to Frederic Pratt c. 1840 when it was described as 'a steam corn-mill ... the most considerable flour-mill in the district; which is chiefly supplied with its large consumption by canal or land conveyance from distant agricultural parts'.[62] It was worked in 1851 by Christopher Dickenson and Charles Cattell[63] and between at least 1854 and 1880 by Dickenson alone.[64] In 1884 it was held by J. and E. Smith.[65]

By the early 19th century there was a windmill at Penkhull in what is now Mill Street on the northwest of the village and another at Hartshill.[66] Both were pulled down in the late 1830's, the site at Hartshill being occupied from 1842 by the new church.[67]

POTTERY INDUSTRY. There was a Roman pottery works on the rising ground above the Trent at Trent Vale near the present Trent Vale Brick Works from c. A.D. 50 until the late 2nd century.[68] There may have been small-scale pottery making at Penkhull by the early 15th century,[69] and the village is said to have possessed three works c. 1600 producing coarse brown ware, one of them belonging to a Thomas

Doody.[70] Butterpots were being made at Stoke by the 1680's,[71] but early in the 18th century there were only two works in the Stoke district, Ward's and Poulson's.[72] By the beginning of the 19th century there were four at Stoke, two at Cliff Bank, and two (one of them unoccupied) in Stoke Old Road.[73] Some 40 years later there were 7 major potworks in the town.[74] In 1959 there were 10 within the area of the former borough, making earthenware and bone china; in addition there were 2 manufacturers of sanitary ware.[75]

The earliest works which can be traced over a long period is that established early in the 18th century by John Alders of Penkhull at Top Square. This lay at the junction of Honeywall and what is now Hartshill Road on the site of the 19th-century St. Andrew's Mission Church. It was later known as the Upper Cliff Bank Works.[76] John (d. 1779) and his brother Thomas (d. 1781) produced there 'mottled and cloudy and tortoiseshell with lead ore and salt glaze and shining black of a very good quality' and also 'blue scratched' domestic ware.[77] By the middle of the century Thomas Alders—John is no longer mentioned—had taken John Harrison of Newcastle-under-Lyme (1716–98) into partnership; from 1751 or 1752 Josiah Wedgwood, having left his brother's Churchyard Pottery at Burslem, worked with them at Cliff Bank for a year or two before joining Thomas Whieldon at Fenton Low.[78] Harrison's son John was working at Cliff Bank by 1783 and remained there until his bankruptcy in 1802.[79] John Davenport of Longport then acquired the works and from 1804 let it to his kinsman William Adams, who produced general earthenware (including blue-printed) and figures[80] and also built up extensive pottery interests elsewhere in Stoke (see below). The Upper Cliff Bank Works remained in this branch of the Adams family until its demolition c. 1840.[81]

The Cliff Bank Works on the opposite side of Hartshill Road at the junction with Shelton Old Road[82] seems to have been occupied in 1740 by Daniel Bird, who made agate knife hafts and buttons besides earthenware. He was known as 'the flint potter' as a result of his having discovered the right proportion of flint and clay needed to prevent the ware from cracking in the oven.[83] Hugh Booth was

[51] Nicholls, *Penkhull cum Boothen*, 41.
[52] W.S.L., D. 1742, bdle. 61.
[53] *Plan for a canal from Longbridge to Wilden by Jas. Brindley revised and approved by John Smeaton, 1760* (in W.S.L., S. 1909, iii); Yates, *Map of Staffs.* (1775).
[54] *Plan for a canal from Longbridge to Wilden.* They were described as steam-driven in 1792: W.S.L., D. 1742, bdle. 61.
[55] O.S. Map 6" Staffs. xviii NW. (1890).
[56] See p. 196.
[57] *Stoke Boro. and District Rate Estimates, 1909*, p. 12 (copy in H.R.L.).
[58] Yates, *Map. of Staffs.* (1775). It may have been the water mill which formed part of the Corbett family's estate in Hanford, Longton, and Stoke in 1595: *S.H.C.* xvi. 145. [59] W.S.L., D. 1742, bdle. 61.
[60] Hargreaves, *Map of Staffs. Potteries.*
[61] Lich. Dioc. Regy., Bp.'s Reg. H, p. 541; White, *Dir. Staffs.* (1834). [62] Ward, *Stoke*, 507.
[63] White, *Dir. Staffs.* (1851).
[64] P.O. *Dir. Staffs.* (1854); *Kelly's Dir. Staffs.* (1880).
[65] *Kelly's Dir. Staffs.* (1884).
[66] Hargreaves, *Map of Staffs. Potteries*; *Staffs. Advertiser*, 25 Mar. 1816, 22 Jan. 1831; Nicholls, *Penkhull cum Boothen*, 26; *Fenn's Stoke Boro. Almanack* (1891).
[67] Nicholls, *Penkhull cum Boothen*, 26. Both windmills were shown on O.S. Map 1" lxxii NW. (1837).

[68] *T.N.S.F.C.* lxv. 140–1; lxvi. 178–9; lxviii. 155–8; lxix. 61–65; xci. 88–92; exhibits at H. Mus.
[69] D.L. 42/4, f. 173a, which mentions Nich. Potter of Penkhull.
[70] Shaw, *Staffs. Potteries*, 65; Ward, *Stoke*, 210.
[71] S.R.O., Q/SR Trans. 1682.
[72] E. Meteyard, *Life of Josiah Wedgwood*, i. 192. Poulson's may have been at Fenton: see p. 217.
[73] Allbut, *Staffs. Pottery Dir.* (1802).
[74] Ward, *Stoke*, 503–5. [75] *Pottery Gaz. Dir.* (1960).
[76] Adams, *Adams Family*, add. and corr. no. 2, p. W, and add. and corr. no. 3, p. 3; see p. 192.
[77] Adams, *Adams Family*, add. and corr. no. 2, p. W; *Staffs. Potteries*, 175; Meteyard, *Wedgwood*, i. 233–4.
[78] Meteyard, *Wedgwood*, i. 233, 234–5; Mankowitz and Haggar, *Eng. Pottery*, 105; Ward, *Stoke*, 429; see pp. 118, 218. In Adams, *Adams Family*, add. and corr. no. 2, p. W, it is stated that Alders let to Harrison.
[79] Mankowitz and Haggar, *Eng. Pottery*, 105.
[80] Ibid. 5; Adams, *Adams Family*, 328, and add. and corr., p. W.
[81] Adams, *Adams Family*, add. and corr. no. 2, p. W. and add. and corr. no. 3, p. 3. It is not mentioned in Ward, *Stoke*, 505.
[82] Adams, *Adams Family*, add. and corr. no. 3, p. 3.
[83] Meigh, 'Staffs. Potters', 28; Jewitt, *Ceramic Art*, 432; Shaw, *Staffs. Potteries*, 63–64.

producing china glazed ware and earthenware at the works in the 1780's and was succeeded in 1789 by his brother Ephraim, who, with his sons Hugh and Joseph, traded as Booth and Sons between at least 1792 and 1802.[84] Hugh and Joseph ran the works between at least 1805 and 1808,[85] and a lease was held by Thomas Ward and Company by 1815 (Ward and Davenport in 1822) and by Thomas Mayer from at least 1826.[86] The firm of William Adams and Sons took over from Mayer c. 1837 and held the works (described in 1841 as 'small, dilapidated and old') until the 1850's. It then passed to Minton, Hollins and Company, who were still the occupants in 1889.[87] The factory was pulled down in 1914.[88]

By 1756 white stoneware was being made at Stoke by R. Bankes and John Turner. It was at this works that in 1762, on Turner's leaving to work at Lane End, Josiah Spode became manager at the age of 29.[89] Spode bought the factory on mortgage from Banks in 1770 and became sole owner six years later.[90] At first he produced tableware, jasperware, Egyptian black, and black-printed ware; he also developed underglaze transfer printing. He was soon experimenting in the production of bone china, but none was sold by him before 1794.[91] He used a 'fire engine' for pumping water back over the flint-grinding water-wheel.[92] His son Josiah, who was already working with his father before succeeding him in 1797, experimented with felspar and in 1805 invented stone china, a felspathic earthenware very like porcelain. He was also among the pioneers in the use of steam power in grinding flint, for he installed a 10-horse power Boulton and Watt engine in 1802 and another of 36-horse power in 1810.[93] He became potter to the Prince of Wales in 1806.[94] Josiah (II)'s son Josiah succeeded in 1827 but died two years later, and in 1833 his executors sold the firm to his partner William Taylor Copeland (1797–1868), son of William Copeland (d. 1826) who had become a partner c. 1800.[95] Thomas Garrett was a partner of W. T. Copeland from 1833 until 1847, and c. 1840 there were some 800 employees at the works.[96] The premises were then extensive, covering some 14 acres; though well run, they were described as old and ramshackle.[97] In 1867 Copeland took his four sons into partnership, and since 1932 the firm

has been styled W. T. Copeland and Sons Ltd.[98] Electric power was introduced in 1923.[99] The pottery has always occupied the same site on the north side of Church (formerly High) Street and several of its early buildings have survived;[1] as well as two ovens they include the ranges to the south-west of the site making up the former 'Printers' Square', and a small round-ended building with an external stone staircase in the entrance courtyard. The original ranges facing Church Street, including the main entrance arch, were demolished in 1938 when the street frontage was set back.[2] A large extension of 1951 with a new façade to Kingsway was built over the site of the former 'Black Bank', a quadrangle of low buildings where black basalt ware is thought to have been made in the early 19th century.[3]

The Big Works stood on the north side of Church Street on the east bank of the Newcastle branch canal opposite the Spode works. It seems to have originated in a pottery sold in 1781 by Elizabeth Webster to Thomas Wolfe (1751–1818) and rebuilt by him.[4] He was making Queen's ware, blue-printed ware, cane, and Egyptian black at this works by 1784,[5] and he is said to have introduced the use of steam power for grinding flint, installing an engine in 1793.[6] He was in partnership with his son-in-law Robert Hamilton from 1800 to 1811 and then worked on his own account until his death.[7] He also added a works on the opposite side of Church Street held by Smith and Jarvis at the beginning of the 19th century.[8] In 1818 Thomas's widow Rachel let the two works to William Adams who began the manufacture of porcelain there, apparently dividing the works on the south side of Church Street for the purpose since this factory consisted in 1827 of a china works and the Bridge Bank Works.[9] The whole undertaking covered some 14 acres in 1840, but the premises were then in a dilapidated condition.[10] The Adams family continued to work the three potteries until 1862 or 1863,[11] and Wolfe Street (the present Kingsway) was run through part of the Big Works in the 1870's.[12] The Bridge Bank Works was still in operation at the end of the century.[13]

Thomas Minton (1766–1836), in partnership with Joseph Poulson and William Pownall of Liverpool,

[84] Mankowitz and Haggar, Eng. Pottery, 28; Ward, Stoke, 499; Jewitt, Ceramic Art, 432; Allbut, Staffs. Pottery Dir. (1802).
[85] Meigh, 'Staffs. Potters', 33.
[86] Ibid. 138, 205; Adams, Adams Family, add. and corr. no. 2, p. W.
[87] Adams, Adams Family, add. and corr. no. 2, p. W; Meigh, 'Staffs. Potters', 144; 2nd Rep. Com. on Employment of Children [431], p. c19, H.C. (1843), xiv.
[88] Adams, Adams Family, add. and corr. no. 3, p. 3.
[89] Mankowitz and Haggar, Eng. Pottery, 206, 225; Jewitt, Ceramic Art, 431–2.
[90] G. B. Hughes, Story of Spode, 5 (copy among W.S.L. pamphs. sub Ceramics).
[91] Ibid. 6, 9; Mankowitz and Haggar, Eng. Pottery, 207.
[92] J. Thomas, 'The Economic Development of the N. Staffs. Potteries since 1750' (London Univ. Ph.D. thesis, 1934), 225, 237, 338.
[93] Ibid. 255, where the first engine is stated to have been of 6 h.p.; Hughes, Spode, 12, 15, 16; Mankowitz and Haggar, Eng. Pottery, 206, 207.
[94] Mankowitz and Haggar, Eng. Pottery, 207.
[95] Hughes, Spode, 16; Mankowitz and Haggar, Eng. Pottery, 60, 206. Wm. Taylor Copeland was Lord Mayor of London in 1835 and Conservative M.P. for Stoke in 1837–65: ibid. 60.
[96] Hughes, Spode, 16; Ward, Stoke, 504.
[97] 2nd Rep. Com. on Employment of Children, p. c13.
[98] Hughes, Spode, 17–18.
[99] Ex inf. Mr. T. R. Copeland (1960).
[1] Some of these can be identified from an earthenware model (see plate facing p. 204) and a plan of 1833 on which the model is based, both in the possession of W. T. Copeland and Sons Ltd.
[2] Ex inf. Mr. Copeland.
[3] Ex inf. Mr. Copeland; foundation stone of new building.
[4] P. W. L. Adams, 'Thos. Wolfe' (T.N.S.F.C. lviii), 34, 36.
[5] Mankowitz and Haggar, Eng. Pottery, 242. John Davenport, later of Longport, is said to have been apprenticed to him: T.N.S.F.C. lviii. 37.
[6] Ward, Stoke, 503.
[7] Mankowitz and Haggar, Eng. Pottery, 242. He was also a partner in a Liverpool pottery firm.
[8] Allbut, Staffs. Pottery Dir. (1802).
[9] Adams, Adams Family, add. and corr. no. 2, p. W; T.N.S.F.C. lviii. 37; Meigh 'Staffs. Potters', 2.
[10] 2nd Rep. Com. on Employment of Children, p. c15.
[11] T.N.S.F.C. lviii, plan facing p. 35; Mankowitz and Haggar, Eng. Pottery, 5; Meigh, 'Staffs. Potters', 2.
[12] Adams, Adams Family, add. and corr. no. 1, pp. E, O.
[13] O.S. Map 6" Staffs. xviii NW. (1900); Meigh, 'Staffs. Potters', 98, 140.

opened a potworks at Eldon Place in 1796.[14] After Poulson's death in 1808 Minton became sole owner but in 1817 took his sons Thomas and Herbert into partnership.[15] Until 1798 only white, cream, and blue-printed wares were made, but porcelain was added from then until 1811; its manufacture was revived in 1821, and felspar china was added soon afterwards.[16] Minton was using water power for grinding his materials from 1796, but in 1819 he installed a 24 horse-power steam engine built by Christopher Kirk.[17] By the 1840's there were two separate earthenware and china factories.[18] Herbert was in partnership with John Boyle from his father's death in 1836 until 1841 and with his wife's nephew Michael Daintry Hollins from 1845; in 1849 Colin Minton Campbell, Herbert's nephew, also became a partner and succeeded his uncle in 1858 as head of the firm which then became Minton and Company; the present name of Mintons Ltd. was taken in 1883.[19] The manufacture of earthenware ceased at the beginning of the Second World War and the earthenware works, by then on the opposite side of London Road from the present bone china works, was sold in 1947.[20] The impressive factory building on the east side of London Road is described elsewhere.[21]

As a condition of increased protection the pottery industry was required by the Import Duties Advisory Committee in 1937 to create a research association.[22] In 1939 the British Ceramic Research Association opened a research station in a converted late-Victorian house in Queen's Road, Penkhull.[23] A large new building was erected in 1947–50 and opened in 1951 by the Duke of Edinburgh.[24] Further offices and laboratories were being built at Hanley in 1959.[25]

The glebe mills and Hanford Mill, all on the Trent, had been converted into flint mills before the end of the 18th century,[26] and by 1834 there were also flint mills in Glebe Street and Cross Street (now Epworth Street).[27] In 1851 there were flint mills in Copeland Street and Wharf Street, the latter evidently the present Portland Mill.[28] There was a flint mill in London Road between at least 1896 and 1908.[29] The early grinding apparatus installed

at the works of Spode, Wolfe, and Minton, has been mentioned above.

OTHER INDUSTRIES. In the 1830's bricks and tiles were made at Trent Vale on the high ground south of Rookery Lane where there had been a kiln in Roman times and where the works of the Trent Vale Brick and Tile Company is now situated. They were also made at a works near the Black Lion Inn, at Spring Fields, where there is still a works, at Hartshill, and at Brick Kiln Lane.[30] Minton's works also was producing tiles by this time, and in 1845 the tile department became a separate business as Minton, Hollins and Company (now Minton, Hollins Ltd.), with a works in Church Street by 1850 and in Shelton Old Road from 1870.[31] The Campbell Brick and Tile Company transferred its production from Fenton to London Road in 1876.[32] There were some fourteen brick and tile works in Stoke in the early 1890's[33] but only four larger works in 1959.[34]

There was quarrying at Penkhull by the later 17th century, and c. 1671 the stone for the repair of Stoke Bridge came from there.[35] In the early 1840's a quarry to the north of Newcastle Lane supplied the stone for the new church at Hartshill.[36] The names Quarry Road and Quarry Avenue in the area between Princes Road and Hartshill Road suggest that there was once quarrying in that part of Penkhull also.

SOCIAL LIFE. In the early 1830's there was a Socratic School at Stoke under the presidency of the curate, Benjamin Vale. Its objects were 'to encourage virtue and discourage vice' by means of lectures, publications, discussions, and the maintenance of a library and 'by pecuniary and honorary awards for correct principles, good conduct, and long service'.[37] The Stoke Athenaeum and Literary and Philosophical Institution was established in 1846 'to diffuse amongst its members knowledge in general' with emphasis on anything relating to local manufactures; it possessed a library, newsroom, and museum, and was housed in the new town hall in Glebe Street.[38] The free library and museum in London Road was built in 1877–8 on land given by Colin Minton

[14] Jewitt, *Ceramic Art*, 396; Mankowitz and Haggar, *Eng. Pottery*, 151, 182.
[15] Jewitt, *Ceramic Art*, 396, 398. Thos. left the firm in 1821 to enter the church; Herbert ceased to be a partner in 1828, although he remained closely connected with the business and succeeded his father in 1836: ibid. 398.
[16] Jewitt, *Ceramic Art*, 398; Mankowitz and Haggar, *Eng. Pottery*, 151.
[17] Thomas, 'Econ. Dev. of N. Staffs. Potteries since 1750', 256, 935–7. [18] Ward, *Stoke*, 504.
[19] Mankowitz and Haggar, *Eng. Pottery*, 32, 41–42, 111, 151. There were 1,500 employees by 1858.
[20] Ex inf. Mintons Ltd. (1960). [21] See p. 182.
[22] M. P. Fogarty, *Prospects of the Industrial Areas of Gt. Brit.*, 328 note. For an abortive attempt by Wedgwood and other potters to set up a co-operative research establishment in 1775 or 1776 see J. Leighton, 'Pots and Potters' (*T.N.S.F.C.* xli), 34–37.
[23] *Staffs. Sentinel*, 1 Feb. 1939; *Programme of Opening* (copy among W.S.L. pamphs.).
[24] *N. Staffs. Focus on Industry and Commerce* (Dec. 1951), 16–17. [25] See p. 168.
[26] See p. 202. There was then another flint mill in Penkhull township on the stream feeding the Newcastle Canal: W.S.L., D. 1742, bdle. 61.
[27] White, *Dir. Staffs.* (1834).
[28] Ibid. (1851); *P.O. Dir. Staffs.* (1872); *Kelly's Dir. Staffs.* (1940).

[29] *Kelly's Dir. Staffs.* (1896, where it is called the Gordon Mills; 1908).
[30] Hargreaves, *Map of Staffs. Potteries*. Tiles were made at Hartshill by 1769: W.S.L., D. o/8/1, p. 256. Parson and Bradshaw, *Dir. Staffs.* (1818), mentions only a works at Hartshill. Ward, *Stoke*, 511, describes the products of the area as 'hard blue bricks, tiles and earthen pipes'.
[31] Jewitt, *Ceramic Art*, 399, 402, 414; Mankowitz and Haggar, *Eng. Pottery*, 111, 151; *P.O. Dir. Staffs.* (1850); J. C. Wedgwood, *Staffs. Pottery and its Hist.* 182, 187.
[32] Jewitt, *Ceramic Art*, 427. The co. was founded in 1875 to carry on the business of Herbert Minton's nephew Robt. Minton Taylor: ibid. For a brief description of the London Rd. factory see p. 182.
[33] *Keates's Potteries Dir.* (1892–3).
[34] Only 4 works are listed in *Pottery Gaz.* (1960).
[35] S.R.O., Q/SR Mich. 1671. Stone for the repair of Hanford Bridge c. 1658 came from 'Beech Clife': ibid. Mich. 1658. There was a 'stone mine' within Newcastle manor in 1559: D.L. 30/237/5 (June 1 Eliz. I).
[36] V. G. Aston, *Penkhull*, 32 (copy among W.S.L. Pamphs. *sub* Stoke).
[37] *Annals of the Socratic Sch. Stoke-upon-Trent, 1830, 1831* (copies in H.R.L.).
[38] R. G. Haggar, 'Some Adult Educ. Institutions in N. Staffs.' (*Rewley House Papers*, iii. no. 6), 6 (copy in H.R.L.), White, *Dir. Staffs.* (1851); see p. 194; and see p. 245 for its 'People's Trips' 1878–91.

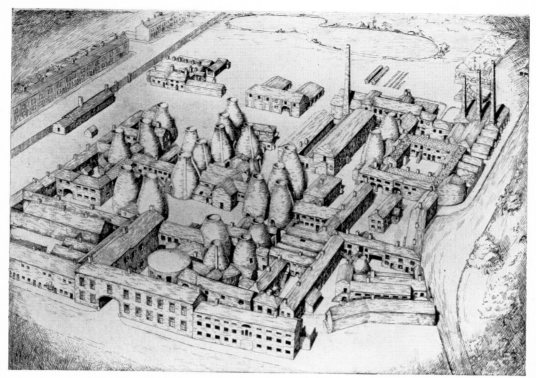

Earthenware model of the Spode Works *c.* 1833

Unveiling of the statue of Josiah Wedgwood outside Stoke Station in 1863

STOKE-UPON-TRENT

VIEW OF PENKHULL VILLAGE
showing the church and the Greyhound Inn

AIR VIEW OF THE LANE DELPH AREA OF FENTON
1937, looking south-east

Campbell.[39] The nucleus of the new library was formed by the collection belonging to Stoke Athenaeum which was transferred there from the town hall.[40] A branch library was opened at Harpfield in 1894 to serve the Hartshill and Basford area.[41]

A school of design was opened at the town hall in Glebe Street in 1847.[42] The accommodation, however, was inadequate, and in 1859 a school of art was opened instead in the Minton Memorial Institute in London Road, the building of which was begun in 1858 and which included also a school of science.[43] After the amalgamation of the art schools of the various towns following on Federation, the Stoke school was used for evening classes in modelling and sculpture, and a few years after the Second World War it became a school of printing.[44]

In the early 19th century Stoke Wakes were still held on the first Sunday of August,[45] the church being dedicated to St. Peter ad Vincula (1 August). By the middle of the century, however, the whole week following this Sunday was 'a popular holiday for pleasure and amusement throughout the whole parish'.[46] In 1850 there was horse-racing on the Monday and Tuesday on a course 'formed for the occasion in Boothen Meadows', a site now occupied by the Michelin tyre factory.[47] Racing continued during the next decade but evidently ceased after 1860, probably because of the bad state of trade in 1861 which reduced the scale of the wakes generally that year.[48] A Stoke Wakes fair is still (1960) held at Hanley during the week following the first Sunday in August.[49]

Stoke City Football Club dates from 1863, the second oldest in the country, and has its ground, Victoria Ground, in Boothen Old Road. It has produced 31 internationals, including Stanley Matthews, the son of a Hanley barber.[50] In 1888 Harry Lockett of Brick Kiln Lane, secretary of the club, became the first secretary of the Football League.[51]

There was a music hall, The Eagle, in Church Street between at least 1880 and 1892.[52] The Gordon Theatre in Wolfe Street (now Kingsway) seating 2,000, was opened in 1900 on the site of the former Crown Theatre.[53] Known as the Hippodrome Theatre of Varieties by 1908,[54] it had been converted into the present Gaumont Cinema by 1924.[55]

A choral festival was held at Stoke in 1833 and raised nearly £900 for the North Staffordshire Infirmary.[56] The Stoke Philharmonic Society had been founded by Dr. Charles Swinnerton Heap by 1877.[57]

An association for the discovery and prosecution of horse-stealers was formed in 1694 for the parish of Stoke with sixteen members.[58] By 1811 Penkhull had an association for the prosecution of felons.[59]

FENTON

THE town of Fenton lies in the south of the Potteries and in 1910 formed an urban district.[1] Historically it consisted of the two townships of Fenton Culvert or Great Fenton and Fenton Vivian or Little Fenton, manorially distinct by the 13th century.[2] The two Fentons are mainly an area of low-lying land. In the northern part of the area there remains much open country which rises to over 600 ft. in the north-east and drops steeply in the north-west from about 450 ft. to the River Trent. In the south, below Grove Road, the land rises to 500 ft.

In 1832 the River Trent formed the boundary of Fenton to the west and the Cockster Brook to the south and the east (the common boundary with Longton), while the northern boundary adjoining the township of Botteslow followed an irregular line with no geographical significance.[3] Fenton Vivian lay north of Fenton Culvert; the boundary between the two townships ran from the River Trent south of Stoke Bridge to join the road from Newcastle to Uttoxeter at the corner of the present Napier Street and then ran in a loop north of the main road to rejoin it at the junction of what are now City Road, Manor Street, and Christchurch Street. It then continued along the main road, Park Street, and Fenpark Road to Pool Dole and thence to the Caverswall boundary.[4]

The names Fenton Low and Culverd's Low (Mole Cop)[5] in the western part of the area suggest primitive burial-places. At Lawn Farm in the north-

[39] Tablet in situ.

[40] Fenn's Stoke Boro. Almanack (1894); Staffs. Sentinel, 10 Sept. 1892. For a description of the building see p. 182.

[41] Fenn's Stoke Boro. Almanack (1894).

[42] R. G. Haggar, A Cent. of Art Educ. in the Potteries, 5–6 (copy in H.R.L.); White, Dir. Staffs. (1851); see p. 195. It was a branch of the Potteries Sch. of Design, the other branch being at Hanley: see p. 171.

[43] Haggar, Art Educ. in the Potteries, 12–13; Kelly's Dir. Staffs. (1892).

[44] Haggar, Art Educ. in the Potteries, 33–34, 36.

[45] Parson and Bradshaw, Dir. Staffs. (1818); Pigot's Nat. Com. Dir. (1828–9).

[46] White, Dir. Staffs. (1851).

[47] Staffs. Advertiser, 10 Aug. 1850. There is still a Racecourse Road off London Road in this area.

[48] Ibid. 12 Aug. 1854, 19 July 1856, 11 Aug. 1860, 10 Aug. 1861; White Dir. Staffs. (1851).

[49] See p. 171.

[50] Stoke Official Handbk. [1958], 55.

[51] Eve. Sentinel, 18 Aug. 1959.

[52] Kelly's Dir. Staffs. 1880, 1892). It does not occur in the edn. of 1884.

[53] Staffs. Advertiser, 17 Mar. 1900; Kelly's Dir. Staffs. (1900).

[54] Kelly's Dir. Staffs. (1908).

[55] Ibid. (1924).

[56] Hordley, N. Staffs. Infirmary, 14; Ward, Stoke, 390; Hanley Jubilee Souvenir (1907), 28.

[57] R. Nettel, Music in the Five Towns, 1840–1914, 34; Hanley Jubilee Souvenir, 32; Woolley's Stoke Boro. Almanack, 1879; Programme of Concert Dec. 1877 (copy in H.R.L., Local Pamphs., vol. 33).

[58] W.S.L., D. 1742, bdle. 56.

[59] Warrillow, Stoke, 387–8.

[1] The urban district included a detached portion to the NE. consisting of a few acres around Lawn Farm: see p. 257, n. 96.

[2] See pp. 211, 212.

[3] T. Hargreaves, Map of Staffs. Potteries and Newcastle (1832). The western part of Fenton is shown on the portion of this map reproduced facing p. 173.

[4] Ibid.; see plan on p. 206.

[5] T.N.S.F.C. lxi. 136; Ward, Stoke, 544; Hargreaves, Map of Staffs. Potteries. Culverd's Low is on the Longton side of the former boundary between Fenton Culvert and Longton south of Grove Road.

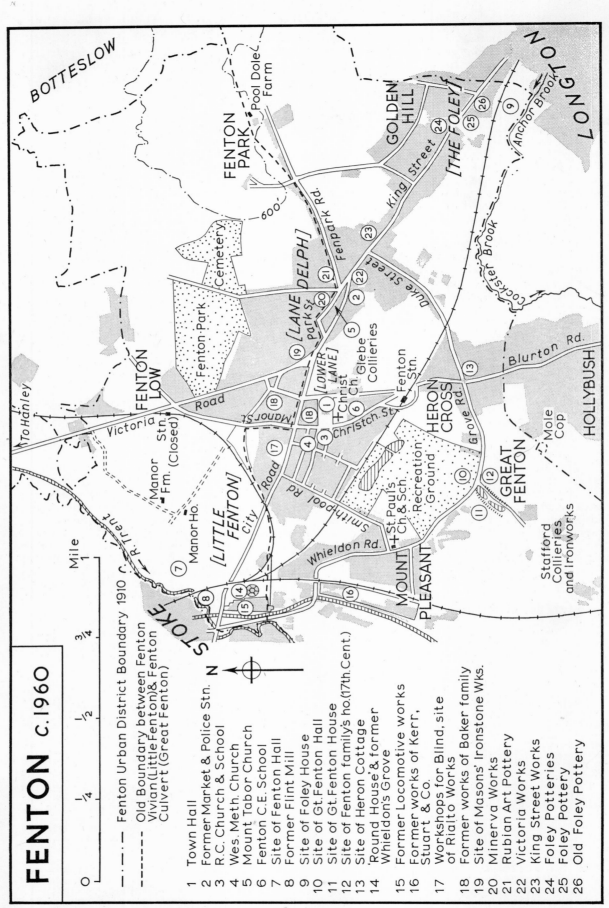

FENTON C.1960

0	¼	½ ¾ 1

Mile

— · — · — Fenton Urban District Boundary 1910
········ Old Boundary between Fenton
Vivian (Little Fenton) & Fenton
Culvert (Great Fenton)

1 Town Hall
2 Former Market & Police Stn.
3 R.C. Church & School
4 Wes. Meth. Church
5 Mount Tabor Church
6 Fenton C.E. School
7 Site of Fenton Hall
8 Former Flint Mill
9 Site of Foley House
10 Site of Gt. Fenton Hall
11 Site of Gt. Fenton House
12 Site of Fenton family's ho.(17th. Cent.)
13 Site of Heron Cottage
14 'Round House' & former
   Whieldon's Grove
15 Former Locomotive works
16 Former works of Kerr,
   Stuart & Co.
17 Workshops for Blind, site
   of Rialto Works
18 Former works of Baker family
19 Site of Masons' Ironstone Wks.
20 Minerva Works
21 Rubian Art Pottery
22 Victoria Works
23 King Street Works
24 Foley Potteries
25 Foley Pottery
26 Old Foley Pottery

The fine stipple indicates built-up areas.

206

east of the area there exists a homestead moat, which, it has been suggested, may have been the site of Fenton Vivian manor house.[6] As a result of the growth of the pottery and mining industries, there were by 1775 three main centres of population: Great Fenton, formerly Fenton Culvert; Little Fenton and Lower Lane; Lane Delph.[7] Lower Lane and Lane Delph lay along the Newcastle–Uttoxeter road and were the most populous parts at this time.[8] In 1818 the Fenton district was said to 'present nothing remarkable' and was described as a kind of suburb of Lane End.[9] By the 1830's, however, the area was noted for 'its many large potteries and handsome houses'.[10]

By this time Lower Lane and Lane Delph were still the largest centres of population and contained two chapels, the only places of worship in the area.[11] Lower Lane itself had been developed around the crossroads formed by the Newcastle–Uttoxeter road and the roads to Bucknall and to Blurton (now Manor Street and Christchurch Street respectively), and this area is still the centre of the town.[12] Lane Delph increased rapidly in buildings and population during the early 19th century, presumably in connexion with the many potworks there, and was described in 1834 as the most populous part of the district.[13] Most of the houses at Lane Delph lay along the main road and in the area around Duke Street and China Street. At the Foley, near the Longton boundary, there were by the 1830's several potworks and some large houses.[14] Apart from this development along the main road there were also some scattered houses at Great Fenton by 1832, including Great Fenton Hall, Great Fenton House, Grove House, and Heron Cottage. Little Fenton manor house, or Fenton Manor as it was called, and Fenton Hall were situated in the north-west of the area, while Whieldon's Grove lay to the south of the main road near Stoke Bridge.[15]

In the next half-century Fenton gradually ceased to be a collection of separate villages and assumed a more urban character. During this period Lower Lane, known as Church Fenton after the building of Christ Church in 1838–9,[16] became by far the largest centre of population. In this area the building between 1840 and 1842[17] of Victoria Road leading to Hanley had been followed by the laying-out of streets leading off it on both sides which in the late 1870's however, were not completely built up.[18] On the north side of the main road and east of the railway line to Bucknall four other streets had been laid out and built up with terraced houses during this period,[19] while Pratt (now Temple) Street and Raglan Street had been built south of these on the

other side of the main road.[20] The engine sheds of the North Staffordshire Railway were built over the Whieldon's Grove estate in the late 1840's[21] and immediately south of them three streets of terraced houses had been built by the late 1870's.[22] The area known as Mount Pleasant lying between Whieldon Road and the railway had been built up by the late 1870's with terraced houses.[23] At Great Fenton part of the area known as Heron Cross had also been built up by the late 1870's, presumably in connexion with the Glebe Colliery which lay to the north.[24] Bourne Street, Clyde (now Tweed) Street and Hill (now Derry) Street had also been laid out by the late 1870's at the south-west of the crossroads but only partially built up. Scattered building of terraced houses between Heron Cross and the centre of Fenton had taken place on the west side of Church (now Christchurch) Street and its continuation Heron Street.[25] A few terraced houses had also been built by the late 1870's along the north side of Duke Street which leads from Heron Cross to Lane Delph.[26] North of Lane Delph several small cottages were built in this period along the north side of the present Fenpark Road and in the present Hulse Street at Pool Dole, perhaps in connexion with the colliery workings nearby.[27]

In the last two decades of the 19th century, there was comparatively little building in Fenton,[28] but in this period a town centre emerged around the town hall, built in 1888 and Christ Church, rebuilt in 1890.[29] Some streets south-west of the town centre, the present Masterson, Alma, Welby, Nelson, Marlborough, Blenheim, Evelyn, and Crawfurd Streets, which had been partially laid out by the late 1870's,[30] had been built up with terraced houses, with small gardens or yards at the rear, by 1898.[31] Houses had also been built along Regent (now Smithpool) Road connecting Mount Pleasant with the present City Road stretch of the Stoke–Uttoxeter road.[32] In the north of the Fentons, at Fenton Low east of Victoria Road, Dimmock, Coburg, and Alfred Streets, which had been laid out by the late 1870's, had been built up with terraced houses by 1898.[33] At Heron Cross the present Hines Street and Chilton Street were laid out and built up in this period,[34] while in the area known as Golden Hill on the north side of the main road, where Queen (now Burnham) Street had been built by the late 1870's,[35] the present Berdmore and Hollings Streets, lying parallel to and east of Queen Street, had also been built up by 1898.[36]

In the first quarter of the present century the only notable housing development in Fenton was at

[6] V.C.H. Staffs. i. 366; Ward, Stoke, 526; see p. 212.
[7] W. Yates, Map of Staffs. (1775), reproduced facing p. 4.
[8] Yates, Map of Staffs.
[9] Parson and Bradshaw, Dir. Staffs. (1818).
[10] White, Dir. Staffs. (1834).
[11] See pp. 288, 293.
[12] Hargreaves, Map of Staffs. Potteries.
[13] White, Dir. Staffs. (1834).
[14] Hargreaves, Map of Staffs. Potteries; see pp. 219, 221.
[15] Hargreaves, Map of Staffs. Potteries; see pp. 209, 210.
[16] Ward, Stoke, 551; see p. 214.
[17] See p. 146.
[18] O.S. Map 6" Staffs. xviii NW. (1890; survey of 1877–9). One of the streets, William St., followed the line of the old Roman road from Longton.
[19] Ibid. These were Herbert Rd. and Hardinge, Pitt, and Wellington Streets.

[20] Ibid. Some houses in Temple St. had been built, however, in the early 19th cent.: see p. 210.
[21] O.S. Map 6" Staffs. xviii NW. (1890); see pp. 209, 214.
[22] O.S. Map 6" Staffs. xviii NW. (1890).
[23] Ibid.
[24] Ibid.; see p. 223.
[25] O.S. Map 6" Staffs. xviii NW. (1890).
[26] Ibid.
[27] Hargreaves, Map of Staffs. Potteries; O.S. Map. 6" Staffs. xviii NW. (1890).
[28] O.S. Map 6" Staffs. xviii NW. (1900).
[29] See pp. 214, 215.
[30] O.S. Map 6" Staffs. xviii NW. (1890).
[31] Ibid. (1900).
[32] Ibid.
[33] Ibid. (1890, 1900).
[34] Ibid. (1900).
[35] Ibid. (1890).
[36] Ibid. (1900).

Golden Hill. Here, adjoining the Longton–Fenton boundary, Goldenhill Road,[37] May Place, Foley Street, and Packett Street had been built up, while behind the streets leading off the main road from Uttoxeter and parallel to the latter Carron Street, Brocksford Street, and Elgin (now Marriott) Street had been laid out and built up.[38] Minor extensions of the other areas of housing had also taken place between 1898 and the early 1920's. Pool Street at Fenton Park was also built up during this period. Warrington Street, parallel to Victoria Road and behind the streets leading off that road on the east side, had been laid out but only partially built up by the early 1920's. Leading off Fenpark Road on the north side, Vivian Road, and St. Matthew, Cowper, Colville, Wallis, and Ashleigh Streets had been laid out but only partially built up. South-east of Heron Cross another block of houses was built by the early 1920's on the site of Heron Cottage, consisting of Grosvenor (now Bracken) Street and Holly Place, while Daisy Place parallel to Holly Place had been laid out but not built up.[39] Fenton Park was opened in 1924 over the site of old coal shafts at Fenton Low.[40]

In recent years the notable changes in Fenton have been the extension of Fenton Municipal Park to Victoria Road in 1957,[41] and the creation of a large recreation ground at Mount Pleasant between Grove Road and the houses in the centre of Fenton. In 1934 the Workshops for the Blind in City Road were erected on the site of a former pottery.[42] In the sphere of housing comparatively little has been done. Three streets, Carling Grove, Newmount Place, and Surtees Grove, have been built at Golden Hill, while the Hollybush council estate which lies mainly in Longton just crosses the boundary into Fenton at Heron Cross. Some demolition of old property has taken place but much still survives, particularly in the Christchurch Street area.

In 1666 there were seventeen persons chargeable to Hearth Tax in Fenton Vivian and sixteen in Fenton Culvert.[43] In 1811 the population of Fenton Culvert was 1,650 and of Fenton Vivian 856[44] and during the 19th century the population figures show a steady rise: in 1831, 2,708 and 1,002 for the two townships,[45] and in 1851, 5,767 for the whole area,[46] and in 1871, 10,299.[47] In 1891 the figure was 16,998.[48] In 1901 the population of the urban district was 22,742.[49] The population of the same area in 1911 was 25,626[50] and in 1921 26,714.[51]

The principal road through Fenton is the road from Uttoxeter to Newcastle which crosses the area

as King Street and City Road. This follows the course of the Roman road called Ryknield Street as far as the junction of Vivian Road and King Street[52] where it inclines westwards and runs directly to Stoke Bridge. The road occurs as a highway in 13th-century records.[53] It was subsequently turnpiked under an Act of 1759;[54] the toll house for this stretch was situated first at Meir and was replaced by a toll house on the Longton boundary at the Foley under an Act of 1763;[55] the latter is still (1960) standing as a small gabled cottage on the south side of the road. In 1794 Thomas Whieldon of Whieldon Hall was licensed to divert this road for 280 yards east of Stoke Bridge to a line slightly north of Whieldon's Grove.[56] By 1832 there was also a toll gate on the main road at the junction of the present City Road and Napier Street.[57] The road was disturnpiked in 1875 and declared a highway and a county responsibility under the Highways and Locomotives (Amendment) Act of 1878.[58]

By 1775 the road from Stoke through Great Fenton ran in a semicircle from its junction with the main road just east of Stoke Bridge down to Great Fenton and then east along the present Duke Street to rejoin the main road at Lane Delph.[59] It was straightened north-west of Great Fenton Hall c. 1800 by John Smith.[60] Another road from the centre of Fenton to Blurton intersecting this road at Heron Cross was turnpiked in 1778.[61] A toll gate was erected at Heron Cross under the Uttoxeter–Newcastle Turnpike Act of 1763.[62] This road was disturnpiked in 1877 and declared a main road under the 1878 Act.[63] By 1775 a road ran northwards from the main road at Lower Lane through Little Fenton to join the road from Stoke to Bucknall west of Fenton Low.[64] By 1832 the roads from Lane Delph to Pool Dole and Fenton Park were in existence.[65]

Victoria Road, running from the Masons' factory on the Uttoxeter–Newcastle road just west of Lane Delph in a straight line to Hanley, was built by 1842 under an Act of 1840, reducing the road distance between the two towns by about a mile.[66] The road from Little Fenton to Bucknall intersected this just below Fenton Low, the northern section of the Fenton–Bucknall road subsequently becoming merely a trackway.[67] Other alterations to the more important roads of Fenton included the diverting of Whieldon Road in the mid-1880's to run west of the canal to the new gasworks,[68] and a minor diversion of Christchurch Street by Fenton Station by the early 1920's.[69]

In the early 19th century Fenton was served by the same coaches as Longton.[70] A tramway from Stoke

[37] Goldenhill Rd. had been laid out by 1898 and at that date had a few houses in it: O.S. Map 6″ Staffs. xviii NW. (1900). [38] Ibid. (1925). [39] Ibid.
[40] Warrillow, Stoke, 382. [41] Stoke Official Handbk. (1960).
[42] Ibid.; see p. 220. [43] S.H.C. 1921, 163–6.
[44] Census, 1811, Staffs. [45] Ibid. 1831, Staffs.
[46] Ibid. 1851, Staffs. [47] Ibid. 1871, Staffs.
[48] Ibid. 1901, Staffs. [49] Ibid.
[50] Ibid. 1911, Staffs. [51] Ibid. 1921, Staffs.
[52] I. D. Margary, Roman Roads in Britain, ii. 41; Ward, Stoke, 12, 13. From this point the Roman road can still be traced as far as Fenton Manor House. [53] See p. 177.
[54] Act for repairing road from Derby to Newcastle-under-Lyme, 32 Geo. II, c. 60.
[55] 3 Geo. III, c. 57. [56] S.R.O., Q/SBe, 27.
[57] Hargreaves, Map of Staffs. Potteries.
[58] See p. 228. [59] Yates, Map of Staffs. (1775).
[60] S.R.O., D. 1742, bdle. 9.

[61] Yates, Map of Staffs. (1775); Act to repair rd. from Lower Lane to Hem Heath, 18 Geo. II, c. 109.
[62] Hargreaves, Map of Staffs. Potteries; 3 Geo. III, c. 57. This Act authorized the trustees to build side gates at Four Lane Ends in the road leading from Lane Delph to Gt. Fenton and Longton or in any other part of the road. The house attached was found to be unfit for human habitation in 1868: H.R.L., Fenton Commrs.' Mins., 7 Jan. 1868. [63] S.R.O., Q/AH, bdle. 3.
[64] Yates, Map of Staffs. (1775).
[65] Hargreaves, Map of Staffs. Potteries.
[66] Ward, Stoke, 553; see p. 146.
[67] Hargreaves, Map of Staffs. Potteries; O.S. Map 6″ Staffs. xviii NW. (1890).
[68] H.R.L., Fenton Local Board Mins. 1881–6, pp. 167, 190, 210, 236; Staffs. Advertiser, 24 May 1884: O.S. Map 6″ Staffs. xviii NW. (1890, 1900); see p. 216.
[69] O.S. Map 6″ Staffs. xviii NW. (1925). [70] See p. 228.

to Victoria Place, Fenton, was constructed in 1881 and extended to Longton in the same year.[71] It was taken over by the British Electric Traction Company (later Potteries Electric Traction Company) which electrified the system and built a new line along Victoria Road from Hanley.[72] The trams were replaced by buses between 1926 and 1928.[73]

By 1802 a post-office had been opened at Lane Delph. The area was served by a horse-post from Newcastle from 1835 until 1854.[74]

The Trent and Mersey Canal, started in 1766 and completed in 1777,[75] crosses Fenton near its former western boundary. By 1832 there was a wharf on the east side of the canal just south of Whieldon's Grove connected with Fenton, Lane Delph, the Foley, and Longton by a mineral line which was still in use in the late 1870's.[76] There was a second wharf on the west side of the canal by 1832, close to Stoke Bridge.[77]

Three railway lines cross the area. The first is the London–Manchester line, the first section of which, from Stoke to Norton Bridge, was opened in 1848. Whieldon's Grove, the house built by the potter, Thomas Whieldon, was used as a temporary station until the opening of Stoke station at the end of 1848;[78] it is now the motive power depot for the Stoke-on-Trent District. The engine sheds of the railway, including the 'monster engine stable' or Round House, were erected in the Whieldon's Grove area. This Round House, which still stands, was then described as 'circular in form, and no less than 200 feet in diameter within the walls. The exterior is composed of massive pilasters of brick work, with a bold stone cornice, surmounted by a parapet, the height being 30 feet from the line of the plinth. Between the pilasters are large Venetian windows,[79] 36 in number. . . . Within this building is another circle 87 feet in diameter, divided into 24 archways, corresponding with compartments for that number of engines. A siding from the railway communicates with the entrance to the "stable".' It was said to be the largest in the country.[80] Goods and carriage sheds were also erected[81] and general maintenance work has been carried on there to the present day. An engine and carriage works was developed later nearby.[82] The second line, from Stoke to Derby, opened as far as Burton-upon-Trent in 1848, has a station at the south end of Christchurch Street dating from the early 1860's.[83] The third railway line, from Stoke to Biddulph, was opened for mineral traffic in 1860 and for passengers in 1864; a station at Fenton Low called Fenton Manor was opened in 1864 and closed in 1956.[84]

BUILDINGS. Few buildings other than cottages have survived from early-19th-century Fenton. The Dog and Partridge Inn near the demolished Smith Square in King Street is a brick building of the cottage type, probably late 18th century in date. A more substantial inn is the 'Royal Oak'[85] at the junction of Christchurch Street and City Road which has three Venetian windows and a pedimented gable above an altered ground floor. The Canning Hotel, now demolished, stood next to the former market in what is now King Street and was evidently a Georgian building of some pretensions.[86] At Great Fenton a row of plastered houses with front gardens, which may date from the early 18th century, still preserve their rural character. At the north end of Duke Street are two detached houses of c. 1800 standing in their own gardens, one of which has a brick stable with 'Gothic' windows. Foley Place near the east end of King Street was probably built in the 1830's or 1840's and is an example of middle-class housing with some attempt at a formal layout, rare in the Potteries at this date. It consists of an L-shaped block of two-storied stucco houses with basements, late Georgian in style. There were originally eleven houses and an inn, the 'Foley Arms,' while a communal garden (now covered by a garage and filling station) was laid out to the west.[87]

Although many of the larger residential houses which were in existence in the early 19th century have been demolished, the former manor house of Fenton Vivian or Little Fenton[88] is still standing on the crest of a hill at the north-west corner of the township, surrounded by several acres of agricultural land. The older part of the house, which Philip Broade was said to have much improved by the early 1840's,[89] appears to date from c. 1800. It is of two tall stories and is built of stucco-covered brickwork on an H-plan; a stone pedimented doorway occupies the centre of the south front. A later wing to the east is still occupied. The drive leads south to entrance gates and a stucco lodge on the main road. Manor Farm, about 100 yards north of the house, has one wing which may be of 17th-century origin and in the farmyard the roof of a cowshed is of the same period.

Before the railway was built across their grounds in 1847–8 there were two houses on the low ground to the south-west of the Manor House, both belonging to the Whieldon family.[90] On the north side of the main road Fenton House or Fenton Hall, a 'very good house' with 'extensive pleasure-grounds, gardens and fish-ponds attached',[91] had been tenanted by William Adams (d. 1829) and later by his widow. It was demolished in 1847 at which time it was a rectangular two-storied building with a front of five bays, a small central pediment and an early 19th-century veranda.[92] South of the road a larger house, known as Whieldon's Grove was probably

[71] *Staffs. Sentinel*, 27 Nov. 1882; Warrillow, *Stoke*, 62.
[72] Warrillow, *Stoke*, 69–75.   [73] See p. 228.
[74] Allbut, *Staffs. Pottery Dir.* (1802); see p. 7.
[75] *S.H.C.* 1934(1), 109.
[76] Hargreaves, *Map of Staffs. Potteries*; OS. Map 6" Staffs. xviii NW. (1890). The present street called Old Tramway off Duke St. indicates part of the course of the mineral line.
[77] Hargreaves, *Map of Staffs. Potteries*.
[78] White, *Dir. Staffs.* (1851); 'Manifold', *N. Staffs. Rlwy.* 33–34; see pp. 180, 214.
[79] The existing three-light windows are square-headed and not 'Venetian' windows as generally understood.
[80] *Staffs. Advertiser*, 22 Apr. 1848.   [81] Ibid.

[82] See p. 223.
[83] 'Manifold', *N. Staffs. Rlwy.* 34; ex inf. Brit. Rlwys. (L.M.R.).
[84] 'Manifold', *N. Staffs. Rlwy.* 50; ex inf. Brit. Rlwys.
[85] It was in existence as an inn by at least 1818: Parson and Bradshaw, *Dir. Staffs.* (1818).
[86] Ward, *Stoke*, 553; foundations of front wall *in situ*.
[87] O.S. Map 1/1,250 Staffs. xviii. 6. 24 (1878).
[88] See p. 212.   [89] Ward, *Stoke*, 549.
[90] Ibid. 550; see p. 213
[91] Ward, *Stoke*, 550–1.
[92] Ibid. 551; Adams, *Notes on some N. Staffs. Families*, annotated view reproduced on fly-leaf; W.S.L., Staffs. Views, iv, p. 191.

built by Thomas Whieldon the potter[93] in the mid-18th century. Its two-storied front of five bays faced west and had a central doorway. About 30 or 40 years later a large north wing was evidently added at right angles to the original house. This had bay windows at both ends and a pedimented doorway flanked by Ionic pilasters in the centre of its principal front.[94] Most of this later wing was cut off when the railway embankment was constructed immediately to the east, the house by this time being empty and in a neglected condition.[95] The west side of the building, which remained standing, was taken over by the railway, in whose hands it still remains.[96] The Ionic doorway has been re-erected in the centre of a former bay window, the bay itself having been raised to two stories. A ground-floor room in the older wing contains an enriched plaster ceiling.

The two dwelling houses originally belonging to the partners and brothers-in-law Ralph Bourne and William Baker[97] are on high ground immediately south of Victoria Place. Both are square two-storied brick buildings with hipped roofs, probably built about 1800. Bourne's house, now occupied as colliery offices, has a central pedimented doorway facing City Road. The front of the other house, approached from Glebedale Road, was faced with stone and altered in the 19th century. It was known at one time as Fenton House and was used by William Meath Baker at least until 1896.[98] It became Christ Church vicarage in the 1920's[99] and in 1960 was being converted into a china factory.

At Great Fenton the three principal houses, said c. 1840 'to distinguish that eminence',[1] have all disappeared. They included Great Fenton Hall on the north side of the present Grove Road (demolished c. 1900),[2] Great Fenton House (demolished after the Second World War),[3] and the house which became known as Great Fenton Hall in the present century (demolished c. 1955).[4] The last two stood to the south of Grove Road and were separated by a large depression or 'fosse' which at one time contained fish-ponds[5] and in which water is still standing. This suggests that one of the two houses occupied an ancient fortified site.

At the south-east corner of the cross-roads at Great Fenton stood Heron Cottage,[6] described in 1829 as a 'small but superb edifice'[7] and c. 1840 as 'agreeable for its seclusion' and having 'the character of an episcopal seat'.[8] It was the home of Charles J. Mason until it was put up for auction at his bankruptcy in 1848. The house was evidently an early-19th-century gabled 'cottage' with Gothic features which included a cloister; Mason added a large red-brick dining-room and a ballroom. Some of its luxurious fittings were damaged by Chartist rioters in 1842.[9] The site was built over by the early 1920's.[10]

The first public buildings in Fenton, which are still standing, were erected on the south side of Market Street (now part of King Street). At the east end of the group the former market, built by C. J. Mason c. 1831,[11] is a small single-storied brick building with a central arched entrance flanked by round-headed windows set in recessed panels, the whole being surmounted by a raking parapet of stone; it is now (1960) used as a garage. The two buildings which adjoin the market on its west side were erected in 1839 or soon afterwards by the newly established Improvement Commissioners on land leased from the Mason family.[12] They are now occupied as a china warehouse, a dwelling-house, and two small shops. The central building, which still carries the words 'Police Station' on a string course above its round-headed doorway, has a two-storied front of five bays with a small central pediment. It contained the commissioners' offices and a large first-floor room used for meetings and as a courtroom; cells with barred windows are still in existence at the rear. The third building, also of two stories, was originally the police inspector's house.[13] At the front is a round-headed doorway, three first-floor windows, and a pedimented gable.

The present town hall in Albert Square, Christchurch Street, was built in 1888[14] and is a large two-storied building of red brick with stone dressings, designed in a combination of the late Gothic and Tudor styles. The main block of six bays has a small central gable and is flanked by lower gabled side wings with oriel windows to the upper floors. The public library (1906)[15] and the police station (1914–15)[16] lie behind the town hall, their entrance fronts facing Baker Street.

The former Athenaeum, erected in 1853 to the designs of Ward and Sons of Hanley,[17] stands at the junction of Christchurch Street and City Road and is now occupied by the District Bank. It is a rectangular building in a heavy Italianate style, the lower story being of stone and the upper of brick with stone dressings. The principal front, which faces Christchurch Street, is of five bays and has a central entrance flanked by stone Doric columns.

Along the main road many of Fenton's earlier terraced cottages have disappeared but a group on the north side of King Street, which includes the Dog and Partridge Inn, is still standing. Immediately to the west a three-sided court known as Smith Square was demolished after the Second World War, as was Meakin's Row, a cul-de-sac off China Street.[18] In Duke Street a single row of old cottages survives and in the former Lower Lane area there are terraces dating from before 1830 both in Temple Street and on the west side of Christchurch Street. All these are built on the usual cottage plan of the period, having two rooms to each floor, but in some

93 See p. 214.
94 W.S.L., Staffs. Views, iv, p. 192; see plate facing p. 228.
95 Ward, Stoke, 49.
96 See p. 209.
97 Shaw, Staffs. Potteries, 68–69. For Bourne and Baker's two pottery works see p. 219.
98 Kelly's Dir. Staffs. (1896).   99 See p. 215.
1 Ward, Stoke, 542.
2 See p. 213.
3 See p. 214.
4 See p. 213.
5 Ward, Stoke, 544.

6 Hargreaves, Map of Staffs. Potteries (1832); O.S. Map 1/1,250 Staffs. xviii. 6. 22 (1878).
7 Shaw, Staffs. Potteries, 19.
8 Ward, Stoke, 554.
9 Haggar, The Masons of Lane Delph, 54, 60, pl. 16.
10 See p. 208.
11 See p. 217.
12 See p. 216.
13 See p. 216.   14 See p. 215.
15 See p. 224.
16 See p. 216; date on building.
17 Keates's Potteries Dir. (1875–6); see p. 224.
18 Warrillow, Stoke, 321.

cases wash-houses have been added later.[19] At the junction of Masterson (formerly Havelock) Street and Christchurch Street a row of five cottages represents one of the few remaining examples in the Potteries of an early type of layout; the front rooms open straight upon the street and the back rooms upon a communal yard which contains a row of three water-closets. On the south side of City Road, between the canal and the railway, a terrace of 20 plain well-built houses behind wooden palings dates from c. 1848 when they were put up for employees of the newly opened railway.[20] These all have projecting wash-houses at the rear and individual yards with back access. At the junction of City Road and Victoria Place a rebuilding scheme was evidently undertaken by W. Meath Baker about 1887,[21] probably for his own workers at the adjacent pottery. Early cottages, some of which were arranged in a three-sided court,[22] were replaced by about 30 terraced houses and a corner shop. A few of the original cottages can still be seen between the later ornate frontages which incorporate much moulded brickwork and terracotta ornament. The houses are of various sizes, some double-fronted and some with passage halls, but all have a two-storied rear wing containing a third bedroom, as well as a water-closet at the end of the yard. A block of about twelve similar houses at the junction of Victoria Place and Hitchman Street also includes a corner shop and is dated 1890 with the monogram 'w.m.b.'

In the mid-19th century sanitary conditions were poor in Fenton[23] and there were several pockets of sub-standard housing. For example, at Mason's Buildings, 'a half-square of about 24 houses', the privies were opposite the house doors and there was 'neither any pavement or drains'.[24] On the other hand, Fenton had the smallest population of the Six Towns and this was spread over a fairly wide area, resulting in less overcrowding than elsewhere. By the end of the century housing conditions in Fenton, which had been the first of the towns to adopt building by-laws, were considered to be the best in the Potteries.[25]

MANORS. In 1086 a virgate of land in Fenton was held of the king by Alward, a king's thegn.[26] This was presumably included in the three virgates in Fenton held of the Crown in 1212 de antiquo jure by William of Erdington.[27] By 1236 this estate was held of Newcastle manor[28] with which the overlordship remained until at least 1650.[29]

William of Erdington held Fenton in 1212 in right of his wife Philippa at a rent of 7s.[30] He still held it in 1236 by which date the rent of 1212 had been increased to 7s. 4d. and 40 days' castle guard had been added to the service of the fief.[31] In 1241 possession of Fenton was given by the king to Vivian of Standon as Philippa's nearest heir.[32] The estate was still rendering 7s. 4d. c. 1249.[33] Vivian died in or before 1250 when Philip Lovel was given custody of the lands and the wardship and marriage of his heirs.[34] Robert, Vivian's heir, was of age and in possession of his estates by 1283 when his right of free warren in his Fenton estates, then first called FENTON VIVIAN, was confirmed.[35] Robert still held Fenton Vivian in 1297, the service to the overlord being then the same as in 1236.[36] By 1310 it had passed to his son Vivian[37] and between 1310 and 1347 to Henry Motlowe.[38] Henry still held it in 1359,[39] but had died before 1367. It is not clear on what terms Henry held the estate since in 1367 and 1368 Vivian of Standon's widow successfully sued the guardians of Henry Motlowe's heirs for dower in one-third of Fenton Vivian.[40] Thomas Roos, guardian of Henry Motlowe's heir, still held the remaining two-thirds of Fenton Vivian in 1369,[41] but in 1374 he was sued for waste there by John Massey and his wife Joan claiming that they held it 'as dower of Isabel' (presumably Isabel, widow of Vivian of Standon) of the inheritance of Joan.[42] John and Joan Massey disseised John son of James Thyknes and Elizabeth his wife of land and tenements in Fenton Vivian which in 1401 were judged to belong to John and Elizabeth, in right of Elizabeth.[43] In 1415 or 1424 John Thyknes held in right of his wife lands and tenements at Fenton Vivian worth 7s. 4d. formerly held by Vivian of Standon.[44]

It appears that the land at Fenton Vivian was divided, for in 1438 John Mountforde son and heir of Elizabeth, daughter of John Boydell, was holding half the manor of Fenton Vivian, but this division of the manor does not seem to have persisted for long.[45] In 1471 a manor of Fenton Vivian was held by Thomas Rogers who, on his death in that year, was succeeded by his son Thomas.[46] This Thomas Rogers died before 1507, having conveyed Fenton to trustees for the benefit of his daughter Elizabeth, wife of William Essex.[47] It was still held in trust for William and Elizabeth Essex in 1513,[48] but between 1547 and 1551 it had passed to their son Thomas Essex.[49] In 1564 his son Thomas Essex leased 3 messuages, one to John Hill,[50] another to Hugh

[19] For the evolution of cottage plans in the Potteries see p. 114.
[20] Local inf.
[21] H.R.L., Fenton Local Bd. Gen. Cttee. Mins. 1887–92, p. 73.
[22] O.S. Map 1/500 Staffs. xviii. 6. 7 (1875).
[23] See p. 216.
[24] R. Rawlinson, Rep. to Bd. of Health on Stoke Par. (1850), 75 (Copy in H.R.L.).
[25] Warrillow, Stoke, 321.
[26] V.C.H. Staffs. iv. 58, no. 290.
[27] Bk. of Fees, 143.
[28] Ibid. 594.
[29] D.L. 42/4, f. 173b; Ward Stoke, app. p. xliv; E. 317/Staffs./38.
[30] Bk. of Fees, 143.
[31] Ibid. 594. The addition of 4d. was in respect of an acre at 'Bothes' (possibly Botteslow): S.H.C. 1911, 146; see p. 246.
[32] Exc. e Rot. Fin. (Rec. Com.), i. 350.
[33] S.H.C. 1911, 146.

[34] Exc. e Rot. Fin. (Rec. Com.), ii. 72.
[35] Cal. Chart. R. 1257–1300, 266.
[36] Cal. Inq. p.m. iii, pp. 288–90; S.H.C. 1911, 245.
[37] S.H.C. vi (1), 277; Cal. Pat. 1307–13, 263.
[38] S.H.C. xii. 74; xiii. 60. Wrottesley notes that Henry Motlowe had been one of the king's justices and had acquired the Standon's estate as a bribe when Vivian of Standon had been indicted for a felony, but gives no authority for this statement: ibid.
[39] Ibid. xii. 173.
[40] Ibid. xiii. 60, 68.   [41] Ibid. 67.
[42] Ibid. 105. In 1373 John and Joan Massey had also sued Ric. Bromley for possession of the manor: ibid. 99, 105.
[43] Ibid. xv. 115.   [44] D.L. 42/4, f. 173b.
[45] Cal. Close 1436–41, 185–6. There is a warranty clause against the Abbot of Westminster and his successors in the grant.   [46] C 140/15.
[47] Cal. Pat. 1494–1509, 533.
[48] S.H.C. xii. 181.   [49] C 1/1216/56.
[50] S.H.C. xiii. 249. This Thos. succeeded his father between 1551 and 1559: C 3/185/3.

Machin,[51] and a third to Joan Brode, widow.[52] By 1614 the estate had passed to William Essex who in that year conveyed it to Andrew Vyse.[53] Vyse is said to have conveyed it to Thomas Broade[54] but Simon Degge was holding a capital messuage called Fenton Hall at his death[55] which was sold in 1734 under the terms of his will to the mortgagee of the estate, William Cotton of Crakemarsh. Cotton sold it in 1735 to Thomas Broade, who, however, may already have purchased the manorial rights as he is then described as of Fenton Vivian.[56] The lordship of Fenton Vivian was divided by 1767; part was held with Botteslow by Thomas Baddeley of Newfield[57] in Tunstall, son of Elizabeth Machin of Botteslow who in 1699 had married Randle Baddeley, and the rest was held in 1789 by Thomas Broade.[58] Thomas Broade and James Caldwell, the latter probably a trustee, held four-fifths of the manor in 1808,[59] while the remaining Botteslow fifth was held in 1807 by John George Child, son of Thomas Baddeley's heir Smith Child, and in 1828 by William Kelsall Tait.[60] By the early 1840's Philip Barnes Broade had inherited four-fifths of the manor and had also purchased the remaining one-fifth, which comprised lands in Botteslow, from Tait.[61]

Philip Barnes Broade was living at Fenton Manor House in 1851[62] but by 1868 it was occupied by Edward Challinor.[63] Thomas William Minton was living there by 1880[64] and continued to occupy it until at least 1884[65] but by 1892[66] it was occupied by Henry Warrington who still lived there in 1912.[67] In 1960 it was partly derelict and was owned by Berry Hill Brickworks Ltd.; the adjacent Manor Farm belonged to the National Coal Board.[68] The homestead moat near Lawn Farm may indicate an earlier manor-house site.[69]

By 1274 the chief rents, pleas, and perquisites of the court of the manor of FENTON CULVERT were held by John de Verdon as part of the Alton barony.[70] The early history of the manor is obscure but it may have formed part of the large estates of Orme (temp. Henry I)[71] whose great-granddaughter Avice de Gresley married Henry de Verdon,[72] who was holding land in Bucknall in 1204.[73] An undated charter of her mother, Aline lady of Darlaston, granting land in Culverds Fenton to her uncle Thomas fitz Orme is witnessed by the *halimot de*

Culverdislow which is evidence of the existence of the manor probably in the late 12th century.[74] In 1274–5 Eleanor widow of John de Vernon sued his son and heir Theobald for one-third of the manor of Fenton Culvert.[75] On the death of the latter in 1316[76] the lands of the Alton barony were taken into the king's hands to await the birth of Theobald de Verdon's fourth child.[77] A daughter was subsequently born and by 1327 the de Verdon lands had been divided between Theobald's four daughters.[78] New extents of the property were made in that year to settle disputes over the partition[79] and in 1328 lands in Fenton were retained in the king's hands as the portion of the youngest daughter Isabel.[80] Isabel had married Henry de Ferrers by 1331 when lands in Fenton were assigned to him by the king.[81] The overlordship of Fenton Culvert manor remained in the Ferrers family until 1520 when it passed to Anthony Fitzherbert.[82] It was still in the hands of the Fitzherbert family in 1619[83] but its later history is unknown.

At an early date the manor appears to have been subinfeudated to the Biddulph family and in the later 12th century Thomas Biddulph made a grant of land in Great Fenton.[84] In the late 12th or early 13th century Francis Biddulph was making grants of land in Fenton Culvert, and was also holding a court there at that time.[85] About the mid-13th century Thomas son of Henry de Bidulf granted William of Fenton Culvert 3 bovates in that vill at a yearly rent subject to suit at his court and to the rent payable to the chief lord of Alton.[86]

In 1563 Richard Biddulph headed the subsidy roll of that year for Biddulph, Bucknall, and Fenton Culvert.[87] In 1633 another Richard Biddulph received a grant of the manor from certain trustees,[88] and by 1639 it had passed to his son John Biddulph.[89] In 1652 quit-rents payable by freeholders in Fenton formed part of the Biddulph estate,[90] and in 1668 these were sold by Richard Biddulph to Thomas Fenton of Fenton Culvert,[91] the transaction apparently bringing to an end the Biddulph tenure of the lordship of Fenton Culvert manor. In 1715 Thomas Fenton sold the quit-rents to Thomas Smith of Great Fenton Hall[92] and he in the same year to Thomas Hunt of Newcastle-under-Lyme.[93] The further history of the manor is not known.

[51] S.H.C. xiii. 249. For the Machins of Botteslow from 1564 see p. 246.
[52] S.H.C. xiii. 249.
[53] Ibid. N.S. iv. 65; W.S.L., D. 1788, P. 67, B. 11.
[54] Ward, Stoke, 549.
[55] A pedigree of the Degge family is given in S. Erdeswick, Staffs., ed. T. Harwood (1844), p. lx.
[56] S.R.O., D. 239/M/2394, 2395 (a, b); D.N.B.
[57] S.R.O., Q/SO, 1767; Ward, Stoke, 87. The Machins' Botteslow estate was still, however, held by them in 1742: see p. 246.
[58] S.R.O., Q/SO, 1789.
[59] C.P. 43/900, rot. 259.
[60] C.P. 43/897, rot. 319; C.P. 43/980, rot. 53. John Child d. in 1811, but his grandfather lived until 1813: Ward, Stoke, 87; see p. 92. For Tait see p. 246.
[61] Ward, Stoke, 549.
[62] White, Dir. Staffs. (1851).
[63] P.O. Dir. Staffs. (1868).
[64] Kelly's Dir. Staffs. (1880).
[65] Ibid. (1884).
[66] Ibid. (1892).   [67] Ibid. (1912).
[68] Local inf. For a description of the 2 houses see p. 209.
[69] See p. 207.

[70] Cal. Inq. p.m. ii, pp. 58–59.
[71] S.H.C. N.S. xii. 7.
[72] Ibid.
[73] Oxfordshire Rec. Soc. Feet of Fines for Oxfordshire, 230.
[74] Ward, Stoke, app. p. lv.
[75] S.H.C. N.S. xii. 64.
[76] Cal. Inq. p.m. vi, p. 35.
[77] S.H.C. 1911, 335.
[78] Cal. Pat. 1327–30, 282.
[79] Cal. Inq. p.m. vii, pp. 68, 78.
[80] Cal. Fine R. 1327–30, 327–8.
[81] Cal. Pat. 1330–34, 152.
[82] B.M. Add. Ch. 57857.
[83] E 134/17 Jas. I Trin./1.
[84] W.S.L., D. 1742, bdle. 1.
[85] Ibid.
[86] S.H.C. N.S. xii. 65.
[87] Ward, Stoke, 541.
[88] Ibid.
[89] C 60/541, p. 33.
[90] Ward, Stoke, 541–2.
[91] W.S.L., Bourne Coll. 15.
[92] Ibid.   [93] Ibid.

OTHER ESTATES. In 1719 Simon Degge mortgaged a messuage called Fenton Hall in Fenton Vivian to Elizabeth Carter. This mortgage was transferred to Robert Cotton in 1723. In 1734 under the terms of Simon Degge's will the premises were sold to William Cotton of Crakemarsh who in 1735 sold them to Thomas Broade of Fenton Vivian.[94] In 1742 Broade sold Fenton Hall and the adjacent lands to John Peate of Lane Delph[95] who built a potworks there. Peate went bankrupt and sold Fenton Hall to Thomas Whieldon in 1748.[96] The Whieldons continued to hold Fenton Hall until 1810 when George Whieldon, then of Knightsbridge, London, leased it for seven years to Robert Hamilton of Stoke-upon-Trent, earthenware manufacturer. By then it was called Little Fenton Hall.[97] In 1824 George Whieldon of Cotton Hall agreed to lease Fenton Hall to William Bishop,[98] who was probably acting for William Adams to whom a seven-year lease was eventually granted in 1827.[99] This lease was renewed in 1834 to Lewis Adams of Fenton, earthenware manufacturer.[1] In 1846 George Whieldon leased the hall to Michael Daintry Hollins of Stoke, china manufacturer, for 14 years.[2] It was demolished in 1847 when the railway was being built.[3]

In 1730 Joseph Hill of Fenton Vivian, a cordwainer, conveyed a house in Fenton Vivian to Thomas Broade.[4] Broade held the house in 1755 when it was still subject to the dower of Rose, widow of Joseph Hill.[5] By 1764 it had passed to Broade's son, also called Thomas, who then sold it to Thomas Whieldon.[6] This was possibly the house in Fenton Vivian sold to Thomas Whieldon in 1764 and then occupied by Thomas Lakyn.[7] Another house in Fenton Vivian near Fenton Hall occupied by Thomas Lakyn was also sold to Whieldon by Broade in the same year.[8]

A chief rent of 40s. was owed by Thomas Crompton to William Essex as lord of Fenton Vivian for land in Fenton Vivian, but Andrew Vyse remitted this rent for £38 in 1614 after his purchase of the manor.[9] In 1628, when the land was sold to Robert Bagnall of Longton, it consisted of various fields in Fenton Park[10] and was still held by him in 1639.[11] By 1670 this estate was owned by John Hewitt. He or his son, also called John, still held it in 1697.[12] Elizabeth Bagnall (d. 1747), daughter of Robert Bagnall, married John Fenton (d. 1746) of Newcastle and subsequently of Fenton Park. Fenton Park descended in the Fenton family, subsequently Fenton

Fletcher Boughey,[13] and was held c. 1840 by Sir Thomas Boughey and Lawrence Armitsted as representatives of the elder line of the Fenton family.[14] The Fenton Park estate, including Fenton Park farm and Yew Tree farm, was the scene of coal mining, from at least the 18th century, and this was still in progress there in the late 1870's.[15]

Great Fenton Hall and the adjoining estate was owned by 1715 by Thomas Smith.[16] About 1840 it was said that the largest part of the township had been owned by the Smith family for upwards of a century.[17] The hall which stood on the north side of the present Grove Road was empty in 1829, the owner John Smith living at Elmhurst, near Lichfield.[18] It was occupied by a tenant of C. J. Smith in 1849[19] and was demolished c. 1900,[20] the site now forming part of Mount Pleasant Recreation Ground.

A John Fenton was holding lands in Fenton Culvert by 1540.[21] In 1666 Thomas Fenton was assessed for tax on five hearths, the second largest number in Fenton.[22] This assessment probably applied to the house which stood on rising ground to the south of what is now Grove Road next to Great Fenton House from which it was separated by a ditch and fish ponds.[23] About 1840 the house was occupied by the widow of John Bourne, the potter.[24] It was then described as 'an old farmhouse, modernised and beautified'.[25] Before its demolition c. 1955 it was apparently a stucco-covered house of Regency character but with an ancient chimney at its north end inscribed with the name 'Thomas Fenton' and a 17th-century date.[26] By the beginning of the 20th century the house, which became known as Great Fenton Hall, was owned by Stafford Coal and Iron Company who used it as offices.[27] A garage for the colliery now (1960) occupies the site; an early-19th-century stucco lodge and outbuildings, however, are still standing.

In the later 12th century Thomas Biddulph granted land in Great Fenton to William of the Hill (del Hull)[28] who presumably took his name from the hill on which Great Fenton stands. Philip of the Hill (de Monte) still held lands in Great Fenton in 1303,[29] but by 1368 lands and a messuage formerly held by Ralph de Hull in Fenton Culvert had passed to John Bron and his wife Sybil.[30] John Browne was holding lands in Fenton Culvert in 1399, including a house and land acquired by a Roger Benet from William Wylat who had received it from Thomas Biddulph.[31] A later John Browne was holding land

[94] S.R.O., D. 239/M 2394, 2395 (a, b); see p. 212.
[95] S.R.O., D. 239/M 2398 (a, b). See p. 231 for Peate's ownership of Gom's Mill in Longton at this date.
[96] S.R.O., D. 239/M 2403.
[97] Ibid. 2414 (a–g).
[98] Ibid.
[99] Ibid. 2414, 2415.
[1] Ibid. 2412.
[2] Ibid. 2430.
[3] See p. 209 where there is also a description of the house.
[4] S.R.O., D. 239/M 2393 (a, b); H. Mus., mortgage transfer dated 24 June 1730, Rogers/Broade/Taylor.
[5] S.R.O., D. 239/M 2405.
[6] Ibid. 2406 (a, b).
[7] Ibid. 2407.
[8] Ibid. 2406 (a, b). The 2 closes called the Little Stoakleys which were sold with the house adjoined the land of Fenton Hall.
[9] W.S.L., D. 1788, P. 67, B. 11.
[10] Ibid.
[11] Ibid. P. 39, B. 4.
[12] Ibid.
[13] Ward, Stoke, 422.
[14] Ibid. 422, 551.
[15] See p. 222.
[16] W.S.L., H. M. Bourne, 15; Ward, Stoke, 542, and pedigree on p. 543.
[17] Ward, Stoke, 542; see pp. 221, 222.
[18] Shaw, Staffs. Potteries, 69.
[19] Tithe Redemption Com., Tithe Maps and Appt., Stoke-upon-Trent (Fenton; 1849).
[20] Local inf.
[21] W.S.L., D. 1742, bdle. 6A.
[22] S.H.C. 1921, 165. Thos. Allen of Gt. Fenton House paid on 10 hearths: see below.
[23] Ward, Stoke, 544.
[24] Ibid.; see p. 219.
[25] Ward, Stoke, 544.
[26] Local inf.
[27] Local inf.
[28] W.S.L., D. 1742, bdle. 1.
[29] Ibid.
[30] Ibid.
[31] Ibid.

in Fenton Culvert in 1540.[32] By 1668 Thomas Allen was holding the capital messuage formerly owned by a Thomas Browne,[33] and in 1666 he had been assessed for tax on ten hearths.[34] In 1728 another Thomas Allen was occupying the capital messuage.[35] Another Thomas Allen was living in the house c. 1840.[36] In 1855 the trustees of the late Thomas Allen leased Great Fenton House to Edward Challinor for ten years.[37] In 1878 the Allens' representatives leased the land and house to the Duke of Sutherland for mining purposes. This lease was surrendered in 1887 but renewed again several times until in 1913 the estate was sold to the Stafford Coal and Iron Company.[38] For some time Great Fenton House was the home of the furnace manager of that company and afterwards of its secretary. By the outbreak of the Second World War it was uninhabited and was used by the Home Guard during the war, being demolished c. 1948.[39]

A house called Millridding or the Folly was owned by Michael Nicholls in 1755 and occupied by John Dixson, father-in-law of Michael Nicholls. There were 66 acres of land attached to the house.[40] The estate passed to John Richardson in 1759 when he purchased the equity of redemption of the mortgage.[41] Foley House, lying south of the railway line and just west of the boundary with Longton, still existed as a farm in the early 1950's.[42]

In 1666 a Richard Nicholls was assessed for tax on three hearths in Fenton Culvert,[43] and in 1755 Michael Nicholls was holding a capital messuage there and 78 acres of land, then said to be usually called Nicholls' farm.[44] This house was tenanted in 1755 by George Thompson and previously by John Matthias.[45] The estate passed to John Richardson in 1760 when he purchased the equity of redemption of Nicholls' mortgage.[46] This appears to have passed to the Allen family[47] who also held Great Fenton House in the mid-19th century.[48]

By 1728 Thomas Allen of Great Fenton House owned Sideway House, the occupier being Thomas Peake.[49] Harry Allen, the owner by 1768,[50] leased it as Sideway House or Sideway House Farm to William Steel in 1785. The farm was then 110 acres in extent.[51] By 1829 Robert Eccles and Benjamin Butter were tenants of the farmhouse, the land remaining in the hands of the Allen family.[52] In 1879 Sideway farm,

then only 60 acres in extent, was bought by Stoke Corporation for development as a sewage farm.[53]

Whieldon's Grove, which lay close to Stoke Bridge and south of the main road to Uttoxeter, was evidently built by Thomas Whieldon, the potter,[54] and occupied by him at his death in 1795. By 1829 it had been abandoned and was then described as a 'dilapidated mansion'.[55] It had been taken over by the North Staffordshire Railway by the late 1840's.[56]

CHURCHES. Until the 19th century the Fenton area lay within the parish of Stoke. Christ Church, in what is now called Christchurch Street, was built in 1838–9.[57] Ralph Bourne (d. 1835) left £3,500 to trustees for the erection and maintenance of the new church. Of this £1,000 was to be used as an endowment and the rest towards the building costs. Over £3,000 more was needed to erect the church, and this was provided by his sister Mrs. W. Baker.[58] In 1841 a new parish was created covering both the Fenton townships except for the part already included in the new Longton parish.[59] The living was a perpetual curacy until 1868[60] when it became a titular vicarage.[61] The right of presentation to the living at first lay with the bishop[62] but was transferred in 1861 to William Baker, nephew of Ralph Bourne the founder of the church.[63] On William's death in 1865 it passed to his brother, the Revd. R. B. Baker, with whom it remained until he died in 1875.[64] It was in the hands of his executors and trustees until 1883 when it passed to his son William Meath Baker of Hasfield Court (Glos.)[65] William died in 1935,[66] and the patronage then passed to the Rector of Stoke[67] with whom it still remains.[68] The benefice received a grant of £200 out of Queen Anne's Bounty in 1842.[69] The church of 1838–9, which stood on the east side of the present Christchurch Street, was a Gothic building of brick with stone dressings; it had an unaisled nave of five bays and two low structures flanking a west tower surmounted by angle pinnacles. The four-light east window was filled with stained glass. The interior, which contained about 1,000 sittings, was fitted with an organ and with galleries supported on iron pillars.[70] In 1890 the present CHRIST CHURCH, a

---

32 W.S.L., D. 1742, bdle. 6A.
33 Ibid.
34 S.H.C. 1921, 165.
35 W.S.L., D. 1742, bdle. 34.
36 Ward, Stoke, 544.
37 W.S.L., D. 1742, bdle. 10.   38 Ibid.
39 Local inf.
40 W.S.L., D. 1742, bdle. 50.
41 Ibid. bdle. 55.
42 O.S. Map 6″ Staffs. xviii NW. (1890); ibid. SJ 94 S.W. (1955).
43 S.H.C. 1921, 165.
44 W.S.L., D. 1742, bdle. 50.
45 Ibid.   46 Ibid.
47 The deeds of the property but not the transfer are in the Allen-Simkin collection deposited in the W.S.L. (D. 1742).
48 See above.
49 W.S.L., D. 1742, bdle. 34.
50 Ibid. bdle. 42.
51 Ibid. bdle. 50.
52 Ibid. bdle. 55.
53 Staffs. Sentinel, 1 Nov. 1898; see p. 196.
54 Shaw, Staffs. Potteries, 67. For Whieldon's other houses see p. 213.

55 Shaw, Staffs. Potteries, 67; see p. 218.
56 See p. 209. For a description of the house see p. 210.
57 Ward, Stoke, 544–5; Lich. Dioc. Regy., Bp.'s Reg. L, pp. 319–31.
58 Ward, Stoke, 545. It is there stated that Bourne devised 2 a. to her son William on trust as the site of the ch. but a memorial tablet in the ch. credits William with the building.
59 Ward, Stoke, 545; see p. 234.
60 Lich. Dioc. Ch. Cal. (1857, and subseq. edns. to 1868).
61 Lich. Dioc. Ch. Cal. (1869).
62 Ward, Stoke, 545; Lich. Dioc. Ch. Cal. (1857, 1860).
63 Lond. Gaz. 1861, p. 4063.
64 Burke, Land. Gent. (1937), 83; Lich. Dioc. Ch. Cal. (1866, 1875).
65 Lich. Dioc. Ch. Cal. (1876, 1882, 1883); Lich. Dioc. Regy., Bp.'s Reg. 34, p. 138; Reg. 37, pp. 347, 438.
66 Burke, Land. Gent. (1937), 83.
67 Lich. Dioc. Ch. Cal. (1937).
68 Lich. Dioc. Dir. (1959).
69 C. Hodgson, An Acct. of the Augmentation of Small Livings by the Governors of the Bounty of Queen Anne (1845), p. ccxcvi.
70 Ward, Stoke, 544–5; W.S.L., Staffs. Views, iv, p. 192 (1841).

larger building to seat 1,900 people, was erected on the same site.[71] It was designed by Charles Lynam[72] in the Decorated style and was built of red brick with stone dressings. At first it consisted of an aisled and clerestoried nave of six bays, a south chapel, a north organ chamber and north vestries, but in 1899 a tall west tower containing eight bells was added.[73] This has paired windows to the belfry stage and a line of white-brick arcading below an embattled parapet. Memorial tablets include one to William Baker (d. 1865), erected by his brother, the Revd. R. B. Baker, and evidently removed from the old church. Its inscription states that William Baker 'built this church, vicarage house, and infant school, gave the organ, and augmented the living'. The vicarage house was originally the square brick house at the end of Glebedale Road opposite the station, now called Glebedale House. Baker's own house at the other end of Glebedale Road became the vicarage in the 1920's, but a house on the opposite side of the road from this is now (1960) being made into the vicarage.[74]

A mission church was founded from Christ Church in 1849 in the former Primitive Methodist chapel in China Street.[75] This was replaced in 1882 by St. Matthew's Mission Church erected in that year at the junction of Park Street and Market Street (now King Street).[76] The church is a cruciform brick building in the Gothic style, with a small central bell turret containing one bell.

Pear Tree Mission, located presumably in the Pear Tree district off Manor Road, was opened from Christ Church in 1874.[77] It was evidently replaced by the school-church built at Fenton Low in 1875–6 and dedicated to St. Michael and All Angels.[78] The present church of St. Michael in Victoria Road, erected in 1887,[79] is a brick building in the Early English style with a bell-cote and one bell. From c. 1913 it has been in the parish of St. Luke's, Hanley.[80]

A mission hall was erected near St. Matthew's Church c. 1888.[81] It continued to be used as a mission hall until at least 1892.[82]

Mount Pleasant Mission Church in what is now Smithpool Road was opened from St. Peter's Church, Stoke, c. 1870.[83] Since at least 1887 it has been known as St. Paul's Mission, Mount Pleasant.[84]

A small mission church at St. Anthony's Row, Victoria Road, on the northern boundary of Fenton was opened c. 1896 from St. Jude's Church, Shelton, to serve the houses near the mines at Berry Hill.[85] A new church, dedicated to St. Margaret and St. Anthony, was built on the site in 1921, the gift of Margaret Hudson of Market Drayton. It was still

in use in 1940,[86] but by 1960 the building was occupied by Edco Supplies.

LOCAL GOVERNMENT AND PUBLIC SERVICES. Both Fenton Culvert and Fenton Vivian lay within the ancient parish of Stoke-upon-Trent and by the early 17th century were combined for the purposes of parish government with Longton and Botteslow to form one of the four 'quarters' into which that parish was divided.[87] Manorially Fenton Vivian was part of Newcastle manor by the early 13th century[88] and was still subject to its leet jurisdiction in the early 19th century.[89]

In 1839 Fenton, like Stoke, Longton, and Trentham, was placed under a body of commissioners with powers of policing, lighting, and generally improving the streets.[90] Local government in Fenton continued to be the responsibility of these commissioners until 1873 when they were superseded by a local board of health consisting of twelve members.[91] The functions of the board were discharged by a number of sub-committees which in 1881 consisted of Finance, Sanitary and General Purposes, Rating, Highways, Joint Gas, Contagious Diseases and Hospital, and Sewerage.[92]

In 1894 the Fentons were constituted an urban district administered by a council of 24 members, six from each of the four wards into which the district was divided.[93] The committees of the council in 1909–10 were General Purposes, Gas, Rate Excuse, Highway and Lighting, Health, Sewage Disposal, Finance, Library, and Education.[94] In 1910 the urban district, as part of the new borough of Stoke-on-Trent,[95] was divided into three wards, each being represented on the Stoke borough council by an alderman and three councillors.[96]

The offices of the Improvement Commissioners were at the police station of c. 1839 in Market Street (now King Street), Lane Delph, and these, having been bought from the Mason family in 1860, were occupied by the newly constituted board of health for a few months in 1873.[97] Later in the year, by agreement with William Meath Baker, the board took possession of the former Athenaeum.[98] In 1888 the present town hall in Christchurch Street was built by Baker and occupied by the board of health, and subsequently the urban district council, as his tenants.[99] In 1897 the urban district council decided to acquire the building by purchase.[1]

By 1335 Fenton Vivian, as a member of Newcastle manor, was represented at the court leet by two frankpledges.[2] These represented Fenton Vivian and

[71] *Kelly's Dir. Staffs.* (1892).
[72] *Keates's Potteries Dir.* (1892–3).
[73] *Kelly's Dir. Staffs.* (1900).
[74] *Keates and Ford's Potteries Dir.* (1867); *Kelly's Dir. Staffs.* (1916 and later edns. to 1940); local inf. (1960); see p. 210.
[75] J. Ward, *Eccl. History of Fenton* (copy in H.R.L.); see p. 297.
[76] Ward, *Eccl. Hist. of Fenton.*
[77] *Lich. Dioc. Ch. Cal.* (1874).
[78] Ward, *Eccl. Hist. of Fenton; Staffs. Advertiser,* 3 Oct. 1891; *Lich. Dioc. Ch. Cal.* (1877).
[79] *Kelly's Dir. Staffs.* (1892); Ward, *Eccl. Hist. of Fenton.*
[80] *Lich. Dioc. Ch. Cal.* (1914); *Lich. Dioc. Dir.* (1959).
[81] *Kelly's Dir. Staffs.* (1892); *Lich. Dioc. Ch. Cal.* (1888).
[82] *Kelly's Dir. Staffs.* (1892).
[83] *Lich. Dioc. Ch. Cal.* (1871).

[84] Ibid. (1887).
[85] *Lich. Dioc. Ch. Cal.* (1896).
[86] *Kelly's Dir. Staffs.* (1924, 1940).
[87] Ward, *Stoke,* 467–8.   [88] See p. 184.
[89] *Staffs. Advertiser,* 10 Oct. 1829.
[90] 2 & 3 Vic. c. 44 (local and personal). For details of the Act see p. 194.
[91] *Keates's Potteries Dir.* (1875–6).
[92] H.R.L., Fenton Local Board Mins., 19 Apr. 1881.
[93] *Staffs. Advertiser,* 5 Jan. 1895.
[94] H.R.L., Fenton U.D.C. Mins. 1907–10, pp. 109–11.
[95] See p. 259.
[96] *Stoke Council Yr. Bk.* (1915).
[97] H.R.L., Fenton Commrs.' Mins. 1842–64, 17 Jan. 1860.   [98] *Staffs. Sentinel,* 6 Dec. 1898.
[99] Ibid. For a description of the building see p. 210.
[1] H.R.L., Fenton U.D.C. Mins., Jan. 1897.
[2] D.L. 30/228/1.

Botteslow jointly in the mid-16th century,[3] but by 1679 each had one frankpledge.[4] Fenton Vivian formed a joint constablewick with Longton and neighbouring places.[5] Fenton Culvert formed a separate constablewick with Bucknall.[6] By 1829 two joint constables for Fenton Culvert and Fenton Vivian were being appointed at the court leet of Newcastle manor.[7]

Under the Act of 1839 the Improvement Commissioners were empowered to raise a police force and in the same year they arranged for the erection of 'a station house, public offices, and buildings for holding of meetings and transacting the business of the Commissioners of the Police and also dwelling rooms for the habitation of the Inspector of Police or Constable and also cells'.[8] As a result of the Chartist riots of 1842, during which the police office was attacked,[9] the commissioners in the following year secured the establishment in Fenton of a branch of the new county force, which leased the police station from the commissioners.[10] Additions to the police office were made in 1846,[11] and a new station was opened in 1915.[12]

In 1839 a stipendiary magistrate for the Potteries area was appointed and sat in alternate weeks at Fenton police office and Stoke. The two Fentons formed one of the six rating districts established to support the new system.[13] At first Fenton was in Hanley County Court District, formed in 1847,[14] but it was transferred to the Stoke County Court District in 1853.[15]

PUBLIC HEALTH. In the sphere of public health the Improvement Commissioners do not seem to have exercised to any marked extent the powers conferred on them by the 1839 Act. The report to the General Board of Health on the Fenton district in 1850 disclosed an unsatisfactory state of affairs, and attention was drawn to the existence of ash pits, communal privies, filthy channels in front of houses, and other sanitary defects.[16] The report recommended that an adequate sewerage scheme for the area with water-pan closets and watertight pipes should be undertaken. As a result of the report a sewerage plan for the area was prepared in 1852,[17] and in the following year sewers were being laid under the commissioners' authority in the China Street district.[18] In 1855 sewers were laid in the area around the junction of Park Street and Market Street (now King Street) and along the main road from Park Street to the post

office,[19] then in High Street.[20] In 1853 scavengers had been appointed whose duties included the removal of ashes, rubbish, and filth, the emptying of privies and cesspools, and the watering of the streets.[21] The commissioners were again faced with the sewerage problem in 1866 when the surveyor attributed the amount of illness in the town to bad ventilation and imperfect drainage.[22] When, however, after an outbreak of typhus in the same year, the commissioners were met with an estimated expenditure of £292 on sewers they elected to spend only 'the minimum and absolutely necessary amount' of £59.[23] In 1883 a sewage disposal works was opened at Blurton[24] and extended three years later.[25] This, however, proved inadequate to the needs of the town, and between 1905 and 1908 the urban district council built a new works on 18 acres of land at Sideway.[26]

Although restrictions were placed on burials in Christ Church and in its graveyard in 1856[27] it was not until 1887 that a cemetery of 16½ acres was laid out.[28] This is situated to the north-east of the town on sloping ground near Fenton Park.

OTHER PUBLIC SERVICES. In the matter of water-supply Fenton in the early 19th century was probably worse off than the other Pottery towns; it was described as being 'almost destitute of water excepting such as falls from the heavens and in summer the want is most severe'.[29] In 1845 the chief bailiff, together with the chief bailiffs of other Pottery towns, approved on behalf of their respective towns a project for a better water-supply, which culminated in the establishment of the Staffordshire Potteries Water Works Company in 1847.[30] Two years later a piped supply was brought to Fenton. From then until the end of 1924 the company, and thereafter the Staffordshire Potteries Water Board, have been responsible for the town's water-supply.[31]

By the early 1840's Fenton was being supplied with gas by the Stoke, Fenton and Longton Gas Company, established in 1839.[32] In 1878 the undertaking was bought by the Stoke Borough Council and the Fenton Local Board and run by a joint committee.[33] In 1883–4, after a dispute between the two authorities, Fenton Local Board erected its own gasworks between the canal and the river Trent.[34] The Fenton Gas undertaking passed under the control of the new county borough in 1910.[35]

3 D.L. 30/237/4.
4 D.L. 30/242/3.
5 S.H.C. x. 93; ibid. 1921, 163–5. The remaining members of the joint constablewick were Hanley, Lane End, Botteslow, and Normacot Grange.
6 Ibid. 1921, 165–7.
7 Staffs. Advertiser, 10 Oct. 1829.
8 H.R.L., Fenton Commrs.' Mins. 1842–64, 1 Nov. 1842. For a description of the buildings see p. 210.
9 H.R.L., Fenton Commrs.' Mins. 1842–64, 1 Nov. 1842.
10 Ibid. 21 Feb. 1843, 7 July 1844.
11 Ibid. 6 Oct. 1846.
12 Staffs. Sentinel, 22 Oct. 1915.
13 Act for more effectual execution of office of J.P., 2 & 3 Vic. c. 15; White, Dir. Staffs. (1851).
14 See p. 159.
15 See p. 195.
16 R. Rawlinson, Rep. to Bd. of Health on Stoke Par. (1850; copy in H.R.L.).
17 H.R.L., Fenton Commrs.' Mins. 1842–64, 9 Mar. 1852.
18 Ibid. Mar. and Dec. 1853.
19 Ibid. 20 Mar., 12 June 1855.
20 White, Dir. Staffs. (1851).
21 Fenton Commrs.' Mins. 1842–64, 15 Feb., 1 Mar. 1853, 18 July 1854.
22 Keates and Ford's Potteries Dir. (1867).
23 Ibid.
24 Warrillow, Stoke, 191; H.R.L., Local Board Mins. 1881–6, pp. 397, 399, 403.
25 Lond. Gaz. 1856, p. 2904.
26 Warrillow, Stoke, 191; H.L. Mins. of Procs. before Sel. Cttee. on Local Govt. Provisional Order (No. 3) Bill, 131.
27 Lond. Gaz. 1856, p. 2904.
28 Kelly's Dir. Staffs. (1892).
29 Pure and Wholesome Water for 100 Years, 1849–1949 10 (copy in H.R.L.).
30 Ibid.
31 Ibid. 12, 13, 19.
32 White, Dir. Staffs. (1851); Warrillow, Stoke, 132; see p. 197.
33 See p. 198.
34 Staffs. Advertiser, 24 May 1884; see p. 198.
35 See p. 266.

In 1882[36] and again in 1889[37] the local board declared its opposition to the introduction of electricity by outside companies on the ground that it had expended large sums on its gas undertaking, that there was no demand for electric light, and that if the demand arose the board itself would obtain the necessary sanction.[38] There was no general supply of electricity to Fenton until 1923.[39]

The establishment of a fire brigade dates from 1859 when the Improvement Commissioners acquired a fire engine. The brigade's offices adjoined the former market house which was offered to them as a fire station but was declined.[40] By 1865 there was an officer acting as Inspector of Nuisances, Lodging Houses, and Fire Brigade, but on his resignation in that year the last two functions were transferred to the Inspector of Police.[41] Fenton retained its own fire brigade until the reorganization of the city's fire service in 1926.[42]

Each of the townships of Fenton Culvert and Fenton Vivian seems to have been individually responsible for the maintenance of its highways, and there were still township surveyors in 1852[43] when legal difficulty arose over a proposal to substitute a district surveyor for them.[44] Separate highway surveyors were still in existence in 1860,[45] but three years later a district surveyor was appointed to act under a newly created Ways and Means Committee.[46] In addition to the supervision of the highways, his duties included drainage inspection, the examination of plans for all new buildings, and the making of contracts.[47]

ECONOMIC HISTORY. In 1086 Fenton was described as waste,[48] but little is known of its economic history until the emergence of coal mining at the end of the 17th century and of pottery manufacture in the early 18th century. Evidence of its agrarian development in the Middle Ages seems to be lacking. In 1540 five free tenants agreed to divide amongst themselves all their lands, meadows, and pastures in the lordship of Fenton Culvert which had not been previously inclosed; the open fields then mentioned were Surbarowe, the Birche, Olde Field, Brantell Field, and Woocrofte Field.[49] Despite the progressive industrialization of the area there still remained in the early 1950's about half a dozen farms[50] but these are rapidly disappearing. The farm at Fenton Manor House is run by the Ministry of Agriculture for testing fluorine deposits in the grass.[51]

MARKET. A small market, with stalls and shambles, was established in Lane Delph c. 1831 by C. J. Mason.[52] It was still in use in the early 1840's when the market was held on Saturday.[53] It had failed by 1851 allegedly because of its proximity to Stoke and Longton markets.[54] In 1839 a pinfold was erected by the Improvement Commissioners behind the adjoining police station, and in 1844 was placed under police superintendence.[55]

MILL. In 1544 Richard Germon of Fenton Culvert leased ground called Broadmeadow, then held by Richard Fenton and Roger Ashe for 45 years, to Thomas Bolton of Penkhull and James Bolton of Fenton Culvert for the building of a mill.[56] It was evidently this mill which was held by the Procter family in 1732[57] but by 1768 it was owned by Harry Allen of Great Fenton House.[58] It was then leased to Edward Bennet of Madeley for 21 years.[59] By 1782 it had become a flint and colour mill and was still in use as such in the 1870's. It was situated on the Trent south of Boothen.[60]

POTTERY INDUSTRY. The earliest known potter at Fenton is Thomas Heath who was working there, probably at Lane Delph, c. 1710 (see below). The member of the Poulson family who was said to be potting at Stoke c. 1710 may in fact be identifiable with William Poulson of Fenton Low (d. 1746), and it is even suggested that Thomas Whieldon took over William's works.[61] Thomas Astbury, a cousin of John Astbury of Shelton, was producing pottery at Lane Delph in the late 1720's, and at the end of the century John's grandson, Richard Astbury, was recorded as a potter at the Foley.[62] Thomas Whieldon of Fenton Low, 'whose name is more intimately mixed up with the early development of the potter's art than that of almost any other man',[63] began working at Fenton Low in 1740. About 1750 John Barker, one of Whieldon's ovenmen in 1749, began to make shining black ware and salt-glazed stoneware at the Row Houses near the Foley. He worked in partnership with his brothers and with Robert Garner, who had been one of Whieldon's apprentices. He later made cream-coloured ware also.[64] There were at least six potters in the Fentons c. 1760[65] but only four were mentioned in 1781, three of them at Lane Delph.[66] There were 13 works in the Fentons some 20 years later[67] and in the early 1840's 2 at Fenton, 6 at Lane Delph and 3 at the Foley.[68] There are now some 11 larger works in the

[36] *Staffs. Advertiser*, 31 Jan. 1882.
[37] Ibid. 21 Nov. 1889.   [38] Ibid.
[39] *Stoke Official Handbk.* (1960).
[40] H.R.L., Fenton Commrs.' Mins. 1842–64, 6 Dec. 1859.   [41] Ibid. 1864–73, 21 Nov. 1865.
[42] See p. 267.
[43] H.R.L., Fenton Commrs.' Mins. 1842–64, 9 Mar. 1852.
[44] Ibid. 26 Mar. 1857.
[45] Ibid. 10 Apr. 1860.
[46] Ibid. 7 July 1863.   [47] Ibid.
[48] *V.C.H. Staffs.* iv. 58, no. 290.
[49] W.S.L., D. 1742, bdle. 6A.
[50] O.S. Maps 6" SJ 84 NE., SJ 94 SW. (1955).
[51] Ex inf. the farmer (1960).
[52] White, *Dir. Staffs.* (1834, 1851). For a description of the building see p. 210.
[53] Ward, *Stoke*, 553.
[54] White, *Dir. Staffs.* (1851).
[55] H.R.L., Fenton Commrs.' Mins. 1842–64, 1 Nov. 1842, 7 May 1844.
[56] W.S.L., D. 1742, bdle. 50.

[57] C.P. 43/598, rot. 379.
[58] W.S.L., D. 1742, bdle. 42.
[59] Ibid. bdle. 50.   [60] See p. 221.
[61] Mankowitz and Haggar, *Eng. Pottery*, 181; J. C. Wedgwood, *Wedgwood Family*, 126.
[62] Meigh, 'Staffs. Potters', 86; Mankowitz and Haggar, *Eng. Pottery*, 10.   [63] Jewitt, *Ceramic Art*, 557.
[64] Ibid. 559–60; Mankowitz and Haggar, *Eng. Pottery*, 15, 94. Garner had m. into the Astbury family: ibid. 10. For the Garners' works in Longton see p. 240. There was still a Barker at Lane Delph in the early 19th cent., but the family had become estab. at Longton by the 1780's: Mankowitz and Haggar, *Eng. Pottery*, 15–16. The Barker Brothers' present Meir Works in Barker St., Longton, was opened in 1882: see p. 243.
[65] Jewitt, *Ceramic Art*, 560.
[66] Mankowitz and Haggar, *Eng. Pottery*, 268. Ward, *Stoke*, 552, mentions Lane Delph as formerly containing some of the oldest potteries in the area.
[67] Allbut, *Staffs. Pottery Dir.* (1802).
[68] Ward, *Stoke*, 551–3.

A HISTORY OF STAFFORDSHIRE

Fenton area, situated in the main to the north and south of King Street. Most of them produce either bone china or earthenware, although in a few cases both are made at the same works.[69]

About 1710 Thomas Heath of Lane Delph was producing a good durable ware, light grey in colour and made from a mixture of clay and 'a species obtained from the coal mines'; he apparently made dipped ware also.[70] One of his daughters married a Mr. Pratt of Fenton,[71] and the William Pratt who was working at Lane Delph in what is now Fenpark Road from at least the early 1780's until his death in 1799 may well have been a descendant of Heath; it is possible, too, that he was working on the same site as Heath.[72] His widow Ellen (d. 1815) and their sons Felix (1780–1859) and John ran the pottery together until 1812.[73] Felix then moved to Fenton,[74] but John continued at his father's works which, as the Lane Delph Pottery producing earthenware, was run by John and William Pratt from 1835 and by John Pratt and Company from the 1850's until 1878.[75] It then passed to Pratt and Simpson who were evidently succeeded in 1882 or 1883 by Wallis Gimson and Company, still the occupants in 1890.[76] By 1892 it was held by Barker, Batty, and Reid and by 1903 by H. K. Barker and Company. It evidently became known as the Rubian Art Pottery during this period.[77] In 1905 or 1906 it passed to the Rubian Art Pottery Company, who were still there in 1932.[78] The extensive site is now (1960) owned by Grimwades Ltd. of Stoke and Shelton, who occupy a small part of it; the firms of Fenton Products, figure-makers, and Casburt's, metalworkers, lease other parts, but most of it is derelict.

Thomas Whieldon (1719–95) opened his works in a small range of low, thatched buildings at Fenton Low in 1740, extending it in 1749.[79] He leased this or another works to William Meir in 1749 or 1750 and to Thomas Broade for eleven years in 1750; Broade assigned the lease to Edward Warburton in 1754.[80] In 1748 Whieldon had bought Fenton Hall from the bankrupt John Peate along with the adjoining potworks built by Peate after his purchase of the Hall estate in 1742,[81] but it is not clear whether it was there or at Fenton Low that Whieldon subsequently worked. He entered into partnership with

Josiah Wedgwood and John Harrison in 1754; Harrison withdrew the same year, but Wedgwood remained until 1759.[82] Whieldon continued in business until c. 1780 and acquired a fortune which has been estimated at £10,000; he was high sheriff in 1787.[83] Part of the works at Fenton Low still stood as cottages in the late 1820's,[84] but it was stated in the early 1840's that the factory was no longer standing.[85] Whieldon's earliest products were agate knife-hafts for the Sheffield cutlers and agate snuffboxes for the Birmingham hardwaremen; about 1750 he began making black ware and figures in salt-glaze and earthenware. His name is chiefly associated with earthenware of a wide range of colours, marbled ware, and tortoiseshell ware. Wedgwood contributed much to Whieldon's fame, but on the other hand Whieldon's formula for cream-coloured ware was the basis of the Queen's ware with which Wedgwood later established his reputation.[86] Among Whieldon's apprentices was Josiah Spode.[87] A flint mill was built on the Trent near Fenton Hall by John Peate after his purchase of the Hall estate in 1742; it was bought by Whieldon in 1749. It had a steam-driven engine of over 24 horse-power by 1825[88] and remained in use until c. 1946.[89] The mill buildings are still (1960) standing.

A works on the site of the present Minerva Works in Park Street was in existence in the early 1760's, owned by the Broade family and in the tenure of James Kent; the Broades were looking for a new tenant in 1764.[90] In 1806 or 1807 it was taken over by Miles Mason (1752–1822),[91] who moved there from the Victoria Works, Market Street (now King Street).[92] His eldest son William (1785–c. 1855) worked with him from c. 1806 until 1811 when he started to make earthenware at a works nearby,[93] and when Miles retired in 1813 it was to his other two sons, George Miles (1789–1859) and Charles James (1791–1856), that the Minerva Works passed.[94] They moved to the works in what is now Victoria Place in 1815.[95] The Minerva Works was in the hands of Pratt, Hassall, and Gerrard by 1827 and passed in 1833 to Richard Hassall and Thomas Green of Bank House, Fenton, son of Thomas Green of the Churchyard Works, Burslem.[96] Hassall retired the same year and Green then bought the works from Francis Broade, entering into partner-

[69] *Pottery Gaz. Dir.* (1960).
[70] S. Shaw, *Staffs. Potteries*, 68, 126; Mankowitz and Haggar, *Eng. Pottery*, 107.
[71] Shaw, *Staffs. Potteries*, 127.
[72] Mankowitz and Haggar, *Eng. Pottery*, 182; Allbut, *Staffs. Pottery Dir.* (1802). The Fenton Potteries opened by Wm.'s son Felix in Fenton (see below) were described in the late 1820's as on the site of the works where T. Heath made dipped pottery: Shaw, *Staffs. Potteries*, 68. It seems more likely, however, that the family's Lane Delph works would have been on the site of Heath's works, Thomas Heath being described by Shaw as of Lane Delph: ibid. 126.
[73] Mankowitz and Haggar, *Eng. Pottery*, 182.
[74] See p. 220.
[75] Meigh, 'Staffs. Potters', 161; Shaw, *Staffs. Potteries*, 70; Ward, *Stoke*, 552.
[76] Meigh, 'Staffs. Potters', 161; Jewitt, *Ceramic Art*, 555; *Keates's Potteries Dir.* (1882–3).
[77] *Keates's Potteries Dir.* (1892–3); Meigh, 'Staffs. Potters', 17.
[78] Meigh, 'Staffs. Potters', 173; *Kelly's Dir. Staffs.* (1932). Meigh, 'Staffs. Potters', 92, mentions Grimwade, Holmes and Co. there in 1907.
[79] Mankowitz and Haggar, *Eng. Pottery*, 239–40; Jewitt, *Ceramic Art*, 557–8.
[80] Jewitt, *Ceramic Art*, 556–7; S.R.O., D. 239/M2404, 2409.
[81] See p. 213.
[82] Jewitt, *Ceramic Art*, 559.
[83] Ibid. 558; Mankowitz and Haggar, *Eng. Pottery*, 239; *S.H.C.* 1912, 291.
[84] Shaw, *Staffs. Potteries*, 67.
[85] Ward, *Stoke*, 550.
[86] Mankowitz and Haggar, *Eng. Pottery*, 239; Jewitt, *Ceramic Art*, 558–9.
[87] Mankowitz and Haggar, *Eng. Pottery*, 239; Jewitt, *Ceramic Art*, 557.
[88] S.R.O., D. 239/M 2402, 2421–4.
[89] Local inf.
[90] R. G. Haggar, *The Masons of Lane Delph*, 22.
[91] Ibid. 21, 22; Mankowitz and Haggar, *Eng. Pottery*, 143, 144.
[92] See p. 220.
[93] Haggar, *Masons*, 29–30, 93–94; Mankowitz and Haggar, *Eng. Pottery*, 143. He moved to another works in 1822, remaining there 2 years.
[94] Mankowitz and Haggar, *Eng. Pottery*, 142–3; Jewitt, *Ceramic Art*, 553.
[95] See p. 220.
[96] Jewitt, *Ceramic Art*, 553; Meigh, 'Staffs. Potters', 91, 161; see p. 133.

ship with W. Richards of Great Fenton from 1834; Richards withdrew in 1847.[97] At first china 'of the commonest kind of blue-figured, white and gold' as well as lustre ware was produced, but Richards introduced the manufacture of 'a variety of ornaments, small ewers and basins, toy mugs and jugs etc.'; French competition put an end to this, and in 1851 Green turned 'to a better class of productions'.[98] Since his death in 1859 the business has remained in the hands of the Green family. It was incorporated as the Crown Staffordshire Porcelain Company Ltd. in 1903, but in 1948, with the growing demand for bone china by name, the company became the Crown Staffordshire China Company Ltd.[99] and now produces nothing but bone china.[1] Part of the works was rebuilt in 1906, and there is an extension of 1950 to the east[2] and another of the same period to the west. A second factory at Heron Cross, which includes a grinding mill, was acquired in 1947.[3]

William Bacchus was making cream-coloured and blue-printed ware at Fenton in the mid-1780's,[4] and his works evidently stood to the north of what is now City Road between Manor Street and Fountain Street where Ralph Bourne and William Baker were working by the end of the century.[5] By the late 1820's Bourne and Baker, in partnership with John Bourne, had acquired an additional works, evidently on the south side of the main road, opposite the first. This seems to have been the site where William Greatbach, son of a Berry Hill farmer and one of Whieldon's apprentices, had made biscuit ware in the 1760's.[6] Both Bourne and Baker had houses, still (1960) standing, on the south side of the road.[7] The business included a flint mill by 1829.[8] With the deaths of John Bourne and William Baker in 1833 the partnership was dissolved, and then for a short time the business was carried on by Ralph Bourne, William Baker the younger, and John Baker.[9] By the early 1840's William Baker was running it alone and was then using 'machinery for the exercise of the potters' operations' in addition to the mill.[10] The business was subsequently carried on by William Baker and Company, makers of printed, sponged, and pearl-white granite ware for export in the early 1880's at the works between Manor and Fountain

Streets; the works on the south side of City Road was by then an encaustic tile works, apparently still in the hands of the Baker family,[11] and is now (1960) occupied by the Ceramic Tile and Pottery Company. Its two-storied front range, dating from the earlier 19th century, has a central arched entrance surmounted by a Venetian window and a pedimented gable. Since at least the early 1920's the other site has been occupied by the flint mill of James Kent Ltd. of the Old Foley Pottery.[12]

The Foley Pottery, described in the 1880's as 'one of the oldest works in the district',[13] was built c. 1790 on the south side of King Street by Josiah Spode for Samuel, his second son (1758–1817). Samuel lived at the Foley Cottage at the north-west corner of the works and is said to have been the last salt-glaze potter in Staffordshire.[14] At his death the house and works passed to Charles Bourne who retired c. 1830.[15] John Hawley had bought the works evidently by 1832, but it was unoccupied some ten years later.[16] He was, however, working there from the early 1840's, and John Hawley and Company were making earthenware there between at least 1862 and 1884.[17] The Foley Pottery was occupied by Barkers and Kent between at least 1889 and 1940,[18] and the building is now (1960) in the hands of John Knox (Stoke-on-Trent) Ltd., wholesale and manufacturing chemists. The cottage still stood at the end of the last century.[19]

A house and potworks at the east end of the Foley was occupied during the last decade of the 18th century by Joseph Myatt, maker of white and printed earthenware and red ware; John Wesley preached in the yard of the house in 1790.[20] The works, which may have been held by the Burrows family between at least 1815 and 1823,[21] was in the hands of Robert Gallimore between at least 1840 and 1850.[22] It was held by Moore and Company as the Old Foley Pottery by 1872, evidently with Samuel Bridgwood as tenant in the mid-1870's; Moore and Company made granite ware for the American market and were succeeded in 1892 by Moore, Leason and Company, still the occupants in 1896.[23] The firm of James Kent Ltd., apparently connected with Barkers and Kent of the Foley Pottery, had succeeded by 1900[24] and are still (1960) working at the Old Foley Pottery. The

[97] Jewitt, *Ceramic Art*, 553; Meigh, 'Staffs. Potters', 91; Haggar, *Masons*, 22.
[98] Jewitt, *Ceramic Art*, 553.
[99] 'The Crown Staffordshire Story' (*Pottery Gaz. and Glass Trade Review*, Oct. 1952).
[1] Ex inf. Mr. S. S. Green, company chairman (1960).
[2] Dates on buildings.
[3] *Pottery Gaz. and Glass Trade Review*, Oct. 1952.
[4] Mankowitz and Haggar, *Eng. Pottery*, 12; Jewitt, *Ceramic Art*, 556; Meigh, 'Staffs. Potters', 9. He apparently m. a widow named Astbury as his 1st wife: Mankowitz and Haggar, op. cit. 12.
[5] Mankowitz and Haggar, *Eng. Pottery*, 30; Shaw, *Staffs. Potteries*, 69.
[6] Meigh, 'Staffs. Potters', 90; Shaw, *Staffs. Potteries*, 68–69; Mankowitz and Haggar, *Eng. Pottery*, 30; Hargreaves, *Map of Staffs. Potteries*. It had evidently been worked by Challinor and Adams around the turn of the cent.: Allbut, *Staffs. Pottery Dir.* (1802); Meigh, 'Staffs. Potters', 52.
[7] See p. 210.   [8] Shaw, *Staffs. Potteries*, 69.
[9] Mankowitz and Haggar, *Eng. Pottery*, 30. Ralph Bourne d. in 1835: see p. 214.
[10] Ward, *Stoke*, 552.
[11] Mankowitz and Haggar, *Eng. Pottery*, 30; Meigh, 'Staffs. Potters', 14; Jewitt, *Ceramic Art*, 554; O.S. Map 6″ Staffs. xviii NW. (1890); monogram 'WMB' (William Meath Baker) on gates.

[12] *Kelly's Dir. Staffs.* (1924); O.S. Map 6″ Staffs. xviii NW. (1925).
[13] Jewitt, *Ceramic Art*, 555.
[14] Ibid.; Ward, *Stoke*, 553; Mankowitz and Haggar, *Eng. Pottery*, 208; Hargreaves, *Map of Staffs. Potteries*; O.S. Map 1/500 Staffs. xviii. 6. 24 (1878).
[15] Meigh, 'Staffs. Potters', 353; Mankowitz and Haggar, *Eng. Pottery*, 29; Jewitt, *Ceramic Art*, 555. Spode d. at Foley Cottage early in 1817: *Staffs. Advertiser*, 1 Feb. 1817.
[16] Meigh, 'Staffs. Potters', 102; Ward, *Stoke*, 553.
[17] Meigh, 'Staffs. Potters', 102; Jewitt, *Ceramic Art*, 555; *P.O. Dir. Staffs.* (1868); *Kelly's Dir. Staffs.* (1884).
[18] Meigh, 'Staffs. Potters', 17; *Kelly's Dir. Staffs.* (1940).
[19] O.S. Map 6″ Staffs. xviii NW. (1900).
[20] Shaw, *Staffs. Potteries*, 72, where it is described as 'at the southern extremity of the Foley'; Jewitt, *Ceramic Art*, 561; Mankowitz and Haggar, *Eng. Pottery*, 272 (giving him at Lane End); Ward, *Stoke*, 553; Allbut, *Staffs. Pottery Dir.* (1802); Wesley, *Journal*, 28 Mar. 1790.
[21] They held 'the Foley Works': Meigh, 'Staffs. Potters', 47.
[22] Ibid. 83.
[23] Ibid. 145; *Keates's Potteries Dir.* (1875–6); Jewitt, *Ceramic Art*, 554.
[24] Meigh, 'Staffs. Potters', 121; *Kelly's Dir. Staffs.* (1892, 1896, 1900).

remains of the 18th-century house have formed part of the west end of the works since at least the beginning of the present century;[25] its upper story was recently removed, but several of the original windows and a moulded stone doorway still survive.

The King Street Works on the north side of King Street to the east of Park Lane was established towards the end of the 18th century by a Mr. Shelley, probably Thomas Shelley of Lane Delph who went bankrupt in 1804.[26] The works was evidently taken over by Jacob Marsh in 1806[27] and had passed to John Carey by 1820.[28] John had been joined by Thomas Carey by 1826, and they remained in partnership until 1842, producing Rockingham ware and ordinary earthenware.[29] The works then passed to a company and in 1850 to John Edwards who in the early 1880's was producing 'semi-porcelain and white granite for the American markets'.[30] In 1859 he patented 'a ring frame or holder' for stacking pottery ready for firing.[31] The firm of John Edwards Ltd. was working there in 1900.[32] The building is now (1960) occupied as a tea warehouse.

The pottery in Market Street (now King Street), later known as the Victoria Works, was occupied from 1796 by Miles Mason and George Wolfe as the tenants of the Revd. John Wolfe.[33] Mason had become a prosperous china and glass merchant in Fenchurch Street, London, in the early 1780's and began to make china at Liverpool in partnership with Thomas Wolfe of Stoke and John Lucock in 1796; the Fenton factory was used for the production of earthenware.[34] Both partnerships were dissolved in 1800, and Mason then began to make porcelain on his own at the Victoria Works, moving in 1802 from Chigwell (Essex) to an 'excellent modern-built sash-window house' adjoining the works.[35] The business evidently prospered, and in 1806 or 1807 he moved to the larger Minerva Works; the Victoria Works was then described as 'new erected'.[36] It was held by Messrs. Ginder from 1807 and by Samuel Ginder and Company between at least 1811 and 1843.[37] Messrs. Wathen and Lichfield held it by 1862, and from 1864 it was in the hands of James Bateman Wathen alone.[38] In 1869 or 1870 he was followed by James Reeves, and a James Reeves was still working there in 1940.[39] The works was held some ten years later by the Victoria Porcelain

(Fenton) Company[40] which still occupies it as part of the Victoria and Trentham Potteries. The house, held by a firm of building contractors c. 1951,[41] was demolished in 1959.[42] Its symmetrical two-storied front had a pedimented doorcase, flanking Venetian windows, and a central pediment at eaves level.[43]

A works on the north side of what is now City Road was evidently held c. 1800 by Harrison and Hyatt.[44] It was occupied from 1812 by Felix Pratt who moved there from Lane Delph and became noted for his distinctively coloured ware.[45] This earthenware works was run by Felix and Richard Pratt from at least 1818 and by F. and R. Pratt and Company between at least 1840 and 1916, and specialized for a time in multi-colour printing; this printing and the Etruscan ware produced at the works won medals at the 1851 Exhibition.[46] It was worked as the Rialto Pottery by the British Art Pottery Company (Fenton) Ltd. between at least 1920 and 1926,[47] but it had been demolished by 1934 when the present Workshops for the Blind were opened on the site.[48]

A works on the east side of what is now Victoria Place was occupied c. 1800 by Bagnall and Hull.[49] The pottery, with a house attached, was bought from Sampson Bagnall by Charles and George Mason of the Minerva Works in 1813. It was then, however, held by Josiah Spode and it was not until his lease expired in 1815 that the Masons moved there from the Minerva Works.[50] Charles had taken out a patent for ironstone china in 1813, and making this china at their new works the Masons 'obtained extensive public favour and an almost exclusive sale on account of its very superior hardness and durability'; they also produced blue-printed earthenware.[51] George retired c. 1829, but Charles, under the name of Charles J. Mason and Company, continued at the works until his bankruptcy in 1848; he was in partnership with Samuel Faraday from c. 1840 until Faraday's death in 1844.[52] The Masons evidently rebuilt or extended the works which stood 'obliquely to the turnpike road and on the line of the canal company's railway'; it was stated in the late 1820's that 'the front warehouse is four stories high, is fire proof, and has the most beautiful façade of any in the district'.[53] This elevation, as shown on tradesman's cards of the period, was punctuated by three

[25] By 1902 the house was used as workshops: J. Ward, *Notes on Wesleyan Methodist Ch. and its Growth in Longton* (copy in H.R.L.).

[26] Jewitt, *Ceramic Art*, 556; Mankowitz and Haggar, *Eng. Pottery*, 201; Allbut, *Staffs. Pottery Dir.* (1802).

[27] Mankowitz and Haggar, *Eng. Pottery*, 141; Meigh, 'Staffs. Potters', 134.

[28] Meigh, 'Staffs. Potters', 48.

[29] Ibid. 49; Mankowitz and Haggar, *Eng. Pottery*, 42; Jewitt, *Ceramic Art*, 556. The Careys also held the Anchor Works in Longton: see p. 242.

[30] Jewitt, *Ceramic Art*, 556. Meigh, 'Staffs. Potters', 74, 75, mentions John and Jas. Edwards at King St. in 1862–4, John Edwards & Co. 1873–9, and Edwards Bros. in 1888.

[31] Jewitt, *Ceramic Art*, 556.

[32] *Kelly's Dir. Staffs.* (1900).

[33] Haggar, *Masons*, 17, 93; ex inf. Mr. R. G. Haggar modifying the information ibid. p. 20.

[34] Haggar, *Masons*, 13–14, 17, 20.

[35] Ibid. 20 and plate facing p. 12. There were some 2 a. of land attached: ibid. 22.

[36] Ibid. 21–22.

[37] Meigh, 'Staffs. Potters', 86.

[38] Ibid. 206.

[39] Ibid. 165, 206; *Kelly's Dir. Staffs.* (1940).

[40] Haggar, *Masons*, 93.

[41] Ibid.

[42] Ex inf. Mr. R. G. Haggar (1960).

[43] Haggar, *Masons*, plate facing p. 12.

[44] Allbut, *Staffs. Pottery Dir.* (1802).

[45] Meigh, 'Staffs. Potters', 160, 161; Mankowitz and Haggar, *Eng. Pottery*, 182; see p. 218.

[46] Mankowitz and Haggar, *Eng. Pottery*, 182–3; Meigh, 'Staffs. Potters', 161; Jewitt, *Ceramic Art*, 555.

[47] Meigh, 'Staffs. Potters', 42; O.S. Map 6" Staffs. xviii NW. (1925). Pratts Pottery Ltd. held the Sutherland Pottery, High St., Fenton, from 1916 until at least 1920 (Meigh, 'Staffs. Potters', 161); this Sutherland Pottery was in existence between at least 1869 and 1922: ibid. 92, 192. For F. and R. Pratt & Co. at the Cauldon Place Works, Hanley, from the 1920's see p. 167.

[48] *Stoke Official Handbk.* (1960), 22.

[49] Allbut, *Staffs. Pottery Dir.* (1802).

[50] Haggar, *Masons*, 45–46.

[51] Ibid. 45; Ward, *Stoke*, 552; Mankowitz and Haggar, *Eng. Pottery*, 144.

[52] Haggar, *Masons*, 35, 37, 55–56, 59–60. Geo. unsuccessfully contested the new boro. of Stoke at the election of 1832: ibid. 37–41.

[53] Ward, *Stoke*, 552; Shaw, *Staffs. Potteries*, 70; Hargreaves, *Map of Staffs. Potteries*.

pedimented gables and had a range of 33 windows to each story; inscribed in large letters below the topmost range were the words 'Patent Iron-Stone China Manufactory'.[54] The factory was described in the early 1840's as of 'recent date and built very commodiously: well ventilated, well drained, but badly provided with accommodation for the sexes'.[55] By 1829 'a steam engine of some peculiarity in its construction', built by Holford of Hanley, was in use,[56] and Mason subsequently installed Potts' improved patent printing machine.[57] Late in 1844 Mason installed an improved version of George Wall's hand- or steam-operated machine for making flat and hollow ware, but fierce opposition from his workers and a mechanical defect caused its withdrawal early in 1845.[58] After Mason's bankruptcy in 1848 the works passed to Samuel Boyle and in 1852 or 1853 to Edward and Charles Challinor of Sandyford, Tunstall, who in the early 1880's were producing ironstone china and white granite, printed, sponged, and common earthenware there.[59] Mason's moulds and engravings were sold after his bankruptcy to Francis Morley of Broad Street, Hanley, and are used by Morley's successors, George L. Ashworth and Brothers Ltd.; Mason himself worked at Daisy Bank, Longton, from 1851 to 1854.[60] In 1891 or 1892 the works passed to Charles Challinor and Company who still held it in 1896.[61] It may have been occupied by William Baker and Company between at least 1916 and 1930,[62] but the site is now occupied by housing of the years between the world wars.

The Foley Potteries were built by John Smith c. 1820, with 'a powerful steam engine and flint mill' which was still in operation in the early 1840's.[63] The premises were then described as 'modern, well constructed, open, roomy and in all respects good'.[64] The works was first occupied by George and Thomas Elkin, John King Knight and John Bridgwood, who produced blue-printed earthenware, the designs on which included Willow and Broseley patterns.[65] Thomas Elkin withdrew in 1833, but the others continued as makers of earthenware, dealers in china, colour grinders, and farmers.[66] Bridgwood retired c. 1840 and Elkin in 1847 or 1848,[67] and Knight was joined in 1853 by Henry Wileman who continued alone after Knight's retirement in 1856.[68]

Wileman's two sons, James and Charles, succeeded him in 1864, but the partnership was dissolved within a few years; James then continued at the earthenware works, and Charles took over the Foley China Works which had been built by their father in 1860.[69] James took over the china works also on Charles's retirement in 1870, and in 1872 went into partnership with J. B. Shelley as Wileman and Company.[70] In the early 1880's the Foley Potteries were producing granite ware, printed ware, lustres, Egyptian, shining black, and cream-coloured ware, mainly for export; the china works was producing china 'of the ordinary useful class for household purposes'.[71] Wileman and Company still seem to have been in business there in 1925.[72] J. Stoddard Goodwin and Company, however, evidently occupied part of the building by 1899 and were still there in 1935.[73] In 1900 the mill was in the hands of the Potter's Mills Ltd.[74] The building is now (1960) divided between the Don Pottery Company, china and earthenware dealers, who were there by 1940,[75] the China and Earthenware Millers Ltd. who run the mill and have their office there, a firm of tile makers, a firm of earthenware factors, and a firm of cabinet makers and upholsterers. The eastern half of the long two-storied range facing King Street and the courtyard behind it probably represent the original works built by John Smith c. 1820; the western half was added at a later period, with a frontage in the same style as the earlier building.[76] The complete range is pierced by two elliptical archways, each surmounted by a Venetian window and a pedimented gable.

The flint mills at Fenton Hall, at the Crown Staffordshire China Company's Heron Cross Works, at Bourne, Baker, and Bourne's works, and at the Foley Potteries have been mentioned above. Great Fenton Mill on the Trent south of Boothen had been converted into a flint and colour mill by 1782 when it was held by Josiah Wedgwood.[77] It was still used as a flint mill in the 1870's.[78]

MINING. Mining in the Fentons can be traced from the end of the 17th century.[79] There was then coal-working in Fenton Culvert, possibly in the Pool Dole area. By the beginning of the 18th century there were mines on the Wood farm in Fenton

[54] Haggar, *Masons*, plates 31, 33, figs. 20 and 21 facing p. 99; Ward, *Stoke*, 552. For Chas. Mason's house at Heron Cross see p. 210.

[55] *2nd Rep. Com. Employment of Children* [431], p. c44, H.C. (1843), xiv.

[56] Shaw, *Staffs. Potteries*, 70.   [57] Haggar, *Masons*, 57.

[58] Mankowitz and Haggar, *Eng. Pottery*, 181; Haggar, *Masons*, 57–59. His house at Heron Cross had been damaged by the rioters in 1842, and he was awarded £900 compensation to be paid by the Hundred of Pirehill North: ibid. 54–55; W.S.L., H.M. Staffs. County I.

[59] Jewitt, *Ceramic Art*, 554; Meigh, 'Staffs. Potters', 37, 51. Edw. was living at Fenton Manor House by 1868: see p. 212.   [60] See pp. 165, 240.

[61] Meigh, 'Staffs. Potters', 51.

[62] *Kelly's Dir. Staffs.* (1916); Meigh, 'Staffs. Potters', 14. The co. had moved to Whieldon Rd. by 1932: *Kelly's Dir. Staffs.* (1932).

[63] Jewitt, *Ceramic Art*, 555–6; Shaw, *Staffs. Potteries*, 71; Ward, *Stoke*, 553. For the Smiths see p. 213.

[64] *2nd Rep. Com. Employment of Children*, p. c80.

[65] Mankowitz and Haggar, *Eng. Pottery*, 83; Jewitt, *Ceramic Art*, 556. Meigh, 'Staffs. Potters', 76, gives Elkin, Knight, and Elkin 1822–3 and Elkin, Knight, and Bridgwood from 1827. Ward, *Stoke*, 553, says that the factory

was built as a china and earthenware works.

[66] Mankowitz and Haggar, *Eng. Pottery*, 83.

[67] Meigh, 'Staffs. Potters', 122, 123; Jewitt, *Ceramic Art*, 556.

[68] Meigh, 'Staffs. Potters', 212; Jewitt, *Ceramic Art*, 556.

[69] Jewitt, *Ceramic Art*, 556, giving 1866 as the dissolution date; Meigh, 'Staffs. Potters', 212, giving 1868. The present Foley China Works on the S. side of King St. has been held by E. Brain & Co. since 1904 (Meigh, op. cit.); they appear, however, to have succeeded Wm. Robinson & Son, and the Robinsons seem to have been working at the Foley since at least 1853: ibid. 170, 171.

[70] Jewitt, *Ceramic Art*, 556; Meigh, 'Staffs. Potters', 212.

[71] Jewitt, *Ceramic Art*, 556.

[72] Meigh, 'Staffs. Potters', 212.

[73] Ibid. 89; *Kelly's Dir. Staffs.* (1908); *Pottery Gaz.* (1935).   [74] *Kelly's Dir. Staffs.* (1900).

[75] Ibid. (1940).

[76] Only the E. half is shown on Hargreaves, *Map of Staffs. Potteries* (1832).

[77] W.S.L., D. 1742, bdle. 42; see p. 217. For another lease in 1796 see D. 1742, bdle. 50.

[78] O.S. Map 6" Staffs. xviii NW. (1890).

[79] About 1550 there were said to be iron mines in Gt. Fenton manor: c1/1216/56

Vivian; their exploitation, apparently confined to the 18th century, was largely the work of the Broade family who acquired a share in them in 1725.[80] By 1728 several small coal and ironstone mines were being worked on the adjoining Fenton Park estate. It is possibly because of these workings that the village along the main road to the south was known as Lane Delph by the later 18th century.[81] There were also several pits at Fenton Low in the north-western part of the area by the second half of the century.[82] New ventures appeared throughout the first three-quarters of the 19th century, encouraged by the needs of the pottery and iron industries, and already c. 1840 John Ward could note that 'the coal and ironstone mines in the Fentons are extensively wrought'.[83] The mineral line which had been built by 1832 from the wharf on the Trent and Mersey Canal south of Whieldon's Grove to Longton ran through the Fentons and was linked with several of the collieries there by branch lines.[84] The only collieries now in operation in Fenton are the Glebe and Stafford Collieries, opened in the 1860's and 1870's respectively. The Stafford Colliery lies to the south-west in the open country near Sideway, but the Glebe Colliery dominates the centre of Fenton with its tips.

The mines on the Fenton Park estate are known to have been worked for 150 years from 1728 by the owners and their tenants.[85] During the early part of this period it was probably the Fentons, then the owners of the estate, who were working there, with eighteen small coal and ironstone mines in operation by 1728.[86] Mining rights on the estate, including Yew Tree farm, had been let to Jeremiah Smith of Great Fenton by the second half of the century[87] and in 1790 were leased to the Fenton Park Company; this consisted mainly of potters, including Josiah Spode and John Harrison.[88] A 30-year lease was granted to a similar group, including Spode, Wolfe and Minton, in 1813.[89] The Fenton Park Colliery was evidently the most notable in Fenton c. 1840 when Ward singled it out for special mention; he also described it as situated 'on and about a commanding eminence, once the pure and peaceful domicile of their [the owners'] ancestry but now the black and noisy seat of Cyclopean labours'. William Taylor Copeland was an important member in the company at this time.[90] There were then eleven pits in operation, employing about 250 men.[91] An adver-

tisement of 1850 offering the lease of the coal and ironstone mines under the Fenton Park estate specified the area as 197 acres, consisting of The Patches, Yew Tree, and Fenton Park farms.[92] Various companies continued to run the colliery, including one of the early 1870's formed by Lawrence Armitsted,[93] and shortly afterwards it was being operated jointly with a neighbouring colliery known as the Victoria.[94] Work had ceased at this new colliery by 1877,[95] and the Fenton Park Colliery itself was closed about two years later.[96] The Broadfield Colliery to the south, in existence by 1832 and closed in the mid-1860's, was evidently worked in conjunction with the Fenton Park Colliery for part at least of this period.[97]

In 1695 Richard Nicholls of Fenton Culvert leased several coal mines to William James of Ashbourne for 99 years. These mines included one in the Ash seam under closes of land in Fenton Culvert called Doles Meadow, the Dolesbank, and the Doles as well as mines on the Woodhouse estate in Longton. James's executors conveyed this lease to Obadiah Lane of Normacot Grange in 1703, and in 1713 Lane's son and heir Nathaniel of Longton Hall entered into partnership with Stephen Wood of the Ash to work all the mines specified in the lease. Lane conveyed, or mortgaged, his share of the mines to Francis Parrott of Talke and John Bourne of Newcastle in 1720, and Parrott assigned his interest to Bourne four years later.[98] This activity was presumably in the Pool Dole area in Fenton where there was mining in the last decade of the 18th century.[99] A Pool Dole Colliery was being worked by William Hulse between the early 1850's and at least the late 1860's.[1] In 1877 Goddard and Sons were mining coal and ironstone there,[2] but the colliery was evidently closed soon afterwards.

John Smith of Golden Hill, Fenton, granted a 22-year lease of mines on Golden Hill and Fieldswood farms in Fenton to Josiah Spode in 1802[3] and was himself mining in the area in 1818.[4] The pits were evidently in the hands of William Hanbury Sparrow between the late 1820's and mid-1850's.[5] The Goddards, who subsequently took over the rest of Sparrow's mines in Fenton (see below), were working the Golden Hill Colliery from 1854 until at least 1872[6] but had suspended operations there by 1877.[7] The Calfcroft Colliery to the south-west of the Golden Hill Colliery in the mid-1870's[8] may have been run in conjunction with it.

80 W.S.L., D. 1788, P. 56, B. 19; P. 66, B.1. It was for Thos. Broade of Fenton Vivian that Jas. Brindley constructed a new 'fire-engine for draining water out of mines' in 1756 or 1757: A. R. L. Saul, 'James Brindley' (T.N.S.F.C. lxxiii), 57. 81 See p. 237.
82 Yates, Map of Staffs. (1775, 1799). A Mr. Warburton of Fenton Low was working the Ash seam somewhere in the area in 1762: W.S.L., D. 1788, P. 56, B. 19.
83 Ward, Stoke, 554.
84 Hargreaves, Map of Staffs. Potteries.
85 For the estate see p. 213.
86 W.S.L., D. 1788, F. 1; P. 25, B. 3.
87 Ibid. F. 1; P. 12, B. 2; P. 56, B. 19.
88 Ibid. P. 56, B. 19; P. 66, B. 1. 89 Ibid. P. 66, B. 1.
90 Ward, Stoke, 554. For a dispute between the Co. and the owners in the 1830's see W.S.L., D. 1788, vol. 142.
91 2nd Rep. Com. Employment of Children [431], p. c44, H.C. (1843), xiv. 92 S.R.O., D. 321/M/B/92.
93 W.S.L., D. 1788, P. 58, B. 12; P. 66, B. 2 and 6; P.O. Dir. Staffs. (1860, 1868, 1872); Slater's Com. Dir. (1862); Jones's Potteries Dir. (1864); Keates and Ford's Potteries Dir. (1865–6, 1867); Keates's Potteries Dir. (1873–4).
94 Keates's Potteries Dir. (1875–6); P.O. Dir. Staffs.

(1876); O.S. Map 6" Staffs. xviii NW. (1890).
95 Rep. Insp. Mines, 1877 [C. 2003], p. 31, H.C. (1878), xx.
96 It occurs in 1877 (ibid.) and in Keates's Potteries Dir. (1879) but not in Kelly's Dir. Staffs. (1880).
97 Hargreaves, Map of Staffs. Potteries; Illus. Lond. News, 1 July 1843, pp. 14–15 (copy in H.R.L.); Rep. Insp. Mines [1994], p. 107, H.C. (1854–5), xv; Jones's Potteries Dir. (1864).
98 W.S.L., D. 788 (32), bdles. 10, 11. For the Longton mines see p. 243.
99 W.S.L., D. 1788, P. 56, B. 19; W.S.L. 39/49.
1 Slater's Dir. Birmingham Dist. (1852–3); Keates and Ford's Potteries Dir. (1876); P.O. Dir. Staffs. (1868). There is now a Hulse St. near Pool Dole Farm.
2 Rep. Insp. Mines, 1877, 31.
3 W.S.L., D. 1788, P. 66, B. 1.
4 Parson and Bradshaw, Dir. Staffs. (1818).
5 S.R.O., D. 321/M/B/64 and 304.
6 Diary of John Hackett Goddard 16 Oct., 11 Dec. 1854 (in poss. of Mr. J. V. Goddard, George L. Ashworth & Bros. Ltd., Hanley); P.O. Dir. Staffs. (1872).
7 Rep. Insp. Mines, 1877, 31.
8 O.S. Map 6" Staffs. xviii NW. (1890).

The Oldfield Colliery was run by William Hanbury Sparrow probably from *c.* 1826 when he opened the nearby Lane End Ironworks.[9] By 1868 the colliery had passed with the ironworks to the Goddards[10] and by the early 1880's was evidently in the hands of Balfour and Company.[11] By 1889 it was being run by the Lane End Works Ltd.,[12] and part of it was closed two years later.[13] It passed subsequently to the Oldfield Colliery Company who, though they were employing 285 men below ground there and 63 above in 1896, closed it in September of that year.[14]

By 1841 Ralph Handley, an iron-master, had a colliery in Duke Street[15] which was known as the Railway Colliery by 1857.[16] It was in the hands of his executors in 1862[17] and evidently ceased to operate about this time.

Of the two Fenton collieries now in existence, the Glebe had been opened by John Challinor and Company by 1868 and remained in their hands until the end of the century when it passed to John Heath and Company.[18] By this time operations were expanding rapidly: 119 men were employed below ground there and 62 above in 1895, 174 and 87 in 1896, and 209 and 94 in 1902.[19] In 1957 400 were employed below ground and 130 above.[20] The Stafford Colliery and Ironworks at Great Fenton was opened about the mid-1870's by the Great Fenton Iron and Coal Company (later the Stafford Coal and Iron Company), largely the creation of the Duke of Sutherland and Messrs. Pender, Charles Homer, and John Bourne, all four of whom were commemorated in the names of the pits at the colliery.[21] There were three pits in operation by 1884, with a fourth being sunk, and five pits by 1891; by 1902 these were employing 1,383 men below ground and 309 above.[22] The three pits in operation in 1957 employed 900 men below ground and 310 above.[23] The Sutherland Pit (3,318 feet) is said to be the deepest in the country and there are still deeper seams below the present workings.[24]

IRON-WORKING. Reference has been made already to the mining of ironstone at many of the collieries in Fenton. In many cases the stone was smelted on the spot. Thus Ralph Handley, who was working the colliery in Duke Street by 1841, was also an ironmaster. At the Foley and Oldfield collieries there were furnaces in the 1850's and 1860's, worked presumably as an adjunct of William Sparrow's Lane End Ironworks nearby;[25] the Sparrow mines and ironworks passed to the Goddards in the late 1860's. The Fenton Park coal and ironstone mines were run at least during the 1860's and early 1870's in conjunction with an ironworks there which then had two furnaces in blast.[26] The present Stafford Colliery and Ironworks at Great Fenton has been engaged in smelting as well as mining from the time of its opening in the mid-1870's; there were two blast furnaces in operation there by 1884, and in 1892 it was described as producing all kinds of pig-iron.[27]

The furnace at Fenton Low opened by Thompson and Massie *c.* 1830 does not appear to have been worked in conjunction with any colliery. It evidently ceased operations *c.* 1840.[28]

OTHER INDUSTRIES. There was a brickworks at Trenthay Sough (presumably in the north-western part of the area)[29] on the Fletcher estate by 1783; between late April and early October that year 266,362 bricks were produced 'for Earl Gower's use'.[30] There was one brickworks in Fenton in 1818, at Lane Delph,[31] but by the middle of the century there were four such works in Fenton.[32] By the early 1890's there were six brick- and tile-makers there.[33] In 1959 bricks were made by D. Duddell Ltd. at the Oldfield Brick and Marl Works and by J. Hewitt and Sons (Fenton) Ltd. who also had a quarry at Fenton Park.[34]

The North Staffordshire Railway Company's locomotive works running south from City Road developed out of the repair and maintenance sheds opened in 1848.[35] At first locomotives were supplied to the company by outside firms, but in 1868 the company's own works began to produce engines.[36] The works was extended before the end of the century and again in the early part of the 20th century to include the production of carriages and wagons.[37] It ceased to be used for this purpose *c.* 1923[38] and the buildings are now (1960) divided between the Mid-

[9] S.R.O., D. 321/M/B/30, 36, 304; Ward, *Stoke*, 573; *Rep. Insp. Mines* [2132], p. 101, H.C. (1856), xviii; *Rep. Insp. Mines* [2433], p. 61, H.C. (1857–8), xxxii; see p. 245.
[10] *P.O. Dir. Staffs.* (1868).
[11] *Keates's Potteries Dir.* (1882).
[12] *Rep. Insp. Mines N. Staffs. 1889* [C. 6015], p. 45, H.C. (1890), xxiii.
[13] Ibid. *1891* [C. 6625], p. 25, H.C. (1892), xxiii.
[14] Ibid. *1894* [C. 7667], p. 56, H.C. (1895), xxii; *1896* [C. 8450], p. 58, H.C. (1897), xx.
[15] *Pigot's Nat. Com. Dir.* (1841); Ward, *Stoke*, 573.
[16] *Rep. Insp. Mines, 1857*, 60.
[17] *Slater's Com. Dir.* (1862).
[18] *P.O. Dir. Staffs.* (1868); *Kelly's Dir. Staffs.* (1896, 1900).
[19] *Rep. Insp. Mines N. Staffs. 1895* [C. 8074], p. 56, H.C. (1896), xxii; *1896*, 56; *Rep. Insp. Mines Stafford, 1902* [Cd. 1590], p. 267, H.C. (1903), xv.
[20] *Guide to the Coalfields* (1960).
[21] *Staffs. Advertiser*, 11 Nov. 1893; *Keates's Potteries Dir.* (1875–6); *Rep. Insp. Mines N. Staffs. 1890* [C. 6346], p. 29, H.C. (1891), xxii; *Trans. N. Staffs. Inst. Mining Engineers* (1884–5), 302–4.
[22] *Trans. N. Staffs. Inst. Mining Engineers* (1884–5), 303, 304; *Rep. Insp. Mines N. Staffs. 1891*, 45; *Rep. Insp. Mines Stafford, 1902*, 267.
[23] *Guide to the Coalfields* (1960).
[24] Warrilow, *Stoke*, 263.

[25] S.R.O., D. 321/M/B/32 and 44; see p. 245. In 1825 Messrs. Sparrow were also running the Foley Limeworks (S.R.O., D. 321/M/B/102), which was in existence by 1794: W.S.L. 39/42.
[26] *Slater's Com. Dir.* (1862); *Jones's Potteries Dir.* (1864); *Keates and Ford's Potteries Dir.* (1865–6, 1867); *P.O. Dir. Staffs.* (1868); S. Griffiths, *Blast Furnaces of Gt. Brit. 1862* (copy in S.R.O., D. 321/M/B/22); S. Griffiths, *Iron Trade of Gt. Brit.* (1873), 256. A disused ironworks near Fenton Park Farm is shown on O.S. Map 6″ Staffs. xviii NW. (1890, surveyed in the later 1870's).
[27] *Keates's Potteries Dir.* (1875–6); *Trans. N. Staffs. Inst. Mining Engineers* (1884–5), 303; *Kelly's Dir. Staffs.* (1892).
[28] Ward, *Stoke*, 574; *Pigot's Nat. Com. Dir.* (1841).
[29] The Trent Hay estate in Shelton township (see p. 153) lay NW. of Fenton.
[30] W.S.L., D. 1788, P. 12, B. 2.
[31] Parson and Bradshaw, *Dir. Staffs.* (1818).
[32] White, *Dir. Staffs.* (1851).
[33] *Keates's Potteries Dir.* (1892–3). There was a brickworks at the Stafford Colliery and Ironworks, Gt. Fenton, in 1884: *Trans. N. Staffs. Inst. Mining Engineers* (1884–5), 303.
[34] *Stoke-on-Trent Classified Telephone Dir.* (Dec. 1959).
[35] See p. 209.
[36] 'Manifold', *N. Staffs. Rlwy.* 58, 90.
[37] O.S. Map 6″ Staffs. xviii NW. (1890, 1900, 1925).
[38] Local inf.

land Carton Works of Board Products Ltd., and the North Staffordshire Steel Foundry of Robert Hyde and Son. The California Engineering Works to the south, in the hands of Hartley, Arnoux and Fanning by 1884, was producing locomotives by 1892.[39] By 1900 the works had passed to Kerr, Stuart and Company who continued in occupation until the late 1920's; they were still supplying the North Staffordshire Railway in 1919.[40] The buildings are now (1960) divided between Doulton Sanitary Potteries Ltd., the Brookfield Foundry and Engineering Company, and Wagon Repairs Ltd.

SOCIAL LIFE. Fenton Mechanics' Institute was founded in 1839 under the influence of the Masons of Lane Delph and their partner Samuel Bayliss Faraday. It then attracted 'a good audience of serious-minded workmen'. It did not, however, flourish and had ceased to exist by 1850.[41]

Fenton Athenaeum was opened in 1853.[42] It was still in use in 1868[43] but had been closed by 1873 when the buildings became the offices of the Fenton Board of Health.[44] In 1889 William Meath Baker adapted the building for use as an Art School;[45] it is now (1960) occupied by the District Bank.

Fenton Free Library was built in 1906 in Baker Street at a cost of £5,300 which was contributed by Andrew Carnegie, the site being given by William Meath Baker. By 1912 it had a lending library of nearly 5,500 volumes and a reference library of about 600 volumes.[46]

LONGTON

LONGTON, which lies in the south-east of the Potteries area, was a municipal borough on the formation of the county borough of Stoke-on-Trent in 1910. As incorporated in 1865 the borough of Longton consisted of the townships of Lane End and Longton[1] but was subsequently extended in 1883 and 1884 to include the areas of East Vale, taken from Caverswall parish, Normacot, taken from Stone parish, and Florence with Dresden, taken from Trentham parish.[2] The earlier history of these last three areas is reserved for treatment in later volumes, but their development as suburbs of Longton will be covered in this article.

The area covered by the townships of Lane End and Longton was roughly 1,000 acres[3] and consisted of three tongues of land radiating from the town of Longton. The largest tongue, about a mile wide and tapering to roughly 440 yards at its south-westerly point, stretched westwards for 3 miles south of Fenton to the Chitlings Brook just beyond the present railway line from Stoke to London. The other two extended north and east; the northerly tongue, just over ½ mile in width, ran for a mile on both sides of the road to Adderley Green and Caverswall, the natural boundary on the east being the Cockster Brook, and the easterly tongue, ¼ mile in width, extended for a mile and a half on both sides of the road to Uttoxeter.[4]

The area, which lies on the edge of the moorlands, is one of low but steep hills and is cut by two valleys. The land drops from an escarpment in the north, called Sandford Hill, to the larger of these valleys, about ½ mile in width. The country rises again on the south to about 450 ft. at Swingle Hill.[5] The second and lesser valley divides this hill from the high ground in the west of the area.[6] The Anchor Brook which rises in the grounds of Park Hall in Caverswall parish flows through the larger of the two valleys, although it is now largely built over. West of the town centre it is joined by a small tributary which flows down from the Golden Hill part of Fenton and formed the boundary between Longton and Fenton in that area. The Anchor Brook then changes its name to the Cockster Brook which likewise formed the boundary between Longton and Fenton as far as the point where it turns south to flow through the second valley.[7] A third brook, the Furnace Brook, was described c. 1840 as rising 'from several powerful springs in the hamlet of Normicot which gush from under the sandstone formation of Meir Heath',[8] and at that date it formed extensive ornamental pools at the edge of the Longton Hall grounds.[9] Now only a sluggish stream, it flows west for some way and joins the Cockster Brook east of Longton Hall. Here the two form the Longton Brook which flows west along the former south-western boundary of Longton township into Trentham parish.

The wider of the two valleys is the route of a Roman road from Derby[10] and has long been one of the main ways of access into North Staffordshire from Derbyshire. It was on this road, roughly at the point where the Anchor Brook and the stream from Goldenhill meet, that the hamlet of Lane End or

[39] Kelly's Dir. Staffs. (1884, 1892); local inf.
[40] Kelly's Dir. Staffs. (1900, 1928); 'Manifold', N. Staffs. Rlwy. 147.
[41] R. G. Haggar, Some Adult Educ. Institutions in N. Staffs. 6.
[42] R. G. Haggar, A Cent. of Art Educ. in the Potteries, 29. For a description of the building see p. 210.
[43] P.O. Dir. Staffs. (1868).
[44] See p. 215.
[45] Haggar, Cent. of Art Educ. 28.
[46] Kelly's Dir. Staffs. (1912).
[1] See p. 235.
[2] S.R.O., D. 593, Longton Boro. Extension Map; see p. 235.
[3] White, Dir. Staffs. (1851).

[4] S.R.O., Q/AH, Map of Boro. of Longton main rds., 1879 (copy of map probably made about the time of the formation of the borough in 1865); Lich. Dioc. Regy., Tithe Maps and Appt., Stoke-upon-Trent (Longton).
[5] The name Swingle Hill occurs on O.S. Map 6" Staffs. xviii SW. (1925).
[6] This includes Mole Cop, probably an ancient burial site, on the Longton side of the former boundary with Fenton: see p. 205.
[7] These streams are clearly shown on O.S. Map 6" Staffs. xviii (1889, 1890).
[8] Ward, Stoke, 558-9.
[9] H. Mus., Heathcote papers, xix, 6, maps of lands of Ric. Edensor Heathcote in Longton.
[10] See p. 228.

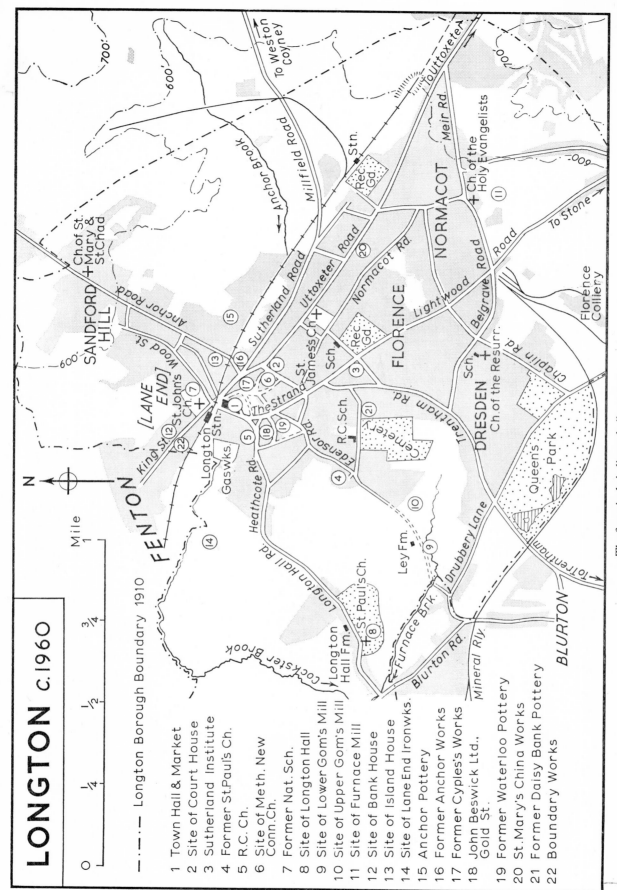

LONGTON c.1960

Mile
0   ¼   ½   ¾   1

N

STAFF. VIII

----- Longton Borough Boundary 1910

1 Town Hall & Market
2 Site of Court House
3 Sutherland Institute
4 Former St.Paul's Ch.
5 R.C. Ch.
6 Site of Meth. New Conn.Ch.
7 Former Nat. Sch.
8 Site of Longton Hall
9 Site of Lower Gom's Mill
10 Site of Upper Gom's Mill
11 Site of Furnace Mill
12 Site of Bank House
13 Site of Island House
14 Site of Lane End Ironwks.
15 Anchor Pottery
16 Former Anchor Works
17 Former Cyples's Works
18 John Beswick Ltd., Gold St.
19 Former Waterloo Pottery
20 St.Mary's China Works
21 Former Daisy Bank Pottery
22 Boundary Works

FENTON [LANE END]

SANDFORD HILL

Ch.of St. Mary & St.Chad

Anchor Road

Wood St.

King St.

Longton Stn.

Gas Wks.

Heathcote Rd.

Longton Hall Rd.

Cockster Brook

St.Paul's Ch.

Longton Hall Fm.

The Strand

St. James's Ch.

Sutherland Road

Millfield Road

Anchor Brook

Ch.of St.

To Weston Coyney

Stn.

Rec. Gd.

Uttoxeter Road

Normacot Rd.

Normacot Road

To Uttoxeter

Meir Rd.

NORMACOT

Ch. of the Holy Evangelists

To Stone

FLORENCE

Lightwood

Belgrave Road

Chaplin Rd.

DRESDEN

Ch. of the Resurr.

Sch.

R.C. Sch.

Cemetery

Trentham Rd.

Edensor Rd.

Rec. Gd.

Queen's Park

To Trentham

Ley Fm.

Furnace Brk.

Drubbery Lane

Blurton Rd.

Mineral Rly.

BLURTON

Florence Colliery

The fine stipple indicates built-up areas.

225

G g

Meare Lane End grew up in the late 17th century[11] under the influence of coal and ironstone mining and ironworking.[12] In 1666 13 houses in Longton were chargeable to Hearth Tax and 12 in Meare Lane End.[13] Meare Lane End was mentioned c. 1680 by Gregory King who noted that there were 5 or 6 houses in Longton itself.[14] Tracks led south-eastward from Meare Lane End to Stone and northward over Sandford Hill to Hanley, Adderley Green, Leek, and the north-east of the county by the 18th century.[15] The turnpiking of the Newcastle to Uttoxeter road under an Act of 1759, of the road to Stone under an Act of 1771, and of the road to Adderley Green under an Act of 1813 greatly facilitated the growth of Lane End.[16] By 1775 there was a nucleus of houses at the junction of the roads and for a short distance along these three roads and along the road to Longton Hall which joined the Stone road just south of the centre of the village. There were in addition a number of scattered houses and numerous coal pits between the Uttoxeter road (then called Meer Lane) and the Stone road.[17] In 1784 Lane End was still small enough to be called a village,[18] although it was fast developing as a community. The first school was built c. 1763[19] and the first church in 1762,[20] and in 1789 the market-square (now Times Square) was laid out at the junction of the Uttoxeter and the Stone roads.[21] By the end of the century there was a network of streets in the centre of the town forming a built-up area bounded by Market Lane (now Transport Lane), the Stone road, the Uttoxeter road, and Commerce Street; the streets in this central area are now called Cornhill Passage, St. Martin's Lane, Cyples Lane, Kingcross Street, and Chancery Lane. By then, also, both sides of the Uttoxeter road had been built up for about half a mile from the town centre.[22] In 1794 a second market-square (later Union Square) was laid out at the north end of Commerce Street.[23]

In the early 19th century Lane End was noted 'for the great irregularity in the position of its buildings of every size and sort from the respectable residence of the manufacturer to the mud and saggar hovel of the pauper scattered over a wide extent of territory'.[24] In the late 1830's the name of the town was changed in popular usage from Lane End to Longton, 'the name "Lane End" being rather offensive to modern ears polite, as conveying an idea of meanness which no longer answered to the respectability of the place'.[25] It was not officially altered until 1848 after the inhabitants had in that year petitioned that the name should be altered to Longton for postal and governmental purposes since the name had frequently been used to denote the town in official documents[26]

During the century considerable changes took place in the centre of the town. Times Square had been enlarged by 1832,[27] and was altered further when the new market and town hall was erected in 1844 extending back to Market Lane (now Transport Lane); it was again altered in 1863 when the present town hall and covered market were built extending back to Market Lane and also west to Stafford Street (now The Strand).[28] In 1832, also, there was a square known as Dragon Square at the junction of the present Cyples Lane, Kingcross Street, and Chancery Lane.[29] This had been partially built over on the Chancery Lane side by 1865[30] and had become merely a road junction by the late 1870's.[31] In 1941 the buildings in the area behind the town hall and market as far back as Kingcross Street were demolished and the ground used for a bus station.[32] The railway station, just west of Times Square, was built in 1848,[33] the line crossing the north end of the square on an iron viaduct. No other major alterations to the layout of the centre of Longton have taken place, although most of the individual buildings in the area were replaced in the later 19th century.

With the rapid expansion of the pottery, coal, and iron industries, early in the 19th century, the town grew quickly. In the area between the town centre and the eastern boundary streets were laid out connecting the Uttoxeter road and the Stone road. Buildings erected along them, though still intermittent and mainly in the Uttoxeter road area c. 1820,[34] had by 1832 become more concentrated.[35] By c. 1865 the area between High Street (the Uttoxeter road, formerly known as Meer Lane) and the stretch of Furnace Road, now known as Normacot Road, had been solidly built up with pottery works and terraced housing as far east as Lovatt (now Calverley) Street.[36] The area between Furnace Road and the southern boundary of the borough was also by this time solidly built up with terraced housing, except for brick-fields and works.[37] By the late 1870's the brick-works opposite St. James's churchyard had been replaced by terraced houses.[38] There were, by c. 1865, allotments south of Furnace Road adjoining the eastern boundary of the borough[39] and these still existed in the late 1870's.[40] The area known as Mount Pleasant, around the present Lawley Street, had also been built up with terraced cottages and potworks by c. 1865.[41] The cottage

[11] Lane End, then called Meare Lane End, occurs on R. Plot, *Map of Staffs.* (1682).
[12] See pp. 243, 244.
[13] *S.H.C.* 1921, 163–4.
[14] Ibid. 1919, 259.
[15] W. Yates, *Map of Staffs.* (1775) reproduced facing p. 4.
[16] See p. 228.
[17] Yates, *Map of Staffs.*
[18] John Wesley, *Journal,* 29 Mar. 1784.
[19] See p. 323.
[20] See p. 233.
[21] White, *Dir. Staffs.* (1834). C. and J. Greenwood, *Map of Staffs.* (1820), shows the market-sq.
[22] Yates, *Map of Staffs.* (1799).
[23] White, *Dir. Staffs.* (1834).
[24] S. Shaw, *Staffs. Potteries,* 72–73.
[25] Ward, *Stoke,* 555.
[26] H.O. 45/OS.8755/1; H.R.L., copy of letter 14 Aug.

1848 authorizing change of name.
[27] T. Hargreaves, *Map of Staffs. Potteries and Newcastle* (1832).
[28] See p. 237.
[29] Hargreaves, *Map of Staffs. Potteries.*
[30] S.R.O., Q/AH, Longton Main Rds. Map. An earthenware manufactory and weighing machine had been built on the site of the former chapel there, closing a road which led from the square to Market Lane.
[31] S.R.O., D. 593, Longton Boro. Extension Map.
[32] Ex inf. City Surveyor (1960).
[33] See p. 228.
[34] Greenwood, *Map of Staffs.*
[35] Hargreaves, *Map of Staffs. Potteries.*
[36] S.R.O., Q/AH, Longton Main Rds. Map.
[37] Ibid.
[38] S.R.O., D. 593, Longton Boro. Extension Map.
[39] S.R.O., Q/AH, Longton Main Rds. Map.
[40] S.R.O., D. 593, Longton Boro. Extension Map.
[41] S.R.O., Q/AH, Longton Main Rds. Map.

hospital and Mount Pleasant mission church were established in Mount Pleasant by 1868.[42] In the present century there has been much demolition in this area, partly in consequence of an underground fire c. 1916, which made many of the houses unsafe,[43] and also for the extension of the factory of Ridgway Potteries Ltd., built on part of the land c. 1944.[44]

East Vale, lying north of the North Staffordshire railway line and east of the Adderley Green road, had been built up with terraced cottages around Goddard and Ford Streets by the late 1870's.[45] By this date streets had been laid out in building plots north and east of this area[46] but these have not been built on.

To the south of Longton, development took place in the later 19th century in the areas known as Florence, Dresden, and Normacot. The area to which the name Florence was given,[47] extending from the Uttoxeter road to Trentham road and belonging to the Duke of Sutherland, was laid out in building plots by 1867.[48] By the late 1870's the southern part of this piece of land, including Kildare, Blantyre, Howard, Ronald, and Leveson Streets, was built up as far as Leveson Street with terraced houses[49] with the exception of Trentham Road where larger detached and semi-detached houses had been built, some before 1867.[50] By 1898 the northern part of Florence had also been built up.[51]

The district to which the name Dresden was given, lying south of Longton borough and south of the road from Normacot to Trentham, was developed by the Longton Building Society[52] by the late 1870's.[53] Most of the streets consist of terraced houses but in Cocknage Road larger detached and semi-detached houses were built. In the area between Park Avenue and the borough boundary, Queen's Park, consisting of 45 acres,[54] given by the Duke of Sutherland to commemorate Queen Victoria's Jubilee,[55] was laid out in 1887 and opened the following year.[56]

Normacot, comprising the triangle of land between the Uttoxeter road, Upper Normacot Road, and Meir Road, lying east of Longton, had been laid out in building plots for the Duke of Sutherland by 1875[57] and much of it built up by the late 1870's.[58] Further houses had been built by 1898.[59] Land between Normacot and Florence was also laid out in building plots for the Duke of Sutherland in 1864,[60] but the building plan was not carried out for some years, the eastern end of the area being built up in the last quarter of the century.[61]

The Greendock area south-west of the town was already developing c. 1820, probably because of its proximity to collieries, along the present Heathcote Road, Edensor Road, and Greendock Street.[62] This development had become more concentrated by 1832.[63] Farther south, houses had also been built by 1820 at Daisy Bank, where a pottery works had been established in the late 1770's.[64] More building took place in the Edensor area between Heathcote and Trentham Roads between 1832 and c. 1865, and also farther east at Daisy Bank where more pottery works and a brick-works had also been established. North of Heathcote Road rows of terraced cottages were built in this period along the line of Marsh Street (now Griffin Street) and Gregory Street running between Heathcote and Foley Roads and around Weston Place at the junction of these two roads.[65] Further streets of terraced cottages had been built by the late 1870's in the area around Gregory Street and Marsh Street.[66] Considerable demolition of houses has taken place in recent years and the terraced cottages in the Greendock area are gradually being pulled down and replaced by small terraces of council houses.

North of the town there was some building along the line of the new road to Adderley Green by 1832 but this was still concentrated along the old road (Wood Street) and also along Caroline Street, which runs parallel to and east of Wood Street.[67] The main road from Uttoxeter to Stoke was built up by 1832 as far as the Fenton boundary.[68] Between 1832 and c. 1865 new building took place in the Ashground mining area to the north of the road. Ashwood, joining Wood Street by the parsonage, was laid out; detached houses with gardens were built on its south side at the east end and terraced houses on the north side at its west end. Farther north and running off the Adderley Green road (now Anchor Road) in a westerly direction Albert Street, Edgefield Road, and Heathcote Street had been laid out, but no houses had been built there.[69] Just south of these, east of and parallel to the Adderley Green road, Pitt Street (now Walpole Street) and Lord Street (now Bartlem Street) had also been laid out but not built up. All these streets had been partially built up with terraced houses by 1879.[70] In Wood Street prefabricated houses were erected on cleared areas after the Second World War.

In 1666 there were 13 persons in Longton and 12 in Lane End chargeable to Hearth Tax.[71] In 1811 the population was 4,930[72] and during the 19th century the population figures show a continued rise: 1821, 7,100;[73] 1851, 15,149;[74] 1871, 19,748.[75] In 1891 the figure was 34,327, which included the added areas

[42] See pp. 234, 237.
[43] Local inf.
[44] Local inf.
[45] S.R.O., D. 593, Longton Boro. Extension Map.
[46] Ibid.
[47] Named after the eldest dau. of the 3rd duke: *Illus. London News*, 23 Jan. 1875; Burke, *Peerage* (1959), 2179.
[48] S.R.O., D. 593, plan of property adjoining the town of Longton and belonging to the Duke of Sutherland, 1867.
[49] Ibid. Longton Boro. Extension Map.
[50] Ibid. plan of property adjoining Longton and belonging to Duke of Sutherland, 1867.
[51] O.S. Map 6" Staffs. xviii SW. (1901).
[52] *P.O. Dir. Staffs.* (1872).
[53] S.R.O., D. 593, Longton Boro. Extension Map.
[54] Warrillow, *Stoke*, 375.
[55] Ibid.
[56] Ibid. 375, 377; *Stoke Official Handbk.* (1960).
[57] S.R.O., D. 593, plan of property adjoining Longton and belonging to Duke of Sutherland, 1875.
[58] Ibid., Longton Boro. Extension Map.
[59] O.S. Map 6" Staffs. xviii SE. (1901).
[60] S.R.O., D. 593, plan of land adjoining Longton laid out for the Duke of Sutherland, 1864.
[61] Ibid., Longton Boro. Extension Map; O.S. Map 6" Staffs. xviii SE. (1901).
[62] Greenwood, *Map of Staffs.*
[63] Hargreaves, *Map of Staffs. Potteries.*
[64] Greenwood, *Map of Staffs.*; see p. 239.
[65] S.R.O., Q/AH, Longton Main Rds. Map.
[66] S.R.O., D. 593, Longton Boro. Extension Map.
[67] Hargreaves, *Map of Staffs. Potteries.*   [68] Ibid.
[69] S.R.O., Q/AH, Longton Main Rds. Map.
[70] S.R.O., D. 593, Longton Boro. Extension Map.
[71] *S.H.C.* 1921, 163–4.
[72] *Census*, 1811, Staffs.   [73] Ibid. 1821.
[74] Ibid. 1851.   [75] Ibid. 1871.

of East Vale, Dresden, Florence, and part of Normacot.[76] In 1901 the population of the borough was 38,815.[77] The population of the same area in 1911 was 37,479,[78] and in 1921, 37,812.[79]

Of the three roads at the junction of which Longton developed, at least two are ancient routes. The road running through Longton from Uttoxeter was used during the Roman occupation.[80] It was probably used continuously thereafter, occurring again as a highway in 13th-century records.[81] It was turnpiked under an Act of 1759.[82] It was disturnpiked in 1875 and declared a highway and a county responsibility under the Highways and Locomotives (Amendment) Act of 1878.[83] The road to Stone occurs in the early 13th century.[84] This was turnpiked under an Act of 1771.[85] The road to Adderley Green followed the course of Wood Street originally. Under an Act of 1813 a new turnpike road to Adderley Green, the present Anchor Road, was built.[86] This road was disturnpiked in 1877[87] and declared a main road under the Highways and Locomotives Act of 1878. The road from Fenton to Blurton, turnpiked in 1778, was also disturnpiked in 1877 and made a main road under the 1878 Act.[88] The road from Meir to Trentham, turnpiked in 1771, runs across the southern part of Longton.[89] Three other roads in the borough, not previously turnpiked roads, were declared main roads and a county responsibility under the 1878 Act: the road from the town centre past Longton Hall which was said to be the most direct route to Heron Cross and Fenton from Longton; the road to Normacot, otherwise known as Furnace Road; and Sutherland Road, the most direct road from Longton to Wetley, Cheddleton, and Leek.[90]

By 1834 four coaches ran through Longton. Three ran daily from the Eagle Inn between Liverpool and London, Burslem and Birmingham, and Longton and Manchester, while the Newcastle to Derby coach ran three times a week stopping at the Crown and Anchor Inn.[91] By 1824 Longton was on the route of a local service between Hanley, Stafford, and Birmingham,[92] and by the middle of the century there was an omnibus service to Hanley and Burslem.[93] In 1881 the North Staffordshire Tramway Company opened a line from Stoke to Longton market-square.[94] A controlling interest in the company was acquired by the British Electric Traction Company (later the Potteries Electric Traction

Company) which electrified and extended the lines within the borough between 1899 and 1905.[95] As in other parts of the Potteries, buses began to operate from 1914, and between 1926 and 1928 replaced the tramway service.[96]

By 1790 Longton had its own postmaster.[97] The town was served by a horse-post and a foot-post from Newcastle from 1835 until the establishment of the head post-office for the Potteries at Stoke in 1854.[98]

A railway line extending from the Trent and Mersey Canal near Stoke to Longton had been built to carry goods by 1832. It was still in use in the late 1870's.[99] On the construction of the North Staffordshire Railway's line from Stoke to Uttoxeter and Burton in 1848, a station was opened at Longton.[1] An omnibus ran twice daily from the station and the Union Hotel to Hanley and Burslem by 1851[2] and to Stoke by 1854.[3] This service continued until at least 1860.[4] Normacot Station was opened in 1882.[5] In 1875 a single-track mineral line was opened by the North Staffordshire Railway from this line at Millfield Junction through Adderley Green to the line from Stoke to Biddulph and Leek south-west of Bucknall. It became a light railway for passenger traffic early in the 20th century but by the mid-1920's was once more a mineral line only.[6] It is now broken into two unconnected parts near Adderley Green. By the late 1870's a mineral line had been built from the Florence Colliery, opened c. 1875, to the main line south from Stoke near Trentham.[7]

BUILDINGS. There are now few buildings in Longton, other than early pottery works, which date from before the middle of the 19th century. Longton Court House, earlier known as the Union Market Hall or the Old Town Hall, survived until 1950.[8] It was built, apparently in 1814, on land at the junction of Market Street and Commerce Street, and was originally 'a handsome brick structure supported by an arched basement'.[9] At the time of its demolition in 1950 it was a two-storied building with a front of five bays, having a central Venetian window beneath a small pediment. The ground floor arches had been filled in and the walls faced with stucco,[10] alterations dating probably from 1856. The site is now occupied by a small public garden. The present town hall and market, fronting upon Times Square, replaced an earlier building in 1863[11] when the site was extended

[76] Census, 1891, Staffs.
[77] Ibid. 1901.
[78] Ibid. 1911.
[79] Ibid. 1921.
[80] I. D. Margary, Roman Roads in Britain, ii. 41; see p. 208. Evidently the Roman road ran along the low ground to the N. of Uttoxeter Rd., the present Sutherland Rd. indicating part of its course through Longton.
[81] S.H.C. xi. 314–15, 322–3.
[82] Act for repairing rd. from Derby to Newcastle, 32 Geo. II, c. 60. The toll house was placed at Meir but under an Act of 1763 moved to Lane End: 3 Geo. III, c. 57.
[83] S.R.O., Q/AH, bdle. 3, and Longton Main Rds. Map; 41 & 42 Vic. c. 77.
[84] S.H.C. xi. 321.
[85] 11 Geo. III, c. 86.
[86] 53 Geo. III, c. 35 (local and personal).
[87] S.R.O., Q/AH, bdle. 3, and Longton Main Rds. Map.
[88] See p. 208.
[89] See n. 85 above.
[90] S.R.O., Q/AH, bdle. 3, and Longton Main Rds. Map.
[91] White, Dir. Staffs. (1834).

[92] See p. 146.
[93] See p. 146.
[94] Kelly's Dir. Staffs. (1884); S.R.O., Q/RUm 486, 619.
[95] Warrillow, Stoke, 69–75.
[96] Ibid. 76–78.
[97] Univ. Brit. Dir. (1791), iv. 111. The same man had a post-office in Anchor Lane by 1802: Allbut, Staffs. Pottery Dir. (1802).
[98] See p. 7.
[99] See p. 209.
[1] Ex inf. Brit. Rlwys., L.M.R.; see p. 209.
[2] White, Dir. Staffs. (1851).
[3] P.O. Dir. Staffs. (1854).
[4] Ibid. (1860).
[5] Ex inf. Brit. Rlwys., L.M.R.
[6] 'Manifold', N. Staffs. Rlwy. 55, 83; T.N.S.F.C. lxi. 136.
[7] O.S. Map 6" Staffs. xviii SW., SE. (1889); see p. 244.
[8] For the various uses to which it was put see p. 237.
[9] Ward, Stoke, 572; see p. 237.
[10] Warrillow, Stoke, 385, plates 10, 11.
[11] See p. 237.

FENTON: WHIELDON'S GROVE *c.* 1845

showing the line of the proposed railway; the road from Stoke to Longton crosses the left-hand side of the picture

LONGTON HALL

(demolished in 1939)

Children collecting coal-cart spillings in Wharf Street in the early 20th century

Former St. John's National School, built in 1822

LONGTON

to include all the ground between Times (formerly Market) Square, Transport (formerly Market) Lane, and The Strand (formerly Stafford Street).[12] Facing Times Square the Town Hall has a long two-storied front of blackened stone incorporating Classical features. The ground floor, which includes a central projecting portico of three bays, is occupied by part of the market; the upper story has blind openings decorated with carved panels and in the centre are Ionic pilasters surmounted by an entablature and pediment. The single-story covered market, which has suffered considerably from subsidence, occupies the rest of the large site behind the town hall and has stone façades in which arched entrances and shop fronts are incorporated. The Sutherland Institute in Lightwood Road (formerly Stone Road), erected in 1897–9 and designed by Wood and Hutchings of Tunstall and Burslem,[13] is a large red brick building, its principal front carrying a continuous terracotta frieze illustrating the pottery industry.

The former National school, built in 1822,[14] is a single-story brick building still standing in St. John's churchyard. The front has hood-moulds to the windows and a central gable below which is a dated tablet. Twin doorways with moulded brick jambs and pointed heads give access to separate school-rooms for boys and girls. Adjoining it on the south side and carrying a date tablet of 1829 is the infants' school, a replica in miniature of the 1822 building.

All the larger dwelling houses in the town dating from before Victorian times had disappeared by 1960. These included the Woodhouse, Island House, and St. John's Parsonage, all well to the north of the town-centre, and Bank House, lying immediately north of Church Street near the Fenton boundary.[15]

Until its demolition in 1939 the most important house in the area was Longton Hall, standing on rising ground two miles south-west of the town and overlooking the Furnace Brook. There was possibly a manor-house at Longton in the Middle Ages and certainly one by the early 17th century.[16] It may have been rebuilt on its present site by the Lane family after they had obtained a lease of the manor in 1702, but Longton Hall as it survived into the 20th century probably owed more to alterations carried out by John Edensor Heathcote about 1778.[17] He is known to have been planning extensive repairs in 1777 when he was employing a 'Mr. Gardner' as architect and was proposing to install a Wedgwood fireplace.[18] The architectural features of the exterior, as shown by surviving drawings and photographs, suggest a building largely remodelled about this time.[19] The house was of three stories and approximately square on plan with a wing extending to the north. On the south side were two projecting bays, rising to the full height of the house, while the west front was adorned with Ionic pilasters, an enriched frieze, and a central pediment.

A large block of stables and other outhouses is still in existence to the north-east of the former house. These may have been begun when the Lane family moved back to the hall in the 1760's,[20] but more probably originated with John Edensor Heathcote later in the 18th century. The Longton Hall porcelain manufactory is thought to have occupied the same site, the kilns standing at the south-west angle of the later stable block.[21] It is likely, therefore, that any buildings connected with the works had disappeared by the end of the 18th century, if not earlier. The existing outbuildings are of red brick and are mainly of two stories; they are arranged round three sides of a rectangular courtyard, its northern end closed by a screen wall having at its centre a water trough in an arched recess. Beyond the wall stands a separate cottage block with a central gable. It would appear that the south range, which has pedimented doorways on its south front and at one time contained a laundry and a brewhouse, was the first to be built. The outer wall of the west range is apparently contemporary,[22] but at some later date—probably between 1824 and 1827 when Richard Edensor Heathcote spent over £5,000 on additional buildings at Longton Hall—the west range was remodelled.[23] Work carried out at the same time seems to have included the levelling of the courtyard, which had formerly sloped towards the south,[24] as well as the erection of the east range and of the cottage block. Richard Heathcote also built the west lodge, a single-story stucco-faced cottage which still stands, and laid out the gardens.[25] A carriageway ran from the lodge through parkland in front of the hall and then in a wide sweep past an ornamental pool and through an Italian garden to the stables. The house was connected to the south-west angle of the stable block by an arcaded wall. Alterations and additions made between 1850 and 1865 included the screen wall at the north end of the stable court, a small coach-house at the south end, and probably an icehouse lying to the south of the other outbuildings.[26]

Longton Hall Lane Farm, lying on the north side of the road opposite Longton Hall stables, is an early-19th-century brick house with outbuildings of the same period. To the west is a cottage probably dating from the early 17th century, now surrounded by modern bungalows. It has been altered and partly brick-faced but one timber-framed wall remains exposed. The only other timber-framed building in the area appears to be Ley Farm which overlooks the Furnace Brook about 500 yards south-east of the Longton Hall site.[27] The house is T-shaped on plan with the upper rooms, lighted by dormer windows, occupying part of the roof space; the walls are faced with later brickwork and roughcast externally.

At the beginning of the 19th century Lane End (later known as Longton) appears to have been a settlement of irregular layout, covering a wide area but with many scattered houses serving individual

[12] See p. 226.
[13] *Staffs. Advertiser*, 28 Oct. 1899; see p. 246.
[14] See p. 324 and plate facing p. 229.
[15] See pp. 231, 232, 233, 240.
[16] See p. 230.
[17] See p. 230.
[18] Meteyard, *Wedgwood*, ii. 373–4; B. Watney, *Longton Hall Porcelain*, 9.
[19] W.S.L., Staffs. Views, vii. 48; see plate facing p. 228. For an estate map (c. 1850) see H. Mus., Heathcote papers, xix. 6.   [20] See p. 230.

[21] Watney, *Longton Hall Porcelain*, 19–20; see p. 239.
[22] Both S. and W. ranges were in existence by 1822: see H. Mus., Heathcote papers, iii. 1.
[23] Ibid. 12; xix. 1. Differences in brickwork indicate the extent of the alterations.
[24] The earlier surface was revealed by excavations (see n. 21); the S. range is built to the old level.
[25] The garden layout is shown on a map of c. 1850 (see n. 19) made after Richard's death.
[26] S.R.O., Q/AH, Longton Main Rds. Map.
[27] See p. 232.

potworks, ironstone mines, and coal pits. As the century proceeded the town became more solidly built-up and the earlier courts and terraces, hemmed in by later streets,[28] soon degenerated into slums. In the Edensor district, in John Street (now Calvin Street), in Locketts Lane, and in the area round St. James's Church conditions in the later 19th century were probably as bad as anywhere in the Potteries.[29] Even after the Second World War a square of thirteen houses at the junction of Normacot Road and Chelson Street was served by only one tap and one water-closet.[30] Two early-19th-century terraces which are still standing on the steeply sloping ground at Millfield, between Uttoxeter Road and Sutherland Road, probably represent some of the better housing of that period. These are built on the 'cottage' plan[31] with two rooms to each floor; back wings, where they exist, appear to be later additions. By 1960 nearly all the poorer housing in Longton had been demolished and the sites were either vacant or, as in the Edensor area, had been used for new streets of council houses.

MANOR. In 1212 an estate in Longton was held in chief in socage by Ranulph de Bevill at a rent of 5s. in succession to his father Ranulph.[32] By 1236 this estate had become part of Newcastle manor, and 40 days' castle-guard service had been added to the obligations of the tenant.[33] Between this date and 1250 a carucate and a virgate out of the estate had been alienated to 7 tenants, and in 1250 William de Bevill, Ranulph's son, granted 3 acres of arable, 1 acre of meadow, and the service due from Longton mill to Trentham Priory.[34] William, however, continued to owe the same service as though no alienation had taken place and in addition paid 9s. 8d. for the part alienated to laymen. Trentham Priory paid 2s. direct to the king for its share.[35] The estate which William retained is first described as the manor of *LONGTON* in the mid-13th century,[36] and the overlordship remained with the manor of Newcastle until at least 1650.[37]

By 1272 William had been succeeded by his son Robert de Bevill[38] who by 1292 was dead, a Ralph de Bevill holding Longton in that year.[39] Ralph had been succeeded by 1297 by a Roger de Bagenholt.[40]

Nothing further is known of the manor of Longton until 1591 when a John Hunt held an estate here.[41] At his death in 1600 the estate included a messuage and croft called the 'Hallecroft'.[42] John was succeeded by a son Thomas, then a minor.[43] In 1649 Thomas, described as an 'ironmonger', was declared bankrupt[44] and the manor of Longton was sold by the Bankruptcy Commissioners in 1650[45] to William Bedwell of 'Feevering' (? Feering), Essex, who in 1651 sold it to Richard Foley of Birmingham, also an ironmaster.[46] The latter died without issue c. 1680 and by will devised the manor of Longton to his uncle, John Foley of London.[47] John Foley died before 1690[48] and left the estate to Thomas Foley of Witley Court, Worcs., created Baron Foley of Kidderminster in 1712. The manor descended in the Foley family[49] until 1773 when it was sold to the Revd. Obadiah Lane, then lessee of the manor.[50]

In 1702 Lord Foley leased the manor to Obadiah Lane of Normacot Grange for 99 years or three lives.[51] Obadiah had been succeeded by 1709 by his son Nathaniel Lane[52] and he in 1720 by his son, the Revd. Obadiah Lane.[53] Obadiah Lane was living at the hall in July 1749.[54] He was still describing himself as of Longton in January 1752[55] but by August of that year had moved to Birmingham.[56] A porcelain works had, however, been established at the hall by 1749 or 1750 and continued until 1760.[57] Obadiah died in 1757,[58] and his son Obadiah acquired a new lease of the manor in 1758,[59] the year in which he became curate of Blurton in the adjoining parish of Trentham.[60] It is highly probable that after his father's death this Obadiah Lane was trying to resume possession of the hall[61] but the Lane family was not again living at the hall until the 1760's.[62] Obadiah Lane resigned the curacy of Blurton in 1772[63] and leased the hall in the same year to Thomas Griffin on an eleven-year lease determinable at the end of five years if the estate were sold.[64]

Lane bought the manor in 1773[65] and put the whole estate up for sale in 1774 or 1775.[66] The hall was sold with other lands c. 1775 to Thomas Fletcher,[67] who sold the hall itself to John Edensor Heathcote in 1778.[68] A year later Obadiah Lane died and the manor was sold in 1784 by the trustees under his will to Sir John Edensor Heathcote,[69] who had already purchased estates in Longton.[70] The

---

[28] Hargreaves, *Map of Staffs. Potteries*; O.S. Map 1/1,250 Staffs. xviii. 11. 7 (survey of 1875–8).
[29] Warrillow, *Stoke*, 320.   [30] Ibid.
[31] See p. 114.   [32] *Bk. of Fees*, 143; see p. 238.
[33] *Bk. of Fees*, 594.   [34] Ibid. 1185; *S.H.C.* xi. 318.
[35] *Bk. of Fees*, 1185. For the priory's estate see p. 232.
[36] *Bk. of Fees*, 1285.
[37] *S.H.C.* vi (1), 266; *Cal. Inq. p.m.* iii, pp. 288–90; C 142/298/58; D.L. 42/4/173*b*; E 317/Staffs./38/8; see p. 184.   [38] *S.H.C.* xi. 321.
[39] Ibid. vi (1), 266.
[40] *Cal. Inq. p.m.* iii, pp. 288–90.
[41] *S.H.C.* xvi. 111.   [42] C 142/287/11; C 142/298/58.
[43] Ibid.
[44] H. Mus., Heathcote papers, iii, unnumbered.
[45] Ibid.   [46] Ibid.   [47] Ibid.   [48] Ibid.
[49] Ibid.; *V.C.H. Worcs.* iv. 372–3; *Complete Peerage*, 'Foley of Kidderminster'.
[50] H. Mus., Heathcote papers, xix. 1.
[51] Ibid. iii, unnumbered.
[52] B. Watney, *Longton Hall Porcelain*, 7; his will was proved in Mar. 1708/9.
[53] Ibid. 8; H. Mus., Heathcote papers, xix, 1; Lichfield Joint Record Office, Lichfield Consistory Wills 1720 (dated 10 Dec. 1719, proved 6 Dec. 1720).
[54] His son, Jonathan, was christened then: *Stoke Par.*

Reg. (Staffs. Par. Reg. Soc.), iii. 533.
[55] S.R.O., Q/SO, Ep. 1751.
[56] W.S.L., D. 788 (32), bdle. 10; Watney, *Longton Hall Porcelain*, 8.   [57] See p. 239.
[58] W.S.L., S.MS. 370. viii, p. 304 (transcript of Dr. Burney's collection of newspapers in the Brit. Mus.), no. 6998.
[59] H. Mus., Heathcote papers, iii, unnumbered.
[60] *Trentham Par. Reg.* (Staffs. Par. Reg. Soc.), list of incumbents of Blurton.
[61] Watney, *Longton Hall Porcelain*, 64, citing indentures.
[62] Obadiah Lane himself may not have lived there as he is described as late of Longton in his marriage settlement 1764 (H. Mus., Heathcote papers, xix. 1), but a Nathaniel Lane of Longton Hall was buried at Trentham in 1768: *Trentham Par. Reg.*
[63] *Trentham Par. Reg.* list of incumbents.
[64] H. Mus., Heathcote papers, xix. 6, sale particulars of the manor of Longton and other estates of Revd. Mr. Lane.
[65] Ibid. xix. i. The purchase price was £4,500.
[66] Ibid. xix. 6, sale particulars.
[67] Ibid.; ibid. 1, schedule of lands purchased by Sir J. E. Heathcote.
[68] H. Mus., Heathcote papers, xix. 1, schedule of lands purchased by Sir J. E. Heathcote.
[69] Ibid. deed of 1784.   [70] See pp. 231, 232.

manor has since descended in the Heathcote family,[71] passing on the death of Sir John Edensor Heathcote in 1822 to his eldest son, Richard Edensor Heathcote,[72] who died in 1850 and was succeeded by John Edensor Heathcote.[73] This John Edensor Heathcote left the estate on his death in 1869 to his sister's son Justinian Heathcote Edwards who took the surname Heathcote in 1870.[74] He died in 1928 and the estate was then broken up.[75] The Heathcote family had ceased to live at Longton Hall c. 1840.[76] In 1847 Richard Edensor Heathcote leased the hall for 21 years to Charles Harvey,[77] a banker of Longton.[78] Harvey sub-let it in 1853 to Henry Wileman,[79] and in 1868 a J. E. Davis was living there.[80] In 1870 Justinian Heathcote Edwards Heathcote agreed to lease the hall to John Balguy;[81] in 1872 he leased it to John Hackett Goddard for fourteen years.[82] After J. H. E. Heathcote's death in 1928 the hall was sold by his executors in 1933 to Messrs. J. and F. Wotton of Bloxwich.[83] It was demolished in 1939,[84] except for the stables and cottages which, with the site, are still owned by Messrs. J. and F. Wotton.[85]

Courts baron were being held for the manor of Longton in the 18th century, the court in December 1758 being held at the Anchor House. The boundaries of the manor were perambulated at the courts of November 1751 and December 1758.[86]

OTHER ESTATES. The Anchor House, mentioned in 1758,[87] was probably situated on the land lying north-east of the centre of Longton called the Anchor Ground, which was held in 1778 by Richard Myatt.[88] In that year the land, and presumably the house, were bought by John Edensor Heathcote.[89] By at least 1834 Anchor House was the home of John Carey, a potter.[90] By mid-century it had been surrounded by a moat and was known as The Moat, being then occupied by Moses Cartwright,[91] as tenant of Harriet Rammage, widow of John Carey. The Heathcote family still owned at least part of the Anchor Ground in 1851.[92] The moat surrounding the house, which by the late 1870's was called Island House,[93] had been drained by the early 1920's.[94] The house has since been demolished.

An estate south-west of Longton Hall and later centring on the mill known as Gom's Mill, can be traced back to 1595 when a Thomas 'Bagnald' was dealing by fine with 2 messuages and various lands in Longton.[95] The Bagnalls still held the estate in 1601.[96] The mill, which had formerly been occu-

pied by Thomas Caldwell, was leased by Joyce Bagnall of Barlaston and her son Randle with some fields in 1632 to Sampson Gomm and his wife Elizabeth for a term of two lives.[97] It was subsequently occupied by an Andrew Stringer and by 1667 was tenanted by Gabriel Clarke, when it was settled, along with a house and lands occupied by Ralph Hattons, by its owner Thomas Proctor of Barlaston as the jointure of the wife of his son John.[98] This estate had passed to John Proctor by 1700, by which date the house formerly tenanted by Ralph Hattons had passed through the tenancy of Thomas Bagnall and was then held by his son, James Bagnall,[99] who still held it in 1728.[1] In 1732 the whole estate, then described as 'two capital messuages known as Gom's Mill and The Fish', was sold by Thomas Proctor, who had succeeded his father John Proctor, to John Peate, a potter of Lane Delph. In addition to the two houses, it consisted of a water corn-mill and a smithy and various lands.[2] There were three tenants of the estate, one of whom was still James Bagnall; the others were John Till and William Brough.[3] By 1745 a kiln had been built at Gom's Mill but the smithy had ceased to be used. There were fourteen fields attached to the mill, and the mill and kiln were apparently being worked by Peate and James Bagnall while the two houses were tenanted by Thomas Elkin and Roger Dale.[4] The estate was sold in 1748 to a Thomas Cotton by the creditors of John Peate.[5] Cotton was acting on behalf of an ironworks partnership but died before executing a conveyance to the partners. Soon afterwards Cotton's son Thomas conveyed the estate to Richard Edward Hall, William Bridge, Anna Kendall, Jonathan Kendall, Samuel Hopkins, and John Smith.[6]

In 1765 a Samuel Hughes purchased the equity of redemption of the mortgage on Gom's Mill[7] and the estate is subsequently found in his hands.[8] Hughes, described as a miller, sold the estate, including a corn mill, to John Edensor Heathcote in 1778 but apparently retained some interest in it until his death in 1796,[9] when he left the Gom's Mill estate to his wife, Mary. Her will, leaving Gom's Mill jointly to her sons Peter and Thomas Hughes, was proved in 1804.[10] By 1808 the property had been acquired by Sir John Edensor Heathcote.[11] A second mill had been erected at Gom's Mill by then,[12] and by 1823 both were tenanted by Booth, Dale, and Deakin, on an annual tenancy.[13] By 1851 both mills, then used for flint grinding, were tenanted by

[71] Burke, *Land. Gent.* (1952), 1200.
[72] Ward, *Stoke*, 562.
[73] H. Mus., Heathcote papers, ii. 14.
[74] Ibid. i, loose papers.
[75] Ibid. ix. 1; ibid. i, loose papers; see p. 232.
[76] Ward, *Stoke*, 562; H. Mus., Heathcote papers, ii. 15. Their seat by this date was Apedale Hall.
[77] H. Mus., Heathcote papers, ii. 15.
[78] Ward, *Stoke*, 560.
[79] H. Mus., Heathcote papers, ii. 15.
[80] *P.O. Dir. Staffs.* (1868).
[81] H. Mus., Heathcote papers, xix. 1.
[82] Ibid. 2.
[83] Ibid. i, loose papers.
[84] Watney, *Longton Hall Porcelain*, 19.
[85] For a description of the buildings see p. 229.
[86] H. Mus., Heathcote papers, xix. 6.
[87] See above.
[88] H. Mus., Heathcote papers, xix. 1.
[89] Ibid.
[90] White, *Dir. Staffs.* (1834); see p. 242.

[91] White, *Dir. Staffs.* (1851); Tithe Redemption Com., Tithe Map and Appt., Longton; see p. 242.
[92] H. Mus., Heathcote papers, ii. 14.
[93] O.S. Map 6" Staffs. xviii SE. (1889).
[94] Ibid. (1925).   [95] *S.H.C.* xvi. 157.
[96] Ibid. 212.
[97] H. Mus., Heathcote papers, iii, unnumbered.
[98] Ibid.; C.P. 25(2)/724, 20 Chas. II Trin.
[99] H. Mus., Heathcote papers, iii, unnumbered.
[1] Ibid. iii, unnumbered.
[2] Ibid. iii, unnumbered; ibid. iii. 12.
[3] Ibid. iii. 12.   [4] Ibid. xx. 3.
[5] Ibid. iii. 12; xxi. 3.
[6] Ibid. iii. 12, abstract of title to Gom's Mill.
[7] Ibid. iii. 12; xix. 1.
[8] Ibid. xix. 1.
[9] Ibid.; ibid. xviii. 11.
[10] Ibid. xviii. 11.
[11] Ibid. xix. 6, survey of the manor of Longton made by Adam MacPhail, 1808.
[12] Ibid.   [13] Ibid. xix. 3; ibid. ix. 1.

Sampson Bridgwood.[14] In 1867 John Edensor Heathcote leased the Upper and Lower Mills, along with Longton Old Mill, to James and Alfred Glover for 32 years.[15] By 1892 the residue of this lease had been vested in the Longton Hall Company, but the Lower Mill had possibly ceased to be used by this date.[16] By 1930 both mills had been closed and the site of Lower Gom's Mill, then occupied by George Breward under the terms of a lease made in 1913, was sold by the executors of Justinian Heathcote Edwards Heathcote to Arthur Adams, described as of Gom's Mill, presumably the Upper Mill.[17]

The two mill pools, that of Lower Gom's Mill lying west of Upper Gom's Mill, were situated on the south-east side of Gom's Mill Road, just north of the present football ground and opposite Ley Farm. They were partly dry by the late 1870's[18] and have now disappeared. The mill buildings have also disappeared, except for a cottage and outbuildings on the site of Upper Gom's Mill. The mill-race is now a slow stream.

The farming land attached to Gom's Mill appears to have been detached from the mill after the sale to the Heathcote family. The capital messuage, formerly known as The Fish, was presumably on or near the site of the present Ley Farm, which, with 51 acres of land, in 1851 was tenanted by James Rae.[19] By the late 1870's it was known as Gom's Mill Cottage, but again as Ley Farm by 1898.[20] In 1928 Ley Farm was sold by the executors under the will of J. H. E. Heathcote to Mrs. Elizabeth Ellen Ray,[21] and in the late 1950's was still in the hands of the Ray family.[22]

In 1250 William de Bevill, then lord of Longton, granted 3 acres of arable land and 1 acre of meadow in Longton and the service due from the mill to the priory of Trentham.[23] In 1251 the priory of Trentham owed 2s. a year for its lands in Longton to the king's manor of Newcastle.[24] Further grants were made by Sybil widow of William de Bevill[25] and in 1272 by Margery widow of Ranulph de Bevill.[26] By 1291 the priory's lands in Longton consisted of a carucate worth 10s.[27] At its dissolution in 1537 the priory held in Longton two farms, one let to Ralph Machin and the other to Margery Bolton and her son John. To the second farm there belonged two pastures called Priors Field.[28] In 1538 the lands of the priory, including land at Longton, were granted

by the Crown to Charles Duke of Suffolk[29] and subsequently in the same year he was given licence to alienate them to Thomas Pope.[30] In 1540 Sir Thomas Pope was licensed to alienate these lands to James Leveson[31] in whose family they subsequently descended.[32] In 1730 the possessions of John Lord Gower included the area known as the Priors Field,[33] lying immediately north-east of the centre of the present town,[34] and two farms, Nicholls' farm and Boulton's farm, both held by John Boulton.[35] In 1783 Lord Gower exchanged a farm in Longton, occupied by John Ford, with John Edensor Heathcote for Hollybush farm lying to the west of Longton.[36] By 1813 further lands totalling 110 acres had been added to the Hollybush estate,[37] presumably as part of the Marquess of Stafford's policy of consolidating and enlarging farms.[38] The farm, which by then had an acreage of 175 acres,[39] was in that year exchanged with Sir John Edensor Heathcote (for lands outside Longton), presumably again as part of the marquess's policy of consolidating his estates.[40]

The Woodhouse, which lay north of Longton to the east of what is now the junction of Anchor Road and Wood Street, occurs in 1649 when it was sold by Thomas Bagnall and Richard Heath of Newcastle-under-Lyme and John Heath of Clavering (Essex) to Henry Goringe of Kingstone parish and Thomas Lovatt of Callowhill in the same parish.[41] In 1652 Simon Degge of Callowhill, William Farmer of Stafford, and Christopher Smyth of Callowhill conveyed it to Alexander Howe of Caverswall.[42] Alexander Howe's daughter and coheir, Sarah, married the Revd. George Newton,[43] who was dealing with the Woodhouse by fine in 1686[44] and settled it on his daughters and coheirs Alice and Elizabeth Newton in 1714.[45] It was sold by the Newtons in 1716 to Richard Hulme of Adderley Green and Thomas Baggaley of Longton.[46] Hulme leased his half immediately to Baggaley for ten years.[47] This moiety was again leased to Baggaley in 1719.[48] In 1729 Thomas Baggaley leased the Woodhouse to Thomas Boulton for 99 years or three lives.[49] Richard Hulme leased his moiety of the Woodhouse to Thomas Boulton in 1743 for 21 years.[50] By 1774 William Boulton had acquired the freehold of the Woodhouse[51] which was sold by the

---

[14] H. Mus., Heathcote papers, iii. 12, rep. on Heathcote estate in Longton; White, *Dir. Staffs.* (1851). For Bridgwood's pottery interests, see p. 241.

[15] H. Mus., Heathcote papers, ii, loose. The Glovers were still holding it in 1873: ibid.

[16] Ibid. i, loose, only Upper Gom's Mill being shown on the plan.

[17] Ibid. xx. 3, register of sales of the Heathcote property.

[18] O.S. Map 6" Staffs. xviii SW. (1889).

[19] H. Mus., Heathcote papers, iii. 12, rep. on Heathcote estate in Longton.

[20] O.S. Map 6" Staffs. xviii SW. (1889, 1900).

[21] H. Mus., Heathcote papers, i, loose.

[22] *Barrett's City of Stoke Dir.* [1959]. For a description of the house see p. 229.

[23] See p. 230.

[24] *Bk. of Fees*, 1185.

[25] *S.H.C.* xi. 320.

[26] Ibid. 321.

[27] *Tax. Eccl.* (Rec. Com.), 252.

[28] S.C. 6/Hen. VIII/3352, m. 4. The rest of the priory's possessions in Longton consisted of rent, including 4 barbed arrows.

[29] *L. & P. Hen. VIII*, xiii (2), p. 492.

[30] Ibid. p. 495.

[31] Ibid. xv, p. 284.

[32] *V.C.H. Staffs.* v. 80.

[33] W.S.L., D. 788 (32), bdle. 10.

[34] O.S. Map 6" Staffs. xviii NW. (1890).

[35] W.S.L., D. 788 (32), bdle. 10.

[36] H. Mus., Heathcote papers, iii. 12; xix. 1; W.S.L. D. 788 (32), bdle. 14.

[37] H. Mus., Heathcote papers, iii. 12.

[38] James Loch, *Short acct. of the improvements to the Marquis of Stafford's estates in Staffs. and Salop. and in Sutherland*, gives an acct. of these improvements.

[39] H. Mus., Heathcote papers, iii. 12.

[40] Ibid.

[41] W.S.L., D. 788 (32), bdle. 10.

[42] Ibid.

[43] H. Mus., Heathcote papers, ii. 17.

[44] W.S.L., D. 788 (32), bdle. 10.

[45] H. Mus., Heathcote papers, ii. 17.

[46] Ibid.; W.S.L., D. 788 (32), bdle. 10.

[47] W.S.L., D. 788 (32), bdle. 10.

[48] H. Mus., Heathcote papers, ii. 17.

[49] W.S.L., D. 788 (32), bdle. 10.

[50] Ibid.

[51] H. Mus., Heathcote papers, ii. 15.

trustees under his will [52] in 1808 to Sir John Edensor Heathcote.[53] The Heathcote family still owned the Woodhouse in the early 1850's[54] when it was occupied by John Wardle.[55]

CHURCHES. Longton and Lane End both lay within the parish of Stoke until the 19th century[56] but by the later 18th century some provision was being made for Anglican worship. A small church was built in 1762, the cost being defrayed by public contributions, the major part of which came from John Bourne of Newcastle.[57] Its position in the Church of England was at first anomalous. Although it was used for Church of England services,[58] it was registered in 1762 as a chapel for Protestant Dissenters,[59] a device adopted presumably in order to legalize its status as a place of worship. It was consecrated in 1764.[60] Later in the century it had become too small for the growing community and was also in a bad state of repair.[61] An Act for rebuilding it was obtained in 1792,[62] and the new building was consecrated in 1795 as a chapel-of-ease to Stoke parish church.[63] In 1802, the stipend of the curate having been augmented from Queen Anne's Bounty,[64] the living became a perpetual curacy under the terms of an Act of 1714.[65] In 1866 a new parish of St. John the Baptist was formed as a district chapelry out of the parish of St. James the Less, Longton.[66] The living has been a vicarage since 1868.[67]

It is not known who held the right of presentation to the church in its early years, but under the Act of 1792 the patronage was vested in the Marquess of Stafford, Sir John Edensor Heathcote, their heirs, and 32 other trustees and their heirs, an arrangement which is said to have produced 'canvassings and contests of a heated, not to say acrimonious, kind.'[68] In 1890 the advowson was conveyed to the bishop[69] with whom it still remains.[70]

The living was endowed in 1764 with four pieces of land lying in Great Fenton purchased by the trustees with money raised by subscription.[71] Further lands, Ackers Edge farm at Stanley (Leek), and Cowall farm at Horton, were later purchased, and the original land was sold.[72] The benefice was augmented from Queen Anne's Bounty in 1802 (£200), 1807 (£200), 1809 (£200), 1810 (£300), 1812 (£200), 1817 (£600), and 1820 (£400).[73] The net annual income of the living during the period 1828–31 was given as £154.[74]

The church of *ST. JOHN THE BAPTIST*, standing immediately north of Times Square, is built of red brick with stone dressings. The nave and west tower date from 1795, the nave walls being continued westwards to flank the base of the tower and to form entrance vestibules which also contain gallery staircases. The nave windows, arranged in two tiers, are slightly pointed and have Gothic glazing-bars; the west doorway in the tower is of typical 18th-century Classical design. Internally the nave contains original galleries on three sides, supported on slender cast iron columns. In 1827–8 the east end of the church was extended in a fashion described soon afterwards as 'disproportionately large for the rest of the structure'.[75] The additions, consisting of a chancel and two transepts, are Gothic in style with steeply pitched roofs, buttresses, and angle pinnacles. The stone embattled parapet was added to the tower in 1832–4 and was designed by T. Johnson.[76] Internally the junction between old and new has been awkwardly managed, the tall eastward extension having open roofs and heavy wood arcading. The traceried east window now contains stained glass of 1921. The north transept now serves as an organ chamber and the south transept as a chapel, the space between them having been included in the chancel. The church was restored in 1889[77] and its fittings all appear to date from the 19th century. Mural tablets include those to George Wood (d. 1817), George Martin (d. 1841), James Meakin (d. 1846) with members of his family, members of the Glover family of Sideway (1852–1901), and the Revd. Thomas Ford (d. 1869), vicar. The registers date from 1764.[78] There were eight bells c. 1840[79] but only seven in 1889, all cast in 1815 by Thomas Mears of London.[80] There were eight again in 1900.[81] The graveyard attached to the first chapel was enlarged in 1765 by the demolition of three cottages.[82] It was again enlarged when the new chapel was built in 1795.[83]

A parsonage-house was built at the north end of Wood Street near the church in 1810 with grants from the trustees of Queen Anne's Bounty and local contributions, the land being given by John Smith.[84] In 1929 the rector moved to a new house in Rutland Street which has remained the rectory-house. The old house was subsequently demolished.[85]

A mission church attached to the church of St. John the Baptist had been opened in Park Hall

[52] Ibid.; W.S.L., D. 788 (32), bdle. 10. Probate of will was granted in 1795.
[53] W.S.L., D. 788 (32), bdle. 10. See pp. 230–1 for the Heathcote family.   [54] H. Mus., Heathcote papers, ii. 14.
[55] White, *Dir. Staffs.* (1851).
[56] See p. 188.
[57] *Order of prayer for chapel near Mear Heath erected in 1762* (1762; copy among W.S.L. pamphlets); S.R.O., Q/SO, Mich. 1762. The date usually given for the erection of the chapel is 1764, the date of the endowment and trust: H. Mus., Heathcote papers, xi. 4; xii. 5; xix. 5.
[58] *Order of prayer for chapel near Mear Heath erected in 1762.*
[59] S.R.O., Q/SO, Mich. 1762. The registration is made by John Bourne, principal founder of the school and of Lane End chapel.
[60] St. John's Reg. (from transcript in W.S.L.).
[61] H. Mus., Heathcote papers, xi. 4; xii. 5; xix. 5.
[62] 32 Geo. III, c. 88.
[63] Lich. Dioc. Regy., Bp.'s Reg. ABCD, pp. 541–7.
[64] C. Hodgson, *An Acct. of the Augmentation of small livings by the Governors of the Bounty of Queen Anne* (1845), p. ccxcvii.

[65] H. Mus., Heathcote papers, xix. 5; Poor Clergy Maintenance Act, 1 Geo. I, c. 10 (printed in Hodgson, op. cit.).
[66] *Lond. Gaz.* 1866, p. 673.
[67] *Lich. Dioc. Ch. Cal.* (1868 and subseq. edns.).
[68] Ward, *Stoke*, 565.
[69] Lich. Dioc. Regy., Bp.'s Reg. 35, agreement and cert., 11 Jan. and 17 Apr. 1890.
[70] *Lich. Dioc. Dir.* (1959).
[71] H. Mus., Heathcote papers, xix. 5.
[72] Ibid. xix. 2, 5.
[73] Hodgson, *Queen Anne's Bounty*, p. ccxcvii.
[74] *Rep. Com. Eccl. Rev.* H.C. 54, pp. 484–5 (1835), xxii.
[75] Inscription at W. end of nave; Ward, *Stoke*, 566.
[76] M. Port, *Six Hundred New Churches*, 64.
[77] *Kelly's Dir. Staffs.* (1940).
[78] Transcript in W.S.L. 1764–90.
[79] Ward, *Stoke*, 566.
[80] C. Lynam, *Ch. Bells Staffs.* 52.
[81] *Kelly's Dir. Staffs.* (1900).
[82] H. Mus., Heathcote papers, xix. 5.
[83] Lich. Dioc. Regy., Bp.'s Reg. ABCD, pp. 541–7.
[84] Ward, *Stoke*, 566.
[85] Ex inf. the rector.

Street by 1868.[86] In 1897 land at Sandford Hill was given to the Church Commissioners by the vicar, George Oliver, for a new church.[87] This had been built by the following year with money raised by voluntary contribution as well as grants from the Diocesan Church Extension Society and the Church Building Society. The northern part of the parish of St. John was then formed into a parish attached to this church.[88] The benefice has remained a perpetual curacy in the gift of the bishop.[89] The church of *ST. MARY AND ST. CHAD* in Anchor Road is in the Early English style and is built of red brick with stone dressings. It consists of an aisled and clerestoried nave of four bays and a chancel flanked by side chapels. A low extension at the west end consisting of two porches and a baptistery dates from 1910.[90] A large school hall with a modern extension lies to the north of it and there is a curate's house in Anchor Road. The plate includes a Spanish chalice of silver which dates from *c.* 1690 and was presented to the Revd. E. F. Woodward in 1919.[91] The church has two bells, one hanging on its south wall, the other in a bell-cote on the roof.

A mission church was opened at Normacot within the parish of St. John the Baptist *c.* 1887. It ceased to be used *c.* 1918.[92]

Land was acquired on the south side of High Street (now Uttoxeter Road) in 1832[93] for a church which was built in 1833–4 by the Church Building Commissioners.[94] Under the Stoke Rectory Act of 1827 it was made parochial in 1839.[95] The living became a rectory and the new district comprised Longton, Lane End, and part of Fenton Culvert.[96] The advowson of the rectory was bought in 1839 by John Carey (d. 1843).[97] It passed subsequently to his widow Harriet (after her remarriage Harriet Rammage), who presented in 1863.[98] She and her husband sold the advowson in that year to Mrs. Matilda Elizabeth Clarke who by will proved in 1886 devised it to the bishop.[99] The right of presentation still lies with the bishop.[1] The living was endowed in 1839, under the Stoke Rectory Act of 1827, with £10,000 from the rectory funds.[2] A grant out of the Common Fund of £177 a year was made in 1872.[3]

The church of *ST. JAMES THE LESS* is a Gothic building of blackened Hollington stone. The design, mainly Perpendicular in style, is by James Trubshaw, architect of St. Peter's Church, Stoke.[4] The building remains structurally unaltered and consists of an aisled and clerestoried nave, a west tower 90 ft. high surmounted by tall angle pinnacles, and a chancel flanked by two low projecting wings, one containing a sacristy, the other a vestry. Internally the nave arcades are of stone and the west bay of the nave is occupied by a stone-built gallery supported on three four-centred arches. The corresponding aisle bays form vestibules with projecting porches beyond them. There were originally side galleries in the aisles and the west gallery supported a small organ.[5] The chancel, which has a five-sided east end, has been extended internally to include the easternmost bay of the nave, while a vestry and an organ chamber occupy the aisle bays to north and south of it. These alterations were probably made in 1889[6] and a low stone screen enclosing the chancel dates from 1904.[7] The font is dated 1858 and the pulpit 1874. In the sanctuary are large mural tablets to John Carey (d. 1843) and Dr. Benjamin Vale (d. 1863), respectively first patron and first rector of the church; the former tablet carries a mourning figure carved in relief. In the aisles are rows of glazed memorial tiles. The church was being restored in 1959. In 1899 there were two bells, one cast by I. Rudhall in 1834 and the other by C. and G. Mears in 1853.[8] Three more have since been added.[9] Nearly two acres were purchased as a burial ground around the church by the commissioners at the expense of the parish of Stoke, various old buildings being demolished for the purpose.[10]

A rectory-house was built by John Carey, the patron, in 1840 in the present Trentham Road. It was described *c.* 1840 as 'a handsome square building in the Italian style . . . agreeably situated in a newly-planted curtilage'.[11] It was wrecked by a Chartist mob in 1842[12] but was still the rectory-house in the 1870's.[13] The rectory-house is now in Clivedon Place.

Mount Pleasant Mission Chapel in the east end of the borough in what is now Lawley Street had been opened from St. James's by 1868.[14] In 1887 a brick building, the former cottage hospital, was given to the mission.[15] This was altered in 1893. It continued in use until at least 1939 but by 1942 was dilapidated and no longer required because the congregation had moved to new housing estates. Authority for sale was given in 1943.[16] The chapel has been demolished but the social hall attached to it still (1959) stands and is used as a store-room.

The Edensor district was constituted a parish in 1846 out of the parish of St. James the Less.[17] Services were at first held in the school there,[18] and the church of *ST. PAUL* was opened in 1854.[19] In 1940 as a result of housing development in the

[86] *P.O. Dir. Staffs.* (1868).

[87] Lich. Dioc. Regy., Bp.'s Reg. U, p. 266; *Guide to Church Congress* (1911), 107–8 (copy in W.S.L.).

[88] Lich. Dioc. Regy., Bp.'s Reg. U, p. 266.

[89] Bp.'s Reg. 36, p. 179; *Lich. Dioc. Dir.* (1959).

[90] Tablet on W. wall.

[91] S. A. Jeavons, 'Church Plate in the Archdeaconry of Stoke-on-Trent' (*Trans. Birm. Arch. Soc.* lxxvii), 67.

[92] *Lich. Dioc. Ch. Cal.* (1888, 1917–18).

[93] Lich. Dioc. Regy., Bp.'s Reg. K, pp. 129–38.

[94] Ward, *Stoke*, 569; White, *Dir. Staffs.* (1851); Lich. Dioc. Regy., Bp.'s Reg. K, pp. 129–38.

[95] Ward, *Stoke*, 459–60, 568, 570; see p. 187.

[96] *Lond. Gaz.* 1839, p. 1103; Lich. Dioc. Regy., Bp.'s Reg. L, p. 332.

[97] Ward, *Stoke*, 568; memorial tablet in St. James's Ch.

[98] Lich. Dioc. Regy., Bp.'s Reg. 32, p. 260.

[99] Bp.'s Reg. T, p. 125.

[1] *Lich. Dioc. Dir.* (1959).

[2] Ward, *Stoke*, 568; see p. 187.

[3] Lich. Dioc. Regy., Bp.'s Reg. Q, p. 599.

[4] Ward, *Stoke*, 568.   [5] Ibid.

[6] Ex inf. R. Scrivener & Sons, Hanley.

[7] Inscription on screen.

[8] Lynam, *Ch. Bells Staffs.* 53.

[9] A. E. Garbett, 'Ch. Bells Staffs.' (*Trans. Old Stafford Soc., 1953–4*), 19.

[10] Ward, *Stoke*, 570.

[11] Lich. Dioc. Regy., Bp.'s Reg. L, p. 21; Ward, *Stoke*, 570.

[12] White, *Dir. Staffs.* (1851); Ward, *Stoke*, 586.

[13] S.R.O., Q/AH, Longton Main Rds. Map.

[14] *P.O. Dir. Staffs.* (1868).

[15] Char. Com. files; local inf.; see p. 237.

[16] Char. Com. files; *Kelly's Dir. Staffs.* (1940).

[17] *Lond. Gaz.* 1846, p. 3545.

[18] White, *Dir. Staffs.* (1851).

[19] *Lich. Dioc. Dir.* (1959).

area a new church was built in the former grounds of Longton Hall. The old church became a food store.[20] The benefice was at first a perpetual curacy[21] and became a vicarage in 1868.[22] The patronage was vested in and remains with the Crown and the bishop alternately.[23] The former church of St. Paul in Edensor Road was still standing in a derelict condition in 1960. It is a stone building in the Decorated style designed by H. Ward and Son of Hanley[24] and consists of chancel, nave, aisles, and north transept; a south porch has been demolished. It has a turret above the transept which formerly contained one bell. The present church of St. Paul, built in 1940,[25] lies slightly east of the site of Longton Hall. It was designed by Wood and Goldstraw, architects,[26] and is a simple brick building with low passage aisles, tall clerestory windows, and a recessed porch at the west end. The present parsonage-house had been built immediately south of the first church by 1860.[27]

A mission centre in Edward Street was opened from St. Paul's, Edensor, c. 1870. About 1891 it was replaced by the present mission church of St. Mark.[28]

The church of *THE HOLY EVANGELISTS* in Belgrave Road, Normacot, was built in 1847 as a chapel of ease to the church of Blurton by the Duke of Sutherland.[29] It was made parochial in 1852.[30] The living was at first a perpetual curacy[31] and a vicarage since 1868.[32] The right of presentation after the creation of the perpetual curacy lay with the dukes of Sutherland until at least 1940.[33] By 1946 it had passed to the Diocesan Board of Patronage[34] with whom it still remains.[35] The church is built of stone in the Early English style. It originally consisted of chancel, nave, south aisle, and north porch, with a central turret. In 1891 a north aisle and vestry were added to the church by George, 3rd Duke of Sutherland.[36] There is one bell.

The church of *THE RESURRECTION* in Chaplin Road, Dresden, was built in 1853 as a chapel of ease to the parish church of Blurton.[37] In 1867 the area became a district chapelry. The benefice was at first a perpetual curacy[38] and after 1868 a titular vicarage.[39] The right of presentation was vested in the incumbent of Blurton[40] with whom it still remains.[41] The church was built in the Early English style from designs by George Gilbert (later Sir Gilbert) Scott. The walls are of red brick with blue-brick diaper ornament and the building consists of an aisled nave, a chancel, and a west porch. A central bell turret was originally faced with Minton tiles. In 1903 the chancel was enlarged, four memorial windows and a new window were placed there, and a west window was erected.[42] A choir vestry was added at the west end of the church as a memorial to those who fell in the First World War[43] and the building was renovated in 1927–30.[44] There is one bell, acquired in 1853.[45]

The present mission church of St. Luke in Cromartie Street, Florence, attached to the church of the Resurrection, was built and licensed in 1884.[46]

The present St. Andrew's Mission Church, East Vale, was opened from St. Peter's, Caverswall, by 1868.[47] It was transferred to the parish of St. James the Less c. 1937.[48] The building, which is of brick in Gothic style, comprises a church and schoolroom.

LOCAL GOVERNMENT AND PUBLIC SERVICES. For the purpose of parish government Longton and Lane End were by the 17th century grouped with Fenton and Botteslow to form one of the quarters of the ancient parish of Stoke-upon-Trent.[49] Longton manor had its own court baron by the mid-18th century, but the area was still subject to the leet jurisdiction of Newcastle manor in the early 19th century.[50]

In 1839 Longton and Lane End, like Stoke, Fenton, and Trentham, were placed under a body of commissioners with powers of policing, lighting, and generally improving the streets.[51] In 1862 the commissioners, having become a Local Board under the Local Government Act of 1858,[52] obtained powers to extend the market-place.[53] A Board of Health was set up for East Vale in 1858[54] and another for Dresden in 1863.[55] The Longton Board of Health District was made a borough in 1865 with a council of 6 aldermen and 18 councillors, 6 for each of the 3 wards, St. John's, St. James's, and St. Paul's.[56] The constitution of the council remained unaltered when the East Vale Board of Health District was added to the borough under an Act of 1883,[57] but when the Dresden Local Board District, Florence, and part of Normacot were added in 1884, the number of wards was increased to five; the council then consisted of 10 aldermen and 30 councillors.[58] In 1873, when the council minutes begin, the committees consisted of Finance, Sanitary,

[20] *Kelly's Dir. Staffs.* (1940); tablet in present church; local inf.
[21] White, *Dir. Staffs.* (1851).
[22] *Lich. Dioc. Ch. Cal.* (1868 and subseq. edns.).
[23] White, *Dir. Staffs.* (1851); *Lich. Dioc. Dir.* (1959).
[24] Port, *Six Hundred New Churches*, 64.
[25] Tablet on church.
[26] Ibid.
[27] *P.O. Dir. Staffs.* (1860).
[28] *Lich. Dioc. Ch. Cal.* (1871, 1892).
[29] Lich. Dioc. Regy., Bp.'s Reg. N, p. 599.
[30] *Lond. Gaz.* 1852, p. 2900.
[31] *Lich. Dioc. Ch. Cal.* (1857).
[32] Ibid. (1868).
[33] Ibid. (1857 and subseq. edns. to 1938); *Kelly's Dir. Staffs.* (1940).
[34] *Lich. Dioc. Dir.* (1946).
[35] Ibid. (1959).
[36] *Kelly's Dir. Staffs.* (1940).
[37] Bill of costs for erection is displayed in the church.
[38] Lich. Dioc. Regy., Bp.'s Reg. 32, p. 325.
[39] *Lich. Dioc. Ch. Cal.* (1869).
[40] Lich. Dioc. Regy., Bp.'s Reg. 32, p. 325.
[41] *Lich. Dioc. Dir.* (1959).
[42] *P.O. Dir. Staffs.* (1868); plaque in church.
[43] Tablets on external walls.
[44] *Kelly's Dir. Staffs.* (1940).
[45] Plaque in church.
[46] Lich. Dioc. Regy., Bp.'s Reg. 35, pp. 18, 19.
[47] *P.O. Dir. Staffs.* (1868).
[48] *Lich. Dioc. Ch. Cal.* (1938).
[49] Ward, *Stoke*, 467–8; see pp. 189, 198.
[50] *Staffs. Advertiser*, 10 Oct. 1829; see pp. 184, 231.
[51] 2 & 3 Vic. c. 44 (local and personal). For details of the Act see p. 194.   [52] 21 & 22 Vic. c. 98.
[53] Act to confirm certain provisional orders, 25 & 26 Vic. c. 25.
[54] Longton Improvement Act, 46 & 47 Vic. c. 62 (local).
[55] Longton Extension Act, 47 & 48 Vic. c. 27 (local). The minute bks. 1863–84 are in H.R.L.
[56] 29 & 30 Vic. c. 24 (local and personal); *Boro. of Longton: Charter of Incorporation* (copy in H.R.L.).
[57] Longton Improvement Act, 46 & 47 Vic. c. 62 (local); H.R.L., Longton Boro. Mins. 1881–4, pp. 231–2.
[58] Longton Extension Act 1884, 47 & 48 Vic. c. 27 (local); *Kelly's Dir. Staffs.* (1884).

Improvement, Market, Rate Appeal, and Gas Contract.[59] By 1909 the following committees had been added: General Purposes, Park Fêtes, Local Pensions, Sewage Farm, Park and Cemetery, Gas and Electricity (replacing Gas Contract), Market and Baths (replacing Market), Plans, Executive, Public Library, and Education.[60] With the creation of the new county borough of Stoke-on-Trent in 1910, the area covered by the old borough of Longton was formed into 4 wards represented on the new council by 4 aldermen and 12 councillors.[61]

The upper floor of the Union Market Hall was used for public meetings until the early 1850's,[62] and the sessions of the stipendiary magistrate were at first held there. A town hall and market in Times Square was built in 1844 but was replaced by the present town hall and market in 1863.[63]

As a member of Newcastle manor Longton was represented at the court leet by two frankpledges by 1335.[64] The representation was still two in the mid-16th century,[65] but by 1679, with the emergence of Lane End township, each had one frankpledge.[66] The area formed a constablewick with Fenton Vivian and neighbouring places, the townships of Longton and Lane End each forming one of the six divisions of that constablewick.[67] A constable and four assistant constables were appointed for Longton and Lane End at Newcastle manor court in October 1829.[68] The Act of 1839 gave the Improvement Commissioners power to appoint constables, but in 1843, after the riots of the previous year, a branch of the new county force was established in Longton with an office in the lower part of the Union Market Hall by 1851.[69] This office was replaced by the present police station in Sutherland Road in 1906.[70]

A stipendiary magistrate for the Potteries area was appointed in 1839, sitting once a week at Longton which formed one of the six rating districts established to support the new system.[71] Sessions were at first held in the Union Market Hall[72] but by 1851 were being held at the Eagle Inn.[73] In 1856 the former Union Market House was opened as Longton Court House.[74] At first within Hanley county court district, formed in 1847, Longton was placed in Stoke district in 1853, and from 1863 regular sessions of the court were held at Longton.[75] By 1868 Longton had its own borough court.[76]

PUBLIC HEALTH. In Longton as elsewhere in the Potteries the main threats to public health in the 19th century arose from poor housing and bad sanitation. By the later part of the century there were particularly bad slums in the Edensor district, in John Street (now Calvin Street), in Locketts Lane, and around St. James's Church.[77] At the end of the century the medical officer of health for the borough was complaining that privies and ashpits were not cleared frequently enough, one of the results being the prevalence of diphtheria; Florence and Normacot were particularly bad in that respect.[78] By then, however, privies were being converted to water-closets at the rate of some 50 a month.[79]

The problem of drainage was already being tackled before the formation of the borough in 1865. By 1859 the Heathcote Road and Edensor Road areas had a certain amount of sewering; the sewage from the second area was conveyed to an open tank near Gom's Mill.[80] Two new sewers were constructed soon after this; they ran the length of the town and after joining together at the market-square, emptied into the Longton Brook near Foley Road.[81] Since the brook flowed into the Trent, Longton thus contributed with the other Pottery towns to the pollution of that river.[82] In 1875 the corporation tackled the problem of sewage disposal by coming to an arrangement with the Duke of Sutherland whereby the duke built a sewer from the borough boundary on to 250 acres of his land at Blurton Waste.[83] At the end of the 19th century the corporation leased Blurton Waste farm from the duke and built a sewage works there.[84] This eventually became inadequate and in 1946 the city's works at Strongford was extended to receive Longton's sewage, part of Blurton Waste farm being released for a new housing estate.[85] The first refuse destructor in the Potteries was erected at Longton in 1877–8.[86]

Restrictions were placed on burials in St. John's Church and churchyard in 1856 and 1879[87] and in St. James's Church and churchyard in 1856 and 1874.[88] The corporation was constituted a burial board in 1875[89] and three years later opened the present cemetery on 10 acres of ground lying on the south side of Spring Garden Road and formerly occupied by allotments called Spring Gardens.[90]

The public baths in Times Square were built in 1880–1.[91] The private baths were still open in 1958, but the swimming baths had been closed several years previously as a result of damage caused by mining subsidence.[92]

Longton Cottage Hospital was opened in Mount

[59] H.R.L., Longton Boro. Mins. 1873–80, 10 Nov. 1873.
[60] Ibid. 1909–10, 9 Nov. 1909.
[61] Stoke Counc. Year Bk. (1915).
[62] See p. 237.
[63] See pp. 229, 237.
[64] D.L. 30/228/1.
[65] D.L. 30/237/4.
[66] D.L. 30/242/3.
[67] S.H.C. x. 93; ibid. 1921, 163–5. The other places were Hanley, Botteslow, and Normacot Grange.
[68] Staffs. Advertiser, 10 Oct. 1829.
[69] White, Dir. Staffs. (1851).
[70] Warrillow, Stoke, 406. The road became known locally as 'Handcuff Alley'.
[71] Act for more effectual execution of office of J.P., 2 & 3 Vic. c. 15.
[72] Ward, Stoke, 572.
[73] White, Dir. Staffs. (1851).   [74] See p. 237.
[75] Lond. Gaz. 1847, p. 1012; 1853, p. 3587; 1863, p. 633; P.O. Dir. Staffs. (1872); Kelly's Dir. Staffs. (1912). By 1868 the district was called Longton District and by 1872 Stoke and Longton: P.O. Dir. Staffs. (1868, 1872).

[76] P.O. Dir. Staffs. (1868). Petty Sessions Mins. for the period 1883–1904 are in the County Record Office.
[77] See p. 230.
[78] Warrillow, Stoke, 318.
[79] Ibid. 316–17.
[80] Ibid. 185.
[81] Ibid.
[82] Ibid. 185–6; see pp. 196–7.
[83] Warrillow, Stoke, 190; Hughes and Harber's Longton Boro. Almanack (1897).
[84] Warrillow, Stoke, 190.
[85] Ibid.; see pp. 264, 269.
[86] Warrillow, Stoke, 190.
[87] Lond. Gaz. 1856, p. 2904; 1879, p. 3537.
[88] Ibid. 1856, p. 2904; 1874, p. 3452. The closing of the graveyard, ordered in 1874, was postponed to 1876 by an order of 1875: 1875, p. 6402.
[89] Ibid. 1875, p. 3990.
[90] Kelly's Dir. Staffs. (1884); Lich. Dioc. Regy., Bp.'s Reg. S, pp. 313–16.
[91] Warrillow, Stoke, 373.
[92] Ibid. 374.

Pleasant (now Lawley Street) in 1868.[93] In 1879 it was moved to a new building on the north side of the same street.[94] This was replaced by the present Cottage Hospital in Upper Belgrave Road built in 1889–90 on land given by the Duke of Sutherland.[95]

OTHER PUBLIC SERVICES. A large reservoir at Meir, supplied by several springs in the sandstone rock, was built in 1817 by George, Marquess of Stafford, to provide water for the town.[96] In 1844 the supply was said to be good and carried to almost all the houses in the town.[97] The Potteries Water Works Company, incorporated in 1847, leased the Meir works from the Duke of Sutherland from 1849 and used it to supply Longton, Fenton, and part of Stoke.[98]

Gas was supplied to Longton by the 1830's from the British Gaslight Company's works at Shelton and by the early 1840's from the Stoke works of the Stoke, Fenton, and Longton Gas Company.[99] The Longton Gas Company was formed in 1858 and opened a works on the site of the present works south-west of Longton station.[1] In 1866 the company received statutory recognition, bought the Stoke, Fenton, and Longton Gas Company's rights in Longton, and began building the present works.[2] The undertaking was taken over by Longton Corporation in 1878[3] and by Stoke-on-Trent Corporation in 1910.[4]

Electricity was supplied to the town by Longton Corporation from 1901.[5] This undertaking too passed to Stoke-on-Trent Corporation in 1910.[6]

Longton had a fire brigade by the mid-1860's. The engine-house was in Commerce Street and the inspector of police acted as superintendent.[7] By 1873 the fire brigade was under the control of the Sanitary Committee.[8] By the mid-1870's the office of superintendent was no longer held by the police inspector.[9]

ECONOMIC HISTORY. Longton's agrarian character was already being modified by the end of the 17th century when coal mining and ironstone working were developing there. In the following century the manufacture of earthenware and, early in the 19th century, of bone china established Longton as an industrial town. Its position at the junction of the Stone and Uttoxeter roads was no doubt an

important contributory factor to its growth as a market-town in the late 18th century.

Trentham Priory was engaged in extensive farming in the Longton area by the mid-13th century. Open-field cultivation then existed, and the field names Okhul, Mill Field, and Brickehull are met with.[10] References to assarting suggest the expansion of arable cultivation, probably at the expense of woodlands.[11] Among woods mentioned was Longton Wood described as lying between Longton and Cockstall and bounded by the main road from Newcastle.[12] The priory also had flocks of sheep in the area.[13] In the 1660's the lord of the manor held a free fishery in Longton Brook.[14]

MARKETS AND FAIRS. In the later 18th century Lane End was described as a market-town and had apparently two market houses,[15] though in 1802 only one, 'a large elegant market hall', is mentioned.[16] This stood at the cross-roads (now Times Square) by the church and was built by subscription in 1789.[17] It consisted of two squares of stalls and shambles for tradesmen and butchers.[18] In 1814 a second market house known as the Union Market was built by a company of shareholders on a piece of ground at the north end of Commerce Street given to the town in 1794 by the devisees of John Turner.[19] Its use as a market, however, seems to have been short-lived for by 1829 the market-place itself was being used only for fairs and the market hall for public meetings.[20] By 1851 the Union Market was stated to be disused and the Union Market Hall, sometimes known as the Old Town Hall, was still being used occasionally for public meetings, while the lower part was the police office.[21] Three years later the assembly room had become a furniture store and auction room.[22] The building became Longton Court House in 1856 and was demolished in 1950.[23]

A new market and town hall was built in Times Square in 1844[24] and rebuilt in 1863.[25] In the later 18th century the market-day was Saturday,[26] and in the mid-19th century there was also a Wednesday market for vegetables in summer;[27] by the end of the century this market had ceased.[28] By the mid-1950's markets were held on Wednesdays, Fridays, and Saturdays.[29]

By 1829 fairs were being held on the days following those held at Newcastle[30] and in the middle of the

[93] Ibid. 359. The building was later occupied by Mount Pleasant Mission: see p. 234.
[94] Hughes and Harber's Longton Boro. Almanack (1897); S.R.O., D. 593, Longton Boro. Extension Map.
[95] Warrillow, Stoke, 360; Farmer's New Boro. Almanack (1890).
[96] Ward, Stoke, 559.
[97] Pure and Wholesome Water for 100 years, 1849–1949 (1949), 8 (copy in H.R.L.).
[98] Ibid. 12. This extensive use of the Meir springs was possibly one reason for the drop in the level of the Furnace Brook, Gom's Mill pools, and Longton pools.
[99] Warrillow, Stoke, 132; see pp. 160, 197.
[1] Warrillow, Stoke, 136; O.S. Map 6" Staffs. xviii SW. (1889).
[2] Warrillow, Stoke, 138; 29 & 30 Vic. c. 125 (local).
[3] Warrillow, Stoke, 141; 40 & 41 Vic. c. 22 (local).
[4] See p. 266.
[5] Warrillow, Stoke, 152; S.R.O., Q/RUm 643.
[6] See p. 266.
[7] Keates and Ford's Potteries Dir. (1865–6).
[8] H.R.L., Longton Boro. Mins. 1873–80, 29 Nov. 1873.
[9] Keates's Potteries Dir. (1875–6).

[10] S.H.C. xi. 321.
[11] Ibid. 314–15, 319–20.
[12] Ibid. 322.
[13] Ibid. 314–15.
[14] C.P. 25(2)/723, 17 Chas. II East.
[15] Univ. Brit. Dir. (1791), iv. 110.
[16] Allbut, Staffs. Pottery Dir. (1802).
[17] White, Dir. Staffs. (1834).
[18] Ibid.
[19] Ibid. (1851). Ward, Stoke, 571–2, gives 1794 as the date of building, stating that in 1814 the other market hall was enlarged.
[20] Shaw, Staffs. Potteries, 75–76.
[21] White, Dir. Staffs. (1851).
[22] P.O. Dir. Staffs. (1854).
[23] Warrillow, Stoke, 399–400. For a description of the building see p. 237.
[24] White, Dir. Staffs. (1851); see pp. 228–9.
[25] P.O. Dir. Staffs. (1868).
[26] Univ. Brit. Dir. (1791), iv. 110.
[27] White, Dir. Staffs. (1851).
[28] Kelly's Dir. Staffs. (1896).
[29] Stoke Official Handbk. [edns. of later 1950's].
[30] Shaw, Staffs. Potteries, 75–76.

century the fair days were 14 February, 29 May, 22 July, and 1 November.[31] In the 1840's woollen cloth, hardware, and pedlary were dealt in at the fairs.[32] By 1860, and possibly earlier, they had become pleasure fairs and were then held on Shrove Tuesday, Easter Tuesday, Whit Tuesday, and Martinmas Tuesday.[33]

MILLS. Before 1212[34] Ranulph de Bevill, lord of Longton, granted the stream which ran down from the vill of Longton, presumably the present Cockster–Longton Brook,[35] and the adjoining bank to the priory of Trentham 'to the use of the mill upon the heath'.[36] This grant was confirmed by his son Ranulph,[37] lord of the manor by 1212.[38] In 1250 William de Bevill, lord of Longton, granted the service due from the mill of Longton to Trentham priory.[39] Between 1277 and 1292 William's son Robert gave the priory the right to erect a mill anywhere within the manor of Longton, with suit of service by all the men of Longton when built.[40] This mill may have been in place of the first. Nothing more is known of Longton mill until 1600 when a water-mill was owned by John Hunt as part of his manor of Longton.[41] It was still held with the manor in 1665 and in 1774 after it had been bought by the Revd. Obadiah Lane.[42] The mill, which for some years had been worked by Ambrose Smith and Obadiah Lane as partners in flint-grinding there, was offered for sale by Lane in 1777, with the benefit of the partnership[43] and was sold in 1778 to Sir John Edensor Heathcote.[44] By this date the mill estate included a cottage in a small field.[45] Richard Edensor Heathcote leased a flint mill and cottage in Longton to William K. Harvey in 1847 on a 21-year lease. In 1867 John Edensor Heathcote leased the mill, along with the two Gom's Mills, to James and Alfred Glover, partners in a flint-grinding business, who continued to use it to grind flint.[46] In 1882 they surrendered the lease of the mill, by this date called Longton Old Mill, and it was immediately leased to Thomas and George Bakewell for ten years.[47] By this date a drying kiln had been built there.[48] The mill was leased in 1899 by John Heathcote Edwards Heathcote to Messrs. J. and E. J. Froggatt for five years.[49] A further lease to the Froggatts for a period of seven years was made in 1904.[50] The mill was sold in 1916 to W. V. S. Gradwell Goodwin by J. H. Edwards Heathcote.[51] By this date it was known as Sideway Mill. Since c. 1920 the mill has been worked by British Glue and Chemicals Ltd. as a bone mill. It is situated on the Longton Brook in the southwest of Longton at the junction of Poplar Lane and the bridle road from Longton to Hanford. There was formerly a large mill pool east of the mill which survived until at least 1898.[52] The mill was still using water-power until soon after the Second World War when the large water-wheel, which was of the overshot type, was removed. Steam-power also was used from at least 1930.[53] The mill is now run by electricity.

By 1632 a corn mill known as Gom's Mill had been erected on the Furnace Brook, south-east of Longton Hall.[54] By 1851 it was in use as a flint mill.[55]

POTTERY INDUSTRY. The pottery industry became established at Longton somewhat later than in the more northern parts of the Potteries, and it was not until the early 19th century that the rise of the bone-china industry helped to bring importance to the town. In the mid-18th century, however, the first porcelain works in Staffordshire was built at Longton Hall. This is also the first known pottery works in Longton. In the second half of the century earthenware and fine stoneware were made at Longton by such men as John Turner, Joseph Cyples, Benjamin Plant, and the Garner family.[56] Thirteen potters at Longton were listed in 1784[57] and 37 c. 1800.[58] In the early 19th century Longton became the centre of the rapidly expanding bone-china industry.[59] By 1851 there were 42 potworks there, a larger number than in any of the other Pottery towns, and only eleven of these made earthenware only.[60] Longton, however, has never been distinguished by the continued presence of great families of potters on the scale of the other towns, its undertakings being on the whole of a smaller size. There were over 60 works in 1959, of which more than half were devoted to the manufacture of bone china. Very few firms were making both china and earthenware; at the Crown Works of John Tams Ltd., in the Strand since 1875, vitrified ware was produced as well as earthenware. In addition the town produces some sanitary ware, electrical porcelain, and glazed tiles.[61]

With its greater number of works Longton presents a more distinctive pottery landscape than any of the other towns. The works are ranged along the principal streets such as Church Street, Uttoxeter Road, and Sutherland Road; they are also clustered in the narrow lanes to the west of The Strand and in the formerly congested area south-east of the market. In the latter district, where there has been extensive demolition of buildings since the Second World War, several smaller pot-banks are now (1960) standing derelict, their structures in some cases

[31] White, *Dir. Staffs.* (1851).
[32] *Parl. Gazetteer* (1844).
[33] *P.O. Dir. Staffs.* (1860).
[34] His son Ranulph was lord of the manor by 1212: see below.
[35] See p. 224.
[36] *S.H.C.* xi. 320.
[37] Ibid.
[38] See p. 230.
[39] *S.H.C.* xi. 318.
[40] Ibid. 321–2. Robt. was dead by 1292 and the gift was to the Prior of Trentham, John de Conyngeston, 1277–96.
[41] C 142/287/11.
[42] C.P. 25(2)/723, 17 Chas. II East; C.P. 25(2)/1411, 14 Geo. III Hil.; see p. 230.
[43] H. Mus., Heathcote papers, xix. 1, 6.
[44] Ibid. xix. 1.
[45] Ibid.
[46] Ibid. ii, loose; see p. 232.

[47] H. Mus., Heathcote papers, xix. 2.
[48] Ibid.
[49] Ibid. i, loose.
[50] Ibid.
[51] Ibid.
[52] O.S. Map 6″ Staffs. xviii SW. (1901).
[53] Local inf.
[54] The ownership of this mill is treated in another section: see p. 231.
[55] See p. 231.
[56] Mankowitz and Haggar, *Eng. Pottery*, 134, 176–7. The Longton Hall Works and the works of Turner, Cyples, and the Garners are treated subsequently in this article.
[57] Ibid. 270.
[58] Allbut, *Staffs. Pottery Dir.* (1802).
[59] Mankowitz and Haggar, *Eng. Pottery*, 134.
[60] White, *Dir. Staffs.* (1851).
[61] *Pottery Gaz. Dir.* (1960). For the Crown Works see Meigh, 'Staffs. Potters', 191; Jewitt, *Ceramic Art*, 542.

probably dating from about 1800. Elsewhere the factories are mainly of the second half of the 19th century. A notable exception is the long two-storied front range of the Boundary Works in Church Street, dated 1819 and possibly the least altered early industrial façade in the Potteries. The design of the three-storied central feature with its arched entrance surmounted by a Venetian window and a pedimented gable was much favoured in all six towns, and persisted in modified forms until the later 19th century.[62] Late examples at Longton are at the works of John Aynsley and Sons in Sutherland Road (1861) and at the St. Louis works in Edensor Road (1876). These entrance blocks, latterly often of three stories, contain warehouses and offices; behind them the lower factory buildings are usually ranged round a court or series of courts. Bottle ovens of varied shapes and sizes have survived, including interior ovens emerging through the roofs as well as the free-standing examples more usual in the other towns. Although Longton lacks the striking canal-side groups found in Burslem or Hanley, recent demolition of houses throughout the town has opened up new views of typical 19th-century pot-banks, themselves likely to disappear within a few years as the electrification of the industry proceeds.

The first known pottery works at Longton is that opened on the site of the present stables block at Longton Hall in 1749 or 1750 by William Jenkinson.[63] It was also the first Staffordshire porcelain works. Jenkinson, who was evidently living at the hall by 1752, went into partnership with William Nicklin of Newcastle-under-Lyme and William Littler of Hanley in 1751, but in 1753 his place in the triumvirate was taken by Nathaniel Firmin of St. Clement Danes, London. Jenkinson withdrew from Longton, evidently to Oswestry, and Littler moved in as manager. A fourth partner, the Revd. Robert Charlesworth of Bakewell, joined the group in 1755, and it was his money which kept the venture going for the next five years. In 1760, however, he withdrew and the factory was closed. The partners brought clays for their porcelain from Cornwall, Devon, and Dorset, and possibly from Derbyshire also, and fragments found on the site show that they made earthenware as well.

John Turner, having worked in partnership with R. Bankes at the works in Stoke which later passed to Josiah Spode, began to work on his own account at Lane End in 1762,[64] evidently in or near High Street (now Uttoxeter Road).[65] His main products were cream-coloured, stone and jasper ware and

dry bodies, and much of his work will stand comparison with the Wedgwood ware which he frequently imitated.[66] From c. 1780 he was making his stoneware from a local clay which he discovered at Greendock.[67] He was a member of the New Hall Company from 1781 to 1782, and in 1784 his firm (Turner and Abbott) was described as 'potters to the Prince of Wales'.[68] On his death in 1787 John Turner was succeeded by his two sons, William and John,[69] who some fifteen years later had two factories on opposite sides of High Street.[70] In 1800 they took out the first patent for 'stone china'.[71] The firm was enlarged to include John Glover and Charles Simpson in 1803, but being dependent on its continental trade it was ruined by the French wars and went bankrupt in 1806.[72] The factory was occupied by Richard Woolley from 1809 until his bankruptcy in 1814.[73] William Turner started again at Fenton in 1807 and returned in 1811 to High Street, Longton, where he was still working in the 1830's.[74]

A pottery between what are now Cyples Lane and Smithy Lane and said to be contemporary with the Wedgwood works at Etruria (opened in 1769), was founded by one of the Cyples family,[75] but the first known potter of that name is Joseph Cyples who was making 'Egyptian black and pottery in general' at Longton in 1784.[76] The family continued to work in Market Street until the late 1840's[77] when Thomas Barlow took it over, continuing there until the late 1880's.[78] The works was held by G. L. Bentley and Company between at least 1898 and 1912[79] and by J. T. Fell and Company (Longton) Ltd. between at least 1923 and 1940.[80] The building, no longer used as a pottery, is now partly derelict. Richard Cyples evidently moved c. 1846 to the works in High Street belonging to the Bridgwoods (see below), and worked there as one of the partnership of Cyples and Bull for a few years.[81]

Samuel Hughes, who bought the Gom's Mill estate in 1765,[82] sold an acre and a half of the land in 1777 to his son-in-law Mark Walklate for the erection of a potworks. Walklate had built a house and works by the following year, but he eventually ran into financial difficulties and in 1786 the house and works, known as Daisy Bank, passed to Hughes.[83] In 1804 the estate passed to Hughes's sons, Peter and Thomas, and in 1811 Peter, having bought Thomas's share, sold the whole to Sir John Edensor Heathcote.[84] The works was in the tenure of John Drewery (or Drury) by 1812 and remained in his family until 1830.[85] It then passed to Ray and Tideswell, who made china and earthenware and in

[62] See plate facing p. 172.
[63] For this section on the Longton Hall Works see B. Watney, Longton Hall Porcelain, passim. For the hall itself see p. 229.
[64] Mankowitz and Haggar, Eng. Pottery, 225.
[65] His sons were working there c. 1802: see below.
[66] Mankowitz and Haggar, Eng. Pottery, 225, 226; Jewitt, Ceramic Art, 559; N. Hudson Moore, Wedgwood and his Imitators, 102–4; The Times, 18 June 1960.
[67] Jewitt, Ceramic Art, 559; Mankowitz and Haggar, Eng. Pottery, 226.
[68] Mankowitz and Haggar, Eng. Pottery, 225 (where the date is given as 1786), 270 (citing a directory of 1784); see p. 166.
[69] Mankowitz and Haggar, Eng. Pottery, 226; Shaw, Staffs. Potteries, 222–3.
[70] Allbut, Staffs. Pottery Dir. (1802).
[71] R. G. Haggar, The Masons of Lane Delph, 65–66.
[72] Mankowitz and Haggar, Eng. Pottery, 225.

[73] Ibid. 52.
[74] Ibid. 225; Shaw, Staffs. Potteries, 75; The Times, 18 June 1960.
[75] Jewitt, Ceramic Art, 540, stating also that they 'are said to be the oldest works in Longton—the first there established'; see p. 166.
[76] Mankowitz and Haggar, Eng. Pottery, 64, 270.
[77] Ibid. 64; Meigh, 'Staffs. Potters', 63–64; Jewitt, Ceramic Art, 540. There were several partnerships in the 1840's.
[78] Meigh, 'Staffs. Potters', 17; Jewitt, Ceramic Art, 540, 542.
[79] Meigh, 'Staffs. Potters', 24.
[80] Ibid. 78; Kelly's Dir. Staffs. (1940).
[81] Meigh, 'Staffs. Potters', 63; Jewitt, Ceramic Art, 542.
[82] See p. 231.
[83] H. Mus., Heathcote papers, xviii. 11.
[84] Ibid.; ibid. ix. 5; see p. 231.
[85] Meigh, 'Staffs. Potters', 71; Jewitt, Ceramic Art, 551.

1833 were succeeded by Ray and Wynne; Richard Ray was working there alone by 1847.[86] In the early 1840's the works was 'a small factory in good condition, with rooms open, large and ventilated'.[87] Charles James Mason, having gone bankrupt at Fenton in 1848, started to work again at Daisy Bank in 1851, leasing the works from J. E. Heathcote, and remaining there for three years.[88] The lease, and later the freehold, of the Daisy Bank Works passed to Hulse, Nixon, and Adderley.[89] On Nixon's death in 1869 the firm became Hulse and Adderley and from 1874, the year after Hulse's death, was run by William Alsager Adderley, who in the early 1880's was making china and earthenware there.[90] The firm of Adderley was still working the Daisy Bank Pottery, in Spring Garden Road, in 1940,[91] but the works is now (1960) occupied as the Gainsborough Works by the sub-standard china department of Ridgway Potteries. The extensive buildings, which include the remains of crate-making shops, date largely from the later 19th century, with considerable additions of the period between the world wars. There were also flint mills on the Gom's Mill estate.[92]

A china works in Church Street (now King Street), said to have been founded by 1780 by John Forrester, was in the hands of the Hilditch family in the early 19th century.[93] John Hilditch was joined by William Hopwood in 1830; John died in 1843 and his son William in 1850, but the firm remained Hilditch and Hopwood until the death of William Hopwood in 1858.[94] His executors continued the business until 1867 when they sold it with the stock and plant to Dale, Page, and Company.[95] They continued at the works until 1876 when as Dale, Page, and Goodwin the firm moved to the New Town Works, High Street.[96] Thomas Bentley and Company, china manufacturers, are also given as occupants of the works between at least the mid-1860's and the early 1870's.[97] If this is correct the buildings must have been divided, a fact which would justify the tentative identification of the factory with the Boundary Works on the south side of King Street, bearing the date 1819. This factory was known as the California Works in the 1860's and 1870's and was held in the mid-1860's by Thomas Hobson and Company,

earthenware manufacturers; china and earthenware were made there in the 1870's.[98] The name had been changed to the Boundary Works by 1897 when the Royal Art Pottery Company was there.[99] Held by Tranter and Bradbury in 1899 and by A. Bradbury and Company between at least 1900 and 1903,[1] the Boundary Works was in the hands of Joseph Peake, maker of Rockingham ware and jet ware, between at least 1905 and 1920.[2] It then seems to have passed to Barlows (Longton) Ltd., a firm of earthenware manufacturers who also held the adjoining Melbourne Works and were still working in King Street in 1940.[3] The Boundary Works is now (1960) occupied as a pottery warehouse by Leo Samuels Ltd.; its front range of 1819, as already described above, is comparatively unaltered and is typical of its period. There was a flint and bone mill attached to Hilditch and Hopwood's works in 1835.[4]

Robert Garner (1733–89) built a works on the north side of King Street on a site now enclosed by Clarence Road and Marsh Road, with a house (Bank House) adjoining to the east.[5] He was evidently the son of the Robert Garner who had been an apprentice to Thomas Whieldon at Fenton and later worked with the Barkers near the Foley.[6] His son, also Robert (born 1766), still held the works in 1821.[7] The works has been rebuilt and is now (1960) occupied by the Co-operative Wholesale Society's Crown Clarence Pottery (earthenware) and by Messrs. Wagstaff and Brunt, china and earthenware dealers, who were there as china and earthenware manufacturers by the 1880's.[8] The house was the home of Charles Harvey, banker and former potter, by the late 1820's[9] but is no longer standing.

The former St. Gregory Works on the north side of High Street is said to have been established by George Barnes in 1794, and it was still in his hands c. 1800.[10] It is probably identifiable with the works in Hog's Lane (now Sutherland Road) held by him in 1823.[11] Apparently in the hands of Chesworth and Blood in 1824,[12] it was held by Wood and Blood by 1827[13] and by Beardmore and Birks from 1830 or 1831 until 1843.[14] It seems then to have passed to Sampson Beardmore who in 1850 was succeeded by George Townsend.[15] Tams and Lowe took over the works in 1864 and were still in possession in 1874.[16]

86 Meigh, 'Staffs. Potters', 165; Jewitt, *Ceramic Art*, 551; Mankowitz and Haggar, *Eng. Pottery*, 188. Ray and Tideswell were in partnership with one of the Drewery family at an unspecified date: Meigh, 'Staffs. Potters', 71.
87 *2nd Rep. Com. Employment of Children* [431], p. c90, H.C. (1843), xiv.
88 Mankowitz and Haggar, *Eng. Pottery*, 9, 143; Jewitt, *Ceramic Art*, 551; Meigh, 'Staffs. Potters', 136; H. Mus., Heathcote papers, xv. 15; see p. 221.
89 Jewitt, *Ceramic Art*, 551–2; Meigh, 'Staffs. Potters', 114.
90 Jewitt, *Ceramic Art*, 551–2; Meigh, 'Staffs. Potters', 4, 113.
91 *Kelly's Dir. Staffs.* (1940).   92 See p. 231.
93 Jewitt, *Ceramic Art*, 545; Mankowitz and Haggar, *Eng. Pottery*, 109; Meigh, 'Staffs. Potters', 105, which also (p. 24) gives Thos. Bentley.
94 Jewitt, *Ceramic Art*, 545; Mankowitz and Haggar, *Eng. Pottery*, 109; Meigh, 'Staffs. Potters', 105.
95 Jewitt, *Ceramic Art*, 545; Mankowitz and Haggar, *Eng. Pottery*, 109; Meigh, 'Staffs. Potters', 110.
96 Jewitt, *Ceramic Art*, 545; Meigh, 'Staffs. Potters', 64, showing them still at the New Town Works in 1892. The New Town Works had been built in 1845 by Jas. Meakin, founder of the Hanley firm of J. and G. Meakin (Jewitt, *Ceramic Art*, 545; Mankowitz and Haggar, *Eng. Pottery*, 146; see p. 164) and was occupied from 1905

by the Blythe Porcelain Co. (Meigh, 'Staffs. Potters', 30), being now (1960) an earthenware works run by the Blythe Pottery (Longton) Ltd.
97 *Jones's Potteries Dir.* (1864); *P.O. Dir. Staffs.* (1872); Meigh, 'Staffs. Potters', 24.
98 *Jones's Potteries Dir.* (1864); Meigh, 'Staffs. Potters', 107; O.S. Map 6″ Staffs. xviii NW. (1890).
99 Meigh, 'Staffs. Potters', 172.
1 Ibid. 37, 196.
2 Local inf. (1960); Meigh, 'Staffs. Potters', 18, 153; *Kelly's Dir. Staffs.* (1908, 1940).
3 See plate facing p. 172.
4 *Pigot's Nat. Com. Dir.* (1835).
5 Mankowitz and Haggar, *Eng. Pottery*, 94; Shaw, *Staffs. Potteries*, 174; Jewitt, *Ceramic Art*, 559–60, identifying Robt. Garner of Bank House and Robt. Garner of Fenton as the same man.   6 See p. 217.
7 Mankowitz and Haggar, *Eng. Pottery*, 94; Meigh, 'Staffs. Potters', 84.   8 *Kelly's Dir. Staffs.* (1884).
9 Shaw, *Staffs. Potteries*, 77.
10 Jewitt, *Ceramic Art*, 548; Allbut, *Staffs. Pottery Dir.* (1802).   11 Meigh, 'Staffs. Potters', 18.
12 Ibid. 53; Jewitt, *Ceramic Art*, 548.
13 Meigh, 'Staffs. Potters', 217.   14 Ibid. 20.
15 Ibid. 196. This also (p. 20) gives Beardmore as at the St. George's Pottery, High St., Longton 1843–8.
16 Jewitt, *Ceramic Art*, 548; Meigh, 'Staffs. Potters', 191.

In 1874 or 1875 William Lowe succeeded,[17] building the Sydney Works to the rear in Sutherland Road in 1879 for the china department.[18] The firm remained in operation until *c.* 1930;[19] the St. Gregory Works has been demolished and the Sydney Works is now a textile factory.

James Chetham (d. 1807) and Richard Woolley (1765–1825) were working in Commerce Street, Longton, by 1796 and became noted for busts and figures in white grained 'pearl' ware.[20] After Chetham's death his widow continued at the factory in partnership with Woolley who moved to the former Turner factory in or near High Street in 1809.[21] The Chethams continued in Commerce Street until the early 1870's; they were in partnership with John Robinson from *c.* 1822 until 1840.[22] The factory passed from the Chethams to H. Aynsley and Company which still makes earthenware there.[23]

A works in Charles Street to the west side of Stafford Street (now The Strand) was built in 1799 by John and Charles Harvey who were succeeded by Hulme and Hawley.[24] Charles and W. K. Harvey, sons of Charles Harvey, had taken over the works by 1835 and added china and gold lustre ware to the earthenware made by the two previous firms; subsequently, however, the Harveys concentrated on printed goods and white granite ware for the export market.[25] They were succeeded in 1853 by Holland and Green who were followed in the early 1880's by Green, Clark, and Clay.[26] By then most of the buildings had been demolished and replaced by shops, but the remainder of the works was held by Green and Clark between at least 1886 and 1891.[27] Harvey and Sons were working a flint mill in Charles Street by the early 1820's, and this had passed to Charles and John Harvey by 1829.[28] Described as in Stafford Street it was held by Charles Harvey in 1851, by Charles Harvey and Son in 1864, and by Holland and Green in the later 1870's.[29]

A works in Stafford Street adjoining the market was occupied by George Forrester between at least 1805 and 1831[30] and was said to be the first with 'a regular plan for the arrangement of the separate places for the distinct processes'.[31] By 1838 it was occupied by Sampson Bridgwood whose family had established a business in Market Street at the beginning of the century.[32] The Stafford Street works was demolished to make way for the new market of 1863, but the Bridgwoods had already opened a second factory at the present Anchor Pottery in Bridgwood Street (formerly Wharf Street) ten years before.[33] The firm began to make bone china at this second works but now (1960) confines its products to earthenware.[34] Sampson Bridgwood, who was working Gom's Mills as flint mills in 1851,[35] had opened the Anchor Mills in Goddard Street adjoining the Anchor Pottery by 1867.[36] About the mid-1890's the Anchor Mills passed to William Lockett and Company[37] and by 1900 were in the hands of the Potters Mills Ltd.[38] Between at least 1908 and 1916 they were held by Stephen Mear[39] and ceased operations in the mid-1950's, being then held by Mellors Mineral Mills Ltd.[40]

The Waterloo Pottery in Flint Street, off Stafford Street, was opened in 1815 by Batkin and Deakin who were still working there in 1822.[41] It was worked by Deakin and Bailey by the late 1820's and by James Deakin and Son from 1833 until at least 1862.[42] Between at least 1864 and 1869 it was held by Lowe and Abberley[43] and in the early 1870's first by James Abberley and then by Brough and Blackhurst, makers of earthenware, who were still there in 1895.[44] The Royal Art Pottery Company was in occupation of the Waterloo Works between at least 1897 and 1915.[45] The works is now called the Royal Art Pottery and has been held by Alfred Clough Ltd. since at least 1940.[46]

A works between St. Martin's Lane and Chancery Lane was occupied by Martin and Shaw in 1815, by Martin, Shaw, and Cope between at least 1816 and 1824 as makers of lustre ware and china, and then by William Martin who was succeeded in the mid-1830's by Thomas Martin, still the occupant in 1847.[47] It was then held by Glover and Colclough until at least 1854[48] when it may have been partially

[17] *Keates's Potteries Dir.* (1875–6).

[18] Jewitt, *Ceramic Art*, 548; inscription on building 'Sydney Works W L 1879'.

[19] Meigh, 'Staffs. Potters', 130; *Kelly's Dir. Staffs.* (1928; 1932, where it is last mentioned).

[20] Mankowitz and Haggar, *Eng. Pottery*, 52, 172.

[21] Ibid.

[22] Ibid.; Meigh, 'Staffs. Potters', 53.

[23] Meigh, 'Staffs. Potters', 9; Mankowitz and Haggar, *Eng. Pottery*, 52; Jewitt, *Ceramic Art*, 542; *Pottery Gaz.* (1960). The factory is now called the Commerce Works. For the firm of John Aynsley see Mankowitz and Haggar, op. cit., 11.

[24] Jewitt, *Ceramic Art*, 542–3; Meigh, 'Staffs. Potters', 101, 102.

[25] Jewitt, *Ceramic Art*, 543; Meigh, 'Staffs. Potters', 101; Mankowitz and Haggar, *Eng. Pottery*, 106.

[26] Jewitt, *Ceramic Art*, 543; Meigh, 'Staffs. Potters', 91, 108.

[27] Jewitt, *Ceramic Art*, 543; Meigh, 'Staffs. Potters', 108.

[28] Allbut, *Newcastle and Pottery Dir.* (1822–3); *Pigot's Nat. Com. Dir.* (1828–9).

[29] White, *Dir. Staffs.* (1851); *Jones's Potteries Dir.* (1864); *Keates's Potteries Dir.* (1875–6, 1879).

[30] Meigh, 'Staffs. Potters', 82; Jewitt, *Ceramic Art*, 552. Meigh, op. cit. 516, states that it was built in 1756 by Roger Wood of the Ash.

[31] Shaw, *Staffs. Potteries*, 75.

[32] Meigh, 'Staffs. Potters', 40–41; Jewitt, *Ceramic Art*, 552; Mankowitz and Haggar, *Eng. Pottery*, 35; Allbut, *Staffs. Pottery Dir.* (1802).

[33] Meigh, 'Staffs. Potters', 41; Jewitt, *Ceramic Art*, 552; Mankowitz and Haggar, *Eng. Pottery*, 35; date 1853 on building.

[34] Mankowitz and Haggar, *Eng. Pottery*, 35; *Pottery Gaz.* (1960).

[35] See pp. 231–2.

[36] *Keates and Ford's Potteries Dir.* (1867).

[37] *Kelly's Dir. Staffs.* (1896). They were still in the hands of Sampson Bridgwood and Son in 1892: *Keates's Potteries Dir.* (1892–3).

[38] *Kelly's Dir. Staffs.* (1900).

[39] Ibid. (1908, 1916).

[40] Local inf. (1960). The site and unused buildings are now owned by Sampson Bridgwood and Son Ltd.

[41] Jewitt, *Ceramic Art*, 550; Meigh, 'Staffs. Potters', 13, 20. Jewitt, loc. cit., mentions that 'the date 1815 occurs on the ovens' and that in the hands of 'Ratkin [*sic*] and Booth' the works was noted for its gold and silver lustre ware.

[42] Meigh, 'Staffs. Potters', 13, 67, 68.

[43] Ibid. 130. For James Abberley and then Thomas Lowe at the Gold St. works see p. 243.

[44] Meigh, 'Staffs. Potters', 1, 43; Jewitt, *Ceramic Art*, 550.   [45] Meigh, 'Staffs. Potters', 172.

[46] *Kelly's Dir. Staffs.* (1940); *Pottery Gaz. Dir.* (1960).

[47] Jewitt, *Ceramic Art*, 547; Meigh, 'Staffs. Potters', 135.

[48] Meigh, 'Staffs. Potters', 86; Jewitt, *Ceramic Art*, 547, where it is stated that Abel Booth succeeded Martin and Cope and that there were subsequently various changes before Glover, Colclough, and Townsend took over.

rebuilt (see below). Named the New Market Works presumably c. 1863 when the new market was completed, it was held by Skelson and Plant (also of the Heathcote Road Pottery) between at least 1868 and 1872[49] and then by George Copestake the elder.[50] It was in the hands of Samuel Radford by 1879 and of Radford and Ward from 1885 until at least 1894.[51] The works presumably formed part of the block situated to the east of the market,[52] and it may well be identifiable with the disused pottery still (1960) standing at the southern end of this block. It has a front on Chancery Lane dated 1854 with the initials 'P M', but the remainder consists of older ranges, that on St. Martin's Lane incorporating two bottle-ovens which project through the roof.

The Anchor Works at the junction of Anchor Road and Sutherland Road was run by Thomas and John Carey from at least 1818 until the dissolution of the partnership in 1842.[53] The works then passed to John Ashwell.[54] Between at least 1845 and 1852 it was held by Broadhurst and Green[55] and between at least 1853 and 1856 by William Green.[56] By 1860 it had passed to Copestake Brothers and from 1871 or 1872 until at least 1889 was in the hands of George Copestake the younger who produced china there.[57] Held by Thomas Morris between at least 1898 and 1903[58] the works was in the hands of Fell and Robinson between at least 1923 and 1930[59] and was occupied as the Pelican Pottery by Messrs. Fell early in 1960 when it was abandoned.[60] Most of the range in Anchor Road, however, has been occupied since c. 1957 as a warehouse by the nearby British Anchor Pottery[61] and has been rebuilt. The remainder of the building, dating probably from c. 1800, consists of a long two-storied range in Sutherland Road, with three bottle-ovens projecting through the roof, and another two-storied range behind and parallel to it. An angle entrance at the junction of the two streets surmounted by a Venetian window has been converted into a shop; by the 1870's the entrance was already in its present position in Anchor Road.[62] By the late 1820's the Careys had a mill for grinding corn and potters' materials in Anchor Road to the north of the Anchor Works; the steam engine was supplied with water from the reservoir surrounding The Moat, the house on the opposite side of the road which was occupied by John Carey by 1834.[63] By 1851 the mill and house were in the hands of Moses Cartwright who was still working the mill in 1860,[64] but by 1864 it was held by the Longton Mills Company, still the occupants in 1900.[65] It has been run by W. G. Ball Ltd., colour manufacturers, since the mid-1950's.[66]

By 1822 William Bradshaw was working a pottery later known as the St. James's Place China Works and situated after the building of St. James's Church opposite its west end. He was succeeded in 1822 by Baggulley and Ball.[67] Robert Gallimore took over in 1831 and produced china in addition to the lustre ware already made at the works; by 1841 he was in partnership with George Shufflebotham.[68] Gallimore retired in 1842, and the business was then carried on by Shufflebotham and William Webberley, who in 1844 dropped the manufacture of lustre ware.[69] After Shufflebotham's death in 1847 Webberley continued at the works on his own account, buying it in 1888 and rebuilding it as 'a commodious "four oven" manufactory' soon afterwards.[70] He worked there until 1892[71] when the factory passed to Coggin and Hill who still held it in the early 20th century.[72] It was held by the Primrose Pottery Company in 1912 and 1913[73] and by Smith, Hodgkinson, and Company in 1915.[74] By 1960 it had been demolished.

A works in what became Victoria Place, off Stafford Street, was built by Ralph Shaw c. 1828 and was subsequently run by him or his tenants. His executors still owned the premises in the early 1880's.[75] Yale and Barker were there in the early 1840's when the works was described as 'a small, well-conducted factory; rooms low, small, and dirty'; Cooke and Griffiths held it in 1850 and 1851 and Walker and Finney from 1853.[76] Joseph Finney was working on his own there in 1858 and began manufacturing china instead of earthenware in the late 1860's; he was still at the works in 1900.[77] Messrs. Cartwright and Edwards, of the nearby Borough Pottery since at least 1869, held the Victoria Pottery also by 1912.[78] When Cartwright and Edwards Ltd. became a subsidiary of Alfred Clough Ltd. in 1955 both works were sold to the Manor Engineering Co. Ltd. The Victoria Pottery was pulled down and the present Victoria Foundry built on the site.[79]

St. Mary's China Works in what is now Uttoxeter Road existed by 1830 and was run by Moore and

[49] Jewitt, Ceramic Art, 551; Meigh, 'Staffs. Potters', 183; P.O. Dir. Staffs. (1868, 1872); see p. 237.
[50] Meigh, 'Staffs. Potters', 60; Jewitt, Ceramic Art, 547.
[51] Meigh, 'Staffs. Potters', 163; Jewitt, Ceramic Art, 547.
[52] O.S. Map 1/2,500 Staffs. xviii. 10 (survey of 1877).
[53] Meigh, 'Staffs. Potters', 49; Mankowitz and Haggar, Eng. Pottery, 42; Jewitt, Ceramic Art, 554; Shaw, Staffs. Potteries, 77; Parson and Bradshaw, Dir. Staffs. (1818).
[54] Jewitt, Ceramic Art, 554; Meigh, 'Staffs. Potters', 8.
[55] Meigh, 'Staffs. Potters', 42.
[56] Ibid. 91.
[57] Ibid. 60, 61; Jewitt, Ceramic Art, 554.
[58] Meigh, 'Staffs. Potters', 146.
[59] Ibid. 78.
[60] Local inf. (1960).
[61] Ibid.
[62] O.S. Map 1/2,500 Staffs. xviii. 11 (surveys of 1877 and 1879).
[63] Shaw, Staffs. Potteries, 77; Pigot's Nat. Com. Dir. (1828–9); Hargreaves, Map of Staffs. Potteries; see p. 231.
[64] White, Dir. Staffs. (1851); P.O. Dir. Staffs. (1860); Harrison and Harrod's Dir. Staffs. (1861).

[65] Jones's Potteries Dir. (1864); Kelly's Dir. Staffs. (1900).
[66] Local inf. (1960).
[67] Meigh, 'Staffs. Potters', 11, 38; O.S. Map 1/2,500 Staffs. xviii. 11 (surveys of 1877 and 1879).
[68] Jewitt, Ceramic Art, 551; Ward, Stoke, 573.
[69] Jewitt, Ceramic Art, 551; Meigh, 'Staffs. Potters', 207. They also held the Gold St. works: see below.
[70] Jewitt, Ceramic Art, 551.
[71] Meigh, 'Staffs. Potters', 207.
[72] Ibid. 56. On p. 106 Meigh gives Hill and Co.
[73] Ibid. 161.
[74] Ibid. 185.
[75] Ibid. 177, 178 showing Shaw and Yale in 1840; Jewitt, Ceramic Art, 547.
[76] Meigh, 'Staffs. Potters', 58, 202, 220; 2nd Rep. Com. Employment of Children, p. c89. Walker and Finney are given in 1853–5 and Thos. Walker in 1856–7.
[77] Meigh, 'Staffs. Potters', 79; Jewitt, Ceramic Art, 547; Keates's Potteries Dir. (1892–3); Kelly's Dir. Staffs. (1900). He was the tenant of Shaw's executors in 1883: Jewitt, loc. cit.   [78] Meigh, 'Staffs. Potters', 51.
[79] Ex inf. Cartwright & Edwards Ltd. (1960), who now occupy the newly built Newborough and Sutherland Potteries west of the former Borough Pottery.

Hamilton until 1859 when Samuel Moore became the sole owner.[80] In the early 1840's it was described as 'a small compact factory, well conducted; good rooms; open, airy, well ventilated'.[81] The present St. Mary's Works on Uttoxeter Road at Mount Pleasant was built by him in 1862 and passed in 1870 to his sons, Bernard and Samuel.[82] Bernard sold the works in 1906 and moved to Wolfe Street, Stoke.[83] The new owner of St. Mary's Works was Thomas Clarke Wild, who had founded the Royal Albert Crown China Works, also in Uttoxeter Road, in 1894, and the business is now (1960) run by his sons who produce Royal Albert bone china at the St. Mary's China Works.[84] There is an addition of the 1880's to the east with numerous extensions beyond made since 1937.[85] The firm was the first to use mechanical firing commercially in the manufacture of bone china.[86]

A works in Gold Street, stated in 1883 to be among the oldest in Longton, was then noted as the place where gold lustre had been discovered and first used for decoration.[87] It was held by Shufflebotham, Webberley, and Hallam in 1846, and after Shufflebotham's death in 1847 it passed from his executors to Hannah and Mary Shufflebotham who still held it in 1858.[88] The Broadhursts held the works from at least 1860 until 1864,[89] and Brough Brothers and Company were working in Gold Street from 1864 until 1870[90] when they were succeeded by James Abberley, himself followed in 1871 by Thomas Lowe; Mrs. Thomas Lowe held the works in 1875.[91] Barker Brothers, of the family that had been working at Longton for about 100 years, were at Gold Street from at least 1876 until 1882 when they moved to the Meir Works, Barker Street, still occupied by Barker Brothers Ltd.[92] Lowe, Ratcliffe and Company succeeded them at Gold Street where they made earthenware until at least 1892.[93] J. W. Beswick was there by 1899,[94] and the firm of John Beswick Ltd. still makes earthenware in Gold Street.[95] The three-storied cement-rendered front of the works probably dates from the first half of the 19th century.

MINING. There was mining at Longton before the end of the 17th century, and the supply of cheap coal in the area is given as one of the reasons for the location of the first porcelain works in Staffordshire at Longton Hall.[96] In 1760 the increasing population included 'colliers, stone-getters, labourers, and

other poor people',[97] and by 1775 the area between the Uttoxeter road, the Stone road, and the Meir–Blurton road was pitted with numerous coal workings.[98] The growth of the town early in the 19th century may be attributed to the extension of mining as well as to the rise of the bone china industry there; indeed the two were presumably connected. By 1832 a mineral line ran from the Trent and Mersey Canal south of Whieldon's Grove, Fenton, to three separate parts of Longton—Anchor Road, The Strand, and Greendock.[99] The mines in the area c. 1840, some of them just to the east of the Longton boundary at Adderley Green and Weston Coyney, included shafts at least 320 yards deep, 'much deeper than the pits in general in the more northerly part of the borough'.[1] Since the end of the last century, however, there has been only one colliery, Florence, in operation within the limits of the 1910 borough.

In 1695 coal-mining rights on the Ash Lands on the Woodhouse estate were leased, with a nearby mine in Fenton Culvert, by Richard Nicholls of Fenton Culvert to William James of Ashbourne. James's executors conveyed them in 1703 to Obadiah Lane of Normacot Grange, also tenant of other mines in the manor by grant of Thomas Foley in 1699.[2] From 1713 Obadiah's son and heir, Nathaniel, was working the Woodhouse and Fenton mines in partnership with Stephen Wood of the Ash in Stoke parish, sharing the use of a 'great gutter' running from the brook below Longton Hall up to Woodhouse Lane.[3] Nathaniel mortgaged his share of the partnership in the Woodhouse mines in 1717 to John Harrison who in 1720 assigned the mortgage to Francis Parrott of Talke and John Bourne of Newcastle, Bourne taking over Parrott's share in 1724.[4] Wood's portion, with other adjoining mines, was leased to John Robinson of Goldenhill nearby in Fenton in 1759.[5] The subsequent history of mining on the Woodhouse estate is not clear; possibly it became absorbed in the operations of the Golden Hill Colliery,[6] but in the 1870's the Speedwall Colliery was in operation to the west of Woodhouse.[7] In 1721 Wood, Bourne, and Parrott were also mining in the nearby Priors Field, Lord Gower's property, and had constructed a gutter there.[8]

The Meir Hay Colliery to the south-east of the Woodhouse was in operation by 1791 and was worked in the 19th century in conjunction with the

[80] Jewitt, *Ceramic Art*, 544.
[81] *2nd Rep. Com. Employment of Children*, p. c88.
[82] Jewitt, *Ceramic Art*, 544; Mankowitz and Haggar, *Eng. Pottery*, 156; date on building.
[83] Mankowitz and Haggar, *Eng. Pottery*, 156.
[84] *Stoke Official Handbk.* (1960), 120, 121.
[85] Ibid. 121; inscriptions on buildings.
[86] *Stoke Official Handbk.* (1960), 121.
[87] Jewitt, *Ceramic Art*, 548.
[88] Ibid. 181. Shufflebotham and Webberley also held the St. James's Works. There were evidently two works in Gold St. in the late 1820's and the 1830's, held by Wm. Jervis and by Hulse, Jaquis, and Barlow: ibid. 114, 116. Joseph Reeves was at Gold St. in 1834 (ibid. 165), Wm. Marsh in 1841 (ibid. 135), and Jas. Colclough in the early 1840's: ibid. 56.
[89] Meigh, 'Staffs. Potters', 42 (Jas. and Sam. in 1860, then Jas. alone).
[90] Ibid. 43.
[91] Ibid. 1, 130. Lowe and Abberley held the Waterloo Works in the 1860's.
[92] Meigh, 'Staffs. Potters', 17; Mankowitz and Haggar,

Eng. Pottery, 15–16. For the Barkers at Fenton see p. 217.
[93] Meigh, 'Staffs. Potters', 130; Jewitt, *Ceramic Art*, 548.
[94] Meigh, 'Staffs. Potters', 25.
[95] *Pottery Gaz.* (1960).
[96] B. Watney, *Longton Hall Porcelain*, 9, 14, 19, 61; see p. 239.
[97] Ward, *Stoke*, 564.
[98] Yates, *Map of Staffs.* (1775).
[99] Hargreaves, *Map of Staffs. Potteries*.
[1] Ward, *Stoke*, 573.
[2] W.S.L., D. 788 (32), bdles. 10, 11. Reference was made to a gutter on the Ash Land brought up there by Ric. Foley: ibid. bdle. 11. Lane was evidently mining in Longton by 1695, agreeing there to extend a gutter draining mines there along to an ironstone mine on Meir Heath: ibid. bdle. 10. For the mine at Fenton see p. 222.
[3] W.S.L., D. 788 (32), bdle. 10.
[4] Ibid. bdles. 10 and 11.
[5] Ibid. bdle. 10.
[6] See p. 222.
[7] O.S. Map 6″ Staffs. xviii NE. (1889).
[8] W.S.L., D. 788 (32), bdle. 11; see p. 232.

Lane End Ironworks opened by William Sparrow in 1826 and closed in 1880.[9] The colliery was closed in 1888.[10] Various other collieries were worked in conjunction with the ironworks. The Foley Colliery (coal and ironstone) to the south in Heathcote Road had been opened by 1826.[11] Also known as the Swingle Hill Colliery after it had passed to J. W. Sparrow in the mid-1860's,[12] it came into the hands of the Goddards (who had already taken over the ironworks) in the early 1870's,[13] and some ten years later it passed to Balfour and Company who closed it in 1888 or 1889.[14] The Lane End Colliery held by Balfour and Company in 1888 and apparently closed about then may be identifiable with the colliery lying to the south-west of the ironworks and in operation by 1832.[15] There was, however, a Lane End Colliery in Heathcote Road to the south-east of the works in the mid-1860's, when it was held by J. W. Sparrow; it had been closed by the mid-1870's and may have been a branch of the other Lane End Colliery.[16] Another colliery to the north of the ironworks seems to have been worked as part of the Sparrow concern from the beginning.[17] A Stone Row Colliery which was described as 'sinking' in 1877 was evidently run in conjunction with the ironworks and seems to have been closed in 1888 or 1889.[18]

The Anchor Colliery in Anchor Road was being worked by Ashwell and Company by 1859.[19] It seems to have been closed about the mid-1870's.[20]

The Cinderhill Colliery at East Vale was run by the Cinderhill Colliery Company (Leighton, Burgess and Williams) by 1865[21] and by Charles Leighton of Fenton Park from the late 1860's.[22] It seems to have been closed in the mid-1870's.[23]

The Longton Hall Colliery (coal and ironstone) was worked by James and Alfred Glover from at least 1867 until 1887 with an ironworks attached by 1872 to smelt the ironstone raised.[24] It was in the hands of their executors in 1888[25] and by 1889 had passed to the Longton Hall Company.[26] This had 121 men working below ground there and 71 above ground in 1895 when the colliery was closed.[27]

The Florence Colliery to the west of the Stone road south of Florence was started by the Duke of Sutherland in 1874.[28] It had been temporarily closed by 1895 but new shafts were opened soon afterwards, and in 1902 572 men were employed below ground there and 215 above.[29] By 1910 the colliery had between 1,500 and 2,000 employees[30] and the three pits in operation in 1957 employed 1,260 below ground and 410 above.[31]

IRON-WORKING. Thomas Hunt who held Longton manor until his bankruptcy in 1649 was described in 1650 as 'buying and selling in the trade of an ironmonger in Longton for the space of 20 years and upwards'.[32] Richard Foley of Birmingham who bought the manor in 1651 was also an 'ironmonger',[33] and he was mining ironstone on Meir Heath by 1679 when the Newcastle manor court ordered him to fill in 'the deep and dangerous pits' there.[34] This activity was presumably connected with the furnace situated to the south-west of the intersection of the Longton–Stone road and the Meir–Blurton road.[35] It was in operation by the mid-17th century[36] and c. 1700 was in the hands of a partnership which included Philip Foley and Obadiah Lane.[37] The furnace was still in existence at the end of the 18th

---

[9] W.S.L. 39/49, note on fly-leaf and *passim*; see p. 245.

[10] W.S.L. 39/49, note on fly-leaf; *Rep. Insp. Mines N. Staffs., 1888* [C. 5779], p. 13, H.C. (1889), xxiv. It was mentioned as in the hands of McLagen and Simpson in 1889: ibid. *1889* [C. 6015], p. 46, H.C. (1890), xxiii. In 1890 it was in the hands of the Park Hall Colliery Co. (ibid. *1890* [C. 6346], p. 28, H.C. (1891), xxii), but it was still 'standing' in 1891: ibid. *1891* [C. 6625], p. 43, H.C. (1892), xxiii. It was marked as disused on O.S. Map 6″ Staffs. xviii SE. (1889). It is possible that the Meir Hay Colliery is identifiable with the Millfield Gate Colliery at the 'head of Hog's Lane', in existence by 1800: Shaw, *Staffs. Potteries*, 229; White, *Dir. Staffs.* (1834); Meigh, 'Staffs. Potters', 18, identifying Hog's Lane as Sutherland Rd. It was run by W. H. Sparrow and Co. in 1868 and 1872: *P.O. Dir. Staffs.* (1868, 1872).

[11] S.R.O., D. 321/M/B/5, 6, 7, 25, 94–103; *Pigot's Nat. Com. Dir.* (1828–9, 1835, 1841); *Rep. Insp. Mines* [1845], p. 143, H.C. (1854), xix.

[12] *Keates and Ford's Potteries Dir.* (1865–6, 1867); S.R.O., Q/AH, Longton Main Rds. Map; O.S. Map 6″ Staffs. xviii SW. (1889). There was a Foley Ash Colliery being worked in conjunction with the Swingle Hill Colliery in 1882: S.R.O., D. 321/M/B/50.

[13] *P.O. Dir. Staffs.* (1872); see p. 245.

[14] *Keates's Potteries Dir.* (1882). It occurs in *Rep. Insp. Mines N. Staffs., 1888*, 13, but not in later reports.

[15] Hargreaves, *Map of Staffs. Potteries*; *Rep. Insp. Mines N. Staffs., 1888*, 13. It is not mentioned in later reports.

[16] *Keates and Ford's Potteries Dir.* (1865–6, 1867); O.S. Map 6″ Staffs. xviii SW. (1889). A Lane End Colliery was worked by John Smith in 1834 and John Chas. Smith in 1851: White, *Dir. Staffs.* (1834, 1851).

[17] Hargreaves, *Map of Staffs. Potteries*, showing the shafts on the Fenton side of the boundary (1832); O.S. Map 6″ Staffs. xviii SW. (1889), showing them on the Longton side with the Fenton shafts disused. The colliery receives no separate mention in directories. For the collieries in Fenton associated with the ironworks, see p. 223.

[18] *Rep. Insp. Mines, 1877* [C. 2003], p. 31, H.C. (1878), xx; S.R.O., D. 261/M/B/50, 53; *Rep. Insp. Mines N. Staffs. 1888*, 13. It is not mentioned in subseq. reports.

[19] *Rep. Insp. Mines, 1859* [2740], p. 79, H.C. (1860), xxiii.

[20] It is shown on O.S. Map 6″ Staffs. xviii NE. (1889) but is not mentioned in *Rep. Insp. Mines, 1877*.

[21] *Rep. Insp. Mines, 1865* [3768], p. 75, H.C. (1867), xvi; *Keates and Ford's Potteries Dir.* (1865–6, 1867).

[22] *Keates and Ford's Potteries Dir.* (1869–70).

[23] It was mentioned in *Keates's Potteries Dir.* (1875–6) but not in *Rep. Insp. Mines, 1877*; nor is it shown on O.S. Map 6″ Staffs. xviii NE. (1889). It was described in 1888 as in the hands of the Weston Coyney Colliery Co. and as 'standing': *Rep. Insp. Mines N. Staffs., 1888*, 13. In 1890 and 1891 it was held by the Park Hall Colliery Co. and was still 'standing': ibid. *1890*, 28; *1891*, 43.

[24] *Keates and Ford's Potteries Dir.* (1867); *Porter's Potteries Dir.* (1887); see p. 245. The Glovers were mining at the Heathcote Hill Colliery in 1865 (*Keates and Ford's Potteries Dir.* 1865–6), which may be the Longton Hall Colliery under another name.

[25] *Rep. Insp. Mines N. Staffs. 1888*, 13.

[26] Ibid. *1889*, 46.

[27] Ibid. *1895* [C. 8074], p. 58, H.C. (1896), xxii.

[28] *Illus. London News*, 23 Jan. 1875.

[29] *Rep. Insp. Mines N. Staffs. 1895*, 55; *1896* [C. 8450], p. 56, H.C. (1897), xx; *Rep. Insp. Mines Stafford, 1902* [Cd. 1590], p. 266, H.C. (1903), xv.

[30] *Staffs. Advertiser*, 13 and 20 Aug. 1910.

[31] *Guide to the Coalfields* (1960).

[32] H. Mus., Heathcote Papers, iii, unnumbered; see p. 230; and see *S.H.C.* xv. 140, for an 'iron-mill' in Longton in 1582.   [33] Ward, *Stoke*; 558, see p. 230.

[34] D.L. 30/242/3.

[35] Ward, *Stoke*, 558; Yates, *Map of Staffs.* (1799).

[36] *S.H.C.* 4th ser. ii. 94.

[37] B. L. C. Johnson, 'Iron Industry of Cheshire and N. Staffs. 1688–1712' (*T.N.S.F.C.* lxxxviii), 32, 33–35, 43; B. Watney, *Longton Hall Porcelain*, 8. The furnace specialized in the casting of forge hammers and anvils at this time. For the connexion of the Foleys and the Lanes with Longton manor see p. 230. Sir John Edensor Heathcote, who bought Longton manor in 1784 (see p. 230), was also an ironmaster: Watney, op. cit. 9.

century,[38] but by 1820 its site was occupied by a water-mill known as Furnace Mill which was still in use in 1872.[39]

The main feature of the history of the iron industry in Longton is the Lane End Ironworks started in 1826 by William Hanbury Sparrow who came from the Wolverhampton area; he also secured a lease of coal and ironstone mines from the Duke of Sutherland.[40] In 1829 the yield of the furnace was 1,367 tons, from 7 January to 14 July 1840 3,804 tons, and from April 1844 to April 1846 15,394 tons;[41] by the early 1840's at least the smelted iron was sent to the South Staffordshire market.[42] The firm of W. H. Sparrow and Son had three furnaces at Longton by the beginning of 1862, although only two were then in blast.[43] The works had passed to T. Goddard and Son by 1868,[44] and by 1873 there were three furnaces in blast.[45] The works remained in the hands of the Goddards until 1880 when it was closed,[46] but the colliery interests passed to Balfour and Company.[47]

By 1872 the Glovers were raising ironstone as well as coal at the Longton Hall Colliery and had an ironworks attached to the colliery.[48] Although the colliery was closed in 1895, the ironworks was still in operation in 1912.[49]

OTHER INDUSTRIES. There was a brickworks at Priors Field at the beginning of the 19th century. Nearly 19,000 bricks were fired there between 30 April and 21 July 1802 and nearly 100,000 between 13 May and 6 October 1803.[50] There were two brickworks at Longton in 1818[51] and by the middle of the century six brick- and tile-works there.[52] Longton was noted as a considerable centre of brick-making in the 1860's,[53] and there were still five brick- and tile-works there in the early 1890's.[54] In 1959 tiles were being made at the Dura Tile and Faience Company's Sutherland Works.[55]

By 1829 James Glover had a brewery in Sutherland Road described in the early 1840's as 'an extensive ale and porter brewery'.[56] By 1860 Ralph Steele had opened a brewery between Caroline and Wood Streets, known as the Crown Brewery by 1880, and malting had become a considerable industry by 1860.[57] The Sutherland Road brewery had been closed by the 1890's,[58] while the Crown Brewery ceased to operate in the first years of the 20th century.[59]

SOCIAL LIFE. A subscription library of 1,000 volumes was established at Longton in 1807, and a newsroom was opened in 1833.[60] These were possibly taken over or superseded by the Longton Athenaeum and Mechanics' Institute, founded in 1840 by 'a few intelligent working men of Longton . . . for mutual improvement'.[61] The members of the Institute met in the upper room of a building known as the Vauxhall schoolroom, but in 1847 the venture came temporarily to an end.[62] In the following year the Institute, with the library of books it had accumulated, moved to a house in Caroline Street,[63] and its membership at this time was about 130.[64] The annual subscription ranged from 10s. to £1 according to the facilities enjoyed.[65] The refounded Institute was predominantly middle-class in character and its committee consisted mostly of iron and coal masters, master potters, and merchants.[66] Free lectures were arranged by the Institute in the town hall but were not well attended.[67] Public lectures were also given at the Working Men's Hall in Church Row, built in 1844, and occasional lectures, concerts, and exhibitions were held in the Union Market Hall.[68] Classes in drawing and design were held from 1852 under the aegis of the Institute and later of the Stoke School of Art.[69]

By 1868 the Institute had moved to a wing of the town hall,[70] built in 1863,[71] where it remained until it ceased to exist in 1891 owing to lack of support.[72] Its membership, which was 230 in 1871, had declined to 136 in 1888.[73] In the early 1860's music was an important activity, and performances by the Longton Sax-horn Band as well as recitals by professionals were given, but losses were incurred owing to lack of support.[74] The one outstanding success of the Institute was its organization during the period 1878–91, in conjunction with Stoke Athenaeum, of annual railway excursions, known as People's Trips.[75]

In 1891, on the adoption by the borough of the Free Libraries Act, the rooms occupied by the

[38] Yates, *Map of Staffs.* (1799).

[39] Greenwood, *Map of Staffs.* (1820); *P.O. Dir. Staffs.* (1872), under Normacot. Ward, *Stoke*, 558, states that the 'mill occupies the place of the water-wheel by which the bellows were worked upon a stream, called Furnace Brook, where large deposits of scoria still exist', and that the furnace had gone out of use at least 80 years before his date of writing (the early 1840's).

[40] Ward, *Stoke*, 573; Shaw, *Staffs. Potteries*, 73. See pp. 223, 244 for Sparrow's mines in Longton and Fenton. Ward gives 1827 as the starting date, but there is a register of furnace disbursements from 1826 in S.R.O., D. 321/M/B/23.

[41] S.R.O., D. 321/M/B/2.

[42] Ward, *Stoke*, 573. The same was true at Burslem by the 1830's: see p. 140.

[43] S. Griffiths, *Blast Furnaces of Gt. Brit., Jan. 1862* (copy in S.R.O., D. 321/M/B/22).

[44] *P.O. Dir. Staffs.* (1868).

[45] S. Griffiths, *Iron Trade of Gt. Brit.* (1873), 256.

[46] W.S.L. 39/49 (note on fly-leaf). It is mentioned in *Keates's Potteries Dir.* (1879), but not in *Kelly's Dir. Staffs.* (1880).

[47] *Kelly's Dir. Staffs.* (1884); see pp. 223, 244.

[48] *P.O. Dir. Staffs.* (1872); see p. 244.

[49] W. Campbell, *Street Map of Stoke, Fenton and Longton* (1907, 1912; copies in H.R.L.); see p. 244.

[50] W.S.L. 39/49.

[51] Parson and Bradshaw, *Dir. Staffs.* (1818).

[52] White, *Dir. Staffs.* (1851).

[53] *P.O. Dir. Staffs.* (1868).

[54] *Keates's Potteries Dir.* (1892–3).

[55] *Stoke Classified Telephone Dir.* (Dec. 1959).

[56] *Pigot's Nat. Com. Dir.* (1828–9); Ward, *Stoke*, 574; White, *Dir. Staffs.* (1851), where the firm is given as Jas. Glover & Sons. The brewery is shown in Wharf St. (now Bridgwood St.) on O.S. Map 1/2,500 Staffs. xviii. 11 (1880).

[57] *P.O. Dir. Staffs.* (1860); *Kelly's Dir. Staffs.* (1880).

[58] Mentioned in *Kelly's Dir. Staffs.* (1884).

[59] Mentioned ibid. (1900).

[60] White, *Dir. Staffs.* (1834).

[61] R. G. Haggar, *Some Adult Educ. Institutions in North Staffs.* (*Rewley House Papers*, iii, no. 6), 10.

[62] Ibid.

[63] Ibid. 11.

[64] White, *Dir. Staffs.* (1851).

[65] Haggar, *Some Adult Educ. Institutions*, 11.

[66] Ibid.   [67] Ibid.

[68] White, *Dir. Staffs.* (1851).

[69] R. G. Haggar, *A Cent. of Art Educ. in the Potteries*, 29.

[70] *P.O. Dir. Staffs.* (1868).

[71] See p. 237.

[72] Haggar, *Some Adult Educ. Institutions*, 14.

[73] Ibid.

[74] Ibid. 13.   [75] Ibid. 14.

Institute in the town hall, comprising a lending library of nearly 6,000 books, reference library, and reading-room, were transferred to the corporation.[76] The Sutherland Technical Institute in Stone Road, which included an art school,[77] was opened in 1899[78] and the library was moved there in that year.[79] The building still (1960) houses the library and the art school.

The Royal Victoria Theatre was erected at Berry Bank in Stafford Street (now The Strand) in 1867[80] and was still in existence in 1892.[81] The Queen's Theatre at the junction of Commerce Street and Chancery Lane was opened in 1888.[82] It was burnt down in 1894 but rebuilt the following year.[83] By 1916 the name had been changed to the Empire Theatre,[84] which was still being used as a theatre in 1940[85] but is now (1960) a cinema.

There was a choral society at Longton by 1824.[86]

BOTTESLOW

BOTTESLOW was a liberty of 593 acres in the ancient parish of Stoke-upon-Trent bounded on the west by the Trent and on the north and east by a small tributary of the Trent; to the south lay the township of Fenton Vivian.[1] It is an upland area lying between 400 and 500 ft. and devoted mainly to farming and coal mining.

Although the termination 'low' may indicate the site of an early burial[2] the first known mention of the area appears to be in 1236 when land at 'Bothes' was part of Fenton.[3] A John of Botteslow occurs in 1327.[4] In 1666 eight persons there were assessed for hearth tax.[5] William Bagnall had the largest assessment, six hearths,[6] and this may represent Berry Hill Farm, the lease of which had been granted to the Bagnalls in 1555.[7] By 1748 the farm was owned by Godfrey Clarke of Sutton (Derb.), and was then the scene of coal mining. It was 193 acres in extent in 1816[8] and is still the largest of the remaining farms in Botteslow.[9] The farmhouse appears to have been rebuilt in the 19th century. The Machin family, assessed on two hearths in 1666, were evidently living at Lower Botteslow Farm by 1564 and were still there in 1742; in the early 19th century it was held by their descendant, William Tait, who had sold it to Philip Broade of Fenton Vivian by the early 1840's.[10] The farmhouse had disappeared by the late 1870's.[11] The house at Botteslow farm to the north, which still (1960) survives, may be partly of 17th-century date. Botteslow consisted of eight farms c. 1840 and was then 'purely agricultural or pasture but abounding with mines, at present little wrought'.[12] Mining began again about this time (see below), and in 1851 Botteslow had a population of 800.[13] A school-church was opened near Berry Hill Farm in 1878 (see below). The area is still open country, but the farms are disappearing, leaving the tips and winding-gear of the Berry Hill Colliery as the predominant feature of the landscape.

The area is crossed by tracks which presumably used to link the various farms. The road from Fenton Low to the Berry Hill Brickworks was originally part of the road between Fenton and Bucknall which lost what importance it had with the opening of Victoria Road from Fenton through the western end of Botteslow to Joiner's Square and Hanley in the early 1840's.[14] It was then noted that Botteslow's 'roads are neglected and founderous'.[15] The railway between Longton, Adderley Green, and Bucknall, a single-track mineral line opened by the North Staffordshire Railway Company in 1875, crosses the north-eastern corner of the area.[16]

Parochially Botteslow was part of the ancient parish of Stoke and manorially part of Fenton Vivian.[17] By 1679 it was represented at the Newcastle court leet by one frankpledge. Earlier it presented jointly with Fenton Vivian.[18] It lay within the constablewick which also included Fenton Vivian, Longton, Hanley, and other neighbouring places.[19] Botteslow became part of the new parish of Stoke Rural in 1894 and of the county borough of Stoke-on-Trent in 1922.[20]

INDUSTRIES. Mining on the Berry Hill estate was in progress before the mid-18th century. In 1748 Godfrey Clarke of Sutton (Derb.), the owner of the estate, leased all coal mines there to Jeremiah Smith of Great Fenton, and reference was made in the lease to existing workings.[21] There was evidently little or no mining in Botteslow in the 1830's, despite

[76] Haggar, *Some Adult Educ. Institutious*, 14.
[77] Haggar, *Art. Educ. in the Potteries*, 29.
[78] *Staffs. Advertiser*, 28 Oct. 1899. For a description of the building see p. 229.
[79] *Kelly's Dir. Staffs.* (1912).
[80] *P.O. Dir. Staffs.* (1868).
[81] *Keates's Potteries Dir.* (1892–3).   [82] Ibid.
[83] *Kelly's Dir. Staffs.* (1896).
[84] Ibid. (1916).
[85] Ibid. (1940).
[86] *Pottery Mercury*, 6 Oct. 1824.
[1] White, *Dir. Staffs.* (1851); T. Hargreaves, *Map of Staffs. Potteries and Newcastle* (1832).
[2] For the other lows in the Fenton area see p. 205.
[3] The township of Fenton then paid rent for an acre at 'Bothes': *S.H.C.* 1911, 146; *Bk. of Fees*, 594; see p. 211.
[4] *S.H.C.* vii (1), 208.
[5] Ibid. 1921, 163.   [6] Ibid.
[7] C 3/185/3. A Thos. Crompton owed rent for lands at Berry Hill and elsewhere in the area in 1614 (W.S.L., D. 1788, P. 67, B. 11), but in 1618 Thos. Bagnall evidently

held the largest estate in Little Fenton and Botteslow: *Stoke Churchwardens' Accts.* (*T.N.S.F.C.* lxxviii), p. A237.
[8] *Staffs. Advertiser*, 18 Mar. 1816.
[9] Local inf.
[10] *S.H.C.* 1921, 163; S. Shaw, *Staffs. Potteries*, 131; Ward, *Stoke*, 526; *Stoke Churchwardens' Accts.* (*T.N.S.F.C.* lxxviii), p. A237; C3/209/76; see p. 212.
[11] It is not shown on O.S. Map 6" Staffs. xviii NW. (1890). For its position see Hargreaves, *Map of Staffs. Potteries*.   [12] Ward, *Stoke*, 526.
[13] White, *Dir. Staffs.* (1851).
[14] See p. 146.   [15] Ward, *Stoke*, 526.
[16] See p. 228.
[17] Ward, *Stoke*, 467–8, 549; see pp. 198, 212.
[18] D.L. 30/242/3.
[19] *S.H.C.* vii (1), 208; ibid. 1921, 163. The other places were Lane End and Normacot Grange.
[20] *Kelly's Dir. Staffs.* (1900); see p. 259.
[21] W.S.L., D. 1788, F. 1. Coal was being supplied from the area to manufacturers at Fenton about the mid-18th cent.: Shaw, *Staffs. Potteries*, 156.

its known mineral wealth,[22] but by 1841 the Berry Hill Colliery south-west of Berry Hill Farm was in operation. The colliery was run by William Taylor Copeland who was at the time also an important member of the Fenton Park Company.[23] Some 20 years later the colliery passed from him to William Bowers who had been working the nearby Holly Bush Colliery south of Berry Hill Farm since at least 1852.[24] After Bowers' death in the late 1870's the Berry Hill and Holly Bush Collieries were taken over by Henry Warrington,[25] and in 1891 his firm was working four pits at Berry Hill and three (coal and ironstone) at Holly Bush.[26] By 1894 the two undertakings had evidently been amalgamated as the Berry Hill Collieries,[27] and the five pits in operation there in 1902 employed 660 men below ground and 232 above.[28] The firm of Henry Warrington and Son was still running the Berry Hill Collieries in 1916,[29] but by 1924 they were in the hands of Berry Hill Collieries Ltd.[30] The four pits in operation in 1957 employed 480 men below ground and 150 above.[31] There was an ironworks attached to the collieries from at least 1868 until the early 20th century.[32]

The Brookhouse Colliery south of Brookhouse Farm was being worked by Forrester and Read in 1841[33] and by Smith and Forrester in 1854.[34] In the early 1860's it passed to Pratt, Crewe and Knox, who worked it with the Botteslow Colliery.[35] F. E. Pratt was in sole control by 1868[36] and ran both collieries until they were closed in the early 1880's.[37] The Lawn Colliery lay to the south-east of the Brookhouse Colliery by the 1870's;[38] the centre of its operations had been moved north into Bucknall by the end of the century and the shafts in Botteslow abandoned.[39]

There was a brick-works on the site of the existing Berry Hill Brickworks by the early 1870's when it was in the hands of William Bowers.[40] It now (1960) belongs to the Berry Hill Brickworks Ltd. which has three other works in the county.[41]

CHURCH. Open-air services were held at Berry Hill Farm from June 1877,[42] and in the following year William Bowers, who was working the Berry Hill and Holly Bush Collieries (see above), opened a school-church to the north of the farm.[43] The mission remained within the parish of St. Peter, Stoke, until 1895 when it was included in the new parish of St. Jude, Shelton;[44] c. 1914 it was transferred to the parish of All Saints, Hanley.[45] It was closed in the late 1940's.[46]

HULTON

THE lordship of Hulton, some 1,400 acres in extent, lay within the parish of Burslem, of which it formed the south-eastern projection. It comprised Sneyd Green, Birches Head, and part of Milton. This long tongue of land slopes down from an altitude of some 600 ft. around Sneyd Green and Birches Head to one of about 400 ft. by the Trent. It then climbs the eastern ridge beyond the river to a height of 700 ft. at Woodhead Farm. The Hot Lane Brook, the Trent, and its tributary the Foxley Brook formed the north-western boundary, and a stretch of the road from Sneyd Green to Bagnall formed the north-eastern boundary in the Milton area.[1] Since Sneyd Green and Birches Head had been transferred to the

boroughs of Burslem and Hanley by 1910, their history is treated in the articles on those boroughs. An account of coal mining there, however, is given in this article. Since Milton lay mainly within Norton-in-the-Moors, its history is reserved for treatment under that parish.

There are remains of an earthwork on the western slope above the Trent to the south of the Birches Head road, and traces of early burials have been found nearer the river.[2] A primitive boat was dug out of the former course of the Trent at Hulton in 1930.[3] The significance of these discoveries, however, has not yet been assessed. Hulton was grouped with Rushton in Domesday Book, and the two vills

[22] Hargreaves, *Map of Staffs. Potteries*; Ward, *Stoke*, 526. Coal mines under Berry Hill farm were to let in 1816: *Staffs. Advertiser*, 18 Mar. 1816.
[23] *Pigot's Nat. Com. Dir.* (1841); O.S. Map 6″ Staffs. xviii NW. (1890).
[24] *Slater's Dir. Birmingham District* (1852–3); *Slater's Com. Dir.* (1862); *Jones's Potteries Dir.* (1864); O.S. Map 6″ Staffs. xviii NW. (1890).
[25] *Kelly's Dir. Staffs.* (1880); Bowers was still listed in *Keates's Potteries Dir.* (1879).
[26] *Rep. Insp. Mines N. Staffs. 1891* [C. 6625], p. 46, H.C. (1892), xxiii.
[27] Ibid. *1894* [C. 7667], p. 52, H.C. (1895), xxii.
[28] *Rep. Insp. Mines Stafford, 1902* [Cd. 1590], p. 265, H.C. (1903), xv.
[29] *Kelly's Dir. Staffs.* (1916).
[30] Ibid. (1924).
[31] *Guide to the Coalfields* (1960).
[32] *P.O. Dir. Staffs.* (1868); W. Campbell, *Street Map of Stoke, Fenton and Longton* (1907; copy in H.R.L.); no ironworks is shown on the 1912 edn. of this map.
[33] *Pigot's Nat. Com. Dir.* (1841).
[34] *P.O. Dir. Staffs.* (1854).
[35] *Slater's Com. Dir.* (1862).
[36] *P.O. Dir. Staffs.* (1868).
[37] *Kelly's Dir. Staffs.* (1880). A Brookhouse Colliery is

mentioned as in the hands of H. H. Williamson in 1862 (*Slater's Com. Dir.* 1862) and of the Chatterley Iron Co. between at least 1877 and 1888: *Rep. Insp. Mines, 1877* [C. 2003], p. 32, H.C. (1878), xx; *Rep. Insp. Mines N. Staffs. 1888* [C. 5779], p. 14, H.C. (1889), xxiv.
[38] O.S. Map 6″ Staffs. xviii NW. (1890).
[39] Ibid. (1900).
[40] Ibid. (1890); *Keates's Potteries Dir.* (1873–4).
[41] *Stoke Official Handbk.* (1960 and the two previous edns.). One of these works is the Clanway Brickworks at Tunstall: see p. 90.
[42] F. E. J. Wright, *The Schs. of the Par. of St. Peter ad Vincula, Stoke-upon-Trent*, 15.
[43] Ibid. 16; *Lich. Dioc. Ch. Cal.* (1885); O.S. Map 6″ xviii NW. (1900).
[44] Wright, *Schs. of Par. of St. Peter*, 16; *Lich. Dioc. Ch. Cal.* (1896).
[45] *Lich. Dioc. Ch. Cal.* (1915).
[46] The last edn. of *Lich. Dioc. Dir.* to mention it is that for 1947–8.
[1] Ward, *Stoke*, 288; T. Hargreaves, *Map of Staffs. Potteries and Newcastle* (1832).
[2] *V.C.H. Staffs.* i. 372; *T.N.S.F.C.* lxv. 152–3; O.S. Map 1/25,000, 33/84 (1951).
[3] R. Nicholls, *Hist. of Stoke and Newcastle*, 13 and illus. facing p. 40.

were there said to have a population of three villeins and three bordars.[4] Granted to the new abbey of St. Mary in 1223, Hulton disappeared as a vill for the rest of the Middle Ages, probably because it became the site of the abbey and of one of its granges.[5] After the dissolution of the monastery in 1538[6] Sneyd Green probably became the centre of the district,[7] and even in the late 1870's the only other area that was at all built up was that part of Milton which lay on the Hulton side of the road from Sneyd Green to Bagnall.[8] The population of Hulton lordship rose from 477 in 1821 to 945 in 1871.[9] The area around the abbey site, now known as Carmountside, has developed only in very recent times. A large house belonging to the Sneyds and Carmountside Farm had been built near the site by the early 17th century.[10] Abbey Farm to the west beyond the Trent was in existence by the early 18th century when it was the home of John Bourne, grandfather of the Primitive Methodist leader Hugh Bourne.[11] It appears to have been rebuilt early in the 19th century, but though mainly of brick it contains stone walling which may possibly be of 17th-century origin.[12] A council estate completed in 1936[13] lies south and east of the abbey site which is itself occupied by the Carmountside Secondary School, opened in 1938.[14] There are still (1960) some post-1945 prefabricated bungalows on the north side of Woodhead Road, and farther north still on the east side of Leek Road is Lawn Cemetery and Crematorium, opened in 1940.[15] Barratt Gardens on the north-eastern edge of the cemetery, with its old people's homes and community centre, dates from the mid-1950's.[16] Although the lordship of Hulton was also called 'Abbey Hilton' by the late 16th century,[17] the modern suburban district known as Abbey Hulton[18] lies south of the former lordship boundary.

The area is crossed by the road from Stoke to Endon which was built by 1842 under an Act of 1840[19] and by the road which runs from Great Chell to Hanley via Sneyd Green, turnpiked in 1770.[20] A road runs from the Carmountside area over the Trent to Birches Head and Hanley and another from Cobridge to Sneyd Green, Milton, and Bagnall. This second road was formerly part of the main road from Newcastle to Leek.[21] The stretch which comprises Holden Lane and Sneyd Street is thought to have been part of a way between Hulton Abbey and its grange at Rushton near Cobridge.[22] 'Abbey Bridge' existed by 1733,[23] and is presumably identifiable with the bridge which carries the Hanley road over the Trent at Abbey Farm. In 1734 it was stated in Hulton manor court that 'a sufficient footbridge' over Foxley Brook was needed,[24] and there was a Foxley Bridge carrying the road from Cobridge to Bagnall over the brook by 1759 when it was in a state of disrepair.[25] It was rebuilt as a carriage bridge c. 1834, by which time it was a county responsibility.[26]

The Caldon branch of the Trent and Mersey Canal, constructed from Etruria to Froghall under an Act of 1776,[27] runs through Abbey Hulton.

The Biddulph Valley railway line from Stoke built in 1858–63 and opened for passenger traffic in 1864[28] runs through Abbey Hulton. The line to Leek, built under an Act of 1863, branches off near Foxley Bridge.[29]

Hulton remained within Burslem parish (though it was never within Burslem borough) until 1894 when it became part of the new civil parish of Milton, itself added to Smallthorne Urban District in 1904.[30] In 1891 166 acres of the Sneyd Green portion of Hulton had been added to Burslem Borough, while in 1905 Birches Head and the rest of Sneyd Green were transferred from Smallthorne to Hanley.[31] Most of the remainder of the former lordship, as part of Smallthorne, was added to the county borough of Stoke-on-Trent in 1922.[32] Hulton had its own manorial and leet jurisdiction[33] and formed a separate constablewick from the rest of Burslem parish.[34] A constable was still appointed at Hulton manor court in 1839. In 1826 an assistant constable or headborough was also appointed. Two assistant constables were appointed in 1831, three in 1835 and subsequent years, and four in 1840.[35] The Burslem police attended the court in October 1839 and were sworn, presumably in connexion with their duties in the Sneyd Green area which was the only portion of the lordship subject to the jurisdiction of the Burslem Improvement Commissioners.[36] Like the other town-

[4] *V.C.H. Staffs.* iv. 50, no. 176.
[5] See pp. 249–50, 251.
[6] See p. 249.
[7] See p. 107.
[8] O.S. Map 6" Staffs. xii NW., SW. (1890); Ward, *Stoke*, 296.
[9] *Census*, 1821, 1871, Staffs.
[10] See p. 249.
[11] J. T. Wilkinson, *Hugh Bourne*, 13, 14, 21; W. Yates, *Map of Staffs.* (1775), reproduced facing p. 4.
[12] It has not proved possible to confirm the present owner's suggestion that the stone for Abbey Farm came from Hulton Abbey.
[13] *City of Stoke Housing 1919 to 1957*, 18, 19, 59.
[14] See pp. 250, 326.
[15] Warrillow, *Stoke*, 341.
[16] See p. 269.
[17] *S.H.C.* xv. 180, 192. It occurs as 'Hilton Abbey' in 1601: ibid. 1935, 369.
[18] See pp. 268, 269.
[19] See p. 178.
[20] See p. 146.
[21] See p. 109.
[22] See p. 105.
[23] U.C.N.S., Sneyd MSS., Ct. R. 1/1 (1733), 1/2 (1784).
[24] Ibid. 1/1 (1734).
[25] S.R.O., Roads Index.
[26] S.R.O., Q/SO 30, f. 101b, Q/SO 31, f. 262a. The

question of the county's liability was referred to the justices of Pirehill North in 1825 (Q/SO 29, f. 104b), and the county surveyor was asked to prepare estimates for repair and rebuilding in 1829 (Q/SO 30, f. 101b); the bridge was not, however, listed by him as a county bridge in 1830: J. Potter, *List of Bridges which Inhabs. of County of Stafford are bound to repair* (1830; copy in W.S.L.). The bridge was of brick with 2 arches by 1864: W.S.L., Hand Morgan Coll., 31/15, County Surveyor's Notebk.
[27] 16 Geo. III, c. 32.
[28] 'Manifold', *N. Staffs. Rlwy.* 50; ex inf. Brit. Rlwys., L.M.R.
[29] 'Manifold', *N. Staffs. Rlwy.* 52.
[30] K. D. Miller, *Brief Chronology of Local Govt. in Stoke-on-Trent* (1955), 20, 31–32; Local Govt. Board Order no. 31,833, confirming Staffs. County Counc. Order 24 July 1894 (copy of each with the Clerk of the Staffs. County Counc.); *Kelly's Dir. Staffs.* (1916), citing Local Govt. Board Order no. 43,817. For the relief of the poor in Hulton see p. 129.
[31] See pp. 105, 142.
[32] See p. 259.
[33] See p. 249.
[34] *L. & P. Hen. VIII*, xiv (1), p. 290; Ward, *Stoke*, app. p. xxiii; *S.H.C.* 1921, 168; 1932, 44; 1935, 210, 352.
[35] *Staffs. Advertiser*, 2 Nov. 1839; U.C.N.S., Sneyd MSS., Ct. R. 1/2.
[36] *Staffs. Advertiser*, 2 Nov. 1839; see p. 125.

ships in Burslem parish Hulton was responsible for the maintenance of its own highways, appointing its own highway surveyor and spending its rates independently of the rest of the parish.[37]

MANOR. *HULTON*, held before the Conquest by Ulviet, had become part of Robert de Stafford's estates by 1086 when, with Rushton, it was assessed at ⅓ hide.[38] The overlordship remained in the Stafford barony until at least 1284 when Hulton and Rushton together formed ⅓ knight's fee.[39]

In 1086 the Saxon tenant Ulviet was still in possession, holding as tenant of Robert de Stafford.[40] By 1167 Hulton was held by Emma, daughter and heir of Ralph fitz Orm and soon afterwards the wife of Adam de Audley.[41] In 1223 Henry de Audley, son of Adam and Emma, granted Hulton to the Cistercian abbey of St. Mary in his foundation charter of that year.[42] The Audleys, however, continued to owe knight service to the Staffords for Hulton until at least 1284.[43]

In 1535 Hulton appears as a manor with demesne, tenants, and courts, worth in all £16 9s. 4d. and organized under a steward, deputy-steward, and bailiff.[44] On its suppression in 1538 the abbey and its possessions passed to the king.[45] In 1539 the site, the demesne in Hulton and Stoke, and a coal mine in 'the field of Hulton' were leased to Stephen Bagot of London[46] who had already purchased the abbey's movables at the Dissolution.[47] In 1543 the Crown granted the manor of Hulton, the site of the abbey, its demesne, and all its other possessions in Hulton, Sneyd, Baddeley, Milton, and Burslem to Sir Edward Aston.[48] Sir Edward's great-grandson Sir Walter Aston conveyed the manor to William Sneyd of Keele in 1611.[49] The manor then remained in the Sneyd family,[50] Ralph Sneyd owning some 1,100 of the 1,400 or so acres in Abbey Hulton in 1838.[51] The 150-acre Abbey farm, the 26-acre Mill farm, and the 78-acre Birches Head farm formed the only land there still owned by the family in 1951 and were

offered for sale on the break-up of the Keele estate in that year.[52]

A house and garden formed part of the demesne of Hulton manor in 1621,[53] and it was presumably there that Ralph Sneyd was living in 1615 when he was described as of Hulton.[54] The house, which evidently stood near the abbey site, was of some size in 1682[55] and was still in existence in the mid-18th century.[56]

The view of frankpledge attached to the manor by 1611 was then stated to cover all or part of Hulton, Milton, Bucknall, Baddeley, and Ubberley, and parts of Burslem, Sneyd, Stoke, and Newcastle.[57] Courts were being held for the manor by 1535,[58] but court rolls and papers survive only from 1733 to 1841; during that period the courts were held at Sneyd Green.[59]

OTHER ESTATES. In 1647 Birches farm, lying within the manor of Hulton to the east of what is now the Birches Head district, seems to have been held by a John Brett.[60] By 1669 it was the home of William Sneyd, second son of William Sneyd of Keele and M.P. for Newcastle-under-Lyme from 1685 to 1687.[61] William continued to live there until his death in 1708,[62] and a 'Mr. Sneyd' was tenant in 1722 and 1723.[63] The farm was occupied by John Prime in 1791,[64] and the Prime family remained there until at least 1854.[65] Birches farm, some 150 acres in extent, was bought from the Sneyds by the present owner, Mr. William Jenks, before the break-up of the Keele estate in 1951; the old farmhouse was rebuilt some time after 1926.[66]

Carmountside farm within the manor of Hulton was held in 1611 by Beatrice Smith, widow, and Roger Smith,[67] probably her son. Thomas Smith was granted the lease by the Sneyds in 1650[68] and was still the tenant in 1672.[69] By 1697 the farm was held by John Heath[70] whose family occupied it until at least 1748,[71] but c. 1758 a Robert Clark was the tenant.[72] The Worthington family lived there during

[37] St. John's, Burslem, Churchwardens' and Overseers' Accts. 1700–95, p. 97; *Staffs. Advertiser*, 26 Mar. 1836; Ward, *Stoke*, 211. The Sneyd Green to Holden Lane stretch of the Milton road was not a public road but the responsibility of the lord of Hulton or his tenant; an attempt to charge its repair on the parish c. 1753 was successfully resisted: Churchwardens' and Overseers' Accts. 1700–95, p. 97.
[38] *V.C.H. Staffs.* iv. 50, no. 176; see p. 116.
[39] *Bk. of Fees*, 974, where with Burslem the 2 vills are said to form 2 parts of a fee; *Feud. Aids*, v. 3, where all 3 form one fee. Burslem was given as ½ fee in 1242 or 1243 and in 1460: see p. 116.
[40] *V.C.H. Staffs.* iv. 50, no. 176; he had also acquired Alward's holding in Burslem: ibid. no. 177.
[41] *S.H.C.* i. 48; ibid. 1923, 297; iv (1), 50; *Complete Peerage*, 'Audley'.
[42] Dugdale, *Mon.* v. 715.
[43] *Bk. of Fees*, 974; *Feud. Aids*. v. 3.
[44] *Valor Eccl.* (Rec. Com.), iii. 107.
[45] *L. & P. Hen. VIII*, xii (2), p. 349; xiii (2), pp. 84, 147, 177; S.C. 6/Hen. VIII/3353, mm. 12–12d.; /3354, mm. 36–37.
[46] *L. & P. Hen. VIII*, xv, p. 557; S.C. 6/Hen. VIII/3353, m. 12d.   [47] *L. & P. Hen. VIII*, xiii (2), p. 254.
[48] Ibid. xviii (1), p. 200.
[49] U.C.N.S., Sneyd MSS., Hulton Deeds; *S.H.C.* N.S. iii. 67; T. & A. Clifford, *Tixall*, 149–51.
[50] C 142/338/86; S.R.O., D. 418/M3, M8–11, M14, M17–20, M24; S.R.O., Index to Gamekeepers' Deps.; S.R.O., Q/RPl 1781, 1801, 1821, 1830; U.C.N.S., Sneyd MSS., Hulton Deeds; ibid. Ct. R. 1/1, 1/2, 7/42; R. Gill, 'Sepulchral

Slabs from Hulton Abbey' (*The Reliquary*, xxv), 114, 115.
[51] Ward, *Stoke*, 289 n.
[52] W.S.L., Sale Cat. E/4/16; see pp. 152, 248, 252.
[53] U.C.N.S., Sneyd MSS., Tunstall Deeds, Wm. Sneyd's Rental 1621.
[54] Ibid., Sneyd Green Deeds.
[55] R. Plot, *Map of Staffs.* (1682); R. Morden, *Map of Staffs.* [c. 1695].
[56] E. Bowen, *Improved Map of Staffs.* (1749).
[57] *S.H.C.* N.S. iii. 67.
[58] *Valor Eccl.* (Rec. Com.), iii. 107.
[59] U.C.N.S., Sneyd MSS., Ct. R. 1/1, 1/2, 7/42.
[60] Ibid., Hulton Deeds.
[61] Ibid.; Burke, *Land. Gent.* (1952), 1803, 2355; *S.H.C.* 1920 and 1922, 160.
[62] *Cal. S.P. Dom.* 1685, 38; U.C.N.S., Sneyd MSS., Hulton Deeds, Abbey Hulton rental 1699; W.S.L. 305/40; Burke, *Land. Gent.* (1952), 1803.
[63] U.C.N.S., Sneyd MSS., Hulton Deeds, Abbey Hulton rentals 1722, 1723.
[64] *Burslem Par. Reg.* ii. 466.
[65] Ibid. 486; iii. 616; U.C.N.S., Ct. R. 1/2, summons to Abbey Hulton court, 1839; White, *Dir. Staffs.* (1834, 1851); *P.O. Dir. Staffs.* (1854).
[66] Ex. inf. Mr. Jenks (1958).
[67] U.C.N.S., Sneyd MSS., Hulton Deeds.
[68] Ibid.   [69] Ibid.; Ward, *Stoke*, app. p. xxviii.
[70] Adams, *Adams Family*, 411.
[71] Ibid. 237, 239; U.C.N.S., Sneyd MSS., Hulton Deeds, 25 Mar. 1721; *Burslem Par. Reg.* i, pp. v and 218; *Stoke Par. Reg.* iii. 529, 545.
[72] *Burslem Par. Reg.* i, p. v.

the earlier 19th century.[73] The house was rebuilt in 1856 on a site farther west which in 1884 was found to be over the chancel of the former abbey church.[74] The farm, some 210 acres in extent c. 1878,[75] still existed in 1930,[76] but the site of the house, and thus of the abbey, has been occupied since 1938 by Carmountside Secondary Modern School.[77]

Carmount Head farm at the southern end of Baddeley Edge above the village of Milton[78] was held of the manor of Hulton in 1611 and 1621 by John Loggun.[79] A messuage and lands called Carmount 'near or adjoining Baddeley Edge' were leased by the Sneyds to Thomas Knight in 1647 in succession to his father John[80] and were evidently the Carmount farm occupied by the Austen family between at least 1699 and 1744.[81] The estate seems to have been occupied in 1760 by John Weatherby, probably the tenant of Woodhead farm also.[82] Joseph Adams was farming at Carmount Head in 1834 and 1839,[83] and by 1848 the 19-acre farm was owned by Benjamin Yardley, the elder, and held by a tenant.[84] Between at least 1876 and 1912 the farm was occupied by John Williamson who on emigrating to Canada c. 1912 sold it to Frank Mayer, still the occupant in 1940.[85] It is now (1958) owned and occupied by Mr. Harold Mayer. The stone-built house and farm buildings appear to date from the 19th century; there is a barn dated 1836.

Holden farm was in the tenure of the Heath family between at least 1611 and 1657,[86] but in 1683 it was evidently occupied by Thomas Beech and his wife Dorothy.[87] Thomas died in that year and in 1689 his widow married William Adams, younger son of Thomas Adams of Birches Head.[88] William

was living at Holden in 1699,[89] but in 1701 he and Dorothy divided the farm and the house with a Thomas Beech who was also living there by then.[90] Thomas was given the parlour, the parlour chamber, the little chamber, the back kitchen, the great entry, use of the well, and a share of the outhouses, but William and Dorothy were to be allowed to bake in the back kitchen.[91] This division continued until at least 1718 when Dorothy died at Holden and possibly until the death of her husband in 1721.[92] The Beeches continued to live at Holden until at least 1754[93] and retained the ownership[94] until 1806 when Thomas Beech sold it to John Sparrow of Bishton (in Colwich) and John Hales of Cobridge.[95] By 1848 the 101-acre Holden farm, held by William Wooliscroft, was owned by Sir George Chetwynd of Brocton (in Baswich) and Grendon (Warws.), who had married one of John Sparrow's daughters and co-heirs.[96] The house, situated north of the road from Sneyd Green to Milton,[97] had been abandoned by 1957 when it was occupied as a temporary Methodist church.[98]

Woodhead farm is situated on the hillside in the eastern part of Abbey Hulton and now within the parish of Norton-in-the-Moors. It was part of the property of Hulton Abbey at the time of its dissolution in 1538 and was then held on a 30-year lease by William Barnett and his family.[99] They were still the tenants in 1543 when the farm was conveyed with the manor of Hulton and other abbey lands to Sir Edward Aston.[1] By 1637 the estate had been divided. One part was then in the tenure of John Weatherby[2] whose family remained tenants there until c. 1839.[3] By 1848 Ralph Sneyd's tenant at this 48-acre farm

[73] Burslem Par. Reg. iii. 814; White, Dir. Staffs. (1834, 1851); U.C.N.S., Sneyd MSS., Ct. R. 1/2, summons to Abbey Hulton court, 1839.
[74] T. M. Leith, 'Records of the Mission of St. Peter, Cobridge' (MS. at St. Peter's R.C. Ch., Cobridge), f. 6a.; R. Gill, 'Sepulchral Slabs from Hulton Abbey' (The Reliquary, xxv), 114–15; T.N.S.F.C. (1885), 99, 100; Lich. Dioc. Regy., Tithe Maps, Burslem (1848); O.S. Map 6″ xii SW. (1890). Other parts of the abbey were uncovered in 1955 and 1959: Eve. Sentinel, 18 Aug. 1959, 5 Feb. 1960.
[75] U.C.N.S., Sneyd MSS., Maps and Plans, Carmountside Farm.
[76] T.N.S.F.C. lxv. 150.   [77] See p. 326.
[78] It is treated as part of the parish of Burslem in the Tithe Appt. and in White, Dir. Staffs. (1834); Hargreaves, Map of Staffs. Potteries, places it on the Norton-in-the-Moors side of the parish boundary. It is now in Norton (Bagnall Rd.).
[79] U.C.N.S., Sneyd MSS., Hulton Deeds, 17 Sept. 9 Jas. I, Wm. Sneyd's Rental 1621. He was prob. the John Loggen who married at Burslem in 1582: Burslem Par. Reg. i. 3.   [80] U.C.N.S., Sneyd MSS., Hulton Deeds.
[81] Ibid. rentals 1699, 1722, 1723; W.S.L. 305/40; Burslem Par. Reg. i. 220.
[82] Burslem Churchwardens' and Overseers' Accts. 1700–95 (at St. John's, Burslem), p. 109; see below.
[83] White, Dir. Staffs. (1834); U.C.N.S., Sneyd MSS., Ct. R. 1/2, summons to Abbey Hulton court, 1839.
[84] Lich. Dioc. Regy., Tithe Maps and Appt., Burslem; the tenant is given as Hodgkinson. Yardley occurs as a farmer in the Norton portion of Milton until 1860: White, Dir. Staffs. (1851); P.O. Dir. Staffs. (1854, 1860).
[85] P.O. Dir. Staffs. (1876); Kelly's Dir. Staffs. (1880 and later edns.) to 1940); ex inf. Mr. Harold Mayer (1958).
[86] U.C.N.S., Sneyd MSS., Hulton Deeds, 1611, 1648; Burslem Par. Reg. i. 31, 35; Ward, Stoke, app. p. xxviii.
[87] Adams, Adams Family, 179, which states that Thos. was of Holden. The subsequent hist. of the tenancy makes this likely, but Thos. is not described as of Holden in the parish registers containing the record of his marriage and burial: Norton-in-the-Moors Par. Reg. i. 121; Burslem Par. Reg. iii. 113.

[88] Adams, Adams Family, 179.
[89] U.C.N.S., Sneyd MSS., Hulton Deeds (rental 1699), Milton Deeds.
[90] W.S.L., D. 1788, P. 32, B. 6. A Thos. Beech 'once of Holden' d. in 1700: Burslem Par. Reg. i. 130.
[91] W.S.L., D. 1788, P. 32, B. 6. This also mentions incidentally 'the old house'.
[92] Adams, Adams Family, 180, 235; Burslem Par. Reg. i. 160, 163, 164, 169, 170. Wm. Adams' place of residence at the time of his death is not given. 'H. Beech' of 'Holdin' occurs in a list of Burslem potters c. 1710 as a maker of butterpots: Adams, Adams Family, 111.
[93] 'Mr. Beech' owed 5s. rent for 'the Holding' in 1722 and 1723 (U.C.N.S., Sneyd MSS., Hulton Deeds, rentals 1722, 1723), whereas in 1699 Wm. Adams owed 2s. 6d. (ibid. rental 1699), and 'Adams or Beech' owed 2s. 6d. in 1707 (W.S.L. 305/40). In 1753 and 1754 Thos. Beech was appointed constable of Hulton manor for Holden, but so was a Wm. Forde in 1733: U.C.N.S., Sneyd MSS., Ct. R. 1/1. Thos. Beech was holding the property in trust for his children in 1741 or 1742 (Adams, Adams Family, 189) and served as churchwarden as holder of the farm in 1742: Ward, Stoke, app. p. xxviii. Jas. Mayott (d. 1743) and Jas. Wright (d. 1753) were both described as of Holden: Burslem Par. Reg. i. 215, 221.
[94] W.S.L., D. 1798, bdle. 185 (a, b).
[95] Ibid. bdle. 173.
[96] Lich. Dioc. Regy., Tithe Maps and Appt., Burslem; Burke, Peerage (1949), 398. Wooliscroft was tenant between at least 1834 and 1854: White, Dir. Staffs. (1834, 1851); P.O. Dir. Staffs. (1854).
[97] Lich. Dioc. Regy., Tithe Maps and Appt., Burslem; Adams, Adams Family, plate facing p. 180; O.S. Map 6″ Staffs. xii SW. (1926).
[98] See p. 293.
[99] S C. 6/Hen. VIII/3353, m. 12.
[1] L. & P. Hen. VIII, xviii (1), p. 200.
[2] U.C.N.S., Sneyd MSS., Hulton Deeds. He was married at Burslem in 1635: Burslem Par. Reg. i. 41.
[3] U.C.N.S., Sneyd MSS., Hulton Deeds, rentals 1699, 1722, 1723; ibid., Burslem Deeds, lease 14 Mar. 1714/15; ibid. Milton Deeds, sale of Handleys Farm 1841, containing

was Benjamin Yardley, the younger.[4] In 1649 the other part was held by John Sneyd, yeoman,[5] and in 1672 by a John Sneyd the younger.[6] It was probably the latter John who was the tenant in 1699[7] and his daughter Jane who died there *c.* 1721.[8] By 1722 this part of the farm was held by Josiah Dean,[9] by him or his son Josiah in 1742[10] and 1764[11], and by Richard Dean in 1806.[12] In 1834 and 1839 the tenant was John Docksey[13] who by 1848 had been succeeded in the 63-acre farm by Ephraim Docksey, still the tenant in 1854.[14] By the late 1870's there was only the one Woodhead Farm, owned by the Revd. Walter Sneyd.[15] It changed hands twice in the early 1950's after the break-up of the Keele estate, passing finally to the present owner, Mr. W. Birch, who farms 133 acres there.[16] The farmhouse was rebuilt in brick in 1865.[17] A fine range of outbuildings forming a three-sided court is of local stone and probably dates from the early 19th century.

ECONOMIC HISTORY. Hulton has always been a predominantly agricultural area, although since the 1930's there has been some suburban development.[18] In the Middle Ages, however, there was a certain amount of industry centring on the abbey, notably tile-making and coal mining, and coal continued to be mined in the area until the late 19th-century.

Hulton was assessed with Rushton in 1086. The two vills then had land for 3 ploughs and the 3 villeins and 3 borders there had 1 plough.[19] There was woodland 1 league long and $\frac{1}{2}$ league broad attached to the vills,[20] and Henry de Audley's endowment of Hulton Abbey in 1223 included what was described as a wood at Sneyd 'within the enclosed hay of Kennermunt' (i.e. Carmount).[21] A grange was established at Hulton soon after the foundation of the abbey,[22] and there were 2 carucates of land attached by 1291.[23] Assized rents from Hulton were producing £1 a year by 1291.[24] By 1535 the estates consisted of demesne (£6), 12 tenancies at

will (£9 15s.), and free tenancies (chief rents of 6s.).[25] In the year following the dissolution of the abbey in 1538 the manor, including Rushton Grange and lands in Burslem and Stoke parishes, was divided into the demesne, consisting of the abbey site at Hulton with 33 acres of arable, 30 of meadow, and 54 of pasture, and Rushton Grange with arable in a field called 'Walfeld', 25 acres of meadow and 156 acres of pasture; 3 free tenancies; 3 tenancies-at-will; 4 customary tenancies; and 10 farms leased for 30, 40, or 42 years.[26] By 1621 the Sneyds' Hulton estate consisted of demesne and 3 free and 23 copyhold tenancies.[27] A return of the 1640's lists 8 tenancies on the demesne and 16 other tenancies.[28] Copyhold leases granted during the 17th and early 18th centuries were normally for 2 or 3 lives or for 21 years, and in addition to the cash rent and the heriot the dues payable often included a rent of 1, 2, 4, or 6 hens at Candlemas, Shrovetide, or Michaelmas.[29]

The endowment of the abbey included a fishery, presumably in the Trent.[30] Traces of the abbey's fishponds near the river on the opposite side of the main road from the abbey site[31] are still visible.

The pinfold of Abbey Hulton manor was mentioned in 1831 when the jurors stated that it had been taken down and that a new one was necessary. A new pound had still not been erected in 1833.[32]

MILL. Henry de Audley's endowment of Hulton Abbey as confirmed by the king in 1256 included a mill[33] which followed the same descent as the manor of Hulton.[34] At the Dissolution in 1538 the mill was held on a 42-year lease by William Craddock[35] who still held it in 1543 when it was described as in Stoke,[36] presumably on the Trent just south of the Burslem boundary where Abbey Mill was situated by 1775.[37] By 1611 it was being worked by Thomas Mellor[38] whose son Richard was granted the lease in 1660.[39] Thomas Adams of Birches Head probably held it at his death in 1681,[40] and Jonathan Adams,

---

reference to indenture of 1744 to which John Weatherby the younger of the Woodhead was a party; ibid., Ct. R. 1/1, 1/2; *Stoke Par. Reg.* iii. 531; White, *Dir. Staffs.* (1834).
[4] Lich. Dioc. Regy., Tithe Maps and Appt., Burslem.
[5] U.C.N.S., Sneyd MSS., Hulton Deeds. He was living in Burslem parish by 1637: *Burslem Par. Reg.* i. 44.
[6] U.C.N.S., Sneyd MSS., Hulton Deeds; *Burslem Par. Reg.* i. 78, 95.
[7] U.C.N.S., Sneyd MSS., Hulton Deeds, rental 1699. If so, he had married again by 1691: *Burslem Par. Reg.* i. 121.
[8] H.R.L., EMT 20; *Burslem Par. Reg.* i. 98.
[9] U.C.N.S., Sneyd MSS., Hulton Deeds, rentals 1722, 1723; *Burslem Par. Reg.* i. 170.
[10] Ward, *Stoke*, app. p. xxviii; W.S.L., Marston Wills, vii, f. 198, will of Joseph Dean of Woodhead, 1737, which mentions Joseph's brother Josiah and among Josiah's sons another Josiah.
[11] W.S.L., M/22A. Josiah Dean, doubtless the son, d. in 1786 or 1787: U.C.N.S., Sneyd MSS., Ct. R. 1/2.
[12] W.S.L., D. 1798, bdle. 173, lease and release of Holden farm, 1806.
[13] White, *Dir. Staffs.* (1834); U.C.N.S., Sneyd MSS., Ct. R. 1/2.
[14] Lich. Dioc. Regy., Tithe Maps and Appt., Burslem; White, *Dir. Staffs.* (1851); *P.O. Dir. Staffs.* (1854).
[15] U.C.N.S., Sneyd MSS., Maps and Plans, Woodhead Farm. The consolidation may date from 1865 when the present house was built: see below.
[16] Ex inf. Mr. W. Birch (1960).
[17] Date on building. The initials 'RS' are presumably those of Ralph Sneyd.   [18] See p. 248.

[19] *V.C.H. Staffs.* iv. 50, no. 176.   [20] Ibid.
[21] Dugdale, *Mon.* v. 715; *Cal. Chart. R.* 1226–57, 453.
[22] *Cal. Chart. R.* 1226–57, 453.
[23] *Tax. Eccl.* (Rec. Com.), 252.   [24] Ibid.
[25] *Valor Eccl.* (Rec. Com.), iii. 107.
[26] S.C. 6/Hen. VIII/3353, mm. 12–12d. The free tenements included one in Newcastle. 'Walfeld' included meadow and pasture as well as arable.
[27] U.C.N.S., Sneyd MSS., Tunstall Deeds, Wm. Sneyd's rental of 1621.
[28] S.R.O., D. 260/M/box 25, bdle. k, Royalist Compositions, f. 75b.
[29] U.C.N.S., Sneyd MSS., Hulton Deeds (including rentals of 1699, 1722, 1723), Sneyd Green Deeds; W.S.L. 305/40, rental of 1707.
[30] *Cal. Chart. R.* 1226–57, 453.
[31] Ward, *Stoke*, 295.
[32] U.C.N.S., Sneyd MSS., Ct. R. 1/2.
[33] *Cal. Chart. R.* 1226–57, 453.
[34] *Valor Eccl.* (Rec. Com.), iii. 107; S.C. 6/Hen. VIII/3353, m. 12; *L. & P. Hen. VIII*, xviii, p. 200; *S.H.C.* N.s. iii. 67; U.C.N.S., Hulton Deeds, Walter Sneyd's Estate in Abbey Hulton 1873, p. 8; W.S.L., Sale Cat. E/4/16; see p. 249.
[35] S.C. 6/Hen. VIII/3353, m. 12.
[36] *L. & P. Hen. VIII*, xviii, p. 200.
[37] Yates, *Map of Staffs.* (1775).
[38] U.C.N.S., Sneyd MSS., Hulton Deeds.
[39] Ibid.; C.P. 25(2)/723, 13 Chas. II East.
[40] B.M. Camp. i. 29; Adams, *Adams Family*, pedigree between pp. 180 and 181. His son and heir John later m. into the Mellor family: ibid.

son of Ralph Adams of Sneyd and Milton, was probably the miller at his death in 1721.[41] By 1792 the mill was used as a flint mill and had been leased by Ralph Sneyd to the New Hall Company of Hanley.[42] The mill, in the tenure of 'that veteran grinder, Mr. Mager Walker' in 1839,[43] was used in the early 19th century for grinding both corn and potters' materials but by 1914 was used solely by potters.[44] It had ceased to be worked by the 1930's.[45] The 26-acre farm attached was sold on the break-up of the Sneyds' estate in 1951 and has recently changed hands again.[46]

INDUSTRIES. There was a coal mine in Lee Field at Hulton worked by the abbey at the Dissolution and immediately afterwards leased by the Crown to a Thomas Foxe at a rent of £1 6s. 8d. With other property of the abbey it was leased to Stephen Bagot of London in 1539 and sold to Sir Edward Aston in 1543.[47] By the mid-17th century Thomas Adams of Birches Head was working a coal mine on his estate at Abbey Hulton,[48] and this branch of the Adams family continued to mine on the Birches Head estate and elsewhere within the Sneyds' manor of Hulton until at least 1777.[49] Under the will of John Adams of Birches Head (d. 1753) a share in the mines at Birches Head passed to his daughter Mary, the wife of Richard Hollins. Her sons inherited this share in 1782.[50] Both the Hollins and the Adams families had an interest in the Abbey Hulton Colliery by 1800 which they then assigned to Walter Sneyd.[51] This colliery was still in operation in 1804.[52] It may be identifiable with the colliery at Sneyd Green which was worked by Walter Sneyd in 1818 and by his son Ralph after him and which was leased by Ralph in 1851 to Francis Stanier of Newcastle and Silverdale. A company formed by Stanier worked it until at least the mid-1870's.[53] In the mid-1860's there were two other collieries in operation at Sneyd Green.[54] About 1840 in fact the village of Sneyd Green was described as largely inhabited by colliers.[55] There was a colliery to the north-west of Abbey Farm in 1832, but it had been abandoned by the 1870's.[56]

There was a tannery at Hulton towards the end of the 13th century belonging to the monks.[57] At some time during the Middle Ages they evidently had a fulling mill there, presumably situated on the Trent[58] and possibly connected with their sheep-farming.[59] The monks also seem to have produced encaustic tiles during the Middle Ages.[60] Early pottery-making in the area is mentioned elsewhere.[61]

There has been an aluminium works on the canal near Foxley Bridge since the end of the 19th century.[62] There was a chemical works on a site to the north on the Hulton and Milton boundary between at least 1867 and 1940.[63]

THE FEDERATION OF THE SIX TOWNS

THE federation[1] in 1910 of the six towns, Burslem, Fenton, Hanley, Longton, Stoke-upon-Trent, and Tunstall, is unique in English local government. The story begins with early attempts at co-operation, c. 1817–c. 1840, continues with the abortive 'county' plan of 1888 and the unsuccessful attempt of 1900–3, and ends with the negotiations during the period 1905–10 which culminated in the union of the towns as one county borough.

Early attempts at co-operation

To the modern observer, with the advantage of hindsight, it seems natural that a geographically compact area whose inhabitants are predominantly engaged in a common industry should be treated as a single unit for the purposes of local government. At the beginning of the last century such a point of view would have been to a large extent unfamiliar. As has been shown above, each of the Pottery towns,

[41] Adams, *Adams Family*, 253, 256; he m. into the Mellor family.
[42] W.S.L., D. 1742, bdle. 61; see p. 167.
[43] Ward, *Stoke*, 290 note; U.C.N.S., Sneyd MSS., Ct. R. 1/2. The tenant in 1851 was Eliz. Hammersley: White, *Dir. Staffs.* (1851).
[44] Adams, *Adams Family*, 237 and drawing facing p. 236.
[45] Ex inf. the owner-occupier, Abbey Mill Farm (1958).
[46] Ex inf. the owner-occupier; see p. 249.
[47] S.C. 6/Hen. VIII/3353, m. 12d; L. & P. Hen. VIII, xv, p. 557; xviii (1), p. 200; see p. 249.
[48] U.C.N.S., Sneyd MSS., Hulton Deeds (20 Sept. 1655).
[49] Adams, *Adams Family*, 186, 189, 191, 200, 201, 208, 210, 215; W.S.L. 305/40; U.C.N.S., Sneyd MSS., Burslem Deeds, Hulton Deeds, Milton Deeds. The royalty required by Ralph Sneyd in a lease of the Tabernors Row in 1752 was '17d. a dozen of coal and slack' and in a lease of the Little Row in 1753 10d. a dozen: Adams, *Adams Family*, 191. There are a few instances of mining at Sneyd Green by other tenants of the Sneyds, in 1671, 1721 and 1754: U.C.N.S., Sneyd MSS., Hulton Deeds, Milton Deeds.
[50] Adams, *Adams Family*, 192, 201.
[51] U.C.N.S., Sneyd MSS., Hulton Deeds.
[52] Ibid. (weekly accts. for last quarter of 1804).
[53] Parson and Bradshaw, *Dir. Staffs.* (1818); *Pigot's Nat. Com. Dir.* (1828–9); Ward, *Stoke*, 210; *Keates and Ford's*

Potteries Dir. (1865–6); *Keates's Potteries Dir.* (1873–4, 1875–6); *Rep. Insp. Mines, 1855* [2132], p. 98, H.C. (1856), xviii; *1857* [2433], p. 59, H.C. (1857–8), xxxii.
[54] *Keates and Ford's Potteries Dir.* (1865–6). This does not, however, mention the Stanier Co.'s colliery.
[55] See p. 108.
[56] Hargreaves, *Map of Staffs. Potteries* (1832); O.S. Map 6″ Staffs. xii SW. (1890).
[57] *Tax. Eccl.* (Rec. Com.), 252.
[58] Pastures called 'Walke myll hyll' and 'Little Walke myll hyll' belonged to Hulton Abbey at its dissolution: S.C. 6/Hen. VIII/3353, m. 12d.
[59] *S.H.C.* xi. 306; *Cal. Chart. R.* 1226–57, 453.
[60] Suggested by finds made in the course of excavations carried out by the City Mus.: ex. inf. the deputy curator (1959). P. W. L. Adams (*Adams Family*, 15) stated that the monks produced tiles but gave no evidence or authority for this.
[61] See pp. 131–2.
[62] *Kelly's Dir. Staffs.* (1892 and later edns.).
[63] *Keates and Ford's Potteries Dir.* (1867); *P.O. Dir. Staffs.* (1868); *Kelly's Dir. Staffs.* (1940); O.S. Map 6″ Staffs. xii SW. (1900, 1926). A vitriol works is shown nearby on the N. side of the boundary on the same editions of this map, xii NW.
[1] The term federation, consecrated by local usage, has been retained, though its accuracy is impugnable: see p. 257.

or villages, as some of them still were, made its own attempt to meet the governmental and administrative problems posed by a rapidly growing population. Local patriotism was strong and communications relatively slow, and it would not have occurred to the people of Tunstall, for example, that in the provision of those services which became ever more urgent as the century advanced, there existed any community of interest with neighbouring Burslem, still less with distant Stoke-upon-Trent. Nevertheless, the germ of co-operation can be discerned in the proceedings of a meeting at Hanley on 12 December 1817 of inhabitants of the pottery towns, when a wordy resolution was passed to the effect 'that in future all public meetings convened by and in the joint names of the majority of the head constables for the time being of Burslem, Hanley, Shelton, Stoke, Fenton, and Lane End shall be understood and considered as regularly convened, and that such head constables be recognized as the authorized agents on such occasions and the proper persons to whom requisitions may be addressed for calling certain public meetings from time to time, the same to be held at Hanley as the most central place of meeting for the Potteries at large'.[2] By this date, clearly, it was recognized that the Potteries had become something more than a geographical expression, that their natural centre was Hanley, and that there were certain matters on which joint consultation was desirable. That these matters were concerned principally with the protection of life and property is deducible from the predominance accorded to head constables and, as will be seen from references to later meetings, it was the feeling that law and order were in jeopardy, owing to the absence of a proper police force, that did more than anything else to promote united action.

The Reform Act of 1832,[3] however, had an important bearing on the idea of unity. By it, Stoke-upon-Trent became a parliamentary borough, comprising the townships of Penkhull with Boothen, Tunstall, Burslem, Hanley, Shelton, Fenton Vivian, Lane End, Fenton Culvert, and Longton, the vill of Rushton Grange, and the hamlet of Sneyd.[4] The Potteries thus became one for the purpose of electing their two members of Parliament. Moreover, a Municipal Corporations Bill, introduced in the House of Lords in August 1833 by the Lord Chancellor, contained a proposal that the new parliamentary boroughs should be granted charters of incorporation.[5] Though the proposal came to nothing, the idea of incorporation aroused considerable interest in the Potteries, and meetings were held to discuss its advantages and disadvantages.[6] At such a meeting at Burslem in July 1836 the opinion was expressed that a charter would be expensive without conferring adequate advantage and that as the parliamentary borough comprised towns entirely independent of each other, incorporation would be productive of endless discord and jealousy, and would give to one town an undue influence over the others.[7] This argument was brought forward many times before the union of the towns was finally accomplished. At the same meeting those who spoke for Burslem claimed that it enjoyed all the advantages of municipal government except that of a resident magistracy, and so they were strongly in favour of the appointment of a stipendiary magistrate for the district.[8]

Two years later the question of incorporation was still being canvassed locally, and in August 1838 the principal inhabitants of Fenton, meeting at the Canning Inn, declared themselves unanimously in favour of incorporating the borough.[9] But meetings at Stoke and Burslem in the following month showed a shift of interest from incorporation to the need for a stipendiary magistrate.[10] About the same time an influential meeting, presided over by the Duke of Sutherland, was of the opinion that there should be a police force for the whole of the Potteries as well as a stipendiary magistrate.[11]

In the following year the public demand for the improvement in the administration of justice resulted in the passing of two Acts of Parliament, the first providing for a stipendiary magistrate for the Staffordshire Potteries[12] and the other 'for establishing an effective police in places within and adjoining to the district called the Staffordshire Potteries and for improving and cleansing the same and better lighting thereof'.[13] Thus in one sphere at least, that of law and order, the people of the Potteries demonstrated to themselves the feasibility and desirability of co-operative effort. Whether these changes commended themselves to all classes of society is doubtful; in May 1839 rioting at Lane End calling for intervention by the military was said to have been occasioned by the introduction of the new police.[14]

For nearly 50 years nothing more was heard of amalgamating the Pottery towns. Each went its own way, developing its own institutions, enlarging in some cases its boundaries, and improving its status. Hanley, with Shelton, became a borough in 1857;[15] Penkhull and Boothen were formed into the borough of Stoke-upon-Trent in 1874,[16] and Longton and Lane End into the borough of Longton in 1865;[17] Burslem became a borough in 1878;[18] while Tunstall and Fenton were administered by local boards of health from 1855 and 1873 respectively[19] and automatically became urban districts in 1894. The borough of Longton was extended by the addition of East Vale in 1883[20] and of Florence and Dresden in 1884.[21] Thus, with the consolidation of these large urban areas, the stage was set for the first real attempt to achieve a true federation of the Pottery towns.

The county plan of 1888

The Local Government Bill proposing the creation of County Councils was introduced on 19 March

[2] H.C. Private Bill Office, Local Govt. Provisional Order (No. 3) Bill, 1908, *Mins. of Proc. before Sel. Cttee.* 2 July 1908, p. 2; K. D. Miller, *Brief Chronology of Local Govt. in Stoke-on-Trent* (Hanley, 1960), 4.
[3] 2 & 3 Wm. IV, c. 65.
[4] *Parl. Gazetteer* (1844).
[5] *Parl. Debs.* 3rd ser. vol. 20, July–Aug. 1833, 821.
[6] Miller, *Brief Chronology*, 5.
[7] *Staffs. Advertiser*, 9 July 1836.
[8] Ibid.
[9] *N. Staffs. Mercury*, 1 Sept. 1838.
[10] Ibid. 8 Sept. 1838.
[11] *Staffs. Advertiser*, 15 Sept. 1838.
[12] 2 & 3 Vic. c. 15.
[13] 2 & 3 Vic. c. 44 (local and personal).
[14] *Staffs. Advertiser*, 11 May 1839.
[15] 20 & 21 Vic. c. 10 (local and personal).
[16] 36 & 37 Vic. c. 216 (local).
[17] 29 & 30 Vic. c. 24 (local and personal).
[18] 39 & 40 Vic. c. 97 (local).   [19] See pp. 95, 215.
[20] 46 & 47 Vic. c. 62 (local).
[21] 47 & 48 Vic. c. 27 (local).

1888[22] and received the royal assent on 13 August of that year.[23] During the intervening period of five months much debate and negotiation took place in the Pottery towns regarding their position in the new local government pattern. With a general consensus of opinion against control of the area by the Staffordshire County Council the idea developed of creating an administrative 'County of the Potteries'.[24] It quickly gained favour and on 2 July a deputation from the six towns submitted the proposal for a separate county to the President of the Local Government Board.[25] On 9 July, however, the House of Commons accepted an amendment conferring county borough status on any town with a population of 50,000, whereas the limit for this purpose had earlier been fixed at 100,000[26] The change meant that Hanley on the passing of the Act would become a county borough and the remaining towns would pass under the control of the Staffordshire County Council. On 13 July the member for North-West Staffordshire attempted to include in the Bill the provision of county status for the district of the Staffordshire Potteries, comprising the four boroughs and the urban sanitary districts of Fenton and Tunstall Boards of Health. He expressed the view that, though Hanley would be entitled to be a county borough, it had given up any idea of self-glorification by agreeing to form a county in conjunction with the adjoining district.[27] Subsequent events proved this view to have been premature. The President of the Local Government Board thought that, in view of the difficulties involved, the proper course was to deal with the matter by Provisional Order, which he undertook to introduce at the beginning of the following session. W. Woodall, M.P. for Hanley, in accepting the assurance, insisted that it would be possible for the towns to preserve their own municipal life while combining for all purposes which had to be provided for in the Bill. At the same time he felt he was bound to protect Hanley by claiming its insertion in the Fourth Schedule (the list of county boroughs).[28] At a conference at Stoke the following day he explained that the county plan was running into difficulty but hoped that the promised Provisional Order would provide a solution; as to the possibility that the whole district might be made into a county borough, he thought it 'a dream which none would ever see accomplished'.[29]

When the Act received the royal assent in August 1888, Hanley was duly scheduled as a county borough. What would Hanley do? It took the corporation some time to make up their minds, and it was not until February 1889 that they finally decided to adopt the status of a county borough, thus effectively killing the county plan and delaying any further move towards amalgamation for several years.[30] The reasons for the decision are not known, but according to a town clerk of Hanley the scheme fell through because of the insistence of Stoke that the headquarters of the proposed new county council should be in that town.[31] Local jealousies were strong in the Potteries at that time—they have not altogether disappeared even now—and it is quite understandable that some such apparent triviality was enough to swing the balance against federation.

Apart from a nugatory effort in April of the same year by Longton to promote a scheme for making Stoke, Fenton, and Longton a county borough,[32] no further attempt to secure the whole or partial union of the Pottery towns was made during the succeeding decade, though the matter was the subject of discussion from time to time.[33]

The unsuccessful attempt of 1900–3

On 20 December 1900, on the initiative of the Stoke Town Council, it was decided to invite the various local authorities to attend a conference 'with a view to federal action'. The invitation was sent to the boroughs of Hanley, Stoke, Newcastle-under-Lyme, Longton, and Burslem, the urban districts of Fenton, Tunstall, Audley, Kidsgrove, and Smallthorne, the rural districts of Stoke and Wolstanton, and the parishes of Milton, Chell, Goldenhill, Chesterton, and Silverdale.[34] The wide area over which the invitation was spread indicates that the county plan was still uppermost in the minds of its promoters and the conference which met on 5 February 1901, by resolving that it was desirable in the interests of North Staffordshire to form a federation of local authorities,[35] was obviously thinking on the same lines. However, legal opinion was adverse to the formation of a new county and propounded the extension of the existing county borough of Hanley to include the remaining Pottery towns.[36] On 21 March 1902 a meeting of representatives of the six towns was held at Burslem, when it was agreed unanimously that the principle of federation of the Pottery towns by the constitution of a county borough should be adopted, 'subject to the resolutions passed by each authority for the preservation of their respective interests'.[37] The towns were determined to have their cake and eat it.

On 29 November 1902 Hanley asked the Local Government Board for an extension of the county borough to include Burslem, Longton, Stoke, Fenton, Tunstall, Smallthorne, Milton, Wolstanton, part of the parish of Goldenhill, Chell, Trentham, Stoke Rural, Caverswall, and the rural district of Stone, but only Longton joined in the representation.[38] Meanwhile in October 1902 Sir Hugh Owen, a former Secretary of the Local Government Board, presented a scheme of financial adjustment—'the bone of contention all through'[39]—to the Federation Committee. Under it the net assets of each town were to be ascertained by deducting outstanding debts and liabilities from the value of its various properties. The net assets which each town should contribute according to its proportion of the rateable value of the new borough were to be calculated; those towns whose net assets showed a deficiency

[22] Local Govt. (Eng. and Wales) Bills (182 and 338), H.C. (1888), iv.
[23] Local Govt. Act, 1888, 51 & 52 Vic. c. 41.
[24] Miller, *Brief Chronology*, 8.
[25] *Newcastle Guardian*, 7 July 1888.
[26] *Parl. Debs.*, 3rd ser. vol. 328, p. 849.
[27] Ibid. p. 1276.   [28] Ibid. pp. 1281, 1283.
[29] *Newcastle Guardian*, 31 July 1888.
[30] Miller, *Brief Chronology*, 9.

[31] *Staffs. Sentinel*, 5 Feb. 1901.
[32] Miller, *Brief Chronology*, 9.   [33] Ibid. 10.
[34] Miller, *Brief Chronology*, 11, 12.
[35] *Staffs. Sentinel*, 5 Feb. 1901.
[36] Miller, *Brief Chronology*, 12.
[37] *H.L. Mins. of Proc. before Sel. Cttee. on Local Govt. Provisional Order (No. 3) Bill* (1908), p. 63.
[38] Ibid. p. 5; Miller, *Brief Chronology*, 12.
[39] *H.L. Mins. of Evid. before Sel. Cttee.* (1908), p. 57.

would compensate, by differential rating, those towns contributing net assets in excess of their proper proportion.[40] Fenton considered that the scheme would inflict financial hardship on them and withdrew forthwith from the committee. The other towns decided to await a report from Alderman F. Geen of Stoke on the detailed financial implications of the Owen proposals, and when this was presented in July 1903, the opposition to federation gathered strength, culminating in September in a poll of the ratepayers of Burslem which showed a large majority against federation (2,670 to 457).[41] Burslem consequently withdrew, to be followed on 24 September by Stoke,[42] with the result that Hanley renounced the representation that it, with Longton, had made to the Local Government Board in November 1902.[43] For the time being the movement towards federation was at a standstill.

The final stage, 1905-10

Nevertheless the idea of federation was not dead, though some time elapsed before it recovered from the set-back it had received in 1903. Its re-emergence into the realm of practical politics was due to the initiative of the Longton town council, which in August 1905, at a conference of the various local authorities, expressed the view that the time was ripe for a reconsideration of the question. Their response was not enthusiastic.[44] Longton then changed its ground and resolved that 'on grounds of sanitation, education, and other matters of common interest it is desirable that the parliamentary borough of Stoke-upon-Trent should be formed into one municipal borough on some equitable basis, and that the other authorities concerned be invited to take the subject into their consideration'.[45] This meant the amalgamation of Longton, Fenton, and Stoke[46] into one county borough, and the scheme was launched in November 1906.[47] The Fenton Urban District Council, however, was not prepared to acquiesce in the plan of its larger neighbours without the backing of its ratepayers.[48] A poll was accordingly taken on 14 January 1907 which showed a decisive vote against the scheme (2,608 to 106).[49] Nevertheless, in the following month Longton and Stoke forwarded their joint representation to the Local Government Board and in accordance with the usual procedure a local inquiry was held the same month at Stoke.[50] Instead of giving a decision on the representation, however, the board on 23 April informed Longton and Stoke of its view that in the interests of economy and efficiency a more comprehensive scheme of federation was desirable and that yet another conference of the six towns should be held without delay.[51] What prompted the board to take this step was the evidence of many people at the inquiry indicating a wish for a larger amount of amalgamation[52] and probably, though this

was not stated, the opposition of Fenton to the Longton-Stoke proposal. All the councils were prepared to accede to the board's suggestion and a conference called by the board and presided over by its president, John Burns, was held at Stoke on 12 July.[53] He made a strong plea that conferences should take place between the six towns with a view to putting forward an agreed scheme for comprehensive federation. The conferences were duly held in the autumn of 1907 and were presided over by Major Norton, an officer of the board, Tunstall alone, the 'versatile and whirligig Tunstall', refusing to participate.[54] The path of negotiation proved to be by no means a smooth one. On 11 November Fenton Council made it clear that it would not commit itself to any scheme unless it commanded the approval of a majority of its ratepayers.[55] In the same month Burslem held a poll, at which 74 per cent. of the electorate voted; the verdict was against federation by 3,240 votes to 2,040,[56] despite the fact that a few days earlier the Duke of Sutherland at a public meeting in the same town had promised to make over his Trentham estate to the new county borough if federation should take place.[57] It is this Burslem poll which is so graphically described by Arnold Bennett in *The Old Wives' Tale*, and was adjudged by the county newspaper as quite unprecedented.[58] In the week preceding the poll meetings were held in different parts of the town, promoted on the one hand by the Association for Promoting the Federation of the Pottery Towns, and on the other by the Burslem Anti-Federation League.[59] On the day of the poll, 25 November, 'excitement was great throughout the town and the workers on both sides made supreme efforts to bring every voter possible up to the booths'. 'A number of motor cars', it was said, 'were requisitioned, chiefly by federationists.'[60] With Burslem, Fenton, and Tunstall standing out, it was Hanley, Longton, and Stoke who, on 30 November, lodged three separate representations with the Local Government Board.[61] Those of Longton and Stoke were identical and included the financial proposals, based on Alderman Geen's scheme of differential rating for a period of 20 years, which had appeared to be acceptable to a majority of the representatives. Hanley's representation differed from the other two in that it asked for a valuation, the taking over of the gas and electricity undertakings, and the imposition of a flat rate for educational purposes.[62] The statutory and other formalities were complied with in respect of the Longton representation only, and so it was upon the latter that the subsequent local inquiry was held.[63]

Before the inquiry opened in January 1908, the position in Tunstall had undergone a change. The Tunstall Council had by the casting vote of its chairman, declared itself opposed to federation,[64] but in a poll taken on 30 December 1907 a substantial

[40] Miller, *Brief Chronology*, 12.
[41] Ibid.
[42] Ibid. 13.
[43] *H.L. Mins. of Proc. before Sel. Cttee.* (1908), 73.
[44] *H.L. Mins. of Evid. before Sel. Cttee.* (1908), 13.
[45] *H.L. Mins. of Proc.* 6.
[46] In 1885 the old parl. boro. of Stoke was divided into Hanley and Stoke, the latter consisting of Longton, Fenton, and Stoke: 48 & 49 Vic. c. 23.
[47] *H.L. Mins. of Proc.* 135.
[48] Ibid. 73.
[49] Ibid.
[50] *H.L. Mins. of Evid.* 13.

[51] Ibid. 14.
[52] Ibid. 13; *H.L. Mins. of Proc.* 75.
[53] *H.L. Mins. of Proc.* 177.
[54] *H.L. Mins. of Evid.* 14.
[55] Ibid.
[56] *H.L. Mins. of Proc.* 30.
[57] Ibid. 31.
[58] *Staffs. Advertiser*, 23 Nov. 1907.
[59] Ibid.   [60] Ibid. 30 Nov. 1907.
[61] *H.L. Mins. of Proc.* 84.
[62] Ibid.
[63] *H.L. Mins. of Evid.* 15.
[64] Ibid. 316.

majority of the ratepayers was shown to be in favour (895 to 641).[65] As a result the council decided to offer no opposition to federation generally, but appointed a sub-committee to secure the best terms it could for Tunstall.[66]

The Local Government Board Inquiry, the last act of the federation drama to be performed on the local stage, took place at Stoke, again under the presidency of Major Norton, on 8, 9, and 10 January 1908. The position of the parties was that Hanley, Longton, and Stoke were in favour of the proposals, whilst Fenton and the county council opposed them. Tunstall, in view of the ratepayers' poll, played a waiting game. Burslem dramatically withdrew from the inquiry at the outset on the ground that the presiding officer had already expressed himself as favourable to the principle of federation. The lines of the inquiry then followed Alderman Geen's scheme, though it was known that Hanley did not favour his method of financial adjustment. To the general surprise Hanley on the second day proposed yet another scheme. Its proposal in brief was that there should be a flat rate and also a differential rate, and that by means of the latter the existing differences should be adjusted within a period of ten years.[67] This scheme was fundamentally the Owen scheme of 1902, and at the inquiry was supported only by Tunstall.[68]

On 23 February 1908 the Local Government Board issued the draft Provisional Order for the federation of the six towns, and the financial scheme incorporated in it differed sharply from those put forward at the inquiry, though in some respects it approached the Hanley scheme.[69] It provided that those towns which, on a valuation, were shown to have a deficiency of assets should pay the amount of their deficiency into a common fund over a period not exceeding 20 years. This involved a complicated valuation of municipal properties, which was anathema to most of the towns.[70] Nevertheless, the Order was accepted by Hanley, Longton, and Tunstall, but opposed by Burslem, Fenton, and Stoke.[71]

In July the Provisional Order Bill[72] was considered by a Select Committee of the House of Commons, and on the 29th of that month the third reading was passed.[73] Various amendments, however, were made by the committee, the chief of them relating to the financial adjustment. Differential rating for ten years was introduced, which meant that during that period the rates of the several towns should be *pro rata* what they had averaged for a period of three years. But those towns which on a valuation were shown to have a deficiency of net assets were, in addition, to make an annual payment to the common fund equal to one-tenth of such deficiency. Thus, if a town had an excess of net assets, it was to pay the same rates, proportionately, as its mean rates for the last three years, but it was to receive no credit for its excess of assets. If, however, a town had a deficiency of assets, it was to contribute rates on the basis of the average

for the three years, plus an annual payment of one-tenth of its deficiency of assets. Clearly, the adjustment would depend largely upon the valuation of each town's properties and liabilities, and the Bill, as amended, provided that in calculating assets all floating capital and floating assets, gas and electricity works, public halls and buildings, parks and recreation grounds, and sewage works were to be included, but not street widenings or improvements. As to gas works, it was provided that after the payment to the general district fund of 5 per cent. on the amount at which the works were valued, the balance, if any, was to be applied in the reduction of the price of gas to consumers. The same provision was to apply to electricity works, except that the 5 per cent. paid to the general district fund was to be 5 per cent. on general expenditure.[74]

The Bill, as passed by the Commons, pleased hardly anybody. It is true that differential rating had been inserted in the Order, though for a period of ten years only, whereas 20 years had been the period favoured at the inquiry,[75] but the bugbear of valuation still remained. The local reaction was strong. Tunstall withdrew as one of the promoters, leaving Hanley and Longton to promote the Bill in the House of Lords.[76] Hanley and Longton did not like the Order, but having given an undertaking in the local conferences to accept the Local Government Board as arbitrators they felt bound to carry out the scheme.[77] Petitions were presented to the House of Lords praying to be heard against the Bill from the Staffordshire County Council, Burslem, Fenton, Stoke, and Tunstall Councils, the Longton Justices, the North Staffordshire Railway Co., and certain Tunstall ratepayers.[78] It was clear that the decisive battle on the federation issue would have to be fought out before the Select Committee of the House of Lords and the final outcome would depend on the way in which that committee handled this delicate and complicated matter.

If the federation enterprise was to achieve a successful conclusion in the Upper House, it was essential that a strong chairman should preside over the proceedings of the committee, one with the ability to grasp the complicated nature of the issues involved, and with the diplomatic skill, allied to force of character, required to inseminate and develop a spirit of compromise. In Lord Cromer such a chairman was found. With a long record of success in diplomatic and administrative fields behind him, he was still, at the age of 67, able to turn to and master the intricacies of local government, to separate the essential from the non-essential, and to convince the contending parties that he was 'the soul of reasonable compromise'.[79] Anyone who reads the voluminous reports of the proceedings and evidence before the Lords' Committee cannot fail to be impressed by the skilful manner in which he handled both counsel and witnesses, and prepared the way for final agreement.

[65] *H.L. Mins. of Evid.* 317.
[66] Ibid.
[67] *Staffs. Advertiser, Potteries Federation Souvenir,* 31 Mar. 1910, p. 32.
[68] *H.L. Mins. of Evid.* 15.
[69] *Potteries Federation Souvenir,* 32; Miller, *Brief Chronology,* 15.
[70] *H.L. Mins of Proc.* 103.
[71] *H.L. Mins. of Evid.* 16.
[72] Bills Public, iii, 1908, Bill (201).
[73] *Parl. Debs.* 4th ser. vol. 193, p. 1942.
[74] *H.L. Mins. of Evid.* 16, 17; *Potteries Federation Souvenir,* 32, 33.
[75] *H.L. Mins. of Evid.* 16.
[76] Ibid.; *H.L. Mins. of Proc.* 20.
[77] *H.L. Mins. of Proc.* 109.
[78] *Staffs. Advertiser,* 17 Oct. 1908.
[79] *D.N.B.* 1901–21.

The House of Lords Committee began its hearing of the Bill on 24 November and was addressed by counsel for the various towns and other interested parties who in varying degrees recited the history of the federation movement and championed the points of view of their respective clients. Of the witnesses heard the most important perhaps, as his evidence was certainly the fullest, was G. C. Kent, the town clerk of Longton, who for many years had been a strong and able protagonist in the cause of federation.[80] Another important witness was Major Cecil Wedgwood, a member of the famous pottery firm, who voiced the support of the manufacturing interest for federation;[81] in 1910 he became the first mayor of the new county borough.[82]

On 10 December the committee announced certain preliminary decisions.[83] In the first place they approved the principle of federation, the adoption of which they considered would be of great advantage to the people of the Potteries. Further, they thought that important modifications to the Bill were necessary and suggested that agreement might be sought on what had been termed the Stoke basis, involving the adoption of two main principles: (a) separate rating areas and differential rates for a fixed period, (b) the abandonment of any attempt to value the assets in each district. The committee reserved to themselves full liberty of action should general agreement be found to be impossible. In accepting the responsibility of overriding both the Local Government Board and the House of Commons, the committee 'put the position back in the *status quo ante*, i.e. the state in which affairs were when the Stoke proposal was put forward', which in its view had the 'enormous advantage of uniting a larger body of public opinion than any other which has so far been advanced'.[84] This announcement was really the turning-point in the long-drawn argument. The committee had declared in favour of federation, it had indicated a possible solution of the financial crux, it had hinted that in the absence of agreement the committee might act on its own responsibility— 'occasions may arise when it is one's duty to ignore public opinion'[85]—and further, the chairman emphasized that, in view of the imminent prorogation of Parliament, agreement, if it was to come, must come quickly.[86]

On 16 December the parties informed the committee that they had reached agreement on the main point.[87] In the intervening period much argument took place on the merits of what was called the Burslem basis as compared with the Stoke basis of differential rating. The former contemplated the introduction of a flat rate for the six towns together with an additional rate levied for ten years on Hanley with the object of making up the deficiency of Fenton, with which the latter would be faced in paying the flat rate.[88] Great opposition was immediately manifested towards this Burslem scheme mainly on the ground that it had been introduced at the last moment and that, on the hypothetical figures produced, Hanley would gain considerably at the expense of its neighbours.[89] When, on 16 December, the heads of agreement between the parties were announced, it was seen that the Burslem basis had been abandoned. These heads of agreement may be summarized as follows. Each district was to pay its own loan charges, except those in respect of gas and electricity; the period of differential rating was to be extended from ten to twenty years; the basis of differential rating was to be in the proportions— Hanley 100, Longton 85, Stoke 87, Burslem 96, Fenton 80, Tunstall 88; differential rates were to apply to all expenditure other than loan charges; there was to be no valuation of any kind; there were special provisions for gas and electricity undertakings; the costs of the six towns in connexion with the Order were to be paid by the new borough.[90]

The Bill as amended by the Commons was redrafted on the above lines and on 19 December it was passed by the House of Lords,[91] and on the same day by the House of Commons.[92] It received the royal assent on 21 December.[93]

The new county borough of Stoke-on-Trent came into existence on 31 March 1910.[94] Although federation was the word commonly used to describe the union of the six towns and Lord Cromer had even spoken of the *animus federandi*,[95] the operation effected by the Act was the amalgamation of the Pottery towns and not their federation in the constitutional sense. The councils of the four boroughs and of the urban districts of Fenton[96] and Tunstall ceased to exist and were replaced by the council of the new borough consisting of 78 councillors representing the 26 wards into which the whole area was divided.[97]

The provisions of the Act need not be considered in detail, as they embody the decisions arrived at in the House of Lords Committee. It should be mentioned, however, that in the article dealing with differential rating the figures as set out above regarding the proportion of the rates leviable were slightly altered to read: Hanley 100, Longton 86, Stoke 87, Burslem 94, Fenton 79, Tunstall 86.[98] As this question of differential rating was, throughout the history of the movement, a matter of prime importance, it may not be out of place to illustrate from the accounts of the new borough how it worked out in practice. The relevant article of the Act provided that for 20 years from 31 March 1910 the general district rate to be levied by the council should be levied on a separate basis in each of the areas; the annual rate was to be fixed at such an amount in the £ as would secure that the total amounts in the £ of all the rates levied in that year in the areas for all purposes (except poor law and payment of loan interest) should bear towards each other the proportions mentioned above.[99] Table I shows in column 3 the differential rating for each of the six towns on the proportional basis laid down in the Act.

[80] *H.L. Mins. of Evid.* 7–48, 55–141.
[81] Ibid. 141–153.
[82] *Potteries Federation Souvenir*, 2.
[83] *H.L. Mins. of Proc.* 367–9.
[84] Ibid. 369.
[85] Ibid. 368.
[86] Ibid. 369.
[87] Ibid. 433.
[88] Ibid. 379–81.
[89] Ibid. 401.
[90] Ibid. 434–6.
[91] *L.J.* cxl. 501.
[92] *C.J.* clxiii. 513.

[93] *L.J.* cxl. 504.
[94] Local Govt. Bd.'s Provisional Order Confirmation (No. 3) Act, 1908, 8 Edw. VII, c. 164 (local).
[95] *H.L. Mins. of Evid.* 355.
[96] A small detached part of the urban district consisting of a few acres around Lawn Farm was not included in the amalgamation. It became part of Stoke in the 1922 extension. [97] 8 Edw. VII, c. 164 (local).
[98] Ibid. art. 33. [99] Ibid.

TABLE I

Rates levied in Stoke-on-Trent, 1910–11[1]

Parishes	Borough rate			General district rate			Total corporation rate 5	Relief of poor, &c. 6	Total rates
	General expenses 1	Local loans 2	Total	General expenses 3	Local loans 4	Total			
	s. d.	s. d.	s. d.	s. d.	s. d.	s. d.	s. d.	s. d.	s. d.
Tunstall and Goldenhill	2 11½	0 7½	3 7	2 6½	1 7	4 1½	7 8½	2 1	9 9½
Burslem	2 11½	1 0½	4 0	2 10	1 1½	3 11½	7 11½	2 2	10 1½
Hanley	2 11½	0 7	3 6½	3 5¾	1 3¼	4 9	8 3½	2 3½	10 7
Stoke	2 11½	0 9	3 8½	2 7½	0 10	3 5½	7 2	2 3½	9 5½
Fenton	2 11½	0 6	3 5½	2 1½	0 8½	2 10	6 3½	2 3½	8 7
Longton	2 11½	1 2½	4 2	2 6½	1 1	3 7½	7 9½	2 4	10 1½

The rates levied in each town for all purposes during the last year of its separate existence were as shown in Table II.

TABLE II

Rates levied in the Six Towns, 1909–10[2]

		s.	d.
Tunstall	Tunstall	8	11
	Chell	8	2
	Goldenhill	8	4
Burslem		8	6
Hanley		9	6
Stoke		9	1
Fenton		7	2
Longton	Longton	9	6
	Florence	8	6
	Dresden	8	8

A comparison with the last column of the previous table shows that amalgamation resulted in increases of the rate poundage as follows: Tunstall (approximately), 1*s.* 3½*d.*; Burslem, 1*s.* 7½*d.*; Hanley, 1*s.* 1*d.*; Stoke, 4½*d.*; Fenton, 1*s.* 5*d.*; Longton (approximately), 1*s.* 3½*d.*

The expense of promoting (or opposing) the Order amounted in all to over £35,000, and, as directed by the Act, the charge was borne by the new county borough.[3] Another financial liability of the new borough, namely the amount of compensation for loss of office to be paid to the six former town clerks, occasioned some difficulty. The original clause of the Act was found to have been so drafted as to give the clerks what was thought to be a disproportionately large sum. A Bill was promoted in the House of Lords to rectify the anomaly but was withdrawn after a settlement had been reached by the parties. Under it the claims of the clerks were to be met by the payment of a total sum of £42,500.[4]

A further difficulty arose in connexion with Section 26 of the 1908 Act. This section provided that accounts should be taken by the new council of all revenue assets and liabilities (except those relating to gas and electricity) vested in the six councils and in levying rates during the first three years of the county borough's existence the balance shown on the account relating to each district should be credited or debited to the district. When the borough accounts were computed it was found that Burslem was in credit to the extent of £16,355 and Fenton £3,071, while the following were in debt to the rating area: Tunstall £2,638, Hanley £14,982, Stoke £1,464, and Longton £342. At first it was proposed to spread the adjustment, in order to relieve Hanley's rate, over a period of ten years, but this was not possible as the period laid down by the Act was three years. In the end the Finance Committee, considering the adjustment artificial, decided to terminate it by crediting Burslem with £1,773 and debiting Hanley with £1,367, Stoke with £134, Tunstall with £241, and Longton with £31.[5]

So much for the complicated financial difficulties with which the birth of the new borough was attended. The amalgamation of the six towns had been accomplished and if the question is asked why the change came about, the answer is probably that in essence it was a desideratum of local government voiced by those, councillors and officials, burdened with the administration of an overlapping area, the various parts of which had reached different levels of governmental progress. Economy and efficiency were the primary objectives, aimed at not only by the local councils but also by the Local Government Board which throughout showed itself a sympathetic and powerful supporter of the idea of amalgamation. Strong support for the movement came too from the business and professional classes[6] and also from the local press, particularly the *Staffordshire Sentinel.*[7] But so far as the population of the area generally was concerned, apart from the single exception of the Burslem poll,[8] the issue aroused no great feeling either for or against federation probably because the rarefied atmosphere of local government finance was one in which it was impossible to arouse any strong popular emotion. Although during the fifty years that have elapsed since the union of the towns Stoke-on-Trent has become one of the great cities of the kingdom—it became a city in 1925[9]—the attainment of full civic unity is still somewhat retarded by the continued existence of local loyalties and feelings.

[1] *Stoke-on-Trent Abstract of Accts. 1910–11*, 277 (copy in H.R.L.).
[2] Ibid.
[3] *Abstract of Accts.* 1911, p. 145.
[4] *Staffs. Advertiser*, 23 June 1910.
[5] *Staffs. Sentinel*, 31 Jan. 1913.
[6] *H.L. Mins. of Evid.* 141–4 (evid. of C. Wedgwood); *Assoc. for Promoting the Federation of the Potteries Towns* (copy in H.R.L.).
[7] *Rendezvous with the Past*, Sentinel Centenary (1854–1954), p. 31.
[8] See p. 255.
[9] *Lond. Gaz.* 1925, p. 4449.

THE COUNTY BOROUGH SINCE 1910

THE county borough as constituted in 1910 comprised an area of 11,142 acres.[1] In 1922 an extension of the boundary took place in an easterly and southerly direction by the absorption of the civil parishes of Chell and Smallthorne and part of Milton (2,464 acres), and part of the parishes of Newchapel (155 acres), Caverswall (1,235 acres), Norton-in-the-Moors (1,012 acres), Stoke Rural (1,934 acres), and Stone Rural and Trentham (2,835 acres).[2] Thus an area of 9,635 acres was added, much of it agricultural land,[3] and the total acreage of the borough rose to 20,777 acres. In 1930 a further 430 acres in Trentham and Barlaston parishes, comprising the area between Strongford Farm and Oldroad Farm, was added for the purpose of constructing the Strongford Sewage Works.[4] In 1930 an attempt to extend the borough boundary westwards to include the borough of Newcastle-under-Lyme proved abortive.[5] In 1946 another attempt to include Newcastle, as well as Kidsgrove and parts of the rural districts of Leek, Cheadle, and Stone, was made, in proposals advanced to the Local Government Boundary Commission.[6] Two years later the report of the commission[7] proposed the union of Stoke, Newcastle, and Kidsgrove with some neighbouring areas into a new one-tier county administered by a single all-purpose authority. The proposal, however, fell through when the Government decided in 1949 to wind up the Boundary Commission.[8]

On 5 July 1925 King George V, when visiting Stoke to lay the foundation stone of the extensions to the North Staffordshire Royal Infirmary, announced the conferment of the title and status of a city upon the borough.[9] On 5 July 1928 the title of mayor was replaced by that of lord mayor.[10]

By the Act of 1908 the county borough was divided into 26 wards for purposes of municipal franchise.[11] Consequent upon the 1922 extension the number of wards was increased to 28.[12] Of the original 26 wards, nos. 1 to 20 and 22 and 25 remained unchanged. Those designated 21, 23, 24, and 26, together with the added areas, were formed into six new wards numbered 21, 23, 24, 26, 27, and 28. In 1954 the wards were reorganized and their number reduced to 24.[13]

Under its original constitution the borough council consisted of 26 aldermen (one for each ward) and 78 councillors (three for each ward).[14] As a result of the 1922 extension the number of aldermen was increased to 28 and of councillors to 84.[15] With the reduction of the number of wards in 1954, the number of aldermen was reduced to 24 and of councillors to 72.[16]

The meeting-place of the new council was, in 1910, a matter of some delicacy. Each of the six towns had its own town hall and the choice of one rather than another as the headquarters of the new council was complicated by feelings of local pride and sentiment. The first meeting of the council on 31 March 1910 was held at the North Stafford Hotel, Stoke, when it was decided that the council should meet at each town in turn.[17] Consequently the April, May, June, July, and September meetings took place at Fenton, Tunstall, Burslem, Longton, and Hanley town halls respectively.[18] But this single experience of peripatetic government was sufficient to emphasize its disadvantages, and, at its meeting in Stoke Town Hall on 27 October, the council agreed that all future meetings of the council and its committees, except Education and Watch, should be located at Stoke, which was also to be the council's administrative headquarters. It was also decided that the Education and Police departments should be housed in Hanley, together with their relevant committees.[19]

In 1910 the committees of the council consisted of Baths, Markets and Fairs, Distress, Education, Electricity Supply, Estates, Public Works and Tramways, Finance, Gas, General Purposes, Health, Housing and Destructor, Highways and Plans, Local Pension, Parks and Cemeteries, Libraries, Museums and Gymnasiums, Sewage Farms and Sewage Works, Stores and Purchase, Water (for two years only), and Watch.[20] By 1958[21] inevitable changes in the committee structure had taken place. Electricity Supply and Gas committees had ceased to exist following the nationalization of these industries. Distress and Local Pensions were no longer the direct concern of the local authority. By 1929[22] Baths and Markets and Fairs had been combined with the Estates Committee which by that year had been curtailed by the disappearance of tramways and the constitution of Public Works as a separate committee, still operating in 1958. By 1958 there were separate committees for Health and Housing and a new committee known as Sanitary and Cleansing. Otherwise the original committees remained unchanged but new ones had been added; these were Architectural, Children's, Reconstruction, Welfare Services, and Smallholdings.[23] By 1939 an Aerodrome Committee had been constituted to administer the municipal airport at Meir[24] and by 1949 an Establishment Committee to supervise the large administrative staff required for the conduct of the city's affairs.[25]

In 1911[26] it was ruled that no committee, except the Watch and Education Committees, should con-

[1] *Census*, 1911.
[2] Provisional Order Confirmation (Stoke-on-Trent) Extension Act, 1921, 11 & 12 Geo. V, c. 103 (local).
[3] *Census*, 1931.
[4] Stoke-on-Trent Extension Act, 1929, 19 & 20 Geo. V, c. 27 (local). [5] See p. 7.
[6] *Staffs. Sentinel*, 21 Nov. 1946.
[7] Rep. of Local Govt. Boundary Com., H.C. 150, p. 743 (1948-9), xviii.
[8] *The Times*, 28 June 1949.
[9] *Lond. Gaz.* 1925, p. 4449.
[10] Ibid. 1928, p. 4898.
[11] Local Govt. Board Provisional Order Confirmation (No. 3) Act, 1908, 8 Edw. VII, c. 164 (local), art. xi.

[12] 11 & 12 Geo. V, c. 103 (local).
[13] *Lond. Gaz.* 1954, p. 5578; detailed scheme in town clerk's office.
[14] 8 Edw. VII, c. 164 (local), art. xi.
[15] 11 & 12 Geo. V, c. 103 (local).
[16] *Lond. Gaz.* 1954, p. 5578.
[17] *Staffs. Advertiser*, 2 Apr. 1910.
[18] Ibid. 30 Apr., 28 May, 2 July, 30 July, 1 Oct. 1910.
[19] Ibid. 29 Oct. 1910.
[20] *Counc. Yr. Bk.* (1910-11).
[21] Ibid. (1958-9).
[22] Ibid. (1929-30). [23] Ibid. (1958-9).
[24] Ibid. (1939-40). [25] Ibid. (1949-50).
[26] H.R.L., Council Mins. 26 Oct. 1911.

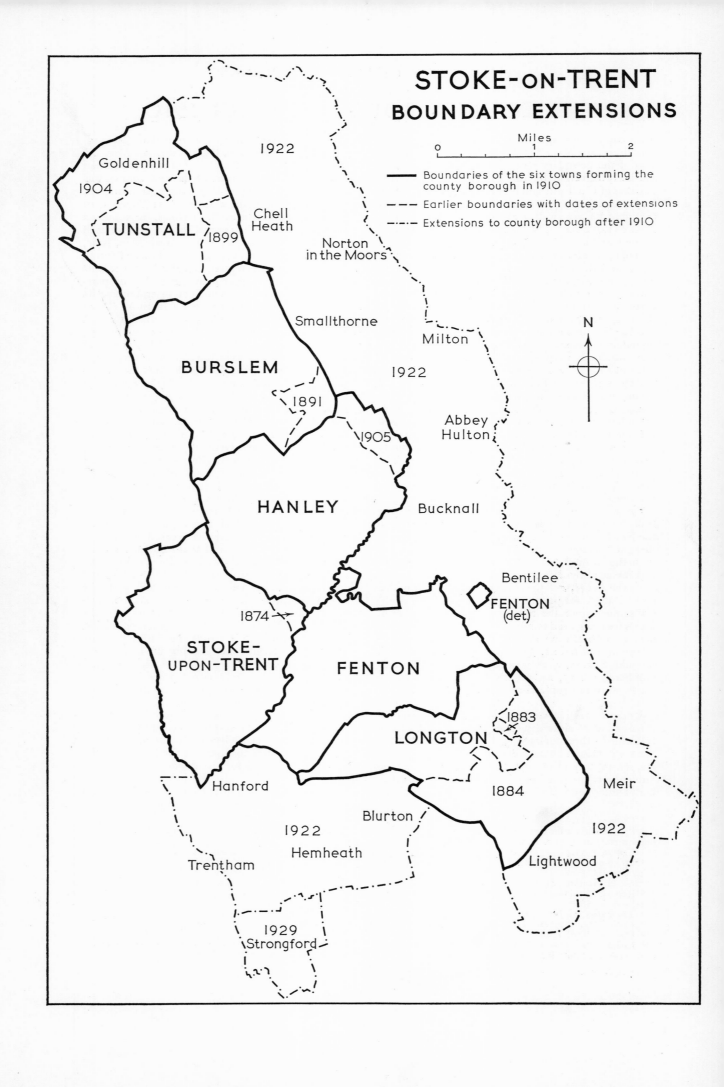

STOKE-on-TRENT
BOUNDARY EXTENSIONS

Miles
0   1   2

—— Boundaries of the six towns forming the county borough in 1910

--- Earlier boundaries with dates of extensions

—·— Extensions to county borough after 1910

N

Goldenhill

1904

TUNSTALL

1899

Chell Heath

1922

Norton in the Moors

Smallthorne

Milton

BURSLEM

1922

1891

1905

Abbey Hulton

HANLEY

Bucknall

Bentilee

FENTON (det)

1874

STOKE-UPON-TRENT

FENTON

1883

LONGTON

Meir

1884

Hanford

Blurton

Lightwood

1922

1922

Hemheath

Trentham

1929
Strongford

sist of more than 26 members, but in the following year[27] the limit was reduced to 18, which still (1959) applies to all committees except General Purposes, Watch, and Education.[28]

In the early years of the new county borough membership of the council does not seem to have had a political complexion but in the 1920's seats were increasingly contested by Labour party candidates.[29] In 1928–9 the council was made up of 66 Independent and 46 Labour members,[30] while in the November 1930 election Labour for the first time secured a small majority over the Independent members (59:53).[31] Labour remained in control of the council until 1937,[32] but in November of that year 60 Independent and non-party members were returned as against 52 Labour members.[33] Elections were suspended during the war but with their resumption the predominance of Labour party members has remained unbroken.[34]

Tables III to VI[35] show the rateable value of the county borough for each year since the amalgamation of the six towns (Table III) and the poundage of the rate for the same period (Tables IV, V, and VI).

TABLE III

Rateable value of county borough since 1910

	£		£		£
1910–11	789,461	1926–7	1,158,371	1942–3	1,280,142
1911–12	818,532	1927–8	1,135,592	1943–4	1,296,246
1912–13	820,003	1928–9	1,182,193	1944–5	1,297,912
1913–14 ⎫ 1914–15 ⎬	858,958*	1929–30	1,214,371*	1945–6	1,306,182
		1930–1	974,618‡	1946–7	1,305,466
1915–16	858,279	1931–2	989,236	1947–8	1,312,178
1916–17	852,249	1932–3	1,005,589	1948–9	1,303,089
1917–18	850,604	1933–4	1,021,632	1949–50	1,330,334
1918–19	848,014	1934–5	1,100,816*	1950–1	1,352,905
1919–20	850,221	1935–6	1,121,097	1951–2	1,368,159
1920–1	891,554	1936–7	1,144,135	1952–3	1,395,243
1921–2	912,734	1937–8	1,177,522	1953–4	1,425,843
1922–3	999,274†	1938–9	1,209,447	1954–5	1,469,538
1923–4	1,033,385	1939–40	1,245,309	1955–6	1,512,194
1924–5	1,018,343	1940–1	1,268,221	1956–7	2,477,054*
1925–6	1,207,561*	1941–2	1,273,826	1957–8	2,420,449

* Denotes a revaluation.
† Includes the added areas (see p. 259).
‡ Shows the effect of derating under Local Government Act (1929).

TABLE IV

Poundage of the borough rate for the period 1911 to 1921

The total rate includes the poor rate, which is shown in italic figures

	Tunstall and Goldenhill		Tunstall		Goldenhill		Burslem		Hanley		Stoke		Fenton		Longton	
	s.	d.	s.	d.	s.	d.	s.	d.	s.	d.	s.	d.	s.	d.	s.	d.
1911–12	9	11½	..		..		10	1½	10	9½	9	8½	8	7	10	2
	(1	*7)*					*(1*	*6)*	*(2*	*0½)*	*(2*	*0½)*	*(2*	*0)*	*(2*	*1½)*
1912–13	9	7	..		..		7	5	11	3	10	1	8	2	10	0
	(1	*2½)*					*(1*	*3⅜)*	*(2*	*0½)*	*(2*	*0½)*	*(2*	*1)*	*(2*	*1)*
1913–14	9	9	..		..		9	6	11	0	9	8½	8	3	9	11½
	(1	*6)*					*(1*	*4½)*	*(2*	*0)*	*(1*	*11½)*	*(1*	*10½)*	*(2*	*1½)*
1914–15	9	6	..		..		10	4	11	0	9	11	8	6	10	6½
	(1	*7½)*					*(1*	*7)*	*(2*	*3½)*	*(2*	*2½)*	*(2*	*1½)*	*(2*	*6½)*
1915–16	9	7	..		..		10	2	11	1	10	1	8	10½	10	6½
	(1	*7½)*					*(1*	*7½)*	*(2*	*5)*	*(2*	*4½)*	*(2*	*5)*	*(2*	*5½)*
1916–17	9	9	..		..		10	3½	11	3	10	2½	8	10	10	4½
	(1	*10)*					*(1*	*8½)*	*(2*	*5½)*	*(2*	*5)*	*(2*	*6)*	*(2*	*4)*
1917–18	10	4½	..		..		11	0½	11	11½	10	8½	9	2	11	0
	(1	*8)*					*(1*	*7½)*	*(2*	*4)*	*(2*	*3)*	*(2*	*3)*	*(2*	*4)*
1918–19	..		11	6	11	7	12	5½	12	8	11	6	9	9	12	1
			(1	*11)*	*(2*	*0)*	*(2*	*0½)*	*(2*	*2)*	*(2*	*1½)*	*(2*	*0)*	*(2*	*5½)*
1919–20	..		14	0½	14	0½	15	3½	16	3	14	7½	12	9	15	0
	..		*(2*	*3)*	*(2*	*3)*	*(2*	*1½)*	*(3*	*0½)*	*(2*	*11½)*	*(2*	*11)*	*(2*	*10)*
1920–1	..		18	10½	18	11½	20	6	22	3½	20	3	17	10½	20	7½
			(2	*11)*	*(3*	*0)*	*(2*	*9)*	*(4*	*4)*	*(4*	*4)*	*(4*	*2)*	*(4*	*3)*
1921–2	..		18	5	18	6	19	10	21	9½	19	11	17	7½	20	2
			(3	*1)*	*(3*	*2)*	*(2*	*10)*	*(4*	*6)*	*(4*	*7)*	*(4*	*5)*	*(4*	*6)*

[27] Ibid. 31 Oct. 1912.
[28] *Counc. Yr. Bk.* (1958–9).
[29] *Staffs. Advertiser*, 6 Nov. 1920, 7 Nov. 1925.
[30] Ibid. 3 Nov. 1928.   [31] Ibid. 8 Nov. 1930.
[32] Ibid. 5 Nov. 1932, 4 Nov. 1933, 3 Nov. 1934, 9 Nov. 1935, 7 Nov. 1936.   [33] Ibid. 6 Nov. 1937.
[34] *Eve. Sentinel*, 11 Oct. 1946; ibid. 12 May 1950; ibid. 13 May 1955.
[35] Figures extracted from *Abstract of Accts. of Corp. for year ended 31 March 1958* (copy in H.R.L.).

TABLE V

Poundage of the borough rate for the period 1922 to 1929

The total rate includes the poor rate, which is shown in italic figures, and which is the same for all rating districts during the whole period

	1922–3		1923–4		1924–5		1925–6		1926–7		1927–8		1928–9		1929–30	
	s.	d.	s.	d.	s.	d.	s.	d.	s.	d.	s.	d.	s.	d.	s.	d.
Poor rate	*(4*	*6)*	*(4*	*1)*	*(3*	*10)*	*(3*	*8½)*	*(5*	*4)*	*(5*	*4)*	*(4*	*5)*	*(4*	*0½)*
Tunstall and Goldenhill .	18	10	17	6	16	8	16	0	17	9½	18	0½	17	2½	16	9½
Burslem	20	5	19	0	18	1	17	7½	19	7	19	11½	19	1	18	7½
Hanley	20	7	19	1½	18	6	17	9	18	8½	20	0½	19	1½	18	9
Stoke	18	11	17	7	16	8½	16	2	17	11½	18	2½	17	5	16	11½
Fenton	16	11	15	8	14	11½	14	3	16	3½	16	7½	15	10	15	6
Longton	19	4	17	11½	17	3½	16	11½	18	7	18	10½	18	0½	17	8½
Newchapel . . .	14	7	13	9	13	8	13	1½	15	2½	15	6	15	3½	15	5½
Chell	14	7	13	9	13	8	13	1½	15	2½	15	6	15	3½	15	5½
Smallthorne . . .	14	7	13	9	13	8	13	1½	15	2½	15	6	15	3½	15	5½
Milton	14	7	13	9	13	8	13	1½	15	2½	15	6	15	3½	15	5½
Norton	14	7	13	6	13	2	12	4½	14	8½	15	3	14	9½	14	8½
Stoke Rural . . .	16	4	15	3	14	11	14	1½	16	5½	17	0	16	3½	15	11½
Caverswall . . .	14	7	13	9	13	8	12	11½	15	6½	16	0	15	11½	15	9½
Stone Rural . . .	13	1	12	3	12	2	11	7½	14	2½	15	0	14	9½	14	11½
Hanford	14	7	13	9	13	8	13	1½	15	5½	16	6	16	3½	15	11½
Trentham	11	7	11	3	11	8	11	7½	14	8½	16	0	16	3½	15	11½

TABLE VI

Poundage of the borough rate for the period 1930 to 1957

From 1930–1 to 1944–5, the Abstracts of Accounts of Stoke-on-Trent Corporation, *from which these tables have been compiled, give the average rate only*

	s.	d.
1930–1	17	2·83
1931–2	16	11·88
1932–3	16	5·88
1933–4	17	1·884
1934–5	16	3·892
1935–6	17	5·895
1936–7	16	11·907
1937–8	17	3·778
1938–9	17	11·799
1939–40	18	7·833
1940–1	18	7·861
1941–2	18	7·889
1942–3	18	1·918
1943–4	18	5·946
1944–5	18	9·973
1945–6	19	6
1946–7	21	0
1947–8	24	6
1948–9	19	0
1949–50	18	6
1950–1	18	6
1951–2	20	0
1952–3	21	8
1953–4	24	6
1954–5	25	6
1955–6	26	0
1956–7	18	10
1957–8	21	6

The amalgamation of the towns in 1910 brought no change in the parliamentary representation, and in the general elections of January and December in that year, Stoke-upon-Trent and Hanley each returned a Labour member.[36] In 1918,[37] however, Hanley lost its separate representation, while Stoke-upon-Trent was allotted three members, one for each of its three divisions, Burslem, Hanley, and Stoke. In December 1918, two Coalition candidates and one Labour candidate were returned,[38] but since 1922 Labour has, apart from a break in 1931–5,[39] remained dominant in the Stoke constituency. Since 1948 the nomenclature of the latter has been Central, North, and South divisions.[40]

The creation of Stoke-on-Trent as a county borough involved no immediate changes in the administration of justice in Burslem, Hanley, Stoke, and Longton, the former boroughs. The 1908 Act provided for the continuance in the new borough of the Hanley Court of Quarter Sessions,[41] and petty sessions continued to be held in the above-mentioned four towns. New borough courts were, however, established in May 1910 at Tunstall and Fenton[42] and each of the six courts had its own justices' clerk. At the same time the stipendiary magistrate held his weekly court at Hanley, Burslem, Tunstall, and Stoke and every alternate week in Longton and Fenton.[43] An exact delimitation of the functions of these two systems of petty sessional jurisdiction had not been attempted, but in 1945 Lord Goddard in his *Report on the Longton Court Inquiry*[44] brought to light certain unsatisfactory features of the existing arrangements. In particular, there was no agreement about the class of case that ought to be taken before the stipendiary magistrate. In other large towns the difficulty did not exist because there was only one clerk to the justices, including the stipendiary magistrate, and he arranged the list of court cases. The

[36] *Dod's Parliamentary Companion.*
[37] Representation of People Act, 1918, 7 & 8 Geo. V, c. 64.
[38] *Dod's Parl. Comp.*   [39] Ibid.
[40] Representation of People Act, 1948, 11 & 12 Geo. VI, c. 65.
[41] 8 Edw. VII, c. 164 (local), art. v.
[42] *Staffs. Advertiser,* 28 May 1910.
[43] *Sentinel Yr. Bk. of Potteries and N. Staffs.* (1928), 91.
[44] Lord Goddard, *Longton Court Inquiry* (H.M.S.O. 1945; copy in H.R.L.).

force of tradition, the recollection of the time when there were separate commissions of the peace, and some feeling of local prestige were, in Lord Goddard's view, probably the reasons why similar arrangements had not been made in Stoke.[45]

As a result of the Inquiry changes were made. It was decided to appoint a full-time magistrate's clerk for the city (but excluding the stipendiary court) and that arrangements should be made with the stipendiary magistrate about the allocation of business between the stipendiary court and the lay magistrates' courts. As a first step towards centralization, the number of magistrates' courts was reduced to four, Tunstall and Fenton being omitted.[46] In the same year the Stipendiary Commissioners were empowered to vary the salaries paid by them to the stipendiary magistrate and his clerk.[47]

THE CITY AND COUNTY BOROUGH OF STOKE-ON-TRENT

Silver, a cross gules fretted with gold; in the first quarter a representation of the Portland Vase; in the second, a kneeling camel proper charged on the body with a silver shield bearing a red cross; in the third, an eagle displayed sable; and in the fourth, a scythe proper; on a chief gules a boar's head torn off, between two Stafford Knots all gold. [Granted 1912]

The population of the county borough in 1911 was 234,553[48] and in 1921 240,428.[49] As a result of the extension of the borough in 1922 and 1930,[50] the population in the intercensal period increased by 27,219, this being the total population of the transferred areas at the 1921 Census.[51] By 1931 the population had increased to 276,639[52] and it is noteworthy that whereas in 1921 the population density per acre was 21·6 persons,[53] that figure had been reduced by 1931 to 13,[54] a result of the development of new housing in the added areas. Between 1921 and 1931 the natural increase of births over deaths was 9·2 per cent. and the loss of population by migration was 5·8 per cent., leaving a net increase of 3·4 per cent. over the 1921 figure (as amended by the intercensal increase).[55] In 1951 the population numbered 275,115. The natural increase of births over deaths

amounted to 11·5 per cent. and the loss by migration to 12·1 per cent., leaving a net decrease over the 1931 figure of 0·6 per cent. The density per acre was still 13 as in 1931.[56]

Arms were granted to the new county borough in 1912.[57] They were made up of devices previously used by the constituent towns, though of these Burslem alone had received a grant.[58] In its coat the Portland Vase appeared. So did a scythe, the emblem of the Sneyds. The fretty cross is supposed to have been derived from a device used by Fenton,[59] and the boar's head from Stoke-upon-Trent.[60] The camel was taken from the crest used by Hanley[61] and the eagle from the Longton crest.[62] Tunstall supplied the Stafford Knots and its unauthorized arms also showed the scythe.[63]

PUBLIC HEALTH. After 1910 the main developments in sewage disposal were located in the Strongford area in the extreme south of the city, and to a lesser extent at Meir on the eastern boundary. The initiation of the Strongford sewage scheme was the result, first, of the deterioration of the Stoke and Fenton sewage works which had been damaged by mining subsidence,[64] and, secondly, of the development of housing estates in the southern part of the city.[65] The need for better sewage disposal facilities had been felt before the First World War and as early as 1912 the Strongford site had been selected,[66] but actual operations had to be postponed until the end of the war.

In 1922 the corporation was required by statute to submit to the Minister of Health a sewage scheme for the borough and, when sanction was given, to carry it out within seven years.[67] After an inquiry in 1927[68] the construction of the first section of the Strongford scheme to serve the Stoke, Fenton, and Trentham districts was begun in 1928.[69] Representatives of Stoke-on-Trent, Newcastle-under-Lyme, Wolstanton United Urban District Council, and the Staffordshire County Council then met in conference, at the suggestion of the Ministry of Health, to discuss the possibility of dealing with the sewage of Newcastle and Wolstanton at the Strongford works.[70] After protracted negotiations it was agreed in 1932[71] that the Newcastle sewage—the borough by that date included Wolstanton[72]—should be received and treated at Strongford. The necessary additions to the works, the construction of the main outfall sewer from Newcastle to the Trent Vale Pumping Station, and the mains thence to Strongford were completed in 1936.[73] In 1938 the city agreed with Stone Rural District Council to receive sewage

[45] Ibid.
[46] *Staffs. Sentinel,* 21 Dec. 1945, 24 Jan. 1946.
[47] Act to amend the Staffs. Potteries Stipendiary Justices Acts 1839 to 1895, 8 & 9 Geo. VI, c. 4 (local).
[48] *Census,* 1911.
[49] Ibid. 1921.
[50] See p. 259.
[51] *Census,* 1931.
[52] Ibid.
[53] Ibid. 1921.
[54] Ibid. 1931.
[55] Ibid.
[56] Ibid. 1951.
[57] T. Pape, 'Early Armorials of the Pottery Towns' (*Cox's Potteries Annual and Yr. Bk.* 1925), 27.
[58] A. C. Fox-Davies, *Book of Public Arms* (1915), 130.
[59] *Cox's Potteries Annual* (1925), 27.
[60] Ibid. C. W. Scott-Giles in *Civic Heraldry* (1953), 330, however, considers that the boar's head was from the arms used by Longton.
[61] Fox-Davies, op. cit. 352.

[62] Scott-Giles, op. cit. 330.
[63] *Cox's Potteries Annual* (1925), 27.
[64] *Inauguration of Sewage Purification Works at Strongford, 1936* (copy in H.R.L.).
[65] See p. 268.
[66] *Sewage Purification Works at Strongford.*
[67] Min. of Health Prov. Order Confirmation (Stoke-on-Trent Extension) Act, 1921, 11 & 12 Geo. V, c. 103 (local).
[68] H.R.L., Sewage Farms and Sewage Works Cttee. Mins. 3 Oct. 1927.
[69] *Strongford Main Drainage Scheme, 1951,* 8 (copy in H.R.L.).
[70] Sewage Farms &c. Cttee. Mins. 5 March 1928.
[71] H.R.L., Mins. of Special Sub-Cttee. re Newcastle-under-Lyme Sewage, 7 Dec. 1932.
[72] See p. 1.
[73] *Sewage Purification Works at Strongford;* and see pp. 34–35.

at Strongford from parts of that area, including the parishes of Barlaston and Swynnerton.[74]

In 1946 sanction was obtained for an extension of the works to deal with the sewage of Longton, the plants at Blurton and Newstead being inadequate.[75] As a result the centralization of the sewage disposal of the district was carried a stage further, and sewage effluent was made available to the Meaford Electricity Power Station, two miles south of Strongford.[76] By 1951 the extension had been completed and the sewage works now occupy an area of 179 acres with ample space for future development.[77] In 1944 the city council agreed to make available the final effluent of the Strongford works to the Meaford Power Station, which came into operation in 1947.[78] Sewage effluent from other sewage works in the city was used for other industrial purposes to the extent, in 1951, of 7 million gallons daily.[79] Protection against mining subsidence was safeguarded by an agreement with the Coal Board in 1946.[80] As a result of the centralization at Strongford of much of the city's sewage, land was released for other uses, 165 acres for 1,200 houses at Blurton and Newstead and 35 acres for the Newstead light industry estate.[81]

The extension of the borough boundary in 1922[82] brought under the control of the corporation the Meir Sewage Works (in Caverswall parish) which previously had been the responsibility of the Cheadle Rural District Council. The works was situated at Calverhay Farm which, together with the adjoining Ivy House Farm, the corporation bought in the same year, providing an area of 19½ acres for sewage development. Extensive house building in the neighbourhood of Meir[83] necessitated an enlargement of the sewage works, which was carried into effect in 1934.[84] Twenty years later the Meir sewage system was incorporated into the larger Blithe Valley Main Drainage scheme, controlled by a Joint Management Committee of 21 members, 10 of whom are appointed by Stoke.[85]

At the time of the amalgamation of the towns the arrangements for indoor sanitation and for the disposal of household refuse could only be described as primitive. In 1911 out of some 48,000 houses in the county borough only about 18,000 were supplied with water closets.[86] In 1914 a fresh attempt to bring about the conversion of privies into water-closets was made, but an application by the council to the Local Government Board for a loan towards the cost of conversion in Longton and Fenton was refused in 1915 on the ground of the war-time financial condition of the country, 'a distinctly retrograde step from

the public health point of view'.[87] After the war the work was resumed, but progress was slow. By 1930, however, out of nearly 60,000 houses, over 35,000 of them had been provided with water closets.[88] In the 1930's the erection of new houses and the demolition of slum dwellings accelerated the final solution of the problem, but, in 1951, there were still 1,501 households without water closets.[89] As late as 1957 the conversion of privies in the outlying areas around Packmoor still awaited the completion of a re-sewering scheme.[90]

In 1911 about one-half of the 48,000 houses in the borough were served by ashpits.[91] By 1930, as part of a scheme for finding work for unemployed workers, covered ashpits, which numbered 19,000 in 1922,[92] had been eliminated, and the whole of the city was served by ashbins.[93]

OTHER PUBLIC SERVICES. In 1910 the water-supply of the county borough was in the hands of the Staffordshire Potteries Water Works Company.[94] To meet increased domestic and trade requirements, the company was empowered in 1912[95] to construct two pumping stations, one at Mill Meece near Stone and the other at Cresswell in the Blithe valley. At the former, in 1914, a pumping engine was erected and in the following year a main was laid from there to Hanchurch reservoir.[96] Expansion of this pumping station took place in 1927-8.[97] The powers acquired under the 1912 Act over the Cresswell works were not at that time assumed.[98] Under the same Act the company was authorized to construct an additional reservoir at Hanchurch which was completed in 1927.[99]

For some years the local authorities in the area served by the Water Company had wished to municipalize the undertaking. The first attempt had been made in 1899[1] and another was made in 1911,[2] but it was not until 1924 that their aim was achieved. In that year the borough councils of Stoke and Newcastle, together with Wolstanton United Urban District Council, promoted a private Bill for the compulsory purchase of the undertaking.[3] The House of Commons Select Committee passed the Bill[4] on the ground that, although the Water Company had fulfilled all its engagements, the community had a right, if it so desired, to own and control its own waterworks, provided that the company was properly compensated.[5] This view would not, at that time, have commended itself to a Conservative House of Lords and it seemed unlikely that the Bill would pass the Upper House.[6] Local efforts were, therefore, initiated to secure agreement between the parties,

74 *Strongford Main Drainage Scheme*, 10.
75 Ibid.
76 Ibid.
77 Ibid. 20.
78 Ibid. 28.
79 Ibid. 32.
80 Ibid.
81 Ibid.; and ex inf. City Sewage Engineer.
82 See p. 259.
83 See p. 268.
84 *Opening of Extensions to Sewage Purification Works (Meir District)*, 4 (copy in H.R.L.).
85 *Blithe Valley Main Drainage Scheme* (1954) (copy in H.R.L.).
86 *Medical Officer of Health Rep. 1922* (copy in H.R.L.).
87 Ibid. *1914, 1915*.
88 Ibid. *1930*.
89 *Census, 1951*.

90 *M.O.H. Rep., 1957*.
91 Ibid. *1922*.
92 Ibid.
93 Ibid. *1930*.
94 See p. 36.
95 Staffs. Potteries Waterworks Act, 1912, 2 & 3 Geo. V, c. 75 (local).
96 *Pure and Wholesome Water for 100 Years, 1849-1949*, 17 (copy in H.R.L.).
97 Ibid.
98 Ibid. 18.
99 Ibid.
1 Ibid.
2 H.R.L., Water Cttee. Mins. 31 Jan. 1911.
3 *Pure and Wholesome Water*, 18.
4 Ibid.
5 *Staffs. Advertiser*, 5 Apr. 1924.
6 *Pure and Wholesome Water*, 18.

and these were successful,[7] so that the Bill went through the necessary stages as an unopposed measure.[8]

Under the Staffordshire Potteries Water Board Act (1924)[9] the undertaking on 1 January 1925 passed under the control of the Water Board consisting of 23 members representative of the local authorities concerned, of whom fifteen were nominated by the borough of Stoke. The area of supply, set out in the Act, comprised, in addition to Stoke and Newcastle, the greater part of North Staffordshire.[10]

In 1928 the board promoted a Bill[11] to revive the powers under the 1912 Act to construct a pumping station at Cresswell, to lay a main from Cresswell to the existing reservoir at Meir, and to obtain powers to lay a gravitation main from Meir Reservoir to Blurton to deliver additional water to the district. At the same time power was sought to protect the Cresswell Pumping Station from the abstraction of underground water in a surrounding protective area and to protect the underground supplies at the board's various pumping stations from possible pollution. Opposition to the former proposal was manifested by the coal-mining interests, with the result that the relevant clause in the Bill was excluded by the House of Lords Committee, which also amended the clauses regarding pollution.[12] Under the 1928 Act[13] the Cresswell works was completed in 1932.[14]

In the 1930's an extensive programme of reconstruction at all the main pumping stations, namely Wall Grange, Meir, Stockton Brook, Hatton, and Mill Meece, was embarked upon, but was interrupted by the outbreak of the Second World War.[15] The increase in house building and the increased use of water for industrial and domestic purposes, including in the latter the installation of baths and water closets, obliged the board to seek new sources of supply. For geological reasons these had to be found outside the board's area and even outside the county. In 1937[16] sanction was obtained for the erection of pumping stations at Peckforton and Tower Wood in Cheshire, for a reservoir on Bulkeley Hill in the same county whence the water would gravitate to a large storage reservoir at Cooper's Green near Audley, for a repumping station near Cooper's Green to enable the water to be repumped from that reservoir to a service reservoir at Bignall Hill, and for trunk mains to connect with the existing trunk mains at Tunstall. The Act also empowered the board to construct wells and boreholes at Greatgate, a reservoir at Heath House in Checkley parish, and trunk mains to connect with the existing trunk main at Draycott-in-the-Moors, through which water is pumped to Meir Reservoir from the Cresswell and Meir works. Most of these enterprises were held up by the Second World War, except for the first stage of the Greatgate scheme which was undertaken in 1942.[17]

Nevertheless during the war the increased demands of munition factories and other activities connected with the war made it imperative that further supplies of water should be obtained quickly. In 1944, in co-operation with the Ministry of Works, tests were made in an old mine-shaft at Draycott Cross.[18] These proved satisfactory so that the Ministry of Health granted the board limited powers under the Defence Regulations to install temporary plant and to lay a pumping main to connect with the existing trunk main.[19] In 1947 Draycott Cross became a permanent part of the board's system,[20] and at the same time sanction was given for the construction of another pumping station also in Draycott-in-the-Moors.[21]

In the immediate post-war period, as supply from the Peckforton works was still not available, the urgency of the water situation called for yet another *ad hoc* effort. The possibility of obtaining water from two abandoned mine shafts, which had been sunk in 1906 at Shaffalong near Cheddleton, was successfully investigated, and in 1949 a pumping plant, water tower, filtration and chemical plant to remove iron and manganese found in the water, and a main connecting with Wall Grange were installed.[22]

In 1948 the protection against the abstraction of underground water, refused in 1928, was granted to the board.[23] In 1949 the area of the board's supply was extended to include the Urban District of Stone and such parts of Kidsgrove Urban District, Newcastle Rural District, and Stone Rural District (except part of Sandon parish) as had not been previously included in the area, together with the parishes of Bagnall and Norton-in-the-Moors. Consequently the constitution of the board was amended to include six additional members representing the four districts.[24]

The board was also empowered to obtain further supplies by the enlargement of surface reservoirs at Deep Hayes and Tittesworth in the Churnet Valley in the neighbourhood of Leek.[25] These had originally been built as compensation reservoirs, Deep Hayes c. 1847 and Tittesworth in 1876,[26] to replace water abstracted by the company from the springs and streams which flowed into the River Churnet, for the benefit of owners of mills in the Churnet Valley. By 1949 the number of these mills had diminished so that the obligation of the board to discharge compensation water was correspondingly reduced[27] and the reservoirs were made available for supply purposes. This decision to collect surface waters represented a departure from the original policy of obtaining naturally purified water from the underground rocks.[28]

Despite the impressive record of development in

[7] *Sentinel Yr. Bk. of Potteries and N. Staffs.* (1928), 118.
[8] *C.J.* clxxix. 364.
[9] Staffs. Potteries Water Board Act, 1924, 14 & 15 Geo. V, c. 68 (local). [10] Ibid.
[11] *Pure and Wholesome Water*, 20.
[12] Ibid.; *Staffs. Advertiser*, 12 May 1928.
[13] Staffs. Potteries Water Board Act, 1928, 18 & 19 Geo. V, c. 75 (local).
[14] *Pure and Wholesome Water*, 20.
[15] Ibid.
[16] Staffs. Potteries Water Board Act, 1937, 1 Edw. VIII and Geo. VI, c. 123 (local).
[17] *Pure and Wholesome Water*, 25.

[18] Ibid. [19] Ibid.
[20] Statutory Rules and Orders 1947, no. 843, Staffs. Potteries Water Order, 1947. [21] Ibid.
[22] Staffs. Potteries Water Order, 1949, S.I. no. 767; *Pure and Wholesome Water*, 26.
[23] Stafford and Derby Area (Conservation of Water) Order, 1948 no. 2454.
[24] Staffs. Potteries Water Board Act, 1949, 12 & 13 Geo. VI, c. 40 (local).
[25] Ibid.
[26] *Pure and Wholesome Water*, 12, 14.
[27] 12 & 13 Geo. VI, c. 40 (local).
[28] *Pure and Wholesome Water*, 33.

the provision of an adequate water-supply there were in 1951 more than 900 households in the city without a piped supply.[29] By 1953, however, it could be stated that 'practically all the houses within the city have a piped supply for domestic purposes [and] only a few persons draw water from standpipes'.[30]

The arrangements for the supply of gas to the Pottery towns have already been outlined.[31] By the Act of 1908[32] the gas undertakings of Burslem Corporation, Longton Corporation, Stoke Corporation, and Fenton Urban District Council passed under the control of the new county borough. Under the Act the revenue of the undertakings was to be applied (a) to meet establishment charges, (b) to pay loan interest, (c) to discharge loans, (d) to form a reserve fund to provide for any extraordinary expenditure, subject to certain limitations. Any residue was to be carried forward to the revenue account for the following year and applied to reducing the price of gas within the borough. Any deficiency on any of the undertakings in any year was to be made good out of the reserve fund, or, if there was no reserve fund or if the fund was insufficient, then out of the district fund of the borough. In the event of the last-named eventuality the deficiency was to be a debt to be repaid to the district fund out of future revenue.[33]

The British Gaslight Company, which supplied Hanley, Tunstall, Newchapel, Smallthorne, and Norton-in-the-Moors, remained outside the scope of the 1908 Act, but the economics of centralized management made it only a question of time before the company was absorbed by the county borough. At the end of the First World War the Gas Committee, faced with the need to spend a large sum of money to bring its gas undertakings up to date, decided to buy out the company and to concentrate the local gas supply at the company's works at Etruria.[34] In March 1922[35] the company agreed to sell its assets as they were at 31 December 1920 to the corporation for £345,000. The corporation was to pay the company the difference between the value of its assets at 31 December 1920 and at the date of transfer, or more if that amount was insufficient to pay the shareholders' maximum dividends for the whole of the period between the two dates. The date of transfer was the next quarter-day following the passing of the Bill (i.e. 24 June 1922). The sale did not include the Directors' Minute Books or any other books and papers 'relating exclusively to shareholders'. The Act provided for the payment of compensation to any company officials discharged by the corporation within a period of five years.[36] The limits of the county borough's undertaking were enlarged to embrace those of the company,[37] and an earlier provision

enabling a gas company at Stone to impinge in a minor way upon the corporation's territory was annulled.[38]

The corporation was empowered to make gas and its by-products, and it might amalgamate and reorganize any of its undertakings as it thought fit. It could also purchase and process residual products of other undertakings up to a maximum of one-third of its own in any one year. It might also acquire by purchase up to 20 acres of land in addition to the existing lands (fully specified in the Third Schedule to the Act), but any land so acquired was not to be used for the manufacture of gas or the processing of its by-products. Full provisions were made for the quality, testing, pressure, and price of the corporation's gas, and the terms in which these were laid down reflect the advance of applied chemistry and physics since the 19th century.[39] After all normal working expenses and loan interest had been allowed for, any surplus profit was to be employed to reduce the price of gas.[40] The price could only be raised if the Minister of Health was satisfied of its necessity for reasons outside the corporation's control.[41]

By September 1924 the corporation had ceased to manufacture gas at Stoke and Fenton, and these undertakings had been connected up with the Etruria works.[42] In 1927 the Longton undertaking was also amalgamated with Etruria.[43] The Burslem gasworks at Longport still remained, and, before it could be connected up with Etruria, statutory authority had to be obtained to lay the pipes between the two places through the Wolstanton United Urban District.[44]

In 1932 the first gas-fired tunnel kilns were laid down by a local pottery manufacturer; by 1936 there were ten such kilns in operation and by 1939 sixty-six.[45] By 1950 the number of gas-fired kilns had increased to 300.[46] These industrial demands necessitated large extensions to the Etruria Works,[47] and in addition an entirely new works was erected on a site adjacent to the main works formerly occupied by the Wagon Repair Company.[48]

In May 1949, following the nationalization of the gas industry,[49] the undertaking passed into the control of the West Midlands Gas Board.[50]

The four electricity undertakings[51] came under the management of the county borough on 1 September 1910[52] as provided by the 1908 Act.[53] A three-fold problem faced the Electricity Supply Committee: the provision of additional electrical power to meet the needs of the district; the linking-up of the four existing works; and the demand for economical generation and distribution. The problem was partly met by the construction of a Central Power House in Hanley together with the adoption of a system of

[29] Census, 1951.
[30] Medical Officer of Health Rep., 1953, 21 (copy in H.R.L.).
[31] See pp. 97, 128, 160, 197–8, 216, 237.
[32] 8 Edw. VII, c. 164 (local)
[33] Ibid. art. xviii.
[34] Sentinel Yr. Bk. of Potteries and North Staffs. (1928), 112.
[35] Stoke-on-Trent Gas (Consolidation) Act 1922, 12 & 13 Geo. V. c. 22 (local), 4th Sched.
[36] Ibid.
[37] Ibid.
[38] Ibid. Pt. II. 7.
[39] Ibid. Pt. V.
[40] Ibid. Pt. VI. 67.
[41] Ibid. Pt. V. 50.
[42] Warrillow, Etruria, 165.
[43] Stoke-on-Trent Corp. (Gas) Act, 1927, 17 & 18 Geo. V, c. 18 (local). [44] Ibid.
[45] Stoke-on-Trent Official Handbk. [1958], 46; Warrillow, Etruria, 177.
[46] Ceramics, May 1955, p. 121.
[47] Stoke Official Handbk. [1958], 46; Warrillow, Etruria, 177; see p. 161.
[48] Ceramics, May 1955, p. 121.
[49] Gas Act, 1948, 11 & 12 Geo. VI, c. 67.
[50] Stoke Official Handbk. [1958], 46.
[51] See pp. 128–9, 161, 198, 237.
[52] Sentinel Yr. Bk. of Potteries and N. Staffs. (1928), 109.
[53] 8 Edw. VII, c. 164 (local), art. xviii.

generation at extra high tension, and three-phase alternating current with a frequency of 50 cycles a second, transmitted by trunk mains to the four existing works and there converted to low tension for local distribution.[54]

After a Local Government Board Inquiry in the summer of 1911,[55] the Central Power House was built and the plant put into operation on 10 April 1913.[56] In the same year the area of supply was extended to cover Wolstanton Ward in Wolstanton United Urban District.[57] Extensions to the Power House were made in 1919, 1922, 1925, 1927, and 1929.[58]

From 1 April 1914[59] the four existing undertakings were combined, but the different systems operated by each proved an obstacle. The original supply system in Hanley was single phase, 100 cycles, alternating current, while the supplies in Burslem, Longton, and Stoke were direct current, although at different voltages. It was not until 1923 that a supply was available in Fenton.[60] In that year also the area of supply was defined as the borough and Wolstanton Ward in Wolstanton United Urban District.[61] The 1923 Act gave the corporation power to supply electricity in bulk to the borough of Newcastle.[62] The work of conversion to the 50 cycles alternating current was not finally completed until 1938.[63]

In 1927 two important developments took place. Eight new houses in Avenue Road, Hanley Park, were electrically equipped for lighting, heating, and other domestic purposes.[64] That year also marked the beginning of the application of electricity to the manufacture of pottery, when two electrical furnaces for the firing of decorated ware were set up.[65] Since the end of the Second World War development in this field has advanced greatly, and in 1957 there were more than 110 electric kilns and ovens in use in the city.[66] Moreover, the making of pottery has been largely mechanized by the use of automatic or semi-automatic electrically driven machines.[67]

The electrical industry was nationalized in 1948[68] and the electricity undertaking came under the control of the Midlands Electricity Board, Stoke being the headquarters of the North Staffordshire Sub-Area of the Board.[69]

In 1910 each of the six towns had its own fire brigade, but as a result of their amalgamation a measure of co-ordination of the fire services of the whole area was introduced. In November of that year all the brigades of the borough, except that of Hanley, were placed under the control of F. Bettany,[70] a former borough surveyor of Burslem, who had captained the Burslem Fire Brigade since 1894.[71] He was made chief officer at a yearly salary of £100.[72] In Hanley the fire brigade was a police responsibility, but in 1913 this brigade, with a station in Stafford Street and manned thereafter by volunteers,[73] passed under the control of the chief officer, and in the same year the erection of a new fire station at the corner of Percy Street and Old Hall Street, Hanley, was approved;[74] this, however, was not opened until 1921.[75] In Stoke, which had never had a permanent home for its fire appliances,[76] a new station in Welch Street was built and opened in 1914.[77]

In 1916 a fire at the Empire Pottery Works, Hanley, brought to light deficiencies in the organization and equipment of the brigade,[78] and one result of the public criticism then aroused was the acquisition of the first motor appliance, which was stationed at Hanley.[79] The other fire stations in the borough continued to use horse-drawn steamer appliances.

In 1926, a major reorganization took place, whereby Hanley became the headquarters of the City Fire Brigade, with sub-stations at Burslem and Longton.[80] The fire stations at Tunstall, Stoke, and Fenton thus ceased to function, and at the same time the horse-drawn appliances were taken out of service.[81] In 1941 the City Fire Brigade became part of the nationalized fire service,[82] but in 1948 the city council resumed control of the brigade,[83] then comprising three fire stations and 89 personnel.[84] The revival of Civil Defence in 1949 placed upon the city council the responsibility for the recruitment and maintenance of an efficient Auxiliary Fire Service.[85] In 1956 a new fire station was built in Hamil Road, Burslem, the old station in Baddeley Street having become inadequate.[86]

When in 1910 the county borough came into existence, the population was about 234,000 contained within an area of a little over 11,000 acres which indicated a population density of 21 to the acre.[87] Overcrowding was consequently rife. Indeed it was even more serious than the density figure suggests because much of the borough area consisted of potworks, tileries, and coal mines and much of the available open land could not be built on owing to the risk of subsidence. The new borough council was naturally reluctant to embark on any major scheme of rehousing which would have meant an increase in the rates, and it was not until the central government

---

[54] *Sentinel Yr. Bk.* (1928), 109.
[55] Ibid.
[56] Ibid.
[57] Stoke-on-Trent Electric Lighting (Extension) Order, 1913, 3 & 4 Geo. V, c. 149 (local).
[58] *Sentinel Yr. Bk.* (1928), 109; *Power House Extensions* (1929; copy in H.R.L.); and ex inf. N. Staffs. Sub-Area Manager, Midlands Electricity Board.
[59] *Cox's Potteries Annual* (1926), 165 (copy in H.R.L.); Stoke-on-Trent Corp. Act (1923), 13 & 14 Geo. V, c. 107 (local).
[60] See p. 217.
[61] Stoke-on-Trent Corp. Act, 1923, 13 & 14 Geo. V c. 107 (local).
[62] Ibid.
[63] *Stoke Official Handbk.* [1958], 50.
[64] *Sentinel Yr. Bk.* (1928), 111.
[65] Ibid.
[66] *Stoke Official Handbk.* [1958], 51.
[67] Ibid.

[68] Electricity Act, 1947, 10 & 11 Geo. VI, c. 54.
[69] *Stoke Official Handbk.* [1958], 50.
[70] *Staffs. Sentinel*, 18 Nov. 1910.
[71] Ibid. 11 Sept. 1913.
[72] H.R.L., Watch Cttee. Mins. 18 Nov. 1910.
[73] *Staffs. Sentinel*, 12 Sept. 1913.
[74] Watch Cttee. Mins. 13 Mar. 1913.
[75] *Staffs. Advertiser*, 10 Dec. 1921.
[76] *Staffs. Sentinel*, 13 Jan. 1914; see p. 198.
[77] *Staffs. Sentinel*, 16 Jan. 1914.
[78] Ibid. 18 Oct. 1916.
[79] Ibid. 27 Oct. 1916.
[80] Watch Cttee. Mins. 14 Jan. 1926.
[81] *Stoke Official Handbk.* [1957], 42.
[82] Fire Services (Emergency Provisions) Act, 1941, 4 & 5 Geo. VI, c. 22.
[83] *Stoke Official Handbk.* [1958], 42.
[84] Ibid.   [85] Ibid.
[86] See p. 129.
[87] *Census*, 1911.

offered financial inducements to local authorities to initiate housing schemes that any progress was made. During the period 1910–18 just under 1,000 new houses were built in the borough,[88] all provided by private enterprise, but in 1919 the generous subsidy provided by the Housing Act of that year[89] spurred the council to set up a Housing Committee[90] to tackle the twin problems of slum clearance and rehousing. Progress was inevitably slow owing to the shortage of building labour and materials, and altogether only 545 houses were built under the so-called Addison Act.[91] The Housing Act of 1923[92] encouraged private builders to build houses for the owner-occupier, while the Housing (Financial Provisions) Act of the following year,[93] by means of a generous subsidy, made it possible for a local authority to erect houses for letting at low rents.

The Housing Act of 1930[94] was the first comprehensive attempt to deal with slum clearance and Stoke was the first local authority in the country to submit a five-year clearance programme to the Ministry of Health.[95] The council was, however, faced with difficulties peculiar to the locality. In the previous year the medical officer of health had pointed out that it was useless to undertake large schemes until more suitable sites could be found; many of the small sites available were quite unsuitable owing to the atmospheric pollution and the congestion of surrounding areas. In his view the incidence of smallpox and infant mortality in the congested areas was proof that the inhabitants must be removed from overcrowded areas and housed away from the smoke; in the event of slum clearance it was impossible to rehouse on the old sites. A peculiarity of the smoke problem in Stoke was that the smoke from the ovens came right down on to the houses and was not carried away by high chimneys.[96] It was no doubt this difficulty of finding suitable housing sites that had prompted the eastward expansion of the borough in 1922.[97]

The Housing Act of 1935[98] imposed on the local authority new duties in relation to the abatement of overcrowding and the redevelopment of congested areas, and in December of that year the number of overcrowded families in Stoke was estimated to be 3,740.[99] In the 1930's much was accomplished by the borough council to meet the challenge of slum conditions, and by the outbreak of the Second World War clearance orders and compulsory purchase orders had been applied to 3,877 houses.[1]

Table VII shows the progress that had been achieved in the period between the world wars in the field of housing and also the substantial contribution made by private enterprise.

The chief housing estates within the original

TABLE VII

Housing in Stoke-on-Trent, 1921–39[2]

Year	By corporation	By private enterprise	Total
1921 . . .	54	..	54
1922 . . .	102	273	375
1923 . . .	224	..	224
1924 . . .	170	47	217
1925 . . .	42	304	346
1926 . . .	404	302	706
1927 . . .	550	379	929
1928 . . .	288	301	589
1929 . . .	232	645	877
1930 . . .	327	402	729
1931 . . .	495	465	960
1932 . . .	604	484	1,088
1933 . . .	676	745	1,421
1934 . . .	601	1,064	1,665
1935 . . .	465	1,059	1,524
1936 . . .	1,117	1,045	2,162
1937 . . .	922	1,626	2,548
1938 . . .	310	1,258	1,568
1939 . . .	515	747	1,262
	8,098	11,146	19,244

borough boundary were Blurton Road (294) and Cowper Street (44), both in Fenton, Etruria Vale (154), Fletcher Road, Stoke (96), Gom's Mill Road, Longton (117), High St. East, Fenton (57), Hollywall Lane, Goldenhill (368), Kingsfield, Basford (56), Leek Road, Hanley (172), Little Chell, Tunstall (74), Lightwood Chase, Longton (266), Newcastle Lane, Penkhull (74), Newhouse Farm, Bucknall (508), Shelton New Road, Stoke (121), Stanfield, Burslem (558), Stoke Lodge, Trent Vale (170), St. Michael's Road, Pitts Hill (90), Swan Lane, Trent Vale (284), Vivian Road, Fenton (257), and Woodlands, Trent Vale (90).[3] The land acquired in the 1922 expansion[4] made possible the erection of the following estates: Abbey Hulton (604), Carmountside (456), Cornhill (358), Back Lane (170) and Wilson Road (158), both in Hanford, Meir (1,388), Sandon Road, Meir (370), and Townsend, Bucknall (262).[5]

In the field of private enterprise mention should be made of the operations of the Sutton Dwellings Trust.[6] In 1926 the trustees acquired by purchase surplus land on the Stoke Lodge site in Trent Vale and 7 acres of adjoining land for the erection of houses.[7] The estate was opened in 1929 and the number of houses built was 310.[8] Collin Road, Forber Road, Freemantle Road, Levita Road, Sutton Drive, and Waterfield Road commemorate the names of trustees. An institute was also built on the estate.[9] In Abbey Hulton, too, from 1933, 403 houses

---

[88] *Med. Officer of Health Reps.*, *1915* (p. 8), *1916* (p. 9), *1917* (p. 7), *1918* (p. 8).
[89] 9 & 10 Geo. V, c. 60.
[90] *City of Stoke-on-Trent Housing, 1919 to 1957*, 8 (copy in H.R.L.).
[91] Ibid. 47.
[92] 13 & 14 Geo. V, c. 24.
[93] 14 & 15 Geo. V, c. 35.
[94] 20 & 21 Geo. V, c. 39.
[95] *Stoke-on-Trent Housing, 1919 to 1957*, 10.
[96] *Annual Rep. of Pub. Health Dep. 1929* (copy in H.R.L.).
[97] See p. 259.
[98] Housing Act, 1935, 25 & 26 Geo. V, c. 40.
[99] *Annual Rep. of Pub. Health Dep. 1935*.

[1] *Stoke-on-Trent Housing, 1919 to 1957*, 51.
[2] Extracted from *Stoke-on-Trent Housing, 1919 to 1957* and *M.O.H. Reps.* (1921–39).
[3] *Stoke-on-Trent Housing, 1919 to 1957*, 18 sqq.
[4] See p. 259.
[5] *Stoke-on-Trent Housing, 1919 to 1957*, 18 sqq.
[6] Founded under the will (dated 1894) of W. R. Sutton of Sutton & Co. Ltd., carriers, for the provision of low-rented model dwellings for the poor in London and other populous parts of the country. At his death in 1900 the assets of the Trust were valued at about 1½ million pounds: *Sutton Dwellings Trust, Rep. for year ended 31 Dec. 1958*.
[7] H.R.L., Housing Cttee. Mins. 7 Jan. 1926.
[8] *Sutton Dwellings Trust Rep.*
[9] Ibid.

were built, the names of the roads, Kyffin Road, Shelley Road, and Taylor Road, again commemorating the names of trustees.[10]

The outbreak of the Second World War slowed down and ultimately put a stop to housing development; during the period 1940–4 the number of new houses erected was: 1940 590; 1941 148; 1942 125; 1943 2; 1944 nil.[11] In 1944 and 1945 the acute housing shortage led to the erection of temporary bungalows by the Ministry of Works[12] and these were made available to the local authority, which was also empowered to acquire the necessary building sites. Temporary bungalows to the number of 662 were erected in the city, mostly on central sites which had been cleared of unfit houses before the war under the slum clearance programme.[13]

At the same time the importance attached by the central government to the provision of permanent houses was manifested by a series of enactments[14] to induce local authorities by the grant of subsidies to resume or initiate building schemes. A noticeable feature of the post-war development in Stoke was the smaller part played by private enterprise as compared with the pre-war period, as shown in Table VIII.

TABLE VIII

Housing in Stoke-on-Trent, 1945–58[15]

Year	By corporation	By private enterprise	Total
1945 . . .	22	6	28
1946 . . .	421	283	704
1947 . . .	599	226	825
1948 . . .	1,203	99	1,302
1949 . . .	783	16	799
1950 . . .	386	87	473
1951 . . .	1,201	81	1,282
1952 . . .	1,407	100	1,507
1953 . . .	2,412	96	2,508
1954 . . .	2,502	157	2,659
1955 . . .	1,998	153	2,151
1956 . . .	2,054	179	2,233
1957 . . .	1,419	169	1,588[16]
1958 . . .	706	189	895
	17,113	1,841	18,954

The principal housing estates erected in the above period within the original borough boundary were Furlong Road (304) and Mill Hill (534), Tunstall; Stonor Street (250) and Windermere Street (50), Cobridge; Hilton Road (248) Harpfields; Riverside Road (122), Springfields (262), and Stone Road (95), Trent Vale; Carron Street (58) and Hollybush (552), Fenton; Anchor Road (256), Heathcote Street (158), Longley Road (544), and Longton Hall Road (120),

Longton. On the land to the east and south of the borough acquired in 1922 and 1930 the following represent the main housing developments: Chell Heath (813), Fegg Hayes; Chorley Avenue (460), Tunstall; Oxford estate (122), Chell; Norton Lane (161), Norton; Wilding Road (64), Ball Green; Woodhead Road (52), Carmountside; Weston Coyney (64); Abbey Lane (94), Longton Road (102), Ruxley Road (94), and Townsmead (266), Bucknall; Bentilee Farm (1,950); Ubberley Farm (636); Whitfield site (220); Lyme Road (340), Meir; Drubbery Lane (62), Blurton; Blurton Farm (1,536); and Newstead Farm (822).[17]

Since the end of the Second World War slum clearance has proceeded,[18] but in 1956 it was estimated that there were still 10,800 houses in the city deemed unfit by modern standards.[19] Redevelopment of the cleared areas was slow and it was not until 1955–6 that the first post-war redevelopment scheme, embracing $57\frac{1}{2}$ acres at Heathcote Road, Longton, on which 421 houses were to be built, was sanctioned.[20] It has been suggested that the extension of the borough to the east had made open agricultural land available for housing expansion and consequently there has been less incentive to redevelop the derelict areas within the older built-up limits.[21]

Another aspect of redevelopment within the limits of the original six towns has been the reconditioning and modernization of houses otherwise structurally sound. The Housing Act (1949),[22] as amended by the Housing Repairs and Rents Act (1954),[23] empowered local authorities to make grants to landlords and owner-occupiers for modernizing their properties. In Stoke, where it was estimated that there were 20,000 houses in this category,[24] the city council, in order to show what could be done, modernized seven houses belonging to the corporation in Gilman Street, Hanley.[25] Up to 31 July 1957 735 grants had been made for the improvement of old houses.[26]

The special housing needs of old people were partially met through the generosity of a local pottery manufacturer, W. G. Barratt, who in 1954 gave £20,000 for the provision of 20 bungalows, together with a social hall, which were built at Carmountside. A further gift of £20,000 by the same donor made it possible for similar provision to be made for old people at Blurton, both sites being provided by the corporation.[27] The city council also helped to solve the problem, e.g. at Hilton Road, Harpfield Estate, and at Mill Hill, Tunstall, where special accommodation has been provided for those who are too old or infirm to care for themselves.[28]

In the post-war period the trend in housing policy has been towards the development of the neighbourhood unit, representing an aggregate of about 10,000

---

[10] Ibid.
[11] *Stoke-on-Trent Housing, 1919 to 1957*, 56.
[12] Housing (Temporary Accommodation) Acts, 7 & 8 Geo. VI, c. 36, 8 & 9 Geo. VI, c. 39.
[13] *Stoke-on-Trent Housing, 1919 to 1957*, 10.
[14] 9 & 10 Geo. VI, c. 20 & c. 48; 12, 13 & 14 Geo. VI, c. 60; 15 & 16 Geo. VI and 1 Eliz. II, c. 53; 2 & 3 Eliz. II, c. 50; 4 & 5 Eliz. II, c. 33.
[15] *Stoke-on-Trent Housing, 1919 to 1957*, 56.
[16] Figures for 1957 and 1958 supplied by town clerk.
[17] *Stoke-on-Trent Housing, 1919 to 1957*, 56.
[18] Ibid. 51–53.
[19] *Housing and Community Development in Stoke-on-*

Trent (Stoke-on-Trent Study Group), 19 July 1956, p. 16.
[20] *Stoke-on-Trent Housing, 1919 to 1957*, 33–34.
[21] Min. of Town and Country Planning, *North Staffs. Plan*, 97.
[22] Housing Act, 1949, 12 & 13 Geo. VI, c. 60.
[23] Housing Repairs and Rents Act, 1954, 2 & 3 Eliz. II, c. 53.
[24] *Stoke-on-Trent Housing, 1919 to 1957*, 54.
[25] Ibid.
[26] Ibid.
[27] Ibid. 45; Warrillow, *Stoke*, 325.
[28] *Housing and Community Development in Stoke*, 8, 9, 18.

people and consisting of a residential area complete with additional buildings, viz. community centre, health centre, churches, schools, shops, public houses, playing fields, and open spaces. Practical effect has been given to this conception in the Ubberley–Bentilee estate on the eastern boundary of the city.[29]

In 1910 there were six full-time libraries[30] in the county borough: Tunstall (Victoria Institute), Burslem (Wedgwood Institute), Hanley (Pall Mall), Stoke (London Road), Fenton (Baker Street), and Longton (Sutherland Institute).[31] They were under the general control of the Libraries Committee of the borough council, but for finance and administration each library was separately administered by its own sub-committee.

These arrangements continued until the beginning of the First World War, but in 1915 a chief librarian was appointed to take charge of all the libraries, though he was required to report to each district sub-committee as well as to the main Libraries Committee. Further steps towards the centralization of the borough's library system were taken in 1920 when it was agreed to pool the different library rates and funds and in 1921 when the district sub-committees were abolished.

In 1929 the Libraries Committee decided to adopt the principle of open access, and in the same year the Longton Library was converted to that system. Tunstall, Fenton, and Stoke Libraries followed in 1931, and Burslem in 1932 on its removal, first proposed in 1914,[32] from the Wedgwood Institute to the first floor of the Old Town Hall. It was not until 1949 that the open-access system was introduced in the Hanley Library.

In 1950 the reference library facilities, hitherto dispersed among the constituent libraries, were centralized in the Hanley Library, and in 1958 a separate reference library, known as the Horace Barks Reference Library, was opened in the former Russell Art Gallery adjacent to the main lending library. The latter, in 1954, had been declared unsafe and was accommodated in Piccadilly Chambers while the Pall Mall building was being repaired. In 1956 the move back to its former building took place.

Provision for young readers, initiated at Hanley,[33] was extended in 1913 with the establishment of junior libraries at Tunstall and Fenton. In 1925–6 a schools library service was instituted. In 1935 the junior library in the Wedgwood Institute at Burslem was reorganized on the open-access system.

The expansion of the county borough in 1922 and the development of housing estates led to the provision of library facilities in the outlying areas. As the need arose, part-time libraries were established; the first, in 1924, was at the Hardman Institute, Milton, converted to the open-access system in 1932. In subsequent years other branch libraries were set up: Brindley Ford (1937), Abbey Hulton (1938), Ball Green (1946), Goldenhill (1946), Packmoor (1946), Chell Heath (1950), Hanford (1955), Bucknall (1955), Blurton (1955), Bentilee (1958), New-

stead (1959), Sandford Hill (1959). At Meir a part-time library service was begun in 1947 at the T.A. Drill Hall, but removal therefrom took place in 1950 when a full-time library was established at the Church Institute, Box Lane.

In 1910 museums[34] existed at Tunstall (Victoria Institute), Burslem (Wedgwood Institute), Hanley (Pall Mall), and Stoke (London Road). Centralization of the art collections of the various towns and of the museums service generally was the chief aim of the newly constituted Libraries, Museums, and Gymnasiums Committee of the council.[35] As a first step a curator was appointed for the county borough. A rearrangement of the collections was undertaken, and in 1912 the museums were reopened by the mayor.[36]

The outbreak of the First World War halted further developments. In 1926 the bequest to the city by Dr. John Russell of an important collection of paintings emphasized the need for adequate accommodation. Part of the Hanley School of Art was acquired for the housing of the collection, but this was no more than a temporary expedient. In the same year a proposal to convert the Old Town Hall, Burslem, into a central art gallery was rejected in favour of the Pall Mall site at Hanley, where the City Art Gallery remained until 1956 (see below).

The museum problem still awaited a solution. As early as 1919 plans for a modern museum and art gallery on the site of the present Essoldo Cinema had been drawn up, but were not proceeded with. Later, similar building plans on the sites of Hope Chapel, Hanley, and Chatterley House, Hanley, proved nugatory. The industrial depression of 1931 put an end to building schemes for the time being. Later in the 1930's the project of a new building was revived, but again the outbreak of war led to its postponement. In September 1939 the contents of all the museums were evacuated to places of safety, and at the end of the war the whole of the evacuated material was returned to Hanley. In 1949 Hanley Art School was acquired from the Education Committee in exchange for three rooms at the Wedgwood Institute, Burslem, and the whole of the Tunstall Museum.

In October 1956 the Museum and Art Gallery, a building of modern design in Broad Street on the site of the former Bell Pottery,[37] was opened, the first new museum to be opened in England since the end of the Second World War. The architect was J. R. Piggott, the City Architect. It contains a notable collection of pottery of all ages and countries, including Staffordshire wares.

In May 1952 Ford Green Hall, a timber-framed building at Smallthorne on the eastern boundary of the city, was opened as a museum devoted primarily to the display of 17th-century furniture and household utensils. The architectural description of the building is reserved for a subsequent volume.

INDUSTRY. The pattern of industrial development in Stoke during the half-century that has elapsed since the amalgamation of the towns has changed

---

[29] *Housing and Community Development in Stoke*, 6.
[30] The following account of the library service is based on information supplied by the Deputy Librarian and by the Reference Librarian, Hanley Pub. Libr.
[31] See pp. 104, 141, 170, 204–5, 224, 246.
[32] H.R.L., Estates, Public Works, and Tramways Cttee. Mins., 20 Feb. 1914.　　　[33] See p. 170.

[34] The following account is based on information supplied by the curator, Mr. G. J. V. Bemrose. For the Arnold Bennett Mus. see p. 142.
[35] See pp. 104, 141, 171, 204, 259.
[36] H.R.L., Pub. Librs., Museums and Gymnasiums Cttee. Mins., 11 Mar. 1912.
[37] See plate on facing page.

HANLEY: CITY MUSEUM AND ART GALLERY
built in 1956

BURSLEM: WEDGWOOD INSTITUTE
completed in 1869

considerably. While the pottery industry has remained predominant, other industries have arisen in the area in the last 50 years. One of the most important has been the manufacture of motor tyres, principally by the Michelin Tyre Company which in 1927 acquired an 80-acre site at Oak Hill between London Road and Campbell Road.[38] In 1921 the Normeir Tyre Company Ltd., a pioneer firm in the repair and remoulding of motor tyres, was established at Meir Bank, then outside the borough boundary, and also at Hanley, and in 1923 at Longton. Additional premises in Liverpool Road, Newcastle, were opened in 1934 and since the end of the Second World War at Tunstall and at Longton (The Strand and Clayton Street).[39]

Light industry, such as the manufacture of electric motors, non-ferrous castings, sewage disposal equipment, sheet metal, and pattern making,[40] has gained a firm foothold in recent years. An oil-blending plant was installed in North Street, Stoke, in 1937 (rebuilt in 1948),[41] while the manufacture of steel tanks began in Fenton in 1949.[42] Glass used in building construction is manufactured at Etruria Road, Hanley, and in the chemical industry at Duke Street, Fenton,[43] while electric lamps, including those for Belisha beacons and totalisator signs, have been manufactured at Newcastle Road, Trent Vale, since 1951.[44]

The extension of the boundaries in 1922 brought within the limits of the county borough additional industrial plants. Such were the Chatterley Whitfield Colliery at Ball Green, Norton Colliery at Ford Green, Berry Hill Collieries in Botteslow, Mossfields Colliery, and Adderley Green Colliery, both at Adderley Green, Park Hall Colliery near Weston Coyney, and Hem Heath Colliery near Trentham; and also the Berry Hill Brickworks, the largest of its kind in North Staffordshire.

Figures compiled in 1952 reveal the pattern of employment in the city. Out of an approximate total of 152,000 employed persons, 62,000 were engaged in pottery and 15,000 in coal mining, a little more than half the total. Of the remainder nearly 6,000 were employed in metal manufacture, including iron and steel milling and rolling and tinplate and steel sheet manufacture; 1,500 in the production of light metal goods; and nearly 5,000 in the engineering and electrical industries, including machine tools, and the manufacture of agricultural, textile, and electrical equipment. One of the larger industries is that of building which employs more than 8,000 persons. With a few exceptions, the factories are small. In 1952 the number of factories was stated to be 428 and one-half of these employed fewer than 100 workers.[45]

ROMAN CATHOLICISM[1]

ROMAN CATHOLICISM in the Potteries area remained weak so long as the district continued one of moorland settlements, its few inhabitants mainly small farmers and potters. It was only from the end of the 18th century, when the population of the district was multiplying rapidly, that Roman Catholics increased in number, helped a few decades later by the beginning of Irish immigration. That Roman Catholicism was able to persist in the area as much as it did during penal times was probably due to the influence of local gentry such as the Biddulphs of Biddulph Grange, the Coyneys of Weston Coyney, and the Draycotts of Paynsley.[2]

The earliest information about the number of Roman Catholics in the area after the Reformation is provided by a return of 1657 which lists 12 at Bucknall, 13 at Cobridge (notably the Bucknalls, a family of potters), 4 at Hanley (3 of them named Maire, another family of potters), 3 at Burslem (including John Daniel, a potter living at the Nook), 2 at

Boothen, and 1 at Meir Heath Furnace; most of the men were described as potters except at Bucknall where they were mainly husbandmen.[3] A return of 1780 lists 134 Roman Catholics in Burslem parish and 102 in Stoke parish.[4] Irish immigration into the Potteries had begun by the 1820's,[5] and by the early 1850's Roman Catholics in the area probably numbered well over 2,000.[6] Just over 100 years later the number is approaching 20,000.[7]

COBRIDGE. The first Roman Catholic centre in the area after the Reformation[8] was established on the Biddulph's Rushton Grange estate at Cobridge.[9] The grange had belonged to the Cistercians of Hulton until the dissolution of the abbey in 1538, and it was bought by the Biddulphs two years later. The Biddulphs were themselves Catholics certainly before the end of the 16th century and had Catholic tenants at the grange by the mid-17th century.[10] There is a tradition that the Biddulphs' chaplain

[38] Stoke Official Handbk. (1960); Stoke-on-Trent Bi-monthly Review, Sept. 1953.
[39] Ex inf. the Co.
[40] Stoke Official Handbk. (1960); N. Beckett, Industrial North Staffs. [1950].
[41] Stoke Bi-monthly Review, June 1953.
[42] Ex inf. Bennis Mechanizations Ltd.
[43] Stoke Official Handbk. (1960).
[44] Ex inf. A. E. I. Lamp and Lighting Co. Ltd.
[45] Staffs. Sentinel Newspapers Ltd. Factual Survey of Stoke-on-Trent (1954).
[1] This article covers the whole area of the present city of Stoke-on-Trent. Parishes are arranged in the chronological order of the foundation of their churches.
[2] Most of the land in the area was owned by the Duchy of Lancaster and the Sneyds of Keele. The latter, however, were Roman Catholics in 1564 and 1648: S.H.C. 1915,

370, 391. An account of these local families is reserved for a general article on Roman Catholicism in a subsequent vol.
[3] S.H.C. 4th ser. ii. 93, 94, 96.
[4] H. L. Main Papers, list of returns of papists, or reputed papists, 5 Mar. 1781. The returns of the dioc. of Lichfield and Coventry are dated 7 Nov. 1780.
[5] Laity's Dir. (1828), 24.
[6] See figures under the various centres.
[7] Birmingham Archdioc. Dir. (1960).
[8] A news sheet of 1642 (B.M., E 149/25) telling of the discovery of a group of laymen and 2 Jesuits at Mass on Mow Cop and their examination before a Justice Biddulph seems to find no corroboration in the Staffs. Quarter Sessions records.
[9] Some encouragement was presumably given by the immunity of the area from tithes and ch. rates: Ward, Stoke, 286.
[10] See p. 116.

ministered to the victims of the plague at Burslem in 1647[11] and another that by 1688 the grange was sufficiently well known as a Catholic centre to be ransacked by a Protestant mob in that year.[12] Cobridge certainly had a relatively strong Catholic community by 1657,[13] and Rushton Grange was a Mass-centre in the 18th century.[14] About 1760 the area received its first resident priest, Thomas Flynn, who, though he used the chapel at Rushton,[15] probably lived at Burslem, and in 1773 Confirmation was administered at the grange by the Vicar Apostolic of the Midland District.[16] Flynn left the area in 1776 and three years later was succeeded by John Corne.[17]

In 1780 Corne began to build a small church on the hill top east of the grange with money subscribed by local Catholics. Work was temporarily suspended owing to the alarm caused by the Gordon Riots, but the church, 21 ft. by 15 ft. with accommodation for 70 people, was opened in 1781.[18] A house for the priest was built to the west.[19] The chapel at the grange ceased to be used and by 1820 was 'a mere thatched shed'.[20] Richard Prendergast, priest there from 1795 to 1813, lengthened the church.[21] In 1816–17 his successor Louis Gerard, of French emigré family,[22] more than doubled the size of the church by adding a nave, 48 ft. by 27 ft., at right angles to the earlier block which thereby became a south transept;[23] he also installed a gallery. This work, the building of the school in 1821–2, and the enlargement of the house in 1831 placed the mission, already very poor, heavily in debt.[24]

The next priest, Roger O'Higgin (1842–5), increased the seating accommodation of the chapel by 70 places, added a sacristy, and established a parish library.[25] Thomas Leith (1851–73) installed gas-lighting in the chapel, house, and school during his first winter at Cobridge, and evening services were held for the first time; in 1855 he built a new sacristy and erected Stations of the Cross.[26] Further alterations were made in 1882,[27] but the church and house eventually became unsafe as a result of mining subsidence. They were pulled down in 1936 and the present church and presbytery opened on the same site in 1937.[28] Designed by E. B. Norris of Stafford,[29] the church is a brick building with wide nave, passage aisles, chancel, and baldachino.

In 1822 Bridgettine nuns from Lisbon opened a convent at Cobridge Cottage situated off Elder Road between the present Grange Street and Mawdesley Street. They moved to Stone c. 1828.[30] The Little Sisters of the Poor, after two years at Druid's Hall, Albion Street, Hanley, moved in 1892 to Cobridge House in Cobridge Road, the home of the Hales family in the 18th and 19th centuries. The nuns bought the house in 1899 and replaced it by the present St. Augustine's Home, built in 1902–3 and extended in 1911 and later. There is now accommodation for about 100 old people at the home.[31]

At first the Cobridge priest served a very wide area covering Leek, Crewe, Market Drayton, Ashley, and Newcastle[32] as well as the Potteries with its rapidly growing population. The gradual establishment of new missions reduced his responsibilities, but in 1827 he could still describe his mission as 'one of the most extensive and in the greatest want . . . about 1,000 souls dispersed in 6 towns and above 20 villages'.[33] By this time, however, the southern part of the Potteries and Newcastle had become part of a new mission centred on Longton. The number served from the Cobridge church was estimated at some 1,300 in the early 1850's,[34] and the average attendance at Sunday Mass there early in 1851 was 600.[35] The missions founded at Tunstall and Hanley in the 1850's removed about 1,000 people from the charge of the Cobridge priest,[36] while the transfer of about 1,500 to the care of the priest of the new mission of Burslem in 1895 reduced the Cobridge mission to about 350. It now (1960) numbers just under 900.[37]

LONGTON. A community of Benedictine nuns exiled from Ghent were settled at Caverswall in 1811 by Walter Hill Coyney of Weston Coyney and his Roman Catholic wife Mary. The nuns opened their chapel for public services and in 1812 their chaplain started a Mass-centre at Normacot. In 1819 he opened a small church dedicated to St. Gregory in

11 Ward, *Stoke*, 216–17; *Stoke Churchwardens' Accts.* (*T.N.S.F.C.* lxxiv), p. A93.
12 Ward, *Stoke*, 280.
13 *S.H.C.* 4th ser. ii. 94.
14 J. O. Payne, *Records of the Eng. Caths. of 1715*, 127; J. Kirk, *Biographies of Eng. Caths. 1700–1800*, 34, 223; Ward, *Stoke*, 280, 287.
15 T. M. Leith, Records of the Mission of St. Peter, Cobridge (MS. at St. Peter's, Cobridge), ff. 33b, 34a, 36a. This was compiled by Leith while he was priest at St. Peter's, 1851–73.
16 Archbp.'s House, Birmingham, Reg. 1768–1811, 9 May 1773, when 35 were confirmed.
17 Leith, Cobridge Mission, ff. 33b, 36a.
18 J. Gillow, *St. Thomas's Priory*, 95; Ward, *Stoke*, 281, 285; 'Cath. Chapels in Staffs.' (*Cath. Mag.* v), 661; Leith, Cobridge Mission, ff. 36a, 43a, 46a, 47a, and plan of ch. on f. 35.
19 Leith, Cobridge Mission, ff. 35b, 43a, 46a.
20 Ibid. f. 34a; S. Shaw, *Staffs. Potteries*, 37.
21 *Cath. Mag.* v. 661. The dates of this and other pastorates are taken from Leith, Cobridge Mission.
22 Leith, Cobridge Mission, f. 61a.
23 Ibid. f. 63a; White, *Dir. Staffs.* (1834); *Cath. Mag.* v. 661; W.S.L., newspaper cutting in S. 603.
24 *Laity's Dir.* (1822, 1825, 1828); Leith, Cobridge Mission, ff. 64b, 65a, 66a; White, *Dir. Staffs.* (1834); see p. 313. The income included a small annuity settled in 1825 and still paid in 1866: Leith, Cobridge Mission, ff. 44a, 86a; Ward, *Stoke*, 285; *Burslem Par. Reg.* iii. 697;

see p. 330. For some account of the financial problems of the mission in the 19th century, see M. Greenslade, *A Brief Hist. of the Cath. Ch. in Stoke-on-Trent*, 19–20 (copy in W.S.L.).
25 Leith, Cobridge Mission, f. 79a.
26 Ibid. ff. 102a, 105a.
27 *Kelly's Dir. Staffs.* (1884).
28 Ex inf. the Parish Priest, St. Peter's (1957); foundation stone by altar, dated 1936; Worship Reg. 56546.
29 Ex inf. the Parish Priest.
30 *Laity's Dir.* (1823, 1826, 1828, 1830); P. W. L. Adams, *Adams Family*, 166, where the nuns are wrongly called Sisters of Mercy; see p. 119.
31 Ex inf. Mr. A. Doran, Hanley (1960). The Hales family seem to have been living there between at least 1674 and 1834: W.S.L. 2/37/42–2/40/42; Ward, *Stoke*, 286; Parson and Bradshaw, *Dir. Staffs.* (1818); White, *Dir. Staffs.* (1834). A Mrs. Alcock was living at Cobridge House by 1851 (White, *Dir. Staffs.* 1851), but the name Hales continues to occur at Cobridge until at least 1900: ibid.; *P.O. Dir. Staffs.* (1854 and later edns. to 1876); *Kelly's Dir. Staffs.* (1880 and later edns. to 1900).
32 Leith, Cobridge Mission, f. 63a.
33 *Laity's Dir.* (1828), 24.
34 Leith, Cobridge Mission, ff. 101a, 103a, 109b, 110a.
35 H.O. 129/15/370/3/1.
36 The Cobridge priest retained responsibility for Roman Catholics in the North Staffs. Infirmary until 1864 to help the overburdened priest at Hanley: Leith, Cobridge Mission, f. 110a. 37 Ex inf. the Parish Priest (1960).

the Greendock area of Longton.[38] The brick building in a simple Gothic style still stands between Gregory and Griffin Streets.[39] The mission was served from Caverswall and Cresswell until 1822 when a resident priest was appointed to St. Gregory's.[40] In 1835 'a low pinnacled tower' and a presbytery, and in 1850 a Lady chapel were added.[41] The present church of St. Gregory in Heathcote Road was built in 1868–9[42] and at its opening Bishop Ullathorne is said to have declared that it should prove 'a great boon to the poor Catholics in this dreary town of sin and mud'.[43] The church, designed by E. W. Pugin, is a tall red-brick Gothic building with blue-brick bands and stone dressings. It consists of an aisled and clere-storied nave, with a west gallery and vestibule, and a high-vaulted chancel. Externally the five-sided east end is roofed in a series of small gables with carved figures standing between them. The windows contain Geometrical tracery, and there is a large rose window at the west end of the nave. The presbytery was built on to the church in 1880.[44] The first church is used as the parish hall; the upper part of the tower has been removed.

A Mass-centre served from St. Gregory's was opened at the Newstead council school in 1958 and transferred to the new Roman Catholic infants' school in 1959.[45]

A small community of Dominican nuns under Mother Margaret Hallahan opened a convent at the Foley between Longton and Fenton early in 1851. On the expiry of the lease in 1854 the convent was moved to Stoke.[46] The Sisters of Charity of St. Paul opened the present St. Gregory's Convent in Trentham Road in 1932.[47]

On the last Sunday of March 1851 260 people heard Mass at St. Gregory's.[48] The Roman Catholic population of the mission was about 2,000 in 1896[49] and had doubled some 30 years later.[50] It is now about 3,000,[51] Meir having been taken out of the parish in 1934.

STOKE. The mission at Stoke was founded in 1838 by the priest at Longton, who in that year began to say Mass at a house in Whieldon Road occupied by a Mr. Maguire.[52] In 1841 the Mass-centre was moved to a joiner's shop in Liverpool Road,[53] and this was replaced by a chapel built in 1843 in Back Glebe Street (otherwise Rome Street) and dedicated to St. Peter's Chains.[54] The chapel continued to be served

from Longton until the appointment of a resident priest in 1850.[55] The building being poor and inadequate, the congregation bought a new site on Cliff Bank in 1852.[56] On condition that a church should be built there this land was offered in the same year to the Dominican nuns who were looking for a site in the Potteries for a new convent and who themselves acquired some of the adjoining land in 1854.[57] Work began on the new church and convent in 1856 and with their opening in the following year the old chapel was sold.[58] The new church, dedicated to Our Lady of the Angels and St. Peter in Chains, was designed by Joseph and Charles Hansom and is an aisled Gothic building of variegated brick to which the chancel was added in 1884–5.[59] The Stations of the Cross from Belgium were given in 1865 by Dr. James Northcote, priest-in-charge 1857–60 and 1881–1907,[60] and the organ was erected in 1905 to commemorate the golden jubilee of his priesthood.[61]

The Dominican convent and girls' school in Harts-hill Road originally occupied a single wing of about half the present frontage and the building below the church (later the presbytery).[62] The west front was added in 1864–5 to house first a boarding-school and from 1869 St. Margaret's Home for Incurables, which the nuns ran in addition to their extensive educational and parochial work.[63] The convent was raised to the rank of a priory in 1866.[64] The choir and chapter-room were built in 1884–5.[65] Cliffville, a house adjoining the convent property, was acquired in 1922; the senior part of the school was then moved there, followed by the junior part in 1929.[66]

The average attendance at Mass in the Stoke church on Sundays in 1850–1 was 144.[67] The Roman Catholic population served by the priest at Stoke was estimated in 1852 as 'upwards of 500 souls', the previously rapid increase being checked by 'the very small and wretched accommodation' afforded by the existing chapel.[68] The population attached to the Church of Our Lady of the Angels in the late 1950's was about 2,300,[69] Fenton and Trent Vale having become separate parishes (see below).

TUNSTALL. The Tunstall mission, the first to be started from Cobridge and covering Tunstall, Goldenhill, Red Street, Kidsgrove, and Norton-in-the-Moors, was founded in 1853 with a school-chapel in Plex Street dedicated to St. Mary. It continued

[38] Greenslade, *Cath. Ch. in Stoke*, 9 (where the chaplain is wrongly called Henry, instead of Robert, Richmond), 32; *Programme of Centenary of Cath. Emancipation, Hanley, 1929*, 15; Archbp.'s House, Birmingham, Longton par. papers, synopsis of conveyance of land 1819.
[39] *Cath. Mag.* v. 394–5; Ward, *Stoke*, 571.
[40] *Cath. Mag.* v. 395; memorial brass in church.
[41] Ward, *Stoke*, 571; *Cent. of Cath. Emanc.* 15.
[42] *Guide to Cath. Truth Conference, Hanley, 1896* (Cath. Truth Soc.), 44; *Staffs. Advertiser*, 16 May 1868; Worship Reg. no. 19157.
[43] B. W. Kelly, *Eng. Cath. Missions*, 259.
[44] Date-stone on presbytery.
[45] Ex inf. the Parish Priest. A site was bought at Newstead for a church and presbytery in 1958 and building was due to start in 1960.
[46] *Our Lady of the Angels, Stoke, Centenary Souvenir*, 4 (copy in H.R.L.); *Centenary of Cath. Emanc.* 35. There is a tradition that there was a convent at Foley Place (see p. 209): ex inf. one of the occupants of Foley Place (1960).
[47] Ex. inf. the Sister Superior (1958).
[48] H.O. 129/15/371/5/2.
[49] *Cath. Truth Conf.* 44.

[50] *Centenary of Cath. Emanc.* 15.
[51] Ex inf. the Parish Priest (1960).
[52] *Centenary of Cath. Emanc.* 35; *Laity's Dir.* (1840).
[53] *Cath. Truth Conf.* 38. The registers date from this year.
[54] H.O. 129/15/371/3/1; Bapt. Reg. 1841–52, title-page.
[55] Bapt. Reg. 1841–52, *passim*.
[56] *Cath. Dir.* (1853), 86; *Centenary of Cath. Emanc.* 35; *Our Lady of the Angels Centenary Souvenir*, 4.
[57] *Centenary of Cath. Emanc.* 35. For the previous convent at the Foley see above.
[58] *Centenary Souvenir*, 4; Worship Reg. no. 8083.
[59] *Cath. Truth Conf.* 38; *Centenary Souvenir*, 4; *Keates's Potteries Dir.* (1873–4). [60] *Centenary Souvenir*, 4.
[61] Brass tablet in church.
[62] *Centenary Souvenir*, 4.
[63] Ibid.; *Centenary of Cath. Emanc.* 36–37.
[64] *Centenary Souvenir*, 4, 6.
[65] Ibid. 4.
[66] Ibid. 4, 5; *Centenary of Cath. Emanc.* 37; see p. 183.
[67] H.O. 129/15/371/3/1.
[68] *Cath. Dir.* (1853).
[69] *Birmingham Archdioc. Dir.* (1960).

to be served from Cobridge until 1854 when it received its own resident priest.[70] The presbytery at first adjoined the chapel[71] but was later moved to a house in Chatterley Road opposite the end of Plex Street, 'a commodious residence with well laid-out grounds', 'castellated walls and strong heavily studded gateways'; the site is now occupied by the Cottage Hotel built in 1875.[72] A new church of St. Mary and a presbytery were erected in Sun Street (now St. Aidan's Street) in 1869[73] and remained in use until 1930 when the present church of the Sacred Heart in Queen's Avenue, begun in 1925, was opened.[74] The Sun Street church was then used as a Sunday school but was sold in 1934 and now houses the main workshop of Taylor's Garage;[75] the Plex Street chapel is now part of the works of the Staffordshire Tea Set Company. Although the architect of the new church of the Sacred Heart was originally J. S. Brocklesby, it was completed by Fr. P. J. Ryan, parish priest 1903–51, who used unemployed parishioners on the building. Of Derbyshire granite and roofed under a series of copper-covered domes, the church is in the Romanesque style and consists of campanile with one bell, north-west tower, clerestoried nave, aisles with side chapels, and apsidal chancel with ambulatory. It is built on a raft foundation to avoid the danger of subsidence. The stained glass, the bench carvings, and some of the ironwork were executed by amateur craftsmen among the parishioners, and the church also contains many furnishings bought abroad by Fr. Ryan. A building in The Boulevard has been acquired as a parish hall and named the Ryan Hall in memory of Fr. Ryan.[76]

A Mass-centre, opened at the primary school, Chell Heath, in 1951, is served from the Sacred Heart Church.[77]

There were some 300 Roman Catholics in the extensive area served by the new mission in 1854,[78] and by the end of the century there were over 1,400 in the Tunstall mission,[79] by then considerably reduced in size by the detachment of Goldenhill and the northern area. The Roman Catholic population is now nearly 2,500.[80]

HANLEY. The priest at Cobridge bought land in Lower Foundry Street, Hanley, in 1857 where in 1860 the church of St. Mary and St. Patrick was opened by William Molloy, Hanley's first resident priest.[81] In the meantime the Cobridge priest had occasionally been saying Mass in a loft over Bath and Poole's carriage-works opposite.[82] The presbytery, however, was built on land between Jasper Street and Regent Street where it was intended to build a new church also, but the poverty of the mission delayed this work for some 30 years. Finally in 1889–91 the present church of the Sacred Heart was built there;[83] it was consecrated in 1911.[84] Built in a Gothic style of brick with stone dressings the church has a clerestoried nave, wide aisles, an apsidal chancel, and a west turret with a bell.[85] The architect was originally H. V. Krolow of St. Helen's and Liverpool, but after his resignation the work was taken over by R. Scrivener and Sons of Hanley.[86] The church in Lower Foundry Street continued in occasional use until its sale c. 1940;[87] it is now (1960) used as a warehouse.

It was originally intended that there should be a convent to the east of the Sacred Heart Church,[88] but the only convent ever established in the parish was that opened by the Little Sisters of the Poor at Druid's Hall, Albion Street, in 1890 with a home for the aged attached. In 1892, however, the sisters moved to Cobridge House.[89]

At its foundation the Hanley mission had a population probably of about 1,000[90] and of some 3,300 by the end of the century.[91] Despite the separation of Birches Head and Abbey Hulton in 1923, the Sacred Heart parish had a population of some 4,500 in 1929.[92] With the resettlement of many Hanley people in new parts of the city in recent years the number has dropped to about 1,800.[93] As there are a number of East European refugees in the city, Mass has been celebrated in the Ukrainian rite on frequent Sundays since c. 1953.[94]

SMALLTHORNE. A chapel was opened at St. Mary's Roman Catholic school in Queen Street (now Brierley Street), Smallthorne, in 1875.[95] It was served from St. Peter's, Cobridge, until 1895 when it was transferred to the new Burslem mission.[96] The present school-church was built in 1905[97] and enlarged in 1934.[98] There has been a resident priest since 1923 and the Roman Catholic population of the parish has remained at about 600 since the late 1920's.[99]

GOLDENHILL. The priest at Tunstall opened a school-chapel dedicated to St. Joseph in John Street (now Brakespeare Street), Goldenhill, in 1871.[1] Goldenhill, including Kidsgrove and Biddulph, became an independent mission with its own priest in 1882, and in the following year an extension at the

70 Leith, Cobridge Mission, ff. 102b, 103a, 104a.
71 Ex inf. the clergy of the Sacred Heart Church (1960).
72 W. J. Harper, Bygone Tunstall, 106 (copy among W.S.L. pamphs. sub Tunstall); date on hotel.
73 Leith, Cobridge Mission, f. 126a; Cath. Truth Conf. 36; Worship Reg. no. 1948.
74 Centenary of Cath. Emanc. 31; Sacred Heart Confirmation Reg., note on title-page.
75 Char. Com. files. The presbytery, still occupied in 1933, was also sold in 1934: ibid.
76 Ex. inf. the clergy.   77 Ex. inf. the clergy.
78 Leith, Cobridge Mission, f. 103a.
79 Cath. Truth Conf. 36.
80 Ex inf. the clergy (1960).
81 Leith, Cobridge Mission, ff. 107a, 108a, 110a; Staffs. Advertiser, 24 Nov. 1860. A school had been opened on an adjoining site in 1858: see p. 318, n. 93.
82 Cath. Truth Conf. 40; ex inf. Mr. A. Doran, Hanley.
83 Cath. Truth Conf. 40; Staffs. Advertiser, 27 July 1889, 12 and 26 Sept. 1891; Greenslade, Cath. Ch. in Stoke, 26.

84 Birmingham Archdioc. Dir. (1960).
85 Only the lower stages of the turret were complete for the opening: Staffs. Advertiser, 12 Sept. 1891.
86 Ibid. 25 July 1889, 12 and 26 Sept. 1891.
87 Ex inf. Mr. Doran; Char. Com. files; Kelly's Dir. Staffs. (1940).
88 Staffs. Advertiser, 25 July 1889.
89 See p. 272.
90 Greenslade, Cath. Ch. in Stoke, 21, 27.
91 Cath. Truth Conf. 42.
92 Centenary of Cath. Emanc. 22.
93 Ex inf. the Parish Priest (1960).
94 Ex inf. the Parish Priest.
95 Leith, Cobridge Mission, f. 131a and plan between ff. 131 and 132.
96 Cath. Truth Conf. 54; Centenary of Cath. Emanc. 28.
97 Centenary of Cath. Emanc. 28; ex inf. the Parish Priest.
98 Ex inf. the Parish Priest.
99 Greenslade, Cath. Ch. in Stoke, 31.
1 Cath. Truth Conf. 46.

north end of the school building was opened as a separate church.[2] The present church of St. Joseph in High Street at the southern end of Goldenhill was built in 1951–3 with a presbytery adjoining, on land bought before the Second World War; the architect was Cecil Barker then of the firm of Wood, Goldstraw and Yorath, Tunstall.[3] The church is built of brick in a modern style and has a low clerestoried nave, passage aisles, and a chancel. At the entrance end of the nave is a domed tower with round-headed windows at the belfry stage where tall stone crosses are incorporated. Internally the pulpit and the piers supporting the nave arcade are built of small unplastered bricks.

The Roman Catholic population of the mission was some 600 by the end of the century,[4] and is now just over 900.[5] Kidsgrove was detached in 1893 and Biddulph in 1956.[6]

FENTON. A Mass-centre was opened in the infants' school in Havelock Street (now Masterson Street) in 1885 and served from Stoke until the appointment of a resident priest in 1922.[7] The present church of Our Lady of Perpetual Succour in Masterson Street was opened in 1923.[8] It is a low brick building designed by E. B. Norris of Stafford[9] and consists of nave, chancel, aisles, and two sacristies.

The Roman Catholic population was estimated as 1,200 in the 1920's and has altered little since.[10]

BURSLEM. A mission including Burslem, Smallthorne, and Wolstanton was formed out of the Cobridge mission in 1895 with the assistant priest from Cobridge as resident priest.[11] At first Mass was said at the Hill Top Pottery in Liverpool Road (now Westport Road),[12] but in 1897–8 a building was erected in Hall Street containing a church dedicated to St. Joseph on the upper floor and a school on the lower.[13] The presbytery in Hall Street was built in 1903.[14] The present church of St. Joseph was built on an adjoining site in 1925–7.[15] Designed in a Romanesque style by J. S. Brocklesby,[16] it is of red and purple brick with campanile, small north-west tower, nave, passage aisles, transepts, and apsidal chancel. The decoration of the ceiling and the work for the stained glass windows were carried out by the young people of the parish under the guidance of Gordon Forsyth, director of the Burslem school of Art; his daughter Maura painted most of the murals.[17] The Sisters of St. Joseph of Peace opened their present convent in Hall Street in 1926.[18] The

new mission had a population of some 1,500 in 1895,[19] but Smallthorne became a separate parish in 1923 and Wolstanton in 1927.[20] The Roman Catholic population of St. Joseph's parish is now (1960) 850.[21]

BIRCHES HEAD. A mission was started at Birches Head in 1915 by the parish priest of Hanley who then opened a chapel dedicated to St. George on the upper floor of a new building between Boulton Street and Gibbins Street, the ground floor being used as a school.[22] The chapel was temporarily closed for a period before 1918 but was otherwise served from Hanley until 1923 when a resident priest was appointed. The present church of St. George and St. Martin was built on an adjoining site in 1927–8. Designed by E. B. Norris of Stafford in the Romanesque style, it has nave, aisles, chancel, and a bell-cote containing one bell.

The Roman Catholic population was 1,100 in 1929 and is now some 1,200, new parishes having been created at Abbey Hulton and Bentilee.

PACKMOOR. In 1920 the priest at Goldenhill opened a Mass-centre at Packmoor in a hut bought from the army camp at Rugeley, and for some years it was served by the chaplains to the Little Sisters of the Poor at Cobridge.[23] In 1932 the priest at Goldenhill bought a plot of ground in Bull Lane, Lane Ends, and built the present brick church of St. Patrick there, designing it himself and using much local voluntary labour.[24] The church was opened in 1935 and served from Goldenhill until 1956 when it was attached to the new parish of the English Martyrs, Biddulph, itself founded from Goldenhill in 1952.[25] There were over 150 Roman Catholics attached to St. Patrick's in the late 1950's.[26]

TRENT VALE. A church dedicated to St. Teresa of the Child Jesus was erected in Stone Road, Trent Vale, in 1928 by the newly opened Michelin Tyre factory. At first served by a French priest, it soon passed into the care of the parish priest at Stoke; a resident priest was appointed in 1935.[27] After considerable extensions by Messrs. Sandy and Norris of Stafford in 1956, the church was reopened and consecrated in September of that year. It is of red brick with nave, transepts, chancel, and campanile. There are now (1960) some 1,100 Roman Catholics in the Trent Vale parish.

The Irish Christian Brothers have had a house at Trent Vale since 1932 with a boys' grammar school attached.[28]

[2] Ibid.; Worship Reg. no. 26129; St. Joseph's Reg. dating from 1882; ex inf. the Parish Priest.
[3] Ex inf. the Parish Priest; foundation stone dated Oct. 1951.   [4] Cath. Truth Conf. 46.
[5] Ex inf. the Parish Priest (1960).
[6] Greenslade, Cath. Ch. in Stoke, 25.
[7] Cath. Truth Conf. 48; Centenary of Cath. Emanc. 17.
[8] Centenary of Cath. Emanc. 17; Worship Reg. no. 48902.   [9] Ex inf. the Parish Priest.
[10] Centenary of Cath. Emanc. 16; ex inf. the Parish Priest (1960).
[11] Worship Reg. no. 34656; St. Joseph's Reg., dating from 20 Jan. 1895; Cath. Truth Conf. 54; ex inf. Mr. A. Doran, Hanley.
[12] Cath. Truth Conf. 54; ex inf. Mr. A. Doran, who attended Mass there.
[13] Ex inf. the Parish Priest (1960); Worship Reg. no. 36503.   [14] Date on building.
[15] Inscription behind Sacred Heart Altar in S. transept, partially blocked by the tabernacle; Worship Reg. no. 50885.

[16] Ex inf. the Parish Priest, St. Joseph's.
[17] Kelly's Dir. Staffs. (1940); ex inf. Mr. R. G. Haggar.
[18] Ex inf. the Sister Superior of St. Joseph's Convent (1958).   [19] Cath. Truth Conf. 54.
[20] See pp. 55, 274.
[21] Ex inf. the Parish Priest (1960).
[22] The information for this section has been supplied (1960) by Canon Martin Power, Parish Priest since 1923, and Centenary of Cath. Emanc. 33–34.
[23] Birmingham Archdioc. Dir. (1958), 222; Worship Reg. no. 47822.
[24] Birmingham Archdioc. Dir. (1958), 222.
[25] Ibid. 220, 222.   [26] Ibid. (1960).
[27] The information for this paragraph has been supplied by the Parish Priest (1960).
[28] Ex. inf. the Parish Priest; Cath. Dir. (1933). The house was previously called High Grove and had been built by 1820: Greenwood, Map of Staffs. (1820); Hargreaves, Map of Staffs. Potteries (1832); O.S. Map 6" Staffs. xviii SW. (1926).

MEIR. In 1934 the priest at Longton bought a house called 'Highfields' in Sandon Road, Meir, with the land attached, and a resident priest was appointed.[29] A church dedicated to St. Augustine of Canterbury was opened at Christmas 1934 in the converted stable block, and the house has remained the presbytery since then. The hall of the new school was used as a church from 1937 until 1949 when the original church building, extended by the addition of a Nissen hut, was reopened as the church. The present church, built of pale yellow brick and designed by Messrs. Sandy and Norris of Stafford, was opened in 1957. The Roman Catholic population of St. Augustine's parish is 1,200.

ABBEY HULTON. The Church of Our Lady and St. Benedict in Abbey Lane was built in 1937–8 by the parish priest at Birches Head.[30] The area became a separate parish in 1941 and has a Roman Catholic population of over 1,300. Bentilee became a separate parish in 1956. A Mass-centre, opened at the Greenway Inn, Baddeley Green, in 1958, is served by the parish priest at Abbey Hulton.

BENTILEE. A Mass-centre was opened by the parish priest of Abbey Hulton in the Clowes Community Hall on the Bentilee housing estate in 1956.[31] The area received its own priest in the same year and became the parish of St. Maria Goretti. A church was begun in 1959. The Roman Catholic population of the parish is 450.

PROTESTANT NONCONFORMITY[1]

IN 1760 John Wesley first visited Burslem, then the largest of the Pottery villages, and six years later the first Methodist chapel was built there. The building of this chapel marks the establishment of the first lasting nonconformist meeting in this area. Before 1766 only isolated vestiges of dissent can be traced. A house in Stoke parish, probably at Seabridge (now in Newcastle), however, belonging to Jane Machin, widow of an ejected minister, had been registered for Presbyterian worship in 1672.[2] The house of Thomas Yardley of Norton had been registered for worship in 1697[3] and there was a Presbyterian or Unitarian meeting in Burslem in 1715.

When Wesley first preached at Burslem the population of the Potteries was still relatively small, not more than 7,500 altogether.[4] It was, however, already expanding and by 1785 according to one estimate had risen to 15,000. Longton showed the steepest rise, with Burslem, Hanley, and Stoke close behind.[5] During the period 1760–85 Wesley and his preachers were frequent visitors to the towns.[6] Methodist chapels were established at Hanley and Longton in 1783, while meetings at Fenton and at Tunstall had been started by 1782, the chapel at Tunstall being built in 1788. The religious revival to which the preaching of Wesley and his associates gave rise thus corresponded with the first rapid expansion of these villages.[7]

Although Methodism was to dominate the nonconformity of the area and undoubtedly led the religious revival of the 1780's,[8] other nonconformist bodies gradually established themselves. In 1780 Captain Jonathan Scott brought Congregational evangelism to Stoke and North Staffordshire,[9] a move that was bitterly resented by Wesley.[10] Con-

gregationalism was established at Hanley and a chapel built there in 1784, followed by others in Burslem, Longton, Stoke, and Milton in the first 25 years of the next century. The Baptists also established themselves in this period; a Particular Baptist chapel was built at Hanley in 1789; a (New Connexion) Baptist chapel at Burslem followed it in 1806; and there was also a meeting of Baptists at Longton in the early 19th century. The Unitarians were also stirring. By 1820 they had a chapel at Longton and by 1825 there was a meeting at Burslem. There was also a small Sandemanian meeting by 1812 at Tunstall.

The two notable schisms in the Methodist movement which resulted in the formation of the Methodist New Connexion and the Primitive Methodist Connexion (later Church) greatly affected the future development of Methodism in the Potteries. The first, which was led by Alexander Kilham, a Methodist minister, found its strongest support in this area; the second started in Tunstall and the moorlands to the north and east of Tunstall. In July 1797, when the annual conference of the Methodist Church was held at Leeds, there were five Methodist chapels in the Potteries, at Longton, Fenton, Hanley, Burslem, and Tunstall, and a regular meeting at Stoke. Support for the Kilhamite demands,[11] the rejection of which at this conference resulted in the formation of the Methodist New Itinerancy or Connexion, had already been shown by the members of Hanley chapel and this had resulted in the temporary closing of the chapel by the trustees. By September 1797, less than two months after the formation of the Methodist New Connexion, there were five societies of this church in the Potteries, at Hanley,

[29] The information in this paragraph has been supplied by the Parish Priest (1960).
[30] The information for this section has been supplied by the Parish Priest (1960). It had originally been intended to buy the site of Hulton Abbey for the new church, but this was used by the city authorities for a school: Greenslade, *Cath. Ch. in Stoke*, 29; see p. 248.
[31] The information for this section has been supplied by the Parish Priest (1960).
[1] This article covers the whole area of the present city of Stoke-on-Trent.
[2] A. G. Matthews, *Cong. Chs. of Staffs.* 92; see p. 77.
[3] Matthews, *Cong. Chs. of Staffs.* 125.
[4] Ward, *Stoke*, 43.

[5] Ibid.
[6] J. Wesley, *Journal, passim*.
[7] Ibid. 8 Mar. 1781.
[8] Wesley, *Journal*, 30 Mar. 1784, says of this revival: 'Indeed the country is all on fire and the flame is still spreading from village to village'.
[9] Matthews, *Cong. Chs. of Staffs*.
[10] Wesley, *Journal*, 26 Mar. 1781.
[11] These affirmed the right of the people to have the sacraments administered to them by their own ministers, to hold services at such times as suited themselves even though these times conflicted with the times of services in the parish ch., and the right of the laity to have some share in Methodist government.

Burslem, Longton, Sneyd Green, and Etruria. Hanley Wesleyan Methodist society was almost extinguished by the New Connexion group there, while Fenton chapel went over to the New Connexion. A chapel at Stoke was added in 1806. Hanley circuit, formed by these societies and those at Newcastle, Silverdale, and Werrington, became increasingly important until by 1812 it was the strongest in the Connexion. It then had over 2,000 members. From the outset the New Connexion in Hanley commanded the support of influential manufacturers, notably the Ridgways of Cauldon Place, Shelton. Bethesda Chapel swiftly became the foremost place of worship in the town. In 1811 the chapel was enlarged to hold 1,000 and within a few months all the seats were let. By 1819 a new chapel had become necessary, which, erected in that year, seated 2,500. Bethesda was still the principal place of worship in Hanley in the mid-19th century[12] and in 1840 one-tenth of the total membership of the Methodist New Connexion was in the Hanley and Longton Circuits.[13]

The Primitive Methodist movement was different in character and origin from the New Connexion. It originated between 1800 and 1810 in the efforts of certain Methodists, notably John and James Bourne, William Clowes, and James Steele, to convert people in the moorland areas north and east of Tunstall. Their methods were extremely revivalistic and the Bournes particularly made great use of field-preaching and the Camp Meeting as a means of spreading Methodism. Their activities aroused the disapproval of the Wesleyan authorities, and one by one these men were expelled from their societies until in 1811 they formed their own itinerancy and gave their church the designation of Primitive Methodist.[14] Tunstall was by this date the centre of the new movement, which spread quickly in the North and the Midlands in the years of depression between 1815 and 1820.[15] In the Potteries it retained its original character of a working-class movement.[16] The chapels, consequently, were short of money, and although the leaders, particularly Hugh Bourne, contributed as much as possible,[17] they themselves had few resources. The new church acquired a large membership and its organization was rapidly developed, one side of which was the establishment of its own printing press or book room at Bemersley in 1822 with James Bourne as book steward and Hugh Bourne as editor.[18] In Tunstall Circuit the Primitive Methodists showed quick appreciation of the need to consolidate their position after the establishment of the first chapels. Tunstall chapel was replaced in 1822 by a larger chapel. Pitts Hill society, established

in 1811, had an early failure, closing within a year, but the society there had been revived by 1823 when a chapel was built. Burslem society acquired a chapel in 1819. Hanley society, established by 1825, proved rather weak, having to compete with Bethesda Chapel, and the first and second chapels both failed and were sold. Penkhull chapel, however, was successfully established in 1815. Then there was a lull. Stoke and Fenton chapels were not established until the 1830's, while Longton had no Primitive Methodist chapel until 1843. In the north of the area, however, the position of the Primitive Methodists was further consolidated when yet another chapel was built at Goldenhill in 1833, and in the early 1840's two more in Burslem were added, at Sneyd Green and Middleport.

The effect of the spread of these two new Methodist churches on Wesleyan Methodism in the area is difficult to gauge. Undoubtedly the denomination was seriously weakened in the Hanley area by the New Connexion and in the Tunstall area by the Primitive Methodists. Yet it appears to have been only a temporary setback, and, although the Primitives and New Connexion were particularly influential in two areas, the Wesleyan Methodists maintained a steady rate of expansion throughout the Potteries. By 1830 there were 5 Primitive Methodist chapels in the Potteries,[19] 10 New Connexion chapels or regular preaching places,[20] and 12 Wesleyan Methodist chapels, a total of 27.[21] There were 4 or 5 Congregational chapels,[22] 2 Baptist chapels, one or two Unitarian meetings[23] and a Presbyterian Church of England church,[24] a total of 34 or 36 Protestant nonconformist places of worship while there were only 4 Anglican churches[25] and 2 Roman Catholic ones.[26]

Between 1831 and 1851 the population of the Potteries rose from about 54,000 to over 88,000.[27] The expansion of the Anglican and Protestant nonconformist churches kept pace with this increase. In 1851 the Primitive Methodists had 10 chapels in the area, the New Connexion 17, the Wesleyan Methodist Church 17, and the Wesleyan Methodist Association 2, a total of 46 Methodist chapels. The Congregationalists formed the next largest nonconformist church with 7 chapels. The Baptists had 4, the Christian Brethren or Barkerites 2 or 3, the Quakers one, the Swedenborgians one, and the Presbyterian Church of England one, a total of 63 or 64 Protestant nonconformist chapels or meeting places. The number of Anglican churches had meanwhile increased to 17.[28] The Roman Catholics built another church and had three churches, at Stoke,

---

[12] Ward, *Stoke*, 396–441. [13] Ibid. 400.
[14] The more detailed history of the origin of this movement is reserved for treatment in an article on nonconformity in the county in a future volume. The information given here is taken from H. B. Kendall, *Hist. of the Primitive Methodist Ch.*; J. Ritson, *Romance of Primitive Methodism* (1909); J. W. Chappell, *In the Power of God* (Burslem, 1901); Hugh Bourne, *Hist. of the Primitive Methodists* (Bemersley, 1823); and various local pamphs.
[15] Kendall, *The Primitive Methodist Ch.* i. *passim*. Derby circuit was formed in 1816, Loughborough and Nottingham following in 1818.
[16] Ward, *Stoke*, 99; thus in Bennett's *The Old Wives' Tale*, Samuel Povey's conversion from the Primitive Methodism of King St., Bursley, to the ranks of the 'proud majority . . . deeply aware of its rightness and correctness' of Duck Bank Wesleyan Chap. (Swan Sq.) was a step into greater respectability and middle-class solidarity.

[17] e.g. Bourne took responsibility for the debt of the Burslem chap. for many years: Chappell, *In the Power of God*, 26–27. [18] *Prim. Meth. Conf. Mins. 1822*.
[19] They were Tunstall, Pitts Hill, Burslem, Hanley, and Penkhull.
[20] They were Tunstall, Burslem, Hanley, Etruria, Stoke, Fenton, 2 at Longton, Bucknall, and Smallthorne.
[21] They were Tunstall, Goldenhill, Norton, Burslem, Sneyd Green, Longport, Etruria, Hanley, Stoke, Fenton, and 2 at Longton.
[22] They were Hanley, Milton, Burslem, Longton, and possibly Stoke.
[23] They were Burslem and possibly Longton.
[24] It was at Hanley.
[25] See pp. 122, 154, 189–90, 233.   [26] See p. 272.
[27] *Census*, 1831, 1851, Staffs.
[28] This fig. includes three temporary churches (see pp. 124, 157, 234) and a mission church (see p. 215).

Cobridge, and Longton.[29] Both the Anglican and nonconformist churches had extended their activities from the centres of the towns to the areas of new development. The Anglicans and the New Connexion had built in the Harpfield–Hartshill area of Stoke, the Wesleyans and Anglicans at Trent Vale;[30] at Longton the New Connexion had three chapels; in Hanley the New Connexion had established new chapels at Eastwood Vale, at Shelton, and in Town Road, while the Wesleyans had a chapel at Northwood. Burslem had perhaps received most attention from the Methodist churches; the Primitive Methodists by this date had 3 chapels there, the New Connexion 4, the Wesleyan Methodists 4, and the Wesleyan Association two.

In the next twenty years the population continued to increase though not so rapidly, Burslem and Hanley showing the greatest growth.[31] The nonconformist churches continued to spread into the areas of new development, though not all of the denominations were still expanding. The Methodist New Connexion had more or less come to a standstill, establishing only one new church in these 20 years, at Dresden in Longton. This denomination had temporarily lost ground, particularly in Tunstall, to the ephemeral Christian Brethren. Also John Ridgway, who had been the driving force behind much of the expansion of the connexion in the first half of the century, had died in 1860. The Wesleyan Methodist Church built five new chapels between 1851 and 1871 but that denomination also had been affected by secessions: the Methodist Reform Church and the Wesleyan Association which joined together in 1857 to form the United Methodist Free Church. The Primitive Methodists, however, had gone from strength to strength in these two decades and had exactly doubled the number of their chapels to a total of twenty in 1871. The United Free Methodist Church had 6 chapels and the Wesleyan Reform Association one, a total of 66 Methodist chapels. The Congregationalists had built 3 new chapels, the Baptists had lost 1 but built 2 more, the Quakers still had 1 meeting, the Christian Brethren had dispersed completely, the Presbyterians still had 1 church, the Unitarians had 1 or 2 churches, and although the Swedenborgians were temporarily inactive, the Latter Day Saints had 1 or 2 churches, making a total of some 85 nonconformist churches. Compared with this over-all increase of 22 chapels, the Church of England had built only 5 new churches,[32] while the number of Roman Catholic churches had increased to five.[33] There were no areas in the Potteries without a church or a chapel,[34] although the figures of chapel membership or attendance available suggest that a smaller percentage of the population than might be expected attended a place of worship. In Longton, for example, if the 1851 census returns

can be trusted, slightly less than one-ninth of the population was attending a nonconformist place of worship, while only one-seventh attended any place of worship.[35] In Hanley and Shelton one-tenth of the population attended nonconformist chapels, and only one-eighth attended any place of worship.[36] The figures for the rest of the Pottery towns are similar. They show that despite the efforts of the nonconformist, Anglican, and Roman Catholic churches to provide places of worship in these rapidly increasing communities, most of the population attended no church or chapel, while, of those who did, the nonconformists were by far the greater in number. Chapel-going as evidence of respectability and the place of the chapel in the social life of the Potteries are well brought out in the Five Towns novels of Arnold Bennett.

In the Potteries the Sunday schools made an important contribution towards both religious and secular instruction and were for most children the only means of gaining secular education. The best known of these was Burslem Sunday School. Founded in 1787 by the Methodists of Burslem, its board of trustees included men of other denominations,[37] and its aim was 'not to promote the religious principles of any particular sect, but, setting aside all party distinctions, to instruct youth in useful learning, in the leading and uncontrovertible principles of Christianity'.[38] It taught reading and writing on Sundays as well as the principles of religion. By 1798 it had nearly 700 pupils[39] and by 1816, including branch schools at Longport and Norton, 1,687 pupils with 182 teachers.[40] In 1828, however, the Wesleyan Methodist Church decided against secular instruction on Sundays and in 1834 the name of this school was changed to the Wesleyan Methodist Sunday School.[41] Two years later, the trustees having determined to restrict the curriculum to religious teaching only, the teachers who opposed this policy were expelled. The latter set up an independent Burslem Sunday School with a branch at Longport.[42] Notwithstanding the Burslem dispute, other branches of Methodism continued to provide secular education in their Sunday schools long after this date. In 1843, for example, about 1,000 pupils at the Methodist New Connexion Bethesda Sunday School in Hanley were being taught reading and writing on Sundays.[43] The Baptist Sunday School in Hanley also taught reading and writing at this date, and although the Independents there were not teaching writing on Sundays, it was taught in the evening on weekdays.[44] This side of the work of the Sunday schools lessened with the establishment of more day schools, and probably, as in the case of Burslem Sunday School, ceased altogether when the provisions of the 1870 Education Act became operative.

The 30 years between 1870 and 1900 was the great

---

[29] See pp. 272–3.   [30] See p. 193.
[31] *Census*, 1871, Staffs.
[32] The Church of England had, however, opened a number of mission centres.   [33] See p. 274.
[34] As there are said to have been in some of the greater cities of Eng.: R. C. K. Ensor, *England 1870–1914*, 140.
[35] The total of nonconformist attendances, taking the highest attendance on the Census day for each chap., was just under 1,650. Attendance at the 2 Anglican chs. was just under 400 and at the R.C. ch. 260.
[36] The total of nonconformist attendances was 2,720 and of Anglican 750.
[37] *Hill Top Centenary. Hill Top Methodist Church*

1837–1937; Burslem Sunday School 1787–1937 (copy in H.R.L.). For example, Enoch Wood, the manufacturer, who was a churchwarden of Burslem, was a trustee of the school: Falkner, *The Wood Family*, 68, 69.
[38] Falkner, *The Wood Family*, 69, quoting the 1808 annual rep. of the school.
[39] *Hill Top Centenary*.
[40] Ibid.
[41] Ibid.
[42] Ibid.
[43] H. Smith and A. H. Beard, *Bethesda Chap. Hanley* (1899), 29–30.
[44] Ward, *Stoke*, 402.

era of chapel building in the Potteries. The towns were still spreading; many new chapels were established in recently developed areas, many of the older chapels were rebuilt. By 1900 the number of Wesleyan chapels had increased to 36; the New Connexion then had 25 chapels, the Primitive Methodists 31 and the United Methodists 8, a total of 100. The Baptists had 9 churches and the Congregationalists 14, the Presbyterians 2 (one Welsh, one English), and the Quakers 1, a total of 126 chapels of the older established denominations.[45] There was also a strong Free Church in Goldenhill, an evangelical splinter from the Church of England there; the Swedenborgian Church had a meeting in Longton about this date; and the Catholic Apostolic Church had established itself at Stoke. This period is remarkable, too, for the growth of evangelical missions, headed by the Salvation Army, and the establishment of Spiritualist churches. The Salvation Army first 'opened fire' in the Potteries in 1881 and by the end of the 1880's had centres in all the Pottery towns. For a short period there was also an organization called the Salvation Navy. Borough Missions, Gospel Missions, and Temperance Missions became numerous. Little is known about their fields of work, but presumably like the Burslem Gospel Mission they concentrated mainly on the poor and overcrowded areas.

These years were marked not only by the building or rebuilding of many chapels but by an increase in congregations. For example, among the Baptist churches, Longton expanded from a membership of 21 in 1862 to 283 in 1890 and Fenton from 15 in 1881 to 40 in 1892. Stoke had a membership of 114 in 1900, and New Street, Hanley, 87. Burslem increased from 44 members in 1862 to 97 in 1900. Membership of Bethesda Chapel, Hanley, stood at 447 in 1897 and there were 982 Sunday school children.[46] Mount Tabor Chapel, Fenton, was said to have a strong congregation in 1900. Comparable attendance figures of other denominations are unobtainable.

The early 1900's were definitely a period of decline for the various Baptist churches in the area, which adopted a limited form of connexionalism in an attempt to consolidate their position. The movement towards unity and consolidation became of national importance for the Methodists. In 1907 the New Connexion Church joined with the United Free Methodist Church. In the Potteries this meant that the surviving three Methodist churches were of more or less equal strength.

Except in Longton the circuits of the two uniting churches were merged,[47] but the union did not result in the closing of chapels in places where each of the churches had previously been established. Two new temporary churches were established by the new church in Fenton but otherwise the union did not result in expansion.

The union in 1932 of the Wesleyan Methodist, Primitive Methodist, and United Methodist Churches brought all the surviving Methodist chapels in the Potteries into the newly created Methodist Church. In Tunstall, Longton, Fenton, and Stoke, the circuits of the three churches were merged,[48] but in Hanley and Burslem remained intact except for alterations in Burslem in 1949 when Swan Bank Wesleyan Chapel became the Central Methodist Church.[49] In Longton the merging of the circuits after the union of 1932 excluded Stafford Street Wesleyan Chapel which then became Longton Central Mission. A few of the larger chapels were closed after the union partly on account of population shift and decline in numbers and partly because of the close proximity of the main chapels of each denomination.[50] There are now (1959) 76 Methodist chapels in Stoke-on-Trent. Only 14 of the former New Connexion chapels are now in use, 4 of the former United Methodist Free Church, one former United Methodist Church, built after the union of these two churches, 24 former Primitive Methodist and 30 former Wesleyan chapels. Three new chapels have been built since Methodist Union in areas of recent development.

The other Free Churches were also facing the same difficulties of decline in membership in the later 1920's and the 1930's and the Methodists were not alone in trying to check this by co-ordinating their activities. In 1934 a Free Church Council was founded in the Potteries under the auspices of the North Staffordshire Federation of Free Church Councils, the first president being the minister of Trinity Presbyterian Church, Hanley. The council has been supported by all the Free Churches but various factors have militated against its success; among them are the overwhelming preponderance of the Methodist Church in the area, which at the time of the formation of the council was much concerned with the problems arising from the Methodist Union; the decline of the Free Churches in the 1930's; the scattered nature of the city; and the comparatively late date at which the council was formed. In recent years, however, the council has effectively co-ordinated the work of the Free Churches in hospital and other chaplaincies and in representation on civic bodies, and has averted a multiplicity of Free Churches in the new housing areas. It has also furthered discussions on Free Church unity and has tried to promote closer relations with the Church of England.[51]

The main trends of the Free Church movement in the Potteries during the last half-century have, therefore, been towards greater co-operation and solidarity, not only within but between denominations. A policy of retrenchment has been forced on the Free Churches through the decline in their numbers, and there are some signs that this has been successful in arresting the regression of the remaining churches.[52] But while the older churches have

45 These figs. are compiled from the detailed treatment of individual chapels.
46 Smith and Beard, *Bethesda Chap. Hanley*, 35.
47 *Kelly's Dir. Staffs.* (1912 and later edns. to 1932).
48 Ibid. (1940); ex inf. the Supt. Ministers (1958); *Meth. Ch. Buildings* (1947).
49 Ex inf. the Supt. Ministers, Burslem (1958).
50 Such as Commerce St. Chap., Longton, Bethel Chap., Burslem, Mt. Tabor Chap., Tunstall, all formerly New Connexion. Clowes Memorial Ch., Burslem, the main Prim. Meth. ch. there, was closed on account of mining subsidence, not for this reason.
51 Ex inf. the Revd. R. R. Bance, Sec. of the Free Ch. Counc., Stoke-on-Trent (1958).
52 e.g. the membership of Meigh St. Bapt. Chap., Hanley, which received part of the dispersed Burslem congregation, has been rising since the Second World War and a new chap. and sch. have been built. Although some of the central Meth. chs. may still show a decline, Harpfield chap. has been steadily gaining with the increasing suburbanization of that area.

been declining in numbers and membership, particularly since 1930, new sects have arisen. These new arrivals have usually been American in origin, and intensely evangelical and fundamentalist. They have often been Pentecostal as well. The Christadelphian Ecclesia was established in 1916, the Church of Christ Scientist in 1913, the Apostolic Church in 1931, the Plymouth Brethren in 1936, the Bethel Evangelistic Society in 1932, the Assemblies of God in 1939, the International Holiness Mission or Church of the Nazarene in 1931, Elim Four Square Gospel Alliance in 1956,[53] and, of a rather different order, the British Israelites in 1934, as well as various missions and the Jehovah's Witnesses. The impact of these new denominations on the membership of the older churches has probably been insignificant and the decline in membership of such churches is presumably attributable to causes general throughout the country.

Apostolic Church

FENTON. An Apostolic church in Foley Street was registered for worship in 1931.[54]

BURSLEM. Three rooms on the first floor of 20A Market Place were registered as an Apostolic church in 1931.[55]

TUNSTALL. The first floor of 50 Goodfellow Road was registered as an Apostolic church in 1908.[56] The church moved to 266 High Street in 1932.[57]

Assemblies of God

LONGTON. A group belonging to the Fellowship of the Assemblies of God had been formed in Longton by 1940 and then met at 135 High Street.[58] In 1944 it moved to Wharf (later Bridgewood) Street,[59] and c. 1954 to the former Primitive Methodist chapel in Alexandra Road[60] where it still met in 1958.

HANLEY. An Assembly of God church in St. John Street was registered in 1952.[61]

BURSLEM. A room at 1 Wycliffe Street was registered for worship in 1953 by the Church of God (Pentecostal), possibly affiliated to the Fellowship of Assemblies of God.[62]

TUNSTALL. The first floor of 101 Roundwell (formerly Well) Street was registered by the Assemblies of God in 1939.[63]

MILTON. A Bethel mission hall in a room under the Archway, 2A Leek Road was registered by the Assemblies of God in 1941.[64] The meeting may have lapsed or moved in 1944 when the rear of 4 Leek

Road was registered as Bethel Hall.[65] In 1950 the group moved to the rear of 2 Leek Road.[66]

NORTON IN THE MOORS, BALL GREEN. A meeting-room of the Assemblies of God in Wilding Road (previously North Street) was registered in 1940.[67] It apparently ceased to be used in 1945[68] but was restarted and again registered in 1946.[69]

Baptist Churches

LONGTON. Before 1820 a room in St. Martin's Lane had been used by Baptists.[70] In 1853, supported by the General Baptist Association, H. Wileman, a master-potter, who had come to Longton from Paddington, reserved the use of the town hall on Sundays for a year in the hope of starting regular Baptist services.[71] These began in the July of the same year, 120 being present in the morning and 200 in the evening on the first day.[72] In November of the following year a church was formally founded.[73] For some years the Court House was used for services which were conducted mainly by lay preachers, but later a regular minister, the Revd. H. Freckelton, was in charge.[74] In 1858 he seceded to the Unitarians and became their minister at Newcastle-under-Lyme.[75] Shortly after this the upper story of a building in Trentham Road, not far from the present chapel, was secured for services.[76] By 1862 the church had 21 members[77] and in 1867 was again served by a regular minister.[78] In 1873 the church was reconstituted and in 1876 the present red-brick Romanesque chapel with blue-brick dressings was erected in Trentham Road.[79] By 1890 Longton church had 283 members and Sunday-school attendance in that year averaged 290.[80] A period of recession for the local Baptist churches followed. To arrest this tendency, a limited form of connexionalism, known as the North Staffordshire Federal Scheme, was introduced in 1905. By this Longton, Newcastle, and Burslem Baptist churches were grouped together with two ministers in charge of them. The scheme was abandoned in 1918 but it apparently proved a successful means of arresting decline and was imitated elsewhere.[81] In the early 1920's Longton church membership rose; it was 133 in 1925.[82] By 1937, however, it had decreased to 122[83] and has steadily declined since; it was 93 in 1946[84] and 73 in 1956.[85] The average Sunday-school attendance has also decreased, from 120 in 1937[86] to 59 in 1946[87] and 76 in 1956.[88]

LONGTON, NORMACOT. In 1883 there was a branch church from Longton Baptist Church at Normacot.[89]

[53] This was established in the 1930's in Newcastle: see p. 59.
[54] G.R.O., Worship Reg. no. 56101.
[55] Ibid. no. 53383.
[56] Ibid. no. 51678.
[57] Ibid. no. 54041.
[58] Ibid. no. 59282.
[59] Ibid. no. 60883.
[60] Ibid. no. 65964; see p. 297.
[61] Worship Reg. no. 63639.
[62] Ibid. no. 63929.
[63] Ibid. no. 59023.
[64] Ibid. no. 59825.
[65] Ibid. no. 60693. This regtn. was not substituted for the former, both being cancelled in 1950 on the second move.
[66] Ibid. no. 62820.
[67] Ibid. no. 59114.
[68] Ibid.
[69] Ibid. no. 61422.
[70] Matthews, *Cong. Chs. of Staffs.* 176.
[71] *Centenary of Longton Bapt. Ch. 1853–1953* (copy in

H.R.L.). The *Bapt. Handbk.* (1862) gives 1834 as the date of foundation.
[72] *Centenary Longton Bapt. Ch.*
[73] Ibid.
[74] Ibid.
[75] G. Pegler, *Hist. of the Old Meeting House, Newcastle-under-Lyme*, 9 (copy among W.S.L. pamphs. *sub* Newcastle).
[76] *Centenary Longton Bapt. Ch.*
[77] *Bapt. Handbk.* (1862).
[78] *Centenary Longton Bapt. Ch.*
[79] Ibid.
[80] *Bapt. Handbk.* (1890).
[81] *Centenary Longton Bapt. Ch.*
[82] Ibid.
[83] *W. Midland Bapt. Assoc. Yr. Bk.* (1937).
[84] *Bapt. Handbk.* (1946).
[85] Ibid. (1956).
[86] *W. Midland Bapt. Assoc. Yr. Bk.* (1937).
[87] *Bapt. Handbk.* (1946).
[88] Ibid. (1956).
[89] Ibid. (1883).

This survived into the following year but had apparently ceased by 1885.[90] In 1897, however, Baptists there were meeting in a hall.[91] The church then had 30 members and there were 200 pupils at the Sunday school.[92] This meeting was still being held in 1900, but had ceased by 1937.[93]

FENTON. In 1877 the North Staffordshire Baptist Association with the help of the British and Irish Home Mission appointed Clarence Chambers as Home Mission Evangelist in the North Staffordshire area. Through his mission work attention was drawn to the possibility of starting a Baptist church in Fenton.[94] In May 1881 a public hall at Fenton was taken for 12 months and in November of that year the church was formally constituted with 15 members and 5 candidates for baptism and church membership.[95] Chambers became its first minister.[96] Under the leadership of W. Bonser, minister 1882–5, the church expanded steadily through its Sunday school, open-air meetings, and cottage meetings.[97] A new schoolroom was completed in 1891 and a new chapel in 1892[98] at the corner of Victoria Street and Brunswick (now Beville) Street. By 1890 membership of the church had risen to 40 and the Sunday-school attendance then averaged 150.[99] In 1892 the church joined the West Midland Baptist Association,[1] but by 1905 was still not in the Baptist Union.[2] The membership remained almost stationary until 1900,[3] but between that date and 1937 rose slightly, being then 56;[4] it dropped again to 46 in 1946[5] and rose sharply in the succeeding ten years to 86 in 1956.[6] The average attendance at Sunday school rose slightly to 196 in 1937,[7] declined to 86 in 1946,[8] but, like the church membership, had increased again by 1956 to 115.[9] Under the North Staffordshire Federal Scheme the minister of New Street Baptist Church, Hanley, became joint minister of that church and Fenton, but since then Fenton has usually formed a joint pastorate with Eastwood Vale Church, Hanley.[10]

STOKE, QUEEN STREET. In 1818 a house in Stoke Lane, occupied by Ellen Ratcliffe, a widow, was being used for worship by a group of Particular Baptists.[11] In 1851 there was a Particular Baptist chapel in Queen (now Rebecca) Street, called Zoar Chapel, but the congregation was very small[12] and its subsequent history oannot be traced.

STOKE, LONDON ROAD. In 1841 a number of Baptists, formerly members of the General Baptist Church, Brook Street, Derby, and of Stoney Street Baptist Church, Nottingham, hired a room over a smithy in Church Street near the later Rialto Ballroom. The room was opened in June 1841 and a church was formed later in the same year with 6 members.[13] In 1851 the room seated 80 and the congregation averaged about 50.[14] In 1850 a site for a chapel in London Road was given by two members of the Church,[15] and the chapel was opened three years later.[16] A new Sunday-school building was added behind and at right angles to the chapel in 1869.[17] The latter was extended in 1879[18] and re-opened in 1880.[19] It seated 500 in 1900 and the membership was 114 with an average attendance of 250 at Sunday school.[20] This church, along with many other nonconformist bodies, showed strong resistance to the 1902 Education Act and the minister was imprisoned for non-payment of the education rate.[21] The membership of the church increased to 131 in 1913,[22] but suffered a serious decline in subsequent years and by 1920 had dropped to 86.[23] Because of serious financial difficulties a plan was then made to merge with Stoke Congregational Church, but no agreement could be reached over which church should be closed.[24] After 1932 the position of the church improved. Membership had increased to 161 in 1937,[25] and to 170 in 1946,[26] but in recent years there has again been a decline, membership numbering only 123 in 1956.[27] Attendance at the Sunday school appears to have steadily declined, averaging 250 in 1900,[28] 175 in 1937,[29] 95 in 1946,[30] and 70 in 1956.[31] The chapel is a rectangular two-story red-brick building, the front of 1879 having stone dressings.[32] The Sunday school is a red-brick building with blue-brick dressings and round-headed windows.

HANLEY, MEIGH STREET. A Particular Baptist Church was formed at Hanley in 1789; the minister in 1790 was John Hinde[33] and a chapel in New (now Goodson) Street was built in that year[34] and registered for worship early in 1791.[35] In 1794 the church had no minister,[36] but by 1798 it again had a regular minister[37] and became a member of the Midland Association of Baptist Churches in 1801.[38] It was closed, however, c. 1803. In 1819 L. J. Abington, a

[90] Ibid. (1884, 1885).
[91] Ibid. (1897).
[92] Ibid. (1900).
[93] It does not appear in the 1937 Yr. Bk. of the W. Midland Bapt. Assoc.
[94] H. S. Langley and W. Lazenby, Fenton Bapt. Ch., a brief historical sketch (copy in Birmingham Ref. Libr.).
[95] Ibid.; Bapt. Handbk. (1890).
[96] Langley and Lazenby, Fenton Bapt. Ch.
[97] Ibid. [98] Ibid.
[99] Bapt. Handbk. (1890).
[1] Langley and Lazenby, Fenton Bapt. Ch.
[2] Bapt. Handbk. (1905).
[3] Ibid. (1900).
[4] W. Midland Bapt. Assoc. Yr. Bk. (1937).
[5] Ibid. (1946).
[6] Bapt. Handbk. (1956).
[7] W. Midland Bapt. Assoc. Yr. Bk. (1937).
[8] Ibid. (1940).
[9] Bapt. Handbk. (1956).
[10] Langley and Lazenby, Fenton Bapt. Ch.
[11] S.R.O., Q/SB, East. 1818.
[12] H.O. 129/15/371/3/1.
[13] 1841–1941: London Rd. Bapt. Ch. Stoke-on-Trent (copy in Birmingham Ref. Libr.); Bapt. Handbk. (1861); H.O. 129/15/371/3/1.

[14] H.O. 129/15/371/3/1.
[15] London Rd. Bapt. Ch.
[16] Ibid.; Worship Reg. no. 1339; Records of an Old Assoc. (1905), 169–70 (copy in W.S.L.).
[17] Bapt. Handbk. (1869).
[18] Tablet in situ; London Rd. Bapt. Ch.
[19] London Rd. Bapt. Ch.
[20] Bapt. Handbk. (1900).
[21] London Rd. Bapt. Ch.
[22] Bapt. Handbk. (1913).
[23] London Rd. Bapt. Ch. [24] Ibid.
[25] W. Midland Bapt. Assoc. Yr. Bk. (1937).
[26] Ibid. (1946).
[27] Bapt. Handbk. (1956).
[28] Ibid. (1900).
[29] W. Midland Bapt. Assoc. Yr. Bk. (1937).
[30] Ibid.
[31] Bapt. Handbk. (1956).
[32] Tablet in situ.
[33] J. Rippon, The Bapt. Annual Reg. (1790), 11.
[34] H.O. 129/15/371/1/1.
[35] S.R.O., Q/SB, Ep. 1791, no. 7. The witnesses to the certificate were O. Buckley, J. Hindle, G. Crompton, John Baddeley, Wm. Pendred, Thos. Booth, and John Fallows.
[36] J. Rippon, The Bapt. Annual Reg. (1794).
[37] Ibid. (1798), 32. [38] Ibid. 554.

deacon of the Baptist Church, Little Wild Street, London, settled in Hanley and bought the chapel in an attempt to revive the Baptist movement there.[39] The chapel was reopened in 1820.[40] In 1843 the chapel seated 400[41] and attendance at chapel in 1851 averaged 190 and at Sunday school 166.[42] In 1870 the chapel had a sub-station at Joiner's Square, Hanley, later Eastwood Vale Church.[43] By 1900 membership of New Street Chapel numbered 87 and Sunday school attendance averaged 180.[44] Membership suffered a decline between the two world wars, being 42 in 1937,[45] but has since steadily risen, numbering 78 in 1946[46] and 107 in 1956.[47] The average attendance at Sunday school has also risen since the Second World War, being 95 in 1946[48] and 141 in 1956.[49] A new church was built in 1952[50] at the junction of Old Hall Street and Meigh Street and is a large brick building with a square tower over the entrance. The church is on the first floor and the schoolroom below. The old chapel which stood in New (now Goodson) Street, on a site facing Burton Place, has been demolished and an extension of the British Home Stores erected there.[51] It was a small brick building of two stories with a vestibule of one story at the front.[52]

HANLEY, EASTWOOD VALE. There was a branch of New Street Baptist Church, Hanley, at Joiner's Square in 1870.[53] The congregation of the Joiner's Square mission subsequently moved to Eastwood Vale[54] where a chapel was erected at the corner of Clifford and Paxton Streets in 1876;[55] a church was formally constituted in 1877.[56] The building was improved c. 1889.[57] The church was still not a member of the Baptist Union in 1905[58] but by 1937 had joined both the Baptist Union and the West Midland Baptist Association.[59] The chapel seated 300 in 1937 when there were 10 full members of the church and also a Sunday-school class of 80.[60] The membership rose during the Second World War to 17 in 1946[61] and has remained more or less constant, being 16 in 1956.[62] Sunday-school attendance averaged 60 in 1946[63] and 55 in 1956.[64]

HANLEY, YORK STREET. A Welsh Baptist church was organized in 1856 and its chapel in York Street, which seated 100, was possibly built at the same date.[65] It was a member of the North Wales Eastern Baptist Association by 1861,[66] and had a membership of 43 in 1862 when Sunday-school attendance averaged 40.[67] By 1900 membership had dropped to 39 and Sunday school attendance to 34.[68] It was not in the Baptist Union in 1905.[69] The society was dispersed c. 1930. By 1936 the chapel was occupied rent-free by the Brethren to whom it was sold in the following year.[70]

BURSLEM. A Baptist group was first founded in Burslem in the early 19th century. Thomas Thompson, a minister, who settled in Newcastle-under-Lyme in 1798 and preached on supply there to 'our Independent brethren' later extended his missionary activities to Burslem and Hanley, finding support at Burslem.[71] He and an inhabitant of Burslem erected a chapel in High Street in 1806[72] and shortly afterwards they with other Baptists, who had come to the area, formally founded a church[73] of Old, Particular, or Calvinistic Baptists.[74] Thompson was invited to be its first minister and was ordained to the church in 1809.[75] By 1838 there was a Sunday class attached to the church with c. 115 pupils.[76] In 1851 the attendance at the chapel averaged 80 and at Sunday school 50.[77] By 1861 the church was a member of the Lancashire and Cheshire Baptist Union;[78] in 1862 it had 44 members and attendance at Sunday school averaged 80.[79] The chapel, which seated 120,[80] was sold c. 1873 to the Burslem Ragged School and a new chapel seating 370, also in High Street, was built.[81] The membership had increased by 1900 to 97[82] and the Sunday-school attendance then averaged 200.[83] By 1937 there were only 57 members.[84] The chapel was burnt down in 1944,[85] but the church continued until 1949, its members, who in that year numbered 46,[86] worshipping either at Hanley or Newcastle.[87] The site of the chapel was then sold, its funds wound up, and the church dispersed.[88] Part of the funds went in 1949 towards the cost of the new manse at Newcastle, part to the building of Hanley New Street Baptist Church, and part in 1952 to the

[39] *Records of an Old Assoc.* [40] Ibid.
[41] Ward, *Stoke*, 402, 403.
[42] H.O. 129/15/371/1/1.
[43] *Bapt. Handbk.* (1870).
[44] Ibid. (1900).
[45] *W. Midland Bapt. Assoc. Yr. Bk.* (1937).
[46] Ibid. (1940).
[47] *Bapt. Handbk.* (1956).
[48] *W. Midland Bapt. Assoc. Yr. Bk.* (1946).
[49] *Bapt. Handbk.* (1956).
[50] Worship Reg. no. 63604; tablet *in situ.*
[51] Local inf.
[52] A photograph of the old chapel is included in the programme for the opening of the new church (copy in W.S.L. pamphs. *sub* Hanley).
[53] *Bapt. Handbk.* (1870).
[54] Ex. inf. the Revd. T. Hough, Minister, Meigh St. Ch., Hanley (1958).
[55] Tablet *in situ.*
[56] *Bapt. Handbk.* (1900).
[57] Ibid. (1899). [58] Ibid. (1905).
[59] Ibid. (1937); *W. Midland Bapt. Assoc. Yr. Bk.* (1937).
[60] *W. Midland Bapt. Assoc. Yr. Bk.* (1937).
[61] Ibid. (1940).
[62] *Bapt. Handbk.* (1956).
[63] *W. Midland Bapt. Assoc. Yr. Bk.* (1946).
[64] Ibid. (1956).
[65] *Bapt. Handbk.* (1861, 1900). The date of the establishment of the ch. is alternatively given as 1868 (Char. Com. files) which may be when the chap. was built.

[66] Ibid. (1861).
[67] Ibid. (1862).
[68] Ibid. (1900).
[69] Ibid. (1905).
[70] Char. Com. files.
[71] Dr. Williams's Libr., Wilson MSS. i. 45. The 'Independent brethren' may have been the worshippers at the Old Meeting House: see p. 64.
[72] Dr. Williams's Libr., Wilson MSS. i. 45; H.O. 129/15/370/3/1; Lich. Dioc. Regy., Bp.'s Reg. E, p. 265. The other witnesses to the regtn. were John Hall, Simon Sollary, and Thos. Fletcher.
[73] Dr. Williams's Libr., Wilson MSS. i. 45.
[74] Char. Com. files; *Supp. Digest of Char. Don.* [C. 70], H.C. (1891–2), lix.
[75] Dr. Williams's Libr., Wilson MSS. i. 45.
[76] Ward, *Stoke*, 245.
[77] H.O. 129/15/370/3/1.
[78] *Bapt. Handbk.* (1861).
[79] Ibid. (1862).
[80] H.O. 129/15/370/3/1.
[81] Char. Com. files; *Bapt. Handbk.* (1900).
[82] *Bapt. Handbk.* (1900).
[83] Ibid.
[84] *W. Midland Bapt. Assoc. Yr. Bk.* (1937).
[85] Char. Com. files.
[86] It drops out of the Yr. Bks. of the W. Midland Bapt. Assoc. in 1950.
[87] Char. Com. files.
[88] Ibid.

cost of the new Sunday school at Newcastle.[89] The first chapel remained the Ragged School until the 1930's but is now used by the Shaftesbury Society which has local preachers here although no permanent minister.[90]

BURSLEM, WATERLOO ROAD. Ebenezer Baptist Church in Waterloo Road, Burslem, was registered for worship in 1902 but the registration was cancelled in 1906.[91]

TUNSTALL. A Baptist chapel was opened in Market (now Tower) Square in 1888, and probably occupied the former New Connexion Chapel there; by 1890 the church had 13 members.[92] It had been closed by 1900.[93]

LATEBROOK. A Baptist church was founded at Latebrook in 1877 and in 1890 seated 150.[94] It then had 22 full members.[95] In 1900 it was still autonomous,[96] but by 1905 it had become a branch of Newcastle Baptist Church.[97] By 1937 it had apparently reverted to its independent status, with a membership of 17 and a Sunday-school class of 72 members.[98] The membership rose slightly during the Second World War and stood at 22 in 1946.[99] Subsequently it dropped, and when the church closed in 1956 there were only 12 members.[1] The chapel is a small brick building in Broadfield Road.

Bethel Evangelistic Society

LONGTON. The Bethel Evangelistic Society registered the Bethel Temple in Dunrobin Street for worship in 1932.[2] Meetings were still being held in 1958.[3]

HANLEY, CAULDON ROAD. Bethel Temple at the junction of Boughey and Cauldon Roads, Hanley Park, was registered for worship in 1930.[4] It apparently left the Bethel Evangelistic Society in 1933[5] and closed the following year.[6]

HANLEY, NEWHALL STREET. In 1932 Bethel Temple in Newhall Street was registered for worship.[7] In 1945 the society acquired the lease of Hope Congregational Church where it still held meetings in 1958.

BURSLEM. A Bethel Mission hall on the first floor of 12 St. John's Square was registered for worship by the Bethel Evangelistic Society in 1931.[8]

TUNSTALL. A Bethel Mission hall at 101 Well (now Roundwell) Street was registered for worship in 1931. The registration was cancelled in 1939.[9]

MILTON. A Bethel Mission hall in Market Street was registered for worship in 1931. The registration was cancelled in 1944.[10]

The Brethren (Plymouth Brethren)

STOKE, TRENT VALE. Swan Lane Gospel Hall, Claytonwood Road, Trent Vale, was registered for public worship by the Brethren in 1939. It had ceased to be used by 1954.[11]

HANLEY. By 1936 the Brethren were occupying the former Baptist Chapel in York Street, Eastwood Vale. In 1937 they bought the chapel.[12]

British Israel World Federation

HANLEY. Two rooms on the second floor of 61 Stafford Street were registered for worship by the British Israelites in 1934.[13]

Catholic Apostolic Church

STOKE and FENTON. A Catholic Apostolic Church in Church Street, Stoke, was registered for worship in 1879,[14] and in 1880 daily services were being held in it.[15] In 1896 a new church was erected at the corner of Whieldon Road and City Road, Fenton.[16] This was still in use in 1940[17] but was probably closed in 1955.[18] The church, which has a Sunday-school building attached to it, is a large brick building and by 1958 was in use as a Gospel Hall. The former church, which for a time was also used as a Gospel Hall, is a smaller brick building and is faced with stone. It stands at the junction of Bowstead and Church Streets and in 1958 was used as a workshop.

Christadelphians or Brethren of Christ

The small Christadelphian Ecclesia in North Staffordshire was formed in 1910 and worshipped originally on the first floor of Sutherland Chambers, High Street, Stoke.[19] After a period at Hanley, it returned to Stoke, where it used no. 9 Majestic Chambers, Campbell Place, in 1935[20] and Lonsdale House, Woodhouse Street, in 1936.[21] It moved to Newcastle c. 1938 and thence to the Co-operative Guildroom, Tunstall, in 1953.[22] In addition to the normal meetings the activities of this group included in recent years a Bible study class which was held for some time in the Moorland Café, Burslem.[23]

Christian Brethren[24]

LONGTON. In 1851 a group of Christian Brethren was using the Vauxhall schoolroom for worship.[25] Attendance was about 40.[26] This group was still meeting in 1859[27] but nothing more is known of it.

STOKE. The Stoke meeting of the Christian Brethren probably started in 1842.[28] In 1851 attendance was small but there was a Sunday school which about

---

[89] Ibid.; *Bapt. Handbk.* (1953).
[90] Local inf.
[91] Worship Reg. no. 38841.
[92] *Bapt. Handbk.* (1890).
[93] Ibid. (1900).
[94] Ibid. (1890).   [95] Ibid.
[96] Ibid. (1900).
[97] Ibid. (1905).
[98] *W. Midland Bapt. Assoc. Yr. Bk.* (1937).
[99] Ibid. (1946).
[1] *Bapt. Handbk.* (1956); ex inf. the Revd. T. Hough, Minister, Meigh St. Ch., Hanley (1958).
[2] Worship Reg. no. 53978.
[3] Local inf.
[4] Worship Reg. no. 52866.
[5] Ibid. no. 54784. The denomination is only given as Free Church in this regtn.   [6] Ibid.
[7] Ibid. no. 53598.
[8] Ibid. no. 53261.
[9] Ibid. no. 53358.
[10] Ibid. no. 53097.

[11] Ibid. no. 58782. The regtn. was cancelled on revision of the official list.   [12] Char. Com. files.
[13] Worship Reg. no. 55612.
[14] Ibid. no. 24373; *Kelly's Dir. Staffs.* (1880).
[15] *Kelly's Dir. Staffs.* (1880).
[16] Worship Reg. no. 35061; *Kelly's Dir. Staffs.* (1896).
[17] *Kelly's Dir. Staffs.* (1896).
[18] Its regtn. was cancelled in that year: Worship Reg. no. 24373.
[19] Ex inf. Mr. A. E. Hill, Hon. Sec., Stoke-on-Trent and Newcastle (Staffs.) Christadelphian Ecclesia (1958); Worship Reg. no. 47228.
[20] Ex inf. Mr. Hill; Worship Reg. no. 55735.
[21] Worship Reg. no. 56727.
[22] Ex inf. Mr. Hill.   [23] Ex inf. Mr. Hill.
[24] In the Potteries this sect was closely associated with Unitarianism: *Unitarian Hist. Soc.* vi. 14–28.
[25] H.O. 129/15/371/5/2.   [26] Ibid.
[27] *Unit. Hist. Soc.* vi. 14–38.
[28] H.O. 129/15/371/3/1. This may only be the date of the building, however.

100 children attended.[29] The society was still in being in 1859,[30] but nothing more is known of it.

HANLEY. There was a Christian Brethren Preacher's Library at Hanley, in Market Street, in 1845; this lasted until at least 1848.[31]

TUNSTALL. Joseph Barker, after his expulsion from the Methodist New Connexion in 1841, started preaching in the shells of three cottages recently built in Tunstall, which formed a Sunday school and preaching-room. About 1842 the Christian Brethren movement reached its height there and greatly decreased the strength of Tunstall Methodist New Connexion Chapel.[32] Nothing further is known about this group.

The Christian Society[33]

BURSLEM. In 1838 there were said to be meetings of the Christian Society in most of the Pottery towns.[34] The group in Burslem used Zoar Chapel,[35] which it bought in that year. Zoar was sold by the Christian Society in 1842 to the Primitive Methodist Connexion.[36] Nothing further is known of this society in the Potteries.[37]

Church of Christ

BURSLEM. Wedgwood Mission Hall in Wedgwood Street was registered for meetings of the Church of Christ in 1890.[38] The group moved to the Church of Christ Meeting House in Macclesfield Street in 1913.[39] This was still in use in 1958.[40]

TUNSTALL. In 1897 the Church of Christ registered the Christian Meeting Room, Goodfellow Street, as a place of worship.[41] This continued in use until 1927 when the Church of Christ, Pinnox Street, was opened.[42] This was still in use in 1940[43] but was closed by or in 1955[44] and the building sold.[45]

Church of Christ Scientist

STOKE. Two rooms, 5 First Floor, Glebe Buildings, Glebe Street, were registered for public worship in 1913 by Christian Scientists.[46]

LONGTON, NORMACOT. A Christian Science meeting-place in Uttoxeter Road was registered for public worship by Christian Scientists in 1937.[47]

HANLEY, SHELTON. In 1940 the First Church of Christ Scientist, Avenue Road (formerly Park Avenue), was registered for public worship.[48]

Church of the Seventh Day Advent

HARTSHILL. An Advent Church in 'The Schoolroom', in The Avenue, Hartshill, was registered for worship in 1940.[49] The registration was cancelled in 1949.[50]

Congregational Churches

LONGTON. The first Congregational church at Longton resulted from a secession from the parish church after the departure of a low-church minister. This group, after using a room in St. Martin's Lane previously used by the Baptists, erected a temporary meeting-house in a court off Market Square and then a chapel in Caroline Street which was opened in 1820. A church was formed at the beginning of 1821. Membership was then 17.[51] In 1841 Sunday-school attendance averaged 200.[52] In the first quarter of 1851 average attendance at the church was 150 in the morning and 250 in the evening and the Sunday-school attendance still averaged 200.[53] In 1957 membership was 59.[54] A new chapel was built in 1905[55] in front of the old chapel. It is a brick building in the Perpendicular style.

LONGTON, DRESDEN. A second Congregational church in Longton came into being when the Staffordshire Congregational Union sent an evangelist to preach at Dresden c. 1868. There was difficulty in finding premises, but in 1869 the Union provided an iron chapel which was described as 'an ornament to the locality'.[56] Part of the proceeds of the sale of Alton chapel went towards the erection of a schoolroom in 1872 which cost £200.[57] A new chapel was erected in Belgrave Road in 1885,[58] replaced by another in 1906.[59] The membership was 25 in 1957 and the chapel then seated 450.[60]

STOKE. About the year 1780 Jonathan Scott, commonly known as Captain Scott, preached in the streets of Stoke, but there is no evidence that a Congregational church resulted immediately from his visits.[61] About the turn of the century interest was aroused and in 1823 a chapel was built in Thomas Street (now Aquinas Street).[62] This meeting was short lived and the chapel was sold before 1834 to the Quakers.[63] In 1833 an attempt was made to revive Congregationalism in Stoke by meetings in a room at an inn, but this was unsatisfactory and the attempt was abandoned.[64] Land was bought for a chapel c. 1838, but subsequently resold.[65] In 1850,

[29] H.O. 129/15/371/3/1. [30] Unit. Hist. Soc. vi. 14–28.
[31] The bks. of the Newcastle Meeting House Libr. were lent to it: Unit. Hist. Soc. vi. 14–28; Pegler, The Old Meeting House, 8.
[32] J. Young, After One Hundred Years: Burslem Circuit (1903), 105–6 (copy in H.R.L.)
[33] This body was formed by the followers of the Revd. Robert Aitken, who seceded from the Church of England: D.N.B.; Ward, Stoke, 36; Chappell, In the Power of God, 32.
[34] Ward, Stoke, 36.
[35] Chappell, In the Power of God, 32; Young, After One Hundred Years: Burslem Circuit (1903), 31–39.
[36] Chappell, op. cit. 32; Young, op. cit. 31–39.
[37] Aitken re-entered the C. of E. in 1840 and the Christian Society probably dispersed about this date: D.N.B.
[38] Worship Reg. no. 32181.
[39] Ibid. no. 45677.
[40] The regtn. has not been cancelled: ibid.
[41] Ibid. no. 35904. [42] Ibid. no. 50842.
[43] Kelly's Dir. Staffs. (1940).
[44] The regtn. was cancelled in 1955: Worship Reg. no. 50842. [45] Char. Com. files.
[46] Worship Reg. no. 45577.
[47] Ibid. no. 57438. [48] Ibid. no. 59402.

[49] Ibid. no. 59145. [50] Ibid.
[51] Matthews, Cong. Chs. of Staffs. 176. The 1851 Census return gives 1819 as the date of erection: H.O. 129/15/371/5/2. The original trust deed is dated 1825: Char. Com. files. [52] Ward, Stoke, 571.
[53] H.O. 129/15/371/5/2.
[54] Staffs. Cong. Yr. Bk. (1957), 2.
[55] Tablet in situ; Worship Reg. no. 41805. The previous chap. was registered in 1861: ibid. no. 14499.
[56] Matthews, Cong. Chs. of Staffs. 227. The building is dated 1868, however, and the original trust deed is dated 1871: Char. Com. files.
[57] Matthews, Cong. Chs. of Staffs. 227–8.
[58] Ibid. 241; Worship Reg. no. 28778.
[59] Matthews, Cong. Chs. of Staffs. 245.
[60] Staffs. Cong. Yr. Bk. (1957).
[61] Matthews, Cong. Chs. of Staffs. 133.
[62] White, Dir. Staffs. (1834); Lich. Dioc. Regy., Bp.'s Reg. G., p. 537.
[63] White, Dir. Staffs. (1834). The Quaker meeting started in 1831, possibly the date of the sale of this building: ex inf. The Librarian, Friends House; see p. 304.
[64] Matthews, Cong. Chs. of Staffs. 225.
[65] Ibid. 225–6.

however, the Congregationalists started to hold services in the town hall[66] and in 1851 formed themselves into a church.[67] Attendance then averaged about 70 people.[68] Shortly afterwards the worshippers moved to a building in Queen Street where they remained until 1855 when Copeland Street Chapel was built.[69] Lecture rooms and class-rooms costing £1,100 were added in 1876.[70] In 1920, because of financial difficulties, amalgamation with Stoke Baptist Church was considered, but the proposal fell through because of disagreement over which church should be closed.[71] This church, which seated 450, was closed in 1937.[72] Proceeds of the sale of the building helped to pay for the erection of the new Congregational church at Clayton.[73]

HANLEY, THE TABERNACLE. Hanley Congregationalism originated in the visits of Captain Jonathan Scott, who preached in the streets of Hanley, and of George Burder who, on one day in 1781, preached in the morning at Burslem, in the afternoon at Hanley, and in the evening at Newcastle.[74] A long room was taken at Hanley and in 1784 a chapel was built called The Tabernacle after George Whitefield's Tabernacle in London.[75] The Sunday school was opened in 1785 by the Tabernacle's first minister, James Boden,[76] who, besides furthering the work of his own chapel, greatly helped in Congregational evangelical work and was responsible for the founding of Stafford Congregational church.[77] This tradition of evangelical work was carried on by The Tabernacle's second minister, James Little,[78] and by 1800 The Tabernacle not only had a good congregation but was also regarded as the centre of Congregational work in the north of Staffordshire.[79] For example, there was a meeting at Hanley in 1799 of all Congregational ministers from Shropshire, Cheshire, and Staffordshire to discuss plans for the maintenance of itinerant preachers and for training ministers. Although this project was not realized,[80] the later North Staffordshire Lay Preachers' Association regarded Hanley Tabernacle as its centre and usually held its meetings there.[81] Later ministers also carried on the tradition of mission work in the surrounding country.[82] In 1840 The Tabernacle was enlarged[83] and in 1851 seated nearly 900.[84] Average attendance was then said to be 400.[85] Sunday-school buildings were added in 1860;[86] in 1883 a new Tabernacle was erected in High Street (now Town Road) opposite the old

Tabernacle,[87] which was then sold.[88] It cost over £16,000 and a further £1,000 was spent in 1893 in enlarging the Sunday schools.[89] The building seats 1,050 and the membership of the church in 1957 was 83.[90] A mission was established in Union Street from The Tabernacle in 1879 (see below). In 1960 the first chapel was in use as a roller-skating rink and the original brick front, dating from 1784, is partly obscured by a modern addition. It still retains, however, a central pediment above a Venetian window and one of its two pedimented doorways. The former minister's house, which adjoins the chapel on the south side, appears to be of the same date or a little later. The present chapel on the opposite side of Town Road is a large red-brick building in the Perpendicular style with stone dressings.

HANLEY, THE TABERNACLE TOWN MISSION. In 1879 Union Street Mission Hall was erected by members of The Tabernacle church.[91] In 1957 there were 40 members.[92] The original red-brick building was extended in 1901.[93] Seating capacity in 1957 was 300.[94]

HANLEY, HOPE STREET. A second Congregational church was formed when a number of members seceded from The Tabernacle after the expulsion of one of the deacons for drunkenness.[95] After worshipping for some years in a temporary building, this group built a chapel for themselves in Hope Street which was opened in October 1812[96] and seated 600.[97] Attendance averaged about 70 in 1851.[98] Alterations and renovations were carried out in 1891.[99] The church declined after 1938, and in 1945 the chapel was let as the Hanley Bethel Temple to the Evangelical Free Church.[1] It is a two-story red-brick building with stone dressings fronting upon New Hall Street. A stone pediment bears the words '1812 Hope Congregational Church 1891', the latter date presumably referring to the alterations of that year. Twin doorways of the original date have semicircular fanlights and are flanked by Tuscan pillars. There is a schoolroom behind, erected in 1835,[2] also of red brick. In 1840 about 300 children attended the school,[3] but in 1851 only about 80.[4]

HANLEY, WELSH, OR CAPEL YR ANNIBYNWYR. A Welsh Congregational church was founded in 1850 in Market Square.[5] It had an average attendance of 70 in 1851.[6] Later a chapel was built in Mayer Street. Its seating capacity in 1957 was 350 and it

[66] Ibid. 226; H.O. 129/15/371/3/1.
[67] Matthews, *Cong. Chs. of Staffs.* 226.
[68] H.O. 129/15/371/3–1.
[69] Matthews, *Cong. Chs. of Staffs.* 226; Worship Reg. no. 14317.
[70] Matthews, *Cong. Chs. of Staffs.* 241.
[71] *London Rd. Bapt. Ch., Stoke-on-Trent* (copy in Birmingham Ref. Libr.).
[72] *Cong. Yr. Bk.* (1938), 414; Worship Reg. no. 14317. The regtn. was cancelled in 1938: ex. inf. Staffs. Cong. Union.
[73] Ex inf. Staffs. Cong. Union; see p. 58.
[74] Matthews, *Cong. Chs. of Staffs.* 133, 136; H. F. Burder, *Memoir of G. Burder*, 22 sqq.
[75] Matthews, *Cong. Chs. of Staffs.* 164; H.O. 129/15/371/1/1; Q/SB, Ep. 1784, no. 3.
[76] Matthews, *Cong. Chs. of Staffs.* 195.
[77] Ibid. 133, 166.
[78] Ibid. 166.
[79] Ibid.
[80] Ibid. 172.
[81] Ibid. *passim.*
[82] e.g. R. W. Newland: ibid. 176, 177, 210, 219.

[83] Ibid. 219.
[84] H.O. 129/15/371/1/1.
[85] Ibid.
[86] Matthews, *Cong. Chs. of Staffs.* 234.
[87] Matthews, *Cong. Chs. of Staffs.* 241. It was then described as a nonconformist cathedral.
[88] Char. Com. files.
[89] Matthews, *Cong. Chs. of Staffs.* 241.
[90] *Staffs. Cong. Yr. Bk.* (1957).
[91] Matthews, *Cong. Chs. of Staffs.* 241.
[92] *Staffs. Cong. Yr. Bk.* (1957).
[93] Tablet *in situ.*
[94] *Staffs. Cong. Yr. Bk.* (1957).
[95] Matthews, *Cong. Chs. of Staffs.* 175–6.
[96] Ibid.
[97] Ward, *Stoke*, 402; H.O. 129/15/371/2/1.
[98] H.O. 129/15/371/2/1.
[99] Matthews, *Cong. Chs. of Staffs.* 242.
[1] *Staffs. Cong. Yr. Bk.* (1938 and later edns. to 1945); board *in situ.*
[2] Ward, *Stoke*, 402; tablet *in situ.*
[3] Ward, *Stoke*, 402.
[4] H.O. 129/15/371/2/1.
[5] *Staffs. Cong. Yr. Bk.* (1957); H.O. 129/15/371/1/1.
[6] H.O. 129/15/371/1/1.

then had 40 members.[7] The chapel is a red-brick building in the Gothic style with a rose window in its front wall. It has a small tower at the side over the porch.

HANLEY, HANLEY PARK. In 1898 an iron tabernacle was erected on land in Cauldon Road, Hanley Park, acquired mainly through the efforts of T. W. Harrison. The following year a church was formed mainly of members transferred from Hanley Tabernacle. The Twentieth Century Fund of the Staffordshire Congregational Union helped to provide a new chapel, with a school, which was opened in October 1901.[8] The iron chapel was moved to Wolstanton.[9] The membership of the church was 25 in 1957[10] and the chapel, which is a building in the Gothic style, seats 450.

BURSLEM. The first Congregational meetings began in the house of a Mr. Bailey at Greenhead c. 1819. Previously there had been a more ambitious scheme of building a chapel in Burslem, but the promoters of it appear to have turned their attention to Hanley Tabernacle, completed in 1784. However, R. W. Newland, minister at Hanley from 1816 to 1839, took great interest in the group at Burslem. He enlisted the help of Thomas Wilson of London, who sent a student to act as pastor under Newland's guidance. After removing for a while to a crate shop at the rear of Navigation Road the worshippers obtained a larger building fronting on the same road and in May 1821 formed themselves into a church.[11] Early in 1825, however, they leased Zoar Chapel, 'The Salt Box', from Aaron Sant, who had purchased it from the Methodist New Connexion, at a rent of £40 yearly.[12] The Congregationalists used Zoar until 1826 when they relinquished it because they could not afford the rent,[13] and moved back to Mr. Bailey's house at Greenhead.[14] In 1828, however, Newland was instrumental in purchasing Zoar for the Congregationalists and they continued to use it until 1838 when a new chapel in Queen Street, erected at a cost of £3,300, was opened.[15] Zoar was then sold.[16] In the first quarter of 1851 the congregation on Sundays averaged 180 in the morning and 160 in the evening, and attendance at Sunday school 60 in the morning and 130 in the afternoon.[17] Wycliffe Hall was opened as a mission church from Queen Street on 1885.[18] Queen Street Church was replaced in 1906 by the present church in Moorland Road, called the Woodall Memorial Church in memory of William Woodall, M.P. This seats 550,[19] and had 128 members in 1957.[20]

Queen Street Church was described in 1841 as 'a handsome structure of brick with very lofty windows'.[21] It had an open vestibule on the ground floor formed by Tuscan columns and pilasters of stone within which were two flights of steps leading to the chapel. The chapel seated 400 and had an end gallery in which there was an organ. The ground floor also contained schoolrooms and a vestry.[22] The William Woodall Memorial Church is a red-brick building with stone dressings.

Wycliffe Hall in Furlong Parade, was built in 1885 at a cost of £3,300 as a mission church and Sunday school attached to Queen Street Congregational Church.[23] It was in use until at least 1916 for services[24] and was used as a Sunday school attached to Woodall Memorial Church after that date. It was abandoned because of a shift in the population to new development areas and was sold in 1942 to Burslem Gospel Mission.[25]

BURSLEM, DALE HALL. In 1867 the Congregationalists registered for worship the former Wesleyan Reform Chapel in Dale Street.[26] It had ceased to be used by 1886.[27]

TUNSTALL. The Revd. W. Moseley, Congregational minister at Hanley Tabernacle, 1802–14, occasionally preached in Tunstall.[28] About 1807 he was offered a site for a chapel but no chapel was built,[29] and it was nearly 50 years before a church was founded. The impetus came from the North Staffs. Itinerant Lay Preachers' Association who discussed the possibility of starting a church in Tunstall at their quarterly meeting held in December 1852 at Hanley Tabernacle.[30] Nield's Assembly Room (the former Methodist New Connexion chapel), Market Place, Tunstall, was rented and the first services were held in July 1853.[31] In 1854 Thomas Bostock of Port Vale Potteries, one of the founder members, tried to interest the Home Missionary Society in Tunstall but a request for one of their ministers was rejected.[32] The church secured its first minister in 1857.[33] Land was acquired in 1856 for a chapel but it was not until 1862 that a school-chapel in High Street was opened.[34] The Sunday school had started in 1855 with about 30 children and by 1862 had an average attendance of 115.[35] A new chapel was completed in 1879 which seats 500.[36] The church, which was frequently without a minister, has had a chequered history. For example, between the end of the Second World War and 1952 there was no minister and the Sunday-school attendance dwindled to about 50 or 60. In

[7] Staffs. Cong. Yr. Bk. (1957).
[8] Matthews, Cong. Chs. of Staffs. 238–9; Kelly's Dir. Staffs. (1912).
[9] See p. 59.
[10] Staffs. Cong. Yr. Bk. (1957).
[11] Matthews, Cong. Chs. of Staffs. 176–7.
[12] J. Young, After One Hundred Years: Burslem Bethel Circuit (1903), 32, 39; Matthews, Cong. Chs. of Staffs. 176–7.
[13] Young, op. cit. 32–39.
[14] Matthews, Cong. Chs. of Staffs. 176–7.
[15] Ibid.
[16] Young, op. cit. 32–39.
[17] H.O. 129/15/570/3/1.
[18] Matthews, Cong. Chs. of Staffs. 241.
[19] Ibid. 245; Staffs. Cong. Yr. Bk. (1957).
[20] Staffs. Cong. Yr. Bk. (1957).
[21] Ward, Stoke, 246.   [22] Ibid.
[23] Kelly's Dir. Staffs. (1896); Matthews, Cong. Chs. of Staffs. 241; Char. Com. files.

[24] Kelly's Dir. Staffs. (1916).
[25] Ex inf. the Revd. J. E. Williams, Minister, Woodall Memorial Ch. (1958); Char. Com. files.
[26] Worship Reg. no. 18087.
[27] Ibid.; see p. 124.
[28] Tunstall Cong. Ch. 1853–1953 (copy in H.R.L.); Matthews, Cong. Chs. of Staffs. 226.
[29] Tunstall Cong. Ch.; Matthews, Cong. Chs. of Staffs. 226.
[30] Tunstall Cong. Ch.; Matthews, Cong. Chs. of Staffs. 226–7.
[31] Tunstall Cong. Ch.; Matthews, Cong. Chs. of Staffs. 226–7. The Assembly Room was registered in 1860: Worship Reg. no. 9827.
[32] Matthews, Cong. Chs. of Staffs. 227.
[33] Tunstall Cong. Ch.
[34] Ibid.; Matthews, Cong. Chs. of Staffs.; Worship Reg. no. 15227.
[35] Tunstall Cong. Ch.
[36] Ibid.

1953, however, attendance was almost twice that number,[37] while in 1957 membership of the church numbered 80.[38] The chapel is a brick building on the west side of High Street.

MILTON. Congregationalism at Milton dates from the beginning of the 19th century.[39] Lay preachers from Hanley preached at Bagnall, Baddeley Edge, and Milton.[40] Jonas Forrister's house was registered as a nonconformist meeting-place in 1806.[41] A small chapel in Eaves Lane was opened in 1808.[42] James Cartledge was largely responsible for the erection of a new chapel which was registered in 1819. About 40 years later Samuel Adams added a schoolroom and in 1880 a new chapel was built on the corner of Market Street (now Millrise Road) and Adam Street.[43] The chapel seated 230.[44] In 1922 after unavailing requests from the Congregational Union that the congregation should conform to the trust deeds, the Union as trustees closed the chapel.[45] The property was sold and by 1937 was used as a Gospel Mission.[46] The sum raised contributed to the building of Clayton Congregational Church.[47]

GOLDENHILL. There has never been a Congregational Church in Goldenhill, but for a time Christ Church was served by Congregational ministers.[48]

Elim Four Square Gospel Alliance[49]

LONGTON. An Elim Four Square Gospel Alliance church at Longton was registered for worship in 1956. It stands in Lightwood Road[50] and is a long weather-boarded building.

Free Church (Undenominational)

GOLDENHILL, CHRIST CHURCH. Christ Church originated in an evangelical secession from St. John's Church, Goldenhill, on the appointment in 1873 of a high churchman to the benefice.[51] When the living became vacant, Bishop Selwyn, himself a high churchman, appointed the Revd. Osmond Dobree, formerly chaplain of a private chapel at Knypersley and a known high churchman. Immediately a petition against the appointment was presented by the parishioners to the bishop and also published in the local press. Dobree offered to withdraw but the bishop refused the offer and instituted him in September of the same year. Only six parishioners were present, however, and even before the institution the schismatics were holding services in private houses. J. Henshall Williamson provided a corrugated-iron church which was erected in what was later called Williamson Street. Services began there in 1874. The first two ministers are believed to have been ordained members of the Congregational Church. On Williamson's death the church was

offered by his widow to the Bishop of Lichfield on condition that there should always be an evangelical curate there, but Bishop Maclagan could not accept the condition. On Mrs. Williamson's death the congregation bought the building and for some time the Congregational minister from Tunstall helped with the services. During the present century, however, the church has had to rely on the services of lay preachers. A new church has been erected since 1944 in front of the old and is a weather-boarded building.

International Holiness Mission or Church of the Nazarene[52]

FENTON. In 1920 the International Holiness Mission, later designated The Church of the Nazarene, registered a mission chapel at the corner of Victoria Road and Church Street for public worship.[53] In 1935 the group moved to Regent (now Smithpool) Road.[54]

SHELTON. In 1931 the International Holiness Mission registered Leek Road Tabernacle, Leek Road, for worship.[55] The Tabernacle is a long single-story wooden hut and was still used in 1958.

Jehovah's Witnesses

LONGTON. In 1940 the Jehovah's Witnesses registered the ground floor of 104 Stafford Street as a Kingdom Hall.[56] The registration was cancelled in 1948,[57] but in 1956 they again registered a Kingdom Hall at 22 Market Street.[58]

STOKE. In 1944 the Jehovah's Witnesses registered the former B.B.C. studio, on the first floor of Majestic Buildings, South Wolfe Street, as a Kingdom Hall. It was re-registered in 1950.[59]

STOKE, BASFORD. The Jehovah's Witnesses registered a building in Victoria Street as a Kingdom Hall in 1940. The registration was cancelled in 1948.[60]

HANLEY. In 1940 the Jehovah's Witnesses registered the first floor of a building in Glass Street as a Kingdom Hall.[61] They moved to 10 Percy Street Chambers in 1945.[62]

BURSLEM and TUNSTALL. In 1943 the Jehovah's Witnesses registered 20 Brick House Street as a Kingdom Hall.[63] In 1949 this group moved to 473 High Street, Tunstall,[64] and in 1952 to 71 Roundwell Street, Tunstall.[65]

SMALLTHORNE. In 1956 the Jehovah's Witnesses registered a building as a Kingdom Hall.[66]

Latter Day Saints

LONGTON. In 1841 the Mechanics' Institute was used by the Latter Day Saints for worship.[67] This

[37] Ibid.
[38] Staffs. Cong. Yr. Bk. (1957).
[39] Matthews, Cong. Chs. of Staffs. 125.
[40] Evangelical Mag. (1810), 491.
[41] Lich. Dioc. Regy., Bp's Reg. E, p. 265.
[42] Evang. Mag. (1809), 131.
[43] Matthews, Cong. Chs. of Staffs. 175, 241; Worship Reg., no. 24889.
[44] Cong. Yr. Bk. (1924), 220.
[45] Ex inf. the Revd. L. Mares, Sec., Staffs. Cong. Union (1958). However, it is still included in the Yr. Bk. for 1924.
[46] Ex inf. the Revd. L. Mares; see p. 304.
[47] Ex inf. the Revd. L. Mares; see p. 58.
[48] See below.
[49] Pastor Geo. Jeffreys, who founded this sect in 1915, preached in the Potteries: local inf.
[50] Worship Reg. no. 65341.

[51] The above account is taken from J. Jack, The Ch. on the Hill, 18–26 (copy in W.S.L.)
[52] This body had only 28 churches in Great Britain in 1952: World Christian Handbk.
[53] Worship Reg. no. 47633.
[54] Ibid. no. 56219.
[55] Ibid. no. 53236.
[56] Ibid. no. 59202.   [57] Ibid.
[58] Ibid. no. 65909.
[59] Ibid. nos. 60803, 62814.
[60] Ibid. no. 59227.
[61] Ibid. no. 59505.
[62] Ibid. no. 61086.
[63] Ibid. no. 60526.
[64] Ibid. no. 63224.
[65] Ibid. no. 63401.
[66] Ibid. no. 65883.   [67] Ward, Stoke, 571.

group had apparently ceased to meet by 1851 as there is no return for it in the census of that year.

STOKE, TRENT VALE. In 1856 the Latter Day Saints registered the premises of John Edwards, previously a joiner's shop, for worship. The group had ceased to meet there by 1876.[68]

HANLEY. A room in Hanley was registered for worship by the Re-organized Latter Day Saints in 1889.[69] In 1892 the group moved to The Saints Mission Hall, 35–36 Bath (now Garth) Street, Hanley.[70] Nothing further is known of it.

HANLEY. Two rooms on the first floor of Florence Chambers, 14 Perry Street, were registered for worship by the Latter Day Saints in 1942.[71]

BURSLEM. There was a meeting of Latter Day Saints at Burslem by 1860.[72] In 1884 the group registered the Gospel Hall, Queen Street, for worship. The registration was cancelled in 1896[73] but the meeting may have ceased by 1892.[74]

Wesleyan Methodist Church

LONGTON, CHAPEL STREET and STAFFORD STREET (now THE STRAND). A building was erected in Longton for Methodist worship in 1783.[75] Wesley first preached there in the following year in the open air, as the meeting-house was too small to hold the congregation.[76] In 1804 a new chapel was built in what became Chapel Street[77] and was subsequently used both for worship and as a Sunday school.[78] As the congregation grew need arose for a new chapel; this was erected in 1842 on land in Stafford Street[79] and in 1851 seated 500.[80] Attendance on 30 March 1851 was returned as 250 in the morning and 400 in the evening.[81] In 1877 alterations, including ornamentation of the interior pillars, were made to the chapel.[82] In 1940 it seated 1,100[83] and is a brick building with Classical features. In 1933 it became Longton Central Mission.[84] Shortly after the building of Stafford Street Chapel, Chapel Street Chapel was converted into Sunday-school buildings. By 1855 new schools had been built at the rear of Stafford Street Chapel and the old chapel was sold.[85]

LONGTON, HIGH STREET (now UTTOXETER ROAD). A second and smaller Wesleyan chapel was erected in High Street *c.* 1812.[86] In 1851 it seated 390 and had an attendance of 170 in the morning and 102 in

the evening of 30 March of that year.[87] Probably by 1853 this chapel had seceded from the Wesleyan Methodist Church and joined the Methodist (or Wesleyan) Reform Church.[88] Its subsequent history is treated below.[89]

LONGTON, EAST VALE. A school-chapel was erected at East Vale in 1875.[90] It was probably rebuilt at a later date, since in 1940 the buildings, standing in Kendrick Street, consisted of a chapel, which then seated 100, and a school-hall.[91] The chapel was still in use in 1958.

LONGTON, HEATHCOTE ROAD. By 1887 the need of a Wesleyan chapel in the thickly populated area known as the Nook was thought to be urgent as services had to be held in cottages in Weston Place.[92] The first part of the chapel in Heathcote Road was then built;[93] a second building was added later.[94] In 1940 the chapel seated 200.[95] It was closed in 1957.[96]

LONGTON, NORMACOT. Wesley Memorial Chapel, Chaplin Road, Normacot, was built in 1892.[97] In 1940 it seated 291[98] and had a membership of 69 in 1942.[99] It was still in use in 1957[1] and is a brick building in the Gothic style with stone dressings.

FENTON, MARKET STREET. Mount Tabor Chapel in Market Street was founded by the Wesleyans in 1762, but, on the formation of the Methodist New Connexion in 1797, seceded to that body.[2]

FENTON, TEMPLE STREET. A Wesleyan Methodist chapel was built in Temple Street in 1812.[3] In 1851 it seated 300 and had an attendance on 30 March 1851 of 65 in the morning and 85 in the evening.[4] A new chapel was erected in 1873[5] which seated 600 in 1940.[6] It had a membership of 166 in 1942[7] and was still in use in 1957.[8]

FENTON, CLARENCE STREET. The ground floor of Nos. 22 and 24 Clarence Street was registered as a Wesleyan mission room in 1920.[9] It was still in use in 1932[10] but had closed by 1935.[11]

STOKE, EPWORTH STREET. In 1799 a group of Methodists, who, it is believed, had a previous meeting-place just off London Road, built a small chapel in Epworth Street (formerly Cross Street and earlier still Chapel Street) at the junction with Market Street.[12] In 1805 additional land adjoining the chapel was acquired. A school and two dwelling-

[68] Worship Reg. no. 7554. The regtn. was cancelled in 1876, on certification of disuse by the Supt. Registrar.
[69] Worship Reg. no. 31895.
[70] Ibid. no. 33076.
[71] Ibid. no. 60149. The regtn. has not been cancelled.
[72] *P.O. Dir. Staffs.* (1860).
[73] Worship Reg. no. 28153.
[74] It ceased to be mentioned in directories then.
[75] S.R.O., Q/SB, East. 1783.
[76] Wesley, *Journal,* 29 Mar. 1784.
[77] Lich. Dioc. Regy., Bp.'s Reg. E, p. 198; J. Ward, *Notes on the Wesleyan Meth. Ch. Longton* (1902; copy in H.R.L.).
[78] *Wes. Meth. Ch. Longton.*
[79] Ibid.; H.O. 129/15/371/5/2.
[80] H.O. 129/15/371/5/2.
[81] Ibid.
[82] *Wes. Meth. Ch. Longton.*
[83] *Meth. Ch. Buildings* (1947), 250.
[84] Ex inf. Sister Grace Simpson, Longton Central Mission (1952).
[85] *Wes. Meth. Ch. Longton.*
[86] H.O. 129/15/371/5/2.
[87] Ibid.
[88] *Handbk. 5th Ann. Conf. United Meth. Free Ch. 1912* (copy in H.R.L.). This incorrectly states that it seceded in 1849 but it was undoubtedly a Wes. Reform Ch. before the

union of 1857 and contd. to be so described in directories for some yrs.: *P.O. Dir. Staffs.* (1860, 1868, 1872, 1876).
[89] See p. 301.   [90] *Wes. Meth. Ch. Longton.*
[91] *Meth. Ch. Buildings* (1947), 250.
[92] *Wes. Meth. Ch. Longton.*
[93] Ibid.; tablet *in situ*; Worship Reg. no. 30391.
[94] *Wes. Meth. Ch. Longton.*
[95] *Meth. Ch. Buildings* (1947), 250.
[96] Worship Reg. no. 30391.
[97] *Wes. Meth. Ch. Longton*; Worship Reg. no. 33495; tablet *in situ*.
[98] *Meth. Ch. Buildings* (1947), 250.
[99] Circuit Plan, 1st Qtr. 1942 (Longton and Fenton Circuit).   [1] Ex inf. the Supt. Minister (1957).
[2] Ex inf. the Supt. Minister, Longton and Fenton Circuit (1942); see p. 293.
[3] H.O. 129/15/371/4/1; Char. Com. files.
[4] H.O. 129/15/371/4/1.
[5] Worship Reg. no. 21269; *Wesleyan Chap. Cttee. Rep. 1876.*   [6] *Meth. Ch. Buildings* (1947), 250.
[7] Circuit Plan, 1st Qtr. 1942 (Longton and Fenton Circuit).   [8] Ex inf. the Supt. Minister (1957).
[9] Worship Reg. no. 47880.
[10] *Kelly's Dir. Staffs.* (1932).
[11] Worship Reg. no. 47880.
[12] *Methodism at Cross St. Chap. Stoke-on-Trent, 1799–1949,* 3; Lich. Dioc. Regy., Bp's Reg. E, p. 153.

houses had been built on this land by 1813.[13] These and the chapel were demolished when a new chapel was built on the site; this was opened in 1816 under the name of Wesley Chapel.[14] In 1851 Wesley Chapel seated 900.[15] Average attendance was then about 80 in the morning and 200 in the evening.[16] In 1958 this chapel had 178 members.[17] The chapel faces into Hide (formerly Market) Street from which it was once approached. In the mid-19th century this entrance was closed, a window placed where the entrance had been, and a new doorway, opening on Cross (now Epworth) Street,[18] made. Two side vestries were added in 1859 and the building was again enlarged c. 1880.[19] The Sunday school building was erected in 1838 and for some years before the erection of Cross Street Board Schools in 1875 was used also as a day school.[20] The chapel is a square red-brick building, its former entrance front having five bays and a central pediment, bearing a date tablet of 1816.

STOKE, TRENT VALE. Wesleyan Centenary Chapel, Trent Vale, was built in 1839[21] and seated 90.[22] In 1851 it had a fairly small attendance, numbers on 30 March being reported as 35 in the morning and 50 in the evening.[23] A new chapel was built in London Road in 1888.[24] In 1940 it seated 196[25] and had 106 members in 1957.[26]

STOKE, COPELAND STREET. A Wesleyan preaching room in Copeland street was registered for worship in 1876. It had ceased to be so used by 1879.[27]

STOKE, QUEEN STREET (now REBECCA STREET). A Wesleyan mission room in Queen Street was registered for worship in 1879[28] and seated 154 in 1881.[29] It had ceased to be used by 1882.[30]

STOKE, PENKHULL. A Wesleyan chapel had been opened in Frederick Avenue, Penkhull, by 1912.[31] It was still in use in 1933[32] but had been closed by 1940.[33]

HANLEY, CHARLES STREET. The first Methodist chapel was opened in Hanley in 1783,[34] and when John Wesley preached there in 1784 he recorded that it was too small to hold the congregation.[35] It lay in Chapel Fields, now Chapel Street, and has

been described as 'an old-fashioned place enough, somewhat after the fashion of the lower rooms of three cottages with the inner walls taken out and, at the end where a pulpit was provided for the speaker, the upper room of the cottage added, by the floor and joists being removed.' 'The pulpit', the same account, continues 'was high for the building and only those in the front room could see the minister's face as he stood with his head and part of his body above the ceiling of the greater part of the room.'[36] Of all the Methodist societies in the Potteries this was the most seriously affected by the formation of the Methodist New Connexion in 1797.[37] It regained ground,[38] however, and in 1819 the makeshift chapel described above was replaced[39] by the present building at the corner of Charles Street and Old Hall Street.[40] A Sunday school was built at the rear of the chapel in 1835[41] which was extended c. 1867.[42] In 1851 the chapel seated 770 and average attendance on Sundays was 310 in the morning and 550 in the evening.[43] Sunday-school attendance then averaged 180.[44] The chapel was enlarged c. 1879 when the present elaborate front in the Renaissance style was added.[45] In 1940 it seated 900.[46] It was formerly the head of Hanley Wesleyan Circuit and in 1958 was head of Hanley Trinity Circuit. The minister of the church benefits under the Robert Sherwin Charity.[47]

HANLEY, ETRURIA. A Wesleyan Methodist chapel was built at Etruria in 1808[48] and stood on the site of the present colour works of Wengers Ltd.[49] In 1820 it was replaced by a new chapel a little higher up the village street.[50] There was a Sunday school attached to this chapel occupying a thatched building that stood on the site of the present church school.[51] In 1851 attendance at the Wesleyan chapel averaged 140 and at the Sunday school 180.[52] The chapel, which stands in Lord Street (now Etruria Road), seated 428 in 1940,[53] and is a brick building with a Classical plastered front surmounted by a pediment and a date tablet. It was still in use in 1958.

HANLEY, NORTHWOOD. A building called Old House, Northwood, was being used by Wesleyan

[13] Cross St. Chap. 1799–1949, 5.
[14] Ibid.; plaque in situ. The 1851 census return, however, gives the date as 1812: H.O. 129/15/371/3/1.
[15] H.O. 129/15/371/3/1.
[16] Ibid.
[17] Circuit Plan, 4th Qtr. 1957 (Stoke-on-Trent Circuit).
[18] Cross St. Chap. 1799–1949, 6.
[19] Wes. Chap. Cttee. Rep. 1880.
[20] Cross St. Chap. 1799–1949, 10.
[21] H.O. 129/15/371/3/1.
[22] Wes. Chap. Cttee. Rep. 1889.
[23] H.O. 129/15/371/3/1.
[24] Ibid.; Worship Reg. no. 30680.
[25] Meth. Ch. Buildings (1947), 251.
[26] Circuit Plan, 4th Qtr. 1957 (Stoke-on-Trent Circuit).
[27] Worship Reg. no. 23148.
[28] Ibid. no. 24394; Kelly's Dir. Staffs. (1880).
[29] Rets. of Accom. 1881, bound with the Chap. Cttee. Reps. at the offices of the Meth. Dept. for Chap. Affairs, Oldham St., Manchester.
[30] Worship Reg. no. 24394.
[31] Kelly's Dir. Staffs. (1912).
[32] Worship Reg. no. 54554.
[33] It is not entered in Meth. Ch. Buildings for that year.
[34] Ward, Stoke, 401.
[35] Wesley, Journal, 30 Mar. 1784.
[36] A. Huntbach, Hanley, 66.
[37] J. H. Beech, Centenary of Burslem Wes. Meth. Circuit (1883; copy in H.R.L.). The writer states that the Hanley society was almost extinguished. The membership of the Burslem Circuit in which Hanley lay dropped from 1,375

[37 cont.] been described as 'an old... [continues]
been described... in 1796 to 860 in 1797, 810 in 1798, 750 in 1800: Wes. Conf. Mins. 1796 to 1800.
[38] The lowest point in the membership of Burslem Circuit was in 1800 and it rose steadily again, being 1,170 in 1820; Newcastle Circuit which was formed in 1802 partly out of Burslem had 730 members in 1820: Wes. Conf. Mins. 1800 to 1820. The pop. of the area was rapidly increasing so that these figs. do not represent members gained from the other Meth. connexions which were also on the increase.
[39] It was demolished by 1843: Ward, Stoke, 401.
[40] Ex inf. the Supt. Minister, Hanley, Trinity Circuit (1958); H.O. 129/15/371/1/3; Char. Com. files; S.R.O., Q/SB, Mich. 1820, certificate of Enoch Keeling, clerk to Josiah Wedgwood.
[41] Ex inf. the Supt. Minister (1958).
[42] Wes. Chap. Cttee. Rep. 1867.
[43] H.O. 129/15/371(1/1.   [44] Ibid.
[45] Wes. Chap. Cttee. Rep. 1879.
[46] Meth. Ch. Buildings (1947), 250.
[47] By will proved 1888 Sherwin left £1,000 for the minister of this chapel: Char. Com. files.
[48] Wes. Conf. Mins. 1808; Lich. Dioc. Regy., Bp.'s Reg. E, p. 400; Warrillow, Etruria, 75, where the date is wrongly given as 1810.
[49] Warrillow, Etruria, 75.
[50] Ibid. 76; S.R.O., Q/SB, Mich. 1820; H.O. 129/15/371/2/1, where the date is wrongly given as 1802; tablet in situ.
[51] Warrillow, Etruria, 78.
[52] H.O. 129/15/371/2/1.
[53] Meth. Ch. Buildings (1947), 253.

Methodists for services in 1851.[54] The congregation was small.[55] The Sunday-school building was opened in 1857[56] and in 1873 the present chapel was built in Keelings Lane.[57] The chapel seated 382 in 1940[58] and was still in use in 1958.[59]

HANLEY, SUN STREET. A Wesleyan chapel had been built in Sun Street by 1860.[60] It was still in use in 1932[61] but had closed by 1940.[62]

HANLEY, HIGH STREET. A Welsh Wesleyan chapel was built in High Street (now Town Road) between 1860 and 1868.[63] It had ceased to be used by 1927.[64]

HANLEY, BOTTESLOW STREET. An iron chapel was erected in Botteslow Street in 1880 by Isaac Dixon, a mineral-water manufacturer.[65] There was a Sunday school by 1890 when permission was given to enlarge it.[66] The present chapel was built in 1906.[67] It seated 200 in 1940[68] and was still in use in 1958.[69]

HANLEY, MILL STREET. A Wesleyan Methodist Church in Mill Street (now Etruria Road), was registered for worship in 1892, but had closed by 1896.[70]

HANLEY, CAULDON ROAD. A Wesleyan chapel was built in Cauldon Road, Shelton, in 1897.[71] In 1940 it seated 400.[72] It was still in use in 1957, when it had 35 members.[73]

HANLEY, ETRURIA ROAD. There was a Wesleyan mission in Etruria Road by 1916.[74] It was probably still in use in 1928[75] but had closed by 1932.[76]

BURSLEM, SWAN BANK. John Wesley first visited Burslem in March 1760.[77] One of the converts, Abraham Lindop, opened his cottage for services.[78] The first chapel was built in 1766.[79] In 1783 Burslem was made head of a circuit.[80] The society was considerably weakened, however, by the formation of the Methodist New Connexion in 1797.[81] In 1801 a new chapel, the present building in Swan Square, was built.[82] This was enlarged in 1816.[83] The society again suffered a setback in 1836 on the division of the Burslem Sunday school.[84] In 1851 it was still the strongest chapel in Burslem and seated 1,290; attendance then averaged 500 in the morning on Sundays and 800 in the evening.[85] The chapel was again extended and improved in 1870 when a

new front with a portico was added.[86] Vestries were added c. 1884.[87] In 1949 the chapel, which has always been the centre of Wesleyan Methodism in the area, became The Central Methodist Church[88] and now (1958) forms a single church circuit.[89] The history of its Sunday school began in 1798.[90] In 1801, when the new chapel was built (see above), the school occupied the old building and also used the Free School in Moorland Road and a house in Hot Lane.[91] In 1805 a new school adjacent to the chapel was erected and had been enlarged by 1809. when the pupils numbered 1,260.[92] After the 1836 dispute,[93] the school was re-opened under the management of the Wesleyan trustees.[94] New Sunday and day school buildings were erected beside the chapel in 1850–1 at a cost of £1,500, of which £400 was granted by the government.[95] The poor of the chapel benefit under Elger Robinson's Charity.[96]

The chapel and schools, which form an impressive range of buildings, were built of brick, but the entrance front was remodelled in stone in 1870. It is in the Renaissance style with a Corinthian order and a tall recessed arch beneath a pediment. Two large angle turrets flank the pediment.

BURSLEM, LONGPORT. A collection was allowed in Burslem Circuit for a chapel at Longport in 1815,[97] probably already erected.[98] In 1851 this chapel seated 222 and attendance on Sundays averaged 50 in the morning and 60 in the evening. There was a Sunday school attached with an average attendance of 60.[99] This chapel was still in use in 1940 when it seated 380[1] but has subsequently been closed, the congregation being merged with that of Alexandra Road Methodist Church (formerly United Methodist).[2]

BURSLEM, SNEYD GREEN. A Methodist chapel was erected in Sneyd Street, Sneyd Green, in 1823, to be used under the terms of the trust as a charity school as well as a chapel. In fact it was only used as a Sunday school and chapel.[3] Attendance at services on 30 March 1851 was reported as 15 in the morning and 25 in the evening, and at Sunday school 84 in the afternoon and 24 in the evening.[4]

[54] H.O. 129/15/371/1/1.
[55] Ibid.
[56] Ex inf. the Supt. Minister, Hanley Trinity Circuit (1958). It was prob. used as a chap. and sch.
[57] Worship Reg. no. 21304; Char. Com. files, where the first trust deed is dated 1872; ex inf. the Supt. Minister (1958).
[58] Meth. Ch. Buildings (1947), 250.
[59] Ex inf. the Supt. Minister (1958).
[60] P.O. Dir. Staffs. (1860).
[61] Kelly's Dir. Staffs. (1932).
[62] It does not occur in Meth. Ch. Buildings for that year.
[63] P.O. Dir. Staffs. (1860, 1868).
[64] Worship Reg. no. 20630.
[65] Wes. Chap. Cttee. Rep. 1881; Huntbach, Hanley, 69.
[66] Wes. Chap. Cttee. Rep. 1890.
[67] Ex inf. the Supt. Minister, Hanley Trinity Circuit (1958).
[68] Meth. Ch. Buildings (1947), 250.
[69] Ex inf. the Supt. Minister (1958).
[70] Worship Reg. no. 33363.
[71] Kelly's Dir. Staffs. (1916); Worship Reg. no. 36583.
[72] Meth. Ch. Buildings (1947), 251.
[73] Ex inf. the Supt. Minister, Stoke-on-Trent Circuit (1957); Circuit Plan, 4th Qtr. 1957.
[74] Kelly's Dir. Staffs. (1916).   [75] Ibid.
[76] It is not mentioned in Kelly's Dir. Staffs. (1932).
[77] Wesley, Journal, Mar. 1760.
[78] Centenary of Burslem Wes. Meth. Circuit (1883).
[79] Ibid.; S.R.O., Q/SB, Ep. 1766; see p. 134.
[80] Burslem Wes. Meth. Circuit.
[81] Ibid.
[82] Wes. Chap. Cttee. Rep. 1870; Char. Com. files.
[83] Wes. Chap. Cttee. Rep. 1870.
[84] See p. 278.
[85] H.O. 129/15/370/3/1.
[86] Wes. Chap. Cttee. Rep. 1870.
[87] Ibid. 1884; Worship Reg. no. 62183.
[88] Ex inf. the Supt. Minister (1958).
[89] Ex inf. the Supt. Minister (1958).
[90] Hill Top Centenary: Hill Top Methodist Church 1837–1937; Burslem Sunday School 1787–1937 (copy in H.R.L.).
[91] Ibid.
[92] Ibid.; Lich. Dioc. Regy., Bp's Reg. E, p. 370; F. Falkner, The Wood Family of Burslem, 68.
[93] See p. 278.
[94] Hill Top Centenary; Staffs. Advertiser, 14 May 1836.
[95] White, Dir. Staffs. (1851).
[96] See p. 330.
[97] Wes. Conf. Mins. 1815.
[98] The census return of 1851 gives c. 1811 as the date of erection (H.O. 129/15/370/3/1); the first deed is dated 1820, but it mentions that the chap. was already built: Char. Com. files.
[99] H.O. 129/15/370/3/1.
[1] Meth. Ch. Buildings (1947), 249.
[2] Ex inf. the Supt. Minister, Burslem Hill Top Circuit (1957).
[3] Char. Com. files; P.W.L. Adams, Adams Family, 157–8.
[4] H.O. 129/15/370/3/1.

The chapel then seated 115[5] and in 1940 170.[6] It was still in use in 1957.[7]

BURSLEM, HOT LANE. A Wesleyan Methodist chapel was erected in Hot Lane in 1840. In 1851 it seated 68. Attendance on 30 March 1851 numbered 22 in the afternoon and at the Sunday school 27.[8] It had ceased to be used by 1868.[9]

BURSLEM, MIDDLEPORT. A Wesleyan Methodist school-chapel had been erected in Newport Lane, Middleport, by 1877.[10] By 1898 it was used solely as a chapel.[11] In 1940 it seated 330[12] and was still in use in 1957.[13] It is a brick building at the corner of Dimsdale Street and Newport Lane.

BURSLEM, WESTPORT. A Wesleyan chapel was erected in Liverpool (now Westport) Road in 1878.[14] In 1940 it seated 280.[15] It was still in use in 1957[16] and is a red-brick building with stone and terracotta dressings. There is also a Sunday-school building.

BURSLEM, STANFIELD. A Wesleyan Methodist chapel was erected at High Lane, Stanfield, in 1890.[17] In 1940 it seated 210.[18] It was still in use in 1957.[19]

TUNSTALL, WESLEY PLACE (now WESLEY STREET). About 1783 a Methodist society was established at the house of Joseph Smith,[20] attached to the Burslem society.[21] By 1775 it had 30 members[22] and in 1787 a fund for a chapel was raised by John Wesley, the site being given by Joseph Smith. The chapel was erected at a cost of £650 and was opened in 1788.[23] Wesley on visiting it in 1790 declared that it was 'the most elegant I have seen since I left Bath'.[24] The chapel, a building in the Gothic style with a turret on its south-east side,[25] was then the only place of worship in Tunstall and the largest Methodist chapel in the Potteries. It stood at the corner of America Street and Temple (now Buren) Street by the windmill.[26] Discontent arose in the early days of the society over Wesley's ruling that only Church of England prayers were to be used.[27] It was more seriously disturbed from 1808 to 1813 by the growth of the Camp Meeting Movement in the area and in 1811 the society expelled its steward and Sunday-school superintendent, James Steele, one of the leaders of this movement and subsequently a foun-

der of the Primitive Methodist Connexion.[28] The establishment of that Connexion, however, was only a temporary setback[29] and by 1834 the chapel was too small for the society. A new chapel in Wesley Place was then begun and officially opened in March of the following year.[30] In 1839 it became head of the newly created Tunstall Wesleyan Circuit.[31] Attendance in 1851 averaged 300 in the morning and 520 in the afternoon.[32] In 1958 it had 176 members.[33] The chapel which seated 740 in 1940[34] is still (1958) largely unaltered. Its brick pedimented front is dated 1834 and has a stone porch of three bays supported on Roman Doric columns. In 1869 it was reseated; in 1890 new windows were inserted and in 1898 an organ was installed.[35]

A Sunday school was started in 1799 which met until 1816 in the chapel. A school building was then erected in America Street. An additional wing was added in 1832, but in 1835 the school moved into the old chapel. In 1838 new schools near Wesley Place Chapel in Farndale Street were opened. Reading and writing were taught in the Sunday school until c. 1844 when a Wesleyan day school was established. A night school for general educational purposes in connexion with the Sunday school was established c. 1834 and lasted until 1874.[36]

In 1950 the chapel benefited under the will of John Dunning Chesters to the extent of £3,000, subject to the life interest therein of his widow.[37]

TUNSTALL, GOLDENHILL. A Wesleyan Methodist chapel was built at Goldenhill in 1822.[38] In 1851 it seated 248 people and had attendances of about 70.[39] In 1868 it was replaced by a new chapel[40] which in 1940 seated 750.[41] This chapel, which lies in High Street, had a membership of 81 in 1958[42] and is a large red-brick building with a portico.

TUNSTALL, SANDYFORD. A Wesleyan chapel in Cartlich Street was built in 1852.[43] It was rebuilt in 1872[44] and enlarged by 1877.[45] It was again rebuilt in 1909[46] and is a large red-brick building at the junction of Cartlich and High Streets. The earlier building in Cartlich Street is of red brick dressed with blue and yellow brick. In 1940 the chapel seated 250[47] and membership in 1958 numbered 36.[48]

[5] Ibid.
[6] Meth. Ch. Buildings (1947), 249.
[7] Circuit Plan, 4th Qtr. 1957 (Burslem Hill Top Circuit).
[8] H.O. 129/15/370/3/1.
[9] See p. 299. The registration was not cancelled, however, until 1879 (Worship Reg. no. 1781), and a Wesleyan Methodist chapel in Hot Lane is mentioned in Keates's Potteries Dir. (1875–6, 1892–3). A Primitive Methodist chapel in Hot Lane is not mentioned in this directory until 1882.
[10] Worship Reg. no. 23791.
[11] Ibid. no. 36801.
[12] Meth. Ch. Buildings (1947), 249.
[13] Circuit Plan, 4th Qtr. 1957 (Burslem Hill Top Circuit).
[14] Kelly's Dir. Staffs. (1884); Worship Reg. no. 25024.
[15] Meth. Ch. Buildings (1947), 249.
[16] Circuit Plan, 4th Qtr. 1957 (Burslem Hill Top Circuit).
[17] Kelly's Dir. Staffs. (1892); Worship Reg. no. 32474.
[18] Meth. Ch. Buildings (1947), 269.
[19] Circuit Plan, 4th Qtr. 1957 (Burslem Hill Top Circuit).
[20] Wesley Place Sunday Sch. Tunstall, Centenary Souvenir 1799–1899. The house of Joseph Smith lay in or near America St. by the windmill: Kendall, Hist. of Prim. Meth. Ch. i. 104; Hargreaves, Map of Staffs. Potteries.
[21] Wesley Pl. Sunday Sch.
[22] Ibid.
[23] Ibid.
[24] Wesley, Journal, 29 Apr. 1790.
[25] Kendall, Prim. Meth. Ch. i. 103.
[26] Wesley Pl. Sunday Sch.
[27] Ibid.
[28] Ibid.; Kendall, Prim. Meth. Ch. i. 106–9.
[29] The membership of the Burslem Circuit in which Tunstall chap. lay dropped from 1,100 in 1812 and 1813 to 970 in 1814 but rose again to 1,173 by 1816: Wes. Conf. Mins. 1812 to 1816.
[30] Wesley Pl. Sunday Sch.; H.O. 129/15/370/2/8; Lich-Dioc. Regy., Bp.'s Reg. I, p. 177; Kelly's Dir. Staffs. (1896); Staffs. Advertiser, 28 Mar. 1835.
[31] Wesley Pl. Sunday Sch.
[32] H.O. 129/15/370/2/8.
[33] Circuit Plan, 1st Qtr. 1958 (Tunstall Circuit).
[34] Meth. Ch. Buildings (1947), 249.
[35] Wesley Pl. Sunday Sch.
[36] Ibid.
[37] Char. Com. files.
[38] H.O. 129/15/370/2/3.
[39] Ibid.
[40] Kelly's Dir. Staffs. (1896); Worship Reg. no. 19017 Wes. Chap. Cttee. Rep. 1868.
[41] Meth. Ch. Buildings (1947), 249.
[42] Circuit Plan, 1st Qtr. 1958 (Tunstall Circuit).
[43] Kelly's Dir. Staffs. (1896).
[44] Tablet in situ.
[45] Wes. Chap. Cttee. Rep. 1877.
[46] Tablet in situ.
[47] Meth. Ch. Buildings (1947), 249.
[48] Circuit Plan, 1st Qtr. 1958 (Tunstall Circuit).

TUNSTALL, KING STREET (now MADISON STREET). In 1871 a Band of Hope mission, otherwise the Wesleyan Home Mission Chapel, was started in Cooper (now Jefferson) Street.[49] Although this was said to be still in use in 1876[50] it was replaced by King Street Chapel and Schools erected in 1873[51] and opened in 1874 to accommodate the growing population at the north end of Tunstall.[52] This chapel seated 850 in 1940[53] and had 178 members in 1958.[54] The chapel is a large brick building in a Romanesque style.

TUNSTALL, CHELL. A Wesleyan Methodist school-chapel at Great Chell was built in 1874.[55] It is a brick building in St. Michael's Road and in 1940 seated 135.[56] It had ceased to be used by 1958.[57]

TUNSTALL, CHURCH STREET. A Wesleyan mission hall in Church Street, Tunstall, was registered for worship in December 1915. It had ceased to be used for this purpose by 1925.[58]

TRENTHAM. A Wesleyan chapel was erected in Barlaston Old Road in 1883.[59] In 1940 it seated 132[60] and was still in use in 1958. A school built at the same date[61] stands on the south side of the chapel.

MEIR. Meir Central Chapel was built in 1870[62] but was subsequently replaced by another chapel in Uttoxeter Road, Meir.[63] This seated 400 in 1940.[64] In 1942 it had 42 members[65] and was still in use in 1957.[66]

ADDERLEY GREEN. In 1862 a Wesleyan Sunday school and chapel was erected at Adderley Green.[67] A new chapel was built in 1925 in Mossfield Road,[68] which seated 200 in 1940.[69] In 1942 it had 27 members[70] and was still in use in 1957.[71]

BUCKNALL, RUXLEY ROAD. A house at Bucknall was being used for Wesleyan Methodist services in 1851, attendance on 30 March of that year being 26.[72] A chapel was built in 1882, called Townsend Chapel, the old one being retained as a Sunday school.[73] Schoolrooms were completed in 1891.[74] The chapel, which was still in use in 1958, seated 120 in 1940.[75] It is a brick building in Ruxley Road.

MILTON. A Wesleyan Methodist chapel was erected at Milton in 1841.[76] In 1851 attendance figures stood at about 50.[77] A new chapel was built in 1862[78] in memory of the Revd. Samuel Leigh.[79] The site was given by Anthony Shaw of Burslem and the architect was George B. Ford of Burslem.[80] Permission was given to build schoolrooms in 1871,[81] but the project fell through, the old chapel still being used by the Sunday school in 1958.[82] The chapel, which stands in Baddeley Road, was extended in 1897 and is built of brick in the Gothic style and in 1940 seated 411.[83] It was still in use in 1958.

SMALLTHORNE. A Wesleyan chapel was built at Smallthorne in 1857.[84] It was replaced in 1867 by a new chapel, the old one being sold.[85] This chapel was enlarged in 1886.[86] In 1940 it seated 400[87] and was still in use in 1957.[88] A Sunday school, behind the chapel, was built in 1872.[89]

BRADELEY. A Wesleyan chapel was built at Bradeley in 1884.[90] In 1940 it seated 216 people.[91] It was still in use in 1957[92] and is a brick building in Brammer Street.

NORTON-IN-THE-MOORS. In 1814 and 1817 there were collections in the Burslem Circuit for a Wesleyan chapel at Norton,[93] which was probably built in 1819[94] in the High Street. A new chapel dedicated to St. John was built in 1893–4 on the opposite side of the road. In 1940 the chapel seated 280[95] and was still in use in 1958.[96] Both chapels are of brick and stand opposite each other in Knypersley Road (formerly High Street), the earlier having Classical features and the later Gothic. The first chapel was in private occupation in 1958.

FEGG HAYES. A Wesleyan Methodist chapel was built at Fegg Hayes in 1874.[97] In 1940 it seated 250.[98] In 1958 membership numbered 22.[99] The chapel is a brick building standing in Fegg Hayes Road (formerly North Parade).

BRINDLEY FORD. A Wesleyan Methodist chapel was built at Brindley Ford in 1861.[1] A Sunday-school building had been added by 1864.[2] In 1940 the

[49] P.O. Dir. Staffs. (1872); H.R.L., Tunstall Wes. Meth. Circuit Plan, 1872.
[50] P.O. Dir. Staffs. (1876).
[51] Kelly's Dir. Staffs. (1896).
[52] Wesley Pl. Sunday Sch.; Worship Reg. no. 22074.
[53] Meth. Ch. Buildings (1947).
[54] Circuit Plan, 1st Qtr. 1958 (Tunstall Circuit).
[55] Worship Reg. no. 21920; tablet in situ.
[56] Meth. Ch. Buildings (1947), 249.
[57] It does not occur on the circuit plan.
[58] Worship Reg. no. 46685.
[59] Tablet in situ.
[60] Meth. Ch. Buildings (1947), 132.
[61] Tablet in situ.
[62] Ex inf. Sister Grace Simpson, Longton Central Mission.
[63] Ex inf. Sister Simpson.
[64] Meth. Ch. Buildings (1947), 251.
[65] Circuit Plan, 1st Qtr. 1942 (Longton and Fenton Circuit).
[66] Ex inf. the Supt. Minister (1957).
[67] Wes. Meth. Ch. Longton.
[68] Tablet in situ.
[69] Meth. Ch. Buildings (1947), 250.
[70] Circuit Plan, 1st Qtr. 1942 (Longton and Fenton Circuit).
[71] Ex inf. the Supt. Minister (1957).
[72] H.O. 129/15/371/1/2.
[73] Ex inf. the Supt. Minister, Hanley Trinity Circuit (1958). [74] Wes. Chap. Cttee. Rep. 1891.
[75] Meth. Ch. Buildings (1947), 250.
[76] H.O. 129/15/372/1/2; ex inf. the Supt. Minister, Hanley Trinity Circuit (1958).

[77] H.O. 129/15/372/1/2.
[78] Ex inf. the Supt. Minister (1958); Wes. Chap. Cttee. Rep. 1866.
[79] Wes. Chap. Cttee. Rep. 1866. The Revd. Sam. Leigh was a native of Milton and first Wes. missionary to Australia and New Zealand.
[80] Ibid. [81] Ibid.
[82] Ex inf. the Supt. Minister (1958).
[83] Meth. Ch. Buildings (1947), 250.
[84] Tablet in situ; Wes. Chap. Cttee. Reps. 1856, 1857.
[85] Wes. Chap. Cttee. Rep. 1867; tablet in situ.
[86] Wes. Chap. Cttee. Reps. 1884, 1886.
[87] Meth. Ch. Buildings (1947), 249.
[88] Circuit Plan, 4th Qtr. 1957 (Burslem Hill Top Circuit).
[89] Tablet in situ.
[90] Wes. Chap. Cttee. Rep. 1886; Worship Reg. no. 27991.
[91] Meth. Ch. Buildings (1947), 249.
[92] Circuit Plan, 4th Qtr. 1957 (Burslem Hill Top Circuit).
[93] Wes. Conf. Mins. 1814, 1817. See p. 300 for an earlier chapel.
[94] Lich. Dioc. Regy., Bp.'s Reg. F, p. 513. This registration cannot be identified conclusively with this chapel.
[95] Meth. Ch. Buildings (1947), 249; tablets in situ.
[96] Circuit Plan, 4th Qtr. 1957 (Burslem Hill Top Circuit).
[97] Tablet in situ; Wes. Chap. Cttee. Rep. 1876 Worship Reg. no. 21988.
[98] Meth. Ch. Buildings (1947), 249.
[99] Circuit Plan, 1st Qtr. 1958 (Tunstall Circuit).
[1] Wes. Chap. Cttee. Mins. 1861.
[2] Ibid. 1864.

chapel, a brick building on the west side of Biddulph Road, seated 260[3] and was dedicated to the Trinity. In 1957 it had 54 members.[4]

. . . . .

HANLEY, GITANA STREET. A Methodist Hall in Gitana (formerly Frederick) Street was registered for worship in 1942.[5]

BURSLEM, STANFIELD. In 1942 a Methodist church in Haywood Road, Stanfield, was registered for worship.[6] It was still in use in 1957.[7]

BURSLEM, SNEYD GREEN. A temporary Methodist church in the abandoned Holden Lane Farm, off Milton Road, was registered for worship in 1957.[8] In 1958 foundations for a new church on an adjoining site were being laid.

ABBEY HULTON. Carmountside Chapel in Abbots Road, Abbey Hulton, was opened in 1940[9] and seats 200.[10] It was still in use in 1958.[11]

Methodist New Connexion

LONGTON, COMMERCE STREET. By September 1797, shortly after the formation of the Methodist New Connexion, there was a society at Lane End.[12] In 1799 a chapel there was registered by George Ridgway.[13] This was an inconvenient building and in 1803 another chapel, called Zion, was built in what is now Commerce Street.[14] This chapel was enlarged in 1812 and in 1822 became head of a new circuit formed out of Hanley Circuit.[15] The chapel was again enlarged in 1822[16] and in 1841 entirely replaced by a new and larger chapel on the same site.[17] It was said to be the strongest nonconformist chapel in Longton at this date.[18] This Zion Chapel seated 1,606 in 1851 and attendance on 30 March of that year was returned as 300 in the morning and 500 in the evening. There was also a Sunday school with an attendance of 300 in the morning and 252 in the afternoon.[19] The chapel continued to be used until 1938,[20] when the society amalgamated with Bourne Chapel.[21] It has since been demolished. It was described in 1841 as a 'building of large dimensions . . . with an ornamental and elegant front of brick and stonework intermixed.'[22] The poor widows of the chapel benefited under William Cook's Charity.[23]

LONGTON, NEW STREET. A Methodist New Con-

nexion chapel was erected in 1827 in New Street. In 1851 it seated 300 and had an attendance of about 40. It was not used solely as a place of worship.[24] It was still in use c. 1865[25] but had closed by 1896.[26] The chapel stood on the south side of the present (1958) Greendock Street midway between Wellington Court and Boulton's Court.[27]

LONGTON, DRESDEN. A New Connexion chapel was built at Dresden in Carlisle Street in 1866.[28] This seated 250 in 1940.[29] It had 28 members in 1942.[30] It was subsequently closed for several years but reopened in 1951.[31] It was still in use in 1958.[32] The chapel is a medium-sized rectangular building of red brick with red- and white-brick buttresses and triangular-headed windows.

LONGTON, NORMACOT. In 1876 Zion Chapel, Longton, established a mission room at Normacot. An iron chapel was erected in Meir Road in 1880. The Duke of Sutherland subsequently gave a site for a new chapel opposite this which was built in 1910.[33] It seated 480 in 1940 and is designated Christ Church.[34] On the closing of Alexandra Road Primitive Methodist Chapel[35] the congregation joined Christ Church. Christ Church was still in use in 1958.[36] The church, which is in the late Gothic style, is cruciform on plan with nave, transepts, and choir. It has a vestibule and stair-turret at the front. The minister's vestry is at the rear and the schools are at the side separated from the church by a corridor.[37] The iron chapel was still standing in 1957 and was used as the junior Sunday school.

LONGTON, EDENSOR ROAD. A Methodist New Connexion chapel was erected in Edensor Road in 1889.[38] In 1940 it seated 250 and had a membership of 29 in 1942.[39] It had been closed by 1957.[40]

FENTON. Mount Tabor Wesleyan Chapel in Market Street was taken over by the Methodist New Connexion in 1797.[41] A new chapel was erected in 1811.[42] In 1851 this seated 350 and had an attendance of 85 in the morning and 203 in the evening.[43] There was also a Sunday school by this date.[44] The chapel was rebuilt in 1869 on a large scale in the Gothic style. In 1900 the society was said to be strong.[45] The chapel seated 900 in 1940[46] and had 166 members in 1942.[47] It was still in use in 1958.[48]

[3] *Meth. Ch. Buildings* (1947), 249.
[4] Circuit Plan, 4th Qtr. 1957 (Tunstall Circuit).
[5] Worship Reg. no. 60022.
[6] Ibid. no. 60192.
[7] Circuit Plan, 4th Qtr. 1957 (Burslem Clowes Circuit).
[8] Worship Reg. no. 66194.
[9] Ibid. no. 59496; ex inf. the Supt. Minister, Hanley Trinity Circuit (1957).
[10] *Meth. Ch. Buildings* (1947), 250.
[11] Ex. inf. the Supt. Minister.
[12] *Handbk. 5th Ann. Conf. United Meth. Ch. 1912* (copy in H.R.L.).
[13] S.R.O., Q/SB, Mich. 1799, no. 114.
[14] *Handbk. 5th Ann. Conf. United Meth. Ch. 1912*; H.O. 129/15/371/5/2. It was not licensed until 1819: Lich. Dioc. Regy., Bp.'s Reg. F, p. 512.
[15] *Handbk. 5th Ann. Conf. United Meth. Ch. 1912.*
[16] Ibid.   [17] Ibid.; H.O. 129/15/371/5/2.
[18] Ward, *Stoke*, 570–1.
[19] H.O. 129/15/371/5/2.
[20] Worship Reg. no. 7153.
[21] Ex inf. the Supt. Minister, Longton and Fenton Circuit (1958); see p. 297   [22] Ward, *Stoke*, 571.
[23] See p. 332.   [24] H.O. 129/15/371/5/2.
[25] S.R.O., Q/AH, Longton Main Rds. Map.
[26] Worship Reg. no. 6477. The registration was cancelled on a revision of the official list of chapels.

[27] It is marked on Hargreaves, *Map of Staffs. Potteries* (1832).
[28] Ex inf. the Supt. Minister, Longton and Fenton Circuit. (1957).   [29] *Meth. Ch. Buildings* (1947), 250.
[30] Circuit Plan, 1st Qtr. 1942 (Longton and Fenton Circuit).   [31] Ex inf. the Supt. Minister (1957).
[32] Ex inf. the Supt. Minister (1958).
[33] H.R.L., Newspaper Cuttings, vol. 5, p. 8.
[34] *Meth. Ch. Buildings* (1947), 250.
[35] See p. 297.
[36] Ex inf. the Supt. Minister, Longton and Fenton Circuit (1958).
[37] H.R.L., Newspaper Cuttings, vol. 5, p. 8.
[38] Tablet *in situ*; *Meth. Ch. Buildings* (1947), 250, gives the denom. as United Meth., and as it does not occur in a list of former United Meth. Free Chs. in 1912 (*Handbk. 5th Ann. Conf. United Meth. Ch. 1912*), it must have been a New Connexion chap.
[39] *Meth. Ch. Buildings* (1947), 250.
[40] Ex inf. the Supt. Minister, Longton and Fenton Circuit (1957).   [41] Ex inf. the Supt. Minister (1957).
[42] H.O. 129/15/371/4/1.   [43] Ibid.
[44] Ex inf. the Supt. Minister (1957).
[45] *Handbk. 5th Ann. Conf. United Meth. Ch. 1912.*
[46] *Meth. Ch. Buildings* (1947), 250.
[47] Circuit Plan, 1st Qtr. 1942 (Longton and Fenton Circuit).   [48] Ex inf. the Supt. Minister (1958).

FENTON, MOUNT PLEASANT. Bethel United Methodist Church, Whieldon Road, Fenton, was registered for worship in 1912.[49] In 1940 it seated 200 and was a wooden building.[50] It has since closed and the congregation has united with that of Jubilee Chapel, Mount Pleasant, Fenton.[51]

FENTON, CARRON STREET. A temporary wooden building, Ebenezer Chapel, was erected by the United Methodist Church in Carron Street in 1920.[52] It held 400 in 1940[53] and was still in use in 1957.[54]

STOKE, HILL STREET. A meeting-house called Mount Zion was registered for worship in 1806.[55] In 1816 Mount Zion Chapel, Hill Street, was built[56] and seated 300 in 1851. Attendance on 30 March of that year was reported as 100 in the morning and 140 in the evening.[57] The chapel was closed in 1939.[58] In 1957 it was in use as a boys' club.[59] The red-brick front of the chapel has two stories and five bays. The two entrance doors are flanked by Tuscan columns. The roof has evidently been lowered.

STOKE, SHELTON NEW ROAD. A Methodist New Connexion chapel founded from Ebenezer Chapel, Newcastle, was built in 1833 in Stoke Road.[60] In 1851 it seated 150 and on 30 March had an attendance of 23 in the morning and 61 in the evening.[61] It was rebuilt in 1897 and renamed Providence Church.[62] In 1940 it seated 220.[63] The chapel has gained in strength as the residential area of Newcastle and Stoke has spread, and in 1957 had 110 members.[64]

HANLEY, BETHESDA. Shortly before the annual Wesleyan Conference of 1797 at Leeds the congregation of Hanley Wesleyan Chapel were locked out of the chapel by the trustees[65] for supporting a resolution embodying the demands made later in the year at the Leeds Conference by the group led by Alexander Kilham. These demands resulted in schism and the formation of the Methodist New Connexion.[66] At its first conference held in 1797 immediately after the separation from the Old Connexion, the New Connexion was asked by William Smith, a prominent Hanley Methodist, to station a minister at Hanley.[67] Smith, Job Meigh, and George and John Ridgway were foremost in forming the

new church at Hanley which began to meet in William Smith's house at Shelton in 1797 immediately on the latter's return from the conference. Shortly afterwards a coach-house in Albion Street was acquired and converted into a meeting-house.[68] The first Bethesda chapel was built on the site of this coach-house in 1798 and seated 600.[69] The group received a regular minister in the same year.[70] During its first twenty-five years Bethesda Chapel grew rapidly. It not only attracted a large proportion of the worshippers of Hanley but Hanley Circuit, of which it was head, became by 1812 the strongest in the Connexion.[71] In 1811 the trustees decided to enlarge the chapel and it was extended at the rear by a semicircular addition. The seating accommodation was thereby increased to 1,000.[72] All seats were let within a few months of the reopening of the chapel. As the chapel was still too small, it was demolished and a new one erected on the same site in 1819.[73] In 1851 this chapel seated 2,500.[74] Attendance on 30 March of that year, the largest for any place of worship in Hanley, was reported as 383 in the morning and 625 in the evening, but was said to average 600 in the morning and 900 in the evening.[75] Meanwhile a Sunday-school building had been erected in 1802, where the chapel-yard vestry now stands.[76] In 1819, before the rebuilding of the chapel, this was replaced by a new school building, which was used for services whilst the rebuilding took place.[77] The schools were enlarged by the addition of another story in 1836.[78] Although Ward, writing c. 1840, stated that more than 1,000 children attended Bethesda Sunday schools,[79] the census of 1851 gave only 250 in the morning and 150 in the evening as an average.[80] In 1859 alterations and additions were again made to the chapel including the erection of a colonnade of Corinthian pillars at the front, and the insertion of a centre window above it with a cornice surmounting the whole.[81] In 1887 various alterations were carried out within the chapel, including the extension of the minister's vestry and the replacement of the windows.[82] In 1897 the chapel had 447 members and 982 children in the Sunday school.[83] In 1940 it seated 1,500.[84] Bethesda was at first head of a circuit covering all New Connexion chapels in

[49] Worship Reg. no. 45355.
[50] *Meth. Ch. Buildings* (1947), 251.
[51] Ex inf. the Supt. Minister, Stoke-on-Trent Circuit (1957).
[52] Ex inf. the Supt. Minister, Longton and Fenton Circuit (1957).
[53] *Meth. Ch. Buildings* (1947), 250.
[54] Circuit Plan, 4th Qtr. 1957 (Longton and Fenton Circuit).
[55] Lich. Dioc. Regy., Bp.'s Reg. E, p. 295.
[56] H.O. 129/15/371/3/1. It was registered in 1819: Lich. Dioc. Regy., Bp.'s Reg. F, p. 513.
[57] H.O. 129/15/371/3/1.
[58] Worship Reg. no. 6475.
[59] Ex inf. the Supt. Minister, Stoke-on-Trent Circuit (1957).
[60] H.O. 129/15/371/3/1; White, *Dir. Staffs.* (1834, and 1851 which wrongly gives 1823 as the date of erection); *Handbk. 5th Ann. Conf. United Meth. Ch. 1912.*
[61] H.O. 129/15/371/3/1.   [62] Stone *in situ.*
[63] *Meth. Ch. Buildings* (1947), 253.
[64] Circuit Plan, 1st Qtr. 1957 (Brunswick and Audley Circuit).
[65] The majority came from Burslem Wes. Chap.
[66] *Handbk. 5th Ann. Conf. United Meth. Ch. 1912;* H. Smith and A. Beard, *Bethesda Chap. Hanley* (copy in W.S.L.), 14–15; W. Salt, *A Memorial of the Wes. Meth. New Connexion* (1822), 27; see p. 276.

[67] *Bethesda Chap. Hanley,* 15.
[68] Ibid. 15–16; Huntbach, *Hanley,* 67.
[69] *Bethesda Chap. Hanley,* 17. It was registered in autumn 1799: S.R.O., Q/SB, Mich. 1799, no. 115.
[70] *Bethesda Chap. Hanley,* 16.
[71] The Wes. Meth. Chap. was seriously weakened by the establishment of Bethesda which attracted almost all its congregation. In 1798 Hanley New Connexion Soc. had only 301 members out of a total of between 5,000 and 6,000, Leeds being the strongest soc. Bethesda and its offshoots grew rapidly; membership stood at over 1,000 in 1815 and over 2,000 in 1821. By 1812 it was the strongest soc. in the connexion: *Meth. New Connexion Conf. Mins. (1798–1820)*; R. Moss, 'Methodism in the Potteries' (London Univ. M.A. thesis, 1949), p. 50.
[72] *Bethesda Chap. Hanley,* 19–22.
[73] Ibid. 22–25; Lich. Dioc. Regy., Bp's Reg. F, p. 512.
[74] H.O. 129/15/371/2/1.
[75] Ibid.
[76] *Bethesda Chap. Hanley,* 26.
[77] Ibid.   [78] Ibid.
[79] Ward, *Stoke,* 403. This section appears to have been written about the end of 1840: ibid. 400.
[80] H.O. 129/15/371/2/1.
[81] *Bethesda Chap. Hanley,* 32.
[82] Ibid. 33.
[83] Ibid. 35.
[84] *Meth. Ch. Buildings* (1947), 250.

BURSLEM: HILL TOP
showing the Methodist Chapel, built in 1837, on the left

HANLEY: THE FORMER BETHESDA SUNDAY SCHOOL OF 1819
showing the graveyard

the area, but, as these multiplied, new circuits were formed: Longton in 1882, Burslem in 1857, and Newcastle in 1872. After the union of 1907, Bethesda became head of the Hanley United Methodist Circuit.[85]

The chapel, which dates largely from 1819, is built of chequered brickwork and has a curved end to the south-east. The front, which has been faced with stucco, has a colonnaded Corinthian portico, a central Venetian window, and much Classical detail applied in 1859. The lofty interior contains the original gallery with its curved front on all four sides. In the gallery there is a mural tablet in memory of Richard Hicks (d. 1844), a founder and trustee of the chapel. There are also mural tablets to members of the Ridgway family, Job Ridgway (d. 1814), Elizabeth his wife (d. 1810), John Ridgway (d. 1860), William Ridgway (d. 1864), George Ridgway (d. 1899).

Bethesda school, separated from the chapel by an extensive graveyard, is a long two-story brick building with a central pedimented feature.[86] The stucco gable-end facing Bethesda Street is surmounted by a pediment and has a tablet commemorating the erection of the school in 1819.

HANLEY, ETRURIA. By September 1797, shortly after the formation of the Methodist New Connexion, there was a society at Etruria.[87] The first chapel was possibly built in 1819.[88] A new building was apparently erected in 1845,[89] the foundation stone of which was laid by John Ridgway.[90] In 1851 it seated 60 people and had a small Sunday school attached. Attendance at the chapel on 30 March of that year was reported as 18 in the morning and 13 in the evening.[91] This chapel, called Salem, was rebuilt in 1886.[92] It seated 250 in 1940[93] and was closed in the same year. The building was sold in 1947.[94] There was also for a time a mission in Cobridge Road in connexion with this chapel.[95]

HANLEY, SHELTON. Bedford Chapel, Bedford Road, Shelton, was built in 1834 by John Ridgway with a schoolroom beneath it.[96] It seated 300 in 1851 and attendance on 30 March of that year numbered 90 in the morning and 80 in the evening.[97] A new chapel was built opposite and named Ridgway Memorial Church in 1867.[98] This seated 426 in 1940.[99] The former chapel was then used by the

Sunday school.[1] The chapel and school were still in use in 1958.[2]

HANLEY, EASTWOOD VALE. A Methodist New Connexion Sunday school, also used as a chapel, was built in Palmerston Street, Eastwood Vale, in 1839.[3] It seated 120 people in 1851 and attendance on 30 March of that year was 60 in the morning and 70 in the evening; a Sunday school was then attached to the chapel.[4] The present chapel, which stands at the corner of Victoria Road and Coteshealth Street, was built in 1909 and named Zion.[5] It seated 300 in 1940[6] and was still in use in 1958.[7]

HANLEY, TOWN ROAD. Providence Chapel, Upper Hanley, was built in 1839[8] on land given by the Duchy of Lancaster.[9] A new chapel was built in 1924[10] and in 1940 seated 440;[11] it was still in use in 1958.[12] The former chapel was described in 1851 as 'the handsomest in the Potteries'[13] and was a brick building with a stone portico supported by Doric columns. A Sunday-school building was built at a right angle to the chapel on its east side.[14]

HANLEY, PORTLAND STREET. A Methodist New Connexion school-chapel was erected in Portland Street in 1876.[15] A separate chapel was built in 1893.[16] This seated 254 in 1940[17] and was still in use in 1958.[18]

HANLEY, JASPER STREET. In 1874 Bethesda Town Mission, presumably attached to Bethesda Chapel, was erected in Jasper Street.[19] This was called the Worthington Town Mission by 1884, and by this date had evidently separated from the Methodist New Connexion.[20]

HANLEY, BUCKNALL OLD ROAD. There was an Ebenezer Methodist New Connexion Mission in Elizabeth Street, Hanley, in 1889.[21] In 1908 this was replaced by Bethesda Mission, Bucknall Old Road.[22] In 1940 the chapel seated 220 and there was a Sunday-school building attached.[23] It was still in use in 1958.[24]

BURSLEM, WATERLOO ROAD. The first Methodist New Connexion meeting in Burslem had started from Bethesda Chapel in the house of a Mr. Rowley in Hot Lane by 1797.[25] This soon became inadequate and in 1798 Job Ridgway built Zoar Chapel, locally known because of its style of building as 'The Salt Box', on land called Kiln Croft, in Princes Row, Nile Street.[26] Zoar was a plain brick building with

[85] *Handbk. 5th Ann. Conf. United Meth. Ch. 1912.*
[86] See plate facing p. 294.
[87] *Bethesda Chap. Hanley*, 16.
[88] Lich. Dioc. Regy., Bp's F, p. 513. It is mentioned in 1834: White, *Dir. Staffs.* (1834).
[89] H.O. 129/15/371/2/1. This date may have been returned incorrectly, however, as Ward, writing *c.* 1840, records a chap. seating 100 with a Sunday sch. attached: Ward, *Stoke*, 400.
[90] Warrillow, *Etruria*, 81–84.
[91] H.O. 129/15/371/2/1.
[92] Warrillow, *Etruria*, 81–84; tablets *in situ*.
[93] *Meth. Ch. Buildings* (1947), 250.
[94] Warrillow, *Etruria*, 81–84. The registration was cancelled in 1957: Worship Reg. no. 54264.
[95] Warrillow, *Etruria*, 81–84.
[96] H.O. 129/15/371/2/1; Ward, *Stoke*, 400; date on building; ex inf. the Supt. Minister, Hanley Trinity Circuit (1958).
[97] H.O. 129/15/371/2/1.
[98] Ex inf. the Supt. Minister.
[99] *Meth. Ch. Buildings* (1947), 250.
[1] Ex inf. the Supt. Minister.
[2] Ex inf. the Supt. Minister.
[3] Ex inf. the Supt. Minister, Hanley Trinity Circuit (1958).
[4] H.O. 129/15/371/2/1.

[5] Ex inf. the Supt. Minister; Worship Reg. no. 45235.
[6] *Meth. Ch. Buildings* (1947).
[7] Ex inf. the Supt. Minister.
[8] *Kelly's Dir. Staffs.* (1884).
[9] White, *Dir. Staffs.* (1851).
[10] Ex inf. the Supt. Minister, Hanley Trinity Circuit (1958).   [11] *Meth. Ch. Buildings* (1947), 250.
[12] Worship Reg. no. 4551.
[13] White, *Dir. Staffs.* (1851).
[14] Ward, *Stoke*, 400.
[15] Ex inf. the Supt. Minister, Hanley Trinity Circuit (1958).
[16] Ex inf. the Supt. Minister.
[17] *Meth. Ch. Buildings* (1947), 250.
[18] Ex inf. the Supt. Minister.
[19] *Kelly's Dir. Staffs.* (1880); tablet *in situ*. The stone was laid by Thos. Worthington.
[20] *Kelly's Dir. Staffs.* (1884); see p. 302.
[21] Worship Reg. no. 31908.
[22] Ex inf. the Supt. Minister, Hanley Trinity Circuit (1958).
[23] *Meth. Ch. Buildings* (1947), 250.
[24] Ex inf. the Supt. Minister.
[25] J. Young, *After One Hundred Yrs.: Burslem Bethel Circuit* (1903), 23 (copy in H.R.L.).
[26] Ibid. 23, 27; S.R.O., Q/SB, Mich. 1799, no. 112.

Classical features and seated 500, having a gallery round three sides.[27] In 1802 a Sunday school was started. Zoar remained the property of the Ridgway family until sold in 1825 by John and William Ridgway to Aaron Sant who subsequently let it to the Independents.[28] Meanwhile John and William Ridgway had acquired a site for a new chapel on the newly constructed highway (Waterloo Road) between Burslem and Hanley, and the chapel was built and opened in 1824.[29] In 1851 this chapel, called Bethel, seated 660; attendance on 30 March of that year was reported as 210 in the morning and 320 in the evening.[30] Also in 1851 a new trust made the chapel independent of Bethesda Chapel, Hanley.[31] Meanwhile the Sunday school had used the chapel for eleven years after the move to Bethel. In 1835 school buildings consisting of three rooms were erected on the north side of the chapel with a minister's house on the south side.[32] In 1853 these and the chapel were repaired and renovated, the main alterations being to the design of the orchestra. Gas lighting was also introduced.[33] In 1877 a school hall, the Dr. Cooke Memorial School, was built on land behind the old schools which had been acquired by the chapel in 1851. This hall was connected with the old schools by a covered passage.[34] A Classical stone vestibule was added to the front of the chapel in 1883 and the shape of the windows was altered by the introduction of circular heads.[35] The chapel was again renovated in 1904 and seated 650 in 1940[36] when it was head of Burslem Bethel Circuit.[37] It was closed in 1955,[38] because of the population shift from the centre of Burslem and its proximity to other large Methodist chapels. In 1960 it was used by Broadhurst Bros., china and earthenware manufacturers. The long two-story stucco front facing Waterloo Road has a central pediment with a date tablet of 1824. The original school and the minister's house form two projecting blocks which flank the main chapel.

BURSLEM, DALE HALL. The chapel at Dale Hall probably originated in a class meeting held at Longport to which William Ford was appointed assistant leader c. 1816.[39] No regular meeting for worship was established, however, until 1825.[40] A chapel, Zion, was erected in Globe Street in 1840 and seated 170 in 1851.[41] Attendance on 30 March 1851 was reported as 42 in the morning and 48 in the evening. A Sunday school was also held in conjunction with the chapel by that date and had an attendance on 30 March of 90 in the morning and 56 in the afternoon.[42] A Sunday-school building was erected in

1852.[43] The chapel was rebuilt on the same site but slightly nearer the road in 1867[44] and in 1940 seated 400.[45] It was apparently closed between 1935 and 1948 and again closed in 1955.[46]

BURSLEM, COBRIDGE. There was a Methodist New Connexion society at Sneyd Green by September 1797.[47] The first Providence Chapel, said to be at Sneyd Green, was registered for worship in 1819.[48] A new chapel was built in 1822 at Cobridge[49] at the corner of Elder Road and Grange Street, then Grange Lane.[50] Attendance on 30 March 1851 was reported as 81 in the morning and 70 in the evening and these were said to be average congregations. The Sunday school had respective attendances of 76 and 20.[51] The chapel was rebuilt in 1884[52] and in 1940 seated 600.[53] It was closed in 1957.[54]

BURSLEM, HOT LANE. In the early 1880's the Methodist New Connexion were stated to have a chapel in Hot Lane,[55] but this is probably a confusion with the Primitive Methodist chapel there.[56]

BURSLEM, MIDDLEPORT. The Methodist New Connexion had a chapel in Brindley Street in 1892.[57] This was still in use in 1896.[58] Its later history is unknown.

TUNSTALL, LASCELLES STREET. In the early 1820's a class meeting of the Methodist New Connexion began in the house of William Evans, 13 Williamson Street. By 1821 there was a regular meeting in Tunstall for worship.[59] The Sunday school usually assembled in the open air in a timber yard belonging to Thomas Walker of Walker Street, Brownhills, or if wet in the joiner's shop there.[60] The congregation also went there after it grew too large for Evans's cottage. John Ridgway acquired land at the top of the new market-square (now Tower Square) from the lord of Tunstall manor in 1823, and a chapel called Mount Tabor was built in 1824.[61] The chapel grew in strength, seating-space being extended by the building of galleries, until the expulsion of Joseph Barker from the New Connexion in 1841.[62] The Connexion then generally lost ground and was greatly disrupted and weakened by the Barkerite opposition in the town.[63] It survived, however, and in 1851 the chapel which seated 420 had a congregation of 80 in the morning and 90 in the evening.[64] About 1851 a religious revival took place; a site was purchased for a new chapel as the old became inadequate, especially for the Sunday school. New schools were built in the same year; the old chapel was sold in 1852 and worship carried on in the upper schoolroom for five years until the new chapel was built in 1857 in Victoria Terrace

[27] Young, *After 100 Yrs.* 27–28.
[28] Ibid. 23–31.
[29] Ibid. 40–46.
[30] H.O. 129/15/370/3/1.
[31] Young, *After 100 Yrs.* 53.
[32] Ibid. 65–71.
[33] Ibid. 53–57.
[34] Ibid. 74.
[35] Ibid. 54–60.
[36] *Kelly's Dir. Staffs.* (1916).
[37] *Meth. Ch. Buildings* (1947), 249.
[38] Worship Reg. no. 11225.
[39] Young, *After 100 Yrs.* 120.
[40] Ibid. It then appeared on circuit plans.
[41] Ibid.; H.O. 129/15/370/3/1.
[42] H.O. 129/15/370/3/1.
[43] Young, *After 100 Yrs.* 121.
[44] Ibid. 122.
[45] *Meth. Ch. Buildings* (1947), 249.

[46] Worship Reg. nos. 11767, 61929.
[47] *Handbk. 5th Ann. Conf. United Meth. Ch. 1912.*
[48] Lich. Dioc. Regy., Bp.'s Reg. F, p. 513.
[49] H.O. 129/15/370/3/1; Ward, *Stoke,* 285.
[50] Ward, *Stoke,* 285.
[51] H.O. 129/15/370/3/1.
[52] *Kelly's Dir. Staffs.* (1884, 1892).
[53] *Meth. Ch. Buildings* (1947), 249.
[54] Worship Reg. no. 29189.
[55] *Kelly's Dir. Staffs.* (1880, 1884).
[56] See p. 299.
[57] *Kelly's Dir. Staffs.* (1892).
[58] Ibid. (1896).
[59] Young, *After 100 Yrs.* 105.
[60] Ibid.
[61] Ibid. 104–5; H.O. 129/15/370/2/8.
[62] For an acct. of the career of Barker, see *D.N.B.*
[63] Young, *After 100 Yrs.* 105–6; see p. 284.
[64] H.O. 129/15/370/2/8.

(now Lascelles Street).[65] This chapel seated 394 in 1940.[66] It was closed in 1953.[67] The chapel is a brick building with a stone Classical front, having a recessed Ionic portico surmounted by a pediment. The lower floor of Mount Tabor Chapel has been converted into a shop but the upper part of the front retains its original Venetian window below the pediment. The poor of the chapel benefited under the charity of Thomas Ford.[68]

TUNSTALL, GOLDENHILL. There was a Methodist New Connexion chapel in Goldenhill between 1892 and 1900.[69]

LIGHTWOOD. In 1831 the Methodist New Connexion took over a chapel, now named Mount Zion, in Stone Road (now Lightwood Road) which is said to have belonged to the Quakers.[70] In 1940 it seated 250[71] and was still in use in 1958.[72] It is a rectangular cement-faced brick building with Classical features. The school building is of red and blue brick.

BUCKNALL. A New Connexion chapel was erected at Bucknall in 1821.[73] In 1851 it seated 150 and had an attendance of 50 in the morning and 70 in the evening on 30 March. By this date there was a Sunday school attached to the chapel which had attendances of 70 in the morning and 30 in the evening.[74] In 1854 the chapel was still owned by a Joseph Hawley.[75] A new chapel was built in 1894 and extended in 1914.[76] In 1940 the chapel, which stands at the corner of Ruxley Road and Heming Place, seated 140[77] and had school buildings attached, situated behind the chapel. The chapel was still in use in 1958.[78]

SMALLTHORNE. Thomas Walker founded a group of the Methodist New Connexion by starting the first Sunday school in the village in his house in the Leek road, directly opposite the present St. Saviour's Church. A few people also met for religious worship there. In 1827 a larger cottage, two doors farther up the street, was rented, and Smallthorne became a regular preaching place for the Methodist New Connexion; a Sunday service was started in 1830.[79] The first chapel was built in 1838, on the site of the present one but facing Lord Street.[80] In 1851 this had an attendance on 30 March of 39 in the morning and 60 in the evening. Sunday school attendance

was 150 in the morning and 30 in the afternoon.[81] In 1874 the foundation stone of the present chapel with the schoolroom beneath was laid by John Ridgway and John Cope.[82] The chapel, a large brick building in Ford Green Road, seated 380 in 1940[83] and was still in use in 1957.[84]

Primitive Methodist Church

LONGTON, LIGHTWOOD ROAD. A Primitive Methodist chapel in Victoria Place[85] was in use by 1843.[86] By 1851 the society had moved to the former Independent Methodist chapel, Ebenezer, in the High Street.[87] This chapel seated 264 in 1851 and attendance on 30 March of that year was returned as 200 in the afternoon and 250 in the evening.[88] There was also a Sunday school by this date.[89] This chapel continued in use until the opening of Sutherland Road Primitive Methodist Chapel c. 1863.[90] In 1901 the society again moved to a new chapel, called Bourne, in Lightwood (formerly Stone) Road.[91] Bourne Chapel seated 600 in 1940[92] and in 1942 had 230 members.[93] It was still in use in 1958.[94] On the closing of Zion Chapel, Commerce Street, in 1938 that society amalgamated with Bourne Chapel.[95] Since then the poor of Bourne Chapel have benefited under William Cook's charity.[96] The first chapel is still standing and is a Romanesque red-brick building with blue-brick dressings.

LONGTON, SANDFORD HILL. The Primitive Methodists bought a site at Sandford Hill in 1863 for a chapel[97] which was completed by 1868.[98] In 1940 it seated 200[99] and had 58 members in 1942.[1] The chapel, which stands in Edgefield Road, was still in use in 1957.[2]

LONGTON, NORMACOT. A Primitive Methodist chapel, called Florence Chapel, was erected in Alexandra Road, Normacot, in 1876.[3] It seated 300 in 1941.[4] It was sold to the Assemblies of God c. 1954.[5] The chapel is of red brick and stone with round-headed windows.

FENTON, CHINA STREET. A Primitive Methodist chapel was opened at Lane Delph between 1834 and 1843.[6] By the latter date it had ceased to be used by the Primitive Methodists and was occupied by the Congregational Methodists.[7] In 1849 it was acquired by the Church of England.[8]

[65] Young, *After 100 Yrs.* 115; *Kelly's Dir. Staffs.* (1896); Worship Reg. no. 11223.
[66] *Meth. Ch. Buildings* (1947), 249.
[67] Worship Reg. no. 35767.
[68] See p. 329.
[69] *Kelly's Dir. Staffs.* (1892, 1896, 1900).
[70] Ex inf. the Supt. Minister, Longton and Fenton Circuit (1957).
[71] *Meth. Ch. Buildings* (1947), 251.
[72] Ex inf. the Supt. Minister (1958).
[73] H.O. 129/15/371/3/1; Lich. Dioc. Regy., Bp.'s Reg. G, p. 234.   [74] H.O. 129/15/371/3/1.
[75] Worship Reg. no. 4455.
[76] Tablets *in situ*.
[77] *Meth. Ch. Buildings* (1947), 250.
[78] Ex inf. the Supt. Minister, Hanley Trinity Circuit (1958).
[79] Young, *After 100 Yrs.* 125.
[80] Ibid.; H.O. 129/15/372/1/4.
[81] H.O. 129/15/372/1/4.
[82] Tablet *in situ*; Young, *After 100 Yrs.* 125; H.R.L., Newspaper Cuttings, 1826–1906, p. 35.
[83] *Meth. Ch. Buildings* (1947), 249.
[84] Ex inf. the Supt. Minister, Burslem Hill Top Circuit (1957).
[85] Victoria Place is now (1958) the junction of Kingcross St. and Cyples Lane.

[86] Ward, *Stoke*, 571.
[87] H.O. 129/15/371/5/2.
[88] Ibid.
[89] Ibid.
[90] Worship Reg. no. 15849.
[91] Ibid. no. 38201.
[92] *Meth. Ch. Buildings* (1947), 250.
[93] Circuit Plan, 1st Qtr. 1942 (Longton and Fenton Circuit).
[94] Circuit Plan, 1st Qtr. 1958.
[95] See p. 293.
[96] See p. 332.
[97] Ex inf. the Supt. Minister, Longton and Fenton Circuit (1957).
[98] Worship Reg. no. 18727; *P.O. Dir. Staffs.* (1868).
[99] *Meth. Ch. Buildings* (1947), 251.
[1] Circuit Plan, 1st Qtr. 1942.
[2] Ex inf. the Supt. Minister (1957).
[3] Tablet *in situ*.
[4] *Meth. Ch. Buildings* (1947), 250.
[5] Ex inf. the Supt. Minister, Longton and Fenton Circuit (1957). The regtn. was cancelled in 1957: Worship Reg. no. 54467.
[6] It does not occur in White, *Dir. Staffs.* (1834) but is mentioned by Ward, *Stoke*, 554.
[7] Ward, *Stoke*, 554.
[8] See p. 215.

FENTON, BOURNE STREET. Heron Cross Primitive Methodist Chapel was built in 1878.[9] In 1940 it seated 180[10] and was still in use in 1957.[11]

FENTON, VICTORIA ROAD. A Primitive Methodist chapel was erected in Victoria Road in 1884. It was rebuilt in 1904.[12] In 1940 it seated 200[13] and was still in use in 1957.[14]

FENTON, WHIELDON ROAD. Jubilee Primitive Methodist Chapel was built in 1860. It was rebuilt in 1867[15] and in 1940 seated 215.[16] The present chapel is a brick cement-faced building with round-headed windows and door.

STOKE, PENKHULL. The first Primitive Methodist chapel in Stoke was built at Penkhull in 1815.[17] It was rebuilt in 1836[18] and in 1851 it seated 184.[19] Attendance on 30 March of that year was reported as 43 in the morning and 61 in the evening, while the Sunday school had an attendance of 66.[20] In 1940 the chapel seated 130[21] and had a membership of 76 in 1957.[22] The chapel which lies in Newcastle Lane at the corner of St. Thomas Place is a small brick building with a plastered front and has a school adjoining it built in 1878.

STOKE, LONSDALE STREET. The second Primitive Methodist chapel in Stoke was built in John (now Leese) Street, off Liverpool Road, in 1834.[23] In 1851 this chapel seated 40, but attendance on 30 March of that year was reported as being 43 in the afternoon and 151 in the evening.[24] By 1860 a new chapel had been built in Queen Street[25] and this in turn was replaced by a chapel in Lonsdale Street in 1878.[26] Lonsdale Street Chapel seated 350 in 1941[27] and had 80 members in 1957.[28]

STOKE, BOOTHEN. A Primitive Methodist chapel was built in New Street, Boothen, between 1868 and 1872.[29] In 1941 it seated 100[30] and had a membership of 32 in 1957.[31]

STOKE, TRENT VALE. A mission room at Trent Vale was registered for worship in 1894. It had ceased to be used by 1899.[32]

HANLEY, ETRURIA ROAD and BRUNSWICK STREET. The first Primitive Methodist chapel in Hanley was built in 1824 in Etruria Road on the site of the present railway station.[33] This chapel was put up for auction in 1829[34] and the congregation probably transferred to a chapel built in Brunswick Street.[35] This was sold in 1850 to 80 working men by Thomas Bundred,[36] who had registered the first chapel for worship[37] and who is variously stated to have been the owner[38] or mortgagee[39] of Brunswick Street Chapel. This became the People's Hall and stood on the site of the present Theatre Royal.[40]

HANLEY, MARSH STREET. A Primitive Methodist chapel had been built in Marsh Street by 1857,[41] probably by the group who had given up Brunswick Street Chapel shortly before 1851. It apparently closed at some time between 1884 and 1892.[42]

HANLEY, NORTHWOOD. A Primitive Methodist chapel, Ebenezer Chapel, was erected in Bold Street, Northwood, in 1865. A school was added in 1876.[43] In 1940 the chapel seated 405.[44] It was still in use in 1958.[45]

HANLEY, PADDOCK STREET. A Primitive Methodist chapel had been built in Paddock Street by 1880.[46] It had probably been closed by 1892,[47] and certainly by 1925.[48]

HANLEY, ETRURIA. A Primitive Methodist chapel was started in Cavour Street, Etruria, by 1892.[49] It closed c. 1905.[50]

BURSLEM, WILLIAM CLOWES STREET. The first Primitive Methodist society in Burslem was founded in 1819, meetings taking place in a disused crate-shop.[51] In 1822 the site of the crate-shop and the adjoining land were acquired for a chapel which was completed in the same year.[52] This chapel which stood on the south side of Navigation Road seated 250 and was a plain brick building with rectangular windows.[53] Six cottages were also built by the trustees on the same site. In 1842 the society acquired the former New Connexion chapel, Zoar, in Nile Street but leased it out for the two ensuing years until the Navigation Street chapel was sold.[54] The chapel had considerable financial difficulties at this period, responsibility for which until 1849 was

9 Ex inf. the Supt. Minister, Longton and Fenton Circuit (1957).
10 Meth. Ch. Buildings (1947), 251.
11 Ex inf. the Supt. Minister (1957).
12 Ex inf. the Supt. Minister, Hanley Trinity Circuit (1958).
13 Meth. Ch. Buildings (1947), 250.
14 Ex inf. the Supt. Minister.
15 Tablet in situ.
16 Meth. Ch. Buildings, 251.
17 Ward, Stoke, 496.
18 H.O. 129/15/371/3/1.
19 Ibid.   20 Ibid.
21 Meth. Ch. Buildings (1947), 253.
22 Circuit Plan, 4th Qtr. 1957 (Stoke-on-Trent Circuit).
23 H.O. 129/15/371/3/1; Lich. Dioc. Regy., Bp.'s Reg. I, p. 177.   24 H.O. 129/15/371/3/1.
25 P.O. Dir. Staffs. (1860).
26 Tablet in situ.
27 Meth. Ch. Buildings (1947), 251.
28 Circuit Plan, 4th Qtr. 1957 (Stoke-on-Trent Circuit).
29 P.O. Dir. Staffs. (1868, 1872).
30 Meth. Ch. Buildings (1947), 251.
31 Circuit Plan, 4th Qtr. 1957 (Stoke-on-Trent Circuit).
32 Worship Reg. no. 34277. The regtn. was cancelled on a revision of the official list.
33 Huntbach, Hanley, 68; Lich. Dioc. Regy., Bp.'s Reg. G, p. 540.
34 Staffs. Mercury, 17 Jan. 1829. Nevertheless it is marked as a chap. on Hargreaves, Map of Staffs. Potteries (1832), and is noted as still in use in 1834 and 1851 by White, Dir. Staffs. (1834, 1851). It may have continued in use for a time but the entry for 1851 is probably an error as it is not noted by Ward and made no ret. in the Census of 1851.
35 Huntbach, Hanley, 68; Ward, Stoke, 402.
36 White, Dir. Staffs. (1851).
37 Lich. Dioc. Regy., Bp.'s Reg. G., p. 540.
38 White, Dir. Staffs. (1851).
39 Huntbach, Hanley, 68.
40 See p. 171.
41 C. J. H. Homer, Plan of Hanley and Shelton, 1857 (copy in S.R.O., Z/M/7).
42 Kelly's Dir. Staffs. (1884, 1892). The regtn. was not cancelled until 1942 (Worship Reg. no. 19721), but as Huntbach, writing just before 1910, does not mention the chap. the directories are probably correct.
43 Ex. inf. the Supt. Minister, Hanley Trinity Circuit (1958).   44 Meth. Ch. Buildings (1947), 250.
45 Ex inf. the Supt. Minister.
46 Kelly's Dir. Staffs. (1880).
47 It is not mentioned in Kelly's Dir. Staffs. (1892).
48 Worship Reg. no. 28729. The regtn. was cancelled on a revision of the official list.
49 Kelly's Dir. Staffs. (1892).
50 Ex inf. the Supt. Minister, Burslem Clowes Circuit (1957).
51 J. W. Chappell, In the Power of God (Burslem, 1901), 17–18.
52 Ibid. 18–19, plate facing p. 17. The regtn., however, was made in 1821: Lich. Dioc. Regy., Bp.'s Reg. G, p. 75, chap. in occupation of Chas. John Abraham.
53 Chappell, In the Power of God, plate facing p. 17.
54 Ibid. 25, 31.

mainly taken by Hugh Bourne.[55] In 1851 Zoar Chapel seated 320 and attendance on 30 March of that year was reported as 66 in the morning and 120 in the evening; Sunday-school attendance was 115.[56] Extensive alterations to the chapel were made in 1854; the porch was built, the chapel raised, and a new roof constructed.[57] In 1859 an adjoining cottage was bought as a caretaker's house.[58] About 1872 a plan was made to build school premises on an adjoining site. These were to be so constructed as to be easily convertible into cottages.[59] In 1876, however, the trustees decided on a more ambitious plan and acquired a site in Church (now William Clowes) Street for a new chapel, to be called Clowes Memorial Church. Zoar was sold in 1878 and Clowes was completed in the same year.[60] In 1898 additional land was purchased for Sunday-school buildings and the foundation stone laid in 1900, the schools and an institute being opened later in the year.[61] In 1940 Clowes seated 648.[62] Mining subsidence in the area seriously affected the whole range of buildings and in 1956 the chapel and Sunday schools were closed and the society disbanded.[63] The designation, Clowes Memorial Church, was then transferred to Hamil Road Chapel whither many of the congregation also went.[64] Clowes Memorial Church and schools have now been demolished but were a long range of red-brick buildings, the chapel being in the Romanesque style.

BURSLEM, SNEYD GREEN. A Primitive Methodist chapel in Sneyd Street, Sneyd Green, was erected in 1841. In 1851 it seated 200 and had an attendance on 30 March of 15 in the morning and 40 in the afternoon.[65] It was rebuilt in 1864[66] and named Bourne Chapel. In 1940 it seated 250,[67] and was still in use in 1957.[68]

BURSLEM, MIDDLEPORT. About 1845 a Joseph Challinor who had been associated with Tunstall Primitive Methodist Chapel moved to Dale Hall. He formed a Primitive Methodist society which met in a small upper-room in Stubbs Street, formerly used as a warehouse.[69] A site for a chapel in Albion (now Harper) Street was acquired in 1847[70] and the chapel was completed in the same year.[71] In 1851 it seated 200 and attendance on 30 March of that year was returned as 42 in the morning and 50 in the evening; Sunday school attendance was 130 in the morning and 40 in the afternoon.[72] A site for a new chapel in Maddock Street was acquired in 1900 and plans in an elaborate Gothic style were drawn up.[73] However, they were never executed, possibly be-

cause of the First World War. The chapel seated 178 in 1940[74] and was still in use in 1958.

BURSLEM, HOT LANE. Hot Lane Chapel was opened from Zoar Chapel.[75] J. Harrison, a member of Zoar, asked for permission to start a Primitive Methodist group in the area as many members of Zoar lived there. About 1867 services began in a cottage. In 1868, however, the Wesleyan chapel in Hot Lane,[76] which had proved a failure, was bought by the Primitive Methodists. The chapel was enlarged in 1869 and again in 1875. In 1876 vestries were added at the rear.[77] The chapel seated 214 in 1940[78] and was still in use in 1957.[79]

BURSLEM, HAMIL ROAD. In 1897 Primitive Methodist services were started in a cottage to serve the rapidly expanding suburb north-east of Burslem Park.[80] Shortly afterwards the group moved to the Board Schools and in August of the same year a small chapel with two vestries was built. More vestries were added in 1901, part of a plan for the eventual replacement of the church.[81] In 1940 the church seated 214.[82] A new church was built in 1941–2 which was still in use in 1957.[83] The designation Clowes Memorial Church was transferred to it on the closing of that church in 1956. It is now the head of Burslem Clowes Circuit.

TUNSTALL, CALVER STREET. In March 1808 a group of revivalists began to meet in the kitchen of the house of Joseph Smith of Tunstall,[84] which was then registered for worship.[85] The houses of Hugh Wood and of William Clowes were both registered in the same year.[86] In 1810 after his expulsion from Burslem Wesleyan Society William Clowes began to preach at the meetings at Joseph Smith's house, and, as Bourne relates, the followers of Clowes 'began to look upon it as their regular place of worship'.[87] James Steele after his expulsion from Tunstall Wesleyan Society in April 1811, followed by a large number of the Tunstall Wesleyan Church,[88] began meetings immediately in a warehouse belonging to John Boden. The Clowes group from Joseph Smith's house joined in this Sunday worship and thus the Tunstall Society was formed.[89] In June 1811 the first chapel was built in the form of a shell of four cottages—'as it could not be known whether the Connexion would be of any long continuance'.[90] While the connexion was co-extensive with Tunstall circuit from 1811 to 1816, this chapel was its head.[91] From the nature of Methodist organization, however, as the church spread and other circuits were formed,[92] this chapel lost in importance connexionally.

[55] Ibid. 26–27.
[56] H.O. 129/15/370/3/1.
[57] Chappell, *In the Power of God*, 35.
[58] Ibid.
[59] Ibid.
[60] Ibid. 48–49; *Clowes Memorial Ch., Burslem* (copy in W.S.L.).
[61] Chappell, *In the Power of God*, 54–55; *Clowes Memorial Ch.*
[62] *Meth. Ch. Buildings* (1947), 249.
[63] *Clowes Memorial Ch.*
[64] Ex inf. the Supt. Minister, Burslem Clowes Circuit (1957).
[65] H.O. 129/15/370/3/1.
[66] *Kelly's Dir. Staffs.* (1896).
[67] *Meth. Ch. Buildings* (1947), 253.
[68] Circuit Plan, 4th Qtr. 1957 (Burslem Clowes Circuit).
[69] Chappell, *In the Power of God*, 39.
[70] Ibid.
[71] H.O. 129/15/370/3/1.
[72] Ibid.   [73] Chappell, *In the Power of God*, 40.

[74] *Meth. Ch. Buildings* (1947), 249.
[75] Ex inf. the Supt. Minister, Burslem Clowes Circuit (1957).   [76] See p. 291.
[77] Chappell, *In the Power of God*, 42; inscription on chapel 'Primitive Methodist Chapel enlarged 1869'.
[78] *Meth. Ch. Buildings* (1947), 249.
[79] Circuit Plan, 4th Qtr. 1957 (Burslem Clowes Circuit).
[80] Chappell, *In the Power of God*, 58.
[81] Ibid. 59.
[82] *Meth. Ch. Buildings* (1947), 253.
[83] Circuit Plan, 4th Qtr. 1957 (Burslem Clowes Circuit).
[84] H. B. Kendall, *Hist. of the Prim. Meth. Ch.* i. 103.
[85] Lich. Dioc. Regy., Bp.'s Reg. E, p. 372.
[86] Ibid. pp. 368, 369.
[87] Kendall, *Prim. Meth. Ch.* i. 104–5; H. Bourne, *Hist. of the Prim. Meths.* (Bemersley, 1823), 33–34.
[88] Bourne, *Prim. Meths.* 35–36.   [89] Ibid. 36.
[90] Ibid. 36–37; Lich. Dioc. Regy., Bp.'s Reg. F, p. 2.
[91] Kendall, *Prim. Meth. Ch.* i. 159.
[92] Ibid. The first new circuit was Derby (1816), followed by Nottingham and Loughborough (1818).

It has, nevertheless, remained one of the great centres of Primitive Methodism, frequently chosen for the annual conference of that church,[93] and was head of Tunstall Primitive Methodist Circuit until the union of 1932.[94]

The chapel itself was replaced in 1822[95] by a new building at the corner of Calver Street and Wellington Place (now Oldcourt Street). This was enlarged in 1832-3 by the addition of extra space on the Calver Street side and the construction of a new front there replacing the plain entrance in Wellington Place.[96] In 1851 the chapel seated 800. Attendance on 30 March of that year was reported as 129 in the morning, 600 in the afternoon and 650 in the evening; Sunday school attendance was 316.[97] The chapel was altered again in 1859-60 and in 1906.[98] In 1940 it seated 1,200[99] and in 1957 had 235 members.[1] There is still a Sunday school attached to the chapel.

TUNSTALL, PITTS HILL. In 1811 Pitts Hill occurred as a preaching place on the first plan of Tunstall circuit[2] but had been dropped by 1812.[3] A chapel was built in 1823 in the High Street[4] and enlarged in 1830.[5] It was either enlarged or rebuilt in 1841[6] and in 1851 seated 340.[7] Attendance at chapel on 30 March of that year was reported as 100, both in the morning and evening, and at Sunday school 110 in the morning and 100 in the afternoon.[8] In 1865 a new chapel was built[9] on the same site[10] but was replaced in 1876 by yet another and larger chapel farther up the road.[11] The 1865 chapel was then presumably used by the Sunday school and in 1894 a further range of Sunday-school buildings was built between that and the new chapel, an arch connecting them with the new chapel.[12] In 1940 the chapel seated 494[13] and in 1957 had a membership of 149.[14] The whole range of buildings are of brick in the Gothic style.

TUNSTALL, GOLDENHILL. In 1807 the house of James Nixon at Goldenhill was registered for worship.[15] The place does not appear on the early circuit plans of the new church, and it was not until 1833 that a chapel was built.[16] This was only ten yards by eight in size[17] but in 1851 seated 90.[18] In 1839 the Sunday school had 18 teachers and 156 children.[19] The congregation at the chapel was said to be 30 in the morning and 60 in the evening on 30 March 1851.[20] In 1855 the society moved to a larger chapel in Dale (now Andrew) Street.[21] A new Sunday-school building was erected in 1876, the previous one becoming the caretaker's house.[22] In 1940 this chapel seated 330[23] and in 1957 had a membership of 76.[24] The chapel and school form a range of red-brick buildings in Andrew Street.

TUNSTALL, SANDYFORD. A Primitive Methodist chapel, called Zion Chapel, was built in Sandyford at the corner of Stewart Road in 1879.[25] It was closed in or before 1941[26] and in 1958 was in use as a builder's store.

HANFORD. A Primitive Methodist chapel was erected in Mayne Street, Hanford, in 1883.[27] In 1940 it seated 84.[28] It was still in use in 1958 and is a small red-brick building.

ABBEY HULTON. A Primitive Methodist chapel was erected in Whitehouse Road, Abbey Hulton, in 1928 in place of an earlier chapel.[29] In 1940 it seated 250[30] and was still in use in 1958.[31]

BUCKNALL. In 1880 a Primitive Methodist chapel was built in what was afterwards known as Chapel Street, Bucknall. A Sunday school was added in 1932.[32] In 1940 the chapel seated 450[33] and was still in use in 1958.[34]

SMALLTHORNE. In 1808 the house of David Leak at Smallthorne was registered for worship.[35] Smallthorne, however, does not appear on the early circuit plans of the connexion. A Primitive Methodist chapel there was registered for worship in 1869.[36] This was rebuilt in 1904.[37] The new chapel seated 235 in 1940[38] and was still in use in 1957.[39] It is a brick building in Sangster (formerly Chapel) Lane.

BRADELEY. A Primitive Methodist chapel in Unwin Street, Bradeley, was built in 1874.[40] In 1940 it seated 250[41] and had 29 members in 1957.[42]

NORTON-IN-THE-MOORS. In 1807 a group led by Hugh and James Bourne registered a chapel at Norton in the Moors.[43] Coming before the definite expulsion of the revivalists from the Methodist Church this was taken over by the latter[44] and the further history of Wesleyan Methodism here has been treated above.[45] Houses at Norton were sub-

[93] *Mins. of Conf., Prim. Meth. Connexion, passim.*
[94] Ex. inf. the Supt. Minister, Tunstall Circuit (1957).
[95] H.O. 129/15/370/2/8.
[96] W. J. Harper, *Bygone Tunstall*, 64; Ward, *Stoke*, 96.
[97] H.O. 129/15/370/2/8.
[98] Harper, *Bygone Tunstall*, 64.
[99] *Meth. Ch. Buildings* (1947), 249.
[1] Circuit Plan, 4th Qtr. 1957.
[2] Kendall, *Prim. Meth. Ch.* i. 114.
[3] Ibid. 134.
[4] Kendall states that the original preaching-place was on the site of the present Sunday-sch. buildings: ibid. 127.
[5] White, *Dir. Staffs.* (1851), under Gt. Chell.
[6] White states that it was then enlarged: ibid. The census ret. gives this as the date of erection, however: H.O. 129/15/370/2/8.
[7] H.O. 129/15/370/2/8.   [8] Ibid.
[9] Tablet *in situ*.
[10] Kendall, *Prim. Meth. Ch.* i. 127.
[11] Tablet *in situ*.   [12] Tablet *in situ*.
[13] *Meth. Ch. Buildings* (1947), 249.
[14] Circuit Plan, 4th Qtr. 1957 (Tunstall Circuit).
[15] Lich. Dioc. Regy., Bp.'s Reg. E, p. 363.
[16] H.O. 129/15/370/2/3/; *Prim. Meth. Mag., 1834.*
[17] J. Jack, *The Ch. on the Hill*, 50.
[18] H.O. 129/15/370/2/3.
[19] Jack, op. cit., 50, quoting the *Prim. Meth. Mag. 1839.*
[20] H.O. 129/15/370/2/3.

[21] Jack, op. cit., 50. *Kelly's Dir. Staffs.* (1896) gives 1853 as the date.   [22] Jack, op. cit. 50.
[23] *Meth. Ch. Buildings* (1947), 249.
[24] Circuit Plan, 1st Qtr. 1957 (Tunstall Circuit).
[25] Tablet *in situ*.
[26] Worship Reg. no. 54112.
[27] Tablet *in situ*.
[28] *Meth. Ch. Buildings* (1947), 253.
[29] Ex inf. the Supt. Minister, Hanley Trinity Circuit (1957); Worship Reg. no. 51032. The previous chap. was probably built by 1884: *Kelly's Dir. Staffs.* (1884), where, however, it is listed under Milton.
[30] *Meth. Ch. Buildings* (1947), 250.
[31] Ex inf. the Supt. Minister.
[32] Ex inf. the Supt. Minister, Hanley Trinity Circuit (1958).   [33] *Meth. Ch. Buildings* (1947), 250.
[34] Ex inf. the Supt. Minister.
[35] Lich. Dioc. Regy., Bp.'s Reg. E, p. 366.
[36] Worship Reg. no. 18942.
[37] Ibid. no. 40954; tablet *in situ*.
[38] *Meth. Ch. Buildings* (1947), 249.
[39] Circuit Plan, 4th Qtr. 1957 (Burslem Clowes Circuit).
[40] Tablet *in situ*.
[41] *Meth. Ch. Buildings* (1947), 249.
[42] Circuit Plan, 4th Qtr. 1957 (Tunstall Circuit).
[43] Lich. Dioc. Regy., Bp.'s Reg. E, p. 249.
[44] Kendall, *Prim. Meth. Ch.* i. 113-14.
[45] See p. 292.

sequently registered for worship by Bourne, that of Enoch Goodfellow in 1808[46] and that of Thomas Mountford in 1811.[47] The Connexion later built a chapel at Norton Green. This is reserved for treatment under Norton-in-the-Moors in another volume.

CHELL HEATH. A Primitive Methodist chapel was built at Chell Heath in 1868.[48] In 1940 it seated 230[49] and in 1957 had 23 members.[50] It is a brick building in Chell Heath Road. The amount raised from the sale of Mount Tabor Chapel, Tunstall, has been given to a fund for a new chapel here.[51] The poor of the chapel have benefited under the charity of Thomas Ford since the closing of Mount Tabor Chapel, Tunstall.[52]

FEGG HAYES. A Primitive Methodist chapel, Lear Memorial Chapel, was built at the corner of East Terrace and Fegg Hayes Road in 1882.[53] It was extended in 1897[54] and in 1940 seated 200. It is a red-brick building and contains a Sunday-school hall as well as a chapel.[55] It was still in use in 1957.

BRINDLEY FORD. A Primitive Methodist chapel was built at Brindley Ford c. 1862. It was rebuilt in 1898.[56] In 1940 this chapel, called Bethel, seated 350[57] and in 1957 had 54 members.[58] It is a red-brick building in Outclough Road.

PACKMOOR. Packmoor Primitive Methodist Chapel was built in 1862.[59] In 1940 it seated 250.[60] It is a red-brick building with blue-brick dressings and stands in Samuel Street.

United Methodist Free Church

LONGTON. In 1851 there was a small chapel belonging to the Wesleyan Association in Longton.[61]

LONGTON, HIGH STREET (now UTTOXETER ROAD). Probably by 1853 the Wesleyan Methodist chapel in High Street[62] had joined in the secession from the Wesleyan Methodist Church which resulted in the formation of the Methodist (or Wesleyan) Reform Church.[63] It was closed in 1937,[64] and in 1957 part was in use as an antique shop and the remainder as a public house.

LONGTON, VICTORIA PLACE. The former Primitive Methodist chapel in Victoria Place had been taken over by the United Methodist Free Church by 1860.[65] It had ceased to be used by this church by 1876[66] and had probably passed to the Wesleyan Reform Church by this date.[67]

FENTON. A Methodist Free Church preaching room at Fenton Park was registered for worship in 1877.[68] A new chapel was erected in Fenpark Road in 1900.[69] This seated 300 in 1940[70] and had 123 members in 1942.[71] It was still in use in 1958.[72]

HANLEY. A United Methodist Free Church in Birch Terrace was registered for worship in 1881.[73] The registration was cancelled in 1906.[74]

BURSLEM, HILL TOP. Members of the Burslem Wesleyan Society who were expelled in 1836 as a result of a dispute over the running of the Sunday school[75] formed themselves into 'The Methodist Society'.[76] For a time they used a warehouse attached to the Churchyard Pottery Works as their chapel and Sunday school, but within a few months they had erected a wooden building called the Tabernacle in Moorland Road.[77] This was replaced by the present chapel and Sunday school at Hill Top, on the corner of Westport Road (formerly Liverpool Road) and Hall Street, built in 1836–7 to the designs of Samuel Sant.[78] Services were at first conducted by the new society's own local preachers and by the Baptist, Congregational, and New Connexion ministers.[79] In 1848, however, the society joined the Wesleyan Methodist Association and in 1849 received its first minister.[80] Attendances at the chapel were stated in 1851 to average 400 in the morning and 800 in the evening.[81] A house was built for the minister in 1862 and new Sunday school accommodation for the girls and infants in 1864.[82] In 1940 the chapel seated 900 and had 3 Sunday-school halls and 23 other rooms.[83] Since the closing of the Burslem Bethel Chapel in 1955 the Hill Top chapel has been the head of the circuit.[84] It is an impressive three-storied brick building with stone dressings. It is entered at first-floor level by a double flight of steps and a seven-bay stone portico with Doric columns. Above the portico the front has central round-headed windows and a pediment.[85]

BURSLEM, LONGPORT. The Burslem Sunday-school dispute resulted in the expulsion of Wesleyans at Longport as well as at Burslem, and they too used the warehouse of the Churchyard Works.[86] In 1838 they erected a chapel and Sunday school in Bradwell Street.[87] Like the Hill Top Society they at first used the ministers of various nonconformist denominations for their services and in 1848 joined the

[46] Lich. Dioc. Regy., Bp.'s Reg. E, p. 364.
[47] Ibid. F, p. 3.
[48] Tablet in situ; Worship Reg. no. 18712.
[49] Meth. Ch. Buildings (1947), 252.
[50] Circuit Plan, 4th Qtr. 1957 (Tunstall Circuit).
[51] Ex inf. the Supt. Minister (1958).
[52] See p. 329.
[53] Tablet in situ. It was registered for worship in the following yr.: Worship Reg. no. 27126.
[54] Tablet in situ.
[55] Meth. Ch. Buildings (1947), 249.
[56] W. J. Harper, Mow Cop and its Slopes, 35.
[57] Meth. Ch. Buildings (1947), 252.
[58] Circuit Plan, 4th Qtr. 1957 (Tunstall Circuit).
[59] Harper, Mow Cop and its Slopes, 35.
[60] Meth. Ch. Buildings (1947), 252.
[61] White, Dir. Staffs. (1851); see p. 278. It made no ret. in the census of that yr.
[62] See p. 288.
[63] Char. Com. files; Handbk. 5th Ann. Conf. United Meth. Ch. 1912 (copy in H.R.L.); see p. 278.
[64] Ex inf. the Supt. Minister, Longton and Fenton Circuit (1957).
[65] See p. 297; P.O. Dir. Staffs. (1860). It was registered by the Meth. Free Ch. in 1862: Worship Reg. no. 15285.
[66] Worship Reg. no. 15285.

[67] See p. 302.
[68] Worship Reg. no. 23179.
[69] Ex inf. the Supt. Minister, Longton and Fenton Circuit (1957).
[70] Meth. Ch. Buildings (1947), 250.
[71] Circuit Plan, 1st Qtr. 1942.
[72] Circuit Plan, 1st Qtr. 1958.
[73] Worship Reg. no. 25547.
[74] Ibid. This chap. may have been closed long before 1906 as it is last mentioned in directories in 1884.
[75] See p. 278.
[76] Hill Top Centenary: Hill Top Methodist Church 1837–1937; Burslem Sunday School 1787–1937 (copy in H.R.L.). [77] Ibid.
[78] Ibid.; Handbk. 5th Conf. U. Meth. Ch. 1912; H.O. 129/15/370/3/1; Ward, Stoke, 243.
[79] Hill Top Centenary.
[80] Ibid.; Handbk. 5th Conf. U. Meth. Ch. 1912.
[81] H.O. 129/15/370/3/1.
[82] Hill Top Centenary.
[83] Meth. Ch. Buildings. (1942), 250.
[84] Ex inf. Supt. Minister, Burslem Hill Top Circuit (1957); and see p. 296.
[85] See plate facing p. 294.
[86] Hill Top Centenary.
[87] H.O. 129/15/370/3/1; Worship Reg. no. 11224.

Wesleyan Methodist Association.[88] In 1851 the average attendance was said to be 60 at chapel and 120 at Sunday school.[89] The present chapel at the corner of Scott Lidgett Road and Station Street was built in 1906.[90] In 1940 it seated 300.[91] It was still in use in 1957.[92]

BURSLEM, DALE HALL. A Wesleyan Reform Chapel in Dale Street, Dale Hall, was registered for worship in 1855.[93] It is not known whether this chapel joined the United Methodist Free Church on the union of 1857 or whether it joined the Wesleyan Reform Union on its formation in 1859. It had ceased to be used by Methodists by 1867 when it was registered by the Congregationalists.[94]

TUNSTALL. A United Methodist Free Church was built in Bank Street, Tunstall, between 1860 and 1868.[95] It had ceased to be used by 1940.[96]

NORTON-IN-THE-MOORS, BALL GREEN. A United Methodist Free Church at Ball Green was registered for worship in 1894.[97] This chapel which lies in North Street seated 264 in 1940 and had 3 school halls.[98] It was still in use in 1957.[99]

Wesleyan Reform Union

LONGTON. On the union of the Methodist (or Wesleyan) Reform Church and the Wesleyan (or Methodist) Association in 1857 to form the United Methodist Free Church, the Methodist Reform Chapel in High Street joined the newly formed church. By 1860, another society had been formed, using the ex-Primitive Methodist chapel in Victoria Place.[1] By 1876, however, this new society appears to have seceded to the minority of the Methodist Reform Church which refused to join in the union of 1857 and formed the Wesleyan Reform Union in 1859.[2] Victoria Place Chapel continued to be used by the Wesleyan Reform Union until at least 1880[3] but had closed by 1884.[4]

Independent Methodists

LONGTON. In 1843 the Independent Methodists were using Ebenezer Chapel, High Street, Longton, later said to have been built in 1841.[5] This had passed to the Primitive Methodists by 1851.[6]

BURSLEM, SNEYD GREEN. An Independent Methodist chapel at Sneyd Green, Burslem, was registered for worship in 1854. It had ceased to be used by 1871.[7]

Missions[8]

LONGTON, HIGH STREET. The Blue Ribbon Gospel Army registered the Blue Ribbon Hall in High Street, Longton, in 1883. It had ceased to meet there by 1896.[9]

LONGTON, TRENTHAM ROAD. An unsectarian Christian mission registered a mission room in Trentham Road at the corner of Stafford Street in 1890. The room ceased to be used in 1901.[10]

LONGTON, NORMACOT. An unsectarian Working Men's Temperance and Christian Mission, also known as the Newhall Christian Mission, was established in Longton by 1890 when a Mission Hall was built in Newhall Road.[11] This mission was still in existence in 1957.

LONGTON, CLAYTON STREET. Victoria Hall in Clayton Street and Stafford Street was registered for worship by unsectarian Christians in 1901. The group had ceased to meet by 1925.[12]

FENTON. A Temperance Mission Hall in Wesley (formerly Elsing) Street, Fenton, was registered for worship in 1908.[13]

STOKE. A Gospel Hall in Bowstead Street, Stoke, presumably the former Catholic Apostolic Church, was registered for worship in 1895.[14] This was succeeded in 1955 by a meeting in two rooms over 1–3 Whitfield Buildings.[15] By 1958 the group was using the former Catholic Apostolic Church at the corner of Whieldon Road and Church Street.[16]

STOKE, LONDON ROAD. A group of unsectarian Christians registered a room in the Library Buildings, London Road, for worship in 1908. It had ceased to meet there by 1925.[17]

STOKE, WELCH STREET and CHAMBERLAIN AVENUE. An Assembly Hall in Welch Street was registered for worship by a group of unsectarian Christians in 1912.[18] In 1932 this group moved to other premises in Chamberlain Avenue.[19]

STOKE, LIVERPOOL ROAD. Stoke Evangelistic Mission registered a room at 17 Liverpool Road for worship in 1949.[20]

HANLEY, PADDOCK STREET. There was a Deaf and Dumb Mission Hall in Paddock Street in 1880.[21]

HANLEY, JASPER STREET. By 1884 the former Bethesda Town Mission Hall in Jasper Street[22] was being used by unsectarian Christians and had been renamed the Worthington Town Mission Hall.[23] It was still being used by this group in 1896.[24]

HANLEY, MARSH STREET. The Christian Mission

[88] *Hill Top Centenary*. A tablet on the building, however, gives 'Wesleyan Sunday School, established 1845'.
[89] H.O. 129/15/370/3/1.
[90] Worship Reg. no. 41737.
[91] *Meth. Ch. Buildings*. (1947), 250.
[92] Circuit Plan, 4th Qtr. 1957 (Burslem Hill Top Circuit).
[93] Worship Reg. no. 6207.
[94] Ibid. no. 18087; see p. 286.
[95] *P.O. Dir. Staffs.* (1860, 1868). It was registered for worship in 1872: Worship Reg. no. 20951.
[96] It does not occur in the survey of Meth. ch. buildings made in that yr.
[97] Worship Reg. no. 34231.
[98] *Meth. Ch. Buildings* (1947), 250.
[99] Circuit Plan, 4th Qtr. 1957 (Tunstall Circuit).
[1] See p. 301.
[2] *P.O. Dir. Staffs.* (1876), where the High St. and Victoria Place Chapels are both incorrectly given as Wes. Reform chapels, but in 1880 the High St. Chap. is correctly given as United Meth. Free Ch. and Victoria Place Chap. as a Wes. Reform chap.: *Kelly's Dir. Staffs.* (1880). Victoria Place Chap. had ceased to be used by the United Meth. Free Ch. by 1876: Worship Reg. no. 15285.

[3] *Kelly's Dir. Staffs.* (1880).
[4] Ibid. (1884).
[5] Ward, *Stoke*, 571.
[6] H.O. 129/15/371/5/2; see p. 297.
[7] Worship Reg. no. 3125.
[8] This does not include missions attached to churches treated elsewhere in this article.
[9] Worship Reg. no. 26930.
[10] Ibid. no. 32230.
[11] Tablet *in situ*; Worship Reg. no. 40177.
[12] Worship Reg. no. 38142.
[13] Ibid. no. 43169.
[14] Ibid. no. 35152; see p. 283.
[15] Worship Reg. no. 65277.
[16] See p. 283.
[17] Worship Reg. no. 43112.
[18] Ibid. no. 45121.
[19] Ibid. no. 53578.
[20] Ibid. no. 60112.
[21] *Kelly's Dir. Staffs.* (1880).
[22] See p. 295.
[23] *Kelly's Dir. Staffs.* (1884).
[24] Ibid. (1896).

Hall in Marsh Street was registered for worship by the Christian Mission in 1895, but ceased to be used by this group in 1906.[25]

HANLEY, GLASS STREET. The Imperial Mission Hall, Glass Street, was registered for worship by a group of unsectarian Christians in 1901. This group had ceased to meet there by 1903.[26]

HANLEY, NEW STREET and MAJOLICA STREET. A Gospel Mission Hall at 4 New Street was registered for worship by Gospel Mission Worshippers in 1903.[27] This was succeeded in 1931 by a Gospel Mission Hall and School in Majolica Street.[28]

HANLEY, BEREH TERRACE. There was a Mission Room in Bereh Terrace by 1912,[29] which was still in use in 1932,[30] but had closed by 1940.[31]

HANLEY, YORK STREET and PERCY STREET. A Gospel Hall in York Street was registered for worship in 1927.[32] In 1952 this group moved to a room on the second floor of the Old Post Office Buildings in Percy Street.[33]

HANLEY, MILL STREET. Hanley Temperance Mission in Mill Street (now Etruria Road) was registered for worship in 1931.[34]

HANLEY, LEEK ROAD. The Railway Mission[35] registered the Railway Mission Hall in Leek Road for worship in 1937.[36] The annual conference of the mission was held there in 1957.[37]

HANLEY, PAGE STREET. A group of unsectarian Christians registered Hanley General Ragged School, Page Street (formerly Port Vale), for worship in 1950.[38]

BURSLEM, COMMERCIAL STREET and FURLONG PARADE. A Gospel Mission Room at 29 Commercial Street was registered for worship by the Gospel Mission in 1883.[39] It moved to other premises in 1897.[40] In 1942 the Mission purchased Wycliffe Hall from the Congregational Church.[41]

BURSLEM, CORPORATION STREET. A Christian Mission Room in Corporation Street was registered for worship in 1882 by the Burslem Home Christian Mission. It had ceased to be used by 1883[42] when this mission registered an assembly room in Newport Street. This had ceased to be used by 1896.[43]

BURSLEM, CORPORATION STREET. The Nazarene Christian Mission registered a mission hall in Corporation Street in 1884. This had ceased to be used by 1896.[44]

BURSLEM, WEDGWOOD STREET. The Rescue and Evangelical Mission registered the Borough Auction Rooms for worship in 1886. The group has since ceased to meet.[45]

BURSLEM, WEDGWOOD STREET. The Borough Mission registered the Borough Auction Room in Wedgwood Street for worship in 1887.[46] In 1890 it moved to new premises in Wedgwood Place.[47]

BURSLEM, HALL STREET. In 1889 a Mr. Wilkinson's bible class in the Hill Pottery Show Rooms at Top of Sytch was registered for worship.[48] In 1924 this group moved to a mission hall in Hall Street. By this date it belonged to the P.S.A. Mission.[49]

BURSLEM, COBRIDGE, and HANLEY, DERWENT STREET. A Gospel Mission in Elder Road, Cobridge, was registered for worship in 1909.[50] In 1925 it moved to premises in Derwent Street, Hanley.[51]

BURSLEM, ALBION ROAD and NAVIGATION ROAD. In 1938 a group of Pentecostal Christians registered rooms at 92 Albion Street as a Peniel Gospel Hall.[52] This group moved to premises at 38 Navigation Road in the following year but ceased to meet in 1940.[53]

BURSLEM, COBRIDGE. Cobridge Park Mission in Waterloo Road, Cobridge, was registered for worship in 1910.[54]

BURSLEM, WATERLOO ROAD. A Mission Hall in Waterloo Road, Burslem, was registered for worship by unsectarian Christians in 1913.[55]

BURSLEM, MARKET PLACE and WATERLOO ROAD. The Order of the Golden Star registered a room at 20a Market Place, Burslem, for worship in 1937.[56] In 1945 this group moved to 74 Waterloo Road, Burslem, but ceased to meet in 1955.[57]

BURSLEM, NAVIGATION ROAD and BATH STREET. The Universal Full Gospel Mission at 32 Navigation Road, Burslem, was registered for worship in 1938.[58] In 1951 it moved to premises at 1 Bath Street, the members of the mission then being described as Pentecostal Christians.[59]

TUNSTALL, MARKET SQUARE. A Mission Hall in Market Square, Tunstall (probably the former Methodist New Connexion chapel),[60] was registered for worship by the Gospel Mission in 1884. This group had ceased to meet by 1896.[61]

TUNSTALL, GOODFELLOW and WELL STREETS. In 1933 a group of unsectarian Christians registered a Free Mission Hall at 50 Goodfellow Street.[62] In 1937 this group moved to part of a building at the corner of Well and America Streets.[63] It ceased to meet in 1951.[64]

[25] Worship Reg. no. 34752.
[26] Ibid. no. 38304.
[27] Ibid. no. 39530.
[28] Ibid. no. 52877.
[29] Kelly's Dir. Staffs. (1912).
[30] Ibid. (1932).
[31] Ibid. (1940).
[32] Worship Reg. no. 51023.
[33] Ibid. no. 63516.
[34] Ibid. no. 53475.
[35] The main object of the mission is preaching the Gospel to railwaymen by means of evangelistic addresses and by holding meetings for prayer and bible study and special missions at large centres: Rlwy. Mission: 1957 Statement of Accts. p. 16.
[36] Worship Reg. no. 5774.
[37] Rlwy. Mission: 1957 Statement of Accts. p. 4.
[38] Worship Reg. no. 62775.
[39] Ibid. no. 26917.   [40] Ibid. no. 35839.
[41] Char. Com. files, where it is stated that the mission works in the very poor part of the town and was only able to purchase the property because of a loan from a sympathizer; see p. 286.

[42] Worship Reg. no. 26730.
[43] Ibid. no. 27243.
[44] Ibid. no. 28012.
[45] Ibid. no. 29742. The regtn. has been cancelled but no date of cancellation inserted.
[46] Ibid. no. 29888.
[47] Ibid. no. 32181; Kelly's Dir. Staffs. (1896), where it is called the Wedgwood Mission Room.
[48] Worship Reg. no. 31441.
[49] Ibid. no. 49415.
[50] Ibid. no. 44000.
[51] Ibid. no. 50096.
[52] Ibid. no. 58364.
[53] Ibid. no. 58772.
[54] Ibid. no. 44259.
[55] Ibid. no. 45800.
[56] Ibid. no. 57730.
[57] Ibid. no. 61130.
[58] Ibid. no. 58337.
[59] Ibid. no. 63137.   [60] See p. 296.
[61] Worship Reg. no. 27864.
[62] Ibid. no. 54782.
[63] Ibid. no. 57796.   [64] Ibid.

MILTON, SHOTSFIELD STREET. A Full Gospel Hall in the grounds of 51 Shotsfield Street, Milton, was registered for worship in 1937.[65]

MILTON, MARKET STREET. In 1937 a Free Gospel Hall, occupying the former Congregational chapel in Market Street (now Millrise Road), was registered for worship.[66] It was reregistered in 1949.[67]

SMALLTHORNE. A Mission Hall, called Maranatha Hall and occupying rooms at 2 Cliff Street, Smallthorne, was registered for worship in 1938 by a group of unsectarian Christians.[68]

Plymouth Brethren. See Brethren.

Presbyterian Church of England

HANLEY. The Presbyterian cause in Hanley originated in a secession from Hope Street Congregational Church.[69] In 1824 some members of that church, led by the minister, W. Farmer, broke away and met for worship in a room at an earthenware manufactory belonging to a Mr. Simpson.[70] Shortly afterwards one of the group, a Mr. Pawley, gave a site for a chapel.[71] The foundation-stone was laid in 1824 and the chapel, called Brunswick Chapel, was opened in the following year.[72] At this point it was still Congregational, W. Farmer remaining as minister until 1839.[73] A Sunday school was built in 1834.[74] In 1840 the church joined the Staffordshire Association of Congregational Ministers and Churches.[75] It remained Congregational until 1846 when, on the resignation of the minister, it seceded to the Presbyterian Church of England.[76] In 1885 a new church was opened in Trinity Street.[77] A new school was opened in 1912.[78] Attendance at the church has varied considerably. There were originally about 50 seceders from Hope Congregational Church.[79] In August 1847 the communicants numbered 47.[80] Average attendance in the first three months of 1851 was 250 in the morning and 300 in the afternoon.[81] The peak was reached in 1909 when membership reached 212.[82] It had dropped by 1919 to 88 but had risen again to 154 in 1958.[83]

Brunswick Chapel was a one-story building with two small vestries and a single-span low ceiling.[84] Trinity Church is a brick building in the Gothic style with a nave and two aisles. A tower, surmounted by a short spire, stands on the east side. The new schools, built in the same style, stand to the east of the chapel. Both face Trinity Street.

Presbyterian Church of Wales

HANLEY. There was a Welsh Presbyterian, or Calvinistic Methodist, chapel in St. John's Street by 1884.[85] It was still in use in 1940, though without a minister,[86] but its registration as a place of worship was cancelled in 1952.[87] It was never in association with the Presbyterian Church of England.[88]

Society of Friends

STOKE. A group of Quakers started a meeting in Stoke in 1831[89] and purchased by 1834 the former Congregational chapel in Thomas (now Aquinas) Street, Stoke, to which a burial ground was attached.[90] The group in 1851 was very small, average attendance being only about 30.[91] By 1951 it was impossible to repair the building satisfactorily because it lay below the level of the hill and it was abandoned in favour of a new meeting-house in Priory Road, Newcastle.[92] The building was later sold to the British Red Cross Society, but the burial ground was retained.[93]

Salvation Army

LONGTON. A Salvation Army barracks in Stafford Street was registered for worship in October 1884.[94] It was probably superseded in December of the same year by a barracks in Stone (now Lightwood) Road, which was closed in 1910[95] on the opening of the Salvation Army Hall in Commerce Street.[96]

FENTON. The Primitive Methodist Chapel in Canning Street was registered for worship by the Salvation Army in 1885,[97] but was superseded in 1912 by the Salvation Army Citadel in Fountain Street.[98]

STOKE. A Salvation Army barracks in Wharf Street was registered for worship in 1895.[99] In 1916 it was superseded by a Salvation Army hall at 30 Cross Street, Stoke.[1] In the same year the group moved back to a building in Wharf Street[2] and in 1932 to the present hall in Fletcher Road, Stoke.[3] The Divisional Headquarters of the Army for North Staffordshire is in Church Street, Stoke.[4]

STOKE, BOOTHEN. A mission room was registered for worship by the Salvation Mission in 1892.[5] The registration was cancelled in 1922.[6]

HANLEY, GLASS STREET. Batty's Circus in Tontine Street was registered for worship by the Salvation Army in 1881.[7] It was probably superseded in 1882 by the Imperial Circus, Glass Street,[8] which in turn

[65] Worship Reg. no. 57135.
[66] Ibid. no. 57136; see p. 287.
[67] Worship Reg. no. 62210.
[68] Ibid. no. 58436.
[69] See p. 285.
[70] *Centenary Souvenir and Hist. Rev., Trinity Presb. Ch., Hanley, 1824–1924*, p. 5; Lich. Dioc. Regy., Bp.'s Reg. G, p. 541.
[71] *Centenary Souvenir*, 5.
[72] Ibid.   [73] Ibid.
[74] Ibid.
[75] Ibid. 6.   [76] Ibid.
[77] Ibid. 11; Worship Reg. no. 28805, previous regtns. nos. 23582, 6718.
[78] *Centenary Souvenir*, 15; *Staffs. Sentinel*, 22 Sept. 1912.
[79] *Centenary Souvenir*, 5.
[80] Ibid. 8.
[81] H.O. 129/15/371/2/1.
[82] Ex inf. the Revd. R. R. Bance, Minister, Trinity Presb. Ch., Hanley (1958).
[83] Ex inf. the Revd. R. R. Bance.
[84] *Centenary Souvenir*, 8.
[85] *Kelly's Dir. Staffs.* (1884, 1896).

[86] Ibid. (1940).
[87] Worship Reg. no. 37252.
[88] Ex inf. the Revd. R. R. Bance (1958).
[89] Ex inf. the Librarian, Friends Ho., London.
[90] White, *Dir. Staffs.* (1834); ex inf. the Clerk, Staffs. Monthly Meeting (1958).
[91] H.O. 129/15/371/3/1; H.O. 129/15/371/1/1. Two identical rets. were made.
[92] See p. 63.
[93] Ex inf. the Clerk, Staffs. Monthly Meeting (1958), and Mr. A. A. Walmesley, who is in possession of the records of the Monthly Meeting.
[94] Worship Reg. no. 28182.
[95] Ibid. no. 28318.   [96] Ibid. no. 44495.
[97] Ibid. no. 28485.   [98] Ibid. no. 45431.
[99] Ibid. no. 34982.   [1] Ibid. no. 46742.
[2] Ibid. no. 49521.   [3] Ibid. no. 53667.
[4] Ex inf. the Divisional Commander, N. Staffs. Div.
[5] The registering body is designated the Salvation Mission.   [6] Worship Reg. no. 33390.
[7] Ibid. no. 25975.
[8] Ibid. no. 26484. The registering body is designated the Salvation Mission.

gave way in 1903 to the present Salvation Army Citadel in Glass Street.[9]

HANLEY, NEW HALL STREET. A Salvation Army barracks in New Hall Street was registered for worship in 1889. It had ceased to be used by 1903.[10]

HANLEY, JOINER'S SQUARE. A Salvation Army hall in Palmerston Street was registered for worship in 1932.[11] It was still in use in 1958.

BURSLEM, CORPORATION STREET. A mission room in Corporation Street was registered for worship by the Salvation Mission in 1883.[12] It had ceased to be used by 1884.[13]

BURSLEM, MOORLAND ROAD. A mission hall in Moorland Road was registered for worship by the Salvation Mission in 1884.[14] It had ceased to be used by 1896.[15]

BURSLEM, MIDDLEPORT. A Salvation Army hall in Brindley Street was registered for worship in 1903. The registration was cancelled in 1906.[16]

BURSLEM, WESTPORT ROAD. A Salvation Army temple in Hall Street was registered for worship in 1903.[17] This was replaced in 1914 by a Salvation Army temple in Newcastle Street,[18] and in 1933 the latter was superseded by the Salvation Army Hall, 12 Westport (formerly Liverpool) Road.[19]

TUNSTALL, SNEYD STREET. A Salvation Army barracks, later designated a hall, in Sneyd Street (now Ladywell Road) was registered for worship in 1882.[20]

TUNSTALL, GOLDENHILL. A Salvation Army hall at 34 High Street was registered for worship in 1933. The registration was cancelled in 1941.[21]

SMALLTHORNE. A Salvation Army hall in Camp Road was registered for worship in 1925.[22]

Salvation Navy[23]

LONGTON. A body known as the Salvation Navy registered a Salvation Lighthouse in Uttoxeter Road, Normacot, in 1882, for public worship. It had ceased to be used by 1896.[24]

BURSLEM. The Salvation Navy registered the Mission Room in Queen Street, Burslem, for worship in 1882.[25] They had probably ceased to meet by 1884,[26] and certainly by 1896.[27]

The Sandemanians (Glassites)

TUNSTALL. In 1812 Anthony Keeling, a leading pottery manufacturer in Tunstall at the beginning of the 19th century, registered his house for worship by Sandemanians.[28] The other witnesses of the certificate were H. Keeling, Thomas Baggaley, John Cap-

per, Charles Stanier, Betty Marsh, John Hilliere, Enoch Keeling, and Charles Timpson.[29] The group is said to have met for some time, even after Keeling's departure from Tunstall, but had ceased by c. 1838.[30]

Spiritualist Churches

LONGTON, KING STREET. An assembly room in the Post Office Building, King Street, was registered for worship by the Spiritualist Society in 1893. It had ceased to be used for this purpose by 1896.[31]

LONGTON, MARKET STREET. The Courier Buildings in Market Street were registered for worship by Spiritualists in 1896. The meeting has since ceased.[32]

LONGTON, MARKET STREET. A room at 5 Market Street was registered for worship by Spiritualists in 1930.[33]

LONGTON, MARKET STREET. Rooms at 22 Market Street were registered for worship by Spiritualists in 1932.[34]

LONGTON, LIGHTWOOD ROAD. A Spiritualist church in Lightwood Road was registered in 1932.[35]

LONGTON, CHURCH STREET and UTTOXETER ROAD. The Christian Spiritualist Mission registered rooms at Portland Chambers, Church Street, for worship in 1932.[36] In 1940 the group moved to rooms at 4 Uttoxeter Road but ceased to meet two years later.[37]

LONGTON, NORMACOT ROAD. Rooms at 196B Normacot Road were registered for worship by Spiritualists in 1934.[38]

LONGTON, BATHURST STREET. A room at 21 Bathurst Street was registered for worship by the Christian Spiritualists in 1935.[39]

LONGTON, STAFFORD STREET. A room at 100 Stafford Street was registered for worship in 1942.[40]

FENTON, MARKET STREET (later KING STREET). A Spiritualist church at 80 Market Street (later 60 King Street) was registered for worship in 1915.[41] In 1921 62 King Street was also registered.[42]

FENTON, KING STREET. A room at 27 King Street was registered for worship by the Christian Spiritualist Church in 1932.[43]

STOKE, WATER STREET. A Spiritualist church in Water Street, Boothen, was registered for worship in 1922.[44]

STOKE, WELCH STREET. Rooms in Welch Street were registered as a Spiritualist church in 1932.[45]

STOKE, WHARF STREET. Rooms at 45A Wharf Street were registered as a Spiritualist church in 1932.[46]

[9] Ibid. no. 39512.
[10] Ibid. no. 31832.
[11] Ibid. no. 53822.
[12] This was definitely the Salvation Army as this name is also used in the regtn. of the Imperial Circus, Glass St.: see above.
[13] Worship Reg. no. 26849.
[14] The registering body is designated the Salvation Mission.
[15] Worship Reg. no. 27853.
[16] Ibid. no. 39973.
[17] Ibid. no. 39984.
[18] Ibid. no. 46073.
[19] Ibid. no. 47090.
[20] Ibid. no. 26606; see p. 104.
[21] Worship Reg. no. 54300.
[22] Ibid. no. 49595.
[23] Nothing is known of this organization but apparently it had no connexion with the Salvation Army.
[24] Worship Reg. no. 26468.
[25] Ibid. no. 26637.

[26] In 1884 the Latter Day Saints registered the Mission Room, Queen St.: see p. 288.
[27] Worship Reg. no. 26637.
[28] G.R.O., Worship Rets., 1852, Staffs.; S.R.O., Q/SO, Epiph. 1812; Ward, Stoke, 93.
[29] S.R.O., Q/SO, Epiph. 1812.
[30] Ward, Stoke, 93.
[31] Worship Reg. no. 33792.
[32] Ibid. no. 35492.
[33] Ibid. no. 52838.
[34] Ibid. no. 53785.
[35] Ibid. no. 53735.
[36] Ibid. no. 53006.
[37] Ibid. no. 59359.
[38] Ibid. no. 54956.
[39] Ibid. no. 56193.
[40] Ibid. no. 60278.
[41] Ibid. no. 46476.
[42] Ibid. no. 48296.
[43] Ibid. no. 54984.
[45] Ibid. no. 53701.
[44] Ibid. no. 48605.
[46] Ibid. no. 54154.

HANLEY, MARSH STREET. Rooms at 53 Marsh Street were registered as a Spiritualist church in 1919. They had ceased to be used by 1921.[47]

HANLEY, TOWN ROAD (later HIGH STREET). A National Spiritualist church in Town Road (later High Street) was registered in 1927.[48]

HANLEY, RATTON STREET. Rooms at 3A Ratton Street were registered as a Christian Spiritualist church in 1934.[49]

HANLEY, LEEK ROAD. A room at 1103 Leek Road was registered as a Spiritualist church in 1957.[50]

BURSLEM, NEWCASTLE STREET. A Spiritual Temple, Newcastle Street, was registered for worship in 1890, but had ceased to be used by 1896.[51]

BURSLEM, MOORLAND ROAD. A Spiritualist church in Moorland Road was registered in 1925.[52]

BURSLEM, MOORLAND ROAD. A Beacon Light Greater World Christian Spiritualist church, occupying rooms at 257 Moorland Road, was registered in 1936.[53]

BURSLEM, LIVERPOOL ROAD. A Central Mission Spiritualist church at 4 and 6 Liverpool Road was registered in 1941.[54]

TUNSTALL, BREWERY and PICCADILLY STREETS. A Spiritualist church at Victoria Terrace, Brewery Street, was registered for worship in 1914.[55] In 1917 the church moved to 1 Piccadilly Street, Tunstall.[56]

TUNSTALL, HIGH STREET and TOWER SQUARE. A room at 41A High Street was registered by Christian Spiritualists in 1935.[57] This group moved to the upper floor of the former New Connexion chapel[58] in Tower Square in 1941 and was still meeting there in 1958.[59]

SMALLTHORNE, CLIFF STREET. Rooms at 2 Cliff Street, Nettlebank, were registered for worship by Spiritualists in 1934 and had ceased to be used for this purpose by 1938.[60]

Swedenborgian (or New Jerusalem) Church[61]

LONGTON and FENTON. There was a New Jerusalem Church in Longton in 1851 which met in an upper room, designated the New Jerusalem School Room, in Market Lane (now Cornhill Passage). It was a weak society, however, attendance at worship on the 30 March 1851 numbering only 16 and at Sunday school 14.[62] By c. 1865 the group had moved to a chapel in Meir View Place at the corner of the present Park Hall Street and Bridgwood Street.[63] The chapel evidently went out of use in the 1890's.[64]

There is then a long gap, with no record of a regular place of worship, until 1926, when a Swedenborgian church in Foley Street, Fenton, was registered for worship. The registration was cancelled, however, in 1931.[65] The chapel in Park Hall Street, which is a simple brick building probably of the early 19th century, still stands and in 1960 was in use as a warehouse.

Unitarian and Early Presbyterian Meeting-Houses

LONGTON. In 1820 Mary Byerley, niece of Josiah Wedgwood, stated in a letter that there was a Unitarian chapel at Lane End with a small congregation. The chapel joined the Shropshire, Cheshire, and Staffordshire Unitarian Association on its foundation in 1824. This meeting lapsed, however, and a second Unitarian church was formed in 1862 in a room at the back of an inn in Queen Street. In 1870 the members built a chapel at Florence, Longton, and in 1874 James Clayton became its first minister. From 1877 to 1895 it shared a minister with the Meeting House, Newcastle. After that Longton had no settled minister. Services continued until April 1903 and in March 1904 the chapel was let to the Spiritualists.[66]

HANLEY. By 1810 there was a Calvinist chapel in Hanley[67] which had ceased to be used by 1812 (see below).

HANLEY, HILL STREET. In 1812, although the penal laws against Unitarians were still in force, Richard Wright, a Unitarian missionary, made the first of many visits to the Potteries and preached in a disused Calvinist chapel at Hanley.[68] In 1820 there were said to be a few Unitarians at Hanley and Shelton.[69] Thomas Cooper became joint minister of Newcastle and Hanley in July 1821 and a room was leased in Hanley.[70] Wright again visited the Potteries in 1821[71] and in 1823 a Unitarian chapel was built in Hill Street, Josiah Wedgwood being among its trustees.[72] In 1824 the chapel became a founder-member of the Shropshire, Cheshire, and Staffordshire Unitarian Association.[73] By 1826 there was a debt of £230 on the chapel and attendances had fallen off partly because of the long absences of the minister, who then left the area.[74] An appeal was made to the Unitarian Association for financial support and Wright again visited the area to help to raise the money.[75] After the departure of the next minister in 1831 the chapel at Hanley closed.[76]

[47] Worship Reg. no. 47460.
[48] Ibid. no. 50626.
[49] Ibid. no. 55254.
[50] Ibid. no. 66431.
[51] Ibid. no. 32554.
[52] Ibid. no. 49665.
[53] Ibid. no. 57037.
[54] Ibid. no. 59893.
[55] Ibid. no. 46188.
[56] Ibid. no. 47074.
[57] Ibid. no. 58162.
[58] See p. 296.
[59] Worship Reg. no. 59731.
[60] Ibid. no. 55594.
[61] The Manchester district was and is a centre of Swedenborgian influence (Oxford Dict. of the Christian Church), which may account for the recurrent appearance of the sect in the Potteries.
[62] H.O. 129/15/371/5/2. The Swedenborgians were said to be meeting at the Vauxhall Schoolroom, Normacot Rd., by 1864: Jones's Pottery Dir. (1864).
[63] S.R.O., Q/AH, bdle. 3. For dating of this map see p. 224, n. 4.

[64] The Swedenborgians are mentioned in Kelly's Dir. Staffs. (1892) but not in the edn. of 1896. Keates's Potteries Dir. (1875–6) gives the meeting-place as the Vauxhall Schoolroom, but the edns. for 1879 and 1892–3 give it as the Anchor Schoolroom, Wharf (now Bridgwood) St.
[65] Worship Reg. no. 50321.
[66] This account is taken from Unit. Hist. Soc. vi. 14–28. The chap. was registered in 1871: Worship Reg. no. 20443. The regtn. was cancelled in 1906.
[67] Ret. of Places of Worship by Abps. and Bps., Parl. Procs. 1811.
[68] Unit. Hist. Soc. vi. 14–28.
[69] Ibid.
[70] Pegler, The Old Meeting House, Newcastle-under-Lyme, 8.
[71] Unit. Hist. Soc. vi. 14–28.
[72] Lich. Dioc. Regy., Bp.'s Reg. G, p. 537.
[73] Unit. Hist. Soc. vi. 14–28.
[74] Pegler, The Old Meeting House, 8; Unit. Hist. Soc. vi. 14–28.
[75] Unit. Hist. Soc. vi. 14–28.
[76] Pegler, op. cit. 8. It was described as disused in 1834: White, Dir. Staffs. (1834).

HANLEY, ETRURIA. In February 1852 the Unitarians started to use the Infants' School, Etruria, for worship.[77] Services were still being held in 1862.[78] The building was taken over by the Etruscan Choral Society in 1945.[79]

BURSLEM. In 1715 there was said to be a regular meeting in Burslem but no settled minister.[80] Richard Wright, the Unitarian missionary, preached at Burslem as well as Hanley in 1812 in a Methodist chapel, the congregation having been warned to expect a Unitarian discourse. Unitarian meetings were being held in the town in 1825, and in 1826 the average congregation was 20. The Burslem meeting ceased in 1847.[81] It has been impossible to identify their meeting-place. There was a second short-lived Unitarian church in Burslem from 1908 to 1912 which used premises in Liverpool Road.[82]

JEWISH CONGREGATIONS

THE practice of the Jewish religion in the Potteries seems to have been concentrated in Hanley. A congregation was formed there in 1873[1] and by 1876 there was a small synagogue[2] identified in 1880 as being in Hanover Street.[3] This continued in use until at least 1916.[4] By 1924 the Synagogue was in Birch Terrace,[5] and this was still in use in 1958.[6] A second synagogue in Glass Street was registered in 1897, the congregation declaring themselves to be Orthodox Hebrew.[7] Nothing further is known directly of this group although Huntbach writing shortly before 1910 stated that the Jews 'had not always been able to agree to worship in one synagogue and at present have two weak causes'.[8] The burial ground in Stoke, on the Stone road close to the boundary with Newcastle, was in existence by the end of the 19th century.[9]

SCHOOLS[1]

Endowed Schools and Grammar Schools

THE first schools in the area seem to have been those set up in the early 17th century by John Weston, Rector of Stoke (d. 1617). One of these was at Stoke, where 40 boys were taught reading, writing, and the catechism. The other was at Shelton, 'near the head of Snape Marsh, at the Row where the Rector did at some time dwell', and here girls were taught to read, spin, knit, and sew.[2] The subsequent history of these schools is unknown, but it may have been the former of the two at which William Adey was licensed in 1732 to teach.[3]

Thomas Allen, Rector of Stoke 1699–1732,[4] founded a school at Meir Lane[5] which continued as a charity school until some date in the mid-18th century. The income then lapsed because the Allen family, genuinely doubting whether the trust was binding, discontinued payment.[6] The endowment was retrieved, however, and in 1832 the school was reopened. In 1835 it was educating about 30 boys, some of them fee-payers.[7] It had closed again by 1840,[8] but was again in existence by 1870 when the Fenton Improvement Commissioners allowed the use of the courthouse as a day and Sunday school for a few weeks.[9] The further history of this charity school is not known.

In 1760 John Bourne, who also founded the churches of Longton and Hanley,[10] endowed a small school and house at Longton[11] where about 30 of the poorest children of Lane End were to be taught.[12] Land for a school-house was settled in trust in 1763 and a school-house erected on it.[13] By 1825 the schoolmaster received a salary of £15 a year and 18 boys were being taught in the school-house by the master and 20 girls in the master's house by his wife. The trustees were then proposing to transfer the endowments to the new St. John's National School.[14] This was apparently done and the school ceased to have a separate existence.[15] The National School closed at some date between 1859 and 1872.[16] By 1873 the Bourne endowment was again applied to a separate school regulated in that year as a secondary school by a Scheme of the Charity Commissioners.[17] At the same time much of the revenue of Dilhorne

---

[77] Pegler, op. cit. 8.
[78] *Unit. Hist. Soc.* vi. 14–28.
[79] See p. 172.
[80] Dr. Williams's Libr., Evans MSS.
[81] *Unit. Hist. Soc.* vi. 14–28.
[82] Ibid.; Worship Reg. no. 43321. The chap. was registered in Oct. 1908, not 1909 as stated in *Unit. Hist. Soc.* vi. 14–28.

[1] *The Jewish Yr. Bk.* (1957), p. 160.
[2] *P.O. Dir. Staffs.* (1876).
[3] *Kelly's Dir. Staffs.* (1880).
[4] Ibid. (1880 and later edns. to 1916).
[5] Ibid. (1924).
[6] Ex inf. the Rabbi, Birch St. Synagogue (1958).
[7] Worship Reg. no. 35899.
[8] A. Huntbach, *Hanley*, 71.
[9] O.S. Map 6" Staffs. xvii NE. (1900).

[1] This article and the accompanying tables covers those schools, except nursery and grammar schools, supported by charitable endowments or out of public funds within the area of the present city.
[2] Ward, *Stoke*, 488–9.
[3] Lich. Dioc. Regy., Subscription Bk. 1730–8. Money was spent on the Stoke school in 1633: *Stoke Churchwardens' Accts. (T.N.S.F.C.* lxxiv), 68, 69, 70, 73.
[4] S. W. Hutchinson, *Archdeaconry of Stoke-on-Trent*, 120.
[5] Ward, *Stoke*, 489; *13th Rep. Com. Char.* H.C. 349, pp. 310–11 (1825), xi.
[6] *13th Rep. Com. Char.* 319.
[7] *Educ. Enq. Abstract*, H.C. 62, pp. 886–7 (1835), xlii.
[8] Ward, *Stoke*, 567.
[9] H.R.L., Fenton Commrs.' Mins. 6 Dec. 1870.
[10] See pp. 154, 233.
[11] *13th Rep. Com. Char.* 311–14.   [12] Ibid.
[13] Ibid. 312.   [14] See p. 324.
[15] White, *Dir. Staffs.* (1851).   [16] See Table IX.
[17] *Staffs. End. Char. (Elem. Educ.)* [Cd. 2729], pp. 49–50, H.C. (1906), xc.

Free School was applied to Longton School, half of the exhibitions at Longton School going to children from the public elementary schools at Dilhorne.[18] Longton School continued on this basis as a secondary grammar school until 1900. The number of pupils at the school gradually decreased, however, and in January 1900 there were only 36.[19] By 1900, too, the liabilities of the school considerably exceeded its assets. The Charity Commissioners recommended that the school be taken over by the Longton Borough Council and conducted as a mixed boys' and girls' school. Pending a decision by the council the school was closed in July 1900.[20] The council agreed to administer the school in conjunction with the Sutherland Technical Institute, situated close to it in the Stone road and under the same head master. Extensive alterations were made to the High School, as it was by then called; in particular, science laboratories were built and the Upper School was recognized as a school of science by the Board of Education.[21] The school was also opened to girls at this date, and in the formation of the curriculum special attention was given to the needs of the local industries of pottery and metallurgy.[22] The close relationship with the Technical Institute continued at least until 1905, the teaching staff being common to both institutions.[23] In 1947 the school, called Longton Grammar School, moved into new buildings in London Road, Meir. The girls had been transferred in 1938 to Thistley Hough School for Girls in Newcastle Lane, Penkhull, opened in that year to provide separate grammar-school education for girls in the south of the Potteries.[24]

At the end of the 17th century there is mention of a school at Hanley *noviter erecta* at which John Strettell *literatus* was licensed in 1698 to teach.[25] This may have been the same school which in 1825 was occupied by Peter Tock, aged 80, who had been in possession of the school since about 1790 and was said to have kept a school there for some time but to have given it up in recent years. Before he acquired the tenancy a man named Gill had kept a school in the house and Tock paid him £15 to give up possession. When Tock first began his school he received £6 a year from the Adams family of Newcastle to educate 10 children free. The last payment was made about 1807[26] and there is no evidence that the school was in existence after that date.

Burslem Free School was started by subscription in 1740,[27] one of the principal contributors being John Bourne of Newcastle, founder of Longton School. The school was to be an English school, not a grammar school, and it was open to all religious denominations, the only stipulation being that pupils whose parents belonged to the Church of England should attend church regularly on Sundays. In 1825 the school premises consisted of a school room and a master's house. By 1823 the buildings had fallen into disrepair, the school master was very old and incompetent, there were no trustees, and no children were admitted free. Some of the inhabitants of Burslem took matters in hand and in 1823 new trustees and a new master were appointed, and the school buildings repaired. The master was to be allowed to teach 30 boys and his wife 20 girls in addition to the free scholars. The trustees, however, in 1825 felt that the funds of the school would be better applied to the National School,[28] but the proposal was not carried out. In 1832 the old school in Liverpool Road was sold and a new school built in Moorland Road. About 1849, however, this became unusable because of mining subsidence and in 1851 the school was being held in a room of the former school building rented from the owner. It was a grammar school by this date with 2 masters and 25 pupils, of whom 14 were taught English free under the terms of the endowment.[29] In 1859 it was said to have been closed for two years[30] but by 1861 was again in use.[31] It had closed by 1868.[32]

Cobridge Free School for 120 children (paying 2d. to 6d. a week each) was built in 1766 by subscription; it was situated at what is now the junction of Sneyd Street, Elder Road, and Leek New Road, and consisted of a school and two dwelling-rooms below. The premises, which were repaired in 1821, were stated to have been conveyed to trustees who, however, were all dead by 1860. The school ceased to be used c. 1850. It was demolished in 1897,[33] but it is still commemorated by an inscribed plinth.

Tunstall Endowed School originated outside the city in an endowment by Dr. Robert Hulme of Oddrode (Ches.) by will dated 1708. In 1825 the school was at Newchapel,[34] the head master being appointed by the Child family of Tunstall.[35] Between 1876 and 1880 it was transferred to Tunstall.[36] It closed between 1884 and 1892.[37]

There was only one endowed school in the area added to the county borough in 1922.[38] This was Bucknall School founded under the will (dated 1719) of William Shallcross of Uttoxeter, by which the testator gave £5 yearly to a school master to teach 12 poor children, provided the freeholders of Bucknall and Eaves built a school-house.[39] The endowment was charged on Blakeloe farm by 1825, the property of John Tomlinson of Cliffville in Stoke.[40] This school subsequently became a National School.[41] Thus out of these old educational foundations in the Potteries only one grammar school, that at Longton, remains at the present time.

A Higher Grade Elementary school was opened by

[18] *Staffs. End. Char. (Elem. Educ.)* [Cd. 2729], pp. 49–50, H.C. (1906), xc.
[19] G. George, *Educ. Organisation in Longton, an experiment in co-ordination and correlation* (copy in H.R.L.).
[20] Ibid.
[21] Ibid.
[22] Ibid.
[23] Longton Educ. Cttee., High Sch. and Institute Sub-Cttee. Mins. 6 June 1905.
[24] Ex inf. City Educ. Dept.
[25] Lich. Dioc. Regy., Subscription Bk. 1692–9.
[26] *13th Rep. Com. Char.* 317–18.
[27] There is, however, record of a school master in Burslem in the early 17th cent.: Wedgwood, *Wedgwood Family*, 260; *T.N.S.F.C.* lxxiv, pp. A68, 69, 70, 74.
[28] *13th Rep. Com. Char.* 259–60.

[29] White, *Dir. Staffs.* (1851).
[30] G. Griffith, *Free Schs. and Endowments of Staffs.* 510.
[31] *Harrison, Harrod & Co.'s Dir. and Gaz. Staffs.* (1861), 421.
[32] *P.O. Dir. Staffs.* (1868).
[33] Griffith, *Free Schs. of Staffs.* 511; Warrillow, *Stoke*, 274–5.
[34] *13th Rep. Com. Char.* 326–8.
[35] Ibid. 326.
[36] *P.O. Dir. Staffs.* (1876); *Kelly's Dir. Staffs.* (1880).
[37] *Kelly's Dir. Staffs.* (1884, 1892).
[38] See p. 259.
[39] *13th Rep. Com. Char.* 316.
[40] Ibid.
[41] See Table XI.

Hanley School Board in 1893.[42] The junior and middle schools followed an advanced elementary course and the boys in the higher school were taught all the normal subjects of a grammar school including Latin and Greek[43] and the girls a more limited course which, however, included Latin.[44] Since the courses in the upper part of the school were those of a grammar school the Board of Education was reluctant to recognize it as an elementary school but eventually did so; it continued as such until 1905 when it was officially closed and reopened as Hanley High School.[45] It remained as a mixed grammar school until 1938 when the girls were transferred to Thistley Hough School for Girls.[46] Hanley High School buildings were condemned in 1940 because of mining subsidence and the school was moved into the new buildings intended for Chell Senior School. From 1948 to 1953 it was run as a bilateral school with Chell Secondary Modern School and in the latter year moved into new buildings in Corneville Road, Bucknall.[47]

Two Roman Catholic grammar schools have been established in the present century. The first, a girls' school, developed out of a school opened by the nuns at the Dominican Convent at Hartshill.[48] A house called Cliffville near the convent was bought in 1922 and the senior part of the school moved there; the junior part followed in 1929.[49] The school acquired aided status under the 1944 Education Act as a girls' grammar school.[50] The second, a boys' school, was established at Trent Vale by the Irish Christian Brothers in 1932.[51]

Elementary Education before 1870

During the earlier 19th century the educational facilities offered by the endowed schools began to be supplemented by schools founded by the various churches and the two schools' societies, the National Society and the British and Foreign Schools Society. The first such school to be founded was the Wesleyan Day School in Burslem in 1814, followed there by a National School in 1817 in connexion with St. John's Church. National Schools were founded in Stoke in 1815 and in Hanley in 1816. In Hanley the National School was quickly followed by a nonconformist school, the British School in Pall Mall, founded by the Ridgway family, who were leaders of the Methodist New Connexion in the area. Longton (St. John's) National School was founded in 1822 and St. James's National School in 1836, but Tunstall and Fenton National Schools were not founded until 1839. By 1850 thirteen National Schools had been established in the various Pottery towns and there was a parish school at Bucknall. In Stoke itself the Church of England was particularly active in this matter. Apart from the main National School, attached to St. Peter's Church, schools had by 1850 been founded at Hartshill, Trent Vale, and Penkhull. There were also two Wesleyan schools, one unsectarian school, one British school, and two Roman Catholic schools in the Potteries area by

1851. Many of these schools owed their existence, not to the churches, but to particular individuals who promoted them and to a great extent maintained them. Such were the British School for boys at Hanley (founded 1819) supported by the Ridgway family, the unsectarian school at Etruria (founded 1846) maintained by the Wedgwood family, particularly Francis Wedgwood,[52] and the National Schools in Stoke, Longton, and Hanley which benefited by a bequest of £3,000 by J. C. Woodhouse, Dean of Lichfield and formerly Rector of Stoke.[53]

During the period 1851–70 a notable feature of education in the Potteries was the great increase in the number of National Schools. Many were built in the small villages or hamlets which developed under the influence of the six towns, such as the infants' school at Line Houses near Tunstall and the school at Sneyd near Burslem. Many more were established as branch schools of the main National School in each town to serve some small, densely populated area of working-class houses. Such were the second National School at Tunstall (St. Mary's School), Cobridge National School in Burslem, St. Paul's National School in Burslem serving the Dale Hall area, Eastwood Vale National School, Hanley, Wellington National School, Hanley, Northwood National School, Hanley, Trinity National School serving the Hope Street area of Hanley, China Street National School, Fenton, Mount Pleasant National School, Fenton, St. John's Branch School at Park Hall Street, Longton, and Mount Pleasant National School, Longton.

Another development of the period was the growth of the Ragged Schools. These schools for very poor children were sometimes a private and sometimes a church enterprise. Two were established in Hanley in 1852, one an evening school (known as the Ragged School from 1856) and the other Bryan Street Ragged School in a building known as the Workmen's Refuge.[54] Another was opened at Ashley Street, Hanley, in 1856[55] and all three were managed by the same master. In 1861 they were amalgamated as the Borough Ragged Schools.[56] In 1861, too, one was opened in Longton[57] and by that year there was one at Burslem.[58]

Private philanthropy also played some part in the provision of elementary education in this period, illustrated not only by the interest of Francis Wedgwood in the British School at Etruria[59] but also by the school built by Lord Granville for his iron and steel workers.[60] By 1870 there were in the Potteries 28 National Schools, 5 Wesleyan schools, 4 other nonconformist, including British, schools, 6 Roman Catholic schools, and 2 non-sectarian schools, Granville School and Etruria Unsectarian School.

Elementary Education 1870–1910

This period covers the establishment of a state system of education in the Pottery district under the various school boards and, after the 1902 Education Act, by the Education Committees of the various

42 Ed. 21/510; date-stone on building; ex inf. City Educ. Dept.   43 Ed. 21/510.
44 Ibid.
45 Ibid.; ex inf. City Educ. Dept.
46 Ex inf. City Educ. Dept.
47 Ex inf. City Educ. Dept.
48 M. Greenslade, *A Brief Hist. of the Cath. Ch. in Stoke-on-Trent*, 35.   49 Ibid.
50 Ibid.   51 Ibid. 37.
52 Ed. 7/112; see Table IX.
53 See Table IX; White, *Dir. Staffs.* (1851); Ward, *Stoke*, 481.   54 Warrillow, *Stoke*, 280–1.
55 Ibid. 281; see Table IX.
56 Warrillow, *Stoke*, 281.
57 Ibid. 282.   58 Ibid.
59 See Table IX.   60 See Table IX.

borough and urban district councils and by the Staffordshire County Council.

Under the guidance of its first chairman, Sir Lovelace Stamer, Rector of Stoke, who was also chairman of the National Schools Board in Stoke,[61] the Stoke School Board co-operated with the latter to provide new church schools and new board schools.[62] The school board district covered a wide area, some of it outside the present city. It extended from Butterton near Whitmore to Stanley Pool near Endon station, the townships included being Seabridge, Clayton, Penkhull-cum-Boothen, Fenton Culvert, Fenton Vivian, Botteslow, Bucknall, and Bagnall.[63] In 1871 the total number of children at school in the district was just over 3,600, most of them in National Schools which educated children of both churchmen and others.[64] It was then estimated that 1,300 more places in schools were needed. The deficiency was met partly by the opening by the board of a number of temporary schools, some in nonconformist Sunday schools.[65] By 1876 there were 6 schools under the Stoke School Board: Mount Tabor, Cross Street, Harpfield, Penkhull, Bagnall, and Clayton.[66] On the formation of Stoke and Fenton Education Committees in 1903 there were 3 board schools in Stoke itself and 3 in Fenton.[67] There was no notable development in elementary education made by either of these two committees between 1903 and 1910. A novel experiment, however, was made in Stoke in 1905, when the senior boys of St. Peter's School and of Boothen School were transferred to a new school, Stoke Central National School.

Longton School Board encountered the difficulty of having too few children in its first school and so it took over the part-time pupils of a private school occupying the former St. John's National School.[68] Later the board proceeded to establish other permanent schools, namely, Cooke Street Schools (1891), High Street Schools (1879), and the Central School (1898), now Queensberry Schools. This board was more enterprising than the Stoke School Board and in 1898 established a Higher Elementary School at Queensberry Road to provide semi-technical and more advanced education.[69] After its formation Longton Education Committee maintained the emphasis on technical education, instanced by its taking over of the High School and the Technical College, which were managed as a joint institution from 1900 by the Technical Education Committee of the borough in conjunction with the county.[70]

Of the other school boards in the area Hanley, which had the largest population, probably faced the most difficult task. In view of its heavy financial obligations in the educational sphere it was officially recognized as a 'necessitous school board' under the Act of 1897. This greatly benefited the board which was already receiving extra grants under Section 97 of the Act of 1870.[71] The work of the board was chiefly directed towards meeting the scholastic needs of the rapidly increasing school population particularly in the late 1880's and in the 1890's. For example, Cauldon Road Schools, erected in 1891 for boys', girls', and infants' departments to serve part of Shelton, were already overcrowded by 1896 because of the rapid growth of the district. The board, therefore, erected a senior mixed school there in that year with accommodation for 620.[72] In 1896 Wharf Lane Schools also had to be extended and in the following year York Street Schools.[73] A similar policy was followed by the Hanley Education Committee after its formation in 1903.[74] In 1906 Broom Street Schools, Wellington Schools, and the Central Board Schools (Glass Street) in Hanley were reorganized into infants', junior, and senior schools, the Central Schools taking the senior boys and Broom Street Schools the senior girls.[75] Thus some of the recommendations of the Hadow Report were put into effect 20 years before its publication.

Hanley School Board, despite financial difficulties, nevertheless made some provision for secondary and adult education. The Higher Elementary School, which later became Hanley High School, has been described above.[76] By the 1890's a number of evening schools existed, administered at first by the board and later by Hanley Education Committee.[77] The curriculum of the evening classes started at the High School in 1894 included theoretical and practical chemistry, mathematics, physics, geometry, geology, botany, and drawing. All these subjects had some relevance to industry,[78] a practice general throughout the Potteries wherever further education was pursued.

Burslem School Board established in 1874 started somewhat later than the other Potteries boards.[79] It was faced with much the same problems as Hanley, a large child population, with resultant overcrowding in its schools.[80] The number of full-time pupils steadily rose until the number in its schools in 1896 was nearly 10,000. It appears to have been a more conservative board than that of Hanley, and, although it made provision for evening continuation classes on an adequate scale, the subjects taught were less advanced.[81] It made no attempt to run a Higher Elementary School and Burslem Education Committee after its formation in 1903 pursued this same policy of adequate elementary education but without attempting what may be termed advanced education, except in the field of art.[82] It should be noted, however, that in the early part of the present century many children from the Potteries area were attending the Orme Schools in Newcastle.

Tunstall came under Wolstanton School Board which has been treated elsewhere.[83] This board established only one school in Tunstall, Forster Street

[61] *Stoke Sch. Bd. Triennial Rep. 1871–4*; F. E. J. Wright, *Schs. of the parish of St. Peter ad Vincula, Stoke.*
[62] Wright, op. cit.
[63] *Stoke Sch. Bd. Triennial Rep. 1871–4*, introd.
[64] Ibid.; Wright, op. cit.
[65] See Table IX.
[66] *Stoke Sch. Bd. Triennial Rep. 1876.*
[67] *Kelly's Dir. Staffs.* (1908).
[68] *Rep. on Sch. Bd. District of Longton, 1871–92*; see Table IX.
[69] See Table IX.
[70] See p. 308.
[71] *Hanley Sch. Bd. Rep. of Proc. 1894–7.*

[72] Ibid.; see Table IX.
[73] *Hanley Sch. Bd. Rep. 1894–7.*
[74] *Kelly's Dir. Staffs.* (1908).
[75] See Table IX.
[76] See p. 309.
[77] Hanley Sch. Bd. Mins. *passim.*
[78] Ibid. 27 Aug. 1894.
[79] *Kelly's Dir. Staffs.* (1896).
[80] Burslem Sch. Bd. Mins. *passim.*
[81] Burslem Sch. Bd. Mins. of Evening Classes Cttee. *passim.*
[82] Burslem Educ. Cttee. Mins. *passim.*
[83] See p. 68.

School, in 1875. In 1890, however, it took over the Wesleyan School and built the new High Street Schools to replace it in 1894. The problems of over-crowding and a large child population were not so great here as in Burslem, Hanley, or Longton, and with the numerous schools already in the area, the demand for board schools was not so imperative.[84] After the Act of 1902 Tunstall had its own education committee which *inter alia* administered Tunstall Technical College, founded in 1890.[85]

Some educational enterprises affecting the whole area were the result of joint action by the various education committees. The Blind and Deaf School at the Mount in Stoke, opened in 1897,[86] falls into this category. In the first decade of the present century all the education authorities adopted the School Meals Act[87] which eventually led to the present system of subsidized school dinners.[88] Tunstall was the last to do so, in 1910; in 1909 the North Staffs. Federation of the Independent Labour Party petitioned the Education Committee to adopt the Act as there were 5,000 unemployed in Tunstall.[89]

1911 to the Present Day

In 1911 Stoke-on-Trent Education Committee was formed. Stoke as a county borough was responsible for education generally in the area, including further education, much of which had previously been the responsibility of the county. The task of welding all the component elements into a comprehensive educational system was undertaken by R. P. G. Williamson, formerly Education Officer for Burslem. In the sphere of higher education the new authority controlled various technical colleges, even-

ing continuation classes, and two grammar schools. In elementary education the most important change came in the late 1920's and early 1930's when the Education Committee decided to follow the principles laid down in the Hadow Report. An over-all plan was drawn up for the establishment of senior schools, involving frequently the separation of boys and girls.[90] The plan was not put into effect in its entirety, the eventual reorganization being carried out in stages and on an empirical basis by the Director of Education and by H.M. Inspectors of Schools.[91] The reorganization was carried out separately in each of the six towns, Tunstall being dealt with in 1929, Burslem and Longton in 1931, Hanley and Stoke in 1931–2, and Fenton in 1932. The schools of Tunstall were divided into two groups, those of Burslem into three, and those of Hanley and Stoke into four each; there was no such division in Longton and Fenton. The changes are shown in Table XI. In some cases the Church of England schools were grouped with local authority schools and in others reorganized in their own groups. The Roman Catholic schools did not join in the scheme. Some were reorganized later on the same lines, but many were still all-age schools at the end of the Second World War.[92]

The Education Act of 1944 made necessary a second reorganization involving the conversion of senior schools generally into secondary modern schools. The growth in the population of the area, the extension of the school-leaving age, and the inadequacy by modern standards of many of the old school buildings necessitated the erection of many new schools after the war.[93]

Table IX

Schools in the Six Towns[94]

Abbreviations: C. = County, C.S. = County Secondary, C.E. = Church of England, R.C. = Roman Catholic, B = Boys, G = Girls, J = Junior, I = Infants, SB = Senior Boys, SG = Senior Girls, JB = Junior Boys, JG = Junior Girls, M = Mixed, SM = Senior Mixed, / = Separate departments

School	Date of opening	Changes in organization	Buildings
TUNSTALL			
Blessed William Southerne R.C. C.S. School,[95] Little Chell Lane	1957		
Central C. Infants' School[96] (formerly Forster Street School), Forster St.	1875	Reorganized 1929 (see Table XI, Tunstall, Group A).	See Central C. Junior School.
Central C. Junior School,[97] Forster St.	1875	Reorganized as JB, JG, 1929 (see Table XI, Tunstall, Group A). Boys' and girls' departments amalgamated 1956.	Opened in Wesleyan Sunday School, Tunstall. New buildings 1880.
Chell C. Infants' School,[98] High Lane, Chell	1878	See Chell C. Junior School for early history. Reorganized as Chell C. Infants' School in 1946–7.	

[84] See Table IX, Tunstall.
[85] See p. 104.
[86] See p. 197.
[87] Educ. (Provision of Meals) Act, 6 Edw. VII, c. 57.
[88] Mins. of the various Educ. Cttees.
[89] Tunstall Educ. Cttee. Mins. 24 Mar. 1909, 9 Mar. 1910.
[90] Copy in City Educ. Offices.
[91] Ex inf. City Educ. Dept.
[92] See Tables IX, XI.
[93] Ex inf. City Educ. Dept.
[94] The list includes all schools, except nursery and grammar schools, existing in 1960; it also includes schools that had closed before 1960.
[95] *Birmingham Arch. Dioc. Dir.* (1959), 234–5.
[96] Ed. 7/112; ex inf. City Educ. Dept.; ex inf. head mistress (1959); 1959 List of Schs.; tablet *in situ*.
[97] Ibid.
[98] Ex inf. City Educ. Dept.; 1959 List of Schs.

School	Date of opening	Changes in organization	Buildings
CHELL C. JUNIOR SCHOOL,[99] High Lane, Chell	1878	Opened as BG/I. Reorganized as JB, JG in 1946–7 (see Chell C.S. School).	Opened in Wesleyan Sunday School. New buildings August 1878. Enlarged 1891.
CHELL C.S. SCHOOL,[1] St. Michael's Rd., Chell	1947	From 1947 occupied premises of Methodist Sunday School. In 1948 some classes at Smallthorne, some at Pitts Hill. In November 1948 Hanley High School became bilateral, this school forming the secondary modern side. In 1953 it was separated from Hanley High School.	Built 1940 for Chell C.S. School but occupied by Hanley High School till 1953.
CHELL WESLEYAN SCHOOL,[2] St. Michael's Rd., Chell	1874–6	Transferred to School Board in 1878 (see Chell C. Junior, Infants' Schools).	
GOLDENHILL C.E. SCHOOL,[3] High St., Goldenhill	1841	Opened as National School for B, G/I. Reorganized 1929 (see Table XI, Tunstall, Group B). Aided status from 1953, controlled status from April 1957.	New infants' school built 1884. All buildings destroyed by fire 1895. New buildings erected 1895. Enlarged 1904.
GOLDENHILL C. INFANTS' SCHOOL,[4] Heathside Lane, Goldenhill	1881	Formerly Goldenhill Wesleyan School. Opened as infants' school, B/G/I from 1884 until 1929 when reorganized (see Table XI, Tunstall, Group B).	Used buildings of Wesleyan Sunday School until 1884 when new buildings erected.
GOLDENHILL C.S. SCHOOL,[5] Heathside Lane, Goldenhill	1929	See Table XI, Tunstall, Group B.	Used part of buildings of former Goldenhill all-age school.
GOLDENHILL R.C. JUNIOR AND INFANTS' SCHOOL,[6] Brakespeare St., Goldenhill	1870	Opened as mixed all-age school. Aided status since July 1951.	Erected 1871.
GOLDENHILL WESLEYAN SCHOOL,[7] High St., Goldenhill	1872	Transferred to School Board 1881 (see Goldenhill C. Infants' School).	Used Sunday school buildings.
HIGHGATE C. JUNIOR AND INFANTS' SCHOOL[8] (formerly High Street School), High St.	1890	Formerly Tunstall Wesleyan Day School (q.v.). Reorganized 1929 (see Table XI, Tunstall, Group A).	Used buildings of Wesleyan Sunday School, John St., until 1894 when High Street Schools built.
HIGHGATE C.S. BOYS' SCHOOL,[9] High St.	1929	Reorganized as such 1929 (see Table XI, Tunstall, Group A).	Using part of buildings of former Highgate all-age school (see Highgate C. Junior and Infants' School).
HOLLY WALL C. JUNIOR AND INFANTS' SCHOOL,[10] Burnaby Rd., Sandyford	1939		
LINE HOUSES C.E. INFANTS' SCHOOL[11]	1850–4	Supplementary to Goldenhill C.E. School (q.v.). Infants only. Closed c. 1870.	
LYNDHURST STREET TEMPORARY SCHOOL[12]	By 1905	Opened by Hulme Trustees as supplementary infants' and junior school to Tunstall C.E. School. Transferred to Education Committee in 1906. Closed on opening of Summerbank Council School.	
MILL HILL C. INFANTS' SCHOOL,[13] Sunnyside Ave., Little Chell	1952		
MILL HILL C. JUNIOR SCHOOL,[14] Sunnyside Ave., Little Chell	1953		
PITTS HILL BOARD SCHOOL,[15] High St., Pitts Hill	1875	Formerly Pitts Hill Primitive Methodist School. Closed 1877 when pupils transferred to Chell Board School (see Chell C. Junior and Infants' Schools).	Used buildings of Pitts Hill Primitive Methodist Sunday School.

[99] Ed. 7/112; 1959 List of Schs.; *Kelly's Dir. Staffs.* (1916); ex inf. City Educ. Dept.
[1] Ed. 7/112; 1959 List of Schs.; *Kelly's Dir. Staffs.* (1916); ex inf. City Educ. Dept.   [2] Ed. 7/112.
[3] J. Jack, *The Church on the Hill* (1944), 41, 43; Ed. 7/112; *Kelly's Dir. Staffs.* (1916); ex inf. City Educ. Dept.
[4] Ed. 7/112; ex inf. City Educ. Dept.; 1959 List of Schs.; *Kelly's Dir. Staffs.* (1916).
[5] Ex inf. City Educ. Dept.; 1959 List of Schs.
[6] Ed. 7/112; ex inf. City Educ. Dept.; 1959 List of Schs.

[7] Ed. 7/112.
[8] Ed. 7/112; ex inf. City Educ. Dept.; 1959 List of Schs.
[9] Ex inf. City Educ. Dept.; 1959 List of Schs.
[10] Ex inf. City Educ. Dept.; 1959 List of Schs.
[11] Jack, *Ch. on the Hill*, 15, 41.
[12] Tunstall Educ. Cttee. Mins., 22 Nov. 1905; 31 Dec. 1906.
[13] Ex inf. City Educ. Dept.; 1959 List of Schs.
[14] Ex inf. City Educ. Dept.; 1959 List of Schs.
[15] Ed. 7/112; Log Bk., Chell C. Infants' Sch., 19 July 1877.

School	Date of opening	Changes in organization	Buildings
PITTS HILL PRIMITIVE METHODIST SCHOOL,[16] High St., Pitts Hill	1872–5	Transferred to School Board 1875 (see Pitts Hill Board School).	Used buildings of Pitts Hill Primitive Methodist Sunday School.
ST. MARY'S C.E. INFANTS' SCHOOL,[17] Lascelles St.	1860	Opened as mixed and infants' school. Reorganized 1929 (see Table XI, Tunstall, Group A). Aided status since June 1953.	The infants' school replaced by new building in 1911 on separate site. Former infants' school then added to boys' department.
ST. MARY'S C.E. SECONDARY SCHOOL,[18] Harewood St.	1929	Reorganized as such 1929 (see Table XI, Tunstall, Group A).	Occupying buildings of former mixed department of St. Mary's C.E. School (see St. Mary's C.E. Infants' School).
SANDYFORD C.E. SCHOOL[19]	1874	Mixed school. Closed 1884–92.	
SUMMERBANK C. INFANTS' SCHOOL,[20] Summerbank Rd.	1909	See Summerbank C. Junior School.	
SUMMERBANK C. JUNIOR SCHOOL,[21] Summerbank Rd.	1909	Opened as all-age school. Reorganized 1929 (see Table XI, Tunstall, Group A).	
SUMMERBANK C.S. GIRLS' SCHOOL,[22] Summerbank Rd.	1929	See Table XI, Tunstall, Group A.	Occupying part of buildings of Summerbank C. School (see Summerbank C. Junior School).
TUNSTALL C.E. SCHOOL,[23] King St.	1839	Controlled by Hulme Trustees. Opened as National School for B/G/I. By 1905 part of infants' school formed Lyndhurst Street Temporary School, Lyndhurst Street. Board of Education recognition withdrawn and school closed and replaced by Summerbank Council School (q.v.) 1909.	Enlarged 1871 and 1898.
TUNSTALL PRIMITIVE METHODIST DAY SCHOOL,[24] Wedgwood St.	1872	Opened as B/G/I. Succeeded a private school which was opened c. 1840. Closed 1880–4.	
TUNSTALL R.C. JUNIOR AND INFANTS' SCHOOL,[25] Oldcourt St.	1853	Opened as mixed all-age school. In 1874 infants made a separate department. Seniors transferred in 1957 to Blessed William Southerne C.S. School, Tunstall. Aided status since Jan. 1952.	Original buildings erected in Plex St. in 1853. Infants' school erected 1874. Oldcourt St. schools built 1902–3.
TUNSTALL WESLEYAN DAY SCHOOL,[26] John St.	1838	Mixed all-age school. Transferred to School Board in 1890 (see Highgate C. Junior and Infants' School).	
BURSLEM			
BURSLEM WESLEYAN DAY SCHOOL,[27] Moorland Rd.	1814	School taken over by School Board 1902.	In Sunday-school buildings erected 1789. New buildings 1850, enlarged in 1884.
COBRIDGE C.E. INFANTS' SCHOOL,[28] Mawdesley St., Cobridge	1857	Opened as B/GI. B/G/I by 1884. Reorganized 1953. Controlled status since May 1948.	
COBRIDGE FREE SCHOOL,[29] Sneyd St.	1766	Closed by c. 1850.	Repaired 1821.
COBRIDGE R.C. JUNIOR AND INFANTS' SCHOOL,[30] Waterloo Rd.	1822	B/GI by 1852. Also night school by then. Reorganized 1957, when seniors went to Blessed William Southerne C.S. School, Tunstall. Aided status from July 1951.	Rebuilt 1905, new buildings opened 1906.

[16] Ed. 7/112.
[17] Ed. 7/112; ex inf. City Educ. Dept.; 1959 List of Schs.
[18] Ex inf. City Educ. Dept.; 1959 List of Schs.
[19] Ed. 7/113; *P.O. Dir. Staffs.* (1876); *Kelly's Dir. Staffs.* (1880, 1884, 1892).
[20] Ed. 7/112; ex inf. City Educ. Dept.; 1959 List of Schs.
[21] Ed. 7/112; ex inf. City Educ. Dept.; 1959 List of Schs.
[22] Ex inf. City Educ. Dept.; 1959 List of Schs.
[23] Ed. 7/113; *Kelly's Dir. Staffs.* (1900); White, *Dir. Staffs.* (1851); Tunstall Educ. Cttee. Mins., 22 Nov. 1905; 21 Mar., 31 Dec. 1906; 1909 *passim*.
[24] Ed. 7/113; *P.O. Dir. Staffs.* (1876); *Kelly's Dir. Staffs.* (1880, 1884).
[25] Ed. 7/112; 1959 List of Schs.; ex inf. the Clergy, Sacred Heart Ch., Tunstall; ex inf. City Educ. Dept.
[26] Ed. 7/112.
[27] Ed. 7/112; Burslem Sch. Bd., Clerk's Rep., 5 Feb. 1902.
[28] Ed. 7/112; *Kelly's Dir. Staffs.* (1884); ex inf. City Educ. Dept.; 1959 List of Schs.
[29] G. Griffith, *Free Schs. and Endowments of Staffs.* 511; Warrillow, *Stoke*, 274.
[30] Ed. 7/112; Burslem Educ. Cttee., Sch. Management Cttee. Mins., 7 Feb. 1906; tablet *in situ*; ex inf. City Educ. Dept.; 1959 List of Schs.

School	Date of opening	Changes in organization	Buildings
Granville C. Junior and Infants' School,[31] Granville St., Cobridge	1854	Opened by Earl Granville and the partners of Shelton Bar Iron Co. Transferred to the Burslem School Board 1890 by Shelton Iron, Steel, and Coal Co. B/G/I until 1899, then mixed and infants until 1931 reorganization (see Table XI, Burslem, Group B).	Rebuilt 1898.
Hamil Road Temporary Branch School,[32] Hamil Rd.	1903	Took juniors from Park Council School 1903-4.	Occupying Primitive Methodist Sunday-school building.
Hill Top C. Junior School,[33] Greenhead St.	1875	Opened as B/G/I. Reorganized 1931 (see Table XI, Burslem, Group B).	Opened in buildings of Burslem Sunday School. New buildings 1878. Enlarged 1879, 1880, 1893.
Hill Top C. Infants' School,[34] Greenhead St.	1875	Reorganized as such 1931 (see Table XI, Burslem, Group B).	Opened in buildings of Burslem Sunday School. New buildings 1878.
Jackfield C. Infants' School,[35] Jackfield St.	1904	Took infants from Park Road School.	
Longport C. Junior and Infants' School,[36] Longport Rd., Longport	1875	Girls and infants until 1893 when it became mixed and infants. Nursery department by 1895. Reorganized Sept. 1940 with Middleport C. Infants' School (q.v.).	Opened in buildings of Wesleyan Sunday School, Longport. New buildings 1878. New school for mixed dept. 1893.
Middleport C. Infants' School,[37] Morton St., Middleport	1877	Opened as B/G/I. In 1883 made B/G/JM/I. By 1895 a nursery department. Reorganized with Longport C.J. School (q.v.) in Sept. 1940.	Extended 1877-8; new infants' school 1878-9. Extended again 1883. Buildings altered 1893 and 1900.
Middleport C.S. School,[38] Morton St., Middleport	1940	Formed on reorganization of Middleport and Longport C.P. Schools (see Middleport C. Infants' School).	Occupying part of former Middleport C. Infants' School.
Moorland C. Junior School,[39] Moorland Rd.	1911	Took children from Burslem Central (Wesleyan) Schools which then closed. B/G/I until 1931 when reorganized (see Table XI, Burslem, Group B).	
Moorland C.S. Boys' School,[40] Moorland Rd.	1931	Arose out of 1931 reorganization (see Table XI, Burslem, Group B).	In buildings of former Moorland C. Junior School.
Moorland C.S. Girls' School,[41] Moorland Rd.	1931	Arose out of 1931 reorganization (see Table XI, Burslem, Group B).	In buildings of former Moorland C. Junior School.
North C. Infants' School,[42] North Rd., Cobridge	1876	Reorganized as such 1931 (see Table XI, Burslem, Group B).	See North C. Junior School.
North C. Junior School,[43] North Rd., Cobridge	1876	Opened as B/G/I. Nursery class by 1895. Mixed and infants from 1903. Reorganized 1931.	Extended 1903.
Park Road School[44]	1896	Infants' dept. opened 1895-6, and mixed dept. in Apr. 1896. In 1903 juniors transferred to Hamil Road School (q.v.). Infants transferred to Jackfield School in 1904 when juniors returned. Reorganized 1931 when school became a junior mixed school for one year, then made senior school only (see Park C.S. School).	In 1904 juniors moved into former infants' school building.

31 Ed. 7/112; Burslem Sch. Bd., Sch. Management Cttee. Mins., 26 Aug. 1890, 25 Sept. 1899; *Kelly's Dir. Staffs.* (1916); ex inf. City Educ. Dept.; 1959 List of Schs.
32 Burslem Educ. Cttee., Clerk's Rep., 14 Dec. 1903.
33 Ed. 7/112; *P.O. Dir. Staffs.* (1876); Burslem Sch. Bd., Clerk's Rep., 5 Oct. 1897; 1959 List of Schs.; ex inf. City Educ. Dept.
34 Ed. 7/112; *P.O. Dir. Staffs.* (1876); Burslem Sch. Bd., Clerk's Rep., 5 Oct. 1897; 1959 List of Schs.; ex inf. City Educ. Dept.
35 Ed. 7/112; Burslem Educ. Cttee. Mins., 15 Feb. 1904; 1959 List of Schs.
36 Ed. 7/112; *Kelly's Dir. Staffs.* (1880, 1916); Burslem Sch. Bd., Clerk's Rep., 5 Oct. 1897; ibid., Sch. Management Cttee. Mins. 21 May 1895.
37 Ed. 7/112; *Burslem Sch. Bd. Review since 1874 and suppl. 1883-1886*, 11; Burslem Sch. Bd., Sch. Management Cttee. Mins., 17 Sept. 1883; ibid., Clerk's Rep., 5 Oct. 1897; Burslem Educ. Cttee., Sch. Management Cttee. Mins., 31 May 1895, 26 Mar. 1900; ex inf. City Educ. Dept.; 1959 List of Schs.
38 Ex inf. City Educ. Dept.
39 Ed. 7/112; ex inf. City Educ. Dept.; 1959 List of Schs.
40 Ex inf. City Educ. Dept.; 1959 List of Schs.
41 Ex inf. City Educ. Dept.; 1959 List of Schs.
42 Ed. 7/112; ex inf. City Educ. Dept.; 1959 List of Schs.
43 Ed. 7/112; Burslem Sch. Bd. Sch. Management Cttee., 21 Mar. 1895; Burslem Educ. Cttee., Clerk's Rep., 4 Dec. 1903; ex inf. City Educ. Dept.; 1959 List of Schs.
44 Ed. 7/112; *Kelly's Dir. Staffs.* (1900); Burslem Sch. Bd., Sch. Management Cttee. Mins., April 1896; Burslem Educ. Cttee., Clerk's Rep., 14 Dec. 1903; ex inf. City Educ. Dept.

School	Date of opening	Changes in organization	Buildings
PARK C.S. SCHOOL,[45] Park Rd.	1931	Formed on reorganization of 1931 (see Table XI, Burslem, Group B).	Using buildings of former Park Road Council School.
PORTLAND HOUSE C. TECHNICAL SCHOOL,[46] Newcastle St.	1948		
ST. JOHN'S C.E. INFANTS' SCHOOL,[47] Cross Hill	1817	Founded as an all-age school. Reorganized 1931 (see Table XI, Burslem, Group A). Controlled status since April 1950.	Rebuilt 1896 on the site of the nearby Churchyard Pottery.
ST. JOHN'S C.E. SECONDARY SCHOOL,[48] Cross Hill	1931	Arose out of reorganization (see Table XI, Burslem, Group A). Controlled status since April 1950.	Using buildings of former St. John's C.E. Primary School (see St. John's C.E. Infants' School).
ST. JOSEPH'S R.C. JUNIOR AND INFANTS' SCHOOL,[49] Pack Horse Lane	1898	Opened as mixed and infants' school. Reorganized 1957, when seniors went to Blessed William Southerne C.S. School, Tunstall. Aided status from June 1951.	School-church till 1927.
ST. PAUL'S C.E. JUNIOR SCHOOL,[50] Sant St., Dale Hall	1836	Opened as mixed school. Closed 1849. Reopened 1857 or 1860. Branch school at the Sytch for infants c. 1876 until c. 1880. Mixed and infants by 1931 when reorganized (see Table XI, Burslem, Group C). Controlled status from May 1949.	Extended 1879. In 1907 infants' school housed in Hope Mission, Shirley St.
SNEYD C.E. SCHOOL[51]	1857, 1868	Parochial School opened 1857. Apparently closed by 1860. Sneyd National School opened 1868 as B/GI. By 1892 mixed and infants. Reorganized 1931 (see Table XI, Burslem, Group A). Controlled status from Nov. 1949. Closed 1957.	Building of first school erected 1825. Building of Sneyd National School erected 1867.
SNEYD GREEN C. JUNIOR SCHOOL,[52] Sneyd St.	1901	Opened as mixed school. Reorganized 1931 (see Table XI, Burslem, Group B).	Erected 1899.
SNEYD GREEN C. INFANTS' SCHOOL,[53] Sneyd St.	1901		
STANFIELD C. TECHNICAL SCHOOL,[54] Moorland Rd.	1932		Extended 1959.
HANLEY			
ASHLEY STREET NATIONAL SCHOOL[55]	1856	Used first as an evening Ragged School. By 1860 in use as day all-age run by C.E. clergy and committee of Shelton National School.	
BEDFORD STREET SCHOOL[56]	1872	Opened by School Board for girls and infants. Closed 1880 when children transferred to new Wharf Lane School (q.v.).	Used Sunday School of Bedford Methodist New Connexion Chapel.
BELMONT C. INFANTS' SCHOOL,[57] Belmont Rd., Etruria	1934	Opened as infants' school to alleviate overcrowding in other schools.	
BETHESDA BOARD SCHOOL,[58] Bethesda St.	..	Formerly Bethesda School. Children transferred to Cannon Street Schools 1880 (see Lindsay C. Infants' School).	Used Bethesda Sunday School.
BETHESDA SCHOOL,[59] Bethesda St.	1860	Run by trustees of Bethesda Methodist New Connexion Chapel. School transferred to School Board in 1872.	Used Bethesda Sunday School.

[45] Ex inf. City Educ. Dept.; 1959 List of Schs.
[46] Ex inf. City Educ. Dept.; see p. 112.
[47] White, *Dir. Staffs.* (1851); *Kelly's Dir. Staffs.* (1900); ex inf. City Educ. Dept.; 1959 List of Schs.; O.S. Map 6″ Staffs. xii SW. (1890, 1900); see p. 133.
[48] Ex inf. City Educ. Dept.
[49] Ed. 7/112; 1959 List of Schs.; ex inf. City Educ. Dept.; see p. 275.
[50] Ed. 7/112; *P.O. Dir. Staffs.* (1860, 1868, 1876); *Kelly's Dir. Staffs.* (1880); Burslem Educ. Cttee. Mins., 4 and 5 June 1906, 2 Oct., 6 Nov., 4 Dec. 1907; ex inf. City Educ. Dept.; 1959 List of Schs.
[51] Ed. 7/112; *P.O. Dir. Staffs.* (1860); *Kelly's Dir. Staffs.* (1892); ex inf. City Educ. Dept.
[52] Ed. 7/112; *Kelly's Dir. Staffs.* (1912); tablet *in situ*; ex inf. City Educ. Dept.; 1959 List of Schs.
[53] Ed. 7/112; *Kelly's Dir. Staffs.* (1912); 1959 List of Schs.
[54] Ex inf. City Educ. Dept.
[55] Warrillow, *Stoke*, 281.
[56] Ex inf. City Educ. Dept.; 1959 List of Schs.
[57] Ed. 7/112; *P.O. Dir. Staffs.* (1872).
[58] Ed. 7/112.
[59] Ed. 7/112; Ed. 7/113.

School	Date of opening	Changes in organization	Buildings
BIRCHES HEAD R.C. SCHOOL,[60] Boulton St., Birches Head	1915	Opened with infants and young children only. After 1925 became complete school up to 14 years old. Still all-age mixed and infants' school. Aided status from June 1951.	
BRITISH SCHOOL,[61] Pall Mall	1818	Boys only. Still in use in 1860. Closed by 1868.	Building now Hanley Ref. Libr.
BRYAN STREET BOARD SCHOOL[62]	1872	Opened as mixed all-age school in 1852 as Hanley Ragged School. Taken over by School Board in 1872. Children transferred in 1880 to York Street Schools (see Clarence C. Junior and Infants' School).	Used building of Hanley Ragged School, which was sold in 1864, and present building erected in 1867–8.
CAULDON C. INFANTS' SCHOOL,[63] Cauldon Rd., Shelton	1891	Formerly infants' department of Cauldon Road Council School (see Cauldon C. Junior School).	See Cauldon C. Junior School.
CAULDON C. JUNIOR SCHOOL,[64] Cauldon Rd., Shelton	1891	Opened by School Board for B/G/I and continued as such until 1932 (see Table XI, Hanley, Group B).	New boys' and girls' school in 1896. Further additions 1902.
CAULDON C.S. BOYS' SCHOOL,[65] Cauldon Rd., Shelton	1932	Arose out of 1932 reorganization (see Table XI, Hanley, Group B).	Using part of buildings of former Cauldon Road Council School (see Cauldon C. Junior School).
CLARENCE C. JUNIOR AND INFANTS' SCHOOL[66] (formerly York Street Schools), York St.	1880	Opened by School Board as B/G/I taking children from Bryan Street Board School and continued as such until 1931 when reorganized (see Table XI, Hanley, Group A).	
CLIFF VALE C. INFANTS' SCHOOL,[67] Valley Rd., Cliff Vale	1940	Opened as infants' school.	
EASTWOOD C. JUNIOR SCHOOL,[68] Franklyn St.	1876	National School transferred to School Board in 1876 as a girls' and infants' school. Boys' department opened in 1880. Continued as B/G/I until 1939 when reorganized (see Table XI, Hanley, Group C).	Used buildings of National School. New buildings 1880.
EASTWOOD VALE NATIONAL SCHOOL,[69]	1861	Opened as school for girls and infants. By 1871 also had boys. Transferred to School Board in 1876 (see Eastwood C. Junior School).	
ETRURIA BRITISH SCHOOL[70]	1851	Opened for B/G. Closed on opening of Etruria Board School 1881 (see Etruria C. Junior School).	Housed in building belonging to the Methodist Chapel. Infants' department, formerly Etruria Unsectarian School, in separate building.
ETRURIA C. JUNIOR SCHOOL,[71] Cavour St., Etruria	1881	Opened by School Board for B/G/I/Babies. Took place of Etruria British School and Etruria Unsectarian School (q.v.). Continued as B/G/I until 1934 when senior boys sent to Cannon Street, Lindsay, and Cauldon Secondary Schools. Infants transferred in 1940 to Cliff Vale School (q.v.). Senior girls transferred 1940 to Wharf Lane Secondary School.	

[60] Ed. 7/112; ex inf. head master (1959); ex inf. City Educ. Dept.; 1959 List of Schs.

[61] Ed. 7/113; Ward, *Stoke*, 395–6; A. Huntbach, *Hanley*, 78; *P.O. Dir. Staffs.* (1860, 1868). For a description of the building see p. 149. [62] Ed. 7/112; Warrillow, *Stoke*, 81.

[63] Ed. 7/112; *Kelly's Dir. Staffs.* (1916); 1959 List of Schs.; ex inf. City Educ. Dept.

[64] Ed. 7/112; *Kelly's Dir. Staffs.* (1916); 1959 List of Schs.; ex inf. City Educ. Dept.

[65] Ex inf. City Educ. Dept.; 1959 List of Schs.

[66] Ed. 7/112; ex inf. City Educ. Dept.; 1959 List of Schs.

[67] Ex inf. City Educ. Dept.; 1959 List of Schs.

[68] Ed. 7/112; ex inf. City Educ. Dept.; 1959 List of Schs.

[69] Ed. 7/112.   [70] Ed. 7/112.

[71] Ed. 7/112; ex inf. City Educ. Dept.; 1959 List of Schs.; ex inf. head master (1959).

School	Date of opening	Changes in organization	Buildings
ETRURIA NATIONAL SCHOOL[72]	1847	In 1875 a mixed and infants' school. It was closed on or before the opening of Etruria Board School in 1881.	
ETRURIA UNSECTARIAN SCHOOL[73]	1847	Opened as infants' school. Subsequently merged with Etruria British School (q.v.).	Building belonged to Francis Wedgwood.
GLASS STREET COUNCIL SCHOOL[74] (formerly Hanley Central Board School)	1892	Opened by School Board for B/G/I. Took oldest boys from Broom Street, Grove, and Wellington Schools in 1906. Continued as B/G/I until 1931 when reorganized (see Table XI, Hanley, Group A).	
GLASS STREET C.S. GIRLS' SCHOOL[75]	1931	Arose out of 1931 reorganization (see Table XI, Hanley, Group A).	Used buildings of former Glass Street Council School.
GROVE C. INFANTS' SCHOOL,[76] Turner St., Northwood	1891	Opened as girls' and infants' school in succession to Northwood Board School (q.v.). In 1902 it became mixed and infants. Reorganized in 1932 (see Table XI, Hanley, Group E).	Opened in buildings in Beaumont St. New buildings in 1902.
GROVE C.S. SCHOOL,[77] Turner St., Northwood	1932	Arose out of 1932 reorganization (see Table XI, Hanley, Group E).	Using part of buildings of former Grove Council School (see Grove C. Infants' School).
HAMILTON C. JUNIOR AND INFANTS' SCHOOL,[78] Barthomley Rd., Birches Head	1913	Opened as all-age school to take overflow from various schools including Mount Street Temporary Council School. Reorganized in 1932 (see Table XI, Hanley, Group E).	
HANLEY C.E. JUNIOR AND INFANTS' SCHOOL,[79] Lichfield St.	1816	Opened as a girls' school. By 1851 it was for B/G/I. Continued as such until 1952 when on the school's becoming controlled the seniors were dispersed to various secondary schools in the area.	Infants' school erected 1862. Rehoused almost completely since 1952 in prefabricated buildings.
HANLEY RAGGED SCHOOL,[80] Bryan St.	1852	School transferred to School Board in 1872 (see Bryan Street Board School).	Used building known as the Workmen's Refuge. New building 1867–8.
HANLEY WESLEYAN SCHOOL[81]	1863	Date of closure unknown.	Used Sunday-school buildings attached to Wesleyan Chapel.
HANLEY C. JUNIOR AND INFANTS' SCHOOL,[82] Broom St.	1879	Opened by School Board for B/G/I taking children from Mount Street Temporary Board School (q.v.). Took oldest girls from Grove, Wellington, and Central Schools from 1906. Continued as B/G/I until 1931 when reorganized (see Table XI, Hanley, Group A).	
HOPE (or TRINITY) NATIONAL SCHOOL,[83] Hope St.	1858	Mixed all-age school. Still open in 1876.	Buildings erected 1858.
LINDSAY C. INFANTS' SCHOOL,[84] (formerly Cannon Street Schools), Cannon St., Shelton	1881	Took children formerly at Bethesda Board School (q.v.). Opened by School Board for B/G/I. In 1904 took oldest girls from York Street, Wharf Lane, Eastwood, Cauldon, and Etruria Schools and oldest boys from Etruria, Cauldon, York Street, and Eastwood Schools. Continued as B/G/I until 1931 when reorganized (see Table XI, Hanley, Group A).	

[72] Ed. 7/112.
[73] Ed. 7/112; *P.O. Dir. Staffs.* (1872) where only the Brit. and Nat. Schs. are given.
[74] Ed. 7/112; Hanley Educ. Cttee. Mins., 16 Feb. 1906; ex inf. City Educ. Dept.
[75] Ex inf. City Educ. Dept.; 1959 List of Schs.
[76] Ed. 7/112; ex inf. City Educ. Dept.; 1959 List of Schs.
[77] Ex inf. City Educ. Dept.; 1959 List of Schs.
[78] Ed. 7/112; ex inf. City Educ. Dept.; 1959 List of Schs.

[79] Ed. 7/112; White, *Dir. Staffs.* (1851); ex inf. City Educ. Dept.; 1959 List of Schs.
[80] Ed. 7/112; Warrillow, *Stoke*, 281.
[81] Ed. 7/113.
[82] Ed. 7/112; Hanley Educ. Cttee. Mins., 16 Feb. 1906; ex inf. City Educ. Dept.; 1959 List of Schs.
[83] Ed. 7/113; *P.O. Dir. Staffs.* (1876).
[84] Ed. 7/112; Hanley Educ. Cttee. Mins., 16 Feb. 1906; ex inf. City Educ. Dept.; 1959 List of Schs.

School	Date of opening	Changes in organization	Buildings
LINDSAY C.S. BOYS' SCHOOL,[85] Cannon St., Shelton	1932	Arose out of 1931 reorganization (see Table XI, Hanley, Group A).	Using buildings of former girls' and boys' departments of Cannon Street Schools (see Lindsay C. Infants' School).
MOUNT STREET TEMPORARY BOARD SCHOOL,[86] Northwood	1873	All-age mixed school. Children transferred to Broom Street Schools in 1880 (see Hanley C. Junior and Infants' School).	Used buildings belonging to Primitive Methodist Chapel.
MOUNT STREET TEMPORARY BOARD SCHOOL,[87] Northwood	1898	Opened as a temporary infants' school.	Used buildings belonging to Primitive Methodist Chapel.
MOUNT STREET TEMPORARY COUNCIL SCHOOL,[88] Northwood	1904	Opened by Education Committee to provide temporary accommodation for children attending Hanley Northwood Junior School. Condemned and closed in 1904. Mount Street School closed in 1907.	Used buildings belonging to Primitive Methodist Chapel.
MOUNT STREET TEMPORARY COUNCIL SCHOOL,[89] Northwood	1910	Opened as temporary infants' school to alleviate position in Northwood area. Closed 1932–3.	Used buildings belonging to Primitive Methodist Chapel.
NORTHWOOD BOARD SCHOOL,[90] Keelings Lane, Northwood	1874	Mixed all-age school. Closed in 1891 on opening of Grove School (q.v.), which took girls and infants.	Housed in building belonging to Wesleyan Chapel.
NORTHWOOD C. JUNIOR SCHOOL,[91] Keelings Lane, Northwood	1932	Opened in 1932 as part of reorganization scheme.	
NORTHWOOD C.E. JUNIOR AND INFANTS' SCHOOL,[92] Keelings Lane, Northwood	1858–9	Opened 1858–9 but closed between 1860 and 1868. Reopened by 1876 and reconstituted in 1882 when more buildings were erected. Then continued from this date as B/G/I until reorganized 1932 (see Table XI, Hanley, Group E). Controlled status from Aug. 1949.	New infants' school erected 1882.
SACRED HEART R.C. JUNIOR AND INFANTS' SCHOOL,[93] Downey St.	1861	Opened as mixed all-age school. In 1891 became B/G/I. In 1900 infants and juniors separated from seniors. Continued as such until 1932, when reorganized (see also Sacred Heart R.C. Secondary School). Aided status from June 1951.	Original school part of church of St. Mary and St. Patrick, Lower Foundry St. In 1868 new buildings erected, part of same range as church. New buildings in Downey St. erected 1893. Extended 1897 and 1958.
SACRED HEART R.C. SECONDARY SCHOOL,[94] Downey St.	1932	Arose out of reorganization. Aided status from Oct. 1952.	Using part of buildings of former Sacred Heart all-age School (see Sacred Heart R.C. Junior and Infants' School).
SHELTON C.E. JUNIOR AND INFANTS' SCHOOL,[95] Wood Terrace, Shelton	1838	National School. Mixed all-age until 1932 when reorganized (see Table XI, Hanley, Group B). Aided status from Oct. 1953.	Buildings erected 1838.
SHELTON C.S. GIRLS' SCHOOL,[96] Wharf Lane, Shelton	1932	Arose out of 1932 reorganization (see Table XI, Hanley, Group B).	Used buildings of former Wharf Lane Council School (q.v.).
TRENT (formerly LEEK ROAD) C. INFANTS' SCHOOL,[97] Leek Rd.	1913	Opened as infants' school. Took junior boys from Wellington School in 1932 and ceased to be infants' school. Became infants' school again in 1940.	
WELLINGTON C. INFANTS' SCHOOL,[98] Wellington Rd. (formerly Cobalt St.)	1891	Formerly Wellington National School (q.v.), transferred to School Board in 1891. Continued as B/G/I until 1932 when reorganized (see Table XI, Group C).	Housed in former National School buildings in Mulberry St. until 1893 when new buildings in Cobalt St. erected.

[85] Ex inf. City Educ. Dept.; 1959 List of Schs.
[86] Ed. 7/11.
[87] Ed. 7/112.
[88] Ed. 7/112; Hanley Educ. Cttee., Gen. Purposes Cttee. Mins., 21 Feb. 1906; Hanley Educ. Cttee. Mins., 27 Feb. 1907.
[89] Ed. 7/112; *City of Stoke on Trent Educ. Yr. Bk.* (1932. 1933).
[90] Ed. 7/112.
[91] Ex inf. City Educ. Dept.; 1959 List of Schs.
[92] Ed. 7/112; *P.O. Dir. Staffs.* (1860, 1868, 1876); ex inf. City Educ. Dept.; 1959 List of Schs.
[93] Ed. 7/112; Worship Reg. no. 14302; *Kelly's Dir. Staffs.*

(1916); ex inf. City Educ. Dept.; 1959 List of Schs. A School had been opened on the Lower Foundry St. site in 1858: M. Greenslade, *A Brief Hist. of the Cath. Ch. in Stoke-on-Trent*, 26, 27.
[94] Ex inf. the head master (1960); ex inf. City Educ. Dept.; 1959 List of Schs.
[95] Ed. 7/112; ex inf. City Educ. Dept.; 1959 List of Schs.
[96] Ex inf. City Educ. Dept.; 1959 List of Schs.
[97] Ed. 7/112; ex inf. City Educ. Dept.; 1959 List of Schs.
[98] Ibid.

School	Date of opening	Changes in organization	Buildings
WELLINGTON C.S. SCHOOL,[99] Wellington Rd.	1932	Arose out of 1932 reorganization (see Table XI, Hanley, Group C).	Used buildings of former boys' and girls' departments of Wellington Council School (see Wellington C. Infants' School).
WELLINGTON NATIONAL SCHOOL,[1] Mulberry St.	1862	Opened as a mixed school; by 1872 for B/G/I. School transferred to School Board in 1891 (see Wellington C. Infants' School).	Opened in buildings belonging to a Mr. Sawyer. School erected later in 1862. Used also as a Sunday School attached to St. Luke's Church, Hanley.
WHARF LANE COUNCIL SCHOOL[2]	1880	Formerly Bedford Street School (q.v.). Opened by School Board for G/I. Continued as such until 1932 when buildings were transferred to the new Shelton Senior School (see Table XI, Hanley, Group B).	

STOKE-UPON-TRENT

School	Date of opening	Changes in organization	Buildings
BOOTHEN C.E. INFANTS' SCHOOL,[3] London Rd.	1859	Reorganized 1932 (see Table XI, Stoke, Group A). Controlled status from Sept. 1955.	Occupied the shell of three cottages. In 1870 replaced by new school-church. A new wing added 1875. In 1877 it ceased to be used as a church. Further additions in 1878. New infants' school 1902.
BOOTHEN C.E. JUNIOR SCHOOL,[4] London Rd.	1859	Formerly part of Boothen National Schools. Reorganized 1932 (see Table XI, Stoke, Group A). Controlled status from March 1956.	See Boothen C.E. Infants' School.
CLIFF VALE C.E. JUNIOR AND INFANTS' SCHOOL,[5] North St., Cliff Vale	1857	Opened as a mixed branch school for young children. Gradually became all-age. Reorganized 1932 (see Table XI, Stoke, Group A). Closed soon after 1941.	Opened in a cottage at Cliff Vale, then in two cottages which were turned into a school-church. Iron school-church built. Burnt down 1865. New building erected 1865. Became school only in 1906. Building still (1960) stands and is used as a builder's yard.
CLOSE C. JUNIOR SCHOOL,[6] Quarry Rd., Hartshill	1933	Opened as new school in 1933 as part of reorganization.	Old house converted into a school.
GARNER STREET COUNCIL SCHOOL,[7] Garner St., Cliff Vale	1898	Infants' school only. Closed c. 1934.	Used the C. of E. mission room.
HARPFIELD C. INFANTS' SCHOOL,[8] Hartshill Rd., Hartshill	1872	Infants' dept. of former Harpfield Council School (see Harpfield C. Junior School). Separate school after reorganization of 1932 (see Table XI, Stoke, Group C).	Using part of 1875 buildings of former infants' department of Harpfield Council School.
HARPFIELD C. JUNIOR SCHOOL,[9] Hartshill Rd., Hartshill	1872	Opened as Kingscroft Board School. Mixed and infants' until 1902, when it became B/G/I. Reorganized 1932 (see Table XI, Stoke, Group C).	Temporary iron buildings on lease at first. New school 1875. School remodelled 1892–5. New boys' school 1902. Now using part of 1875 building.
HARPFIELD C.S. SCHOOL,[10] Hartshill Rd., Hartshill	1932	Arose out of 1932 reorganization (see Table XI, Stoke, Group C).	Using former buildings of boys' dept. of Harpfield Council School (see Harpfield C. Junior School).
HARTSHILL C.E. JUNIOR AND INFANTS' SCHOOL,[11] Vicarage Rd., Hartshill	1836	Founded by Herbert Minton. Mixed school until 1932 when reorganized (see Table XI, Stoke, Group C). Controlled status from April 1948.	New buildings 1851.

[99] Ex inf. City Educ. Dept.; 1959 List of Schs.
[1] Ed. 7/112.
[2] Ed. 7/112; 1959 List of Schs.; ex inf. City Educ. Dept.
[3] Ed. 7/112; Wright, *Schs. of the Parish of St. Peter ad Vincula*, 10–11, 17; ex inf. City Educ. Dept.; 1959 List of Schs.
[4] Ibid.
[5] Ed. 7/112; Wright, op. cit. 8–10, 20; ex inf. City Educ. Dept.
[6] Ex inf. City Educ. Dept.; 1959 List of Schs.
[7] *Stoke Sch. Board Triennial Rep., 1898–1900*; Ed. 7/112; ex inf. City Educ. Dept.
[8] Ed. 7/112; ex inf. City Educ. Dept.; 1959 List of Schs.
[9] Ed. 7/112; *Stoke Sch. Board Triennial Rep., 1892–95*; ex inf. City Educ. Dept.; 1959 List of Schs.
[10] Ex inf. City Educ. Dept.; 1959 List of Schs.
[11] Ed. 7/112; Ward, *Stoke*, 497; ex inf. City Educ. Dept.; 1959 List of Schs.

School	Date of opening	Changes in organization	Buildings
HONEYWALL C. JUNIOR AND INFANTS' SCHOOL,[12] Cross St. (formerly Epworth St.)	1872	Opened as B/GI. In 1881 juniors formed into separate dept. using Wesleyan Sunday School. Reorganized 1932 (see Table XI, Stoke, Group C). Closed 1960.	Opened in buildings of Wesleyan Sunday School, Cross St. New buildings 1876. In 1881 used Wesleyan Sunday School as annexe for junior school. New junior school building 1884.
OAK HILL C. INFANTS' SCHOOL,[13] Rookery Lane, Oak Hill	1932	All infants transferred to this from Oak Hill Council School (see Oak Hill C. Junior School) on reorganization of 1932 (see Table XI, Stoke, Group D).	Wooden buildings erected 1932.
OAK HILL C. JUNIOR SCHOOL,[14] Rookery Lane, Oak Hill	1924	Junior mixed only until Nov. 1925. Then all-age. Reorganized 1932 (see Table XI, Stoke, Group D).	Now using 1938 buildings.
OAK HILL C.S. SCHOOL,[15] Rookery Lane, Oak Hill	1932	Arose from reorganization of 1932 (see Table XI, Stoke, Group D). Received seniors of Hanford C.E. School in 1938.	Using 1932 buildings; extended in 1938.
PENKHULL C. INFANTS' SCHOOL,[16] Trent Valley Rd., Penkhull	1876	Formerly Penkhull National School (q.v.). Mixed and infants' till 1932 when reorganized (see Table XI, Stoke, Group D).	Enlarged 1889, 1897, and 1914.
PENKHULL C.S. SCHOOL,[17] Prince's Rd., Penkhull	1932	Arose out of 1932 reorganization (see Table XI, Stoke, Group D).	Occupying part of buildings of Penkhull Council School.
PENKHULL NATIONAL SCHOOL,[18] Trent Valley Rd., Penkhull	1844	Opened as boys' and girls' school. Transferred to School Board in 1876 (see Penkhull C. Infants' School).	
ROMAN CATHOLIC SCHOOL,[19] Back Glebe St.	1850	Closed probably by 1859.	Used church.
ST. PETER'S C.E. JUNIOR AND INFANTS' SCHOOL,[20] Wharf St.	1815	Opened as B/G/I. Endowment of £3,000 by Dean Woodhouse 1830, shared by this school, St. Mark's School, Shelton, and St. John's School, Hanley. Reorganized in 1905 as SB, SG, JM, I. SB in new Boothen Rd. buildings. Reorganized again in 1932 (see Table XI, Stoke, Group A). Aided status from April 1952.	New boys' school in Boothen Old Rd. in 1904 (see Stoke Central National School).
ST. PETERS' C.E. SECONDARY BOYS' SCHOOL,[21] Boothen Old Rd.	1932	Arose out of 1932 reorganization (see Table XI, Stoke, Group A). Aided status from April 1952.	Using buildings of former Central National School.
ST. PETER'S C.E. SECONDARY GIRLS' SCHOOL,[22] Wharf St.	1932	Arose out of 1932 reorganization (see Table XI, Stoke, Group A). Aided status from April 1952.	Using part of buildings of former St. Peter's National School (see St. Peter's C.E. Junior and Infants' School).
ST. PETER'S R.C. GIRLS' SCHOOL,[23] Knowl St.	1859	Opened for girls and infants. Run by the Dominican Sisters. Reorganized 1931 (see Table XI, Stoke, Group B).	Rebuilt 1877. Extended 1924.
ST. THOMAS'S R.C. BOYS' SCHOOL,[24] Knowl St.	1876	Reorganized 1931 (see Table XI, Stoke, Group B).	Original buildings in Lonsdale St. Knowl St. buildings opened 1915.
ST. THOMAS'S R.C. JUNIOR AND INFANTS' SCHOOL,[25] Knowl St.	1931	Arose out of 1931 reorganization (see Table XI, Stoke, Group B). Aided status from June 1951.	Occupying buildings of former St. Peter's R.C. Girls' School (q.v.).
ST. THOMAS'S R.C. SECONDARY SCHOOL,[26] Knowl St.	1931	Arose out of 1931 reorganization (see Table XI, Stoke, Group B). Aided status from Dec. 1951.	Occupying buildings of former St. Thomas's R.C. Boys' School (q.v.) and part of former buildings of St. Dominic's High School.

[12] Ed. 7/112; *Kelly's Dir. Staffs.* (1916); *Stoke Sch. Board Triennial Rep., 1883–6;* ex inf. City Educ. Dept.; 1959 List of Schs.

[13] Ex inf. City Educ. Dept.; 1959 List of Schs.

[14] Ed. 7/112; ex inf. City Educ. Dept.; 1959 List of Schs.

[15] Ex inf. City Educ. Dept.; 1959 List of Schs.

[16] Ed. 7/112; *Stoke Sch. Board Triennial Rep., 1886–9; Kelly's Dir. Staffs.* (1900); ex inf. City Educ. Dept.; 1959 List of Schs.

[17] Ex inf. City Educ. Dept.; 1959 List of Schs.

[18] Ed. 7/112; ex inf. City Educ. Dept.

[19] M. Greenslade, *Brief Hist. of Cath. Ch. in Stoke-on-Trent,* 35 (copy in W.S.L.); see p. 273.

[20] Ed. 7/112; Wright, *Schs. of St. Peter ad Vincula,* 6, 19–20; ex inf. City Educ. Dept.; 1959 List of Schs. For a descrip. of the buildings see p. 180.

[21] Ex inf. City Educ. Dept.; 1959 List of Schs.   [22] Ibid.

[23] Ed. 7/112; ex inf. City Educ. Dept.; *Kelly's Dir. Staffs.* (1880); 1959 List of Schs.   [24] Ibid.

[25] Ex inf. the head master; 1959 List of Schs.

[26] Ex inf. the head master, St. Thomas's R.C. Junior and Infants' Sch.; 1959 List of Schs.

School	Date of opening	Changes in organization	Buildings
ST. TERESA'S R.C. JUNIOR AND INFANTS' SCHOOL,[27] Stone Rd., Trent Vale	1937	Aided status from Jan. 1952.	
SPRINGFIELD C. INFANTS' SCHOOL,[28] Springfields Rd., Oak Hill	1953		
SPRINGFIELD C. JUNIOR SCHOOL,[29] Springfields Rd., Oak Hill	1953		
STOKE CENTRAL NATIONAL SCHOOL,[30] Boothen Old Rd.	1905	Took senior boys from St. Peter's C.E. School and Boothen C.E. School (q.v.). Reorganized 1932 as St. Peter's C.E. Boys' Secondary School (see Table XI, Stoke, Group A).	Enlarged 1894.
TRENT VALE C.E. JUNIOR AND INFANTS' SCHOOL,[31] Newcastle Rd., Trent Vale	1845	Mixed and infants' until 1932 when reorganized (see Table XI, Stoke, Group D). Aided status from June 1953.	
TRENT VALE TEMPORARY COUNCIL SCHOOL,[32] London Rd., Trent Vale	1909	Infants' school only, now closed.	

FENTON

School	Date of opening	Changes in organization	Buildings
FENTON C.E. JUNIOR SCHOOL,[33] Christchurch St.	1839	Opened as Fenton National School for B/G/I. Reorganized 1932 (see Table XI, Fenton). Aided status from Dec. 1952.	Original school built in churchyard. New infants' school erected 1864. In 1867 boys using the Athenaeum.
FENTON C. JUNIOR AND INFANTS' SCHOOL,[34] Brocksford St.	1897	Formerly Queen Street Board School. Opened as mixed and infants' school. Reorganized 1932 (see Table XI, Fenton).	
FENTON C.S. BOYS' SCHOOL,[35] Brocksford St.	1932	Arose out of 1932 reorganization (see Table XI, Fenton).	Erected 1897 using part of former Fenton Council School (see Fenton C. Junior and Infants' School).
FENTON LOW C.E. INFANTS' SCHOOL[36]	1876	Infants only. Replaced by Manor Street Council School in 1910.	Mission church.
FENTON R.C. JUNIOR AND INFANTS' SCHOOL,[37] Masterson St.	1885	Opened as infants' school. Expanded to all-age school later, possibly in 1895–6. Aided status from June 1956.	Extended 1895–6, 1916, 1927.
FENTON WESLEYAN DAY SCHOOL,[38] Raglan St.	1871	Taken over by School Board as Raglan St. Board School in 1894.	Building completed 1867.
GLEBE C. INFANTS' SCHOOL,[39] King St.	1872	See Glebe C. Junior School.	See Glebe C. Junior School.
GLEBE C. JUNIOR SCHOOL,[40] King St.	1872	Formerly Market Street Board School. Opened as mixed and infants' school. Reorganized 1932 (see Table XI, Fenton).	Used Methodist New Connexion, Mount Tabor Sunday School. New buildings 1878.
HERON CROSS C. JUNIOR SCHOOL,[41] Grove Rd., Heron Cross	c. 1894	Formerly Wesleyan Day School. Mixed and infants' school until 1932 when reorganized (see Table XI, Fenton).	Opened in Wesleyan School building. New buildings erected 1894. New infants' school erected 1911.
HERON CROSS C.S. SCHOOL,[42] Grove Rd., Heron Cross	1932	Arose out of 1932 reorganization (see Table XI, Fenton).	Erected 1894, part of buildings of former Heron Cross Council School (see Heron Cross C. Junior School).
MANOR C. INFANTS' SCHOOL,[43] William St.	1910	Took children from Fenton Low C.E. Infants' School (q.v.).	
MANOR C.S. GIRLS' SCHOOL,[44] Manor St.	1932	Arose out of 1932 reorganization (see Table XI, Fenton).	Erected 1932.

[27] Ex inf. City Educ. Dept.; 1959 List of Schs.
[28] Ibid. [29] Ibid.
[30] Ed. 7/112; Wright, *Schs. of St. Peter ad Vincula,* 19–20; ex inf. City Educ. Dept.; 1959 List of Schs.
[31] Ed. 7/112; *Kelly's Dir. Staffs.* (1912); ex inf. City Educ. Dept.; 1959 List of Schs.
[32] Ed. 7/112; *Kelly's Dir. Staffs.* (1912).
[33] Ed. 7/112; ex inf. City Educ. Dept.; 1959 List of Schs.
[34] Ibid.
[35] Ex inf. City Educ. Dept.; 1959 List of Schs.
[36] Ed. 7/112.
[37] Ed. 7/112; *Cath. Emanc. Centenary Celebrations, Hanley, 1929;* ex inf. City Educ. Dept.; 1959 List of Schs.
[38] Ed. 7/112.
[39] Ed. 7/112; ex inf. City Educ. Dept.; 1959 List of Schs. [40] Ibid.
[41] Ed. 7/112; *Kelly's Dir. Staffs.* (1896); ex inf. City Educ. Dept.; 1959 List of Schs.
[42] Ex inf. City Educ. Dept.; 1959 List of Schs.
[43] Ed. 7/112; ex inf. City Educ. Dept.; 1959 List of Schs.
[44] Ex inf. City Educ. Dept.; 1959 List of Schs.

School	Date of opening	Changes in organization	Buildings
MOUNT PLEASANT C.E. JUNIOR AND INFANTS' SCHOOL,[45] Smithpool Rd., Mount Pleasant	1858	Opened as branch school of St. Peter's C.E. School. Reorganized 1932 (see Table XI, Stoke, Group A). Aided status from April 1952.	Opened in carpenter's shop in Bridge St. In 1859 moved to a former dissenting meeting house. Iron school-church erected 1861. New school church built, twice enlarged, 1867–77.
TURNER MEMORIAL C.E. INFANTS' SCHOOL,[46] Fenpark Rd.	1865	Formerly China Street National School. Managed by Trustees of Allen's Charity. Young children, under 10 years old, and infants only. Reorganized 1932 (see Table XI, Fenton). Aided status from Dec. 1952.	Building erected 1840. New building 1896.
ST. JOHN'S BRANCH NATIONAL SCHOOL,[47] Pool Dole	By 1872	Closed by 1876.	
LONGTON			
ALEXANDRA C. JUNIOR AND INFANTS' SCHOOL,[48] Uttoxeter Rd.	1886	Formerly called Normacot Board School and Uttoxeter Road County Junior School. Opened as B/G/I. Reorganized 1931 (see Table XI, Longton).	
COOKE STREET C.S. GIRLS' SCHOOL,[49] Edensor	1931	Senior mixed from 1931 to 1935, when boys transferred to Queensberry Senior School for Boys.	Occupied buildings of former Cooke St. Council School until c. 1938 when moved to new buildings in Edensor Rd. (see Edensor C.S. School).
DRESDEN C.E. INFANTS' SCHOOL,[50] Belgrave Rd., Dresden	1853	See Dresden C.E. Junior School.	See Dresden C.E. Junior School.
DRESDEN C.E. JUNIOR SCHOOL,[51] Belgrave Rd., Dresden	1853	Started as mixed all-age school. Infants made separate department in 1865. Benefited under Betton's Charity. Reorganized 1931 (see Table XI, Longton). Controlled status from Jan. 1953.	New infants' school 1865. Another new infants' school 1914 when previous infants' building taken over as mixed dept.
EAST VALE C.E. SCHOOL,[52] Palmer St., East Vale	1870	Mixed all-age school. Closed 1904.	School-church.
EDENSOR C.E. INFANTS' SCHOOL,[53] Edward St., Edensor	1868	Former mixed school became infants' only in 1868. Moved 1949 on buildings' being condemned, forming an infants' department of Edensor C.E. Junior School (q.v.) for a time. Had ceased by 1959.	Housed in old part of Edward St. building. Building enlarged 1877. Condemned as school 1949.
EDENSOR C.E. JUNIOR AND INFANTS' SCHOOL,[54] Cooke St., Edensor	By 1851	Opened as mixed all-age school by 1851. Reorganized 1931 (see Table XI, Longton). In 1948 became a controlled school and moved into buildings in Cooke St. formerly used by the Electricity Board. Infants' school formed department of this school for a time after 1949.	New buildings erected 1868 in Edward St. Condemned in 1949 when moved to buildings in Cooke St. (formerly Cooke St. Council School).
EDENSOR C.S. SCHOOL,[55] Edensor Rd.	1932	Boys' school till c. 1938 when became mixed.	Extended c. 1938 to accommodate girls from Cooke St. C. Secondary (q.v.).
FLORENCE C. INFANTS' SCHOOL,[56] Lilleshall St., Florence	1886	See Florence C. Junior School.	See Florence C. Junior School.
FLORENCE C. JUNIOR SCHOOL,[57] Lilleshall St., Florence	1886	Founded as B/G/I. Reorganized 1931 (see Table XI, Longton).	

[45] Ed. 7/112; Wright, Schs. of St. Peter ad Vincula, 7–8; ex inf. City Educ. Dept.; 1959 List of Schs.
[46] Ed. 7/112; Kelly's Dir. Staffs. (1916); ex inf. City Educ. Dept.; 1959 List of Schs.
[47] P.O. Dir. Staffs. (1872, 1876).
[48] Ed. 7/112; ex inf. City Educ. Dept.; 1959 List of Schs.
[49] Ex inf. City Educ. Dept.
[50] Ed. 7/112; Kelly's Dir. Staffs. (1916); ex inf. City Educ. Dept.; 1959 List of Schs.
[51] Ibid.
[52] Ed. 7/112; Ed. 21/511; Longton Educ. Cttee., Subcttee. Mins., 29 June 1903.
[53] Ed. 7/112 and 113; ex inf. City Educ. Dept.
[54] Ed. 7/112 and 113; White, Dir. Staffs. (1851); ex inf. City Educ. Dept.; 1959 List of Schs.
[55] Ex inf. City Educ. Dept.; 1959 List of Schs.
[56] Ed. 7/112; ex inf. City Educ. Dept.; 1959 List of Schs.
[57] Ibid.

School	Date of opening	Changes in organization	Buildings
FREE SCHOOL[58]	c. 1763	Founded by John Bourne with endowment of Golden Lion Inn and 2 cottages. Amalgamated with St. John's National School.	
GRAFTON C. INFANTS' SCHOOL,[59] Marlborough St.	1892	See Grafton C. Junior School.	See Grafton C. Junior School.
GRAFTON C. JUNIOR SCHOOL,[60] Marlborough St.	1872	Opened as boys' school. Small attendance; therefore arrangement to take 137 boys from private school of Josiah Ball (at St. John's Church), all half-timers, as latter school overcrowded. Ball subsidized by Board to make up loss of fees. Girls' and infants' depts. opened Dec. 1892. Reorganized 1931 (see Table XI, Longton).	Opened in Sunday-school buildings of Zion Chapel. In Dec. 1873 St. John's schoolrooms taken over, Ball's lease of them having fallen in. New buildings erected 1892.
HEATHCOTE C. INFANTS' SCHOOL[61] (formerly Cooke Street School), Cooke St., Edensor	1891	Replaced Longton Wesleyan Day School, taken over by Board Sept. 1891. M/I until 1931 reorganization (see Table XI, Longton).	Held in Wesleyan Day School buildings until 1893 when Cooke St. School erected.
HIGH STREET SCHOOLS,[62] Uttoxeter Rd.	1879	Opened as B/G/I. Reorganized 1931 as infants' school only (see Table XI, Longton). Infants' school transferred to part of Alexandra Road School premises in 1949 on the High St. premises' being condemned. School closed 1956.	
INDEPENDENT SCHOOL,[63] Caroline St.	By 1854	Still open 1860. Closed by 1868.	
INDEPENDENT CHAPEL BOARD SCHOOL,[64] Caroline St.	1873	Temporary school for boys. Open for short period only.	Using Congregational Sunday-school buildings.
LONGTON C.E. SCHOOL,[65] Webberley Lane	1836	Benefited under will of Dr. J. C. Woodhouse. Opened as B/G/I. After 1868, B/G/I until 1931 when reorganized (see Table XI, Longton). Became controlled Oct. 1952.	In 1868 boys' department housed in Methodist New Connexion Sunday School, Commerce St.
METHODIST NEW CONNEXION SCHOOL,[66] Commerce St.	1851, 1872	Opened in 1851 but closed by 1854. Reopened by 1872. Moved to New St. by 1876. Closed by early 1880's.	
MOUNT PLEASANT NATIONAL SCHOOL,[67] Mount Pleasant (now Lawley St.)	1866	Opened as mixed school. Closed 1873.	School-church.
NORMACOT C.E. INFANTS' SCHOOL,[68] Meir Rd., Normacot	1853	Opened as mixed all-age school, boys' and girls' depts. forming a separate school by at least 1895. Reorganized 1931 (see Table XI, Longton). Controlled status from July 1951. Junior school closed c. 1954.	New buildings 1876 (enlarged 1886) for boys and girls. New infants' school 1895. The 1876 buildings and enlargements of 1886 demolished c. 1954.
QUEENSBERRY ROAD CENTRAL SCHOOL,[69] Normacot Rd.	1901/2	In 1901 boys' department of Queensberry Road Board School was recognized as a Higher Elementary School and girls' department as a Higher Standard School. In 1902 both recognized as a Higher Elementary School. In 1921 these departments of Queensberry Road Schools were recognized as a Central School. Reorganized 1931 (see Table XI, Longton). See also Queensberry Road Council School.	Using part of buildings of Queensberry Road Board School.

[58] *13th Rep. Com. Char.* 311–15; White, *Dir. Staffs.* (1851); Ward, *Stoke*, 567; see p. 307.
[59] Ed. 7/112; *Rep. on Sch. Bd. District of the Boro. of Longton, 1871–1892*; ex inf. City Educ. Dept.; 1959 List of Schs.
[60] Ibid.
[61] Ed. 21/513; Ed. 7/112; *Rep. on Sch. Bd. District, 1871–92*; ex inf. City Educ. Dept.; 1959 List of Schs.
[62] Ed. 7/112; *Rep. on Sch. Bd. District, 1871–92*; ex inf. City Educ. Dept.; 1959 List of Schs.
[63] *P.O. Dir. Staffs.* (1854, 1860, 1868).
[64] Ed. 7/112.
[65] Ed. 7/112; White, *Dir. Staffs.* (1851); *Kelly's Dir. Staffs.* (1916); ex inf. City Educ. Dept.; 1959 List of Schs.
[66] White, *Dir. Staffs.* (1851); *P.O. Dir. Staffs.* (1872); *Keates's Potteries Dir.* (1875–6, 1879). It is not mentioned in 1882: ibid. (1882).
[67] Ed. 7/112.
[68] Ed. 7/112; *Kelly's Dir. Staffs.* (1896); ex inf. City Educ. Dept.; 1959 List of Schs.
[69] Ed. 7/112; Ed. 20/126; ex inf. City Educ. Dept.

School	Date of opening	Changes in organization	Buildings
QUEENSBERRY ROAD COUNCIL SCHOOL,[70] Normacot Rd.	1898	Opened by School Board as an all-age boys', girls', and infants' school. Reorganized 1901–2 when part of school was recognized as a Higher Grade School. The rest remained an all-age Elementary School until 1931 when reorganized (see Table XI, Longton). See also Queensberry Road Central School.	
QUEENSBERRY C.S. SCHOOLS,[71] Normacot Rd.	1931	Opened as a senior school in 1931 upon reorganization (see Table XI, Longton) and became separate secondary schools for boys and girls after 1945.	Used buildings of former Queensberry Road Council School and Queensberry Road Central School.
ROMAN CATHOLIC SCHOOL,[72] Gregory St.	By 1834	Closed by 1852 and reconstituted as St. Gregory's R.C. School (see below).	Building enlarged in 1841.
ST. GREGORY'S R.C. SCHOOL,[73] Spring Garden Rd.	1852	Opened as boys' school only. Infants' department added in 1853. Girls' department opened in 1857. Reorganized 1937, when seniors were transferred to St. Gregory's R.C. Secondary School. Aided status from March 1953.	Opened in buildings of former R.C. school, Gregory St. Infants' school built in 1853. New buildings erected in 1893 in Cemetery Rd. (now Spring Garden Rd.).
ST. GREGORY'S R.C. SECONDARY SCHOOL,[74] Spring Garden Rd.	1937	Took seniors from all R.C. schools in the area. Aided status from July 1953.	
ST. JOHN'S BRANCH SCHOOL,[75] Park Hall St.	By 1868	Mixed school. Closed by 1876.	
ST. JOHN'S NATIONAL SCHOOL,[76] St. John's Churchyard	c. 1825	Old Free School amalgamated with St. John's National School after Charity Commissioners' Rep. of 1825. School then opened. Closed at some date between 1859 and 1872. Building occupied by a private school run by Josiah Ball by 1872 (see Grafton C.J. School).	Buildings erected 1822, but school could not open for lack of funds. Land given by the Marquess of Stafford.
WESLEYAN DAY SCHOOL,[77] Stafford St.	1855	Mixed school. Taken over by School Board in 1881 (see Heathcote C. Infants' School).	Used Wesleyan Sunday School buildings.
WOODHOUSE C. INFANTS' SCHOOL,[78] Anchor Rd., Sandford Hill	1876	Opened as B/G/I, and continued as such until 1931 when reorganized (see Table XI, Longton). See also Woodhouse C. Secondary School.	Extended 1896.
WOODHOUSE C.S. SCHOOL,[79] Anchor Rd., Sandford Hill	1931	Arose out of reorganization in 1931 (see Table XI, Longton).	Using 1876 part of buildings of former Woodhouse Council School.

[70] Ed. 7/112; ex inf. City Educ. Dept.
[71] Ex inf. City Educ. Dept.; 1959 List of Schs.
[72] Ed. 7/112; White, *Dir. Staffs.* (1851).
[73] White, *Dir. Staffs.* (1851); *Kelly's Dir. Staffs.* (1916); S.R.O., D. 593, Longton Boro. Extension Map; ex inf. City Educ. Dept.; 1959 List of Schs.
[74] Ex inf. City Educ. Dept.; 1959 List of Schs.
[75] *P.O. Dir. Staffs.* (1868, 1876).

[76] *13th Rep. Com. Char.* 311–15; White, *Dir. Staffs.* (1851); Ward, *Stoke,* 567; G. Griffith, *Free Schs. and Endowments of Staffs.* (1860), 522. For a description of the building see p. 229.
[77] Ed. 7/112.
[78] Ed. 7/112; ex inf. City Educ. Dept.; 1959 List of Schs.
[79] Ex inf. City Educ. Dept.; 1959 List of Schs.

TABLE X

Schools in Area Added to County Borough in 1922[80]

For abbreviations see Table IX

School	Date of opening	Changes in organization	Buildings
ABBEY HULTON C. INFANTS' SCHOOL, School Rd., Abbey Hulton	1936		
ABBEY HULTON C. JUNIOR SCHOOL, School Rd., Abbey Hulton	1900		
ABBEY HULTON R.C. JUNIOR AND INFANTS' SCHOOL, Abbey Lane, Abbey Hulton	1938	Aided status from June 1951.	
ADDERLEY GREEN C. JUNIOR AND INFANTS' SCHOOL, Anchor Rd., Adderley Green	1884	Opened by Caverswall School Board for B/G/I. Continued as such until reorganized 1931 (see Table XI, Longton).	Extended 1893.
BALL GREEN C. INFANTS' SCHOOL, Whitfield Rd., Ball Green	1930	Opened in first instance as a temporary school.	
BENTILEE C. INFANTS' SCHOOL, Beverley Drive, Ubberley	1956		
BENTILEE C. JUNIOR SCHOOL, Beverley Drive, Ubberley	1957		
BERRY HILL C. INFANTS' SCHOOL, Arbourfield Drive, Bucknall	1958		
BLURTON C.E. SCHOOL	1872	Opened for B/G/I. Closed 1959 when only infants there. Aided status from March, 1953.	Building erected 1834.
BLURTON C. INFANTS' SCHOOL, Poplar Drive, Blurton	1948		
BLURTON C. JUNIOR SCHOOL, Poplar Drive, Blurton	1948		
BLURTON C.S. SCHOOL, Beaconsfield Drive, Blurton	1956		
BRADELEY C. INFANTS' SCHOOL, Chell Heath Rd., Bradeley	1900	Opened as mixed and infants' school. In 1936 reorganized as senior and infants' school. Juniors went to Smallthorne (see Bradeley C.S. School and Smallthorne C. Junior School).	
BRADELEY C.S. SCHOOL, Chell Heath Rd., Bradeley	1936	Arose out of reorganization (see Bradeley C. Infants' School).	Using part of buildings of former Bradeley Council School.
BRINDLEY C. MIXED AND INFANTS' SCHOOL, Outclough Rd., Brindley Ford	1863	Opened as a Wesleyan school. Transferred to School Board by 1885.	Originally used Methodist Sunday-school buildings. New buildings 1885.
BROOKHOUSE GREEN C. INFANTS' SCHOOL, Wellfield Rd., Ubberley	1954		
BROOKHOUSE GREEN C. JUNIOR SCHOOL, Dawlish Drive, Ubberley	1955		
BUCKNALL C.E. JUNIOR AND INFANTS' SCHOOL,[81] Guy St., Bucknall	c. 1721	Founded under the will of William Shallcross of Uttoxeter (proved 25 May 1721). School reconstituted in 1868. By 1871 the school was for B/G/I. It was reorganized in 1932, the seniors being transferred to Bucknall Senior School, now Bucknall C.S. School. Controlled status from June 1953.	First schoolhouse built c. 1721. In bad condition by 1868 when new school was built on site 150 yards away. New girls' and infants' school completed in 1871.
BUCKNALL C. INFANTS' SCHOOL, Malthouse Rd., Bucknall	1877	Opened by School Board for B/G/I. Reorganized as an infants' school after 1932.	
BUCKNALL C.S. SCHOOL, Malthouse Rd., Bucknall	After 1932	Arose from reorganization of Bucknall Council School.	Uses part of buildings of former Bucknall Council School (see Bucknall C. Infants' School).

[80] For the basis on which this table has been compiled see p. 311, n. 94. Unless there is a note to the contrary, the information for the schools in this section is drawn from one or both of the following sources: the City Educ. Dept.; 1959 List of Schs. For the older schools early information is taken from Ed. 7/112.
[81] Additional inf. from *Staffs. End. Char. Elem. Educ.* [Cd. 2729], pp. 114–15, H.C. (1906), xc.

School	Date of opening	Changes in organization	Buildings
BURNWOOD C.S. SCHOOL, Chell Heath Rd., Chell Heath	1958		
CARMOUNTSIDE C. INFANTS' SCHOOL, Woodhead Rd., Abbey Hulton	1938		
CARMOUNTSIDE C. JUNIOR SCHOOL, Woodhead Rd., Abbey Hulton	1935		
CARMOUNTSIDE C.S. SCHOOL, Beard Grove, Abbey Hulton	1939		
CHAPEL STREET TEMPORARY SCHOOL,[82] Chapel St., Bucknall	1940		Used premises belonging to chapel.
CHELL HEATH C. INFANTS' SCHOOL, Sprink Bank Rd., Chell Heath	1949		
CHELL HEATH C. JUNIOR SCHOOL, Sprink Bank Rd., Chell Heath	1950		
FEGG HAYES C. INFANTS' SCHOOL, Oxford Rd., Fegg Hayes	1956		
GRANGE C. INFANTS' SCHOOL, Harrowby Rd., Meir	1939		
GRANGE C. JUNIOR SCHOOL, Harrowby Rd., Meir	1939		
HANFORD C.E. SCHOOL, Church Lane, Hanford	1952	Opened as a mixed all-age National School. Seniors sent to Oak Hill C.S. School in 1938. Controlled status from Jan. 1951.	
HEM HEATH C. INFANTS' SCHOOL, Magdalen Rd., Blurton	1958		
HEM HEATH C. JUNIOR SCHOOL, Magdalen Rd., Blurton	1959		
HOLDEN LANE C. INFANTS' SCHOOL, Ralph Drive, Sneyd Green	1958		
MEIR C. INFANTS' SCHOOL, Uttoxeter Rd., Meir	1877		Occupying buildings of former Meir Council School (see Meir C. Junior School).
MEIR C. JUNIOR SCHOOL, Colclough Rd., Meir	1877	Opened as mixed and infants' Board school. Continued as such until 1931 when school reorganized (see Table XI, Longton).	New buildings in 1931.
MEIR C.S. SCHOOL, Colclough Rd., Meir	1931	Erected as part of 1931 reorganization (see Meir C. Junior School).	
MEIR ST. AUGUSTINE'S R.C. JUNIOR AND INFANTS' SCHOOL, Sandon Rd., Meir	1937	Aided status from June 1951.	
MILTON C. INFANTS' SCHOOL, Leek Rd., Milton	1874		Housed in Bagnall Road Sunday School until 1912.
MILTON C. JUNIOR SCHOOL, Leek Rd., Milton	1874	Opened as a girls' and infants' school. Became boys' school also 1890-6. Reorganized in 1932.	Housed in buildings of Wesleyan Sunday School.
MILTON C.S. SCHOOL,[83] Leek Rd., Milton	1932	School formed on reorganization of Milton Council School in 1932.	Using 1912 part of former Milton Council School buildings (see Milton C. Junior and Milton C. Infants' Schools).
NEWSTEAD C. INFANTS' SCHOOL, Waterside Drive, Blurton	1954		
NEWSTEAD C. JUNIOR SCHOOL, Waterside Drive, Blurton	1954		
NEWSTEAD R.C. SCHOOL, Springside Place, Blurton	1954		
NORTON C. JUNIOR AND INFANTS' SCHOOL, Norton Lane, Norton-in-the-Moors	1848	Succeeded school established in 1797. Opened as a parochial and National school. Had endowments from Hugh Ford (d. 1730) and Charlotte Sparrow (endowment given in 1851). School was for B/G/I until 1936 when reorganized as junior and infants' school, seniors going to Smallthorne Senior School. New county school succeeded church school in 1953.	Original boys' and girls' school erected 1848, and infants' school 1849. In 1953 the school was closed and a new county school erected.

[82] Ex inf. Mr. McPhail, City Educ. Dept.   [83] Additional inf. from the head master (1960).

School	Date of opening	Changes in organization	Buildings
PACKMOOR C. JUNIOR AND INFANTS' SCHOOL, Samuel St., Packmoor	1949		
PINEWOOD C. JUNIOR AND INFANTS' SCHOOL, Pinewood Crescent, Meir	1953		
ROUGH CLOSE C.E. JUNIOR AND INFANTS' SCHOOL, Lightwood Rd., Rough Close	1850	Mixed all-age school until 1931 when reorganized, seniors going to various senior schools in Longton. Aided status from June 1953.	Opened in mission church erected in 1850. New buildings, 1896.
ST. MARIA GORETTI'S R.C. INFANTS' SCHOOL,[84] Aylesbury Rd., Bentilee	1958		
SMALLTHORNE C. INFANTS' SCHOOL, Regina St., Smallthorne	1876	Opened as B/G/I school. Continued as such until 1936 when reorganized as infants' and junior schools.	Opened in Sunday-school buildings of Salem Chapel. New buildings erected in 1878.
SMALLTHORNE C. JUNIOR SCHOOL, Regina St., Smallthorne	1876	See Smallthorne C. Infants' School.	See Smallthorne C. Infants' School.
SMALLTHORNE NATIONAL SCHOOL[85]	1855	Opened as mixed all-age school. Became infants only by 1927. Closed shortly after.	
SMALLTHORNE R.C. JUNIOR AND INFANTS' SCHOOL, Brierley St., Smallthorne	1871	Opened as all-age school. Aided status from July 1951.	Original buildings in Queen St. (now Brierley St.). New buildings in 1904, extended 1934.
SUTHERLAND C. INFANTS' SCHOOL, Beaconsfield Drive, Blurton	1954		
SUTHERLAND C. JUNIOR SCHOOL, Beaconsfield Drive, Blurton	1954		
TOWNSEND C. INFANTS' SCHOOL, Werrington Rd., Bucknall	1949		
TOWNSEND C. JUNIOR SCHOOL, Werrington Rd., Bucknall	1950		
TRENTHAM C.E. SCHOOL,[86] Stone Rd., Trentham	c. 1674	Boys' school opened under will of Lady Katherine Leveson (d. 1674). Girls' school opened as a private school, c. 1856. By 1876 also an infants' school, all three run as Trentham Church schools. School reconstituted in 1877–8. Seniors sent to Oak Hill Secondary School in 1938. Controlled status from Jan. 1953. School due to be closed in 1960.	Buildings in 1876 belonged to Duke of Sutherland. Boys' school erected c. 1674. Girls' school erected c. 1856. New buildings in 1877.
WILLFIELD C.S. SCHOOL, Lauder Place North, Ubberley	1956		

TABLE XI

Reorganization of Schools, 1929–1932

For abbreviations see Table IX

TUNSTALL

Group A (1929)	
Forster Street (B/G/I)	Tunstall High Street (J/I)
High Street (M/I)	Highgate Senior (SB)
St. Mary's C.E. (B/G/I)	St. Mary's C.E. (I)
	St. Mary's C.E. Senior (SM)
Summerbank Council (BG/I)	Summerbank C.J. (J/I)
	Summerbank Senior (SG)
Group B (1929)	
Goldenhill C.E. (M/I)	Goldenhill C.E. (J/I)
Goldenhill Council (B/G/I)	Goldenhill C.I. (I)
	Goldenhill Senior (SM)

BURSLEM

Group A (1931)	
St. John's C.E. (B/G/I)	St. John's C.E. (I)
	St. John's C.E. Senior (SM)
Sneyd C.E. (M/I)	Sneyd C.E. (JM)
Group B (1931)	
Granville Council (M, I)	Granville C.J. (J, I)
Hill Top Council (B/G/I)	Hill Top C.J. (J, I)
Moorland Road (B/G/I)	Moorland Road C.J. (J/I)
	Moorland Road Senior (B/G)
North Road Council (B/G/I)	North Road C.J. (J/I)

[84] Ex inf. the Parish Priest (1960).
[85] Additional inf. supplied locally.

[86] Additional inf. from *Staffs. End. Char.* 122–3.

Reorganization of Schools, 1929–1932 (cont.)

BURSLEM *(cont.)*

Park Road Council (SM/JM) — Park Road C.J. (J/I) [Changed in 1932 to Jackfield C.I. and Park Road Senior (SM)]

Sneyd Green Council (M, I) — Sneyd Green C.J. (J/I)

Group C (1931)

Longport Council (M, I) — Longport C.J. (J/I)

Middleport Council (SB/SG/JM, I) — Middleport C.J. (I) / Middleport Senior (SM)

St. Paul's C.E. (M, I) — St. Paul's C.E. (J/I)

HANLEY

Group A (1931)

Broom Street Council (B/G/I) — Hanley C.J. and I (JM/I)

Cannon Street Council (B/G/I) — Cannon Street C.I. [now Lindsay C.I.] (I) / Cannon Street Senior [now Lindsay C.S.] (SB)

Glass Street Council (B/G/I) — Glass Street Senior (SG)

York Street Council (B/G/I) — York Street C.J. [now Clarence C.J. and I] (JM/I)

Group B (1932)

Cauldon Road Council (B/G/I) — Cauldon C.I. (I) / Cauldon C.J. (JM) / Cauldon Senior (SB)

Shelton C.E. (M, I) — Shelton C.E. (JM, I)

Wharf Lane Council (B/G/I) — Shelton Senior (SG)

Group C (1932)

Eastwood Vale Council (B/G/I) — Eastwood Vale C.J. [all-age until 1939 when seniors transferred to Wellington Senior]

Leek Road (now Trent) Council (I) — Leek Road C.I. (I)

Wellington Council (B/G/I) — Wellington C.I. (I) / Wellington Senior (SM)

Group D (1932)

Grove Council (M/I) — Grove C.I. (I) / Grove Senior (SM)

Hamilton Road Council (M, I) — Hamilton C.J. (JM, I)

Northwood C.E. (B/G/I) — Northwood C.E. (JM, I) / Northwood C.J. (JM)

STOKE

Group A (1932)

Boothen C.E. (M, I) — Boothen C.E. (I) / Boothen C.E. (JM)

Cliff Vale C.E. (M, I) — Cliff Vale C.E. (JM, I)

St. Peter's C.E. (SB/SG/JM, I) — St. Peter's C.E. (JM, I) / St. Peter's Secondary Boys (SB) / St. Peter's Secondary Girls (SG)

Mount Pleasant [Fenton] C.E. (M, I) — Mount Pleasant C.E. (JM, I)

Group B (1931)

St. Peter's R.C. (G, I) — St. Thomas's R.C. (JM, I)

St. Thomas's R.C. (B) — St. Thomas's R.C. Secondary (SM)

Group C (1932)

Hartshill C.E. (M, I) — Hartshill C.E. (JM, I)

Harpfield Council (B/G/I) — Harpfield C.J. (JM, I) / Harpfield C.S. (SM)

Honeywall Council (B/G/I) — Honeywall Council (JM, I)

Group D (1932)

Oak Hill Council (M, I) — Oak Hill C.I. (I) / Oak Hill C.J. (JM) / Oak Hill C.S. (SM)

Penkhull Council (M, I) — Penkhull C.I. (I) / Penkhull C.S. (SM)

Trent Vale C.E. (M, I) — Trent Vale C.E. (JM, I)

FENTON

(1932)

Fenton C.E. (B/G/I) — Fenton C.E. (JM)

Heron Cross Council (M/I) — Heron Cross C.J. (M/I) / Heron Cross C.S. (SM)

Market Square (now Glebe) Council (M/I) — Glebe C.I. (I) / Glebe C.J. (JM)

Queen Street Council (M/I) — Fenton C.J. and I (JM/I)

Fenton C.S. (SB) to which all senior boys transferred except those from Heron Cross.

Turner Memorial C.E. (J/I) — Turner Memorial C.E. (I)

Manor C.S. (SG) to which all senior girls transferred except those from Heron Cross.

LONGTON

(1931)

Adderley Green Council (B/G/I) — Adderley Green C.J. and I. (JM/I)

Alexandra Road Council (B/G/I) — Alexandra Road C. (JM/I)

Cooke Street Council (M/I) — Cooke Street [now Heathcote] C. (I) / Cooke Street Senior (SM)

Dresden C.E. (M, I) — Dresden C.E. (JM/I)

Edensor C.E. (B/G/I) — Edensor C.E. (JM/I)

Florence Council (B/G/I) — Florence Council (JM/I)

Grafton Road Council (B/G/I) — Grafton C.I. (I) / Grafton C.J. (JM)

High Street Council (B/G/I) — High Street C. (I)

Longton C.E. (B/G/I) — Longton C.E. (JM/I)

Meir Council (M/I) — Meir C.I. (I) / Meir C.J. (JM) / Meir C.S. (SM)

Normacot C.E. (B/G/I) — Normacot C.E.I. (I)

Queensberry Road Central (SB/SG) — Queensberry Senior for Boys (SB)

Queensberry Road Council (B/G/I) — Queensberry Senior for Girls (SG)

Woodhouse Council (B/G/I) — Woodhouse C.I. (I) / Woodhouse C.S. (SM)

CHARITIES FOR THE POOR

TABLE XII

Founder	Instrument	Endowment	History

TUNSTALL[1]

Founder	Instrument	Endowment	History
Mrs. Adderley of Blake Hall[2]	Will of 1692	50s. rent-charge for poor of Tunstall.	Lapsed through failure to collect by 1818.
William Baddeley[3] (d. 1734)	Will	£30 to provide 15s. for poor of Tunstall and 15s. for poor of Chell on St. Thomas's Day.	It seems that Thomas Child, executor of William Baddeley and trustee of his £30, added another £20; by 1824 £4 interest was distributed in cash to poor of Tunstall at Shrovetide; lapsed by 1958.
John Cartlich[4] (d. 1734)	Will	£50 to be laid out in land to produce rent of £2 for distribution to poor of Tunstall at Shrovetide.	
Thomas Ford of Tunstall[5]	Will proved 1902	£200, interest to be distributed to poor members of Methodist New Connexion Church in Tunstall.	Since closing of Mount Tabor Chapel in Tunstall in 1953 (see p. 297), income has been paid to Chell Heath Methodist Chapel Poor Fund.
John Nash Peake of Congleton (Ches.)[6]	Will proved 1905	£500, interest to be distributed to poor of Tunstall at Christmas at discretion of his executors and the chief bailiff of Tunstall; charity to be called the Nash Peake Fund.	In 1956 these charities were distributed at Christmas in the form of 137 tickets worth £27 8s. Under terms of the will the Roxburgh Fund is vested in the city authorities. Income of Nash Peake Fund 1956–7 £20 9s. 10d. interest on stock, that of Roxburgh Poor Fund £9 interest on stock.
Eliza Roxburgh of Weston-super-Mare (Som.)[7]	Will proved 1913	£200, interest to be distributed to poor of Tunstall; charity to be called the Roxburgh Poor Fund.	
John Chesters[8]	Will proved 1950	£100, income to be distributed to Methodist residents of the Old People's Homes in Stanley Street.	It was to become payable after death of his widow (still living in 1955).

BURSLEM[9]

Founder	Instrument	Endowment	History
John Colclough[10] (d. 1666)	Will	£5 rent-charge to provide 20 1d. loaves each Sunday after morning service; residue in money on 2 Feb.	By 1824 the Sunday bread still distributed, but rest of money given in bread soon after Christmas; lapsed 1938.
John Wedgwood[11]	Will proved 1705	£5, interest to provide bread every Christmas Day.	Charged by his daughter Katherine Egerton, by will proved 1756, on land in Burslem; the form of her settlement invalid under Act of 9 Geo. II, and payment lapsed about end of 18th century.
Revd. Mr. Orme (probably Edward Orme, curate of Burslem 1688–1707, or Edward Orme of Newcastle d. 1705)[12]	Will	£10.	No effects for payment of legacy.
Thomas Leigh of Jackfield[13] (d.1720)	Will	£40, interest to be distributed to poor at discretion of executors.	Lapsed by 1786.

[1] The charities covering the whole of Wolstanton ancient parish of which Tunstall was part are reserved for treatment in a subsequent volume.
[2] 13th Rep. Com. Char. 329.
[3] Ibid. 329–30, where a different interpretation of the history is given; Wolstanton Par. Reg. i. 278; ex inf. the Vicar, Christ Church.
[4] Ibid.
[5] Char. Com. files; ex. inf. the Superintendent Minister, Tunstall Circuit (1958).
[6] Char. Com. files.
[7] Ibid.
[8] Ibid.
[9] The area comprises the old poor law parish of Burslem: see p. 125.
[10] 13th Rep. Com. Char. 260–1; J. C. Wedgwood, Wedgwood Family, 78, 80, 84; Charities Acct. 1851–1925, at St. John's, Burslem; Char. Com. files. Colclough left a further £10 for poor householders of Burslem: Wedgwood, op. cit. 83.
[11] Abstract of Rets. of Charitable Donations, 1786–8, H.C. 511, pp. 1134–5 (1816), xvi (2); 13th Rep. Com. Char. 261; Wedgwood, Wedgwood Family, 119, 123.
[12] Char. Donations, 1786–8, ii. 1136–7; Burslem Par. Reg. i, p. x; Newcastle Par. Reg. i. 267.
[13] Char. Donations, 1786–8, ii. 1134–5, which, however, mentions a trustee in whom the charity was then vested; 13th Rep. Com. Char. 262; Burslem Par. Reg. i. 168.

Founder	Instrument	Endowment	History
Revd. William Adams[14] (d. 1722)	Will	£10, interest to be distributed to poor of Hulton on St. Thomas's Day.	No effects for payment of legacy.
Hugh Meare[15] (d. 1742)	Will	£20, interest to be distributed to poor.	Lapsed by 1788 through insolvency of borrower.
R. (probably Richard) Cartwright[16] (probably d. 1754)	Will	£20, to provide 5s. worth of bread four times a year.	Lent to overseers towards cost of new workhouse (see p. 130) and 20s. charged on poor-rates; charged on land at Harriseahead by 1919 and lapsed on sale of land soon afterwards.
Katherine Egerton[17]	Will proved 1756	£2 10s. rent-charge for distribution to poor.	Settlement invalid under Act of 9 Geo. II, and charity never paid.
Ralph Shaw[18]	Will—between 1720 and 1759	£5, interest to be distributed to poor.	No effects for payment of legacy.
Joseph Bucknall[19]	Will proved 1789	£200, interest to be distributed to poor of Cobridge at Christmas.	£225 settled by Jacob Warburton (will of 1825) as Bucknall's executor to provide £10 for poor of Cobridge under Bucknall's will and £1 5s. for the Roman Catholic priest at Cobridge. From c. 1837 trustees paid whole to the priest who distributed £10 to the Catholic poor. Payment suspended by trustees c. 1870, and under scheme of 1880 the charity, represented by £299 4s. 1d. stock, was vested in the vicar and churchwardens of Cobridge who were to distribute the income in kind at Christmas among poor of Cobridge irrespective of creed. This charity is still (1958) paid.
Randle Keay[20]	Will of 1817	£500 to provide bread for poor attending parish church on first Sundays of February, May, and August and on 1 November (founder's birthday) or Sunday following; also £4 to rector for supervising distribution and preaching on each occasion on practical charity.	Became payable 1846, but only £300 available; applied also to new ecclesiastical Districts of Burslem as created. By 1958 income of £7 15s. distributed in general comforts at discretion of Rector of St. John's; charity sermons, still preached in 1932, have since lapsed.
Howard Haywood[21]	Will proved 1875	£30,000 to be applied to sick poor of Burslem and immediate neighbourhood in such a way that his name and that of his brother Richard should be for ever associated with it.	Howard and Richard Haywood Hospital built 1886–7 in Moorland Road; replaced by present hospital in High Lane built 1927–30. Endowment increased by other gifts.
Elger Robinson of Burslem[22]	Will proved 1904	Stock (£313 17s. in 1937), interest to provide coal at Christmas for poor widows and other poor attending Swan Bank Wesleyan Chapel; in memory of his daughter Louisa (d. 1889).	By 1958 22 gifts of 10s. were being made each year towards cost of coal.
Harriet Bates of Endon[23]	Will proved 1912	£300 stock, residue of interest, after deducting cost of maintaining grave of herself and her husband, to provide income for poor of Cobridge.	Stock sold 1913 for £325.
Col. Sir William Warrington Dobson of Seighford Hall[24]	Will proved 1942	£1,000, income to be used to continue the treat given to poor children of Burslem by Sir William and his late wife (tea and concert before Christmas to about 1,200 children from elementary schools of Burslem).	Income accumulated during war; treats subsidized until 1948 by Parker's Brewery (Sir William's firm).

[14] *Char. Donations, 1786–8*, ii. 1134–5, which mentions a current trustee but adds 'no effects'; *13th Rep. Com. Char.* 262; *Burslem Par. Reg.* i. 172.

[15] *Char. Donations, 1786–8*, ii. 1136–7; *Burslem. Par. Reg.* i. 214, burial of Hugh Mare of Cobridge Gate.

[16] *13th Rep. Com. Char.* 261–2; *Char. Donations, 1786–8*, ii. 1134–5, identifying him as Ric. Cartwright, who also gave money for the sch. (see p. 308); Char. Acct. 1851–1925; Char. Com. files; *Burslem Par. Reg.* i. 250.

[17] *13th Rep. Com. Char.* 261; Wedgwood, *Wedgwood Family*, 122, 123. She also gave £3 to be distributed to the poor of Burslem after her funeral: ibid. 122.

[18] *Char. Donations, 1786–8*, ii. 1136–7. Several persons of the name Ralph Shaw died between 1720 and 1759:

Burslem Par. Reg. i. 165, 179, 183, 250, 260, 267.

[19] Char. Com. files; Ward, *Stoke*, 285–6; Adams, *Adams Family*, 287; ex inf. the Vicar of Cobridge (1958). The priest's share, £1 from 1858, was still paid in 1866: T. M. Leith, Records of the Mission of St. Peter, Cobridge (MS. at St. Peter's, Cobridge), f. 44a.

[20] Char. Com. files; Char. Acct. 1851–1925; ex inf. the Rector of St. John's (1958).

[21] Char. Com. files; *Haywood Charity Hospital* (copy in H.R.L.); see p. 128.

[22] Char. Com. files; ex inf. the Superintendent Minister, Burslem Central Mission (1958).

[23] Char. Com. files.

[24] Ibid.

Founder	Instrument	Endowment	History
Mrs. E. A. Smith[25] (d. 1957)	Will	£100 to be applied by Rector of St. John's to poor of his parish.	Capital held by rector in 1958 for disbursement in general comforts as required.

STOKE-UPON-TRENT PARISH[26]

Founder	Instrument	Endowment	History
Robert Bagnall of Fenton Vivian[27]	Deed of 1674 or 1675	£100 for purchase of a £5 annuity to be distributed to poor of Botteslow, Fenton Vivian, Fenton Culvert, Longton, and Meare Lane End on 24 June and 1 Nov.	Laid out in purchase of £5 rent-charge; by 1822 distributed in cash and bread to poor of these townships; from 1843 distributed in clothing (in February by 1847) by rectors of Stoke and Longton; by 1957 added to Stoke parish bread and clothing fund as £2 15s. rent-charge.
Revd. Mr. Orme (probably Edward Orme, curate of Burslem 1688–1707, or Edward Orme of Newcastle d. 1705)[28]	Will	£1 interest on £20 for poor of parish.	Lapsed by 1824.
Robert Whilton[29] (d. 1729)	Will	£1 rent-charge to provide bread twice a year, half to be distributed to poor of Eaves liberty in Bucknall chapel and half to poor of rest of parish in Stoke church.	By 1824 distributed to widows in cash and bread at Stoke and Bucknall; from 1843 distributed in clothing; lapsed 1860 through failure to collect but revived 1902; lapsed again by 1958.
Thomas Finney of Blurton[30]	Will of 1761	£3 p.a., settled as interest on £60 by executor, for poor widows living near Stoke church.	At first distributed in money to widows, from 1843 in clothing; embezzled by a trustee 1888.
George Broom of Hanley[31] (d. c. 1799)	Will	£1 rent-charge for poor of Hanley.	Distributed in bread by 1824; still in force 1865.
Ephraim Chatterley of Shelton[32]	Deed of 1803	£8 8s. rent-charge (or net profit from land concerned) for bread for poor of Hanley and Shelton on Christmas Day and Good Friday.	By 1885 the income (£10) was distributed in bread at Christmas and Easter by the incumbents of Hanley, Shelton, Northwood, Hope, Wellington, and Etruria; under a scheme of 1895 the income (£24 0s. 8d. interest on stock, the land having been sold 1889) was to be used for the general benefit of the poor of the borough; paid to the North Staffs. Deaf and Dumb Society 1950–3; allowed to accumulate 1954–6.
William Ridgway of Northwood[33]	Not known	Almshouses in Keelings Lane for 'decayed widows' by 1832.	The history of the almshouses after c. 1840 is not known. A small side lane off Eastbourne Road near its junction with Keelings Lane is still called Widows Row and runs close to the site of the former almshouses.
John Bourne[34]	Deed of 1834	Land in Fenton, the income to be distributed to poor of parish on St. Thomas's Day.	Some years before 1902 two-thirds of the income (£27 rent in 1894; £24 12s. 8d. interest on stock by 1902, the land having been sold 1895) was allotted to the poor of Fenton; under a scheme of 1902 the income was assigned to the poor of the ancient parish; still in force 1935–6.
Revd. John Woodhouse (d. 1833)[35]	Deed of 1836 in fulfilment of will	£100 to provide bread for poor of Penkhull and Boothen at Christmas.	Distributed to poor of Stoke town as well as of Penkhull and Boothen by 1840; still distributed in bread in 1879; by 1957 paid to Stoke church schools account.

[25] Ex inf. the Rector of St. John's (1958).

[26] The area comprises the old poor law parish of Stoke-upon-Trent: see p. 198.

[27] *13th Rep. Com. Char.* 315–16; tablet in St. Peter's, Stoke; Charities Acct. 1814–58 (in St. Peter's Vestry); St. Peter's Vestry Mins. (from 1887), p. 202.

[28] *Char. Donations, 1786–8,* 1136–7; *Burslem Par. Reg.* i, p. x; *Newcastle Par. Reg.* i. 267. It is not mentioned in *13th Rep. Com. Char.*

[29] *13th Rep. Com. Char.* 315; Char. Acct. 1814–58, where it is also called Dean's Dole from the name of the tenant of the estate; Char. Com. files; ex inf. the Rector of Stoke (1958).

[30] *13th Rep. Com. Char.* 314; R. Nicholls, *Stoke Ch.* 98; Char. Acct. 1814–58.

[31] *13th Rep. Com. Char.* 318; *Staffs. End. Char.* H.C. 91, pp. 48–49 (1868–9), xlv.

[32] *13th Rep. Com. Char.* 318; Char. Com. files.

[33] Ward, *Stoke,* 382; Hargreaves, *Map of Staffs. Potteries.*

[34] Char. Com. files. If this is John Bourne of Fenton who d. 1838 (see p. 219), the deed presumably gave effect to a devise under his will.

[35] Tablet in St. Peter's; Char. Acct. 1814–58; Char. Com. files; *Stoke Par. Mag.* (Jan. 1880), 4; St. Peter's Vestry Mins. (from 1887), p. 202.

Founder	Instrument	Endowment	History
John Tomlinson of Cliffville[36] (d. 1838)	Will	£5 p.a. to provide bread for poor of Penkhull, Boothen, and Stoke town on 1 Jan.	By 1958 income £3 6s. 6d. interest on stock; two-thirds added to bread and clothing account, one-third to Stoke church schools account.
William Cook of Longton[37]	Will proved 1873	£100, interest to be distributed every Christmas Day to 10 poor widows, members of the Methodist New Connexion Zion Chapel in Longton.	Since the amalgamation of Zion and Bourne Chapels the money has been paid at Christmas to 10 widows, members of Bourne Chapel.
Thomas Gilbert[38]	Will proved 1878	£280 to mayor and corporation to provide food for aged poor over 60 of Hanley borough during subsequent 21 years.	£152 still remained in 1901 but this had been spent by 1904.
William Carter[39]	Will proved 1881	£150 to provide bread for poor of Stoke-upon-Trent parish.	By 1958 the income, £3 13s., was added to parish bread and clothing fund.
Samuel Owen, Rector of Bucknall 1878–91 (d. 1891)[40]	Presumably will	Not known.	By 1960 the income, £34 6s., was distributed to old and needy of Bucknall parish at Christmas and other times.
William Webberley of Meir[41]	Will proved 1893	£500, interest to be distributed to poor widows on St. Thomas's Day by rector and churchwardens of St. James's.	By 1958 distributed by rector on St. Thomas's Day to elderly women of parish in financial need.
Henry Hill of Meir[42]	Will proved 1895	£1,000, interest to be distributed in money or kind on 22 Dec. (founder's birthday) to 50 or more aged poor of borough of Longton as Henry Hill's Christmas Gift.	Laid out in land 1896; a further £28 8s. 2d. stock added 1942; by 1958 disbursed in sums of 4s. in Longton area of city.
George Mountford of Stoke[43]	Will proved 1898	£500 to provide annual dinner for aged poor of Stoke borough, to be selected by a committee of the borough council.	Became payable 1906; in 1937–8 £18 spent on dinner, £2 7s. 6d. on tea, and £1 7s. 1d. on tobacco; still in force 1958.
George Burton of Stoke[44]	Will proved 1907	£215 for aged persons attending Stoke church.	Implemented under scheme of 1922; in 1958 the income, about £18 interest on stock, distributed in gifts at rector's discretion.
Marion Telwright[45]	Will proved 1913	£100, income to be distributed by the rector or churchwardens of Bucknall to the poor on 1 January.	By 1960 the income, £3 16s. 8d., was distributed to old and needy of Bucknall parish at Christmas and other times.

[36] White, Dir. Staffs. (1851), 227; Char. Acct. 1814–58; Char. Com. files; Vestry Mins. (from 1887), p. 202; ex inf. the rector.

[37] Char. Com. files; ex inf. the Superintendent Minister, Longton and Fenton Circuit (1958); see p. 297.

[38] Staffs. End. Char. (Suppl.), H.C. 70, pp. 24–25 (1892), lix; A. Huntbach, Hanley, 76; Char. Com. files; Hanley Boro. Counc. Yr. Bks. (1901–2, 1904–5).

[39] Char. Com. files; ex inf. the rector.

[40] Char. Com. files; ex inf. the Rector of Bucknall (1960);

S. W. Hutchinson, The Archdeaconry of Stoke-on-Trent, 126.

[41] Char. Com. files; ex inf. the Rector of St. James's (1958).

[42] Char. Com. files; ex inf. the lord mayor's secretary (1958).

[43] Char. Com. files; ex inf. the lord mayor's secretary (1958).

[44] Char. Com. files; Vestry Mins. (from 1887), p. 202; ex inf. the rector.

[45] Char. Com. files; ex inf. the Rector of Bucknall (1960).

INDEX

NOTE: The arrangement of the index in general reflects the arrangement of the volume summarized on p. 80. Thus all places within one of the six Pottery towns in 1910 are identified to the relevant town; all other places are identified to their ancient parish. Individual potbanks, however, are grouped together under the entry 'Potbanks'; individual brick- and tile-works and mines are also grouped under separate entries. General references to various industries are indexed under place headings. General references to Protestant nonconformity are indexed under the relevant place; in the case of Newcastle-under-Lyme and the six towns there are also entries for individual sects.

The following abbreviations have been used, sometimes with the addition of the letter *s* to form the plural: adv., advowson; agric., agriculture; Alex., Alexander; And., Andrew; Ant., Anthony; assoc., association; Benj., Benjamin; boro., borough; bp., bishop; cast., castle; chant., chantry; chap., chapel; char., charity; Chas., Charles; Chris., Christopher; ch., church; coll., college; Ctss., Countess; Dan., Daniel; d., died; econ. hist., economic history; Edm., Edmund; Edw., Edward; Eliz., Elizabeth; fam., family; fl., flourished; Fred., Frederick; Geo., George; Geof., Geoffrey; Gilb., Gilbert; Hen., Henry; Herb., Herbert; hosp., hospital; ho., house; Humph., Humphrey; hund., hundred; inc., inclosure; ind., industry; Jas., James; Jos., Joseph; Kath., Katherine; Lawr., Lawrence; loc. govt., local government; man., manor; Marg., Margaret; m., married; Mat., Matthew; Mic., Michael; *n*, note; Nat., Nathaniel; Nic., Nicholas; nonconf., nonconformity; par., parish; parl. rep., parliamentary representation; Pet., Peter; Phil., Philip; pop., population; Prot., Protestant; rly., railway; Ric., Richard; riv., river; Rob., Robert; Rog., Roger; Rom. Cath., Roman Catholicism; s., son; Sam., Samuel; sch., school; Sim., Simon; soc., society; Steph., Stephen; Thos., Thomas; U.D., Urban District; Vct., Viscount; Wal., Walter; w., wife; Wm., William.